Teaching Students with Severe Disabilities

Third Edition

David L. Westling
Western Carolina University

Lise Fox
University of South Florida

Upper Saddle River, New Jersey
Columbus, Ohio

Library of Congress Cataloging-in-Publication Data
Westling, David L.
Teaching students with severe disabilities / David L. Westling, Lise Fox.—3rd ed.
p. cm.
Includes bibliographical references and index.
ISBN 0-13-110553-1
1. Children with disabilities—Education—United States. 2. Youth with disabilities—Education—United States. 3. People with disabilities—Service for—United States. 4. Special education—Vocational guidance—United States. I. Fox, Lise. II. Title.
LC4031.W47 2004
371.9'0973—dc21
2003054910

Vice President and Executive Publisher: Jeffery W. Johnston
Acquisitions Editor: Allyson P. Sharp
Editorial Assistants: Penny Burleson and Kathleen S. Burk
Production Editor: Linda Hillis Bayma
Production Coordination: Linda Zuk, WordCrafters Editorial Services
Design Coordinator: Diane C. Lorenzo
Photo Coordinator: Sandy Schaefer
Cover Designer: Bryan Huber
Cover image: SuperStock
Production Manager: Laura Messerly
Director of Marketing: Ann Castel Davis
Marketing Manager: Amy June
Marketing Coordinator: Tyra Poole

This book was set in Times by Carlisle Communications, Ltd. It was printed and bound by Courier Westford, Inc. The cover was printed by The Lehigh Press, Inc.

Photo Credits: pp. 2, 20, 30, 226: Tom Watson/Merrill; pp. 59, 80, 100, 202, 415: Anthony Magnacca/Merrill; pp. 123, 152, 193, 262, 453, 480, 528: Scott Cunningham/Merrill; pp. 164, 292, 393, 500, 512: Barbara Schwartz/Merrill; pp. 181, 316: Todd Yarrington/Merrill; p. 340: Anne Vega/Merrill; pp. 362, 530: Lise Fox; p. 401: Laima Druskis/PHCollege.

Pearson Education Ltd.
Pearson Education Singapore, Pte. Ltd.
Pearson Education Canada, Ltd.
Pearson Education—Japan
Pearson Education Australia PTY, Limited
Pearson Education North Asia Ltd.
Pearson Educación de Mexico, S.A. de C.V.
Pearson Education Malaysia, Pte. Ltd.

10 9 8 7 6 5 4 3 2 1
ISBN 0-13-110553-1

Preface

It was almost 30 years ago, in 1975, that the 94th Congress of the United States passed P.L. 94-142, which said that every child in the United States has a right to public education. For 100 or so years before 1975, states had required that children go to school, usually until they were 16. But the states' laws allowed some children to be excluded if local school boards deemed that they would not learn sufficiently. In most states, therefore, many young people whom we now refer to as having severe disabilities were excluded from public education programs. If they did go to school, it was almost always in a separate building from where other children were in school. If a student's disability was significant, the student was not even allowed to attend these separate schools. Parents had few options: keep their child at home, find a private special school (usually one run by a parents' group or organization), or place their child in a residential institution.

To some, this may seem like ancient history. To us, as well as to many others who have had a long-standing interest in the well-being of persons with severe disabilities, we were there. We were there when many school systems, not with some degree of reluctance, began to offer educational programs for students with significant disabilities.

Of course, the learning settings were not exactly what we might have desired but, nevertheless, public education began to occur. In our area, the educational arrangement for teaching students with very significant disabilities was the top floor of the residential institution in which they had lived for most of their lives. (The special school in the area, which was serving students with more moderate disabilities, said there was not enough room. Later it built a special wing for "the severe/profound.") So every morning students would be taken to the top floor, where a few special education pioneers would try their best to teach these students something that would presumably make their lives better. Some of the instruction was good and relevant; some was of little relevance. But, all in all, it was a learning experience for everyone.

If you look at the field of education for students with severe disabilities from a historical perspective, you might characterize it as an ever-moving, broader-growing, outward-spiraling effort to assist people to become fuller participants in the mainstream world. In the early 1970s and to some extent in the 1960s, innovative researchers were looking for ways to help people with disabilities become more able. What they were working on were relatively basic, albeit important, skills. They were working primarily in institutions, and they were teaching toileting skills, how to bathe and groom, how to get dressed, how to use feeding utensils—essentially, how to take care of oneself in the world. Most of what they were doing was of interest only to people who read professional journals, but they were starting to lay important groundwork for the development of relevant, functional educational programs.

In the latter 1970s and beyond, the earth really began to move with regard to what many professionals, including researchers, policymakers, administrators, teachers, and, most important, parents, began to study, say, and do with and for persons with severe disabilities. Students who were more able, though still labeled "trainable," were now being taught basic reading and other academic skills, totally segregated schools began to be considered inappropriate, and many students were moved into regular school buildings with peers without disabilities, although generally still separated. Students began to go into the community to learn how to function in the nonschool world, to eat in restaurants, to shop in stores, and to work at jobs. We learned about how best to teach new skills and learned better how to ensure the generalization of these new skills. Ultimately, we began to learn how to really include students with severe disabilities in general education classrooms, how to foster social relationships, and how to provide meaningful instruction to students with disabilities who were taught with their nondisabled peers.

As professionals who have been around for awhile, we have had the opportunity, like many of our colleagues, to observe many significant and even dramatic changes in the lives of people with severe disabilities. But, while we take some pleasure in seeing what has occurred in the last 30 or so years, we have to remember two critical points.

First, students with severe disabilities and their families today are not part of this history. They don't look back at the innovations and trends and consider themselves better off today, because they were not part of what was happening 20 or 30 years ago. Their context is only the present, only now. And their judgment of what is occurring today is made solely on the quality of life that they are experiencing vis-à-vis the lives of others in their communities. Therefore, the fact that the field has moved forward can never really give them much satisfaction with regard to how supports and services are perceived today.

The second important point is that we know how to do things better than we are actually doing them. In most public school systems, students with severe disabilities (labeled as mentally retarded, autistic, multiply handicapped, or deaf–blind) are still educated in separate facilities. Many are not given an appropriate education by well-qualified general and special education teachers. Many times ineffective teaching approaches are used, and often students don't learn what they might have learned under different circumstances. Furthermore, most students with severe disabilities are still not adequately prepared for participation in an integrated postschool world.

But, as we have said, we are in a position to know that conditions have improved. And we are hopeful that they will continue to do so. Perhaps the work we have done here will be of some help, and perhaps progress will come soon enough to benefit some of the persons who need better services today.

About the New Edition

As with previous editions, we have tried to produce a current text with useful information that can be easily comprehended and applied by the reader who is developing instructional programs. Recognizing that there is always a gap between research and practice, we wanted to write the book in such a way that the reader could understand and use research findings in the real world. Although we know this is often difficult, nevertheless we think it is possible and hope that the content and style of presentation make it probable. As we studied the research literature to provide what we hope is a comprehensive text, we also relied on our own experience, values, and common sense to direct us. We have also learned a great deal from many persons with disabilities, their parents, and their teachers, which we think has increased the relevance of our work.

Since the last edition was published, several important issues have arisen or been given greater emphasis. We have tried to capture the essence of these issues and address them in the text where appropriate. In addition to other topics covered in earlier issues, more attention has been given to the following:

- Research continues to document conditions about individuals with severe disabilities and their learning potential. We address this topic in Chapter 1.
- Access to the general curriculum is a matter that many researchers and practitioners have given more attention to in recent years, and we have addressed this beginning in Chapter 2 and in other relevant chapters in the text. Akin to this is the participation of students with severe disabilities in literacy learning, which we discuss in some detail.
- Likewise, the use of alternate assessments to hold schools responsible for the education of students with severe disabilities has been given greater coverage. States, school districts, schools, and individual teachers are searching for ways to accurately assess and document students at the end of the year. We have tried to shed some light on this topic.
- Appropriate roles of paraprofessionals have been given much consideration. The roles of these individuals are very important, but some have warned that these roles have to be better defined and understood. Chapter 3 takes a broad look at this issue.
- In Chapter 4 we devote much more attention to multicultural issues. The condition remains that most teachers of students with severe disabilities are White females, but the students they teach come from very diverse backgrounds. We felt it was important to look at this issue in more depth in order to better shape practice.
- One of the most significant practices emerging in recent years is the promotion of more self-management by persons with severe disabilities to improve skill acquisition, maintenance, and general-

ization. We have discussed and explained this practice in different areas of the text.

- Finally, we have developed an entirely new chapter (Chapter 19) on assistive technology (AT). Although the full potential of AT has not yet been realized for the large majority of persons with severe disabilities, there is enough promise so that readers need to know about AT to help them to move forward in this area.

This book reflects the knowledge and understanding of individuals with severe disabilities that we have gained from the research and our relationships with students with disabilities, their families, and the teachers who support them. These relationships have inspired us and fueled our commitment to this endeavor. We are very appreciative of the support and encouragement offered by our loved ones, friends, and colleagues as we worked on this revision. As always, the feedback that we received from those who used or read the text or parts of it has been helpful. At the risk of forgetting someone who has given us constructive feedback, we would like to thank Karena Cooper-Duffy, Bill Ogletree, Glen Dunlap, Bobbie Vaughn, and many students for their ideas and support. We would also like to thank Allyson Sharp, our editor at Merrill/Prentice Hall, and Penny Burleson, her assistant, for the ideas and ongoing prompts that they provided to improve the text and keep us on track in revising it. Also, thanks go to the reviewers of the second edition who made suggestions for this edition, including Marquita Grenot-Scheyer, California State University; Helen Hammond, University of Texas at El Paso; and Tony Russo, Marywood University. To the extent that we were able to incorporate the recommendations, our gratitude is expressed to all who made them. For any shortcomings, we accept responsibility and hope that readers will understand.

The lives of people with severe disabilities and their families are complex and difficult to fully comprehend by anyone who is not an intimate part of them. So too are the challenges of those who try with all their effort to provide appropriate service. We know that our roles in this process are small. But we hope that what we have offered in this text will be useful and will contribute in some way to the continued improvement of educational and related services for persons with severe disabilities.

D. L. W.
L. F.

Educator Learning Center: An Invaluable Online Resource

Merrill Education and the Association for Supervision and Curriculum Development (ASCD) invite you to take advantage of a new online resource, one that provides access to the top research and proven strategies associated with ASCD and Merrill—the Educator Learning Center. At **www.EducatorLearningCenter.com** you will find resources that will enhance your students' understanding of course topics and of current educational issues, in addition to being invaluable for further research.

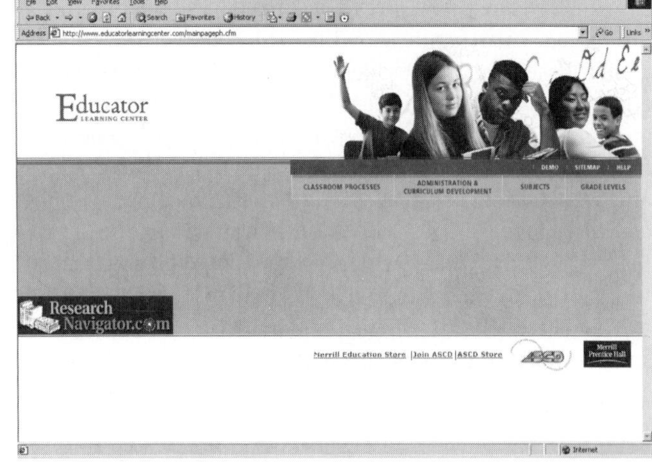

How the Educator Learning Center will help your students become better teachers

With the combined resources of Merrill Education and ASCD, you and your students will find a wealth of tools and materials to better prepare them for the classroom.

Research

- More than 600 articles from the ASCD journal *Educational Leadership* discuss everyday issues faced by practicing teachers.
- A direct link on the site to Research Navigator™ gives students access to many of the leading education journals, as well as extensive content detailing the research process.
- Excerpts from Merrill Education texts give your students insights on important topics of instructional methods, diverse populations, assessment, classroom management, technology, and refining classroom practice.

Classroom Practice

- Hundreds of lesson plans and teaching strategies are categorized by content area and age range.
- Case studies and classroom video footage provide virtual field experience for student reflection.
- Computer simulations and other electronic tools keep your students abreast of today's classrooms and current technologies.

Look into the value of Educator Learning Center yourself

Preview the value of this educational environment by visiting **www.EducatorLearningCenter.com** and clicking on "Demo." For a free 4-month subscription to the Educator Learning Center in conjunction with this text, simply contact your Merrill/Prentice Hall sales representative.

Discover the Companion Website Accompanying This Book

The Prentice Hall Companion Website: A Virtual Learning Environment

Technology is a constantly growing and changing aspect of our field that is creating a need for content and resources. To address this emerging need, Prentice Hall has developed an online learning environment for students and professors alike—Companion Websites—to support our textbooks.

In creating a Companion Website, our goal is to build on and enhance what the textbook already offers. For this reason, the content for each user-friendly website is organized by topic and provides the professor and student with a variety of meaningful resources. Common features of a Companion Website include:

For the Professor—

Every Companion Website integrates **Syllabus Manager**™, an online syllabus creation and management utility.

- **Syllabus Manager**™ provides you, the instructor, with an easy, step-by-step process to create and revise syllabi, with direct links into Companion Website and other online content without having to learn HTML.
- Students may log on to your syllabus during any study session. All they need to know is the web address for the Companion Website and the password you've assigned to your syllabus.
- After you have created a syllabus using **Syllabus Manager**™, students may enter the syllabus for their course section from any point in the Companion Website.
- Clicking on a date, the student is shown the list of activities for the assignment. The activities for each assignment are linked directly to actual content, saving time for students.
- Adding assignments consists of clicking on the desired due date, then filling in the details of the assignment—name of the assignment, instructions, and whether it is a one-time or repeating assignment.
- In addition, links to other activities can be created easily. If the activity is online, a URL can be entered in the space provided, and it will be linked automatically in the final syllabus.
- Your completed syllabus is hosted on our servers, allowing convenient updates from any computer on the Internet. Changes you make to your syllabus are immediately available to your students at their next logon.

For the Student—

- **Overview and General Information**—General information about the topic and how it will be covered in the website.
- **Web Links**—A variety of websites related to topic areas.
- **Content Methods and Strategies**—Resources that help to put theories into practice in the special education classroom.

- **Reflective Questions and Case-Based Activities**—Put concepts into action, participate in activities, examine strategies, and more.
- **National and State Laws**—An online guide to how federal and state laws affect your special education classroom.
- **Behavior Management**—An online guide to help you manage behaviors in the special education classroom.
- **Message Board**—Virtual bulletin board to post and respond to questions and comments from a national audience.

To take advantage of these and other resources, please visit the *Teaching Students with Severe Disabilities,* Third Edition, Companion Website at

www.prenhall.com/westling

Brief Contents

Contents

PART 4

Specific Instructional and Management Procedures 261

PART 1

Initial Considerations

CHAPTER 1

Students with Severe Disabilities: Definitions, Descriptions, Characteristics, and Potential

In this chapter, definitions and concepts of severe disabilities and the traditional categories covered by this term are discussed. In addition, descriptions of learning characteristics, personal–social characteristics, and physical conditions often associated with severe disabilities are provided. The chapter concludes with a discussion of the potential of students with severe disabilities who are given appropriate forms of instruction and support.

Defining Severe Disabilities

The term *severe disabilities* has been defined somewhat differently by different people and agencies. Generally, however, it implies a condition in which the development of typical abilities is in some way adversely affected (Abt Associates, 1974; Baker, 1979; Brimer, 1990; Justen, 1976; Sailor & Haring, 1977). Unlike most other people, individuals with severe disabilities are often challenged by significant weaknesses in general learning abilities, personal and social skills, and/or sensory and physical development. The general ability to demonstrate the skills necessary to maintain oneself independently in typical life environments is reduced for persons with severe disabilities; and often the condition requires assistance and ongoing support from individuals without disabilities, including family members, friends, teachers, and professionals.

Traditional categories of persons usually referred to as having a severe disability include those who have been classified as moderately, severely, or profoundly mentally disabled;[1] those who are autistic (or demonstrate autistic-like behaviors); and those who have multiple disabilities that include mental disabilities. Persons with severe disabilities have also been described as exhibiting uncommon behavioral characteristics, such as self-stimulatory behavior, or as lacking in typical abilities, such as self-care or verbal communication skills (Abt Associates, 1974). Others have defined the condition of severe disabilities as one in which more extensive services are required for the person to achieve maximum potential (Justen, 1976; Sailor & Haring, 1977). In other words, these individuals are lacking in the abilities and skills necessary to achieve complete independence (Baker, 1979; Brimer, 1990).

TASH, an organization supporting "equity, opportunity and inclusion for people with disabilities" (formerly *The Association for Persons with Severe Handicaps*), defined the condition of severe disabilities with regard to necessary support:

> These people include individuals of all ages who require extensive ongoing support in more than one major life activity in order to participate in integrated community settings and to enjoy a quality of life that is available to citizens with fewer or no disabilities. Support may be required for life activities such as mobility, communication, self-care, and learning as necessary for independent living, employment and self-sufficiency. (Adopted by TASH, December, 1985, revised November, 1986; reprinted in Meyer, Peck, & Brown, 1991, p. 19)

Similarly, the American Association on Mental Retardation (AAMR) in its most recent characterization of mental retardation, a condition that often results in severe disabilities, considered it as a human manifestation in which different levels of support are required. According to the AAMR: "Mental retardation is a disability characterized by significant limitations both in intellectual functioning and in adaptive behavior as expressed in conceptual, social, and practical adaptive skills. This disability originates before age 18" (American Association on Mental Retardation, 2002).

Since 1992, AAMR ceased making distinctions using the traditional subclasses of mental retardation (e.g., mild, moderate, severe, or profound), but instead proposed that an individual who is diagnosed as being mentally retarded must be described within a multidimensional context that provides a comprehensive description of the person and the necessary supports (see Figure 1–1).

The theoretical model of mental retardation presented in Figure 1–1 has five dimensions: (1) intellectual abilities, (2) adaptive behavior, (3) participation, interactions, and social roles, (4) health, and (5) context; these are mediated by a support system to affect an individual's functioning. That is, the impact of all the dimensions on the individual is influenced by the support that buffers the person's life. Furthermore, in a reciprocal manner, the functioning level of the individual may affect the supports that are required for successful functioning. The model implies that a person's functioning is not due solely to characteristics of the individual, but also to the supportive context in which the person must operate. Thus AAMR looks at mental retardation not as a deficiency, but in terms of needed supports. The AAMR states five assumptions "essential" to the application of its definition:

1. Limitations in present functioning must be considered within the context of community environments typical of the individual's age peers and culture.

[1]The term *mental disabilities* is preferred by some to the more traditional term *mental retardation*. We will interchange the terms in this text.

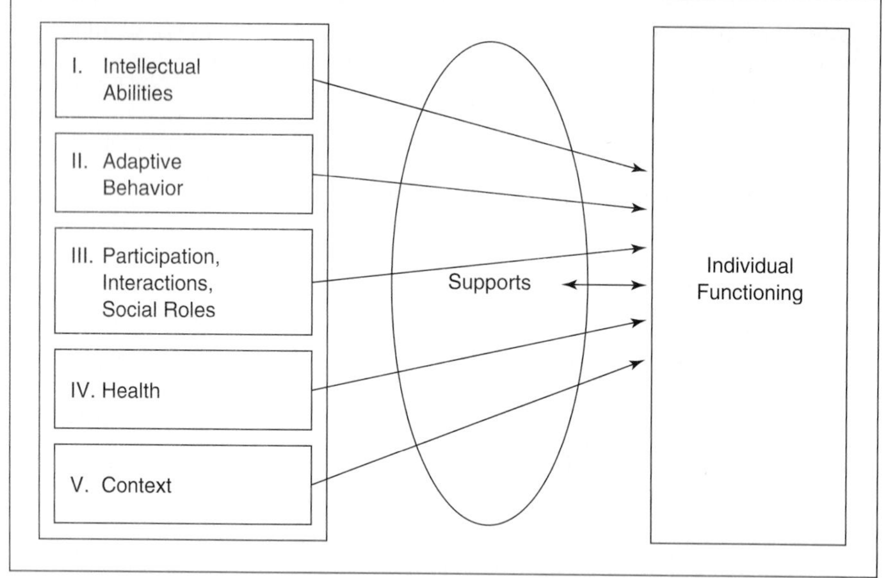

Figure 1–1 Theoretical Model of Mental Retardation

Source: American Association on Mental Retardation, 2002. *Mental retardation: Definition, Classification, and System of Support* 10th edition. Washington, DC: Author. Reprinted with permission.

2. Valid assessment considers cultural and linguistic diversity, as well as differences in communication, sensory, motor, and behavioral factors.
3. Within an individual, limitations often coexist with strengths.
4. An important purpose of describing limitations is to develop a profile of needed supports.
5. With appropriate personalized supports over a sustained period, the life functioning of the person with mental retardation generally will improve.

In contrast, the traditional levels of mental retardation are still maintained in the American Psychiatric Association's (APA) *Diagnostic and Statistical Manual of Mental Disorders,* 4th Edition, Text Revision (DSM-IV, 2000). These levels and their corresponding approximate IQ ranges include mild (50–70), moderate (35–50), severe (20–35), and profound (below 20–25) mental retardation. Although we agree with the concept of mental retardation used by the AAMR, we will use the traditional classification system in this text in an attempt to improve communicative clarity.

It is important to understand that there is not a homogeneous population of students with severe disabilities. Instead, many individuals who may be characterized as having severe disabilities are, in fact, quite different from each other. The common bond among the members of this population is that their general functioning is below that exhibited by about 99% of the rest of the population; thus they need more support than 99% of the population to participate in society and enjoy a quality of life similar to most others. Even so, it is critical that, as people who are concerned about the well-being of persons with severe disabilities, especially as professionals or professionals-to-be, we be sensitive to their individuality. Kay Drais, whose daughter Jessica has Down syndrome, expressed her opinion about "impairment" in "An open letter from my heart to educators." She wrote (1995):

> I do not see Jessica as impaired. I see her as different than most of us in general terms, but different is not impaired. Synonyms for impaired are defective, damaged, ruined, incapacitated, mutilated—synonyms for different are distinct, non-uniform, differing, dissimilar, unusual, uncommon. I prefer to believe, and my heart very clearly tells me, that my daughter is uncommon, not defective.

With this caveat in mind, in the following sections of this chapter, more detail about the nature of severe disabilities is provided by looking at the traditional categories and groups of students with severe disabilities and by examining significant characteristics that are displayed by many members of this population. We realize the danger of negative stereotypes being associated with these descriptions and urge readers not to draw erroneous conclusions about the potential of these individuals. We hope that these descriptions will not be interpreted as being demeaning or derogatory, nor as suggesting that people with severe disabilities are without many positive qualities. Nevertheless, it is important to acquire information pertinent to the population that is referred to as having severe disabilities. To provide a more complete picture and allow the reader to see some of the potential of students with severe disabilities, findings about the abilities and achievements of students with severe disabilities are discussed at the end of this chapter.

Mental Disability Categories and Syndromes

In many parts of society, including community agencies and school systems, several different categories may be used to refer to students with severe disabilities. Brief discussions of some of the more prevalent conditions are presented here.

Moderate, Severe, and Profound Mental Disabilities

Prior to the 1992 AAMR definition (and still within the DSM-IV manual), persons diagnosed as being mentally disabled were placed in subcategories based primarily on their measured level of intelligence, that is, their IQ range (Grossman, 1973, 1977, 1983; Heber, 1959, 1961). More recently, the AAMR created a new multidimensional classification system that eliminated the subcategories and instead requires an evaluation of individuals in multiple areas to determine strengths, weaknesses, and optimal levels of support. Although no longer a part of the AAMR system, the traditional system will likely be used for many years to come. Therefore, a brief discussion of the traditional terms and what they imply is presented next.

Persons with *moderate mental disabilities* score above 35 to 40 and below 50 to 55 on traditional intelligence tests. Generally, individuals who fall within this classification are capable of learning many basic skills in the areas of communication, self-help, functional academics (or in some cases more advanced academics), domestic skills, community functioning skills, and vocational skills. For example, many adults with a moderate mental disability are able to manage all their own daily self-care needs; prepare some foods for themselves and others; demonstrate adequate body control, including good gross and fine motor development; participate in common conversations; have some basic functional reading skills; interact cooperatively or competitively with others; make purchases in a grocery store, use money with fair accuracy; and carry out many occupational routines. An individual classified as moderately mentally disabled might also be capable of self-initiation and show an ability to assume a degree of responsibility (Grossman, 1983). Based on some concepts of severe disabilities, not all persons who have a moderate mental disability would be considered to have a severe disability.

Historically, individuals have been classified as having a *severe mental disability* if their level of adaptive behavior is relatively lower than that described for persons with moderate mental disabilities and if their measured IQ is between 20 to 25 and 35 to 40 (Grossman, 1983). Ability examples of adults with severe mental disabilities include being able to eat adequately with a fork or spoon (but may need help with cutting); dressing and bathing with some supervision; using the toilet independently; and washing hands and face without help (but may have to be told or reminded to do so).

The individual's physical ability is generally good and he or she is probably able to walk, run, hop, skip, dance, and maybe skate, sled, or jump rope. The person with a severe mental disability probably does not possess many academic skills, such as reading, but may be able to recognize some words and common signs. He may know that money is of value, but may not be able to state the specific value of coins. McLean, Brady, and McLean (1996) conducted a large-scale investigation of the communication abilities of individuals classified as severely mentally disabled and found their abilities in this area to be very diverse. The majority of adults and nearly half of the children could communicate symbolically and many used multisymbol or multiword expressions. McLean et al. found that the use of symbolic communication increased among older individuals.

An individual diagnosed as being *profoundly mentally disabled* falls within the most severe range of mental disability. Often these individuals are referred to as having "the most severe" disabilities or "significant disabilities" and have IQs below 20 to 25 points and developmental ages under 12 months on a standardized test of intelligence, if they are testable at all. It is difficult to provide a typical profile of an individual with a profound mental disability because there is such an extreme degree of variability among the individuals so classified. Some persons are capable of relatively independent functioning in common self-care activities, such as eating and toileting, and may also possess functional skills in other domains of development, such as vocational and domestic skills. Others in this group do not speak, have very limiting sensory and motor impairments, are nonambulatory, and tend not to be very attentive or responsive to environmental stimuli (Thompson & Guess, 1989). Many of these persons, however, demonstrate the ability to learn and are capable of at least partial participation in normal daily activities.

Some studies of individuals classified as profoundly mentally disabled have revealed the complex and variable nature of these individuals. For example, Guess and his colleagues have investigated behavior states of persons with profound mental retardation. These states are a description of the individual's condition that affects the ability to interact with the environment (Guess et al., 1988, 1990; Guess, Roberts, et al., 1993; Guess, Siegel-Causey, et al., 1993; Guess & Siegel-Causey, 1995; Guy, Guess, & Ault, 1993). In these studies, researchers have shown that the behavior state directly affects alertness and responsiveness and indirectly affects learning and development. Individuals with profound mental disabilities can be described according to their behavior state at a given time. States include sleep states (asleep-inactive, asleep-active), indeterminate states (drowsy, daze), preferred awake states (awake inactive-alert, awake active-alert), and other awake states (awake-active/stereotypy, crying/agitated). Using these states, the researchers have been able to develop individual profiles and have noted the consistency of state patterns of individuals across observations. These researchers have developed a procedure to analyze states and environmental conditions with the intent of maximizing the learning of students with profound disabilities (Ault, Guy, Guess, Bashinski, & Roberts, 1995).

For most individuals classified as having moderate, severe, or profound mental disabilities, the etiology of their conditions is identifiable. Batshaw and Shapiro (2002) identified etiological categories and percents of conditions associated with them. These are presented in Table 1–1.

Syndromes of Mental Disabilities and Other Conditions Associated with Severe Disabilities

Many individuals who have a mental disability exhibit clusters of similar physical and behavioral characteristics and have common etiologies. When this occurs, these people are said to have a certain *syndrome* of mental disability. There are hundreds of recognized syndromes and obviously not all can be discussed here. However, several that are likely to be encountered by professionals working with individuals with severe disabilities are briefly described. The reader interested in more information about certain syndromes should turn to more complete references on this topic (e.g., Batshaw, 2002; Dykens, Hodapp, & Finucane, 2000). Hodapp and Fidler (1999) argue that knowledge of the characteristics associated with specific syndromes could be very useful in designing educational interventions.

Table 1–1 Identifiable Etiologies in Children with Severe Mental Retardation

Chromosomal disorders	22%
Genetic syndromes	21%
Developmental brain abnormalities	9%
Inborn errors of metabolism (or neurodegenerative disorders)	8%
Congenital infections	4%
Familial retardation	6%
Perinatal causes	4%
Postnatal causes	5%
Unknown	21%

Source: "Mental Retardation." In M. L. Batshaw (Ed.), *Children with Disabilities* (5th Ed., pp. 287–305), by M. L. Batshaw and B. Shapiro, 2002. Reprinted by permission of author. Baltimore: Paul H. Brookes.

Down Syndrome

Down syndrome (DS) is one of the most common syndromes associated with mental disability. It has an incidence of about 0.92 per 1,000 live births, with a much higher incidence among women older than 45, about 1 in 20 (Roizen, 2001). Over 90% of the time it occurs due to the presence of an extra chromosome 21. Children with DS are usually smaller than average and have slower physical, motor, language, and mental development. Some do not fall within the range of mental disabilities, but most are in the mild to moderate range and some are classified as severely mentally retarded (Benke, Carver, & Donahue, 1995; Pueschel, 1990, 1992; Roizen, 2001). Although, as Pueschel (1992) points out, persons with DS are like people without disabilities in many ways, certain physical features are characteristic of the syndrome and can be used for clinical diagnosis. These usually include a flattening of the back of the head; slanting eyelids; small folds of skin at the inner corners of the eyes; depressed nasal bridge; smaller ears, mouth, hands, and feet; and decreased muscle tone.

According to Roizen (2001), children with Down syndrome have an increased risk of abnormalities in almost every organ in the system. Typical medical complications are listed in Table 1–2. In the first 5 years of life, 87% of children with Down syndrome without congenital heart disease survive, as do 76% *with* congenital heart disease. More than half of individuals with Down syndrome will survive into their 50s, and 13.5% will be alive at 68.

In terms of behavioral characteristics, Roizen (2001) reported that children with Down syndrome have language delays that become apparent between 18 months and 2 years of age; but receptive language is generally better than their expressive language. Although children with Down syndrome are often characterized as being amiable and happy, they actually have temperament profiles much like

Table 1–2 Medical Complications in Down Syndrome

Disorder	*% Affected*
Congenital heart defect	66
Endocardial cushion defect	19
Ventricular septal defect	15
Atrial septal defect	14
Other	18
Ophthalmic disorders (often more than one)	60
Refractive errors	35
Strabismus	27
Nystagmus	20
Blepharitis	9
Tear duct obstruction	6
Cataracts	5
Ptosis	5
Hearing loss	66
Endocrine abnormalities	50–90
Subclinical hypothyroidism	30–50
Overt hypothyroidism	4
Diabetes	0.4
Growth problems	50–90
Obesity	60
Short stature	50–90
Orthopedic abnormalities	16
Subclinical atlantoaxial subluxation	15
Symptomatic atlantoaxial subluxation	1
Dental problems, periodontal disease, malocclusion	60–100
Gastrointestinal malformations	5
Celiac disease	5
Epilepsy	6
Leukemia	0.01
Skin conditions	50
Alzheimer's disease after 40 years	15–20

Source: "Down Syndrome," by N. J. Roizen, 2001. In M. L. Batshaw (Ed.), *Children with Disabilities* (5th Ed., pp. 307–320). Baltimore: Paul H. Brookes Publishing Co. Reprinted with permission.

those of other children. Nevertheless, small percentages may demonstrate aggression, ADHD, oppositional disorders, stereotyped behaviors, phobias, autistic-like characteristics, eating disorders, self-injurious behaviors, or Tourette syndrome. According to Hodapp and Fidler (1999), persons with DS perform better on visual versus auditory processing tasks. Their visual memory is better than their auditory memory, and they can generally do well on learning sight word reading, even when they are young. They have relatively lower rates of maladaptive behavior when compared to other persons with developmental delays.

Fragile X Syndrome

In recent years, fragile X syndrome (FXS) has been recognized as the most commonly inherited genetic syndrome that results in mental disabilities, with its overall prevalence being estimated at 1 in 1,000 males. Almost 5% of children with mental retardation receiving special education may be diagnosed as having FXS (Meyer & Batshaw, 2001). FXS is transmitted on the sex-linked (or X-linked) chromosome of the mother to a child and is manifested more often by boys than by girls. When inherited by boys, about 80% of them will have mental disabilities ranging from mild to severe. Girls are affected less often (about 30% of the time), and usually their disabilities are mild learning disabilities, not general mental disabilities (Edelson, 1995a; Hagerman, 1994).

Meyer and Batshaw (2001) summarize much of the research literature on characteristics of persons with FSX. Physical characteristics of males with FXS include a long, narrow face; prominent jaw and forehead; large, protruding ears; high, arched palate; hyperextensible joints; flat feet; and enlarged testicles. Many tend to be hypotonic and lack coordination. They may grow rapidly, but tend to have short stature as adults. Individuals with FXS have various medical conditions, including ophthalmic disorders (strabismus, myopia, ptosis, nystagmus), orthopedic disorders (flat feet, scoliosis, loose joints), serous otitis media, mitral valve prolapse, and seizure disorders.

According to Meyer and Batshaw, learning is easier for persons with FXS when the whole task is presented at once, instead of teaching separate parts of a task. They are weak in communication and social skills, but relatively strong in daily living skills. They often have a delightful sense of humor. There are usually speech and language delays, and often echolalia occurs. Their speech is also often cluttered and perseverative. They also tend to have difficulty with auditory memory and receptive language. Behaviorally, these individuals tend to have stereotyped behaviors, such as hand flapping, lack of eye contact, tactile defensiveness, hyperactivity, and inattention. Some may exhibit aggression and anxiety. The behaviors of children with FXS are often considered similar to those who are classified as having pervasive developmental disorders. Although less than 7% of the children with autism have been found to have the FXS mutation, a significant percentage of individuals with FXS (15% to 28%) meet the American Psychiatric Association diagnosis for autism. Although the autism–fragile X syndrome link has been debated, many FXS children demonstrate characteristics like children with autism. Individuals with FXS often benefit from a structured learning environment, with instructions that are concrete, clear, and accompanied by visual cues and prompts (Meyer & Batshaw, 2001).

Fetal Alcohol Syndrome

Fetal alcohol syndrome (FAS) and the less severe condition, alcohol-related neurodevelopmental disorder (ARND) (formerly referred to as fetal alcohol effects), form the largest class of birth impairments that are 100% preventable (The Arc, 1992; Wunsch, Conlon, & Scheidt, 2001). The condition results from mothers consuming alcohol during their pregnancy, although the precise amount of alcohol consumption required to cause the condition is not known. Furthermore, Wunsch et al. point out that it is difficult to isolate the influence of specific substances on fetal development, because often multiple influences are possible. For example, a woman using one drug such as alcohol may also be smoking, using other drugs, receiving inadequate nutrition, and not receiving adequate prenatal medical care.

The most critical impact on the unborn child occurs during the first trimester of pregnancy when the alcohol may affect the way cells grow and are organized. During this time the brain will be particularly sensitive, and the alcohol can diminish the number of brain cells that develop. Consumed in the later stages of pregnancy, alcohol can result in fetal distress, reduced growth, poor central nervous system development, or miscarriage. FAS occurs in about one in every 750 live births and ARND in about 1 in every 100 births. The incidence in women who continuously abuse alcohol is much higher, with about 30% of their births resulting in FAS (Chavez, 1995).

According to Wunsch et al. (2001), FAS is a "delineated diagnosis resulting in neurobehavioral abnormalities including developmental delay, growth problems, and other physical effects" (p. 111). The diagnosis of FAS is defined by four criteria: maternal drinking during pregnancy, a characteristic facial appearance, growth retardation, and brain damage. School age children may show difficulties in learning and behavior. The diagnosis ARND may be applied if there are signs of neurodevelopmental problems without the other criteria being present. FAS and ARND account for about 5% of congenital anomalies and about 10% to 20% of all cases of mild mental disabilities, but the range of intelligence may be from normal to more severe levels of mental disability.

Children with FAS may have a small head, narrow eye slits, a flat mid-face, and a low nasal bridge. In addition to having a mental disability or developmental delay, as babies they may have sleeping problems, be restless and irritable, and have sucking problems. Developmental delays generally become apparent in the first 2 years of life, particularly in the areas of speech and language. Verbal learning may be most impaired. Intellectual problems may also be seen in planning, sequencing, self-monitoring, and goal-directed behavior. Developing appropriate social interactions can be a problem, and deficits in adaptive behavior may occur. Behavior and emotional problems may also occur (Wunsch et al., 2001).

Prader–Willi Syndrome

The most commonly recognized characteristics of individuals with Prader–Willi syndrome (PWS) are their propensity for overeating, low muscle tone, and obesity (Batshaw, 2002; Scott, Smith, Hendricks, & Polloway, 1999). The condition is not inherited, but is due to a chromosomal anomaly on chromosome number 15 and occurs in about 1 of every 10,000 births. Shortly after birth, infants with PWS will show extreme hypotonia (weak muscle tone), a weak cry, poor sucking and swallowing, and little interest in food. Between ages 1 and 3 years, they will develop insatiable appetites, become very preoccupied with food, will want to eat continuously, and develop life-threatening obesity. At this time they will start to show delayed psychomotor activity, cognitive delay, and emotional–behavioral problems (Scott et al., 1999).

The syndrome often results in a moderate mental disability, but measured IQs have ranged from 40 to over 100. In addition to being overweight, individuals with PWS are short, have small hands and feet, have underdeveloped sexual characteristics, and may exhibit behavior problems. The child with PWS is likely to have delayed motor development and will walk later than most children. Speech and language problems are also common, with articulation often being noted as a problem. As they get older, especially when they enter puberty, behavioral problems often occur, including fluctuations in mood and temper tantrums. Efforts to inhibit eating and access to food often spur temperamental outbursts. They may also be stubborn and at times can become very depressed. They may also have impaired speech and experience language delays (Scott et al., 1999).

According to Lacy (1996), people with Prader–Willi have a three-part problem with food: they are always hungry, they gain weight easily, and they cannot exercise as easily as others. Therefore, it is very important to manage food intake and limit it to three balanced meals and one snack per day with low-caloric foods. Because of the individual's insatiable desire to eat, without strict control, obesity will develop. Since individuals with PWS do not exhibit the typical growth spurt that occurs during adolescence for most people, the proportion of weight to height will continue to increase. The problem of being overweight during adulthood will be much greater than in childhood and will be more difficult to manage.

Intervention for individuals with PWS should focus on weight management and educational development, with a later focus on transition planning. If weight can be managed, a normal life expectancy may be possible. If weight is not adequately managed, obesity may lead to lung and heart disease, diabetes, high blood pressure, and other disorders. It must be understood that weight management can be very challenging. Individuals with PWS have been known to obtain food in a number of ways, including stealing, raiding the refrigerator in the middle of the night, taking food from classmates, and searching through waste containers. Their hunger is painful and constant and leads to an unceasing pursuit of food. Weight gain is caused not only by overeating, but by a low metabolic rate, lethargy, and a low energy level. Lacy recommends early control of food during the childhood years. Moderate exercises are also recommended. Because the individual typically has poor muscle tone and weak muscles, low-impact exercises such as walking, swimming, and jumping rope are recommended (Prader–Willi Syndrome Association—USA, 1998).

Angelman Syndrome

Individuals with Angelman syndrome usually are severely to profoundly mentally disabled. As with Prader–Willi syndrome, the condition occurs due to a chromosomal anomaly in which a portion of chromosome 15 is missing (Edelson, 1995a). The prevalence of this condition is very rare, perhaps 1 in 25,000, but as a relatively new syndrome (it was first identified in 1965), there may be many individuals with the condition who have not been diagnosed. Some of the characteristics of the syndrome include jerky body movements and stiff-legged walking. Individuals with this syndrome tend to have common facial features, such as a wide smiling mouth, a thin upper lip, and deep-set eyes. They often have fair hair and skin and light blue eyes. About 80% of the time they have epilepsy.

Diagnosis of the condition often occurs during infancy when feeding problems and poor sleeping patterns occur. Individuals with Angelman syndrome sometimes exhibit behaviors that are similar to autism (see later discussion), such as little or no speech, hand flapping, short attention spans, and motor delays. Sometimes they are hyperactive and may engage in hair pulling and biting. In contrast to individuals with autism, however, they may be very sociable, happy, and affectionate. Sometimes they show an unusually happy disposition and laugh frequently. Many children with the syndrome require far less sleep than does a normal child. They seem to enjoy the company of others, but often do not interact with them directly (Angelman Syndrome Support Group, United Kingdom, no date).

Dual Diagnosis (Mental Retardation and Mental Illness)

As we use the terms in this textbook, it is important to understand that mental disabilities (or mental retardation) and mental illness are different conditions. Most people with mental retardation do not exhibit mental illness, and vice versa. Having a severe disability, even a severe or profound degree of mental disability, does not mean that an individual is mentally ill. Having said that, however, it is possible for some individuals to have a *dual diagnosis*—to have both a cognitive disability and some form of mental illness, and, in fact, individuals with mental retardation experience a higher rate of psychiatric disorders than do persons with typical development. Because of the developmental disability, however, it is sometimes difficult to discern the presence of a mental illness. These individuals form a very heterogeneous group (Reber, 2001).

The cause of most psychiatric disorders among individuals with mental retardation is likely a complex interaction of biological (including genetic), environmental, and psychosocial factors. Reber (2001) notes,

> When one considers the psychosocial contribution to the cause of psychiatric disorders, the chronic stress and limited opportunities inherent in the life experiences of most children with mental retardation cannot be overemphasized. Phenomena such as ridicule and rejection by peers and society at large; repeated experience of failure at school; limited opportunities to participate in the recreational, social, cultural, and community learning experiences of peers; confused and prejudicial responses to emerging sexuality; and foreclosed or vague future plans all tend to make a person feel ashamed, inadequate, dependent, and without self-esteem. (p. 350)

Conditions such as family disturbances or social adversity would have a greater impact on individuals with cognitive limitations because of their inability to understand the circumstances of the situation, weaker problem-solving abilities, greater need for support, and less ability to cope with stress.

According to Reber (2001) and Reiss (1993), various types of mental illness may affect people with mental disabilities. These include:

- *Mood disorders*. It is estimated that 5% to 15% of persons with mental retardation are affected by mood disorders, including dysthymia (chronic low-grade depressive symptoms), major depression, mania, and bipolar disorder (manic depression). Symptoms of mood disorders can include sleep or appetite problems, noncompliance, social withdrawal, aggression, irritability, self-injury, or crying spells.
- *Anxiety disorders*. The prevalence of anxiety disorders may be as high as 25% among persons with mental retardation. These disorders are characterized by displays of emotional uneasiness, arousal, fear, and a need to escape. Anxiety disorders include phobias, separation anxiety disorder, social phobia, panic disorder, generalized anxiety disorder, and obsessive–compulsive disorder (OCD).
- *Psychosis*. Psychosis represents the most extreme form of psychiatric disorders and includes schizophrenia, severe depression, mania, and delirium. The symptoms of psychosis include confused thinking, delusions, and hallucinations.
- *Posttraumatic stress disorder*. A stressful experience that presents the possibility of harm or death and that is associated with feelings of intense fear and helplessness may lead to recurrent recollections of the experience, nightmares, and intense emotional distress when the person is in circumstances that are reminders of the event. This condition is diagnosed as posttraumatic stress disorder.

One difficulty with the determination of mental illness among persons with intellectual disabilities is differentiating whether the problem observed is a function of the mental disability or the mental illness. Because many persons with cognitive disabilities do not have adequate verbal abilities to describe or explain their symptoms, interviews with family members and caregivers and careful observation are often required to reach a diagnosis of a particular psychiatric disorder. Standardized rating scales that indicate the occurrence of atypical behaviors along with functional behavioral assessments are useful to determine the behavioral patterns of the individual and to then develop an intervention plan. Interventions consider both the developmental level of the individual and the specific psychiatric diagnosis. Comprehensive interventions may incorporate one or more forms of intervention, including an appropriate educational program, communication or language therapy, psychotherapy, behavioral intervention, and the use of different medications (Reber, 2001).

There are often discrepancies in estimations of the prevalence of persons with dual diagnosis, which range from about 10% to 40% of persons with mental disabilities (Borthwick-Duffy & Eyman, 1990; Reiss, 1990, 1993). The majority of persons who are dually diagnosed fall into the range of mild to moderate mental disabilities, tend to be older rather than younger persons, are about equally male and female, and come from different ethnic and racial backgrounds (Jacobson, 1990; Reiss, 1993).

Autism

Autism is classified as a pervasive developmental disorder (PDD). Besides autism, other PDDs include Asperger's syndrome (discussed below), pervasive developmental disorder–not otherwise specified (PDD–NOS), Rett syndrome, and childhood disintegrative disorder (CDD). The common condition associated with all PDDs is impaired social reciprocity. Additionally, there are generally weaknesses in communication, repetitive behaviors (such as stereotypies or self-injurious behaviors), very narrow interests, limited imagination or play behavior, and ritualistic behaviors (Towbin, Mauk, & Batshaw, 2001; Wetherby & Prizant, 2000). Towbin et al. states, "The cause of PDDs [is] developmental brain abnormalities with significant genetic influence. It appears unlikely that autism is the result of infections, adverse nutrition, or maternal stress" (p. 371). The terms *autism spectrum disorders* and *pervasive developmental disorders* are used synonymously (Wetherby & Prizant, 2000).

Individuals who are diagnosed as autistic are often considered to have a severe disability, but the range of ability within this syndrome is broad. The majority of persons with autism are classifiable as being mentally disabled (because of a low measured IQ), but this is not always the case. Some individuals with autism might function at or near a level of independence. Although their physical features often do not suggest that they have a severe disability, their disability is manifested in the nature of their language and by their personal and social behavior. While there is a range of autistic characteristics, individuals who are diagnosed as autistic show problems in three main areas: social interaction, communication, and stereotyped behavior problems (American Psychiatric Association, 1994). They behave in a manner that shows little emotion and excludes much of the rest of the social world.

According to the Autism Society of America (2002), autism is the most common of the pervasive developmental disorders, affecting an estimated 2 to 6 per 1,000 individuals. This means that approximately 1.5 million Americans are currently believed to have some form of autism, and the number is increasing at a rate of 10% to 17% per year. The condition is four times more prevalent in boys than girls and is equally distributed across racial, ethnic, and socioeconomic levels.

A notable aspect of most persons with autism is their lack of social reciprocity. They often do not interact with others with the type and degree of emotionalism that typically occurs between two people. They appear to lack an awareness of the existence or the feelings of others and do not look to others for comfort during times of distress or discomfort. They do not learn many social skills, such as waving bye-bye, through imitation. Often children with autism do not engage in social play with other children and have difficulty forming close peer relationships or friendships (American Psychiatric Association, 1994; Volkmar, 1987).

Some persons who are diagnosed as autistic demonstrate behavioral characteristics that functionally increase the severity of their disability. For example, some display stereotyped movements such as hand flicking, spinning, or complex body movements. Or they may show an uncommon preoccupation with some particular item or items (or parts of items) for which there does not seem to be any reason. They may, for example, insist on carrying around a blanket or a particular book, or they may show unusual fascination with items by continuously touching them, feeling them, spinning them, or smelling them. There is apparently no limit to the types of items that may be of interest.

Following strict routines or being rigid in many daily activities may also be important to individuals who are autistic. As a part of this *insistence on sameness,* they tend to want aspects of their environment to be arranged in a certain order and daily events to proceed in a predictable manner. In their regular activities their interests and attention do not vary. For example, they may insist on eating a certain food or watching a certain television show at a set time. If there is some variation in this routine, the person may become very upset, even to the point of having a temper tantrum.

Persons with autism often show a severe lack of language development. Those with the most severe degree of disability may not communicate at all, although these are the minority. However, even those who do communicate do so in a limited or abbreviated fashion, usually showing various abnormal speech and language characteristics. For example, their body language does not express the typical features that appear in normal communication. They may not make or sustain eye contact, vary their facial features, use gestures, or change their body posture when conversing. These unique communicative characteristics can often be traced back to the individual's infancy. Very early in life the child may have begun to show a lack of responsiveness when held and talked to by parents or others (Paul, 1987).

Persons with autism also generally show atypical characteristics in the production, form, and content of their speech. Speech sounds may have inappropriate volume, pitch, rate, rhythm, or tone; be monotonous; have a melodylike quality; or be high pitched. The speech that is produced may be stereotyped or repetitive, and the individual may use inappropriate parts of speech, saying, for example, "You go to the store?" when he means "I want to go to the store." In other cases the meaning of the speech that is produced may be difficult to interpret, especially for someone who does not know the individual. Sometimes these individuals say particular sentences or phrases over and over, which the context of the statements does not appear to warrant. Usually, persons with autism will not participate in conversations of normal length and quality. They seem to be incapable of "reading" the social situation or participating actively in it.

An interesting hypothesis that has recently been proposed about people with autism is referred to as the *theory of mind* (Baron-Cohen, 1995; Frith, 1997). According to this theory, people with autism have difficulty understanding the perspective of other people. They do not understand that others have different plans, thoughts, and points of view. They also have difficulty understanding that others have beliefs, attitudes, and emotions. Furthermore, according to this theory, they cannot comprehend that a person might not know the answer to something and become upset when they ask a question that cannot be answered.

There is no consistent, identifiable cause of autism. Early theories attributed autistic characteristics to emotional distress that occurred between mothers and infants during early infancy, but these theories were never substantiated. As noted by Edelson (1995b), more recent research suggests that there are a variety of possible biologic or biochemical causes of autism. Studies of twins and of autistic children of autistic fathers indicate that genetics may play a role. It has also been found that the rubella virus and the cytomegalovirus affecting the mother in the first trimester increase the occurrence of autism. Finally, there is speculation that toxins and pollutants in the environment may increase the chance of a child being autistic. Edelson cites a finding about a small town in which homes that were downwind of a factory that made sunglasses had an above average number of cases of children with autism. It has also been noted that the incidence of autism is higher among the population of persons with known brain injuries and occurs more often with children who have identifiable chromosomal anomalies (Schor, 1990).

Asperger's Syndrome

Initially we must make the point that individuals with Asperger's syndrome (AS) are not considered to have a severe disability in that they are very capable of independent functioning. However, we include a discussion of these individuals here because of the unique challenges that they face and because, as Marks, Schrader, Longaker, and Levine (2000) indicated, they are often brought to the attention of special education teachers in an effort to find ways to meet those needs.

Asperger's syndrome is classified as a PDD. AS was originally identified in Austria in the 1940s by Hans Asperger, a psychiatrist, but has not been widely discussed in the American special education literature until recently. Although studied in Europe for about the last 20 years, AS has only recently become more recognized in the United States and is now listed and characterized in the *Diagnostic and Statistical Manual IV* of the American Psychiatric Association (DSM-IV). Safran (2001) speculated that AS will become more widely recognized by special education professionals in the United States because it may have a relatively high, albeit unrecognized, prevalence rate. In Sweden, it is now estimated to be 0.7% of the general population, suggesting a large number of unidentified individuals in schools who may need support services.

As might be expected, persons with AS have a number of characteristics similar to persons with autism. The most important distinction between children with AS and those with autism is usually intelligence level: persons with AS typically have average to above average intellectual abilities, whereas most persons with autism demonstrate significantly low levels of measured intelligence and adaptive behavior. Still, a differential diagnosis between children with AS and those with high-functioning autism is sometimes difficult to make.

Even though intelligent and often academically gifted, individuals with AS have social interactions that are atypical in many ways and that present them with many difficulties. They seem to have a lack of interest in what's going on around them, they may engage in stereotypic behavior, and they have a tendency to be absorbed in their own interests regardless of others' responses. They often fail to use body language to express themselves, do not share interests with others, and do not engage in emotional reciprocity. They have difficulty reading facial cues or understanding the feelings of others and in learning to model appropriate social behavior, possibly because they do not understand this behavior. They may engage in long pedantic speeches about esoteric topics and fail to recognize that the person to whom they are speaking does not have any interest in the topic. Other pertinent characteristics include speech peculiarities, motor clumsiness, and nonverbal communication problems (limited gestures, clumsy body language, and inappropriate expressions).

Sometimes persons with AS may exhibit violent behavior, which may be due to an inability to understand others' feelings or to a lack of empathy for others. Sometimes depression occurs, which may be due to a recognition of their difference from other persons. They may also become easily stressed because of their inflexibility. Worst of all, because of their uncommon behavior and social characteristics, they may face peer rejection throughout their lives (Bock & Myles, 1999; Safran, 2001).

Marks et al. (2000) interviewed three adolescent students with Asperger's syndrome, their parents, and their teachers to gain greater knowledge of their lives and the difficulties that they encountered. They found that the individuals had similarities and differences. All had deficits in social interactions, social communication, and social imagination. Each had unique and narrow interests that bordered on obsessions and excluded interests in other areas. Unlike persons with autism, their intense areas of interests were more with ideas (e.g., social fairness, getting good grades, measuring objects) than with objects. Within their schools, they were all socially isolated and lonely. They were very able academically, but because their interests were narrow, two of the three did not perform as well in school as they could have. The third had an obsession with getting good grades and was considered an ideal student. When threatened with less than a perfect grade, however, this student would become panicked and threaten to leave school.

The social isolation of these adolescents and their lack of friends were not due to a disinterest in friendships, but were a result of their misunderstanding of what constituted appropriate social skills. They did not know how to interact with other persons their own age. They would either ignore them or would go to extremes to try and gain attention and social recognition. In either case, they were isolated by their peers. Marks et al. (2000) suggest that what they found indicated two directions that should be taken with regard to individuals with Asperger's syndrome. First they suggest that the students should be specifically instructed in the development of social skills. Second, their classmates should be educated about the characteristics of Asperger's syndrome and be helped to understand the behavior of their classmates with this condition.

Dual Sensory Impairments

The least common classification of disability is dual sensory impairment or the inadequate functioning of both the visual and auditory systems. Nationally, only 1,840 deaf–blind students between the ages of 6 and 21 were reported to the federal government as being served in the public schools during the 1999–2000 school year (U.S. Department of Education, 2001). This low prevalence rate translates to only 3 of every 1,000 children with disabilities being classified as deaf–blind.

It is important to understand that people with dual sensory impairments vary greatly in their development and functioning, and even though all would need some degree of support, not all persons so classified are considered to have a severe disability. Over 90% of persons who are deaf–blind have some functional vision and/or hearing, and many are of average or above average intelligence, as was Helen Keller (Fredericks & Baldwin, 1987). Our concern, then, will be directed more toward persons with dual sensory impairments that are relatively more severe and who simultaneously function with a degree of mental disability. In this most severe form, the person has very limited social and communicative abilities and needs many structured learning opportunities to acquire various daily living skills.

A significant characteristic of persons with severe deaf–blindness is that they often attempt to create a degree of self-stimulation, because normal sources of environmental stimulation are lost or diminished due to the nature of the disability. To create the stimulation, there is a turning inward to oneself and the production of self-stimulatory behavior. It may appear that the individual is passive, noncompliant, or unresponsive to overtures from people or the environment in general. There may be a lack of interaction with others, and often inappropriate repetitive or stereotyped behavior, such as hand flapping, finger flicking, or head rocking, will occur. It is important to realize that this behavior is probably occurring to satisfy the need for sensory–physical stimulation, which is a basic need of all persons (Smithdas, 1981; Van Dijk, 1985).

There are several causes of multiple sensory impairments. One of the most well-known is rubella, or German measles. If a woman contracts the disease when she is in the early stages of pregnancy, particularly in the first 8 weeks, there may result some degree of hearing and visual loss as well as other disabilities, including mental disabilities, congenital heart lesions, neurological disorders, and seizure disorders (Bleck, 1982b; Van Dijk & Nelson, 1996–97). During the mid-1960s, prior to the development of immunization against rubella, a large number of children were born with multiple disabling conditions some months after a rubella epidemic. Today, because people are usually immunized against this disease when they are children, it is a less common source of multiple disabilities.

More common today than rubella as a cause of deaf–blindness is Usher syndrome. This syndrome is due to an autosomal-recessive genetic disorder, which means that both parents must be carriers of the condition but will not manifest it themselves. The child with Usher syndrome will be born deaf and will gradually acquire other disabilities, including blindness and mental disability. Genetic research has determined that at least 10 subtypes of Usher syndrome exist. They are characterized by variations in the progressive loss of vision (Scacheri, 2002; Van Dijk & Nelson, 1996–97).

It is not adequate to treat a student with a dual sensory impairment as a blind person who also has a hearing loss or as a deaf person who also has a visual loss. The unique condition of this disability requires that the individual be considered holistically and that a transdisciplinary model of intervention be developed (Downing & Eichinger, 1990; Orelove & Sobsey, 1996). Consideration needs to be given to the degree of residual vision and hearing that exists in order to maximize the functional use of these abilities.

Besides dual sensory impairments, persons with severe disabilities often have multiple disabilities. For example, a person with a profound mental disability is likely to have cerebral palsy and epilepsy associated with her cognitive disability, as well as having single or dual sensory impairments. When an individual has multiple impairments, it is essential that a holistic approach be used to develop an appropriate educational program. To better understand the different conditions that contribute to multiple disabilities, there is a separate discussion later in this chapter under Physical Characteristics.

Characteristics of Persons with Severe Disabilities

The descriptions presented in the previous sections should clearly indicate that students with severe disabilities have diverse characteristics, abilities, and needs. This is true both within and between different traditional categories. However, some traits occur with relatively high frequency and these deserve close attention. Understanding these traits will help us to better understand the needs of individuals with severe disabilities and how to address these needs. Key characteristics of students with disabilities are discussed in the following sections. We will examine the learning, personal–social, and physical characteristics that bear on the lives of these individuals.

Learning Characteristics

Students who are classified as having a severe disability have significantly more difficulty learning than do most other individuals. Although many students with very challenging disabilities or unique needs such as dual sensory impairments, multiple physical disabilities, Asperger's syndrome, or even autism may have normal or above average intelligence, our concern is with those who have limited cognitive ability. Quantitative measures (i.e., IQ scores) as well as qualitative indicators (such as the ability to demonstrate independent adaptive behavior) indicate that they are functioning below average in cognitive ability. In practical terms this means that they are weak in certain learning characteristics, resulting in greater amounts of time being required to learn skills, greater difficulty in learning more complex skills, and overall fewer skills being learned as compared to others (Brown et al., 1983). While it must be stressed that it is possible for many skills to be learned, the number and type of skills will not be comparable to those learned by most individuals. This fact has implications for the necessary relevance of skills that teachers and others teach. Relevant learning characteristics have been explained in more detail in various references (Bierne-Smith, Ittenbach, & Patton, 2002; Brown et al., 1983; Ellis, 1963, 1979; Mercer & Snell, 1977; Westling, 1986).

Attention to Stimuli, Dimensions, and Cues

A significant learning difficulty experienced by many students with severe disabilities is determining what particular part of the environment or what particular stimulus or aspect of the stimulus should be attended to. In other words, they may have difficulty in learning what feature of an item or situation gives the information necessary for correct action. An example of this would be looking at a set of keys and learning which key to select to open a particular door. In a period of time before the selection becomes automatic (i.e., is learned), the learner must decide first which dimension of the keys should be considered (size? color? shape? position?) and then which cue within the selected dimension indicates the correct choice (large or small? bronze or silver? jagged or smooth? middle, right, or left?). Learning this two-step system takes longer for persons with cognitive disabilities.

Observational and Incidental Learning

Observational learning is learning through watching and imitating a model, that is, another person. Incidental learning is learning something that was not taught directly, but that might be learned if attended to. Students with severe disabilities benefit from these forms of learning less well than do students who do not have disabilities. Part of the reason for this may be their weakness in attending, as described above. Another reason may be the environment and the instructional programs in which they have been placed. In other words, there may have been little opportunity for observing and imitating others or experiencing many interesting situations.

Memory

Remembering skills and information that have been learned previously also presents a challenge to persons with severe disabilities. The major problems in this area appear to be related to being inadequately exposed to the learning condition initially, having insufficient opportunity to practice or use the information or skill after it is initially learned, and then not using strategies adequately to pull the information from long-term memory for use when needed. As a result of this learning characteristic, important skills that are not adequately practiced over an extended period of time usually need to be taught again.

Skill Synthesis

Most individuals who do not have intellectual disabilities learn separate skills such as reading, writing, and arithmetic and then pull these skills together in an organized, useful way to undertake a particular activity, such as grocery shopping. For students who have cognitive disabilities, however, the ability to synthesize information and skills is very limited. They often fail to see the relation of one bit of information to another. Therefore, we cannot teach isolated skills and expect them to be cohesively organized for application. Instead, more specific instruction is necessary, and relevant skills must be taught in clusters to better ensure meaningfulness.

Generalization

One of the most significant learning weaknesses of students with severe cognitive disabilities is their weak ability to generalize acquired skills—to apply what was learned in one situation to another situation (Haring, 1988). Generalization is usually considered the demonstration of skills among different people, using different objects or materials, in different settings, and at different times. It is not usually sufficient to learn how to do something in one isolated location and nowhere else if the skill is expected to be demonstrated in a new situation. Because the ability to generalize is often very important, specific instructional strategies must usually be undertaken to get it to occur (Fox, 1989).

Self-Regulation

Because students with severe cognitive disabilities often do not apply what they have learned to other environments or situations, it may be concluded that they have difficulty in self-regulation or identifying the appropriate action that should be taken under a certain condition (Whitman, 1990). To self-regulate, an individual must monitor his own behavior, evaluate it as being correct or incorrect, and then self-reinforce or withhold reinforcement. This obviously represents a sophisticated task, and research on how to improve this process for students with mental disabilities holds much promise (Agran, Fodor-Davis, Moore, & Martella, 1992; Hughes & Agran, 1993; Hughes, Hugo, & Blatt, 1996). One important suggestion is that persons with mental disabilities may be weak in this ability because of the degree of external regulation that has typically been provided for them. With more opportunity and with specific training efforts, they may be able to improve in the ability to regulate or manage their own behavior.

Personal–Social Characteristics

It is important to stress again the individuality of students with severe disabilities when we consider issues related to their personal behavior and their relations with other students. There are many who have relatively normal lives, replete with friends and social activities, while others may have fewer social relations and more personal difficulties. Some personal problems experienced by persons with severe disabilities may be closely related to their intellectual development, the way that they interact with others, or their physical development. But many may also be explained by their learning history, environmental influences, and the attitudes of others in society.

Friendships and Personal Relations

The quality of life of persons with disabilities is related to the network of friends and acquaintances that they develop in their schools, workplaces, and communities. Some studies have shown that persons with disabilities have relatively little in the way of social relations with other individuals, both with and without disabilities (Crapps, Langone, & Swain, 1985; Davis & Rogers, 1985; Sullivan, Vitello, & Foster, 1988). In contrast, others have reported more favorable social behavior patterns, including the development of acquaintances, friends, and best friends (Kennedy, Horner, & Newton, 1989; Strully & Strully, 1985). The best predictor for the development of relations with others by persons with severe disabilities may be the same as for those who are not disabled: opportunity, understanding, and common interests.

Studies of the social interactions between people with severe disabilities and nondisabled persons have shown that individuals with disabilities are generally isolated until they or the persons without disabilities have been taught or prompted to interact (Gaylord-Ross & Peck, 1984). However, the opportunity for social interaction is certainly important. In an observational study, Brinker (1985) found that students with and without severe disabilities had more positive social interactions than did homogeneous groups of students with severe disabilities. The persons without disabilities provided more positive social responses for the social bids of the students with disabilities. In a study of developing social relations between adults with and without mental retardation, Green, Schleien, Mactavish, and Benepe (1995) asked participants without disabilities to explain the evolution of their relationships. They found that initially the nondisabled adults were very cautious about committing themselves to the relationships. However, after they spent more time with their peers with mental retardation, their relationships matured, often becoming more like typical friendships. Better relationships occurred when the pairs were more likely to have common interests. In other cases, the nondisabled adults assumed the role of service providers.

Love and Sexuality

The existence of a severe disability does not necessarily affect the sexual attraction or tendencies of an individual in one way or another. There is no evidence to indicate that sexual desires are reduced or heightened as a result of a disability. However, because of relatively lower rates of social interactions and increased rates of physical disabilities, many persons with severe disabilities have less opportunity for engaging in sexual activity. Nevertheless, advocates have called for the rights of people with mental disabilities with regard to sexual expression to be respected. The Arc (formerly the Association for Retarded Citizens) has taken the following position (The Arc Delegate Body, 1996):

> The Arc recognizes and affirms that individuals with mental retardation are people with sexual feelings, needs and identities, and believes that sexuality should always be seen in the total context of human relationships. The Arc believes that people with mental retardation have fundamental rights as individuals to: have privacy; love and be loved; develop friendships and emotional relationships; learn about sex, sexual exploitation, sexual abuse, safe sex and other issues regarding sexuality; exercise their rights and responsibilities in regard to privacy and sexual expression and the rights of others; marry and make informed decisions concerning having children; and develop expressions of sexuality reflective of age, social development, cultural values and social responsibility. The Arc further advocates that on an individual basis people with mental retardation who have children receive proper supports to assist them in rearing their children. The Arc also believes that the presence of mental retardation regardless of severity must not, in itself, justify either involuntary sterilization or denial of sterilization to those who choose it for themselves.
>
> The Arc supports programs which encourage people with mental retardation to develop expressions of their sexuality that reflect their age and social development, acknowledge the values of their families and are socially responsible. The Arc believes education should be available for people of all ages to assist in and, where appropriate, teach expressions of sexuality and responsible sexual behaviors with respect for the rights of others.

Unfortunately, persons with moderate to severe cognitive disabilities too often have little knowledge about sex and its implications (Scotti, Speaks, Masia, Boggess, & Drabman, 1996). Two critical issues related to the sexual functioning of persons with severe disabilities are sexual abuse and the transmission of HIV/AIDS or other sexually transmitted diseases. There is evidence that people with cognitive disabilities are at great risk for both (Marchetti & McCartney, 1990; Scotti et al., 1996).

Challenging Behaviors

Some students with severe disabilities, particularly those with the most severe disabilities, exhibit challenging behaviors, including stereotyped behaviors (repetitive behaviors such as hand flapping), self-injurious behaviors (such as head banging), aggressive behaviors (such as hitting other people), or noncompliance. The cause of these behaviors is often difficult to interpret, and several theories have been developed in an attempt to explain them.

The most recent theories and research have considered the context in which inappropriate behavior occurs and the possible motivation for the behavior. In some cases, it may occur as a basic form of communication, that is, to express discontent, dislike, or the need for help. In others, it may occur in order to escape from a demanding situation, one in which the individual does not want to participate. Other possibilities also exist, leading several authors to suggest the need to functionally analyze the environment to determine factors that may be causing or maintaining the unusual behavior (Evans & Meyer, 1985; Horner & Carr, 1997; Horner et al., 1990; Koegel, Koegel, & Dunlap, 1996). This approach has proved to be effective in improving abberant behaviors such as kicking, hitting, spitting, throwing, running away, and laying down on the floor (Dunlap, Foster-Johnson, Clarke, Kern, & Childs, 1995; Dunlap, Kern-Dunlap, Clarke, & Robbins, 1991; Umbriet & Blair, 1996).

Physical Characteristics

Often people with severe disabilities are not in good general physical health. Although most of the research is with individuals who are mildly or moderately mentally disabled, it has shown that fitness levels are generally below those of the general population. Because the lifestyles of people with mental disabilities tend to be inactive, they are more likely to develop hypokinetic (low movement) diseases such as high blood pressure, obesity, brittle bones, depression, and general tiredness (Rimmer, 1996). Individuals with severe disabilities may also have physical disabilities or health disorders along with their cognitive disabilities. Jacobson and Janicki (1985) examined the characteristics of 22,256 persons with severe or profound mental disabilities residing in the state of New York. They found that cerebral palsy, convulsive disorders (epilepsy), cardiovascular (heart) diseases, respiratory diseases, eating disorders, and growth impairments affected many individuals in the population they studied. These conditions are briefly described next. Although not found with great frequency, spina bifida and hydrocephaly might also be present in the population of people with severe disabilities.

Cerebral Palsy

Cerebral palsy is a neurological disorder resulting from the inability of the brain to control the voluntary muscles in a normal fashion, thus interfering with normal movement and posturing abilities. Depending on which region of the brain is damaged, different forms of this condition occur and affect different areas of the body (Pellegrino, 2002).

The most common form of cerebral palsy is *spasticity,* which represents about 60% of all forms of cerebral palsy. The condition is characterized by muscle stiffness (or hypertonia) and originates in the pyramidal tract of the central nervous system (Best, 2001; Dunn, 1996; Healy, 1990; Pellegrino, 2002). Individuals who have spasticity have limited range of motion due to severe muscle contractures affecting their hands, elbows, hips, knees, and feet. They might also have misformed spines and hip dislocations.

About 20% of the population with cerebral palsy exhibit the form commonly known as *athetosis,* which is also referred to as *dyskinesia,* meaning unwanted or involuntary movement. This form of the disorder appears when neurologic damage has occurred outside the pyramidal tract (extrapyramidal). It is characterized by either slow, writhing movements or abrupt, jerky movements, which may occur in facial muscles, the wrists and fingers, the trunk of the body, or in one or more extremities.

Rigid cerebral palsy, or rigidity, is a relatively rare type of cerebral palsy and is often classified as a form of spasticity (Bleck, 1982a). The least common type of cerebral palsy is *ataxia,* which accounts for approximately 1% of the prevalence of the general disorder. Ataxia occurs primarily due to damage to the cerebellum and is characterized by a lack of balance and uncoordinated movement (Best, 2001; Bleck, 1982a).

A final diagnosis often applied to persons with cerebral palsy is *mixed.* As the term implies, more than one form of the disorder exists simultaneously when the mixed diagnosis is applied. Most often the mix includes spasticity and athetosis. Spasticity and ataxia may also occur together. As many as 30% of the persons diagnosed with any particular form of cerebral palsy also show evidence of another form. Physical disabilities, including those due to cerebral palsy, are described clinically by the particular limbs that are affected. The different conditions are described in Figure 1–2.

Figure 1–2 Clinical Terms for Effects of Physical Disabilities

- Monoplegia: only one limb is affected.
- Diplegia: the lower limbs are severely affected, the trunk and the upper limbs to a lesser extent.
- Hemiplegia: only the limbs on one side of the body are affected.
- Paraplegia: only the legs are affected.
- Quadriplegia: major involvement of all four limbs, as well as the neck and the trunk.

Cerebral palsy, particularly in the spasticity form, is the most common type of physical disability to be found within the population of persons with severe disabilities. From 50% to 60% of persons with cerebral palsy are also classified as mentally disabled (Pellegrino, 2002). The mental disability may range from mild to moderate, severe, or profound. It is often difficult to specifically assess the degree of cognitive ability in persons with severe cerebral palsy because their motor disability often interferes with life experiences and their ability to communicate what they know.

Epilepsy

Epilepsy is a disorder of the brain that results in recurrent seizures (Epilepsy Foundation of America, 1997; Weinstein, 2002). There are different types of seizures, but the most severe form, generalized tonic–clonic seizures (formerly referred to as grand mal), occurs most often among persons with severe disabilities. Epilepsy is not a disease but a symptom of irregular activity within the brain. Seizures may have several known causes, but in many cases the cause is unknown.

When a generalized tonic–clonic seizure occurs, the first visible sign is usually that the person appears to lose awareness. She then ceases to engage in present activity, loses consciousness, and falls to the floor. She becomes tonic (stiff); then clonic (jerking) movements occur. When this happens the person becomes less rigid and shakes or jerks arms, legs, or both. At some point during the seizure, the individual may lose control of bowels or bladder, cry, or expel saliva from the mouth. After a few minutes of the seizure activity, the person usually becomes drowsy and disoriented or falls into a deep sleep that may last from several minutes to several hours (Weinstein, 2002; Wolraich, 1990b).

Although the tonic–clonic seizure is the most common among persons with severe disabilities who have seizures, other types may also occur. These include complex partial seizures (known previously as psychomotor or temporal lobe seizures) and absence seizures (previously called petit mal seizures). During complex partial seizures, which originate in the temporal lobe of the brain, the person may carry out complex behaviors such as undressing or saying something over and over again, even though there is an altered state of consciousness. In absence seizures, which are very brief, lasting perhaps 1 to 10 seconds, the person experiences a loss of consciousness, but otherwise remains fixed. Sometimes it is assumed that the individual is daydreaming (Berg, 1982).

Prescribed anticonvulsant drugs might be used to control the occurrence of seizures. The specific medicine depends on the nature of the disorder and the individual's reaction to it. Since the mid-1990s, several new anticonvulsant drugs have been released, including Felbatol, Neurontin, Lamictal, Keppra, Trileptal, Gabitril, Topamax, and Zonegran. Weinstein (2002) states that these drugs may be more precisely prescribed and thus result in fewer side effects. Several studies have noted the high frequency of anticonvulsant drugs used by students with the most significant disabilities in public schools and residential facilities (e.g., Davis, Cullari, & Breuning, 1982; Fox & Westling, 1986; Tu, 1979).

Cardiovascular Disorders

Many persons with severe disabilities have congenital heart disease. The causes are sometimes unknown, but they are often found to be the same factors that result in the primary disability, for example, chromosomal anomalies, viruses during the first trimester of pregnancy, genetic factors, chronic alcoholism, and excessive radiation. Roizen (2002) reported that children with Down syndrome could have various congenital heart defects, including an endocardial cushion defect, ventricular septal defect, and atrial septal defect (see Table 1–2).

Numerous other cardiac conditions may affect persons with severe disabilities, including the occurrence of narrowed valves within the heart; a hole in a wall of the heart that allows blood to leak into another part of the heart; a lack of separation of the heart's chambers; arteries that are too narrow, causing the heart to pump harder; underdevelopment of part of the heart; the mixture of deoxygenated with oxygenated blood due to various defects; the abnormal development of major veins; and the attachment of arteries to the wrong part of the heart (Baum, 1982; Blackman, 1990a). These conditions result in shortness of breath, fatigue, poor growth and development, chest pain, blueness of the lips and nail beds (cyanosis), fainting, chest deformity, and rapid heartbeat. Additionally, as a result of some forms of congenital heart defects, congestive heart failure may occur. This means the heart may not pump adequately, causing fluids to build up in the lungs, liver, and other organs (Baum, 1982).

Many children with heart defects die at birth or in the first year of life; others live fairly normal lives either with or without specific medical intervention (e.g., surgery or medicine). Most persons with heart defects must avoid too much activity, although otherwise normal involvement and participation in life are encouraged. The particular problem for persons with severe disabilities who have a congenital heart disease may be the degree of tiredness or fatigue that they experience during the normal routine of the day. The opportunity for frequent rest periods should help alleviate this problem while still allowing involvement in many typical activities.

Respiratory Disorders

Persons with severe disabilities often have respiratory disorders such as asthma, bronchitis, apnea, bronchopulmonary dysplasia, cystic fibrosis, respiratory distress syndrome, and chronic colds, flu, or pneumonia. Additionally, breathing difficulties may occur due to weakened muscles that result from cerebral palsy, muscular dystrophy, or spinal muscular atrophy (Blackman, 1990b; Bleck & Nagel, 1982). Various respiratory disorders result in wheezing, breathing difficulties, and excess mucus. Persons with these conditions may need to undergo regular postural drainage, suctioning, and oxygen therapy and receive prescribed medication. Avoiding high activity levels also will be necessary.

Some individuals who are severely disabled and who have chronic respiratory problems are considered *technology dependent* or *technology assisted* (Bigge, 1991). These terms suggest that, without some regular form of intervention using technical equipment, these persons would not be able to survive. The types of equipment used with persons with respiratory disorders include continuous or periodic ventilation to assist breathing (a ventilator using a battery-operated electric motor pushes air into the lungs); the provision of concentrated oxygen, using an oxygen tank or oxygen concentrator; or suctioning to remove excess mucus from the lungs, using manual suction or an electric suctioning machine. Some persons who have respiratory difficulties have a tracheostomy (an opening in the trachea), which allows breathing to occur more easily or accommodates the ventilator or suctioning device.

Eating Problems

For most individuals, eating abilities progress in a normal fashion, beginning with reflexive sucking, progressing to normal chewing and swallowing, and maturing with the use of eating utensils. Persons with severe disabilities might develop eating problems that call for special attention if they are to consume enough nutrients to ensure adequate growth and maximum cognitive development. The most critical time for this concern is the infant, toddler, and early childhood years.

A variety of problems can either result in inadequate eating or hinder the normal digestive process. Cerebral palsy may result in defective oral–motor functioning, causing a weak suck, poor lip closure, jaw thrusting, lack of tongue control, and difficulty in chewing and swallowing (Alexander, 2001; Curry, 1990). The increased muscle tone of individuals with spasticity may consume greater than normal calories and thus compound the problem. If, in addition, a child has a respiratory disorder or a cardiac disease, he may lack the energy to participate in the feeding process. This is clearly problematic because lack of adequate nutrition will result in even less stamina.

Some children exhibit voluntary or involuntary resistance to eating by tantrums, gagging, or regurgitating. Gastroesophageal (GE) reflux (vomiting because of a weak muscle connecting the stomach and the esophagus) can be corrected by surgery. In other cases, these behaviors may occur as a response to an unpleasant eating experience, because of a strong preference or dislike for different foods, because of changes in the environment or the routine, or because of hunger (Curry, 1990).

Growth Impairments

Children with severe disabilities often do not demonstrate normal rates of growth and in fact are often small for their age. There are several possible causes for this. One is that the child may not receive adequate nutrition. Because of eating difficulties and frequent illnesses that are often associated with developmental disabilities, a child may not receive the amount of food that is normally consumed. In other cases, such as in cerebral palsy, oral–motor development may be impaired. In still others, malabsorption of food and/or diarrhea may be a factor (Curry, 1990).

Some growth impairments are related to specific syndromes or to prenatal conditions that also result in mental disabilities. For example, Down syndrome and Cornelia de Lange's syndrome are characterized by slow growth; generally, individuals with these syndromes are below average in size. Additionally, rubella, cytomegalic inclusion disease, syphilis, and toxoplasmosis are all prenatal viral infections that can result in both mental disabilities and physical retardation (Horton & Rimoin, 1982).

Spina Bifida

Spina bifida is a congenital disorder in which the spine does not develop normally during the first trimester of fetal development; it sometimes occurs in individuals with severe disabilities, but may also occur without adversely affecting cognitive development. The most serious and most common form of spina bifida is *myelomeningocele.* When this condition occurs, the spinal cord (myelo) and its covering membrane (meninges) pouch out of the opening in the vertebrae. It is often accompanied by hydrocephalus and flaccid paralysis of the lower trunk. Besides lacking leg use, the person who has a myelomeningocele will lack bladder and bowel control, lack skin sensation in the lower body, and may have scoliosis (Liptak, 2002).

Hydrocephaly

Hydrocephaly accompanies the myelomeninges form of spina bifida 90% to 95% of the time it occurs, although it may also occur without the spinal disorder. Hydrocephaly occurs when the cerebrospinal fluid is not absorbed normally by the body and instead is trapped in the ventricles of the brain and causes the brain, and thus the head, to become enlarged. Brain cells and nerve fibers become compressed, sometimes leading to some degree of mental disability, often mild. A shunt or tube may be surgically inserted into the ventricles, allowing the fluid to drain into the cavity of the abdomen or, less often, into the heart (Wolraich, 1990a). Occasionally, shunts cause infections that must be treated.

Hydrocephalus often results in motor, language, or perceptual disabilities and seizure disorders. Usually, the condition is treated immediately upon its discovery during the first year of life, using the shunting procedure. Delayed treatment results in the condition becoming more serious, including a more serious degree of intellectual disability.

Other Physical Characteristics

Persons with severe disabilities may have various other physical problems; these involve bowel and bladder control, partial or complete loss of hearing or visual ability, congenital limb malformations or absences, juvenile

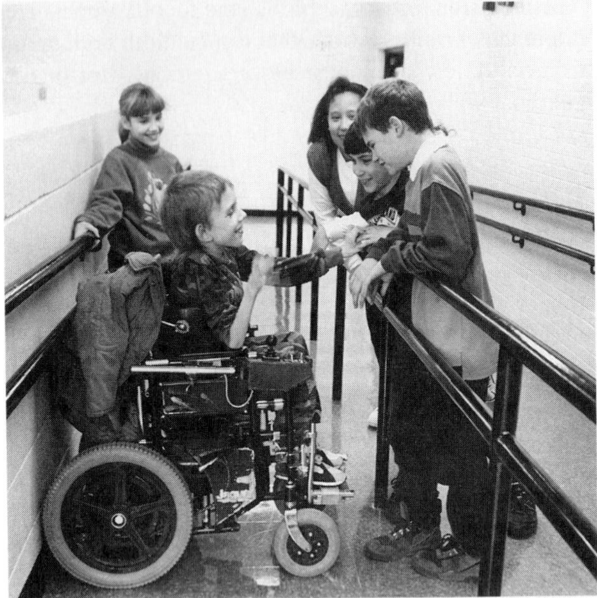

The development of a network of friends is a benefit of inclusive schooling.

rheumatoid arthritis, and susceptibility to infection. Like the other physical conditions discussed above, these present substantial challenges to persons with severe disabilities.

Learning Potential of Persons with Severe Disabilities

Given the learning characteristics, the personal–social difficulties, and the physical challenges described in the previous sections, it would certainly be easy to conclude that there is little that persons with severe disabilities can learn, little that they can do. However, many studies and reports have demonstrated that this is not true. From experience and research, we have learned that, given adequate opportunities, supports, and appropriate forms of instruction, many persons with severe disabilities can *learn* and *participate* in many life activities. When their involvement is limited or when full participation is not possible, partial, yet meaningful, participation is the goal (Baumgart et al., 1982; Ferguson & Baumgart, 1991).

The potential areas of learning for students with severe disabilities are far too numerous to present here. However, it is important that the reader acquire at least an idea of skill potential and how the skills are learned. The areas of achievement discussed below are of great importance and are those in which research has demonstrated that students with severe disabilities can make substantial progress. We will briefly look at successful methods for teaching language skills, social skills, domestic and daily living skills, recreational and leisure skills, community skills, and skills for working in vocational settings. More details about providing instruction in these areas and others are presented throughout the text.

Language and Communication Skills

Students with severe disabilities often exhibit diverse language skills, and sometimes their communication can be very limited (Kernan & Sabsay, 1996; McLean et al., 1996; Ogletree, Wetherby, & Westling, 1992; Reichle, 1997). It has been found, however, that different techniques and communication systems can result in the successful development and use of language (Reichle, 1997). Some of these techniques include using environmental events to increase the probability that the person with the restricted language will exercise his verbal language skill. Other tactics include teaching the student to use signs or gestures or to communicate using pictures or symbols.

A very functional manner in which language has been taught to persons with severe disabilities requires that teachers, parents, and others identify naturally occurring opportunities, such as arriving or departing from school, eating, or dressing, and use these opportunities to prompt and reinforce the occurrence of language activity. Another natural strategy is skill clustering—teaching related skills in a natural sequence that will be functionally useful to the student, including a particular language skill. For example, the individual may be taught the steps necessary for entering a room, removing a coat, and then asking for a particular game to play (Caro & Snell, 1989; Halle, 1987; Johnson, Baumgart, Helmstetter, & Curry, 1996).

These language-training tactics attempt to develop necessary environmental conditions, primarily the responsiveness of other persons in the environment, in order to develop and increase natural speech. However, for some persons with severe disabilities, other methods of language or communication production are necessary because speech does not occur. Alternatives that have been successful include nonsymbolic or gestural communication, manual signing, and the use of static symbols or photographs. Usually, the symbols will be attached to laptrays, communication boards, or even electronic communication devices that produce synthetic speech. Based on the individual's unique characteristics, the most suitable communication system will be developed (Johnson et al., 1996; Mirenda et al., 1990; Sigafoos & Iacono, 1993).

Communication instruction has been successful in increasing the frequency of language use, enlarging the number of language skills a student has, increasing the spontaneous and natural use of language in different environments, and providing alternative approaches to language production. After learning appropriate forms of language, some students with severe disabilities have reduced their display of maladaptive, inappropriate, stereotyped, or self-injurious behaviors. These behaviors often serve as an attempt to communicate, but when other more acceptable forms of communication are introduced, they are no longer necessary (Carr & Durand, 1985; Durand & Carr, 1991).

Whatever communication system is most appropriate, a major goal is to increase the responsiveness of key persons in the environment to the attempts of these individuals to use language. Language is important because it allows us to exert some influence over our environment and on the action of the people who are around us. Because this is true, we must work to increase our attention to the attempts by students with severe disabilities to communicate with us and then reinforce these attempts. When this has been done, communication skills have generally improved.

Social Skills

The quality of our lives is related to the nature of our interaction with other people. Learning social skills allows us to live with others and to have different types and degrees of relationships with them. These relationships are important to most people and are no less important to persons with severe disabilities. However, because their abilities and circumstances often reduce their opportunities for normal social relations, it is important that they participate in environments in which social behaviors and relations typically occur and that they be taught the skills necessary to participate meaningfully in these environments.

The social behaviors of students with severe disabilities have often been restricted by their segregation into environments that include only other persons with severe disabilities. In contrast, the development of social skills can improve if they are given the opportunity to interact with nondisabled students. In a study that examined the effect of integrating persons with and without severe disabilities, Brinker (1985) found that there was more social behavior in the mixed groupings; that the students with severe disabilities made more positive social bids to the nondisabled students than to other students with severe disabilities; that those without disabilities made more positive social bids to the students with disabilities than did other students with disabilities; and that nondisabled students were more responsive to the social bids of the students with disabilities than were their peers with disabilities. All this suggests that social behaviors by students with severe disabilities are likely to increase in the presence of students without disabilities. The findings of Hunt, Farron-Davis, Beckstead, Curtis, and Goetz (1994) also support this notion. Hunt et al. compared children with severe disabilities who were enrolled in full-inclusion regular classrooms with others in separate special classrooms on several different measures. Among other significant findings, they reported that the children in the regular classes were more often engaged in daily events, initiated social contacts more often, and engaged in more reciprocal social interactions.

To improve the skills necessary for people with severe disabilities to experience a full range of social relations, different forms of intervention might be necessary. Some that have been successful include direct instruction of social skills, teaching peers to initiate social interactions, and teaching social skills within the context of other functional behaviors. Research has shown that it is possible to use verbal directions, prompting, modeling, and role playing to teach skills such as initiating interactions, acknowledging others' initiations, and elaborating on interactions and expanding them. As a result, students who have severe disabilities have been able to learn how to interact in a meaningful way with their nondisabled peers (Haring, 1991).

While learning specific social behaviors is important, it is more important to develop relations with nondisabled people that range from acquaintances to friendships. Research reports suggest that people with severe disabilities can do so when given the opportunity (Kennedy et al., 1989; Strully & Strully, 1985) and that people without disabilities can learn to accept people with disabilities for their unique characteristics as individuals (Green et al., 1995). In part, this is likely due to the ability of many people without disabilities to look past a person's mental and physical restrictions and toward the positive aspects of the person. It must be realized, however, that such occurrences are more likely to increase if we teach persons with severe disabilities how to interact with others in a socially desirable fashion and allow them opportunities to be in socially productive situations.

Domestic and Daily Living Skills

After 1967 the number of people with mental disabilities residing in large residential institutions began to decrease and, simultaneously, community-based residential programs

began to expand. Today there are more options for where persons with severe disabilities may live, including private homes, group-living homes, and apartments in which they can live independently or semi-independently.

A great deal of research has demonstrated the ability of people with severe disabilities to acquire the skills necessary for self-care and daily living in their living environments (Browder & Snell, 1993; Snell & Farlow, 1993). These studies have shown that many people with moderate, severe, or profound mental disabilities can learn to use the toilet, bathe themselves, brush their teeth, shave, manage their menstrual care, dress themselves, eat appropriately, and perform most other self-care skills. They can also learn to do such things as wash their own clothes, use the telephone, clean their room, prepare meals, and perform other routine chores.

A portrayal of the typical domestic abilities of adult persons with mental disabilities was reported by Sullivan et al. (1988). In their observational study, they described the activities of a group of six men with moderate mental disabilities over a 6-month period. The men resided in a group-living home and were observed as they engaged in their normal daily activities. Based on their extensive observations, Sullivan and her colleagues concluded that the men demonstrated skillful behaviors in virtually all their daily routines, including personal care, domestic skills, and using appropriate manners and social behaviors.

Where a person lives and how she functions there is important. Natural homes are favored over institutional environments and provide the opportunities necessary for persons with severe disabilities to function more independently.

Recreational and Leisure Skills

Leisure and recreational activities are an important element of life for most people, and they are even more important for people with severe disabilities. Engaging in these activities is essential because it provides an opportunity to participate in an integrated world, to demonstrate age-appropriate skills and social behavior, and to make constructive use of free time. Thus an important goal for persons with severe disabilities—and a significant component of their instructional program—should be to develop appropriate leisure and recreational activities. Research has shown that many people with severe disabilities can make much progress in acquiring skills in this life domain (Dattilo, 1991; Nietupski, Hamre-Nietupski, & Ayres, 1984).

Early studies found that persons with severe disabilities often engaged in no purposeful recreation and that their idle hours were spent in passive activities such as watching television. While to a certain degree this may be considered normal and acceptable, if it is the *only* way an individual spends free time, it may be less than desirable. Based on an apparent need for more suitable free-time skills, researchers developed a variety of instructional strategies and related interventions that have allowed persons with severe disabilities to develop more typical and enjoyable pursuits and to share many of the features of freedom.

Hoge and Dattilo (1995) compared the recreational activities of 100 adults with and 100 adults without mental retardation matched for age, gender, ethnicity, area of residency, and marital status. Using structured in-depth interviews, they found that, like adults without mental disabilities, those with mental disabilities participated in a core of leisure activities, although far fewer than their nondisabled peers. The most common free-time activity for both groups, as might be expected in today's society, was watching television. Among the other 10 most frequent activities experienced by both groups were travel or scenic car trips, listening to the radio, eating out, visiting family or friends, and listening to tapes. The adults with mental retardation also enjoyed talking on the phone, going for a walk, shopping, and going to the movies. Other activities that children with moderate, severe, or profound mental disabilities have been able to learn include riding a tricycle; using a trampoline; playing tic-tac-toe, checkers, and other table games; and playing with toys such as Legos, Lite-Brite, Marble Rollway, and remote-control vehicles (Nietupski et al., 1984). Other activities learned by adolescents and adults with mental disabilities have been doing physical fitness exercises; using a camera; playing Frisbee, darts, pinball, and video games; and buying soft drinks from a vending machine (Nietupski et al., 1984).

Community Skills

A major effect of normalization, deinstitutionalization, and community living is that persons with severe disabilities are able to make use of many of the facilities that exist throughout neighborhoods, towns, and cities. Many studies show that they can be taught the functional skills necessary for using such places as grocery stores, restaurants, department stores, laundromats, and community recreational facilities. Studies also demonstrate that many adolescents and adults with severe disabilities can learn to cross the street safely, use public transportation, and withdraw money from automatic teller machines, as well as other skills that allow them to participate in communities (Morse, Schuster, & Sandknop, 1996; Snell & Browder, 1986; Test & Spooner, 1996; Westling & Floyd, 1990).

Aveno (1987) surveyed 436 community residences of persons with various severe disabilities to learn about the ways in which they participated in the community. Among the activities in which they engaged the most were using health-care services; walking, biking, or strolling in their wheelchairs; using restaurants; attending churches and synagogues; using grocery stores and supermarkets; using department stores; going to the barber shop or the beauty shop; visiting parks and zoos; and engaging in various recreational events, including going to parties and dances, swimming, bowling, and attending movies, concerts, and plays. It is thus apparent that many persons with severe disabilities desire to take advantage of the many aspects of community life.

Teaching functional skills in community settings obviously requires a different instructional arrangement than has been used in the past by public school programs (Brown et al., 1983; Hamre-Nietupski, Nietupski, Bates, & Maurer, 1982). Teachers must take their students out of the schools and into community settings and conduct their instruction in the stores, restaurants, and other places in which the students will ultimately need to function. This will call for different public school staffing arrangements and instructional schedules and obviously will be a challenge for many educators and school administrators. However, the benefit will outweigh the additional effort because the students will be able to live much fuller, more normal lives in the community after learning how to operate in different settings.

Vocational Skills

Most adults are employed. Prior to the 1970s, the closest most people with severe disabilities came to employment was working in sheltered workshops. These workshops hired only people with disabilities and paid them far below the minimum wage (sometimes about one tenth of it) to perform relatively simple tasks like folding letters and stuffing envelopes. While there are still such workshops today, there is clearly a different trend, one that encourages supported employment (or supported work) for people with severe disabilities in regular, integrated working environments (Callahan & Garner, 1997; Rusch & Hughes, 1990; Wehman & Kregel, 1985).

The realization that people with severe disabilities could work in the regular world with different degrees of support occurred during the 1970s after several researchers, using the principles of applied behavior analysis, provided *illustrations of competence* by teaching people with moderate, severe, and profound mental disabilities to perform complex assembly tasks (Bellamy, Peterson, & Close, 1975; Gold, 1972). Following this work, individual case studies began to appear in the literature, demonstrating that individuals with severe disabilities could learn to do jobs in community settings instead of in sheltered workshops (Rusch, Connis, & Sowers, 1978; Wehman, Hill, & Koehler, 1979). For more than a decade, supported employment models have been used in most states (Callahan & Garner, 1997; Shafer, Wehman, Kregel, & West, 1990).

A number of studies have been conducted that demonstrate the viability of supported employment, both in terms of the successful employment of people with disabilities and the financial benefit to both the person and the rehabilitation system. It has been shown that many persons with severe disabilities can perform various jobs, that they can get paid at least minimum wage for performing these jobs, and that they do not have to rely on sheltered workshop employment, which relies in turn on public funding (Rusch & Hughes, 1990). For example, a study by Wehman, Hill, Wood, and Parent (1987) reported on the employment of 21 persons with severe mental disabilities (i.e., IQs under 40) over an 8-year period in various community settings. Although many demonstrated behavior difficulties that interfered with their work (e.g., worked slow, poor social skills), most demonstrated positive characteristics as well (reliable attendance, good attitude) and remained employed for extended periods of time, earning at least minimum wage. The jobs were as entry-level service workers such as dishwashers and janitors. At the time of the study, as a group, these workers earned more than $230,000. One worker, whose IQ was 36, averaged more than $500 a month for more than 7 years (Wehman et al., 1987). Studies such as this demonstrate that having a severe disability need not preclude one from developing adequate vocational skills to function in the world of work.

Conclusion

People with severe disabilities are a heterogeneous group that have been placed in various traditional categories of disability. Regardless of the categorical placement, these individuals differ from one another, just as much as any two people without disabilities differ, perhaps even more. This variability makes it difficult to draw many general truths about people with severe disabilities. Nevertheless, certain characteristics and conditions seem to explain their strengths and weaknesses. It is important to have knowledge of these in order to realize the types of services that need to be provided, although the specific needs of individuals can only be individually determined. When we know the learning difficulties experienced by people with severe disabilities, we can develop ways to provide instruction and support, and we can evaluate the effectiveness of these ways. By realizing some of the problems that they face when interacting with others as well as when they are alone, we can help both the individual with disabilities and members of society to improve their behavior and accept each other. And by being aware of the many physical conditions that challenge those with severe disabilities, we can assist with their needs and find ways for them to have a fuller degree of participation and a better quality of life.

Prior to the last 30 years, most people with severe disabilities were, in fact, denied the opportunity to participate in the world. They resided in institutions or were segregated in separate schools. But in the United States and many other parts of the world, these conditions are rapidly changing. The last 10 to 20 years have seen tremendous advances in the knowledge we have about people with severe disabilities and how to educate them and assist them in learning to live. We are now better equipped to improve their functioning in many areas, such as using language, living in the community, and working on a job. All this, and much else, offers a hope, if not a promise, that their lives will be better today and tomorrow than were the lives of persons with severe disabilities in past years.

Questions for Reflection

1. Several different concepts and definitions have been used for the term *severe disabilities.* What are some other ways to explain this condition?
2. Because people with severe disabilities are unique persons, is it appropriate to group them all together under one label? Why or why not?
3. Does the new definition of *mental retardation* by the American Association on Mental Retardation improve the concept of this condition or make it more difficult to understand?
4. Given the learning characteristics shared by many people with severe disabilities, what would be one way to improve their learning potential?
5. How important is it for people to be able to generalize their skills? For which skills is generalizing most important? Are there any for which it is not important?
6. Many people with severe disabilities have significant physical problems or disabilities. Should we assume that people with very severe physical disabilities also have cognitive disabilities?
7. Unfortunately, some people with severe disabilities have relatively few friends. What could be done to improve this situation?
8. Research shows that there is much potential for learning by individuals with severe disabilities. What additional areas of research might be important to expand on this knowledge?

References

Abt Associates. (1974). *Assessment of selected resources for severely handicapped children and youth: Vol. 1. A state of the art paper.* Cambridge, MA: Author. (ERIC Document Reproduction Service No. ED 134 614.)

Agran, M., Fodor-Davis, J., Moore, S. C., & Martella, R. C. (1992). Effects of peer-delivered self-instructional training on a lunch-making work task for students with severe disabilities. *Education and Training in Mental Retardation, 27,* 230–240.

Alexander, R. (2001). Feeding and swallowing. In M. L. Batshaw (Ed.), *Children with Disabilities* (5th Ed., pp. 504–535). Baltimore: Paul H. Brookes.

American Association on Mental Retardation. (2002). *Mental retardation: Definition, classification, and systems of supports* (10th Ed.). Washington, DC: Author.

American Psychiatric Association. (1994). *Diagnostic and statistical manual of mental disorders* (4th ed.). Washington, DC: Author.

Angelman Syndrome Support Group, United Kingdom. (No date). *What is Angelman Syndrome?* [Online]. Available: http://www.angel.rdg.ac.uk/#whatisAS.

Ault, M. M., Guy, B., Guess, D., Bashinski, S., & Roberts, S. (1995). Analyzing behavior state and learning environments: Application in instructional settings. *Mental Retardation, 33,* 304–316.

Autism Society of America. (2002). *What is autism?* [Online] Available: http://www.autismsociety.org.

Aveno, A. (1987). A survey of activities engaged in and skills most needed by adults in community residences. *Journal of the Association for Persons with Severe Handicaps, 12,* 125–130.

Baker, D. (1979). Severely handicapped: Toward an inclusive definition. *AAESPH Review, 4*(1), 52–65.

Baron-Cohen, S. (1995). *Mindblindness: An essay on autism and theory of mind (learning, development, and conceptual change).* Cambridge, MA: MIT Press.

Batshaw, M. L. (Ed.). (2002). *Children with disabilities* (5th Ed.), Baltimore: Paul H. Brookes.

Batshaw, M. L., & Shapiro, B. (2002). Mental retardation. In M. L. Batshaw (Ed.), *Children with disabilities* (5th Ed., pp. 287–305). Baltimore: Paul H. Brookes.

Baum, D. (1982). Heart disease in children. In E. E. Bleck & D. A. Nagel (Eds.), *Physically handicapped children: A medical atlas for teachers* (pp. 313–324). Orlando, FL: Grune & Stratton.

Baumgart, D., Brown, L., Pumpian, I., Nisbet, J., Ford, A., Sweet, M., Messing, R., & Schroeder, J. (1982). Principle of partial participation and individualized adaptations in educational programs for severely handicapped students. *Journal of the Association for the Severely Handicapped,17*(2), 17–27.

Bellamy, G. T., Peterson, L., & Close, D. (1975). Habilitation of the severely and profoundly retarded: Illustration of competence. *Education and Training of the Mentally Retarded, 10,* 174–186.

Benke, P. J., Carver, V., & Donahue, R. (1995). *Risk and recurrence risk of Down syndrome* [Online]. Miami, FL: University of Miami School of Medicine Department of Pediatrics. Available: http://www.nas.com/downsyn/benke.html [Feb. 3, 1997].

Berg, B. O. (1982). Convulsive disorders. In E. E. Bleck & D. A. Nagel (Eds.), *Physically handicapped children: A medical atlas for teachers* (pp. 171–180). Orlando, FL: Grune & Stratton.

Best, S. J. (2001). Physical disabilities. In J. L. Bigge, S. J. Best, & K.W. Heller (Eds.), *Teaching individuals with physical, health, or multiple disabilities* (4th Ed., pp. 34–64). Upper Saddle River, NJ: Merrill/Prentice Hall.

Bierne-Smith, M., Ittenbach, R., & Patton, J. R. (Eds.). (2002). *Mental retardation* (6th ed.). Upper Saddle River, NJ: Merrill/Prentice Hall.

Bigge, J. L. (1991). *Teaching individuals with physical and multiple disabilities* (3rd ed.). Upper Saddle River, NJ: Prentice Hall.

Blackman, J. A. (1990a). Congenital heart disease. In J. A. Blackman (Ed.), *Medical aspects of developmental disabilities in children birth to three* (2nd ed., pp. 81–87). Rockville, MD: Aspen.

Blackman, J. A. (1990b). Respiratory distress syndrome. In J. A. Blackman (Ed.), *Medical aspects of developmental disabilities in children birth to three* (2nd ed., pp. 243–245). Rockville, MD: Aspen.

Bleck, E. E. (1982a). Cerebral palsy. In E. E. Bleck & D. A. Nagel (Eds.), *Physically handicapped children: A medical atlas for teachers* (pp. 59–132). Orlando, FL: Grune & Stratton.

Bleck, E. E. (1982b). Rubella syndrome. In E. E. Bleck & D. A. Nagel (Eds.), *Physically handicapped children: A medical atlas for teachers* (pp. 431–432). Orlando, FL: Grune & Stratton.

Bleck, E. E., & Nagel, D. A. (Eds.). (1982). *Physically handicapped children: A medical atlas for teachers.* Orlando, FL: Grune & Stratton.

Bock, S. J., & Myles, B. S. (1999). An overview of characteristics of Asperger syndrome. *Education and Training in Mental Retardation and Developmental Disabilities, 34,* 511–520.

Borthwick-Duffy, S. A., & Eyman, R. K. (1990). Who are the dually diagnosed? *American Journal on Mental Retardation, 94,* 586–595.

Brimer, R. W. (1990). *Students with severe disabilities: Current perspectives and practices.* Mountain View, CA: Mayfield.

Brinker, R. P. (1985). Interactions between severely mentally retarded students and other students in integrated and segregated public school settings. *American Journal of Mental Deficiency, 89,* 587–594.

Browder, D. M., & Snell, M. E. (1993). Daily living and community skills. In M. E. Snell (Ed.), *Instruction of students with severe disabilities* (4th ed.). Upper Saddle River, NJ: Merrill/Prentice Hall.

Brown, L., Nisbet, J., Ford, A., Sweet, M., Shiraga, B., York, J., & Loomis, R. (1983). The critical need for nonschool instruction in educational programs for severely handicapped students. *Journal of the Association of the Severely Handicapped, 8,* 71–77.

Callahan, M. J., & Garner, J. B. (1997). *Keys to the workplace: Skills and supports for people with disabilities.* Baltimore: Paul H. Brookes.

Caro, P., & Snell, M. E. (1989). Characteristics of teaching communication to people with moderate and severe disabilities. *Education and Training in Mental Retardation, 24,* 63–77.

Carr, E. G., & Durand, V. M. (1985). Reducing behavior problems through functional communication training. *Journal of Applied Behavior Analysis, 18,* 111–126.

Chavez, E. (1995). Fetal alcohol syndrome: Teachers guide and resource booklet. Available: http://www.lcsc.edu/education/fas/index.html.

Crapps, J., Langone, J., & Swain, S. (1985). Quantity and quality of participation in community environments by mentally retarded adults. *Education and Training of the Mentally Retarded, 20,* 123–129.

Curry, P. A. S. (1990). Feeding problems. In J. A. Blackman (Ed.), *Medical aspects of developmental disabilities in children birth to three* (2nd ed., pp. 125–139). Rockville, MD: Aspen.

Dattilo, J. (1991). Recreation and leisure: A review of the literature and recommendations for future directions. In L. H. Meyer, C. A. Peck, & L. Brown (Eds.), *Critical issues in the lives of people with severe disabilities* (pp. 171–193). Baltimore: Paul H. Brookes.

Davis, R. R., & Rogers, E. S. (1985). Social skills with persons who are mentally retarded. *Mental Retardation, 23,* 186–196.

Davis, V., Cullari, S., & Breuning, S. (1982). Drug use in community foster homes. In S. Breuning & A. Poling (Eds.), *Drugs and mental retardation* (pp. 359–376). Springfield, IL: Charles C. Thomas.

Downing, J., & Eichinger, J. (1990). Instructional strategies for learners with dual sensory impairments in integrated settings. *Journal of the Association for Persons with Severe Handicaps, 15,* 98–105.

Drais, K. (1995). *An open letter from my heart to educators* [Online]. Available: http://www.nas.com/downsyn/let2ed.html [no date].

Dunlap, G., Foster-Johnson, L., Clarke, S., Kern, L., & Childs, K. E. (1995). Modifying activities to produce functional outcomes: Effects on problem behaviors of students with disabilities. *Journal of the Association for Persons with Severe Handicaps, 20,* 248–258.

Dunlap, G., Kern-Dunlap, L., Clarke, S., & Robbins, F. R. (1991). Functional assessment, curricular revisions, and severe behavior problems. *Journal of Applied Behavior Analysis, 24,* 387–397.

Dunn, W. (1996). The sensorimotor systems: A framework for assessment and intervention. In F. P. Orelove & D. Sobsey (Eds.), *Educating children with multiple disabilities: A transdisciplinary approach* (3rd ed., pp. 35–78). Baltimore: Paul H. Brookes.

Durand, V. M., & Carr, E. G. (1991). Functional communication training to reduce challenging behavior: Maintenance and application in new settings. *Journal of Applied Behavior Analysis, 24,* 251–256.

Dykens, E. M., Hodapp, R. M., & Finucane, B. M. (2000). *Genetics and mental retardation syndromes: A new look at behavior and interventions.* Baltimore: Paul H. Brookes.

Edelson, S. (1995a). *Fragile X syndrome* [Online]. Center for the Study of Autism, Salem, OR. Available: http://www.autism.org/fragilex.html.

Edelson, S. (1995b). *Overview of autism* [Online]. Center for the Study of Autism, Salem, OR. Available: http://www.autism.org/overview.html.

Ellis, N. (Ed.). (1963). *Handbook of mental deficiency: Psychological theory and research.* New York: McGraw-Hill.

Ellis, N. (Ed.). (1979). *Handbook of mental deficiency: Psychological theory and research* (2nd ed). Hillsdale, NJ: Erlbaum.

Epilepsy Foundation of America. (1997). *Epilepsy facts & figures.* Available: http://www.efa.org/education/facts.html.

Evans, I., & Meyer, L. (1985). *An educative approach to problem behaviors: A practical decision model for interventions with severely handicapped learners.* Baltimore: Paul H. Brookes.

Ferguson, D. L., & Baumgart, D. (1991). Partial participation revisited. *Journal of the Association for Persons with Severe Handicaps, 16,* 218–227.

Fox, L. (1989). Stimulus generalization of skills and persons with profound mental handicaps. *Education and Training in Mental Retardation, 24,* 219–229.

Fox, L., & Westling, D. L. (1986). The prevalence of students who are profoundly mentally handicapped receiving medication in a school district. *Education and Training of the Mentally Retarded, 21,* 205–210.

Fredericks, H. D., & Baldwin, V. (1987). Individuals with sensory impairments: Who are they? How are they educated? In L. Goetz, D. Guess, & K. Stremel-Campbell (Eds.), *Innovative program design for individuals with dual sensory impairments* (pp. 3–14). Baltimore: Paul H. Brookes.

Frith, U. (1997). Autism. *Scientific American, 7*(1), 92–99.

Gaylord-Ross, R., & Peck, C. A. (1984). Integration efforts for students with severe mental retardation. In D. Bricker & J. Fuller (Eds.), *Severe mental retardation: From theory to practice* (pp. 185–207). Reston, VA: Division on Mental Retardation of the Council for Exceptional Children.

Gold, M. (1972). Stimulus factors in skill training of the retarded on a complex assembly task: Acquisition, transfer, and retention. *American Journal of Mental Deficiency, 76,* 517–526.

Green, F., Schleien, S., Mactavish, J., & Benepe, S. (1995). Nondisabled adults' perceptions of relationships in the early stages of arranged partnerships with peers with mental retardation. *Education and Training in Mental Retardation and Developmental Disabilities, 30,* 91–108.

Grossman, H. J. (Ed.). (1973). *Manual on terminology and classification in mental retardation.* Washington, DC: American Association on Mental Deficiency.

Grossman, H. J. (Ed.). (1977). *Manual on terminology and classification in mental retardation.* Washington, DC: American Association on Mental Deficiency.

Grossman, H. J. (Ed.). (1983). *Classification in mental retardation.* Washington, DC: American Association on Mental Deficiency.

Guess, D., Mulligan Ault, M., Roberts, S., Siegel-Causey, E., Thompson, B., & Bronicki, G. J. (1988). Implications of biobehavioral states for the education and treatment of students with the most profoundly handicapping conditions. *Journal of the Association for Persons with Severe Handicaps, 13*(3), 163–174.

Guess, D., Roberts, S., Siegel-Causey, E., Ault, M., Guy, B., Thompson, B., & Rues, J. (1993). An analysis of behavior state conditions and associated environmental variables among students with profound handicaps. *American Journal on Mental Retardation, 97,* 634–653.

Guess, D., & Siegel-Causey, E. (1995). Attractor dimensions of behavior state changes among individuals with profound disabilities. *American Journal on Mental Retardation, 99,* 642–663.

Guess, D., Siegel-Causey, E., Roberts, S., Guy, B., Mulligan Ault, M., & Rues, J. (1993). Analysis of state organizational patterns among students with profound disabilities. *Journal of the Association for Persons with Severe Handicaps, 18,* 93–108.

Guess, D., Siegel-Causey, E., Roberts, S., Rues, J., Thompson, B., & Siegel-Causey, D. (1990). Assessment and analysis of behavior state and related variables among students with profoundly handicapping conditions. *Journal of the Association for Persons with Severe Handicaps, 15,* 211–230.

Guy, B., Guess, D., & Ault, M. (1993). Classroom procedures for the measurement of behavior state among students with profound disabilities. *Journal of the Association for Persons with Severe Handicaps,18,* 53–60.

Hagerman, R. (1994). *Fragile X syndrome. The Arc's Q&A on Fragile* X [Online]. Available: http://TheArc.org/faqs/fragqa.html.

Halle, J. (1987). Teaching language in the natural environment: An analysis of spontaneity. *Journal of the Association for Persons with Severe Handicaps, 12,* 28–37.

Hamre-Nietupski, S., Nietupski, J., Bates, P., & Maurer, S. (1982). Implementing a community-based educational model for moderately/severely handicapped students: Common problems and suggested solutions. *Journal of the Association for the Severely Handicapped, 7,* 38–43.

Haring, N. G. (Ed.). (1988). *Generalization for students with severe handicaps: Strategies and solutions.* Seattle, WA: University of Washington Press.

Haring, T. G. (1991). Social relationships. In L. H. Meyer, C. A. Peck, & L. Brown (Eds.), *Critical issues in the lives of people with severe disabilities* (pp. 195–217). Baltimore: Paul H. Brookes.

Healy, A. (1990). Cerebral palsy. In J. A. Blackman (Ed.), *Medical aspects of developmental disabilities in children birth to three* (2nd ed., pp. 59–66). Rockville, MD: Aspen.

Heber, R. (1959). A manual on terminology and classification in mental retardation. *Monograph Supplement of American Journal of Mental Deficiency* (No. 64).

Heber, R. (1961). Modifications in the manual on terminology and classification in mental retardation. *American Journal of Mental Deficiency, 65*(4), 499–500.

Hodapp, R. M., & Fidler, D. J. (1999). Special education and genetics: Connections for the 21st century. *Journal of Special Education, 33,* 130–137.

Hoge, G., & Dattilo, J. (1995). Recreation participation patterns of adults with and without mental retardation. *Education and Training in Mental Retardation and Developmental Disabilities, 30,* 283–298.

Horner, R. H., & Carr, E. G. (1997). Behavioral supports for students with severe disabilities: Functional assessment and comprehensive intervention. *Journal of Special Education, 31,* 84–104.

Horner, R. H., Dunlap, G., Koegel, R. L., Carr, E. G., Sailor, W., Anderson, J., Albin, R. W., & O'Neill, R. E. (1990). Toward a technology of "nonaversive" behavioral support. *Journal of the Association for Persons with Severe Handicaps, 15,* 125–132.

Horton, W. A., & Rimoin, D. L. (1982). Short stature and growth. In E. E. Bleck & D. A. Nagel (Eds.), *Physically handicapped children: A medical atlas for teachers* (pp. 451–468). Orlando, FL: Grune & Stratton.

Hughes, C., & Agran, M. (1993). Teaching persons with severe disabilities to use self-instruction in community settings: An analysis of the applications. *Journal of the Association for Persons with Severe Handicaps, 18,* 261–274.

Hughes, C., Hugo, K., & Blatt, J. (1996). Self-instructional intervention for teaching generalized problem-solving within a functional task sequence. *American Journal on Mental Retardation, 100,* 565–579.

Hunt, P., Farron-Davis, F., Beckstead, S., Curtis, D., & Goetz, L. (1994). Evaluating the placement of students with severe disabilities in general education versus special classes. *Journal of the Association for Persons with Severe Handicaps, 19,* 200–214.

Jacobson, J. W. (1990). Do some mental disorders occur less frequently among persons with mental retardation? *American Journal on Mental Retardation, 94,* 596–602.

Jacobson, J. W., & Janicki, M. P. (1985). Functional and health status characteristics of persons with severe handicaps in New York State. *Journal of the Association for Persons with Severe Handicaps, 10,* 51–60.

Johnson, J. M., Baumgart, D., Helmstetter, E., & Curry, C. A. (1996). *Augmenting basic communication in natural settings.* Baltimore: Paul H. Brookes.

Justen, J. E. (1976). Who are the severely handicapped? A problem in definition. *AAESPH Review, 1*(5), 1–11.

Kennedy, C. H., Horner, R. H., & Newton, J. S. (1989). Social contacts of adults with severe disabilities living in the community: A descriptive analysis of relationship patterns. *Journal of the Association for Persons with Severe Handicaps, 14,* 190–196.

Kernan, K. T., & Sabsay, S. (1996). Linguistic and cognitive ability of adults with Down syndrome and mental retardation of unknown etiology. *Journal of Communication Disorders, 29,* 401–422.

Koegel, L. K., Koegel, R. L., & Dunlap, G. (Eds.). (1996). *Positive behavioral support: Including people with difficult behavior in the community.* Baltimore: Paul H. Brookes.

Lacy, M. (1996). Some common sense answers to dietary management. *Wavelength, 5*(2). Available: http://www.visibleink.inter.net/wavelength.htm [no date].

Liptak, G. S. (2002). Neural tube defects. In M. L. Batshaw (Ed.), *Children with disabilities* (5th Ed., pp. 467–492). Baltimore: Paul H. Brookes.

Marchetti, A. G., & McCartney, J. R. (1990). Abuse of persons with mental retardation: Characteristics of the abused, the abusers, and the informers. *Mental Retardation, 28,* 367–371.

Marks, S. U., Schrader, C., Longaker, T., & Levine, M. (2000). Portraits of three adolescent students with Asperger's syndrome: Personal stories and how they can influence practice. *Journal of the Association for Persons with Severe Handicaps, 25,* 3–17.

McLean, L. K., Brady, N. C., & McLean, J. E. (1996). Reported communication abilities of individuals with severe mental retardation. *American Journal on Mental Retardation, 100,* 580–591.

Mercer, C. D., & Snell, M. E. (1977). *Learning theory research in mental retardation: Implications for teaching.* Columbus, OH: Charles E. Merrill.

Meyer, G. A., & Batshaw, M. L. (2001). Fragile X syndrome. In M. L. Batshaw (Ed.), *Children with disabilities* (5th Ed., pp. 321-331). Baltimore: Paul H. Brookes.

Meyer, L. H., Peck, C. A., & Brown, L. (Eds.). (1991). *Critical issues in the lives of people with severe disabilities.* Baltimore: Paul H. Brookes.

Mirenda, P., Iacono, T., & Williams, R. (1990). Communication options for persons with severe and profound disabilities: State of the art and future directions. *Journal of the Association for Persons with Severe Handicaps, 15,* 3–21.

Morse, T., Schuster, J. W., & Sandknop, P. A. (1996). Grocery shopping skills for persons with moderate to profound intellectual disabilities: A review of the literature. *Education and Treatment of Children, 19,* 487–517.

Nietupski, J., Hamre-Nietupski, S., & Ayres, B. (1984). Review of task analytic leisure skill training efforts: Practitioner implications and future research needs. *Journal of the Association for Persons with Severe Handicaps, 9,* 88–97.

Ogletree, B. T., Wetherby, A., & Westling, D. L. (1992). Profile of the prelinguistic communicative behaviors of children with profound mental retardation. *American Journal on Mental Retardation, 97,* 186–196.

Orelove, F. P., & Sobsey, D. (1996). *Educating children with multiple disabilities: A transdisciplinary approach* (3rd ed.). Baltimore: Paul H. Brookes.

Paul, R. (1987). Communication. In D. J. Cohen & A. M. Donnellan (Eds.), *Handbook of autism and pervasive developmental disorders* (pp. 61–84). New York: John Wiley.

Pellegrino, L. (2002). Cerebral palsy. In M. L. Batshaw (Ed.), *Children with disabilities* (5th Ed., pp. 443–466). Baltimore: Paul H. Brookes.

Prader–Willi Syndrome Association—USA. (1998). *Basic facts and medical alert.* Available: http://www.pwsausa.org/.

Pueschel, S. M. (1990). *A parent's guide to Down syndrome: Toward a brighter future.* Baltimore: Paul H. Brookes.

Pueschel, S. M. (1992). Down syndrome: *The ARC's Q&A on Down syndrome.* Available: http://thearc.org/faqs/mimrqa.html.

Reber, M. (2001). Dual diagnosis: Mental retardation and psychiatric disorders. In M. L. Batshaw (Ed.), *Children with disabilities* (5th Ed., pp. 347–363). Baltimore: Paul H. Brookes.

Reichle, J. (1997). Communication intervention with persons who have severe disabilities. *Journal of Special Education, 31,* 110–134.

Reiss, S. (1990). Prevalence of dual diagnosis in community-based day programs in the Chicago metropolitan area. *American Journal on Mental Retardation, 94,* 578–585.

Reiss, S. (1993). *Mental illness in persons with mental retardation.* Available: http://thearc.org/welcome.html.

Rimmer, J. H. (1996). *Physical fitness in people with mental retardation.* Available: http:thearc.org/faqs/fitness.html.

Roizen, N. J. (2002). Down syndrome. In M. L. Batshaw (Ed.), *Children with disabilities* (5th Ed., pp. 307–320). Baltimore: Paul H. Brookes.

Rusch, F. R., Connis, R. T., & Sowers, J. (1978). The modification and maintenance of time spent attending to task using social reinforcement, token reinforcement, and response cost in an applied restaurant setting. *Journal of Special Education Technology, 2,* 18–26.

Rusch, F. R., & Hughes, C. (1990). Historical overview of supported employment. In F. Rusch (Ed.), *Supported employment: Models, methods, and issues* (pp. 5–14). Sycamore, IL: Sycamore Press.

Safran, S. P. (2001). Asperger syndrome: The emerging challenge to special education. *Exceptional Children, 67,* 151–160.

Sailor, W., & Haring, N. (1977). Some current directions in the education of the severely/multiply handicapped. *AAESPH Review, 2*(2), 67–86.

Scacheri, C. (2002). Syndromes and inborn errors of metabolism. In M. L. Batshaw (Ed.), *Children with disabilities* (5th Ed., pp. 749–773). Baltimore: Paul H. Brookes.

Schor, D. P. (1990). Autism. In J. A. Blackman (Ed.), *Medical aspects of developmental disabilities in children birth to three* (pp. 7–10). Rockville, MD: Aspen.

Scott, E. M., Smith, T. E. C., Hendricks, M. D., & Polloway, E. A. (1999). Prader–Willi syndrome: A review and implications for educational intervention. *Education and Training in Mental Retardation and Developmental Disabilities, 34,* 110–116.

Scotti, J. R., Speaks, L. V., Masia, C. L., Bogges, J. T., and Drabman, R. S. (1996). The educational effects of providing AIDS-risk information to persons with developmental disabilities: An exploratory study. *Education and Training in Mental Retardation and Developmental Disabilities, 31,* 115–122.

Shafer, M. S., Wehman, P., Kregel, J., & West, M. (1990). National supported employment initiative: A preliminary analysis. *American Journal on Mental Deficiency, 95,* 316–327.

Sigafoos, J., & Iacono, T. (1993). Selecting augmentative communication devices for persons with severe disabilities: Some factors for educational teams to consider. *Australia and New Zealand Journal of Developmental Disabilities, 18* (3), 133–146.

Smithdas, R. (1981). Psychological aspects of deaf–blindness. In S. Walsh & R. Holzberg (Eds.), *Understanding and educating the deaf–blind/severely and profoundly handicapped* (pp. 38–42). Springfield, IL: Charles C. Thomas.

Snell, M. E., & Browder, D. M. (1986). Community-referenced instruction: Research and issues. *Journal of the Association for Persons with Severe Handicaps, 11,* 1–11.

Snell, M. E., & Farlow, L. J. (1993). Self-care skills. In M. E. Snell (Ed.), *Instruction of students with severe disabilities* (4th ed., pp. 380–441). Upper Saddle River, NJ: Merrill/ Prentice Hall.

Strully, J., & Strully, C. (1985). Friendship and our children. *Journal of the Association for Persons with Severe Handicaps, 10,* 224–227.

Sullivan, C. A. C., Vitello, S. J., & Foster, W. (1988). Adaptive behavior of adults with mental retardation: An intensive case study. *Education and Training in Mental Retardation, 23*(1), 76–81.

Test, D. W., & Spooner, F. (1996). *Innovations: Community-based instructional support.* Washington, DC: American Association on Mental Retardation.

The Arc. (1992). *Facts about alcohol use during pregnancy* [Online]. Available: http://thearc.org/faqs/fas.html.

The Arc Delegate Body. (1996). *Sexuality* [Online]. Available: http://thearc.org/posits/sex.html.

Thompson, B., & Guess, D. (1989). Students who experience the most profound disabilities: Teacher perspectives. In F. Brown & D. H. Lehr (Eds.), *Persons with profound disabilities: Issues and practices* (pp. 3–41). Baltimore: Paul H. Brookes.

Towbin, K. E., Mauk, J. E., & Batshaw, M. L. (2001). Pervasive developmental disorders. In M. L. Batshaw (Ed.), *Children with disabilities* (5th Ed., pp. 365–387). Baltimore: Paul H. Brookes.

Tu, J. B. (1979). The survey of psychotropic medication in mental retardation facilities. *Journal of Clinical Psychiatry, 40,* 125–128.

Umbriet, J., & Blair, K. (1996). The effects of preference, choice, and attention on problem behavior at school. *Education and Training in Mental Retardation and Developmental Disabilities, 31,* 151–161.

U.S. Department of Education. (2001). Twenty-third annual report to Congress on the implementation of the Education of the Handicapped Act. Washington, DC: Author.

Van Dijk, J. (1985). An educational curriculum for deaf–blind multi-handicapped persons. In D. Ellis (Ed.), *Sensory impairments in mentally handicapped people* (pp. 374–382). San Diego, CA: College-Hill Press.

Van Dijk, J., & Nelson, C. (1996–97). Syndromes, behavior, and educational intervention. *Deaf–Blind Perspectives, 4*(2).

Volkmar, F. R. (1987). Social development. In D. J. Cohen & A. M. Donnellan (Eds.), *Handbook of autism and pervasive developmental disorders* (pp. 41–60). New York: John Wiley.

Wehman, P., Hill, J. W., & Koehler, F. (1979). Placement of developmentally disabled individuals into competitive employment: Three case studies. *Education and Training of the Mentally Retarded, 14,* 269–276.

Wehman, P., Hill, J. W., Wood, W., & Parent, W. (1987). A report on competitive employment histories of persons labeled severely mentally handicapped. *Journal of the Association for Persons with Severe Handicaps, 12,* 11–17.

Wehman, P., & Kregel, J. (1985). A supported work approach to competitive employment of individuals with moderate and severe handicaps. *Journal of the Association for Persons with Severe Handicaps, 10,* 3–11.

Weinstein, S. (2002). Epilepsy. In M. L. Batshaw (Ed.), *Children with disabilities* (5th Ed., pp. 493–523). Baltimore: Paul H. Brookes.

Westling, D. L. (1986). *Introduction to mental retardation.* Upper Saddle River, NJ: Prentice Hall.

Westling, D. L., & Floyd, J. (1990). Generalization of community skills: How much training is necessary? *Journal of Special Education, 23,* 386–406.

Wetherby, A. M., & Prizant, B. M. (2000). Introduction to autism spectrum disorders. In A. M. Wetherby & B. M. Prizant (Eds.), *Autism spectrum disorders: A transactional, developmental perspective* (pp. 1–7). Baltimore: Paul H. Brookes.

Whitman, T. L. (1990). Self-regulation and mental retardation. *American Journal on Mental Retardation, 94,* 347–362.

Wolraich, M. (1990a). Hydrocephalus. In J. A. Blackman (Ed.), *Medical aspects of developmental disabilities in children birth to three* (2nd ed., pp. 175–179). Rockville, MD: Aspen.

Wolraich, M. (1990b). Seizure disorders. In J. A. Blackman (Ed.), *Medical aspects of developmental disabilities in children birth to three* (2nd ed., pp. 251–257). Rockville, MD: Aspen.

Wunsch, M. J., Conlon, C. J., & Scheidt, P. C. (2001). Substance abuse: A preventable threat to development. In M. L. Batshaw (Ed.), *Children with disabilities* (5th Ed., pp. 107–122). Baltimore: Paul H. Brookes.

CHAPTER 2

Philosophy and Best Practices for Educating Students with Severe Disabilities

This chapter presents a philosophy for providing educational services to students with severe disabilities. It then discusses historical events that led to what we believe are the current best practices for providing special education to students with severe disabilities. These practices include teaching functional, age-appropriate skills in inclusive settings, promoting self-determination, and supporting access to the general curriculum to the extent possible. The chapter concludes with a rationale for the practices that we propose, a definition of special education, and the conditions that should characterize it.

A Philosophy of Services

As we begin to consider the nature of the most appropriate educational services for students with severe disabilities, we must do so in light of the type of life we believe that they should have. When examining this issue from a historical perspective, we must conclude that the quality of the lives of people with severe disabilities has often been poor, and the corresponding educational programs and other services that have been offered have been equally less than desirable. If we as professionals, advocates, family members, or friends of people with severe disabilities believe that they should have a higher quality of life, we must ensure the provision of correspondingly high-quality educational and related services.

Given the challenges faced by people with severe disabilities, which were described in Chapter 1, the purpose of this chapter is, first, to provide the philosophy that will permeate the instructional strategies and tactics presented throughout this text, and then to outline the currently accepted best practices for teaching students with severe disabilities, that is, practices that reflect the stated philosophy. We offer the following philosophy:

A Philosophy for Providing Services to Students with Severe Disabilities

> Students with severe disabilities should be provided with a quality of education that is no less than that offered to other students. The education should be individually designed to meet their needs, but should not serve to isolate or segregate them from other people. It should begin as soon in life as possible after the recognition that there is a disability. As an integral part of the early intervention service, family involvement and support should occur. The education should continue through the school years and until the person is adequately prepared to enter the adult world as a participating, self-determining individual, which should be the ultimate goal of an educational program. Special education and related services should maximize the learning, growth, and development of the individual, while having the least possible degree of unnecessary or extraordinary intrusiveness. It should strive to reduce external control and dependence and increase internal regulation and independence. Simultaneously, special education should attempt to assist all nondisabled persons in understanding and developing a world that accommodates persons with severe disabilities.

Teachers and key professional personnel must recognize that each individual is of value and has the potential to learn. No student, with or without a severe disability, will learn if the persons responsible for promoting learning do not believe it is possible. It is therefore critical that teachers of these students have confidence in their ability to profit from instruction, regardless of the severity of their disability. The progress of a student with a severe disability will be directly related to the quality of education provided.

The Evolution of Philosophies and Practices for Teaching Students with Severe Disabilities

Since educational and related services began to be offered to persons with severe disabilities about two centuries ago, the philosophies that have guided professional practices have varied. Early in the 19th century, because practitioners thought that mental disabilities could be cured by exercising the nervous system, their instructions consisted primarily of sensory and motor exercises. Later, toward the end of the century, professionals began to change their opinions. Deciding that cures were not possible, they felt that it would be better to protect and care for the needs of people with severe disabilities. The focus shifted from instruction to care and management.

As the 20th century approached, Western society was swept by what has been referred to as the "genetic scare." There was great concern that persons with "inferior genes" would have a degrading effect on the quality of the human race. As a result of this type of thinking, people with mental and other disabilities were warehoused in distant, large residential institutions so that they would not pose a threat to the gene pool of society. Beginning with the turn of the century, then, the guiding philosophy was not to teach and not even to care for persons with cognitive disabilities, but to protect society from them. This sorrowful and inhumane reasoning led to equally sorrowful and inhumane living conditions for most persons with mental and other severe disabilities.

Before the 1950s there was little in the way of services for most persons with mental disabilities except for being housed in institutions. Other services that were available were provided by parents' organizations and private groups. It was not until the 1950s and 1960s that public schools began to provide instruction for persons with moderate and severe mental disabilities, and it was not until several years later, during the mid-to late 1970s, that children and youth with the most severe and profound mental disabilities began to receive public school services. This first occurred when Public Law (P.L.) 94-142 (now called the *Individuals with Disabilities Education Act, IDEA*) was passed in 1975. The reasons given by the public school personnel for these exclusionary practices were that schools were intended to teach academic skills and that persons not capable of learning at least the three Rs should not be served.

When students with severe disabilities were finally accepted into public school systems, instructional practices were often guided by an ability-level philosophy. Students' developmental levels (i.e., mental ages, IQs, social quotients) were determined, and they were taught skills that were considered to be attainable within these levels. Instructional activities for students with moderate and severe mental disabilities, even those in their adolescent years, consisted of arts and crafts, preacademic and primary-level academic skills, language development, self-care skills, gross and fine motor skills, and prevocational skills. Regardless of the students' ages, most classrooms resembled kindergarten or nursery school classes.

When programs were developed for students with profound mental disabilities, instructional programming was intended to inch them forward on scales of normal human development. Teachers would attempt to increase the number of trials during which a student would make eye contact or put a block in a box, because this was the next step in the normal progression of human development according to the developmental scales. Positive reinforcement (usually a small amount of food) was used to reinforce correct responses, and behavioral performances were recorded and charted on graph paper. Little thought was given to the usefulness of the behavior or how it would improve the student's life.

Current best practices for providing services to persons with severe disabilities did not spontaneously emerge, but evolved from different sources of influence over a period of time. During the late 1960s, the concept of *normalization* was introduced (Nirje, 1969, 1972; Wolfensberger, 1972). This policy called for agencies to provide persons with mental disabilities with living and learning experiences that were as normal as possible. Skills to be taught were those that would allow greater independence and life patterns that were parallel to those of people without disabilities. Under the normalization principle, it was intended that the instructional procedures for teaching these skills also were to be as close to normal as possible.

At about the same time, the *deinstitutionalization* period began. This period was characterized by a decline in the number of persons living in large residential institutions and an increase in the number living with their families and in smaller community-based residences. Community facilities were intended to be homelike and included foster homes, group homes, intermediate-care facilities, and sheltered apartments. Much effort was made to move individuals out of large residential institutions into smaller facilities located in regular communities, where services traditionally provided only in the institutions were to be provided.

As normalization and deinstitutionalization were occurring and public school programs were emerging, the focus gradually began to shift from simply providing services to improving the quality of instruction and related services. Many instructional programs lagged behind what was being proposed and implied by the normalization and deinstitutionalization movements. Students were *not* being educated for lives that were to be as normal as possible. They were *not* being educated for living with their families and in communities and being a part of these social systems. Often they were being taught activities that would not be of use to them, even though they may have been able to learn them and may have enjoyed doing them. In the worst cases, teachers were simply providing baby-sitting or custodial care and not teaching anything at all.

The question of the value and relevance of much special education was first raised in the 1960s about special education for students with mild mental disabilities. The most often cited paper was one written by Lloyd Dunn (1968), a prominent professor of special education at Peabody College. Dunn stated that too many minority children were being placed in self-contained special classes for students with mild mental disabilities and that this practice was discriminatory and did little good for the students. Dunn proposed that many of these students should not be considered mentally disabled, that general education should be able to serve them, and that so much special education was not justifiable. Following Dunn's paper, special education programs and related practices for students with mild mental disabilities started to change. But similar concerns about the practices of educating students with more severe disabilities did not begin to surface until a few years later, after the passage of P.L. 94-142.

Contemporary Best Practices for Students with Severe Disabilities

Within the last 30 years, approaches to educating individuals with moderate or more severe cognitive disabilities have changed dramatically, and they are still changing today. Three discernible movements have emerged, each with clusters of recommended practices. In order of time, the first to evolve was the call to include persons with severe disabilities in the mainstream of life and to teach them functional, practical, and chronologically age-appropriate skills so that they could be more successful in that mainstream (Brown, Nietupski, & Hamre-Nietupski, 1976). This position has continued and forms the basis for many of today's practices.

The second movement came to the forefront in the early 1990s and had at its core the goal of improving the abilities of people with cognitive disabilities so that they would have greater personal control over their own lives and make their own decisions to the extent possible. This self-determination movement extended the previous position and has also become a significant theme in the education of students with cognitive disabilities (Wehmeyer, 1992). Often associated with improved self-determination is the ability to make personal choices, regulate one's own life, and be a self-advocate, all of which should lead to an improved quality of life.

The most recent movement, spurred by school reform movements and the 1997 amendments to IDEA, is to provide students with disabilities access to the general curriculum to whatever extent they are capable of participating in it (Wehmeyer, Lance, & Bashinski, 2002; Wehmeyer, Lattin, & Agran, 2001) and to include them in statewide accountability evaluations through the use of alternate assessments (Browder, 2001; Browder & Spooner, 2003; Kleinert, Kearns, & Kennedy, 1997; Ysseldyke & Olsen, 1999). This movement stretches beyond the inclusion of students with severe disabilities in regular classrooms and the teaching of functional skills and calls for them to be engaged in general education learning activities whenever possible. It also holds schools accountable for the progress of these students, just as it does for students without disabilities. Some have noted that, while this aspect of reform is important, it should not negate the value of providing students with severe disabilities the opportunity to learn functional skills (Billingsley & Albertson, 1999). The details and implications of the three movements are described in the following sections.

Inclusion and Functional Instruction

In 1976 Brown and his colleagues published a paper that set the tone for much of what has evolved into current best practices for educating students with severe disabilities (Brown et al., 1976). They proposed the following:

- Students with severe disabilities should be educated in regular schools with students who do not have disabilities. "Placement in large multipurpose institutions, sustained maintenance at home, and/or sustained placement in self-contained classes within segregated schools is generally restrictive. The community must create other more educationally tenable developmental environments" (p. 3).
- The exclusive use of homogeneous ability grouping of students with severe disabilities should be avoided. Development and learning are more likely to occur if there is opportunity to interact with persons of different ability levels. "If severely handicapped students are to be expected to function effectively in heterogeneous community environments, as many preceding developmental experiences as possible should represent that heterogeneity" (p. 5).
- Teachers must directly teach the skills that students with severe disabilities are expected to learn and teach them in the settings in which they need to be performed. Referring to a "zero degree inference strategy," the authors wrote, "Teachers of severely handicapped students can rarely, if ever, infer that because a student performs a particular skill in an artificial setting, he or she can also perform that skill in other more natural settings" (p. 6).
- All educational efforts for persons with severe disabilities should be judged as they relate to the "criterion of ultimate functioning," that is, the ability to participate as fully as possible in integrated adult environments. Any activity that does not contribute to this type of personal development should not be pursued. We need to ask questions such as "Is this activity necessary to prepare students to ultimately function in complex heterogeneous community settings?" and "Could students function as adults if they did not acquire the skill?" (p. 9).
- Teaching procedures for students with severe disabilities should be natural. Instruction should be delivered to groups of students, as opposed to an overreliance on one-to-one instruction. Massed practice of behaviors in artificial circumstances (e.g., putting a block in

> a box for 10 consecutive trials) should be avoided in favor of distributed teaching of functional skills throughout the school day. Skills should be learned and practiced in different settings, with different people, and under different conditions so that the learner will be better able to use the skills in natural settings. Instructional materials and settings should be real. "However cumbersome, time consuming, inconvenient, or expensive it may be to do so, the pegs, felt squares, pictures of money, tokens, pictures, edible consequences, and many, if not all, of the commercially available kits and irrelevant paper-and-pencil tasks should be faded out" (p. 14).

Since the publication of the paper by Brown et al., many subsequent authors have described or summarized related best practices in papers and books, sometimes emphasizing one or more of the components of Brown et al. (e.g., Ayres, Meyer, Erevelles, & Park-Lee, 1994; Certo, Haring, & York, 1984; Downing & Eichinger, 2002; Ford et al., 1989; Fox et al., 1986; Horner, Meyer, & Fredericks, 1986; McDonnell, Hardman, McDonnell, & Kiefer-O'Donnell, 1995; Meyer, 1987; Meyer, Eichinger, & Park-Lee, 1987; Rainforth & York-Barr, 1997; Sailor et al., 1989; Salisbury & Vincent, 1990; Snell, 1988; Strain, 1990; Westling, 1989; Williams, Fox, Thousand, & Fox, 1990). These writings have outlined practices covering services for all ages of persons with severe disabilities, from infancy through adulthood, and have presented the perspectives of parents, teachers, administrators, and advocates. Together they elaborate on, discuss, and study many of the best practices for providing services to people with severe disabilities based on the initial writing of Brown et al. In the following sections some of these practices are discussed in more detail.

Inclusion and Integration

Where students with severe disabilities go to school is important and can affect the skills that they develop, their attitudes, and the attitudes of others toward them. It can also influence the involvement of parents in the formal schooling process. For many years now the argument has been made that students with severe disabilities should receive their education in general school placements and in regular classrooms. Still, in many school systems and locations in our country, this does not occur, and some have argued against universal inclusion for all students with cognitive disabilities (Hilton & Smith, 1994; Smith & Puccini, 1995). Nevertheless, inclusion has become a dominant model of service delivery, and it is anticipated that it will continue into the future (Putnam, Spiegel, & Bruininks, 1995). Following are suggested guidelines for placing students with severe disabilities in inclusive settings. Strategies and tactics for achieving inclusive programs are discussed in Chapter 10.

- Students should be placed in regular schools for their education. The most preferred school will be the one that they would attend if they did not have a severe disability, that is, the home school appropriate for their chronological age.
- Students should be placed in regular classrooms and given necessary supports for functioning successfully in these classrooms.
- If a student is to spend any portion of the day in a special classroom, the primary or homeroom classroom in the school should be a regular classroom. The student should be placed in a special classroom or another setting only if appropriate learning opportunities to achieve individual objectives are not possible in the regular classroom with appropriate supports and services.
- Placement in regular education schools and classrooms should be based on the natural ratio of people with severe disabilities to people who do not have severe disabilities. Typically, no more than 1% of a school's population will have severe disabilities, and there will be no more than one child with a severe disability in a regular classroom.
- Various tactics may be used in regular classes to promote successful inclusion, such as cooperative learning, the use of peer tutors, the judicious use of paraprofessionals, adapted curricula and materials, and collaborative problem solving.
- Students with severe disabilities will be better able to participate in classes that are activity based and those that have more hands-on activities, such as home economics, industrial arts, art, physical education, and the like. As students become older, learning activities outside the classroom, and often outside the school, will become more appropriate. Because this has the potential of segregating students, care must be taken to use this form of instruction judiciously and to involve nondisabled peers when possible.
- If students are placed in separate special classrooms, they should have access to peers throughout the day, attend all special events with their peers, and have opportunities to learn in other settings besides the special class.

- The special education teacher should work with the regular education teacher to develop activities that promote appropriate learning for students with severe disabilities and that foster social interactions between students with and without severe disabilities.
- Students without disabilities may play different roles in interacting with the students with disabilities. They may participate with them in cooperative learning activities, provide them with physical assistance when such is required, and serve as tutors on certain learning tasks. Most importantly, they may become friends. It is more appropriate for teachers to support relationships of interdependence than hierarchical roles.
- The regular classroom teacher should be a part of the instructional team for the child with disabilities along with the special educator and the related services professional. This educator should participate in IEP planning, work with parents, and, of course, instruct students. It is important that all school personnel, especially classroom teachers, accept the philosophical position that students with severe disabilities do not "belong" to the special education teacher, but are a part of the school population, even though they have need for special attention.
- Paraprofessionals may be an important source of support for students with severe disabilities in regular classrooms. However, there are risks associated with the overuse of paraprofessionals: they may not be appropriately qualified, may be given undue responsibilities, and may serve to isolate the student from the classroom teacher and peers.
- Administrators should provide support for inclusion by providing adequate time for teachers to meet and plan for students in inclusive classrooms and by showing positive support for inclusion.

Social Integration

In concert with the goal of instructional inclusion is the social integration of students with and without disabilities. Being physically included does not necessarily mean one will be socially included, and yet this is an essential goal. Social integration is an extremely important component of educational programs for students with severe disabilities, because social skills are very difficult for them to learn, especially when they are segregated from good models of social behavior. They need every opportunity to develop social skills in socially integrated environments. More than any other cluster of skills, social skills affect the degree to which persons with severe disabilities are accepted and are able to participate in normal life routines and thus enjoy a good quality of life. The practices described below are suggested as optimal ways to improve social skills through social integration. Further discussions of strategies and tactics in this area are presented in Chapters 10, 11, and 12.

- All current and future age-appropriate environments for social interaction should be identified and targeted for instruction. These environments will certainly include the regular classroom and school and the home, but may also include different community settings and vocational settings, depending on the age of the student.
- Specific social skills that are to be taught should be identified for students. These may include appropriate behaviors to be developed or increased and/or undesirable social behaviors to be reduced and replaced with more appropriate behaviors.
- During all instructional activities and in all instructional environments, social skills should be taught. This suggests that a great deal of incidental teaching is appropriate.
- Barriers and facilitators of social integration in natural environments should be identified. These may include particular individuals, physical structures, or personal characteristics of the individual with severe disabilities.
- The teacher should provide information to nondisabled individuals so that they might better understand the behavior of students with severe disabilities and should assist them in developing appropriate ways to interact with these students.
- Teachers and other professionals who work with and interact with students who have severe disabilities should be encouraged to set social behavior standards for them similar to those set for other students without disabilities of the same ages. In other words, inappropriate social behavior should not be tolerated simply because the student has a disability.
- Prompts for appropriate social actions should be subtle but direct enough to improve the behavior. Prompts should be faded as soon as possible in order to allow natural environmental stimuli to influence the student's behavior.

- Efforts to improve the *quality* as well as the *quantity* of social interactions between persons with and without disabilities should be continuous.

Functional, Age-Appropriate Skills

Even though students with severe disabilities may participate in and benefit from some or all of the elements of the general curriculum (see the discussion in the following section), public school instruction should continue to play a vital role in teaching students valuable, age-appropriate functional skills. Functional skills, such as crossing a street or making a sandwich, are those that allow a person to be successful in their typical daily lives. Instruction in this area should not be sacrificed because of the inclusion of students in regular schools and classrooms or because they are participating in the general curriculum.

Specific functional objectives must be developed for most students with severe disabilities, and these must be written into the student's individual educational program (IEP). To have a framework in which to teach these objectives, the teacher must plan a series of daily activities, including activities in the regular classroom, and use a number of instructional methods to help students to achieve their specific objectives within these activities. The points presented in the following list suggest preferred practices related to teaching functional skills. Many of the chapters in the text elaborate on these practices.

- Skills should not be taught as isolated behavioral targets, but as integrated clusters that build on each other and that allow students to have greater access to more activities and environments.
- All objectives should focus on increasing the independence, participation, or self-determination of the individual or on making the individual less dependent and less isolated within the home, school, and community.
- Students should not be excluded from instructional activities because they cannot learn a complete skill independently. Instead, objectives may be developed that allow students to have meaningful *partial participation.*
- Although the student should have ample opportunity to enjoy incidental learning through participation and partial participation in class activities, the most important skills to be learned must be identified as instructional objectives, and instructional programs and data collection systems must be developed to ensure that they are learned in a timely manner.
- Objectives should be written so that they describe specific observable behaviors and include criteria so that the student's skill level on a particular objective can be readily determined. Objectives should be written that target initial acquisition of skills and also skill maintenance and generalization.
- Instructional programs for each student's specific objectives should be written to describe setting, materials, prompts, expected behavior, consequences for correct performance, correction procedure for incorrect performance, and the data collection or recording system.
- Settings, tasks, and materials used for instruction should be those found in natural environments, not artificially developed.
- Important skills that contribute to functioning in all life domains, such as language, ambulation and mobility, motor skills, and social skills, should be taught within functional contexts, that is, the school, home, or community.
- For specific objectives, student performance data must be recorded and should be carefully observed. Decisions to change instruction should be based on students' performance as reflected in the data. Different forms of data collection, including quantitative and qualitative forms, may be useful.

Nonschool, Community-Based Instruction

Although the inclusion of students with disabilities in all regular education activities is greatly valued, there is often a need to provide instruction for students with severe disabilities outside school contexts in order that functional and age-appropriate skills can be learned and generalized to natural settings. Sometimes this may be done with peers with and without disabilities learning together, and this is preferred.

Community-based instruction (CBI) takes students from classrooms and school grounds and into community settings where they can learn necessary skills. The intention of CBI is to teach students to be more independent and self-reliant in community settings. It is important even for students with the most severe disabilities to learn to participate as much as possible in community settings. The ideas listed below are recommended when providing community-based instruction. More in-depth discussion of this topic is presented in Chapter 18.

- The best and most natural way to teach community skills is in real community settings. Teaching skills in simulated settings can be helpful, but simulations will usually not be effective without additional instruction and assessment in actual community settings.
- There are community skills that are differentially important for different age groups. Young children, for example, may not need to shop for groceries, but they may need to learn to cross the street safely.
- An ecological inventory of community sites should be conducted to determine the skills needed for the site. These skills may then be broken down and taught through appropriate instructional procedures.
- The student with disabilities and his family members should be involved in selecting the community sites for which skills are needed and the specific objectives for these sites. Family members and friends may also participate in community learning activities whenever possible.
- Probes of performance ability on community skills must be taken in community settings to determine if the student has actually learned the skill. Skills should not be considered learned until they have been adequately demonstrated in the targeted environments.
- The "community" in community-based training suggests that the skills be demonstrated in the community where the student lives. It is most appropriate for skills to be taught and tested in the community settings that will be used in real life.

Participation in the General Curriculum and in Alternate Assessments

The 1997 IDEA amendments called for students with disabilities to have access to the general curriculum and also to be assessed using standardized alternate assessment systems in order that their progress may be evaluated like other students in public education. Reinforcing this policy, many professionals now believe that students with severe disabilities will be better served if they are given the opportunity to engage in more traditional academic activities, such as literacy instruction and other areas of the general curriculum (Jorgeson, 1999; Katims, 2000; Kliewer & Biklen, 2001; Kliewer & Landis, 1999; Ryndak, Morrison, & Sommerstein, 1999; Tashie, Jorgenson, Shapiro-Barnard, Martin, & Schuh, 1996). This means that not only should students with severe disabilities be included in general education classrooms, but that they should participate in learning in the same curricular areas as students without disabilities (Agran, Alper, & Wehmeyer, 2002; Wehmeyer et al., 2001). Additionally, their progress must be evaluated using alternate standardized state assessment systems. The implication is that the general curriculum, as well as the student's IEP, should both be driving forces for what students should be learning and that learning outcomes must be documented.

Engagement in the General Curriculum

For some students with severe disabilities, participating in the general curriculum may open a door that until now has been inappropriately shut. It could improve and expand the quality of their education. But it also raises a question about the extent to which many students will be able to participate or benefit from the general curriculum.

To address this question, Agran et al. (2002) surveyed 200 special education teachers of students with severe disabilities. Their purpose was to determine the extent to which the teachers' students participated in the general curriculum and factors related to their participation. Analyzing the responses they received from 84 (42%) of those surveyed, Agran et al. found that most teachers were *not* supportive of their students with severe disabilities participating in the general curriculum. Even though 81% of the teachers reported that their students were included in general education classrooms for all or part of the school day, 63% thought participation in the general curriculum was more important for students with mild disabilities, rather than those with severe disabilities, and only 47% said that there was a plan in their school district to increase access to the general curriculum for students with severe disabilities. Only 35% of the teachers said that they actively coplanned with the general educator to better ensure the success of the students with severe disabilities in the general curriculum. The respondents ranked social skills and communication skills as being among the most important for participating in the general curriculum and indicated that challenging behaviors and resistance from general educators and building administrators were the most significant barriers to general curriculum participation.

Decision Making Regarding the General Curriculum

Notwithstanding the findings of this study, it may well be beneficial for some students to participate in the general curriculum, and to deny them this opportunity could be a serious error. Wehmeyer et al. (2001) noted that some students with cognitive disabilities could benefit from some or all of the general curriculum, but that many persons with cognitive disabilities would not be able to do so. Wehmeyer et al. offered a decision-making model to assist IEP teams in determining the extent to which a student should participate in the general curriculum. In the model, they propose that a series of questions be raised that would allow team members to identify the extent and manner to which the students with cognitive disabilities might participate in the general curriculum.

A copy of the model is contained in Figure 2–1. As it shows, the decision-making process begins with an assumption that two directives will influence the decision of what constitutes a student's formal curriculum (what the student is to be taught). The first is the locally (or state) determined general curriculum; the second is the unique learning needs of the student. With the recognition of these two influences, the first question to ask is if the general curriculum is appropriate for the student with disabilities without any modification. If the answer is yes, then the general curriculum will become the student's curriculum, as the figure shows. However, if the answer is no, the next question is whether assistive technology has been considered. As we discuss in Chapter 19, many types of assistive technology may help the student to participate in the general curriculum. If appropriate, the IEP team may consider providing assistive technology devices and services in order to allow the student to participate in some or all of the general curriculum.

If assistive technology has been considered and it is thought that the regular curriculum is still not entirely appropriate, then the curriculum may be *adapted* in a way that will allow the student to participate. A curriculum adaptation consists of a modification to the way in which information is represented to the student and the manner in which the student engages in the learning process. An adapted curriculum does not change the fundamental content of the curriculum, but presents it in a way that the student can comprehend it and participate in. For example, the student might not be able to read a history textbook, but can

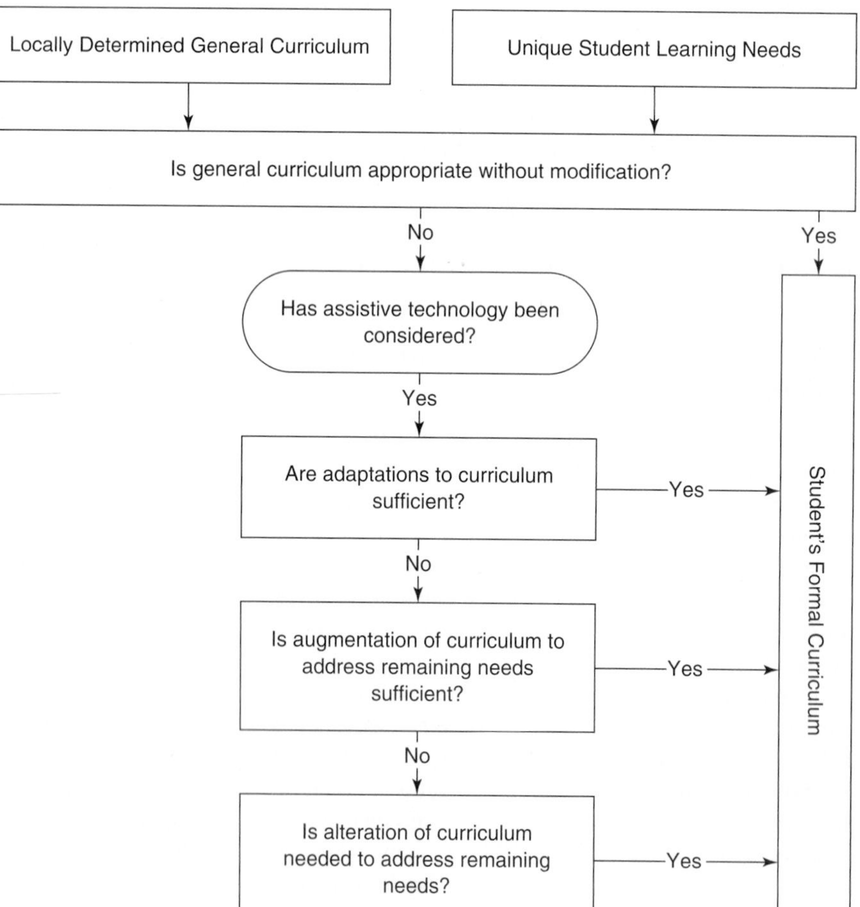

Figure 2–1 A Model to Gain Access to the General Curriculum
Source: "Achieving Access to the General Curriculum for Students with Mental Retardation: A Curriculum Decision-making Model," by M. L. Wehmeyer, D. Lattin, & M. Agra, *Education and Training in Mental Retardation and Development Disabilities, 36* (4), 327–342. Copyright 2002 by the Division of Mental Retardation and Developmental Disabilities/CEC. Reprinted by permission.

arrive at the same general understanding by watching a video or listening to a presentation by another student. Or, instead of writing a paper about a particular battle, the student, with assistance, might be able to search for pictures on the Internet and develop a PowerPoint presentation using them. Again, the content of the curriculum is essentially the same, but the input to the student and the output by the student may be modified. If this is sufficient to meet the student's needs, then the student can participate in some or all of the general curriculum using an adapted mode.

If the IEP team decides that the student's needs are not sufficiently addressed even with an adapted curriculum, Wehmeyer et al. propose that the general curriculum be augmented to meet additional needs of the student. An *augmented* curriculum is one that is enhanced or expanded in some way to teach not only the content of the general curriculum, but also the skills necessary to better enable the student to *participate* in the general curriculum. One type of curriculum augmentation, as Wehmeyer and his colleagues note, is teaching the student self-regulation skills. For example, it may be necessary that the student learn the appropriate communication and social skills to become engaged in general curriculum activities. The teacher may determine that the best way to approach this is to teach the student how to manage his own behavior so that he can be a meaningful, successful participant in general curricular activities. If this is identified as a part of what the student needs to learn to benefit from the regular curriculum, then the regular curriculum has been *augmented* with additional instructional targets that allow the student to better participate in it.

However, even with adaptations to the general curriculum and/or augmenting the instruction of the curriculum to help a student to engage in it, many students with cognitive disabilities, especially those with more severe disabilities, will not be able to benefit from it in any meaningful way or there will be higher-priority needs that must be addressed. When such a condition exists, the IEP team must decide on an alternative curriculum for the student, such as one that focuses on teaching more real-life functional skills. This does not necessarily imply that the student cannot learn many important skills in a general education setting or that the student cannot enjoy various aspects of the general curriculum; it means, however, that the key learning targets for the student will lie outside the general curriculum.

Universally Designing the Curriculum

To some extent, the nature of the curriculum itself will be a factor in whether some individuals with disabilities may participate in it. It is possible to design commercial or teacher-made curricular materials that allow individuals with various abilities to participate (Center for Applied Special Technology (CAST), 1999–2002; Council for Exceptional Children, 1999; Hitchcock, Meyer, Rose, & Jackson, 2002; Wehmeyer et al., 2002). Wehmeyer et al. (2002) proposed that the principles of "universal design" be used in schools to allow greater access by students with cognitive disabilities to the general curriculum. These principles, developed by the Center for Applied Special Technology (1999–2002), propose that there are three essential qualities of a universal curriculum:

1. *Multiple means of representation:* Alternative means of presentation reduce perceptual/learning barriers and can adjust to the different ways that students recognize things. Digital format is the most flexible means for presenting curricular materials because it makes material transformable, transportable, and recordable.
2. *Multiple means of expression:* Students can respond with preferred means of control. Different strategic and motor systems of students can be accommodated.
3. *Multiple means of engagement:* Students' interests in learning can be matched with the mode of presentation/response; this can better motivate more students.

If the way in which the material is presented, the way the student can respond, and the way the student can be engaged are variable, then it is much more likely that students with severe disabilities will be more able to participate in some or all of the curriculum.

The extent to which all or the majority of students with severe disabilities will be able to participate and learn in the general curriculum is not fully known at this time. However, it would be unjust to dismiss this possibility as irrelevant, as many students with severe disabilities show evidence of developing and using various forms of literacy skills (Kliewer & Biklen, 2001; Kliewer & Landis, 1999; Ryndak et al., 1999). Thus this movement clearly warrants continued attention. We discuss it more in Chapter 17 when we address teaching academic skills.

Alternate Assessment

Regardless of a student's specific curriculum, if the student with disabilities is part of a public school system that mandates assessment of its students for the purpose of school accountability, which most states now do, the IDEA amendments of 1997 require that students with disabilities must be included as part of the assessment process. If the student has a disability that prohibits her from participating meaningfully in the standard assessment process, even if accommodations are allowed, then the student must be assessed using an alternate means of assessment. This assessment may be conducted in various ways (Ysseldyke & Olsen, 1999), but the alternate assessment portfolio appears to be the approach that has been used the longest and studied the most (Kleinert & Kearns, 1999; Kleinert et al., 1997; Kleinert, Kennedy, & Kearns, 1999; Turner, Baldwin, Kleinert, & Kearns, 2000).

By requiring that students with severe disabilities be given access to the general curriculum and participate in alternate assessment systems, there is an expectation that higher standards will result in higher levels of performance (Browder & Spooner, 2003). At this time, more research is needed to definitely determine if this outcome will result. There is, however, evidence that better outcomes on alternate assessment portfolios are correlated with better practices in schools. Analyzing data from 60 students distributed across 34 schools in Kentucky, Turner et al. (2000) studied the relationship between student outcomes as assessed by Kentucky's alternate portfolio assessment system, the quality of the students' IEPs, and the quality of the services offered to the students within the schools. They found a significant correlation between the quality of programs (based on the PQI Checklist evaluation; Meyer, Eichinger, & Downing, 1992) and the quality of the portfolios, but not between the quality of the IEP (based on criteria developed by Hunt, Goetz, & Anderson, 1986) and the portfolios. Turner et al. suggest that the results imply that better school programs for students with severe disabilities will result in better outcomes for the students as reflected in their portfolio assessment scores. They explain that, although all the students' IEPs may not have reflected that their objectives were entirely indicative of best practice, the overall rating of programs was clearly associated with improved performance as indicated by the portfolios. We discuss alternate portfolios in more detail in Chapter 9.

Self-Determination as an Educational Outcome

For the last several years, many people, including parents of children with disabilities, advocates, teachers and other professionals and, most importantly, individuals with cognitive disabilities themselves, have believed that self-determination by people with disabilities is critical to experiencing life satisfactorily. If we accept this as an important educational outcome, then our educational programs and all the services provided by professionals should be guided toward this outcome. Furthermore, we must support individuals with cognitive disabilities in the development of the relevant and necessary skills that will allow them to have greater control over their lives (Wehmeyer, 1992, 1996).

The desire for people with cognitive disabilities to develop greater self-determination had its origins in the previously discussed normalization movement of the 1960s and is related to other social trends affecting the lives of people with disabilities, most notably self-advocacy and disability rights (Ward, 1996). The self-advocacy movement, led by groups such as People First, encourages the self-organization of people with cognitive and other disabilities in order that they might learn to speak for themselves, make their own decisions, defend their rights as citizens, and help others who cannot speak for themselves. The disabilities rights movement, which originated like other civil rights movements in the 1960s, is concerned with gaining concrete benefits and opportunities in society, such as equal employment opportunities and the right to be integrated as full members of society (Ward, 1996). The Americans with Disabilities Act (ADA) and the Individuals with Disabilities Education Act (IDEA) have affirmed many of the rights that were sought by people with disabilities.

Self-determination, sometimes referred to as empowerment, can be (1) viewed as an educational outcome, (2) defined in relation to the characteristics of an individual's behavior, and (3) achieved through life-long learning, opportunities, and experiences (Wehmeyer, 1996). Self-determination has been defined as *"acting as the primary causal agent in one's life and making choices and decisions regarding one's quality of life, free from undue external influence or interference"* (Wehmeyer, 1992 [emphasis added]). For self-determination to occur, according to Wehmeyer (1996; and Wehmeyer, Kelchner, & Richards, 1996), an individual must exhibit four essential characteristics:

1. *Autonomy:* acting according to one's own preferences, interests, and abilities, independently and free from undue external influences
2. *Self-regulation:* deciding what strategies and tactics to use in particular situations, in setting goals for oneself and working to achieve these goals, in problem solving, and in monitoring one's own performance in these tasks
3. *Psychological empowerment:* a belief that one has control over important circumstances, that is, an internal locus of control, and a belief that one has the skills to achieve the desired outcomes and that by applying these skills the desired outcome will occur

4. *Self-realization:* the individual has a reasonably accurate knowledge of himself, his strengths, and his limitations and acts in a way that capitalizes on this knowledge

These conditions of a self-determined person are graphically displayed in Figure 2–2 (Wehmeyer, 1996).

For these essential characteristics to develop within an individual and thus lead to self-determination, important life experiences are necessary. Unfortunately, these are often lacking in the lives of people with mental disabilities. Wehmeyer (1996) referred to these critical experiences as *component elements of self-determined behavior.* They include the following:

- Choice making
- Decision making
- Problem solving
- Goal setting and attainment
- Self-observation, evaluation, and reinforcement
- Internal locus of control
- Positive attributions of efficacy and outcome expectations
- Self-awareness
- Self-knowledge

Why should self-determination be considered a primary goal for students with cognitive disabilities? First, many people with moderate to severe disabilities and those who are concerned about the quality of their lives believe that for too long they have had too little influence over their own lives and conversely have had their lives controlled too much by others. In an ongoing cycle, the control exerted by others has led to greater dependency and less independence. Second, we all desire a satisfactory quality of life. Although quality of life may be an elusive concept, it is certainly something that everyone wants and that everyone wants to define and control for oneself. It means we can be in charge of our own relationships, have our basic needs satisfied, and make important decisions for ourselves. Third, because there has been insufficient emphasis on self-determination, much of what we have done previously in special education has led to very limited lives for adults with mental disabilities.

Figure 2–2 Depiction of Essential Characteristics of Self-Determination

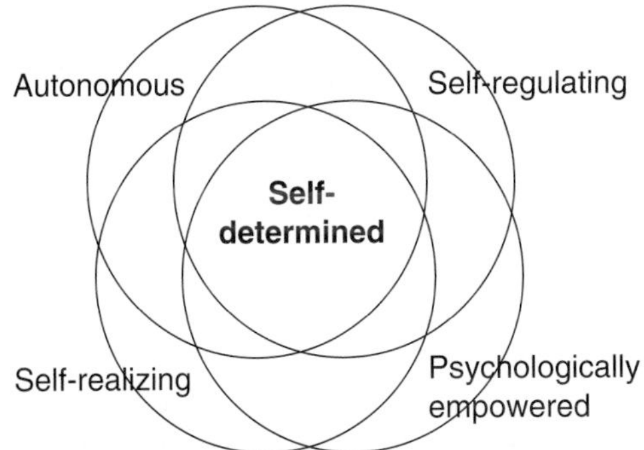

Source: Wehmeyer, M. L. 1996. *Self-Determination across the Life Span: Independence and Choice for People with Disabilities.* Baltimore: Paul H. Brookes. Reprinted by permission of the author.

To an extent, this condition still exists. Wehmeyer, Agran, and Hughes (2000) conducted a national survey that was responded to by more than 1,200 high school-level special education teachers (out of 9,762 mailed out) to determine what teachers thought about the importance of teaching self-determination skills to their students with disabilities. They found that most of the respondents (60%) were familiar with the construct of self-determination and felt it important to teach skills such as decision making, problem solving, and choice making. Most teachers thought such skills would be especially important for students during the postschool years. Somewhat disturbing, though, were findings that many teachers did not think that their students would benefit from instruction in self-determination strategies, only 22% of the teachers stated that all their students had self-determination strategies on their IEPs, and teachers of students with severe disabilities were less likely to focus on self-determination than were teachers of students with mild disabilities, even though both groups of teachers had the same level of knowledge about the term self-determination. The authors pointed out that this latter finding is unfortunate. They noted that "The fact that someone may not become completely independent in his or her decision-making capacity does not mean that he or she cannot become less dependent or more involved in decisions that impact his or her life" (p. 65).

Those teachers polled by Wehmeyer et al. (2000), as well as others, should realize that there is a need to place more emphasis on teaching students to become more self-determined. Several studies clearly make this point. In a study of 282 adolescents with mental disabilities, Wehmeyer (1994) found that these individuals, as a group, lacked some of the psychological characteristics necessary for self-determination. Their *self-efficacy* (belief in your own ability to perform certain behaviors) decreased as they got older and their *locus of control* (belief that one's actions are related to certain outcomes) was more external than internal as compared to the same characteristic within people without mental disabilities. This indicated that the adolescents believed something other than their own actions affected their lives. Wehmeyer concluded that "it appears that students with mental retardation hold perceptions of self-determination which are not conducive to becoming the causal agent in one's own life" (p. 16). We should keep in mind that such perceptions can be created by the experiences that we have had that influence our own lives. This point was made clear in the following study.

Wehmeyer and Metzler (1995) reported that a survey of over 4,000 adults with mental disabilities and other developmental disabilities indicated that very often they were given little say in basic life events, even though decisions about these events bore directly on their quality of life. For example, 66% of the adults had no say in where they lived, 88% were not able to choose the staff person that worked with them, 77% did not choose their own roommate, and 56% had no choice in their job or daily activity. A majority were not given the opportunity to do their own banking, pay their own bills, or consent to their own medical treatment. Wehmeyer and Metzler conclude that the study strongly suggested that "people with mental retardation are not likely to be self-determining." However, they state that, although there were numerous possibilities for this condition, "environments that are overly structured or protective and do not place emphasis on opportunities to make meaningful choices and decisions and solve problems are contributors" (p. 117).

Stancliffe and Wehmeyer (1995) also conclude that, even though there is evidence that many people with mental disabilities can make effective choices, there are generally few opportunities for them to do so. Furthermore, they point out that, as adults, people with moderate or severe cognitive disabilities do not fare well in employment, residential opportunities, or social integration. These conditions lead to the conclusion that we must do a better job of teaching people with cognitive disabilities to have greater control over their own lives and give them the skills and experiences to develop this control. If we can do so, our educational efforts may result in better outcomes. Consider two additional studies.

Wehmeyer et al. (1996) collected data from 407 individuals with mental disabilities who were self-advocates. The data they collected evaluated their autonomy, self-regulation, locus of control, self-efficacy, outcome expectancy, and self-realization. They then examined the degree to which each of these individuals demonstrated self-determination by measuring how much influence they had over different aspects of their lives, such as where they lived, where they worked, what they did with their free time, and so on. They found that those individuals who had higher levels of self-determination also had higher measures of autonomy, self-awareness, self-regulation, and locus of control. The degree of their disability correlated only a little with the degree of their self-determination ability, suggesting that cognitive limitations are not a major factor in acquiring self-determination abilities.

Wehmeyer and Schwartz (1997) further examined the effect of self-determination by following up on the status of individuals with mental retardation who had left high school in the previous year. While in high school, the individuals' self-determination abilities and locus of control had been assessed, and the individuals were then categorized into two groups based on whether they had high or low levels in these areas. About 1 year later, follow-up data were collected on various life conditions. The researchers found that although virtually all the individuals continued to live with their parents, those with higher measured levels of self-determination while in high school expressed more than twice as often the desire to leave home and live elsewhere. They also found that significantly more persons with higher self-determination levels had jobs and maintained their own savings and checking accounts.

Improving Self-Determination Ability

Because of findings such as these, Wehmeyer and others have proposed that policies and practices be adopted in homes and schools that are intended to improve the self-determination ability of people with mental disabilities (Brotherson, Cook, Cunconan-Lahr, & Wehmeyer, 1995; Brown & Cohen, 1996; Doll, Sands, Wehmeyer, & Palmer, 1996; Reid, Parsons, Green, & Browning, 2001; Sands & Wehmeyer, 1996). Among their proposals is a strong position that developing the component elements that lead to self-determination must begin early in life. As Brown and Cohen stated, "If self-determination is deemed an important outcome for adults with severe disabilities, it is critical that opportunities to be self-determining be made available early in life" (p. 22).

The psychological characteristics and behaviors that are necessary for self-determination have been documented as occurring among typical individuals in an age-related developmental sequence (Doll et al., 1996). However, they must occur in an appropriate social context, and the opportunity must be made for them to be practiced. This provides us with possible forms of intervention that may occur at different times of life in order to affect the occurrence of self-determination and related skills. Doll et al. provide information about typical self-determination development and also some ways that parents, teachers, and others might encourage development of self-determination among children and adolescents with cognitive disabilities. Several examples are listed below.

Early Childhood (Ages 2 to 5). During this period the focus should be on helping the child to recognize personal preferences and be aware of alternative options. A strong degree of trust is necessary between the child and the caregiver so that the child has enough freedom to make the choice. Ample opportunities should be given to make choices within structured situations, but the child must be told that some choices can be harmful. Helping the child to think about the consequences of choices made in the past may improve planning and decision making. It may also be possible to help the child to become aware of others' views by encouraging thinking about how others might choose in certain situations. Some examples as to how these situations might occur include the following:

- Offer choices with two alternatives: "Do you prefer a red or blue shirt?"
- Provide choices that might result in positive or negative outcomes: "What would you like to do in the next 10 minutes?"
- Provide feedback about the consequences of past choices: "What happened the last time you grabbed Jessica's crayon?"
- Provide a chance to plan for near-future activities: "What would be good for lunch tomorrow?"
- Promote self-evaluation by inviting comparisons with a model: "Look at how your picture is like mine."

Early Elementary (Ages 6 to 8). At about this age, children's thinking and reasoning begin to improve, and normally they can identify more varied solutions to their problems. They are also better judges of their own strengths and weaknesses and will select their strategies accordingly. At about six, children can set their own goals and work to achieve them, but they continue to need a lot of adult praise to stay on task and to continue to make improvements. They also can benefit from frequent evaluation of their work and can understand what helped or hindered their progress. Children at this age can usually benefit from the following:

- Allow them to choose from several different strategies to accomplish a task: "Do you think you should put the plates on the table first or the silverware or the napkins?"
- Encourage them to reconsider recently made choices in light of the consequences that occurred: "Remember yesterday when you decided you would only wear a sweater instead of your jacket and you were cold? Do you think it was a good idea?"
- Encourage them to think out loud about how they will solve a problem: "Tell me how you're going to decide who gets to come to your party."
- Provide opportunities for them to discuss how they learn best: "Would you rather practice your writing on paper or on your chalkboard? Which do you like better?"
- Let children at this age evaluate their work: "Look at how you colored your map. Do you think it's as nice as you could make it?"
- Help children at this age to set simple goals and reflect on whether they reached them. "You said you were going to help Mom do the laundry this weekend. Did you do that?"

Late Elementary (Ages 9 to 11). Within this age range, children usually begin to set personal goals and to take actions to reach these goals. As they get information, they can change their behavior in response. They can recognize when they need help and will ask for it. Often they realize when extra effort on their part will improve outcomes and understand how others are likely to react to their behavior or activities. All this will have a bearing on their behavior. However, they are limited in that the possible consequences about which they will be most aware will be those that are most salient, and they may not attend to the less apparent possible effects of their behavior. Parents, teachers, and others can be helpful during this period by providing opportunities and support, such as the following:

- Provide assistance in systematically analyzing decisions and possible outcomes. Writing the problem and sketching possible results can be helpful.
- Also use structured analysis to help the student to understand the results of past behaviors and what alternatives might have been selected.
- Give students the opportunity to write down personal goals for home or school and then review the goals regularly to discuss progress toward achieving them.
- Help the individual to understand the perspectives of others, such as teachers or coaches who have

reprimanded them. Help them to guess what the adult is thinking or feeling.

- Provide guidance in self-evaluating tasks and what could be done to improve performance.

Secondary (Ages 12 to 18). Normally, individuals at this age can achieve a sophisticated level of self-determination and the psychological abilities that allow it to occur. They can make systematic decisions similar to adults, determine the value of the information that they have to make decisions, and understand the consequences of their choices. They can revise their strategies in light of their successes or failures and generalize successful problem-solving strategies to other situations. They can understand the impact of their actions on others, but their rational behavior will often give way to emotional reactions, this being a primary barrier to being a fully self-determined person. Support for the continued development of self-determination can be provided through the following:

- Provide opportunities for them to make important decisions about their daily activities and about longer-term goals, for example, diet, academic goals, and career possibilities.
- Encourage adolescents to see the links between their daily decisions and their ability to achieve important goals for themselves, such as diet, exercise, and physical condition.
- Help them to see how long-term goals can be broken down into smaller tasks that will ultimately lead to the goals.
- Help them to recognize their strengths and weaknesses and how to set and achieve goals in light of this information. "It's great that you love animals, but since science is not one of your strengths, maybe you want to look into animal care instead of vet school."
- Encourage students to recognize different sources of support and to seek it when necessary. "Don't you think your boss might be able to show you how to clean those parts better? How do you think you could get him to do that?"

Self-Determination and Students with Very Significant Disabilities

Determining personal preferences is not something that we often think is possible for individuals with very significant disabilities, but in many cases it is not only possible, but important to promote. For example, Reid et al. (2001) offered adults with profound disabilities who were working in a small publishing shop the opportunity to choose whether to work with adaptive devices or to work without them. The devices helped them to work more independently by requiring less assistance from a support person. The workers nearly consistently chose to use the devices and thus relied on less support from their supervisor. Even though they could not talk, their preference was clearly expressed.

Doll et al. (1996) stressed that, although we cannot always know how well individuals with very severe cognitive disabilities can exercise self-determination, often the greater problem is with the *opportunity and support* for self-determination, more than the person's ability. Likewise, Brown and Cohen (1996) suggested that often teachers develop instructional objectives that focus more on the student responding to the teacher than on responding to the situation based on a self-conducted analysis of the situation and the need to respond. When developing instructional goals and objectives, consideration should be given to this issue.

It is clear that individuals with the most significant disabilities will be less likely than other individuals to express their preferences, wants, or interests, at least in a traditional sense. There are two ways that this challenge can be addressed. In the first, individuals who are very close to the person with very severe cognitive disabilities, such as parents, siblings, and teachers, may determine their wishes through close, personal observation and an interpretation of their behavior (Brown, Gothelf, Guess, & Lehr, 1998). Those who make these determinations are in critical positions, because they may be more influenced by what *they* want for the person, than by what the person would determine for herself. A primary way to undertake this approach is through the process of *person-centered planning,* an alternative planning system that is discussed in Chapter 5. Only by focusing on promoting self-determination to the extent appropriate within a context of interdependence might a person providing support also support self-determination (Brown et al., 1998).

A second approach to interpreting self-determination by persons with significant disabilities is through a *preference assessment* procedure. These procedures, which are discussed in Chapter 7, require closely observing the person's positive and negative reactions as they are presented with different items and activities. These reactions allow the observer to determine items and events that are preferred and those that are not. Reid, Everson, and Green (1999) found that only some of the preferred leisure items that were identified in several person-centered planning processes were actually preferred by individuals with profound multiple disabilities when they were presented to them in a preference assessment procedure.

Other Best Practices

In addition to the major practices described in the previous section, several others warrant our attention. These are also generally recognized as important components of quality programs for students with severe disabilities.

Collaboration with Other Professionals and Parents

The effectiveness of services for students with severe disabilities will be maximized if professionals and paraprofessionals collaborate with each other, as well as with parents and family members. In this way, services can be coordinated and goals and objectives can be developed that address students' needs holistically. Successful collaboration should reflect the practices described below. This topic is discussed in greater detail in Chapters 3 and 4.

- All persons participating in the collaborative process, including parents, professionals, and paraprofessionals, are of great importance with regard to the contribution that they can make.
- All participants should be aware of the knowledge and expertise of other members of the collaborative team.
- Representatives of various disciplines participate in the collaborative process. The needs of the student imply that professionals should participate.
- Decisions are made through a consensus of the group.
- Skills that are to be developed by various specialists (such as physical and occupational therapists) should be related to the functional skills needed by the student.
- All disciplines should share knowledge and skills with all others so that these can be applied to different needs and in different situations.
- Various degrees and types of participation are appropriate for parents, and their right to choose how they want to be involved in their child's education must be respected, especially within their cultural conditions. To the extent that they desire to participate, parents may be given the necessary instruction for joining in the instructional process as it occurs in the home and community.
- Parents should have frequent opportunities to visit the school and participate in activities with their child.
- Communication among parents, teachers, and other members of the school system is extremely important. A system should exist for regular parent–school communication.
- In addition to teaching their children, schools must recognize that they are a primary source of information for parents on other matters of support for their child. Parents should be provided with information about community services.

Assessment and Planning

For the most relevant instruction to be provided to the student with severe disabilities, professionals and parents must cooperatively determine students' current skills, determine what skills are needed, consider the extent to which the student can participate in the general curriculum, prioritize what is to be learned, and plan the specific objectives that should be achieved by the student. There are several types of assessment, but the most relevant forms involve the parents (and sometimes the student) and indicate what the student can do and what skills he needs to function in important environments. Based on this information, different types of plans can be developed, including Individual Family Service Plans (IFSP) for infants and toddlers with disabilities and their families and IEPs for school-age students. Person-centered plans, such as personal futures planning, can also be useful. Assessment and planning are covered in Chapters 5 and 6. Some of the associated best practices are listed here.

- Planning should be a collaborative process with input from parents, professionals, and the student whenever possible. Friends of the student can also provide meaningful information. All these persons can make important suggestions on appropriate objectives for students.
- To aid in this planning process, consideration should be given to functioning in all life domains, including areas of human activity that occur in *the school, home, community, recreational settings, and work environments.* Conducting *ecological inventories* in these settings and in their subenvironments is one way to determine what students need to function. Other methods include reviewing previous records, using adaptive behavior scales, and directly observing the student.
- Consideration should also be given to participation in the general curriculum. It may be determined that the student may benefit by being meaningfully

engaged in some or all of the curriculum followed by other students. In this phase of planning, consideration must be given to the role of assistive technology and the extent to which it may help to support the student's participation.

- The student's current skill level in different settings and his needs should prescribe which specific skills should be listed as objectives for the student on the IEP. In addition to current environments, future environments should be considered when identifying specific objectives.
- Planning for major moves or transitions should occur well in advance of the transition, with attention being given to the needs of the person with disability and to the nature of the future setting or service. The transition out of the school system and into the adult world, including employment and often new residential arrangements, is often considered one of the most important. Planning for this transition should begin when the student is in early adolescence. All types of transition planning should be initiated at least a year prior to the change.
- Special focus should be on planning to move the learner to the least restrictive environment if she is not already there. This plan will include actions that are necessary for achieving as much inclusion as possible.

Early Intervention and Preschool Programs

An early intervention program is an extremely important service that should be provided to infants and toddlers with disabilities. This should be followed by participation in a preschool program when the child is 3 years old. Since most children with severe disabilities are identifiable at birth or very early in life, it is possible to begin intervention early; to do so is critical to maximizing later development. Early intervention and preschool programs reduce the impact of the disability, promote the child's normalized development as much as possible, support the family in meeting the child's needs, and help to coordinate all the available sources of support for the child and the family. Complete discussion of early intervention and preschool programs is presented in Chapter 20. Early intervention and preschool programs should have several characteristics, including the following:

- Screening for children with disabilities, referral to programs, and initiation of services should all occur as soon as possible after atypical development has been identified.
- Support of the family is an integral component of early intervention. The family's strengths and needs should be identified on the IFSP, and unique intervention plans should be developed accordingly.
- In addition to family involvement, the extended family and other members of the family's social network should be considered a part of the support system for the child. Professional assistance should be provided to buttress the natural system of family support, not to supplant it.
- The early intervention program should be developmentally based in that it encourages and fosters integrated development as opposed to "training" isolated skills. Children should be encouraged to make choices, be actively involved in the learning process, and learn how to effectively influence what happens in their environment.
- Frequent assessment should occur, and learning activities should be planned as a result of these assessments.
- Because an important goal should be the introduction of the child into a normal kindergarten, the program should prepare the child for that environment and work with the family to plan a transition into the new program.
- Program evaluation should occur on a regular basis, with input from parents, teachers, and administrators on the satisfactory outcome of the program.

Related Services

Related services are those that students receive in addition to their normal instructional services that allow them to fully benefit from their educational program. Typical related services for students with severe disabilities include speech, communication, or language therapy; physical therapy; and occupational therapy. Students may also require services from school psychologists or behavioral specialists, nurses, social workers, rehabilitation engineers, rehabilitation counselors, and job coaches.

Appropriate related services should be listed on each student's IEP (or, for preschool children, the IFSP) and should be an integral part of the educational process. They should be provided in a collaborative fashion, as described below. Detailed information about the responsibilities of different professionals and their collaboration is given in Chapter 3, which also discusses the appropriate roles of paraprofessionals.

- Like instruction, related services should be offered through a collaborative model that includes various professionals, paraprofessional, and students' parents.
- Related services providers should be a part of the student's instructional team and contribute to the planning process and other key aspects of instruction in addition to the therapy service being provided.
- Professionals should share knowledge about procedures with each other to increase the quality of services provided to students. There should be communication about students' specific needs and interventions and how each person who works with the student can contribute holistically to the student's development.
- *Role release* will allow different professionals to provide some services that were traditionally only provided by certain therapists. This principle states that some functions of various professionals (e.g., speech therapists) can be carried out by others (e.g., teachers) so that appropriate services can be provided more often and in different relevant contexts.
- All related services should be offered in the most natural, least restrictive environment possible. Providing related services in contrived environments such as small speech therapy rooms should generally be avoided except when therapists believe the restricted setting will better allow the student to accomplish new, difficult tasks that cannot be learned in more open environments.
- If it is necessary to isolate the student for some aspect of a particular therapy, as indicated in the previous statement, the therapy should continue in the most natural setting as soon as possible.
- Therapy goals should be integrated into the student's other objectives, and vice versa. The more opportunity the student has to practice a particular skill, the better is the chance for it to be learned, and learned sooner.
- The therapist's expertise will be especially useful to teachers in explaining the student's limitations on certain tasks and how to circumvent or overcome them and the student's level of development and how to improve it. For example, an occupational therapist could explain the best way for the child to hold an eating utensil for self-feeding, while a language therapist could help to identify the vocabulary most necessary for immediate acquisition.

Improvement of Challenging Behavior

Some individuals with severe disabilities, particularly those with the most severe disabilities (i.e., profoundly mentally disabled), demonstrate various forms of challenging behavior. These may include stereotyped acts, self-injurious behaviors, noncompliance with requests, and aggressive acts. Various theories have been put forth to explain these behaviors, but in recent years researchers have started to find positive, nonaversive behavioral supports that offer solutions for improvement in this area. Listed below are several basic guidelines for improving inappropriate behavior. Detailed discussion of methods for using positive behavioral supports is provided in Chapter 12.

- Although there often seems to be no readily apparent reason for stereotyped or self-injurious behavior, in many cases it is possible to identify the conditions under which the behavior occurs. Systematic observation can help us to form hypotheses about influencing factors and conditions.
- Although aversive stimuli (i.e., punishment) may result in rapid decrease in the behavior, their use is opposed because it subjects the individual with severe disabilities to abnormal and sometimes inhumane treatment. Additionally, the effects of punishment tend to be short-lived and do not generalize.
- In contrast to punishment, efforts should be made to identify through a functional analysis the conditions under which the behavior occurs and either change these conditions or teach the individual a more appropriate way to respond to them.
- Although the challenging behavior will be the behavior of greatest concern, attention also must be given to the effect of the intervention on collateral behaviors and on the occurrence of the behavior in different situations, with different people, and at different times.
- Data must be taken in order to learn precisely about the influence of the intervention on the behavior of concern.

From Policy and Research to Best Practices

What we consider to be the best practices for teaching students with severe disabilities today differ from many of the practices that existed years ago, practices that, although they continue in some places, are now judged to be inappropriate by many professionals, parents, and persons with disabilities. What, then, makes some activities and procedures preferred over other approaches? We believe there are four bases of support for many of the practices that we have outlined above: changing *social values*, which lead to *legal policies*, along with the *consensus of professionals and others* and *empirical research*. Let's consider these briefly.

Social Values

The values of any society change with the passing of time. Most of us have different attitudes toward different dimensions of the world and its people than those that were held by our ancestors. Our values are reflected in our attitudes toward the environment, health care, quality of life, public education, minorities, and other aspects of society. For some individuals, society's values have changed and are changing too fast; for others, change seems to occur too slowly. But most of what changes in society's practices is shared by most members of the society; otherwise the changes would not occur.

One major change that has evolved over the last 30 or 40 years is the value that our society places on the rights of the individual. In the United States there has always been a basis for individual rights in our Constitution; however, the interpretation of these rights was often limited. This was clearly the case in the era of slavery and for many years beyond. However, for most of Western society, the world has gradually improved. Not too long ago, even after the end of slavery, we accepted without question or criticism the separation and derogation of persons for their race, religion, national origin, or gender. Because of normal variations in human characteristics, people were denied human rights that were extended to others.

As history will note, however, beginning in the 1960s, significant positive changes in the course of our society appeared. Civil rights legislation was passed, "separate but equal" schools for different races were ruled unconstitutional by the Supreme Court, and racial integration in society began to occur. Such changes as these, and many more, took place because the values of our society changed.

It is important to recognize all this because we must understand that values related to the education and treatment of people with disabilities do not exist in a social vacuum. If we did not value the rights of minorities, most likely the quality of education for persons with severe disabilities would not be where it is today. In fact, it is possible to draw parallels between the integration of minority students and the integration of students with severe disabilities (McDonnell & Hardman, 1989).

Although research has demonstrated the importance of many best practices, Peck (1991) discussed the need for linking values and science in social policy decisions affecting persons with severe disabilities. The traditional reliance on research data is now being supplemented by consideration for values, particularly by organizations such as TASH, which promotes "equity, opportunity and inclusion for people with disabilities." Peck suggested that "knowledge gained through scientific research should affect and be affected by knowledge from other sources, including personal and cultural values" (p. 2). To the extent that certain practices are in accord with the general values of society, we can expect that they will be considered as best practices for educating persons with severe disabilities.

Legal Policies

Typically, society expresses its values through the laws that are written by its representatives. Since the 1970s a series of federal laws has been passed that supports many of the best practices listed earlier. Several of these and their requirements are highlighted in the sections that follow.

P.L. 94-142: The Education for All Handicapped Children Act

Passed in 1975, P.L. 94-142 was considered landmark legislation that included many requirements for developing and improving educational services for students with disabilities. These included the following:

- It gave *all* students with disabilities, including those with the most severe disabilities, the legal right to a free, appropriate public education (FAPE).
- It also required that numerous related services be provided (such as transportation, physical therapy, psychological services, etc.) pertinent to the student's development.
- The law provided for students with disabilities to be educated in the "least restrictive environment" (LRE). This requirement placed the responsibility on the public schools to show reason why a particular student has to be placed in a more restrictive setting (such as a

special school or class) as opposed to a less restrictive setting (such as the regular classroom).

- P.L. 94-142 also required that each student have an IEP, that this plan state the annual goals and short-term objectives for the student, that an evaluation system be used at least once a year to monitor the student's progress, and that the student's parents be given the opportunity to participate in the educational planning process.
- The law guaranteed due process if disagreement occurred on decisions about placement and other educational matters. In other words, if the parents (or the student) disagreed with the action of the school system, a method of appeals that led to the federal court system could be used to resolve the conflict.

P.L. 99-457: The Education of the Handicapped Act Amendments of 1986

This law expanded on what was required by P.L. 94-142. Its most important contribution was the creation of two new programs. The first was a *mandatory* requirement that children with disabilities between the ages of 3 and 5 be provided with free educational programs in the public schools. In other words, the requirements of P.L. 94-142 were extended to cover children beginning with their third birthday. The second program was a discretionary program to serve children between birth and age 2: the Handicapped Infants and Toddlers Program. This federal program is extremely important for children with severe disabilities, because appropriate early intervention can reduce the impact of the disability. Under the Handicapped Infants and Toddlers Program, several best practices were legislated. These included the following:

- The development of an IFSP for each family and child served
- Multidisciplinary assessment of the child during the development of the IFSP
- A multidisciplinary early intervention program
- The employment of a case manager to guide the family through the service system

P.L. 101-476: The Individuals with Disabilities Education Act (IDEA)

IDEA was originally signed into law in October 1990 by the first President George Bush. It renewed the provisions of previous laws and made the following changes and additions:

- It changed the language of the previous "Education of the Handicapped" laws to "Individuals with Disabilities." The intention was to direct the focus first toward the individuality of persons with disabilities and then to note their unique challenge.
- IDEA allocated funding to support special projects that address the needs of students with severe disabilities in integrated settings and placed a priority on programs that improved the chances for the successful integration of students with severe disabilities into educational programs for nondisabled students (National Association of State Directors of Special Education, 1990).
- The law also included the requirement that a statement of the transition services be included in the student's IEP no later than at age 16 in order to result in better outcomes for individuals with disabilities as adults.

P.L. 105-17: Individuals with Disabilities Education Act Amendments of 1997 (IDEA 97)[1]

The most recent special education federal law was signed by President William Clinton on June 4, 1997. In this amendment of IDEA, Congress noted much of what had been learned in the previous two decades as a result of the research and experience that had evolved from federal legislation. In the findings of the act, they wrote that "over 20 years of research and experience has demonstrated that the education of children with disabilities is more effective" when there are "high expectations," when the student has "access to the general curriculum to the maximum extent possible," when parents and families have "meaningful opportunities to participate in the education of their children at school and at home," when special education is "a service for children rather than a place where they are sent," and when special education and related services and supports are provided in "the regular classroom to such children whenever appropriate."

Based on these findings, IDEA 97 was strengthened in several ways relative to the education of students with severe disabilities (NICHCY News Digest, 1998):

- Students with disabilities must be assessed in mandated state and local assessment programs that are required for students without disabilities. This better ensures the accountability of states and districts to provide the maximum appropriate education for

[1]As our text goes to press, IDEA is scheduled for congressional review and reauthorization, which may result in changes in the current law.

these students. Students for whom the standard assessment procedure is inappropriate, even with modifications, including most students with severe disabilities, must be assessed through an alternate assessment procedure. This assessment is discussed in Chapter 9.

- Parent participation rights have been improved to ensure parent involvement in decisions about student eligibility for special education and student placement in special education programs. Parents are entitled to provide input about their child during the evaluation procedure.
- A full review of existing records and documents is necessary preceding initial evaluations to determine an individual's eligibility and educational needs. This review is to be undertaken by the IEP team. Additional assessment may occur if needed following this review. The evaluation must directly assist in the determination of educational needs, including gathering information about how the student may be involved in the regular curriculum.
- The IEP must show greater participation in the general curriculum and the regular classroom or explain why this is not occurring. It must include a statement about how special education and related services and any necessary supplementary aids and services needed by the student will allow participation in the general curriculum and in extracurricular and nonacademic activities and with other students with and without disabilities. There is a clear intention to strengthen the connection between special education and the general curriculum. The IEP team must include professionals, parents, and, when appropriate, the student. A general educator must also serve on the IEP team.
- The IEP must list positive behavioral interventions that will occur to improve any inappropriate student behavior. The IEP must also list any assistive devices and services that will benefit the student.
- The IEP must explain why a child is not participating in the general education curriculum and is separated from students in regular education to the extent that this occurs.
- For older students, beginning at 14 years of age and annually thereafter, the IEP must include a transition plan that focuses on service needs and instruction in relevant areas such as vocational education. For students within 1 year of reaching the age of majority (21 in most states), the IEP must include a statement that the student has been informed of her rights under the law when this age is reached.

P.L. 101-336: Americans with Disabilities Act of 1990 (ADA)

The ADA is also considered to be landmark legislation because it guarantees civil rights to all U.S. citizens with disabilities. The following provisions are made under the law (Council for Exceptional Children, 1990):

- Persons with disabilities cannot be discriminated against in hiring practices by companies that employ 15 people or more. In addition, the employer is expected to make "reasonable accommodations" in the workplace if it will help the person with a disability to perform the job.
- In the area of public transportation, the ADA requires that all new vehicles be accessible to people with disabilities.
- Public accommodations must also be accessible. It is illegal to exclude persons with disabilities from services used by the general public, such as hotels, restaurants, grocery stores, schools, and parks. If necessary, "reasonable" modifications must be put in place in order to better accommodate these persons.
- The law also covers all public buildings, such as government facilities.

The relation of ADA to many of the best practices that are listed above is apparent: both are intended to foster the *inclusion* of persons with disabilities, rather than excluding them. Both also have as a goal the maximization of an individual's human potential. The educational practices presented in this chapter will help persons with severe disabilities to better enjoy the rights ensured them by the ADA.

Consensus of Professionals and Others

Many of the best practices that we have listed in this chapter can be defended as such because they are supported by the opinions of a large number of professionals, parents, advocates, and persons with disabilities. Three studies that used survey research methodology to find general consensus among different individuals about many of the practices that we have discussed are discussed below (Ayres et al., 1994; Meyer et al., 1987; Williams et al., 1990).

Meyer et al. (1987) analyzed responses from 254 persons to a questionnaire listing what they considered to be

122 best practices related to the education and treatment of persons with severe disabilities. Each item was scored by the respondents on a scale of 0 (not a consideration) to 20 (a very important consideration), with intermediate points at 5 (not an important consideration), 10 (undecided), and 15 (an important consideration).

In a later similar study, Ayres et al. (1994) asked a sample of special education teachers from five different states who taught students with severe disabilities in regular schools to rate the importance of 79 items taken from the 122-item best practices list used by Meyer et al. (1987). The teachers were nominated to participate in the study because they were considered by administrative personnel to be excellent teachers. On separate 5-point scales, they were asked to indicate (1) their own knowledge or skill related to each best practice quality indicator, (2) the degree of presence of the indicator within their program, and (3) the difficulty implementing the indicator. Of the 140 teachers who were asked to participate, 92 (66%) returned the questionnaire and 83 were included in the final analysis.

In a third study, Williams et al. (1990) used a similar procedure, although it was limited to the state of Vermont. Their target responders included parents, special education administrators, special education teachers, general education teachers and principals, and related service providers. The special education teachers and administrators received a 64-item questionnaire; the other groups received abbreviated versions containing only selected items from the longer list. The responders were asked two types of questions: Does the item represent a best practice? and Is the item a current practice? Williams et al. received responses from 212 persons.

All studies had important results. In each study, most of the questionnaire items offered by the researchers as possible best practices (which were very similar to many of the items listed in this chapter) were rated positively by the respondents. They were rated as being somewhere between important and very important (Meyer et al., 1987), used in educational programs by prominent teachers (Ayres et al., 1994), or simply considered appropriate best practice (Williams et al., 1990). However, there was some disagreement from different subgroups of the respondents as to the relative value of particular best practice indicators. For example, Meyer et al. found that items related to integration were rated higher by severe disabilities experts and parents than by the other groups, although the directors of special education gave a higher rating to the items in this factor than that given by the other groups. In the Vermont study, Williams et al. (1990) found that differential responses to questions about placing students with severe disabilities in regular classrooms or in special classrooms were closely related to whether the special education teachers and parents responding actually had experience with one setting or another. Those who had experience with regular classroom placements more often considered this placement as a best practice. In an important finding, Ayres et al. (1994) reported that their responding teachers considered the best practice indicators to be largely within their skill repertoire and present in their programs, but the degree of their presence within a program was related to the degree of difficulty in implementing them. In other words, there was no question of their importance or of the teachers' ability to carry out the best practice quality indicator, but difficulties related to the operation of their schools or school systems presented problems. The two major factors that the teachers cited as related to implementing best practices were insufficient time and inadequate administrative support.

By examining these studies, we see that many practices suggested in this chapter and elsewhere as being most appropriate for the education of students with severe disabilities are supported by a strong degree of consensus. Of course, this consensus is not universal nor is there the implication that these practices are applied ubiquitously. As the study by Ayres et al. implies, variation in the actual implementation of best practices will likely depend on the degree to which policy makers and administrators in individual settings support them.

Research Findings

The final basis for arguing that a particular practice is best (or at least better or preferred) is if research has been conducted to demonstrate its effectiveness. Two types of research may be conducted to test if particular interventions or practices yield improved results as compared to other approaches. One is *group research,* in which groups are treated differently, and the differential effects are observed and measured using valid and reliable standardized measures (Campbell & Stanley, 1963; Leary, 2000). The other is *single-subject research,* in which one or a few individuals are sequentially treated under varying experimental conditions, and their responses under these conditions are directly measured (Alberto & Troutman, 2002; Poling, Methot, & Lesage, 1995; Tawney & Gast, 1984). Another type of research, qualitative or ethnographic research, does not manipulate experimental variables, but may imply the influence of different conditions within environments through multiple forms of data collection such as interviewing, reviewing documents, and participating in daily activities as a participant–observer (Bogdan & Biklin, 1998; Patton, 2002).

During the last 10 to 15 years, research evidence has accumulated to support many of the practices discussed in this chapter. Research findings and reviews of much of this research are available on many topics, including:

- Effects of early intervention (Fox & Hanline, 1993; Guralnick, 1990; Westlake & Kaiser, 1991)
- Inclusive school placements (Downing & Eichinger, 2002; Giangreco & Putnam, 1991; Halvorsen & Sailor, 1990; Hunt & Goetz, 1997; York & Reynolds, 1996)
- Curriculum and instructional practices (Ault, Wolery, Doyle, & Gast, 1989; Cipani & Spooner, 1994; Snell, 1988; Wolery, Ault, & Doyle, 1992)
- Integrated use of related services (Dunn, 1991; Orelove & Sobsey, 1996)
- Development of communication skills (Alvares, Falor, & Smiley, 1991; Haring & Ryndak, 1994; Kaiser, Yoder, & Keetz, 1992; Mirenda, Iacono, & Williams, 1990; Reichle, 1997; Reichle & Sigafoos, 1994)
- Improving challenging behaviors (Carr et al., 1999; Didden, Duker, & Korzilius, 1997; Durand & Crimmins, 1988; Horner & Carr, 1997; Koegel, Koegel, & Dunlap, 1999)
- Transitional planning and supported employment (Agran, Test, & Martin, 1994; Rusch, Chadsey-Rusch, & Johnson, 1991)
- Community-based instruction (Spooner & Test, 1994; Westling & Floyd, 1990)
- Home–school partnerships (Singer & Irvin, 1991; Snell & Beckman-Brindley, 1984)
- Development of self-determination (Sands & Wehmeyer, 1996; Wehmeyer, 1992, 1996)

What has been learned from these areas of research has provided much of the information that will be presented throughout the rest of this text. Although there is apparently a substantial amount of research to support many of the practices that have been recommended, not all best practices are fully supported by research, nor would we expect them to be. The role of social science is probably better for the evaluation of social policy than for its invention (Peck, 1991). Thus some practices included on our list and elsewhere may not have evolved from research and, in fact, should not need to be subjected to research in order to provide a defense for them. (Does allowing women to vote make the country a better place? Should minority individuals be free to live and work where they want?) Obviously not all questions of social practice should be subjected to research. Instead, the more appropriate role of research is to improve practices that are socially valued.

We have advanced to a point where there is relatively clear direction about what, when, where, and how we should be doing to provide the best, most humane services to persons who have severe disabilities. Because this is an evolving field, we can expect additional practices to be developed, given consideration, and perhaps added to those discussed in this chapter.

Although the best practices have been identified, as stated earlier, we must not conclude that they have been fully implemented. A majority of students with various disabilities in the United States are still served primarily in separate classes, separate schools, or residential facilities. Most of these students are classified as autistic, mentally retarded, multihandicapped, or deaf–blind (U.S. Department of Education, 2002). A study by Williams et al. (1990) in Vermont reported that, while approximately 90% of the special educators surveyed agreed with most of the best practices on their list, each practice was implemented for all students by only 20% to 60% of the teachers. Likewise, teachers surveyed by Ayres et al. (1994) reported that some administrative constraints made it difficult to implement many best practices.

Why do these conditions exist? There are no doubt several reasons. The long-time existence of separate special schools and the funding formulas used in many states may impede the integration of children with severe disabilities. Additional factors may include the lack of preservice or in-service training for teachers (including both general and special educators) that would provide them with the skills to implement more appropriate practices, the lack of administrative support, inflexible scheduling of time and instructional activities, poor or nonexistent interagency agreements, the lack of sufficient funds, and the low quality of many general education programs (Williams et al., 1990).

The responsibility of current and future professionals, administrators, parents, and citizens is to work to improve the status quo and move forward to the implementation of the most appropriate instructional and related practices, not only for students with severe disabilities, but for all public school students. If this is achieved, the benefits will be realized not only by persons with severe disabilities, but by society as a whole. The remaining chapters of this text are devoted toward achieving this end.

The Meaning of Special Education

We began this chapter by stating our philosophy of special education. As we conclude, the following definition is proposed for special education for students with severe disabilities. As can be seen, it is based on the previously presented philosophy.

Definition of Special Education

Special education for persons with severe disabilities consists of an instructional process by which students with cognitive, social, and sometimes physical limitations are able to maximize their potential in such a way that they can enjoy a quality of life and a level of self-determination similar to that enjoyed by persons who do not have disabilities. As a result of this process, these persons would be able to experience a life in their home and community very much like that experienced by others of the same chronological age. Special education is not made special by the nature of the instructional materials used or by being provided in "special" settings where there are only other students with severe disabilities. It is made special by the nature of the skills that are taught and the methods used to teach them. Special education should consist of the supportive educational programs necessary to best ensure that a student with severe disabilities lives a normal life and learns normal behaviors to the degree she or he is most capable.

Conclusion

A high-quality special education program should be characterized by the following 12 features:

1. Students should be treated with dignity. The language and the attitudes of the teachers and others should reflect the value of the students as human beings. The professionals and paraprofessionals providing services should respect the humanity of the individual students whom they are teaching. They should also believe in the value of teaching them.
2. Students should be allowed to determine for themselves as much as possible in accordance with their chronological age and life circumstance. They should be encouraged to make choices, self-regulate, and solve their own problems to the extent that they can.
3. There should be a pervasive attitude that all students are capable of learning meaningful skills that will move them away from dependence and toward independence, away from isolation and toward involvement.
4. All students should be involved in the normal routines and schedules of the school along with the students who do not have disabilities. Interactions with students who do not have disabilities should occur in normal patterns throughout the school day.
5. Meaningful learning activities should be planned, and each student should be working toward individually prescribed objectives within these activities. Objectives should be taught that allow the student to function as well as possible in all current environments and to be prepared for operating in future environments. Instruction directed toward the achievement of specific objectives should be distributed throughout the day in a natural fashion, not presented in an artificial, massed array.
6. Instruction should occur in the most natural and least restrictive settings, including regular classes to the extent possible, and in different settings within the school, community, and home. Placement in special classes should be generally avoided.
7. Materials used and instructional activities should be natural. They should be items and activities used in everyday life and not materials especially designed for special education, with the exception of technologically sophisticated devices designed to assist in areas such as communication or mobility.
8. Instructional procedures should be as precise as necessary, yet as natural as possible. The procedures should be those that best ensure that learning will occur, but that show respect for the dignity of the individual and thus are not overly intrusive.
9. Student performance data on key, specific objectives should be collected on a regular basis in order to assess the student's progress.
10. Instruction should focus on skill acquisition, maintenance, and generalization. Targeted skills should not be checked off a checklist when completed, but should become a part of the repertoire of functional skills possessed by the student.
11. Specific efforts to improve the knowledge and attitudes of other students and school employees toward people with severe disabilities should be made. Teachers should encourage students and other professionals, paraprofessionals, and nonprofessionals in the school to interact appropriately with

students who have disabilities. Friendships between students with and without disabilities should be encouraged.

12. Parents should be acknowledged as the student's primary teachers and should be included in the educational program to the degree that they wish. Most important, parents should be involved in the educational planning process.

Questions for Reflection

1. Of the best practices listed, which would you consider to be the most important? Why?
2. Why has self-determination come to be considered an important focus area for students with cognitive disabilities in recent years?
3. What are your views regarding participation by students with severe disabilities in the general curriculum?
4. Are there any best practices discussed in this chapter that you disagree with? Why?
5. Could you suggest other important practices that should be included when providing services to people with severe disabilities?
6. What are the reactions of some professional educators to the practices discussed in this chapter? How about nonprofessionals?
7. Of the various ways by which we conclude that certain practices are preferred, which do you think is most important? Why?
8. From the point of view of a student with a severe disability, which of the practices described in this chapter would be considered most important?
9. What do you believe is the teacher's role in implementing best practices?

References

Agran, M., Alper, S., & Wehmeyer, M. (2002). Access to the general curriculum for students with significant disabilities: What it means to teachers. *Education and Training in Mental Retardation and Developmental Disabilities, 37*(2), 123–133.

Agran, M., Test, D., & Martin, J. E. (1994). Employment preparation of students with severe disabilities. In E. C. Cipani & F. Spooner (Eds.), *Curricular and instructional approaches for persons with severe disabilities* (pp. 184–212). Boston: Allyn and Bacon.

Alberto, P. A., & Troutman, A. C. (2002). *Applied behavior analysis for teachers* (6th ed.). Upper Saddle River, NJ: Merrill/Prentice Hall.

Alvares, R., Falor, I., & Smiley, L. (1991). Research on nonlinguistic communication functioning of individuals with severe or profound handicaps. In L. Sternberg (Ed.), *Functional communication: Analyzing the nonlinguistic skills of individuals with severe or profound handicaps* (pp. 18–37). New York: Springer-Verlag.

Ault, M. J., Wolery, M., Doyle, P. M., & Gast, D. L. (1989). Review of comparative studies in the instruction of students with moderate and severe handicaps. *Exceptional Children, 55,* 346–356.

Ayres, B. J., Meyer, L. H., Erevelles, N., & Park-Lee, S. (1994). Easy for you to say: Teacher perspectives on implementing most promising practices. *Journal of the Association for Persons with Severe Handicaps, 19,* 84–93.

Billingsley, F. F., & Albertson, L. R. (1999). Finding a future for functional skills. *Journal of the Association for Students with Severe Disabilities, 24,* 298–302.

Bogdan, R. C., & Biklen, S. K. (1998). *Qualitative research for education, an introduction to theory and methods* (3rd ed.). Boston: Allyn and Bacon.

Brotherson, M. J., Cook, C., Cunconan-Lahr, R., & Wehmeyer, M. L. (1995). Policy determining choice and self-determination in the environments of persons with severe disabilities across the lifespan. *Education and Training in Mental Retardation and Developmental Disabilities, 30,* 3–14.

Browder, D. M. (2001). *Curriculum and assessment for students with moderate and severe disabilities.* New York: Guilford Press.

Browder, D. M., & Spooner, F. (2003). Understanding the purpose and process of alternate assessment. In D. L. Ryndak & S. Alper, *Curriculum and instruction for students with significant disabilities in inclusive settings* (2nd Ed.). Boston: Allyn and Bacon.

Brown, F., & Cohen, S. (1996). Self-determination and young children. *Journal of the Association for Persons with Severe Handicaps, 21,* 22–30.

Brown, F., Gothelf, C. R., Guess, D., & Lehr, D. H. (1998). Self-determination for individuals with the most severe disabilities: Moving beyond chimera. *Journal of the Association for Persons with Severe Handicaps, 23,* 17–26.

Brown, L., Nietupski, J., & Hamre-Nietupski, S. (1976). Criterion of ultimate functioning. In A. Thomas (Ed.), *Hey, don't forget about me!* Reston, VA: CEC Information Center.

Campbell, D. T., & Stanley, J. C. (1963). Experimental and quasi-experimental designs for research on teaching. In N. L. Gage (Ed.), *Handbook of research on teaching.* Chicago: Rand-McNally.

Carr, E. G., Horner, R. H., Turnbull, A. P., Marquis, J. G., McLaughlin, D. M., McAtee, M. L., Smith, C. E., Ryan, K. A., Ruef, M. B., & Doolabh, A. (1999). *Positive behavior support for people with developmental disabilities: A research synthesis.* Washington, DC: American Association on Mental Retardation.

Center for Applied Special Technology (CAST). (1999–2000). Available: http://www.cast.org.

Certo, N., Haring, N., & York, R. (Eds.). (1984). *Public school integration of severely handicapped students.* Baltimore: Paul H. Brookes.

Cipani, E., & Spooner, F. (1994). *Curricular and instructional approaches for persons with severe disabilities.* Boston: Allyn and Bacon.

Council for Exceptional Children. (1990). Americans with Disabilities Act of 1990: What should you know? *Exceptional Children, 57*(2) (Supplement).

Council for Exceptional Children. (1999). *Universal design: Ensuring access to the general education curriculum.* Research Connections in Special Education.

Didden, R., Duker, P. C., & Korzilius, H. (1997). Meta-analytic study on treatment effectiveness for problem behaviors with individuals who have mental retardation. *American Journal on Mental Retardation, 101,* 387–399.

Doll, B., Sands, D. J., Wehmeyer, M. L., & Palmer, S. (1996). Promoting the development and acquisition of self-determined behavior. In D. J. Sands & M. L. Wehmeyer (Eds.), *Self-determination across the lifespan: Independence and choice for people with disabilities* (pp. 65–90). Baltimore: Paul H. Brookes.

Downing, J. E., & Eichinger, J. (2002). Educating students with diverse strengths and needs together: Rationale for inclusion. In J. E. Downing (Ed.), *Including students with severe and multiple disabilities in typical classrooms* (2nd Ed., pp. 1–16). Baltimore: Paul H. Brookes.

Dunn, L. (1968). Special education for the mildly retarded—Is much of it justifiable? *Exceptional Children, 35*(1), 5–24.

Dunn, W. (1991). Integrated related services. In L. H. Meyer, C. A. Peck, & L. Brown (Eds.), *Critical issues in the lives of people with severe disabilities* (pp. 353–377). Baltimore: Paul H. Brookes.

Durand, V. M., & Crimmins, D. B. (1988). Identifying the variables maintaining self-injurious behavior. *Journal of Autism and Developmental Disorders, 18,* 99–117.

Ford, A., Schnorr, R., Meyer, L., Davern, L., Black, J., & Dempsey, P. (Eds.). (1989). *The Syracuse community-referenced curriculum guide for students with moderate and severe disabilities.* Baltimore: Paul H. Brookes.

Fox, L., & Hanline, M. F. (1993). A preliminary evaluation of learning within developmentally appropriate early childhood settings. *Topics in Early Childhood Special Education, 13,* 308–327.

Fox, W., Thousand, J., Fox, T., Williams, W., Lewis, P., Reid, R., & Creedon, S. (1986). *Proposed state guidelines for the education of students with moderate/severe handicaps.* Burlington, VT: Center for Developmental Disabilities, University of Vermont.

Giangreco, M. F., & Putnam, J. W. (1991). Supporting the education of students with severe disabilities in regular education environments. In L. H. Meyer, C. A. Peck, & L. Brown (Eds.), *Critical issues in the lives of people with severe disabilities* (pp. 245–270). Baltimore: Paul H. Brookes.

Guralnick, M. J. (1990). Major accomplishments and future directions in early childhood mainstreaming. *Topics in Early Childhood Special Education, 10(2),* 1–17.

Halvorsen, A., & Sailor, W. (1990). Integration of students with severe and profound disabilities: A review of the research. In R. Gaylord-Ross (Ed.), *Issues and research in special education* (vol. 1, pp. 110–172). New York: Teachers College Press.

Haring, T. G., & Ryndak, D. (1994). Strategies and instructional procedures to promote social interactions and relationships. In E. C. Cipani & F. Spooner (Eds.), *Curricular and instructional approaches for persons with severe disabilities* (pp. 289–321). Boston: Allyn and Bacon.

Hilton, A., & Smith, T. E. C. (1994). Inclusion as a philosophy which leads to loss of vision: A response to Rainforth's philosophy versus student need? *Education and Training in Mental Retardation and Developmental Disabilities, 29,* 253–255.

Hitchcock, C., Meyer, A., Rose, D., & Jackson, R. (2002). Providing access to the general curriculum: Universal design for learning. *Teaching Exceptional Children, 35*(2), 8–17.

Horner, R. H., & Carr, E. G. (1997). Behavioral support for students with severe disabilities: Functional assessment and comprehensive intervention. *Journal of Special Education, 31,* 84–104.

Horner, R. H., Meyer, L. H., & Fredericks, H. B. D. (Eds.). (1986). *Educating learners with severe handicaps: Exemplary service models.* Baltimore: Paul H. Brookes.

Hunt, P., & Goetz, L. (1997). Research on inclusive educational programs, practices, and outcomes for students with severe disabilities. *Journal of Special Education, 31*(1), 3–29.

Hunt, P., Goetz, L., & Anderson, J. (1986). The quality of IEP objectives associated with placement on integrated versus segregated school sites. *Journal of the Association for Persons with Severe Handicaps, 11,* 125–130.

Jorgeson, C. M. (1999). *Promoting access to the general education curriculum for high school students with significant dis-*

abilities. Paper presented at the International TASH Conference, Chicago, December 1999.

Kaiser, A. P., Yoder, P. J., & Keetz, A. (1992). Evaluating milieu teaching. In S. F. Warren & J. Reichle (Eds.), *Causes and effects in communication and language intervention* (pp. 9–47). Baltimore: Paul H. Brookes.

Katims, D. S. (2000). Literacy instruction for people with mental retardation: Historical highlights and contemporary analysis. *Education and Training in Mental Retardation and Developmental Disabilities, 35,* 3–15.

Kleinert, H. L., & Kearns, J. F. (1999). A validation study of the performance indicators and learner outcomes of Kentucky's alternate assessment for students with significant disabilities. *Journal of the Association for Persons with Severe Handicaps, 24,* 100–110.

Kleinert, H. L., Kearns, J. F., & Kennedy, S. (1997). Accountability for *all* students: Kentucky's alternate portfolio assessment for students with moderate and severe cognitive disabilities. *Journal of the Association for Persons with Severe Handicaps, 22,* 88–101.

Kleinert, H. K., Kennedy, S., & Kearns, J. F. (1999). The impact of alternate assessments: A statewide teacher survey. *Journal of Special Education, 33,* 93–102.

Kliewer, C., & Biklen, D. (2001). "School's not really a place for reading": A research synthesis of literate lives of students with severe disabilities. *Journal of the Association for Persons with Severe Handicaps, 26,* 1–12.

Kliewer, C., & Landis, D. (1999). Individualizing literacy instruction for young children with moderate to severe disabilities. *Exceptional Children, 66,* 85–100.

Koegel, L. K., Koegel, R. L., & Dunlap, G. (1999). *Positive behavioral support: Including people with difficult behavior in the community.* Baltimore: Paul H. Brookes.

Leary, M. R. (2000). *Introduction to behavioral research methods* (3rd Ed.). Boston: Allyn and Bacon.

McDonnell, A. P., & Hardman, M. L. (1989). The desegregation of America's special schools: Strategies for change. *Journal of the Association for Persons with Severe Handicaps, 14,* 68–74.

McDonnell, J., Hardman, M. L., McDonnell, A. P., & Kiefer-O'Donnell, R. (1995). *An introduction to persons with severe disabilities: Educational and social issues.* Boston: Allyn and Bacon.

Meyer, L. (1987). *Program quality indicators: A checklist of most promising practices in educational programs for students with severe disabilities* (rev. ed.). Syracuse, NY: Syracuse University Division of Special Education and Rehabilitation.

Meyer, L., Eichinger, J., & Downing, J. (1992). *The Program Quality Indicators (PQI): A checklist of most promising practices in educational programs for students with severe intellectual disabilities.* Syracuse, NY: Syracuse University Division of Special Education and Rehabilitation.

Meyer, L., Eichinger, J., & Park-Lee, S. (1987). A validation of program quality indicators in educational services for students with severe disabilities. *Journal of the Association for Persons with Severe Handicaps, 12,* 251–263.

Mirenda, P., Iacono, T., & Williams, R. (1990). Communication options for persons with severe and profound disabilities: State of the art and future directions. *Journal of the Association for Persons with Severe Handicaps, 15,* 3–21.

National Association of State Directors of Special Education. (1990). *Education of the Handicapped Amendments of 1990 (P.L. 101-476): Summary of major changes in Parts A through H of the act.* Washington, DC: Author.

NICHCY News Digest. (1998). *The IDEA Amendments of 1997, 26* (rev. ed.), 1–40.

Nirje, B. (1969). The normalization principle and its human management implications. In R. B. Kugel & W. Wolfensberger (Eds.), *Changing patterns in residential services for the mentally retarded.* Washington, DC: President's Committee on Mental Retardation.

Nirje, B. (1972). The right to self-determination. In W. Wolfensberger (Ed.), *Normalization* (pp. 176–193). Toronto: National Institute on Mental Retardation.

Orelove, F. P., & Sobsey, D. (1996). *Educating children with multiple disabilities: A transdisciplinary approach* (3rd ed.). Baltimore: Paul H. Brookes.

Patton, M. Q. (2002). *Qualitative research and evaluation methods* (3rd ed.). Thousand Oaks, CA: Sage Publications.

Peck, C. A. (1991). Linking values and science in social policy decisions affecting citizens with severe disabilities. In L. H. Meyer, C. A. Peck, & L. Brown (Eds.), *Critical issues in the lives of people with severe disabilities* (pp. 1–15). Baltimore: Paul H. Brookes.

Poling, A. D., Methot, L. L., & Lesage, M. G. (1995). *Fundamentals of behavior analytic research.* New York: Plenum Publishing.

Putnam, J. W., Spiegel, A. N., & Bruininks, R. H. (1995). Future directions in education and inclusion of students with disabilities: A Delphi investigation. *Exceptional Children, 61,* 553–576.

Rainforth, B., & York-Barr, J. (1997). *Collaborative teams for students with severe disabilities: Integrating therapy and educational services* (2nd ed.). Baltimore: Paul H. Brookes.

Reichle, J. (1997). Communication intervention with persons who have severe disabilities. *Journal of Special Education, 31,* 110–134.

Reichle, J., & Sigafoos, J. (1994). Communication intervention for persons with developmental disabilities. In E. C. Cipani & F. Spooner (Eds.), *Curricular and instructional approaches for persons with severe disabilities* (pp. 241–262). Boston: Allyn and Bacon.

Reid, D. H., Everson, J. M., & Green, C. W. (1999). A systematic evaluation of preferences identified through person-centered planning for people with profound multiple disabilities. *Journal of Applied Behavior Analysis, 32,* 467–477.

Reid, D. H., Parsons, M. B., Green, C. W., & Browning, L. B. (2001). Increasing one aspect of self-determination among adults with severe multiple disabilities in supported work. *Journal of Applied Behavior Analysis, 34,* 341–344.

Rusch, F., Chadsey-Rusch, J., & Johnson, J. R. (1991). Supported employment: Emerging opportunities for employment integration. In L. H. Meyer, C. A. Peck, & L. Brown

(Eds.), *Critical issues in the lives of people with severe disabilities* (pp. 1–15). Baltimore: Paul H. Brookes.

Ryndak, D. L., Morrison, A. P., & Sommerstein, L. (1999). Literacy before and after inclusion in general education settings: A case study. *Journal of the Association for Persons with Severe Handicaps, 24,* 5–22.

Sailor, W., Anderson, J. L., Halvorsen, A. T., Doering, M. A., Filler, J., & Goetz, L. (1989). *The comprehensive local school: Regular education for all students with disabilities.* Baltimore: Paul H. Brookes.

Salisbury, C. L., & Vincent, L. J. (1990). Criterion of the next environment and best practices: Mainstreaming and integration 10 years later. *Topics in Early Childhood Special Education, 10*(2), 78–89.

Sands, D. J., & Wehmeyer, M. L. (Eds.). (1996). *Self-determination across the life span: Independence and choice for people with disabilities.* Baltimore: Paul H. Brookes.

Singer, G. H. S., & Irvin, L. K. (1991). Supporting families of persons with severe disabilities: Emerging findings, practices and questions. In L. H. Meyer, C. A. Peck, & L. Brown (Eds.), *Critical issues in the lives of people with severe disabilities* (pp. 271–312). Baltimore: Paul H. Brookes.

Smith, T. E. C., & Puccini, I. K. (1995). Position statement: Secondary curricula and policy issues for students with mental retardation. *Education and Training in Mental Retardation and Developmental Disabilities, 30,* 275–282.

Snell, M. (1988). Curriculum and methodology for individuals with severe disabilities. *Education and Training in Mental Retardation, 23,* 302–314.

Snell, M. E., & Beckman-Brindley, S. (1984). Family involvement in intervention with children having severe handicaps. *Journal of the Association for Persons with Severe Handicaps, 9,* 213–230.

Spooner, F., & Test, D. (1994). Domestic and community living skills. In E. C. Cipani & F. Spooner (Eds.), *Curricular and instructional approaches for persons with severe disabilities* (pp. 149–183). Boston: Allyn and Bacon.

Stancliffe, R., & Wehmeyer, M. L. (1995). Variability in the availability of choice to adults with mental retardation. *Journal of Vocational Rehabilitation, 5,* 319–328.

Strain, P. S. (1990). LRE for preschool children with handicaps: What we know, what we should be doing. *Journal of Early Intervention, 14,* 291–296.

Tashie, C., Jorgenson, C., Shapiro-Barnard, S., Martin, J., & Schuh, M. (1996). High school inclusion. *TASH Newsletter, 22*(9), 19–22.

Tawney, J. W., & Gast, D. L. (1984). *Single subject design in special education.* Upper Saddle River, NJ: Merrill/Prentice Hall.

Turner, M. D., Baldwin, L., Kleinert, H., & Kearns, J. F. (2000). The relation of a statewide alternate assessment for students with severe disabilities to other measures of instructional effectiveness. *Journal of Special Education, 34*(2), 69–76.

U.S. Department of Education. (2002). *Twenty-third annual report to Congress on the implementation of the Individuals with Disabilities Education Act.* Washington, DC: Author.

Ward, M. J. (1996). Coming of age in the age of self-determination: A historical and personal perspective. In D. J. Sands & M. L. Wehmeyer (Eds.), *Self-determination across the life span: Independence and choice for people with disabilities* (pp. 3–16). Baltimore: Paul H. Brookes.

Wehmeyer, M. L. (1992). Self-determination and the education of students with mental retardation. *Education and Training in Mental Retardation, 27,* 302–314.

Wehmeyer, M. L. (1994). Perceptions of self-determination and psychological empowerment of adolescents with mental retardation. *Education and Training in Mental Retardation and Developmental Disabilities, 29,* 265–278.

Wehmeyer, M. L. (1996). Self-determination as an educational outcome: Why is it important to children, youth, and adults with disabilities. In D. J. Sands & M. L. Wehmeyer (Eds.), *Self-determination across the life span: Independence and choice for people with disabilities* (pp. 17–36). Baltimore: Paul H. Brookes.

Wehmeyer, M. L., Agran, M., & Hughes, C. (2000). A national survey of teachers' promotion of self-determination and student directed learning. *Journal of Special Education, 34*(2), 58–68.

Wehmeyer, M. L., Kelchner, K., & Richards, S. (1996). Essential characteristics of self-determined behavior of individuals with mental retardation. *American Journal on Mental Retardation, 100,* 632–642.

Wehmeyer, M. L., Lance, G. D., & Bashinski, S. (2002). Promoting access to the general curriculum for students with mental retardation: A multi-level model. *Education and Training in Mental Retardation and Developmental Disabilities, 37*(3), 223–234.

Wehmeyer, M. L., Lattin, D., & Agran, M. (2001). Achieving access to the general curriculum for students with mental retardation: A curriculum-decision making model. *Education and Training in Mental Retardation and Developmental Disabilities, 36,* 327–342.

Wehmeyer, M. L., & Metzler, C. A. (1995). How self-determined are people with mental retardation? The national consumer survey. *Mental Retardation, 33,* 111–119.

Wehmeyer, M. L., & Schwartz, M. (1997). Self-determination and positive adult outcomes: A follow-up study of youth with mental retardation or learning disabilities. *Exceptional Children, 63,* 245–255.

Westlake, C. R., & Kaiser, A. P. (1991). Early childhood services for children with severe disabilities: Research, values, policy, and practice. In L. H. Meyer, C. A. Peck, & L. Brown (Eds.), *Critical issues in the lives of people with severe disabilities* (pp. 429–458). Baltimore: Paul H. Brookes.

Westling, D. L. (1989). Leadership for the education of students with mental handicaps. *Educational Leadership, 46*(6), 19–23.

Westling, D. L., & Floyd, J. (1990). Generalization of community skills: How much training is necessary? *Journal of Special Education, 23,* 386–406.

Williams, W., Fox, T. J., Thousand, J., & Fox, W. (1990). Level of acceptance and implementation of best practices in the education of students with severe handicaps in Vermont. *Education and Training in Mental Retardation, 25,* 120–131.

Wolery, M., Ault, M. J., & Doyle, P. M. (1992). *Teaching students with moderate to severe disabilities: Use of response prompting strategies.* New York: Longman.

Wolfensberger, W. (1972). *The principle of normalization in human services.* Toronto: National Institute on Mental Retardation.

York, J. L., & Reynolds, M. C. (1996). Special education and inclusion. In J. Sikula, T. J. Buttery, & E. Guyton (Eds.), *Handbook of research on teacher education* (2nd ed., pp. 820–836). New York: Simon & Schuster/Macmillan.

Ysseldyke, J., & Olsen, K. (1999). Putting alternate assessments into practice: What to measure and possible sources of data. *Exceptional Children, 65,* 175–185.

CHAPTER 3

Collaboration among Professionals and Paraprofessionals

To work effectively, teachers must collaborate with other professionals and paraprofessionals. This chapter presents information about these groups, their functions and roles, and how they can work together on collaborative teams. Special attention is given to the structure of transdisciplinary teams, a service delivery arrangement that is considered to be especially suitable for providing services to students with severe disabilities. Considerable attention is also given to the role of the paraprofessional, a position that has been discussed a great deal in recent years because of its prominence in the education of students with severe disabilities, especially in inclusive classrooms.

The Meaning of Collaboration

The most effective teachers of students with severe disabilities, including special and general educators, work collaboratively with other teachers, with related services professionals, and with paraprofessionals. Every workday, teachers attend meetings, discuss problems, plan strategies, give and receive directions, offer advice, coteach, and in many other ways interact cooperatively with other key persons. To be effective team members, special educators must understand the roles of general educators, physical therapists (PTs), occupational therapists (OTs), communication disorder specialists (also called speech therapists or speech pathologists), and often other professionals. Paraprofessionals (also referred to as paraeducators, teacher aids, or teacher assistants) spend much time directly instructing and assisting students with disabilities, as well as performing other roles, and are also considered important team players. Together, these individuals and the student's parents comprise a collaborative team that functions to provide an appropriate education for students with severe disabilities. In this chapter we discuss professionals, paraprofessionals, and effective teaming. In the following chapter we will consider parents, families, and their various cultural conditions.

Although all professionals and paraprofessionals who provide educational and related services to students with disabilities share a general goal—to improve the skills, abilities, and lives of the students about whom they are concerned—they will vary in their perceptions, knowledge, experiences, and preparation. They may have different attitudes and philosophies about disabilities and about the type of services that should be provided and hold different expectations about students' abilities. It will not always be easy for service providers to maintain good working relations. Yet the better the cooperation, the greater will be the success of the overall program and, therefore, the learning and life quality of the students with severe disabilities.

Collaboration is more than different individuals simply working together, working on the same project, or being agreeable with each other. Instead, *collaboration* is the process by which people with different areas of expertise work together to identify needs and problems and then find ways to meet the needs and solve the problems. Collaboration may occur between as few as two people, such as between a general educator and a special educator; but more ideally *collaborative teams* consisting of several professionals, paraprofessionals, and parents work together on behalf of individual students. Within this structure, all members of the collaborative team are expected to cooperatively contribute their expertise to the process. Collaboration should be applied to identifying students' needs, planning to meet these needs, and creating and delivering instruction and other services to meet the needs.

Recognition of the need for collaboration has occurred in recent years because of the complexity of the needs of students with disabilities. This complexity calls for the knowledge and skills of many different persons if maximum learning and development are to occur (Cook & Friend, 2002; Downing, 2002; Orelove & Sobsey, 1996; Pugach & Johnson, 1990, 2002; Rainforth & York, 1997; Vandercook & York, 1990). As noted by a number of authorities, successful collaboration is characterized by several features, including the following:

- *Concern with mutual goals.* Individuals working collaboratively are concerned about the same goals for the student. The first step in collaboration, therefore, is often deciding what particular goals or objectives are appropriate for the student.
- *Recognition of diverse areas of expertise.* Those involved in collaborative processes recognize their own knowledge and skills, as well as the expertise of others. This does not imply that one person is relegated to dealing with only one aspect of the student with disabilities, but that team members will rely on the consultation of particular persons for particular types of information and directions.
- *Sharing of expertise.* Having different areas of expertise also implies that team members are willing to openly share their expertise with each other. If all team members are concerned about achieving the same goals, each team member will provide all that she can to help to achieve these goals.

- *Equality of team members.* All team members, including parents and professionals, are considered to be of equal importance to the collaborative process and are expected to work with the same goals in mind. No one team member can claim greater importance in this process than another.
- *Decision making by consensus.* The collaborative process calls for decisions about curriculum, instruction, and related services to be made through consensus. Groups deal with issues and resolve them in a way in which there is close to uniform agreement among the decision makers.
- *Shared responsibility and accountability.* Those engaged in collaboration accept that they each share a part of the responsibility for the success or lack of success for an individual student. No one person assumes more responsibility than another; all are held accountable together.

Pugach and Johnson (2002) maintain that professionals who are successful collaborators have several personal or professional characteristics that contribute to their roles as collaborators. These characteristics should be considered important by those teaching or planning to teach students with severe disabilities.

- *Collaboration is recognized as a complex process.* Much joint effort must be directed toward providing effective education for diverse learners, especially those with disabilities. Individuals willing to put forth this effort are more likely to be effective collaborators.
- *Creativity generated by working together is acknowledged.* Collaboration generates results that are greater in number and superior to those generated by individuals. People who value the multiple possibilities generated through group processes will be more likely to work effectively within the process.
- *Collaboration is enjoyed.* Even though collaboration can be difficult, ultimately the effect can be worthwhile, and many people will enjoy the social nature of this professional activity. Quality collaboration requires respect and trust, and these are very reinforcing to many people.
- *Professional experience and growth are realized through collaboration.* Besides yielding a greater benefit for the student, collaboration provides intellectual stimulation and growth for those who participate. Continuous intellectual stretching will improve the quality of the professional in various areas.
- *Collaborators are reflective professionals.* Teachers and other professionals need to be aware of the quality and effectiveness of their work. Collaboration should require this to happen, because interaction with others brings one's own practice to the foreground for consideration by self and others.

Collaboration can take different forms. As will be noted in Chapter 5, collaboration is critical during the process of planning instructional goals, objectives, and services for students with severe disabilities. Collaboration also occurs during the day-to-day delivery of services. Teachers can provide one-to-one consultation to each other, can coteach, or can work in larger teams (Pugach & Johnson, 2002). One of the most effective ways in which professionals can work together is through *collaborative problem solving* (CPS) (Cook & Friend, 2002; Hobbs & Westling, 1998; Pugach & Johnson, 2002; Salisbury, Evans, & Palombaro, 1997). CPS is a systematic process that is used first to identify problems or barriers related to unique challenges associated with inclusion or other important educational practices and then to create practical solutions to these problems. Salisbury and her colleagues described the use of CPS in an elementary school that was in the process of implementing inclusion for students with severe disabilities. In the CPS process that they developed, teachers and students initiated a CPS procedure whenever a problem was recognized. The process required five steps: identify the issue, generate possible solutions, screen possible solutions, choose a solution to implement, and evaluate the solution. Over the course of 2 years, Salisbury et al. documented 48 CPS sessions that helped to improve the inclusion of children with disabilities and noted that there were many more undocumented applications of the CPS process. In a study on the same topic, Hobbs (1997) found that teachers working collaboratively were able to better define problems and create more possible solutions than when they worked alone.

Collaborating with Other Professionals

The success of educational programs for students with severe disabilities may be directly related to the success with which various professionals collaborate with each other. Many professionals provide direct or indirect services to students with severe disabilities. Some of the professionals most commonly involved are described in the following sections. Understanding their roles will be an important part of having a successful collaborative team.

Special Educators

The special educator has been referred to as an educational synthesizer (Bricker, 1976), which suggests a person who brings together the resources of his own knowledge and skills and those of other professionals to deliver the most effective education possible for each student. The special educator is responsible for participating in the planning process and conducting a substantial portion of the student's assessment. On a daily basis, this professional is responsible for providing direct instruction to students with disabilities (and often other students when working in inclusive classrooms), communicating with other professionals and paraprofessionals, and giving them assistance and advice for conducting instructional activities. He or she also serves as the primary liaison between the school and the students' parents. Additionally, the special educator should serve as an advocate for students with severe disabilities.

The skills required by a special educator of students with severe disabilities are numerous. Fox and Williams (1992) suggested that these teachers must have at the core of their activity a value system that acknowledges the dignity of individuals with severe disabilities and the appropriateness of providing an education that fosters a high-quality inclusive lifestyle. Special educators who work with general educators in inclusive classrooms will be more successful in their collaborative efforts if they adhere to a few important guidelines. They must provide effective interpersonal support (have good rapport, be enthusiastic, be flexible) and task-related supports for individual students. They also must be present when necessary, but understand that their presence is not always necessary. And, of course, they must participate in planning and implementing instruction (Janney, Snell, Beers, & Raynes, 1995).

General Educators

It would not be feasible to include students in regular classrooms and other general educational classes and environments without the cooperation and support of general educators. It is probably because of this that general education teachers must now serve on IEP teams. Although it cannot be assumed that these professionals have the depth of knowledge about the nature of severe disabilities that the special educator has (although some may), it can be expected that with support and adequate preparation they can provide instruction to students with severe disabilities in their classrooms and elsewhere.

General educators have the primary responsibility for teaching subject matter to students who can acquire information primarily through verbal and written instruction and other kinds of learning experiences. In this process they plan lessons, prepare materials, organize instructional activities, and use instructional media and materials to teach the content of specific subject matter from the elementary level through high school. When students require alternative forms of instruction or have learning goals that fall outside the norm, as do students with severe disabilities, the general educator often needs help to find ways to instruct that benefit all students.

To be successful as inclusive teachers, general educators must have an open mind about the possibilities of students with disabilities; plan, teach, and problem solve collaboratively; and help students with disabilities to feel that they belong (Janney et al., 1995). It can be expected that many general educators will be supportive of inclusion. However, given their duties with students without disabilities, they will often find the additional challenge of teaching students with disabilities to be very trying. Their attitudes toward inclusion will likely be more positive if they have enough time for collaborative planning, receive necessary instruction in teaching students with disabilities, have adequate assistance from special education teachers and paraprofessionals, are provided with adequate material resources, and have reduced class sizes (Scruggs & Mastropieri, 1996).

Physical and Occupational Therapists

The physical therapist (PT) is a health-care professional who has been educated to work with individuals who have physical disabilities. The PT possesses expertise in evaluating, planning, and intervening in posture and balance, preventing bodily misformations, and improving gross motor functioning, including ambulation. This professional provides exercises and positioning techniques to help to align the spine, legs, and feet; fits students with positioning equipment and braces or prostheses; provides range of motion, relaxation, sensory stimulation, and postural drainage procedures; and develops methods that allow the student to function as independently as possible (Bigge, Best, & Heller, 2001; Orelove & Sobsey, 1996).

The PT can provide exercises that allow the student to increase the appropriate use of her body and its parts and can prevent further limitations that may occur through misalignments, contractions, or primitive reflexes that persist. Equally important from the perspective of the teacher is the application of the PT's knowledge to help the student to participate in various common daily activities, such as eating, dressing, and participating in recreational activities. By attending to concerns such as these, the PT helps the student to function in a more normal life routine.

The occupational therapist (OT) possesses knowledge and skills similar to the PT, but has an orientation toward purposeful activities or tasks that have meaning for the individual (Dunn, 1991). Practically speaking, OTs are more able to assist in using fine motor skills related to daily living activities (Orelove & Sobsey, 1996). For example, if a student with cerebral palsy is attempting to learn to eat independently using a spoon, an OT can provide specific suggestions on the type of utensil to use, how to place the plate or bowl for the best access, how to help the student to learn to scoop the food, and how to improve oral–muscular control if necessary.

Most OTs and PTs have been trained in clinical models that call for in-depth evaluation of the physical development and needs of the individual, followed by specific intervention to improve functioning or inhibit deterioration. Although, traditionally, these therapists have worked in isolated settings with individuals with disabilities, more recent practices consist of integrated therapy models. This approach is intended to bring the expertise of the therapist into areas of functional needs.

Communication Disorders Specialists

Most individuals with severe disabilities need special attention focused on communication skills: improving verbal language, developing and applying language skills to satisfy environmental needs, developing alternative or augmentative communication systems, or developing relatively basic forms of communication to express satisfaction or dissatisfaction, comfort or discomfort, or yes or no. Specialists in communication disorders (speech–language therapists, speech pathologists) can provide expertise in this area if they have received appropriate training.

The communication disorders specialist evaluates the student's language ability and needs and cooperates with other team members to suggest appropriate language–learning goals. Traditionally, the language specialist has provided direct therapy, but more recent approaches require the specialist to work through the teacher and others to help the student to develop and improve functional language skills for use in natural environments (Caro & Snell, 1989; Mirenda, Iacono, & Williams, 1990).

School Administrators

All public school districts have well-developed administrative structures with various administrators serving in different roles. School administrators, both from the central school district office (superintendent, assistant superintendent, and director of special education, among others) and within the school (principal, assistant principal, and department heads), are responsible for developing policies, making decisions, and implementing programs. Without question, their commitment is vital to having successful, high-quality programs for students with and without disabilities. Individually and as a group, they make critical decisions on factors such as financing, service delivery arrangements, placement of students, IEP development procedures, community- and home-based instruction, and staff development needs.

While their positions allow administrators to be very influential, like other professionals, they are held accountable for their actions. It is their responsibility to see that federal and state laws for educational services for students with disabilities are followed. They must also be responsive to parents, advocacy groups, and professional organizations. As the potential for quality services for students with severe disabilities continues to increase, so too does the demand for these services. Most successful administrators form strong alliances with these groups and individuals to develop high-quality programs.

School Psychologists

The traditional role of the school psychologist has been to conduct assessments to determine the present level of functioning of students with disabilities. To be eligible for special education services in most school districts, students must score below predetermined criteria on standardized tests of intelligence and adaptive behavior. The school psychologist is the professional responsible for conducting these assessments, collecting other relevant types of information, and preparing a written report on the cognitive and behavioral functioning of the individual. For students with multiple disabilities and the most severe disabilities, traditional forms of intellectual assessment may have little meaning. Likewise, because of a restricted range of ambulation and mobility, formal adaptive behavior assessment may have little meaning. Nevertheless, such assessments may be required to allow the individual to receive services.

Many school psychologists are trained in the area of applied behavior analysis and can analyze the relation between a student's behavior and environmental activities. With such analysis, plans may be developed to increase adaptive behavior and decrease less desirable forms of behavior using positive behavioral supports and interventions (see Chapter 12). Serving in the role of behavior analyst, the school psychologist may directly observe the student in the classroom and may also ask the teacher(s) to provide information about the student's behavior. A strong cooperative relationship between teacher and psychologist can improve the quality of intervention used to facilitate a student's learning.

School Nurse

The school nurse is probably the professional most available to provide information and treatment for a student's medical needs. Because many students with severe disabilities have sensitive physical conditions, the expertise of a nurse can be very valuable. This individual can provide direct treatment and also demonstrate to others how to respond to seizures, provide first aid when needed, give medication, and perform catheterization, suctioning, and tube feeding for students who need these services (Orelove & Sobsey, 1996).

Special and general educators should take advantage of the nurse's expertise by requesting in-service training and informal information related to medical needs. Teachers working with students with severe disabilities for the first time should arrange to receive an orientation from the nurse about general health-care practices. When new students arrive, the teacher should seek medical information from the nurse about the unique characteristics or needs of each student.

Other Professionals

The above list of professionals is extensive, but there are actually many other professionals who may work on collaborative teams and play important roles. Their involvement will usually depend on the extent and nature of specific students' disabilities. Some of these include social workers, vision specialists, orientation and mobility specialists, audiologists, physicians (in pediatrics, neurology, ophthalmology, orthopedics, or urology), and dentists. Additionally, the school guidance counselor, nutritionists and dietitians, respiratory therapists, pharmacists, rehabilitation engineers, bus drivers, music therapists, recreational therapists, and media specialists may be part of the collaborative team (Orelove & Sobsey, 1996).

Structuring Transdisciplinary Collaborative Teams

In the formation of collaborative teams, there are different possible structures, all of which are not equal in terms of their potential success. Three common team models exist: the *multidisciplinary model*, the *interdisciplinary model*, and the *transdisciplinary model*. Of these, the transdisciplinary team is considered to be most effective for providing services to students with severe disabilities (Orelove & Sobsey, 1996; Rainforth & York, 1997).

The multidisciplinary model is the oldest model of professionals working with individuals with disabilities. Each professional, primarily the teacher, the communication disorders specialist, the PT, and the OT, works separately and in isolation with each student. Based on their own specific expertise, each conducts an assessment, plans a program of intervention, implements the program, and evaluates the student's performance in the program (Campbell, 1987; Orelove & Sobsey, 1996). The major advantage of this model is that it offers students the expert knowledge and skills of many professionals. Beyond this, it has few advantages and several disadvantages. One major drawback is that it does not call for interaction or cooperation among professionals; it does not require professionals to go beyond what is considered their primary area of expertise. Another major problem is that services provided under the multidisciplinary model are delivered in isolation, using a *pull-out* model that takes the student out of relevant learning environments in order to provide brief episodes of therapeutic intervention. Many professionals feel that the multidisciplinary model is inadequate because it falls short of meeting the needs of students with severe disabilities. The approaches taken by different professionals are often in opposition to each other, and implementation beyond that provided by individual therapists is inadequate (Orelove & Sobsey, 1996).

The interdisciplinary model is a more sophisticated team approach that exceeds the multidisciplinary model in its ability to provide a more coordinated program. The primary characteristic of this model is the sharing of information by professionals at team meetings (Campbell, 1987; Orelove & Sobsey, 1996), which has the effect of improving organization and ensuring that all service needs are met. Although the interdisciplinary model allows professionals of different disciplines to come together and make coordinated decisions about the educational and therapeutic needs of the student, it suffers many of the problems associated with the multidisciplinary model. Assessments and programs are carried out in isolation from each other, interventions are tied to the orientations of the individual disciplines, and all efforts are not necessarily going in the same direction. Although communication between professionals is an improvement over the multidisciplinary model, the interdisciplinary model is still a clinical–medical, deficit-remediation model that works toward the improvement of select, isolated goals. Greater focus among the professionals working with the student is needed, which is provided by the third model, the transdisciplinary team.

The transdisciplinary team model extends the potential effectiveness of the previous team models and is considered by many the preferred method of coordinating services and improving the functioning of students with severe disabilities (Bricker, 1976; Campbell, 1987; Dunn, 1988, 1991; Lyon & Lyon, 1980; Orelove & Sobsey, 1996; Rainforth & York, 1987, 1997; Sears, 1981; Sternat, Messina, Nietupski, Lyon, & Brown, 1977). As its name implies, the transdisciplinary model provides coordinated services across disciplines, rather than isolated services within disciplines. Table 3–1 compares the major features of the transdisciplinary model with the multidisciplinary and interdisciplinary models. Under the transdisciplinary model, one professional, usually the teacher, is responsible for coordinating and implementing most of the services, including those traditionally in the domains of other professionals. The teacher must be in regular contact with all the other professionals involved and, to the extent possible,

Table 3–1 Comparison of Three Team Models

	Multidisciplinary	*Interdisciplinary*	*Transdisciplinary*
Assessment	Separate assessments by team members	Separate assessments by team members	Team members and family conduct a comprehensive developmental assessment together
Parent participation	Parents meet with individual team members	Parents meet with team or team representative	Parents are full, active, and participating members of the team
Service plan development	Team members develop separate plans for their discipline	Team members share their separate plans with one another	Team members and the parents develop a service plan based upon family priorities, needs, and resources
Service plan responsibility	Team members are responsible for implementing their section of the plan	Team members are responsible for sharing information with one another as well as for implementing their section of the plan	Team members are responsible and accountable for how the primary service provider implements the plan
Service plan implementation	Team members implement the part of the service plan related to their discipline	Team members implement their section of the plan and incorporate other sections where possible	A primary service provider is assigned to implement the plan with the family
Lines of communication	Informal lines	Periodic case-specific team meetings	Regular team meeting where continuous transfer of information, knowledge, and skills are shared among team members
Guiding philosophy	Team members recognize the importance of contributions from other disciplines	Team members are willing and able to develop, share, and be responsible for providing services that are a part of the total service plan	Team members make a commitment to teach, learn, and work together across discipline boundaries to implement the unified service plan
Staff development	Independent and within their discipline	Independent within as well as outside of their discipline	An integral component of team meetings for learning across disciplines and team building

Source: Early Intervention Team Approaches: The Transdisciplinary Model, by G. Woodruff & M. J. McGonigel, 1988. In J. B. Jordan, J. J. Gallagher, P. L. Huntinger, & M. B. Karnes (Eds.), *Early Childhood Special Education: Birth to Three,* p. 166, Reston, VA: Council for Exceptional Children. Reprinted by permission.

incorporate the necessary therapies into students' daily learning routines.

Assessment and Planning

Implementing the transdisciplinary model in daily educational practice begins with team members participating in the assessment and planning process. Although therapists may conduct some forms of assessment in isolation, they also analyze the student's performance in natural settings. They do this by examining the environments in which the student needs to operate (this is called an *ecological inventory*) and then determine what modifications, adaptations, or skills are needed in these environments. They then observe the student's performance within the targeted environments to determine key skills that need to be learned. If necessary, they will follow up with more in-depth assessment in more traditional clinical settings. The teacher and other team members share information with each other about their observations to answer the following questions (Campbell, 1987):

- What skill will be selected for instruction in each targeted functional skill domain?
- What types of adaptive positioning equipment, adaptive materials, or other devices will be used to enable skill performance?
- What strategies will be used to teach certain skills?
- When and where will instruction be implemented and by whom?
- How will the effects of instruction be measured and reviewed? (p. 109)

Providing Integrated Therapy

Although some isolated forms of therapy may continue, a primary function of therapists operating within the transdisciplinary model is to provide direct theurapeutic services to students in classrooms and natural settings. The *integrated therapy approach* is considered a significant complement to the transdisciplinary model (Rainforth & York, 1997). Throughout the day, there are natural opportunities for the student to exercise skills necessary to the development of physical and communicative functioning. At these times, therapists (PT, OT, speech) can provide direct therapy within the contexts in which the skills will be needed. This allows the student to benefit from therapy throughout the day and simultaneously to participate in various learning activities. Many activities can incorporate both educational goals and therapeutic goals.

Role Release by Professionals

Another important characteristic of the transdisciplinary model is *role release*. This aspect of the model allows different professionals to provide some of the services traditionally offered by other professionals. For role release to be successful, professionals must share information with each other about their activities and explain how certain procedures are carried out (Lyon & Lyon, 1980). Thus the teacher will perform some of the functions of the communication disorders specialist, the physical therapists, and the occupational therapists, and the therapists will perform some instructional functions of the teacher. This feature of the transdisciplinary model makes the participating professionals more of a team than those working in other models. But for the model to be implemented, it is necessary for therapists to broaden their traditional roles. Three therapy approaches may be used appropriately within the transdisciplinary team model: direct service, monitoring, and consultation (Dunn, 1988, 1991).

Direct service from a therapist to a student is the most traditional form of intervention provided by a therapist and has usually been provided through pull-out practices. Although it is more desirable for therapy to be provided within natural learning environments, in some circumstances it is necessary for the therapist to work individually with a student in a nondistracting environment. This would be the case when *ongoing* clinical judgment is required during exercises. Even when this is necessary, however, the therapeutic target should be relevant to the student's educational needs and transferred to natural learning environments for practice when possible.

There are many needs of students for which therapists can provide primarily a *monitoring* service as teachers, parents, and paraprofessionals provide the therapeutic intervention. When monitoring, the therapist is exercising the role release option. She is most involved in the initial assessment and planning and in teaching the teacher and others how to implement the program in natural environments. The therapist maintains regular contact with the teacher (usually at least twice a month) to determine if any changes are needed in the intervention. From a therapeutic point of view, monitoring is appropriate under certain circumstances: if the therapist feels the student's health and safety will be protected, if the teacher or another person implementing the procedure can be taught to do it without assistance, and if the teacher or other person can also be taught to independently identify signs that call for the procedure to be discontinued (Dunn, 1988).

Consultation is a final form of service provided by the therapist in a transdisciplinary model. It may be provided for individual students (case consultation), for other professionals' needs (colleague consultation), or for the generic needs of a school system (system consultation). Obviously, in the transdisciplinary model, consultation is the most desirable form of involvement by a therapist. When all therapists involved are serving primarily in consultative roles, there is opportunity for diverse expertise to be cooperatively applied to students' needs.

Collaborating Effectively as a Transdisciplinary Team

For the transdisciplinary team to function effectively, team members must undertake certain roles and responsibilities. These may be generic or discipline specific (Rainforth & York, 1997). Generic roles include participating in decision-making activities about each student, contributing to problem-solving efforts, sharing knowledge and skills, supporting the contributions of others, and continuing to learn about successful methods for ensuring participation of the students in their family, school, and community lives. Discipline-specific roles are generally unique to the different members of the transdisciplinary team. For any group of professionals to function as a transdisciplinary team, it is important for each team member to be aware of the functions and expertise of other team members.

Working on a team, especially a transdisciplinary team, is not easy for many professionals. Sharing expertise, role release, and collaboratively consulting in a collegial manner obviously have much merit, but individual characteristics of team members can sometimes provide a hindrance. If true team functioning is to work, it will take commitment and practice. Pugach and Johnson (2002) have provided several suggestions for effective team functioning. These are described next.

Team Membership

Teams whose members are able to resolve conflicts, can communicate clearly, are stable and open, and are willing to take risks will be the most effective teams. These individual characteristics are most desirable in team members, although it is not often that professionals can select the team members with whom they work.

Meeting Place and Time

A major impediment to team functioning is having adequate time to meet and a suitable location. The location should be comfortable and conducive to group discussion. Administrators should allow adequate time for meetings to be built into team members' schedules. Typically, these meetings should occur at least once a week, before or after school hours.

Group Facilitator

Although all members are expected to participate and function as collaborators, one person must be designated as the facilitator of the group. This may be an administrator or a teacher. The special education teacher providing support to students in inclusive settings is often the facilitator. The facilitator should have broad knowledge of the issues and be able to maintain a positive and cooperative atmosphere during collaborative meetings. Being able to communicate clearly is an extremely important skill, as is the ability to resolve conflicts among members and to promote group rapport.

Format

Meetings should be well organized with an agenda of scheduled topics. For example, student(s) who will be discussed and the instructional challenges that they present should be outlined on the agenda. Meeting formats should be established by the facilitator with input from other team members.

Goal Setting

Teams will work together better if they can agree on their goals. The more clearly stated the goals of the team, the more efficiently they will be able to work. Sometimes it is necessary for the facilitator to keep the team on task so that goals will be achieved through consensus of the team members. The goals that are set should be practical and attainable, and members should be especially sensitive about setting goals that place an undue burden on the parents and family of the student.

Conflict Resolution

Teams must be able to resolve conflict through arbitration and mediation. Conflicts can best be resolved by clearly identifying the conflicting issues, discussing the points for and against a particular position, and agreeing through negotiation and consensus if possible or through a vote of the team members if necessary. Conflicts should be resolved professionally and without personal attacks.

Collaborating with Paraprofessionals

In recent years, paraprofessionals (or paraeducators) have taken a major role in the education of students with severe disabilities. Paraprofessionals have often worked closely with teachers in self-contained special classes, but more and more they are being used when students with disabilities are placed in general education classrooms (Giangreco & Doyle, 2002; Giangreco, Edelman, Broer, & Doyle, 2001). It is very likely that a teacher will have more daily contact and a more direct relationship with a paraprofessional than with the other previously described members of the collaborative team. This has many implications. Therefore, in the remaining pages of this chapter we provide an extensive discussion of the role of paraprofessionals with teachers and students.

Recent Developments in the Use of Paraprofessionals

Paraprofessionals in education began to appear in the 1950s due to a shortage of teachers following World War II. In the 1960s and 1970s, several of the War on Poverty programs, such as Head Start and Title 1 (later Chapter 1), increased the use of paraprofessionals in educational programs. Guaranteed educational services for students with disabilities that resulted from the passage of P.L. 94-142 in the mid-1970s again led to an increase in the use of paraprofessionals (French & Pickett, 1997). In more recent years, the use of paraprofessionals has increased dramatically, with many of these persons providing services to students with severe disabilities. Several factors have had an influence on the recent increase, especially these:

- Increases in the numbers of students with disabilities in public schools
- Increases in the number of children in early childhood education programs and the number of older individuals receiving transition services
- A constant shortage of certified special education teachers
- Increases in the number of students with disabilities in general education classrooms and general educators' perception that paraprofessional assistance is essential to serve these students (French & Pickett, 1997; Giangreco, Edelman, Broer, & Doyle, 2001).

To study the professional–paraprofessional relationship in special education, French (2001) conducted a survey of special education teachers in Colorado. She found that 75% of the teachers who responded to her survey supervised paraprofessionals as part of their duties. On average, teachers generally supervised between one and two paraprofessionals, but, as might be expected, teachers of students with severe disabilities supervised more paraprofessionals, typically between two and four, and teachers of students with multiple disabilities often had even more paraprofessionals working with them. High percentages of the teachers reported that the primary roles of the paraprofessionals were to assist the special education teacher (91%), to assist individual students (82%), and to assist general education teachers when students with disabilities were included in general education classrooms (71%). With regard to this last duty, Werts et al. (1996) found that general education teachers identified the presence of a paraprofessional in the classroom as one of the most important sources of support to facilitate inclusion of students with disabilities.

Historically, no uniform training has been required for persons serving as paraprofessionals beyond a high school diploma. Under the No Child Left Behind Act of 2001 (P.L. 107-110), however, paraprofessionals working in public education are required to have 2 years of college training, although the nature of the coursework was not specified in the law. In a large study of more than 700 special education paraprofessionals, Riggs and Mueller (2001) found that 20% of their respondents held bachelors degrees and 14% were certified teachers. They also reported that all the paraprofessionals felt that they needed more training for their duties.

Based on their review of the literature, Giangreco, Edelman, Broer, and Doyle (2001) concluded that under the most appropriate circumstances, paraprofessionals effectively increase learning by students with disabilities. When paraprofessionals are taught to use specific instructional procedures, students have been shown to learn skills, and the paraprofessionals have reported satisfaction at the opportunity to learn new skills for teaching the students. However, these studies have been limited to relatively few students and have not focused broadly on the use of paraprofessionals as teachers (Giangreco, Edelman, Broer, & Doyle, 2001).

Roles and Duties of Paraprofessionals

Paraprofessionals work in special and regular classes with students with severe disabilities, performing many instructional functions similar to those carried out by teachers, as well as several noninstructional duties. The primary differences between teachers and their assistants are (1) teachers must hold at least a 4-year degree from a college or university, whereas paraprofessionals traditionally have not been required to have college training; (2) teachers are considered to be the primary planners and decision makers for their students, although paraprofessionals may make suggestions; and (3) teachers, with other professionals on the collaborative team, are responsible for developing instructional programs and are held accountable for students' learning and well-being, even though paraprofessionals may often provide direct instruction.

Paraprofessionals are often assigned a range of duties. Although there is no concrete list of responsibilities, there appears to be a general consensus that duties of the following nature are appropriate for paraprofessionals *under the direction and supervision of the teacher* (Boomer, 1980, 1982; Frith & Lindsey, 1980; Giangreco, Broer, & Edelman, 1999; Giangreco & Doyle, 2002; McKenzie & Houk, 1986):

- Supervise individuals and small groups in classrooms, other school settings, and community settings
- Position, lift, and carry students with physical disabilities
- Carry out self-care, feeding, dressing, and toileting programs
- Help to prepare materials and arrange the classroom for learning activities
- Be responsible for keeping the classroom neat and orderly and clean material and equipment when necessary
- Assist in preparing materials, bulletin boards, adaptive equipment, classroom furniture, and the like
- Collect student performance data
- Help to implement positive behavioral support plans and respond to inappropriate behavior appropriately
- Intervene in medical emergencies and contact an appropriate individual for emergency medical services
- Communicate positively with students with and without disabilities and with professional and paraprofessional personnel
- Assist students with mobility needs and transportation
- Provide instruction and assistance to individuals or groups
- Engage in clerical tasks to free teachers to spend more instructional time with students

When paraprofessionals are assigned to work with students with disabilities included in general education classrooms, they are in a position to have a very positive influence, or sometimes a negative impact. They may serve in a beneficial role by helping students to learn successfully and adapt to an inclusive environment. However, many times paraprofessionals may be misused or overused in the delivery of services, and this presents a problem. A common approach to inclusion, one often cited by teachers as being a critical need (Werts et al., 1996), is to assign a one-to-one paraprofessional to work full time with a student with a disability, especially when the disability is severe. While the support may be considered useful, it may also be detrimental. According to Giangreco et al. (1999), a constant one-to-one paraprofessional may:

- Increase the student's dependence on an adult
- Interfere with the involvement of the teacher with the student
- Impede the development of peer relationships
- Adversely impact gender identification
- Reduce the development of personal control

In light of these possibilities, a critical question is "When are paraprofessionals a necessary support for students with disabilities?" Giangreco et al. (1999) propose that the assignment of a paraprofessional to a student with disabilities be a short-term intervention plan and that a systematic decision-making process be used by the collaborative team to make decisions about the placement of a paraprofessional for a more extensive period of time. Further discussion of the use of paraprofessionals to provide direct instruction in inclusive classrooms is provided later.

Teachers' Roles with Regard to Paraprofessionals

The responsibility for maximizing learning by students with severe disabilities rests with the members of the collaborative team. The day-to-day duty of implementing the appropriate learning activities rests primarily with the special educator, the general educator, and, to some extent, the other members of the team. In fulfilling these responsibilities, professionals are the decision makers who determine, with the parents, the appropriate goals and objectives, the instructional strategies, and the related therapeutic needs of students with disabilities. Working in this framework, teachers must design the daily learning activities for classrooms and other environments, monitor students' progress through data collection and evaluation, and continue to collaborate with other team members.

For paraprofessionals to be employed correctly, the responsibilities of the teacher must be expanded from solely providing direct service to overseeing the service of one or more paraprofessionals working side by side with her in the classroom. So, in addition to student-focused responsibilities, the professional must also assume responsibility for directing, supervising, and evaluating the activity of the paraprofessional. Often this task presents more of a challenge to new teachers than does directly teaching students, and many teachers are not adequately prepared for this role (Wallace, Shin, Bartholomay, & Stahl, 2001). Nevertheless, it is an important responsibility and must be undertaken by the teacher with the same level of effort as directly teaching students with disabilities.

Assigning Duties. An individual working as a paraprofessional needs to perform a variety of tasks assigned by the teacher, such as those listed previously. It is important for the teacher to determine the paraprofessional's ability to perform certain tasks, and, if important skills are found to be lacking, the teacher should either explain and demonstrate to the assistant how these tasks are to be done or ensure that adequate training is provided (Giangreco, Edelman, & Broer, 2001). French (1999) proposes that teachers may assign paraprofessional duties based on consideration of laws, risks, and ethics. In various states, laws have been implemented to specify what paraprofessionals can and cannot do. In addition to these laws, individual school boards have identified situations in which paraprofessionals may or may not act independently based on the risks to which students may be exposed. French warned that, if a paraprofessional is not adequately trained to perform a duty with a student, it is unethical for a teacher to assign the paraprofessional to perform that duty. French also stressed that it is inappropriate for the teacher to assign duties to paraprofessionals that he himself would not do and instead recommended that teachers and paraprofessionals should share selected duties. Nevertheless, French (2001) found that the respondents stated that most often paraprofessionals working with students with more severe disabilities are assigned duties that are not undertaken by the teachers, such as dressing and changing clothes, feeding, and toileting or diapering students.

As shown earlier, there are many appropriate tasks for a paraprofessional to perform. It will be helpful and may offset future conflicts if these tasks or other specific responsibilities are written down and discussed with the paraprofessional at the beginning of employment with a teacher. In some school districts, paraprofessional requirements may already have been developed and these may be sufficient. However, it is important that paraprofessionals have a clear understanding of their duties regardless of who specifies these duties. Even if there are schoolwide or districtwide policies, the teacher may wish to develop an individual assignment protocol for the paraprofessional unique to the needs of her program (McKenzie & Houk, 1986).

Supervising and Evaluating. Studies have shown that many paraprofessionals are not adequately supervised or evaluated (French, 2001; Riggs & Mueller, 2001; Salzberg & Morgan, 1995, Wallace et al., 2001). This condition can sometimes result in the individual performing unacceptably. To avoid this, the teacher must be prepared to appropriately direct the paraprofessional and assess the quality of service provided. The following four guidelines will be helpful when fulfilling these responsibilities.

1. A clearly written statement of the paraprofessional's job responsibility facilitates supervision and evaluation because there is little doubt by either the teacher or the teacher's assistant about what is expected. Given that there is mutual understanding of what the paraprofessional is to do, the job of supervising and evaluating can be very objective, with job performance serving as the basis.
2. To further facilitate supervision and evaluation, regular weekly meetings between the teacher and the paraprofessional should be scheduled. This not only allows the teacher to evaluate the assistant's performance, but also allows the assistant to be involved in planning future activities for the students. Also, by scheduling regular meetings, discussions between the professional and paraprofessional are not limited to the times when the teacher is not satisfied with his assistant.
3. If the paraprofessional is not performing a task correctly, the teacher should be very explicit as to what must be done. Again, the teacher may refer to the written job requirements. If this is not sufficient, the teacher may need to demonstrate how to perform the task. The teacher should make sure that the assistant has the opportunity to perform the task under close supervision and direction in order that she can do so independently in the future.
4. Regular feedback, both written and verbal, provides a paraprofessional with reinforcement for doing a job correctly or with information about what areas of job performance are in need of improvement. During weekly scheduled meetings, verbal evalua-

tions may be sufficient; however, written evaluations should also be provided, although they may come less often. Although schools or school districts may require teachers to provide annual written evaluations about paraprofessionals, more frequent notices about performance may be useful, particularly when new professional–paraprofessional relations are being established.

Because paraprofessionals are such an integral part of the teacher's daily activities, it is important for both, as well as for the students, that harmonious personal relations be maintained. Most often there are no problems in this area, but there are potential sources of conflict. If the assistant has duties that are not clearly explained or that he does not know how to perform, if less pleasant duties are not shared equally by teacher and assistant, if the supervision by the teacher is critical in a nonconstructive fashion, or if the respective roles of the two are not clearly defined, personal conflicts may occur. The appropriate approach to supervision and evaluation as discussed above will help, but conflicts may still sometimes occur.

Although these conflicts cannot always be avoided, some efforts may be helpful. To begin with, once again, the teacher must reinforce the fact that final decisions about operations in the classroom rest with her. This position needs to be taken early and often, but it must be presented diplomatically. The fact is that the paraprofessional is not employed or paid sufficiently to have this responsibility. So while input should be invited and welcomed, the paraprofessional must understand that ultimate decision making is the teacher's responsibility. Teachers should learn about and use the unique strengths of paraprofessionals, who have varied backgrounds and experiences that allow them to provide unique types of assistance (French & Pickett, 1997). Discovering, using, and reinforcing the personal contributions of individuals will improve their self-esteem and make them more pleasant team players. It may also result in better service to the students, because there may be some tasks at which the assistant may be more adept than the teacher.

Critical Issues Related to the Use of Paraprofessionals

During the last few years, several authorities have raised important questions about the use, or more correctly, the overuse and possible misuse, of paraprofessionals in providing educational services to students with severe disabilities. These questions have focused primarily on two issues: (1) the overreliance on paraprofessionals and (2) the lack of preparation by teachers for training and supervising paraprofessionals.

Extensive Reliance on Paraprofessionals

Giangreco and Doyle (2002) contend that the extensive use of paraprofessionals is a two-edged sword. On the one hand, they provide a valuable service; on the other, without the paraprofessionals having appropriate training and skills, students will receive less appropriate services. Giangreco and Doyle stated, "Although we have no doubt that paraprofessionals will continue to have vital and valued roles in special education, confusion about their changing roles has led to a situation in which some students with disabilities receive their special education services primarily or exclusively from paraprofessionals" (p. 2). They pose serious questions about the soundness and effectiveness of such an approach:

- Is it appropriate that the less-trained individual be assigned to work with the most challenging students?
- Is it fair for students with disabilities to be served by paraprofessionals when students without disabilities are served by fully trained and certified teachers?
- Is it fair to pay paraprofessionals a relatively low wage and expect them to carry out the same duties as teachers with regard to planning, adapting, and instructing?

The problem is especially acute when paraprofessionals are placed one on one with students in general education classrooms. Brown et al. (1999) commented, "Assigning a paraprofessional to a student with disabilities in a regular education setting too often inhibited, prevented, or excused others from sharing the responsibility for educating all children and from developing a meaningful array of relationships with schoolmates who did not have disabilities" (p. 251). They further maintained that, because of the learning needs and complex challenges of students with the most severe disabilities, they are in "dire need of continuous exposure to the most ingenious, creative, powerful, competent, and interpersonally effective and informed professionals" (p. 252). Giangreco and his colleagues (1999) charged that there appears to be a double standard when students without disabilities are instructed by fully certified and qualified teachers, while students with disabilities are taught by the noncertified, inadequately prepared personnel. Even though paraprofessionals may be fully committed to their jobs and the students that they teach, they are, nevertheless, not as well qualified as a trained teacher with an appropriate teaching credential. Giangreco, Edelman, Broer, and Doyle (2001) raised more critical questions:

- Are the roles and duties paraprofessionals are asked to perform appropriate?
- Are they adequately trained for their roles?
- Are they appropriately supervised?
- Are they truly assisting qualified personnel, or are they functioning as the primary instructors and decision makers for some students with disabilities?
- Are models of service delivery that rely heavily on paraprofessionals effective and, if so, under what conditions?

Two studies document the extensive use of paraprofessionals in inclusive classrooms and address a number of concerns that have been raised (Marks, Schrader, & Levine, 1999; Riggs & Mueller, 2001). Marks and his coworkers interviewed 20 paraprofessionals who worked exclusively in one-on-one situations with students with disabilities placed in regular classrooms, all of whom exhibited challenging behaviors. The paraprofessionals took on many roles, but the most significant was providing support to students so that their placement in an inclusive setting would be successful. Their responsibilities were extensive: they provided instruction in academic and social skills, made curricular modifications, managed students' behavior, and maintained working relations with others in the schools. Marks et al. found that the paraprofessionals considered themselves to be responsible for the success of the included students and felt that often no one else, especially the general educator, shared this responsibility. In fact, some of the paraprofessionals viewed their major role as not allowing the student with disabilities to "bother" the teacher so as not to be a "burden." Clearly, such staffing patterns represent undesirable arrangements in that, even though "included" physically, the student is not viewed by the teacher as an integral part of the class. Other findings by Marks et al. were these:

- The paraprofessionals felt that they were considered experts by others in the school both about the children with disabilities and about inclusion. Some respected them for their role, but others did not understand why the children or the paraprofessionals who worked with them were in the school.
- The paraprofessionals often had the major responsibility for making on-the-spot curricular adaptations and instructing or tutoring the students with disabilities so that the teacher's lesson would make sense to them.
- Often the paraprofessionals were considered by others in the school as the expert about the student's disabilities and what would work effectively with him or her. Other times they were the synthesizer who had to take in suggestions and information from multiple sources, interpret it, and apply it in a way meaningful to the student's daily learning routine.
- Many times the paraprofessional found himself or herself in an advocacy role for inclusion, defending the practice to others in the school.

In their study, Riggs and Mueller (2001) also gathered a range of information about paraprofessionals working in regular classrooms with students with disabilities. Twenty-three paraprofessionals were interviewed, another 758 responded to a 100-item survey, and 20 completed time log diaries to indicate their activities. Key findings for the roles of paraprofessionals were the following:

- All the paraprofessionals spent the majority of their time providing direct instruction to students, and 70% of them provided instruction for at least three quarters of their work time.
- All the paraprofessionals felt that they needed more training for their duties, but reported that their school districts provided little orientation or training. Fewer than 40% had any type of orientation in key areas (student characteristics and programs, discipline, health and safety, etc.).
- Of the training received, most of it was on the job training or consisted of advice and assistance from other paraprofessionals. Only 17% had training before starting their positions, and only 8% to 12% received any training through in-service workshops or courses. Although a majority said training was available, 70% said that it was irrelevant to what they were doing.
- The greatest areas of training needs were in behavior management and curriculum modifications and adaptations.
- Nearly half of the respondents were not given a written job description before they began working.
- Most of the paraprofessionals were unclear about policies related to their supervision and evaluation and considered most of the evaluations by their supervising teachers to be informal.

- Twenty-five percent of the respondents indicated that they received no daily supervision on the tasks that they carried out most often.
- Many of the paraprofessionals felt that they were not sufficiently supported, as indicated by a lack of differential pay for different training or experience and for attending meetings about students.
- Other problems included being assigned to work with too many students or in too many classrooms, insufficient time for planning and communication, and inflexible schedules. Many also felt a lack of mutual respect and that their opinions on student issues were not appreciated.

The studies by Riggs and Mueller (2001) and Marks et al. (1999), among others (e.g., Giangreco, Edelman, & Broer, 2001), seem to suggest that the line between the duties of paraprofessionals and professionals has been blurred. It seems that paraprofessionals, at least in some cases, are being used to a greater extent and in more ways than many consider appropriate for nonprofessionals. They are making judgments about instructional needs and are assuming the primary role of teaching and managing behavior. To the extent that such patterns of paraprofessional use are common, this would truly raise the question as to whether students are receiving the quality of services called for by IDEA. Although most would agree that paraprofessionals may work on many tasks under the direction and supervision of a certified teacher, many contend that paraprofessionals are taking on too many roles that should be reserved for teachers. With regard to paraprofessionals working closely with students in general classrooms, Giangreco and Doyle (2002) expressed strong concern and specifically admonished that paraprofessionals should not work in isolation and be responsible for making critical curricular and instructional decisions, nor should they serve to isolate or segregate students within inclusive settings. They wrote:

> The teacher should explicitly discuss the paraprofessional's roles and responsibilities relative to (a) instructional and non-instructional tasks, and (b) students with and without disabilities. The (general teacher) or special educator should take the lead in planning the instruction, describing and demonstrating how to implement the planned instruction. Then the teacher and the paraprofessional should establish a time when the two will meet to discuss ongoing responsibilities. (p. 10)

This concern was also expressed by French and Pickett (1997). They stated that there is a "substantial overlap" of the instructional duties and roles of professionals and paraprofessionals and that the division of responsibilities, in many cases, is nonexistent or unclear. They wrote:

> With the emphasis on inclusion in general education classrooms and the increased employment of paraeducators as assistants to students with profound disabilities, those with complex health-support needs, those who need academic support, those with challenging behaviors, [or] those making transition from school to work or to post secondary education, the roles of paraeducators are becoming more and more like those of professionals. (p. 65)

Preparation of Teachers for Training and Supervising Paraprofessionals

As critical as is the role of the paraprofessional and the appropriate use of this individual, one would think that an important part of teacher preparation would be in working with these persons. But generally this is not the case. Salzberg and Morgan (1995) conducted a review of the literature to determine the skills most appropriate for teachers to work effectively with paraprofessionals. The skills that they identified as being most important included:

- Evaluating the performance of paraprofessionals
- Identifying the roles and responsibilities of paraprofessionals
- Communicating effectively with paraprofessionals
- Integrating the paraprofessional into the instructional setting
- Managing and supervising the paraprofessional

However, they noted that teachers are typically not adequately prepared to work with paraprofessionals. This need for teacher preparation was also raised by French and Pickett (1997), who stated that, although special educators are generally responsible for supervising paraprofessionals, they usually have no preparation to do so in their teacher education programs. This can result in both the professional and the paraprofessional not doing their jobs as effectively as possible.

The lack of training of teachers to work with paraprofessionals was also discussed by Wallace et al. (2001), who received surveys from 266 teachers, 211 paraprofessionals, and 92 administrators in a midwestern state that identified the types of competencies (knowledge and skills) needed by teachers to supervise paraprofessionals. They asked what was important for teachers to be able to do and also how often they actually carried out these activities with the paraprofessionals. Seven key areas were rated as being important or very important: communicating with paraprofessionals, planning and scheduling, providing them with instructional support, modeling for them, being an advocate them, training them, and managing their activities. Unfortunately, all the groups surveyed reported a gap between what teachers should be doing and what they were actually doing, and the teachers most often said this was because they were not sufficiently prepared to work with paraprofessionals.

The inadequate preparation of teachers for supervising paraprofessionals is clearly reflected in the fact that many paraprofessionals do not feel that they receive appropriate supervision. Although the high level of responsibility often assigned to paraprofessionals might imply that they generally receive appropriate training for their duties, they most often do not. In fact, most receive little or no training before beginning their jobs and acquire on-the-job experience as they progress, but with little guidance or supervision (Giangreco & Doyle, 2002; Giangreco, Edelman, & Broer, 2001; Giangreco, Edelman, Broer, & Doyle, 2001). Two studies identified the lack of training and supervision of paraprofessionals as a serious problem.

Using qualitative research methods, Giangreco, Edelman, and Broer (2001) investigated the views of paraprofessionals, professionals, and administrators working in four schools about the recognition given to paraprofessionals and the understanding of the type of work that they perform. They found that paraprofessionals who were given a thorough orientation to classroom and school activities felt more valued and respected, because it then seemed that the job was important enough for the professional to explain the system to them. But usually, Giangreco and his colleagues found, there was no systematic orientation process. They also found that the ability of the paraprofessionals to carry out instructional tasks varied widely. Some paraprofessionals were better qualified than others to perform instructional duties because of their educational level (some had college degrees and even teaching certificates); but these individuals were the most likely to feel that they were doing "teacher work" for salaries far below those of teachers, and this led to personal dissatisfaction. On the other hand, some paraprofessionals were given instructional tasks for which they felt ill equipped. This usually happened when a paraprofessional was assigned to one student with a disability in a general education classroom as opposed to when the paraprofessional was assigned to a whole classroom.

Recommendations Regarding the Appropriate Use of Paraprofessionals

It should be clear that although paraprofessionals can provide very significant services their use should not be without limits or guidelines. Practicing professionals, including teachers in general and special education, related services personnel, and most importantly, administrators, should do all that they can to make sure that the ways in which paraprofessionals are used are appropriate for their skill level and employment status. Additionally, paraprofessionals should be given the recognition, direction, and supervision that they require to do their jobs as well as possible. Often this will be the responsibility of the teacher and, when it is, the teacher must be adequately prepared to assume it. The following specific recommendations are intended to increase the appropriate utilization of paraprofessionals who work with students with severe disabilities.

Making the Paraprofessional a Meaningful Part of the Team

At the beginning of the year or at the point when an individual is employed as a paraprofessional, Giangreco and Doyle (2002) recommend that efforts be taken to make sure that the new paraprofessional feels a part of the team. Some ways to do this are relatively easy:

- Provide the paraprofessional with a space of his or her own in the classroom (e.g., desk, work area, mailbox, etc.)
- Put the paraprofessional's name on the door along with the teacher's.
- Orient the paraprofessional to the classroom materials and make sure that she or he has access to all of them.
- Orient the paraprofessional to the school and those locations most often visited by the teacher, and introduce him or her to other school personnel.
- Review written school and district policies with the paraprofessional and make sure to discuss key issues such as confidentiality and safety issues.

Beyond these actions, the teachers need to show their respect for the paraprofessional and his position by clearly delineating the responsibilities and duties of the paraprofessional and those of the teacher. Then the teacher needs to provide regular supervision, evaluation, and feedback for the paraprofessional to help this person to know how well the job is being done or not done. As Giangreco and Doyle (2002) argued, respect for the role of the paraprofessionals is important and can best be achieved through orienting and instructing them, providing them with plans for their work, and providing adequate supervision. This indicates that the work that they do is important enough to warrant the attention and support of the teacher. They also feel respect when they are a full member of the classroom team and are given the opportunity to provide input into classroom decisions.

Using the Paraprofessional in Inclusive Classrooms

When assigned to facilitate inclusion, it is important that paraprofessionals not work in isolation and not be responsible for making critical curricular and instructional decisions, nor should they serve to isolate or segregate students within inclusive settings. Instead they should work under the close supervision of fully qualified general and special education teachers. Teachers should make sure that the paraprofessional understands his assignments and duties and provide sufficient input for the paraprofessional to carry them out. In inclusive settings, the general educator should be the teacher of *all* students, even if paraprofessionals are used to help to support individual students. It is preferable for the paraprofessional to work with all students within the general classroom and not just with those with disabilities.

Sometimes paraprofessionals must maintain close proximity to students with disabilities to provide personal care, safety, or instructional support. However, the degree of proximity should be no more than is necessary and should be faded whenever possible. When paraprofessionals maintain continuously close proximity, there is less interaction between the student with disabilities, the classroom teacher, and peers without disabilities. Reduction of paraprofessional proximity may be feasible through the involvement of peers and classroom volunteers, as well as through changes in instructional formats, such as the increased use of cooperative learning and coteaching arrangements. Paraprofessionals working in inclusive classrooms should be assigned *to the classroom, not to the student*, and should provide assistance to various students (Giangreco & Doyle, 2002).

Despite common opinion, it may not always be necessary for a one-to-one assistant to be present to achieve successful inclusion. In fact, as previously stated, this arrangement can have several drawbacks. Giangreco, Broer, and Edelman (1999) raised the question "When are paraprofessionals a necessary support for students with disabilities?" and proposed that the assignment of a paraprofessional to a student with disabilities be a short-term intervention plan and that a systematic decision-making process be used by the collaborative team to make decisions about the placement of a paraprofessional for a more extended period of time. Ten guidelines were proposed for use in deciding the appropriate degree of use of a paraprofessional for a student with a disability.

1. *Rely on collaborative teamwork.* All team members should have sufficient knowledge about the characteristics and needs of the student, the learning context, and the instructional program to contribute to the decision-making process. Team decision-making reduces the risk of an error occurring because of individual decision-making.
2. *Build capacity in the school to support all students.* The greater the ability of various personnel in the school (students, teachers, administrators, and paraprofessionals) to support individual students with special needs, the less need there is for select individuals to provide ongoing support. Increased capacity of personnel could also better ensure that paraprofessionals are used to work with all students and not solely those with disabilities.
3. *Consider paraprofessional support individually and judiciously.* Because the effect of paraprofessional overuse may be negative, their assignments to students with disabilities should be determined on a case-by-case basis.
4. *Clarify the reasons why paraprofessional supports are being considered.* If the reason for the assignment of a paraprofessional is unclear, such an assignment may merely shift responsibility for a challenging aspect of a student's educational program to the paraprofessional without adequately addressing the challenge.
5. *Seek a match between identified support needs and the skills of the person to provide the support.* Two key points are related to this guideline. First, a paraprofessional who will be working with a student with disabilities must be appropriately oriented and trained to carry out assigned duties. Second, other individuals in the school may be more appropriate for providing certain types of support to the student. These persons should not be overlooked. They may allow for less reliance on a paraprofessional.

6. *Explore opportunities for natural supports.* Other individuals, such as cafeteria workers, office staff, or custodial staff, may be sources of more natural supports for students with disabilities. Peers may also offer natural supports. One might ask, "Who would provide support if there were no paraprofessional to do so?"
7. *Consider school and classroom characteristics.* In some cases, changes in the physical characteristics of a school or classroom may reduce the need for paraprofessional assistance. Removing barriers, using adaptive equipment or assistive technology devices, or changing the location of materials or equipment may reduce the reliance on paraprofessionals.
8. *Consider special educator and related services caseloads.* Sometimes it may be possible to make systemic changes, such as reducing the caseloads of special educators and related services therapists. This would allow professionals instead of paraprofessionals to spend greater amounts of time with students with disabilities.
9. *Explore administrative and organizational changes.* Schedules of paraprofessionals may be made more flexible so that they can provide assistance to different individuals at different times of the day. Students may need supports at some times during the day, but not at others.
10. *Consider if paraprofessional support is a temporary measure.* If it is determined that paraprofessional support is necessary, consider it as a temporary arrangement until other supports can be arranged.

Matching Paraprofessionals and Their Duties

Paraprofessionals will have a variety of personal characteristics, experiences, and educational backgrounds. To fully realize the benefit of having a paraprofessional, teachers should be able to identify the strengths of the paraprofessionals that they work with and consider these when assigning responsibilities. Paraprofessionals have a desire to be respected and to have their contributions acknowledged. Many paraprofessionals consider the opportunity that they have for input on the classroom team an indication of how much they are valued. Since they often spend more time with a student than anyone else, they feel that they know the student best and therefore their thoughts and ideas should be taken into consideration. Often the gratitude of administrators and teachers is expressed through giving the paraprofessionals symbols, tokens, and small gifts. Although these tokens and gifts may be appreciated, paraprofessionals often feel that they are more appreciated when they are recognized as providing a significant contribution (Giangreco, Edelman, & Broer, 2001).

Giangreco, Edelman, and Broer (2001) suggested that it is important that there be a match between what professionals and paraprofessionals expect of the latter. When there is a mismatch, the paraprofessional will be less satisfied with her job responsibilities. Some teachers expect paraprofessionals to teach and some paraprofessionals want to. In these cases, when given noninstructional assignments, some paraprofessionals feel that they are being given insignificant work. On the other hand, when some paraprofessionals are given instructional assignments, especially assignments that they have not been trained to do, they feel that they are being asked to do a teacher's job for which they are not adequately compensated. Three matches are important: (1) all team members should understand and agree on the duties of a paraprofessional, which are likely to vary among paraprofessionals and therefore must be individually determined; (2) there should be a match between duties and the paraprofessional's skills, training, and support to engage in these roles; and (3) differentiated roles and duties should be reflected in different levels of compensation (Giangreco, Edelman, Broer, & Doyle, 2001).

Conclusion

The professional responsibilities of a teacher of students with severe disabilities extend beyond the provision of direct services to these students. The teacher must collaborate with other professionals by serving as a member of a transdisciplinary team and usually must also work daily with one or more paraprofessionals. The importance of the relationship between the special educator and these other individuals cannot be overstated. If the teacher does not work effectively with others, less than optimal services will be delivered to the students.

For several years, it has been acknowledged that many different professionals possess skills that can make substantial contributions to the development and learning of individuals with severe disabilities. Special and general educators, occupational and physical therapists, and specialists in communication disorders have the most frequent contact with students, but others also play important roles. It is not enough that the expertise of these persons be applied to the individual; it must be applied in a collaborative fashion, with the professionals each playing an important role on the transdisciplinary team. At times this role will call for the direct application of unique skills; at other times there will be role release. The transdisciplinary model is the model that, to date, appears to offer the greatest benefit to students with severe disabilities.

Paraprofessionals have played an important role in special education for several decades. Although often not formally trained, they have usually worked alongside teachers, providing instructional and noninstructional support for students with disabilities. There has always been an assumption that these persons should perform their duties under the close direction and supervision of the teacher who is responsible for making decisions about curriculum, instruction, and behavior management. With the advent of inclusion for students with severe disabilities in the last 15 to 20 years, it has been observed that many paraprofessionals are operating as the primary instructor in one-on-one relationships with students in regular classrooms. This has resulted in some criticism of the arrangement and warrants close attention and modification. Nevertheless, paraprofessionals will continue to play important roles for years to come, and educators are responsible for ensuring that their activities are appropriate and commensurate with their backgrounds and skills.

Questions for Reflection

1. Which professional disciplines (in addition to special educators) do you believe are most important for providing services to students with severe disabilities? Why?
2. Give a few examples of how professional collaboration might benefit students with severe disabilities.
3. What would be different for a teacher working on a transdisciplinary team than for a teacher working independently or on a multidisciplinary team?
4. In what ways might professionals best learn from each other?
5. How would you characterize the type of relationship that should exist between a paraprofessional and a teacher?
6. Should paraprofessionals who work with students with severe disabilities receive formal training? What should it include?
7. Should paraprofessionals be considered to have the same status on transdisciplinary teams as the specially trained professionals? Why or why not?
8. Can you suggest ways to improve team functioning? What do you believe is the greatest barrier to successful collaborative teaming?

References

Bigge, J. L., Best, S. J., & Heller, K. W. (2001). *Teaching individuals with physical, health, or multiple disabilities* (4th Ed.). Upper Saddle River, NJ: Merrill/Prentice Hall.

Boomer, L. W. (1980). Special education paraprofessionals: A guide for teachers. *Teaching Exceptional Children, 12,* 146–149.

Boomer, L. W. (1982). The paraprofessional: A valued resource for special children and their teachers. *Teaching Exceptional Children, 14,* 194–197.

Bricker, D. (1976). Educational synthesizer. In M. A. Thomas (Ed.), *Hey, don't forget about me!* (pp. 84–97). Reston, VA: Council for Exceptional Children.

Brown, L., Farrington, K., Knight, T., Ross, C., & Ziegler, M. (1999). Fewer paraprofessionals and more teachers and therapists in educational programs for students with significant disabilities. *Journal of the Association for Persons with Severe Handicaps, 24,* 250–253.

Campbell, P. H. (1987). The integrated programming team: An approach for coordinating professionals of various disciplines in programs for students with severe and multiple handicaps. *Journal of the Association for Persons with Severe Handicaps, 12,* 107–116.

Caro, P., & Snell, M. (1989). Characteristics of teaching communication to people with moderate and severe disabilities. *Education and Training in Mental Retardation, 24,* 63–77.

Cook, L., & Friend, M. P. (2002). *Interactions: Collaboration skills for school professionals* (4th Ed.). Boston: Allyn and Bacon.

Downing, J. E. (2002). *Including students with severe and multiple disabilities in typical classrooms* (2nd Ed.). Baltimore: Paul H. Brookes.

Dunn, W. (1988). Models of occupational therapy service provision in the school system. *American Journal of Occupational Therapy, 42,* 718–723.

Dunn, W. (1991). Integrated related services. In L. H. Meyer, C. A. Peck, & L. Brown (Eds.), *Critical issues in the lives of people with severe disabilities* (pp. 353–377). Baltimore: Paul H. Brookes.

Fox, L., & Williams, D. G. (1992). Preparing teachers of students with severe disabilities. *Teacher Education and Special Education, 15,* 97–107.

French, N. K. (1999). Paraeducators and teachers: Shifting roles. *Teaching Exceptional Children, 32*(2), 69–73.

French, N. K. (2001). Supervising paraprofessionals: A survey of teacher practices. *Journal of Special Education, 35,* 41–53.

French, N. K., & Pickett, A. L. (1997). Paraprofessionals in special education: Issues for teacher educators. *Teacher Education and Special Education, 20,* 61–73.

Frith, G., & Lindsey, J. D. (1980). Paraprofessional roles in mainstreaming multihandicapped students. *Education Unlimited, 2*(2), 17–20.

Giangreco, M. F., Broer, S. M., & Edelman, S. W. (1999). The tip of the iceberg: Determining whether paraprofessional support is needed for students with disabilities in general education settings. *Journal of the Association for Persons with Severe Handicaps, 24,* 281–291.

Giangreco, M. F., & Doyle, M. B. (2002). Students with disabilities and paraprofessional supports: Benefits, balance, and band-aids. *Focus on Exceptional Children, 34*(7), 1–12.

Giangreco, M. F., Edelman, S. W., & Broer, S. M. (2001). Respect, appreciation, and acknowledgement of paraprofessionals who support students with disabilities. *Exceptional Children, 67,* 485–498.

Giangreco, M. F., Edelman, S. W., Broer, S. M., & Doyle, M. B. (2001). Paraprofessional support of students with disabilities: Literature from the past decade. *Exceptional Children, 68,* 45–63.

Hobbs, T. (1997). *Planning for inclusion: A comparison of individual and cooperative procedures.* Unpublished doctoral dissertation, Florida State University, Tallahassee.

Hobbs, T., & Westling, D. L. (1998). Promoting successful inclusion through collaborative problem solving. *Teaching Exceptional Children, 31*(1), 12–19.

Janney, R. E., Snell, M. E., Beers, M. K., & Raynes, M. (1995). Integrating students with moderate and severe disabilities into general education classes. *Exceptional Children, 61,* 425–439.

Lyon, S., & Lyon, G. (1980). Team functioning and staff development: A role release approach to providing integrated services for severely handicapped students. *Journal of the Association for the Severely Handicapped, 5,* 250–263.

Marks, S. U., Schrader, C., & Levine, M. (1999). Paraeducator experiences in inclusive settings: Helping, hovering, or holding their own. *Exceptional Children, 65,* 315–328.

McKenzie, R. G., & Houk, C. S. (1986). The paraprofessional in special education. *Teaching Exceptional Children, 18,* 246–252.

Mirenda, P., Iacono, T., & Williams, R. (1990). Communication options for persons with severe and profound disabilities: State of the art and future directions. *Journal of the Association for Persons with Severe Handicaps, 15,* 3–21.

Orelove, F. P., & Sobsey, D. (1996). *Educating children with multiple disabilities: A transdisciplinary approach* (3rd Ed.). Baltimore: Paul H. Brookes.

P.L. 107-110: *No Child Left Behind Act of 2001.* Available: http://www.ed.gov/legislation/ESEA02/index.html.

Pugach, M. C., & Johnson, L. J. (1990). Meeting diverse needs through professional peer collaboration. In W. Stainback & S. Stainback (Eds.), *Support networks for inclusive schooling: Interdependent integrated education* (pp. 123–137). Baltimore: Paul H. Brookes.

Pugach, M. C., & Johnson, L. J. (2002). *Collaborative practitioners, collaborative schools* (2nd Ed.). Denver, CO: Love Publishing Co.

Rainforth, B., & York, J. (1987). Integrated related services in community instruction. *Journal of the Association for Persons with Severe Handicaps, 12,* 190–198.

Rainforth, B., & York, J. (1997). *Collaborative teams for students with severe disabilities: Integrating therapy and educational services* (2nd ed.). Baltimore: Paul H. Brookes.

Riggs, C. G., & Mueller, P. H. (2001). Employment and utilization of paraeducators in inclusive settings. *Journal of Special Education, 35,* 54–62.

Salisbury, C. L., Evans, I. M., & Palombaro, M. M. (1997). Collaborative problem-solving to promote the inclusion of young children with significant disabilities in primary grades. *Exceptional Children, 63,* 195–209.

Salzberg, C. L., & Morgan, J. (1995). Preparing teachers to work with paraeducators. *Teacher Education and Special Education, 18,* 49–55.

Scruggs, T. E., & Mastropieri, M. A. (1996). Teacher perceptions of mainstreaming/inclusion, 1958–1995: A research synthesis. *Exceptional Children, 63,* 59–74.

Sears, C. J. (1981). The transdisciplinary approach: A process for compliance with Public Law 94-142. *Journal of the Association for the Severely Handicapped, 6,* 22–29.

Sternat, J., Messina, R., Nietupski, J., Lyon, S., & Brown, L. (1977). Occupational and physical therapy services for severely handicapped students: Toward a natural public school service delivery model. In E. Sontag, J. Smith, & N. Certo (Eds.), *Educational programming for the severely and profoundly handicapped* (pp. 263–266). Reston, VA: Council for Exceptional Children, Division on Mental Retardation.

Vandercook, T., & York, J. (1990). A team approach to program development and support. In W. Stainback & S. Stainback (Eds.), *Support networks for inclusive schooling: Interdependent integrated education* (pp. 95–122). Baltimore: Paul H. Brookes.

Wallace, T., Shin, J., Bartholomay, T., & Stahl, B. J. (2001). Knowledge and skills for teachers supervising the work of paraprofessionals. *Exceptional Children, 67,* 520–533.

Werts, M. G., Wolery, M., Snyder, E. D., & Caldwell, N. K. (1996). Teachers' perceptions critical to the success of inclusion programs. *Journal of the Association for Persons with Severe Handicaps, 21,* 9–21.

CHAPTER 4

Parents, Families, and Cultural Issues

To provide effective education programs for students with severe disabilities, teachers must work in partnership with the family. The importance of parent involvement in the education of children and youth is well established in the research literature and the values foundation of schooling in the United States (Epstein, 1983). When parents are involved in a child's educational program, there is an increase in student achievement and an improvement of student attitudes toward school (Caplan, Choy, & Whitmore, 1992; Henderson & Berla, 1994; Olmstead & Rubin, 1983).

Promoting Family Involvement

The promotion of the involvement of the family in the education of students with severe disabilities is as important as the promotion of family involvement in general education. Comprehensive school efforts offer mechanisms for involvement that are traditional (open house, PTO, festivals and fairs, attending sports and performances, classroom volunteers, and parent–teacher conferences) and more innovative (strategic planning committees, share-your-career day, mentor programs, parent-to-parent support groups). Teachers of students with severe disabilities should be aware of their schools' efforts to promote parent involvement and assist the parents of students with disabilities in becoming involved. The inclusion of the family in the school community will help to support efforts to include the student within the classroom.

Table 4–1 offers multiple ideas for ways that parents of students with disabilities (and without disabilities) can be meaningfully involved in the school community. As you consider these ideas, it is critical to remember that each family will choose how much to be involved in their child's school. A family's willingness to be involved is often directly related to the other demands in their lives. Each family should be encouraged to participate as much as it chooses, and mechanisms for participating in different ways should always be available.

The importance of family involvement is even more critical in the provision of educational programs to children who have severe disabilities. Students with severe disabilities are often reliant on their families for physical mobility, health and self-care, and communication access, in addition to the supports that all families provide to children. Families often rely on schools for access to information, services, and knowledge about promoting the independence of their children. Moreover, the family and school personnel must work in partnership to develop and implement an educational program that is individualized and effective and supports the student in achieving maximum independence. The importance of establishing a collaborative relationship with the family cannot be overestimated. This chapter will provide information on the development of collaborative relationships with the families of your students. It will also describe the importance of cultural awareness and the provision of culturally competent services within relationships with families of students with severe disabilities.

The Meaning of Collaboration

Collaboration refers to a process of interaction in which the partners share resources and knowledge and work together in achieving a common goal (Turnbull & Turnbull, 2001). Collaboration involves a bidirectional relationship,

Table 4–1 Promoting Parent Involvement

Parenting	Parents may be assisted with the basic obligations of parenting and providing home support for learning
Communicating	Parents receive and respond to communication from the school about children's progress and school events
Volunteering	Parents are provided with opportunities to volunteer in the classroom, for school events, in the school resource areas (e.g., clinic, library, office), and from home in support of the school (e.g., phone tree)
Extending learning in the home	Parents are provided with activities to extend the learning that occurs in the classroom to the home
Decision making	Parents are provided with opportunities to participate in school governance and policy development
Collaborating with community	Parents are involved through community efforts and partnerships with the school

Source: Based on "School/Family/Community Partnerships: Caring for the Children We Share," by J. L. Epstein, 1995, *Phi Delta Kappan,* 701–712.

rather than a unidirectional or hierarchical relationship. In collaborative relationships, partners are influenced by each other, bring unique strengths and gifts to the table, and actively work toward the establishment of a relationship that results in valued outcomes.

Establishing a collaborative relationship with the families of your students should be considered essential to the provision of a quality educational program. When families and teachers work together, the student is more likely to be successful in all environments. Collaboration is not easy! It will involve many hours of meeting, discussing, considering, and listening. Effective collaborative relationships are built on a foundation of trust, mutual respect, and a common interest, elements that take time to establish. As a professional, you will find that you must enter into relationships with the families of your students with an open mind and a willingness to learn. Professionals who view collaboration with families as their opportunity to provide information and guide the family without regard for what the family brings to the relationship will not be successful. Consider these two brief scenarios and reflect on the quality of the relationship that the teacher has with the family and the potential for achieving meaningful outcomes for the student.

> Kirsten remembers that it is Ms. Gomez's 50th birthday and makes a note to help José develop a birthday greeting for his mother on his augmentative communication device. Ms. Gomez has had a difficult year with health issues and caring for her elderly mother, who was diagnosed with a terminal illness. José has also presented challenges this year with his transition to high school. Kirsten is relieved that the team finally was able to effectively support José and address his problem behaviors at home and school. It took a lot of meeting together, comparing his mother's observations of behavior at home with behavior at school and working on a plan that could be used in all environments. José now uses his augmentative communication device at school and home and with his friends. The team was able to establish a circle of support for José with a lot of involvement of his ninth-grade peers. Kirsten reflects that the peers were really important in the development of José's support plan; they are with him at school, a friend helps him home from the bus stop, and friends make sure that he has company after school and on weekends. Ms. Gomez has really appreciated the support of the peers and makes sure that they know that they are valued by inviting them to stay for dinner on the weekends and taking an interest in their activities and achievements.

> Emily has a list of phone calls to make to the families of her students. It's IEP time again and she needs to make sure that the families are invited to attend. Her IEPs are scheduled for three straight days next week. She has a substitute teacher scheduled already and has assigned each family an appointment time. After confirming the IEP meeting, Emily will send each family a note about the IEP and a worksheet so that the families can begin to think about their goals for their children. Emily will come to the meeting with notes on her goals for the student already prepared. She likes to be well prepared for these meetings so that they can be conducted efficiently. She is secretly hopeful that the Jordan family will not be available for the IEP meeting. She has had a difficult time with the Jordan family. It seems like they are constantly asking for changes in their child's instructional program and asking questions about what is happening at school. Every week there have been phone calls or notes from the family. It frustrates Emily that she has to take time away from her students or planning their activities to address the Jordans' concerns.

Establishing Partnerships with the Family

A primary goal for the educator is to establish a partnership with the family. In consideration of this goal, the teacher first needs to consider the question of how family is defined. Family may be defined in many different ways. Students may come from single-parent homes and have no siblings or live in homes with both the nuclear and extended family. The family will define who is in the family unit. Teachers should question the parent who is important in raising the child and making decisions in the family system and become aware of who may be living with the student. Teachers need to consider the entire family system, because it is the family system that influences and supports the student's development, participation, and success in school. In addition, the entire family system is affected by the child's disability, health status, development, and progress in school.

A partnership will develop only if there is mutual respect and trust among the partners (Rao, 2000; Turnbull & Turnbull, 2001). The teacher's role begins with seeking an understanding of the family system, considering the strengths and needs of the family, and creating opportunities to build a relationship with the family. As the teacher reaches out to establish a partnership, it is important to realize that the development of a relationship with the teacher may not be of primary importance to the family. Families may have competing needs and demands (economic, housing, mental health, health issues) that take priority over actively pursuing the development of a relationship with their child's teacher. If this occurs, the response of the teacher should not be to view the family as unwilling, but to continue to offer opportunities for partnership and to support the family by providing connections to services or agencies that may help the family to meet their most pressing needs.

Our first concern as collaborative professionals must be working effectively with parents and families. We need to recognize that parents of children with disabilities generally know what is best for their children, and their role on the collaborative team, and particularly their interaction with their child's teacher, will have a positive effect on their child's education. *All teachers* should communicate with parents to inform them of such matters as their educational philosophy, approaches, and practices and also to listen to their concerns about the needs of their children. When the student in question has a severe disability, parent–teacher communication is even more critical.

Teachers and other professionals should see parents of students with severe disabilities as consumers of services. When considering parents from this viewpoint, professionals should ask: What do parents want? Although parents' needs are different, many studies of parents' wishes and desires have been conducted and can provide insight to professionals. Studies have examined the views of parents of individuals with moderate, severe, and profound mental disabilities within a variety of areas. Some of the more important areas are discussed in the following sections. Many of these studies have been more fully described in a review by Westling (1996).

What Parents Want Their Children to Learn

Given the diversity among students with severe disabilities, as well as the diversity of their parents, it can be expected that parents will desire different curricular goals and have different concerns. To some extent, research has shown that different instructional priorities are related to students' ages and the severity of their disability (D'Amato & Yoshida, 1991; Epps & Myers, 1989; Hamre-Nietupski, Nietupski, & Strathe, 1992). Most parents seem to believe that instruction in functional skills, especially domestic and vocational skills, is very relevant for their children. However, many parents of students with moderate mental disabilities consider functional academic skills to be very important, more important even than the development of social skills and friendships. On the other hand, parents of students with more severe or profound mental disabilities rate the development of social skills and the acquisition of friendships higher than learning functional skills (Hamre-Nietupski et al., 1992).

As discussed in Chapter 2, children with disabilities are entitled to have an individual educational program (IEP) and receive a free and appropriate education in the least restrictive environment. Parents want their children to develop to their maximum potential, but particular areas of emphasis vary. Teachers should be sensitive to this point and attempt to teach students those skills that are perceived by parents to have the greatest relevance. Sometimes, from the teacher's perspective, parents under- or overestimate their children's abilities, with the teacher then becoming critical of the parents. Instead, teachers should try to understand the views and desires of the parents and work cooperatively with them.

What Kind of School Parents Want

As discussed in Chapter 3, a dominant issue in the field of special education today is the inclusion of students with disabilities, including those with moderate, severe, and profound mental disabilities, in regular classrooms and schools. When parents are questioned about their position on inclusion, a number are in favor of it, but many harbor concerns and prefer separate classrooms or schools for their children (Hanline & Halvorsen, 1989; McDonnell, 1987; Mlynek, Hannah, & Hamlin, 1982; Reichart et al., 1989; Williams, Fox, Thousand, & Fox, 1990).

Studies reveal that critical concerns about inclusion for most parents are the comfort and safety of their children and the provision of quality educational programs and related services. Many parents perceive that their children will be safer and better cared for in separate programs and that they will receive more intense educational and related services. Unless parents believe that their children will be safe and will receive a quality education in inclusive settings, many will be hesitant about placing their children in these settings. Interestingly, studies have found that the large majority of parents of students who have actually *experienced* inclusive programs tend to be satisfied and feel comfortable with them (Hanline & Halvorsen, 1989; McDonnell, 1987; Mlynek et al., 1982; Reichart et al., 1989; Williams et al., 1990). Apparently, their children have been safe and accepted and the program quality did not suffer. Nevertheless, many parents continue to support separate placements and will probably continue to do so until they are convinced that inclusive programs can be supportive of their children (Westling, 1996).

The Importance of Social Development, Relationships, and Friendships

Not surprisingly, parents are often concerned about the nature of their children's personal behavior and social relationships. Typically, concerns about friendship and acceptance by others rank only slightly below concerns about health and safety (Westling, 1997; Westling & Plaute, 1999). Some parents place greater value on the development of friendships and social relationships than on the acquisition of specific skills (Hamre-Nietupski et al., 1992). Obviously, this issue will also bear on their decision as to where to send their child to school and where in public they will allow their child to go. They want their child to be happy, to have friends, and to not be teased, ridiculed, or mistreated because of their disability; and they want to avoid embarrassing circumstances for themselves or others that their child's behavior may cause (Turnbull & Ruef, 1996).

Some parents believe the best way for their children with disabilities to have friendships is to attend schools only with other children with disabilities. Others believe that it is more appropriate for their children to attend inclusive schools where they can have the opportunity to become friends with children with and without disabilities. Guralnick, Connor, and Hammond (1995) compared the views of parents of preschool children with disabilities who attended integrated schools with those whose children attended special schools on the topic of social relationships and social learning benefits. They found that both groups of parents placed great value on developing appropriate social skills and, most interestingly, both groups felt that the setting in which their children were placed was conducive to developing social skills, promoting peer relations, and positively affecting self-esteem. However, most of the parents of children in the integrated settings believed that the presence of children without disabilities was an added value and that their children benefited specifically because of their social interactions with them. Nevertheless, a sizable minority (40%) feared rejection of their child because of his social behavior.

A particular area of concern for parents is their child's behavior (Fox, Vaughn, Wyatte, & Dunlap, 2002; Turnbull & Ruef, 1996). Turnbull and Ruef (1996) studied the perspectives of parents on their children's problem behaviors and reported that parents identified two major domains: dangerous behavior and difficult behavior. Dangerous behavior included actions such as aggression toward others, destroying property, or engaging in self-injurious behavior. Difficult behavior was described as "creating constant demands for supervision, making the child stand out from others, and provoking others' embarrassment or annoyance" (p. 248) and included behavior such as hand flapping and loud, inappropriate vocalizations. Overall, parents were much more concerned about difficult behavior, especially in public, and how it would be perceived by others. They noted that even though the behavior may have been episodic, the worry was constant. In a qualitative study of culturally diverse families whose children had disabilities and problem behavior, researchers found similar themes regarding family perspectives about their child's problem behavior (Fox et al., 2002). In addition, they documented that problem behavior affects all aspects of the family lifestyle, including how family roles were defined, family routines and activities, and the sense of emotional well-being of the child's primary caregiver. Fox et al. (2002) recommend that efforts in behavioral support include the family as a partner and consider the broad impact that problem behavior may have on the family system when designing supports and interventions. Procedures for addressing challenging behaviors are discussed in Chapter 11.

Involvement by Parents

Since 1975, when P.L. 94-142 became law, all children with disabilities have been required to have an IEP, and their parents have had the right to participate in this planning process. Beyond this mandated form of planning, more involved planning processes have been developed, calling for participation by the student, her parents, other family members, teachers, and friends, that focus on creating inclusive and quality life conditions for the individual with disabilities (see Chapter 4). These planning processes are more elaborate and require more time and commitment by parents and others. But to what degree and in what ways do parents wish to be involved in planning and other activities related to their child, such as direct instruction in the school or home? A number of researchers have investigated the question of the type and degree of desired parental involvement in school programs (Gallegos & Gallegos, 1988; Leyser, 1985; Lynch & Stein, 1987; Meyers & Blacher, 1987; Salisbury & Evans, 1988; Williams et al., 1990; Yanok & Derubertis, 1989).

Based on these studies, several tentative conclusions can be drawn. Parents of children with mental disabilities usually want to be more involved than parents of children in general education, and they usually are. They believe that they have more opportunity to influence their child's educational program and that these opportunities are important. Most parents will be involved in the IEP process, but some will want additional forms of involvement, such as participation in parent groups. Finally, most, if not all, parents of children with mental disabilities desire regular communication with the school.

Needs during the Adolescent and Adult Years

As children with moderate to severe or profound mental disabilities grow toward adolescence and adulthood, their parents are faced with unique challenges and dilemmas with which most other parents do not have to contend (Thorin, Yovanoff, & Irvin, 1996). For example, parents want their children to become more independent, but they also continue to worry about their safety and well-being; they want their grown child to have a social life, but they want to reduce their involvement in his life. Dealing with these dilemmas and continuing to meet their children's needs often place extraordinary stress on parents.

Studies clearly indicate that when children with severe disabilities become adolescents and adults their parents face their greatest challenges in providing for their needs (Black, Molaison, & Smull, 1990; Epps & Myers, 1989; Heller & Factor, 1991; Sherman, 1988). For example, Epps and Myers (1989) found that parents were generally not very positive about the future of their children. Most believed that as an adult their child would continue to live at home, and 20% thought that they would need to place their child in an institution. Less than 4% thought that full-time or part-time employment was feasible. Black et al. found that parents of adults with mental disabilities sought residential arrangements, day-care programs, social skills training for their adult children, respite care services, financial assistance, behavior management, and psychological services. More than half of those needing services said that their need was urgent. The frequency of inappropriate behavior, the perceived level of required supervision, and other family circumstances correlated with the parents' urgency of request for residential placement. In a similar study, Sherman also examined conditions of families with adult children with mental disabilities. He found that parents who sought residential settings had adult children who were older and had more severe disabilities and behavior problems.

Providing Culturally Competent Education and Support

The demographics of the school population are rapidly changing. In 1999, the U.S. Census Bureau reported that 57 million children were enrolled in the schools. Of these students, 64% were White; 16% were Black; 5% were Asian, Pacific Islander, and other; and 15% were Hispanic (Proctor & Dalakar, 2002). Immigration accounts for many of these changes, with 20% of the students having at least one parent who was foreign born. These students were also economically diverse, with 52% of students coming from homes with annual incomes of at least $40,000 and 21% coming from homes with annual incomes of less than $20,000.

Change in the diversity of school populations has important implications for how schools are structured and how teachers provide instruction. Schools are increasingly challenged to meet the needs of a diverse school population and to promote the involvement of families from a variety of cultural, linguistic, and economic backgrounds (Kalyanpur & Harry, 1999; Parette & Petch-Hogan, 2000; Salend & Taylor, 1993). Since most teachers are from White middle-class families, understanding the conditions and needs of many minority or culturally different families is somewhat challenging. Yet, if teachers are to collaborate with *all* parents, they must be able to interact and communicate with them in ways that are not entirely foreign or aversive to them from *their* cultural perspective (Lynch & Hanson, 1998). Studies have shown that very often the profession of special education has been unsuccessful at involving minority parents and families of different cultural backgrounds in the collaborative process, particularly when the families are poor (Gallegos & Gallegos, 1988; Leyser, 1985; Lynch & Stein, 1987). This strongly states that there is need for improvement.

A study of Korean American families offers an illustration of the impact of cultural and linguistic differences in developing partnerships with educators (Park, Turnbull, & Park, 2001). In this study, qualitative interviews were used to develop themes that reflected the experiences of 10 families who had children with disabilities. These families reported that their limited English proficiency was a major barrier in developing meaningful partnerships with professionals. The families also reported feelings of racial discrimination, and of professionals treating their children differently because of their ethnicity. The families shared stories of how their values and practices were different and that these differences made it challenging to develop partnerships with the teacher. One mother shared that she did not interact with her child during a home visit because she was taught to not express affection to her children in front of others. She was upset to find that her actions were interpreted by the visitors as problematic and that she was considered to be uninvolved with her children. Another theme that developed from family responses was the feeling that the families lacked the prerequisites needed to establish partnerships. These families reported that they did not have reliable allies or connections with their children's teachers, that they did not have information on the nature of the services that they should be expecting or their parental rights, and that they did not have the advocacy skills needed to support their children.

Needs of Minority and Poor Families

To better understand the nature of families from minority cultures and/or families that are poor, and therefore to be better able to communicate and collaborate with them, we must begin by examining ourselves and our biases (Kalyanpur & Harry, 1999). Do we appreciate the fact that not all people live by the same economic and cultural standards? Are we sensitive to the idea that how we live and what we value will not be the same for different people? If we do not recognize our own biases, we probably will never understand why we cannot communicate effectively with those who are different. The development of cross-cultural competence requires a great deal of personal openness and self-reflection. As professionals work with families and students from cultures that are different from their own, they have to have a willingness to accept alternative perspectives and set aside some of their own beliefs (Barrera & Corso, 2002; Chen, Downing, & Peckham-Hardin, 2002; Kalyanpur & Harry, 1999; Lynch & Hanson, 1998). Some ways to improve collaboration with parents and families of different cultural backgrounds include the following (Dennis & Giangreco, 1996; Lynch & Hanson, 1998; Parette & Petch-Hogan, 2000):

- *Develop self-awareness about your own cultural identity and recognize your own values, beliefs, and customs.* To understand different cultural perspectives, it is necessary first to know your own heritage and how it influences your perceptions. Seek new understanding and knowledge of cultural norms. Through reading, formal education, or informal experiences with others from a different culture, professionals can actively seek to gain knowledge about the culturally based practices of others. It is important to learn about and respect values and beliefs that vary from your own.
- *Appreciate the uniqueness of each family.* Within cultures, different families may be structured in different ways, sometimes including extended family members or unofficially adopted children. It should also be understood that, within cultures, families will be different from each other. It should never be assumed that being a part of a cultural system totally dictates the way that people live or what they need.
- *Try to understand the communication styles within different cultures.* Some cultures tend to be less verbal and rely more on shared experiences and unspoken understandings when they are communicating, whereas others are more verbal. Sometimes it is necessary for the professional to slow down, to listen more, and to adopt a communicative style more like the family's.
- *Develop awareness of cultural norms.* The pace of a conversation, facial expressions, eye contact, proximity, touching, body language, gestures, and other personal behaviors differ in different cultures. By knowing about these and attempting to adhere to them in a sensitive manner, professionals may develop better collaborative relations with minority families.
- *Be aware of the nature of the influence of professionals.* Some families will have had negative experiences with professionals and may be actively or passively uncooperative. On the other hand, some may defer their own judgment to that of the professional and not be willing to express their own opinion.
- *Learn from families.* By asking parents and family members to provide feedback about formal and informal interactions, professionals can better learn to adjust their own personal styles.

The ethnicity and culture of a family often result in different personal, social, and religious characteristics, all of which can bear on how family members react to a child with disabilities and interact with a formal system such as special education (Kalyanpur & Harry, 1999). In the following section we provide examples of differences in cultural perspectives that may affect the education of students with severe disabilities. This information is presented with the caveat that every family is unique and that professionals should not make any assumptions about a family's priorities, concerns, or resources. This information is presented to illustrate ways that culture can influence the relationship between the home and school and the educational program for the student.

Verbal and Nonverbal Communication

Researchers have identified cultures as being different in the amount of information that is provided through words in a verbal exchange as opposed to nonverbal communication, the context of the situation, and body language (Gudykunst, Ting-Toomey, & Nishida, 1996; Lynch & Hanson, 1998). Low-context cultures include as much verbal information as possible, are focused on communication in precise and direct ways, and get to the point quickly. High-context cultures draw meaning from the context of the interaction and attend to the subtle nonverbal cues as holding important meaning in an interaction. Low-context cultures have been identified as Anglo-European and American, and high-context cultures include Asian, Native American, Arab, Latino, and African American. The differences in verbal communication seem to reflect differences in collectivist cultures versus individualistic cultures.

In individualistic cultures, people may tend to talk more and use talk to establish relationships in social and professional contexts. In addition, they are more likely to use persuasion and openly disagree with others. Persons from collectivist cultures are apt to be more comfortable with silence, to tolerate ambiguity in talk, to be less definitive, and to use indirect modes of communication such as storytelling. These differences are also reflected in the pragmatics of a conversation with individualists, who often assert a topic and spend a disproportionate amount of time engaged in a monologue. Collectivists are uncomfortable when turn taking in the conversation is not equitable.

Differences in communication style can also occur through nonverbal behavior. For example, in Anglo-European culture, establishing eye contact is expected and valued. In other cultural groups, there may be specific rules about who you make eye contact with and the meaning of eye contact. For example, among some Asian or Middle Eastern groups, eye contact may be seen as disrespectful or shameful (Lynch & Hanson, 1998). Other differences may be noted in proximity (being too close or far from the speaker), touching, greetings, and gestures.

These differences can be very important in the teacher's attempt to establish a relationship with the family and to build rapport. Thus it is important to gain general knowledge of the traditions of the cultural backgrounds of the families that you support. The following scenario demonstrates how differences in communication style can cause discomfort for the family and the teacher.

> Emily was looking forward to her home visit with Angela Begay. Angela's son, A. J., is Navajo and was recently transferred to the elementary school where Emily provides special education consultation to the classroom. When Emily arrived at the home, Mrs. Begay offered her a cup of coffee and a muffin. Emily declined as she had recently eaten lunch. Mrs. Begay then sat at the kitchen table in silence, looking out the kitchen window. Emily began to get nervous with the silence and decided to go ahead and explain the reason for the visit. Emily chattered as Mrs. Begay seemed to alternate between listening and looking out the window. After several minutes, Emily told Mrs. Begay, "I think that A. J. should continue to go to the third grade for social studies and science and that I can provide the teacher with some ideas for supporting his inclusion." Mrs. Begay did not respond initially and then said "O.K." The home visit lasted an uncomfortable 30 minutes and then Emily left.
>
> Emily wondered if Mrs. Begay was angry with her for some reason or if she may not have understood what Emily was saying. Mrs. Begay had been offended by Emily's refusal of coffee and a snack and was put off by Emily's enthusiastic monologue.

Differences in Beliefs, Values, and Parenting Styles

In addition to differences in communication styles, differences in beliefs and values may pose dilemmas or challenges for the special educator (Barrera & Corso, 2002; Chen et al., 2002; Kalyanpur & Harry, 1999; Salend & Taylor, 1993). For example, Native Americans value the collective and the extended family (Joe & Malach, 1992). Extended family members may play important roles in decision making or discipline for the child. There may be differences in cultural groups relating to child discipline. Many African American families feel strongly about child discipline and are more restrictive than the permissive styles of White middle-class families (Delpit, 1995; Willis, 1992). There may be cultural values about the topics that are appropriate to discuss and traditions about the course of the conversation. For example, many Asian families have difficulty with public disclosure of family problems. Professionals may need to approach discussing problems by first establishing rapport and discussing other topics before having a frank discussion of the child's problems.

Beliefs about parenting are also culturally embedded and may clash with the teacher's perspectives. For example, Korean parents start toilet training very early (as early as 3 months) and may request that toileting be worked on at school at an age that is not recommended in American culture. A child's independence in developing her own social opportunities is not highly valued by Middle Eastern cultures and may not occur until after puberty. These differences are typically not problematic unless they are a factor in a disagreement about appropriate educational goals and activities for the student or if professionals make judgments about the family based on differences. In the final section of this chapter, we will provide professionals with a process for discussing and reconciling differences with families.

Needs of Families with Multiple Risks

Many families, especially poor families, can be described as families with multiple risks (Hanson & Carta, 1996). They may have one or more children with disabilities, but other problems in their lives are often more significant. These problems are reflected in many of the statistics that appear in today's newspapers. Consider the following facts about families and children in the United States (Child Welfare League of America, 2003, Children's Defense Fund, 2003; Proctor & Dalaker, 2002):

- In 2001, there were 32.9 million poor people living in the United States; 16.6% of the people who are poor are children.
- In 2002, 878,955 children were reported to be abused or neglected.
- In 1999, 3,365 children were killed by firearms—nine each day.
- In 2002, more than half a million children were in foster care.
- In 2002, 9.2 million children were not covered by health insurance.

Statistics such as these reflect some of the dire conditions in which many American families live. In such conditions, human survival and coping are put to the test. Poor and undereducated caregivers, trying to raise children while living in poor and nonsupportive communities permeated by violence and hopelessness, present needs that cannot typically be met by the fragmented educational, social, and health-care systems. The needs of families whose lives are affected by both poverty and disability are an increasing concern. A study of the 14-year period from 1983 to 1996 documents that there is a growing relationship between poverty and risk for disability, with the prevalence of disability rising among families who are poor (Fujiura & Yamaki, 2000). Families that exist in such conditions will clearly have more pervasive needs than does an otherwise safe and intact family with a child with a severe disability. Their problems will be so extensive that collaborating with special education and other school professionals will have a relatively low priority, if it is a priority at all. Hanson and Carta (1996) state that, because the problems of these families come from more than one source, more than one source of intervention is required to address their needs. Among these services are good prenatal care, accessible health and nutrition programs, and effective family support programs to help to prevent abuse and neglect. Early-intervention preschool programs can increase readiness for school, and, of course, the schools must be responsive to the needs of the children and their families.

Special educators must realize that it may be difficult to gain the participation of parents living in such conditions on collaborative teams for purposes of planning and decision making. Carrying through on plans within their homes may also be difficult (Hanson & Carta, 1996). Often, professionals respond to this lack of involvement by condemning the parents for not caring for their children, but this is likely an erroneous conclusion. More correct may be the fact that the parents are simply overwhelmed by their circumstances. Some of the strategies and tactics discussed later for improving parental involvement may be effective but, regardless, educators should understand the situations in which some people live and refrain from making judgments.

Providing Support to Parents

There is a high probability that parents of children with severe disabilities experience more distress and personal and family difficulties than other parents, particularly if there is no adequate formal or informal support to assist them with the unique challenges that they face (Singer & Irvin, 1991). This is not necessarily true for all parents of individuals with severe disabilities, and it is not our intention here to stereotype these parents. In fact, in many cases the child with a severe disability improves the mental and emotional health of a family and results in much happiness (Taunt & Hastings, 2002; Turnbull, Guess, & Turnbull, 1988). A study conducted by Scorgie and Sobsey (2000) indicated that many parents report positive changes in their lives as a result of having a child with a disability. These changes included personal growth (e.g., assuming new roles, developing new skills), improved relationships with others and changes in their interpersonal interaction skills (e.g., stronger marriages, expansion of social networks, appreciation of the value of others), and strengthening of their philosophical values (e.g., changes in perceptions about what is important). However, such a positive outcome is more likely if parents have adequate internal and external sources of support. Such support can typically come from spouses, partners, teachers, physicians, or other children in the family, as well as from educational and habilitation programs (Herman & Thompson, 1995).

The conditions that often result in parents' difficulties, such as emotional distress, are generally related to the accessibility of different forms of support. Services such as health care for the child with severe disabilities, appropriate educational services, respite care (care of the individual with severe disabilities for short periods of time), financial assistance, in-home assistance (to help with problems related to caregiving or behavior problems), counseling and training in coping skills, as well as support from family, friends, or other parents of individuals with severe disabilities serve to reduce stress within families (Herman & Thompson, 1995; Singer & Irvin, 1991). Singer, Irvin, Irvine, Hawkins, and Cooley (1989) described an "intensive support" program that offered the following services:

- Case management to help parents to find and deal with various community agencies and to coordinate the services of these agencies.
- Respite care of up to 3 hours a week of free, in-home care for their child.
- Weekly 2-hour classes for parents on coping skills that created a "supportive environment" and "encouraged parents to assist one another, to show warmth and respect, and to use active listening skills" (p. 314).
- Community involvement activities for the children, provided by volunteers. (The children were taken to such settings as public swimming pools, malls, and video arcades. This was in addition to the in-home respite care.)

Singer et al. (1989) found that, as a result of this level of intervention, the parents reported a lower level of distress than did a group of parents receiving less intensive support. The effect was still positive a year later when the researchers conducted a follow-up study.

While this type of program would obviously be beneficial, less formal sources of support can also be very helpful. Programs such as Project SHaRE (Source of Help Received and Exchanged) (Dunst, Trivette, Gordon, & Pletcher, 1989) are based on the notion that it is better for parents and families to help themselves and each other through an assistance bartering system than to rely exclusively or even primarily on formal support systems. According to Dunst and his colleagues (Dunst, Trivette, & Deal, 1988; Dunst et al. 1989), personal social networks have several advantages. They serve as buffers against stress, enhance well-being, and lessen the likelihood of emotional and physical distress. When families have strong personal support systems, these sources of support may reduce the time demands placed on the parents by the child; promote positive caregiver–child interactions, improve parent perceptions of child functioning, and indirectly influence positively several dimensions of a child's behavior.

Unfortunately, at times sufficient personal support is not available or parents perceive this to be the case. When this occurs, parents are more susceptible to ill health and have a difficult time adapting to stress. Singer and Irvin (1991) state that parents and families of individuals with severe disabilities become isolated because (1) their caregiving has left them fatigued, (2) they have limited free time, (3) they encounter misunderstandings and negative reactions regarding their child, and (4) their child is often excluded from normal social settings and experiences. When formal services are provided, those that are more *family-centered* (professionals serve the needs of the parents, and services are based on parents' rather than professionals' plans) than *professionally centered* (professionals are experts who determine family needs) are likely to be better regarded by families and provide the parents with a better sense of self-efficacy and personal control (Trivette, Dunst, Boyd, & Hamby, 1995).

Table 4–2 provides a list of the supports often needed by families. Schools and teachers often play an important role in assisting families in accessing these supports. While these supports would not be directly provided by the school, they are often available in the community and may be listed in a resource or referral guide. Parent-to-parent supports are available in most communities through family advocacy and support organizations. In many communities, there are established groups called *Parent to Parent*. These groups match a family with a veteran parent who has been in similar circumstances. The veteran parent provides support and training and assists the family in accessing resources. In other organizations or support groups, parents gain advocacy skills and information and receive social support from their involvement in groups where they can meet families in similar circumstances.

There is also an important need for family education and advocacy skill development. In every state, a Parent Training and Information Center (PTI) has been federally

Table 4–2 Family Support Services and Resources

Parent-to-parent support
Family education and advocacy
Sibling support
Respite care
Case coordination
Economic support
Housing support
Transportation support
Medical care
Social support

established to provide education and training to parents of children with disabilities. These organizations provide training opportunities and materials that will be helpful to teachers and the families that they support. Other family organizations, many of which are specific to the disability (e.g., ARC, the Autism Society) can be a wonderful resource for family information and training.

An important, although often neglected, area of family support is based on sibling issues. In many communities Sibshops are offered for siblings of children with disabilities (Meyer & Vadasy, 1994). *Sibshops* are workshops designed to assist siblings with processing their feelings and concerns about their siblings with disabilities. In addition to Sibshops, several books address family and sibling issues and may be helpful for the families that you support.

Respite care refers to assistance in caring for a child with a disability. When respite care is provided, families can have time away from the child and a break from the demands of child care. Respite care is available in many communities through the health and human services agency or through community service organizations.

When families have complex needs, they may also use the services of a case coordinator. The role of the case coordinator is to assist the family in accessing supports and services. Case coordination services may be provided by a school social worker, a local service agency, or a state program for persons with disabilities. Some families in your program may need assistance with basic needs, such as economic support, housing, medical care, and transportation. These supports are typically provided through state or community agencies that have targeted programs and specific eligibility criteria. Teachers and school personnel should seek to gain a list of these programs and be willing to assist families in identifying programs to meet their needs. Often a family just needs assistance with identifying the agency or the phone number of a person to call for assistance.

The Role of Teachers When Collaborating with Parents

Although services such as counseling and case management are usually provided by other professionals on the collaborative team (e.g., counselors, psychologists, and social workers), the teacher is most likely the professional with whom the parent has the greatest amount of direct contact. Additionally, the teacher is the primary link between the collaborative team (and the public school) and the parent. Teachers and other professionals who are perceived by parents as being most helpful are those with a pleasant disposition, those who are knowledgeable about their child's problems, those who treat parents as equals and involve them in making decisions, and those who are specific and practical when discussing how to address the child's needs (Singer & Irvin, 1991).

Communicating with Parents

An open line of communication is the most important feature of teacher–parent relations. Parents can provide important information on a daily basis and likewise want to receive regular reports from the teacher. Parents and teachers who share information better understand how to interact with the student on matters ranging from communicative acts to medical problems.

Teachers and parents may communicate with each other using any medium that is mutually satisfactory. Parents who drop their children off and pick them up at the end of the school day have frequent natural opportunities to talk with the teacher. Phone calls can also be used as long as there is agreement about when and where to call. Teachers should know whether calls to the parent's place of employment are acceptable and should let parents know if they (the teachers) are willing to accept calls at home and, if so, during what hours. (Of course, emergency phone calls about a student's well-being should be made whenever the need arises.) Recent communication devices such as e-mail, telephone answering machines, and fax machines make communication easier and may be of use between some parents and teachers.

The oldest and probably most commonly used form of communication between teachers and parents is the daily log or journal, which is usually a spiral-bound notebook that goes between the home and the school with the student. In it, the teacher writes a brief report of the day's activities, focusing on any special positive highlights of the day (e.g., "Emily selected a book in the library") or difficulties that occurred (e.g., "Samuel had a seizure this morning; you may want to talk to his doctor about his blood levels"). When the book is returned by the student on the next school day, it may include a note from the parent indicating any current problems that the student may be having and suggesting implications for the teacher ("Jamey did not sleep well last night, he may be tired today," or "Lucretia had a big breakfast at home, she probably won't eat anything at school this morning"). Teachers should send the notebook home each day, preferably with some positive message. Even if parents do not write a response, they will at least have the opportunity to do so, and a useful line of communication will be kept open with relatively little effort.

Offering Help to Parents

Teachers often become aware that parents are facing unique difficulties associated with having a child with severe disabilities. When offering help, professionals should realize that certain forms of help-giving can have positive effects, while others can be negative (Dunst et al., 1988). Giving help should never undermine the family's use of its own resources to solve its problems, which can result in reduced self-efficacy. Instead of solving the problem, the professional should encourage the parents to explore ways to solve it so that they can see themselves as successful problem solvers. Of course, the help-giving professional should never be patronizing or convey the notion that the parents seeking help are inferior or incapable of dealing with the problematic situation (Dunst et al., 1988).

Dunst et al. (1988) also advised that the act of giving help should not foster a sense of indebtedness. This could interfere with the recognition of problems and might inhibit the person from seeking assistance in the future. Unsolicited help is likely to be harmful. Advice or help from someone who is not well known by the individual or from whom the individual does not want advice is not likely to be well received. Nor will help be well received if it does not match the real need that an individual has or believes that he has. Help-giving is likely to be most effective if it emphasizes building strengths within the family, rather than remediating weaknesses.

With these understandings, there are several ways in which a teacher can serve as a source of support for parents. However, two points must be remembered. First, no one should assume that all parents of children with severe disabilities have personal problems related to their children. Some do and some do not, but creating situations that do not exist is detrimental to the students and their parents. Second, the teacher or other professional must realize that she can be helpful in some ways, but not in all ways. For the most part, the objective when working with parents is to find ways to support them as they try to meet their own needs. Some commonly occurring stressful situations for parents and ways in which teachers can assist include the following:

- Parental difficulties are more likely to occur at times of transition or during major life events (e.g., divorce, moving into a new school area).Teachers should be understanding of parents' needs at this time.
- Smaller, more common events can also cause stress (e.g., the car breaking down, the checkbook running low). Teachers should not contribute to them by sending home "special requests" that may require extra effort.
- Teachers should inform parents of community sources of support, particularly respite care. Other support services could provide health care, financial assistance, and counseling. The school social worker can help to identify these services.
- There may be parent support organizations within communities, and teachers should provide parents with information about them.
- Teachers may assist parents by helping them to form informal networks with parents of other students that they teach.
- Parents should be encouraged by teachers to talk with other family members, friends, and relatives about their child and look to them as sources of informal support.
- Teachers should place a high priority on improving those aspects of the child's behavior that parents indicate are the most difficult or challenging.

While it is helpful for families if some of the conditions that cause stress and personal difficulties can be reduced, it is also helpful if they can learn to accept the conditions that cannot be changed, realizing that all is not "their fault" and that all cannot be fixed. As Singer and Irvin (1991) stated, "Efforts to improve the situation have to be balanced with ways of accepting it" (p. 283). Teachers and other professionals can provide important support by acknowledging this.

Providing Culturally Competent Instruction

Cultural competence has been defined as "a set of congruent behaviors, attitudes, and policies that come together in a system, agency, or among professionals and enables that system, agency, or those professionals to work effectively in cross-cultural situations" (Cross, Bazron, Dennis, & Isaacs, 1989, p. 13). Cultural competence is an essential element of providing education and human services to diverse populations. Cultural competence implies an active effort to ensure that organizations and individuals provide services and supports in a manner that is culturally competent (Barrera & Corso, 2002).

Cultural competence is reflected in how schools and classrooms are organized and operated and how personnel interact with each other, their students, the students' families, and the community. School personnel who are culturally competent are accepting and respectful of differences, engage in continual self-assessment of their own culture and their biases that may affect their interactions with others, seek to learn about other cultures, and adapt services, supports, and interactions that support students and families who are culturally and linguistically diverse. Schools and school personnel that are culturally competent incorporate the following elements into their structure and interactions (Hernandez, Isaacs, Nesman, & Burns, 1998):

- *Valuing diversity.* Understanding and accepting the perspectives, actions, and values of other cultures
- *Cultural self-assessment.* Assessing the policies and practices that may be barriers to supporting and engaging diverse cultures
- *Cross-cultural dynamics.* Recognition of differences in communication styles, etiquette, and interactions
- *Institutionalization of cultural knowledge.* Providing training and awareness to staff about cultural differences and norms and practices to support diverse cultures
- *Adaptation to diversity.* Enacting policies and procedures to ensure institutional cultural competence and culturally relevant supports and services

Cultural competence is an action-oriented concept that implies a continual commitment to ensuring that your behavior, classroom, and school are accepting and supportive of students, families, and colleagues who are culturally diverse. A teacher who is culturally competent makes a conscious effort to be reflective about his assumptions and the perspectives of others. In the following section, examples of actions and behaviors will illustrate cultural competence within the school and classroom and in interaction with others.

The School and Classrooms

It often requires an active effort to create schools and classrooms that are welcoming to the diverse cultures of their students and families (Montgomery, 2001; Parette & Petch-Hogan, 2000; Salend & Taylor, 1993). Schools are typically staffed by the majority-culture, middle-class professionals who do not share the cultural or linguistic background of their students. In schools with cultural competence as a goal, the school environment and personnel use strategies to ensure that their students and families feel supported and respected and that efforts are made to consider their values, needs, and perspectives.

Actions that schools may take include the following:

- An emphasis on recruiting diverse staff to meet the needs of the diverse school population
- Access to translation services for meetings and conferences that involve families
- Posting of school signs in the languages of the school population
- Provision of essential school family information materials in multiple languages
- Provision of ongoing staff development on issues related to cultural competence
- Outreach to promote the involvement of community cultural leaders to assist the school in addressing issues of cultural competence
- Recruitment of family leaders who represent the diverse cultures of the school to participate on school policy planning and social committees

In addition, schools may need to change policies or traditional practices to ensure that teachers can meet with families in their homes or community settings or that meetings and conferences are held at times when families are able to attend.

Classrooms should also reflect a commitment to promote cultural diversity and cultural competence (Montgomery, 2001). Classroom environments should display pictures, posters, and materials that represent the cultures and ethnic backgrounds of the students in the school. Books and media resources (videos, computer programs) should reflect the diversity of the school population. Opportunities may be provided for families to share their cultural background and transitions with the children and other families. Field trips and projects should support students in learning about their own cultural or ethnic history, as well as the history of others. Celebrations should include the holidays that are unique to culturally diverse children and families in addition to those celebrated by the majority culture. When holidays are celebrated, there needs to be an awareness that the symbols and traditions associated with a holiday may not be meaningful for all students. Students should not be required to participate in nonacademic activities such as holiday celebrations that may not be culturally relevant. Table 4–3 provides a list of instructional practices that promote cultural competence.

Table 4–3 Culturally Competent Instructional Practices

1. Learn as much as possible about each family's culture and values. Do not make cultural assumptions based on faith, race, or country of origin.
2. Network with community agencies, organizations, and leaders that can provide you with cultural guidance and family support and facilitate rapport and relationship development with the families of your students.
3. Make no assumptions about English fluency and literacy. Offer the service of translators. Ask families for their language preference in communication with the school.
4. Create a physical environment that embraces diversity and reflects the community. Visual displays, films, and literature should include individuals from diverse cultures and differing abilities engaged in everyday activities.
5. Use materials and activities that come from the family cultures of your students. For example, dominoes may be a family game specific to a student, or you may have a student from a Latino home who prefers listening to the Spanish radio station.
6. Be aware of how your culture, beliefs, and practices influence the nature of instructional activities that you develop or plan. Actively promote the inclusion of other traditions and avoid assumptions that all families engage in majority-culture activities or celebrations (e.g., Christmas, Halloween).
7. Develop an understanding of how each family may view disability, gender roles, decision making, child independence, and discipline. Engage in a respectful dialogue to understand the unique views of the family system and its priorities for the child.
8. Encourage family participation in school activities regardless of English proficiency. Personally invite families to events or to volunteer; provide explanations of the purpose of events or activities that may be unfamiliar, such as book fairs or the PTO meeting; and help families to network with each other at school events.
9. Work actively to create a school environment that embraces diversity and supports all families. Examine and work collaboratively to change school policy, activities, and culturally insensitive behavior of individuals.

Interactions with Students and Families

A teacher's interactions with students must also reflect an awareness of the students' cultural or linguistic differences. Teachers should attempt to learn to use key words from the languages of students who do not speak English to better communicate with them. Students with severe disabilities who are from linguistically diverse homes may have a receptive vocabulary that is not English. In addition, teachers should become familiar with the routines and activities that their student may be exposed to at home or in their communities and reflect these perspectives within the curriculum. For example, a student from a Hispanic home and community may be more responsive to Spanish popular music or be more engaged in table games when dominoes are an option for a leisure activity. The best way for teachers to become informed about the cultural and linguistic backgrounds of their students is through interactions with the family. Teachers who are knowledgeable about the family culture of their students will find that being culturally responsive in the classroom is an easier task.

The teacher bears the primary responsiblity to develop a relationship with the family. If teachers approach this obligation with fear, biases, intolerance, or superiority, it is difficult to establish a reciprocal relationship. The development of a relationship will be much more successful if the teacher approaches the family with an acceptance of differences in beliefs, values, and traditions.

It is important that the teacher approach a relationship with a family from a different culture with some knowledge of the family's culture. However, it is also important to realize that each family will be unique (Lynch & Hanson, 1998). A third-generation Asian American family may have very different perspectives and values from an Asian family that has recently immigrated. It is very important in the early stages of developing a relationship with a family to be open to differences in communication style, nonverbal communication, decision making, and family values. Teachers who are not sensitive to the possible differences may find themselves frustrated with the family because they do not understand their behavior and perspectives. The following examples demonstrate the difference between two teachers' interactions with the families of their students.

> Ms. Hartsfield was anxious about her meeting with the Medi family. She really enjoyed teaching their daughter Priya, but had not had a conference with the family. She wasn't even sure of how much English they spoke. When the family came to her classroom, she was relieved to find out that both parents spoke beautiful English. She introduced herself and began sharing an update on Priya's progress. Priya's mother kept looking away while Ms. Hartsfield was speaking. Ms. Hartsfield wondered if Priya's mother was upset about the information that she was sharing. Ms. Hartsfield ended her discussion by asking Priya's mother what instructional goals were important to the family so that they could be addressed in the

classroom. Mrs. Medi hesitated and then turned to her husband who responded. After a brief discussion, Mr. Medi stood up and thanked Ms. Hartsfield for her time. The parents then left the meeting. As Ms. Hartsfield reflected on the conference, she felt badly for Priya's mother. She felt as if she was dominated by Mr. Medi. She decided to make a special effort to communicate with Priya's mother and to encourage her to become more involved in the classroom.

Mr. Brady was looking forward to his meeting with the Perez family. He had agreed to meet them at the neighborhood center. The Perez family preferred to meet there and could take advantage of an on-site child-care program for their three children. Mr. Brady greeted the family in Spanish and was warmly greeted by Mrs. Perez and her mother, Mrs. Morales. Mrs. Perez was a single parent of three children and lived with her mother. When Mr. Brady presented his update on Emil's progress, he was careful to begin by discussing Emil's strengths before presenting some of the current challenges. Emil was having a lot of problem behavior in the classroom, and Mr. Brady wanted to begin a process of functional behavioral assessment and positive behavior support. Mrs. Perez was Puerto Rican, but fluent in English. Her mother, however, only spoke Spanish. The meeting took some time because Mrs. Perez would translate for her mother everything that was relayed by Mr. Brady. Mr. Brady was patient with the process because he knew that Emil's grandmother had to approve most of the decisions that were made. The meeting went well and resulted in a plan to conduct a functional assessment on the behavior problems that Emil was having at home and in the community. Mrs. Perez thanked Mr. Brady as the meeting ended and gave him a hug. Mr. Brady left the meeting satisfied with the outcome and reflecting on how happy he was that he had enlisted the support of the Perez family. He was excited to be working in partnership with them to develop appropriate supports for Emil.

These two examples of a teacher's interactions with the family demonstrate that knowledge and support of the family culture are of primary importance. What will happen if Ms. Hartsfield pursues pushing Priya's mother to be active in the classroom? How might the cultural background of Ms. Hartsfield be influencing her perceptions? What did Mr. Brady do to facilitate the comfort and participation of the Perez family? Table 4–4 provides strategies that the teacher may use to promote the participation and comfort of families.

Table 4–4 Building Partnerships with Culturally and Linguistically Diverse Families

1. Strive to develop a trusting and respectful relationship with the student's family. Become aware of the family's language preferences, family goals, and family roles.
2. Network with other professionals and access information that can inform you on the customs, beliefs, and traditions of the family's cultural or ethnic background. Understanding the norms of cultural groups will be helpful, although you must also realize that each family is unique in its construction, history, and perspectives.
3. Structure IEP meetings so that the family is comfortable and understands the process. Arrange for an interpreter if needed. Adjust the process to ensure that the family can participate and feels respected throughout the process.
4. Seek to understand the family's preferences for who makes family decisions, perspectives about the student's disability, values about the student's independence, and approach to discipline. Realize that families may have very different perspectives about disability, the goals of schooling, and their involvement in their child's education.
5. Understand and respect family roles and lines of authority. In many families (e.g., some Asian or Latin), the teacher must involve the extended family or family members who hold positions of authority.
6. Use formal titles when interacting with the family and in your communication.
7. Identify a liaison from the community to help you to establish a relationship with a family that is hard to reach. Some families may be more comfortable communicating with the school through a respected community leader (e.g., minister or physician).
8. Be flexible about where meetings and family conferences are held. Some families are uncomfortable in the school setting and may be more comfortable in a community-based site such as a community center or church.
9. Arrange for child care and/or transportation for families who may not be able to access these resources to attend IEP meetings and school conferences.
10. Provide updates on the student's successes and progress in a manner that matches the family's preferences. Some families may prefer a face-to-face interaction, while others may be more comfortable with a phone call or e-mail. Provide the updates in the family's preferred language.
11. Be aware of cultural differences for communication and interacting. Some forms of nonverbal communication, such as physical proximity, touching, eye contact, gestures, and facial expression, have different meanings in different cultures.

When Culture Intersects with Instructional Decisions

On occasion, cultural perspectives conflict with instructional decisions and goals. Families may have a perspective that is culturally driven, and the teacher may have a perspective that reflects the values of the dominant culture and mainstream education practices (Barrera & Corso, 2002; Chen et al., 2002). These types of situations are very difficult for many teachers. Kalyanpur and Harry (1999) describe a four-step process for building collaborative relationships. They recommend an adoption of this approach whenever the teacher is engaged in discussions with a family regarding differences in cultural practices or values.

The four steps are briefly presented in Table 4–5. Step 1 involves the teacher examining the cultural values that are embedded in her interpretation of what is needed for the student. At this step, the teacher should question why he believes that his recommendation is important. For example, the teacher who believes that it is important for a high school student to have a supported employment experience when the family wants the student to stay on campus should question if the importance of supported employment is driven from her cultural perspective about the importance of work and independence.

Step 2 is to determine if the family holds the same values and assumptions or if they have a differerent perspective. The family may not feel that work is a pressing need for their child and may not be worried about their child's employment post-high school. In their view, their child can continue to live with them and should not have to worry about work.

Step 3 is to acknowledge the differences identified and provide an explanation of the cultural assumptions that serve as the foundation of your recommendation. For example, the teacher may explain the cultural value of work in the community and the need to provide support now so that the student will be ready for supported work after high school.

Step 4 is a discussion about how to come to a resolution that adapts your recommendations to the values of the family. In this step, you collaborate with the family to develop an alternative solution that is acceptable to you and is respectful of the family's values and perspectives. In the example of supported employment for the high school student, the teacher decides that the family perspective is important and that the other goals that the family has for their son are equally important. The teacher agrees that supported employment does not have to be an experience provided to the student.

Conclusion

The professional responsibilities of a teacher of students with severe disabilities extend beyond the provision of direct services to these students. The teacher must collaborate with the parents and families of the students. The importance of the relationship between the special educator and these other individuals cannot be overstated. If the teacher does not work effectively with others, less than optimal services will be delivered to the students.

Understanding the unique circumstances of parents and families of students with severe disabilities not only allows the teacher to better form appropriate goals and objectives for students, but also helps him to approach the educational process with an empathetic perspective. This is not to imply that the teacher should have an attitude of pity toward the parents or feel that they are superhuman because their child has a severe disability. In fact, the opposite is true. The better the interactions are between parents and teachers, the more likely it is that teachers will realize the unique characteristics of the parents and how the impact of their child affects each individually.

The provision of culturally competent instruction and supports demonstrates the teacher's acceptance of the diversity of the student population and their families.

Table 4–5 A Process of Cultural Reciprocity

1. **Where am I coming from?** Think about the cultural values and assumptions that are embedded in your recommendations.
2. **Is the family coming from the same place?** Find out if the family has the same views and beliefs. Identify the values and perspectives of the family that may be different.
3. **Get it all on the table**. Provide the family with an explanation of the assumptions, values, and perceptions that drive your recommendations. Acknowledge the different perspectives of the family.
4. **Come to a mutual decision**. Collaborate with the family to come to an agreement about actions that support the needs of the student without compromising the values of the family.

Source: Based on *Culture in Special Education: Building Reciprocal Family–Professional Relationships,* by M. Kalyanpur and B. Harry, 1999. Baltimore: Paul H. Brookes.

To build optimal relationships with students and their families, a teacher must be willing to question her own cultural assumptions, examine the assumptions that underlie professional practices and policies, and actively seek to develop an understanding of the diverse cultures of her students and their families. Teachers who commit themselves to the ongoing process of cultural competence will find that their relationships with their students, the families of their students, and their colleagues are enhanced by a deeper understanding of diversity and differences.

Questions for Reflection

1. What have you perceived as important needs of parents and families of students with severe disabilities?
2. What type of relationship do you believe should exist between professionals and parents?
3. What are some ways that professionals can gain a better understanding of parents' needs and concerns?
4. Why do professionals often expect more from parents of children with severe disabilities than from other parents?
5. What are some creative ways for professionals and parents to meet and work together on a regular basis?
6. What are some actions that you may take as a classroom teacher to ensure that all families are welcome in the school and that the development of partnerships with families is supported?
7. Reflect on an experience that you may have had when you were the minority (e.g., visiting another country, joining a group of people who all share an experience or attribute). What emotions did you experience? What did others do to try to help you to feel more comfortable? What lessons can you draw from these experiences in supporting families who come from minority cultures or circumstances?

References

Barrera, I., & Corso, R. (2002). Cultural competency as skilled dialogue. *Topics in Early Childhood Special Education, 22,* 103–113.

Black, M. M., Molaison, V. A., & Smull, M. W. (1990). Families caring for a young adult with mental retardation: Service needs and urgency of community living requests. *American Journal on Mental Retardation, 95,* 32–39.

Caplan, N., Choy, M., & Whitmore, J. K. (1992). Indochinese refugee families and academic achievement. *Scientific American,* 36–42.

Chen, D., Downing, J. E., & Peckham-Hardin, K. D. (2002). Working with families of diverse cultural and linguistic backgrounds: Considerations for culturally responsive positive behavior support. In J. M. Lucyshyn, G. Dunlap, & R. Albin (Eds.), *Families and positive behavior support: Addressing problem behavior in family contexts* (pp. 133–154). Baltimore: Paul H. Brookes.

Child Welfare League of America. (2003). *National Fact Sheet 2003* [Online]. Available: http://www.cwla.org/advocacy/nationalfactsheet03.html (2003, May 1).

Children's Defense Fund. (2003). *Children in the states: 1998 United States profile* [Online]. Available: http://www.childrensdefense.org/states/all_states.pdf (2003, May 1).

Cross, T. L., Bazron, B. J., Dennis, K. W., & Isaacs, M. R. (Eds.), (1989). *Towards a culturally competent system of care: Vol. I. A monograph on effective services for minority children who are severely emotionally disturbed.* Washington, DC: Georgetown University, Child Development Center, Child and Adolescent Service System Program, Technical Assistance Center.

D'Amato, E., & Yoshida, R. K. (1991). Parental needs: An educational life cycle perspective. *Journal of Early Intervention, 15,* 246–254.

Delpit, L. D. (1995). *Other people's children: Cultural conflicts in the classroom.* New York: New Press.

Dennis, R. E., & Giangreco, M. F. (1996). Creating conversation: Reflections on cultural sensitivity in family interviewing. *Exceptional Children, 63,* 103–116.

Dunst, C., Trivette, C., & Deal, A. (1988). *Enabling and empowering families: Principles and guidelines for practice.* Cambridge, MA: Brookline Books.

Dunst, C. J., Trivette, C. M., Gordon, N. J., & Pletcher, L. L. (1989). Building and mobilizing informal family support networks. In G. H. S. Singer & L. K. Irvin (Eds.), *Support for caregiving families: Enabling positive adaptation to disability* (pp. 121–141). Baltimore: Paul H. Brookes.

Epps, S., & Myers, C. L. (1989). Priority domains for instruction, satisfaction with school teaching, and postschool living and employment: An analysis of perceptions of parents of students with severe and profound disabilities. *Education and Training in Mental Retardation, 24,* 157–167.

Epstein, J. (1983). *Effects on parents of teacher practices in parent involvement.* Baltimore, MD: Center on Families,

Communities, Schools and Children's Learning, Johns Hopkins University.

Epstein, J. L. (1995). School/family/community partnerships: Caring for the children we share. *Phi Delta Kappan*, 701–712.

Fox, L., Vaughn, B. J., Wyatte, M. L., & Dunlap, G. (2002). "We can't expect other people to understand": Family perspectives on problem behavior. *Exceptional Children, 68*, 437–450.

Fujiura, G. T., & Yamaki, K. (2000). Trends in demography of childhood poverty and disability. *Exceptional Children, 66*, 187–201.

Gallegos, A., & Gallegos, R. (1988). The interaction between families of culturally diverse handicapped children and the school. In H. S. Garcia & R. Chavez (Eds.), *Ethnolinguistic issues in education* (pp. 125–132). (ERIC Document Reproduction Service No. ED 316 044.)

Gudykunst, W. B., Ting-Toomey, S., & Nishida, T. (1996). *Communication in personal relationships across cultures*. Thousand Oaks, CA: Sage.

Guralnick, M. J., Connor, R. T., & Hammond, M. (1995). Parent perspectives on peer relationships in integrated and specialized programs. *American Journal on Mental Retardation, 99*, 457–476.

Hamre-Nietupski, S., Nietupski, J., & Strathe, M. (1992). Functional life skills, academic skills, and friendship/social relationship development: What do parents of students with moderate/severe/profound disabilities value? *Journal of the Association for Persons with Severe Handicaps, 17*, 53–58.

Hanline, M. F., & Halvorsen, A. (1989). Parent perceptions of the integration transition process: Overcoming artificial barriers. *Exceptional Children, 55*, 487–492.

Hanson, M. J., & Carta, J. J. (1996). Addressing the challenges of families with multiple risks. *Exceptional Children, 62*, 201–212.

Heller, T., & Factor, A. (1991). Permanency planning for adults with mental retardation living with family caregivers. *American Journal on Mental Retardation, 96*, 163–176.

Henderson, A. T., & Berla, N. (1994). A new generation of evidence: The family is critical to student achievement. St. Louis, MO: Danforth Foundation; and Flint, MI: Mott (C. S.) Foundation.

Herman, S. E., & Thompson, L. (1995). Families' perceptions of their resources for caring for children with developmental disabilities. *Mental Retardation, 33*, 73–83.

Hernandez, M., Isaacs, M. R., Nesman, T., & Burns, D. (1998). Perspectives on culturally competent systems of care. In M. Hernandez & M. Isaacs (Eds.), *Promoting cultural competence in children's mental health services* (pp. 1–28). Baltimore: Paul H. Brookes.

Joe, J. R., & Malach, R. S. (1992). Families with Native American roots. In E. W. Lynch & M. J. Hanson (Eds.), *Developing cross-cultural competence: A guide for working with young children and their families* (pp. 89–120). Baltimore: Paul H. Brookes.

Kalyanpur, M. & Harry, B. (1999). *Culture in special education: Building reciprocal family–professional relationships*. Baltimore: Paul H. Brookes.

Leyser, Y. (1985). Parent involvement in school: A survey of parents of handicapped students. *Contemporary Education, 57*(1), 38–43.

Lynch, E. W., & Hanson, M. J. (Eds.). (1998). *Developing cross-cultural competence: A guide for working with young children and their families (*2nd ed.*)*. Baltimore: Paul H. Brookes.

Lynch, E. W., & Stein, R. C. (1987). Parent participation by ethnicity: A comparison of Hispanic, Black and Anglo families. *Exceptional Children, 54*, 105–111.

McDonnell, J. (1987). The integration of students with severe handicaps into regular public schools: An analysis of parents' perceptions of potential outcomes. *Education and Training in Mental Retardation, 22*, 98–111.

Meyer, D. J., & Vadasy, P. F. (1994). *Sibshops: Workshops for siblings of children with special needs*. Baltimore: Paul H. Brookes.

Meyers, C. E., & Blacher, J. (1987). Parents' perceptions of schooling for severely handicapped children: Home and family variables. *Exceptional Children, 53*, 441–449.

Mlynek, S., Hannah, M. E., & Hamlin, M. A. (1982). Mainstreaming: Parental perceptions. *Psychology in the Schools, 19*, 354–359.

Montgomery, W. (2001). Creating culturally responsive, inclusive classrooms. *Teaching Exceptional Children, 33*(4), 4–9.

Olmstead, P. P., & Rubin, R. I. (1983). Linking parent behaviors to child achievement: Four evaluation studies from the parent education follow-through programs. *Studies in Educational Evaluation, 8*, 317–325.

Parette, H. P., & Petch-Hogan, B. (2000). Approaching families: Facilitating culturally/linguistically diverse family involvement. *Teaching Exceptional Children, 33*(2), 4–10.

Park, J., Turnbull, A. P., & Park, H. (2001). Quality of partnerships in service provision for Korean American parents of children with disabilities: A qualitative inquiry. *Journal of the Association for Persons with Severe Handicaps, 26*, 158–170.

Proctor, B. D., & Dalaker, J. (2002). *Poverty in the United States: 2001*. U.S. Census Bureau, Current Population Reports, P60-219. Washington, DC: U.S. Government Printing Office.

Rao, S. S. (2000). Perspectives of an African American mother on parent–professional relationships in special education. *Mental Retardation, 38*, 475–488.

Reichart, D. C., Lynch, E. C., Anderson, B. C., Svobodny, L. A., DiCola, J. M., & Mercury, M. G. (1989). Parental perspectives on integrated preschool opportunities for children with handicaps and children without handicaps. *Journal of Early Intervention, 13*, 6–13.

Salend, S. J., & Taylor, L. (1993). Working with families: A cross-cultural perspective. *Remedial and Special Education, 14*(5), 25–32, 39.

Salisbury, C., & Evans, I. M. (1988). Comparison of parental involvement in regular and special education. *Journal of the*

Association for Persons with Severe Handicaps, 13, 268–272.

Scorgie, K., & Sobsey, D. (2000). Transformational outcomes associated with parenting children who have disabilities. *Mental Retardation, 38,* 195–206.

Sherman, B. R. (1988). Predictors of the decision to place developmentally disabled family members in residential care. *American Journal on Mental Retardation, 92*(4), 344–351.

Singer, G. H. S., & Irvin, L. K. (1991). Supporting families of persons with severe disabilities: Emerging findings, practices, and questions. In L. H. Meyer, C. A. Peck, & L. Brown (Eds.), *Critical issues in the lives of people with severe disabilities* (pp. 271–312). Baltimore: Paul H. Brookes.

Singer, G. H. S., Irvin, L. K., Irvine, B., Hawkins, N., & Cooley, E. (1989). Evaluation of community-based support services for families of persons with developmental disabilities. *Journal of the Association for Persons with Severe Handicaps, 14,* 312–323.

Taunt, H. M., & Hastings, R. P. (2002). Positive impact of children with developmental disabilities on their families: A preliminary study. *Education and Training in Mental Retardation and Developmental Disabilities, 37,* 410–420.

Thorin, E., Yovanoff, P., & Irvin, L. (1996). Dilemmas faced by families during their young adults' transitions into adulthood: A brief report. *Mental Retardation, 34,* 117–120.

Trivette, C. M., Dunst, C. J., Boyd, K., & Hamby, D. W. (1995). Family-oriented program models, help-giving practices, and parental control appraisals. *Exceptional Children, 62,* 237–248.

Turnbull, A. P., & Ruef, M. (1996). Family perspectives on problem behavior. *Mental Retardation, 34,* 280–293.

Turnbull, H. R., Guess, D., & Turnbull, A. (1988). *Vox populi* and Baby Doe. *Mental Retardation, 26,* 127–132.

Turnbull, A. P., & Turnbull, H. R. (2001). *Families, professionals, and exceptionality: Collaborating for empowerment* (4th ed.) Upper Saddle River, NJ: Merrill/Prentice Hall.

U.S. Census Bureau. (2001). School enrollment in the United States—Social and economic characteristics of students. Available: http://148.129.75.3/.

Westling, D. L. (1996). What do parents of children with moderate and severe disabilities want? *Education and Training in Mental Retardation and Developmental Disabilities, 31,* 86–114.

Westling, D. L. (1997). What parents of young children with mental disabilities want: The views of one community. *Focus on Autism and Other Developmental Disabilities, 12*(2), 67–78.

Westling, D. L., & Plaute, W. (1999). Views of Austrian parents about special education services for their children with mental disabilities. *Education and Training in Mental Retardation and Developmental Disabilities, 34,* 43–57.

Williams, W., Fox, T. J., Thousand, J., & Fox, W. (1990). Level of acceptance and implementation of best practices in the education of students with severe handicaps in Vermont. *Education and Training in Mental Retardation, 25,* 120–131.

Willis, W. (1992). Families with African American roots. In E. W. Lynch & M. J. Hanson (Eds.), *Developing cross-cultural competence: A guide for working with young children and their families* (pp. 121–150). Baltimore: Paul H. Brookes.

Yanok, J., & Derubertis, D. (1989). Comparative study of parental participation in regular and special education programs. *Exceptional Children, 56,* 195–199.

PART 2

Preparing to Teach

CHAPTER 5

Planning Instructional Programs for Students with Severe Disabilities

This chapter discusses the need for developing appropriate educational plans for students with severe disabilities. The requirements for the content of individual educational programs, transition plans, and individual family service plans are presented. The chapter concludes with a discussion of some of the shortcomings of the required plans and a discussion of person-centered plans that allow more complete plans to be developed by parents and collaborative teams.

Planning for Students with Severe Disabilities

To provide an appropriate education for students with severe disabilities, the collaborative team of professionals and the student's parents must work in unison to develop effective educational plans. The plan that is developed, which will typically cover a 1-year period, must take into consideration the characteristics of the individual, including strengths and needs, the environments in which she currently functions and will function in the near future, and the types of skills necessary for functioning in these environments. The plan should also reflect skills that can be learned or changes that can be made in environments to positively affect the individual's quality of life.

Plans will contain goals and objectives for the student; sometimes the dreams that the student, family, and friends would like to see realized; and the instructional activities and learning experiences that should occur to reach the desired ends. To fully develop the educational plans, the teacher and other professionals must each conduct assessment activities. The different forms of assessment, discussed in Chapter 6, contribute important information about the student and his functional abilities that lead to the formation and re-formation of educational plans. In this chapter we will discuss the process of planning and the types of plans that must be developed. In the next chapter we will discuss assessment procedures, or the types of information-gathering actions, that must be taken to fully develop plans.

In the field of special education, the term *instructional plan* refers primarily to *individual educational programs* (IEPs). Within these, *transition plans* must be developed when students are in their adolescent years. *Individual family service plans* (IFSPs) must be developed for families of infants and toddlers who receive services. These plans are required by IDEA 97 (P.L. 105-17). In addition, there are alternative planning approaches, referred to as person-centered plans, that are very helpful; they identify the needs and desired life conditions for persons with severe disabilities. Person-centered plans may be viewed as ways of strengthening required plans, rather than supplanting them.

Planning and Quality of Life

Prior to the 1970s, teachers of students with disabilities were not required to plan individually for students as part of their instructional duties. Although accountability was considered an important component of special education, it was not until P.L. 94-142 was passed in 1975 that professionals were required to write formal individual educational programs for students receiving special education services. Smith (1990) noted that since IEPs were mandated a general reluctance has developed among many professionals to write them and to use them as functional documents. Instead, many have moved toward processes that allow information about the student from formal assessment instruments to be fed into a computer program and generated into a document that satisfies the requirements of laws and regulations.

For some students, this process may be satisfactory, especially when the student's problems are primarily in learning academic skills. However, this type of planning is not appropriate for students with more severe disabilities whose instructional and service needs are beyond what can be determined through pencil-and-paper assessment. In contrast, it has been suggested that the quality of life desired for an individual with severe disabilities should direct the development of educational and service delivery plans (Dennis, Williams, Giangreco, & Cloninger, 1993; Halpern, 1993; Schalock, 1990a, 1994). The commitment to this idea by the persons involved in the planning process will translate directly into how well the student will be taught, how well he will learn, and how well he will be accepted. Thus the quality of life that the person enjoys will be directly related to the quality of the plan.

Quality of life is not easy to conceptualize or measure (Schalock, 1990b), yet it has become a central point of focus in many processes of planning for individuals with disabilities. In a paradigm shift that places more emphasis on inclusion, equity, empowerment, and community-based supports, service providers have come to realize that their instruction and other service activities should lead to more satisfactory life conditions (Schalock, 1994). Because indicators of quality of life will vary from one person to the next, precisely what these life conditions should be cannot be prescribed. One important condition will certainly be for the individual to be as self-determining as possible (as discussed in Chapter 2). This would imply that the person has the opportunity to exert personal control and make choices and decisions. Most likely, other indicators of quality of life can be observed in the individual's home or community living arrangement, financial and employment conditions, possessions, health and safety status, and integration with and natural supports by family, friends, and associates (Schalock, 1994).

To improve an individual's quality of life, educational and other plans should focus on three factors: home and community functioning, employment (for adults), and health and safety. Social indicators of a good quality of life include observable conditions such as good health, friendships and relationships, safety, pleasant leisure-time pursuits, and meaningful participation in the community. Psychological indicators consist more of the individual's subjective reactions to life experiences, for example, the expression of personal satisfaction and happiness (Schalock, 1990b, 1994). Planners should incorporate quality enhancers into plans to improve the development of quality of life indicators. Schalock (1994) has outlined how quality enhancement techniques can be used to improve these factors. Some of these are shown in Table 5–1.

As practitioners develop plans with the intention of improving quality of life, they should do so with an open mind, particularly with regard to the meaning of quality of life in different cultures and families. They should consider the individual holistically, including his individual values and needs, the values and needs that are common to all human beings, and those that are culturally specific (Dennis et al., 1993). These considerations can be applied to the development of required plans, but are especially well suited for the alternative planning approaches discussed later in this chapter.

Ideally, planning for students with severe disabilities involves the entire transdisciplinary, collaborative team. Parents, professionals, paraprofessionals, and the individual with disabilities should join together both mentally and physically to plan for the person's needs. Some person-centered plans also encourage siblings, friends, extended family members, and advocates to join in the planning process to discuss what the individual should learn and what actions can be taken to improve her quality of life.

Individual Educational Programs[1]

IEPs are the legally required planning tools for school-age students with disabilities. According to IDEA 97, the IEP is a written document for each student classified as having a disability and must include the following eight components (P.L. 105-17):

1. Present level of educational performance
2. Annual goals and short-term objectives (or benchmarks)

[1]As this edition goes to press, IDEA is being considered for reauthorization. Much of this content could change based on congressional actions.

Table 5–1 Quality Enhancement Techniques

Quality of Life Factor	*Enhancement Techniques*
Home and community living	• Allow for choices, decision making, and environmental control.
	• Interface with the person's social support system.
	• Maximize use of natural supports such as family, friends, neighbors.
	• Stress normalized and integrated environments, social interactions and community activities.
	• Emphasize family-professional partnerships
	• Promote positive role functions and lifestyles
Employment	• Facilitate employment, work status, and nonemployment volunteerism.
	• Foster co-workers as natural supports
	• Promote stable, safe environments that reduce stress.
Health functioning	• Emphasize physical fitness, wellness, nutrition, and healthy lifestyles.
	• Provide health care coverage and access.
	• Use prosthetics to facilitate communication, mobility, and self-help.
	• Maintain as low a psychotropic medication level as possible.

Source: "Quality of Life, Quality Enhancement, and Quality Assurance: Implications for Program Planning and Evaluation in the Field of Mental Retardation and Developmental Disabilities," by R. L. Schalock, 1994, *Evaluation and Program Planning, 17,* pp. 121–131. Reprinted by permission of Elsevier Science.

3. Special education and related services and supplementary aids, services, and modifications necessary for the student
4. An explanation of the extent, if any, to which the student will participate with nondisabled students in regular classrooms and schools
5. A statement of individual modifications in the administration of statewide or districtwide assessments needed for the student to participate in the assessment; or a statement of why the student will not participate and what alternate assessment will be used
6. Projected date for beginning services, supports, and modifications; and the frequency, location, and duration of services and modifications
7. Beginning at age 14, a statement of transition service needs that focus on the student's course of studies and, beginning no later than age 16, an individual transition plan that includes interagency responsibilities
8. How the student's progress on individual goals and objectives will be measured and how the student's parents will be informed of the progress

According to the law, the IEP must be written at least once a year, but may be modified more often if necessary. As has been stated, it is highly desirable that a collaborative transdisciplinary team working with parents develop and implement the plan. Notwithstanding this recommended practice, the law *requires* that certain individuals participate in writing the IEP. Members of the IEP team must include the following:

1. The parents of the student
2. At least one regular education teacher if the student is to participate in a regular school environment
3. At least one special education teacher
4. A local education agency representative who is knowledgeable about the student's unique service needs, the general curriculum, and the availability of resources in the school district
5. A person who can interpret the instructional implications of the evaluations that have been conducted
6. If the parents or school district wishes, other persons, including related services personnel, who have knowledge or special expertise about the student
7. Whenever appropriate, the student with the disability

Although the importance of parental participation in the IEP process cannot be overstated, research has shown that parents often do not get involved to the extent desirable (Gilliam & Coleman, 1981; Shevin, 1983). There may be many explanations for this. Parents may perceive the meeting as a formal experience in which they do not have the knowledge of many of the "experts" and thus are reticent about participating. As noted in Chapter 4, this may be especially true of minority parents. To improve parental participation, schools can implement several practices. Some of the following may be useful (Goldstein, 1993; Goldstein & Turnbull, 1982):

- Contact parents personally before the meeting; don't rely only on the formal written notice to prompt their attendance.
- Send questions that may come up about the student to the parents before the meeting; avoid putting them on the spot at the IEP conference.
- Have a school staff member greet the parents when they arrive; don't leave them standing or sitting and uncertain of how long they will have to wait.
- Appoint an interpreter, someone responsible for explaining to the parents anything that is not clear to them.

Like the parents, the special education teacher's role in the IEP process is very important. She is expected to provide input for all aspects of the IEP but, most importantly, the teacher should be able to offer relevant information about the student's current abilities, suggest appropriate goals and objectives, state an opinion about the need for related services, and discuss ways to include the student with severe disabilities in classrooms and settings with students who do not have disabilities. The following sections provide more detail about select components of the IEP and their appropriate development for students with severe disabilities.

Current Performance Levels

This section of the IEP must specify the student's present level of ability, including strengths and needs. Various assessment activities undertaken by the teacher and other professionals (discussed in the next chapter) with input from the student's parents will help to develop critical information about the student's current performance level. Most often, the student's ability level in important life domains (domestic skills, community skills, leisure and recreational skills, and vocational skills), as well as in areas such as communication, social behaviors, and academic abilities, will be stated in this section of the IEP.

Many transdisciplinary team members can provide information about the student's current performance level. The parents may discuss the student's abilities and activities in the home, neighborhood, and community. General and special education teachers should discuss the student's functioning in different areas during the school day. A communication disorders specialist, a physical therapist, and/or an occupational therapist may also provide input about the student's abilities if they have worked with the student over the course of the year or have evaluated the student before the IEP meeting. Other professionals, such as a visual disabilities specialist or an audiologist, may also be present at the meeting to explain the student's abilities within their areas of expertise. A school psychologist may report the student's IQ, developmental level,[2] or behavioral characteristics.

Annual Goals and Short-Term Objectives

The student's annual goals and short-term objectives are based on current performance level and his learning needs in immediate and future environments as perceived by parents and other team members. Each member of the team must consider available assessment data and give thought to factors such as the student's age and any pending changes in the living, schooling, or working environment. The goals and objectives to be developed must be functional and chronological-age appropriate, and they should be written to include learning in major life domains (community, domestic, recreational and leisure, and vocational) and key social, communicative, and academic skills. As discussed earlier in Chapter 2 and later in Chapter 17, consideration must also be given to the student's potential participation in the general curriculum. In addition to the unique needs being addressed in the IEP, it must also discuss if and in what ways the student can participate in the general curriculum of the school district or state.

The type, complexity, and difficulty level of specific goals and objectives must be individually determined and geared toward the needs and abilities of each student. As a general guide, we should always think in terms of the types of goals and objectives that will improve the student's quality of life (Halpern, 1993; Schalock, 1990a, 1994). Students whose disabilities fall within the moderate mental disabilities range might have goals such as learning independent grocery shopping and functional academic skills or developing appropriate literacy skills. Such skills may allow greater independence and community participation or may enhance the student's quality of life. In comparison, a student with a very severe disability, for example, one who is profoundly mentally disabled, may have goals that will increase her degree of participation in other ways. Lehr (1989) proposed that goals for students with the most severe disabilities should be based on four continuums (see Figure 5–1). The goals would move the student *away from* being dependent, not participating, being difficult to care for, and being unpleasant to be around, and *toward* independence, full participation, being easy to care for, and being pleasant.

The distinction between annual goals and short-term objectives is significant. Annual goals are usually broadly worded statements that describe a desired outcome in a certain learning area. For example, a goal may be for a student to learn to shop in a grocery store independently. Another may be for a student to cooperate appropriately when being dressed by extending limbs and leaning forward. Stated in this fashion, the goal is clear enough for another to know what the student is to learn. In contrast, writing that the student is going to "learn community skills" or "participate in daily activities" is too vague; we would not have a good idea of what we want to achieve within a year's time.

Another way to judge if the annual goal has adequate clarity is if it gives enough information for specific short-term objectives to be written. In contrast to the annual goals, short-term objectives, often referred to as behavioral objectives, must be very specific. Short-term objectives are the building blocks of annual goals; the objectives, when learned, indicate that the goal has been achieved.

A behavioral or short-term objective written in sufficient detail states *who* is going to do *what, under what conditions,* and *how often, for how long,* or *how quickly* it should happen. For example, an objective might be written for the goal of improving communicative–social skills with other students at school. The objective might be stated as follows: "Bill will greet at least one classmate by

Figure 5–1 Curricular Goal Continuums for Students with Profound Mental Handicaps

Dependence	◄-------►	Independence
No participation	◄-------►	Full participation
Difficult to care for	◄-------►	Easy to care for
Unpleasant	◄-------►	Pleasant

Source: Persons with Profound Disabilities: Issues and Practices (p. 218) by F. Brown & D. H. Lehr (Eds.), 1989, Baltimore: Paul H. Brookes Publishing Co., P.O. Box 10624, Baltimore, Maryland 21285-0624. Reprinted by permission.

[2]Although IQ and developmental level may not be relevant for developing an educational program, it must be determined every 3 years to establish the student's eligibility and will therefore be reported at some annual meetings.

looking and smiling at the classmate or demonstrating some other appropriate social behavior within 10 seconds after he enters a classroom or another setting in the school where there are classmates."

In this example, Bill is *who;* looking and smiling at a classmate or demonstrating some other similar behavior is *what;* and when he comes into a classroom with other students is the *condition* under which the behavior should occur. Within 10 seconds after coming into the room expresses *how quickly* the behavior should occur.

In addition, there must be a learning criterion or multiple criteria for judging when the objective has been learned. How often or on how many days must Bill greet classmates before we decide that he has adequately learned this skill? How well does the skill have to be learned before we decide that we do not have to formally instruct Bill to greet others and collect data on his behavior? How many different classmates does he need to greet? In how many different school settings does he need to greet classmates?

Obviously, there is no correct answer or absolute standard for determining these criteria or the performance standards for many other behavioral objectives. Instead, we may consider how well others without disabilities can perform the action called for in the objective and make necessary modifications in the criteria. In other words, how often and in how many places do students without disabilities demonstrate this behavior? Based on this type of information, the criteria for achievement might be like the following: "Bill will greet a classmate at least 4 out of 5 days a week." Or "Bill will greet at least 3 of the 4 students he comes into contact with daily for 2 weeks."

A point worth noting about writing behavioral objectives is that they should focus more on function than on form. In many situations, how the behavior looks or is accomplished is not as important as whether it achieves the intention of the action. For example, it really would not matter whether Bill looked and smiled, waved his hand, or said "Hi." What *is* important is that some social greeting occurred and had an effect on the student's environment. In this example, we would expect that the student who was greeted would respond to Bill. If the behavior serves the function for which it is intended and does so by being topographically formed in a reasonable fashion (one that approaches normalcy as much as possible), the behavior called for in the behavioral objective will have been satisfactorily demonstrated.

When writing goals and objectives for students with severe disabilities, the IEP team should consider some important guidelines about their structure. Notari-Syverson and Schuster (1995) described five characteristics of goals and objectives that should be present:

1. *Functionality.* The skill increases the student's ability to interact in the environment and to do things that would have to be done by another if the student did not learn the skill.
2. *Generality.* The skill can be used in different settings, with different materials, and among different people and may be adapted to different needs, rather than isolated to a specific task.
3. *Ease of integration within the instructional context.* The goal and corresponding objectives should be incorporated into daily routines and taught in natural contexts.
4. *Measurability.* For the purpose of evaluation, the skill should be clearly defined and measurable.
5. *Hierarchical relationship between goals and objectives.* Objectives should lead to the achievement of goals, and multiple goals and objectives should lead consistently to a greater complexity of skills.

A question often asked is "How many goals and objectives should be written on an IEP?" The answer is that there is no specific number. Generally, at least one goal should be written for each major life domain, including domestic, community, recreational–leisure, and vocational skills (if appropriate) and for each major academic curricular area in which the student is participating. Additional goals may also be written to address areas such as social skills, communication skills, daily living skills, and motor skills.

Special Education, Placement in the Regular Classroom, and Related Services

The IEP must state the nature of special education, related services, and supplementary aids to be provided to meet the student's needs, as well as state the modifications and supports that will be provided. Together these services, supports, and modifications are intended (1) to help the student advance toward achieving her annual goals and objectives, (2) to allow the student to be involved and progress in the general education curriculum to the extent appropriate and to participate in extracurricular and nonacademic activities, and (3) to allow the student to be educated and participate with other children with and without disabilities. If the student is *not* to participate with nondisabled children in the regular classroom, the law requires that the IEP include a written explanation as to why this is the case.

In designing the most appropriate instructional arrangements for a particular student, the IEP planning team faces an important task: determining the most appropriate placement for a student. As discussed in Chapter 2, many professionals generally accept as best practice the placement of students with severe disabilities into regular classrooms and schools, in contrast to placement in special classes or segregated, special schools. It is generally difficult to defend special school placement for any student based on educational needs, because a variety of studies have shown that students with disabilities progress well in inclusive settings (Brinker, 1985; Evans, Salisbury, Palombaro, Berryman, & Hollowood, 1992; Hunt, Farron-Davis, Beckstead, Curtis, & Goetz, 1994) and that students without disabilities not only do not suffer from inclusion, but often benefit from it (Hendrickson, Shokoohi-Yekta, Hamre-Nietupski, & Gable, 1996; Peck, Donaldson, & Pezzoli, 1990; Sharpe et al., 1994). In some cases, professionals may find that parents feel that their child will be safer in special school environments (Hanline & Halvorsen, 1989; McDonnell, 1987; Westling, 1996), and they may support the parents in this choice. In such cases, placement in a special school will occur. However, there is no evidence that special schools are any safer than other schools. Therefore, unless there is contrary evidence, it is suggested that students with severe disabilities be placed in regular schools for their education. Under ideal circumstances, this should be the school that they would attend if they did not have a disability, which will give them the opportunity to go to school with their brothers and sisters and neighborhood friends (Brown et al., 1989).

Assuming that the regular home school is the school placement, the planning team must also address where services should occur within the school. Here, again, parents will often have a strong preference. Should the student be placed in a special education class? Should the student be in a regular classroom? How much time should students spend in different instructional settings? (Brown et al., 1989; Brown et al., 1991). It is our position that students should be served in regular classes as much as possible. However, the issue of placement is complex. Brown et al. (1991) offer some useful guidelines. These are summarized in Figure 5–2. In

Figure 5–2 Guidelines for Placing Students in Regular Classrooms

1. *Chronological Age.* Placement in regular classrooms for individually determined amounts of time is generally more appropriate for children in elementary schools. As students get older, learning in nonschool settings becomes more important.
2. *Related Services.* There are many instances when therapeutic services can be delivered in the regular classroom. In other instances there may be times when the student and therapist work in private.
3. *Number of Environments in Which a Student Functions.* Students with severe disabilities must learn to function in a number of environments besides the regular class. If experience in these environments is not provided through the educational program, they may not occur.
4. *Personnel Qualities.* Many regular education classroom teachers are very competent and will operate classrooms in which the student with severe disabilities can learn important skills. Other teachers will have less competence. Time spent with competent persons should be maximized; time with incompetent persons, regardless of the setting, should be minimized.
5. *Effects on Social Relationships.* The regular classroom offers a rich environment for the development of social relationships. Students should not be removed from this environment without protecting the social relationships that exist.
6. *Parent/Guardian/Student Priorities.* Parents, guardians, or students who place a high priority on developing social relations with nondisabled peers should spend more time in regular classroom settings.
7. *Probability of Acquisition.* If there is a low probability that the student with severe disabilities will acquire certain knowledge and skills being taught because of their complexity, abstractness, or difficulty, then it is acceptable for the student to be in another setting for more appropriate activities.
8. *Functionality.* Many functional skills cannot be incorporated into the regular classroom program. Many important functional skills must be taught in home, community, and work environments.
9. *Preparation for Post-School Life.* As the student approaches graduation, skills that are important for adulthood must be given greatest priority. Many skills taught in regular high school classes will not be as useful for students with severe disabilities as those taught elsewhere.

Source: Adapted From "How Much Time Should Students with Severe Intellectual Disabilities Spend in Regular Education Classrooms and Elsewhere?" by L. Brown, P. Schwarz, A. Udvari-Solner, E. F. Kampschroer, F. Johnson, J. Jorgensen, & L. Gruenewald, 1991, *Journal of the Association for Persons with Severe Handicaps, 16,* pp. 39–47. Adapted by permission of TASH, Baltimore, MD.

Chapter 10, information is provided for creating inclusive environments in general education classrooms.

The types of related services and how they will be provided must also be addressed in the IEP. As discussed in Chapter 4, various professionals besides the special educator will be responsible for providing services to maximize each student's potential. The most common related services required by students with severe disabilities are speech therapy, physical therapy, and occupational therapy. The evaluation of the student by the professionals in these areas will indicate the type and amount of service that each should provide.

Of course, it will not suffice for each professional to provide his or her service in an isolated manner. On the contrary, an important consideration in the offering of related services is the degree to which they are integrated with each other and with the entire educational program, which is why the transdisciplinary model was proposed in Chapter 3. Under this model, for example, it might be agreed by the team that a certain functional objective, such as selecting one's own clothing, is important for a student to achieve. Particular team members would then help design instructional strategies that allow the student to acquire such a skill, given his sensory, motor, or cognitive abilities. As Campbell (1987) stated, "Methodologies from each discipline are integrated into one instructional program to minimize the impact of limitations in vision, hearing, movement, and cognition, on a student's performance of cognitive skills" (p. 109).

Access to the General Curriculum and Participation in District and State Assessment Programs

As discussed in Chapter 2, IDEA 97 mandated two new requirements for students with disabilities: participation in the general curriculum to the extent possible and participation in state assessment programs. Since these requirements are discussed extensively in Chapters 2, 9, and 17, the reader is referred to those chapters for discussion of these topics. Here it is important to note that the goals and objectives on the IEP should indicate the extent to which the student will participate in the general curriculum and that the student will be assessed in the local or state assessment system, as required by law.

Projected Date for the Initiation of Services and the Duration of the Services

Services for students with severe disabilities are most often initiated by the time the child is 3 years old, if not before, and then continue on an annual basis in the form called for by the IEP. One important feature of the law's requirement for an annual (or more frequent) review and rewriting of the IEP is that it provides an opportunity for the IEP team to reconsider the student's goals, objectives, and placement. The fact that the IEP must be reviewed and renewed at least once a year should not be interpreted to mean that changes cannot be made at other times. Whenever there is reason to believe that placement in a less restrictive environment is possible or that other objectives are more appropriate, changes can be made. The specification of an annual review simply states that IEPs cannot be developed for more than 1 year at a time.

Annual Evaluation Procedures

The IEP must state how the student's performance will be evaluated on an annual basis. Although students with mild disabilities often have their performance evaluated by means of standardized tests, including those taken by nondisabled students within a school district, such tests do not appropriately evaluate the performance of students with severe disabilities. Instead, the IEP should state that the student's performance will be evaluated based on the degree of completion of individual goals and objectives. The various data collection systems discussed in Chapter 9 are helpful in documenting the student's progress.

In addition to performance on specific objectives, related services professionals may evaluate the student on speech, language, and communication development and on motor development. Progress may be reported using developmental assessment instruments specific to these areas.

When considering the importance of developing and using IEPs, attention must also be given to what individualized planning *should not be.* A plan for teaching students with severe disabilities should not be seen as a restriction on what should be taught or what activities someone may participate in. If, for example, a trip from New York to California is planned with designated stops at points in between, the traveler would be certain to visit all those points. This doesn't mean, though, that all other areas of interest along the way would be ignored, because this might limit learning and probably a lot of fun as well. It is the same when using an instructional plan: it should guide instructional actions, but not limit them. Keep this point in mind as various types of plans are considered.

Transition Plans

When students with disabilities reach adolescence, IDEA 97 requires that a plan be developed to facilitate the transition from school to adult life. This plan, the individual transition plan (ITP), is to be written as part of the IEP. By the time the student is 14 years old, the IEP must include a statement about transition services, focusing on the high school courses that the student should take, such as participation in academic, supported employment, or domestic skills courses, in preparation for the postschool years. When the student reaches 16 years of age (or earlier if the IEP team thinks it is appropriate), the statement of need for transition services must include a statement of the responsibilities to be taken on by different community agencies and the necessary linkages to the agencies. Key consideration when planning for the postschool years are opportunities for employment and residence in the community. Of equal importance is planning that allows the individual to have a satisfactory level of personal fulfillment and to perform typical adult roles such as mobility within the community, participation in recreational activities, having personal relationships, having spiritual fulfillment, and participating as a citizen in civic activities (Halpern, 1993).

Making the transition from childhood into adulthood is a difficult process for individuals with severe disabilities and their parents. This is the reason why ITPs must be incorporated into the IEP during the adolescent years. Studies have shown that many parents do not believe that their children with mental disabilities will, as adults, be able to work or live in community settings and believe that they will have to live in institutions or group living homes and spend their days in sheltered workshops or adult activity centers (Epps & Myers, 1989). In fact, parents often find that there is a lack of quality adult community-based residential programs and other service provisions for adults with severe disabilities (Black, Molaison, & Smull, 1990). Individuals with more severe disabilities who also exhibit behavior problems are those for whom normalized adult residential programs are most difficult to find (Sherman, 1988).

The importance of the ITP as a required component of the IEP is underscored by the fact that many parents of individuals with severe disabilities have difficulty planning independently for the future of their children. Campbell and Essex (1994) questioned 32 parents whose children with mental disabilities ranged in age between 3 and 51 years about their planning procedures. They found that few parents had made plans about their child's future. Their main reasons were that they lacked information about services in the community and that too many professionals had expressed different opinions about what they should do. Similarly, Brotherson et al. (1988) studied the individual planning processes of parents about the future of their adolescent children with disabilities. Not surprisingly, they reported that the parents' greatest planning topic was determining residential options. The frequency of planning activities correlated significantly with family functioning, indicating that better functioning families were more likely to engage in planning procedures. Lynch (1991) also asked parents about planning activities but, more specifically, about their participation in transition planning. Only 12 of the 50 parents questioned said that their child had transition plans. Unfortunately, high levels of disagreement were also found on what the child would do after high school and on what services were available for the child as an adult in the postschool years. Lynch concluded that many parents had not been involved in transition planning and that many were ill informed about this process.

Given the results of such studies, the ITP must accomplish two major goals. It must identify the skills that the student must learn before leaving school to allow her to function most effectively as an adult, and it must simultaneously identify the postschool services that must be available to the individual with severe disabilities (McDonnell & Hardman, 1985; Wehman, 1990). Additionally, the development and implementation of a successful ITP must involve all members of the transdisciplinary team and different agencies and, *most critically,* the parents must have the opportunity to participate. Besides the usual members of the team, the ITP team should include a vocational education teacher, a vocational rehabilitation counselor, a local representative of the appropriate state human services agency (such as the Department of Mental Health, Developmental Disabilities, or Mental Retardation) who will assume case management responsibilities, and representatives of private organizations such as The Arc (formerly the Association for Retarded Citizens) that may serve as vendors for supported employment or residential programs.

Functioning as a team, this group must design an ITP; then individuals on the team must assume specific roles that allow the plan to be implemented. Steps in this process have been outlined by several authors (McDonnell & Hardman, 1985; McDonnell, Wilcox, & Hardman, 1991; Wehman, 1990; Wehman, Wood, Everson, Marchant, & Walker, 1987). They can be summarized as follows:

1. Identify students needing an ITP.
2. Identify personnel who will serve on the ITP team.
3. Identify adult service agencies that will be required to provide services and make certain that each is represented on the ITP.
4. Identify the skills needed to be learned by students prior to leaving school and how these skills will provide important benefits to the individual (such as

socializing with friends, living and working in the least restrictive environment, and continuing to develop personal skills). Gather this information from parents, teachers, and therapists.

5. Schedule transition planning meetings at times when key persons can attend. These meetings should be a part of the IEP planning meeting.
6. At the meeting, discuss with the student his or her plans and desires for postschool life; ask parents about their views of their adolescent child's future; ask agency representatives to discuss services that they can provide and possible options; ask teachers and therapists to discuss specific skills that they will help the student to develop to maximize participation as an adult.
7. Based on the above, write the formal ITP including (a) the services to be provided by specific agencies before and after the student leaves school, (b) the skills to be learned, (c) the individuals responsible for carrying out specific tasks, (d) the time line for completing different steps in the task, and (e) a system for monitoring achievement of the different tasks.
8. Subsequent to writing the initial ITP, plan follow-up meetings on an annual basis to report the achievement of tasks by different agency representatives of the ITP team. Make changes in assignments if tasks have not been satisfactorily completed.
9. Schedule an exit meeting and interview the parents and the student within 6 months of the time that the student will leave the school system. At this meeting, reconfirm the roles to be played by adult service agencies and organizations in the community after the individual with severe disabilities leaves the school and enters adult life.

It is important that various services and activities do not infringe on the benefits of other services. For example, the ITP planning committee should investigate and report to the parents if the level of income to be earned by their adolescent or adult child will threaten supplemental security income (SSI) and associated medical benefits if the student is receiving them (McDonnell & Hardman, 1985). The committee should also provide parents with information about trusts and wills and the long-term care of their adult child after their death.

After the ITP has been developed, schools should begin its implementation while the student is in school. Instruction should be provided on specific vocational skills in actual vocational settings. Leisure activities should be taught and practiced. Functional domestic and community skills should be taught in the most appropriate real settings, including those outside the school. Practicing transportation skills in the community is very important. Contacts should be made with various agencies, and necessary entry forms should be submitted to them at the earliest date. If possible, adult services from agencies such as vocational rehabilitation should begin while the student is still in school. Any problems associated with implementing any aspect of the ITP should be noted and corrected. The purpose is for the student and the agencies to be fully prepared when it is time for the student to leave the school and enter the adult world. Furthermore, according to IDEA 97, students must be informed of their rights at the age of majority (21 in most states) 1 year before reaching this age.

The development of ITPs, now required by federal legislation, should do a great deal to facilitate successful adult lives for persons with severe disabilities. However, how these plans are developed and implemented may vary widely, and some plans will assuredly not be as successful as others. To better ensure success in the transition process, Wehman (1990) recommended the following:

- Plan in the context of the local community. Understand the resources available and plan with them in mind.
- Strive for meaningful input from students and their parents. Let them know what their options are, what they could be, and how they can achieve what they want.
- Establish clear agreements between agencies so that the resources of all are being shared fairly and directed toward specific outcomes.
- Place vocational rehabilitation counselors in the school settings to facilitate communication and cooperation.
- Develop good relationships with local businesses. They can provide input into what students need to learn, provide job sites, and support programs for individuals with disabilities.
- Use families, relatives, and friends of students with disabilities as sources of employment or for help in finding employment. Many follow-up studies have found that these persons play very important roles in helping to secure employment.

Individual Family Service Plans

IFSPs were first required under P.L. 99-457, Part H, as a significant element of the Handicapped Infants and Toddlers Program. More recently, the IFSP has been again required in P.L. 105-17, IDEA 97, under Part C. The law gives states discretionary authority, but does not mandate them, to serve infants and toddlers with disabilities under 3 years of age. If states implement this plan, the governor of the state must designate a lead state agency responsible for administering the early intervention program. This agency will be responsible for identifying the children and their families in need of services. In addition to conducting a multidisciplinary assessment to determine the strengths and needs of the infant or toddler, the law requires that there be a "family-directed assessment of the resources, priorities, and concerns of the family and the identification of the supports and services necessary to enhance the family's capacity to meet the developmental needs of the infant or toddler" [P.L. 105-17, Sec. 636(a)(2)]. This evaluation process is to be used by the multidisciplinary team and the parents to develop an IFSP for the family of each child served. The IFSP must include these eight components:

1. A statement of the infant's or toddler's present level of development in various areas (e.g., physical, cognitive, communication, social–emotional, etc.)
2. A statement of the family's resources, priorities, and concerns related to enhancing the infant's or toddler's development
3. A statement of the major outcomes expected to be achieved for the infant or toddler and the family; the criteria, procedures, and time lines used to determine the degree of progress toward outcomes; and whether modifications or revisions in the outcomes or services are necessary
4. The specific early intervention services necessary to meet the needs of the child and family, including the frequency, method, and intensity of delivering services
5. A statement of natural environments where the services will be provided and a justification of the extent, if any, to which the services will not be provided in a natural environment
6. The projected date for initiating services and the anticipated duration of services
7. The identification of the service coordinator from the profession most immediately relevant to the infant's, toddler's, or family's needs; this person is responsible for implementing the plan and coordinating services from participating agencies
8. The procedures for transition from the early intervention program to the preschool program

P.L. 105-17, Part C, and particularly the IFSP requirement clearly recognize the importance of the family in providing services to infants and toddlers, specifies that it is the family that will be the service recipient as opposed to the child alone, and recognizes that family representation is an essential element of the decision-making team (Krauss, 1990). *Family-oriented services* emerged in recent years from the recognition of the significance of families in the development of children, particularly very young children. It makes little sense to intervene in the life of a young child in isolation from the physical and social ecology in which the child exists. When service systems support families as well as their children and work collaboratively with them, both the child and the family benefit (Turnbull & Turnbull, 1990).

Family-oriented services imply that an agency providing services exhibits certain characteristics (Murphy, Lee, Turnbull, & Turbiville, 1995). An agency offering family-oriented services recognizes that the family is a constant in the child's life and that agencies and their personnel will fluctuate. It attempts to protect the family's integrity and strengthen its functioning. Facilitating parent and professional collaboration at all levels is critical, as is sharing unbiased and complete information with parents on an ongoing basis. Being family oriented also means recognizing families' strengths and individualities, respecting parents' methods of coping with their needs, and respecting their rights to choose their level of participation and decision making and the service delivery method.

One of the most significant features of the law requires that a case manager or service coordinator be provided for each family and that this person be named in the IFSP. Often the difficulties that families face can be multiplied by the need to interact with many different agencies and professionals. Undoubtedly, this is an especially critical issue with a very young baby or toddler and at a time in their lives when parents are most likely to be unfamiliar with different agencies and services. Therefore, to reduce the need for parents to organize and manage all the services, the law requires that a designated service coordinator carry out these functions.

Because this individual will have the most direct contact with the parents and child, her ability to work collaboratively is critical. Dinnebeil and Rule (1994) conducted a study of experts, service coordinators, and parents to determine the critical characteristics of service coordinators that would enhance or detract from collaboration with parents. Their findings were as follows:

Positive Collaborative Characteristics

- Respects family's attributes
- Emphasizes family strengths
- Shows patience
- Encourages and supports
- Is an open communicator and good listener
- Builds rapport
- Has a high level of self-confidence
- Is tactful and honest
- Is a good team builder
- Is well-informed, provides information
- Is prompt in follow-up

Negative Collaborative Characteristics

- Doesn't use family-centered approach
- Emphasizes family weaknesses
- Is rushed at meetings
- Tries to remove the problem
- Has paternalistic attitude
- Displays emotional detachment
- Lacks self-confidence
- Uses protective dishonesty
- Prescribes to families
- Is judgmental
- Is cold, rude

In addition to these considerations about the approach of the service coordinator, the very practice of focusing on the family, despite its merits, has some potential pitfalls (Beckman & Bristol, 1991; Krauss, 1990). The IFSP requirement for assessment and possible intervention within the family is potentially troublesome because of its intrusiveness. We might question why we should determine a family's resources, priorities, and concerns. To what extent should professionals evaluate a family because one of its members has a disability? Also, what types of intervention are appropriate for a family and when and how should they be provided? Beckman and Bristol (1991) discussed the need for sensitivity, particularly with regard to family and cultural diversity.

Many infants with disabilities are born to families outside the majority population, yet most of the professionals who respond to their needs are of the majority culture. As discussed in Chapter 4, the challenge for professionals is that they must understand and accept some practices that are different from their own. The service provider must acquire a sensitivity that will allow her to work effectively with a minority family without judging the family by her own cultural standards. Consideration of the family's cultural influences is, if anything, perhaps more important when the child is very young and the family is initially experiencing the child's disability. Parents' and family members' interpretation of the condition and their reaction to it will vary among families, and this variation may be affected by cultural ideas and ideologies. Working to develop a document as personal and sensitive as an IFSP requires deft professional skills. Understanding manners appropriate for particular cultures, interacting with the families less formally in preconference meetings, allowing the parents to decide when and where the conference should be held, and allowing them to invite family, friends, or support persons to attend the conference with them can be helpful (Hyun & Fowler, 1995). The family outcomes and intervention procedures written into the IFSP must take into consideration the family's cultural background and give special consideration to who the primary caregiver is, who the decision maker is, and the family's beliefs about disabilities. Most importantly, the written outcomes must be valued by the family (Hyun & Fowler, 1995).

When early interventionists collaborate with families to identify their priorities and concerns, regardless of the family's cultural values, they must avoid treating the family as if it has a disability. Some professionals have suggested that formal family assessments should be bypassed in favor of having informal discussions with family members to determine if specific needs can be met to support the family in its efforts to support the child (Slentz & Bricker, 1992; Winton & Bailey, 1988, 1990). This approach is intended to reduce a perception that the family must be treated. As Krauss (1990) noted, "Families may chafe at the realization that because their child has Down syndrome or was born with a low birthweight, they, too, must be evaluated if their child is to receive services" (p. 390).

Finally, professionals need to choose carefully the types of family outcomes that they specify on the IFSP. In some instances, more goals are to be carried out by family members than by the professionals. It must be recognized that families vary greatly in the amount of extraordinary effort that they can make because their child has a severe disability. More appropriate than stating several responsibilities that parents or families must achieve may be stating as goals on the IFSP what parents may expect from professionals (Beckman & Bristol, 1991).

Concerns about Plans and Alternative Approaches to Planning

Federal law requiring formal plans should be understood for what they are intended to accomplish. Instead of treating an individual based on a disability classification, these plans direct professionals to examine individual needs and to develop intervention goals and objectives accordingly. Unfortunately, some professionals view these plans as laborious and bureaucratic. Instead of viewing them as opportunities for thinking carefully about what would be of benefit to specific students, they have sought ways to reduce the time that they must invest in them (Smith, 1990).

Why is this? There may be several reasons. One is simply that teachers would rather spend their time with students than with paper, and this is understandable. Most professional educators enjoy working with children or adolescents, and many have specifically entered this field because they dislike meetings and paperwork. Additionally, teachers may not see the need for plans. It may be difficult to make progress without knowing where you are heading, but many teachers feel that they know their students well enough and do not need to put on paper the goals and objectives for each individual student. Finally, it could be hypothesized that writing IEPs is not an activity that has been highly valued by many school systems. A federal law requiring such plans does not necessarily result in school districts liking them. What may be more true is that schools consider the task necessary for compliance with federal law. This will bear on the teachers' attitudes toward writing IEPs.

If planning is truly to be of value, there must be a greater commitment to it, not only by teachers, but also by other professionals, parents, and administrators. To arrive at this commitment, it is necessary to ask some critical questions about the planning process itself and to consider ways in which it could be improved. Some important questions and proposed answers are presented next.

Who owns the plan? Does it belong to the school system or other service agency (or agencies)? The parents? The person with the severe disability? It can be argued that the parents, the family, and the student with severe disabilities are the rightful owners of the individual plan that is developed. It is theirs because their lives are the ones that it is intended to affect. The service agency should be viewed as assisting families to the degree necessary to write the plan, but the plan should be seen as belonging to the individual and the family. Ownership is an important factor, and this should be understood by those who participate in the process. If families of individuals with severe disabilities and the individuals themselves accept that it is their plan, they will be more likely to address its development with deliberation. Also, if professionals understand that the plan is owned by the service consumer, they may give it more respect and appreciate their own role in assisting in its development.

What is an appropriate time frame for planning? One year? Three years? The school years? A lifetime? Currently, IEPs must be written for 1 year at a time. This is certainly better than week-to-week planning, but it should be realized that the 1-year requirement is somewhat arbitrary. It is simply tied into the traditional school year calendar. It may be more beneficial to parents and their children to project for a longer period of time, to think farther into the future. This is clearly the intention of the transition plan, yet this longer-term planning does not begin until the student is into his adolescent years. Many parents of children with severe disabilities approach life one day at a time because they feel that is about all they can handle. Certainly, each family must approach life in a way that it can best manage. However, many parents would like to know what the future holds and how they and their child with a severe disability can be best prepared for it. Although no one can say precisely what time frame should be used in planning, it is suggested that in many cases it should be beyond 1 year.

Who should be involved in the planning? Who knows the most about the individual and has the "natural" responsibility for her? The law already states who is *required* to be a part of the planning team, but there may be other significant persons in the life of the child with disabilities who should also be included. Siblings, grandparents, neighbors, friends, ministers, and others who have a personal relationship with the individual and who care about what happens in her life could make an important contribution to developing individual plans.

What should affect the content of the plan? Existing programs and services, or those that are possible? Agency philosophy or family, culture, and personal values? Particular goals and objectives and, more broadly, the student's lifestyle can be affected by the circumstances surrounding the learning process. For example, many might agree that a particular student needs to learn age-appropriate recreational activities. In one situation, however, the student may be bound to learn activities in the context of a special school with only other students with disabilities. In another school district, the student may have the opportunity to learn the skills with nondisabled peers in community recreational facilities.The plan that is developed, the one owned by the individual with severe disabilities and his family, should not be encumbered by current limitations in agencies' programs, practices, or philosophy. Certainly, it may take time for service providers to make changes but, even so, this should not inhibit persons from making plans that suit their needs and desires for a quality life. This would be contrary to some of society's most cherished principles, particularly those that deal with the rights of persons to pursue happiness and lead productive lives. Instead, it is proposed that the plans developed should influence what is available to the individual with disabilities, instead of vice versa.

Person-Centered Plans

Given these views, it is important to consider alternative approaches to planning. These are viewed as alternatives not because they are intended to replace current planning requirements, but because they can add significantly to the quality of planning. These plans are referred to as *person-centered plans.* Three person-centered planning processes are discussed in the remainder of this chapter.

Personal Futures Planning

Personal futures planning, developed by Mount and Zwernik (1988), is a radical departure from traditional planning approaches. It was developed based on the work of O'Brien and Lyle (1987) and is intended to provide a positive approach for planning life activities for persons of various ages who have disabilities. Its primary goal is to help groups of people who are personally close to the person with disabilities to plan ways in which this individual can "develop personal relationships, have positive roles in community life, increase their control of their own lives, and develop the skills and abilities to achieve these goals" (Mount & Zwernik, 1988, p. 1). The plan is intended to be dynamic, changing as changes occur in the individual's lifestyle. A critical aspect of personal futures planning is that it does not focus on a person's deficits (what she cannot do), but rather on the individual's gifts, talents, skills, and opportunities. The plan is also person centered in that it continually focuses on the individual (referred to as the *focus person*) for whom the future plan is being developed. In this way, the plan is not limited by current services, but by what would be necessary to allow the individual to participate fully in society.

The personal futures planning system recognizes three basic problems associated with traditional planning: It begins with an assessment that highlights the person's deficits, it establishes goals that are part of the existing service system, and it relies primarily on professional judgment and decision making. In contrast, the futures planning system offers an interactive style that involves people who are closest to the focus person and emphasizes the planning process more than the product. It has five important characteristics (Mount & Zwernik, 1988):

1. It describes capacities and opportunities in people and environments.
2. It seeks ideals.
3. It involves people who interact on a daily basis with the person with a severe disability.
4. It encourages experimentation with new courses of action.
5. It prompts people to act and to accept commitments to be involved in improving the quality of life for the person with the disability.

The three steps that comprise the personal futures planning process are (1) developing a personal profile of the focus individual, (2) developing a plan for the person, and (3) forming a network of support, with the people in it making a commitment to support the individual in various ways to ensure the success of the plan. Each component is explained briefly next.

In the first step of the process, the person with the disability and a few people who know and care about him come together for an interactive interview conducted by a facilitator to develop the *personal profile.* The facilitator is the person who will direct the group to address the key issues contained in the personal profile. At this meeting, the group is directed to discuss key information about the individual and his capacities upon which a plan can be built. First, basic information is gathered. This is not about results of formal assessments, but about the person's background, positive and negative experiences, major moves, critical events, current situation, family issues, general health concerns, and relationships in the community. Second, information is gathered about the focus person's quality of life, including accomplishments, routines, and lifestyle patterns. Considered in this part of the personal profile are such areas as community participation and relationships with others, choices and rights, respect for the person by others, and the skills that the person has that allow others to view him in a positive manner.

In developing the final section of the personal profile, the third type of information gathered is a list of what the individual enjoys and prefers and what is not enjoyable to him. The main questions to be addressed are these: What images does this person have for the future? What unrecognized dreams and hopes does this person have? What does this person want in life?

During the discussion, the facilitator uses colored pens to sketch the personal profile of the individual on large pieces of paper. Vivid symbols and words make the profile come alive. This description is then used as a basis for the futures planning. Similar sketches are developed showing relationships, places visited, choices, preferences, and so forth.

Following the meeting to develop the personal profile, another meeting is arranged to write the *personal future plan* for the individual. In addition to those who were present for sketching the personal profile, key people in the focus person's life should be in attendance. These should include family, friends, professionals, and others with whom the target person spends a great deal of time. Once again, the facilitator directs the meeting. If the person with the disability can communicate, he should be at the meeting as well. Mount and Zwernik also recommend that an advocate for the individual be present. The process for developing the future plan consists of seven steps:

1. *Reviewing the personal profile.* The first step is for the group to look at the profile that has been developed and add other relevant information that has not been considered.
2. *Reviewing trends in the environment.* This consists of thinking about anything that may occur in the near future that might have a bearing on the individual (e.g., graduation from high school).
3. *Finding desirable images of the future.* This is the key element of the plan; persons at the meeting present their ideas about the future. During this brainstorming session, participants are asked to imagine ways for the person to have more positive experiences than were identified in the personal profile. Ideas are clustered by the facilitator into major areas such as home, work, school, community activities, relationships, and so forth.
4. *Identifying obstacles and opportunities.* The clusters in step 3 are ranked by the group in terms of their importance; then obstacles and opportunities are identified, beginning with the first area and continuing to each subsequent area. The group discusses ways to overcome obstacles, turning them into opportunities.
5. *Identifying strategies.* These strategies are the concrete *action steps* to be taken to implement the visions created in step 3. At this step, each member of the planning group must make a commitment to assist with particular efforts.
6. *Getting started.* Mount and Zwernik recommend identifying five specific strategies that can be implemented right away. It is important to accomplish some parts of the plan immediately, even though they may be only small steps. Once these activities have been identified, a time for the next meeting should be agreed on.
7. *Identifying the need for system change.* Sometimes existing systems (public schools, agencies) do not include structures or conditions that support a person's future plan. In this case, a commitment must be made to change the system or work around the existing obstacle. Regardless, it is important that system barriers be recognized.

The final component of personal futures planning is *building a network of support persons* who will meet regularly to plan and implement strategies and tactics to improve the quality of life of the focus person. This group is referred to as a *circle of support.* It includes family members, friends, neighbors, and others who are close to the person with disabilities.

Mount and Zwernik outlined several elements that they felt resulted in a strong support network. These included focusing on the individual and her dreams, instead of directing the person toward something that the support network wants; starting small and avoiding taking on too much at one time; and including at least one person in the support group who has good ties to the community and can serve as a bridge for the focus person to move outward toward more community involvement. The circle of support is an essential element for making the future plan work for the individual with disabilities. As long as there is personal support, changes will occur, even though they may be gradual.

McGill Action Planning System

The McGill action planning system (MAPS) (Forest & Lusthaus, 1987; Vandercook, York, & Forest, 1989) is another comprehensive planning process that clearly goes beyond what is required by law for individual plans. In many ways it is similar to the personal futures planning system. The primary difference is that the personal futures system may be more appropriate for adults, whereas MAPS focuses specifically on providing information for developing IEPs for school-age individuals.

MAPS targets full inclusion and participation in the regular classroom and other mainstream educational settings. Its primary purpose is to foster relationships for improving the quality of life of the individual with severe disabilities, as well as his social skills and cognitive development. It calls for the involvement of a team that includes the individual with disabilities, family members, friends without disabilities, and general and special education personnel. During the planning sessions, all these individuals gather in one setting to discuss the educational and life needs of the individual with severe disabilities. An important feature of MAPS is the inclusion of the targeted individual's chronological-age peers on the planning team. Because of this, the MAPS process is usually not undertaken unless there has been an opportunity for the student with disabilities to have had integrated experiences long enough to begin developing relationships.

As with the previously described system, a facilitator coordinates the planning session(s) by asking questions, encouraging open discussion, and writing down the key thoughts of those participating. According to Vandercook et al. (1989), this person must be "committed to building an integrated school community in which the individual is valued and provided the support necessary to be a member of the class with same age peers" (p. 207). The facilitator should be a good listener and one who can encourage interaction among those participating in the process. She is responsible for prodding group members to broaden their view of the community and also getting them to offer creative ideas that will allow the individual with disabilities to be a successful participant in integrated settings. Most important, the facilitator must be able to convince all those involved in the MAPS process that their contribution is critical.

Although the process is flexible, seven questions serve to guide the discussion. These questions, presented one at a time by the facilitator, are as follows:

1. What is the individual's history?
2. What is your dream for the individual?
3. What is your nightmare?
4. Who is the individual?
5. What are the individual's strengths, gifts, and abilities?
6. What are the individual's needs?
7. What would the individual's ideal day at school look like and what must be done to make it happen?

After each question is asked, those present are asked to respond, and their responses are recorded by the facilitator. There are no rules as to what types of responses should occur. In fact, participants are encouraged to be creative, especially in discussing the individual's potential and future and ways to foster inclusion.

The MAPS procedures usually require about 3 hours, and sometimes more than one session is needed. This can be contrasted with more typical IEP sessions, which may be over in less than 30 minutes. However, as can be easily understood, the depth of the planning using MAPS is much greater. Table 5–2 demonstrates the priority needs of a student as identified by family, friends, and educators using MAPS, and Table 5–3 displays a modified schedule for the student as she "moves toward an ideal school day."

Choosing Options and Accommodations for Children

COACH (choosing options and accommodations for children) is a system developed for assessment and planning that begins with the identification of priority learning outcomes by family members and the student with disabilities, converts these desired outcomes into IEP goals and objectives, and then devises educational supports that will allow the student to achieve these objectives in inclusive educational environments (Giangreco, Cloninger, & Iverson, 1998). The COACH system is based on six principles:

1. Pursuing valued life outcomes is an important aspect of education.
2. The family is the cornerstone of relevant and longitudinal planning.
3. Collaborative teamwork is essential to quality education.
4. Coordination among support service providers is essential to appropriate education.
5. Using problem-solving methods improves the effectiveness of the educational plan.
6. Special education is a service, not a place.

COACH allows for the development of goals that are considered to be *cross-environmental* (communication, socialization, personal management, leisure–recreation, and applied academics) and those that are *environment-*

Table 5–2 Catherine's Priority Needs Identified by Family, Friends, and Educators

Family	*Friends*	*Educators*
For others to know she is not helpless Music and time to listen to it Affection To be with people To change environments and surroundings often Healthy foods	More friends Support to get more places and learn things there A lot of opportunity to walk and use her hands As an adult, to live in a small home with friends in a community where she is accepted Teachers to accept her To learn to hang onto the book when a friend is reading with her	More friends Support to get more places and learn things there A lot of opportunity to walk and use her hands Opportunity to let people know what she wants and a way to communicate that with more people To increase the opportunity and skill to make more choices Affection People to know how to: deal with her seizures, help her stand up, and accept and deal with her drooling

Source: "The McGill Action Planning System (MAPS): A Strategy for Building the Vision" by T. Vandercook, J. York, & M. Forest, 1989, *Journal of the Association for Persons with Severe Handicaps, 14*(3), 205–215. Copyright 1989 by The Association for Persons with Severe Handicaps. Reprinted by permission of TASH, Baltimore, MD.

Table 5–3 Tuesday Morning Schedule for Catherine: Moving Toward the Ideal School Day

Time	*Catherine's Day (current)*	*3rd Grade Day (current)*	*Possibilities for Change (proposed)*
9:00–9:30	Take off coat Use restroom Adaptive P.E.	Pledge of Allegiance Seat work directions Spelling	Breakfast (could eat with nondisabled peers if school arrival coincided)
9:30–10:00	Breakfast Work on lip closure, holding the spoon, choosing objects she wants	Reading Group I Others do seat work, write stories, read silently	Switch center (in 3rd grade reading) Transition to center, reaching, touching picture, activating tape player
10:00–10:45	Switch center Transition to center, reaching, touching picture, activating tape player using microswitch (leisure activity)	Physical education (10:00–10:20) Mousercize, Exercise Express, use restroom Reading Group II (10:25–10:45)	Physical education (with 3rd grade) Skills related to maintaining ambulation and mobility (weight shifting, balance reactions, strength exercise) Cooperation with peer partner Rest time
10:45–11:10	Reading Group III (with 3rd grade) Makes transition to floor, responds to greeting from peer, reaches for peer's hand, holds onto book, looks at book, closes book, makes transition to standing	Reading Group III	Maintain current activity with 3rd grade
11:10–11:30	Library (with 3rd grade) Return book, choose book, look at it, check it out, return to class	Library	Maintain current activity with 3rd grade

Source: "The McGill Action Planning System (MAPS): A Strategy for Building the Vision" by T. Vandercook, J. York, & M. Forest, 1989, *Journal of the Association for Persons with Severe Handicaps, 14*(3), pp. 205–215. Copyright 1989 by The Association for Persons with Severe Handicaps. Reprinted by permission.

specific (for participating in activities in home, school, community, and vocational settings). The COACH system is divided into two parts: (A) determining a student's educational program (steps 1 to 6) and (B) strategies and processes to implement a COACH-generated educational program (steps 7 to 10). These 10 major components of COACH are presented in Figure 5–3. The most critical are the first three.

Figure 5–3 Major Components of COACH

Part A: Determining a Student's Educational Program

Step 1: Family Interview
Purpose: to determine family-selected learning priorities for the student through a series of questions asked by an interviewer

Step 2: Additional Learning Outcomes
Purpose: to determine learning outcomes beyond family priorities

Step 3: General Supports
Purpose: to determine what supports need to be provided to *or for* the student

Step 4: Annual Goals
Purpose: to ensure the family's priorities are reflected as IEP goals

Step 5: Program at a Glance
Purpose: to provide a concise summary of the educational program

Determine Least Restrictive Educational Placement and Related Services

Step 6: Short-Term Objectives
Purpose: to develop short-term objectives to achieve annual goals

Finalize IEP Document

Part B: Strategies and Processes to Implement a COACH-Generated Educational Program

Step 7: Organizing and Informing the Instructional Planning Team
Purpose: to organize team functioning and ensure IEP implementation

Step 8: Scheduling for the Student with Disabilities in the Classroom
Purpose: to develop a schedule of activities that meets student needs

Step 9: Planning and Adapting Instruction
Purpose: to develop and implement instructional plans that address student needs and participation in class activities even when IEP goals differ from those of classmates'

Step 10: Evaluating the Impact of Educational Experiences
Purpose: to evaluate educational plans to determine their impact on learning outcomes and valued life outcomes

Source: Choosing Options and Accommodations for Children: A Guide to Planning Inclusive Education (2nd Ed.), by M. F.Giangreco, C. J. Cloninger, and V. S. Iverson, 1998. Baltimore: Paul H. Brookes (p. 45). Reprinted with permission.

The first step of the COACH planning process, the *family interview*, uses a structured interview with family members to identify valued life outcomes, that is, outcomes that are considered by family members to be most critical. These outcomes can then be converted to IEP goals. During the family interview, family members are asked questions and presented with options to help them to determine what they consider to be priority goals for the student.

In the next step, *additional learning outcomes* are considered by the collaborative planning team consisting of professionals. Some of these may be other learning outcomes that were targeted during the family interview but not identified to be IEP goals. This process is included so that professionals have an opportunity to consider goals in addition to those that were considered by family members, so that some items "do not accidentally fall through the cracks" (p. 97). Another part of step 2 is to consider aspects of the general curriculum that would be appropriate for the student to participate in. In doing this, the team considers how the curriculum might be adapted or modified.

In step 3, necessary *general supports* for the student are considered. General supports identify what other people need to do to help the student achieve identified goals. General supports are those that are required across all areas of learning. Giangreco et al. (1998) characterize the general supports in an important way. Whereas the family-identified goals and additional learning goals represent desired changes in the student's ability or behavior, the general supports section of the plan states the type of behavior or behavior change that those in the student's environments must demonstrate in order for the student to be successful. Five areas of support are included with the general support section:

1. Addressing personal needs: feeding, dressing, giving medication, helping with personal hygiene needs, and so forth.
2. Addressing physical needs: positioning and handling the student, helping the student move from place to place, managing special equipment such as braces or wheelchairs.
3. Addressing sensory needs: accommodations that are necessary if the student has visual or hearing impairments, such as adjusting distance, location, lighting, and so forth.
4. Teaching others about the student, including other faculty, staff, and students.
5. Providing access and opportunities to a variety of integrated locations inside and outside the school.

After developing all the components of the plan, the team identifies the most inclusive educational setting in which the student can be served, with the first preference being the regular classroom. The team also decides what types of related services will be necessary and how these should be delivered. Subteams may be used to develop short-term objectives, support plans, and lesson adaptations.

Like the other alternative planning approaches, COACH is family and student centered. The authors warn that the process should not be undertaken unless the team is "willing to accept and use the priorities of the family." They also suggest that the COACH system interview be limited to family members and the individual with disabilities. The authors propose that the presence of too many people at the family interview can interfere with the participation of the parents. The team member who conducts the interview reports the priorities to other team members.

COACH is a well-designed, structured package for assessing students' needs and planning a comprehensive educational program. Professionals are guided through a process that begins with parent input and ends in an educational program to be carried out in inclusive environments. It is most helpful for developing IEPs and ITPs.

The Value of Person-Centered Planning

Although somewhat limited, research tends to be supportive of the process of person-centered planning. Research on COACH has demonstrated that professionals and parents believe it is congruent with many best practices for teaching students with severe disabilities (Giangreco, Cloninger, Dennis, & Edelman, 1993). Additionally, when used as intended, professionals and parents report that COACH leads to the identification of valued life outcomes and goals for achieving them, includes parents and professionals as equal partners in the planning process, and makes educational programs for students in inclusive settings more relevant to their needs (Giangreco, Edelman, Dennis, & Cloninger, 1995).

Miner and Bates (1997) studied the effects of participating in an adapted version of personal futures planning. They evaluated the extent to which parents and students participated in subsequent IEP conferences after they had been involved in the person-centered planning process. They found that parents who had participated with their son or daughter in the personal futures planning activities spoke more at the IEP conferences than those who did not and also more often indicated that the IEP conference processes and outcomes were "more favorable" than previous conferences.

Using a focus group approach, Everson and Zhang (2000) interviewed 10 persons who had participated in five different person-centered planning groups (i.e., two members from each group). Participants in the interview had all completed training in person-centered planning in the previous year, and Everson and Zhang had followed up to learn about their subsequent experiences in using the planning procedure. They found that shortly following the training session each person began her involvement in person-centered planning activities and that as the planning groups continued to meet they became stronger, the number of participants increased or stabilized, and they became more successful.

However, Everson and Zhang identified several challenges associated with the person-centered planning process. For example, in many cases, initially, the focus person was unable or unwilling to express what was needed or wanted, which led other members to make best guesses on behalf of this individual. Sometimes this condition improved and the focus person began to more clearly state personal preferences, sometimes correcting the ideas about himself or herself that had been provided by other members of the group. Sometimes this meant that the group had to restart the process, which was considered to be "okay" by most participants.

In some cases, those interviewed identified the focus person, or the individual's behavior, as presenting problems during the planning sessions. Sometimes inappropriate behavior was said to interfere with the participation, such as touching and hugging others who were present. Other times the focus person's lack of communication skills was seen as a boundary. There were also problems sometimes associated with different points of view expressed by members of the planning groups. Sometimes relatives did not agree with each other about their vision of the person's future, some being overly optimistic, others being very pessimistic. Other problems were of a logistical nature. Scheduling meeting times was problematic for all the groups, and many group members found it difficult to maintain a continuing commitment to participate in the process.

Even with such difficulties, however, those who were interviewed felt as though the process was beneficial to the focus person. They especially felt that the process led to increased participation in community and social activities. Another positive aspect considered by most was the opportunity for the focus person to be involved in his or her own planning activities. The process led to more respect for the individual and a greater effort to understand his or her dreams. All felt that the process brought positive changes into the life of the person and expressed a strong intent to continue it into the future.

Finally, it should be noted that, although person-centered plans can provide a helpful basis for future directions, participants may not always be able to accurately identify preferred and nonpreferred items and activities. Reid, Everson, and Green (1999) took leisure items and activities identified through a person-centered planning process for four individuals with profound multiple disabilities and, using a preference assessment system (see Chapter 7 for a description of this process), observed whether they were actually preferred by the individuals. They found that of 24 items identified in the person-centered planning process as being preferred (which represented only 35% of all preferences identified in the plans), during the actual preference assessment, only eight (33%) were found to be "highly preferred" (they were approached at least 80% of the time over several sessions), and ten (42%) were found to be "moderately preferred." The finding implies that direct observation in a preference assessment procedure may be necessary to validate the items and activities that are identified as being preferred in a person-centered planning process.

Conclusion

Individuals who experience severe disabilities will be the subject of considerable planning efforts. By law, during their lifetime as recipients of human services, these individuals will have individual family service plans, individual educational plans, individual transition plans, and perhaps other plans written on their behalf. If these are written with appropriate collaboration and deliberation, they will serve a critical role in helping agencies to identify and carry out services. Unfortunately, as Smith (1990) pointed out, too often this is not the case. Too often plans are developed solely to comply with the requirements of federal laws.

This condition is, of course, not satisfactory. To improve it, person-centered planning approaches have been developed that are intended to lead to more meaningful outcomes. You are encouraged to explore these planning systems in more depth to understand fully what they offer and how they can be implemented. Even though they have been recognized to have some limitations when investigated through different research procedures, it is suggested that they can have an important role in increasing the meaningfulness of the plans required by law.

Questions for Reflection

1. Why do you believe (or not believe) that formal educational planning for individual students with severe disabilities is necessary?
2. Is it possible for teachers to do a good job teaching without developing individual plans? Without specifying goals and objectives?
3. What do you believe is the most important part of any educational plan?
4. What requirements of the IEP would you like to see changed? Would you add any? Remove any? Why?
5. Do you think it is necessary that a general educator be included as part of the planning team for the IEP?

6. Why specifically require a transition plan within the IEP when the student reaches adolescence?
7. Why is it important to have IFSPs for providing services to infants and toddlers with disabilities?
8. If you had a young child with a disability, what would be your reaction to having professionals inquire about your family's condition?
9. What type of alternative planning system would you like to see developed or what type would you like to develop?
10. Do you think we can eliminate formal plans and just use the alternative planning approaches?

References

Beckman, P. J., & Bristol, M. M. (1991). Issues in developing the IFSP: A framework for establishing family outcomes. *Topics in Early Childhood Special Education, 11*(3), 19–31.

Black, M. M., Molaison, V. A., & Smull, M. W. (1990). Families caring for a young adult with mental retardation: Service needs and urgency of community living requests. *American Journal on Mental Retardation, 95,* 32–39.

Brinker, R. P. (1985). Interactions between severely mentally retarded students and other students in integrated and segregated public school settings. *American Journal of Mental Deficiency, 89,* 587–594.

Brotherson, M. J., Turnbull, A. P., Bronicki, G. J., Houghton, J., Roeder-Gordon, C., Summers, J. A., & Turnbull, H. R. (1988). Transition into adulthood: Parental planning for sons and daughters with disabilities. *Education and Training in Mental Retardation, 23,* 165–174.

Brown, L., Long, E., Udvari-Solner, A., Davis, L., VanDeventer, P., Ahlgren, C., Johnson, F., Gruenewald, L., & Jorgensen, J. (1989). The home school: Why students with severe intellectual disabilities must attend the schools of their brothers, sisters, friends, and neighbors. *Journal of the Association for Persons with Severe Handicaps, 14,* 1–7.

Brown, L., Schwarz, P., Udvari-Solner, A., Kampschroer, E. F., Johnson, F., Jorgensen, J., & Gruenewald, L. (1991). How much time should students with severe intellectual disabilities spend in regular education classrooms and elsewhere? *Journal of the Association for Persons with Severe Handicaps, 16,* 39–47.

Campbell, J. A., & Essex, E. L. (1994). Factors affecting parents in their future planning for a son or daughter with developmental disabilities. *Education and Training in Mental Retardation and Developmental Disabilities, 29,* 222–228.

Campbell, P. H. (1987). The integrated programming team: An approach for coordinating professionals of various disciplines in programs for students with severe and multiple handicaps. *Journal of the Association for Persons with Severe Handicaps, 12,* 107–116.

Dennis, R. E., Williams, W., Giangreco, M. F., & Cloninger, C. J. (1993). Quality of life as context for planning and evaluation of services for people with disabilities. *Exceptional Children, 59,* 499–512.

Dinnebeil, L. A., & Rule, S. (1994). Variables that influence collaboration between parents and service coordinators. *Journal of Early Intervention, 18,* 349–361.

Epps, S., & Myers, C. L. (1989). Priority domains for instruction, satisfaction with school teaching, and post-school living and employment: An analysis of perceptions of parents of students with severe and profound disabilities. *Education and Training in Mental Retardation, 24,* 157–167.

Evans, I. M., Salisbury, C. L., Palombaro, M. M., Berryman, J., & Hollowood, T. M. (1992). Peer interactions and social acceptance of elementary-age children with severe disabilities in an inclusive school. *Journal of the Association for Persons with Severe Handicaps, 17,* 205–212.

Everson, J. M., & Zhang, D. (2000). Person-centered planning: Characteristics, inhibitors, and supports. *Education and Training in Mental Retardation and Developmental Disabilities, 35,* 36–43.

Forest, M., & Lusthaus, E. (1987). The Kaleidoscope: Challenge to the cascade. In M. Forest (Ed.), *More education/integration* (pp. 1–16). Downsview, Ontario: G. Allen Roeher Institute.

Giangreco, M. F., Cloninger, C. J., Dennis, R. E., & Edelman, S. W. (1993). National expert validation of COACH: Congruence with exemplary practice and suggestions for improvement. *Journal of the Association for Persons with Severe Handicaps, 18,* 109–120.

Giangreco, M. F., Cloninger, C. J., & Iverson, V. S. (1998). *Choosing options and accommodations for children: A guide to planning inclusive education* (2nd ed.). Baltimore: Paul H. Brookes.

Giangreco, M. F., Edelman, S. W., Dennis, R. E., & Cloninger, C. J. (1995). Use and impact of COACH with students who are deaf–blind. *Journal of the Association for Persons with Severe Handicaps, 20,* 121–135.

Gilliam, J. E., & Coleman, M. C. (1981). Who influences IEP decisions? *Exceptional Children, 47,* 642–644.

Goldstein, S. (1993). The IEP conference: Little things mean a lot. *Teaching Exceptional Children, 26,* 60–61.

Goldstein, S., & Turnbull, A. P. (1982). Strategies to increase parent participation in IEP conferences. *Exceptional Children, 48,* 360–361.

Halpern, A. S. (1993). Quality of life as a conceptual framework for evaluating transition outcomes. *Exceptional Children, 59,* 486–498.

Hanline, M. F., & Halvorsen, A. (1989). Parent perceptions of the integration transition process: Overcoming artificial barriers. *Exceptional Children, 55,* 487–492.

Hendrickson, J. M., Shokoohi-Yekta, M., Hamre-Nietupski, S., & Gable, R. (1996). Middle and high school students perceptions on being friends with peers with severe disabilities. *Exceptional Children, 63,* 19–28.

Hunt, P., Farron-Davis, F., Beckstead, S., Curtis, D., & Goetz, L. (1994). Evaluating the effects of placements of students with severe disabilities in general education versus special classes. *Journal of the Association for Persons with Severe Handicaps, 19,* 200–214.

Hyun, J. K., & Fowler, S. A. (1995). Respect, cultural sensitivity, and communication: Promoting participation by Asian families in the individualized family service plan. *Teaching Exceptional Children, 28* (1), 25–28.

Krauss, M. W. (1990). New precedent in family policy: Individualized family service plan. *Exceptional Children, 56,* 388–395.

Lehr, D. H. (1989). Educational programming for children with the most severe disabilities. In F. Brown & D. H. Lehr (Eds.), *Persons with profound disabilities: Issues and practices.* Baltimore: Paul H. Brookes.

Lynch, P. S. (1991). *Parents' perceptions of their involvement in planning the transition from school to work for their children with disabilities.* Paper presented at the 1991 Southeastern Educational Research Association Annual Meeting, San Antonio, TX. (ERIC Documentation Service No. ED 332 020.)

McDonnell, J. (1987). The integration of students with severe handicaps into regular public schools: An analysis of parents' perceptions of potential outcomes. *Education and Training in Mental Retardation, 22,* 98–111.

McDonnell, J., & Hardman, M. (1985). Planning the transition of severely handicapped youth from school to adult services: A framework for high school programs. *Education and Training of the Mentally Retarded, 20,* 275–286.

McDonnell, J., Wilcox, B., & Hardman, M. L. (1991). *Secondary programs for students with developmental disabilities.* Boston: Allyn and Bacon.

Miner, C. A., & Bates, P. E. (1997). The effect of person centered planning activities on the IEP/transition planning process. *Education and Training in Mental Retardation and Developmental Disabilities, 32,* 105–112.

Mount, B., & Zwernik, K. (1988). *It's never too early, it's never too late.* (A booklet about personal futures planning.) St. Paul, MN: Metropolitan Council.

Murphy, D. L., Lee, I. M., Turnbull, A. P., & Turbiville, V. (1995). The family-centered program rating scale: An instrument for program evaluation and change. *Journal of Early Intervention, 19,* 24–42.

Notari-Syverson, A. R., & Shuster, S. L. (1995). Putting real life skills into IEP/IFSPs for infants and young children. *Teaching Exceptional Children, 27*(2), 29–32.

O'Brien, J., & Lyle, C. (1987). *Framework for accomplishment.* Decatur, GA: Responsive Systems Associates.

Peck, C. A., Donaldson, J., & Pezzoli, M. (1990). Some benefits nonhandicapped adolescents perceive for themselves from their social relationships with peers who have severe handicaps. *Journal of the Association for Persons with Severe Handicaps, 15,* 241–249.

P.L. 105-17. *The Individuals with Disabilities Education Act Amendments of 1997.*

Reid, D. H., Everson, J. M., & Green, C. W. (1999). A systematic evaluation of preferences identified through person-centered planning for people with profound multiple disabilities. *Journal of Applied Behavior Analysis, 32,* 467–477.

Schalock, R. L. (Ed.). (1990a). *Quality of life: Perspectives and issues.* Washington, DC: American Association on Mental Retardation.

Schalock, R. L. (1990b). Attempts to conceptualize and measure quality of life. In R. L. Schalock (Ed.), *Quality of life: Perspectives and issues* (pp. 141–148). Washington, DC: American Association on Mental Retardation.

Schalock, R. L. (1994). Quality of life, quality enhancement, and quality assurance: Implications for program planning and evaluation in the field of mental retardation and developmental disabilities. *Evaluation and Program Planning, 17,* 121–131.

Sharpe, M. N., York, J. L., & Knight, J. (1994). Effects of inclusion on the academic performance of students without disabilities: A preliminary study. *Remedial and Special Education, 15,* 281–287.

Sherman, B. R. (1988). Predictors of the decision to place developmentally disabled family members in residential care. *American Journal on Mental Retardation, 92*(4), 344–351.

Shevin, M. (1983). Meaningful parental involvement in long-range educational planning for disabled children. *Education and Training of the Mentally Retarded, 18,* 17–21.

Slentz, K. L., & Bricker, D. (1992). Family guided assessment for IFSP development: Jumping off the family assessment bandwagon. *Journal of Early Intervention, 16,* 11–19.

Smith, S. W. (1990). Individualized education programs in special education—From intent to acquiescence. *Exceptional Children, 57,* 6–14.

Turnbull, A. P., & Turnbull, H. R. (1990). Families, professionals, and exceptionalities: A special partnership (2nd ed.). Upper Saddle River, NJ: Merrill/Prentice Hall.

Vandercook, T., York, J., & Forest, M. (1989). The McGill Action Planning System (MAPS): A strategy for building the vision. *Journal of the Association for Persons with Severe Handicaps, 14,* 205–215.

Wehman, P. (1990). School to work: Elements of successful programs. *Teaching Exceptional Children, 23,* 40–43.

Wehman, P., Wood, W., Everson, J., Marchant, J., & Walker, R. (1987). Transition services for adolescent age individuals with severe mental retardation. In R. N. Ianacone & R. A. Stodden

(Eds.), *Transition issues and directions.* Reston, VA: Council for Exceptional Children/Division on Mental Retardation.

Westling, D. L. (1996). What do parents of children with moderate and severe mental disabilities want? *Education and Training in Mental Retardation and Developmental Disabilities, 31,* 86–114.

Winton, P. J., & Bailey, D. B. (1988). The family-focused interview: A collaborative mechanism for family assessment and goal-setting. *Journal of the Division for Early Childhood, 12,* 195–207.

Winton, P. J., & Bailey, D. B. (1990). Early intervention training related to family interviewing. *Topics in Early Childhood Special Education, 10,* 50–62.

CHAPTER 6

Conducting Assessments to Determine Instructional Needs

This chapter addresses approaches to determine the instructional needs of students with severe disabilities. The information gathered will assist in the planning processes discussed in Chapter 5. They include reviewing previous records, interviewing parents, using adaptive behavior scales and activities–skills checklists, conducting ecological inventories and direct observations of the student, and conducting assessments in the related areas of language, physical functioning, social skills, self-determination, and, when appropriate, traditional academic skills.

Approaches to Assessment

The abilities and skills of students with severe disabilities may be assessed for different reasons. Most importantly, however, assessments are conducted to determine what skills should be taught and what forms of instruction and services are needed in order for the skills to be learned (Browder, 1991, 2001; Rainforth & York-Barr, 1997). Equally important is how well the educational program and related services are working in order that the student will progress adequately. This calls for regularly monitoring the progress of students, a process described in Chapter 9.

As was seen in Chapter 5, different types of plans can or must be written. In this chapter, the discussion of assessment provides information that will help parents, teachers, and other team members to make decisions about what the student needs to learn. Thus the assessment procedures discussed here complement the previously described planning processes. In addition, however, it should be understood that assessment, as discussed here, is not intended to be deficit oriented and should not be conducted simply for the purpose of pointing out what the student cannot do. Also, the types of assessment discussed should not result in a label or category designation. Most important, assessment is not being proposed to suggest a student's limitations in potential development. Instead, the intention of assessment is to help with the planning process.

To that end we will present various types of information-gathering procedures that will prove helpful. The information gathered may include information about the student that comes from other people or reports; information about the student's needs as suggested by participation in natural, inclusive environments; and direct observations of the student within these environments. More formal or *diagnostic* assessments also may be conducted by individual team members, including physical or occupational therapists, speech therapists, or teachers. However, these should generally be completed after more ecologically relevant assessments have been conducted in natural, functional settings and should supplement the information gathered through observations in these settings (Rainforth & York-Barr, 1997).

The specific assessment processes that will be discussed include the following:

- Collecting information from existing records
- Interviewing parents to determine educational goals
- Using adaptive behavior scales to determine instructional needs
- Using activities and skills lists to help to decide students' needs
- Conducting ecological inventories and directly observing students in natural settings
- Assessing related skills by team members to determine needs in areas such as communication and language, physical functioning, social skills, self-determination, and, when appropriate, in traditional academic areas (with adaptations if necessary)

Although it is ultimately the responsibility of the planning team to decide which type or types of assessment should be used, it is suggested that generally the more information the team has, the better its decisions will be when developing individual plans. Also, each member of the team will have an important role in the assessment process. However, a very significant role will be that of the teacher, who will collect much of the information directly and coordinate much of the rest of the process. Each assessment method in the list above is discussed in the following sections.

Collecting Information from Existing Records

An important activity that should be undertaken before determining instructional objectives is to review the student's existing records, especially her previous IEP (Browder, 1991). When a teacher will be working with a new group of students, this review should take place very early, during the preplanning days before students arrive (Westling & Koorland, 1988). Keep in mind, however, that not all the information in a student's cumulative folder will be useful. IQ scores, developmental screening test scores, and irrelevant goals and objectives may not provide the type of information that is helpful in forming new goals and objectives.

Useful information includes the objectives that the student has attempted to achieve in the past, information about whether they were achieved, and how well the student has maintained them and/or demonstrated their generalized use. Skills that have not been mastered may be viable candidates for continued instruction. Those that have been learned may need to be considered for maintenance (so that they will not be forgotten by the student, perhaps as a part of a new objective) or generalization (so that the skills may be used or applied across different people, times, places, and/or conditions). Chapter 8 discusses ways to promote skill maintenance and generalization.

In addition to previous objectives, the teacher should look for other pertinent data about the student, which includes information about his medical or physical condition, medicines taken, dietary restrictions, allergies, ongoing challenging behavior (particularly self-injurious behaviors or aggressive acts), evidence of likes and dislikes, physical and sensory abilities, and communication skills (Gage & Falvey, 1995). This type of information might not only result in the development of instructional goals and objectives, but it may also caution the teacher to be on the lookout for specific needs when the students arrive.

Interviewing Parents to Determine Educational Goals

Person-centered approaches to planning for students with severe disabilities, such as COACH, MAPS, and personal futures planning, call for the integral involvement of parents in determining skills that are appropriate for the student to learn. As a part of the team, parents can provide critical information about the student's current abilities and daily activities and about what the student needs to learn, particularly in the home and community.

To learn about parent views, the teacher (and/or other professionals) will need to interview parents. This may be a part of one of the planning systems described in the previous chapter, or it may be a less formal activity. Regardless, when interviewing parents, teachers and other professionals should adhere to the guidelines offered in Figure 6–1 in order to gather information with the least amount of intrusion into the privacy of the family.

During the interview with the student's parents, the two major questions are "What can your child do?" and "What do you want your child to learn?" These questions may be asked in different ways and using different formats. Two examples are presented in Figures 6–2 and 6–3. Figure 6–2 is a sample of open-ended questions about what the student does at different times at home (Neel & Billingsley, 1989). In Figure 6–3, the parent is given the opportunity to rate the importance of possible skills for the student to learn at school (Rainforth & York-Barr, 1997).

The questions to ask the parents should be developed by the teacher and other professional members of the collaborative team. A variety of commercially produced adaptive behavior scales and curriculum–activity guides may be used to help to direct the questioning. These products are described in the following two sections.

Figure 6–1 Suggestions for Interviewing Parents

1. Make an appointment with the parents at a time that is convenient for them and at a location of their choice, usually the school or their home.
2. Try to determine the familial and cultural values that exist within the family and show respect for them.
3. Attempt to build a relationship of trust, honesty, and openness with the family.
4. In order to facilitate the parents' opportunities to participate, if they wish, try to arrange child care for their child or children during the time of the meeting.
5. Avoid using professional jargon and displaying an air of arrogance. Show respect for the parents and be very open to their thoughts and opinions. Listen more than talk.
6. Arrive on time for scheduled meetings and only stay for a reasonable amount of time, usually no more than an hour.

Figure 6–2 Sample of Parent Interview Using Open-Ended Questions

Source: IMPACT: A Functional Curriculum Handbook for Students with Moderate to Severe Disabilities (pp. 146–148), by R. S. Neel and F. F. Billingsley, 1989, Baltimore: Paul H. Brookes Publishing Co. Reprinted by permission.

What Does Your Child Do Most of the Time?

This section is designed to give us an idea about the number and types of activities your child participates in during the week. We are interested in where, when, and with whom your child interacts. We especially want to know the problems you and your child face on a day-to-day basis. Be sure to add any additional comments you feel will help us understand what goes on during a typical week. This information will be used to aid us in designing a functional program for your child.

What does your child usually do between school and dinner?

____

____

____

Which of these activities does your child do:

Independently ______________________________

With members of the family ________________________

____

With friends and/or neighbors _______________________

____

What special problems, if any, occur during those times?

____

____

____

What does your child usually do between dinner and bedtime?

____

____

____

Which of those activities does your child do:

Independently ______________________________

With members of the family ________________________

____

With friends and/or neighbors _______________________

____

Before selecting any one or more to use, however, the professional team should review them and determine their appropriateness for the student in question.

Using Adaptive Behavior Scales

Information about adaptive behavior skills, or skills that are especially useful for daily functioning, can be collected using one or more commercially produced adaptive behavior scales. These scales provide a broad overview of the student's skills and abilities in many areas of daily life. There are many such scales, and some will be more useful than others. Usefulness depends largely on the types of items contained on the scale and how well they apply to the student being evaluated. Typical items include daily living skills, some community skills, and functioning in specific ability areas, such as demonstrating appropriate social behaviors, communicating, motor abilities, and applying basic academic skills. Descriptions of specific adaptive behavior scales and their contents have been given by Bierne-Smith, Ittenbach, and Patton (2002), Browder (1991, 2001), Bruininks, Thurlow, and Gilman (1987), Cone (1987), and Leland (1991). Among the most commonly used scales are the second edition of the *AAMR Adaptive Behavior Scales* (*ABS*), including the Residential–Community versions (ABS-RC:2) (Nihira, Leland, & Lambert, 1993) and the School version (ABS-S:2) (Lambert, Nihira, & Leland, 1993). Other scales that are often used are the *Vineland Adaptive Behavior Scales* (Sparrow, Balla, & Cicchetti, 1984), *Scales of Independent Behavior* (Bruininks, Woodcock,

Figure 6–2 Continued

What special problems, if any, occur during those times?

____

____

____

What does your child usually do on weekends?

____

____

____

Which of those activities does your child do:

Independently ______________________________

With members of the family __________________

____

With friends and/or neighbors _______________

____

What special problems, if any, occur during those times?

____

____

____

Does your child play with other children? ____ Yes ____ No

If yes, with whom?

____

____

____

What activities does your family do for entertainment *at home*?

____

____

____

____

Weatherman, & Hill, 1985), and the *Pyramid Scales* (Cone, 1984).

No formal training is usually required for the use of adaptive behavior scales, although it is very important that each scale be carefully reviewed before use. Each item may be directly rated (using the scale's designated rating system) by someone who is very familiar with the student, such as a parent or a caregiver. Alternatively, the scale may be filled out by the teacher while interviewing a person who is knowledgeable about the student's ability.

Although adaptive behavior scales do not always identify the most important skills to be taught, they do provide an important dimension of understanding about a student with severe disabilities (Browder, 2001). In essence, most adaptive behavior scales yield a profile of the "hills and valleys" that portray the student's overall strengths and weaknesses. If the instrument truly assesses adaptive behavior, and this is behavior that allows the person to function within a typical environment, it would be important to know two things: areas that are lower than others that need special attention, especially if they interfere with the person's integration and participation in society, and areas that are strengths and that can help to identify skills that fit within a range of social acceptability (Leland, 1991).

Cone (1987) suggested that five factors be considered when an adaptive behavior scale is used to make instructional programming decisions:

1. The scale should be relevant to different environments.
2. It should have a comprehensive listing of behaviors.
3. It should have items linked to instructional activities.

Figure 6–2 Continued

What activities does your family do for entertainment *away from home*?

____
____
____
____

Which, if any, of these activities does your child enjoy?

____
____
____
____

When your child does participate in one of the activities that the family uses for recreation, does he or she participate in a special way, or with special rules, that are only understood by the members of the family? ____ Yes ____ No

If yes, please describe the special adaptations that you have made.

____
____
____

What, if any, are some of the problems you have with your child during vacation (when there is no school)?

____
____
____

What are some of the ideas you have that might make these times easier for your child and you?

____
____
____

4. The items and their rating should be specific enough to help to determine initial programming decisions.
5. The instrument should be helpful in determining the scope, sequence, and content of instruction. (p. 129)

Of greatest importance is whether the items reflect the typical abilities of the students in the program. A common criticism of adaptive behavior scales is that they do not have items suitable for assessing students with the most severe disabilities, that is, those with profound mental disabilities or severe multiple disabilities. For some of these students, the items are far beyond their behavioral repertoire and so they receive a completely flat profile. Information of this nature is not of much use.

After selecting an appropriate scale, the teacher must carefully read the directions and give particular attention to the scoring system that is used. Typically, a scale that reflects different performance levels is provided. For example, the Vineland has five levels of item rating: yes, usually (score 2); sometimes or partially (score 1); no, never (score 0); no opportunity (N); and don't know (DK). Each item on the scale is scored to reflect the most correct status of ability or knowledge about ability.

After the adaptive behavior assessment using the instrument has been completed, the test may be scored. Because many adaptive behavior scales are norm referenced (the student's score may be compared to a standardization sample) and contain other technical properties such as validity and reliability, the scores for different sections, as well as the overall score, can be compared to the normative sample. This comparison allows the evaluator to develop the profile (draw the hills and valleys) referred to earlier. This may provide useful information, but the most applicable information will be that determined by analyzing

Figure 6–3 Sample of Parent Interview Using a Rating Scale

What Is Important for Your Child to Learn at School?

Parents want their child to go to a classroom where he or she will make progress. Children can make progress in different areas, and some areas may be more important than others. The list below contains different areas your child may progress in next year. Please circle the number to the right of the phrase to show how important it is for *your* child to progress in this area next year.

	NA	Not at all					extremely	RANK
1. Learn basic concepts such as colors, numbers, shapes, etc.	0	1	2	(3)	4	5	6	____
2. Learn prereading and reading skills such as letters.	0	1	2	3	(4)	5	6	____
3. Learn to use a pencil and scissors.	0	1	(2)	3	4	5	6	____
4. Learn to listen and follow directions.	0	1	2	3	4	(5)	6	____
5. Learn to share and play with other children.	0	1	2	3	4	5	(6)	1
6. Learn to be creative.	0	1	2	(3)	4	5	6	____
7. Learn more communication skills.	0	1	2	3	4	5	(6)	3
8. Learn confidence and independence.	0	1	2	3	4	(5)	6	____
9. Learn to work independently.	0	1	2	3	4	(5)	6	____
10. Learn to climb, run, and jump.	0	(1)	2	3	4	5	6	____
11. Learn self-care skills such as toileting, dressing, feeding.	0	1	2	3	4	5	(6)	2
12. Learn to follow classroom rules and routines.	0	1	2	3	(4)	5	6	____

Using the above list, place the numbers 1, 2, and 3 next to the three most important areas for your child to progress in next year.

Source: Salisbury, C. L., Dunst, C. J. Home, School, and Community Partnerships: Building Inclusive Teams. In B. Rainforth & J. York-Barr, 1997, *Collaborative Teams for Students with Severe Disabilities: Integrating Therapy and Educational Services* (2nd ed.), Baltimore: Paul H. Brookes Publishing Co. Reprinted with permission.

individual items, which will help the teacher to identify potential instructional objectives.

Using Curriculum and Activity Guides

A number of curriculum and activity guides have been developed that can greatly assist teachers and planning teams in determining appropriate functional objectives for students with severe disabilities. Four such guides are *COACH* (Giangreco, Cloninger, & Iverson, 1998), which was described in the previous chapter for use as a planning instrument; *The Syracuse Community-Referenced Curriculum Guide* (Ford et al., 1989); *Community Living Skills: A Taxonomy* (Dever, 1988); and *The Activities Catalog: An Alternative Curriculum for Youth and Adults with Severe Disabilities* (Wilcox & Bellamy, 1987).

These guides are very different from earlier ones designed for students with severe disabilities, which presented lists of discrete behaviors sequenced according to the order of normal development in infants, toddlers, and children without disabilities. Instead, the most recent guides present an array of activities and skills that are functional and appropriate for the chronological age of the learner. The primary utility of these guides is to provide the teacher or service agency, working cooperatively with the student and his parents, with a broad array of activities in various domains. The guides can be used to help to determine appropriate objectives for students through parent interviews. Key aspects of each of the guides are presented next.

COACH (Choosing Options and Accommodations for Children, Giangreco et al., 1998) was discussed in Chapter 5. However, it is listed here because, as a part of its planning process, it presents parents with a variety of possible learning needs that may be appropriate for their child with severe disabilities. COACH integrally relates the processes of assessment and planning by asking parents to evaluate their child's abilities on key skills and then rate the importance of learning the skill. To set the framework for this evaluation, the COACH system directs parents as well as professionals to consider important life values.

COACH helps parents and professionals to identify learning needs, to prioritize them, and to determine when they should be taught, where they should be taught, and what supports will be required for the student. It is a comprehensive planning system based on learning priorities determined by parents and professionals. Figure 6–4 displays one of the forms used in COACH to identify a student's abilities (in this example, language skills are listed) and to determine whether the skill needs to be worked on by the instructional team. Refer to Chapter 5 and to Giangreco et al. (1998) for additional information about COACH.

Community Living Skills (Dever, 1988) is a list of functional community goals intended to allow the learner to live more independently. The skills are appropriate for a wide range of persons of different ability levels and are useful in both public schools and adult service agencies.

The goals are presented within five major domains: personal maintenance and development, homemaking and community life, vocational, leisure, and travel. Each domain contains four major goals and several subgoals. Under each subgoal, several relevant skills are presented. One goal in each domain is dealing with glitches, which is intended to teach the learner how to react when what is expected does not occur. The domains, goals, and subgoals were developed based on common weekday routines and special routines for weekend days and other "uncommon" days (e.g., payday). The analysis of the routines led to the development of the goals and subgoals in the taxonomy, most of which are clearly beneficial for persons living independently in the community. Figure 6–5 shows the taxonomy of *Community Living Skills*, including all the major goals and subgoals within the different domains.

The Activities Catalog, according to its authors (Wilcox & Bellamy, 1987), was developed to avoid the "readiness trap" by offering functional activities appropriate for learning by adolescents and young adults with severe disabilities. Instead of listing discrete skills to be identified as objectives, the catalog identifies whole activities as units of instruction. The critical feature of an activity is that it results in a natural effect or outcome. Table 6–1 provides illustrations of activity goals and distinguishes them from isolated skills.

A major feature of *The Activities Catalog* is that it provides an assortment of choices for teachers, parents, and persons with disabilities to select for learning or participation. Wilcox and Bellamy point out that it is not important for the student to be able to learn all the skills in an activity, but to be able to participate in an activity and enjoy it. It is also not expected that the individual will learn each activity, but that the catalog will serve as a convenient selection tool for reviewing various appropriate learning possibilities and selecting those that at the time seem to be the most suitable for learning.

The activities in the catalog are divided into three content domains: leisure, personal management, and work. These domains are further divided into different categories that reflect a commonsense grouping related to the benefits and functions of the activities.

The Syracuse Community-Referenced Curriculum Guide (Ford et al., 1989) is another guide that offers an array of functional activities appropriate for learning by persons with severe disabilities. The guide includes scope and sequence charts that cover the major community living areas: self-management and home living, vocational, recreation and leisure, and general community functioning. There are also sections on functional academic skills, including reading and writing, money handling, and time management. Finally, there are three sections on embedded activities: social skills, communication skills, and motor skills. Figure 6–6 shows the scope and sequence for the major community living areas in the *Syracuse Curriculum*.

The primary philosophy guiding the *Syracuse Curriculum* is that many typical school or general education activities are applicable to the needs of students with moderate and severe disabilities, but there are others that they must learn that often do not appear in the normal curriculum. These latter skills, therefore, are the ones presented in the guide.

Like the other guides, the *Syracuse Curriculum* does not suggest that it includes all that a student needs to learn or that all its contents should be taught to students with severe disabilities. The authors state that the guide "provides a framework for decision making that should be applied to individuals on a student-by-student basis. We would expect individualized decisions to vary considerably depending on a range of factors, including the stu-

Figure 6–4 COACH Assessment of Instructional Priorities in the Area of Communication

Source: Choosing Options and Accommodations for Children: A Guide to Planning Inclusive Education, 2nd ed., by M. F. Giangreco, C. J. Cloninger, & V. S. Iverson. Baltimore: Paul H. Brookes. Reprinted with permission.

COACH 2

COMMUNICATION

Step 1.2

Mark only one box to indicate if the family wants to discuss this set of learning outcomes in:
Step 1 (Family Interview; priority this year?) ☐; Step 2 (Additional Learning Outcomes) ☐; Skip for Now ☐

Currently, in what ways does the student communicate?
Expressively: ____________________
Receptively: ____________________

#	Learning Outcomes	Step 1.3 Circle Score	Step 1.3 Needs Work?	Step 1.4 Rank up to 5 Priorities
1	Expresses Continuation or "More" (e.g., makes sounds or movement when desired interaction stops to indicate he or she would like eating, playing, etc., to continue)	E P S	N Y	
2	Makes Choices When Given Options	E P S	N Y	
3	Makes Requests (e.g., for objects, food, interactions, activities, assistance)	E P S	N Y	
4	Summons Others (e.g., has a way to call others to him or her)	E P S	N Y	
5	Expresses Rejection/Refusal (e.g., indicates when he or she wants something to stop or does not want something to begin)	E P S	N Y	
6	Expresses Greetings and Farewells	E P S	N Y	
7	Follows Instructions (e.g., one step, multistep	E P S	N Y	
8	Sustains Communication with Others (e.g.,) takes turns, attends, stays on topic, perseveres)	E P S	N Y	
9	Initiates Communication with Others	E P S	N Y	
10	Responds to Questions (e.g., if asked a question, he or she attempts to answer)	E P S	N Y	
11	Comments/Describes (e.g., expands vocabulary for events, objects, interactions, feelings)	E P S	N Y	
12	Asks Questions of Others	E P S	N Y	
		E P S	N Y	

Comments:

Scoring Key: (use scores for Step 1.3 alone or in combination):
E = Early/Emerging skills (1%–25%) P = Partial skill (25%–80%) S = Skillful (80%–100%)

dent's age, present ability to participate in community living activities, personal and parental preferences and so forth" (Ford et al., 1989, p. 4).

Assessment of students' needs through parent interviews using commercially produced guides such as those described in this section consists of similar procedures regardless of the guide. The decision-making process described here is based on the procedures presented in the guides reviewed in this section.

The first step of the process is for the parents or caregivers to become familiar with the pertinent contents of the curriculum guide(s). Gaining knowledge of the contents alone can be an important learning activity that will prompt thoughts about possible learning outcomes. Copies

Figure 6–5 Taxonomy of Community Living Skills

DOMAIN P: Personal Maintenance and Development

I. The learner will follow routine body maintenance procedures
   A. Maintain personal cleanliness
   B. Groom self
   C. Dress appropriately
   D. Follow appropriate sleep patterns
   E. Maintain nutrition
   F. Exercise regularly
   G. Maintain substance control

II. The learner will treat illnesses
   A. Use first aid and illness treatment procedures
   B. Obtain medical advice when necessary
   C. Follow required medication schedules

III. The learner will establish and maintain personal relationships
   A. Interact appropriately with family
   B. Make friends
   C. Interact appropriately with friends
   D. Cope with inappropriate conduct of family and friends
   E. Respond to sexual needs
   F. Obtain assistance in maintaining personal relationships

IV. The learner will handle personal glitches
   A. Cope with changes in daily schedule
   B. Cope with equipment breakdowns and material depletions

DOMAIN H: Homemaking and Community Life

I. The learner will obtain living quarters
   A. Find appropriate living quarters
   B. Rent/buy living quarters
   C. Set up living quarters

II. The learner will follow community routines
   A. Keep living quarters neat and clean
   B. Keep fabrics neat and clean
   C. Maintain interior of living quarters
   D. Maintain exterior of living quarters
   E. Respond to seasonal changes
   F. Follow home safety procedures
   G. Follow accident/emergency procedures
   H. Maintain foodstock
   I. Prepare and serve meals
   J. Budget money appropriately
   K. Pay bills

III. The learner will coexist in a neighborhood and community
   A. Interact appropriately with community members
   B. Cope with inappropriate conduct of others
   C. Observe requirements of the law
   D. Carry out civic duties

IV. The learner will handle glitches in the home
   A. Cope with equipment breakdowns
   B. Cope with depletions of household supplies
   C. Cope with unexpected depletions of funds
   D. Cope with disruptions in routine
   E. Cope with sudden changes in the weather

Source: Community Living Skills: A Taxonomy (pp. 26–27) by R. B. Dever, 1988, Washington, DC: American Association on Mental Retardation. Copyright 1988 by the American Association on Mental Retardation. Reprinted with permission.

of the guide being used may be shared with the parents and caregivers, and the contents (or selected portions) may be shown to the student with disabilities if appropriate.

The next step should be for those who are familiar with the student to rate the student's skill level on the items in different sections or across different domains of the curriculum guide. The rating should be a system that reports the performance or ability of the student on the activity or skill. As an example, the *Syracuse Curriculum* allows each skill to be rated using one of the following:

- Needs assistance on most steps
- Needs assistance on some steps
- Performs all steps independently

It also allows the student's skill use to be rated in terms of whether he possesses the related social skills to perform the task and whether he demonstrates certain critical features in conjunction with the use of the skills (initiates as needed? makes choices? uses safety measures?). Finally, it allows a note to be made regarding the priority goal area.

Figure 6–5 Continued

DOMAIN V: Vocational

I. The learner will obtain work
   - A. Seek employment
   - B. Accept employment
   - C. Use employment service

II. The learner will perform the work routine
   - A. Perform the job routine
   - B. Follow work-related daily schedule
   - C. Maintain work station
   - D. Follow employer rules and regulations
   - E. Use facilities appropriately
   - F. Follow job safety procedures
   - G. Follow accident and emergency procedures

III. The learner will coexist with others on the job
   - A. Interact appropriately with others on the job
   - B. Cope with inappropriate conduct of others on the job

IV. The learner will handle glitches on the job
   - A. Cope with changes in work routine
   - B. Cope with work problems
   - C. Cope with supply depletions and equipment breakdowns

DOMAIN L: Leisure

I. The learner will develop leisure activities
   - A. Find new leisure activities
   - B. Acquire skills for leisure activities

II. The learner will follow leisure activity routines
   - A. Perform leisure activities
   - B. Maintain leisure equipment
   - C. Follow leisure safety procedures
   - D. Follow accident and emergency procedures

III. The learner will coexist with others during leisure
   - A. Interact appropriately with others in a leisure setting
   - B. Respond to the inappropriate conduct of others

IV. The learner will handle glitches during leisure
   - A. Cope with changes in leisure routine
   - B. Cope with equipment breakdowns and material depletions

DOMAIN T: Travel

I. The learner will travel routes in the community
   - A. Form mental maps of frequented buildings
   - B. Form mental maps of the community

II. The learner will use conveyances
   - A. Follow usage procedures
   - B. Make decisions preparatory to travel
   - C. Follow travel safety procedures
   - D. Follow accident and emergency procedures

III. The learner will coexist with others while traveling
   - A. Interact appropriately with others while traveling
   - B. Respond to the inappropriate conduct of others while traveling

IV. The learner will handle glitches during travel
   - A. Cope with changes in travel schedule
   - B. Cope with equipment breakdowns
   - C. Cope with being lost

COACH uses a similar procedure. Each skill is rated on the following scale:

R—Resistant to assistance from others

E—Early/emerging skill (1% to 25%)

P—Partial skill (25% to 80%)

S—Skillful (80% to 100%)

Once the skill level is determined, COACH calls for a determination on whether the skill should be taught and what level of priority it should be given.

Prioritization should be the next step regardless of the guide used. This is generally done by reviewing the ratings of the different items and establishing through parent and professional consensus the student's instructional priorities. The most important aspect of this phase of the process is that those skills that will be most immediately useful or enjoyable to the student are given top consideration. As Wilcox and Bellamy (1987) stated, the skills should be directed toward "building and maintaining a desirable lifestyle."

After interviewing parents or caregivers (or even previous teachers) and using adaptive behavior scales and activity and skills guides, the planning team has another source for determining potential objectives. This approach, analyzing the environments in which the student

Table 6–1 Illustrations of Skills and Activities from *The Activities Catalog*

Isolated Skills	*Activity Goals*
Given any price tag less than $15, Jason will count out bills and coins to equal that amount. John will match pictures, line drawings, rebuses to functional objects (e.g., clothing items, food items, classroom materials).	Tom will demonstrate the ability to shop at three different supermarkets: Safeway (2427 River Road), U Mart (416 Santa Clara Street), and Fred Meyer (3000 River Road) for up to 15 specific-brand grocery items. Picture cards will be used as the grocery list. Performance includes travel to the store, selecting items, paying for the purchase using a next-dollar strategy, and transporting purchases back to school.
Heidi will learn to sign 25 functional words and word phrases (e.g., hamburger, milk, fries, I want, thank you) on request. Bianca will improve self-care skills in the areas of eating and meal preparation. Michael will independently cross uncontrolled intersections during low traffic periods.	Joe will use a communication notebook to order lunch at two fast-food restaurants (McDonald's and Arby's). Performance includes travel to the restaurant, entering, waiting in line as necessary, indicating desired lunch (sandwich, beverage, fries, dessert), paying using a next-dollar strategy, transporting food to table, eating, cleaning up, and returning to next activity.
Cindy will name, locate female body parts. Bob will demonstrate mature catching and throwing patterns using a variety of sizes and weights of balls. Diane will demonstrate appropriate use of makeup. Jackie will independently wash her hair once a week.	Susan will use the YMCA twice weekly after school. Performance includes travel to the "Y," locating the correct locker room, finding a locker, changing clothes, using the weight room for at least 10 minutes, using the sauna, showering, dressing, and traveling home.
Bill will increase his understanding of areas of career interest relevant to his vocational potential. Matt will improve the social and communication skills needed for community vocational functioning.	Dan will participate as a member of a work crew responsible for after-school cleanup. Performance includes arriving for work on time, greeting coworkers, putting on appropriate clothing, independently completing jobs designated by activity cards, changing out of work clothes, and returning home on designated bus.
Jeff will improve and maintain fine motor skills, bilateral coordination, spatial orientation, and equilibrium. Rob will increase his vocational skills and abilities. Allen will demonstrate an increased awareness of work values.	Shawn will participate in the Food Service Program at the Erb Student Union. Job cluster includes bussing tables, washing dishes, washing pots and pans, and shelving clean dishes and pans. Training will monitor social interactions, speed and quality prompts, and performance according to schedule.

Source: The Activities Catalog: An Alternative Curriculum for Youth and Adults with Severe Disabilities (p. 13) by B. Wilcox and T. G. Bellamy, 1987, Baltimore: Paul H. Brookes Publishing Co. Reprinted with permission of the author.

functions or may function and then observing the student's functioning within the environments, is discussed next.

Conducting Ecological Inventories and Directly Observing Students in Natural Settings

One of the most important ways to determine potential instructional and therapeutic needs of students with disabilities, as well as to determine current functional skills, is to analyze the student's current (and future) environments to determine the activities that are required within the environments and to subsequently observe the individual as she operates within the environments. The analysis of the activities required within a particular setting is called an *ecological inventory* (Brown et al., 1979), and it is seen as perhaps the most valid basis for instruction and the provision of related service therapies (cf. Downing, 2002; Falvey, 1995; Orelove & Sobsey, 1996; Rainforth & York-Barr, 1997). An ecological inventory is intended to delineate the types of performance and skills that would be expected by a person without a disability in the environment. Following this analysis, the ability of the student with the disability to function in the environment is directly observed to determine instructional needs and therapeutic interventions that will improve the student's skill level within the environment.

To conduct an ecological inventory, the teacher, the parents, and the rest of the collaborative team must first identify environments or learning areas of interest, that is, those in which the student operates presently or may operate in the future. These will very likely include environments within the home, community, school, workplace, or leisure or recreational settings. Often, all these domains are appropriate. Next, the specific settings within the domains are identified, for example, the kitchen at home, the

Figure 6–6 Scope and Sequence of the Community Living Areas

Community living areas		Age and grade levels					
			Elementary school				
		Kindergarten (age 5)	Primary (ages 6-8)	Intermediate (ages 9-11)	Middle school (ages 12-14)	High school (ages 15-18)	Transition (ages 19-21)
Self-management and home living	Eating and food preparation						
	Grooming and dressing						
	Hygiene and toileting						
	Safety and health						
	Assisting, taking care of others						
	Budgeting/planning/scheduling						
	Household maintenance						
	Outdoor maintenance						
Vocational	Classroom/school jobs and community work experiences						
	Neighborhood jobs						
	Community jobs						
Recreation/leisure	School and extracurricular						
	Alone–home and in the neighborhood						
	Family/friends – home and in the neighborhood						
	Family/friends – community						
	Physical fitness						
General community functioning	Travel						
	Community safety						
	Grocery shopping						
	General shopping						
	Eating out						
	Using services						

Source: The Syracuse Community-Referenced Curriculum Guide for Students with Moderate and Severe Disabilities (p. 6) by A. Ford, R. Schnorr, L. Meyer, L. Davern, J. Black, and P. Dempsey (Eds.), 1989, Baltimore: Paul H. Brookes Publishing Co. Reprinted with permission.

department store in the community, the regular classroom or school cafeteria, the grocery store where the person shops or works, and/or the neighborhood recreational center. After specific environments have been identified, the subenvironments of greatest significance are identified along with the important actions that are to occur in them, for example, using the microwave to prepare a meal or the dishwasher to wash dishes, selecting clothes in the clothing department of the store, bagging groceries at the checkout counter, selecting food items in the cafeteria, or shooting pool in the recreation center. Once the key subenvironments and corresponding activities have been identified, the latter may be given consideration as *instructional objectives* (see Chapter 7), and the student's current skill level within them will be observed and recorded.

The ecological inventory is conducted to determine the types of activities an individual with severe disabilities might learn to perform in the settings. It is necessary to list all the actions that the individual must perform to successfully operate either partially or fully within the setting. Some of these may be identified by the team for immediate instruction; others may be considered appropriate for instruction at a later time.

When interviewing parents to determine students' instructional needs, the teacher can determine sites where ecological inventories will be necessary. The teacher should ask for information about learning needs necessary in the home and also about needs for participating with the parents and family members in places outside the home.

A variation of the ecological inventory to determine environmental needs is an analysis of *routines* (Dever, 1988). This is similar to ecological inventories except that the focus is on typical activities that occur during a day, rather than activities within particular environments. Dever suggested that if we identify the routine of a typical independent individual we may be able to teach those skills to make another person more independent. Therefore, he proposed that routines be developed such as the one presented in Figure 6–7. This type of information may complement or broaden the data gathered through an ecological inventory. For example, if it is known that on a daily basis the individual can dress herself except for buttoning her shirt and zipping her pants (two things her mother says she must always do), these tasks might become important learning objectives.

After relevant environments or routines have been identified, the student's performance within the environments should be observed and recorded. Direct observations of students in natural environments may occur during unstructured periods or when planned, structured activities are arranged. Observations of students in natural environments during unstructured activities are made by teachers at times when there is no attempt by the teacher or another person to prompt the student to demonstrate a particular skill or activity. Previously identified relevant environments and subenvironments are used to observe the student's current functional level within the settings. During observations, notes or records should be taken that can be used to answer several important questions about the student's general functional abilities:

1. How well does the student perform in the domains, environments, subenvironments, and activities that were identified through the ecological inventory process? Is total participation possible or should some form of partial participation be the learning goal?
2. What types of leisure activities does the student enjoy and with whom does he spend leisure time? Do any particular toys, games, or activities seem to be especially interesting or reinforcing?
3. How does the student express herself in different settings and with different people? Is the individual's language functional? Is communication adequate or is it difficult to understand the person's meaning or intention? Is an alternative form of communication used?
4. How are relationships with nondisabled peers manifested? Are there appropriate social behaviors? Are there friendships?
5. Does the student have limitations related to his physical or sensory abilities? Is he ambulatory or mobile? How much are arms and hands used? Are orthotic devices used or do they appear necessary?
6. Does the student exhibit any type of inappropriate behavior, such as self-injurious or aggressive acts? Do these occur in any particular circumstances? Do they appear to be related to communicative attempts or to express particular feelings?

Another approach to analyzing a student's skills is for the teacher or other team members to arrange for structured activities within environments, such as folding clothes in the laundry room, and record performance data during these activities. The purpose of this form of assessment is to pinpoint specific instructional targets by seeing exactly what the student can and cannot do on particular tasks. This type of direct assessment is important because information obtained using the previously described procedure may not be specific enough or may not have given the individual enough of an opportunity to perform the task. This would imply that her true ability may not be known.

Figure 6–7 A Weekday Routine

Source: Community Living Skills: A Taxonomy (p. 29) by R. B. Dever, 1988, Washington, DC: American Association on Mental Retardation. Copyright 1988 by the American Association on Mental Retardation. Reprinted with permission.

1. Rise
2. Toilet
3. Groom self
4. Check weather conditions and select workday clothing
5. Dress
6. Make bed
7. Prepare breakfast
8. Eat breakfast
9. Prepare sack lunch
10. Clear table and wash dishes
11. Tidy kitchen
12. Brush teeth
13. Select outerwear for weather conditions
14. Check lights and appliances
15. Leave and secure house
16. Travel to work

•
•
•

(Perform work routine)

•
•
•

17. Travel home (see also payday routine)
18. Collect mail
19. Store outerwear
20. Exercise
21. Select evening clothing (for chore/leisure routine)
22. Bathe
23. Groom and dress
24. Store dirty clothing (and linen, if applicable)
25. Tidy bathroom
26. Set table
27. Prepare supper
28. Eat
29. Clear table and wash dishes
30. Tidy kitchen
31. Tidy living room
32. Perform chore/leisure routine
33. Toilet and dress for bed
34. Set alarm
35. Sleep

For the purpose of forming potential instructional objectives, the most appropriate time to conduct observations during either unstructured or structured activities would be before the student begins to be served by the teacher, if this is possible. For example, if a student is moving into a new school program, such as from an elementary school to a middle school, it would be appropriate for the future teacher to go to the elementary school and observe the child in various applicable school environments. In addition, the teacher could arrange with the parents to observe the child in the home and in community settings visited by the family. Other possible observational settings include previously identified settings, such as a friend's house; a neighborhood playground, park, or recreational setting; or the school bus.

When determining the student's performance abilities within settings, records should be made of what the student can and cannot do. During unstructured times, the best form of initial assessment is *anecdotal recording*, a relatively simple process in which the observer makes written notes about the targeted individual's behavior. During the observation, careful and continuous attention is given to the acts of the student, and nearly all that occurs is written down. Because the observer–recorder should not be a part of the ongoing action, an unobtrusive posture and position of observation should be taken whenever possible.

During structured activities, the purpose of the observation is to determine the student's actual ability on specific skills. The level of competence or skill deficiency demonstrated indicates whether the targeted behavior or skill should be considered for instruction. To conduct this assessment, the teacher needs to plan an activity that provides the opportunity for the student to demonstrate the skills to be assessed. In most cases, this means that the student will be enrolled in the teacher's class and the teacher will develop activities for the student in order to observe and record performance on specific tasks as the activities occur naturally during the school day. This does not mean that all the opportunities for skill demonstration should occur in one location. Instead, the skill should be assessed where it will ultimately need to occur.

Structured assessment procedures must allow the student adequate opportunity to demonstrate whether the particular behavior, skill, or some parts of the skill can be performed, which implies that there must be more than a one-time evaluation. Typically, the teacher will collect three to five days of performance data on the target behavior to validate the student's actual ability level. These data points are referred to as *baseline* data because they indicate the student's current performance level before instruction. They will be displayed on graph paper so that the teacher may determine precisely which parts of the task the student can do and which need to be learned (see Chapter 9).

The types of performance opportunities and the type of data to be collected depend on the type of behavior that is being observed. Given the heterogeneous characteristics of persons with severe disabilities, it is understandable that there will be a range of behaviors, skills, and activities that will need to be assessed and ultimately taught. This range of instructional needs varies depending on severity and need. For students with the most severe disabilities, we may be looking for their ability to partially participate in an activity, to make a choice, or to reduce dependency (Lehr, 1989; Orelove & Sobsey, 1996). Older or more capable students may be assessed to determine how well they can cook a meal or wash their clothes at a laundromat. Although the behaviors are different, the principles of direct assessment apply equally.

For the purpose of baseline data collection, as well as continuous measurement during instruction (as discussed in Chapter 9), we may consider each learning target as having one of four topographies or forms: *simple, discrete behaviors; continuous, ongoing behaviors; complex, chained skills* (comprised of multiple behaviors); or *functional routines* (also comprised of multiple behaviors, but occurring when natural cues and reinforcers are in effect). Methods for collecting data on student performance on these types of behaviors include event recording, rate measures, partial interval and whole interval recording, momentary time sampling, latency recording, duration measures, and task analytic assessment. Since these data collection methods are explained in detail in Chapter 9, they are not discussed here. However, the four forms of behaviors that may be identified for baseline and ongoing assessment are explained below.

Simple, Discrete Behaviors

Behaviors within this group include simple movements that usually occur in and across different situations. Examples include smiling, eye contact, touching, holding, lifting, and so forth. These often appear in clusters with other behaviors, and the teacher may have several behaviors in one cluster that should be assessed. As is explained in Chapter 9, event recording, rate measures, partial interval recording, momentary time sampling, and sometimes latency measures are used to measure these types of behaviors.

Continuous, Ongoing Behaviors

For some objectives or potential objectives, it is important not only to know that they occur, but also to know for how long they occur. For example, how long can a student work at a particular job or engage in a fitness activity? When such behavior is of concern, an appropriate measure, such as duration measures or whole interval recording, is used (see Chapter 9).

Complex, Chained Skills

Several possible instructional targets for evaluation require the student to perform a chain of related behaviors in order to complete a task. Folding laundry, playing a pinball machine, setting a table, and vacuuming a room are a few examples of tasks that can be broken down into multiple individual behavior components. Breaking down a particular task in this way is referred to as *task analysis*. When a student's ability to perform all the steps in such a multicomponent task is evaluated, it is called a *task analytic assessment* (Browder, 1991, 2001). Assessment of students on such tasks requires that the teacher observe how well the student does on each component of the task and also what type of assistance the student needs to complete the task. Procedures for doing this are discussed in Chapter 9.

Functional Routines

Functional routines are similar to task analyses in that they contain several behaviors in a chain that are to be evaluated as they occur in the chain. However, according to Neel and Billingsley (1989), routines differ in some important ways from traditional task analyses. First, routines are more complete acts in that they require all relevant behaviors necessary to "have access to a particular activity or event in the natural context" (Neel & Billingsley, 1989, p. 50). In other words, it is not sufficient during assessment only to determine whether the student can make a sandwich. Instead, it is necessary to observe the student when she is hungry and see if the student begins by going into the kitchen, finding the appropriate ingredients, arranging them for use, and then making the sandwich and eating it. As such a routine occurs, we may expect the student to use cognitive skills, communication skills, social skills, and motor skills.

Second, routines are initiated by a natural cue in the environment, instead of by the teacher's direction to initiate the task (unless this is a natural cue). In addition, routines are finished when the student experiences the natural consequence that serves as a reinforcer for the entire event, which Neel and Billingsley refer to as a "critical effect." In our example, this would be eating the sandwich and thus reducing the hunger that prompted the entire sequence. It is this idea of a critical effect that Neel and Billingsley suggest is the major difference between teaching through routines and the use of most task analyses.

Routines may be relatively brief or they may be elaborate. Although Neel and Billingsley recommend that the typical routine should have about 15 steps, the concept of the routine is broader than that of the task analysis. Because of the defining characteristics of a routine, we might envision routines that range from getting off the school bus and coming into the classroom to one that calls for a student to get on a bus, go to the grocery store, shop, and return home on the bus. While it is apparent that this would be extensive and we may need to break it into subroutines, it does possess the critical components of a routine.

Recording the student's performance on each step of a routine can be the same as recording performance on steps in a task analysis. Again, these procedures can be found in Chapter 9.

For the teacher to accurately monitor the student's progress, he should record the correct occurrences of the behavior, using the unit of measure most appropriate, and then transfer this information onto graph paper. Although the process of recording, graphing, and interpreting student performance should be started during initial assessment, it is also an important aspect of instruction (see Chapter 7) and checking for maintenance and generalization (see Chapter 8). The discussion of this topic is presented separately in Chapter 9.

Assessing Related Skills

As was discussed in Chapter 3, collaborative, transdisciplinary teaming is essential to offering the best possible educational service to students with severe disabilities. During the process of determining actual and potential skills in natural environments, different members of the team should participate in observing and recording a student's performance. Physical and occupational therapists should observe to assess sensory and motor skills and required interventions and supports (Rainforth & York-Barr, 1997); communication disorders specialists should determine language forms, functions, and opportunities for the use of language within natural environments (Brady & Halle, 1997; Sigafoos & York, 1991).

Related skills, such as communication and motor skills, are referred to as such because they may be related to most functional targets that will be taught. Ford et al. (1989) referred to them as "embedded skills." Although they are not taught in isolation from other skills, it is still necessary to have a clear understanding of a student's abilities and needs in these areas so that they can be given the appropriate attention when teaching any and all functional skills. In this way, the student can learn to function more independently in her environment by working on the specific functional activity and the related skill that is a part of it.

In addition to communication skills and motor skills, during the assessment process the collaborative team may want to consider other related skills for evaluation and subsequent intervention. Social interaction skills, self-determination skills, and academic skills may warrant special evaluation for some students with severe disabilities. Special assessment of related, potentially relevant skills is discussed in the following sections.

Communication Skills

Determining current and needed functional communication skills will measure the ability of the individual with severe disabilities to influence the behavior of other people. The assessment of communication skills must be a team effort led by the specialist in this area and must include information provided by parents, teachers, and other professionals and paraprofessionals. Each will contribute to the understanding of the student's abilities and needs.

Assessment of communication requires information about three areas (Neel & Billingsley, 1989; Noonan & Siegel-Causey, 1990; Sigafoos & York, 1991):

1. *Communicative functions*. What does or will the student need to express to participate more fully in current and future environments? In what way does the student currently attempt to control the environment? What would be important for him to learn to be able to do so?
2. *Communicative form*. How does the student communicate now? Is this system adequate? Is it understood by others in the student's environment?
3. *Communicative context and situations*. What does the student communicate about and with whom does she communicate? What aspects of the environment stimulate communication?

To answer these questions, several different types of evaluation are helpful, including commercially available assessments, communication–language samples, analog probe assessments, oral–motor assessment, and behavioral assessment (Brady & Halle, 1997; Noonan & Siegel-Causey, 1990). The speech–language therapist conducts the first three forms of assessment, a physical or occupational therapist may conduct the oral–motor assessment, and the teacher is in the best position to conduct a behavioral assessment by using the anecdotal recording system described previously. For very specific language behaviors, the teacher may also use event recording or take frequency measures.

Motor Skills

A significant number of students with severe disabilities have physical disabilities, or perhaps multiple disabilities, that present extraordinary challenges to their participation in many life activities. Their motor skills may be both delayed and disorganized. Very often students with disabilities of this nature have cerebral palsy in addition to a moderate, severe, or profound mental disability (Rainforth, Giangreco, & Dennis, 1989). It is very important, therefore, that their motor skills be assessed and that the assessment lead to functional improvements in participatory skills. In the assessment of motor skills and physical abilities, the first requirement is to determine the functions that the student must acquire that require motoric involvement. That is, in various areas of functioning, what type of physical movement or participation must the student develop to achieve more independence (Browder, 1991)?

The evaluation conducted by the therapist should provide the teacher and others with this type of information. The physical and/or occupational therapist, like the teacher, is concerned about functional performance and therefore observes the student during normal activities. Additionally, in-depth evaluations are conducted in the areas of self-help and general motor development. The outcome of the assessment by the PT or OT will identify motor skill deficits, suggest environmental modifications to improve participation, and perhaps restructure the job or task so that the intended function can be achieved.

Although therapists, like teachers, are very concerned with functioning, they are also concerned with the underlying physical dysfunctioning associated with functional performances. Because of this, the therapist conducts evaluations of reflexes and reflex patterns, the conditions of muscle tone, range of motion, motor patterns, limb length discrepancy, limb girth (circumference), muscle strength, sensation, gait, posture, and sensory integration (Bigge & Best, 2001; Dunn, 1996). As a result of these assessments, information is provided that will help the student to maintain health and increase participation in current and future integrated environments (Rainforth & York-Barr, 1997).

Self-Determination Skills

Acquiring skills necessary to be a self-determining individual is important for many people with severe disabilities just as it is for people without disabilities. Parents, teachers, and other members of the collaborative team should seek to determine the extent to which an individual exercises skills in self-determination and the opportunities that exist for using these skills. Obviously, an examination of the individual and her lifestyle will shed light on self-determination opportunities and activities. However, in addition to less structured observations, formal assessments have been recently developed to assist professionals in examining skills and opportunities in this area (Martin & Huber Marshall, 1996a & b; Wehmeyer, 1995). Although these assessment instruments have been used primarily with students who have mild disabilities, they may be useful for examining the self-determination skills of some individuals with more severe disabilities, especially if they are administered in one-to-one settings with the administrator reading and explaining the items and recording the student's responses.

The Arc's Self-Determination Scale was designed for two purposes: (1) to assess students' strengths and weaknesses in self-determination and thus to facilitate their involvement in their own educational planning and (2) as a tool for research on the development of self-determination

(Wehmeyer, 1995). It can be used by teachers and team members to help to develop educational goals related to the improvement of self-determination skills and the development of opportunities for self-determination. The scale was developed so that it could be read by a student who has acquired a fourth-grade reading level or could be read to the student by the teacher. If used with students with more significant disabilities, administration of the assessment tool allows a wide latitude of accommodations to be provided, including explaining the meaning of words contained within the test items and recording the student's response if the student has insufficient writing skills.

The Arc Scale contains four sections: *Autonomy*, which measures perceived independence; *Self-regulation*, which measures the ability to arrive at appropriate solutions to problems; *Psychological Empowerment*, which measures the individual's belief in his own ability; and *Self-realization,* which measures self-knowledge and self-awareness. Across the domains there are a total of 72 questions to which the examinee is asked to respond with either a forced-choice response or a created response, depending on the section.

The *ChoiceMaker Self-determination Transition Assessment* (Martin & Huber Marshall, 1996a) is an assessment instrument that is keyed to the *ChoiceMaker Self-determination Transition Curriculum* and also allows teachers to evaluate students' personal expressions of choices (Martin & Huber Marshall, 1996b). The teacher rates students in such areas as the ability to express interest in daily living activities, future employment, and community participation, as well as the opportunities available at school for the student to make such expressions. Although the instrument and the corresponding curriculum are designed primarily for older students to assist in the process of transition into adulthood, many of the items are also useful for assessing self-determination expressions and opportunities for younger individuals.

Social Skills

The acceptance of individuals with severe disabilities often depends on the quality of their social behavior. Students whose social behavior is more appropriate and closer to the norm of similar-age individuals without disabilities are more likely to be accepted. Appropriate social skills have been related to successful inclusion and integration, job retention, friendships, social networks, and a satisfactory quality of life (Storey, 1996). For these reasons, during the evaluation process it is often important to look specifically at the social skills of students.

Although a great deal of relevant knowledge about social skills can be discovered through direct observation, the use of formal instruments can also be helpful. Social skills rating scales have been developed for use by teachers, parents, or other adults and can serve various functions, such as assessing the social behavior of an individual across different settings or over time. The instruments allow ratings on a number of social behaviors related to appropriate functioning.

A number of formal social skills assessment instruments may be useful. Demaray et al. (1995) reviewed six of these and, based on their analyses, determined that the *Social Skills Rating System* (*SSRS*, Gresham & Elliott, 1990) was the most comprehensive. The SSRS allows separate evaluations by teachers, parents, and students and contains different norms for individuals at the preschool, the elementary school, and the high school level. Relevant to many students with disabilities, it has scales in the areas of social skills and problem behaviors and subscales in cooperation, assertion, and self-control. The evaluation of a student's social skills in different areas by multiple raters results in a more valid assessment (Storey, 1996).

Although scores from scales and subscales may be useful, as are the results of most assessment instruments, such as adaptive behavior scales, teachers of students with severe disabilities should be more concerned about individual item ratings than about global measures. Close examination of individual items is more likely to provide useful information for targeting instructional goals and behaviors.

The van Dijk Approach to Assessment

Although all the previous assessment procedures have great utility for most individuals with severe disabilities, some persons are functioning at such a level that a more intense and direct assessment approach may be necessary. An approach to assessing young children with very severe, multiple disabilities was developed by Jan van Dijk of the Netherlands for use primarily with children with dual sensory impairments (deaf–blindness). The van Dijk method relies on a period of interaction between the assessor and the child (about 1 to 2 hours) in order to determine the child's functioning in several key areas of development. The assessment begins with an interview with a parent or caregiver and then continues with playlike activities of interest to the child during which the assessor notes the child's abilities. Based on this knowledge, IFSPs or IEPs can be written with activities to enhance further learning

Table 6–2 van Dijk Approach to the Assessment of Individuals with Severe Multiple Disabilities

Biobehavioral state

What is the individual's current state?
Is the individual able to control or modulate his or her state?
How much time does the individual spend in an alert state?
What range of states does the individual show and what is the transition pattern between states?
What variables affect the individual's state?

Orienting response

What factors elicit an orienting response?
How does the individual exhibit an orienting response?
What sensory channels appear to be associated with the orienting response (sensory information that triggers the response and the senses utilized)?

Learning channels

How does the individual appear to take in information?
How does the individual react to sound?
How does the individual react to vision?
How does the individual react to touch?
Does the individual use more than one sense at a time?
Does the individual exhibit engagement or disengagement cues in response to particular sensory information?

Approach–withdrawal

What are the individual's engagement cues?
What are the individual's disengagement cues?
What appears to motivate the individual?
What does the individual seem to turn away from?

Memory

Does the individual habituate to familiar stimuli?
How many presentations of stimuli are necessary and for how long before there is habituation?
Does the individual attend again if the features of the stimulus change?
Are reactions differentiated?
Does the individual react differently to familiar and unfamiliar people?
Does the individual appear to have object permanence (understands that something still exists even if it is not currently visible)?
Does the individual associate a preceding event with one that follows?
Does the individual appear to anticipate an upcoming event?
Does the individual react when there is a mismatch to expectations?
Does the individual demonstrate functional use of objects?
Is the individual able to learn a simple routine?
Is the routine that is learned remembered?

Interactions

Does the individual orient to a person?
Does the individual exhibit secure attachment with important individuals in his or her life?
Does the individual engage in turn taking when he or she begins the interaction?
How many turns are taken before disengagement?
In response to a partner's interaction, does the individual add more to turn-taking interaction?

Communication

Does the individual demonstrate communicative intent through the use of signals, vocalizations, gestures, and the like?
What are the communications used?
Are signals used with consistency?
Does the individual use differentiated communications?
Describe the communications and their probable meanings.
When presented with options, does the individual make choices?
Does the individual use conventional gestures?
Can the individual use one item or symbol to stand for an activity or object?
Does the individual demonstrate understanding of communication symbols (auditory, visual, or tactual)?
Does the individual use symbolic communication? Describe.

continued

Table 6–2 Continued

Problem solving

Does the individual demonstrate cause and effect?
Does the individual demonstrate an understanding of means and ends or the use of an intermediate step to solve a problem?
Does the individual demonstrate understanding of the function of common objects?
How does the individual approach a problem?
Does the individual maintain attention and persist?

Source: "A Framework for Understanding Young Children with Severe Multiple Disabilities: The van Dijk Approach to Assessment," by C. Nelson, J. van Dijk, A.P. McDonnell, and K. Thompson, 2002, *Research and Practice for Persons with Severe Disabilities, 27,* pp. 97–111. Reprinted by permission of TASH, Baltimore, MD.

and development (Nelson, van Dijk, McDonnell, & Thompson, 2002).

The interactions between the evaluator and child begin with establishing a trusting relationship and progress with a series of interactions that are built on the child's interests and successes. The evaluator is interested in determining the child's underlying developmental abilities with regard to (1) ability to maintain and modulate behavioral state, (2) preferred learning channel, (3) means of processing information and stimuli, (4) ability to accommodate new experiences with existing schemes, (5) ability to learn, remember, and anticipate routines, (6) approach to problem-solving situations, (7) ability to form attachments and interact socially, and (8) communication modes and skills (Nelson et al., 2002). Table 6–2 contains the questions that the evaluator wishes to answer based on the child's actions during the session.

There is no standard protocol, and there is no intention that the evaluation proceed in any particular order. More important is that a holistic understanding of the child's current level of development in the different areas occur in order that activities may be developed to expand the child's current abilities in these areas. As the evaluator interacts with the child, he or she is seeking to find answers to the questions that appear in Table 6–2. Until the evaluator becomes skilled at what to look for and remember, a second person may need to take notes or the session may be videotaped. Figure 6–8 provides a description of the assessment process used with "Leroy" and Table 6–3 gives a succinct list of findings and implications.

The van Dijk assessment model is particularly useful for young children (0 to 8 years) whose current status calls for the development of basic abilities in cognition, language, and social skills. The other forms of assessment discussed in this chapter are useful for teaching many skills, but may become more relevant for some children when accompanied by van Dijk's assessment process. Based on assessment findings, teachers and other team members can develop learning activities and use systematic instruction in rich, inclusive environments that will maximize the child's development.

Traditional Academic Skills

The academic skills that teachers of most students with severe disabilities are interested in assessing include reading, writing, and arithmetic (primarily money handling and time management) (Ford et al., 1989). Although acquisition and application of skills in these areas may not be possible or may not be the most important area of instruction for some students with severe disabilities, for others it would be inappropriate not to teach certain academic skills. As we discuss in Chapter 17, some students with severe disabilities are capable of learning some useful and interesting academic skills, and such skills may enrich the quality of their lives and increase their ability to participate more fully in normal environments. Teachers should not make assumptions about the student's ability in this area, but should undertake a careful analysis to determine the extent that academic skills should be taught.

The first step in the assessment of academic skills for students with severe disabilities is to develop an estimation of the type of academic curricular focus appropriate for the student. This is based on five primary considerations about the student:

1. *What is the age of the student and how much time does she have remaining in school?* The younger the student, the more likely it is that she will benefit from instruction in academic skills. The skills that are taught are relatively simple during the first few years of school, and the student may be at an age when cognitive abilities and academic objectives coincide maximally. As the student gets older and the number of years left in school decrease, there must be more concern about how well particular skills will serve her in the adult world. The functionality of the

Figure 6–8 van Dijk Assessment of Leroy

"The assessment began with a favored electronic toy. The teacher stacked colored rings on a column and when all rings were in place, she pressed on the top and music sounded and the column lit up. Leroy smiled and reached out to the toy as soon as the music played. When the music stopped, he took the teacher's hands and placed them on top of the toy. She pressed and the music began again. This time, she moved her hands out of reach, and Leroy banged on the top of the toy. Sometimes this activated the music, but if it failed, he promptly went to the teacher's hand to get her to activate the music for him. As he tired of this toy, the teacher substituted a new musical toy. After a brief round of playing with the new toy, Leroy lay down on his back. When the teacher joined him, Leroy rolled over on his stomach, when the teacher did the same, Leroy laughed and rolled again on his back with arms out to his side and the teacher again followed his lead. After a few turns of this, he closed his eyes. The teacher let him rest for a couple of minutes, but then held out her hands and helped him stand up. Leroy began stomping his feet from side to side and the teacher took his hands and began stomping with him and singing a song from a popular television show. Leroy smiled and continued this new dance. When she stopped, he took her hands and initiated the dance steps. After several such stops and starts, Leroy went over and kicked at the slide. The teacher helped him to hold on to the rail and climb the first step, but he whimpered and climbed back down and led his teacher to the water wheel and Leroy watched intently as the wheel moved. When it stopped, he took her hands to get her to do it again. She did it several times and then stood back. Leroy splashed some more and then moved closer to the wheel until his splashing moved it. The teacher moved back in and the two took turns splashing the wheel. Leroy picked up the bright red cup in the table and poured the water on the teacher's hand. She picked up the cup and did likewise, dumping her water on his hands. After several turns, she dumped her cup of water on the water wheel and Leroy followed suit. Later, Leroy put his mouth to the water in the table. His teacher asked him if he wanted a drink and he picked up the cup and led his teacher to the closet where juice is kept and she promptly took the cup and gave him a new cup of juice in exchange. Each time he handed her the cup, she poured a little bit of juice in it and handed it back." pp. 100–101

Source: "A Framework for Understanding Young Children with Severe Multiple Disabilities: The van Dijk Approach to Assessment," by C. Nelson, J. van Dijk, A.P. McDonnell, and K. Thompson, 2002, *Research and Practice for Persons with Severe Disabilities, 27,* 97–111. Reprinted by permission of TASH, Baltimore, MD.

skills that are taught becomes critical at some time between the beginning of the middle school years and the high school years.

2. *What amount of success has the student had thus far in learning academic skills?* If a good attempt has been made to teach the student academic skills, but she has made little progress, this is an indication that instruction should take another form or be terminated. In this area, as in other curricular areas, the value of what is being taught must be questioned and the success or lack of success must be judged. All students with severe disabilities can benefit from instruction, but we must decide what are the most appropriate objectives. Through the experience that the teacher and other teachers have had with the student, the decision must be made whether to continue or move to other areas of instruction.

3. *What type of academic skills are needed for functioning in relevant environments and also for leisure and recreational activities?* Given the student's current and near-future life situation, different types of academic instruction will be useful. For example, a student who is learning to participate in community activities (e.g., shopping for groceries or clothes) needs certain skills, whereas other skills may be needed for leisure activities (e.g., reading magazines, looking at books, reading the television or movie listings). If there is difficulty teaching academic skills for one type of activity, it still may be appropriate to teach for another.

4. *What is the relative value or significance of academic skills when compared to other skills? Are there other skills that will increase independence?* If a student cannot brush his teeth, pull up his pants, or use appropriate social responses, and also lacks basic academic skills, which is more important to teach? The answer to this is simply based on which type of skills will allow the person to be more independent and be viewed more as a valued member of society. Academic skills may be important, but if the individual does not have an adequate repertoire of more basic skills, he is more likely to be shunned by others. On the other hand, many persons with severe disabilities have many functional, generalizable self-care and other daily living skills.

Table 6–3 Summary Form of Leroy's Assessment Using the van Dijk Method

Observation Area	*Strengths in Observed Area*	*What the Individual Is Ready for in Observed Area*	*Next Steps*
Behavioral state	Leroy frequently becomes very sleepy at school and often sleeps during the day. Increased activity elevates his state, but when overstimulated he turns away and begins to yawn.	Leroy's mother notes that sleep–wake patterns at home are somewhat erratic. It is sometimes difficult to get him to go to sleep and then it is difficult to wake him up.	Keep a diary of Leroy's sleep patterns. Begin a regular bedtime routine and engage in routine bedtime activities that help with transitioning to sleep state. Reduce stimulation in response to Leroy's looking away. Use movement to arouse him when he becomes drowsy during the school day.
Orienting response	Leroy orients to a variety of stimuli, including visual stimuli, sounds, voices, and motion.	Consistency in orienting to someone saying his name.	Throughout the day, look for natural opportunities to say his name and then reinforce turning or looking toward you by engaging in favorite turn-taking games.
Learning channels	Leroy uses vision, hearing, and touch to take in information. He must get close (within 2 feet) to see. He appears to have difficulty with depth perception and is afraid of climbing up or down.	Continue to explore the environment using a variety of learning channels.	Allow Leroy to feel steps with his hands before climbing. Help him to establish firm footing and teach him to use handrails. Rotate centers to encourage exploration (e.g., bubbles in sensory table, listening center).
Approach and withdrawal	Smiles and maintains eye contact to show engagement and reaches out to touch what he is interested in. He shows withdrawal by turning away or covering his eyes.	Ready to build routines using the music and rhythms he enjoys. Leroy is ready to refine engagement and disengagement cues so that they will be more readily recognized.	Build routines based on rhythm and reinforce imitation of the routines. Encourage participation with peers in music and rhythm activities. Respond consistently to cues. Try using switch that says "I'm finished."
Memory	Habituates to stimuli and reorients to changes. Has differentiated reactions, anticipates upcoming events, reacts to mismatch, and learns simple routines.	Ready to associate objects with activities, increase functional use of objects, and search for items not present.	Increase functional use of objects in centers such as the kitchen center. Begin associating objects with activities, beginning with favorite activities, and build slowly. Model searching for lost objects.
Interactions	Orients to people and seems to have secure attachments to important people in his life. Begins interactions and engages in turn taking during those interactions. Takes up to six turns in enjoyed activity. Will add more to the interaction.	Ready to expand number of routines that he will engage in, supported by turn taking with peers.	Provide opportunities to add new schemes to routines by following his lead in turn taking and then adding new schemes to be imitated. Provide opportunities to take turns with peers in the context of favorite activities. Provide peer training to encourage peers to follow his lead in turn taking. Use adult reinforcement at first.
Communication	Consistently uses a variety of gestures, vocalizations, and facial expressions to communicate. Guides adults to what he wants. Chooses among preferred activities, toys, food, and people. Is beginning to use objects to communicate.	Ready to begin using objects to represent preferred activities and to make choices by pointing or handing objects representing activities or toys. Increase nonsymbolic conversational turn taking. Ready to begin using conventional gestures to communicate.	Help others in environment to recognize and respond to his nonsymbolic communications. Select an object to represent going outside and going home and begin a simple calendar system. Select two favorite activities for a choice board; encourage Leroy to make a choice by handing an object to another. Model and shape use of conventional gestures such as nodding head and beckoning.

Source: "A Framework for Understanding Young Children with Severe Multiple Disabilities: The van Dijk Approach to Assessment," by C. Nelson, J. van Dijk, A.P. McDonnell, and K. Thompson, 2002, *Research and Practice for Persons with Severe Disabilities, 27*, pp. 97–111. Reprinted by permission of TASH, Baltimore, MD.

For them, it may be more appropriate to teach academic skills to the extent that they can be learned.

5. *What are the wishes of the student and the student's parents on instruction in academic skills?* This is the final question, but certainly not the least important. Students may express an interest in learning academic skills in some form, and this should not be ignored. Parents may say that it is *their* responsibility to teach functional skills and that it is their wish that the school system teach their child academic skills. In cases like this, consideration should certainly be given to their wishes, especially if the student does indeed demonstrate that many skills have been taught in the home by the parents.

After careful consideration of these questions, the teacher, along with the parents and other members of the planning team, will likely choose one of four forms or types of academic curriculum for the student (Browder & Snell, 1993; Ford et al., 1989):

1. The general education curriculum
2. The general education curriculum adapted to focus on the most essential skills
3. A sequenced functional skills curriculum
4. An embedded functional skills curriculum

These approaches and instructional methods in different areas of academic instruction are discussed in Chapter 17. How assessments should be conducted within each area is explained next.

Assessment of students on a *general education curriculum* may be done using commercially produced tests that are appropriate for students with mild disabilities or for nondisabled students, such as the Peabody Individual Achievement Test (Markwardt, 1997); tests of specific skills such as the Woodcock Reading Mastery Test (Woodcock, 1997) and the KeyMath Diagnostic Test (Connolly, 1997); school district checklists of academic skills; or curriculum-based assessment using grade-level curriculum material (Deno, 1985; Howell, Fox, & Morehead, 1994; Salvia & Hughes, 1990).

For students with multiple sensory and/or physical disabilities, evaluation of academic skills may require adaptations to the normal procedures so that speaking and writing are not required. In cooperation with specialists in communication disorders, physical disabilities, and sensory disabilities, the teacher may modify these tests to allow the student to respond to multiple-choice items by pointing to the correct response in an array of options, by using eye glances to indicate her response, by matching objects and symbols, or by signaling yes and no (perhaps with eye blinks or other facial expressions). When using such adaptations of standard procedures, several test sessions will be required to complete the assessment (Bigge & Best, 2001).

Some students with severe disabilities will work on academic skills by pursuing a *general education curriculum adapted to focus on the most essential skills*. Such modifications in the curriculum allow the teacher to focus on those parts of the curriculum that are more essential and applicable to everyday life (Ford et al., 1989). It would be expected that the student could achieve about a second-grade reading level, which would allow for both functional reading and pleasure reading. The student would also have functional mathematics computational skills and be able to learn to use time skills to read schedules, use a calendar, and tell time from a clock face or a digital clock or watch. Students who do not appear to be making adequate progress in the general curriculum may be appropriate candidates for the adapted curriculum.

A *sequenced functional skills curriculum* calls for an instructional emphasis that helps the student to acquire academic skills that will have a direct bearing on life's daily needs. As Ford et al. (1989) ask, "If a student . . . could learn to handle money, manage time, and read and write some of the words that are encountered in everyday life, would that not be a more desirable outcome than his or her having acquired a few rudimentary math and reading skills that were never developed to a point of becoming useful?" (pp. 90–91). A decision should be made to pursue a functional skills curriculum when too much time is spent on academic skills that will not lead to a degree of usefulness. Students who develop skills at this level could read functional words and phrases such as those found in recipes and menus, write short notes and lists, use number lines and calculators to shop for items, and understand time from clocks and watches. Instruction of these skills occurs in the classroom during normal periods of reading, writing, and math. The skills learned are then practiced in applied settings outside the classroom.

Ford et al. (1989) have provided a series of inventories for use in determining key skills appropriate for students to learn at this curricular level. Similar information could be gathered from ecological inventories with a particular focus on the academic skills that appear in them.

The fourth level of academic instruction is an *embedded functional skills curriculum*. For these skills, no time is spent in the classroom on direct instruction. Instead, instruction occurs when the skills are needed naturally during other activities—it is embedded within the instruction in other areas. Students may interpret the meaning of words, pictures, or line drawings as they occur in various contexts; they may enjoy looking at pictures and drawings; they can pay for objects by matching coins to a money card or by using a predetermined amount of money; and they may use picture symbols to follow schedules (Ford et al., 1989). Determining the academic skills to teach students at this curricular level is the same as stated earlier.

Conclusion

The assessment of persons with severe disabilities as described in this chapter provides a starting point for deciding what skills should be taught. The process does not end here, but is ongoing. Not only must the teacher continuously monitor the student's learning on specific objectives, but she must also stay abreast of the environmental needs of the student.

As students get older, change schools, change interests, visit different places in their community, acquire new responsibilities, get new jobs, and so on, their learning needs change. The teacher must communicate with the student (when possible), with parents or caregivers, and with other team members to determine what the student should be learning at a given time.

The student's needs, having been determined through different forms of assessment, will ultimately be discussed and prioritized through the planning processes discussed in Chapter 4.

Questions for Reflection

1. What do you believe is the most important way for determining what students with severe disabilities need to learn? Are any approaches discussed in this chapter more important than others?
2. In what ways might reviewing existing records be detrimental to assessment and planning procedures? Can you design a checksheet to use when gathering information from previous records?
3. What do you believe would be the most useful type of information that parents could provide? Why have parents' views often been neglected?
4. Do you believe that the norm-referenced status of a student based on an adaptive behavior scale is useful information? Why or why not?
5. With several fellow students or colleagues, review the curriculum and activity guides referenced in this chapter and discuss their strengths and weaknesses.
6. What are various ways to determine locations where ecological inventories should be conducted for students of different ages with severe disabilities (e.g., elementary school age, high school age, etc.)?
7. Direct observations of students during structured activities take up a great deal of time. In what ways might a teacher conduct such observations in the most efficient manner?
8. How could the expertise of different professionals be used during unstructured observations and observations during structured activities?
9. Collaboration by professionals during assessment procedures requires a great deal of cooperation and organization. What ways can you think of to facilitate this process?

References

Bierne-Smith, M., Ittenbach, R., & Patton, J. R. (Eds.). (2002). *Mental retardation* (6th ed.). Upper Saddle River, NJ: Merrill/Prentice Hall.

Bigge, J., & Best, S. (2001). Task and situation analysis. In J. L. Bigge, S. J. Best, & K. W. Heller (Eds.). *Teaching individuals with physical, health, or multiple disabilities* (4th ed., pp. 121–148). Upper Saddle River, NJ: Merrill/Prentice Hall.

Brady, N. C., & Halle, J. W. (1997). Functional analysis of communicative behaviors. *Focus on Autism and Other Developmental Disabilities, 12*, 95–104.

Browder, D. M. (1991). *Assessment of individuals with severe disabilities: An applied behavior approach to life skills assessment* (2nd ed.). Baltimore: Paul H. Brookes.

Browder, D. M. (2001). *Curriculum and assessment for students with moderate and severe disabilities*. New York: Guilford Press.

Browder, D. M., & Snell, M. E. (1993). Functional academics. In M. E. Snell (Ed.), *Instruction of students with severe disabilities* (3rd ed., pp. 442–479). New York: Macmillan.

Brown, L., Branston-McLean, M. B., Baumgart, D., Vincent, L., Falvey, M., & Schroeder, J. (1979). Using the characteristics of current and subsequent least restrictive environments as factors in the development of curricular content for severely handicapped students. *AAESPH Review, 4*, 407–424.

Bruininks, R. H., Thurlow, M. L., & Gilman, C. J. (1987). Adaptive behavior and mental retardation. *Journal of Special Education, 21*(1), 69–88.

Bruininks, R. H., Woodcock, R. W., Weatherman, R. F., & Hill, B. K. (1985). *The scales of independent behavior*. Allen, TX: DLM Teaching Resources.

Cone, J. D. (1984). *The pyramid scales*. Austin, TX: PRO-ED.

Cone, J. D. (1987). Intervention planning using adaptive behavior instruments. *Journal of Special Education, 21*(1), 127–148.

Connolly, A. J. (1997). *KeyMath Revised/NU: A diagnostic inventory of essential mathematics*. Circle Pines, MN: American Guidance Service.

Demaray, M. K., Ruffalo, S. L., Carlson, J., Busse, R. T., Olson, A. E., McManus, S. M., & Leventhal, A. (1995). Social skills assessment: A comparative evaluation of six published rating scales. *School Psychology Review, 24*, 648–671.

Deno, S. (1985). Curriculum-based measurement: The emerging alternative. *Exceptional Children, 52*, 219–232.

Dever, R. B. (1988). *Community living skills: A taxonomy*. Washington, DC: American Association on Mental Retardation.

Downing, J. E. (Ed.). (2002). *Including students with severe and multiple disabilities in typical classrooms* (2nd ed.). Baltimore: Paul H. Brookes.

Dunn, W. (1996). The sensorimotor systems: A framework for assessment and intervention. In F. P. Orelove & D. Sobsey (Eds.), *Educating children with multiple disabilities: A transdisciplinary approach* (pp. 35–78). Baltimore: Paul H. Brookes.

Falvey, M. A. (Ed.). (1995). *Inclusive and heterogeneous schooling: Assessment, curriculum, and instruction*. Baltimore: Paul H. Brookes.

Ford, A., Schnorr, R., Meyer, L., Davern, L., Black, J., & Dempsey, P. (Eds.). (1989). *The Syracuse community-referenced curriculum guide for students with moderate and severe disabilities*. Baltimore: Paul H. Brookes.

Gage, S. T., & Falvey, M. A. (1995). Assessment strategies to develop appropriate curricula and educational programs. In M. A. Falvey (Ed.), *Inclusive and heterogeneous schooling: Assessment, curriculum, and instruction* (pp. 59–110). Baltimore: Paul H. Brookes.

Giangreco, M. F., Cloninger, C. J., & Iverson, V. S. (1998). *Choosing options and accommodations for children: A guide to planning inclusive education* (2nd ed.). Baltimore: Paul H. Brookes.

Gresham, F. M., & Elliott, S. N. (1990). *The social skills rating system*. Circle Pines, MN: American Guidance Service.

Howell, K. W., Fox, S. L., & Morehead, M. K. (1994). *Curriculum-based evaluation: Teaching and decision-making* (2nd ed.). Pacific Grove, CA: Brooks/Cole.

Lambert, N., Nihira, K., & Leland, H. (1993). *AAMR adaptive behavior scale—School* (2nd ed.). Austin, TX: PRO-ED.

Lehr, D. H. (1989). Educational programming for young children with the most severe disabilities. In F. Brown & D. H. Lehr (Eds.), *Persons with profound disabilities: Issues and practices* (pp. 213–237). Baltimore: Paul H. Brookes.

Leland, H. (1991). Adaptive behavior scales. In J. L. Matson & J. A. Mulick (Eds.), *Handbook of mental retardation* (2nd ed., pp. 211–221). New York: Pergamon Press.

Markwardt, F. C. (1997). *Peabody individual achievement test—Revised*. Circle Pines, MN: American Guidance Service.

Martin, J. E., & Huber Marshall, L. H. (1996a). ChoiceMaker: A comprehensive self-determination transition program. *Intervention in School and Clinic, 30*, 147–156.

Martin, J. E., & Huber Marshall, L. H. (1996b). *ChoiceMaker self-determination transition assessment*. Longmont, CO: Sopris West.

Neel, R. S., & Billingsley, F. F. (1989). *IMPACT: A functional curriculum handbook for students with moderate to severe disabilities*. Baltimore: Paul H. Brookes.

Nelson, C., van Dijk, J., McDonnell, A. P., Thompson, K. (2002). A framework for understanding young children with severe multiple disabilities: The van Dijk approach to assessment. *Research and Practice for Persons with Severe Disabilities, 27*, 97–111.

Nihira, K., Leland, H., & Lambert, N. (1993). *AAMR adaptive behavior scale—Residential and community* (2nd ed.). Austin, TX: PRO-ED.

Noonan, M. J., & Siegel-Causey, E. (1990). Special needs of students with severe handicaps. In L. McCormick & R. Schiefelbusch (Eds.), *Early language intervention: An introduction* (pp. 383–425). Upper Saddle River, NJ: Merrill/Prentice Hall.

Orelove, F. P., & Sobsey, D. (1996). *Educating children with multiple disabilities: A transdisciplinary approach*. Baltimore: Paul H. Brookes.

Rainforth, B., Giangreco, M., & Dennis, R. (1989). Motor skills. In A. Ford, R. Schnorr, L. Meyer, L. Davern, J. Black, & P. Dempsey (Eds.), *The Syracuse community-referenced curriculum guide for students with moderate and severe disabilities* (pp. 211–230). Baltimore: Paul H. Brookes.

Rainforth, B., & York-Barr, J. (1997). *Collaborative teams for students with severe disabilities: Integrating therapy and educational services* (2nd ed.). Baltimore: Paul H. Brookes.

Rynders, J. E., & Horrobin, J. M. (1990). Always trainable? Never educable? Updating educational expectations concerning children with Down syndrome. *American Journal on Mental Retardation, 95*, 77–83.

Salvia, J., & Hughes, C. (1990). *Curriculum-based assessment: Testing what is taught*. Upper Saddle River, NJ: Prentice Hall.

Sigafoos, J., & York, J. (1991). Using ecological inventories to promote functional communication. In J. Reichle, J. York, & J. Sigafoos (Eds.), *Implementing augmentative and alternative communication* (pp. 61–70). Baltimore: Paul H. Brookes.

Sparrow, S. S., Balla, D. A., & Cicchetti, D. V. (1984). *Vineland adaptive behavior scales*. Circle Pines, MN: American Guidance Service.

Storey, K. (1996). Social validation issues in social skills assessment. *International Journal of Disability, Development and Education, 43*, 167–174.

Wehmeyer, M. L. (1995). *The Arc's self-determination scale: Procedural guidelines.* Arlington, TX: The Arc of the United States.

Westling, D. L., & Koorland, M. A. (1988). *The special educator's handbook.* Boston: Allyn and Bacon.

Wilcox, B., & Bellamy, T. G. (1987). *The activities catalog: An alternative curriculum for youth and adults with severe disabilities.* Baltimore: Paul H. Brookes.

Woodcock, R. W. (1997). *Woodcock reading mastery tests—Revised.* Circle Pines, MN: American Guidance Service.

PART 3

General Instructional Procedures

Chapter 7
Teaching Students to Acquire New Skills

Chapter 8
Teaching Skills for Generalization and Maintenanace

Chapter 9
Evaluating Student Progress

Chapter 10
Supporting Students within Inclusive Classrooms

CHAPTER 7

Teaching Students to Acquire New Skills

Instructional procedures for teaching students with severe disabilities to learn new skills are discussed in this chapter. The chapter begins with a brief overview of appropriate general instructional strategies and then continues with specific procedures to be used for skill acquisition, including prompting methods, nondirect instruction, stimulus modifications, using natural cues, reinforcement and error correction, and procedures for increasing compliance.

Elements of Effective Instruction

Effective instruction of students with severe disabilities calls for the use of strategies and tactics that lead to the acquisition of new behaviors or skills. Special and general education teachers who teach students with severe disabilities must use both sound general teaching strategies and effective, specific instructional tactics if the students are to have successful learning experiences. The planning and assessment procedures explained in previous chapters should lead parents, teachers, and other members of the team to arrive at a minimum set of objectives for the student. These will be the primary targets for instruction. Additionally, of course, instruction on nontargeted objectives may occur throughout the day, often through the use of nondirect instructional procedures, to enrich the student's educational experience (Giangreco, Cloninger, & Iverson, 1998).

This chapter begins with a brief overview of how to develop instructional or behavioral objectives, followed by a discussion of appropriate general teaching practices. Next, the operant learning paradigm is briefly reviewed to provide a context for the major section of the chapter: specific tactics for teaching students with severe disabilities how to learn new skills. The chapter concludes with a format for writing instructional plans for specific objectives. In the two chapters that follow, ways to achieve skill maintenance and generalization of acquired skills are explained (Chapter 8) and procedures for documenting student learning through portfolio assessments and continuous direct measures are discussed (Chapter 9).

Types of Objectives to Teach

Appropriate instructional objectives for students with severe disabilities are usually those that students were unable to demonstrate adequately when they were observed during assessment activities or that appeared to be important based on other types of information. Deciding on the objectives to be targeted for instruction is a critical decision that calls for the consensus of all team members. The format for writing behavioral objectives was presented in Chapter 5 within the discussion of IEPs. In addition, you will recall from Chapter 6 that we identified four types or categories of behaviors appropriate for assessment and direct instruction: *simple, discrete behaviors; continuous, ongoing behaviors; complex, chained skills;* and *functional routines.* Depending on the student's needs and abilities, the objectives that are written will be one or more of these types. If necessary, you should review the structure of these behavioral objective forms as discussed in Chapter 6. The following are some examples:

- Jesus will shake his head up and down to indicate when he wants an offered item or activity 90% of the time that something is offered. He will do this throughout the school day in different locations with different people for five continuous days (simple, discrete behavior).
- Sara will take an item in her hand when it is offered to her 80% of the time for three consecutive days (simple, discrete behavior).
- Joan will hold her head erect for 5 minutes when engaged in cooperative learning activities with her fellow fourth graders during social studies and language arts class throughout the semester (continuous, ongoing behavior).
- Huan will remain actively involved in physical education exercises for 20 minutes after the exercises begin every day during PE class (continuous, ongoing behavior).
- Mac will play the pinball machine at the recreation center, completing all the necessary steps, until the game has been completed two days a week after school (complex, chained skill).
- Rhonda will fold all the laundry after it has been taken out of the dryer both in her training apartment and at home when requested by her father or mother (complex, chained skill).
- Alexis will complete all necessary bathroom activities after appropriately using the toilet, including pulling up pants, flushing the toilet, and washing and drying hands. She will do this in any location where she must use the bathroom (functional routine).
- When Jeff is hungry after school, he will prepare an appropriate snack, eat it, and clean up after he has finished (functional routine).

As you read each of the above objectives, notice that each states *who* the learner is and *what* he or she is expected to be able to do, *under what conditions,* and *how often.* All objectives should include these dimensions. In some cases it is also important to add a time dimension stating *how long the behavior should occur* or *how quickly.*

Of course, these characteristics do not tell what is or is not an appropriate objective. That decision must be made through the assessment and planning process. As part of this process, when parents and professionals are considering the importance of objectives, they should try to answer the following questions:

- Is the skill functional in that it will allow the student to have more independence, less dependence, greater participation, or a better quality of life?
- Is the skill appropriate for the chronological age of the individual?
- Is the skill something that the student will use in his present living condition or in the near future?
- Is the skill something that will help the student to be better accepted by others?
- Will the skill allow the individual to live and participate in more life environments?
- Is the skill considered important by the individual with severe disabilities and by those close to the person?

Rosales-Ruiz and Baer (1997) discussed the concept of the behavioral cusp. The *behavioral cusp* is "a behavior change that has consequences for the [learner] that go beyond the change itself, some of which may be considered important" (p. 537). For example, a child who has learned to walk is not only able to walk, but is able do things that he would not be able to do otherwise, such as play with his siblings and get desired objects. Thus the walking has more value than the simple act of walking itself. Bosch and Fuqua (2001) expanded on the concept. They said that meeting certain criteria would help to determine behaviors that could be considered as cusps and thus behaviors that should be given priority for instruction. These included:

- *Access to new reinforcers, contingencies, or environments.* For example, a person that learns to safely cross a street can have access to restaurants, shopping centers, and movies.
- *Generativeness.* The behavior may serve as a prerequisite to other learning or be a component of a more complex learning process. For example, learning to read words on a simple recipe may facilitate using the recipe to bake a cake.
- *Competition with inappropriate responses.* Some targeted behaviors may replace inappropriate behaviors. For example, learning to request a toy may alleviate the need to hit someone to gain access to the toy.
- *Number and relative importance of people affected.* How much does the response benefit other people? A child who is taught to eat appropriately in the cafeteria may increase the mealtime pleasure of peers sitting nearby.
- *Social validity.* If the behavior is one that is acceptable to the society in which the person lives, it will be more valued.

Any objective that might result in learning a behavioral cusp would certainly be one that should be targeted for instruction.

Function Over Form

For many objectives, if not for all, more concern should be placed on the student achieving a critical effect instead of demonstrating a behavior in a way that is typical for people without disabilities. In other words, function is more important than form. This is especially important in complex, chained behavioral objectives or functional routines in which multiple steps are necessary for achieving the objective. Brown, Evans, Weed, and Owen (1987) made a distinction between *fixed* and *substitutable* routines and the specific behaviors that comprise them. Although some skills, such as "brushing teeth," require very specific behaviors to occur (although not necessarily in a particular order), other skills may have different forms and yet achieve the same *function.* For example, "spending leisure time with a friend" may have the form of listening to CDs together, walking in the park, playing cards, or hanging out at the recreational center. Each will achieve the same function, but each will take a different form.

Extending the Objective

Although behavioral objectives represent the most critical learning targets for students, they should not be limited or taught in an isolated fashion. Instead, *extension* activities can be added, particularly to task-analyzed behaviors or skills (Brown et al., 1987). Extension activities such as *initiating* the activity, *preparing* for the activity, *monitoring the quality* of one's performance, *monitoring the tempo* of performance, *problem solving* if necessary, and *terminating* the activity when appropriate may be applied to extend different core skills to increase a student's opportunity for participation. Additionally, during many activities it is possible for the student to work on enrichment skills or related skills in communication, social interaction, expression of choice, or other forms of self-determination (Brown et al., 1987).

Partial Participation

In some cases it is appropriate for objectives to reflect a desire for a student to learn how to at least partially participate in some activities (Baumgart et al., 1982; Ferguson & Baumgart, 1991). Simply because a student cannot learn to cook a meal, put on a sweater, or engage independently in activities in a community recreational center does not mean that she cannot participate in some part of the activity or participate using a form different from that used by others. By employing even simple, discrete behaviors (e.g., reaching, touching, holding, or looking), the student may participate in a wide variety of activities. Suppose, for example, that third-grade students are making a cake as part of a lesson on foods and are working within cooperative groups. Each student may have a particular assignment to perform. If a child has a severe disability it may be difficult for him to perform the activities that the other children are doing, but it may be possible to participate by holding a utensil or a bowl, pouring an ingredient, or pressing the switch on an electric mixer. The student may be able to make such actions alone or with the assistance of the teacher, the teacher's assistant, or another student. Regardless, this form of participation by the student can represent an important aspect of the educational experience, contribute to the group activity in a meaningful way, and allow the student to practice a relevant objective.

Four strategies can assist teachers in making partial participation meaningful for students, especially for students with the most severe or multiple disabilities (Ferguson & Baumgart, 1991). First, the student should be engaged in an *active* manner, rather than in a passive way. Even though a student may have limited movement and a restricted repertoire of skills, objectives may be developed for abilities and skills to be used in different ways. Second, the teacher must make sure that the type of participation, albeit partial, is *responsive to a multiple-perspective view* of the student's needs. In other words, the perspectives should be family- and community-based and related to the daily life of the student. Teachers should monitor the student's learning from the view of others. This can be done by asking key people about how the student is performing and whether, in their view, her quality of life is being positively affected. Third, teachers should *avoid piecemeal participation* (i.e., the student is partially participating only some of the time) by devising daily schedules that continuously involve the student. Finally, the teacher or another person should always *be as involved as necessary* to ensure that participation occurs. In some cases, as discussed later in this chapter, it will be appropriate for the teacher to reduce assistance, but this should not be done if it jeopardizes the student's opportunity to be involved.

Good General Teaching Practices

All teachers should realize that there are research-based, effective teaching strategies that should be used regardless of whether students have disabilities, regardless of the instructional objectives, and regardless of the particular characteristics or ages of students. Use of these practices will improve the learning of students without disabilities, at-risk students, and students with mild or severe disabilities. In other words, *good general teaching practices will benefit all students.* The following are summarized from many research-based teaching practices reviewed by Cotton (1995, 1998), Sikorski, Niemiec, and Walberg (1996), the U.S. Department of Education (1986), and Wolery, Ault, and Doyle (1992).

- *Carefully plan instruction.* Identify goals and objectives, instructional activities, and resources, and plan integrated instructional activities. Modify instruction to help students with unique learning needs.
- *Manage instructional time efficiently.* The more time a student spends engaged in instructional activities, the more he is likely to learn. Teachers, therapists, and aides must coordinate their time to maximize students' learning time. Daily activities should be planned in advance so that every minute is used in the most productive way.
- *Manage student behavior effectively.* Teachers should develop simple rules and reinforce students for appropriate behavior. Students should learn that they must participate in learning activities and not behave in ways that are socially unacceptable.
- *Design instructional groups that meet students' learning needs.* Use whole-group instruction when

introducing new concepts; use smaller groups to ensure that all students are learning. Use heterogeneous cooperative learning groups.

- *Carefully present instructional stimuli and procedures.* Teachers must give clear directions and other forms of input, review previously learned skills, keep instruction occurring at a steady pace, and make smooth transitions from one activity to another.
- *Establish smooth, efficient classroom routines.* Begin class quickly and purposefully with assignments and activities, having materials and supplies ready for students. Handle administrative matters and other noninstructional needs quickly and efficiently with a minimum of disruption to the instructional process.
- *Provide frequent feedback to the student.* Performance will improve if the student knows if he is performing a task correctly; the teacher needs to provide reinforcement for correct responses and correct those responses that are not.
- *Monitor students' performance.* Teachers must have a system that allows them to track the performance of students on the objectives that they should be working toward achieving. When a student is not making satisfactory progress, a change is needed in the objective or in the instructional method being used.
- *Review and reteach material as necessary.* Provide regular, focused reviews of key concepts and skills. Don't allow learned knowledge and skills to be forgotten. Regular review will assist with retention.
- *Integrate workplace readiness skills into instruction.* Communicate to students the importance of meaningful employment during adulthood. Focus on problem-solving skills as preparation for participation in the world of work.
- *Have appropriately high expectations for students.* What teachers believe about students' learning ability can have a bearing on how much or how little students can learn. It is sometimes assumed that when a student has a severe disability many skills cannot be learned. Although some limitations exist, a positive attitude toward students' learning ability may increase what is actually learned.
- *Interact with students in a positive, caring way.* Show concern about students' problems and pay attention to their interests and accomplishments. Be aware of students' lives, both in and out of the classroom. Make sure that you clearly communicate your care to the students.

These approaches to daily instruction and teacher–student interaction will increase the productivity of the teacher's teaching and the students' learning, and all professional educators should employ them to increase the effectiveness of their teaching. Sikorski et al. (1996) provide an observation form that can be used by schools or individual teachers to monitor the occurrence of effective classroom practices. Many of the items included are particularly relevant to teaching students with severe disabilities.

In addition to these preferred *general* teaching practices, *specific* teaching practices have been found to be effective for students with severe disabilities. Before examining them, however, a general paradigm for learning, an operant paradigm, should be considered to provide a context for the specific tactics that will be discussed.

How Behaviors and Skills Are Learned

Many theories and concepts have been developed to explain learning: what it is, how it occurs, how it is impaired, and the conditions that are associated with it. We cannot discuss all these at this time. However, when we consider learning specific skills by persons with severe disabilities, it may be useful to do so within the paradigm of *operant learning* (Alberto & Troutman, 2002; Wolery et al., 1992).

Operant learning considers behavior to occur primarily as a function of the external environment. Particular behaviors, whether they are motoric or verbal, simple or complex, occur because of a history of reinforcement. This means that the behavior has occurred and has been followed by a positive consequence, resulting in an increase in the probability that the behavior will occur again in the future (Alberto & Troutman, 2002; Sailor & Guess, 1983). Learning is defined as a change in behavior. The operant learning condition is depicted by the following formula:

> behavior + consequence (positive) = high probability of future occurrence

An example might be greeting people by saying hello, because just about every time we say hello to someone, it is positively reinforced by that person saying hello to us. If there were not such a response, there would be a lower probability that we would say hello in the future. Virtually any behavior that exists in an individual's behavioral repertoire has been reinforced on several occasions (the exception to this is physiologically based behavior such as a seizure), which is to say that the person has learned the behavior.

But it is also obvious that not only do previously reinforced behaviors occur with regular frequency, but they usually occur under certain conditions and not others. These conditions exist in the environment and present themselves before the behavior and are therefore called *behavioral antecedents.* Since some tend to trigger or prompt certain behaviors and not others, they can be referred to as *discriminative stimuli.* The addition of this component to the behavioral formula changes it to the following:

> antecedent (discriminative stimuli) + behavior + consequence = high probability of future occurrence when antecedent is present

This suggests that a particular behavior is more likely to occur when the corresponding antecedent (discriminative stimulus) is present and when there is a positive consequence that follows the behavior. Extending the example used above illustrates this condition.

The greetings we usually extend are to particular people that we know or they occur in certain situations when greetings are appropriate. For example, if we are walking down the street and we see someone we know, we will probably say hello. Or if we walk into a clothing store and see a salesperson, again it is likely that we will say hello. Under both circumstances the behavior is appropriate and most often will be reinforced with a response from the other person. In contrast, if we are walking down a busy avenue, we are not likely to greet everyone we see. Essentially, we *attend to* and *discriminate* the relevant conditions under which certain behaviors should occur and those that indicate that behaviors should not occur. We learn to make these discriminations based on multiple experiences that teach us the relationship between antecedents, behaviors, and consequences.

All the above clearly applies to behaviors that exist, but what is the origin of a new behavior or new skill? If we stop to think about all that we know and know how to do—daily living skills, socially interacting with others, communicating, performing academic exercises, and so on—we realize that, despite the presence of a broad skill repertoire, at some earlier time these skills did not exist.

Normally, individuals learn their many skills in several ways. One way is through *differential reinforcement* of existing behaviors only when they occur under certain environmental circumstances. At the outset, these behaviors may not have any intention or purpose, but when they occur in certain contexts and are reinforced in these contexts, they become *learned* behaviors; that is, they become controlled or influenced by certain stimuli. Take, for example, the infant who randomly says "dada." This behavior reflects normal development, but occurs initially without any particular intention. However, the parents will generally reinforce the behavior only when it is appropriate, for example, when daddy is present, or is expected, or is wanted. On the other hand, when it is not appropriate for the situation, the parent(s) will say "No, that's not daddy." Sooner or later the child will learn to say "dada" under the appropriate circumstances. When a behavior is appropriately influenced to occur or not occur by environmental conditions, both antecedents and reinforcers, *stimulus control* has been established and the behavior has been learned.

New behaviors also result from differential reinforcement of behaviors of a somewhat different form. Taking again the example of the baby saying "dada," we can see that this rough form of the word ultimately takes on the more accepted form of "daddy." Part of the reason this occurs is because those around the child will *differentially reinforce* more correct responses. At first "dada" is accepted and reinforced; but as the baby grows older, forms of the word that are closer to the norm will be reinforced, while less mature forms will be corrected or ignored. Ultimately, a new behavior will be formed: saying "daddy."

Another way in which initial learning occurs is through the observation and imitation of others. The ability to follow a model is very important for learning verbal skills, social skills, and many other things. The learner attends to what another is doing, imitates it under a similar circumstance, is reinforced, and ultimately demonstrates the behavior or skill after the model is no longer there. Since reinforcement has occurred in the presence of certain stimuli, these stimuli take over as the environmental elements that influence the subsequent occurrence of the behavior. Development of imitation is critical to early learning, but also continues throughout life. Future teachers, for example, learn many of their teaching behaviors by observing and imitating the teaching of veteran teachers.

People can also develop new skills by being verbally directed to perform the skills. Appropriate directions tell what to do, when to do it, and/or how to do it. Sometimes the verbal directions may also tell why. If a skill has not been learned (e.g., how to solve an algebra problem), the verbal direction must tell the student first to "solve the problem" and then will explain how the problem-solving behavior is to occur, that is, how the student should respond given the elements of the problem. The ability to acquire skills from others through the use of language is what makes humankind such a remarkable and accomplished species. When we broaden this form of input to include written language as well as spoken language, we have indeed an extremely useful mechanism for people to learn new skills and behaviors. After acquisition of these skills, the same antecedent–behavior–consequence paradigm maintains the subsequent occurrence and continuation of the behaviors.

Finally, some new skills may be learned through direct physical contact and guidance. Young children learning to use a knife to cut up their food may need to have someone guide their hand, directing them through a slicing motion. As the child becomes a little more skillful, verbal directions may be sufficient, for example, "Turn the knife over and slice back and forth. Press down hard." A person learning to skate is another case in which direct physical contact may be necessary during the initial stage of skill acquisition, and this guidance may occur until the person learns to skate appropriately.

As people grow older, they usually develop an adequate ability to learn new skills through verbal input (either oral or written) and/or modeling and rely less and less on physical contact to guide them through a specific movement. However, in some circumstances some form of physical contact may help in the initial learning process, especially when the behavior being learned is physical. For example, a coach might tell or show a new football player how to block, but might also need to physically position the player to get the best performance. In most situations, however, most persons can learn most skills by watching them occur and/or by receiving verbal directions.

Instructional Tactics for Teaching New Skills to Students with Severe Disabilities

The operant paradigm provides a functional model in which to develop instructional practices for teaching new skills to individuals with severe disabilities. Various cues or prompts will serve as antecedents for behaviors to be learned, and positive reinforcement will be used, often differentially, as a consequence following desirable forms of the behaviors. As the behavior develops, the instructional strategy will be to move away from obtrusive and artificial stimuli and reinforcement as much as possible and toward maintenance of the behavior by natural stimuli and reinforcers. Numerous instructional strategies and tactics can be used to take an individual from a level of not being able to perform a specific act or skill to being able to do so with some degree of independence. The facility with which the student learns depends on both the learning ability of the student and the teaching ability of the teacher. Clearly, students who have severe disabilities will not be able to learn as efficiently as students who do not have disabilities or those who have relatively mild disabilities. Nevertheless, all students are capable of learning and at least part of their success depends on how well they are taught. Instructional tactics that lead toward success are discussed in the following sections.

Instructional Prompts

Several prompting tactics are useful for teaching students new behaviors. Prompts may be defined as "any teacher behaviors that cause students to know how to do a behavior correctly. In a more precise sense, response prompts are teacher behaviors presented to increase the probability of correct responding" (Wolery et al., 1992, p. 37). In reference to the operant paradigm, we might think of the difficulty in learning experienced by a student with a severe disability as a low probability of attending to a particular stimulus (or a group of stimuli), responding in a normally acceptable manner, or being reinforced in the normal fashion. Response prompting is intended to help the student to make the correct response in the presence of a particular discriminative stimulus so that reinforcement can occur. Several forms of prompts may be used. Again, however, keep in mind that these prompts are intended to assist the student in *initially* acquiring a behavior; they should give way to less intrusive or more natural stimuli as learning improves over time.

Gestural Prompts

Some behaviors may be prompted with hand motions, pointing, head nodding, or other nonverbal prompts that are intended to provide a supplemental cue to a student so that she will perform a behavior that is appropriate for a particular situation and that is normally prompted by a natural cue in this situation. A student learning to bus tables in a restaurant who does not notice a table that needs to be cleared could be prompted by a job coach using a slight nod of the head. Normally, the cluttered table would serve as a natural stimulus, but in this case the additional prompt may be required to get the student to act. Similarly, a student who has removed his coat but does not know where it should be placed could be easily prompted by a gesture to hang the coat on a hook.

Gestures are events that commonly occur among people without disabilities. For this reason, using a gesture as a prompt is a tactic that a teacher can do easily and in a natural fashion. If gestures are used as behavioral prompts, however, the teacher must be aware of their limitations. A gesture may not work; it may not exert sufficient stimulus control over the student to initiate the desired behavior. This suggests that a more direct form of prompting should be used. Another problem, one that is exactly opposite, is that the gesture may exert too much control. When this occurs, the student may become overly reliant on the artificial cue and respond appropriately only after seeing the teacher give the gestural prompt, instead of responding to the natural cue. Because this type of prompt dependency may occur for other types of prompts as well, teachers must attempt to eliminate all artificial prompts through systematic instructional procedures.

Verbal Prompts

The use of a specific verbal statement that tells a student what to do and how to do it (as opposed to simply telling a student to do something) is a verbal prompt. If, for example, a student is learning to play checkers, the person teaching him or her might say, "When my piece is right next to yours like that, you need to jump it. Go ahead and jump my piece now." It is important to note that verbal prompts are specific to the performance of particular behaviors. A verbal statement that is more general, like "let's play checkers," would be considered a suggestion or direction, but not a verbal prompt.

Wolery et al. (1992) point out that there are five types of verbal prompts: those that tell how to do a behavior, those that tell how to do part of a behavior, those that give a rule to follow, those that give a hint, and those that provide options. When a verbal prompt is given, it must be clear, as natural as possible, and effective (i.e., the student must be able to respond correctly to the prompt). It is understandable that some students with severe disabilities may not have acquired a level of receptive language sufficient to allow them to respond to a verbal prompt. In such cases, the teacher must use other forms of prompts along with the verbal prompt until the student can respond to the verbal prompt.

Prerecorded Auditory Prompts

Many times students with severe disabilities must rely continuously on verbal directions from a teacher, job coach, or another individual to assist them in completing a task. The constant presence of others reduces the independence of the learner and increases the cost of instruction. One way to counter both of these problems is to use prerecorded auditory prompts. This is done by conducting the task analysis of the skill to be learned and then audiotape recording the prompts necessary for the student to complete the task. Based on a review of research, Post and Story (2002) suggest that the following steps be used in auditory prompting systems.

1. Create a task analysis by breaking down the targeted task into sequential performance steps.
2. Create a written script of these steps for recording on a cassette tape. Designate a script reader who is known and liked by the individual, or experiment with various readers for a positive effect. Choose precise wording tailored to individual's language usage.
3. Make the recording. Wait time between prompts should be determined by observation of the individual's work pace. Adjusting the length of intervals between prompts may take some experimenting.
4. Prompts of encouragement or embedded music to provide positive reinforcement may be inserted into the wait time between instructional prompts. This step may be used if the prompt system is designed to stay on (not be turned off to perform the instruction and turned on again to listen to the next instructional step).
5. Model the physical operation of the tape player with the headsets and have the individual practice wearing and operating the equipment. Many players are designed so that they may be worn attached to a belt, apron, or vest pocket. An individual's favorite tape-recorded music may be used for this step.
6. Modify operational buttons on the tape player, if necessary.
7. Once it is determined that the individual can put on, operate, and remove the tape-recording equipment, introduce the recorded cassette with the script containing the task analysis.
8. Instruct the individual to press the on button, listen to the step, and then turn off the player and perform the step. If there is difficulty in performing the step,

have the individual speak the step out loud before performing it. It may be necessary to model or prompt with verbal or physical support.

9. Monitor the individual's use of the system until he or she has demonstrated competence and independence with system operation and task performance.
10. Once the specific task has been learned, the prompt system may be removed or gradually eliminated. Some individuals may prefer to continue to use the prompt system according to their need or comfort level. If the auditory prompt system is removed, it can easily be reintroduced if learning fades.

Pictorial (Two-Dimensional) Prompts

In some situations, students may be prompted to perform a particular behavior through the use of pictures or other two-dimensional stimuli (e.g., words, symbols, and signs). Depending on the situation in which these visual prompts may be required, they may be formatted or arranged in different ways. Copeland and Hughes (2000) used job picture books to increase the performance of two adolescents with severe disabilities, a boy with autism and a girl with moderate mental retardation. Each of the students had jobs (the boy in a cafeteria, the girl in a hotel), but they relied too much on prompting by trainers to complete their duties successfully. Copeland and Hughes created picture books to allow the students to prompt themselves independently for each step in their tasks and monitor their own performance. The picture books consisted of photographs representing each step in the students' task analyses. The students were taught to self-initiate by first pointing to the picture of the step in the task, then completing the step, and then turning the page in the book to indicate to themselves that the step was completed and it was time to do the next step.

Pictorial prompts have advantages and disadvantages. They have the potential for being used without the intervention of another person. In some cases they can be used in a very unobtrusive fashion and can be made available to the student in ways that only he needs to be aware of. However, the student must initially learn to attend to the two-dimensional prompt when it is appropriate to do so and remember to attend when necessary; otherwise, picture prompts will not serve adequately as stimuli. Finally, the student must be able to interpret the prompt. In other words, the visual images that are presented must not be of a level of complexity that is too difficult for the student to respond to appropriately.

Model Prompts

Imitation is a natural form of learning, and some behaviors that need to be learned may be prompted by an instructor's (or peer's) modeling or demonstration of the behavior. A teacher attempting to teach a 5-year-old how to put on a coat might do so by demonstrating how to do it as the child watches or may have a competent peer demonstrate the process. Because the prerequisite to modeling is attending, the teacher would have to be certain that the child is looking or paying attention. In addition to visual models, verbal models may also be used and are particularly useful in teaching speech and language skills.

Model prompts alone may not be effective for some students with severe disabilities who do not readily imitate the actions of others. In such cases, model behavior may be combined with other forms of prompts to cue the occurrence of a behavior.

Partial and Full Physical Prompts

If a student does not respond with the appropriate physical movement called for by a natural stimulus (e.g., the student is thirsty, there is a glass of water on the table, the student does not lift the glass and take a drink of water) or does not respond when other prompting techniques are used, such as those just described, physical prompts may be used to teach the student how to respond. These prompts may be partial or full.

For the preceding condition, a full physical response would require that the instructor place her hand over the student's hand and guide the student's hand to grasp the glass, pick it up, take a sip of water, and then return the glass to the table. The use of the full prompt is the most intrusive and controlling prompt, because the person providing the prompt is performing the behavior, not the student himself. Generally, full physical prompts should be used only when it does not seem that the student will respond to less direct methods of prompting.

Like full physical prompts, partial physical prompts require the teacher to touch the student, but the touch may be a nudge, a tap, guidance partially through the movement, or contact on a part of the arm (the wrist, the forearm). It is less manipulative and less intrusive than fully guiding the hand. Sometimes full prompting is used until the student begins to show some volitional movement; then it is faded to partial physical prompts.

Full and partial physical prompts should always be paired with less intrusive prompt forms, particularly verbal or gestural prompts. When the physical prompts are gradually eliminated or faded, it may be necessary to continue to cue the behavior with the less intrusive prompts. The pairing technique may facilitate this because, as the physical influence is diminished, the verbal or gestural prompt may gain stimulus control.

Mixed Prompts

Various types of prompts may be mixed or combined to better ensure the occurrence of a behavior (e.g., verbal + physical, verbal + model, pictorial + verbal). Combinations of prompts seem more natural and are often more effective. When using such combinations, however, teachers should remain cognizant of what types of prompts are being used so that they can fade components of the multiple prompts systematically. Mechling and Gast (1997) demonstrated the use of a combined auditory–visual self-prompting system to teach four elementary school-age students with moderate mental disabilities to complete domestic chores, such as putting dishes in a dishwasher and sorting groceries. The prompting device, a *Digivox,* used digitized recorded speech that prompted the students to perform different parts of the task when they pressed a certain symbol, picture, or photograph overlaid on an area of the device. Probes that compared their performance with and without the self-prompted directions clearly indicated that activating the verbal prompts resulted in an increase in correct responses.

Applying Prompts during Skill Acquisition Training

To the extent that it is possible, the ultimate goal of an instructor using any of the types of prompts described is to eliminate the artificial, teacher-made prompts so that the student will respond to the natural environmental conditions (stimuli) by demonstrating the behavior or skill when it is typically required (Ford & Mirenda, 1984). Sometimes complete elimination of artificial prompts is possible; sometimes only partial elimination can be achieved. Nevertheless, prompt reduction is the goal, for which several methods can be used.

Over a number of years researchers have developed and studied different ways that students with severe disabilities can learn to acquire new skills through prompt reduction methods. These methods are designed to initially prompt behaviors, but then to eliminate the prompts. Reviews and additional information about the tactics are available from several sources (Ault, Wolery, Doyle, & Gast, 1989; Billingsley & Romer, 1983; Demchak, 1990; Doyle, Wolery, Ault, & Gast, 1988; Schoen, 1986; Wolery et al., 1992; Wolery & Gast, 1984). As will be seen in the explanations provided next, these tactics arrange prompts in different combinations to get behaviors and skills to occur independently.

Before considering these techniques, two important concepts must be understood: *target stimuli* and *controlling stimuli* (Wolery et al., 1992). A target stimulus is the discriminative stimulus that is expected to *ultimately* control the occurrence of a behavior or group of behaviors after training has been completed. It may be a verbal direction or cue from an individual (e.g., "Put all your toys away"; "Set the table"), or it may be a natural environmental condition that normally cues the occurrence of behavior (e.g., walking across a street at an intersection when the signal says "walk"; smiling or waving at someone when she smiles or waves at you).

In many instructional practices with students with severe disabilities, teachers have identified verbal directions as the target stimulus. In other words, it has been their primary intention to teach the student to respond in a certain way when told what to do. While this is appropriate for some behavioral objectives, for many others it is better if the target stimulus is a natural aspect of the environment, one that would normally be a discriminative stimulus in the natural environment. Learning to respond appropriately to such a stimulus makes it possible for the student to ultimately function as normally and independently as possible in the natural environment, which often means doing what is appropriate without being told to do so. Therefore, whenever possible, teachers should identify the natural aspects of the environment that normally prompt behavior and consider these as the target stimuli to which they wish to have the student respond.

In contrast to the target stimulus, a controlling stimulus is one that *controls a student's responsiveness* to the target stimulus *given the student's current skill or ability level.* In other words, at the start of training the student may not have learned to respond to the target stimulus, so a controlling stimulus, one that the student *can* respond to, is used either simultaneously with the target stimulus or shortly after it to get the behavior to occur. For example, a student with a severe disability may not have learned to brush her hair when she looks in a mirror and sees that it is mussed (the natural target stimulus). However, when the teacher points to the hair and tells the student she needs to brush it while she is looking in the mirror, and she does so, then the verbal direction serves as a controlling stimulus. Ultimately, however, we want the reflection in the mirror (the target stimulus) to be sufficient to get the student to brush her hair.

Further examples of target and controlling stimuli are presented in the tactics described next. In each case, the goal is to ultimately eliminate the controlling stimulus so that the target stimulus will have the desired effect.

Constant Time Delay

One of the most effective and easy-to-use practices for teaching new skills to students with severe disabilities is constant time delay (CTD). Using CTD, the instructor first provides an *attentional cue* such as "are you ready?" and then presents a *task direction* (the target stimulus, a verbal or nonverbal environmental stimulus indicating what behavior is to occur) such as "read the sign." The instructor's intention is for the student to read the sign that is being presented to him. The direction "read the sign" is followed by a *delay period* of a few seconds (usually 4 to 5), followed by an effective *controlling stimulus* that will have enough impact to result in the completion of the behavior by the learner. The controlling stimulus may be a verbal model, a gesture, a physical prompt, or any other appropriate prompt, but, most important, it must have enough control over the student's behavior so that the behavior that was called for by the target stimulus (task direction) will occur when the controlling prompt is given (Snell & Gast, 1981). In the example given, we might assume that the controlling stimulus is the teacher reading the sign, followed by the student imitating the teacher's verbalization.

During the first several trials or sessions, the delay period may be eliminated (i.e., a zero-second delay period is used) to provide initial instruction. In other words, the teacher would say "read the sign" and then immediately say "walk." This is done so that a correct response may be virtually guaranteed during early learning. After these initial trials, the delay period (typically 4 or 5 seconds) is inserted between the direction and the controlling prompt. Usually, CTD is used to teach single, discrete behaviors such as reading sight words, saying the name of an object, or pointing to an object within an array of objects.

During instruction, if the target behavior does not occur within the allocated delay period following the target stimulus, the prompt, or controlling stimulus, is delivered by the teacher. After the prompt is given and the behavior occurs, the student is reinforced. As learning begins to occur, the student will perform the task (say the word, point to the object) during the delay period. Whenever this happens, the controlling stimulus prompt is withheld and the student is reinforced immediately. This procedure allows the student to learn that the initial task direction is calling for a particular behavior to occur. After multiple sessions of instruction the student learns the relation between the initial direction (target stimulus), the behavior, and the reinforcement, and the controlling prompt is no longer required.

Another example of using a CTD procedure is a teacher who wishes a student to ask for a particular item using verbal language. Initially, the teacher presents the item (perhaps a toy or something to eat) by holding it out to the student and saying, "Would you like to have the toy?" Let's assume that the target response for the student is "Toy." For the first 5 or 10 trials, after presenting the item and asking the question, the teacher immediately provides a verbal prompt or a model ("Say toy" or simply "toy"), waits for the student's response, and reinforces the student when it occurs. Once the student is responding correctly and consistently under the zero-second delay period, the teacher moves to a 4-second delay, inserting the interval between the first question (task direction) and the prompt. This gives the student time to respond appropriately before the prompt and to be reinforced by receiving the toy.

For time delay to be effective, the student must be able to wait for the prompt if he does not know the correct response. In our example, the student would need to have imitative ability. This is not always necessary; it simply depends on the type of response that is desired, but generally verbal responses require that the student be able to imitate the model. An alternative would be to teach the student to point to (or touch) the desired item following a direction to "show me what you want." Since the desired response in this case is physical, the teacher could use full or partial physical guidance or a physical model, instead of a verbal model. In all other ways the procedure remains the same; that is, after correct responding occurs through the use of no time delay, the fixed time interval is inserted between the direction and the prompt. Again, when the behavior occurs during the interval, there is no need to provide the prompt and the student is reinforced. The prompt is used when the behavior does not occur or occurs incorrectly.

Several studies have demonstrated the effective use of CTD. Schoen and Ogden (1995) taught three children of mixed ability to read individual sets of sight words. Two of the children were considered to be at risk and one was moderately mentally disabled. The instruction occurred within a group in a regular classroom. In another study, Zhang, Gast, Horvat, and Dattilo (1995) taught four young adults classified as severely to profoundly mentally disabled to engage in meaningful adult recreational skills (bowling, throwing, putting) using a CTD procedure. The controlling prompt consisted of a combination of verbal description plus physical assistance. Collins,

Branson, and Hall (1995) used peer tutors to teach sight words that were on the labels of cooking products using CTD. Participants were four adolescents with moderate mental disabilities. Probes for both acquisition and generalization demonstrated that the participants learned how to read the words through CTD. Miracle, Collins, Schuster, and Grisham-Brown (2001) taught five adolescent peers without disabilities to teach sight words to four students with moderate to severe mental disabilities using CTD. The progress of the students with disabilities on these words was compared to their progress on different sets of grocery words taught by the teacher using the same procedure. The results showed that three of the four students learned the words as well from their teenage peers as they did from the teacher. In a review of research on teaching sight words, Browder and Xin (1998) found that CTD was the most effective teaching tactic used.

Progressive Time Delay

Progressive time delay is very similar to constant time delay, but it may be more effective for students with severe disabilities (Wolery et al., 1992). The only difference between constant and progressive time delay is that the progressive procedure gradually increases the delay period between the initial task direction and the prompt. Instead of going immediately from a zero-second time delay to a 4- or 5-second delay period, as in CTD, the progressive procedure requires that the instructor follow the zero-second trials by introducing several 1-second trials, followed by several 2-second trials, then 3-second trials, 4-second trials, and so forth. Because the delay period is gradually increased, it is more likely that the student will not be lost between the initial task direction and the controlling prompt.

Except for the variation of the time interval between the task direction and the prompt, the progressive time delay procedure is just like the constant time delay procedure—the most important ingredient is that the controlling stimulus must be effective enough to influence the student to perform the behavior if she does not do so within the allowed number of seconds following the initial direction. When increasing the number of seconds of delay, care should be taken to make the increases gradually. Although no hard rule governs the amount of time by which to increase the delay period, usually 1- or 2-second increments are appropriate. Increases in the delay intervals may occur after each session of instruction, after a certain number of trials, or after a certain number of trials in which correct responses occur.

The maximum amount of delay time is also somewhat arbitrary: "Should I increase up to 4 seconds?" "Up to 6 seconds?" "To 8 seconds?" Again, there is no rule to determine this. The teacher must judge the task to be learned and the student who is learning the task to decide on the maximum amount of delay time that would be acceptable in an environment in which the behavior normally occurs. If, for example, the situation called for a student to look at the price on a grocery item and enter that amount into a handheld calculator, the teacher would have to ask, "How much time is sufficient from when the student sees the price and when it is punched into the calculator?" If the teacher decides that the response should occur within 5 seconds, then the final amount of wait time would be 5 seconds. In the trials leading up to that time, the teacher would allow for perhaps 10 trials of zero-time delay, 10 for a 1-second delay, 10 for a 2-second delay, and so on. If the target behavior did not occur before the wait time was over, the teacher would prompt the student to respond, using a prompt such as "When you see the price, you need to punch it in on the calculator. Do it now."

System of Least Prompts

Both constant time delay and progressive time delay are based on the premise that the behavior will occur following a particular target stimulus or task direction; if it does not occur within the allowed period of time, then it will be prompted, using a single prompt that is virtually guaranteed, that is, a controlling stimulus. The system of least prompts [SLP, sometimes called least-to-most prompting, or least intrusive prompts (Orelove & Malatchi, 1996), or increasing assistance (Downing & Demchak, 1996)] also uses a brief waiting period following the initial stimulus, but then provides the student with a hierarchy of prompts that moves progressively from having a minimal influence to having a maximum, controlling influence (the controlling stimulus). The intention is to provide a prompt on each trial with only the minimum intensity necessary to get the behavior to occur. This skill acquisition training system is one of the most commonly used for teaching individuals with severe disabilities and, in contrast to time delay, has been used more often to teach chained tasks (task-analyzed skills) than discrete behaviors (Doyle et al., 1988).

As the teacher moves from one step to the next in a task analysis or functional routine, she presents the target stimulus and, if no response occurs, the next stimulus, and then the next, until finally a controlling stimulus is used. Having completed this step, the teacher moves on to the next step in the chain and repeats the hierarchical process. This continues until instructions have been provided for all steps (whole-task instruction). The following example demonstrates how the system of least prompts is applied to teach a complex, chained task.

Suppose that a teacher wants to teach a student to use a drip coffeemaker to make coffee. The teacher begins by writing a task analysis of the coffee-making process, for example:

1. Remove the container of coffee from the cupboard.
2. Remove the coffee filters from the cupboard.
3. Plug in the coffeemaker.
4. Remove the filter tray from the coffeemaker.
5. Place a coffee filter in the filter tray.
6. Place three scoops of coffee from the container into the filter in the filter tray.
7. Return the filter tray to the coffeemaker.
8. Fill the water container with 8 cups of water.
9. Pour the water into the opening in the coffeemaker.
10. Make sure that the coffee pot is located beneath the filter tray containing the coffee.
11. Turn on the switch.
12. Return the material to the cupboard.

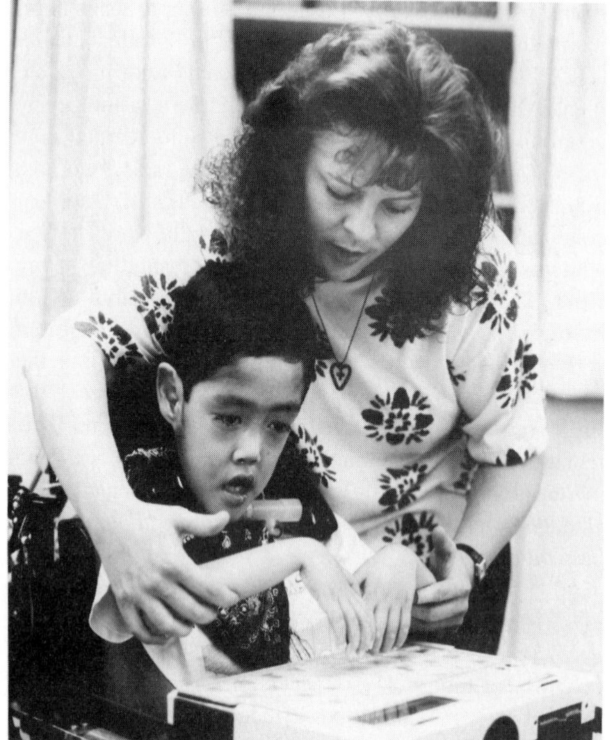

Physical prompts assist the student with severe disabilities to perform and practice new skills.

Following this, the teacher determines a least-to-most hierarchy of prompts. In this case, the teacher uses the following:

1. No prompt (completion of prior step is to serve as the cue to do the next step)
2. Verbal direction (will tell the student what to do)
3. Partial physical prompt (will nudge the student's hand in the direction of the action that should occur)
4. Full physical assistance (will fully guide the student through the behavior that is to occur)

The teacher begins instruction at a time that is appropriate for making coffee and in a location where coffee making should occur, let's say in the home economics room. The teacher might say something like "Why don't you make some coffee for us?" and then wait for the student to start making the coffee. (This would be a natural cue to start the process.) From this point the teacher observes, prompts, and reinforces as appropriate and necessary.

If the student does not begin to remove the coffee container from the cupboard within an allotted period of time (e.g., 4 seconds), the teacher gives the verbal prompt appropriate for the first step in the task analysis, such as "Get the coffee." If the student does not respond, the teacher repeats the verbal direction and simultaneously provides a partial physical prompt by moving the student's hand toward the coffee. Finally, if necessary, the teacher repeats the verbal direction and fully guides the student through the step in the task analysis. For each step in the task analysis, the teacher proceeds in the same fashion, progressing through the prompt hierarchy only to the extent necessary for the student to complete the step. Once the student has successfully completed a step, regardless of the prompt required to do so, the teacher provides reinforcement.

An important consideration is the specific prompts listed in the hierarchy and how many there should be. The prompts to be used are determined by the teacher. They should be natural for the situation, with each prompt being a little more intrusive than the preceding one. The final prompt, which is the controlling stimulus, must be as direct and intrusive as necessary to get the behavior to occur. Often this is full physical assistance, but it does not have to be if the teacher knows from experience that the student will respond consistently to another prompt form, such as a model or a clear verbal direction. The types of prompts that can be used in the hierarchy are those described earlier and include:

- Gestural prompts (e.g., pointing)
- Verbal prompts (e.g., "Put your toys away.")
- Pictorial prompts (e.g., written or drawn directions)
- Model prompts (e.g., demonstrating how to tie a shoe)
- Partial physical prompts
- Full physical prompts

Different types of prompts might be included in the hierarchy or the same type of prompt. Table 7–1 displays possible combinations of prompt types. Usually, no more than three or four prompts are used in the sequence in addition to the target stimulus.

At each level of prompt, the target stimulus must be repeated to allow the student to learn the association between the stimulus and the prompt. In situations such as the coffee-making example, the completion of the previous step in the task should serve as the stimulus for the next step to occur and thus would always be present. Beyond this stimulus, however, the teacher could include the verbal prompt alone and then say the verbal prompt again at each of the subsequent prompt levels (partial and full physical assistance). Ultimately, however, the teacher wants the student to complete each step *without* the verbal or the physical prompts.

When using the system of least prompts (or other behavior acquisition methods) to teach chains of behaviors, it is preferred to teach the whole task at each teaching opportunity. In past experiments, researchers have taught single steps in the task analysis (using backward or forward chaining) and, as each was learned, additional steps were added. However, whole-task teaching has generally been shown to be more effective and is a more natural teaching approach (Kayser, Billingsley, & Neel, 1986; Zane, Walls, & Thvedt, 1981). Of course, learning occurs more rapidly if there are more opportunities for learning. In our example, the student might be given the opportunity to make coffee twice a day instead of just once.

Most-to-Least Prompts

The most-to-least prompting system, which is essentially the opposite of the system of least prompts, is another tactic that may be used to establish new behaviors. Also known as the *decreasing assistance* procedure (Downing & Demchak, 1996), this tactic calls for the teacher to begin teaching a new behavior by simultaneously providing both a target stimulus *and* a controlling prompt on the first set of trials. (This is the same as the time delay procedure when there is a zero-second delay.) When the student has experienced the behavior after being exposed to the stimulus and the controlling level of prompting, subsequent prompts with lesser degrees of control or intrusiveness are used, each being paired with the target stimulus. As the influence of the controlling prompt is gradually lessened over subsequent trials, the target stimulus increases its controlling effect. The advantage of this instructional model is that it can eliminate most errors that tend to occur in the early learning trials. For this reason this instructional method is often used with individuals with very severe or profound disabilities, with the first prompt level being full physical assistance (the controlling prompt) in combination with a verbal direction (the target stimulus).

Use of the most-to-least model requires that the teacher establish a hierarchy of prompts, just as in the least-to-most procedure. However, instead of starting with the least intrusive prompt and going to the prompt ultimately required to cause the behavior to occur within a single trial, the teacher establishes a criterion for correct

Table 7–1 Combinations of Prompt Types at Levels in the System of Least Prompts Hierarchy

Level	*Different Type Each Level*	*Multiple Types Each Level*	*Single Type Each Level*
1	Target stimulus	Target stimulus	Target stimulus
2	Target stimulus + Verbal prompt	Target stimulus + Verbal prompt + Gestural prompt	Target stimulus + Physical prompt at shoulder
3	Target stimulus + Model prompt	Target stimulus + Verbal prompt + Model prompt	Target stimulus + Physical prompt at wrist
4	Target stimulus + Physical prompt	Target stimulus + Verbal prompt + Model prompt + Physical prompt	Target stimulus + Physical prompt hand on hand

Source: Teaching Students with Moderate to Severe Disabilities: Use of Response Prompting Strategies (p. 101) by W. Wolery, M. J. Ault, & P. M. Doyle, 1992, New York: Addison Wesley Longman, Inc. Copyright © 1992. Reprinted by permission of Addison Wesley Longman, Inc.

performance at each level of prompting (e.g., 80% correct for a certain number of trials). When this criterion is achieved, the teacher (at the following instructional session) moves to the next prompt on the hierarchy, which is less intrusive than the previous one. This process continues until the student can complete the behavior when only the target stimulus has been given.

One potential disadvantage of the most-to-least model is the possibility that the student may be learning faster than the prompting hierarchy requires, and thus the teacher may be using a more intrusive prompt than is necessary. To resolve this problem, Wolery et al. (1992) suggested that periodic probes be provided to see if the student can perform the required task at less intrusive prompt levels or when only the initial direction or target stimulus is given. Probes are opportunities for the student to perform the skill given only the target stimulus and no other input from the instructor. A student who demonstrates the behavior or skill adequately under the probe condition, that is, to the level of satisfaction specified in the instructional or behavioral objective, would not need further instruction to acquire the skill.

To better understand how the most-to-least intrusive procedure is implemented, consider an example of a student learning to feed herself with a spoon. Using the most-to-least method, the teacher first conducts a task analysis of self-feeding with a spoon and then decides on the prompts to be included in the hierarchy, such as the following:

1. Full physical assistance (will fully guide the student through the behavior that is to occur)
2. Partial physical prompt (will nudge the student's hand in the direction of the action that should occur)
3. Verbal direction (will tell the student what to do)

Note that these prompts are like those listed in the previous example, but their order is reversed; instead of going from least to most, they go from most to least. The teacher decides on the criterion for moving from one prompt (more intrusive) to another (less intrusive). She may decide, for example, that she will require a minimum of 2 days of correct performance with a minimum of four opportunities (or trials) per day for each step in the task analysis.

When the teacher has made the relevant decisions and is ready to begin training, she approaches the student, provides the necessary material for eating with a spoon, and in some way tells the student that he should begin eating. Then, for each step in the task analysis, the teacher simultaneously gives an appropriate, predetermined verbal direction ("pick up your spoon") and physically guides the student through the task, using full physical assistance, the first level of assistance in the prompting sequence listed earlier. The teacher provides this level of assistance on each step of the task analysis until criterion has been achieved on the step, using the present prompting system. If criterion for a task analysis step is achieved after eight trials (let's assume it was 80% correct responding with the prompt), the student can move forward to the next less intrusive level of assistance (partial physical guidance) on the next learning opportunity. (Each step in the task analysis must be treated independently of other steps when deciding to move forward to lesser levels of assistance.) The process continues until each step of the task analysis occurs when only the target stimulus is being used, which is, in this example, a verbal direction.

It should be noted that the criterion for success is somewhat arbitrary. In this example the teacher or the collaborative team decided that 80% correct performance on eight attempts over 2 days was necessary before moving to a lesser level of assistance. However, it might have been decided that 70% or 100% is necessary. Depending on the target behavior, the usual criterion of successful performance is set between 80% and 100%.

Antecedent Prompt and Test Procedures

In all the preceding tactics, the order of instructional events has consisted of providing a prompt after the task direction or target stimulus (constant time delay, progressive time delay, system of least prompts) or during the presentation of the task direction (most-to-least procedure). Antecedent prompt and test procedures allow for the delivery of the prompt preceding a test or probe. This is to determine if the student can perform the task as the prompt indicated (Wolery et al., 1992). Typically, this consists of telling, showing, or physically guiding the student to do something and then testing the student to see if the task has been learned. According to Wolery et al., there are three prompt and test procedures: antecedent prompt and test, antecedent prompt and fade, and graduated guidance.

The *antecedent prompt and test* procedure calls for the simultaneous presentation of a controlling prompt (one that ensures that the student will correctly perform the task) and the target stimulus to which the student is to respond. Several trials or opportunities are presented for the student to perform the target task under this condition, and then the prompt is totally removed and only the stimulus is presented. Under this test (or probe) condition, the student is observed to see if the control of the behavior is shifted to the stimulus, that is, if the behavior occurs in the presence of the stimulus instead of the stimulus and the prompt. An example of this procedure follows.

> Rodney is requested to separate plastic containers from glass containers so that they may be recycled. To teach Rodney how to do this, his job coach says, "Rodney, put the glass containers over here (indicating one bin) and the plastic ones over here (indicating the second bin)." Then the job coach begins separating the items while Rodney watches. As he works, the job coach says, "plastic here, glass here." After the job coach separates many items, he stops (removes the prompt) and tells Rodney to do it (provides the target stimulus). As Rodney performs the task, the job coach reinforces correct separation.

In this example, the prompt was totally dropped, but in some cases it is possible to gradually fade the prompt until the student is being tested on the activity without the presence of the prompt. This is the *antecedent prompt and fade* procedure. Initially, the controlling prompt is presented along with the stimulus, but then it is gradually withdrawn or reduced in intensity while the stimulus remains present. Ultimately, the prompt is entirely removed and the stimulus is sufficient to cause the behavior to occur. Unlike the most-to-least procedure, the fading of the controlling prompt is not previously specified, but occurs based on the teacher's judgment about whether the student is capable of responding with a less intrusive prompt.

An example of the antecedent prompt and fade procedure could be seen in a student learning to feed herself with a spoon and requiring assistance to complete all the steps of lifting the spoon, scooping the food, putting the spoon in her mouth, and so forth. The teacher provides a full physical guidance prompt of holding the student's hand and fully guiding it through the required movement. Obviously, this would be a very intrusive, fully controlling prompt. If, after only a few successful trials of doing this, the teacher were to terminate all prompting, the student would most likely not be able to complete the movement, or at least not all of it. Instead, the teacher decides to fade the prompt by gradually providing less assistance when it is perceived that the child is making more independent movements. The teacher might fade assistance in several ways. She may provide assistance on some attempts, but not all; she may provide assistance through the initial portion of the movement, but allow the student to complete more and more of the latter portion; or she may provide physical support at the hand for several trials, then at the wrist, at the forearm, at the elbow, and so forth. The important feature of the system is that the prompt is faded gradually until the student acquires enough prompted experience to successfully complete the movement independently.

Graduated guidance is very similar to the antecedent prompt and fade procedure except that the teacher is making moment-to-moment decisions about the amount of support that the student needs to complete any particular part of the movement (Downing & Demchak, 1996; Wolery et al., 1992). For example, if the teacher were teaching a student how to reach for an object, she might place her hand over his and gradually move it toward an object, but in the process feel the student beginning to reach and thus "back off" her physical guidance. She would keep her hand near the student's (i.e., "shadow" the student's movement), but physically guide the student only when needed. Graduated guidance is often used with students with very severe disabilities to teach correct movements for particular skills.

Nondirect Instruction of Skills

It is clear that the prompting procedures and their implementation as described in the previous sections target instruction of specific skills or behaviors and require very precise and direct instructional applications. Using these approaches, teachers or instructors work directly with students to accomplish their instructional targets. We can consider these methods to be *direct* instructional methods. To be effective, much of the instruction of students with severe disabilities requires that these methods be used. There are, however, circumstances in which students can learn new skills or information with less direct or intense instructional approaches. Two such approaches are observational learning and incidental learning. We can refer to these as *nondirect* instructional practices.

Observational Learning

In many learning environments, especially in regular classrooms, students with severe disabilities have the opportunity to observe the behavior and learning of other students. Because one of the purposes of inclusion is to improve skills through association with nondisabled peers, it is important that observational learning be encouraged. *Observational learning* is considered to be nontargeted learning that occurs because the student observes someone else engaged in the task. Different tactics help learning through observation to occur. These include working with students in small groups while demonstrating how to do part of the task, but not directing the students to do the task; directly teaching one student within the group while directing the noninstructed student's attention toward the student who is performing the task; and providing reinforcement to the student being directly instructed as other students are observing.

In the previously described study by Shoen and Ogden (1995) in which CTD was used to teach sight words, observational learning was used to teach members of the group the words of other group members. Working with three students with mixed ability, Schoen and Ogden used CTD as the principal instructional method. However, the children were also cued to look at the words being learned by each other and to listen as they were read to, that is, to learn through observation of the other students. The two at-risk students learned not only their words, but 100% of the words taught to the others. The child with moderate mental retardation learned the words taught directly to him through CTD, but *over half of the words* of the other students were also learned through observation without direct instruction.

Werts, Caldwell, and Wolery (1996) examined the observational learning ability of three students with disabilities, one with moderate mental retardation, one with autism, and one with severe mental retardation. They wanted to know if the students with disabilities, who were enrolled in general education classrooms, could observe a student without disabilities performing (and simultaneously verbalizing) a task and then perform the task themselves. Using chained tasks with 7 to 10 parts (e.g., spelling their name using letter tiles, playing an audiotape, using a calculator, sharpening a pencil), they found that the students with disabilities were successful. This not only reinforces the notion of observational learning as a way to acquire new skills, but also reinforces the use of nondisabled peers in general education classrooms as effective models for learning.

In a final example, Smith, Collins, Schuster, and Kleinert (1999) taught table-cleaning skills to four adolescents with moderate to severe mental disabilities. To do this, they developed three task analyses. One was for preparing the materials, the second was for actually cleaning the tables, and the third outlined putting away the cleaning materials. Students were taught to clean the tables using the system of least prompts, and all were successful in learning to do so. But the students were also asked to observe as the instructor prepared the materials for cleaning the table and as the instructor put them away. While completing these tasks, the instructor described each step in the tasks. Pre- and postassessments were conducted to determine if the students had been able to learn the preparation and putting away tasks without direct instruction in doing so. For preparing materials, during the pretest, on average, students were able to complete only one step in the task analysis, but during the posttest, they were able to complete at least 13 of the 15 steps. This also held true for the task of putting materials away. Before observing, they could complete less than one step on average, but after observing they could complete 11 to 13 of the steps in the task analysis.

These studies demonstrate that if students with moderate to severe mental retardation are asked to observe a particular task as it is being performed and the task is verbally described, they may be able to complete the task without more direct and systematic instructions.

Incidental Learning

Incidental learning occurs when a teacher is using a form of direct instruction (such as CTD or SLP) to teach the critical components of a task, but incidentally provides additional information to the learner by embedding it within the task, such as when providing an attentional direction, the target stimulus, the controlling prompt, or the reinforcer. In other words, the information is not being provided to directly assist the student in learning the skill, but typically for acquiring information related to the skill. Consider the following examples.

Gast, Doyle, Wolery, Ault, and Farmer (1991) compared the use of progressive time delay and the system of least prompts to teach sight words (recipe words) to four students with moderate to severe mental disabilities and simultaneously assessed the effectiveness of teaching related information (the meaning of the recipe words) in an incidental manner. This was done by embedding the related information within the prompt hierarchy or in the reinforcement provided following correct response of the targeted behavior. The incidental information was presented by either showing an action picture representing the word just read by the student or using a gesture to represent the action of the word just read. For example, if the student saw and read the word "stir," the teacher would say "yes, that's right, this is stir," while showing an action picture or a gesture of "stir." Besides learning to read most of the sight words (three students learned them all, one learned half), the students learned 75% of the information taught incidentally regardless of the method used.

Collins et al. (1995) used peer tutors to teach sight words that were on the labels of cooking products using CTD. Participants were four adolescents with moderate mental disabilities. Incidental instruction was provided to teach the definitions of the words by the peer tutor stating the meaning of the word when reinforcing the student for reading the word correctly. Probes for both acquisition and generalization demonstrated that the participants learned how to read the words through CTD and learned the meanings of many of the words through the less structured incidental teaching method.

Singleton, Schuster, and Ault (1995) reported teaching two students with moderate mental disabilities community signs using simultaneous prompting procedures. A picture of the community sign was held up and simultaneously the teacher said "What sign?" and immediately provided the answer, that is, the controlling prompt. If the student correctly repeated the answer within 5 seconds, the teacher praised the student and, when doing so, also gave the meaning of the sign ("Good job! Exit means go out!"). This was done without actually requiring the student to state the meaning of the sign during the instructional session. In probes that were conducted at times separate from instructional sessions, the researchers found that the students learned to see and say all the sign words and also learned incidentally the meaning of the words that had been embedded in the reinforcement. This study was also important because it demonstrated observational learning as well as incidental learning; that is, the students learned from each other's learning opportunities. They learned to read many of the words *and to state the definitions* that were taught to the other student.

Fiscus, Schuster, Morse, and Collins (2002) used constant time delay in an effort to teach four children with moderate to severe cognitive disabilities to prepare snacks at school. As they were teaching the food preparation skills, they embedded different types of instructive feedback into the prompting and feedback components of the instruction and then assessed how well the students acquired what was incidentally taught. During the prompting, if it was necessary for the teacher to use a controlling prompt, the teacher would read a sentence directing the student to complete the task while pointing to the words as she read them and then model the step for the student. When delivering a consequence, either reinforcing the student for a correct response or correcting an error, the teacher would again read the words in the sentence as she was pointing to them. Afterward she would record the student's response and then give the second type of instructive feedback, which was to show the student a kitchen utensil (one not used by the student to prepare the snack) and say the name of the utensil. At the completion of the study, three of the four students had learned to prepare three snacks. The students were also tested to determine if their reading skills and utensil recognition skills had improved. Again three of the four students had learned either to read some of the words (although none learned to read them all) or to recognize them when presented in an array with distracter words. All four students learned to name or recognize the cooking utensils.

Both observational learning and incidental learning hold great practical value for at least three reasons. First, they can maximize the efficiency of instruction because they can be used at different times without direct instruction. It is as if there is no cost for the instruction. Second, they take advantage of natural learning opportunities. In classrooms, on the playground, or in the community, there are always opportunities for learning through which the teacher can either direct students to observe others or convey the relevant information. Even though they are not planned, teachers can and should take advantage of these opportunities. And, third, they can be very useful in inclusive classrooms in which students with multiple ability levels are being taught. These advantages call for use of these tactics whenever the chance to do so occurs.

Modifying Stimulus Materials

In some learning situations it is possible to modify stimulus materials to increase the probability of correct responding. This may occur when students are learning to discriminate between materials or when they are learning to manipulate materials in a particular way. Two techniques may be used: *stimulus shaping* and *stimulus fading* (Ault et al., 1989; Schoen, 1986).

Stimulus Shaping and Fading

Stimulus shaping consists of the gradual changing of the shape (or topography) of a particular stimulus from one that the student responds to correctly to one that the student cannot respond to correctly at the start of training, but needs to learn to respond to by the end of training. *Stimulus fading* involves changing a particular element of a stimulus gradually (one that the student is responsive to) so that the normally controlling element of a stimulus (one that the student is not initially responsive to) will ultimately influence the student's behavior. Some examples will clarify these procedures.

In many daily activities, individuals are required to make discriminations, for example, selecting a bowl over a plate to hold ice cream because the latter will not hold the ice cream as well. Selecting a heavy coat to wear when a light sweater would suffice may result in being hot and uncomfortable or carrying the coat around instead of wearing it. The ability to discriminate which item is most appropriate for a particular need or situation is sometimes difficult for persons with cognitive disabilities because they do not know what particular aspect of the item warrants their attention. It may be helpful to take steps to better ensure that correct discriminations occur.

A practical way to improve discrimination ability is to use stimuli or cues that the student can easily recognize to identify the different items or materials that are to be selected. As the student learns to make the discrimination based on the more familiar cues, they can be faded or shaped so that the student's attention gradually shifts to the relevant dimensions and cues of the stimulus. The following is an example.

Wood, Frank, and Hamre-Nietupski (1996) wanted to teach middle school students with moderate to severe cognitive disabilities to open their own locks. They used picture prompts and redundant cues to teach this very functional skill. First, they developed a sequence of picture prompts to demonstrate the steps to use to open the locks. These prompts were placed in plastic wallet-size inserts. Then red marks were placed on the locks in appropriate spots to serve as redundant cues that would be easier to find than the cues that were normally available on a lock (i.e., the numbers). Modeling, verbal directions, and, when necessary, physical prompts were used along with the prompts and red mark cues during instruction. The picture prompts were eliminated after students achieved a prespecified criterion and then, later, the red marks were also eliminated when students demonstrated a high enough level of performance with their use. All the students learned to open their locks independently.

Stimulus shaping can be used in situations in which it is possible to gradually change the features of a particular stimulus. For example, suppose that it is desired that a student learn to select spoons instead of forks for eating dessert. To do this, normally the student would have to attend to the *shape* of the two items and then make the choice. In this situation, the shape is considered the *relevant dimension* of the stimuli because it possesses the information that identifies the correct item. But if the student does not attend well to shape, errors will occur. Assume, however, that the student has a better ability to discriminate between large and small than between the shapes of objects. One way to get the student to learn the shape discrimination more easily would be to initially allow discrimination based on the size dimension instead of the shape dimension. To do this, the teacher would make all the spoons large (e.g., by using large tablespoons) and the forks small (e.g., salad forks). This would make the discrimination easier because, instead of attending to shape, the student could attend to size. Once the student learns to select the correct item (the spoon for dessert), the relevance of the size dimension can be decreased, with the aim of shifting the student's attention to the shape dimension. This can be done in three stages: by first replacing the salad forks with dinner forks, then replacing the tablespoons with long-handled teaspoons, and finally replacing the long-handled spoons with regular spoons appropriate for eating dessert. Throughout the process, the verbal direction to "get the spoon" is used. At each stage, the student is given enough opportunities to perform until an adequate criterion of success is achieved.

Stimulus shaping is difficult in many cases because it requires the gradual changing of some dimension of the stimulus. Therefore, it is often easier to use stimulus fading. Consider again the previous situation. If the student cannot attend well to shape, but is able to attend to the dimension of color, the teacher might simply mark the forks with red and the spoons with blue, and then, over several trials, *fade* the colors gradually so that the student's attention is shifted from the color dimension to the shape dimension. The effect would be the same, but stimulus fading may be an easier process for this learning task as well as for others.

Modifying Material Difficulty

Materials can be modified to make some manipulation tasks easier in the early stages of learning and then slowly changed to make the tasks more difficult in later stages. In the final stage, the material will be of a nature that is normally required for a task. Learning to dress oneself is a good example. When a child with a severe disability is first learning to button a shirt, the small buttons on the shirt may be extremely difficult to manipulate. When the teacher is just beginning to teach the task, a higher probability of success may be possible if larger buttons and correspondingly larger buttonholes are provided during early learning trials. As the child begins to achieve criterion in early phases, learning to successfully use the material that is easier to handle, the material can gradually be changed, going through several stages, until finally the child can successfully button the buttons that she will use in daily life.

Although the sequential modification of materials can be a helpful tactic for acquiring many skills that require materials to be used, there is an important caveat for teachers and others. If the materials in use appear to be inappropriate for the age of the individual in a particular situation and call negative attention to the individual's disability, it will not be appropriate to use them. For example, it would not be appropriate for an adolescent to wear a coat in public that had oversized buttons on it simply because he could better manipulate these buttons. Instead, for such occasions, assistance with normal-size buttons would be preferred, or another material that is easy to manipulate and also age appropriate, such as Velcro, might be used.

Use of Natural Cues

As discussed earlier in the chapter, in all objectives, it is very important to remember one thing: the ultimate accomplishment for the student when learning new behaviors or skills is to respond appropriately to the natural cues available in the environment (Dever, 1988; Ford & Mirenda, 1984). For example, individuals usually put on their socks and shoes in the morning after putting on their other clothes and before going to breakfast. Most people do not put on shoes and socks only when given a verbal direction, a gesture, a model, or a physical prompt to do so. Because of their relative general learning limitations, persons with severe disabilities often require systematic instruction, using the tactics described previously, when initially learning some skills, but this does not mean that these artificial prompting techniques should be continued without end. If we consider the environment to be full of natural stimuli that call for certain behaviors to occur, we would hope that these stimuli would assume their normal function for individuals with severe disabilities. But how is this to occur?

The most important consideration is that skills must be taught in the presence of natural stimuli. Usually, this means teaching in those environments where the stimuli exist and considering the natural stimuli to be the ultimate cue, or target stimulus, in our sequence. Even though prompting may occur in several ways, whenever possible all prompts should ultimately be eliminated so that the student responds to naturally existing stimuli. Consider the following example.

Suppose that there is an objective for a student to learn to order a hamburger at a fast-food restaurant. An instructional plan is designed to use the system of least prompts by (1) asking if she would like to order a hamburger, (2) suggesting to the student that she order a hamburger, and (3) directly telling the student to order a hamburger. The problem with this sequence is that normally there would not be someone around to complete even step (1) of the least-to-most system. Therefore, there should be one step that precedes (1). That is, the student must be in the location, smelling the food, seeing the large menu on the wall (reading ability is not important here), and having the counter attendant ask, "Can I help you?" These are all natural cues that the student must learn to attend and respond to if the behavior (ordering a hamburger) is going to occur in the natural setting.

Unless such conditions can be arranged for learning all functional objectives, the student may learn to respond only when there is an initial artificial prompt. When certain conditions inhibit training in the natural environment, it is important that relevant conditions be incorporated into the training situation. Nietupski, Hamre-Nietupski, Clancy, and Veerhusen (1986) offered several suggestions for creating simulated learning conditions to enhance training that cannot occur in the natural environment. These suggestions include taking inventories of community settings to determine the range of stimuli, using various simulations, changing simulations that do not improve performance in the natural environment, using simulations to provide for intensive practice that cannot be provided in natural environments, and providing training in simulations close in time to when the skill will be practiced in the natural environment.

Although it is clearly desirable for students with severe disabilities to respond to natural cues, some students will not be able to do so, or at least not be able to do so in all circumstances. For these students, it is more important that they participate in some meaningful manner, even if uncommon prompting and support must be continued indefinitely, than not to participate at all (Ferguson & Baumgart, 1991). Still, when possible, teachers should work to develop appropriate skills and behaviors that occur when natural stimuli are present.

Reinforcing Correct Responses

Only if behaviors are reinforced will they tend to recur. This is referred to as the *law of effect,* and it is true for all individuals, whether they have a disability or not. Therefore, when individuals with severe disabilities exhibit appropriate behaviors, regardless of the stimulus that prompts the behaviors, the behaviors must be reinforced. If they are not, ultimately they will cease to occur. In the initial stages of learning, when a skill is first being acquired, reinforcement should occur immediately after each appropriate or desired behavior, or at least after most behaviors. Once the behavior has been established, a thinner schedule of reinforcement can be used; that is, not every instance of the behavior will be reinforced. (For a complete discussion on schedules of reinforcement, the reader is referred to Alberto and Troutman, 2002.)

Selecting Reinforcers

In the general population, different people like different things and effective reinforcers are not the same for everyone. This can also be said about reinforcers used as consequences for specific behaviors of persons with severe disabilities. Therefore, it is necessary to discover what will serve as an effective reinforcer for each student and then use that reinforcer during instruction for skill acquisition.

Wolery et al. (1992) suggested four tactics for selecting effective reinforcers. The first is to use reinforcers that are effective for other students. The second is to identify possible reinforcers by asking parents, family members, and others who know the student what they believe to be most desirable or favored by the student. This could be done during assessment and planning. Third, the student may be observed over a period of time to determine what objects she seeks, holds, or manipulates for a period of time or what activities are preferred. Finally, reinforcers may be identified by a preference assessment procedure, as discussed next.

The most desirable types of reinforcers to use are those that are most natural for the behavior and those that occur in the natural environment. For example, the reinforcer that typically keeps one involved in performing personal grooming behaviors is the reaction of others, such as someone saying, "You look nice today." The difficulty with relying solely on natural reinforcers is that they may not occur often enough to maintain the behavior, particularly when the behavior is first being learned and/or the student may not fully comprehend the meaning of some social or verbal reinforcers. The teacher or another person may need to supplement the natural schedule of reinforcement by using other items and activities that are selected based on the individual likes of the student. This calls for conducting preference assessments.

Preference Assessments

Determining what is preferred by an individual with severe disabilities is useful when deciding what to use as a reinforcer for the person. But knowing a person's preferences can have other important implications as well, and because many persons with severe disabilities, especially those with the most severe disabilities, cannot communicate effectively, it is often difficult to know what their preferences are, for example, what they prefer to eat, what type of leisure activities are desired, the order in which they wish to do their chores, or whom they would like to associate with. To discover this information, teachers should conduct systematic preference assessments (Hughes, Pitkin, & Lorden, 1998; Lohrmann-O'Rourke, Browder, & Brown, 2000).

Systematic preference assessment consists of presenting different items or events to an individual and observing his or her reaction to the items. Preferred items generally will be identifiable because the person will exert more effort to acquire the item, exhibit longer periods of interaction with the item, or perhaps show facial expressions that indicate that the item is desirable. Lohrmann-O'Rourke, et al. (2000) maintain that knowledge of such preferences is important for three reasons. First, if we know what is preferred by someone, we can offer him these preferred items or events within his current context and thus contribute to his exercise of self-determination. Second, if we are cognizant of what an individual prefers, acknowledging and acting on these preferences can contribute to an enhanced lifestyle. Instead of a person simply acquiescing to what is presented by a teacher, parent, or caregiver, we can better ensure that the conditions, materials, and events that are provided are those most enjoyed by the individual. Finally, if we understand an individual's preferences, we may be able to incorporate these conditions into instructional programs, using them to develop the conditions in which instruction occurs or using preferred items or activities as reinforcers for work that has been achieved. For these reasons, conducting systematic preference assessments is an important undertaking if we are to provide successful instruction and improve an individual's quality of life.

Lohrmann-O'Rourke et al. (2000) propose that the following four key components be included in the process of conducting valid systematic preference assessments:

1. *Expanding the options in the preference assessment.* Possible items to offer during a preference assessment may include those that occur in the individual's natural environment, those recommended by parents or caregivers, those that occur in routines or activities that the person engages in, or those that might occur within a setting in which the person might learn new skills and which appeal to individuals without disabilities in these settings. Sometimes brainstorming with others who work with the individual may be helpful. If patterns of potentially preferred items begin to emerge (for example, if it seems that small items that have tactile appeal appear promising), then this information may be used to expand the list by adding similar items to it. According to Lohrmann-O'Rourke et al., most research suggests that persons with very severe disabilities prefer concrete instead of symbolic stimuli. Therefore, instead of using symbols that represent items or events, it is better to use real things or activities. If an entire event cannot be presented (for example, a specific employment option),

Lohrmann-O'Rourke et al. recommend using a portion of the event in the assessment process.

2. *Deciding when and where to conduct preference assessments.* For some types of items, preference assessments may be conducted by offering one after the other in a massed preference assessment procedure. Another way is to conduct the assessment in a more natural way by distributing the presentation of items or events throughout the day in natural contexts. In this way, after the individual indicates the preferred choice, the item can be delivered in a normal manner or the person can engage in the preferred activity. For example, if attempting to determine whether a person prefers country music or modern jazz, the evaluator may play a little of each while observing the individual's reaction to the different music. If this evaluation occurs during different times of leisure and a preference becomes clear (for example, the person smiles more during one type of music), it would be very natural to offer the preferred music for the person to enjoy during the leisure period.

   Preference assessment should be ongoing, because what is preferred may change across time. As Lohrmann-O'Rourke et al. noted, "Offering continuing opportunities to sample new options is responsive to personal changes across time and reduces the risk that known available options will become stagnant. . . . When the options available lose their value, individuals may respond by failing to engage in activities or emitting problem behaviors to communicate their dissatisfaction" (p. 48).

3. *Deciding who presents the sampling options.* Although there is no clear research, generally, it is expected that a person who has had a long-term relationship with the individual with a severe disability, or one with whom the person is most comfortable, will be able to gain the most reliable response and recognize reactions that indicate what is preferred and what is not. When a new teacher or another person comes into the life of the person with a severe disability for the first time, it may be better initially to rely on a caregiver or a more familiar person to conduct the preference assessment or, if this is not possible, to ask those most familiar with the person to recommend preferred items or activities.

4. *Methods for presenting the sampling options.* Three formats have been used most often to conduct preference assessments: single-stimulus presentations, paired-stimulus presentations, and group presentations. In the first, a single item or event is presented at a time and the response is monitored. Subsequent items are presented in a similar manner, that is, one at a time. For each, a record is made of the person's reaction. In a paired-stimulus format, preference is determined by presenting two choices at once and noting which of the two is selected, attended to, reached for, or the like. By forming different pairs of possible choices, it is possible to determine over several trials the options that are preferred and those that are not. Finally, possible preferred items may be presented in groups of three or more for the target person to select from. As preferred items are selected, they are set aside into a preferred pool, and another item is added to the group. When one is selected from the new group, it too is placed in the preferred pool. This process continues until the individual doesn't seem to have any interest in what remains. This method may help to determine a hierarchy of preferred items.

Perhaps the most important aspect of conducting a preference assessment is determining what particular response of an individual is indicative of a preferred item, event, or activity. Lohrmann-O'Rourke et al. suggest that it is important to focus on well-defined, observable, discrete responses. Such responses may include moving one's body, arm, or hand toward an item; activating a microswitch; touching an item; manipulating the item; or using the item in a meaningful way. Other responses may indicate that an item is *not* preferred, for example, trying to avoid an item, pushing it away, or not responding to it at all.

In an important review, Hughes, Pitkin, and Lorden (1998) analyzed 27 studies that were conducted to determine the preferences or choices of persons with severe to profound disabilities. Their purpose was to determine the ways in which researchers interacted with these individuals to learn which items, activities, or events they desired. Hughes et al. found that researchers assessed choices by relying on different types of responses made by the individuals with severe or profound disabilities. In all, there were six classes of responses: (1) activating a microswitch, (2) approach toward a stimulus,(3) verbalizations, signing, gestures, vocalizations, or affect, (4) physical selection of a stimulus, (5) task performance, and (6) time engaged with a stimulus. They also found that researchers sometimes assessed preference of choice by the effect of stimuli on collateral behaviors that accompanied or followed the choice or preference response. These included task performance, time engaged with a stimulus, changes in inappropriate behaviors, verbal requests, affective displays, or consuming a preferred food item.

Hughes et al. reported that to determine the individual's choice or preference researchers needed between 7 and 123 assessment sessions. During most of these sessions, either one or two items were presented. These items could be classified into nine groups: (1) edibles, (2) music, (3) sensory reinforcers, (4) toys, (5) social reinforcers, (6) video displays, (7) vocational tasks, (8) everyday activities, and (9) computer games. In most cases, stimuli were presented by placing the items on a table, a wheelchair tray, or another surface. In a few studies, the researcher demonstrated the use of the item, and in a few the participant was questioned about the preferred item. Preferences were often found to change over time and vary among participants.

Hughes et al. made several important points with regard to the research that has been conducted on choice and preference determination. They noted that few studies were conducted in integrated settings with nondisabled peers, few were conducted in the context of daily routines or activities, and none looked at persons making major decisions, such as where to live, where to go to school, or moving to a new home. Hughes et al. stated, "If expressing preferences and making choices are expected to serve a function in people's lives and extend their self-determination, quality of life, and community participation, opportunities to exercise these skills must be incorporated into the environments in which people live, work, recreate, and attend school, and throughout their day-to-day activities" (p. 313).

Using Food and Drink as Reinforcers

During the relatively brief history of teaching persons with severe disabilities, particularly those with the most severe disabilities, food and drink items have often been used as reinforcers. Even though they have typically been effective when used this way, for several reasons this is not a good idea. First, individuals have a natural right to food and drink when they are hungry and thirsty; to deliver them contingently seems to diminish this right. Second, dietary concerns may admonish against the use of food as reinforcement. This may include possible allergic reactions to certain foods. Third, the student may learn to respond only in the presence of food and become overly responsive when food is available. For example, the student may hold out his hand continuously in the presence of food. Fourth, the responsiveness of the student may decrease after snacks, lunch, and other natural eating opportunities. Although the potency of food as a reinforcer for many individuals cannot be denied, for these reasons the teacher should search for and use other reinforcers.

Delivery of Reinforcement

The way in which reinforcers are delivered following a behavior is as important as the reinforcer itself. Reinforcement must come immediately after the correct behavior (regardless of the prompt level required) so that the student learns the association between the stimulus, the behavior, and the reinforcer. If reinforcement is delayed, this association may not occur. It is also important to tell the student, in a natural way, why she is being reinforced. For example, "you look really nice, your hair looks good" may provide reinforcement and also tell why the student is being reinforced. Also, when reinforcing students, teachers and others should be sincere in their expressions. All learners, even those with severe disabilities, recognize insincerity. Finally, and of great importance, the delivery of supplementary reinforcement in natural, nonschool environments should be paired with the natural reinforcement and be presented in an unobtrusive fashion, one that does not call attention to itself. As the natural reinforcer begins to acquire more influence, the supplemental reinforcement should be reduced and eliminated (Ford & Mirenda, 1984).

Correcting Errors

As one may expect, there will be errors when new behaviors or skills are first acquired. The instructional tactics described in this chapter are designed to reduce the occurrence of these errors and sometimes even eliminate them altogether. For example, the most-to-least prompting system has a very low error-producing rate because it requires an initial controlling prompt that exerts much control over the student's behavior when it is first being learned. This tends to reduce student errors. This is also the case with time delay when the controlling prompt occurs at the zero-second delay interval.

Types of Errors

Even though instructional tactics are intended to result in few student errors, errors (or no responses) will occur, and they will occur in different forms, including the following:

- The behavior does not occur when the target stimulus is presented. This may happen either after prompts have been eliminated or before the prompt can be delivered (unprompted, no response error).

- An incorrect behavior occurs when the target stimulus is presented. This may happen after prompts have been eliminated or before the prompt can be delivered (unprompted error).
- The behavior does not occur when the target stimulus and the prompt are presented together (prompted, no response error).
- An incorrect behavior occurs when the target stimulus and the prompt are presented together (prompted error).

As can be seen, there are both prompted and unprompted errors, as well as errors of no response. In contrast, there are prompted and unprompted correct responses. A prompted correct response occurs when the student performs the correct behavior when a prompt is used, whatever its form. An unprompted correct response occurs only when the target stimulus is provided.

Error Correction Procedures

When incorrect responses occur, the teacher may use several possible *correction procedures* depending on the nature of the error and the instructional tactic being used. Generally, the purpose of any correction procedure is to cause the behavior to occur correctly when a student either does not respond or gives an incorrect response, whether prompted or unprompted.

If a *time delay* procedure is being used (either constant or progressive), it is important that the prompt that is delivered at the end of the delay interval be a controlling prompt to which the teacher is certain the student will respond. If errors occur when using time delay, they are most likely to do so during the delay interval, between when the target stimulus occurs and when the teacher intends to use the prompt. This is considered an unprompted error. When this occurs, the teacher should use a verbal direction, a gesture, and/or a physical prompt to interrupt the incorrect behavior and then provide the target stimulus again.

If a pattern of responding incorrectly before the prompt is given develops, the teacher may need to introduce *wait training* (Wolery et al., 1992), which is done by switching to the progressive time delay procedure and gradually moving from a zero-second delay to 1-second delay, 2-second, and so forth. To improve the chance of the student's learning to wait, Wolery et al. suggested using special tasks that are too difficult for the student to perform without a controlling prompt so that the student must wait for the prompt before responding.

When an error occurs after the controlling prompt is delivered using a time delay procedure, whether the error is an incorrect behavior or no response at all, this indicates that the controlling prompt is not "controlling" enough to get the behavior to occur. In this case, a more effective prompt is necessary.

When an error occurs using the system of least prompts, regardless of the level or type of prompt being provided (including no prompt at the first delivery of the target stimulus), the appropriate correction procedure is to repeat the target stimulus and go immediately to the next, more intrusive prompt on the hierarchy. If the error is an incorrect behavior, the teacher should interrupt the movement and provide the next prompt. If the error is no response within the allotted time interval, the teacher should repeat or re-present the target stimulus and the next more intrusive prompt. The final prompt used in the sequence must be a controlling prompt; if its use does not result in a correct response, a stronger, more effective controlling prompt is required.

Errors are also possible with the most-to-least prompting procedure; they include both prompted and unprompted errors and no responses. Since the first level of assistance provided is assumed to be a controlling prompt, errors at this time indicate that the prompt is inadequate and needs to be changed to exert more influence. If errors occur at subsequent, less intrusive levels of prompting, the teacher should either revert to the most intrusive prompt to correct the error or to a prompt more intrusive than the one at which the error occurred, but less intrusive than the controlling prompt.

Regardless of the prompting system used, when an error occurs on a particular trial, the teacher should implement an error correction procedure. Whatever form of reinforcement is being used should be withheld, and the correction of the error should be carried out in a matter-of-fact manner without any anger or hostility shown toward the student. Before going on to the next trial, the teacher might pause briefly (10 to 20 seconds) before repeating the target stimulus.

Increasing Compliance

On some occasions, students with disabilities (like students without disabilities) are reluctant to comply with instructions to learn something or participate in some activities. Often they have activities that they prefer and others that they do not. Vaughn and Horner (1997), working with two students with severe mental retardation and one with autism, found that the students' preference for the task that they were requested to do clearly affected the occurrence of problem behaviors such as hitting, pinching, scratching, throwing materials, or noncompliance. They interviewed the teachers to find out which tasks were considered to be preferred and which were nonpreferred and confirmed the results of the interview through direct observation. When students were presented with nonpreferred tasks, their rates of problem behaviors increased; when more preferred tasks were presented, problem behaviors decreased. When given a choice (which they indicated by selecting a representative symbol), the students chose their preferred activities more than 90% of the time.

When students resist learning certain tasks, the teacher might first question the relevance of the task. If the task is clearly one of importance, however, then efforts may be undertaken to reduce the student's resistance or noncompliance. Research suggests that participation in less desirable or low-probability activities can be positively influenced. One way to do this is to precede the less desirable task with several (three to five) more desirable (or high probability) activities. These activities have a history of earning the individual reinforcement, and when they occur before requesting or prompting the low-probability behavior, they tend to increase the chance that the latter will occur (Mace et al., 1988). The student builds what has been referred to as *behavioral momentum* as he engages in the more desired tasks. After several episodes of positive responding, the teacher may request that the less desired task be undertaken and then switch immediately back to more desired activities. This process may continue until the student becomes less resistant. In a variation on this, Kennedy, Itkonen, and Lindquist (1995) found that by making a series of unrelated social comments ("It's a beautiful day") prior to making low-probability requests, compliance with the request increased.

Writing an Instructional Program

An instructional program must be written for every behavioral objective for students with severe disabilities. This program is a comprehensive description of the plan of instruction for a particular objective. It begins with the behavioral objective (and task analysis or functional routine, if appropriate) and the material and setting used to teach the skill. It then states all the elements of the instructional process that have been discussed in this chapter as they will be used in the instruction of the objective. This includes a statement of the skill acquisition training procedure with the levels of prompting if they are part of the procedure, the reinforcement procedure, and the error correction procedure. (Plans for maintenance and generalization of the behavior, as well as for data collection and recording, should also be included. See Chapters 8 and 9 for discussion of these topics.) Figure 7–1 provides an example of an instructional plan for a student who is learning how to clean a bathroom in a motel. As can be seen, the teacher has developed a complete description of the instructional plan that will be followed to teach the student to clean a bathroom.

A complete plan of instruction for each student with a severe disability should include at least six written instructional programs such as the one presented in Figure 7–1. This is not intended to imply that this is all that the student will learn, because there should be much opportunity for observational learning and incidental learning; but it is a precise way of detailing how the student will acquire certain behaviors or skills that have been prioritized by the collaborative team. The plan for each objective is to be developed regardless of the exact nature of the objective to be taught, whether the objective is to teach simple, discrete behaviors or complex skills with task analysis or functional routines.

Conclusion

For each skill or behavior to be learned by a student, a variety of skill acquisition training techniques might be used. The teacher should select procedures that seem to be most effective for getting the job done. Although it is not possible to say which specific procedure will be effective for which student or skill to be learned, Wolery et al. (1992) provide the following suggestions:

- Teachers should study the research literature to determine the effectiveness of different techniques.
- Teachers should select tactics that have the least potential for harming the student and are the least likely to call attention to the student when being used in public settings.
- The tactics used should be those that require the least amount of intrusiveness or restrictiveness and that seem to be the most natural for the situation.
- Consideration should be given to the student and to what has been effective with the student in the past. Students respond differently to prompting systems; the more the teacher knows about students, the better she may be able to select effective instructional systems.

Figure 7–1 Instructional Plan for Cleaning a Bathroom

Student: James

Behavioral object: James will clean the bathroom in the motel where he is working by completing all of the steps of the task analysis. He will begin 10 seconds after he enters the bathroom and will complete the entire task within 10 minutes.

Setting and materials: Any bathroom within the motel where James is learning to work.

Task analysis/functional routine:

1. Gather all towels, bath mats, and wash cloths and place them in the laundry cart in the hallway.
2. Gather old soap and trash basket and empty into the container in the hallway.
3. Turn on the cold water and wet the inner portion of the bathtub.
4. Sprinkle cleanser in the bathtub.
5. Use sponge to wipe the bathtub thoroughly.
6. Rinse tub and dry.
7. Sprinkle cleanser in toilet bowl and on the outside of the toilet.
8. Wipe inside and outside of the toilet.
9. Use second damp cloth to wipe cleanser off toilet.
10. Sprinkle cleanser on sink.
11. Wipe sink clean.
12. Rinse sink.
13. Clean mirror with glass cleaner and cloth.
14. Damp-mop bathroom.
15. Put clean towels, bath mats, and wash cloths in bathroom.

Instructional procedure:

(Including prompting sequence)

Use the system of least prompts for each step in the task analysis beginning when James enters the bathroom. Wait 5 seconds between prompts.

1. No prompt.
2. Gesture by pointing to the materials of the activity to occur. (Point to the tub and the cleanser and the cloth.)
3. Verbally suggest the step in the task analysis that is to be completed, using an indirect statement. ("What are you supposed to do with the sink now?")
4. Tell James what step in the task analysis he is to do. ("Throw away the old soap and the trash.")

Reinforcement: During the first 3 days of training, reinforce James after each step in the task analysis is completed correctly by saying "looks good" or something similar. On the next 3 days, reinforce only after every other step. Continue reducing comments until a point is reached where James is congratulated for a good job after he has finished the entire task. If the amount of time required for task completion is greater than called for in the objective, reinforce more often for faster performance.

- Teachers should select the simplest system that will be effective. It is best to avoid developing elaborate instructional systems that will be difficult to implement if simpler systems will work just as well.
- Finally, teachers should be concerned with using only systems that are socially valid. This means that the method of instruction should be acceptable to the student, parents, members of the community, other professionals, and instructional team.

During the process of instruction, the teacher must respond to behaviors appropriately by using correction procedures when errors occur and by reinforcing appropriate behaviors. However, as this is done, the teacher should remember that the importance of the task is likely to be more effective in motivating the student than the reinforcement and error correction procedures. Thus, again it is suggested that objectives be written to develop important skills that will decrease dependence, increase independence, and improve the student's quality of life.

Questions for Reflection

1. How important is it for all team members to agree on the objectives for a student? What if they do not?
2. Why must objectives be stated in specific terms? When developing objectives, why is *function* often more important than *form*?
3. Develop some sample objectives that allow for partial participation. Explain in what ways these would be meaningful for the student.
4. Are there any additional good general teaching practices that can be added to those discussed in this chapter?
5. How would you describe the purpose and structure of the prompting techniques presented in this chapter?
6. Describe some observational and incidental learning opportunities that might exist within a regular elementary classroom.
7. Why is it desirable that students learn to respond to natural cues and consequences? What should the teacher do if this does not occur?
8. Do you believe there are circumstances in which it would be appropriate to use food or drink as reinforcement for students with severe disabilities?
9. Besides identifying possible reinforcers, why are preference assessments important?

References

Alberto, P. A., & Troutman, A. C. (2002). *Applied behavior analysis for teachers* (6th ed.). Upper Saddle River, NJ: Merrill/Prentice Hall.

Ault, M. J., Wolery, M., Doyle, P. M., & Gast, D. L. (1989). Review of comparative studies in the instruction of students with moderate and severe handicaps. *Exceptional Children, 55,* 346–356.

Baumgart, D., Brown, L., Pumpian, I., Nisbet, J., Ford, A., Sweet, M., Messing, R., & Schroeder, J. (1982). Principle of partial participation and individualized adaptations in educational programs for severely handicapped students. *Journal of the Association for the Severely Handicapped, 7*(2), 17–27.

Billingsley, F. F., & Romer, L. T. (1983). Response prompting and the transfer of stimulus control: Methods, research, and a conceptual framework. *Journal of the Association for the Severely Handicapped, 8,* 3–12.

Bosch, S., & Fuqua, R. W. (2001). Behavioral cusps: A model for selecting target behaviors. *Journal of Applied Behavior Analysis, 34,* 123–125.

Browder, D. M., & Xin, Y. P. (1998). A meta-analysis and review of sight word research and its implication for teaching reading to individuals with moderate and severe disabilities. *Journal of Special Education, 32,* 130–153.

Brown, F., Evans, I. M., Weed, K. A., & Owen, V. (1987). Delineating functional competencies: A component model. *Journal of the Association for Persons with Severe Handicaps, 12,* 117–124.

Collins, B. C., Branson, T. A., & Hall, M. (1995). Teaching generalized reading of cooking product labels to adolescents with mental disabilities through the use of key words taught by peer tutors. *Education and Training in Mental Retardation and Developmental Disabilities, 30,* 65–75.

Copeland, S. R., & Hughes, C. (2000). Acquisition of a picture prompt strategy to increase independent performance. *Education and Training in Mental Retardation and Developmental Disabilities, 35*, 294–305.

Cotton, K. (1995). *Effective schooling practices: A research synthesis 1995 update.* Portland OR: Northwest Regional Educational Laboratory.

Cotton, K. (1998). *Education for lifelong learning: Literature synthesis.* Portland OR: Northwest Regional Educational Laboratory.

Demchak, M. (1990). Response prompting and fading methods: A review. *American Journal on Mental Retardation, 94,* 603–615.

Dever, R. B. (1988). *Community living skills.* Washington, DC: American Association on Mental Retardation.

Downing, J. E., & Demchak, M. (1996). First steps: Determining individual abilities and how to best support students. In J. E. Downing (Ed.), *Including students with severe and multiple disabilities in typical classrooms* (pp. 35–61). Baltimore: Paul H. Brookes.

Doyle, P. M., Wolery, M., Ault, M. J., & Gast, D. L. (1988). System of least prompts: A literature review of procedural parameters. *Journal of the Association for Persons with Severe Handicaps, 13,* 28–40.

Ferguson, D. L., & Baumgart, D. (1991). Partial participation revisited. *Journal of the Association for Persons with Severe Handicaps, 16,* 218–227.

Fiscus, R. S., Schuster, J. W., Morse, T. E., & Collins, B. C. (2002). Teaching elementary students with cognitive disabilities food preparation skills while embedding instructive feedback in the prompt and consequent event. *Education and Training in Mental Retardation and Developmental Disabilities, 37*(1), 55–69.

Ford, A., & Mirenda, P. (1984). Community instruction: A natural cues and corrections decision model. *Journal of the Association for Persons with Severe Handicaps, 9,* 79–87.

Gast, D. L., Doyle, P. M., Wolery, M., Ault, M. J., & Farmer, J. A. (1991). Assessing the acquisition of incidental information by secondary-age students with mental retardation: Comparison of response prompting strategies. *American Journal on Mental Retardation, 96,* 63–80.

Giangreco, M. F., Cloninger, C. J., & Iverson, V. S. (1998). *Choosing options and accommodations for children: A guide to educational planning for students with disabilities* (2nd Ed.). Baltimore: Paul H. Brookes.

Hughes, C., Pitkin, S. E., & Lorden, S. W. (1998). Assessing preferences and choices of persons with severe and profound mental retardation. *Education and Training in Mental Retardation and Developmental Disabilities, 33*, 299–316.

Kayser, J. E., Billingsley, F. F., & Neel, R. S. (1986). A comparison of in-context and traditional instructional approaches: Total task, single trial versus backward chaining, multiple trials. *Journal of the Association for Persons with Severe Handicaps, 11,* 28–38.

Kennedy, C. H., Itkonen, T., & Lindquist, K. (1995). Comparing interspersed requests and social comments as antecedents for increasing student compliance. *Journal of Applied Behavior Analysis, 28,* 97–98.

Lohrmann-O'Rourke, S., Browder, D. M., & Brown, F. (2000). Guidelines for conducting socially valid systematic preference assessments. *Journal of the Association for Persons with Severe Handicaps, 25*, 42–53.

Mace, F. C., Hock, M. L., Lalli, J. S., West, B. J., Belfiore, P., Pinter, E., & Brown, D. K. (1988). Behavioral momentum in the treatment of noncompliance. *Journal of Applied Behavior Analysis, 21,* 123–142.

Mechling, L. C., & Gast, D. L. (1997). Combination audio/visual self-prompting system for teaching chained tasks to students with intellectual disabilities. *Education and Training in Mental Retardation and Developmental Disabilities, 32,* 138–153.

Miracle, S.A., Collins, B.C., Schuster, J.W., Grisham-Brown, J. (2001). Peer versus Teacher-delivered instruction: Effects on acquisition and maintenance. *Education and Training in Mental Retardation and Developmental Disabilities, 36,* 373–385.

Nietupski, J., Hamre-Nietupski, S., Clancy, P., & Veerhusen, K. (1986). Guidelines for making simulations an effective adjunct to in vivo community instruction. *Journal of the Association for Persons with Severe Handicaps, 11,* 12–18.

Orelove, F. P., & Malatchi, A. (1996). Curriculum and instruction. In F. P. Orelove & D. Sobsey, *Educating children with multiple disabilities* (3rd ed., pp. 377–409). Baltimore: Paul H. Brookes.

Post, M., & Story, K. (2002). Review of using auditory prompting systems with persons who have moderate to severe disabilities. *Education and Training in Mental Retardation and Developmental Disabilities, 37*(3), 317–327.

Rosales-Ruiz, J., & Baer, D. M. (1997). Behavioral cusps: A developmental and pragmatic concept for behavior analysis. *Journal of Applied Behavior Analysis, 30*, 533–544.

Sailor, W., & Guess, D. (1983). *Severely handicapped students: An instructional design.* Boston: Houghton Mifflin.

Schoen, S. (1986). Assistance procedures to facilitate the transfer of stimulus control: Review and analysis. *Education and Training of the Mentally Retarded, 21,* 62–74.

Schoen, S. F., & Ogden, S. (1995). Impact of time delay, observational learning, and attentional cuing upon word recognition during integrated small-group instruction. *Journal of Autism and Developmental Disorders, 25,* 503–519.

Sikorski, M. F., Niemiec, R. P., & Walberg, H. J. (1996). A classroom checkup: Best teaching practices in special education. *Teaching Exceptional Children, 29*(1), 27–29.

Singleton, K. C., Schuster, J. W., & Ault, M. J. (1995). Simultaneous prompting in a small group instructional arrangement. *Education and Training in Mental Retardation and Developmental Disabilities, 30,* 218–230.

Snell, M. E., & Gast, D. L. (1981). Applying time delay procedure to the instruction of the severely handicapped. *Journal of the Association for the Severely Handicapped, 6*(3), 3–14.

Smith, R. L., Collins, B. C., Schuster, J. W., & Kleinert, H. (1999). Teaching table cleaning skills to secondary students with moderate/severe disabilities: Facilitating observational learning during instructional downtime. *Education and Training in Mental Retardation and Developmental Disabilities, 34,* 342–353.

U.S. Department of Education. (1986). *What works: Research about teaching and learning.* Washington, DC: Author.

Vaughn, B. J., & Horner, R. H. (1997). Identifying instructional tasks that occasion problem behaviors and assessing the effect of student versus teacher choice among these tasks. *Journal of Applied Behavior Analysis, 30,* 299–312.

Werts, M. G., Caldwell, N. K., & Wolery, M. (1996). Peer modeling of response chains: Observational learning by students with disabilities. *Journal of Applied Behavior Analysis, 29,* 53–66.

Wolery, M., Ault, M. J., & Doyle, P. M. (1992). *Teaching students with moderate to severe disabilities: Use of response prompting strategies.* New York: Longman.

Wolery, M., & Gast, D. L. (1984). Effective and efficient procedures for the transfer of stimulus control. *Topics in Early Childhood Special Education, 4,* 52–77.

Wood, B. A., Frank, A. R., & Hamre-Nietupski, S. (1996). How do you work this lock? Adaptations for teaching combination lock use. *Teaching Exceptional Children, 28*(2), 35–39.

Zane, T., Walls, R. T., & Thvedt, J. E. (1981). Prompting and fading guidance procedures: Their effect on chaining and whole task teaching strategies. *Education and Training of the Mentally Retarded, 16,* 125–135.

Zhang, J., Gast, D., Horvat, M., & Dattilo, J. (1995). The effectiveness of a constant time delay procedure on teaching lifetime sport skills to adolescents with severe to profound intellectual disabilities. *Education and Training in Mental Retardation and Developmental Disabilities, 30,* 51–64.

CHAPTER 8

Teaching Skills for Generalization and Maintenance

For new behaviors or skills to be useful, students must learn how to apply the skills in new situations or locations and must retain the skills over a period of time. This chapter describes procedures that will help to achieve skill generalization and maintenance. The use of nondisabled peers as mediators to improve generalization and maintenance is discussed as a viable approach because of the development of more inclusion programs in recent years.

The Importance of Generalization and Maintenance

In Chapter 7, methods for skill acquisition, that is, methods that are designed to help students to initially acquire new behaviors or skills, were discussed. Teaching students to acquire new skills requires the systematic use of cues, prompts, positive reinforcement, and correction procedures. However, it should be realized that acquiring a new skill, or learning how to perform a particular task in one situation or under one limited set of conditions, very often is not sufficient for functional activity. In addition, students must learn to use skills as often as needed and in all appropriate and necessary situations. Conversely, students must also learn *not* to do something or exhibit behaviors in situations or environments when they are inappropriate or unnecessary. When individuals can apply skills in different environments or situations or under different circumstances from those they first learned, this is referred to as skill *generalization*. When students can use skills at times beyond the point that they were originally learned, it is referred to as behavioral *maintenance* or generalization across time.

A well-recognized learning weakness of individuals with cognitive disabilities is their poor ability to apply learned skills to new situations, that is, in new environments, with different people, using different materials, or at different times (Fox, 1989; Haring, 1987, 1988; Horner, Dunlap, & Koegel, 1988). For example, a student might acquire shopping behaviors, but fail to shop correctly when taken to a grocery store; a student might learn to correctly use a communicative act at school, but not at home or in the community; a student may exhibit appropriate social behavior at home, but not in the community. A similar problem occurs when the student has successfully learned a skill in one school year, but during the next year seems to have forgotten what was learned. This problem is often a concern expressed by teachers of students with severe disabilities.

Unfortunately, this learning weakness of many students with severe disabilities is often compounded by the fact that teachers and others do not always plan adequately to use effective instructional tactics that can better result in generalization and maintenance (Billingsley, 1984). Instead, they often work on a skill until initial acquisition has occurred (usually in the classroom) and then, considering it learned, check it off the IEP or the curriculum checklist. The following year a new teacher has to reteach the skill or behavior and the cycle starts anew. The essence of the problem is that the behavior was not learned sufficiently; the student did not learn how to use what was learned with different people, or beyond the site, or beyond the time of initial acquisition. In short, the behavior did not adequately generalize and was not maintained.

This is often an unnecessary instructional shortcoming. Even though many students with cognitive disabilities do not automatically generalize and maintain what they have learned, it is possible to improve their chances of doing so by using more effective instructional procedures. These procedures have been developed through research conducted over more than 20 years (Black & Langone, 1995; Donnellan & Mirenda, 1983; Fox, 1989; Haring, 1987, 1988; Haring et al., 1985; Horner et al., 1988; Horner, McDonnell, & Bellamy, 1986; Horner, Sprague, & Wilcox, 1982; Rutherford & Nelson, 1987; Scruggs & Mastropieri, 1994; Westling & Floyd, 1990; White et al., 1988).

In this chapter, strategies and tactics for achieving generalization and maintenance are discussed. Most of the attention is placed on generalization because most of the research has been conducted in this area. It should be realized that, since maintaining skills over a period of time may be considered a form of generalization, information relevant to promoting skill generalization is also applicable to maintaining behaviors.

Strategies That Have Been Used to Achieve Skill Generalization

In broad terms, *generalization* is "appropriate responding in untrained situations" (Haring, 1988). A student who has learned a generalized skill is able to demonstrate the skill not only in the original situation and under conditions in which it was initially acquired, but also in a variety of situations and conditions when it is appropriate to do so. These "situations and conditions" could include *different persons, different objects or materials, different settings and stimuli, different reinforcers, and different times of the day* (Haring, 1988). Albin and Horner (1988) point out that it is equally important for a particular behavior *not* to occur when it is not appropriate.

In an early paper, Stokes and Baer (1977) examined many applied behavior analysis research articles in which there was an attempt to measure the occurrence of generalization. Drawing from these studies, they identified nine methods that were used to achieve generalization and their relative degrees of success. In addition to the strategies identified by Stokes and Baer, additional methods for promoting generalization were identified by later authorities (Chandler, Lubeck, & Fowler, 1992; White et al., 1988). All these strategies are described in Table 8–1. In the following sections we consider the strategies in some detail.

Train and Hope

The *train and hope* approach is the least likely to result in generalization. White et al. (1988) concluded that individuals with severe disabilities would generalize only about 25% of the skills taught with this approach. In examining generalization of community skills, Westling and Floyd (1990) determined that about 30% of the time learners with severe disabilities were able to generalize acquired skills without specific efforts being made to help them to do so. In 6 of the 25 studies (about 25%) on the generalization of skills by individuals with the most severe disabilities reviewed by Fox (1989), it was found that some degree of generalization occurred when only the train and hope model was used. Likewise, Scruggs and Mastropieri (1994), in their quantitative analysis of interventions, reported that the train and hope approach resulted in the lowest level of generalization outcome.

It is not clear why in some circumstances some individuals with severe disabilities are able to generalize their skills without specific preparation to do so and others are not. Westling and Floyd (1990) speculated that the successful persons may have had some relevant experiences prior to the experimental studies that helped them to generalize. Fox (1989) and, earlier, Stokes and Baer (1977) suggested that instructional models that appear to be only train and hope approaches may actually, perhaps inadvertently, include efforts to improve generalization even though they are not reported. Regardless, the fact is clear that if teachers simply teach a skill, using one of the skill acquisition methods described in Chapter 7, generalization will not often occur.

Arranging Consequences during Initial Training to Improve Generalization

In the list of generalization strategies contained in Table 8–1, three pertain to behavioral consequences: *introducing natural maintaining contingencies, using indiscriminable contingencies,* and *training to generalize.* Another strategy, *sequential modification*, uses reinforcement to reteach a skill under different conditions if initial train and hope instruction does not result in generalization.

The use of reinforcement as a consequence following the occurrence of a behavior is known to be among the most powerful of the interventions (Scruggs & Mastropieri, 1994). But relatively few studies have examined the effectiveness of the different reinforcement strategies thought to promote generalization with learners who have severe disabilities. Those that have, however, have reported moderate success. White et al. (1988) found that, when students with severe disabilities were taught skills that were functional and thus more likely to be reinforced in the natural environment, they were more likely to generalize them than when the skills were nonfunctional and thus not likely to be frequently used or reinforced. The analysis of research conducted by Chandler et al. (1992) led to the same conclusion. In fact, Chandler et al. found that one of the most successful factors for achieving generalization was the use of functional target behaviors. White et al. (1988) cautioned, however, that the student must have enough opportunity in the natural environment to practice the skill, that the student must be proficient enough with the skill for it to result in the natural reinforcer, and that reinforcement must be available for successful performance. Without these conditions, the application of natural reinforcement may not be effective.

Another effective consequent strategy for promoting generalization is the use of indiscriminable contingencies. In the studies that Chandler et al. reviewed, they found that this was an important distinction between studies in which generalization occurred more often and those in which it occurred less often. White et al. noted that this strategy calls for a continuous schedule of reinforcement (one in which every instance of the behavior is reinforced) to be gradually replaced by intermittent, unpredictable, and more natural occurrences of reinforcement. (Intermittent reinforcement is discussed later in this chapter.) In their review of studies that included school-age students with various, albeit mostly mild, disabilities, Scruggs and Mastropieri (1994) found that the use of indiscriminable contingencies was one of the most powerful interventions resulting in generalization.

Table 8–1 Strategies Identified to Promote Generalization

Strategy	*Description*
Train and Hope	The train and hope approach teaches someone to acquire a skill and then hopes that it will generalize. In other words, there is no specific programming to promote generalization. Using train and hope, the teacher focuses on teaching a behavior to the level of acquisition and then expects that it will generalize to those environments and conditions in which it will be needed. This is the approach least likely to be successful.
Sequential Modification	Teaches the individual to generalize if she fails to do so following initial acquisition training. After a train and hope approach has been used and a follow-up test for generalization in another setting, time, or other condition is presented to the learner, *if generalization does not occur,* training is conducted in the novel setting, at the new time, or under another desirable new condition.
Introduce to Natural Maintaining Contingencies	Teaches an individual a skill during the acquisition period that will later be reinforced by natural contingencies in the environment in which the behavior will occur, instead of through the artificial reinforcers that were used during acquisition training. Since initial training often occurs in an environment other than the one in which the behavior or skill is needed, generalization to the criterion environment may be improved if the reinforcers in that environment can be applied to the behavior as it is being learned initially.
Train Sufficient Exemplars	Because the lack of generalization is associated with training in limited settings or under limited conditions, improved generalization should occur if training occurs under several sufficient conditions with various stimuli. An example would be teaching an individual to put on a sweater. Instead of teaching with only a long-sleeved crew-neck sweater, sleeveless sweaters, v-neck sweaters, cardigan sweaters, and other types would also be used (White et al., 1988).
Train Loosely	To avoid having the person learn to respond under strict stimulus conditions, variations in stimuli, responses, and reinforcers are allowed. This may be considered an "informal technique" with "relatively little control over the stimuli presented" (Stokes & Baer, 1977, p. 357).
Use Indiscriminable Contingencies	A behavior is much more likely to continue to occur if the learner is reinforced on an intermittent schedule of reinforcement. If the individual does not know when reinforcement will occur, or in what settings, or under what stimulus conditions, he is likely to demonstrate the behavior with greater frequency and also in different settings and conditions. The behavior is less likely to be forgotten.
Program Common Stimuli	Generalization to a new setting will be more likely to occur if the training setting contains stimuli that are also contained in the generalization setting. "Programming common stimuli" refers to having in the training environment those stimuli that will appear in the environment(s) in which it is desirable for the learned behavior to occur. To use this approach, a teacher would attempt to strictly re-create many of the conditions in the initial teaching environment that would appear in the generalization environment(s). This is often difficult to accomplish.
Mediate Generalization	This requires teaching a co-behavior with the target behavior during initial training so that the co-behavior can facilitate (mediate) the new behavior during generalization training. For example, the learner may learn to *say* the particular behavior that is to occur, or to *self-manage* or *self-instruct,* so that she may remind herself what to do in the new setting.
Train to Generalize	This approach differentially reinforces the student for behaviors that occur outside of the initial setting or condition and stops reinforcement when the behavior occurs only under the original condition. In this way the student learns that it is the generalized behavior that is to occur.
Teach Functional Target Behaviors	This strategy suggests that generalization will be more likely if the instructional targets (behaviors or skills) are relevant and functional. If they are, they are more likely to occur and be reinforced in the natural environment. On the other hand, if something is being taught that has little practical utility for the learner, it will cease to occur when the individual is no longer in the training environment.
Specify a Fluency Criterion	The degree of successful generalization may depend on how fluently or proficiently someone performs a task at the time of initial learning. Thus some researchers have studied the relationship between teaching the student to acquire a particular skill performance fluency criterion and later generalization. Skills that the student learns to perform faster and with greater ease during initial teaching may generalize better.
Teach in the Natural Setting	This strategy calls for teaching in at least one natural setting in which the skill will be used. The emphasis proposed on nonschool, community-based training (Brown et al., 1983; Falvey, 1995) is based on the premise that teaching that occurs in natural environments is likely to generalize to other natural environments.
Use General Case Programming	General case programming applies the practice of using several exemplars of a very specific nature. It calls for the teacher to identify the "universe" of desired generalization conditions, identify the variations of the relevant stimuli and responses in the universe, and then teach the student to respond appropriately under all appropriate stimulus conditions. Although it is a complex procedure, it has met with a great deal of success in achieving generalization (Westling & Floyd, 1990; White et al., 1988).

The train to generalize method for attempting to improve generalization skills has not been used a great deal except in combination with other approaches to improve generalization. Thus its individual effectiveness is difficult to determine. In their review, White et al. (1988) found that only 10% of the individuals with whom this procedure was used generalized well as a result. Similarly, Chandler et al. (1992) found that the approach was used more often in unsuccessful studies of generalization than in successful ones.

Few studies have used the process of sequential modification with students with severe disabilities. As described in Table 8–1, this approach is used when train and hope fails to achieve some degree of desired generalization. In one example in which this approach was used, Duker and Jutten (1997) attempted to teach gestural yes–no responding to three adults with profound mental disabilities. Using most-to-least physical prompting, they were successful in initially teaching the skills, but reported that generalization did not spontaneously occur across persons or settings. Therefore, they successfully retaught the responses (using sequential modification) under the desired generalization conditions. Scruggs and Mastropieri (1994) found that the sequential modification procedure, that is, reinstructing individuals under the desired generalization condition, was one of the most powerful forms of intervention in terms of outcome. However, they noted that this form of intervention may be considered more reteaching of the same skill under a different condition than generalizing by the learner. They proposed that when the generalized outcomes are "finite and known" this method may be preferred.

Arranging Antecedents during Initial Training to Improve Generalization

Much research has been conducted to determine the impact of arrangements made *before* the demonstration of the behavior or skill, that is, the effect of behavioral antecedents on subsequent skill generalization. As the term is used here, behavioral antecedents include the *setting* where the instruction occurs, the use of *sufficient exemplars, training loosely* (i.e., providing various cues or prompts), *programming common stimuli in the teaching and generalization settings*, and using the *general case method.*

Providing instruction in the natural environment, particularly in nonschool, community environments, has often been recommended for students with severe disabilities (Brown et al., 1983; Falvey, 1995; see Chapter 18). The assumption is that students who are taught in the natural environment will be able to learn functional skills and generalize them to other natural environments. However, if the teacher provides instruction only in one natural environment, without undertaking additional activities to promote skill generalization, it may not occur. White et al. (1988) stated, "An analysis of the overall impact of those studies indicates that merely shifting the location of instruction without incorporating other strategies to facilitate generalization will not be effective for many students. In studies with severe subjects, training in the natural setting is only as effective as train and hope" (p. 21).

In their analysis of studies on the generalization of community skills, Westling and Floyd (1990) came to a similar conclusion. They reported that instruction in *simulated* community conditions could be effective in achieving generalization, but that the degree of generalization improved if this activity was paired with *actual* community site-based instruction. They also found that instruction in multiple community settings was generally more effective than instruction in single community settings.

The use of sufficient exemplars may also be considered an aspect of instruction important for improving generalization. Teaching skills using this method requires providing enough exemplars until the concept or induction is formed. Using sufficient exemplars is defined by White et al. (1988) as the sequential introduction of new target stimuli within an environment. These authors found only three studies using this procedure with individuals who had severe disabilities. In these studies, about half of the subjects with severe disabilities generalized well as a result of using this approach. Chandler et al. (1992) found that the use of sufficient exemplars as a strategy to improve generalization of social behaviors was approximately equal in more successful and less successful studies, but from their analysis, Scruggs and Mastropieri (1994) determined that the use of multiple exemplars was often associated with strong generalization outcomes.

One problem with simply employing multiple exemplars is that they may not be adequately representative of the stimuli that will exist in various generalization circumstances. For the stimuli to be effective, therefore, there must be some criteria for their selection. Without such, simply using multiple stimuli may not be likely to result in effective generalization. The general case method (discussed later) provides very specific criteria for the selection of the exemplars.

Training loosely allows for unplanned variation in both the stimuli used to prompt the skill or behavior during initial training and the form of the behavior as exhibited by the learner. It has had only modest success in promoting generalization by individuals with disabilities and those without (Chandler et al., 1992; White et al., 1988). Programming common stimuli, which means to ensure that stimuli that exist in the generalization settings will also be in the initial training setting, has resulted in somewhat more success than training loosely when teaching individuals with severe disabilities (White et al., 1988). Part of the effectiveness of this approach depends on how similar the common stimuli are in the training condition compared to the generalization condition. If there is much similarity, generalization will probably be more successful than if there is little (Westling & Floyd, 1990).

Based on the analyses of the available research, the general case method is considered the most successful antecedent training strategy for promoting generalization (Fox, 1989; Westling & Floyd, 1990; White et al., 1988). This approach uses multiple exemplars that are representative of the universe of conditions or settings in which the learner is to successfully demonstrate the learned skill and also teaches any necessary variations in the skills that must be used under relevant generalization conditions (Albin, McDonnell, & Wilcox, 1987; Horner, McDonnell, & Bellamy, 1986; Horner et al., 1982). In the various reviews of studies, this approach was consistently reported to result in high levels of generalized performance. It has been employed with much success in developing generalized skills in areas such as purchasing food in fast-food restaurants (McDonnell & Ferguson, 1988), operating of vending machines (Sprague & Horner, 1984), purchasing groceries (McDonnell et al., 1984), selecting grocery items (Horner, Albin, & Ralph, 1986), and street crossing (Horner, Jones, & Williams, 1985). Because the general case method has been more successful than others, it is described in more detail later in this chapter.

Using Peers to Improve Generalization

A number of studies have reported the use of chronological-age nondisabled peers as facilitators in both initial learning and promoting and testing the generalization of new skills. Given the desire to provide instruction in more natural and inclusive environments, this is a very positive if tentative finding. Essentially, the use of multiple peers as models or mediators during instruction can provide the learner with multiple exemplars for learning and generalizing in such critical areas as communication and social skills development (Black & Langone, 1995). Learners with severe disabilities can model the behavior of peers, be prompted by peers, or interact with them in ways that may lead to more generalized performance. Several factors may be at work in such arrangements. In addition to the effect of using multiple peers as multiple exemplars, peers might also provide looser training or use indiscriminable contingencies. The age similarity between peers (as opposed to the dissimilarity between students with disabilities and their teachers) *may* be an influential factor. A few studies in which nondisabled peers have been used to mediate learning and generalization are briefly described next.

Goldstein and Cisar (1992) conducted a study in which nine preschool children played in three triads; two in each triad did not have disabilities and one had autism (or autismlike behaviors). The children were first taught to engage in sociodramatic play activities and were then observed daily as they did so. Sociodramatic scripts, like little plays, were used to teach the children to play different parts, with each learner's part corresponding to his language and developmental levels. The objective was to generate theme-related verbal and nonverbal social behavior both specific to the play and related to it, while simultaneously decreasing unrelated social behavior and nonsocial utterances. The children with disabilities increased theme-related target behavior and decreased unrelated social behavior. To test generalization, new triads were formed with each child in a triad with two others with whom he had not been before. Under the generalization condition, performance continued as it had with the original groups.

McMahon, Wacker, Sasso, Berg, and Newton (1996) recruited nondisabled peers to teach fellow students with mild or moderate mental disabilities to play recreational board games and appropriate social skills. In this study, four students with cognitive disabilities (three mild, one moderate), all 8 years old, were taught to play cooperative board games by same-age students without disabilities. The peer-mediated procedure used several strategies to promote generalization of social skills, including using mutually reinforcing cooperative play material, limited adult prompting for peer trainers, and the use of peer reinforcement as a natural contingency. Generalization was evaluated across play materials, social situations, and peers. Four peers served as initial trainers, and other students without disabilities were used to assess generalization. Initiations, instructional interactions, and social interactions for both disabled and nondisabled students were measured. The peer trainers were taught how to teach the students with disabilities to play cooperative board games using prompting, praising, and correcting.

According to McMahon et al. (1996), all the students with disabilities learned to play the games and also increased the frequency of their social interactions. As students learned the games, there were less instructional interactions and more social interactions. The social interactions generalized across settings, other materials, and other children.

Working in a group home with adults with mental disabilities, Farmer-Dougan (1994) employed adult peers with mild mental disabilities to teach appropriate requesting behaviors during the preparation of lunch to adults with moderate to severe mental disabilities or autism. The peer tutors were taught to "occasion appropriate verbal responses using incidental teaching." The incidental teaching required that the tutor watch for an initiation (such as reaching for the mayonnaise), remove the desired item, and, if necessary, ask for the correct response ("ask nicely"), wait for the correct response ("mayonnaise please"), and reward for the correct response (give the mayonnaise). A time delay of 5 seconds and, if necessary, modeling were used by the tutor to prompt a response. The tutors used incidental teaching to teach appropriate responding during lunch making, but tutors also generalized the use of the incidental teaching tactic to dinner time. The learners increased their appropriate responses and overall verbalizations and maintained them after the incidental teaching sessions were over.

Self-Mediation during Generalization Training

An approach studied more in recent years that has met with a relative degree of success is the use of self-mediated events to help generalization to occur. In an earlier review, Liberty (1987) noted that most generalization strategies are based on the control of environmental stimuli, either antecedents or consequences, by someone other than the learner. In contrast, she proposed that self-control by the learner through the use of mediational techniques (e.g., reminding oneself what is being done and what is to be done later) may be an effective method to improve skill generalization. In her review, Liberty examined the effect of *self-control* on 34 skills by various individuals, some with severe disabilities and some without. She found that the use of this strategy improved the generalization ability for 90% of the persons without severe disabilities and for 50% of those with severe disabilities. The analysis by Chandler et al. (1992) of the social behavior of young children also found that the use of mediators was an effective strategy in that it was used more often in studies that resulted in successful generalization than in those that were not as successful. In contrast, Scruggs and Mastropieri (1994) rated self-mediated or self-managed interventions as being relatively ineffective.

Some more recent studies using this technique offer good examples. In addition to using a self-instructional strategy, many of these studies also incorporated the use of peers. Agran, Fodor-Davis, Moore, and Martella (1992) attempted to teach adolescents with moderate to severe mental disabilities how to make sack lunches in a cafeteria using peers with mild disabilities as instructors and embedding self-instructional procedures into the task of making the lunches. First, the peers with milder disabilities were taught and then they taught the students with more severe disabilities how to take orders from customers and make sack lunches according to the orders received. Thus the task consisted not only of making the lunches (sandwiches, chips, cookies), but also interacting verbally with the customers to know what type of sandwich they wanted. Working according to a task analysis, the learners were taught to verbalize the chain in the task that had just been completed, then state the next task to be completed, and then what would be preferred for the next task. For example, they would say, "Did condiments, meats are next, 'which meat would you like?'" Two of the three students learned to complete the task using the self-instructional process, but the third required picture prompts to follow the sequence. Conditional probability analysis showed that correct responses in the lunch-making task increased as a function of self-instruction.

In another study, Hughes, Harmer, Killian, and Niarhos (1995) used a multiple-exemplar self-instructional strategy to increase conversations between young adults and adolescents with moderate mental retardation and nondisabled peers. The multiple exemplars consisted of *several* peers teaching the use of a self-instructional social skills strategy using different types of conversational initiations in different settings. Generalization was assessed by examining conversational skills with different peers. Prior to instruction, the four targeted students generally did not initiate or respond to conversational initiations by others, nor did they maintain eye contact. Instruction was provided by several different peers without disabilities, and generalization of conversational initiations and responses was tested in different locations with other peers, with and without disabilities, who were not included in the instruction. The multiple peers who provided instruction taught the students with disabilities to *prompt themselves* to engage in conversation. In each conversational situation, treating their lack of conversation as a problem that needed to be solved, they taught them to identify the problem by stating "I want to talk" and then by stating the appropriate response, "I need to look and talk." Then they were to engage in initiating a conversation and were given a pool of topics from which to choose. After the conversation they were to self-evaluate, "I did it, I talked!" and to self-reinforce, "I did a good job."

Following instruction, conversational initiations increased, as did the total number of intervals in which conversations occurred and the amount of eye contact. The amount of conversing and eye contact fell within the normal ranges for nondisabled adolescents and young adults. The use of several different peers as instructors and several different settings for instruction (multiple exemplars) served to increase the generalization of the skills.

In another study of the use of self-instruction, Hughes, Hugo, and Blatt (1996) taught five adolescents classified as severely mentally disabled to make toast and respond appropriately when problems occurred during the toast-making sequence. Using self-instruction, they first learned to solve one problem and then applied self-instruction to solve four other different types of problems (multiple exemplars). This led to their ability to generalize their problem-solving skills to uninstructed problems.

In this study, Hughes et al. (1996) used a combination of self-instruction training and training with multiple exemplars. First, students were taught to self-instruct to solve an initial problem by following a four-step problem-solving sequence. For example, the initial problem for some students was that the toaster was turned upside down. Therefore, the student was taught to (1) state the problem ("won't go in"), (2) state the response ("turn it"), (3) self-evaluate ("fixed it"), and (4) self-reinforce ("good!"). This procedure was taught by the instructor first modeling the appropriate response while describing verbally what she was doing, then having the student perform the response while the instructor instructed aloud, and then having the student perform the response while instructing herself aloud. After learning to solve an initial problem, four other problems (the multiple exemplars) were presented that required different operations. After learning how to respond to these problems, students were able to respond to topographically similar yet different problems. The study demonstrated the effectiveness of a combination of self-instruction and multiple exemplars on developing generalized problem-solving skills.

Realizing that relatively minor problems can impede progress, Bambara and Gomez (2001) applied a self-instructional program to help three men with moderate to severe cognitive disabilities learn how to handle problematic situations. The men were taught that when they encountered a snag in what they were working on (e.g., taking a shower, cleaning the bathroom, or cooking), they were to self-instruct on a four-step process to help themselves to resolve the dilemma before turning to an attendant to solve the problem for them. The steps that they were to verbalize were these:

1. State the problem ("no soap")
2. State three alternative solutions ("look in the cabinet," "look on the floor," "ask a staff person to help")
3. Self-report and evaluate the response ("looked in the cabinet, no soap," "looked on the floor, found it.")
4. Self-reinforce when the problem is solved ("good")

Bambara and Gomez taught the men on a training set of problems in real situations and then tested them both in the same settings with untrained problems and in novel settings, routines, and activities. They used a model–lead–test direct instruction procedure in which they first showed them how to respond to the problem, then led them through a response by proving verbal prompts, and then let them practice without help. If a mistake was made, they increased the amount of direction and practice opportunities.

The researchers looked at both how well the problems were solved and the extent to which the men learned to use the self-instruction steps. During self-instruction training, the men learned rather quickly how to solve their problems (i.e., they learned to search for and find missing items) and they also maintained their problem-solving skills over a period of time. Most importantly, they learned to generalize their self-instructional skills to new untrained problem situations in novel routines. The researchers concluded that their "results demonstrated that self-instructional training could successfully enhance independent problem solving in problem situations involving more than one alternative solution" (p. 396).

Summary of the Effectiveness of Generalization Strategies

Six of eight strategies examined by White et al. (1988), when used in isolation, produced statistically better results than the success generally achieved using the train and hope approach (e.g., 25%). These included using natural contingencies, indiscriminable contingencies, programming common stimuli, using sufficient exemplars, training loosely, and using the general case method. Training in the natural environment did not produce better results than the train and hope approach, nor did using mediation techniques. However, in the latter case, White et al. looked at relatively few subjects (six) in few studies (two), and this low number probably precluded finding statistically significant differences. In contrast, Liberty (1987) found the use of mediational techniques to be effective for about half of the persons with severe disabilities with whom they were tried. As shown in the previous section, although the studies are relatively few, self-mediation appears to be possible for use in achieving learning and generalization with at least some individuals with severe disabilities.

Chandler et al. (1992) found that in studies that resulted in the most successful generalization, the most common strategies used were addressing functional target behaviors, using indiscriminable contingencies, and specifying a fluency criterion. In contrast, these strategies were used in relatively few of the studies that resulted in the least amount of generalization success. Chandler et al. also analyzed most and least successful combinations of generalization strategies. They found that the most successful combinations of two promotion strategies included the following: addressing functional target behaviors and using indiscriminable contingencies, using indiscriminable contingencies and teaching mediation strategies, and addressing functional target behaviors and teaching mediation strategies. The studies analyzed by Chandler et al. that used three or four generalization promotion strategies most often included some combination of addressing functional target behaviors, specifying a fluency criterion, using indiscriminable contingencies, and using mediational strategies.

Scruggs and Mastropieri (1994) conducted a quantitative analysis of a subset of studies that had been reviewed previously by Rutherford and Nelson (1987). Most of the studies in their review were of students without disabilities or with mild disabilities, including learning disabilities and behavioral disabilities. Therefore, the extent to which their findings are appropriate for teaching students with more severe disabilities is somewhat questionable. Nevertheless, among their highest rated methods for achieving generalization were indiscriminable contingencies, peer mediation, multiple exemplars, and fading reinforcement.

As can be seen, the practitioner has many useful generalization strategies when teaching skills to students with severe disabilities. In the planning process, it is important to realize the significance of generalization and plan for it prior to the beginning of instruction. Without such planning, the instruction may help the student to acquire a particular skill, but the usefulness of the skill may be limited to the situation in which it was learned.

Applying Generalization Strategies

Implementing various methods to assist in the achievement of generalization by persons with severe disabilities is an important aspect of instruction by teachers. Fortunately, as seen from the previous descriptions, the practicing teacher has several strategies that can be used to help the student to progress beyond the level of skill acquisition. Stokes and Osnes (1988) suggested three principles that they considered to be important for achieving generalization. The first was to take advantage of natural communities of reinforcement, meaning that within an individual's environment there exist natural reinforcers (generally social reinforcers) that may be successfully applied to promote generalization of particular skills. Second, it was proposed that instructors should train diversely (or train loosely). Stokes and Osnes acknowledged that more tightly controlled training activities may influence behaviors more quickly during the acquisition phase of learning, but suggested that more variation in stimuli may ultimately result in better generalization. They suggested that only the least amount of control necessary for successful acquisition be applied. Finally, as a principle for instruction, Stokes and Osnes suggested that functional mediators that could be applied to the generalization settings or conditions be used during initial instruction. They stated that these could be either physical stimuli, such as objects, or stimuli "carried by" the learner, such as verbal self-instructions.

Tactics of Generalization Programming

Based on the available research literature and the principles proposed by Stokes and Osnes (1988), the following tactics are proposed for teaching students with severe disabilities to generalize important skills.

Teach Relevant Skills

As has been stated throughout this text, the primary focus of instruction for students with severe disabilities should be teaching skills that can be applied to improve their lives. But adding even more value to this recommendation is the likelihood that teaching relevant or functional behaviors also means that these behaviors will be more likely to generalize. This is because such behaviors are more likely to result in reinforcement than are behaviors that are irrelevant or nonfunctional.

Modify Environments Supporting Maladaptive Behaviors

Functional and appropriate behaviors are less likely to occur if inappropriate behaviors are occurring. Thus, it is important that reinforcement be available for appropriate behavior, but not for maladaptive behavior. More information on decreasing inappropriate behavior in a positive fashion is presented in Chapter 12.

Recruit Communities of Natural Reinforcers

As the earlier principle stated, natural reinforcers should be used to promote generalization. However, because the occurrence of these reinforcers in the natural environment may be less than sufficient, the learner with severe disabilities may be taught to seek reinforcement for positive generalized behavior by prompting members of his environment to provide it by asking such questions as "How am I doing?"

Use Sufficient Stimulus Exemplars

To improve generalization, Stokes and Osnes suggested that one of the most important things that can be done is to vary the instructional materials and settings. It is also helpful to use various persons during the training process.

Use Sufficient Response Exemplars

To allow for more functional success, Stokes and Osnes suggested that variations in the nature of the behavior being learned be reinforced so that it may be more applicable to all the different generalization situations. This is referred to as *response generalization.*

Use Indiscriminable Contingencies

It is easy for particular behaviors or skills being learned by individuals with severe disabilities to be linked to particular reinforcers and schedules of reinforcement. To enhance generalization, therefore, contingencies of reinforcement should become progressively less discriminable. Stokes and Osnes suggested that the sooner this happens in the instructional process, the better it will be for the student.

Use Common Physical and Social Stimuli

When the learner moves beyond the initial learning environment and into the generalization environment, her success in the new environment will be related to the stimuli in the new environment that were present in the previous environment. Such stimuli may be physical, such as signs, furniture, or equipment, or social, such as friends, peers, and siblings.

The application of the above principles and tactics from the onset of the instruction for particular skills or behaviors is of extreme importance. Stokes and Osnes (1988) summarized:

> Generalization programming needs to be built in to any serious behavior management program from the beginning of any behavior change procedure. If the focus of attention and effort turns to issues of generalization only *after* a successful but well-discriminated behavior change, it may be too late. *It may be more complicated to work on such programming from the outset, but it is probably more efficient in the long run.* (p. 15 [emphasis added])

Incorporating Peers into Generalization

These principles and the previously cited research examples suggest that teachers can use peers without disabilities to effectively influence the learning and generalization of skills by students with severe disabilities. This does not have to always be done in a formal tutor–tutee relationship, but can be done in more natural conditions and settings. Communication skills and social skills might be the primary types of objectives for which peers could serve as mediators, but other types of skills might also be learned (Wolery & Schuster, 1997).

When using peers to promote skill generalization, teachers should adhere to certain guidelines. First, it is important to keep in mind that other principles of learning and generalization be followed. This implies that peer involvement, although it can be informal and nondirective, needs to be based on valid practices. Therefore, peers will need to know what skills are targeted for learning by the student with severe disabilities. They should also understand and be able to use basic prompting techniques. Constant time delay and least-to-most prompting may be relatively easy to teach and can be very effective. Peers also need to understand the value of reinforcement, especially social reinforcement delivered in a natural and sincere way.

The value of peers in promoting skill generalization rests on two additional important tactics. First is the use of multiple peers. If we want students with severe disabilities to learn to interact appropriately with a variety of people, they need to learn to do so with a representative group. Therefore, the more experience that they have with different individuals, the more likely they are to socially and communicatively interact appropriately with unknown individuals. The second point is equally important: interactions should occur in multiple settings. Multiple peers providing influence in one classroom is good, but multiple peers mediating appropriate behavior throughout the day and in a number of different settings is preferred.

A number of studies, including those cited previously in this chapter as well as many others (cf. Wolery & Schuster, 1997), indicate that teachers and other members of the collaborative team working in inclusive settings should use peers without disabilities to their advantage. In an observational study, Janney and Snell (1996) observed how teachers influenced the activities of peers without disabilities in inclusive classroom settings as they interacted with peers with moderate or severe disabilities. They found that the teacher-promoted interactions could be classified in four ways: (1) having the children without disabilities provide assistance to those with disabilities, (2) encouraging students to positively interact in ways in which the student with the disability was treated as "just another student" who was expected to behave and participate like other students, (3) encouraging the students to interact in age-appropriate ways, and (4) "backing off" to allow typical child interactions. Besides these types of interactions, teachers may find that nondisabled peers can also be effective mediators to promote learning and generalization. In their discussion on the generalization of relevant social skills, Black and Langone (1995) proposed that "If students with mental retardation do not interact with non-disabled peers on a regular basis, they will not understand the rules of social behavior that operate in these settings. Students with mental retardation need to learn appropriate skills through direct experience with their peers in school and the workplace" (p. 5).

Using Self-Instruction to Promote Generalization

As some studies have shown, teachers can also help to achieve generalization with at least some students with severe disabilities by teaching self-instructional practices. Hughes and Agran (1993) discussed the relevance of using self-instruction to help individuals to learn skill acquisition, generalization, and maintenance, stressing the importance of self-instruction, particularly in community and other settings where there was no teacher or other support person to direct the individual in completing a task. They noted that self-instruction may serve as a form of mediating for generalization because the person learns to prompt himself to complete a task.

The self-instruction process may be learned as part of a chain of behaviors that is initiated when the person recognizes that action should occur. Hughes and Agran (1993) recommended the use of a modified version of the self-instruction system originally used by Meichenbaum and Goodman (1971). According to this recommendation, the student learns to (1) state a task-related problem ("I don't know what to wear"), (2) state a possible response ("Guess I'll wear the red dress"), (3) evaluate the response ("Hey, that looks pretty good), and (4) self-reinforce ("I did a good job choosing"). Meichenbaum and Goodman provide a protocol to teach self-instruction that includes the following:

- A teacher performs a task, instructing aloud as the student observes.
- The student performs the task while the teacher instructs aloud.
- The student performs a task while self-instructing aloud.
- The student performs the task while self-instructing with a whisper or covertly.

If students have adequate language skills to self-instruct (whether verbally or nonverbally) and if the self-instruction process generalizes from the instructional setting to new settings, then self-instruction can serve as a mediator to increase correct responses in new settings. It may also serve to maintain the skill over a period of time. Hughes and Agran (1993) suggested that, when teaching self-instruction, all four parts of the self-instructional procedure be used (state the problem, state a possible response, evaluate the response, reinforce oneself). They also stated that self-instruction alone may not be sufficient and that it should be combined with other direct instructional procedures and taught as part of an instructional package.

To increase the likelihood that self-instruction generalizes across settings, Hughes and Agran recommended that during the instructional procedure multiple exemplars be used, that students be told to use the procedure as if they were in real settings, and that students be reminded to use the procedure when in real situations. Finally, they warned that, although individuals may be more successful at a task if they follow a self-instructional sequence, overt verbalizations to oneself may appear atypical. Therefore, covert verbalizations or engaging in self-instruction as part of a conversational pattern with another person may be preferred.

Today, because many students with cognitive disabilities are in inclusive settings, there is an important need for them to learn and generalize appropriate social behavior. To do this, they need support, but in inclusive settings often no individual is present to provide this support. And without adequate direction, they may not exhibit types of behaviors or skills that foster their acceptance by other people. One way to help individuals with cognitive disabilities to maintain and generalize socially appropriate skills is to teach them to use self-monitoring techniques. Hughes et al. (2002) demonstrated the effectiveness of self-monitoring and prompting with four students with mild to moderate cognitive disabilities enrolled in general high school classes.

Each of the four individuals exhibited a particular behavioral deficit that inhibited inclusion in his or her high school class. Mia held her head down and would not look people in the eye; Vondre would not socially respond to individuals; Jamal would not use his textbook in his auto mechanics class to complete in-class assignments; and Michael did not initiate verbal interactions with his peers.

To counter these behavioral limitations, Hughes et al. taught each student to use a self-monitoring tactic to remind himself or herself about the correct way to respond. Mia learned to look at or touch a picture prompt card to keep her head upright. When selling cookies, Vondre learned to look at money placed in his hand and then look at the customer and say thank you. Jamal learned to follow a written guide that directed him step by step on how to use his textbook to look up the names of automotive tools and mark them on his paper. After completing each step, he learned to check it off. And Michael learned to look at a picture prompt book to prompt himself to make a conversational interaction.

During the baseline phase, all target behaviors were very low for all students and no self-monitoring activities occurred. After only two to three sessions of teaching the students to use the self-monitoring methods, the students were able to generalize them to natural settings in the schools and their targeted behaviors increased noticeably. Coinciding with this change in the students' behavior was the recognition of their improvement through a social validation procedure. Teachers and classmates noted the positive change in the students' behavior and indicated how much more pleasant it was to work and interact with them.

Applying Decision Rules about Generalization Strategies

Although broad application of the principles and tactics suggested above would seemingly increase the likelihood of generalization, Liberty and her colleagues offered an alternative. They have suggested *decision rules* that would allow practitioners to determine the most appropriate strategies to use to help students with severe disabilities learn to generalize skills (Liberty, 1988; Liberty, Haring, White, & Billingsley, 1988). These decision rules rest on four assumptions:

1. Generalization must be a target of instruction, and criteria for measuring generalization and the conditions under which generalization is expected should be specified in the IEP.
2. Direct assessment of student performance in the target generalization situations is required to make decisions about generalization.
3. Some learners with severe disabilities may generalize some skills before, during, or after instruction without the need for special strategies.
4. If a learner does not generalize a skill once it has been acquired, special strategies are needed.

The decisions about which strategies might be used to improve generalization are based on answers to a series of questions asked about the student's performance. These questions, the procedures used to acquire the answers, and the next step or decision to make based on the answers are discussed next.

The first question to be answered is whether the skill has generalized in all desired situations when assessed in initial probes. This implies that these situations have been identified through the planning process and that probes have been taken in the different situations to see if the skill is present. It would obviously not be necessary to plan a generalization instructional strategy if the individual already could demonstrate the behavior or skill under all desirable conditions, situations, or settings. Assuming that the answer to this item will most often be no (the student cannot demonstrate the behavior in a generalized fashion), the next question is whether the student has acquired the skill. In other words, in a single instructional setting, has the student been able to demonstrate the skill to a level of satisfaction? If not, the instructor is to continue instruction leading toward skill mastery using acquisition training procedures such as described in Chapter 7.

If the student is able to demonstrate the skill under a single condition, the next issue is to what extent is generalization desired. This is an important consideration. There will be times when only limited or no generalization is necessary. For example, since a person usually uses only one toothbrush, how necessary is it to teach generalized toothbrushing? When only a few specific locations or conditions are necessary to ensure functional performance and extensive generalization will not improve the quality of life, it will most likely be sufficient to teach the individual to operate only in those select settings or under the desired specific conditions. When this is the training need, a sequential modification approach, that is, reteaching the skill under a new condition or in a new situation, will be adequate and appropriate.

If a sequential modification approach is not sufficient, Liberty et al. (1988) suggest that the next issue to be considered is the existence of competing reinforcers. In other words, the individual's behavior may be affected by reinforcement for inappropriate behavior or simply be reinforced for not performing the desired target objective. If this is the case, the contingencies of reinforcement must be changed so that the student is not reinforced when demonstrating nontargeted behavior and is reinforced when the behavior occurs. Reinforcement may also be a problem if the student does not appear to be motivated to perform the behavior or task in the generalized settings or conditions even though she has done so in the past or has come close to doing so. When the situation is "she can do it if she wants to; she just doesn't want to," then reinforcement strategies to improve generalization should be considered. These strategies could include providing natural reinforcers while eliminating reinforcers used for initial instruction, teaching the person to use a mediational strategy to provide self-reinforcement, teaching the person to ask for reinforcement ("Do you think I did a good job on this?"), and reinforcing generalized behavior.

If the problem in achieving generalization is not related to reinforcement, but to adequately attending and responding to correct stimuli ("Did the student respond partially correctly during at least one response opportunity?"), Liberty et al. refer to this as a "discrimination function problem" and offer accommodating solutions. These include varying the stimuli, using multiple exemplars, or using the general case method. Finally, the option of the student's not generalizing at all is presented; if this is the outcome, a "generalization training format" is suggested that calls for increasing proficiency, using natural reinforcers and natural schedules of reinforcement, and using natural stimuli while fading training stimuli.

Using the General Case Method

The general case method, or general case programming, has proved to be one of the most successful methods for promoting generalization by persons with severe disabilities. Because of the complexity of its procedures and the extensiveness of the successful research associated with it, it warrants a more detailed report.

The general case method was developed by Horner and his colleagues and has been explained in several publications (Albin & Horner, 1988; Albin et al., 1987; Horner, McDonnell, & Bellamy, 1986; Horner et al., 1982). The strategy requires that the practitioner undertake a process to ensure that the skills acquired can be demonstrated in any environment or under any condition in which they are needed. The six steps of the general case method are described next.

Step 1: Define the Instructional Universe

The first step of the general case method is to define the instructional universe. This means that the teacher must determine all the locations, persons, conditions, and/or other situations in which the student is expected to demonstrate a particular learned skill and also what type of variation in the skill may be necessary. Certainly, this could be an extensive task, but it directs the teacher to answer this question: Under what circumstances is the skill expected to occur and what different forms could it take? For example, the parents and the teacher may decide that it is desirable for the student to shop in all the convenience stores within a three-block radius of her home and be able to buy any combination of snacks up to two dollars. These stores and the various items within them would then be considered the *instructional universe* of convenience stores in which the student would be expected to generalize. Other examples of instructional universes could include cleaning all the tables in a restaurant that are ready to be cleaned, but not cleaning those that people are using; selecting clothing that would be appropriate for the weather; and selecting and using a board game from those available in the apartment.

In general case method instruction, teaching occurs in situations that provide the range of conditions that are present in the generalization setting.

Step 2: Define the Range of Relevant Stimulus and Response Variation

In this step, the teacher must consider all relevant aspects of all the settings or conditions in the instructional universe in which generalization is to occur and also the variations in actions that may need to occur. There must be an identification of aspects of the environment that are likely to influence the successful performance of the learner, how these will vary, and the ways in which the learner will respond to the different stimuli. In reference to a convenience store, for example, the teacher may note where the entrance doors are located (center or side), where the checkout counter is located (middle of the store or side), whether the store serves food, and so on. Several important stimuli may exist within the store, and the teacher must know what they are and how the student must respond to them. Table 8–2 provides an illustration of an activity analysis for fast-food restaurants (Albin et al., 1987). As can be seen, there are five considerations:

1. The generic responses are identified.
2. All discriminative stimuli that could prompt the target responses are listed.
3. The possible variations of stimulus classes are listed.
4. Ways in which the learner might respond are outlined.
5. There is a list of anticipated problems, errors, and exceptions.

Step 3: Select Examples for Teaching and Probe Testing

Having identified relevant stimuli and response variations, the teacher must select one set of examples from the instructional universe for use in teaching and one set for probe testing. Both sets must reflect the range of conditions that exist within the universe and all behaviors that may be required. Again considering the convenience store, the teacher selects some that have the door on the side and others that have the door in the center; some that have the checkout counter in the center of the store and some that have it on one side of the store; some that serve food and some that do not; and so on. It is not necessary that the teacher select *all* stores for instruction, but the ones that are selected must together adequately represent all the variations of important stimuli and responses. The list is then divided equally, with some stores being used for teaching and others for testing. Each list must reflect an adequate array of stimulus conditions and requisite behaviors.

In teaching the generalization of some skills, it is important to have two types of teaching examples: positive examples and negative examples (Albin & Horner, 1988). Positive examples are used to teach the learner the conditions appropriate for when the behavior *should* occur; negative examples are presented so that the learner will know *when not* to engage in the action. The table-clearing situation suggests the type of occasion when both negative and positive teaching examples are necessary. Typically, in circumstances when it is possible for the student to "overgeneralize," there should be adequate examples of the negative conditions or stimuli in order to teach the student not to do so. Albin and Horner (1988) point out that the greater the differences are between the positive and negative stimuli, the easier it will be for the learner to make the discrimination. However, smaller differences will lead the learner to ultimately become more precise in his discrimination ability. Therefore, they suggest that in initially teaching discrimination–generalization tasks the teacher start with positive and negative samples that are very different and then reduce their differences over progressive instructional opportunities.

Additional guidelines for selecting instructional examples were provided by Albin et al., 1987:

1. Select the smallest number of teaching examples that will sample the full range of stimulus and response variation in the instructional universe.
2. Select teaching examples that provide equal amounts of new information to the learner.
3. Provide adequate negative teaching examples (that teach the learner what not to do).
4. Select examples that vary irrelevant stimuli (characteristics that do not provide information about whether or not the behavior should occur).
5. Select examples that include significant exceptions.
6. Select examples that are logistically feasible.

Step 4: Sequence the Teaching Examples

Having selected appropriate examples for instruction, the teacher must sequence these in an appropriate order for instruction. Albin et al. (1987) offered five guidelines for sequencing instruction.

1. Teach multiple components of an activity within a training session (do not teach isolated components).
2. Present variations within individual sessions. Teach as many of the examples as possible within training sessions.

Table 8–2 Illustration of Activity Analysis for Using a Fast-Food Restaurant

Generic Response Components	*Discriminative Stimuli*	*Range of Stimulus Characteristics*	*Response Variation*	*Anticipated Problems/ Errors/Exceptions*
1. ENTER	Door	Door type (single, double, automatic)	Push or pull door Walk through automatic door	Door location varies
	People entering or exiting	People present (entering before, entering after)	Follow others in/out Wait Push or pull and hold open for others	Student may hold door for too many people
2. APPROACH COUNTER	Counter	On the right On the left Straight ahead after entering	Walk to counter at register	Separate order and pick-up counters
	Register	Tan register on counter		Visibility of register varies Shape of register varies
	People waiting in line	One too many people waiting in line	Walk to end of line and move up with the line	
	Entry lane	Railings for entrance lane	Walk through lane	
3. ORDER	Verbal request for order	Can I help you? What will it be? Yes. Can I take your order? Have you been helped? What would you like? Will that be to stay or go?	Show communication notebook for a drink or lunch Verbally order Request condiments if desired Answer "stay" or "go"	Other employees behind counter not taking orders
	Clerk at counter	Clerk at register eye contact with customer		Number of people in restaurant varies with time of day
	Item choices	Drinks only Preselected choices in prosthetic Hamburger, french fries, cola, etc		Menu changes with time of day
4. PAY	Displayed cost	Amounts .15–$4.99 Color of numerals on register Red or green LED Readout location Near top of register No readout	Count out X + 1 dollars and hand to counter person Money from wallet and/or pocket	
	Verbal cue	.XX Cents		Other prices being stated in close proximity
5. OBTAIN ORDER	Order payment made	Clerk may say "Thank you" Give receipt or number Put money in register Give direction to move to next window	Step aside and wait for order to come up Move to pick-up window and wait for order	Other orders will come up before student's order
6. EAT	Requested items in hand	Tray (no tray, single item)	Pick up order Locate condiments, get what is needed	Food or drinks may be dropped or spilled
	Empty table	Table (2 chairs, 3 chairs, 4 chairs) Table (empty)	Locate table, sit down, and eat	No empty tables
7. EXIT	All finished eating	Food and beverage gone	Bus table if required	Other customers may or may not bus table
	Time up	Time management prosthetic (watch or clock)	Exit building	

Source: "Designing Intervention to Meet Activity Goals" by R. W. Albin, J. J. McDonnell, & B. Wilcox (pp. 63–88), in B. Wilcox & G. T. Bellamy (Eds.), *The Comprehensive Guide to the Activities Catalog,* 1987, Baltimore: Paul H. Brookes Publishing Co. Reprinted by permission.

3. Juxtapose the most similar positive and negative examples to improve discrimination ability.
4. Use cumulative programming. If all teaching examples cannot be taught in one session, work on a few at a time, adding new examples to already learned examples in each new session.
5. Teach the general case before teaching exceptions.

Step 5: Teach the Sequence That Was Developed

The instructional activities required employ the methods of skill acquisition described in Chapter 7. The important aspect required by the general case method is the use of appropriate stimuli to ensure proper generalization.

Step 6: Test Using the Nontrained Probe Examples

To determine if generalization has occurred, the teacher must examine the student's performance under each relevant condition initially identified.

The general case method of teaching is complex because it forces the teacher, the parents, and other members of the collaborative team to consider various settings or conditions in which the behavior or skill needs to occur. Then it asks that all the relevant variations be identified, taught, and tested. Although the process is complicated, it provides the most empirically validated method for achieving generalization. Teachers may wish to consider various methods for achieving generalization, but the general case method is likely to be the most effective, if not the simplest, to implement. Certainly, it provides a framework for thought about the factors that affect generalization and for this reason at least merits attention.

Teaching Skill Maintenance

Maintenance refers to a behavior or skill continuing to occur for as long as it is needed without having to be taught again, for example, learning to ride a bicycle, then being able to use that skill whenever it is required or desired. A student with a severe disability who maintains a behavior or skill for a long period of time (e.g., more than a year) has the advantage of being able to apply the skill when it is needed. Maintenance is often considered to be *generalization across time.* Several strategies may improve the chance of this occurring.

For students with severe disabilities to maintain learned skills over a long period of time, they must learn the skills to a functional degree of usefulness and then use the skills in many situations over a long period of time. Generally, the strategies that can be used to teach skill generalization also help to achieve skill maintenance. The error often made is that a skill is learned, and even generalized to some degree, but then is not practiced sufficiently beyond the initial learning period. Or a skill is learned, but not well enough for it to be practical or used after the teaching sessions have ended. To avoid these problems, several strategies are suggested. They should be used in addition to strategies that will facilitate skill generalization (Alberto & Troutman, 2002).

Skill Overlearning

Students should learn the skill to an adequate level of performance and then continue practicing the skill beyond that point, a practice referred to as *overlearning.* This suggests that an appropriate criterion statement for an objective should be the correct performance of the behavior or skill many times after the first time it is performed. Alberto and Troutman (2002) suggested that overlearning opportunities be at least 50% of the opportunities necessary for the student to initially learn the objective.

Learning through Distributed Practice

Another way to help to make sure that the skill is maintained is to practice it during distributed learning sessions. Instead of working with a student to see some skill practiced 10 times successively in a very short period of time (i.e., massed practice), practice is spread out across the day. When the student is given many opportunities to practice a skill at different times, instead of all at once, the skill is likely to be maintained for a longer time after it has been initially learned.

Intermittent Reinforcement

As discussed in Chapter 7, providing the student with reinforcement after the completion of a particular behavior increases the chance of that same behavior recurring in the future when similar stimuli are present. During acquisition training, it is important to reinforce the behavior nearly every time it occurs so that the student can learn the connection between the stimulus conditions, the behavior, and the reinforcer. However, for a behavior to strengthen (i.e., to be more resistant to extinction), the teacher should use positive reinforcement on an intermittent basis after the behavior has been well established.

There are four main intermittent schedules of reinforcement: fixed ratio and variable ratio (FR and VR) schedules and fixed interval and variable interval (FI and

VI) schedules. Ratio schedules reinforce the behavior based on a count of the behavior. For example, the teacher may determine that for every five dishes washed correctly the student will receive a reinforcer. This would be a ratio schedule of reinforcement; more precisely, it would be a *fixed* ratio five (FR:5) schedule, because the reinforcement would be delivered following every fifth dish washed. If the reinforcement delivery schedule was calculated so that the reinforcer was delivered *on an average* of every five dishes washed, but not precisely on each fifth dish, this would be a *variable* ratio five (VR:5) schedule of reinforcement.

Interval schedules of reinforcement are based on time instead of the number of behaviors occurring. Consider again the student learning to wash dishes. If the teacher or job coach decided to reinforce the student after a 2-minute period of dishwashing without regard to the number of dishes washed, this would be an interval schedule of reinforcement. The reinforcer would be delivered after the first dish was finished, following a 2-minute period; this would be referred to as a fixed interval 2-minute (FI:2 min.) schedule. Variable interval schedules are like variable ratio schedules except that the reinforcement delivery is based on an average amount of time passage, instead of an average number of behaviors occurring. For example, the student washing dishes would be reinforced on a schedule that has an average of 2 minutes passing between reinforcement delivery.

All intermittent schedules have the effect of making behavioral occurrences more frequent simply because the learner must exhibit more behavior before being reinforced. They also make the behavior less vulnerable to extinction. Variable schedules are more effective than fixed schedules because the learner does not know when the reinforcement is coming (an *indiscriminable contingency*) and thus tends to work more to get it. Use of intermittent schedules of reinforcement can be of great practicality in building strong behavioral and skill repertoires. As the behavior develops more and more, the schedules can be "leaned out" so that more and more behavior (or time) must occur before the reinforcement. This again will produce stronger behaviors more likely to be maintained over longer periods of time.

Building on Learned Skills

Another strategy that may help to prevent the loss of learned skills is to incorporate the newly acquired skills into different, new skills. Likewise, skills can be linked together through different activities. For example, a student may have learned to participate in home economic activities by holding utensils or being responsible for mixing various ingredients. These activities may help to achieve the student's need to hold items with her hand and improve fine motor skills. These same motor skills can be practiced during different classroom activities, art activities, physical education, or some leisure-time activities. The more opportunities for practice that the student is given, the greater the likelihood that the behavior will be maintained.

Another way to consider the application of this guideline is by inserting newly learned skills into existing tasks or routines. For example, a student may know how to go into a movie and enjoy watching it, but may not know how to use public transportation. Learning to ride a bus or subway may be targeted for instruction and, once it has been satisfactorily learned, should be included in the routine of going to a movie. It has also been noted that students who sometimes are not compliant when it comes to learning new skills become more cooperative when existing skills are inserted into the instructional sequence being used to teach the new skills (Wolery & Schuster, 1997).

Using a Maintenance Schedule

Students with severe disabilities may learn skills that, although functional, may be used infrequently or on an irregular basis. Going to a dentist's office, using a sanitary napkin, and responding to a fire alarm are examples of skills that may be considered important by parents and other team members. However, skills such as these are easy to forget if they are not practiced often enough.

Obviously, some of these skills will be naturally practiced on a regular basis, and it is very likely that they will be maintained. Others, however, should be placed on a maintenance list and practiced on a regular timetable, say once a month, after they have been learned initially. If this provision is not made, the skill is likely to be forgotten, which would indicate the need for reteaching it and then practicing it more often.

Using the Skill at Home and Elsewhere

If a skill has been identified as an important target for instruction, there is probably a need for it outside the classroom or other initial learning environments, and it might be expected that the skill would be practiced in settings and at times when it is needed. If this is the case, the additional practice is likely to help to maintain the skill. Skills that are not useful or helpful to an individual with severe disabilities are likely to neither generalize nor be maintained. This point is made so that, during the initial identification of skills for instruction, efforts are made by all involved to agree that practice outside the primary learning environment is encouraged and coordinated with learning new skills.

Skills can be maintained through regular practice after initial training. Varying the location or other conditions of the practice setting also helps to ensure that generalized use of the skill is being maintained. A major error often made is that a skill is learned to an acceptable level of criterion as specified within the instructional objective, but then is not adequately practiced and is forgotten. This is certainly a common problem, but one that teachers should avoid if possible.

Writing Instructional Programs to Include Generalization Training and to Promote Maintenance

In Chapter 7, an outline was provided for writing instructional plans for individual objectives (see Figure 7–1). The suggested plan was to include the objective, setting and material, a task analysis or elements of a routine, an instructional procedure, and reinforcement and error correction procedures. It is now proposed that the plan include a description of how generalization be taught and how the behavior or skill might be maintained over a period of time.

The first step toward teaching skills that will generalize and be maintained is to *plan* adequately. Generally, it is not sufficient to plan to teach a particular skill to an individual with severe disabilities; the plan should also include provisions for generalizing the skill. Whether the skill is an individual behavior that allows the student to participate more, a complex chained skill, or a routine, such as going shopping in department stores, adequate planning will include a strategy for generalization. This requires that parents, teachers, and the rest of the collaborative team raise questions about where the skill needs to occur, with what people, under what conditions, at what times, with what variations and exceptions, and with what behavioral changes. Addressing questions such as these will result in objectives that include generalized outcomes (Billingsley, 1988; Billingsley, Burgess, Lynch, & Matlock, 1991).

The objective presented as an example in Figure 7–1 can be redesigned to include generalization and maintenance in its format. The intention was for the student to be able to clean a bathroom by completing each step in a task analysis. But could it be concluded that if a student successfully cleaned one bathroom this objective would have been achieved? Based on the criteria presented in the original objective, the answer would be yes. However, two facts should be apparent. The first is that satisfactorily cleaning one bathroom does not indicate that the student can clean all the bathrooms in several motels, or even in one motel. Second, unless the student can learn to clean all the motel bathrooms requiring cleaning, it cannot be expected that he will be successful at a job that requires this skill. Therefore, the objective should be rewritten to reflect the appropriate degree of generalization required. For example:

> James will clean all the bathrooms in the motel where he is working. . . . *or*
>
> James will clean all the bathrooms in the six motels on the interstate highway.

In this way, generalization becomes an expected part of the objective. Once the need for generalization has been established and written into the objective, a generalization plan can be incorporated into the instructional plan. To do this, the various strategies discussed in this chapter should be reviewed to see what method might be helpful in achieving generalization, for example, the general case method. The plan for achieving generalization would then require following the six steps called for by that strategy.

In addition to generalization, the question of skill maintenance must be considered when the planning is being done. Once again, to use the previous example, the plan might include a statement that the student will be able to successfully clean the bathrooms over a 1-year period of time:

> James will be able to continue cleaning bathrooms successfully for 1 year without additional instruction after initial learning and successful generalization.

If the student were to work cleaning hotel bathrooms for that period of time (1 year), there would be no special difficulty in monitoring the maintenance of the skill. However, for other objectives, continued practice after the initial learning has been achieved would be specified. This would state the number of times per week, month, or semester, for example, that it would be necessary for the student to practice the behavior and in what locations or under what circumstances. As this practice was done, the teacher would record the student's performance. Appropriate procedures for continuously monitoring students' performance are discussed in Chapter 9.

Conclusion

People without cognitive disabilities acquire certain skills in their lives either through direct instruction or incidental learning. In the process, they also learn new and different circumstances in which it is appropriate to apply the skills and, conversely, circumstances in which the skills do not apply. The learning and generalization continue throughout their lives, and important skills are maintained for a long time.

People with cognitive disabilities have learning abilities that are not as efficient. It takes longer periods of time for them to learn and then they often do not know the circumstances in which to use the skills that they have learned, or they forget how to use the skills before they have been practiced enough. For many years, teachers and parents have been frustrated by the fact that students did not remember or did not apply previously learned skills to new or different situations.

Part of the problem of such shortcomings is due to the learner, but part is also due to the instructional process. The train and hope strategy is not effective for achieving generalization or for helping to maintain the newly learned skill for most students. Parents and professionals must actively plan and implement strategies that will ensure that generalization and maintenance occur to a desired degree.

Some of the current best practices are likely to result in more generalization and maintenance. The fact that there is much greater focus on skills that are functional or interesting is very important and will do much more to ensure that what is taught will be reinforced in the natural environment. In addition, teaching in nonschool natural environments will be helpful. Although teaching in only one such environment does not necessarily result in generalization, multiple sites of the appropriate variety are likely to do so. Using natural reinforcers and natural schedules of reinforcement also helps generalization and maintenance to occur more often. But foremost in importance is the idea that generalization and maintenance are important and desirable outcomes, no less important than initial skill acquisition. Given this assumption, during initial training there must be a plan that will achieve these components of the instructional objective. The strategies and tactics presented in this chapter are intended to help to achieve this outcome.

Questions for Reflection

1. Why is generalization so difficult to achieve when only the train and hope approach is used? How might student characteristics be related to this result?
2. What type of reinforcement procedures might best result in generalization and maintenance? Why?
3. What are some of the pros and cons related to using self-instruction as an approach to achieving generalization?
4. How effective do you think peers might be in helping students with severe disabilities learn to generalize their communication and social skills?
5. What are the most important decisions that must be made using the decision rules?
6. Why has research found the general case method to be so successful? What would be the most difficult aspect of this method for a teacher to implement?
7. How would the relevance or functionality of a behavior help to achieve maintenance and generalization?
8. How can successful generalization of a skill also help to achieve successful maintenance?
9. Describe a plan that would allow a teacher to work on generalization and maintenance.

References

Agran, M., Fodor-Davis, J., Moore, S. C., & Martella, R. C. (1992). Effects of peer-delivered self-instructional training on a lunch-making work task for students with severe disabilities. *Education and Training in Mental Retardation, 27,* 230–240.

Alberto, P. A., & Troutman, A. C. (2002). *Applied behavior analysis for teachers* (6th Ed.). Upper Saddle River, NJ: Merrill/Prentice Hall.

Albin, R. W., & Horner, R. H. (1988). Generalization with precision. In R. H. Horner, G. Dunlap, & R. L. Koegel (Eds.),

Generalization and maintenance: Life style changes in applied settings (pp. 99–120). Baltimore: Paul H. Brookes.

Albin, R. W., McDonnell, J. J., & Wilcox, B. (1987). Designing intervention to meet activity goals. In B. Wilcox & G. T. Bellamy (Eds.), *The comprehensive guide to the Activities Catalog* (pp. 63–88). Baltimore: Paul H. Brookes.

Bambara, L. M., & Gomez, O. N. (2001). Using a self-instructional training package to teach complex problem-solving skills to adults with moderate and severe disabilities. *Education and Training in Mental Retardation and Developmental Disabilities, 36,* 386–400.

Billingsley, F. F. (1984). Where are the generalized outcomes? (An examination of instructional objectives). *Journal of the Association for Persons with Severe Handicaps, 9,* 186–192.

Billingsley, F. F. (1988). Writing objectives for generalization. In N. G. Haring (Ed.), *Generalization for students with severe handicaps: Strategies and solutions* (pp. 123–128). Seattle: University of Washington Press.

Billingsley, F. F., Burgess, D., Lynch, V. W., & Matlock, B. L. (1991). Toward generalized outcomes: Considerations for writing instructional objectives. *Education and Training in Mental Retardation, 26,* 351–360.

Black, R. S., & Langone, J. (1995, October). *Generalization of work-related social behavior for persons with mental retardation.* Paper presented at the 1995 DCDT International Conference, Raleigh, NC. (ERIC Document Reproduction Service No. 389 132.)

Brown, L., Nisbet, J., Ford, A., Sweet, M., Shiraga, B., & York, J. (1983). The critical need for non-school instruction in programs for severely handicapped students. *Journal of the Association for the Severely Handicapped, 8,* 71–77.

Chandler, L. K., Lubeck, R. C., & Fowler, S. A. (1992). Generalization and maintenance of preschool children's social skills: A critical review and analysis. *Journal of Applied Behavior Analysis, 25,* 415–428.

Donnellan, A. M., & Mirenda, P. L. (1983). A model for analyzing instructional components to facilitate generalization for severely handicapped students. *Journal of Special Education, 17,* 317–331.

Duker, P. C., & Jutten, W. (1997). Establishing gestural yes–no responding with individuals with profound mental retardation. *Education and Training in Mental Retardation and Developmental Disabilities, 32,* 59–67.

Falvey, M. A. (Ed.). (1995). *Inclusive and heterogeneous schooling: Assessment, curriculum, and instruction.* Baltimore: Paul H. Brookes.

Farmer-Dougan, V. (1994). Increasing requests by adults with developmental disabilities using incidental teaching by peers. *Journal of Applied Behavior Analysis, 27,* 533–544.

Fox, L. (1989). Stimulus generalization of skills and persons with profound mental handicaps. *Education and Training in Mental Retardation, 24,* 219–229.

Goldstein, H., & Cisar, C. L. (1992). Promoting interaction during socio-dramatic play: Teaching scripts to typical preschoolers and classmates with disabilities. *Journal of Applied Behavior Analysis, 25,* 265–280.

Haring, N. G. (Ed.). (1987). *Investigating the problem of skill generalization: Literature review III.* Seattle: University of Washington, Washington Research Organization.

Haring, N. G. (Ed.). (1988). *Generalization for students with severe handicaps: Strategies and solutions.* Seattle: University of Washington Press.

Haring, N. G., Liberty, K., Billingsley, F., White, O., Lynch, V., Kayser, J., & McCarty, F. (1985). *Investigating the problem of skill generalization* (3rd Ed.). Seattle: University of Washington, Washington Research Organization.

Horner, R. H., Albin, R. W., & Ralph, G. (1986). Generalization with precision: The role of negative teaching examples in the instruction of generalized grocery item selection. *Journal of the Association for Persons with Severe Handicaps, 11,* 300–308.

Horner, R. H., Dunlap, G., & Koegel, R. L. (Eds.). (1988). *Generalization and maintenance: Life style changes in applied settings.* Baltimore: Paul H. Brookes.

Horner, R. H., Jones, D. N., & Williams, J. A. (1985). A functional approach to teaching generalized street crossing. *Journal of the Association for Persons with Severe Handicaps, 10,* 71–97.

Horner, R. H., McDonnell, J. J., & Bellamy, G. T. (1986). Teaching generalized skills: General case instruction in simulation and community settings. In R. H. Horner, L. H. Meyer, & H. D. Fredericks (Eds.), *Education of learners with severe handicaps: Exemplary service strategies* (pp. 289–314). Baltimore: Paul H. Brookes.

Horner, R. H., Sprague, J., & Wilcox, B. (1982). Constructing general case programs for community activities. In B. Wilcox & G. T. Bellamy (Eds.), *Design of high school programs for severely handicapped students* (pp. 61–98). Baltimore: Paul H. Brookes.

Hughes, C., & Agran, M. (1993). Teaching persons with severe disabilities to use self-instruction in community settings: An analysis of the applications. *Journal of the Association for Persons with Severe Handicaps, 18,* 261–274.

Hughes, C., Copeland, S. R., Agran, M., Wehmeyer, M., Rodi, M. S., & Presley, J. A. (2002). Using self-monitoring to improve performance in general education high school classes. *Education and Training in Mental Retardation and Developmental Disabilities, 37*(3), 262–272.

Hughes, C., Harmer, M. L., Killian, D. J., & Niarhos, F. (1995). The effects of multiple-exemplar self-instructional training on high school students' generalized conversational interactions. *Journal of Applied Behavior Analysis, 28,* 201–218.

Hughes, C., Hugo, K., & Blatt, J. (1996). Self-instructional intervention for teaching generalized problem-solving within a functional task sequence. *American Journal on Mental Retardation, 100,* 565–579.

Janney, R. E., & Snell, M. E. (1996). How teachers use peer interactions to include students with moderate and severe disabilities in elementary general education classrooms.

Journal of the Association for Persons with Severe Handicaps, 21, 72–80.

Liberty, K. (1987). Behavior-control of stimulus events to facilitate generalization. In N. G. Haring (Ed.), *Investigating the problem of skill generalization: Literature review III* (pp. 1–16). Seattle: University of Washington, Washington Research Organization.

Liberty, K. (1988). Characteristics and foundations of decision rules. In N. G. Haring (Ed.), *Generalization for students with severe handicaps: Strategies and solutions.* Seattle: University of Washington Press.

Liberty, K. A., Haring, N. G., White, O. R., & Billingsley, F. (1988). A technology for the future: Decision rules for generalization. *Education and Training in Mental Retardation, 23,* 315–326.

McDonnell, J., & Ferguson, B. (1988). A comparison of general case in vivo and general case simulation plus in vivo training. *Journal of the Association for Persons with Severe Handicaps, 13,* 116–124.

McDonnell, J. J., Horner, R. H., & Williams, J. A. (1984). Comparison of three strategies for teaching generalized grocery purchasing to high school students with severe handicaps. *Journal of the Association for Persons with Severe Handicaps, 9,* 123–133.

McMahon, C. M., Wacker, D. P., Sasso, G. M., Berg, W. K., & Newton, S. M. (1996). Analysis of the frequency and type of interactions in a peer-mediated social skills intervention: Instructional vs. social interactions. *Education and Training in Mental Retardation and Developmental Disabilities, 31,* 339–352.

Meichenbaum, D., & Goodman, J. (1971). Training impulsive children to talk to themselves: A means of developing self-control. *Journal of Abnormal Psychology, 77,* 115–126.

Morse, T., Schuster, J. W., & Sandknop, P. A. (1996). Grocery shopping skills for persons with moderate to profound intellectual disabilities: A review of the literature. *Education and Treatment of Children, 19,* 487–517.

Rutherford, R. B., & Nelson, C. M. (1987). Generalization and maintenance of treatment effects. In J. C. Witt, S. N. Elliott, & F. M. Gresham (Eds.), *Handbook of behavior therapy in education* (pp. 277–324). New York: Plenum.

Scruggs, T. E., & Mastropieri, M. A. (1994). The effectiveness of generalization training: A quantitative synthesis of single subject research. In T. E. Scruggs & M. A. Mastropieri (Eds.), *Advances in learning and behavioral disabilities* (vol. 8, pp. 259–280). Greenwich, CT: JAI Press.

Sprague, J. R., & Horner, R. H. (1984). The effects of single instance, multiple instance, and general case training on generalized vending machine use by moderately and severely handicapped students. *Journal of Applied Behavior Analysis, 17,* 273–278.

Stokes, T. F., & Baer, D. M. (1977). An implicit technology of generalization. *Journal of Applied Behavior Analysis, 10,* 349–367.

Stokes, T. F., & Osnes, P. G. (1988). The developing applied technology of generalization and maintenance. In R. H. Horner, G. Dunlap, & R. L. Koegel (Eds.), *Generalization and maintenance: Life style changes in applied settings* (pp. 5–19). Baltimore: Paul H. Brookes.

Westling, D. L., & Floyd, J. (1990). Generalization of community skills: How much training is necessary? *Journal of Special Education, 23,* 386–406.

White, O. R., Liberty, K. A., Haring, N. G., Billingsley, F. F., Boer, M., Burrage, A., Connors, R., Farman, R., Fedorchak, G., Leber, B. D., Liberty-Laylin, S., Miller, S., Opalski, C., Phifer, C. & Sessoms, I. (1988). Review and analysis of strategies for generalization. In N. G. Haring (Ed.), *Generalization for students with severe handicaps: Strategies and solutions.* Seattle: University of Washington Press.

Wolery, M., & Schuster, J. W. (1997). Instructional methods with students who have significant disabilities. *Journal of Special Education, 31,* 61–97.

CHAPTER 9

Evaluating Student Progress

This chapter is devoted to the importance of evaluating the educational progress of students with severe disabilities. The emergence of alternate assessment as a critical aspect of school reform and its application to students with severe disabilities is discussed. Attention is given to the use of portfolios in statewide alternate assessment systems and also to directly measuring student progress.

The Importance of Evaluating Student Progress

In the discussion of effective teaching practices in Chapter 7, it was stated that effective teachers regularly and continuously monitor the learning of their students. Directly monitoring and evaluating the learning and behavior of students with severe disabilities has been a hallmark of the educational process for these students for many years. Through the direct measurement of skills, teachers, therapists, parents, and researchers can identify whether sufficient progress is occurring on a day-to-day basis and, when necessary, make modifications in instructional tactics, reinforcement, the curriculum, or other important variables.

In more recent years, documenting the progress of all students, including students with severe disabilities, has taken on even greater significance because of educational reform movements. The No Child Left Behind Act of 2001 (P.L. 107-110) calls for states to use standardized end-of-year tests to determine whether students, and thus the schools which they attend, have made adequate progress. In some states, referred to as high-stakes states, the progress of students determines whether students pass to the next grade, whether teachers and administrators receive pay raises, or even whether the school is allowed to continue to operate. Students with disabilities, including those with severe disabilities, have not been ignored in this process. In addition to the direct measures that have been used through the years to improve instructional procedures, students are now to be assessed at the end of the year to determine if their progress has been significant enough to meet statewide standards.

As this recent requirement continues with the intention of improving educational outcomes, it is important to realize that simply assessing students with severe disabilities at the end of the year will generally not be sufficient to provide teachers with the feedback that they need to improve student learning (Browder, 2001; Browder & Spooner, 2003). Although this may meet the legal demands for accountability and is becoming ubiquitous throughout the country, more frequent assessment processes will lead to better decisions about instructional procedures. This, in turn, will be more likely to contribute to better annual evaluation outcomes for students.

In this chapter, we address three major themes. First, because of its recent importance, we look at the requirements for conducting end-of-year legally mandated alternate assessments for students with severe disabilities. This type of assessment is required under the IDEA Amendments of 1997 for all students who cannot meaningfully participate in standard statewide assessment systems. Second, we describe portfolio assessments such as used by many states to meet the requirement of alternate assessments for students with severe disabilities. Third, we describe direct measurement procedures that have been used for several decades to collect data on students' performance. In examining this material, readers will see how the type of data collected can help them to make decisions about instructional targets and procedures. We conclude the chapter by discussing how these measures could well be merged with portfolio assessments to document the adequacy of student progress, given the nature of the support and resources devoted to the improvement of students' skills.

Alternate Assessment Requirements for Students with Severe Disabilities

During the 1990s, the identification and assessment of educational outcomes (or outcomes-based education, OBE) became a major aspect of school reform in general education (Spady, 1992). Beginning in this period, many states adopted educational outcomes or standards for public school students in elementary and secondary schools. Unlike historical reform practices that focused more on variables such as how long the student was in school, what classes were taken, and performance on standardized tests, outcomes-based reforms focused on what students *know and can do* as a result of their education.

Typically, this type of reform effort begins with the identification of particular skills or benchmarks that are to be learned at specific times (such as in certain grades) in the student's educational career. Nearly all states now have standardized curricula that specify the minimal skills that students are expected to achieve by the end of the year. The benchmarks or standards are specified so that school districts can provide appropriate instruction and learning experiences for students to achieve. Also, the states require that students be evaluated at the end of the year using a standard state-designed assessment instrument to determine the extent to which the skills have been achieved. In high-stakes states, the outcomes on the end-of-year tests can have significant impact on the operation and funding of local schools. States may require that a student's progression to the next grade be made contingent on satisfactory demonstration of key benchmarks, or they may reward schools with additional financing for good progress by students. In some states, schools may be placed on sanctions if too many students fail to make sufficient progress.

As discussed in Chapter 2, many professionals in the field of special education have supported including students with disabilities in state-mandated testing and, in fact, this is required by law (Hardman, McDonnell, & Welch, 1997; Kleinert, Haig, Kearns, & Kennedy, 2000; Kleinert, Kearns, & Kennedy, 1997; Sailor, 1997; Ysseldyke & Olsen, 1997; Ysseldyke & Olsen, 1999; Ysseldyke, Olsen, & Thurlow, 1997; Ysseldyke, Thurlow, & Shriner, 1992). There are several reasons why so many professionals support this position. Most importantly, it is believed that if schools are not held accountable for educating students with disabilities, the quality of instruction for these students will not be on par with the quality of instruction for students without disabilities. Additionally, if inclusion of students with disabilities is a desired outcome and if they are to be given access to the general curriculum, also called for by law, then they must also be included in the assessment processes that result in judgments about the quality of schools.

Students with disabilities may be included in a state's standardized assessment of educational outcomes in one of three ways. They may be evaluated in the same way as all other students, they be evaluated with adaptations or accommodations that allow them to take the tests, or they may participate through alternate assessment procedures. *Alternate assessments* are developed by states to be used when students cannot take part meaningfully in the typical educational outcomes or benchmarks assessment process, even when provided with accommodations or adaptations. Most students with severe disabilities will participate in alternate assessments, but legally this must be an IEP team decision (Browder & Spooner, 2003).

What Is to Be Included in Alternate Assessments

There are two critical issues regarding alternate assessments: what should be tested and how should it be tested. Naturally, the alternate assessment content should be designed to be relevant to students' curriculum. For students with severe disabilities, this suggests that areas such as progress in functional skills, progress related to inclusion, personal and social participation, and self-determination should be assessed. But students with severe disabilities also have the right to participate in the general curriculum, so aspects of this curriculum might also need to be assessed through the alternate system.

Ysseldyke and Olsen (1997, 1999) proposed that areas in which alternate assessment data be collected are those that are typically contained in curricula guides for students with severe disabilities: academic and functional literacy, personal and social adjustment, contribution and citizenship, responsibility and independence, and physical health. Based on discussions with teachers in focus groups, Ysseldyke and Olsen reported that the following were important considerations for alternate assessments:

1. The focus should be on authentic skills and on assessing experiences in real-life environments.
2. Integrated skills should be measures across domains.
3. Multiple measures should be taken across time.
4. The assessment should include not only an assessment of the student's skills, but an assessment of the extent to which schools provide adequate support in terms of "assistive devices, people, and other supports that allow students to function as independently as possible" (p.184).
5. The best way to judge the value of alternate assessments is the extent to which they result in better decisions about ways to most effectively serve students.

Although Ysseldyke and Olsen (1999) indicated that alternate assessments should focus primarily on functional skills, not all experts agree, and different states are assessing different types of skills. Browder and Spooner (2003) reported that states are using three different schemes to determine the content of alternate assessments: assessment of functional skills such as are contained in a life skills curriculum; assessment based on the state's academic content areas, specifically testing "critical functions" (an interpretation of the skill so that it could be carried out by a student with a severe disability); and a combination of academic critical functions and functional skills. Functional skills such as contained in life skills curricula are those we have often considered important for students with severe disabilities. In contrast, academic skills assessment uses the areas defined for learning by all students and interprets them in a way that indicates "critical functions" or "indicators" for students with severe disabilities. For example, in the statewide assessment system used in

Kentucky, one skill for all students to demonstrate is "accessing information—students use research tools to locate sources of information and ideas relevant to a problem." For students with severe disabilities, the corresponding critical function of this expectation is "requests assistance" (Kleinert & Kearns, 1999).

Tables 9–1 and 9–2 contrast the orientation of two states with regard to content. In Table 9–1, Maryland's outcomes for students with severe disabilities are indicated. As can be seen, these are listed in areas of more traditional instruction for students with severe disabilities (i.e., personal management, community, etc.) In Table 9–2, Kentucky's academic expectations are listed. As indicated in the previous example, these include skills linked to the academic expectations for general education students (Ysseldyke, Olsen, & Thurlow, 1997). It should be noted that in addition to the academic expectation indicators Kentucky's alternate assessment also includes performance indicators, which assess more functional skills (Kleinert & Kearns, 1999).

Relatively little systematic research has been conducted to determine the appropriate content that should be included in an alternate assessment system. One study of importance was conducted by Kleinert and Kearns (1999). They reported that the Kentucky alternate portfolio assessment system for students with severe disabilities contains two sections. The first section asks for evidence of the student's performance on *performance indicators.* These indicators are based on best practices for teaching students with severe disabilities and primarily call for an assessment of functional skills. One example of an item in this section is "student performs specifically targeted skills in portfolio

Table 9–1 Examples of Maryland's Content Domain Outcomes for Students with Severe Disabilities in Independence Mastery Assessment Program

Content Domain	*Indicators*
Personal Management: Students will demonstrate their ability in the following areas: personal needs, appropriate health and safety practices, managing household routines, and participating in transition planning with adult service providers.	Eating and feeding self. Dressing appropriately for activities, season, and weather.
Community: Students will demonstrate their ability to access community resources and get about safely in the environment.	Shopping or browsing for variety of items. Demonstrating safe pedestrian skills.
Care/Vocational: Students will demonstrate their ability to participate in transitioning to employment and in various employment opportunities.	Arriving at work appropriately dressed and on time. Completing assigned duties with appropriate productivity and quality.
Recreation/Leisure: Students will demonstrate their ability to participate in recreational and leisure activities.	Engaging in hobbies. Participating in clubs or organizations.

Source: Issues and Considerations in Alternate Assessments (NCEO Synthesis Report 27), by J. E.Ysseldyke, K. Olsen, & M. Thurlow, 1997, Minneapolis: National Center on Educational Outcomes, University of Minnesota. Reprinted by permission.

Table 9–2 Examples of Kentucky's Academic Expectations for Students with Moderate and Severe Disabilities in the Alternate Portfolio System

Academic Expectation	*Indicator(s)*
Accessing Information: Students use research tools to locate sources of information and ideas relevant to a specific need or problem.	Requests assistance.
Reading: Students construct meaning from a variety of printed materials for a variety of purposes through reading.	Reads environmental, pictorial print.
Quantifying: Students organize information by quantifying real, whole, rational, and/or complex numbers.	Counts; uses one-to-one correspondence.
Writing: Students communicate ideas and information to a variety of audiences for a variety of purposes through writing.	Constructs printed, pictorial messages; uses personal signature.
Constancy: Students understand the tendency of nature to remain constant or move toward a steady state in a closed system.	Predicts next event.

Source: Issues and Considerations in Alternate Assessments (NCEO Synthesis Report 27), by J. E. Ysseldyke, K. Olsen, & M. Thurlow, 1997, Minneapolis: National Center on Educational Outcomes, University of Minnesota. Reprinted by permission.

entries"; another is "student plans, monitors, and evaluates own performance." The second section is referred to as *academic expectations.* In this section (formerly referred to as learner outcomes), 28 competency areas are identified that are a subset of the 57 academic expectations for students without disabilities. These are based on the state's academic benchmarks. In the Kentucky alternate portfolio system, for each academic expectation, there is a corresponding *critical function indicator.*

To determine the content validity of Kentucky's alternate portfolio assessment, Kleinert and Kearns (1999) asked 80 experts in the area of severe disabilities to rate the importance of each item from both sections, that is, how important they felt it was for students with severe disabilities to acquire the skill indicated by the item. Of the 80 questioned, 44 (55%) responded to the survey. All the items received ratings that were sufficiently high to establish their validity. However, the range of ratings by the experts on some items indicated that there was not uniform agreement on the importance of each. For example, some evaluators thought that some students with severe disabilities could learn at a higher level than indicated by the critical function of the academic expectation. Nevertheless, the Kleinert and Kearns study demonstrated that it is possible to establish validity for an alternate portfolio assessment system.

An important point from the results of this study is that reaching universal agreement on what students with severe disabilities should be taught is almost impossible. As explained in Chapter 1, there is a great deal of heterogeneity among this population, and individualization of goals and objectives is the only way a quality education can be provided. Thus determining what should be included on a standardized assessment will be a never ending challenge. Nevertheless, it appears that alternate assessments will continue to be a requirement and we will have to continue to find the most appropriate content to include on them (Browder & Spooner, 2003). Of course, there is a positive side to this. Regardless of the specific content, student outcomes on the alternate assessment serve as a substitute for outcomes on typical assessments and must be analyzed along with the data of other students to hold schools accountable for adequate progress of all students (Ysseldyke & Olsen, 1997).

How Alternate Assessments Are to Be Conducted

The second issue is how students should be assessed to determine their level of achievement. The format of alternate assessments may be determined by individual states. Ysseldyke and Olsen (1999) proposed that four types of assessment methods are appropriate:

- *Observations:* Watching the student exhibit the behavior.
- *Interviews and surveys:* Gathering information from people who know the student.
- *Record reviews:* Using a structure procedure to extract information.
- *Tests:* Putting a challenge in front of the students and having them solve the problem.

Although alternate assessments may be constructed in various ways, a way gaining popularity in many states is the *alternate portfolio assessment* system (Browder, 2001; Browder & Spooner, 2003; Kleinert et al., 1997; Kleinert et al., 2000; Ysseldyke & Olsen, 1997; Ysseldyke & Olsen, 1999; Ysseldyke et al., 1997; Ysseldyke et al., 1992). Using an alternate portfolio, information about student performance is gathered over a period of time and placed in the student's portfolio. This information is intended to demonstrate the student's ability level on key mandated outcomes. Following the collection of the information, the portfolio is evaluated to determine the success of the student in achieving the desired outcomes.

Because portfolios are becoming more commonly used to evaluate the performance of students with severe disabilities in alternate assessments, we discuss this procedure next.

Portfolio Assessment Procedures

Before being used as mechanisms for alternate assessments, portfolios were originally developed to assess learning and development by young children. Assessment portfolios are collections of evidence reflecting the development and learning of individuals over a period of time. They are a "means of assessment that provides a complex and comprehensive view of student performance in context" (Grace & Shores, 1992, p. 5). Portfolio assessment allows a wide variety of different types of material to be stored in one place so that the teacher (or in some cases an independent evaluator) can judge the progress of a student qualitatively as well as quantitatively. Ideally, portfolio assessment is intended to provide information that will be useful for making decisions about student performance in a variety of curricular areas (Meisels & Steele, 1991; Paulson, Paulson, & Meyer, 1991).

Portfolio Content

Portfolios serve as an ongoing vehicle of authentic assessment. Therefore, they should only include evidence of authentic outcomes and assessment of real-life activities. Particularly with regard to students with disabilities, the matter of portfolios is based on the assumption that students will live in real-life settings and work on real-life activities. Therefore, they need to learn skills that have relevance beyond the classroom, and evidence of these skills should be entered into the portfolio for assessment (Wesson & King, 1996). Often it is desirable for the teacher and student to compose the portfolio together. This allows both to have a voice in important contents that are to be evaluated to reflect progress. When used as an alternate assessment vehicle, items must be entered into portfolios that are related to individual, school, district, and state goals, objectives, or benchmarks. The portfolio should be a selective collection, and the items included should help to make instructional decisions. The portfolio should also be multifaceted and include different types of evidence or data about a student's learning. It should be organized by instructional area and in chronological order and should be accessible for easy use and updating as necessary (Wesson & King, 1996). Examples of information appropriate for student portfolios include the following (Meisels & Steele, 1991; Wesson & King, 1996):

- Samples of the student's written work
- Logs of activities completed by the student
- Photos of the student's completed art or work products or actual samples
- Written records about the student's thoughts and ideas that the student has commented on
- Anecdotal records about the student's performance on different activities
- Videotapes of the student engaged in certain activities
- Checklist of skills completed by the student (such as from a particular curriculum or adaptive behavior assessment)
- Teachers' notes or anecdotal records
- Charts or graphs of the student's progress on particular skills (such as described later in this chapter)

Meisels and Steele (1991) suggested that no less than once or twice a month teachers should gather evidence to be included in the portfolio. They also recommended that the students be given the opportunity to help to select the information to be included, with the teacher prompting the students to select items that were especially pleasing or difficult for them. Most important, the included items should reflect the student's progress on individually developed goals or objectives (Grace & Shores, 1992). Portfolios may also reflect students' critique of their own learning, such as how important the work or the skill is to them, whether they would do something different, or how they will continue to use a skill in the future.

Meyer and Janney (1989) suggested several types of items that could easily be included in portfolios to document the progress of students with severe disabilities. These are less formal records that teachers may keep to monitor the progress of students. They include schedules of students' activities, daily logs, and incident records. These are briefly explained next.

Schedule of Student Activities. Since various instructional efforts and interventions are often intended to broaden the activities and inclusive opportunities available to students with severe disabilities, a weekly schedule of students' activities can be used to monitor progress. Meyer and Janney explained that "a diary of student activities completed by program staff before, during, and after the intervention can be used to document broad changes in the nature of the student's school day and staff perceptions of the behavior change" (p. 265). Using such a schedule would allow one to see the types of activities that the student is engaged in, grouping arrangements, staff assignments, the amount of time that the student is included, and the level of success achieved. In analyzing student progress based on a weekly schedule, the teacher would look to see if the student has been involved in more integrated learning opportunities, fewer one-to-one teaching arrangements, and more varied instructional groupings, with a higher number of activities being rated as more successful.

Daily Log. Another relatively simple approach to monitoring student progress proposed by Meyer and Janney is the daily log. Entries into this log can reflect several kinds of data; some of these may be listed as prompts on preprinted log forms to remind the record-keeper to address them. They might include the following or similar entries.

- Overall, what kind of day did the student have? Circle one of the following: A very good day; okay; not sure; not okay; a very bad day.
- How well did the student do on tasks in school today? Circle one of the following: A very good day; okay; not sure; not okay; a very bad day.

- How well did the student do on tasks in the community today? Circle one of the following: A very good day; okay; not sure; not okay; a very bad day.
- Comment briefly on the day's events and the student's behavior. Note any incidents that occurred that seemed important to you (positive and negative).
- Describe tasks or activities that the student enjoyed or worked well on.
- Describe tasks or activities that the student did *not* enjoy or work well on.

For the log to be as true an indicator of student performance as possible, Meyer and Janney recommended that log entries be made 2 days a week and that these days be preselected randomly to avoid bias on when to make an entry.

Incident Record. The third form of measurement recommended by Meyer and Janney is the incident record, a document designed to record serious problems such as self-injury or other challenging behaviors. The incident record includes information relevant for conducting a functional analysis of the problematic behavior (see Chapter 12 for an explanation of this procedure) and the following objective information:

- A description of the behavior, how intense it was, and how long it lasted
- The activity taking place when the behavior occurred
- Where the behavior occurred
- Professional staff and other students present when the behavior occurred
- What was happening immediately before the behavior occurred
- What happened immediately following the behavior that may have been a consequence of the behavior. (For example, How did people react? Were task demands reduced? Could anything else have served as a reinforcer for the behavior?)

The recorder could also add subjective information to the record, such as these: Why do you think the incident occurred? How do you think the behavior could have been prevented or handled differently?

Evaluating Portfolio Contents

When evaluating the contents of portfolios, teachers will want answers to one or both of these questions: Is there sufficient evidence that the student is making adequate progress? Or, if the portfolio is used as an alternate assessment, Is there sufficient evidence that the student is achieving the standard that has been specified by the school, district, or state?

The first question implies that the student is being compared to himself over a period of time. Behavioral charts (as discussed later in this chapter) or anecdotal records might reveal this performance, as will displays of projects or other permanent products. Many teachers like to use videotapes of particular skills, such as self-feeding, with additions being made to the tapes on a regular basis. Audiotapes of episodes of conversations might serve the same purpose. Reviews of this material should occur frequently enough so that necessary changes can be made, but with enough time between reviews to allow adequate opportunity for growth. Every 4 weeks might be the briefest amount of time that should pass and every 3 months is recommended as the maximum.

Many states have established standards for alternate assessments. Tables 9–1 and 9–2 reflect examples of outcomes on alternate assessments from Maryland and Kentucky (Ysseldyke et al., 1997). In such cases the content, or what the content must reflect, will be preestablished. Although specified evidence must be included, additional material might also be in the portfolio, for example, material that reflects attainment of IEP objectives.

One of the most difficult aspects of portfolio assessment is the objective evaluation of the content (Kleinert et al., 1997; Kleinert et al., 2000; Ysseldyke et al., 1997). Two tactics may be helpful in improving objectivity. One is to prespecify what the evidence should look like. Then, when the evaluation of actual material is conducted, the judge's subjectivity can be reduced. The second strategy is to use two judges with the intention of achieving agreement. This attempt at reliability should improve objectivity.

An example of portfolio evaluation was provided by Hanline and Fox (1994). They documented the progress of the children over a period of 1 year, collecting information for inclusion in the portfolios at the beginning, middle, and end of the year. They examined and evaluated photos of block construction and of free-form art products, results of systematic observations of sociodramatic play during both outdoor and indoor play periods, and systematic observations of social and cognitive play behavior during fluid play periods (i.e., with water and sand). Based on their observations, they noted the developmental progress of the children, which was determined by changes in the quality of block construction and art products; an improvement in motor skills, spatial awareness, and symbolic abilities; an increase in social interactions; and an increase in dramatic play. Hanline and Fox (1994) reported that the type of information included in the portfolio assessment proved to be especially useful when communicating with parents about the students' progress.

The Value and Limitations of Portfolios as Alternate Assessments

Kentucky was one of the first states in which an alternate portfolio was developed as an alternate assessment for students with severe disabilities (Kleinert et al., 1997) and serves as a good example of the use of portfolios as alternate assessment systems for students with severe disabilities. According to Kleinert et al. (1997), under the Kentucky Educational Reform Act (KERA), Kentucky instituted an alternate assessment system for students with moderate and severe cognitive disabilities that used a structured portfolio system. Assessment of all students, including those with and without disabilities, occurred on the same schedule as assessments of students without disabilities. The scores derived from the evaluation of the alternate portfolios are weighted the same as the scores of nondisabled students with regard to determining school accountability. This ensures that the progress of *all* students is tied to the state-mandated school reward and sanctioning outcome. Thus the accountability for the quality of education for students with severe disabilities is of no less importance in Kentucky than the quality of education for nondisabled students.

The Kentucky alternate portfolio was designed to reflect the broad learning goals of all students, but with different outcomes for students with severe disabilities. A state advisory committee was used to determine the contents of the portfolio. Subsequently, Kleinert and Kearns (1999) conducted a study to determine experts' opinions about the relevance of what is assessed and found that the instrument was valid.

In another study of the Kentucky system, analyzing data from 60 students distributed across 34 schools in Kentucky, Turner, Baldwin, Kleinert, and Kearns (2000) studied the relationship among student outcomes as assessed by Kentucky's alternate portfolio assessment system for students with severe disabilities, the quality of the students IEPs, and the quality of the services offered to the students within the schools. They proposed that, in addition to knowing if students were achieving satisfactorily, alternate assessments should also indicate whether sufficient structures and supports are available within schools for students to attain the desired level of achievement.

The portfolios were judged and graded by using the evaluation rubric established by the Kentucky public schools. The IEPs were evaluated using criteria developed by Hunt, Goetz, and Anderson (1986), which examined objectives to determine if they reflected best practices, such as teaching age-appropriate skills, teaching in natural environments, and including students in activities with nondisabled peers. The quality of the programs provided to students was determined by evaluating the programs using the *Program Quality Indicator* (PQI) Checklist developed by Meyer, Eichinger, and Downing (1992). The PQI Checklist allows an evaluator to assess a school program for students with severe disabilities to determine if quality practices are used in the school, such as student opportunity to make choices, instruction in different situations, opportunity to engage in active learning opportunities, and social interaction with nondisabled peers.

Turner et al. (2000) found a significant correlation between the quality of programs (based on the PQI Checklist evaluation) and the quality of the portfolios ($r = .45$), but did not find a significant correlation between the quality of the IEP and the portfolios. They suggested that the results implied that better school programs for students with severe disabilities would result in better outcomes for the students as reflected in their portfolio assessment scores. They explained that, although all the students' IEPs may not have reflected that their objectives were entirely indicative of best practice, the overall rating of programs was clearly associated with improved performance as indicated by the portfolios.

The findings by Turner et al. suggest that programs considered to demonstrate best practices result in greater achievement by students. They also found that portfolio scores were *not* correlated with the severity of the disability, indicating that the flexibility of the content allowed for individualization. Very important, Turner et al. reported that use of the portfolios affected teachers' instructional styles. Because choice-making and the use of individual schedules had been specified, teachers reported that they provided students with more opportunities to achieve these desired outcomes. In these ways they were increasing the self-determination opportunities of students. However, there were difficulties related to using the alternate portfolios. Teachers sometimes reported difficulty documenting performance, supporting friendships between students with and without disabilities, and having enough time to work on the portfolios. A lack of inclusive opportunities inhibited performance on some standards.

Two studies have reported the views of teachers who were experienced in using alternate assessments

(Kampfer, Horvath, Kleinert, & Kearns, 2001; Kleinert, Kennedy, & Kearns, 1999). Their findings are very relevant.

Kleinert et al. (1999) surveyed Kentucky teachers who completed alternate assessment portfolios to determine their views with regard to the portfolios. Of the 508 teachers surveyed, 331 responded (62.5%). A positive finding was that the majority of the respondents agreed or strongly agreed that it was important for all students, including students with severe disabilities, to be included in the statewide assessment system (54.8%), and saw a benefit to having their own students included (52.9%). However, less than a majority agreed or strongly agreed that the alternate portfolio assessment made it easier to include their students in school activities (34%), include them in regular classrooms (30.7%), or provide community-based instruction (43.5%). About 30% of the teachers offered a number of written comments that were critical of the alternate portfolio assessment system. Among those that were most notable were these:

- Completing the portfolios takes time away from teaching.
- The process is more an evaluation of the teacher than of the student.
- Some of the evaluation items included in the alternate assessment system are not appropriate for all students.
- Teacher creativity and work is a greater factor in determining the ultimate score than is the student's learning.
- The scoring system for the portfolio is too subjective, must be done on one's own time, and is too stressful.
- Some of the documentation, such as taking photographs of the student in certain situations, is not a natural part of the learning routine.
- There is a need for more scoring training.
- The assessment procedure doesn't really benefit the students.

Kleinert et al. (1999) concluded, "These findings, especially the written teacher comments, indicated some serious issues that must be addressed as local districts and whole states strive to develop alternate assessment systems for students who are unable to participate in the regular assessment process" (p. 98). They felt that, with regard to the desired impact of the alternate assessment system to positively influence what and how teachers teach, the survey provided "limited evidence for changes in instructional practices . . . " (p. 98).

In the second study, Kampfer et al. (2001) also surveyed teachers in Kentucky who used the alternate portfolio assessment system. Four hundred teachers were sent surveys and 206 responded (51.5%). They were asked a number of questions about the process for completing the portfolio assessments and the amount of effort required. Some of the major findings included these:

- Portfolio entry, that is, deciding what to put in the portfolio, required the most time and effort.
- Alternate portfolio assessment items that required moderate to extreme effort included facilitating social relationships, documenting students' progress, developing natural supports for students, and accessing multiple settings.
- Teachers reported that on average the use of portfolios provided "some" benefit to the student (a rating of 1.9 out of 4.0).
- They also reported that portfolio elements were embedded into instruction a moderate amount of time (3.3/4.0), and that there was a "moderate" amount of student involvement in portfolio development (3.1/4.0).
- Finally, teachers said they spent *25 to 35 hours* outside their instructional day to complete *one* portfolio.

Kampfer et al. found high, statistically significant correlations between the score on the portfolio and several variables, including how much the student was involved in developing the portfolio, how much the development of the portfolio was embedded in instruction, and how much the portfolio was perceived as being a benefit to the student. There were also significant correlations, although not as high, between portfolio scores and the number of hours spent developing the portfolios, the number of years teaching, and the number of years developing portfolios. Overall, as revealed in their comments, the teachers responded negatively to the process. They "overwhelmingly wrote about the time-consuming nature of this type of assessment" (p. 369), stating that "there is 'an enormous amount' of paperwork involved in the development of the Alternate Portfolio" (p. 369). They also said that "this time-consuming process tended to take away from other students who were not completing a portfolio that school year" (p. 369). Other areas of complaints by the teachers included the subjective nature of the scoring, the validity of the portfolio for assessing the effectiveness of a program, and the lack of support and assistance that they received from administrators and teachers in general education in completing the portfolio assessments.

As these studies indicate, although including students in statewide assessments to hold schools accountable for their learning is viewed as having much merit, the procedures required to create and evaluate alternate portfolios are very demanding and time consuming. Kleinert et al. (2000) recognized this condition and other problems, such as difficulty in establishing reliable scoring procedures, but they maintained that the procedure has merit. They proposed that more support be provided for the development of alternate portfolios and that greater stress be placed on evaluating the services provided to students, as well as on the students themselves.

Long before alternate assessments were mandated or portfolio assessments were proposed for use with students with severe disabilities, continuous direct measures of behaviors and skills were taken to assess student progress. In light of the requirement for alternate assessments, there has been less attention to these measures in recent years. However, we feel that they continue to be very important. They can greatly assist teachers in analyzing students' progress and thus in making decisions about the adequacy of instructional procedures. In many ways, they are of greater value than end-of-year assessments. In the remaining sections of this chapter, these measures are discussed.

Continuous Direct Assessment

Continuous direct measurement of the progress of students allows teachers, parents, and other professionals to know if important goals and specific instructional objectives are being met. Continuous direct assessment is a system that measures each student's progress on specific behaviors or skills on a regular and frequent basis. It provides data that allow the teacher and others to know if adequate progress is being made, if certain teaching strategies are working, if there is a need to change to other approaches that may be more successful, or if there is a need to develop new instructional objectives. During all phases of the instructional process, including baseline (after an instructional target has been identified but before instruction), initial skill acquisition, and generalization and maintenance, the student's progress is monitored and performance data are recorded. Review of the data allows important decisions to be made.

There are important conceptual differences between continuous direct assessment and alternate portfolio assessments, but in some ways the two are very complementary. As was stated, an alternate assessment evaluates the student to determine how well the student is achieving previously stated benchmarks. Alternate assessment does not specify precisely when measurement is to be made, but it generally occurs at the end of an academic year. Continuous assessment is not necessarily linked to standards that are desired for all students, but more often measures the achievement of a student on particular objectives that have been designated on the IEP. Furthermore, the measures are taken on a more regular basis. In continuous assessment, measurement of specific behavior often occurs once a day or several days per week. *Direct measurement,* or measurement that requires a quantitative unit of measure of an observed behavior (such as the number of positive social comments that occur within a period of time), is often used.

There are different ways to approach the task of continuous direct assessment, but all require the teacher to regularly observe and record the student's performance. The data must be written down so that the teacher can observe over a period of time (days, weeks, or months) whether progress is sufficient without having to rely on memory to make decisions about instruction. Although some teachers often neglect the task of data collection, available research suggests that teachers who collect student performance data make better decisions about instruction (Farlow & Snell, 1989; Fuchs & Fuchs, 1986). This means that students learn more because less time is spent on ineffective teaching practices.

Using continuous direct measurement, the teacher or another observer makes a record of the student's performance either during instruction, during probe periods (attempts by the student to perform the task without instruction), or at other times when the behavior may be expected to occur. After collecting data during an observation session, the teacher then transfers the written data to a graph or chart. By adding data points on a daily (or frequent) basis and using lines to connect the points, the teacher (as well as others, such as the student or the parents) can easily observe the student's progress on a particular behavior or skill over a period of time. This type of continuous measurement system has been used for many years in the fields of applied behavior analysis and special education (Alberto & Troutman, 2002; Browder, 1991, 2001; Brown & Snell, 1993; Sailor & Guess, 1983; White & Haring, 1980).

Types of Behaviors and Units of Measure

As discussed in Chapter 6, direct measurement of student performance begins as part of the initial assessment process. It requires that the teacher first identify the topographical types of behaviors that will be measured and then use an appropriate unit of measure. The behaviors were described as being *simple, discrete; continuous, ongoing; complex, chained skills;* or *functional routines.* Respectively, these could be objectives such as touching to indicate choice, jogging for a period of time, assembling a model car, or shopping for clothes in a department store. The units of measure that could be used include event recording, rate, partial interval recording, momentary-time sampling, and latency for simple, discrete behaviors; duration measures and whole interval recording for continuous, ongoing behaviors; and task analytic recording for both complex, chained and functional routine types of objectives.

Defining the Behavior

Before direct measurement of student performance, it is very important that the behaviors to be observed and measured be precisely defined. Once the measurement process begins, the teacher must take the same type of measure from day to day. If one day the teacher interprets the behavior to have occurred because it was demonstrated in a particular way, but on another day the form of the behavior is different, yet still counted as occurring, the measurement system will not be consistent. This type of inaccuracy could result in the behavior being counted at some times but not at other times, defeating the purpose of direct measurement. Thus a primary rule is to adequately define (or pinpoint) the behavior so that there is no mistake about when it occurs and when it does not. This is true for all types of behaviors to be measured, including one-component behaviors (simple, discrete and continuous, ongoing) and multiple-component behaviors (complex, chained and functional routines). With multiple-component behaviors, each component or part of the chain must be specified well enough so that accurate and consistent measurement can occur.

To know if a behavior has been well enough defined, the teacher may provide the definition to another person (another professional or paraprofessional) and ask her to record the occurrence of the behavior simultaneously with the teacher for a brief period of time. If the two people arrive at the same result, then the measurement system is said to be *reliable.* Reliability is always higher when the behavior being measured is well defined.

Observation of the Behavior

When the behavior has been identified and adequately defined, the teacher (or another trained individual) observes the student at predetermined times and circumstances to note the occurrence of the behavior or skill. The time and circumstance depend on the instructional objective and the daily schedule. For some behaviors, the teacher may need to observe for an extended period of time, perhaps an hour or maybe even an entire day. For example, a student may be working on a social skill such as offering a toy to another child or asking for a favorite item instead of grabbing it. In this type of situation, it would be important for the teacher to observe for at least enough time so that the behavior has an adequate opportunity to occur. In addition, some functional routines may require a couple of hours or longer to complete (e.g., planning a dinner menu and shopping in a grocery store). In circumstances such as these, much time would have to be spent in direct observation. Other behaviors or skills, however, may require less time. Putting on one's coat, reading sight words, or sweeping a kitchen, for example, can be completed in a relatively brief period and thus require relatively little observation time.

The most desired frequency of observing a student's behaviors is on a daily basis, but this is not likely to happen, especially for behaviors that take longer to observe. With these, once or twice a week may be all that is possible.

Recording the Data

Behavioral data may be recorded in several ways. In each, the basic process requires that the teacher make a written note or place a mark on a data collection sheet and then transfer the mark to a corresponding graph or chart. The type of data collected depends on the unit of measure being used. Procedures for different types of data collection are explained in the following sections.

Event Recording

Discrete behaviors are those with clear beginning and ending points, such as various social, communicative, or motor behaviors. They can be recorded as they occur throughout a typical day or within a certain period of time during the day. The teacher can make marks on a piece of paper to note the occurrence or may use other simple tactics, such as counting on a golf counter strapped to the wrist, changing paper clips from one pocket to another, or using any other simple technique that will allow an accurate count to be kept.

The teacher (or another capable person, such as the paraprofessional) may need to count several behaviors of one student or several behaviors of several students. This process can be facilitated by using a data collection form such as that shown in Figure 9–1. As can be seen in the

Figure 9–1 Date Collection Form for Event Recording

Date 6/5/04

Student / Behavior(s)		Number of Events	Length of Observation	Total
Jill	Raises hand for help	~~||||~~ |||	1 hr.	8
	Responds to classmate's greeting	|||	1 hr.	3
Ricardo	Looks toward someone calling his name	||||	30 min.	4
	Points toward desired object	~~||||~~ ||||	30 min.	9
Andrea	Throws objects	||	30 min.	2
	Comes to seat when requested	|||	30 min.	3
Nino	Passes an item when requested			20 min.	1
	Touches classmate	~~||||~~	20 min.	5
	Pinches classmate	|||	20 min.	3

figure, the teacher wishes to monitor several behaviors for each student. It may be assumed that each of these represents one of the objectives that is included in the student's IEP or that has been noted by the teacher, parent, or other member of the team to require some type of intervention for improvement. The teacher is recording the number of times that the events occur within a specified amount of time in order to have an accurate record of each student's progress on each behavior.

Rate Measures

Any behavior that may be counted during event recording may also be measured in terms of rate. *Rate* is defined as the number of behaviors that have occurred divided by the number of minutes of observation, or simply behaviors per minute. The use of rate as a measure results in a consistent unit of measure (behaviors per minute) being calculated, recorded, and analyzed. It is like speed measured using the unit *miles per hour:* the speed is not affected by either the actual number of miles driven or the number of hours. Using rate, the amount of time spent recording the behavior may vary, but the unit of measure is consistent from day to day.

To measure a behavior using rate, the teacher begins by noting the starting time, counts the target behavior and records the number of occurrences, and writes the ending time of the observation period, noting the total number of minutes of observation. Finally, the teacher divides the number of behaviors that occurred by the number of minutes. The result is the rate of the behavior or behaviors per minute. It should be noted that unless the behavior is occurring at a high rate (more than one behavior per minute) the result of the calculation will be a number less than 1.

Figure 9–2 displays the collection of rate data for the same behaviors displayed in Figure 9–1 for event recording. Note the different amounts of time that were used during the counting period and how the count was divided by time to result in the rate data.

Partial-Interval Recording

Interval recording notes whether a behavior occurred within a specific interval of time. The time of the intervals may vary according to the frequency of the behavior and the flexibility of the observer in recording the data. Intervals may be 1 minute, 5 minutes, 10 minutes, and so on, even up to a half-hour or an hour. Typically, strings of contiguous intervals are arranged so that the observer may note the occurrence of the behavior over a period of time. For example, there may be twelve 5-minute intervals linked together during a 1-hour period. The teacher will need to judge the occurrence of the behavior and determine the interval length as well as the number of intervals in a way that will show the occurrence of the behavior in its truest form. There are two forms of interval recording: partial interval and whole interval. Partial interval is discussed here because it is more appropriate for recording discrete (as opposed to continuous, ongoing) behaviors. Whole-interval recording will be discussed later.

Partial-interval recording means that the observer records the behavior as occurring if it occurs at least once at any time during the present observation interval. As shown in Figure 9–3, unlike the previous recording forms

Figure 9–2 Data Collection Form for Rate Data

Date 4/3/04

Student / Behaviors		Number of Events	Beginning/ Ending Time	Total Minutes	Number / Minute = Rate
Jill	Raises hand for help	𝍸 III (8)	9:30–10:15	45	8/45 = .18
	Responds to greeting	III (3)	9:30–11:30	120	3/120 = .02
Ricardo	Looks toward someone calling his name	IIII (4)	8:00–9:30	90	4/90 = .04
	Points toward desired object	𝍸 IIII (9)	9:00–10:00	60	9/60 = .15
Andrea	Throws objects	II (2)	8:30–11:30	180	2/180 = .01
	Comes to seat when requested	III (3)	10:00–11:00	60	3/60 = .05
Nino	Passes an item when requested	I (1)	2:00–2:20	20	1/20 = .05
	Touches classmate	𝍸 (5)	2:00–2:20	20	5/20 = .25
	Pinches classmate	IIII (4)	2:00–2:20	20	4/20 = .20

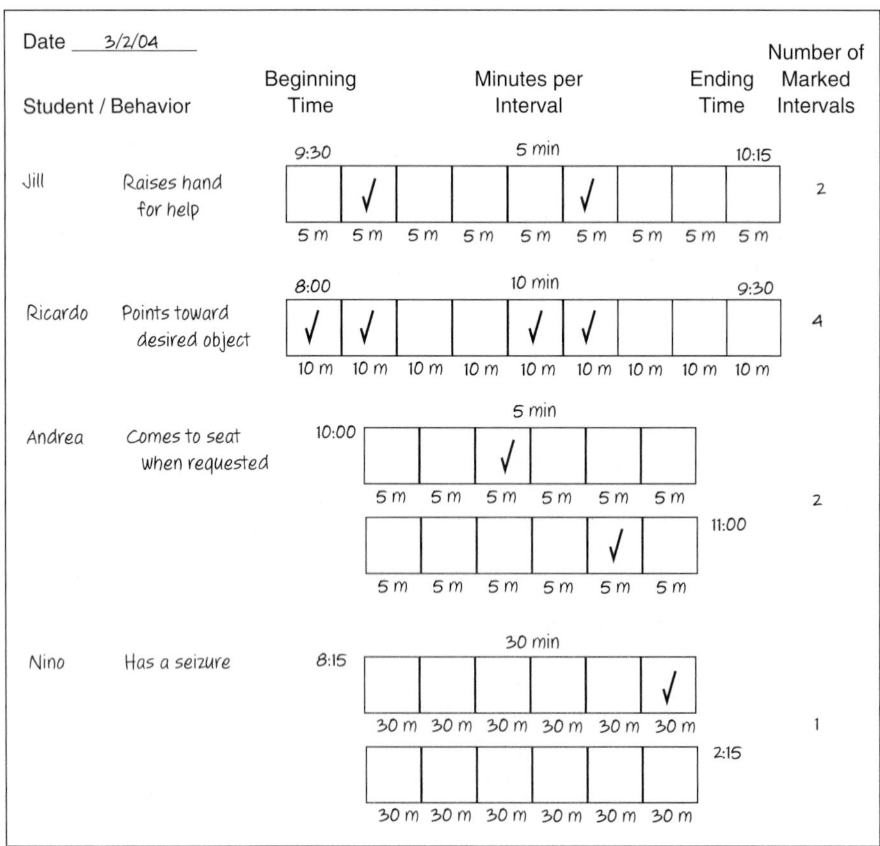

Date 3/2/04

Student / Behavior		Beginning Time	Minutes per Interval	Ending Time	Number of Marked Intervals
Jill	Raises hand for help	9:30	5 min (9 intervals: 5 m each; ✓ in intervals 2 and 6)	10:15	2
Ricardo	Points toward desired object	8:00	10 min (9 intervals: 10 m each; ✓ in intervals 1, 2, 5 and 6)	9:30	4
Andrea	Comes to seat when requested	10:00	5 min (12 intervals: 5 m each; ✓ in intervals 3 and 11)	11:00	2
Nino	Has a seizure	8:15	30 min (12 intervals: 30 m each; ✓ in interval 6)	2:15	1

Figure 9–3 Partial Interval Data Recording Form

for event recording and rate measures, each simple, discrete behavior being observed is given a series of small cells representing time intervals. (Again, these intervals can be of any appropriate length, as shown in Figure 9–3.) At the end of the interval period, if the behavior has occurred at least once at some time during the interval observation period, the observer or teacher makes a check mark in the cell. Afterward, the observation begins again and continues to the end of the next interval and again a mark is made if the behavior occurs. It is important that only one mark be made per cell regardless of the actual number of behaviors that occurred. Herein lies both the advantage and the disadvantage of partial interval recording. The teacher only needs to know if the behavior occurred once and therefore does not need to record each individual occurrence of the behavior, as with event recording or rate recording, but because of this recording rule, the teacher sees only an *estimate* of behavior occurrence. Thus, if Jill raises her hand once, twice, or more during the 5-minute interval (see Figure 9–3), the data in the particular cell would show only one mark.

Momentary Time Sampling

Another recording system that provides only an estimate of the actual occurrence of a particular behavior is momentary time sampling. This technique uses an interval cell system just as does partial interval recording as shown in Figure 9–3, but the rule for making a mark in the cell is different. Instead of making the mark if the behavior occurs at least once at any time in the interval, the mark is made only if the behavior is occurring precisely at the time that the interval ends. If it occurs at any other time during the interval, but is not occurring at the time that the interval ends, no mark is made. For momentary time sampling to be useful, the behavior must be occurring often enough so that on at least some occasions it occurs at the time that the observer is allowed to record it.

Latency Measurement

Measures of latency are not often used, but in some cases could be a useful unit of measure. Latency is the period of time between when a stimulus occurs or is presented and when the behavior occurs that the stimulus is intended to prompt. If an individual is particularly slow at responding to a cue and it is considered important to decrease the time interval between the cue and the response, one might wish to measure the latency of the response.

Measuring latency requires that a count of seconds be made between the cue and the response. This can be done by simply counting or by using a stopwatch or a watch with a second hand. At each opportunity, after the cue occurs the teacher measures and records the response time. An example of when this measure might be used is when a student is learning to respond to natural inquiries in the community during a shopping trip. The store clerk or counter attendant might ask, "May I help you?," and the student would be expected to respond in a reasonable amount of time. In such a situation the teacher counts the number of seconds that elapsed between the natural cue ("May I help you?") and the response. Figure 9–4 shows a data collection form that could be used to record latency.

Duration Measures

Unlike previous measures, duration is useful for measuring how long a continuous, ongoing behavior lasts. Like event recording and rate measures, duration is a direct measure of the actual behavior, not an estimate like interval recording or momentary time sampling.

Several instructional objectives may target increasing the amount of time that a student can be engaged in an activity, such as working on a particular job, playing at a recreational activity, or exercising during a physical activity. When these types of objectives occur, measures of duration are appropriate because they indicate to the teacher if progress is being made; positive behaviors should show an increase in duration, whereas negative behaviors should show a decrease in duration. Figure 9–5 displays an example of a data sheet used for recording the duration of a behavior.

The most precise way to observe and record the duration of a behavior is to use a stopwatch or, if this is not possible, a watch with a second hand. As with all behaviors, it is important that the behavior being measured for duration be accurately defined with a clear beginning and end so that the observer knows when the record should begin and when it should end.

Whole-Interval Recording

Whole-interval recording is like partial-interval recording except for one important difference. For the observer to place a mark in the cell, the behavior must occur *continuously* throughout the interval, instead of at least once during the cell interval. This is why whole-interval recording is a better measure of continuous, ongoing behaviors. Only if the behavior continues to occur for the entire time of the interval is the mark made. When it is not possible to use duration recording, it may be possible to use whole-interval recording to provide an estimate of the length of time of a behavior.

Figure 9–4 Latency Data Recording Form

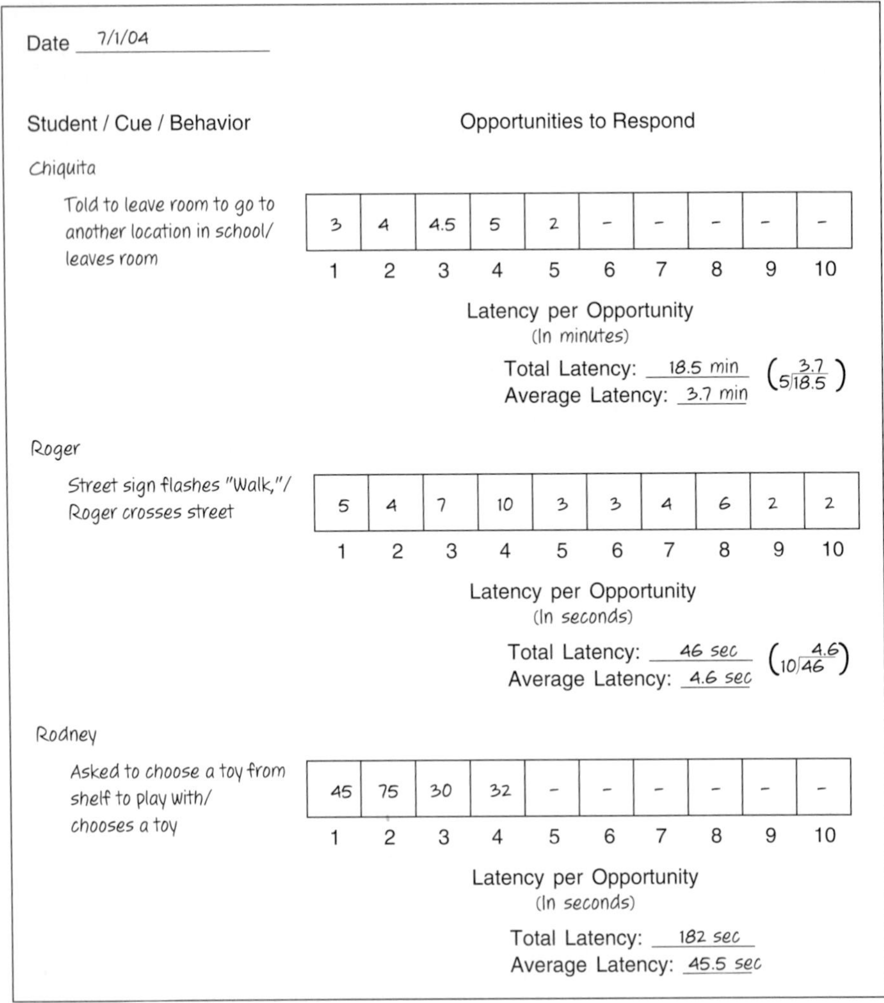

Date 7/1/04

Student / Cue / Behavior — Opportunities to Respond

Chiquita

Told to leave room to go to another location in school/ leaves room

1	2	3	4	5	6	7	8	9	10
3	4	4.5	5	2	–	–	–	–	–

Latency per Opportunity (In minutes)

Total Latency: 18.5 min (5)18.5 = 3.7
Average Latency: 3.7 min

Roger

Street sign flashes "Walk,"/ Roger crosses street

1	2	3	4	5	6	7	8	9	10
5	4	7	10	3	3	4	6	2	2

Latency per Opportunity (In seconds)

Total Latency: 46 sec (10)46 = 4.6
Average Latency: 4.6 sec

Rodney

Asked to choose a toy from shelf to play with/ chooses a toy

1	2	3	4	5	6	7	8	9	10
45	75	30	32	–	–	–	–	–	–

Latency per Opportunity (In seconds)

Total Latency: 182 sec
Average Latency: 45.5 sec

Using a measure of duration, the teacher would know exactly how long a behavior occurred. Using whole-interval recording, however, the observer can only record the behavior (make a mark in the interval) if the behavior occurred throughout the entire interval. The disadvantage of whole-interval recording is that if the behavior occurs for up to 99% of the time represented by the interval it is not recorded. Obviously, this can result in a false picture of accomplishment. For example, a student learning to shovel snow (a relatively continuous behavior) may be observed using a whole-interval recording system with intervals set at 2 minutes. Each time 2 minutes pass during which the student has continuously shoveled the snow a mark is made in an interval cell. During any 2-minute period, if the student pauses, the cell is not marked because the behavior was not continuous. The process continues through all the intervals for which recording was planned.

Even though the need for a continuous display of the behavior may be considered a major disadvantage of the whole-interval recording system, the advantage of it is that it does not require continuous measurement using a stopwatch or second hand as is required for duration recording. For this reason, whole-interval recording may be a useful data recording system in some situations. The same form as used for partial-interval recording is used for whole-interval recording (see Figure 9–3), but the difference is the rule stipulated above for marking the cell.

Task Analytic (Multiple-Component) Recording

Each previously discussed unit of measure was developed for recording individual behaviors, either simple, discrete behaviors or continuous, ongoing behaviors. However, many of the skills that are taught to individuals with severe disabilities have multiple components. As

Figure 9–5 Duration Data Recording Form

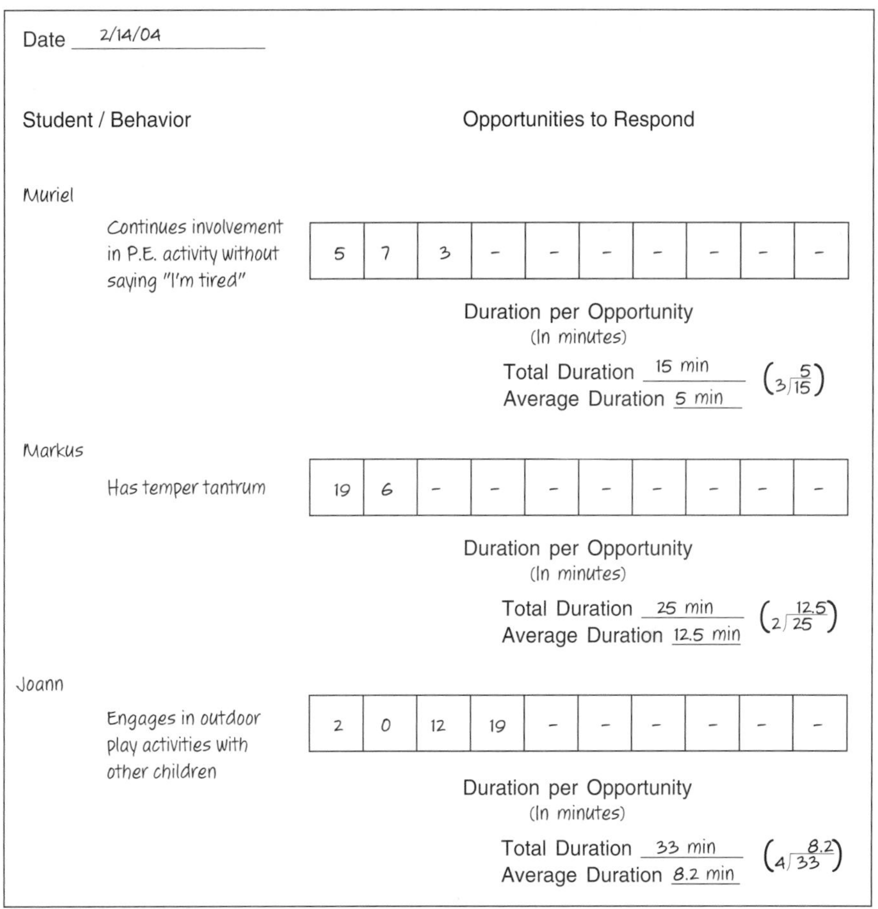

Date 2/14/04

Student / Behavior — Opportunities to Respond

Muriel

Continues involvement in P.E. activity without saying "I'm tired"

5	7	3	-	-	-	-	-	-	-

Duration per Opportunity (In minutes)

Total Duration 15 min
Average Duration 5 min ($3 \overline{)15}$ = 5)

Markus

Has temper tantrum

19	6	-	-	-	-	-	-	-	-

Duration per Opportunity (In minutes)

Total Duration 25 min
Average Duration 12.5 min ($2 \overline{)25}$ = 12.5)

Joann

Engages in outdoor play activities with other children

2	0	12	19	-	-	-	-	-	-

Duration per Opportunity (In minutes)

Total Duration 33 min
Average Duration 8.2 min ($4 \overline{)33}$ = 8.2)

explained in Chapter 6, they are either complex, chained skills or functional routines. Thus it is necessary to have a measurement system that allows the teacher to record students' performance on objectives that have several components or behaviors chained together. The measurement process begins by constructing a task analysis or list of the individual behaviors that constitute the entire action. Such a list is presented in Figure 9–6 for putting on pants, an objective that may need to be taught to a student with severe disabilities.

During the continuous assessment process, the student's performance on each component of the instructional target is recorded. Typically, recording of the student's performance occurs at least once a day. (In the case of learning to put on pants, the most normal time to teach this is probably during physical education.) The data collection form used is based on the task analysis and includes all the steps of the behavior and spaces for recording the student's performance. Figure 9–7 shows the data collection form used for recording how well the student puts on pants. (Note that the steps have been abbreviated.) All other multiple-component instructional objectives use a similar form.

As can be seen in Figure 9–7, all the steps are listed with spaces for recording performance on each step during each day. There is also a section on the bottom of the form to indicate the type of prompt or other assistance that was required for each step.

During the baseline period, as discussed in Chapter 6, the teacher is interested simply in whether the student can perform any of the steps independently and records this performance on the data collection form. During instruction, however, the teacher wants to know not only which steps the individual can demonstrate independently, but also what level or type of assistance is necessary to get the student to complete each step when he cannot do so independently. This is usually done by constructing a least-to-most prompting sequence, as discussed in Chapter 7, and listing the sequence on the recording form (see Figure 9–7).

To begin the instructional sequence, the teacher waits until the environmental circumstances provide a natural cue for putting on pants or, if necessary, gives a general

Figure 9–6 Task Analysis of Putting On Pants

1. Get pants from closet, drawer, or wherever they are located.
2. Place pants within reach of a place where you can sit (near a chair, the bed, a stool, etc.).
3. Sit down on the chair, bed, or stool.
4. Pick up the pants from the nearby location.
5. Adjust the pants so they are being held in front of you with two hands holding the pants at the waist with one hand on each side of the pants.
6. Bend over as much as possible and lower the pants down to almost floor level.
7. Push one foot through the appropriate pants leg.
8. Push the second foot through the other pants leg.
9. Pull the pants up as high as possible while sitting.
10. While still holding on to the pants, stand up.
11. While standing, pull the pants up all the way around the waist.
12. Button the pants.
13. Pull up the pants zipper.
14. If appropriate, find a belt for the pants.
15. Adjust the belt so that it can be inserted into the first loop on the pants.
16. Pass the belt through each loop on the pants.
17. Buckle the belt.

verbal direction for the student to put on the pants. If the student does not begin the first step (getting the pants and bringing them to the location where they are to be put on), the teacher provides a gesture, such as pointing to the pants. If the student does not respond in 4 to 5 seconds, the teacher moves to the second level of assistance, which calls for a specific verbal cue. Again the teacher waits for the student to respond. If there is still no response or an incorrect response is initiated, the teacher proceeds to an even greater level of assistance, which in this case would be providing partial physical assistance. Finally, if the student is not responsive to this level of assistance, the plan calls for the teacher to provide total physical guidance.

Each multiple-component objective follows the same type of format. As discussed in Chapter 7, the instructional assistance plan varies depending on the objective and the student. Regardless of the plan, on each day or during each instructional session, the teacher records after each step the level or type of input that was necessary for the student to successfully complete the behavior. As shown in Figure 9–7, levels of assistance are coded and the codes can be used to show how the student performed on each day or during each session. If the student was unable to perform a step regardless of the level of assistance, an × could be used to indicate that the step was not completed.

Data Collection during Baseline

Baseline is the time when the teacher observes the student's ability to demonstrate certain behaviors or perform skills that have been identified as being instructional objectives, but before providing instruction for the student to learn the objective. As discussed in Chapter 6, the instructional objectives may have been identified by the teacher, parents, and other members of the collaborative team. Baseline observations are then conducted for each objective to confirm that the student cannot actually perform the targeted behavior or skill. In single-subject research designs, it is the relative improvement in the individual's behavioral performance beyond the baseline level during the intervention phase that is used to confirm the effectiveness of the intervention (independent variable) on the target behavior (dependent variable). In the instruction of students with severe disabilities, however, baseline may be considered more a demonstration of the student's need for instruction in a particular area than a way to demonstrate that the instruction affected the behavior.

Collecting baseline data requires that the teacher place the student in situations in which the behavior has the opportunity to occur and record the occurrence of the behavior, using one of the methods described earlier. A low or zero

Figure 9–7 Data Recording Form for Multiple-Component Behaviors (Putting on Pants)

Objective: Josh will put on his pants independently by completing all of the steps listed in the task analysis independently for at least three days in a row.

Steps	M	T	W	Th	F	M	T	W	Th	F
1. Get pants.	PP	VC								
2. Place pants within reach.	PP	PP								
3. Sit down.	VC	G								
4. Pick up the pants.	FP	PP								
5. Adjust the pants.	FP	FP								
6. Lower the pants to floor level.	PP	FP								
7. Push one foot through.	FP	X								
8. Push the second foot through.	FP	FP								
9. Pull the pants up while sitting.	PP	VC								
10. Stand up.	G	VC								
11. Pull pants up around the waist.	PP	PP								
12. Button the pants.	FP	PP								
13. Pull up the zipper.	FP	FP								
14. If appropriate, find a belt.	VC	VC								
15. Adjust the belt.	PP	FP								
16. Pass the belt through each loop.	FP	FP								
17. Buckle the belt.	FP	FP								

Days or Sessions

Prompts or Assistance:

NA: No assistance. Student completes step following completion of previous step with no assistance from teacher.
G: Gesture. Student completes step following a gesture from the teacher indicating what the student should do.
VC: Verbal cue. Student completes the step after the teacher provides a cue as to what to do, e.g., "pull them up!"
PP: Partial physical assistance. Student completes the step after teacher provides partial physical assistance.
FP: Full physical. Student completes the step only after teacher completely physically guides the student through it.
X: The student did not perform the step correctly with any level of assistance.

Direction: Use least-to-most assistance with delay of 4 to 5 seconds before moving to greater level of assistance.

measure of the behavior over several days suggests that instruction should be given. During experimental research, a minimum period of baseline is usually considered to be 3 to 5 days or until the baseline is stable (shows little variability). This is also a good rule of thumb for collecting baseline data for instruction unless the baseline data is very low or nonexistent. In this case, common sense suggests that instruction should be initiated sooner to avoid wasting time.

Data Collection during Instruction

Data collection and instruction should usually occur simultaneously. For simple, discrete and continuous, ongoing behaviors, the time of observation to record the data is when instruction can be provided for the targeted behavior. For example, suppose that the objective is for a student to use words to ask for certain objects. Each time that the student needs something, the teacher uses event recording to note if the student makes an appropriate verbal request. The teacher keeps nearby a data collection form such as the one shown in Figure 9–1 on which to record the data. Because part of the objective is to increase such verbal statements, the instructional plan that has been developed may call for time delay or least-to-most prompting or other tactics for skill acquisition (see Chapter 7) to be used when there is a natural opportunity for the student to demonstrate the behavior. When the behavior is demonstrated correctly, reinforcement is provided. After such a sequence of events, the teacher records the student's performance on the data collection sheet.

When there is opportunity for the behavior to occur at any time, as in the case just described, the teacher should implement the instructional plan whenever possible. Sometimes, however, the recording that is done is limited to a representative portion of the day, for example, from 9 to 10 A.M. This allows the teacher to collect representative data for analysis, but does not require her to record data during every occurrence of the behavior.

What is important is that enough time be allotted for data collection so that the record can reflect the results of the intervention. In a large way, this will depend on how often the behavior can and does occur. Behaviors or skills that have the opportunity to occur at high frequencies require less time for observation and recording because only short time periods are required to see occurrence—essentially, a snapshot of the student's performance is taken. On the other hand, low-frequency behaviors require longer observation periods because they cannot always be detected in short periods of time. For example, a student who is learning to control angry outbursts may demonstrate such outbursts only once or twice a day. Monitoring would have to take place throughout the entire day to record the occurrence of the behavior.

Multiple-component behaviors, complex chains, or functional routines that are broken down into their component parts are taught at specific times, with the entire skill being taught in its natural sequence. In this process, data collection can be recorded during the instructional process as described above and as displayed in Figure 9–7. However, data should also be collected during noninstructional probe sessions.

Data Collection during Probe Sessions

Probes are opportunities for the student to demonstrate the behavior or skill in natural circumstances without teacher assistance, instruction, or reinforcement. A probe may be thought of as a test to see how well the student has learned the skill. During probe sessions, the teacher observes the student in the context in which the behavior normally occurs and records her performance on each component of the skill. The type of form displayed in Figure 9–7 could be used, but the teacher only records whether or not each step of the behavior was demonstrated correctly. Since it is a probe, the teacher should not provide different types of instructional input. Essentially, probes are conducted in the same way that baseline data are collected, without any form of instruction.

Data Collection during Generalization

One special form of probe that must be conducted tests how well generalization has occurred. As discussed in Chapter 8, skill generalization is often an important goal for individuals with severe disabilities. To find out how well the student can perform learned tasks in different situations, probes should be conducted in targeted generalization conditions or settings.

The data collection procedures discussed in the previous sections may be used to assess students' efforts to generalize their skills. However, there are some considerations that the teacher should keep in mind. First, as discussed in Chapter 8, it is necessary to determine what adequately constitutes appropriate generalization sites or conditions for the purpose of assessment, and this should be done when objectives are being written. Natural times and natural places must be used. In addition, the number of times that the generalized skill is assessed, the people present when the condition is assessed, and the stimuli in the environment should all be normal for the condition. The teacher should keep in mind that the purpose of a generalization probe is to determine if the student can demonstrate the behavior in the real world (White, 1988). More recently, the term *authentic assessment* has been used with this form of assessment.

As with other probes, generalization probes are conducted without the use of any of the instructional cues or prompts used in the training phase. However, stimuli that are natural to the environment are allowed because they will be present when the learner is expected to demonstrate the behavior after training. If artificial prompts or supports are provided by a teacher or another individual during observations in generalized settings, this should be noted on the data collection form, because it would not be accurate to conclude that the student could independently perform the skill.

One concern about the collection of data during generalization probes is the presence of the person who conducted the initial instruction of the skill, usually the teacher (Westling & Floyd, 1990; White, 1988). The problem is that this person may serve as an unrecognized prompt and/or reinforcer for the individual learning the task. Even though this occurs unintentionally, it nevertheless inhibits the teacher from knowing if the student possesses the skill and can perform it independently. For this reason, it is often useful to have someone present whom the student does not know to observe the student and report on how well the behavior or skill was demonstrated in the natural environment. White (1988) suggests that if someone else does this observation the teacher should clearly inform that person what to look for, define examples of the behavior, and explain how to collect data on the behavior.

Graphing Direct Measurement Data

The data that are recorded using the units of measures on the forms represented in Figures 9–1 through 9–5 and 9–7, as already explained, provide the teacher with significant information about the progress of students on their individual objectives and therefore the effectiveness of instruction. However, to be able to interpret progress (or the lack of it), the teacher must look at student data occurring over many learning opportunities. One way to do this would be to examine all the daily data collection forms over many days. A more efficient way would be to transfer the raw data onto graphs or charts and observe students' progress, using these graphic displays. In this way the teacher may discern important trends on particular skills.

Graph paper with four or five squares to the inch may be used to construct simple graphs to display each student's performance on particular behaviors or skills that have been observed and recorded on the data collection forms. Figure 9–8 displays such a chart with the vertical axis and the horizontal axis drawn at right angles to each other and with spaces to add other pertinent information (name, target skill, etc.).

The horizontal lines on the graph represent the unit of measure that is being used for the targeted behavior or skill. The appropriate label to place beside the vertical axis thus depends on the unit of measure of what is being observed and measured. Based on the types of measures that have been discussed, the following units of measure may be appropriate and used to label the horizontal lines:

- The number of certain events that occur during the day
- The rate of certain events (number per minute)
- The number of intervals in which the behavior appeared at least once (partial intervals)
- The number of momentary observations at which the behavior was observed (momentary time sampling)
- The total or average latency that occurred between a certain cue and the initiation of the behavior (in minutes or seconds)
- The total or average duration of the behavior (in minutes or seconds)

Figure 9–8 Graph Paper Used to Chart Student Performance on Individual Objectives

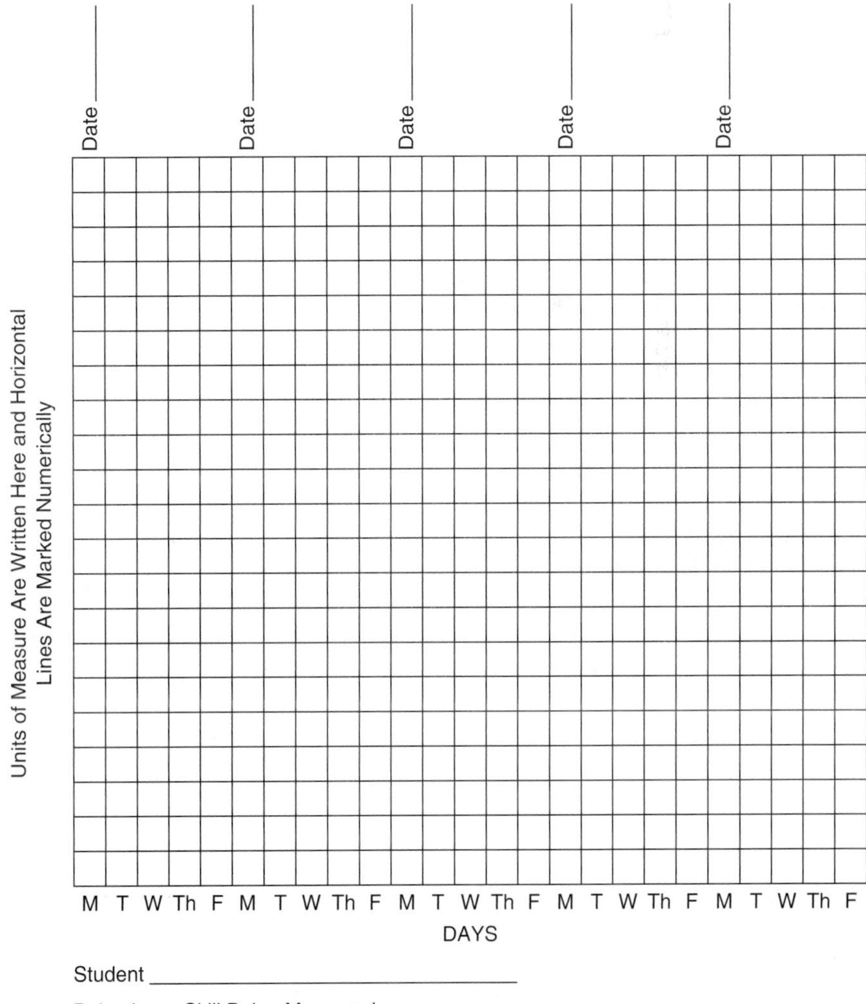

- The number of intervals in which the behavior occurred continuously (whole intervals)
- The number (or percentage) of steps in the task analysis or routine successfully completed

After the appropriate unit of measure is written on the side of the chart, each horizontal line is given a numerical value so that the entire possible range of performance levels can be recorded on the graph. For example, a behavior that is likely to occur no more than 10 times during a day would require the horizontal lines to be numbered from 1 to at least 10. Similarly, a task analysis or routine with 15 steps would require the numbering of lines 1 to 15.

Under the bottom horizontal line on the graph, the word *Days* is written, and each ascending vertical line represents a particular day and should be labeled beneath accordingly, that is, *M, T, W, Th, F.* If it is possible to collect data on the weekend, *S* and *Su* should also be included. At the conclusion of the instructional day, the teacher or the paraprofessional transcribes the data collected on the data form to a corresponding graph by using a pencil to place a dot at the intersection of the current day line (vertical line) and the unit of measure line (horizontal line). As each dot is placed, a straight line is drawn between it and the previous dot. If the previous dot was on the preceding day, obviously, this will be only a short line. However, if several days have passed since data were collected, the days that were missed will have nothing marked on them, and the line will go from the present data point to the last previous data point. Figure 9–9 displays six graphs, on each of which a different unit of measure has been used. Graphs constructed by the teacher would be similar.

Interpreting the Graphs

During the baseline period, data points representing the student's performance prior to instruction are placed on the first few vertical lines. These data are analyzed in order to make decisions about instruction. Uniformly low performance indicates that instruction is warranted. Data points that are high or ascending suggest that the student already has learned much of the skill and instruction that is necessary to achieve mastery and then maintenance and generalization.

After collecting, recording, and graphing baseline data points are completed, subsequent data points are added after the beginning of the instructional phase. When there is a change from baseline condition to the instructional phase condition, a straight vertical line is drawn between day lines. This *phase change* line indicates that there has been an important change and, by observing the following data points, the teacher will know if the change (in this case going from baseline conditions to instructional conditions) has resulted in improved performance by the student. Any changes in important aspects of the environment that might affect the student's performance should also be indicated with phase change lines. Typical important phase changes include changes in reinforcement, the location or time of instruction, the materials, and so forth. The critical purpose of this technique is that the person examining the graph will see what happens to the student's performance during different phases of instruction and/or observation.

When the graphic display of the data is examined, various patterns may emerge and the teacher must know how to interpret them to make instructional decisions. A pattern that usually occurs at the beginning of instruction shows a very low level of performance [see Figure 9–9 (a) and (b)], meaning that few steps in the task analysis or routine are being recorded, few events are occurring, or there is a low rate of behavior. The teacher should realize that this is typical and should continue instruction for several days to see if performance starts to improve. If this occurs, the teacher is on the right track with regard to instructional practices.

When the data points on the graph are ascending but have not reached their highest possible level, learning is occurring [see Figure 9–9 (c) and (d)]. Over several days the student has steadily demonstrated more correct steps, longer durations, or higher rates of performance. When this occurs, it indicates that the teacher should continue under current conditions until criterion performance (as specified in the behavioral objective) is achieved. Ultimately, the student may show a uniformly high level of performance across all days of direct assessment. When this is the case, the teacher should conclude that the target skill has been learned and does not require further instruction. It is being demonstrated adequately, at least under the conditions in which it is currently being taught and assessed. For example, the teacher may see that a student smiles often throughout the day and therefore concludes that this does not need to continue as an instructional objective. The teacher then works on skill maintenance and generalization, as discussed in Chapter 8.

The data pattern that indicates that something is very wrong with the teacher's instructional practice is one in which the student is showing a gradual decrease in performance [see Figure 9–9 (e) and (f)]. In other words, across several days there is a drop in data points. This may suggest several conditions. The cues or prompts are not working effectively, the reinforcement is not effective, or perhaps something else in the student's life, something not a part of instruction, is affecting learning. The teacher must take note of this pattern and attempt to find methods to improve student performance. Of course, if the goal is for a decrease in the measure to occur, as it

Figure 9–9 Charts of Student Performance on Individual Objectives

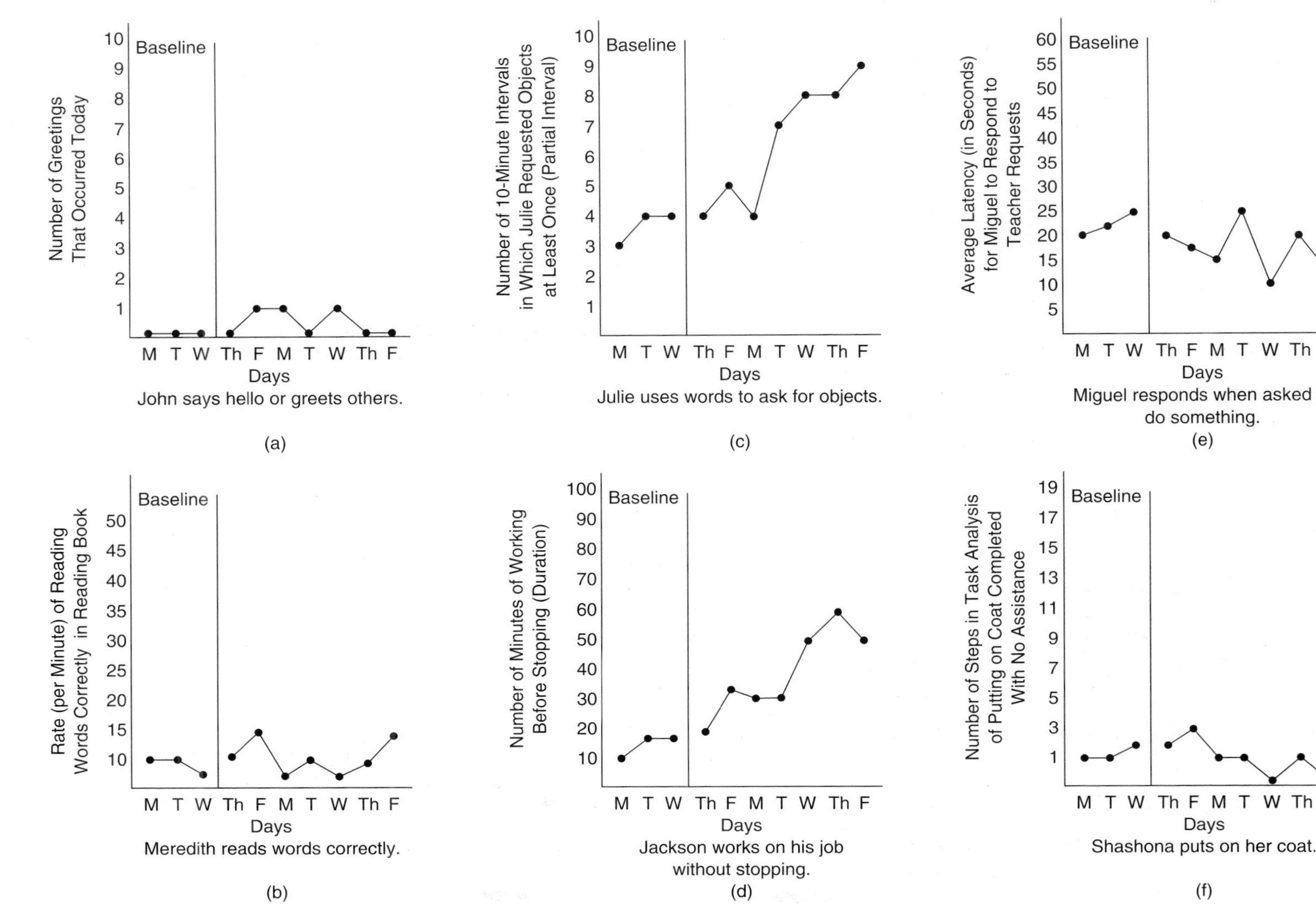

would be in Figure 9–9 (e), then this pattern would be desirable.

Direct measurement of students' behaviors and skills offers a complex yet thorough method for documenting progress on instructional objectives or the need for changes in the instructional process.The use of these procedures allows teachers and others to note whether students are learning and, if they are not, whether new forms of intervention can be more effective. Direct measure of behavior has a long history in special education and is used successfully by many special educators (Farlow & Snell, 1989).

Conclusion

A well-documented practice of effective teachers is measuring and evaluating the progress of their students. For many years, directly and continuously measuring the progress of students with disabilities has been considered to be a basic tenet of special education. This practice leads to more effective instruction because the teacher must observe the student and make a record of behavioral change or the lack of it.

In addition to the use of direct measurement to judge the progress of students, there is also the impact of the current era of educational accountability. Accountability mandates that students' academic and/or functional skills be evaluated in a way that determines their ability to meet state standards. Many propose the use of alternate portfolio assessment to document learning by students with severe disabilities. As we have seen, portfolios can incorporate a variety of information, including the direct measures of students' performance that have been used through the years. If carried out correctly, portfolio assessments should help the teacher to make sound decisions to provide effective instruction and should also document the effect of the instruction. Unfortunately, the use of portfolios as required alternate assessment forms has not been well received by all teachers. Policy makers and researchers may need to find more efficient ways for alternate assessments to be constructed if they are to serve the purpose for which they are intended.

Questions for Reflection

1. Should students with severe disabilities be included in statewide assessments of educational outcomes? Why or why not?
2. By specifying educational outcomes or standards for students with disabilities, are we usurping the significance of IEPs?
3. Should the assessment of students with severe disabilities be more frequent than the assessment of students without disabilities? Why?
4. What are some advantages and disadvantages of quantifying human behavior for the purpose of assessment?
5. Why would a measure of the rate of behavior usually be preferred to event recording?
6. Why can partial- and whole-interval recording and momentary time sampling be considered only estimates of true behavioral occurrences?
7. Would you prefer to use continuous and direct methods of recording student performance or less direct methods that might be reflected in a portfolio? Why?
8. What are some ingredients that could be included in an assessment portfolio for adolescents with severe disabilities?
9. Can you think of alternatives to the portfolio assessments now being used to assess students on the achievement of state standards?

References

Alberto, P. A., & Troutman, A. C. (2002). *Applied behavior analysis for teachers* (6th Ed.). Upper Saddle River, NJ: Merrill/Prentice Hall.

Browder, D. M. (1991). *Assessment of individuals with severe disabilities: An applied behavior approach to life skills assessment* (2nd Ed.). Baltimore: Paul H. Brookes.

Browder, D. M. (2001). *Curriculum and assessment for students with moderate and severe disabilities.* New York: Guilford Press.

Browder, D. M., & Spooner, F. (2003). Understanding the purpose and process of alternate assessment. In D. L. Ryndak & S. Alper, *Curriculum and instruction for students with significant disabilities in inclusive settings* (2nd Ed.). Boston: Allyn and Bacon.

Brown, F., & Snell, M. E. (1993). Measurement, analysis, and evaluation. In M. E. Snell (Ed.), *Instruction of students with severe disabilities* (4th Ed.). Upper Saddle River, NJ: Merrill/Prentice Hall.

Farlow, L. J., & Snell, M. E. (1989). Teacher use of student instructional data to make decisions: Practices in programs for students with moderate to profound disabilities. *Journal of the Association for Persons with Severe Handicaps, 14,* 13–22.

Fuchs, L. S., & Fuchs, D. (1986). Effects of systematic informative evaluation: A meta-analysis. *Exceptional Children, 53,* 199–208.

Grace, C., & Shores, E. F. (1992). *The portfolio and its use: Developmentally appropriate assessment of young children.* Little Rock, AR: Southern Association on Children under Six.

Hanline, M. F., & Fox, L. (1994). The use of assessment portfolios with young children with disabilities. *Assessment in Rehabilitation in Exceptionalities, 1*(1), 40–57.

Hardman, M. L., McDonnell, J., & Welch, M. (1997). Perspectives on the future of IDEA. *Journal of the Association for Persons with Severe Handicaps, 22,* 61–76.

Hunt, P., Goetz, L., & Anderson, J. (1986). The quality of IEP objectives associated with placement on integrated versus segregated school sites. *Journal of the Association for Persons with Severe Handicaps, 11,* 125–130.

Kampfer, S. H., Horvath, L. S., Kleinert, H. L., & Kearns, J. F. (2001). Teachers' perceptions of one state's alternate assessment: Implications for practice and preparation. *Exceptional Children, 67,* 361–374.

Kleinert, H. L., Haig, J., Kearns, J. F., & Kennedy, S. (2000). Alternate assessments: Lessons learned and roads to be taken. *Exceptional Children, 67,* 51–56.

Kleinert, H. L., & Kearns, J. F. (1999). A validation study of the performance indicators and learner outcomes of Kentucky's alternate assessment for students with significant disabilities. *Journal of the Association for Persons with Severe Handicaps, 24,* 100–110.

Kleinert, H. L., Kearns, J. F., & Kennedy, S. (1997). Accountability for *all* students: Kentucky's alternate portfolio assessment for students with moderate and severe cognitive disabilities. *Journal of the Association for Persons with Severe Handicaps, 22,* 88–101.

Kleinert, H. L., Kennedy, S., & Kearns, J. F. (1999). The impact of alternate assessments: A statewide teacher survey. *Journal of Special Education, 33,* 93–102.

Meisels, S. J., & Steele, D. M. (1991). *The early childhood portfolio collection process.* Ann Arbor: Center for Human Growth and Development, University of Michigan.

Meyer, L., Eichinger, J., & Downing, J. (1992). *The Program Quality Indicators (PQI): A checklist of most promising practices in educational programs for students with severe intellectual disabilities.* Syracuse, NY: Syracuse University Division of Special Education and Rehabilitation.

Meyer, L. H., & Janney, R. (1989). User friendly measures of meaningful outcomes: Evaluating behavior interventions. *Journal of the Association for Persons with Severe Handicaps, 14,* 263–270.

Paulson, F. L., Paulson, P. R., & Meyer, C. A. (1991). What makes a portfolio a portfolio? *Educational Leadership, 48,* 60–63.

Sailor, W. (1997). Invited commentary. *Journal of the Association for Persons with Severe Handicaps, 22,* 102–103.

Sailor, W., & Guess, D. (1983). *Severely handicapped students: An instructional design.* Boston: Houghton Mifflin.

Spady, W. C. (1992). It's time to take a close look at outcome-based education. *Communique, 20*(6), 16–18.

Turner, M. D., Baldwin, L., Kleinert, H., & Kearns, J. F. (2000). The relation of a statewide alternate assessment for students with severe disabilities to other measures of instructional effectiveness. *Journal of Special Education, 34*(2), 69–76.

Wesson, C. L., & King, R. P. (1996). Portfolio assessment and special education students. *Teaching Exceptional Children, 28*(2), 44–48.

Westling, D. L., & Floyd, J. (1990). Generalization of community skills: How much training is necessary? *Journal of Special Education, 23,* 386–406.

White, O. (1988). Probing skill use. In N. G. Haring (Ed.), *Generalization for students with severe handicaps: Strategies and solutions.* Seattle: University of Washington Press.

White, O. R., & Haring, N. G. (1980). *Exceptional teaching.* Upper Saddle River, NJ: Merrill/Prentice Hall.

Ysseldyke, J. E., & Olsen, K. (1997). *Putting alternate assessments into practice: What to measure and possible sources of data (NCEO Synthesis Report 28).* Minneapolis: National Center on Educational Outcomes, University of Minnesota.

Ysseldyke, J., & Olsen, K. (1999). Putting alternate assessments into practice: What to measure and possible sources of data. *Exceptional Children, 65,* 175–185.

Ysseldyke, J. E., Olsen, K., & Thurlow, M. (1997). *Issues and considerations in alternate assessments (NCEO Synthesis Report 27).* Minneapolis: National Center on Educational Outcomes, University of Minnesota.

Ysseldyke, J. E., Thurlow, M. L., & Shriner, J. G. (1992). Outcomes are for special educators too. *Teaching Exceptional Children, 25*(1), 36–50.

CHAPTER 10

Creating Inclusive Educational Environments

In this chapter, strategies for organizing and supporting the instruction of students with severe disabilities within inclusive programs are presented. The chapter begins by providing information on practices that are related to successful school inclusion and the facilitation of acceptance of the student with severe disabilities. The second section of the chapter describes procedures that may be used for organizing and managing instruction. The final section addresses scheduling issues and the role of the special educator in the school.

Teaching in Inclusive Environments

An important task for teachers is to organize instruction in a manner so that the needs of every student are met. The IEP provides direction to the teacher on the goals of instruction and the support services that can be provided, but the teacher must determine how, where, and when instruction will occur. In this chapter, guidelines for organizing instruction in inclusive school settings is provided. The chapter begins with an explanation of the importance of inclusive schooling and then provides strategies for developing optimal inclusive environments. The next section of the chapter moves from the big picture of inclusive schooling to the specifics of when and where to provide instruction on individual goals. The chapter ends with a description of the changing role of the special educator in programs that are moving toward inclusive education.

The Importance of School Inclusion

A variety of terms have been used over the last two decades to describe the education of students with disabilities with their nondisabled peers. When students with severe disabilities were primarily educated in separate special schools, *integration* was the term used to describe the successful placement of students with disabilities into regular schools. In situations in which students with disabilities attended the regular school but were primarily instructed in separate special classes, the term *mainstreaming* was used to describe the placement of students with disabilities in general education classes. In both integration and mainstreaming, students with disabilities were viewed as newcomers to the school or class who had to be accommodated.

Since the mid-1980s professionals and parents have worked to achieve education programs that include all students without the presumption that some students do not belong or must be labeled to receive support services. *Inclusion* describes much more than the acceptance of students with disabilities into the mainstream. Inclusive education programs do not focus on the accommodation of students with disabilities into a general education setting, but are focused on the restructuring of schools to accept and provide for the needs of all students. *Inclusive education* is used to describe the development of schools where every student belongs and is supported (Stainback & Stainback, 1990; Villa & Thousand, 2000). In inclusive education, mainstreaming and integration are viewed as intermediary steps to the ultimate goal of teaching all students together. In inclusive programs, specialized instruction and support are provided to any student who is in need of support.

The Individuals with Disabilities Education Act (IDEA) provides for a continuum of services for all students with disabilities that includes segregated school programs that enroll only students with disabilities. Although IDEA includes a presumption that students with disabilities will have access to general education programs and nondisabled peers, students with severe disabilities may be instructed in a variety of educational arrangements. Educational programs for students with severe disabilities may be provided in segregated special schools, in self-contained classrooms located at a regular school with minimal contact with nondisabled students, in self-contained classrooms with informal and formal opportunities for interaction with nondisabled students, or in inclusive schools. There is great variability between and within states. In this text, practices are presented for educating students within inclusive programs because they represent best practice for students with severe disabilities and also apply to more restrictive settings. Teachers who educate students in self-contained classrooms or special schools may find that their role as the primary educator of students with severe disabilities is more explicitly defined, but they may also feel isolated from the support of colleagues in general education.

It is important for the teacher to understand why inclusion is best practice. The teacher who is trained in practices needed to support students with severe disabilities in the inclusive school should be prepared to articulate the benefits of inclusive schooling to school and community members who may be unaware of its importance. The rationale for educating students with disabilities with nondisabled students is based on legal, moral, and educational grounds (Bricker, 1978).

Legal Rationale

The Education for All Handicapped Children Act (P.L. 94-142) of 1975, now known as the Individuals with Disabilities Education Act (P.L. 105-17), was the culminating legislation of a struggle to legally mandate the education of all students with disabilities. Included in the mandate was the provision that students with disabilities should be educated with their nondisabled peers. This provision requires that (20 U.S.C. 1415 [5][B]):

> To the maximum extent appropriate, handicapped children, including children in public or private institutions or other care facilities, are educated with children who are not handicapped, and that special classes, separate schooling, or other removal of handicapped children from general educational environment occurs only when the nature or severity of the handicap is such that education in regular classes with the use of supplementary aids and services cannot be achieved satisfactorily.

The passage of P.L. 94-142 marked a time in history when there was a philosophical shift in the way that society regarded people with disabilities. Prior to this time, students with disabilities were educated in segregated settings if they were educated at all. The prevailing theme in educational and social services was that individuals with disabilities needed to be sheltered and protected from others in society. When the efforts of parents, professionals, and legal advocates pushed issues regarding the inclusion of people with disabilities into public view, the shift in philosophy about the need to include and integrate persons with disabilities followed, closely paralleling the civil rights movement, in which society was forced to confront issues surrounding the inclusion of minorities (McDonnell & Hardman, 1989).

The right to be educated with students who are not disabled is supported by litigation and has been affirmed by several court decisions (*Greer by Greer* v. *Rome City School District, Holland* v. *Sacramento City School District,* and *Oberti* v. *Board of Education of Clementon School District).* The decision made in 1993 by the U.S. Court of Appeals for the Third Circuit in the case of *Rafael Oberti* v. *Board of Education of Clementon, New Jersey,* used guidelines established by both *Holland* v. *Sacramento City School District* and *Greer by Greer* v. *Rome City School District* to uphold the right of students with disabilities to be included in general education classes with students who are not disabled. In the Oberti case, the court found that the school district violated the rights of Rafael Oberti, an 8-year-old with Down syndrome, when it refused to allow him to attend regular classes in his neighborhood school. The district had argued that Rafael's behavioral problems and immaturity made placement in a regular class inappropriate and recommended placement in a segregated, self-contained special class for students classified as multihandicapped. The Obertis contended that Rafael would not have presented such severe behavior problems had he been provided with adequate supplementary aids and services in the regular class as stipulated in the Individuals with Disabilities Education Act.

In the Oberti decision, the Court of Appeals established that the school district must seriously consider including the student with disabilities in the regular class with supplementary aids and services and modifications in the curriculum. In addition, the Oberti decision directs the court to carefully consider the unique benefits that the student with disabilities may obtain from an integrated setting that are not available in a segregated setting. The promise of greater academic progress in a segregated setting may not warrant the exclusion of a student from the regular classroom.

The legal mandate for inclusion was strengthened in the 1997 reauthorization of the Individuals with Disabilities Education Act (P.L. 105-17) with a shift to a presumption that a student would be educated with children without disabilities by requiring that school districts provide an explanation for the extent to which the student with disabilities is not educated in the general education setting. In addition, the amendments include language that places greater emphasis on the participation of students with disabilities in the general education curriculum. IEPs must include a statement about the special education and related services, as well as supplementary aids or services, that the student needs to be involved and progress in the general education curriculum and to be educated with nondisabled students. In addition, the attendance of a general educator in the IEP meeting is now required.

Philosophical Rationale

The legal mandates for inclusion are based on the philosophical or moral value held by our society that the segregation of persons because of a physical attribute is not appropriate. We have made a philosophical commitment to the equal rights of all human beings. The inclusion of students with disabilities into their neighborhood schools is an application of equality. Inclusion is also based on the concept of normalization (Nirje, 1969) for persons with disabilities. Normalization has been described as making available the patterns and conditions of everyday life to people with disabilities. The concept of normalization serves as a criterion for service providers when decisions are made about designing interventions for people with disabilities. The placement of students with disabilities into the school that they would attend if they were not disabled is the application of the concept of normalization.

Educational Rationale

In addition to the philosophical and legal reasons for the inclusion of students with disabilities, there are important educational reasons. Many special educators view an inclusive educational environment as interdependent with a quality program for students with disabilities (Snell, 1988). The regular school environment offers such students a rich setting in which to learn skills in natural contexts. Because students with severe disabilities have slow rates of learning and difficulty retaining and generalizing what is learned, they must be taught personally relevant skills that are useful in a variety of present and future environments. The need for functional skill attainment illuminates the importance of providing instruction in integrated environments, for it is in these types of environments that students with severe disabilities must learn to function (Snell, 1988). The general education setting offers a diverse and stimulating natural context for the instruction of important communication and social interaction skills that cannot be easily replicated in a special education classroom (Downing & Eichinger, 2002). When students with disabilities are in classrooms with only other students who have intensive learning needs, there are many occasions when the student must wait for adult assistance or attention. In the inclusive classroom, the student's nondisabled peers are available for interaction, assistance, and instruction. The educational rationale for inclusion is supported by research that substantiates its benefits in providing for the instructional and social interaction needs of students with severe disabilities. In addition, there is evidence that inclusion has a positive impact on nondisabled students.

Benefits of Inclusion

Instructional Benefits

In addition to the logical arguments for the appropriateness of educating students with severe disabilities in an inclusive environment, there is empirical evidence that confirms the practice as beneficial (Halvorsen & Sailor, 1990; Hunt & Goetz, 1997; McGregor & Vogelsberg, 1998; Ryndak, Morrison, & Sommerstein, 1999). Brinker and Thorpe (1984) investigated the educational impact of integration on the achievement of learners with severe disabilities and found that the rate of interaction with nondisabled students was a significant predictor of the number of IEP objectives achieved by a student with severe disabilities. Integrated settings have also been linked to increased social and communication skills (Gaylord-Ross & Peck, 1985; Strain & Kerr, 1981). Social and communication skills are learned by interacting with other individuals. Students who attend schools where all their peers have communication and social skill deficits do not have as many opportunities for interaction as students who are educated with peers who are not disabled. Frequent interaction opportunities are essential to communication and social skill development. Episodic interactions with nondisabled peers may not offer enough practice for achieving skill mastery (Snell & Eichner, 1989). Some educators may question if students with severe disabilities can receive adequate instructional time when in inclusive classrooms. A study conducted by Helmstetter, Curry, Brennan, & Sampson-Saul (1998) demonstrated that the amount of one-on-one instructional time was equivalent in both settings, with more instructional opportunities evident in the general education classroom. Students in the special education classroom spent a greater amount of time waiting for interaction with an adult or being left alone within an activity (watching television) that did not include instructional opportunities.

The value of full inclusion programs over special class placement with opportunities for integration was supported in research conducted by Hunt, Farron-Davis, Beckstead, Curtis, and Goetz (1994). These researchers compared the program quality and student outcomes of 16 programs in the state of California. Their study found that there was a significant difference in the quality of IEPs written for students with the more severe disabilities who were in general education programs versus special classes. In addition, they found that students with the more severe disabilities were more actively engaged in full inclusion programs. Equally important was their finding that students with more severe disabilities placed in full inclusion programs initiated and engaged in more social interactions than students in special classes.

Social Interaction Benefits

Most important, the general education environment offers an opportunity for students with severe disabilities to build friendships with nondisabled peers. The development of friendships may be seen as an outcome of schooling, although it is not explicitly addressed in the curriculum for general education students. Students with severe disabilities who have difficulties with communication, social, and motor skills may not develop friendships without the provision of supports.

The development of friendships by students with severe disabilities is viewed by many parents and professionals as essential to the quality of life, happiness of the student, and community inclusion (Logan et al., 1998; Stainback & Stainback, 1987; Strully & Strully, 1989). Numerous accounts by parents and professionals describe the advantages of inclusion for the student with severe disabilities in the development of friendships (Forest & Lusthaus, 1989; Peck, Donaldson, & Pezzoli, 1990; Staub, Schwartz, Gallucci, & Peck, 1994; Strully & Strully, 1985). Clearly, opportunities for friendship formation with nondisabled students are restricted when students with severe disabilities are segregated from their nondisabled peers. In a study conducted by Fryxell and Kennedy (1995), students with severe disabilities who were placed in general education classrooms had higher levels of social contact with nondisabled children and had larger friendship networks comprised primarily of nondisabled schoolmates. In a study that compared the experiences of students with severe disabilities who were educated full time in general education classes to students with severe disabilities in self-contained classes, the authors noted important differences in social interaction and social support (Kennedy, Shukla, & Fryxell, 1997). Students in the general education classes experienced more frequent social interactions and more social support during interactions and had larger and more durable friendship networks.

Impact on Nondisabled Peers

When inclusion occurs, students with disabilities are not the only ones to benefit. The most important benefit to nondisabled students and to society in general is that the inclusion of students with disabilities in the school positively influences the attitudes of nondisabled students toward people with disabilities (Fisher, Pumpian, & Sax, 1998; Gaylord-Ross & Peck, 1985; Hughes et al., 2001; Voeltz, 1980; Voeltz, 1982). The current school population will be the next generation of adults (e.g., bus drivers, grocery store clerks, apartment managers, doctors, lawyers, architects, and parents of children with disabilities) who will interact with people with disabilities in the community. Their exposure to individuals with disabilities and subsequent positive attitudes should result in a generation of citizens who understand and accept peers with disabilities (Brown et al., 1983).

In addition to promoting positive attitudes toward people with disabilities, nondisabled students who have had direct and sustained contact with students with severe disabilities have experienced other benefits. Peck et al. (1990) interviewed 21 adolescents who had contact with students with moderate and severe disabilities in their school programs. Using qualitative analysis of the interviews, the researchers found that the high school students perceived the following six benefits from their social relationships with peers who had severe disabilities (Peck et al., 1990):

1. *Self-concept:* growth in their understanding and appreciation of their own personal characteristics.
2. *Social cognition:* growth in their understanding of the feelings and beliefs underlying the behavior of other people.
3. *Reduced fear of human differences:* reduced anxiety and fear of people who look or behave in an unusual fashion and/or increased confidence in their ability to respond appropriately and effectively in interpersonal interactions with such people.
4. *Tolerance of other people:* increased acceptance of the feelings, behavior, and personal limitations of other nondisabled people, including family and friends.
5. *Development of personal principles:* relationships with students with disabilities contribute to reflection and/or action toward the further formation of, clarification of, or commitment to personal moral or ethical principles.
6. *Experiencing relaxed and accepting friendships.* (p. 244)

These outcomes were substantiated by a study of 166 high school students who responded to a survey on the experiences, difficulties, and perception of benefits of the interactions of nondisabled students with students who had severe disabilities (Helmstetter, Peck, & Giangreco, 1994). In addition, the researchers found that positive outcomes for nondisabled students were more likely to occur when students had opportunities for sustained contact and personal interaction with classmates who had severe disabilities. There is also evidence that the positive effects on attitudes of nondisabled students will last over time. Kishi and Meyer (1994) conducted a 6-year follow-up study on the attitudes of high school students who had participated in an elementary school program designed to promote social interactions between typically developing students and students with severe disabilities. The researchers examined attitudes and self-concept and conducted personal interviews with three groups of students. These groups were (1) students who had participated in the structured social interaction program, (2) students who had enrolled in schools where there was a social interaction program but had not participated, and (3) students who had attended schools where they had no contact with students who had severe disabilities. Analysis of the data revealed that students who had participated in the social interaction program and those who attended schools that included students with severe disabilities were more positive and accepting of persons with disabilities than students in the no-exposure group.

It is also important to note that inclusion has not been shown to be harmful to the learning outcomes of nondisabled students. An investigation by Hollowood, Salisbury, Rainforth, and Palombaro (1994) examined the time allocated for instruction and the engaged time of students in elementary classrooms where a student with severe disabilities was included and in classrooms that did not include a student with severe disabilities. They found that there was no difference in the time allocated for instruction and the level of engagement of students between the classrooms. Sharpe, York, and Knight (1994) examined the academic performance and behavior of elementary students without disabilities who were members of a class that included a child with severe disabilities and compared these outcomes with students in classes that did not include a student with severe disabilities. The results of their study indicated that there were no differences in academic achievement and classroom behavior as measured by achievement tests and grades on report cards.

Although there is a wealth of evidence that inclusive educational programs are desirable, change from segregated special programs to a more progressive model of instruction has not occurred as rapidly as many advocates, parents, and professionals would like. It is important to remember that school systems are large bureaucracies that do not respond quickly to innovation and reform. The development of an inclusive school is not simply the adoption of a new curricular approach; it involves major school restructuring that goes far beyond meeting the needs of students with disabilities. Salisbury (1991) describes the inclusive elementary school as "a value that is manifested in the way we plan, promote, and conceptualize the education and development of young children" (p. 147).

Despite the slow and uneven pace with which some school districts are moving to inclusive models of education, there is little question among professionals and researchers that progress toward the widespread adoption of inclusive schooling will continue to occur. Schools across the country are concerned with the ability of public schools to meet the needs of a diverse at-risk school population. The inclusive schooling movement should be viewed as a school restructuring innovation that can meet the needs of all students, not just students with disabilities (Bauer & Brown, 2001; Baumgart & Giangreco, 1996; Villa & Thousand, 2000). In the following section, the inclusive education model is described, and practices that should be implemented for successful inclusion are presented.

The Inclusive Education Model

The term *full inclusion* has been used to describe educational programs for which a student's primary placement is in general education. This means that all students report to a regular homeroom or have a primary placement in a grade-level classroom. The schedule of classes for the remainder of the day depends on the student's IEP and is developed by the IEP team. The principle of natural proportion—the distribution of individuals with disabilities in a school that reflects the natural diversity in the community—is adhered to by the enrollment of students with severe disabilities in individual schools and in involvement with the regular class (York, Vandercook, MacDonald, & Wolff, 1989). Full inclusion programs are based on the philosophy that every student is a genuine member of the school community and that the school community has a responsibility to meet all students' needs (Williams, Villa, Thousand, & Fox, 1989). General educators work in partnership with special educators in providing for the individual needs of students with disabilities.

Some advocates of inclusive schooling wish to eliminate the use of the term full inclusion because it suggests that inclusion is an entity that is measurable and that can occur partially or fully. They believe that if inclusive programs truly support every student's individual needs, a range of supports will be provided that may involve full-time general education classroom placement or instruction in the community or other settings. In this chapter, inclusive schooling is defined as providing the supports necessary to promote the learning of every student in the neighborhood or home-zone school without the use of separate special education classrooms.

The partnership of general and special educators is essential to the success of the inclusion model (Halvorsen & Neary, 2001; Stainback & Stainback, 1990; Villa & Thousand, 2000). The development of an IEP for a child in an inclusion program requires the collaboration of a variety of people as a team (Giangreco, 1996; Halvorsen & Neary, 2001; Janney & Snell, 2000; Vandercook & York, 1990).

This team is not composed of only the classroom teacher and the student's parents, but also may include the student, important family members, a support teacher with training in instructional adaptations and in meeting the needs of students with disabilities (i.e., a special educator), an administrator or a designee, support personnel from related services, and classmates of the student.

The mission of the team is to identify, evaluate, and implement the supports and adaptations needed by the student with disabilities for meaningful inclusion in the school community. Stainback and Stainback (1989) suggest that a person be designated as a *support facilitator* to enhance the success of inclusion programs. The support facilitator would most likely be a trained special educator whose role is to promote natural networks of support for the student with disabilities (particularly friendships), locate needed instructional resources (curricula, assessments, equipment, consultants), and provide direct help as a team teacher.

The primary placement of students with severe disabilities in general education classes is an idea that has been received with controversy (Brown et al., 1989). People who have resisted this model are concerned that the placement of students with severe disabilities full time in general education is too radical a model and that general educators will receive it with resistance, that students with severe disabilities will not be provided with the appropriate supports and services that they need in a regular class, that special education is better configured in ratio and technology to meet the needs of these students, and that the curricula provided to students in general education is often inappropriate for students with disabilities (Brown et al., 1989). Proponents of full inclusion argue that it is better for a student to belong in a regular class and leave for some periods than to be an outsider who comes in, that adjustments can and should be made in classroom ratio and the resources needed to support the student with disabilities, and that general education class placement does not preclude instruction in more relevant environments and activities when necessary (Brown et al., 1989).

The decision about classroom placement is made by the student's educational or IEP team. These individuals are given the responsibility to discuss the student's instructional needs and to develop an instructional plan that will promote the achievement of identified instructional goals. In many communities, placement decisions are shaped in part by the philosophy of the school program or district and their history in educating students with severe disabilities. For example, in a community in Vermont, all students with severe disabilities may be educated in general education. In other communities, a range of placement options (e.g., resource support, self-contained special classes) may be considered by the IEP team. While it is a reality that IEP teams approach placement decisions with different orientations based on community practices, IDEA stipulates that "the removal of children with disabilities from the general educational environment occurs only when the nature or severity of the disability is such that education in regular classes with the use of supplementary aids and services cannot be achieved satisfactorily" (IDEA, 1997).

Facilitating School Acceptance: Structures for Successful Inclusion

An important challenge to implementing an inclusive educational program is ensuring school acceptance of students with disabilities. Strategies must be used to promote an environment of acceptance and inclusion. The school district, individual schools, and school personnel must prepare for and work together to achieve this goal (Halvorsen & Neary, 2001). It is also necessary to use strategies to facilitate peer interactions. Nondisabled students who have been denied exposure to people with disabilities may not know how to interact with their peers with disabilities or may enter into interactions with fears and biases that hinder the development of personal relationships.

In successful inclusion programs, inclusion is viewed as a schoolwide effort, not just another specialized program of exceptional student education. Strategies that have been used to foster school inclusion are listed in Figure 10–1 and are introduced in the next section. It is important to note that every school community is unique and that strategies that work in some settings may not be applicable to others.

Classroom Placement

For inclusion programs to be successful, the school must accept students with disabilities as members of the school community. Students with disabilities should be placed in a grade-level classroom or homeroom with nondisabled peers. When students are placed in a separate classroom, a message may be transmitted to the school community that students with severe disabilities don't really belong in the regular classroom, although they may be invited to join their nondisabled peers by special arrangements. A classroom that is used to instruct students with severe

Figure 10–1 School Inclusion Strategies

Place students with disabilities in general education homerooms and classrooms.

Specialized instruction should occur in environments that are also used by nondisabled peers.

Provide for initial and ongoing ability awareness activities.

Provide information to everyone in the school community about the importance of inclusion.

Model positive and respectful interactions with students with disabilities.

Use curriculum infusion to increase student and teacher knowledge about supporting students with disabilities.

Develop collaborative teams to support school inclusion and individual student support.

Involve the parents of all students in supporting inclusion.

Develop peer tutoring, special friends, and peer networks to support the inclusion of students with disabilities.

Facilitate the interactions and friendship development of students with disabilities and their nondisabled peers.

disabilities separately from a grade-level class should not be identified as a special class; rather, it may be a designated room that is used as a resource for students who have a variety of needs, for example, students in a Title 1 program or those who need individualized tutoring (Snell, Lowman, & Canady, 1996). If the classroom serves a variety of students, students with severe disabilities would not ever be excluded from what was provided to the general school population.

Awareness Training

In successful inclusive schools, the entire school population is aware of the need to support students with disabilities. Information about students with disabilities can be presented to nondisabled students through awareness training (Halvorsen & Neary, 2001; Sailor et al., 1989). Some awareness activities that have been used are instructional puppet shows, movies about persons with disabilities, reading books about disabilities, disability simulation exercises, and workshops in classrooms. When presenting awareness training activities, it is important to conduct them in ways that promote positive images of persons with disabilities. The purpose of the awareness training is not to generate sympathy or charitable feelings toward the student with disabilities, but to encourage an understanding of their capabilities and needs (accessibility, adaptations, assistance). Teachers should carefully review films, movies, books, and awareness kits to make sure that the language used is appropriate and that a desirable image of persons with disabilities is portrayed.

Awareness training should become part of the school's effort to provide a multicultural, antibias curriculum—an approach to instruction that directly addresses issues of stereotyping, bias, and discrimination (Sapon-Shevin, 1996). In such a curriculum students are taught to understand and value diverse cultures and differences and to recognize and combat racism, sexism, and handicapism. Students do not learn these concepts in an isolated fashion with a thematic or unit focus on a particular cultural group or difference; rather, they are provided with information on diversity in an integrated curriculum. Teachers who embrace a multicultural, antibias approach seek to provide realistic images of people from diverse backgrounds in relevant, everyday situations. This approach provides an awareness of disability by including wall displays and books that picture persons with disabilities engaging in everyday activities, instructional materials such as books and toys (dolls, play props) that include persons with disabilities, and instructional activities that help students to understand the concepts of disability, accessibility, and handicapism.

Awareness training may be one component of developing an inclusive school, but it should not represent the only effort (Fritz, 1990). Awareness activities should be ongoing and conducted in conjunction with all the other strategies listed in Figure 10–1. Awareness should not be encouraged for students only; it will also be necessary for the special educator or designated professional involved in the inclusion effort to educate general educators and the parents of students in the school about inclusion and students with severe disabilities. For many general educators, inclusion is a new idea that may be initially met with apprehension.

Professionals with knowledge of inclusion can provide in-service training to colleagues, lead faculty discussions on the issues related to inclusion, disseminate relevant literature about inclusion from special education resources and journals and magazines that are familiar to general educators (e.g., *Young Children, Elementary School Journal, Phi Delta Kappan*), and provide presentations to the parent–teacher organization. In building an awareness of the importance of inclusion, educators have found that showing videos depicting successful inclusion efforts or providing presentations from teachers and families of successful inclusion stories can be beneficial.

Teacher Modeling

In addition to formal presentations on the importance and implementation of inclusion, the special educator should provide modeling of appropriate interactions with students who are disabled. The attitude of the special educator, the person who is presumed to be the expert, influences the way that others will view these students. If the special educator appears to be protective of the students or apologetic for their presence, others in the school will react accordingly. The teacher should emphasize the positive attributes of students with disabilities, model social interactions with them, and use appropriate and normalizing language when talking about them. For example, if the special educator refers to them as the "handicapped students" or speaks to them using the tone of voice and phrasing used with young children, others in the school will think that students with disabilities should be treated in a protective or condescending manner.

The special educator will be in a highly visible position in an inclusive school program as she works within multiple general education classrooms and as a collaborative team member with a diverse group of professionals. It is important that other teachers and personnel within the school view the special educator in a positive manner. Special educators who are highly regarded by the other teachers and school personnel often find greater support for their efforts to include students with disabilities. Showing appreciation of the efforts of others (through notes, comments, newsletter stories) is one mechanism that may foster positive impressions. Special educators should also integrate themselves in the school community by becoming active in school committees or the parent–teacher organization or by becoming a faculty sponsor of student groups and clubs.

Collaborative Teaming

The education of students and staff about the importance of inclusion is only the beginning for success. Awareness and curriculum infusion activities must be accompanied by some type of formal mechanism to provide ongoing support and problem solving as students with disabilities are integrated into the school. One method for providing such support is the use of collaborative teams (Fox & Williams, 1991; Giangreco, 1996; Stainback & Stainback, 1990; Thousand & Villa, 1990). In collaborative teaming, team members work together as equal partners to achieve a common goal. The team assists with school inclusion by developing solutions to problems and challenges and strategies to support the school goal of inclusion.

In schools where inclusion is a relatively new concept, a school planning team should be formed to develop a plan to improve the educational program for meeting the diverse needs of all students (Fox & Williams, 1991; Halvorsen & Neary, 2001; Schaffner & Buswell, 1996). Members of the community, instructional personnel, administrators, and families should be involved in the team, whose tasks may include developing a shared vision and mission statement for inclusive schooling, assessing school practices and identifying areas for improvement, and developing action plans that provide for the changes needed to promote the inclusion and appropriate instruction of all students in the school.

Collaborative Student Support Teams

In addition to the school planning team, each student with disabilities should be supported by a collaborative team whose task is to ensure that an appropriate and effective instructional program is provided to the student (Fox & Williams, 1991; Giangreco, 1996; Villa & Thousand, 2000). The collaborative student support team is composed of the special educator, related service providers, general educators, the family, and other individuals who provide essential supports to the student with disabilities. The tasks of the collaborative team are to assess and develop the supports needed by the student with severe disabilities by determining the skills that should be taught to the student; designing accommodations to meet the student's individual needs, including access to the general education curriculum; monitoring the student's progress; and designing supports to assist the student with transitions.

Fox and Williams (1991) recommend that the collaborative team meet each week for an hour, using a structured agenda with time limits for each topic discussion to facilitate an efficient teaming process. Because it is likely that the special educator or inclusion facilitator will initiate the collaborative teaming process, it is important for the special educator to remember that the team members must share equal roles in the planning process. This activity should not be solely led by the special educator. The goal is for all team members to actively participate in the support of students with intensive needs.

Community and Family Involvement

A school inclusion program will not work well without community support and involvement. The parents of all students in the school must be aware of the goals of inclusive schooling and may also help to implement the integration program. In some schools, parents have conducted disability awareness activities, shared their views of inclusion with students, and served as volunteers with inclusion activities. There may be initial resistance or anxiety in the community when inclusion is first discussed, so it is important to give community members an opportunity to express their fears and for professionals to provide reassurance. In time, most families will see the positive aspects of the program.

Peer Programs

Because the physical placement of students with disabilities in regular schools and classrooms may not be enough to promote social interaction between nondisabled students and their peers with disabilities, there must also be an effort to promote such interaction. The importance of promoting true class membership for students with severe disabilities is an area of concern for professionals and researchers (Evans, Salisbury, Palombaro, Berryman, & Hollowood, 1992; Farley, 1996; Hunt, Alwell, Farron-Davis, & Goetz, 1996; Schnorr, 1997). Peer tutoring and peer interaction are two commonly identified programs that have been successfully used by many schools to promote social interaction between students with severe disabilities and their schoolmates. Peer tutors are students who volunteer to assist other students in achieving their instructional goals; in peer interaction programs, volunteers are recruited to interact with students who are disabled in fun and leisure activities. These programs may be useful in offering a structured vehicle for encouraging initial social interactions, although the ultimate goal is for the development of natural supports and true friendships. Strategies for fostering peer interactions are discussed in detail in the following section.

Making Inclusion Work: Essential Supports

Providing a quality, inclusive educational program to students with severe disabilities involves time, careful planning, and very difficult work. Teachers in one study identified training, the need for assistance from the collaborative team, and assistance (i.e., paraprofessional support) within the classroom as critical to successful inclusion (Werts, Wolery, Snyder, & Caldwell, 1996). In this section, information is provided on three areas that are critical to the success of inclusive education: facilitating peer acceptance, collaborative teaming, and meaningful instructional arrangements.

Facilitating Peer Acceptance

As students with severe disabilities have been provided with opportunities to become members of a classroom community, teachers have gained important knowledge and experience in fostering peer interactions. In a study conducted by Janney and Snell (1996), general education teachers were observed to determine the strategies that they employed to promote peer interaction. Teachers were observed encouraging nondisabled students to assist their peers with disabilities, but also establishing restrictions on when helping was appropriate. For example, a peer may be encouraged to help a student during free time or transitions, while being prohibited from providing help during a test or while a new lesson is being introduced. Teachers also explicitly provided instructions on how to help students. Teachers were observed instructing peers on ways to support a child with physical disabilities without hindering the child's independent movement. Teachers were also observed promoting the membership of the student with severe disabilities as "just another student" and were observed instructing students to interact with the student with disabilities in an age-appropriate manner. Teachers were also sensitive to the need for students to have time and opportunity to interact without adult interference. The teachers were observed helping to initiate a social interaction and then fading out of the situation.

These types of strategies were also evident in a study conducted by Salisbury, Gallucci, Palombaro, and Peck (1995), who interviewed and observed elementary general education teachers who included students with moderate and severe disabilities full time in their class. They found that these teachers used five themes or strategies to facilitate social interactions. The first strategy included actively facilitating social interaction through the use of cooperative groupings within instruction, using collaborative problem solving to work together to solve interpersonal issues, peer tutoring, and structuring time and opportunities for the students to mingle or "connect." A second theme was to "turn it over to the kids" by involving the students in the decision making about how to promote a peer's inclusion in the classroom. The third theme of strategies included the efforts of teachers to build a sense of community in the classroom where acceptance and concern for all students were promoted. The fourth theme included the explicit efforts of the teacher to model acceptance of the student with disabilities. For example, teachers described modeling appropriate expectations and interactions including being on the student's eye level and waiting for a response. Finally, teachers described the many ways that their school was structured (collaborative teaming, multiage classrooms) that supported their efforts to promote inclusion.

The studies described above offer a view of how some general education teachers have fostered peer interactions. Strategies for facilitating peer interaction in inclusion settings that have appeared in the literature are listed in Figure 10–2 and discussed next.

Figure 10–2 Strategies for Facilitating Peer Interaction

Environmental Arrangement
Teacher Mediation
Peer-Mediated Interactions
Peer Tutoring
Special Friends
Peer Support Networks

Environmental Arrangement

A first step to promoting interactions between the two groups of students is to examine the environment for interaction opportunities and to create opportunities through environmental arrangement. Those times in the school day when students have opportunities to be social (e.g., recess, lunchroom, gym, music class, media center) should be used to facilitate interactions. The teacher also may want to create activities that promote joint participation; for example, a teacher may help students to develop a collaborative enterprise (such as selling popsicles or school supplies) that offers opportunities for peer interaction and a shared goal. Teachers can make use of adapted materials, toys, and games such as computers with electromechanical switches; video games, remote control, or electromechanical switch toys; or race car sets that can be operated by the student with disabilities and are also attractive to nondisabled students. Providing the student with disabilities with an interesting toy or activity (e.g., bubbles and giant bubble wand, kite, classroom pet) when on the playground is an effective way to encourage other students to approach the student with disabilities.

Teacher Mediation

When students approach peers with disabilities, the teacher can use facilitation procedures to assist with the interaction. These procedures include modeling social interactions, prompting peers to initiate and interact with the student with disabilities, prompting the students with disabilities to initiate and maintain interactions with their peers, and providing reinforcement to both sets of students for appropriate social interaction. These procedures may be used when opportunities for interactions occur, or the teacher may want to use peer tutoring or Special Friends programs to schedule interaction time.

Peer-Mediated Interventions

Many researchers have been successful at facilitating social interaction by providing nondisabled students with prompts and reinforcement to interact with their peers with disabilities (Hendrickson, Strain, Tremblay, & Shores, 1982; Kamps et al., 2002; Kohler & Fowler, 1985; Lancioni, 1982). This is typically done by providing the peer with a brief training program in social interaction prompting techniques and teaching the student with disabilities to respond and initiate back to the nondisabled peer so that true social reciprocity results (Odom & Strain, 1986). Procedures that have been used in peer mediation that may be successful include teaching peers to reciprocate to the initiations of students with disabilities (Odom & Strain, 1986), training peer mentors in methods to adapt play activities for the students with disabilities (Knapczyx, 1989), and providing training to peers in ways to use prompts to encourage untrained peers to interact with the target student (Sasso, Hughes, Swanson, & Novak, 1987).

Peer Tutoring

Peer tutoring programs involve the recruitment of nondisabled students to instruct or tutor students with severe disabilities. Most peer tutoring programs (Donder & Nietupski, 1981; Kohl, Moses, & Stettner-Eaton, 1983; Kohl & Stettner-Eaton, 1985; Lancioni, 1982; Staub, Spaulding, Peck, Gallucci, & Schwartz, 1996) have focused on training nondisabled students as instructors of the students with disabilities.

Peer tutors have been used to teach a variety of skills, including playing games, performing classroom jobs, preparing a snack, cooking, using cafeteria skills, and operating a tape player or record player. It is important for peer tutors to be trained by the teacher on how to work with the student with disabilities and to be provided with information on how to appropriately prompt and reinforce their tutees. Training for peer tutors usually includes information presented prior to the tutoring, modeling and instruction by the teacher with the student and peer tutor, and feedback to the tutor on his performance (Sailor et al., 1989). Peers have also been used as student aides to assist students with severe disabilities to participate in their general education junior high school classroom (Staub et al., 1996). The responsibilities of the student aides were to fulfill the roles of monitoring the behavior, providing help, being a friend, and teaching the student with severe disabilities.

Some researchers have expressed concern that peer tutor relationships are hierarchical in nature and may inhibit true friendship formation (Meyer & Putnam, 1987; Voeltz, 1980; Voeltz, 1982). Others (Sailor et al., 1989) contend that peer tutor and Special Friends programs are very similar and that friendships have evolved from relationships that began as tutorials. Haring, Breen, Pitts-Conway, Lee, and Gaylord-Ross (1987) used a pretest–posttest experimental design to examine the effects of peer tutoring and peer buddy (i.e., special friend) participation on the attitudes and social exchanges of the nondisabled peer toward persons with disabilities. They found that there were no significant differences in attitude or interaction styles for the two groups except that the nondisabled students who served as peer buddies were more likely to initiate a social interaction toward an unfamiliar peer with autism.

Peer Interaction Programs

Voeltz (1984) described a peer interaction program, Special Friends, in which students with disabilities and nondisabled students were encouraged to develop "positive, mutually rewarding relationships . . . that will generalize to nonschool environments and maintain over time" (p. 176) and that will develop the social competence of the child with disabilities.

The first activity of the Special Friends program was a short slide and tape presentation that was about the Special Friends program and the students with disabilities. The slide show was presented to all the classes in the school, and students were told that they could volunteer for the Special Friends program in about a week. The volunteers then attended eight 15- to 30-minute weekly group sessions. Examples of session titles were "What Is a Disability?", "How Do We Communicate?", and "How Can We Play Together?" Each Special Friend volunteer spent free-time periods and recess with a selected peer with disabilities. The interactions of the Special Friend were structured by the special educator to promote social peer exchange.

A follow-up study was conducted on the nondisabled students who participated in the Special Friends program to detect if differences would be evident when these students were compared to students who did not volunteer as a special friend or to students who had had no contact with students with severe disabilities in their schooling. Kishi and Meyer (1994) found that students who had participated in the program had more accepting attitudes than students who had no contact with peers with severe disabilities. Unfortunately, the maintenance of friendships between the nondisabled student and the student with disabilities did not occur over time. This may be due, in part, to the administrative decision to cluster the secondary students with severe disabilities at a high school that was different from the school that their elementary peers attended. The researchers also found that students remembered their interactions with their peers with disabilities as helping and instructional, despite the explicit goal in the design of the program to avoid fostering hierarchical relationships. Kishi and Meyer (1994) raised important questions about the use of formal peer programs and the need to develop strategies to facilitate the development of interactions that are "egalitarian, mutually beneficial, and socially normalized." They caution about the use of peer interaction programs that may promote caregiving interactions and interfere with the development of reciprocal peer relationships.

A study conducted by Cole, Meyer, Vandercook, and McQuarter (1986) lent support to the idea that the teacher should be nonintrusive in facilitating peer relationships. The researchers compared two approaches to peer interaction. One group of nondisabled peers received social instruction; the other received friendly comments as they interacted with a student with severe disabilities. The nondisabled peers in the social instruction group were prompted to engage in cooperative play; in the friendly comments group, peers were rewarded for attendance, encouraged to practice the game, or received friendly comments about miscellaneous unrelated topics. Initially, the social instruction group showed higher levels of social interaction as measured by a revised version of the Social Interaction Observation System (Voeltz, Kishi, & Brennan, 1981), but by the middle of the study these differences disappeared, and by the end of the study the friendly comments group was more interactive. The authors postulate that high rates of teacher intervention may lead to habituation of the cooperative play behavior of peers.

Peer interaction programs have also been successfully implemented within the complex environment of the high school. Hughes et al. (1999) describe their efforts to recruit high school peers to support the inclusion of their peers with disabilities. The peers were recruited through posters and flyers distributed throughout the school. Students who were most likely to volunteer were students who had a greater history of contact with persons who have disabilities (e.g., family member with a disability, family friend with disability, class included peer with disability) (Carter, Hughes, Copeland, & Breen, 2001). Volunteers were provided with an orientation session that included disability awareness, program expectations, communication strategies, instruction on how to promote social interactions, and strategies for preventing and responding to inappropriate behavior. In addition, the peer buddies were provided with a peer buddy manual that gave information on disabilities and the peer buddy program. Students who volunteered as peer buddies assisted their peers with disabilities within instructional activities and during noninstructional times. Peers who participated reported that they were comfortable with their dual roles as helpers and friends and reported changes in their personal growth and attitudes toward individuals with disabilities (Hughes et al., 2001).

Both peer tutor and peer interaction programs have proved to be successful strategies for promoting peer social relationships. Teachers should note that these programs were developed in the era of integration programs (i.e., when students with severe disabilities were clustered in self-contained special classrooms) and were initially used to bring together two student populations that had very limited exposure to each other. Schools in the present decade may wish to implement peer buddy programs to provide systematic support to students with disabilities and may consider implementing an expanded program to ensure that any student with a special need or concern may be provided with peer assistance. General guidelines for implementing these programs are presented in Figure 10–3.

Peer Support Networks

In some programs, educators collaborate with student peers in designing ways to support the student with disabilities in the regular school (Ford & Davern, 1989; Forest & Lusthaus, 1989; Stainback & Stainback, 1990; Vandercook & York, 1990). This procedure, building peer networks, has been a key component of inclusion programs. The peer network is a group of students who are actively involved in encouraging, supporting, and helping the student with disabilities to become a member of the school community.

The peer support network is classroom based and is comprised of volunteers who have a genuine interest in supporting the student with disabilities. Forest and Lusthaus (1989) described the Circle of Friends process that they have used to establish peer networks. A facilitator visits the classroom before a student is integrated and talks to the other students about the arrival of the student with disabilities and the apprehensions that some adults have about the experience. She elicits from the students that some of the fears may be that the student won't be treated well or have friends. The facilitator then draws four concentric circles on the chalkboard with a stick figure in the center, gives each student a worksheet with the circles, and asks the students to fill in the circles with the people who are in their lives, using the first circle for people closest to them, the second circle for friends, and so forth. The facilitator completes the circle on the chalkboard, shares it with the group, and asks the students to share their circles. Then she draws the circles and describes a fictional person who has only a mother in the first circle and then service workers (doctor, teacher, therapist) in the last. The facilitator asks the students how that person must feel and then uses this example to discuss the student who is arriving and how the student will need a network of people to welcome him to the classroom. She explains that she hopes that friendships will evolve from the network, but she says that for the moment the network should concentrate on ways to welcome the new student.

The peer support network can be used to brainstorm ways to include students with disabilities in the general education curriculum and extracurricular activities.

Figure 10–3 Guidelines for Implementing Peer Tutor/Special Friends Programs

1. Obtain permission from school administrator.
2. Give program presentation to faculty members.
3. Provide faculty and parents with written materials describing the program.
4. Develop participation criteria with teachers who wish to be involved.
5. Make presentations in individual classrooms to recruit students.
6. Send permission forms and parent letter home with students wishing to participate.
7. Develop schedules with students and classroom teachers. You may wish to assign students to support students with severe disabilities in general education classes, individualized instruction, community-based instruction, lunchtime, or playground activities.
8. Meet individually with Peer Tutor/Special Friend to discuss role in the classroom, expectations desired, etc. Develop a contract with student if appropriate.
9. Allow student several warm-up visits to observe and meet students with disabilities.
10. Meet with Peer Tutor/Special Friend to discuss students and activities with which he or she would like to assist.
11. Train Peer Tutor/Special Friend in procedures he or she should use, review student's likes and dislikes, communication system, when to ask for assistance, and how to assist physically; model interactions with the student with disabilities for the Special Friend/Peer Tutor.
12. Provide ongoing feedback to the Special Friend/Peer Tutor and his or her classroom teacher.
13. Promote the activities of the program in the school.

Because peers are more knowledgeable about what is current fashion or is "in," they can be a good resource for helping the student with disabilities to fit in socially with peers. In some programs, the peer support network works formally with other team members in the development of instructional goals and activities.

Collaborative Teaming

The Role of the Collaborative Team

The goal of the collaborative student support team is to design and implement an educational program in which individual students achieve their educational goals (Halvorsen & Neary, 2001; Rainforth, York, & MacDonald, 1992). The student support team should be composed of people who are responsible for meeting the daily instructional needs of the student with severe disabilities. Thus, membership on the team may range from the special educator teaming with related service personnel to the special educator in the role of inclusion facilitator teaming with a variety of general educators and related service providers. The issues that the student support team addresses may include designing individual curriculum adaptations, designing instructional plans, assessing a student's communicative strengths and needs, developing a behavior support plan, developing strategies to promote the development of peer relationships, developing an instructional schedule that ensures appropriate adult support within different school environments and activities, and monitoring the progress of the student.

The special educator or inclusion facilitator is often given the role of team coordinator. It is essential that team meetings be structured so that the process is efficient and rewarding to all team members. A first step in developing the team is to engage in a discussion about the purpose of the team and to develop a shared vision about the desired outcomes of the teaming effort (Giangreco, 1996; Rainforth et al., 1992). The group should also decide on a decision-making process, determine the process that will be used for problem solving (e.g., see Chapter 3), decide on a process for developing the meeting agenda, and develop a commitment to a regularly scheduled meeting time. Other strategies that facilitate an efficient teaming process include beginning and ending meetings on time, taking minutes at the meeting so that decisions on next actions and the persons responsible are recorded, limiting meeting times to 30 to 60 minutes, and distributing an agenda to team members prior to a meeting.

Providing Supports in General Education

One critical task of the student support team is to design instructional arrangements and supports for students in the general education classroom to meet the students' instructional needs and to ensure access to the general education curriculum (Agran, Alper, & Wehmeyer, 2002). The support of the collaborative team is essential in determining the ideal arrangement for the student, her peers, and the teacher. Inclusion does not mean the instruction of the student with disabilities in a one-to-one situation on content that is different from what is taught to nondisabled students. The goal for instruction should be the inclusion of the student with disabilities in the general education curriculum (Wehmeyer, Lattin, & Agran, 2001). The collaborative team should begin by first considering the general education curriculum in concert with the student's unique learning needs. For some students, the use of assistive technology will ensure the ability of the student to participate in the general education curriculum without further accommodations. However, most students with severe disabilities will need curricular modifications to ensure access and participation.

The team must decide how the student will access the general education curriculum. For students with severe disabilities, some or all of the following options may be applicable (Wehmeyer et al., 2001):

Curriculum adaptations. The student can participate in the general education curriculum, but may need modifications in the presentation of instruction, expected performance, response modes, changes in materials, and the like.

Curriculum augmentation. The student needs additional instruction or strategies to participate in the curriculum.

Curriculum alterations. The student needs additional content that is not found in the general education curriculum. Students with severe disabilities may need instruction in basic social, communication, daily living, and motor skills that are not found in the general education curriculum.

Developing Curriculum Modifications

The development of curriculum modifications is an important topic for the student support team. Often it takes the collective creativity of a group that is committed to supporting an individual student to develop meaningful strategies that result in active student engagement in the curriculum. The process of discussing and designing curriculum modifications together provides all team members with a deeper understanding of the student's abilities and instructional needs and the process used to think about the support of the student within the general education curriculum. Once the team has tackled a few of the more difficult situations requiring curriculum modifications, individual team members should be more skilled at developing strategies on their own.

A curriculum adaptation or modification is any change or adjustment in the environment, instruction, or materials that enhances the performance of a student within an instructional activity (Udvari-Solner, 1994). Curriculum adaptations are aimed at promoting the participation of the student with severe disabilities within the general education classroom and minimizing the differences between the student with disabilities and his peers. When considering curriculum adaptations, the collaborative team will need to consider the following:

1. Information on the target student's abilities, strengths, interests, learning modalities, and support needs.
2. The teaching format, instructional arrangements, instructional environment, curriculum scope and sequence, instructional materials, instructional pacing, student performance modes, and outcomes that are used in the general education classroom or within the instructional activity that is being considered.
3. The performance and support needs of the student within the instructional context determined through direct observation.

Once information is gathered on the nature of the instructional activity and the challenges that are presented for the student with disabilities, the team may brainstorm possible modifications. The collaborative team may consider modifications in the way that the instruction is delivered, the type or amount of work, or the student response mode. These modifications could include simplifying work, providing less work, providing instruction through a different modality, and using hands-on materials or activities. In addition, the expected student response may be changed by expecting less, expecting a less sophisticated response, or responding in a different modality. In addition, the team may want to consider changes in who provides instruction, where instruction occurs, and the pace of instruction or expectations for duration of engagement. Modifications should be selected

Figure 10–4 Considerations for Curriculum Adaptations

1. *Change the Instructional Grouping or Arrangement*—Use different instructional groupings to promote the student's participation. Groupings to consider include teacher-directed small groups, cooperative learning groups, student-directed small groups, peer tutors, one-to-one instruction, and independent seat work.
2. *Change the Teaching Format*—Use different teaching techniques. Techniques may include lecture and demonstration, whole class discussion, games, role-playing or simulations, activity-based lessons, and experiential lessons.
3. *Change the Environmental Conditions*—Change the physical conditions of the learning environment to meet the physical or sensory needs of the student.
4. *Change the Curricular Goals or Learning Outcomes*—Individualize the learning objectives or outcomes expected within the context of the instructional activity to meet the ability level of an individual student.
5. *Change the Instructional Materials*—Use materials that may be easy to manipulate or understand or that meet the abilities and preferences of the student with disabilities.
6. *Change the Level or Type of Personal Assistance*—Provide higher level of assistance, attention, guidance, instructional prompts, or the support of a peer.
7. *Create an Alternative Activity*—Provide an alternative activity that is related to the curricular content, is meaningful for all of the students involved, and requires limited adult supervision. Alternative activities should only be created when other adaptations are not possible.

Source: Adapted from *Curricular Adaptations: Accommodating the Instructional Needs of Diverse Learners in the Context of General Education* (monograph), by A. Udvari-Solnar, 1992, Kansas State Board of Education—Services for Children and Youth with Deaf–Blindness Project.

that ensure active learning and student success and that minimize the differences between the student with disabilities and her peers. Figure 10–4 lists areas to consider when developing curriculum modifications, and Figure 10–5 provides a list of sample curriculum modifications that may be considered by the team.

The collaborative team needs to determine what general modifications are desired for the student in all activities in a particular class or modifications that have applicability for all settings. For example, a student may need to have the response mode changed to drawing or pointing to a picture, rather than verbally communicating a comprehension response. Or another student may need to have instructions provided on an audiotape or by a peer who can simplify the lesson into three action steps. These types of modifications have general utility for a variety of activities and are developed by the collaborative team based on their knowledge of the student, the student's strengths and interests, and the demands of the classroom. As these plans are developed, it is helpful to put them in writing so that all members of the team can access a document that summarizes the strategies that should be used. In Figure 10–6 an example of the general modifications plan for Kyla is provided.

In addition to general modifications or plans for curriculum adaptations, the collaborative team may need to address curriculum modifications as new units or activities are introduced in the general education curriculum. The special educator should anticipate the need to make modifications and accommodations for the student with severe disabilities and provide leadership in ensuring that ongoing planning occurs. Figure 10–7 provides the modifications for Kyla within a social studies unit.

Scheduling Support Personnel

In inclusive education programs, the role of the special educator is expanded to include more consultation and collaborative activity. The expansion of the special educator's role, or rather the transformation of the role of the special educator to a support facilitator, means that the role of directly instructing the student with severe disabilities becomes the responsibility of other instructional team members. The student support team must examine all the instructional situations to determine who will be responsible for instruction within specified activities. When doing this, they must not assume that the paraprofessional will shoulder most of the responsibility for instruction. Instead, they must determine ways to accommodate the needs of the student with severe disabilities within instructional activities so that he is being taught by the general educator along with nondisabled peers.

Figure 10–5 Sample Curriculum Modifications

Traditional Curricular Activities	***Modifications***
Write spelling word in response to verbal direction	Mark correctly spelled word when presented with distractors
	Match spelling word to drawing or photograph
	Shorter spelling assignment
	Different set of spelling words
Read passage and respond to comprehension questions in writing	Listen to passage and mark phrases that include key points or events
	Look at picture book on same topic and respond to verbal questions using yes–no response
Conduct independent research on topic using resource materials and write report	Participate in cooperative learning group research activity and project completion
	Create collage on poster of pictures related to the topic
	Watch video or listen to audiotape on topic and develop report by arranging key points or events in order
Listen to lecture presenting new concept and complete assigned seatwork	Work independently with peer tutor on related topic or IEP goal
	Listen to modified lecture on audiotape and complete simplified assignment
Silent reading	Read or look at chosen library book on an appropriate level
	Listen to book read by peer or volunteer
	"Read" stories created from sequenced photos of home or school activities
Complete math worksheet	Complete simplified worksheet using calculator
	Complete counting or matching task using manipulatives
	Use computer to work on one-to-one correspondence or other math skills

The intent of inclusive education is not to bring the traditional special education perspective of instructing students with severe disabilities into the regular classroom, but to offer the advantages of the regular classes to the student with severe disabilities, such as opportunities to learn to interact with peers, to learn the common components of the routines in a regular classroom, and to learn about subject areas (e.g., social studies, science) that may not be part of the curriculum in a self-contained special education classroom (York, Vandercook, Caughey, & Heise-Neff, 1989). The success of inclusive schooling hinges on the provision of adequate supports to the students with disabilities so that they may be active and successful learners. Educators often fall into the trap of thinking about support as an additional person who will take on the responsibility for an activity or a student. If the realization of support is an additional person who shadows the student with disabilities, this person can end up being a barrier to the student's social inclusion in the classroom.

It is helpful to view supports from the perspective of what the student needs, rather than assigning personnel to students. Needs may include teaching support, prosthetic support, and interpretive support (Ferguson, Meyer, Jeanchild, Juniper, & Zingo, 1992). Teaching support, the instruction of skills and concepts, may be provided by peers, general educators, related service personnel, paraprofessionals, or special educators. Prosthetic support, such as adaptive equipment, correct positioning, physical assistance, and adaptations of activities and materials, may be needed by students with severe disabilities so that they can learn effectively. Such supports will always be needed by the student and are most effective when everyone in the school is familiar with them (Ferguson et al.,

Figure 10–6 General Modification Form

General Modifications

Student Name: Kyla | *Class: 4th Grade Language Arts* | *Date: 09/10*
Teacher: Lentini | *Consulting Teacher: Shahan*
Implementation Date: 09/15
Review Date: 11/15

Activity	Adaptations
Listen to lecture and complete written assignment from text	Work with peer tutor on arranging three-word sequence strips (represented by photos) and stating sentence Use computer program to find visual in response to verbal cue
Write in journal	Paste photos in journal; label photos for peer using communication device; peer writes labels or captions for photos in journal
Work with small group to create culminating project on unit lesson	Participate in cooperative learning group in culminating project. Practice embedded skills of choice making, taking out materials, putting materials away, photo identification, turn taking, and transferring from wheelchair to chair independently with peer instructional support
Write story, poem, letter, essay	Work with teacher or peer tutor on arranging word sequence strips; pasting photos in journal; working with teacher or peer on identifying personal identification information
Read silently and complete assignment of comprehension questions	Look at selected book or photo books of class activities. Respond to simple identification questions by pointing to a picture or using communication device.

Embedded Skill Instruction: choice making, taking out materials, putting materials away, photo identification, turn taking; and transferring from wheelchair to chair independently with peer instructional support, using walker to ambulate, using communication device for simple requests and greetings, recognizing personal identification information, and providing it to others on request.

1992). Interpretive supports are those provided to the general educator or peers who do not have intimate knowledge of the student with disabilities and who may need assistance in designing or adapting activities to facilitate the student's learning and social inclusion. Interpretive supports are usually provided by the special educator or related service personnel.

As students are integrated into general education classes, there will be times in the day when the teacher is not with them. It is important that appropriate techniques be used in such situations and that others who interact with them know these strategies. Before a student with severe disabilities is left under the supervision of another adult (general educator, paraprofessional) or typical peer, the teacher should review the goals of the student, instructional strategies to be used, and any specialized positioning or handling techniques that are necessary. The teacher may want to develop a manual for the adult that includes a scheduling matrix focusing on the period of time that the student is with them, photos of the student in the correct position or being assisted with movement, and guidelines for emergencies.

Often the teacher finds that some of the day is spent in activities that are not traditionally regarded as instructional, but that are related to the student's physical and health needs. Students who are not toileting independently need to be assisted with toileting or changed. Students who are not eating independently need to be assisted at mealtimes. Some students may need specialized health-care procedures such as suctioning, postural drainage, and catheterization. Other students have to be assisted in changing physical positions and in being placed in adaptive equipment. It is critical that these activities, which can consume so much of the day, become

Figure 10–7 Unit Modification Form

Unit Modifications

Student Name: Kyla | *Class: 4th Social Studies* | *Date:11/01–12/01*

Teacher: Lentini | *Consulting Teacher:* Shahan

Unit: Florida's First People

Activity	Adaptations
Lecture with time-line entries	During lecture, Kyla will look at primary picture book on Florida's First People. Kyla will work on goals of using her walker to come to front of room and handing marker to peer to write on time line.
Read from text and respond to written questions	Kyla will match pictures from the First People book to identical pictures.
Read from text and participate in whole-class quiz game	Kyla will listen to audiotape during silent reading. Kyla will walk to front of room with walker and click mouse to project quiz question during game.
Read from text and respond to multiple-choice, true–false questions	Kyla will complete worksheet by marking through pictures that did not appear in her First People book.
Guest lecture from Museum of Florida History	Kyla will listen with other students and pass materials to peers as they are distributed by guest lecturer. Kyla will use communication device to thank speaker and give him small thank you gift.
Watch film	Kyla will use walker to move from her chair to bean bag seat. Kyla will watch film with peers.
Quiz on time line	Kyla will work with teacher on identifying her personal identification information.
Museum field trip with scavenger hunt	Kyla will attend field trip with peers. Kyla will hold scavenger hunt list on clip board and will mark through items when located by her team.
Group project to depict daily activities of Florida's First People	Kyla will be member of group using cooperative learning structure. Practice embedded skills of choice making, taking out materials, putting materials away, photo identification, turn taking and independently transferring from wheelchair to chair or chair to walker with peer instructional support

Embedded Skill Instruction: choice making, taking out materials, putting materials away, photo identification, turn taking, and transferring from wheelchair to chair independently with peer instructional support, using walker to ambulate, using communication device for simple requests and greetings, recognizing personal identification information and providing it to others on request.

instructional routines. For example, Naomi is a student who is learning to extend her arms and make choices. She also must stand in a standing frame for 20 minutes a day. Her teacher has integrated her therapy routine of standing in the standing frame into a leisure activity. When Naomi is placed in the standing frame, which is next to a table, she works on extending her arms and making choices by using a mechanical switch to activate several toys while she interacts with a peer for the 20 minutes.

Many students with severe disabilities receive related services such as occupational therapy, speech therapy, and physical therapy. The traditional model of service delivery has been for the therapist to pull the student out of the regular classroom to work on therapy goals in isolation from other skills. A more desirable arrangement is to integrate therapy into the situations where the student is working on meaningful, functional skills (Sternat, Messina, Nietupski, Lyon, & Brown, 1977). Dunn (1991) defined functional integration as the most desirable integrated therapy arrangement. When functional integration occurs, "professionals apply therapeutic strategies to an individual's life environments" (Dunn, 1991, p. 354). An ideal arrangement would be to have the therapist work in the classroom or in community training sites alongside the educator. In this arrangement the therapist can train the educator in strategies and techniques that can then be applied in other activities and throughout the school day. Block scheduling, by which the therapist works in one classroom or school for an extensive amount of time (e.g., 2 hours), enables the therapist to work on therapy goals as they are embedded in routine activities (Rainforth et al., 1992). When block scheduling is used, the therapist reduces the frequency of student–therapist contacts, but increases the number of environments and activities in which facilitation can occur.

When the therapist is with the teacher, it is important to maximize the time for the best therapeutic benefits. This does not mean that the therapist should spend this time in direct therapy with a student. On the contrary, a more appropriate use of the time may be for the therapist to consult with the teacher, address new concerns, examine data on treatment plans, demonstrate techniques, conduct evaluations, and develop therapeutic programs. These tasks involve providing direct therapy, but, more important, they include training the educator and others to use specialized techniques.

Meaningful Instructional Arrangements

The acceptance of students with disabilities is a critical component of a successful inclusive education program. In addition to being accepted in school, the student with disabilities must be learning efficiently. Techniques for teaching students with severe disabilities were presented in Chapter 7. In this section, the methods for organizing and arranging instruction are discussed.

When students with severe disabilities were first taught in the public schools, teachers often used a developmental perspective to determine instructional goals. These goals were based on the development of young children and were usually not relevant to life in the community. The instructional procedures used were based on principles of operant conditioning and often involved artificial cues (teacher verbal instruction) and consequences (e.g., material or food reinforcers). The use of materials designed for preschoolers (stacking rings, shape sorters, etc.) and rigidly designed systematic instruction procedures were not uncommon in the 1970s. Typically, skills that were targeted for instruction were taught using a one-to-one instructional format that involved many instructional trials on the skill presented in a massed fashion within a contrived context. For example, a student may have been taught to sign "drink" using 30 trials for instruction and conducting instruction in the classroom where a drink was not present.

It did not take many years for researchers and teachers of students with severe disabilities to realize that a developmental approach to skill selection would not lead to the acquisition of important life skills by learners with severe disabilities. As a result, the use of ecological inventories became a common method to identify skills that are relevant to the current and future activities of the student. The use of ecological inventories to determine functional curriculum content for the student is only one piece of the puzzle, however. Teachers were also challenged with determining a method for conducting instruction so that it was effective, functional, and meaningful for the student with severe disabilities.

Basic Principles of Instructional Arrangement

Several principles of instruction for educating students with severe disabilities are applicable to students of all ages in all instructional situations. These principles should be considered as the foundation of appropriate practice and be evident regardless of the targeted goals, curriculum, or educational placement.

One of the most important of these principles is to provide students with severe disabilities with instruction in meaningful contexts; instruction should be conducted within relevant daily activities, rather than in isolated or contrived instructional situations. Another critical principle is to provide instruction on skills that are functional for the student; skills should be taught that will be useful to the student in both current and future environments.

Functional Skill Instruction

Because students with severe disabilities are able to learn a restricted number of skills and need intensive support to learn them, teachers must carefully select the skills that are taught. Functional skill instruction has been used to describe the instruction of skills that are related to independent living in the community. Many teachers select functional skills by examining the routines of nondisabled adults and selecting skills and activities from those repertoires without reflecting on the value of the selected skills to the individual student with severe disabilities. For example, teaching a student to operate a sewing machine has little value for the student who is unlikely to use a sewing machine at home or in the future.

Independence in daily living skills must not be the only test of functional skill instruction. Teachers, working in collaboration with the student's support team, must examine the student's individual situation. Instruction should result in the acquisition of skills, but also must assist students in the achievement of valued life outcomes (Giangreco, Cloninger, & Iverson, 1993; Meyer, 1991), such as living in the community, having a network of social relationships, choice and self-determination, having an active lifestyle, and being healthy (Giangreco et al., 1993). When valued life outcomes are used as a defining guideline of functional instruction, skills such as taking turns with peers (needed for building a social network) and learning a community job skill (needed for an active lifestyle) may be important instructional targets, and skills such as sorting silverware or stuffing envelopes may not relate to the achievement of a valued life outcome and, although they appear to be functional, may not be relevant to an individual student.

Embedded Instruction

Students with severe disabilities need repeated trials of instruction to acquire and achieve fluency on new skills. One approach to providing multiple trials of instruction is to mass the trials together or to drill a concept or skill focusing on the acquisition of one skill at a time. This approach ensures that intensive instruction is delivered, but may not provide the student with contextual information that is important to meaningful skill acquisition and generalization. For example, if a student is taught to open a screw-on lid by opening the jar many times in a row, the student may learn the task within that isolated context but be unable to open a screw-on lid when cooking, working, or engaging in grooming activities. An embedded instructional approach offers a mechanism to distribute trials of instruction within activities and routines throughout the school day. To embed instruction, the teacher selects routines and activities that offer opportunities to teach trials of targeted skills. Many trials of instruction are still offered, but they are distributed over the school day and taught within meaningful contexts.

Scheduling instruction by developmental domains contributed to the use of massed practice and the instruction of skills without linking them to related skills. It was not uncommon 10 years ago to see a class schedule (in self-contained special education classrooms) that consisted of 9:00, fine motor skills; 9:30, communication time; 10:00, gross motor skills; and so forth. When instruction was scheduled by domains, the teacher might teach a goal, such as signaling a request, only during that time of day. In the distributed trial format, a student might be taught to signal a request (with an augmentative communication system or using a natural gesture) during morning arrival, small group instruction, free-choice leisure time, lunch, and any other time of the day when requesting is appropriate.

A review of the literature by Mulligan, Guess, Holvoet, and Brown (1980) offered convincing evidence that distributed trial training is preferred to massed trial training. Research also substantiates that distributed trial instruction results in a decrease in nonresponding to tasks (Dunlap & Koegel, 1980) and higher response rates (Mulligan, Lacy, & Guess, 1982).

Skill Clustering

Current educational approaches recognize that teaching skills in isolation does little to promote the use of these skills in meaningful contexts. Skills should be taught with related skills from other domains. For example, peer interaction skills should be taught at the same time that a student is learning to purchase lunch in the cafeteria. Guess and Helmstetter (1986) described the instructional format as horizontal, rather than the vertical format that had been traditionally used. For example, in the traditional model a student was taught communication skills separately from motor skills, although communication is typically used in combination with motor or some other skill domain. In a skill cluster model, a communication skill is taught in combination with the related motor skill; for example, a student raises his head, looks at his communication partner, and says "Hi."

Multiple Exemplars

Instruction is distributed within activities throughout the day, with multiple examples of materials, in multiple locations, using different responses, and with multiple instructors. The use of varied stimuli in skill acquisition increases the likelihood that the skill will be generalized by the learner (Stokes & Baer, 1977). In the traditional instructional model, instruction occurred using the same stimuli until mastery was achieved. Efforts were not made to ensure generalization and, typically, generalization was not achieved (Stokes & Baer, 1977). This issue and other strategies that may be used to promote generalization were presented in Chapter 8.

Natural Cues and Consequences

In an effort to make instruction more meaningful for the student, the training of nonfunctional skills and activities has been abandoned, and skills are taught in ways that result in meaningful skill acquisition. For example, you can teach a student to throw away a piece of paper that you have just crumpled and given to her with the verbal cue of "throw it away," followed by a piece of cereal as a reinforcer, or you can teach her to throw a paper towel away after she has dried her hands with it. Instructing skills in a functional manner (natural cues and consequences) results in the acquisition of skills that can be used in meaningful activities in response to naturally occurring stimuli.

Choice Making

Providing learners with choices is identified as an important component of teaching students with severe disabilities, but there is no room for providing opportunities for choice making when instruction is highly controlled. Professionals in the field have expressed their concern about the conspicuous lack of choice-making opportunities for students with disabilities (Guess & Siegel-Causey, 1985; Shevin & Klein, 1984). Central to the argument of why choice making is an essential component of instruction is that it is a right of all members of our society. In addition to acknowledging the learner's humanness, choice making enhances instruction and may increase student motivation. The opportunity for choice making is also an opportunity for communicative expression; every time the student is offered a choice, there is an opportunity to use whatever form of expressive communication the student possesses. Students who choose the activities that they engage in, the people that they work with, and the materials that they use are likely to be more motivated and engaged in instruction.

Meaningful Environments

When students with severe disabilities were first educated in the public schools, their instruction took place in the special education classroom. This is somewhat compatible with the concept of normalization; that is, students learn in school, therefore students with disabilities should learn in school. But the need to teach students with severe disabilities functional life skills necessitates instruction in settings other than the classroom. If a student needs to learn to prepare a simple snack, purchase items at a grocery store, play a game with a friend, or ask for assistance from a store clerk, it is not likely that he can learn these skills in the special education classroom. Students need to learn skills in the real-life setting where they will be required to use the skill.

Providing Individualized Instruction

The collaborative student support team is challenged to develop an instructional plan that will accommodate instruction on individualized goals within the classroom and in other school environments. Thus the team needs to examine the goals that have been targeted for an individual student and determine how these goals will be individually addressed within the general curriculum. One mechanism for considering how goals will be taught is the use of a scheduling matrix (Giangreco et al., 1993; Guess & Helmstetter, 1986). The matrix, shown in Figure 10–8, is a format for examining a student's individual goals and the activities of the day to determine when skills will be taught.

To develop a scheduling matrix, the teacher and other team members first list the activities of the instructional day in the order that they occur. In an inclusion classroom, the activities scheduled for the regular class are listed on the matrix with the addition of any individualized events planned for the target student. In a special education classroom where there is mainstreaming into the regular class, typical peers coming into the special education class, and community-based instruction, all these events will be listed on the matrix. Although the class schedule may change or may not be finalized at the outset of the school year, filling out the matrix prior to instruction is essential. It should be viewed as a worksheet to assist the teacher with planning instruction, rather than as a rigorous schedule that cannot be changed. The matrix can be revised and readdressed by the teacher or the student support team as the student schedule changes or as goals are changed.

If the teacher determines the activities that will occur (rather than following the regular class routines), it is important to naturalize the order of activities (e.g., clean up after snack time) and to make sure that the locations of activities are natural to the activities (e.g., dressing skills in the locker room). The location of the activity should be listed under each activity.

The next step is to list the student's instructional goals across the top of the matrix and then fill in the individual cells of the matrix. Some teachers simply determine if the skill can be functionally taught during the activity and put an × in the cell. Another procedure is to write in materials or events that will be used to teach the skill. The teacher may want to also list choices that can be made in each cell. A completed scheduling matrix is shown in Figure 10–9.

Skill clusters, sequences of two or more related target skills, are built from the scheduling matrix. In Figure 10–9,

Figure 10–8 Scheduling Matrix

student ______________
teacher ______________

		skills to be taught
Activity (location)	Time/ Instructor	

the teacher has indicated that she can instruct Amy on the simple, discrete behaviors of greeting and extending her elbow and the continuous, ongoing behavior of holding her head up during arrival time. A skill cluster that includes these skills is the following:

> *Teacher Cue:* Teacher greets Amy by saying "Hi, Amy."
> *Student Response:* Amy responds by *vocalizing a greeting* and *raising her head.*
> *Teacher Cue:* Teacher prompts Amy to hang up her backpack by pointing to hook and placing backpack in hand.
> *Student Response:* Amy responds by *extending elbow* holding backpack.

This skill cluster could be repeated in music class, where Amy is prompted by a peer to say hello and must extend her elbow to receive the instrument mallet.

There are skills that are not clustered, but are task analyzed, or that naturally involve massed practice. The skill of brushing one's teeth or preparing a simple snack involves many chained steps that should be task analyzed. The task of stapling together the school assembly program is one that naturally involves massed practice.

The scheduling matrix addresses the organization of instruction for the skills and activities listed as educational goals on a student's IEP. These goals are targeted for the achievement of valued life outcomes and should be specifically addressed, using systematic instructional techniques. Students with severe disabilities will be exposed to much more instructional content than what is listed on the IEP. In the general education classroom, the student with severe disabilities may participate in a social studies lesson on Martin Luther King or a science class on the influence of gravity on matter. The content in these activities may not appear on the IEP or the matrix, although the student may be learning some of the content

Figure 10–9 Activities–Skills Matrix for Amy

student Amy
teacher Lisa

Activity (location)	Time/ Instructor	greet	raise head	extend elbow	use photo book for request	stand in standing frame	take turns	mechanical switch
		skills to be taught						
arrival	8:30 peer	X	X					
homeroom	8:45 Mike	X	X	X	X			
computer	9:00 Chris	X	X		X		X	X
special (art, music)	9:30 Lisa	X	X	X			X	
snack leisure	10:15 10:45 Lisa	X	X	X	X	X	X	X
library	11:15 Beth	X	X	X	X			X
lunch	12:00 peer	X	X		X		X	
community	1:00 Lisa/peer	X	X	X				
project	2:00 S.T/Lisa/peer		X	X	X		X	X
clean-up	2:30 Lisa/peer	X	X		X			
departure								

with her peers. In these situations, the student with severe disabilities may also be working on the acquisition of skills such as working cooperatively with peers, attending to a group presentation, or following two-step directions. The purpose of the scheduling matrix is to provide the teacher and the student support team with a mechanism to examine the activities of the day and the IEP and to determine when the targeted goals will be instructed.

Peer Interaction during Instruction

The primary advantages of inclusive educational programs are the opportunities for intensive and sustained interactions with nondisabled peers. These interactions should not be viewed as occurring exclusively during noninstructional times; peer interactions can and should be promoted during instruction as well. The collaborative team should examine classroom practices to determine if different instructional arrangements can result in the meaningful participation and inclusion of students with severe disabilities. Two strategies that might be used as alternatives to traditional instructional practices are partial participation and cooperative learning groups.

Partial Participation

An important strategy for facilitating social interaction is the use of partial participation (Baumgart et al., 1982; Ferguson & Baumgart, 1991) in designing instructional activities. The principle of partial participation means that students are not excluded from activities because of their inability to complete them independently. The application of this principle in fostering interactions between students guides the teacher to look for ways to adapt activities or their components to allow the student with severe disabilities to participate. A student who cannot understand the rules of a game does not have to be excluded from playing if he can do part of the game with or without assistance. In applying the principle of partial participation to interactions, the teacher looks for activities that students without disabilities engage in and enjoy with their peers and then develops adaptations or strategies so that the student with disabilities can also participate. For example, the seventh-grade students usually play an informally organized soccer game at lunch and recess. Chris, a seventh-grader with disabilities, loves to watch, but is unable to keep up with his peers. His teacher asks the students if they can find some way that Chris can be included. His peers suggest that Chris throw in the foul balls. In another class, Amy watches her peers using a computer to write a report for social studies. Amy does not comprehend the content of a report on the rain forest but, with assistance, can use a mouse to operate a computer. The teacher adapts the lesson criteria for her, and Amy (with the assistance of a peer) uses the computer to put together a picture report on the same topic.

Cooperative Learning Groups

Cooperative learning (Johnson & Johnson, 1989; Putnam, 1998) is a technique that has proved successful in promoting interaction between students with and without disabilities in instructional activities. Cooperative learning is different from academic lessons that are structured competitively (students work against each other to achieve a goal and are graded on a curve that compels them to work harder and perform better than their peers) or lessons that are structured individualistically (students' goal achievements are independent of one another and students work at their own speed to achieve a preset criteria). In cooperative learning, students' goal achievements are positively correlated, and students only achieve their goal if all students in the learning group also reach their goals (Johnson & Johnson, 1989).

Elements of Cooperative Learning. Five critical elements are essential to cooperative learning (Johnson & Johnson, 1989). The first is that students clearly perceive their positive interdependence. Positive interdependence is achieved by goal interdependence, that is, structuring of the task so that the members of the group realize that they can attain their goals only if other members of the group also attain their goals. In addition to goal interdependence, teachers may also use reward interdependence (group members receive the same reward for completing a joint task), resource interdependence (group members must combine their individual resources to complete the task), or role interdependence (members are assigned interconnected roles that the group needs to complete the task).

The second element is that students work in small groups that are structured in a way to facilitate interaction and discussion (Johnson & Johnson, 1989). The third element is individual accountability. By assessing each group member and reporting to the group and individual, all members know that they must contribute to the process and also know which group members will need support to complete the assignment. The fourth element is the use of interpersonal and small-group skills. Collaborative social skills are taught to students so that they will be able to function effectively in cooperative learning groups.

The last element is the use of group processing to focus on the behaviors needed to enable the cooperative group to function. In group processing, members describe to each other member actions that are helpful and unhelpful and receive feedback on participation from their peers.

Designing a Cooperative Lesson. The first step in designing a cooperative lesson is to decide on the lesson objectives. Two types of objectives should be specified: an academic objective and a collaborative skills objective. Once the objectives are determined, the teacher determines the most effective group size (usually two to six students) and assigns students to groups, making sure that the groups are heterogeneous. The classroom may need to be rearranged to accommodate a cooperative group structure. The cooperative group needs to sit close together in a seating arrangement that allows members to share materials and engage in face-to-face discussion. The lesson materials are distributed in ways that promote the notion that this is a group effort—by giving each member part of the materials that are needed to complete the activity or lesson or by giving only one copy of the materials to the group so that they will have to work together. The teacher should assign roles to group members to promote interdependence. Roles that are typically assigned are the following: checker (who makes sure everyone can correctly explain how the group arrived at the answer), summarizer (who reports the group's conclusions), facilitator (who makes sure that group processes are followed and that everyone participates), recorder (who writes down the conclusions), evaluator (who collects evaluation data on the participation of group members), and accuracy coach (who corrects mistakes made in members' explanations or summaries).

Presenting the Cooperative Lesson. The teacher first presents a cooperative lesson by explaining the academic task and how the students will work collaboratively in their groups to produce a product or report. She explains the criteria for success and specifies the appropriate behaviors for the cooperative lesson (e.g., taking turns, talking quietly).

When the cooperative groups begin working, the teacher moves from group to group, observing students' work and assisting with problems. When monitoring groups that include students with severe disabilities, the teacher may have to intervene and model ways to prompt the participation of the student with disabilities or to adapt the task. He may also have to intervene in groups in which students are having problems in collaboration and suggest ways for the group to work together. When the lesson is complete, each student should be able to describe what he learned. The teacher assesses the quality and quantity of the work and provides feedback to the students; and, finally, the learning group performs a self-assessment on the group's ability to work collaboratively and productively.

There is a wealth of research on the effectiveness of cooperative learning (Johnson, Johnson, & Maruyama, 1983; Slavin, 1984) and some data on the application of cooperative learning to successfully instruct students with mild disabilities in the mainstream (Madden & Slavin, 1983). Several studies have demonstrated the application of cooperative learning to individuals with severe disabilities. Eichinger (1990) found that when students with severe disabilities participated in cooperative goal-structured activities they were more socially interactive with their peers than in individualistic goal-structured activities. Cooperative activities were cooking and art activities in which students were each given a part of the materials needed to reach the goal. Hunt, Staub, Alwell, & Goetz (1994) examined the performance of students with multiple severe disabilities within academically structured cooperative learning groups and demonstrated that the students with disabilities independently demonstrated their instructional targets within the activities and then generalized these skills within different cooperative learning activities.

Putnam, Rynders, Johnson, and Johnson (1989) used the Social Interaction Observation System (SIOS) developed by Voeltz et al. (1981) to examine the social interaction behaviors of children with moderate to severe mental handicaps and their nondisabled peers working on a science lesson. One group of children was instructed in collaborative skills; the other was not. Students who had been instructed in collaborative skills were trained to use cooperative skills and given feedback on their use. Nondisabled students in this group showed a significant superiority in orienting to the students with disabilities, in commenting to the students with disabilities, and in cooperative participation. There were no overall differences in the frequency of social behavior directed toward the nondisabled students by the students with disabilities in the two groups.

Effective Instruction in the General Education Classroom

Inclusive education presents challenges to traditional approaches for instructing students with severe disabilities. The technology for instruction in severe disabilities has been based on a student-centered model of providing systematic instruction on individually relevant instructional goals (McDonnell, 1998). This model of instruction is particular to special education classrooms and is less evident within general education environments, although leading researchers in general education are calling for curriculum reforms to provide effective instruction to an increasingly diverse student population. McDonnell (1998) calls for a broader view of teaching by both special and general educators to consider the importance of interventions that are specific to an individual student's instructional needs and compatible with the entire classroom system. He suggests that special educators resist the urge to create an individually tailored special education microcosm around one child who is in the inclusive environment and examine the instructional strategies that can benefit both the general education students and the student who is included.

McDonnell (1998) discusses the use of effective teaching behaviors, heterogeneous student groups, cooperative learning, and peer tutoring as empirically sound strategies that will meet the instructional needs of the general education student population and promote inclusion. Effective teaching behaviors include (1) designing lessons to promote active student engagement and opportunities for responding, (2) designing lessons to match student skill level and ensure a high level of success, (3) presenting new information systematically by linking it to previously mastered skills or ideas, and (4) providing immediate feedback to students about their responses. Heterogeneous grouping is effectively used to assist students in relating to a mixed peer group and to promote acceptance of the diversity of student abilities in a classroom. Research does not support the superiority of within-ability grouping on student achievement (Slavin, 1996). Cooperative learning, as described in the previous section, offers a highly effective instructional approach that supports the social and academic goals of individual students. Peer tutoring has also been supported in both the special and general education research literature as an effective instructional strategy. All these strategies should be familiar to the general educator and offer effective instructional contexts for the inclusion of the student with severe disabilities. The collaborative team should discuss the teaching approaches used by the general educator and examine the fit of the student's instructional needs to teaching strategies that are already being used for whole-class instruction.

An instructional opportunity for inclusion that has recently become prevalent in the general education curriculum is service learning. *Service learning* refers to an instructional activity that provides students with an opportunity to learn academic skills and provide service to others (Fenstermaker, 1990; Fertman, 1994). A service learning project may be to clean up and plant new plantings in a community park or to prepare and serve food at a homeless shelter. Service learning projects may consist of providing direct service to individuals in need, indirect service, or community action (e.g., cleaning up a park).

Service learning projects offer an opportunity for a student with severe disabilities to receive instruction on embedded goals and participate in the general education curriculum (Gent & Gurecka, 1998). For example, if a service learning project is to build an animal habitat for a local nature park, the project would include researching the habitat needs of the animals, planning the construction, building the habitat, reflecting on the learning process, and celebrating the outcome. The student with severe disabilities could participate by practicing embedded skills (e.g., communication, social interaction, mobility) and may also learn some of the basic concepts that are lessons for all the students related to the animal habitat needs and construction safety. In one study related to the use of service learning for including students with severe disabilities, the researchers contrasted the condition of service learning group participation to a condition in which nondisabled students provided a service to students with disabilities by helping with Special Olympics (Burns, Storey, & Certo, 1999). Nondisabled students in the service learning group had more positive attitudes toward their peers with disabilities, and the peer with a disability was able to have a more equal role in the activity.

Implementing Inclusive Instruction

Inclusive instruction involves bringing together the many components of appropriate practice and support that have been discussed in this and earlier chapters. The collaborative team should realize that inclusive instruction is a complex endeavor composed of many variables. An example of one child's inclusive instructional program is provided in this section to help you to understand how the elements of inclusive education fit together.

Paul is a 10-year-old student with severe disabilities who is being educated in the elementary school that he would attend if he were not disabled. He attends a regular fifth-grade class and is the only student labeled severely disabled in the class, although the classroom of 28 students also includes 5 students who are labeled mildly disabled.

He is supported by a support facilitator who is certified as a teacher of students with severe disabilities and who provides instructional support for the 5 students with moderate and severe disabilities in Paul's school of 520 students. The support facilitator provides some instruction to Paul, coordinates the activities of Paul's student support team, and provides consultation to Paul's classroom.

Paul's student support team is composed of the support facilitator, his fifth-grade teacher, his mother, the speech therapist, and the paraprofessional in his class. The team developed the following IEP goals for Paul:

1. Paul will indicate a choice by visually scanning objects offered by peers or a teacher and directly selecting his preference.
2. Paul will spontaneously sign an approximation of "finished" to indicate a desire to change activities.
3. Paul will point to a picture from an array of four options to indicate a request for an object or activity.
4. Paul will increase his social interaction with nondisabled peers during free-play situations from 33% to 50% of observed intervals.
5. Paul will take out materials independently upon natural verbal cues in the classroom and on the playground.
6. Paul will increase the number of turns to 50% above baseline level within a 10-minute play sequence with a nondisabled peer.
7. Paul will prepare a simple snack (place cookie on plate, place chips in bowl, put juice in cup) independently.

8. Paul will independently move through the cafeteria food line with peers at breakfast and lunch.
9. Paul will throw a ball to a peer in a play sequence.
10. Paul will make a purchase in the community by handing the cashier a predetermined amount of money and waiting to receive his change.
11. Paul will use a stamp of his name to identify his work, check out library materials and work, and sign in on the computer log book.
12. Paul will independently select a computer program from a choice of three and place the disk in the drive.

Once the instructional goals were determined, Paul's team examined the activities of his classroom to pinpoint when instruction could occur. In the design of Paul's instructional day, the team made recommendations for the use of cooperative learning, large-group instruction, peer instruction, community-based instruction, and activity-based instruction. Examples of how these approaches are applied to Paul's IEP goals are given next.

Cooperative Learning

Paul is placed in a group of five fourth graders. They have been given a science assignment to plan a day's menu and to calculate the number of calories and the grams of fat, protein, and carbohydrates that their menu includes. The students will work in cooperative groups to decide on the menu, cut out magazine pictures that illustrate the item selections, and display the menu and nutritional information on a poster. The group will then complete a worksheet on nutrition and diet.

In the group, Paul will work on the following IEP goals: visually indicating a choice when a peer holds up two pictures; spontaneously signing "finished" after he glues a picture to the poster board; going to the shelf and getting magazines to bring to the group; and stamping his name on the group worksheet.

Large-Group Lesson with Individualized Goals

A group of 28 students are learning about the solar eclipse. Paul is assisting a student who is making an eclipse viewer. The goals Paul works on in this activity are pointing to an array of pictures to show the peer what he wants to do next (tape, glue, cut); taking turns with the peer; taking out materials independently; and signing "finished."

Peer Instruction

During the free-play part of physical education class, a peer throws a ball with Paul. Paul works on his IEP goals of increasing social interaction, increasing turn taking, throwing a ball, and signing "finished." The peer has been coached on how to redirect Paul to the activity and how to prompt him to sign "finished." When they return to class, the peer reports to the teacher how many turns Paul took before he wanted to quit playing.

Community-Based Instruction

Paul and three classmates go to the community shopping center across the street from school. Paul's classmates have been given a social studies assignment to interview people in management roles about their expectations of employees. This assignment is part of a 9-week unit on careers and job skills. Paul accompanies his peers and, with the supervision of a paraprofessional, receives instruction and practice on his goals of visually indicating a choice and making a purchase.

Activity-Based Instruction

Every day during math, Paul is assigned to work in the computer area. Five other students are allowed to work in the computer area each day; they are allowed to use a program for math drills or can work on developing a program. Paul keeps the computer log book; after he stamps his name on the log, the other students sign in. Paul is prompted by a peer to select the computer program that he wishes to work on and is assisted with turning on his terminal. When Paul stops working on the computer, a peer prompts him to sign "finished" and then assists him with taking the disk out and selecting another program.

The Changing Role of the Special Educator

In the special education classroom, the role of the special educator is fairly easily determined; he or she is the primary person to provide instruction, train and supervise paraprofessionals, and collaborate with families, and typically is the team coordinator of the transdisciplinary team. In inclusive education programs, the special educator's role is changed; he or she becomes a support person for the student with disabilities and other educators. The titles of support facilitator, consulting teacher, method and resource teacher, and inclusion facilitator have been used in inclusive education programs, rather than the title of special educator.

The role of the special educator in an inclusive education program is collaboratively determined by the student support team. However, it is likely that as special educators move into inclusive education programs that have been newly designed they will be the lead professionals; they will coordinate the efforts to support the student with severe disabilities, including such activities as scheduling and information sharing with related service personnel, maintaining ongoing contact with the student's family, managing student paperwork, training and supervising paraprofessionals, facilitating information exchange between team members and other school personnel, securing and maintaining adaptive equipment, and adapting instructional materials (Giangreco et al., 1993).

Inclusive education programs should be viewed within a dynamic framework. The role of the special educator will change as other team members become comfortable with the model and take on new responsibilities. It is highly unlikely that a school can transform itself from one with segregated special education classrooms to an inclusive school overnight; the process of restructuring the school will be gradual. The flexibility of special education personnel will be required as schools attempt to move to inclusionary practices.

Two case studies are provided to illustrate the different roles that the special educator may assume as a teacher of students with severe disabilities in two very different inclusion programs.

Case Study 1: Sarah

Sarah was hired as the teacher of a class for students with severe disabilities in a regular elementary school. This was the first integrated class for her school district and was implemented in response to the advocacy efforts of parents and professionals. To accommodate the students, a portable classroom was placed on the school grounds.

On the first day of the preschool planning week, Sarah requested 20 minutes to discuss her program at the faculty meeting. During this session she explained who she is and why students with severe disabilities are being placed on the campus, gave information about the need to create an environment of inclusion on the campus, and requested that teachers who might be interested in working with her or having their students participate in a special friends or peer tutor project meet with her later that afternoon in the lounge. That afternoon, two teachers came to the lounge and talked with Sarah about the inclusion of her students. They discussed the need to enlist more teacher involvement and the development of awareness activities. One teacher offered to work with the PTO in the development of some schoolwide awareness efforts. Both teachers expressed interest in a Peer Tutor/Peer Buddy program.

Sarah wrote up a description of the Peer Tutor/Peer Buddy program and put a copy in each teacher's mailbox on the second day of planning week. She invited the teachers to meet with her for a coffee break in her room to discuss the program on the last day of the planning week. Five teachers attended the meeting. Sarah explained the program and offered to come to the teachers' classrooms to do an awareness workshop and to recruit volunteers. The teachers helped her to develop permission forms and provided her with the times when their students would be able to come to her class for Peer Tutor/Peer Buddy activities. At this time Sarah would have liked to request that her students attend some of the activities in the regular classes, but sensed that this might be moving too quickly for some of the teachers.

School began and Sarah was able to do workshops in the five classrooms and to begin her Peer Tutor/Peer Buddy programs. She made a short presentation in the faculty meeting, asking if some of the classrooms would volunteer to be a "buddy classroom" to her students to find ways to include one of her students in special activities and field trips, and to find times in the day (reading, project time, sharing) when her student could be integrated. Sarah was pleased to have enough teachers volunteer that each of her students would have a "buddy classroom."

The PTO came through with a committee that wanted to develop the awareness training program. They consulted Sarah about their plans and she guided their selection of films and literature. She also gave them a short lesson in using language that is sensitive to persons with disabilities.

By the middle of the school year the Peer Tutor/Peer Buddy program was going well, and there had been several awareness training activities. Sarah had worked hard to make sure that the classroom teachers' efforts were appreciated by writing articles for the school newsletter and sending thank you notes to helpful parents and faculty. But Sarah was concerned that her students were still not perceived as full members of the school community and were seen as a special project.

She asked three of the teachers with whom she had worked closely to meet with her to talk about these concerns. They recognized that the students with severe disabilities were still seen as outsiders and discussed with Sarah some remedies to the problem. They met again and developed a plan that they intended to present to the principal for discussion and implementation. Included in the plan was the assignment of every student with severe disabilities to a regular classroom at the beginning of the next school year, the movement of Sarah's classroom into the main building, the movement of a special area class into the portable classroom, and the formation of an inclusion committee as one of the formal school committees for the next school year.

Case Study 2: Ray

Ray is a first-year special educator in a school that is implementing a full inclusion program. Ray received some training in integration in his university coursework and interned in a classroom for students with moderate and severe disabilities on a regular school campus. He is very skilled in working with students with severe disabilities and came highly recommended, but he had no direct experience in full inclusion.

Ray was assigned responsibility for coordinating the education program for six students with moderate and severe disabilities of different ages in a regular elementary school. Each student was assigned to a regular classroom teacher who teamed with Ray, the related services professionals, and the parents in the development of each student's IEP.

On the first day of preschool planning, Ray was given the school folders of the students he would be assisting. He reviewed the folders and scheduled home visits with each student's family. That afternoon all the teachers who would be including students with disabilities and the special educators who were hired as support facilitators met to discuss the logistics of the program. At this meeting it was decided that a letter explaining the full inclusion program should be sent to all the parents and that the usual formal awareness activities would not be conducted in school assemblies, but rather in individual classrooms in more subtle ways.

During the remainder of the planning week, Ray divided his time between becoming acquainted with the students he would be supporting and assisting their teachers in developing schedules and adapted lessons for inclusion. All but one of the teachers had been assigned a paraprofessional to assist in the increased demands of including students with disabilities. The teacher who did not receive paraprofessional support was fairly experienced in mainstreaming students with disabilities and would be including a student who is independent in his mobility and self-care skills.

On the first day of school, Ray positioned himself at the bus arrival area to make sure all his students found their way to their homerooms. By prior arrangement, the fifth-grade students were available to help all new students find their way around school. Ray hooked each of his students up with a fifth grader and requested that he or she be assisted to the proper homeroom. When the first bell rang, Ray moved to classroom 6. He had promised to show the teacher how to position a student in an adapted chair. After he demonstrated the transfer and positioning, he stayed in the classroom and assisted the student in the social studies lesson that was being taught. In second period, he went to classroom 18 to pick up Manny, a student who was learning to dress independently. Because it took Manny a longer time to change into his PE clothes, Ray took him to the gym locker room about 15 minutes before the rest of the class came down. By the time the other boys arrived, Manny was ready to put on his T-shirt, which he did independently. The rest of Ray's morning was spent in the classrooms of the other three students conducting assessments of their performance in the regular class that would be used in working with student support teams in designing instructional programs. The speech therapist asked Ray to come with her to the cafeteria so that she could teach him some of the techniques that she uses to promote expressive communication and socialization with two of the students.

In the afternoon, Ray spent time in three classrooms, observing lessons and writing down ideas for adaptations. When the students went home for the day, he wrote a note to each of the grade-level teachers, suggesting activity adaptations and offering assistance. He developed a schedule of his activities for the rest of the week and provided it to all the teachers that he works with. He also made notes about things he wanted to work on in the next few weeks: developing peer support networks for each student, working with the teacher in developing a data collection system to monitor instructional goals, and collaborating with the speech therapist on developing expressive communication systems that can be used at home and at school for two of the students.

Conclusion

The nature of instruction for students with severe disabilities has changed dramatically in the last 25 years. The teacher of students with severe disabilities must be aware of much more than just what he or she wants to plan for the special education classroom. Instruction must be designed to take place in a variety of relevant environments for each individual student, in activities that are meaningful for the student and that have a direct relationship to the student's present and future lifestyle. The curriculum has shifted from a developmental, isolated model to a functional, inclusive one. Teacher roles have also shifted. The special educator working with students with severe disabilities today must be able to plan, develop, and implement instruction in many different settings while working with a variety of people.

The instruction of students with severe disabilities in regular schools and regular class environments is an achievable and beneficial arrangement. Probably the greatest inhibitor to successful inclusion is the prevailing attitude of adults that students with disabilities do not belong and need specialized settings for instruction. Attitudinal barriers can be overcome. The special educator's best defense in response to resistive attitudes is to show that students with disabilities can belong and to find creative ways to develop inclusive school communities.

Questions for Reflection

1. What evidence do you see in the media that the acceptance of persons with disabilities is gaining widespread attention?
2. How do teacher education programs inhibit or promote the ability of teachers to provide inclusive education programs?
3. Do you feel that inclusive education programs are more appropriate for students of a specific age range? What ages? Why?
4. What personal characteristics might enhance a special educator's success as an inclusion facilitator?
5. Do you feel that some skills cannot be taught in a regular classroom? What are they? Could they be taught with nondisabled peers?
6. What do you think are the most significant challenges in implementing an inclusive program for special educators? General educators? School administrators?

References

Agran, M., Alper, S., & Wehmeyer, M. (2002). Access to general curriculum for students with significant disabilities: What it means to teachers. *Education and Training in Mental Retardation and Developmental Disabilities, 37,* 123–133.

Bauer, A. M., & Brown, G. M. (2001). *Adolescents and inclusion: Transforming secondary schools*. Baltimore: Paul H. Brookes.

Baumgart, D., Brown, L., Pumpian, I., Nisbet, J., Ford, A., Sweet, M., Messina, R., & Shroeder, J. (1982). Principle of partial participation and individualized adaptions in education programs for severely handicapped students. *Journal of the Association for the Severely Handicapped, 7*(2), 17–27.

Baumgart, D., & Giangreco, M. F. (1996). Key lessons learned about inclusion. In D. H. Lehr & F. Brown (Eds.), *People with disabilities who challenge the system* (pp. 79–97). Baltimore: Paul H. Brookes.

Bricker, D. (1978). A rationale for the integration of handicapped and nonhandicapped preschool children. In M. Guralnick (Ed.), *Early intervention and the integration of handicapped and nonhandicapped children* (pp. 3–26). Baltimore: University Park Press.

Brinker, R. P., & Thorpe, M. E. (1984). Integration of severely handicapped students and the proportion of IEP objectives achieved. *Exceptional Children, 51,* 168–175.

Brown, L., Long, E., Udvari-Solnaer, A., Schwarz, P., VanDeventer, P., Ahlgren, C., Johnson, F., Gruenewald, L., & Jorgensen, J. (1989). Should students with severe intellectual disabilities be based in regular or in special education classrooms in home schools? *Journal of the Association for Persons with Severe Handicaps, 14,* 8–12.

Brown, L., Nisbet, J., Ford, A., Sweet, M., Shiraga, B., York, J., & Loomis, R. (1983). The critical need for nonschool instruction in educational programs for severely handicapped students. *Journal of the Association for the Severely Handicapped, 8,* 71–77.

Burns, M., Storey, K., & Certo, N. J. (1999). Effect of service learning on attitude towards students with disabilities. *Education and Training in Mental Retardation and Developmental Disabilities, 34,* 58–65.

Carter, E. W., Hughes, C., Copeland, S. R., & Breen, C. (2001). Differences between high school students who do and do not volunteer to participate in a peer interaction program. *Journal of the Association for Persons with Severe Handicaps, 26,* 229–239.

Cole, D. A., Meyer, L. M., Vandercook, T., & McQuarter, R. J. (1986). Interactions between peers with and without severe handicaps: The dynamics of teacher intervention. *American Journal of Mental Deficiency, 92,* 160–169.

Davern, L., & Ford, A. (1989). Scheduling. In A. Ford, R. Schnorr, L. Meyer, L. Davern, J. Black, & P. Dempsey (Eds.), *The Syracuse community-referenced curriculum guide for students with moderate and severe disabilities* (pp. 247–255). Baltimore: Paul H. Brookes.

Donder, D., & Nietupski, J. (1981). Nonhandicapped adolescents teaching playground skills to their mentally retarded peers: Toward a less restrictive middle school environment. *Education and Training of the Mentally Retarded, 16,* 270–276.

Downing, J. E., & Eichinger, J. (2002). Educating students with diverse strengths and needs together: Rationale for inclusion. In J. E. Downing, *Including students with severe and multiple disabilities in typical classrooms: Practical strategies for teachers* (pp. 1–16). Baltimore: Paul H. Brookes.

Dunlap, G., & Koegel, R. L. (1980). Motivating autistic children through stimulus variation. *Journal of Applied Behavior Analysis, 13,* 619–627.

Dunn, W. (1991). Integrated related services. In L. H. Meyer, C. A. Peck, & L. Brown (Eds.), *Critical issues in the lives of people with severe disabilities* (pp. 353–378). Baltimore: Paul H. Brookes.

Eichinger, J. (1990). Goal structure effects on social interaction: Nondisabled and disabled elementary students. *Exceptional Children, 56,* 408–416.

Evans, I., Salisbury, C., Palombaro, M., Berryman, J., & Hollowood, T. M. (1992). Peer interactions and social acceptance of elementary-age children with severe disabilities in an inclusive school. *Journal of the Association for Persons with Severe Handicaps, 17,* 205–212.

Farley, L. (1996). A quartet of success stories: Making inclusion work. *Educational Leadership, 53,* 51–55.

Fenstermaker, B. (1990). Infusing service learning into the curriculum. In J. C. Kendall (Ed.), *Combining service and learning: A resource book for community and public service,* (Vol. 1, pp. 194–197). Raleigh, NC: National Society for Internships and Experiential Education.

Ferguson, D. L., & Baumgart, D. (1991). Partial participation revisited. *Journal of the Association for Persons with Severe Handicaps, 16,* 218–227.

Ferguson, D. L., Meyer, G., Jeanchild, L., Juniper, L., & Zingo, J. (1992). Figuring out what to do with the grownups: How teachers make inclusion "work" for students with disabilities. *Journal of the Association for Persons with Severe Handicaps, 17,* 218–226.

Fertman, C. I. (1994). *Service learning for all students.* Bloomington, IN: Phi Delta Kappa Foundation.

Fisher, D., Pumpian, I., & Sax, C. (1998). High school students: Attitudes about and recommendations for their peers with significant disabilities. *Journal of the Association for Persons with Severe Handicaps, 23,* 272–282.

Ford, A., & Davern, L. (1989). Moving forward with school integration. In R. Gaylord-Ross (Ed.), *Integration strategies for students with handicaps* (pp. 11–31). Baltimore: Paul H. Brookes.

Forest, M., & Lusthaus, E. (1989). Promoting educational equality for all students. In S. Stainback, W. Stainback, & M. Forest (Eds.), *Educating all students in the mainstream of regular education* (pp. 43–57). Baltimore: Paul H. Brookes.

Fox, T. J., & Williams, W. (1991). *Implementing best practice for all students in their local school.* Burlington: Vermont Statewide Systems Support Project, Center for Developmental Disabilities, The University Affiliated Program of Vermont.

Fritz, M. F. (1990). A comparison of social interactions using a friendship awareness activity. *Education and Training in Mental Retardation, 25,* 352–359.

Fryxell, D., & Kennedy, C. (1995). Placement along the continuum of services and its impact on students' social relationships. *Journal of the Association for Persons with Severe Handicaps, 20,* 259–269.

Gaylord-Ross, R., & Peck, C. A. (1985). Integration efforts for students with severe mental retardation. In D. Bricker & J. Filler (Eds.), *Severe mental retardation: From theory to practice* (pp. 185–207). Reston, VA: Council for Exceptional Children, Division on Mental Retardation.

Gent, P. J., & Gurecka, L. E. (1998). Service learning: A creative strategy for inclusive classrooms. *Journal of the Association for Persons with Severe Handicaps, 23,* 261–271.

Giangreco, M. F. (1996). *Vermont interdependent services team approach: A guide to coordinating educational support services.* Baltimore: Paul H. Brookes.

Giangreco, M. F., Cloninger, C. J., & Iverson, V. S. (1993). *Choosing options and accommodations for children: A guide to planning inclusive education.* Baltimore: Paul H. Brookes.

Greer by Greer v. *Rome City School District,* 950 F.2d 688 (11th Cir. 1991).

Guess, D., & Helmstetter, E. (1986). Skill cluster instruction and the individualized curriculum sequencing model. In R. H. Horner, L. H. Meyer, & H. D. Fredericks (Eds.), *Educating learners with severe handicaps: Exemplary service strategies* (pp. 221–248). Baltimore: Paul H. Brookes.

Guess, D., & Siegel-Causey, E. (1985). Behavioral control and education of severely handicapped students: Who's doing what to whom? and why? In D. Bricker & J. Filler (Eds.), *Severe mental retardation: From theory to practice* (pp. 230–244). Reston, VA: Council for Exceptional Children.

Halvorsen, A., & Neary, T. (2001). *Building inclusive schools: Tools and strategies for success.* Boston: Allyn and Bacon.

Halvorsen, A., & Sailor, W. (1990). Integration of students with severe and profound disabilities: A review of the research. In R. Gaylord-Ross (Ed.), *Issues and research in special education* (vol. 1, pp. 110–172). New York: Teachers College Press.

Haring, T. G., Breen, C., Pitts-Conway, V., Lee, M., & Gaylord-Ross, R. (1987). Adolescent peer tutoring and special friend experiences. *Journal of the Association for Persons with Severe Handicaps, 12,* 280–286.

Helmstetter, E., Curry, C. A., Brennan, M., & Sampson-Saul, M. (1998). Comparison of general and special education classrooms of students with severe disabilities. *Education and Training in Mental Retardation and Developmental Disabilities, 33,* 216–227.

Helmstetter, E., Peck, C. A., & Giangreco, M. F. (1994). Outcomes of interactions with peers with moderate or severe disabilities: A statewide survey of high school students. *Journal of the Association for Persons with Severe Handicaps, 19,* 263–276.

Hendrickson, J. M., Strain, P., Tremblay, A., & Shores, R. E. (1982). Functional effects of peer social initiations on the interactions of behaviorally handicapped children. *Behavior Modification, 6,* 323–353.

Holland v. *Sacramento City School District,* 786 F. Supp. 874 (E.D. Cal. 1992).

Hollowood, T. M., Salisbury, C. L., Rainforth, B., & Palombaro, M. M. (1994). Use of instructional time in classrooms serving students with and without severe disabilities. *Exceptional Children, 61,* 242–253.

Hughes, C., Copeland, S. R., Guth, C., Rung, L. L., Hwang, B., Kleeb, G., & Strong, M. (2001). General education students' perspectives on their involvement in a high school peer buddy program. *Education and Training in Mental Retardation and Developmental Disabilities, 36,* 343–356.

Hughes, C., Guth, C., Hall, S., Presley, J., Dye, M., & Byer, C. (1999). They are my best friends: Peer buddies promote inclusion in high school. *Teaching Exceptional Children, 31,* 136–142.

Hunt, P., Alwell, M., Farron-Davis, F., & Goetz, L. (1996). Creating socially supportive environments for fully included students who experience multiple disabilities. *Journal of the Association for Persons with Severe Handicaps, 21,* 53–71.

Hunt, P., Farron-Davis, F., Beckstead, S., Curtis, D., & Goetz, L. (1994). Evaluating the effects of placement of students with severe disabilities in regular education versus special classes. *Journal of the Association for Persons with Severe Handicaps, 19,* 200–214.

Hunt, P., & Goetz, L. (1997). Research on inclusive educational programs, practices, and outcomes for students with severe disabilities. *Journal of Special Education, 31*(1), 3–29.

Hunt, P., Staub, D., Alwell, M., & Goetz, L. (1994). Achievement by all students within the context of cooperative groups. *Journal of the Association for Persons with Severe Handicaps, 19,* 290–301.

Individuals with Disabilities Education Act Amendments of 1997 (IDEA) (1997), 20 U.S.C. 1400 et seq.

Janney, R. E., & Snell, M. E. (1996). How teachers use peer interactions to include students with moderate and severe disabilities in elementary regular education classes. *Journal of the Association for Persons with Severe Handicaps, 21,* 72–80.

Janney, R. E., & Snell, M. E. (2000). *Modifying schoolwork.* Baltimore: Paul H. Brookes.

Johnson, D. W., Johnson, R. T., & Maruyama, G. (1983). Interdependence and interpersonal attraction among heterogenous and homogenous individuals: A theoretical formulation and a meta-analysis of the research. *Review of Educational Research, 53,* 5–54.

Johnson, R., & Johnson, D. (1989). Cooperative learning and mainstreaming. In R. Gaylord-Ross (Ed.), *Integration strategies for students with handicaps* (pp. 233–248). Baltimore: Paul H. Brookes.

Kamps, D., Potucek, J., Dugan, E., Kravitz, T., Gonzalez-Lopez, A., Garcia, J., Carnazzo, K., Morrison, L. & Kane, L. G. (2002). Peer training to facilitate social interaction for elementary students with autism and their peers. *Exceptional Children, 68,* 173–188.

Kennedy, C. H., Shukla, S., & Fryxell, D. (1997). Comparing the effects of educational placement on the social relationships of intermediate school students with severe disabilities. *Exceptional Children, 64,* 31–47.

Kishi, G. S., & Meyer, L. H. (1994). What children report and remember: A six-year follow-up of the effects of social contact between peers with and without severe disabilities. *Journal of the Association for Persons with Severe Handicaps, 19,* 277–289.

Knapczyx, D. R. (1989). Peer-mediated training of cooperative play between special and regular class students in integrated play settings. *Education and Training in Mental Retardation, 24,* 255–264.

Kohl, F. L., Moses, L. G., & Stettner-Eaton, B. A. (1983). The results of teaching fifth and sixth graders to be instructional trainers with students who are severely handicapped. *Journal of the Association for the Severely Handicapped, 8,* 32–40.

Kohl, F. L., & Stettner-Eaton, B. A. (1985). Fourth graders as trainers of cafeteria skills to severely handicapped students. *Education and Training of the Mentally Retarded, 20,* 60–68.

Kohler, F. W., & Fowler, S. A. (1985). Training prosocial behaviors to young children: An analysis of reciprocity with untrained peers. *Journal of Applied Behavior Analysis, 22,* 77–83.

Lancioni, G. E. (1982). Normal children as tutors to teach social responses to withdrawn mentally retarded school mates: Training, maintenance, and generalization. *Journal of Applied Behavior Analysis, 15,* 17–40.

Logan, K. R., Jacobs, H. A., Gast, D. L., Murray, A. S., Daino, K., & Skala, C. (1998). The impact of typical peers on the perceived happiness of students with profound multiple disabilities. *Journal of the Association for Persons with Severe Handicaps, 23,* 309–318.

Madden, N. A., & Slavin, R. E. (1983). Mainstreaming students with mild handicaps: Academic and social outcomes. *Review of Educational Research, 53,* 519–569.

McDonnell, A. P., & Hardman, M. L. (1989). The desegregation of America's special schools: Strategies for change. *Journal of the Association for Persons with Severe Handicaps, 14,* 68–74.

McDonnell, J. (1998). Instruction for students with severe disabilities in general education settings. *Education and Training in Mental Retardation and Developmental Disabilities, 33,* 199–215.

McGregor, G., & Vogelsberg, R. T. (1998). Inclusive schooling practices: Pedagogical and research foundations. Pittsburgh: Allegheny University of Health Sciences.

Meyer, L. H. (1991). Guest editorial—Why meaningful outcomes? *Journal of Special Education, 25,* 287–290.

Meyer, L. H., & Putnam, J. (1987). Social integration. In V. B. VanHasselt, P. Strain, & M. Hersen (Eds.), *Handbook of developmental and physical disabilities* (pp. 107–133). New York: Pergamon.

Mulligan, M., Guess, D., Holvoet, J., & Brown, F. (1980). The individualized curriculum sequencing model (I): Implications from research on massed, distributed, or spaced trial learning. *Journal of the Association for the Severely Handicapped, 5,* 325–336.

Mulligan, M., Lacy, L., & Guess, D. (1982). The effects of massed, distributed, and spaced trial sequencing on severely handicapped students' performance. *Journal of the Association for the Severely Handicapped, 7,* 48–61.

Nirje, B. (1969). The normalization principle and its human management implications. In R. Kugel & W. Wolfensberger (Eds.), *Changing patterns in residential services for the mentally retarded* (pp. 179–195). Washington, DC: President's Committee on Mental Retardation.

Oberti v. *Board of Education of Clementon School District,* 789 F. Supp. at 1327. (1993).

Odom, S. L., & Strain, P. S. (1986). A comparison of peer-initiation and teacher-antecedent interventions for promoting reciprocal social interaction of autistic preschoolers. *Journal of Applied Behavior Analysis, 19,* 59–71.

Peck, C. A., Donaldson, J., & Pezzoli, M. (1990). Some benefits nonhandicapped adolescents perceive for themselves from their social relationships with peers who have severe handicaps. *Journal of the Association for Persons with Severe Handicaps, 15,* 241–249.

Public Law 94-142, *Education for All Handicapped Children Act of 1975,* 20 U.S.C. 14121415 (5)(B), 1975.

Putnam, J. W. (1998). *Cooperative learning and strategies for inclusion: Celebrating diversity in the classroom.* Baltimore: Paul H. Brookes.

Putnam, J. W., Rynders, J. E., Johnson, R. T., & Johnson, D. W. (1989). Collaborative skill instruction for promoting positive interactions between mentally handicapped and nonhandicapped children. *Exceptional Children, 55,* 550–557.

Rainforth, B., York, J., & Macdonald, C. (1992). *Collaborative teams for students with severe disabilities.* Baltimore: Paul H. Brookes.

Ryndak, D. L., Morrison, A. P., & Sommerstein, L. (1999). Literacy before and after inclusion in general education settings: A case study. *Journal of the Association for Persons with Severe Handicaps, 24,* 5–22.

Sailor, W., Anderson, J. L., Halvorsen, A. T., Doering, K., Filler, J., & Goetz, L. (1989). *The comprehensive local school.* Baltimore: Paul H. Brookes.

Salisbury, C. L. (1991). Mainstreaming during the early childhood years. *Exceptional Children, 58,* 146–154.

Salisbury, C. L., Gallucci, C., Palombaro, M. M., & Peck, C. A. (1995). Strategies that promote relations among elementary students with and without severe disabilities in inclusive schools. *Exceptional Children, 62,* 125–137.

Sapon-Shevin, M. (1996). Celebrating diversity, creating community. In S. Stainback & W. Stainback (Eds.), *Inclusion: A guide for educators* (pp. 255–270). Baltimore: Paul H. Brookes.

Sasso, G. M., Hughes, G. G., Swanson, H. L., & Novak, C. G. (1987). A comparison of peer initiation interventions in promoting multiple peer initiators. *Education and Training in Mental Retardation, 22,* 150–155.

Schaffner, B., & Buswell, B. E. (1996). Ten critical elements for creating inclusive and effective school communities. In S. Stainback & W. Stainback (Eds.), *Inclusion: A guide for educators* (pp. 49–65). Baltimore: Paul H. Brookes.

Schnorr, R. F. (1997). From enrollment to membership: "Belonging" in middle and high school classes. *Journal of the Association for Persons with Severe Handicaps, 22,* 1–15.

Sharpe, M. N., York, J. L., & Knight, J. (1994). Effects of inclusion on the academic performance of classmates without disabilities: A preliminary study. *Remedial and Special Education, 15,* 281–287.

Shevin, M., & Klein, N. K. (1984). The importance of choice-making for students with severe disabilities. *Journal of the Association for Persons with Severe Handicaps, 9,* 159–166.

Slavin, R. E. (1984). Review of cooperative learning research. *Review of Educational Research, 47,* 633–650.

Slavin, R. E. (1996). Education for all: Contexts of learning. Lisse, France: Swets & Keitlinger Publishers.

Snell, M. E. (1988). Curriculum and methodology for individuals with severe disabilities. *Education and Training in Mental Retardation, 23,* 302–314.

Snell, M. E., & Eichner, S. J. (1989). Integration for students with profound disabilities. In F. Brown & D. H. Lehr (Eds.), *Persons with profound disabilities: Issues and practices* (pp. 109–138). Baltimore: Paul H. Brookes.

Snell, M. E., Lowman, D. K., & Canady, R. L. (1996). Parallel block scheduling: Accommodating students' diverse needs in elementary school. *Journal of Early Intervention, 20,* 266–277.

Stainback, S., & Stainback, W. (1990). Inclusive schooling. In W. Stainback & S. Stainback (Eds.), *Support networks for inclusive schooling* (pp. 3–23). Baltimore: Paul H. Brookes.

Stainback, W., & Stainback, S. (1987). Facilitating friendships. *Education and Training in Mental Retardation, 22,* 18–25.

Stainback, W., & Stainback, S. (1989). Practical organizational strategies. In S. Stainback, W. Stainback, & M. Forest (Eds.), *Educating all students in the mainstream of regular education* (pp. 71–87). Baltimore: Paul H. Brookes.

Staub, D., Schwartz, I. S., Gallucci, C., & Peck, C. (1994). Four portraits of friendship at an inclusive school. *Journal of the Association for Persons with Severe Handicaps, 19,* 314–325.

Staub, D., Spaulding, M., Peck, C. A., Gallucci, C., & Schwartz, I. S. (1996). Using nondisabled peers to support the inclusion of students with disabilities at the junior high school level. *Journal of the Association for Persons with Severe Handicaps, 21,* 194–205.

Sternat, J., Messina, R., Nietupski, J., Lyon, S., & Brown, L. (1977). Occupational and physical therapy services for severely handicapped students: Toward a naturalized public school service delivery model. In E. Sontag (Ed.), *Educational programming for the severely and profoundly handicapped* (pp. 263–278). Reston, VA: Council for Exceptional Children.

Stokes, T. F., & Baer, D. M. (1977). An implicit technology of generalization. *Journal of Applied Behavior Analysis, 10,* 349–367.

Strain, P. S., & Kerr, M. M. (1981). *Mainstreaming of children in schools: Research and programming issues.* New York: Academic Press.

Strully, J. L., & Strully, C. F. (1985). Friendship and our children. *Journal of the Association for Persons with Severe Handicaps, 10,* 224–227.

Strully, J. L., & Strully, C. F. (1989). Friendships as an educational goal. In S. Stainback, W. Stainback, & M. Forest (Eds.), *Educating all students in the mainstream of regular education* (pp. 59–68). Baltimore: Paul H. Brookes.

Thousand, J. S., & Villa, R. A. (1990). Sharing expertise and responsibilities through teaching teams. In W. Stainback & S. Stainback (Eds.), *Support networks for inclusive schooling* (pp. 95–122). Baltimore: Paul H. Brookes.

Udvari-Solnar, A. (1992). *Curricular adaptations: Accommodating the instructional needs of diverse learners in the context of general education* (monograph). Kansas State Board of Education—Services for Children and Youth with Deaf–Blindness Project.

Udvari-Solnar, A. (1994). A decision-making model for curricular adaptations in cooperative groups. In J. S. Thousand, R. A. Villa, & A. I. Nevin (Eds.), *Creativity and collaborative learning: A practical guide to empowering students and teachers* (pp. 59–77). Baltimore: Paul H. Brookes.

Vandercook, T., & York, J. (1990). A team approach to program development and support. In W. Stainback & S. Stainback (Eds.), *Support networks for inclusive schooling* (pp. 95–122). Baltimore: Paul H. Brookes.

Villa, R. A., & Thousand, J. S. (2000). *Restructuring for caring and effective education: Piecing the puzzle together.* Baltimore: Paul H. Brookes.

Voeltz, L. M. (1980). Children's attitudes toward nonhandicapped peers. *American Journal of Mental Deficiency, 84,* 455–564.

Voeltz, L. M. (1982). Effects of structured interactions with severely handicapped peers on children's attitudes. *American Journal of Mental Deficiency, 86,* 380–390.

Voeltz, L. M. (1984). Program and curriculum innovations to prepare children for integration. In N. Certo, N. Haring, & R. York (Eds.), *Public school integration of severely handicapped students: Rational issues and progressive alternatives* (pp. 155–183). Baltimore: Paul H. Brookes.

Voeltz, L. M., Kishi, G., & Brennan, J. (1981). *The social interaction observation system (SIOS).* Honolulu: University of Hawaii.

Wehmeyer, M. L., Lattin, D., & Agran, M. (2001). Achieving access to the general curriculum for students with mental retardation. *Education and Training in Mental Retardation and Developmental Disabilities, 36,* 327–342.

Werts, M. G., Wolery, M., Snyder, E. D., & Caldwell, N. K. (1996). Teachers' perceptions of the supports critical to the success of inclusion programs. *Journal of the Association for Persons with Severe Handicaps, 21,* 9–21.

Williams, W., Villa, R., Thousand, J., & Fox, W. L. (1989). Is regular class placement really the issue? A response to Brown, Long, Udvari-Solnaer, Schwarz, VanDeventer, Ahlgren, Johnson, Gruenewald, & Jorgensen. *Journal of the Association for Persons with Severe Handicaps, 14,* 333–334.

York, J., Vandercook, T., Caughey, E., & Heise-Neff, C. (1989). Regular class integration: Beyond socialization. In J. York, T. Vandercook, C. MacDonald, & S. Wolff (Eds.), *Strategies for full inclusion* (pp. 117–120). Minneapolis: University of Minnesota, Institute on Community Integration.

York, J., Vandercook, T., MacDonald, C., & Wolff, S. (1989). *Strategies for full inclusion.* Minneapolis: University of Minnesota, Institute on Community Integration.

PART 4

Specific Instructional and Management Procedures

CHAPTER 11

Teaching Communication Skills

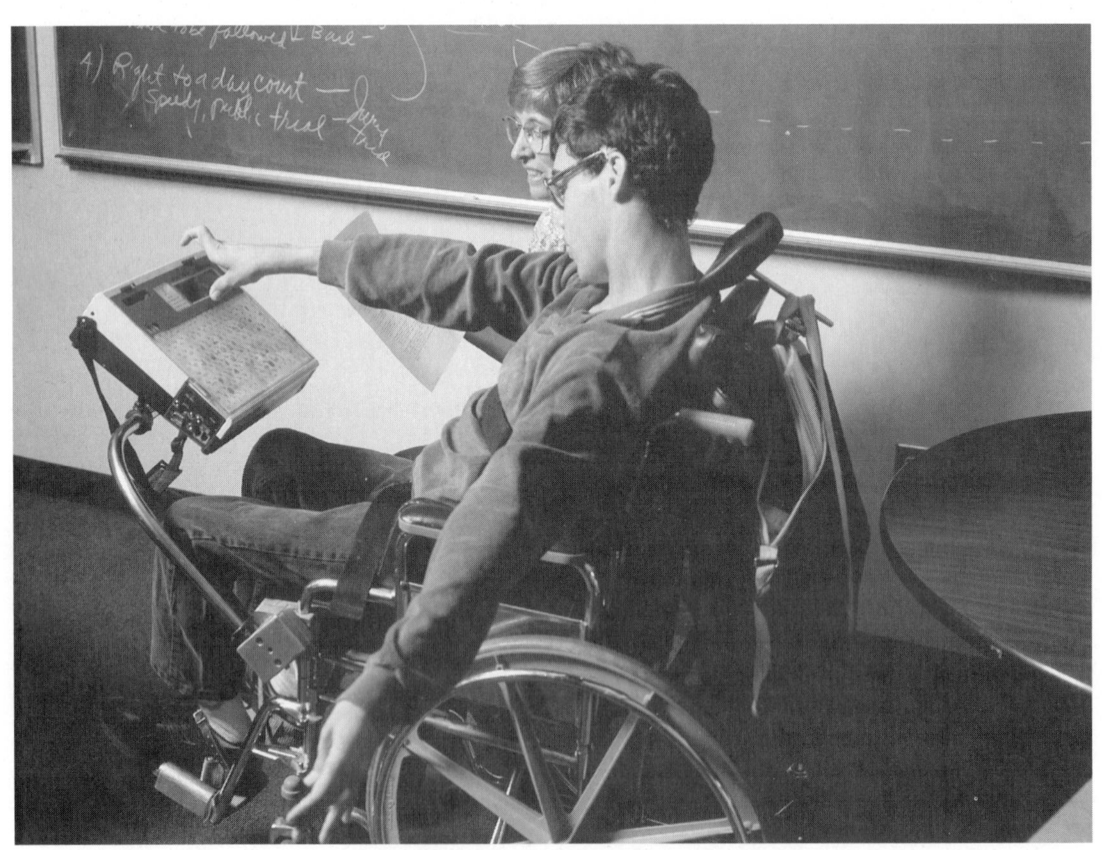

In this chapter, communication skill development is discussed and methods for assessing a student's communication abilities are presented. Information is provided to guide the teacher in how to match a communication system to a student's abilities and techniques for the instruction of communication skills.

The Instruction of Communication Skills

The skill of communication is one of the most important and most difficult to teach students with severe disabilities. The difficulty stems in part from practitioners' lack of knowledge about designing communication interventions and the myriad problems associated with the student's disability. Successful communication is a result of the integration and performance of cognitive, social, and motor skills. Students with severe disabilities are likely to display difficulties in some or all of these areas.

Access to communication services and supports is viewed by educators and advocates as essential to the achievement of meaningful lifestyle outcomes by individuals with disabilities (National Joint Committee for the Communication Needs of Persons with Severe Disabilities 1992, 2002; TASH, 2002). In 1992, the National Joint Committee for the Communication Needs of Persons with Severe Disabilities established a Communication Bill of Rights that included the following rights:

Each person has a right to:

- request desired objects, actions, events, and people
- refuse undesired objects, actions, or events
- express personal preferences and feelings
- be offered choices and alternatives
- reject offered choices
- request and receive another person's attention and interaction
- ask for and receive information about changes in routine and environment
- receive intervention to improve communication skills
- receive a response to any communication, whether or not the responder can fill the request
- have access to augmentative and alternative communication and other assistive technology services and devices at all times
- be in environments that promote one's communication as a full partner with other people, including peers
- be spoken to with respect and courtesy
- be spoken to directly and not be spoken for or talked about in the third person while present
- have clear, meaningful, and culturally and linguistically appropriate communications (National Joint Committee for the Communicative Needs of Persons with Severe Disabilities, 1992)

These rights offer guidelines for the development of communication interventions, supports, and systems. Collaborative teams should examine these rights as they begin to discuss communication intervention goals, communication systems, and the supports that should be in place to support a learner with communication intervention needs.

The knowledge and technology related to communication skill instruction has grown significantly in the last decade. Important milestones that have been achieved include a shift in assessment practices from identifying appropriate candidates for communication instruction to a belief that communication instruction is appropriate for all students, a shift from a focus on the development of isolated speech and language skills to the development of functional communication, and an understanding of the importance of multimodal communication (Mirenda & Iacono, 1990; Reichle, 1997). Researchers and practitioners have also become more aware of the importance of social interactions and the role of communication partners in providing communication opportunities (Bricker, 1993; Butterfield & Arthur, 1995; Goldstein, Kaczmarek, & English, 2002; Jackson, 1993; Reichle, 1997).

Current practice in communication and language instruction uses knowledge of the development of communication to guide interventions that are functional for the student within social contexts (Bricker, 1993; Downing, 1999; Jackson, 1993; Reichle, 1997). Intervention practices have broadened to examine the critical importance of the social use of communication skills, including prelinguistic communication behavior. In the past, interventions were targeted toward the production of spoken language and the use of symbols to communicate. Communication interventions are informed by understanding the early development of communication and language skills, although interventions are developed in a manner to be maximally useful and functional for the student within social exchanges.

The following six tenets have been proposed as fundamental to understanding and developing communication interventions for individuals with severe disabilities

(National Joint Committee for the Communicative Needs of Persons with Severe Disabilities, 1992):

1. Communication is social behavior.
2. Appropriate communication functions enable productive participation in interactions with others.
3. Communication acts can be produced in a variety of modes.
4. Effective communication intervention must fully utilize naturally occurring interactive contexts.
5. Service delivery must involve family members working collaboratively with a cadre of professionals and paraprofessionals.
6. Effective intervention must modify the physical and social elements of environments to invite, accept, and respond to communicative acts.

The instruction of communication skills is a complex and dynamic process. Students who have severe cognitive impairments may also have additional physical and sensory disabilities that make the development of effective receptive and expressive communication systems complicated. The communicative abilities of students with severe disabilities span a broad continuum, from learners who are nonverbal and nonintentional to students who may have more complex, spoken communication (McLean, Brady, & McLean, 1996). The speech therapist, the teacher, and other collaborative team members spend a significant amount of time assessing a student's communicative behavior and trying different types of interventions and communication systems to help the student to achieve success. The areas of knowledge that are essential to appropriate instruction in communication are communication skill development and assessment, augmentative communication systems, instructional strategies, and generalization procedures.

Communication Skill Development

In the past, developmental milestones were used as a guide in examining the development of communication skills by individuals with severe disabilities. Emphasis was placed on the development of expressive and receptive communication skills, with a focus on the acquisition of language. Students with disabilities were assessed using communication inventories or language assessments based on normal developmental milestones and then taught the skills indicated as deficits by the assessment. This resulted in the instruction of language skills that were often not functional for the student with disabilities. For example, a student might have been taught to imitate speech sounds or to label photographs of objects. Instruction in language targets often occurred in isolated, structured contexts that did not resemble the interactions in which communication skills would be used. For example, a student may have been taught to sign words in response to a picture instead of within a conversational exchange. In addition, the focus on teaching language skills excluded instruction for the learner who was at a prelinguistic or nonsymbolic level of language development.

Early Communication Development

In the late 1970s researchers in communication development began to focus on the normal development of prelinguistic skills (i.e., communication skills that develop before speech) with infants and toddlers (Alvares, Falor, & Smiley, 1991). More recently, researchers interested in children with disabilities have applied the research on prelinguistic communication development of infants and toddlers to students with severe disabilities (Siegel-Causey & Guess, 1989; Wetherby & Prizant, 1989; Wetherby, Warren, & Reichle, 1998). An important result of the study of prelinguistic communication has been a focus on the pragmatics of communication. *Pragmatics* can be defined as the use of communication indexes within the social context. What has been learned from the research on the development of prelinguistic communication skills is that these skills develop within the context of a social relationship, predictably the relationship between the primary caregiver and the child. The application of a pragmatic orientation requires the evaluation of communication skills by examining the social context in which the exchange occurs, and it often results in targeting both the learner and the communication partner for intervention (Alvares et al., 1991).

The interest in pragmatics was very important in understanding the communication skill development of learners with severe disabilities. In the past, when language researchers and practitioners were concerned with the structure of language, rather than the social aspects of communication, students with severe disabilities who were not talking were often not included in intervention. In addition, there was very little guidance in the literature for ways to assist the skill development of students who were at a nonsymbolic or prelinguistic stage of development.

Intentionality

Researchers have been particularly interested in the development of intentionality in the prelinguistic communication exchanges of children and their caregivers.

Intentionality may be defined as "the deliberate pursuit of a goal" (Wetherby & Prizant, 1989, p. 77). A child who exhibits intentionality is one who knows that, if a message is sent to the listener, the listener will receive and act on it. A common approach to identifying intentionality is to use behavioral criteria (Bates, 1979; Harding & Golinkoff, 1979). Behavioral evidence that may signal intentionality includes alternating eye gaze between the goal and the listener, persistent signaling or changing the signal until the goal is met, awaiting a response from the listener, and indicating satisfaction when the goal is met (Wetherby & Prizant, 1989).

Bates (1979) proposed a three-stage model for describing the development of communication and intentionality. The first stage of the model, the perlocutionary stage, occurs from birth until there is evidence of intentionality in the child's communicative utterances or gestures. In this stage the child has an effect on the listener without intending to. An example of communication at the perlocutionary stage is the interpretation by the caregiver that an infant's crying means that the infant wants to be held. The second stage of the model, the illocutionary stage, occurs when the child uses gestures and sounds to intentionally affect the listener. An example of a communication expression at the illocutionary stage is a toddler's pointing to a carton of juice to indicate to his caregiver that he wants a drink or repeating a vocalization (i.e., not words) until his caregiver provides his favorite toy. The third stage of the model, the locutionary stage, occurs when language emerges and the child communicates with words.

The Bates (1979) framework offers useful distinctions between communicative stages, but does not fully explain the development of intentionality. A child with disabilities may evidence intentionality when reaching for a toy that is on a shelf to signal a request to a caregiver, but may also cry or shift her eye gaze during a play activity without intentionality. It would be difficult to determine if this child is in the perlocutionary or illocutionary stage. Wetherby and Prizant (1989) discuss the emergence of intentionality as occurring along a developmental continuum, rather than only being present or absent. In their model, they describe intentionality as developing from children who have no awareness of the goal to an ability to send a message and then repair or change the form of the signal if their needs are not met. For example, when a child in the early perlocutionary stage cries, a caregiver might respond by interpreting the cry to mean that the child wants to be picked up. A child in the illocutionary stage who has an awareness that the listener will respond to a message and has the capacity to plan a message may pull the caregiver to the refrigerator to request a bottle and, if the goal is not met, may begin patting the refrigerator or vocalizing. Thus the child has persisted in signaling and has changed the signal form for achieving the desired goal.

Communicative Means and Functions

The development of the child's ability to signal by examining intentionality is one important aspect of communication development to consider. In addition, the interventionist should consider the child's ability to use different means of communication (forms of the communication signal such as crying, vocalizing, gesturing, or talking) to express himself. Wetherby and Prizant (1989) explain that sophistication in the means to express intentionality develops in a horizontal direction during the prelinguistic stage. In this stage, typically developing children progress from nonverbal to verbal means of communication within the three major categories of communication functions that are described in Figure 11–1.

In learners with severe disabilities, means used for communicative functions can range from nonverbal, idiosyncratic behavior (eye poking, slapping) to a variety of conventional means (pointing, words) that are more easily understood by the communication partner. These communicative means are used to express the communicative functions of behavioral regulation (to request objects or actions, to protest), social interaction (to attract and maintain someone's attention for affiliative purposes), and joint attention (to direct someone's attention to an object or entity) (Wetherby & Prizant, 1989).

Teachers can use information on the development of intentional communication and the description of communication functions to understand the communication behavior of students with severe disabilities who are in the prelinguistic or nonsymbolic stage of communication development (Reichle, Halle, & Johnson, 1993). This framework assists the teacher in analyzing the range of means (the form of communication) and functions (the reason for communicating) and the level of intentionality the student exhibits. For example, when Andy, a 10-year-old student with severe disabilities, wants a drink he brings his cup to his mother and looks at her and at the refrigerator. If she does not get a drink immediately, he cries, but does not engage in any additional behavior such as pulling her to the refrigerator or pointing to the refrigerator. Andy also pushes away objects that he does not want and shakes his head back and forth. If the object is not removed immediately, he bangs his forehead on the table or on his knee. In examining Andy's behavior from the Wetherby and Prizant (1989) framework, the teacher can conclude that Andy uses bringing his cup to his mother as a request function and uses shaking his head and banging his forehead as a protest. Both of these functions fall into

Figure 11–1 Communicative Functions Emerging in the First Two Years

I. *BEHAVIORAL REGULATION:* Acts used to regulate the behavior of another person for purposes of obtaining and restricting an environmental goal

- –to request an object or action
- –to protest an object or action

II. *SOCIAL INTERACTION:* Acts used to attract or maintain another's attention to oneself for affiliative purposes

- –to request a social routine
- –to greet or call another person
- –to show off
- –to request another's permission
- –to acknowledge another's action or utterance

III. *JOINT ATTENTION:* Acts used to direct another's attention to an object, action, or utterance for purposes of focus on an entity or event

- –to label or comment on an object or event
- –to clarify a previous utterance
- –to request information about an object or event

Source: "Communicative Profiles of Handicapped Preschool Children: Implications for Early Identification," by A. M. Wetherby, D. G. Yonclass, and A. A. Bryan, 1989, *Journal of Speech and Hearing Disorders, 54*(2), pp. 148–158. Adapted by permission.

the category of behavior regulation. In examining the level of intentionality, the teacher can conclude that Andy shows an ability to use alternative plans to achieve his goal by changing his signal (crying, head banging) after an unsuccessful attempt to achieve that goal.

Assessment Issues

Before communication intervention begins, the educator must determine the student's current repertoire of communication behavior. It is essential to know what current communicative functions are exhibited by the learner, what means are used to express these functions, under what conditions different communicative means and functions are exhibited, and what level of intentionality is present in communicative attempts. In addition, the educator will want to assess the student's capabilities in motoric skills, sensory functioning, cognitive functioning, and receptive language comprehension.

Communication Skill Assessment

A traditional approach to assessment involves the administration of standardized language or communication inventories that are based on normal development and focused on expressive and receptive language skills. However, these instruments are rarely helpful in examining the communication skills of students with severe disabilities (Butterfield, Arthur, & Sigafoos, 1995; Schuler, Peck, Willard, & Theimer, 1989), who may be at a prelinguistic level in communication development or who may not have the physical capacity to speak. The process for assessing the communication skills of students with severe disabilities involves an array of informal and nonstandardized procedures.

Several inventories have been developed for evaluating the communication behavior of students with severe disabilities, including the Communication Programming Inventory (Sternberg & McNerney, 1988), the Communication Intention Inventory (Coggins & Carpenter, 1981), and the Communication Interview (Schuler et al., 1989). In addition to these measures, Neel and Billingsley (1989), Wetherby and Prizant (1989), Siegel-Causey and Downing (1987), and Donnellan, Mirenda, Mesaros, and Fassbender (1984) offer formats for determining a student's communication abilities.

The procedures for determining the current communication abilities of a student may involve the direct assessment of skills in a traditional skill checklist format such as the Communication Programming Inventory (Sternberg & McNerney, 1988), the use of an interview procedure like that shown in Figure 11–2 (Schuler et al., 1989), or the collection of a communication sample (Wetherby & Prizant, 1989). The communication

Figure 11–2 Communication Interview

CUE QUESTIONS	*Crying*	*Aggression*	*Tantrums, Self Injury*	*Passive Gaze*	*Proximity*	*Pulling Other's Hands*	*Touching, Moving Other's Face*	*Grabs, Reaches*	*Enactment*	*Removes Self, Walks Away*	*Vocalization, Noise*	*Active Gaze*	*Gives Object*	*Gestures, Pointing*	*Facial Expression*	*Shakes "no" / Nods "yes"*	*Intonation*	*Inappropriate Echolalia*	*Appropriate Echolalia*	*One-Word Speech*	*One-Word Signs*	*Complex Speech*	*Complex Signs*
1. Requests for affection/interaction: WHAT IF S WANTS																							
adult to sit near?																							
peer to sit near?																							
nonhandicapped peer to sit near?																							
adult to look at him?																							
adult to tickle him?																							
to cuddle/embrace?																							
to sit on adult's lap?																							
other:																							
2. Requests for adult action: WHAT IF S WANTS																							
help with dressing?																							
to be read a book?																							
to play ball/a game?																							
to go outside/to store?																							
other:																							
3. Requests for object, food, or things: WHAT IF S WANTS																							
an object out of reach?																							
a door/container opened?																							
a favorite food?																							
music/radio/tv?																							
keys/toy/book?																							
other:																							
4. Protest: WHAT IF																							
common routine is dropped?																							
favorite toy/food taken away?																							
taken for ride w/out desire?																							
adult terminates interaction?																							
required to do something doesn't want to?																							
other:																							
5. Declaration/Comment: WHAT IF S WANTS																							
to show you something?																							
you to look at something?																							
other:																							

Source: "Assessment of Communicative Means and Functions through Interview: Assessing the Communicative Capabilities of Individuals with Limited Language," by A. L. Schuler, C. A. Peck, C. Willard, and K. Theimer, 1989, *Seminars in Speech and Language, 10,* pp. 51–62. Reprinted with permission from Thieme Medical Publishers, Inc.

interview developed by Schuler et al. provides questions that can be asked of a person familiar with the student with disabilities to determine the student's communicative means and functions. The functions (reasons) of communication that are examined are requests for objects, actions, and interaction; protests; and comments. Across the top of the interview is a listing of different communicative means that range from the idiosyncratic and problematic, such as a tantrum or aggression, to the conventional, such as using complex speech. The assessor probes the person familiar with the student or completes the interview by observing the student and determining what means are used for each communicative function.

Wetherby and Prizant (1989) offer guidelines for an informal procedure that may also assist in determining a student's communicative means and functions. They describe a procedure that uses "communicative temptations" to elicit communicative behavior. An example of a communicative temptation is to eat a desired food item in front of a child without offering the child some, which may elicit request behavior. Another example is to show the child a toy that requires activation, activate the toy without letting the child see how it was done, and then hand the child the toy when it has stopped. This may elicit a request for help or a comment from the child. A communication sample can be collected by videotaping the reactions of the child to a series of communicative temptations. The videotape can be analyzed later to determine the communicative means, functions, and levels of intentionality that the child displays. Other temptations that may be used are presented in Figure 11–3.

It is important for the teacher to realize that students with severe disabilities may express communicative functions using means that are viewed as aberrant or problematic behavior. A student who has not developed a conventional signal for protest may engage in aggression or self-injury to communicate a signal for "no" or "stop." Methods for discerning the communicative functions of problem behavior and the procedures for intervention are discussed at length in Chapter 12. In fact, the most current work in intervening with problem behavior suggests that an understanding of pragmatics is important in behavior intervention (Carr, McConnachie, Levin, & Kemp, 1993; Donnellan et al., 1984).

Assessing the communication abilities of the student is essential to the development of intervention strategies. In addition to understanding the learner's capacities, the interventionist should also seek to understand what communication demands and supports are provided by the student's environments.

Ecological Assessment

Ecological inventories (as described in Chapter 6) can be used to collect information about the unique communicative demands and opportunities of the environments that the student will encounter (Downing, 1999). This information will assist the interventionist in understanding the communicative needs of the student, what modes of communication may be needed (e.g., sign language vs. communication book), and how the learner currently functions in these situations. In addition to information on the activities and skills needed in various subenvironments, information should also be collected on the communicative demands and opportunities of various environments and the communicative functions, vocabulary, and modes needed by the learner to communicate effectively in these environments (Sigafoos & York, 1991). For example, an ecological inventory of a fast-food restaurant might indicate that the learner must be able to respond to "May I help

Figure 11–3 Communicative Temptations

Source: "The Expression of Communicative Intent: Assessment Guidelines," by A. M. Wetherby and B. M. Prizant, 1989, *Seminars in Speech and Language, 10,* pp. 77–90. Reprinted with permission from Thieme Medical Publishers, Inc.

1. Eat a desired food in front of the child without offering any to the child.
2. Activate a wind-up toy, let it deactivate, and hand it to the child.
3. Give the child a book and encourage him or her to look at the book and turn the pages, then repeat this with a second book.
4. Open a jar of bubbles, blow bubbles, then close the jar tightly and give the closed jar to the child.
5. Initiate a familiar and unfamiliar social game with the child until the child expresses pleasure; then stop the game and wait.
6. Hold a food item or toy that the child dislikes out near the child to offer it.
7. Place a desired food item in a clear container that the child cannot open while the child is watching; then put the container in front of the child and wait.

you?" by placing an order. If the learner uses sign language for most of his communication expression, he may need to be taught an alternative mode (such as picture cards) to effectively meet the communication demand in this setting.

Rowland and Schweigert (1993) describe the use of ACE (Analyzing the Communicative Environment), which may be used to assess the properties of student activities and the extent to which an activity is encouraging communication for a particular student. Items on ACE guide the observer to consider the instructional activity, the student's communication system, the nature of the adult interaction with the student, the peer group dynamics of the activity, the materials used within the activity, and the opportunities for communication offered within the activity. ACE offers a heuristic for examining the nature of functional activities and their conduciveness for communication by a particular student. When teachers apply ACE, changes may be targeted for activities that will strengthen their potential for teaching and maintaining communication skills.

Selecting a Communication Mode

When information has been collected on the student's communicative repertoire and opportunities for communication interaction, the collaborative team should determine whether the student's current communication system is understandable to others, socially acceptable, and not a part of an existing behavior repertoire that is inappropriate (Reichle, 1991). If the behavior is understood by others and socially appropriate, the collaborative team may choose to focus on the expansion of means or vocabulary and the level of intentionality that the learner displays in her present mode of communication. If the behavior is not understandable or socially acceptable, the focus of the intervention may be to replace the current mode of communication with a more conventional and acceptable form (Reichle, 1991).

For many students with severe disabilities, speech is not the most effective mode of communication (Romski & Sevcik, 1993). Determining that a student should use an augmentative or alternative communication system or that the focus in the intervention should be increasing language skills is a decision that must be made by the collaborative team, including the family. The speech therapist, physical therapist, audiologist, and occupational therapist may be able to contribute essential information on the student's language, sensory, and motoric abilities to guide decision making. A poor prognosis for the effectiveness of natural speech is evident if the student has physical difficulty in the production of speech sounds as evidenced by the evaluation of oral reflexes, eating patterns, vocal patterns, and neuromuscular status of the oral mechanism; if the student has not developed speech by 5 years of age; if the student is unable to imitate words verbally; and if the student has a hearing impairment (Musselwhite & St. Louis, 1988). Some students may be using limited speech to express some functions. The interventionist should consider the efficiency of speech for the student's communication repertoire. Perhaps an additional mode of communication expression is necessary to allow the student to expand the range of functions and the level of intentionality that he can express.

The decision to teach the use of an alternative or augmentative mode of communication should not be viewed as giving up on the student's eventual use of language. Researchers have found that the use of augmentative communication does not inhibit speech production (Romski & Sevcik, 1992). The goal for the collaborative team is to develop a communication intervention plan that allows the student with severe disabilities to express herself and to affect others. Unlocking the student's access to the social world, using whatever strategy necessary, is of primary importance.

Augmentative and Alternative Communication

For students who will not be using natural speech or who need an additional mode of communication to communicate effectively, the interventionist needs to select an appropriate augmentative or alternative system of communication. Augmentative systems involve the use of aids that supplement existing vocal communication skills; alternative systems are methods of communication that are used by a person without vocal ability (Lloyd, Fuller, & Arvidson, 1997; Mustonen, Locke, Reichle, Solbrack, & Lindgren, 1991). The many types of symbols, methods, techniques, and systems that can be used for augmentative and alternative communication can be classified as either gestural or graphic modes of communication (Mustonen et al., 1991).

The selection of an augmentative or alternative system depends in part on the student's motor, cognitive, and sensory abilities (Johnson, Baumgart, Helmstetter, & Curry, 1996). A student who does not appear to understand symbolic representation of objects is an unlikely candidate for a complex symbol system. A student with vision impairments will need a communication system with enhanced visual symbols, tactile cues, or auditory feedback. A student with limited fine motor skills is not an appropriate candidate for sign language instruction. Knowledge of the student's capabilities in motor, visual, and cognitive skills will assist the collaborative team in selecting an appropriate system. A communication system should be developed with symbols placed in the student's reach or visual field. A communication system must be designed specifically for the student with knowledge of the whole individual and a commitment to continuous modification until success is met.

Teaming with Families

Family involvement in the communication assessment, system selection, and goal identification is absolutely essential to the development of the student's communication system (Parette, Brotherson, & Huer, 2000). Family participation and buy-in to the intervention approach and communication system to be used increases the likelihood that intervention may be successful. If family members are not involved in the process, the team runs the danger of selecting a communication system or device that will not be used in the home or community.

Family and cultural considerations must also be a part of the decision-making process for selecting a communication system. In a study conducted with 58 families who were culturally diverse, the families expressed the following for their involvement in decision making concerning augmentative and alternative communication (Parette et al., 2000):

- Families desire clear, accurate, trustworthy, and straightforward communication from the professionals on the team;
- Families wish to be key informants in the assessment process and for professionals to recognize the family's life-long relationship with their child;
- Families want professionals to recognize the cultural importance of other members (elders, extended family members) of the family and to welcome their involvement in the process;
- Families want professionals to establish rapport with their children prior to assessment activities;
- Families are concerned about their child's continued access to a device;
- Families want professionals to show sensitivity to the individual child and to regard the child as an individual (rather than a type of disability) and to respect cultural preferences in the selection of symbols for the device. For example, Navajo families want symbols and colors used that are appropriate to their clan;
- Families want teams to discuss issues such as the transportation, maintenance, and storage of the device; and
- Families want information, support, and training on the use of the device, including support from other families who are using communication devices. Some families also expressed a preference to have information, support, and training provided in their native language.

Gestural Communication

Gestural communication ranges from the use of natural gestures to indicate communicative functions to formal sign language systems. Children and adults use a variety of natural gestures to communicate. Pointing is a natural gesture that directs attention to an object or event for the purpose of requesting or commenting. Another natural gesture frequently used is holding an object out to the communication partner for the purpose of showing. Handing a person an object, such as an empty cup or a favorite book, is a natural gesture that is used by young children to signal a request (e.g., a drink or a story). Pulling a communication partner toward an activity or an object is another natural gesture that may serve as a request or a comment. A well-recognized natural gesture that is used in adulthood is head nodding to signal a yes or no response. These natural gestures work effectively to communicate one's needs and may be potential targets for acquisition by students with severe disabilities. If a student with severe disabilities grabs objects that he wishes to have, it may be possible to shape the grabbing into pointing to indicate requests. For example, the interventionist could reinforce this behavior for the student by providing the object contingently on the reach. Then the interventionist could model or physically assist the student in pointing to desired objects that are out of reach and reinforce the behavior by providing the object. The same type of process could be used if a student moves her face away when shown an undesired toy or food item, shaping the head turning into a head shaking to indicate no.

For some learners, gestural communication may take the sophisticated form of sign language. Sign language and sign systems have been developed to offer nonverbal communicators a symbol set for communication. American Sign Language (Ameslan), a sign language system used by persons who are deaf, involves signals for letters (finger spelling) and words or phrases. Ameslan has its own semantic and syntactic rules, many of which differ from English. Signing Exact English (Gustason, Pfetzing, &

Zawolkow, 1972) draws its basic signs from Ameslan, but uses English word order and includes signs to represent syntax (arrangement of words to convey meaning) and morphology (the structure of words). Amer-Ind is a gestural set that is derived from the gestures used by American Indians (Skelly, 1979). Amer-Ind signs are more understandable to others with guessability (ability for the naive to interpret the sign), ranging from 50% (Vanderheiden & Lloyd, 1986) to 80% (Skelly, 1979).

The ease with which signs are learned depends on several features of the sign language or system. The easiest signs to learn are those that take two hands to produce with physical contact between the hands, are symmetrical, are produced within the communicator's visual field, and resemble their referents (Dennis, Reichle, Williams, & Vogelsberg, 1982; Doherty, 1985). For example, the sign for "more" is easier to learn because both hands touch, they make the same shape, and the sign is displayed in front of the learner's body. Although sign language has the advantage of not needing any equipment to communicate and offering an unlimited vocabulary potential, it also has several disadvantages in its potential use by learners with severe disabilities. It depends on understanding by the listener. The majority of people in the community are not trained in manual sign language and would have difficulty interpreting communication by sign language. In addition, the production of sign language requires a level of manual dexterity that many individuals with severe disabilities do not have. Signs are also dynamic displays of language, rather than graphic symbols, which are static. Because they are dynamic, the learner with severe cognitive impairments may be unable to maintain a mental representation of the communication utterance when attempting to form the sign symbol. Although sign language is frequently taught as an augmentative system, few studies have shown that learners with severe disabilities acquire generalized sign language systems that involve more than one- or two-word utterances or generalization.

Aided Systems

The use of an aided system of communication is an effective communication alternative for many students with severe disabilities. Aided systems include a range of alternatives, from the use of objects and pictures to communicate to complex electronic communication devices. When selecting an aided communication system, the interventionist must consider if the student is capable of using a representational communication system, the type of symbols to be used, the format in which the symbols are displayed, and the method the learner uses to select the symbol for communication expression.

Symbol Selection

Symbols used in aided communication systems vary in symbol guessability, ease of acquisition, and how well the symbol use is generalized and maintained in non-training settings. Real objects or tangible symbols have been successfully used by individuals with severe disabilities and vision impairments for communication (Rowland & Schweigert, 1989; Stillman & Battle, 1984). Tangible symbols are permanent, manipulable, and tactually discriminable; require simple motor responses for use; and have an obvious relationship to the object that they represent (Rowland & Schweigert, 1989). An example of the use of a tangible symbol may be the presentation of a block to indicate a desire to play with blocks or the presentation of a cup to indicate a desire for a drink. Because the use of real objects limits the expandability and portability of a communication system, miniature objects or parts of objects can be used with a student who is capable of representational thought. For example, a student may use a piece of a milk carton to indicate a request for milk or a tiny spoon to indicate a request for cereal. Students can also be taught to associate unrelated symbols to activities or objects by attaching the tangible symbol. For example, the teacher could glue a sandpaper shape to a game box and provide the student with a similar sandpaper shape to use as a request for the game.

Representations of objects, activities, places, and expressions by photographs, product logos, and line drawings have also been used for expressive communication. Several types of line-drawn symbol systems have been developed for augmentative and alternative communicators. Picsyms (Carlson, 1984) are black line-drawn symbols that represent 1,800 words. Rebus symbols, line drawings that represent words or parts of words, have been used to teach reading skills to young children and children with mental disabilities (Woodcock, Clark, & Davies, 1969). Rebus symbols are easier to learn, remember, and decode than spelled words (Clark, Davies, & Woodcock, 1974).

Blissymbols are another type of pictographic system developed for use as an international communication system (Silverman, 1980). There are approximately 100 symbols, which represent general concepts or ideas. When symbols are combined with other elements, the meaning of the symbol is changed. For example, when the symbols for person, mouth, and musical note are combined, the representation would mean the concept "singer" (Silverman, 1980). Symbols used in the Bliss system are pictographic (the referent is shown in an outline drawing), ideographic (the idea is represented with shapes associated with the referent), and arbitrary (Mustonen et al., 1991). Because Blissymbols are not easily intelligible to untrained communication partners, they are displayed with the written language equivalent.

Many commercially available computer programs provide graphic programs for the development of symbol systems. Catalogs from vendors who specialize in speech and language materials or assistive devices are good sources for identifying programs. In addition, many teachers have access to digital cameras. Photographs taken with a digital camera can be modified on the computer for the development of communication boards or displays.

The learnability of graphic symbol sets has been investigated by researchers (Hurlbut, Iwata, & Green, 1982; Mirenda & Locke, 1989; Sevcik & Romski, 1986). Empirical evidence indicates that a hierarchy of difficulty from easiest to most difficult to learn appears to be real objects, color photographs, black-and-white photographs, miniature objects, black-and-white line drawings, rebuses, and Blissymbols.

Symbol Display and Organization

There are several ways for communication symbols to be displayed, organized, and carried by the communicator. Communication wallets can be designed by placing the symbols on cards that are inserted into the vinyl credit card sleeves of a wallet (Mustonen et al., 1991). Symbols on laminated cards can be put on a ring that can be attached to the learner's belt loop or carried.

Communication books allow for a greater number of symbols to be stored, but are less portable than wallets. A communication book can easily be made from a photo album or three-ring binder. Symbols are displayed and arranged in a format that facilitates quick access by the learner. For example, a communication book may be arranged by symbols that the learner uses at home, school, and work or by symbols representing people, objects, foods, and activities. A more portable version of a communication book can be made by reducing the size of the book so that it can be carried by the learner in a pack attached to the waist.

Communication boards, flat surfaces on which the symbols are placed, are frequently used by individuals who spend most of their time in a wheelchair. The communication board can be placed directly on the lap tray. Communication boards that are specific to an area or activity may also be used. For example, a communication board may be designed for use just at the lunch table with symbols of items the student typically requests; another student may have a communication board specific to a vocational task. With the use of these mini-boards in activities that involve specified vocabulary, more symbols are made available to the learner.

Communicating with Symbols

When developing a communication system, the teacher should examine the system and determine whether the student will be able to gain the attention of a listener effectively. If the student does not have a reliable mechanism to call for the listener's attention, the teacher should consider adding a component to the communication system. Examples of methods that a learner might use include vocalizing, pressing a buzzer, and pressing an icon that activates a message (e.g., "I want to tell you something"). Once the listener's attention has been gained, the learner can select a communication symbol.

Learners who use a graphic system to communicate must have a means to indicate their selection of a symbol to their communication partners. Touching or pointing to the symbol is called *direct selection;* it can be done by using the hand or finger, but can also be accomplished through directed eye gaze, by using another body part (toe, elbow, etc.), or by using a pointer attached to the body (mouthstick, head pointer). If the learner is physically capable of direct selection, it is the preferred method of indicating the symbol (Mustonen et al., 1991).

Scanning is a technique that can be used by learners whose physical impairments prevent direct selection. In scanning, the learner indicates a selection by signaling to the listener that the desired symbol has been reached. One version of scanning, auditory scanning, is the use of "twenty questions" (Shane & Cohen, 1981). In "twenty questions" the learner uses a signal to respond to questions that the listener asks to determine what the learner is trying to communicate. In manual scanning, the listener touches the symbols sequentially until the learner signals to stop, thereby indicating the symbol selection. For learners with many symbols, group/item scanning or page/item scanning also may be used. In group/item and page/item scanning, the learner uses scanning first to indicate the set of symbols (arranged by topic, environment, etc.) and then the item selection. For example, Jacob uses page/item scanning with a communication book. His communication partner opens the book to a menu page. On that page is a symbol for toys, positions, food, activities, and people. The communication partner points to each symbol and asks "Do you want ____ ?" Jacob blinks when the desired symbol is touched. The communication partner then turns to the page in the communication book that has symbols for the selected topic. The communication partner begins scanning these symbols until Jacob indicates his selection by blinking.

Encoding is a type of scanning that may be useful for students who are able to memorize and perform complex representational and sequencing skills (Miller & Allaire, 1987). In encoding, the learner memorizes a coded vocabulary and then communicates a message by using the code. For example, the learner uses eye gaze to point to a code system of numbers, colors, or letters displayed around the edge of the board. The student may eye point to the color red, which means that she wishes to use the red group of words and messages, and then eye points to the numbers, which means that she wishes to use the word in the red group with the designation 5.

Scanning may also be used with electronic communication devices. Because such devices continue to become more affordable, students with the cognitive capacity to use the encoding system described earlier are increasingly more likely to use them. Electronic scanning is accomplished through the use of a switch that controls the scanning. For many devices, the switch activates a light that moves through the symbol array until the switch is hit again. A variety of patterns can be used for scanning. In linear scanning, the cursor moves across the row of symbols one symbol at a time in a left-to-right movement. In circular scanning, the cursor moves in a circular fashion around the display. In row/column scanning, the cursor moves down a column until it is stopped and then moves across the selected row of symbols. Directed scanning can also be accomplished with switches or a joystick controlling the cursor. In directed scanning, the learner uses the joystick to move the cursor directly to the symbol being selected.

A variety of switches can be used to control the cursor of an electronic device for scanning. Electromechanical switches allow the learner to control the movement of the cursor by interrupting the electrical current that operates the machine. They work the same way that a light switch works, allowing a person to turn the light on or off. Push switches are activated by physical pressure and can be designed for activation by almost any body part. Common push switches are push buttons, push plates, paddles, joysticks, and squeeze bulbs. Position switches are activated by a change of position in space and usually are made of a globule of mercury in a tube that opens and closes the switch when the learner moves the body part to which it is attached. Pneumatic switches (sip and puff, suck and blow) are activated by blowing or sucking on the end of a tube. Sound-controlled switches are activated by sound energy that is converted to electrical energy by a microphone and can be designed so that only a particular sound at a particular intensity activates them (Silverman, 1980). Light-controlled switches work by directing a beam of light to a photoelectric cell or by interrupting a beam of light (Silverman, 1980).

In the last 10 years, the cost of electronic devices has dropped and practical applications have increased, including watches that store data, electronic date books, and even wallet-size computers. There has also been a boom in the development of electronic aids for communication. The advantages of electronic devices include the capacity to produce speech, visual displays, and written output; the capacity to produce a message beyond the student's capability (e.g., the symbol for *play* results in the phrase "can I play with you?"); the capability to store messages; and the ease with which scanning can be used with the system (Mustonen et al., 1991).

Electronic devices that offer speech output are in many ways preferable to the use of manual signs or cardboard communication boards (Romski & Sevcik, 1993). The use of the speech output allows the communication partners within an exchange to immediately comprehend the message when a symbol is activated. This is particularly important for the student when communicating with partners who may not be familiar with the communication device. The device provides the student with a spoken modality, while maintaining the visual symbol that allows the student to scan and select a message.

Electronic devices that offer voice output may be characterized as single-level, multilevel, and comprehensive devices (Mirenda, 1999). In single-level devices, a small number of messages are accessed in relatively inexpensive devices that are simple to operate and program. These devices might be used to program an important request (e.g., "I need help" or "I need a break") or to record messages each day or within the class period to promote active participation in classroom activities (e.g., a fact to contribute to class discussion). Multilevel devices are more complex to program and hold more messages. These messages are programmed on levels that require manual adjustment of the device to the new level or access to the multiple levels through user input. The most sophisticated electronic devices, the comprehensive devices, are typically used by individuals without significant cognitive disabilities who wish to access numerous messages efficiently, have the need for significant memory and storage capacity, and wish to interface with computers or other devices.

As teams begin the selection of devices or communication systems, the following considerations should guide the process (Quist & Lloyd, 1997):

- *Parsimony.* The device should be as simple as possible and still meet the user's communication needs and goals.
- *Minimal learning.* The system or device should be immediately usable by the student with minimal instruction.
- *Minimal energy.* The device should require minimal physical effort and not result in student fatigue.
- *Minimal interference.* The device must not interfere with or distract the student from ongoing activity and participation in daily activities.
- *Best fit.* The device should fit the personality and preferences of the student.
- *Practicality and use.* The device should be easy to use in all environments, affordable, and easy to maintain.

The provision of electronic devices is considered an assistive device that is regulated by the Individuals with Disabilities Education Act (IDEA). Under IDEA, the IEP team must consider the need of the student for assistive technology services or devices while developing the IEP. In IDEA, assistive devices are defined as "any item, piece of equipment, or product system, whether acquired commercially off the shelf, modified, or customized, that is used to increase, maintain, or improve the functional capabilities of a child with a disability" (IDEA, 1997).

Selecting an Alternative or Augmentative Communication Mode

There has been much discussion in the literature on candidacy for augmentative communication and on decision rules for selecting communication modes. Decision rules often involve a dichotomous system that separates speech potential from alternative modes and then suggests the type of alternative system that may be most appropriate (Reichle & Keogh, 1986). Decision rule strategies typically consider the student's physiological capacity for speech, success with vocal training, and cognitive level of functioning (Chapman & Miller, 1980; Shane & Baskir, 1980). Alpert (1980) and Reichle (1991) discuss the risks of decision rules by pointing out that some learners may have the physiological capacity for speech, but may not have the potential for functional communication through a speech mode, and yet are not introduced to nonspeech modes until vocal communication training has failed.

Reichle (1991) feels that there are no cognitive prerequisites to communication and that there is no evidence to suggest that instruction in an alternative system will inhibit speech. Reichle (1991) offers the flow chart in Figure 11–4 to describe the questions that must be asked in establishing and monitoring the augmentative or alternative system that is selected.

The first step in developing an augmentative or alternative communication system is to conduct an ecological analysis in an effort to determine the environments, activities, and situations that demand communicative behavior from the learner (Reichle, 1991). The ecological inventory also assists in examining the behavior of the learner's communication partners and may pinpoint changes that they can make to facilitate the communicative efforts of the learner.

An examination of the learner in different environments will yield information on how he currently meets communication obligations and opportunities. The communication situations that the learner is exposed to and his communicative effectiveness in these situations will guide the interventionist in determining the communicative intents that should be taught.

The intents selected for instruction come from the communicative functions of behavior regulation, social interaction, and joint attention (see Figure 11–1), which emerge in the first 2 years of typical development (Wetherby, Cain, Yonclass, & Walker, 1988). The ecological inventory may reveal that students have idiosyncratic or unconventional means for some of these functions. For example, a student may hit her face to request a drink or throw materials to communicate a protest. When students have idiosyncratic means, the goal is to teach a socially acceptable, interpretable means for the communication function. The ecological inventory may also reveal that the student is not exhibiting behavior that can be interpreted as communication. In such a case, the behavioral regulation functions would be the first area on which to focus when establishing communication behavior.

In the selection of communication targets for instruction, the preferences of the family must also be considered by the team. In a study of parents of young children, parents were asked to discuss their priorities for communication skill development and the overall importance of a list of communication skills (Stephenson & Dowrick, 2000). The skills that parents ranked as most important were asking for objects, drawing attention to pain or discomfort, asking someone to do something, rejecting objects or actions, and making a choice. Parents' reasons for these rankings included parent and child frustration with the child's inability to ask for objects or actions, parent concerns for the child's safety, the need for the child to be

Figure 11–4 Decisions Involved in Designing Augmentative or Alternative Communication Systems

Source: "Defining the Decisions Involved in Designing and Implementing Augmentative and Alternative Communication Systems" by J. Reichle, in *Implementing Augmentative and Alternative Communication* (p. 40) by J. Reichle, J. York, and J. Sigafoos, 1991, Baltimore: Paul H. Brookes Publishing Co., Reprinted by permission.

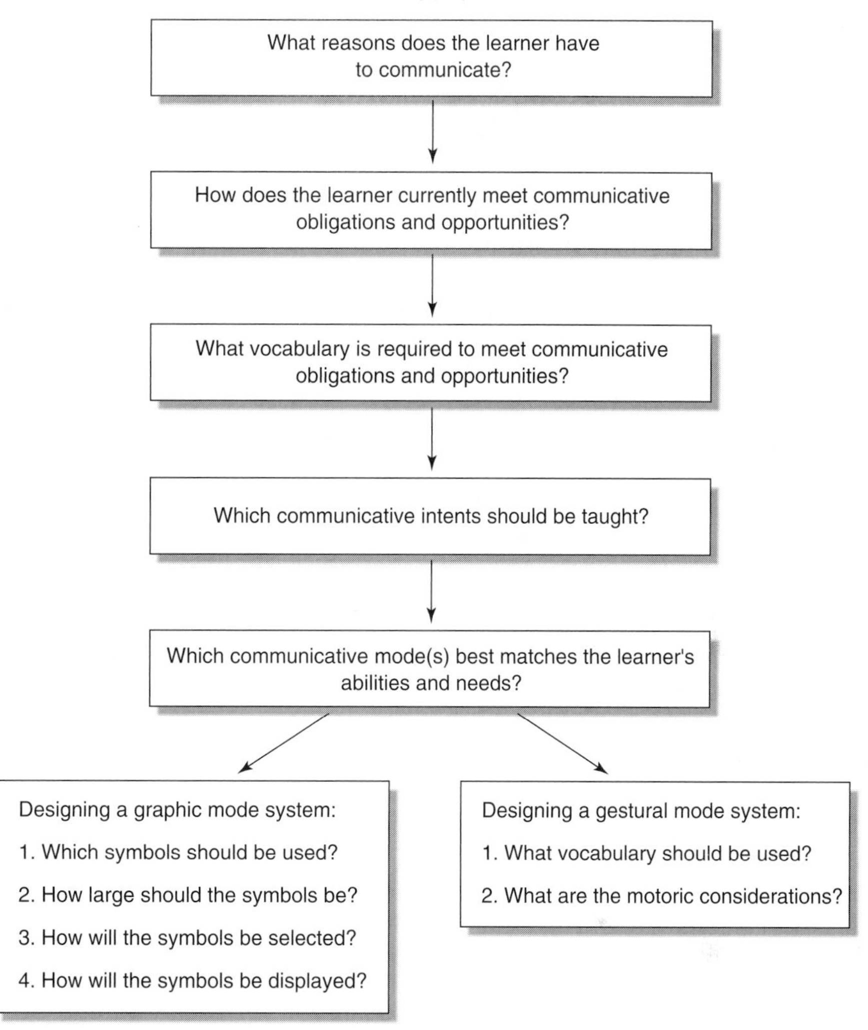
Reichle
What reasons does the learner have to communicate?
How does the learner currently meet communicative obligations and opportunities?
What vocabulary is required to meet communicative obligations and opportunities?
Which communicative intents should be taught?
Which communicative mode(s) best matches the learner's abilities and needs?
Designing a graphic mode system:
1. Which symbols should be used?
2. How large should the symbols be?
3. How will the symbols be selected?
4. How will the symbols be displayed?
Designing a gestural mode system:
1. What vocabulary should be used?
2. What are the motoric considerations?

able to object to the actions of others and have the ability to draw attention to himself, and the importance of communication for social interaction and social acceptance.

When selecting the mode of communication, it is likely and often desirable for mixed modes to be taught (Reichle, 1991). The selection of mode depends on the demands of the environments and the intent that is being taught. For example, if a learner wants to be able to request a certain type of sandwich at a fast-food restaurant, the most efficient mode of communication may be to hand the cashier a picture card describing the sandwich (e.g., Big Mac, please), but the same learner may be taught to use a natural gesture to express rejection or no. The use of two different modes for the same vocabulary is discouraged (Reichle, 1991). If two modes are taught for one word, the learner may become confused about which mode to use and should work on expanding rather than duplicating vocabulary.

The work of selecting and designing a communication system is never complete. The approach selected should build on the student's current skills and needs and expand to meet more needs over time (Johnson et al., 1996; Mirenda & Iacono, 1990). Communication interventions from this perspective are "always ongoing and dynamic" (Mirenda & Iacono, 1990, p. 12).

Initiating an Augmentative System

Once the collaborative team has identified an initial communication system to be taught to the student, a plan is developed that describes how the student will be taught, how communication partners will be trained, and how evaluation (data collection) of the student's progress will occur. The instructional strategies listed in the next section of this chapter should be used to teach the child to use the system.

The collaborative team should discuss and then describe how the system (i.e., communication book, electronic device, manual signing) will be taught by identifying a prompting sequence that will be used in teaching the student. Equally important is the identification of a training process for the student's communication partners, who must learn how to identify the student's communicative signals, arrange contexts to elicit a communicative response, expand on the student's utterance, and respond to the student's spontaneous communication (Johnson et al., 1996).

If the student does not currently use an augmentative system, the instructional team may wish to begin by teaching a restricted vocabulary (Romski & Sevcik, 1993). Initially, the student may be asked to learn the use of one or two symbols before additional vocabulary is added to the device. In selecting the initial symbols to teach, the interventionist should consider the selection of vocabulary that (1) is used in multiple environments and activities, (2) matches a communicative behavior in the student's repertoire, (3) results in a reinforcing response or activity, and (4) provides the student with a more efficient and effective mode of communication.

Expanding the Communication System

Once a communication system is established for a student, the collaborative team should think about how to expand the use and effectiveness of the system (Johnson et al., 1996). Periodically, the collaborative team should review the current system and consider the following:

1. Is there a way to modify the current system to increase its portability, durability, and attractiveness?
2. Does the system (or other modes) offer a vehicle for effective communication exchanges in all the environments and activities of the student?
3. Is the system easily interpreted and used by communication partners in all the environments of the student?
4. Are there more efficient ways to develop and expand the symbols (e.g., through software programs) used in the system?
5. How may the system be used in additional environments and with new communication partners?
6. What new content should be added to the system? Are there additional forms of communication that should be considered?
7. How can more complex messages be communicated by the student?

The communication system must be regarded as dynamic and should be changed to meet the student's increased abilities, access to new activities, and accessibility to new technology. If the student does not appear to be motivated to use the current communication system, the collaborative team should consider the following:

1. Are the represented communicative functions important to the student?
2. Can the student physically manipulate (e.g., select the symbol, see the selection) the communication system efficiently?
3. Are communication partners responsive to the student's communicative attempts?
4. Can the vocabulary on the system be used in multiple environments?

The collaborative team should be poised to adapt and change the communication system using evaluation data to guide them as they assess the effectiveness of the system. A periodic, formal review of the system that includes input from school personnel and the family is recommended.

Facilitated Communication

There have been reports of the success of a controversial method of aided communication called facilitated communication (Biklen, 1990), which involves the use of a letter board or keyboard (computer, typewriter, communicator). In this method the learner is provided with physical support under the forearm or hand to isolate the index finger and make a selection of a letter. One report describes the successful application of this method with 21 students labeled autistic (Biklen & Schubert, 1991). The researchers report that with facilitated communication students with autism were able to communicate by spelling words and sentences and that many of them revealed unexpected literacy and numeracy skills through their typing. Biklen (1990) has hypothesized that facilitated communication allows individuals with autism to overcome the neuromotor difficulties that they have in communication, as well as lack of confidence when communicating.

The term *facilitated communication* was introduced by educator Rosemary Crossley (Crossley & McDonald, 1980), who initially used the method to assist individuals with cerebral palsy and later discovered its application for individuals with autism (Biklen, 1990). Biklen and Schubert (1991) describe the basic elements of the method as (1) physical support under the hand or forearm, (2) initial training and introduction through a series of activities and choices, (3) assisting the learner to maintain focus by ignoring excess behavior and reminding the student to look at the keyboard or resume typing, (4) providing support for typing but not testing the student for competence, (5) providing initial set work (fill in the blank, questions, etc.) to help the student to develop fluency with the method, and (6) fading the physical support over time.

The research on facilitated communication has been controversial. Descriptive reports have supported the validity of facilitated communication (Biklen, 1990; Biklen & Schubert, 1991; Broderick & Kasa-Hendrickson, 2001; Sabin & Donnellan, 1993), and limited research has validated that messages from individuals who are facilitated are authored by the individual who is supported, rather than the facilitator (Cardinal, Hanson, & Wakeham, 1996; Sheehan & Matuozzi, 1996). Other researchers have demonstrated that facilitators may be controlling the communicative responses of the supported individuals (Moore, Donovan, & Hudson, 1993; Regal, Rooney, & Wandas, 1994; Vazquez,1994).

The controversy about facilitated communication is, in part, a reaction to the manner in which facilitated communication was initially promoted and discussed in the media. In many ways, facilitated communication was promoted as a method of communication that would instantly "unlock" the communication abilities of the individual with disabilities and allow the person to prove her hidden cognitive abilities. In reality, facilitated communication should be regarded as a legitimate approach for providing an aided communication system to some individuals. Many users of facilitated communication have been able to demonstrate their ability over time to communicate with only minimal or no support from a facilitator (Weiss, 2002).

Instructional Strategies

In recent years there has been a focus on the instruction of communication skills in natural contexts, which developed in response to operant training interventions that employed one-to-one, massed-trial instructional formats and failed to result in generalized and spontaneous language use (Goetz & Sailor, 1988). The use of natural contexts for communication instruction necessitates that the natural environment promote communication, that communication partners in the environment facilitate communication expression, and that specific procedures be developed and used to prompt and consequate communication use (Jackson, 1993; Johnson et al., 1996; Reichle, 1997).

It is essential that opportunities for communication expression be provided in the student's daily environments. Typical children develop language without planned and systematic intervention, but students with severe disabilities do not. It is only through an intensive and systematic effort that communication interventions are successful for many students with severe disabilities. Unfortunately, teachers often lose sight of the importance of repeated practice in natural contexts. They work with a student and an augmentative communication system in the classroom and then neglect to take it out to the playground, or they teach communication gestures at school without providing the student's family with a vocabulary list of gestures so that they can be used at home. It is critical that repeated practice on communication targets be provided and that communication systems be used in every environment.

An intervention plan designed to promote the communication skills of a student with disabilities is not focused solely on the development of skills by the student; it should also be aimed at creating an environment that encourages and supports the student's communication efforts.

Interaction Style

Communication partners (teachers, caregivers, peers) of the student with severe disabilities need to interact with the student in a manner that facilitates communication use (Johnson et al., 1996). Conversational partners must be able to identify the communicative signals of the student and respond consistently. In classrooms, peers and adults should be trained to understand the idiosyncratic communicative behaviors of each student. When students communicate, the partner must expand on the communicative signal to provide a more advanced communicative model. For example, if a student reaches for an object and states the object name for a request, the peer or adult should be ready to acknowledge the communicative message and expand on the utterance, for example, "Juice, you want some more orange juice." Communication partners also must be attentive to providing opportunities for non-prompted communication. Often, teachers use a high amount of verbal cues by asking questions or displaying prompts. Teachers should be attentive to providing opportunities for the student to initiate communication, instead of waiting for a cue from the instructor.

The Communication Support Checklist (McCarthy et al., 1998) may be used by teams to examine programs and practices to ensure that the communication rights of students with severe disabilities are respected and supported, to determine if the setting supports meaningful communication in natural contexts, to validate that recommended practices for assessment and intervention are being implemented, and to ensure that professionals on the team have the knowledge and skills needed for effective communication support. School teams may wish to use the Communications Support Checklist as a periodic assessment tool to remind team members of the critical features needed to support communication programming and to develop an action plan for making changes in the environment, staff training, or professional practices.

Halle (1984) discussed ways in which caregivers are not facilitative by preempting language use. *Preempting* refers to ways that caregivers limit the communication opportunities available to the student. Environmental preempting is arranging the physical environment so that toys, materials, and activities are freely provided to students in a way that eliminates the need to make requests. Nonverbal preempting occurs when caregivers give materials, toys, and activities freely without expecting communication from the student. Verbal preempting occurs when caregivers use specified prompts and cues for communication that eliminate the opportunity or need for a student to initiate communication.

Methods to inhibit preempting in the classroom or at home include the following:

1. *Time delay.* Wait silently with an expectant look for the child to initiate a request or indicate a need (Halle, 1984). For example, the teacher begins passing out cookies to the student's peers and uses time delay to elicit a request from the target student by holding the cookie and looking expectantly at him.
2. *Sabotage.* The caregiver withholds an essential tool or material that makes completing the activity impossible and creates an opportunity for communication expression. For example, the teacher gives a child a bowl of ice cream but does not provide a spoon or gives a student a toy but withholds the electromechanical switch (Halle, 1984).
3. *Out of reach.* Place desirable toys and materials within the student's sight but out of reach to elicit a request (Halle, 1984).
4. *Inadequate portions.* Provide only small portions of materials or food so that the student will have to request more (Ostrosky & Kaiser, 1991).
5. *Choice making.* Choices of materials, food, and activities present the child with an opportunity to use communication skills for requesting (Ostrosky & Kaiser, 1991).
6. *Assistance.* Provide toys (e.g., battery-operated game, windup toy) that require assistance to activate and result in the need for requesting help (Ostrosky & Kaiser, 1991).

These strategies provide opportunities for students to practice and strengthen the communication skills or behaviors that they have learned. They do not replace the instructional techniques described later in this chapter.

Social Exchanges

Many students with severe disabilities do not socially initiate and seem to lack the basic skills necessary for a social exchange. Before these students can learn to communicate effectively, they need to develop the basic pattern of back-and-forth turn taking with a partner (MacDonald & Gillette, 1986). Turn-taking interactions are difficult to establish when adults do not see the need for becoming social partners with students who are disabled. Strategies that adults may use to build social interactions are playing in routines, taking turns, using wait time, imitating the student's actions and sounds, progressively matching the student by acting like the student and adding one step, playing in the student's world, being animated and interested, and responding acceptingly to any social behavior (MacDonald & Gillette, 1986). The goal for adults is to become sensitive communication partners who facilitate and expand on the communication attempts of the student.

Once the student is communicative, adults must engage in an interactional style that encourages the building of language and conversation. Often adults dominate the communication interactions by talking at a student without expecting a response or by focusing on questions and commands (MacDonald & Gillette, 1986). It is critical that the adult allow the student to be both initiator and responder in communicative exchanges. Some strategies that can be used at this stage are commenting on what the student is experiencing, keeping on a student's topic, keeping the student on your topic, showing the student that you expect her to communicate, and using open-ended comments (MacDonald & Gillette, 1986). These concerns are also pertinent to students who use augmentative communication devices. It is important that communication partners (i.e., teachers, adults, and peers) use the augmentative system when interacting with the student. For example, if the student has an electronic device with "This is fun" programmed, a peer should be encouraged to use the device while communicating "This is fun" to the student who uses the device. The value of acceptance of all forms of communication is portrayed when all of the communicative partners use the augmentative system (Romski & Sevcik, 1993).

Students who are language users may need assistance with how to use language within social exchanges. The knowledge of words is only one element of effective communication. Students must know how to initiate and maintain a communication exchange, stay on topic, use social conventions for interrupting a speaker and asking questions, use social courtesies, ask for clarification, and use appropriate body posture and nonverbal relational skills. Table 11–1 is a list of social skills that may be important instructional targets. Social skills that should be targeted for intervention may be determined by observing the student within naturally occurring conversational exchanges and pinpointing issues or difficulties that are evident within these exchanges.

Interacting with Learners Who Are Nonsymbolic

Siegel-Causey and Guess (1989) developed an intervention approach for learners who are nonsymbolic communicators and function with limited intentionality. Their approach stresses the reciprocal nature of communication exchanges and is intended to enhance the learners' understanding and expand their use of nonsymbolic communication. These strategies were developed after examination of the wealth of research literature on the communication development of infants, which reveals the types of behaviors that caregivers use to facilitate the early nonsymbolic communication behaviors of infants.

Siegel-Causey and Guess (1989) recommend that the strategies listed in Table 11–2 be used in natural contexts and functional, relevant activities to facilitate nonsymbolic communication. The five strategies of developing nurturance, enhancing sensitivity, increasing opportunities, sequencing experiences, and utilizing movement can be used by the interventionist to create an environment that expects communication and promotes reciprocal exchanges between the student and others.

Developing nurturance is used to create in the student a sense of trust that others in the environment will be responsive, warm, and caring. Adults develop nurturance by responding to students warmly, focusing on students' interests, and expanding on students' initiations (Siegel-Causey & Guess, 1989).

Enhancing sensitivity is accomplished by the interventionist becoming aware of the learner's nonsymbolic behavior and early communicative efforts. Interventionists enhance sensitivity by becoming aware of and responding contingently to a learner's behavior and individual level of communication.

Table 11–1 Critical Social Skills for Communication Exchanges

Establish eye contact
Establish appropriate proximity
Maintain appropriate body posture during conversation
Speak with appropriate volume, rate, and latency
Maintain attention during exchange
Initiate greetings
Respond to greetings
Initiate partings
Respond to partings
Discriminate appropriate times to greet or part
Answer questions
Ask questions
Make requests
Respond to requests
Ask for information
Provide information
Ask for clarification
Respond to requests for clarification
Extend social invitations
Respond to social invitations
Deliver refusals
Respond to refusals
Use social courtesies (please, thank you, apology)
Maintain topic
Initiate a new topic

Increasing opportunities is accomplished by providing learners with many opportunities for interaction with others. Strategies that may be used to increase opportunities are to provide choices, create needs for requests, and use time delay (Siegel-Causey & Guess, 1989).

Sequencing experiences refers to the use of routines, games, and turn-taking exchanges that provide learners with the opportunity to participate in reciprocal dialogues. Routines provide the learner with a context in which they learn turn-taking skills and how to initiate, maintain, and terminate interactions.

Utilizing movement is intended to convey to students with severe disabilities that their movements may be used for communication. Adults can use the movements of students by matching student movement with language, modeling the use of movement (gestures, pointing) for communication, and responding to student movement that is communicative.

Table 11–2 Intervention Guidelines and Strategies Illustrated in Dialogues

Guidelines	*Strategies*
Developing nurturance	Provide support, comfort, affection Create positive setting for interactions Expand on child-initiated behavior Focus on individual's interest
Enhancing sensitivity	Recognize nonsymbolic behaviors Respond contingently Recognize individual's readiness for interaction Respond to individual's level of communication
Increasing opportunities	Utilize time delay Provide choices Create need for requests Provide opportunities to interact
Sequencing experiences	Establish routines Utilize patterns in games Provide turn-taking opportunities Encourage participation
Utilizing movement	Respond to movements as communicative behaviors Use movements matched to the level of the learner's actions Select movements that accommodate the learner's immediate ability to respond and interact within particular contexts or moments Use movements as communicative behaviors

Source: Enhancing Nonsymbolic Communication Interactions among Learners with Severe Disabilities (p. 56) by E. Siegel-Causey and D. Guess, 1989, Baltimore: Paul H. Brookes Publishing Co., Reprinted by permission.

Designing Instructional Strategies

Providing a supportive environment is important to facilitate communication development, but it is not enough. Specific instructional goals must be selected, and instructional strategies must be used to strengthen and expand the individual's communication ability. This is not to suggest that language interventions should adopt a didactic approach to instruction. Communication interventions must be conducted in contexts and activities that are meaningful for the student and employ both natural cues and consequences (Bricker, 1993).

Because of the importance of the natural context to communication development, instruction must take place in a variety of environments throughout the day. This approach has direct implications for the manner in which the speech–language therapist delivers services. One approach to the delivery of therapy that uses natural contexts for communication instruction is integrated therapy, which is the use of therapeutic intervention methods in real-life situations across the student's day (Rainforth, York, & MacDonald, 1992). In this model (as discussed in Chapter 3), the therapist provides some direct therapy, but is primarily involved in consultation. The therapist works with the student in daily activities (rather than taking the student to another environment for instruction) so that the classroom teacher is able to observe techniques that are used and to work collaboratively with the therapist. The therapist demonstrates intervention methods and assists the teacher in the evaluation of instructional needs and student performance.

Many of the instructional strategies described in Chapter 7 may also be applied to the instruction of communication skills. Response prompting procedures (most-to-least prompt system, least-to-most prompt system, graduated guidance, and chaining) and stimulus prompting procedures (stimulus shaping and stimulus prompting) can be used to teach the acquisition of communication skills.

Table 11–3 provides examples of the use of response and stimulus prompting procedures in the instruction of a request function. A more detailed discussion of the features and applications of these training procedures is presented in Chapter 7.

Naturalistic Teaching Procedures

A set of naturalistic teaching procedures, referred to as milieu teaching procedures, was developed specifically to promote communication and language

Table 11–3 Stimulus and Response Prompting Procedures

Method		*Application*
Most-to-least prompting procedure to teach a "want" symbol	Step 1:	The teacher places desired object in front of student. The teacher provides full physical assistance to the student to touch the "want" symbol. The teacher provides the desired object to the student.
	Step 2:	The teacher places desired object in front of student. The teacher provides a physical prompt by touching the student's hand and the symbol to cue the student to touch the "want" symbol. If the student touches the symbol, the teacher provides the object. If the student does not touch the symbol, the teacher applies Step 1 and provides the object.
	Step 3:	The teacher places desired object in front of student. The student touches the "want" symbol to receive object. If student does not touch symbol, the teacher applies Step 2.
Least-to-most procedure to teach a natural gesture for request	Step 1:	The teacher presents desired object and waits for the student to use gesture. If student produces gesture, the teacher provides object. If student fails to produce gesture, the teacher applies Step 2.
	Step 2:	The teacher presents desired object and gives student physical prompt to produce gesture by pushing hand toward object. If student produces gesture, the teacher provides object. If student fails to produce gesture, the teacher applies Step 3.
	Step 3:	The teacher presents desired object and gives student full assistance to produce gesture. The teacher provides object after assisting the student to produce gesture.
Graduated guidance to teach a student to touch a symbol for "drink" to receive a drink	Step 1:	The teacher presents the drink. The teacher uses hand over hand assistance to guide the student to touch the drink symbol, using as much assistance as necessary. The teacher provides the drink.
	Step 2:	The teacher presents the drink and reduces the assistance to touching the student's wrist but returns to hand over hand assistance if needed by the student.
	Step 3:	Over successive trials the teacher reduces assistance by shifting from support to the wrist to support to the forearm, elbow, shoulder, and finally to no support at all. Support is increased and faded according to the subtle movements of the student. The teacher provides the drink after the symbol has been touched.
Backward chaining to teach a student to touch a symbol of a toy	Step 1:	The teacher presents a highly desired toy to the student and, as the student reaches for the toy, provides the symbol so that the student touches the symbol immediately prior to touching the toy.
	Step 2:	The teacher places the symbol on the table in front of the toy and prompts the student (using least to most or most to least) to touch the symbol prior to receiving toy.
	Step 3:	The teacher places the symbol on the student's lap tray and prompts the student to touch the symbol prior to receiving toy.
	Step 4:	The teacher presents the toy and waits for response of student to touch symbol prior to receiving toy.
Interrupted behavior chain to teach the use of a communicating book symbol for "eat"	Step 1:	The teacher selects snack routine as chain sequence for interruption because it occurs twice a day, causes moderate levels of distress when interrupted, and results in student trying to complete the sequence.
	Step 2:	The teacher interrupts the snack routine by holding the snack item on the table until the student points to the symbol for "eat." If the student touches the symbol within 5 seconds, the teacher provides the snack. If the student does not touch the symbol, the teacher models touching the symbol and then provides physical guidance to the student. If the student touches the symbol, the teacher provides the snack item. If the student fails to touch the symbol, the snack item is removed and the procedure is tried again in 5 minutes.

skill development. These procedures, which include the use of time delay (Halle, Marshall, & Spradlin, 1979), mand-model (Warren, McQuarter, & Rogers-Warren, 1984), and incidental teaching (Hart & Risley, 1975), share the common features of (1) being based on the child's interest, (2) embedding brief episodes of instruction within naturally occurring contexts, (3) being focused on explicit skill goals, and (4) providing natural consequences (Kaiser, Yoder, & Keetz, 1992).

Milieu procedures have been shown to be effective in the instruction of sign language, one-word responses, multiword phrases, and spontaneous speech (Kaiser et al., 1992). Naturalistic strategies have also been used to teach students with severe disabilities how to use an electronic, speech-output communicative device (Kaiser, Ostrosky, & Alpert, 1993; Romski & Sevcik, 1993). There is also theoretical and correlational evidence that modified milieu procedures may be effective with prelinguistic communicators (Warren & Yoder, 1998; Yoder & Warren, 1993). Table 11–4 describes milieu teaching procedures to teach a request function by natural gesture and a communication board; descriptions of the steps for each milieu procedure follow.

Time Delay

To use time delay, the interventionist must identify the response desired by the student. For example, the teacher wants to teach a student to make a request for more by saying the word *more*. The teacher should identify occasions when the student is likely to need to use the target utterance, such as activity time or snack time. The teacher first establishes joint attention with the student and then introduces a time delay. During snack time, the teacher shows the student the cookie container (establishing joint attention) and waits for a response (time delay). If the student produces the desired behavior, the teacher consequates the response with praise, verbal expansion, and the requested item. If the student fails to produce the behavior, the teacher can provide a correction by modeling the desired response (e.g., "say more") or "manding" (instructing) the behavior (e.g., "tell me what you want"). Providing the model may be more appropriate if the student is not sure of the desired response; the mand may be more useful for students who know the answer.

Mand-Model Procedure

The mand-model procedure was developed to assist students who know language responses to generalize their use to new contexts (Warren et al., 1984). In this procedure, the teacher identifies the desired response and then arranges materials in a way to promote child interest. When a student expresses interest in the material, the teacher mands (verbally instructs) the student to respond. For example, if the teacher wants the student to use object labels with *want* to make requests, she may say "Tell me what you want." If the student fails to respond with the desired utterance, the teacher then models the desired response (e.g., "want ball"). If the child provides the appropriate response, the teacher provides praise, an

Table 11–4 Using Milieu Procedures to Teach Communication Skills

Procedure	*Natural Gesture*	*Communication Board*
Time delay	The teacher holds up a cup of juice that the student wants and looks expectantly at the student. When the student makes eye contact with the teacher, the teacher waits for 5 seconds (time delay). If the student does not gesture for the drink, the teacher models the action.	The teacher holds up a toy that the student wants and looks expectantly at the student. When the student makes eye contact with the teacher, the teacher waits 5 seconds (time delay). If the student does not touch the appropriate icon, the teacher models or mands the action.
Mand-model	The teacher is playing with a favorite toy of the student. The student moves to the teacher and looks from the toy to the teacher. The teacher says "What do you want?" The child looks from the toy to the teacher. The teacher says "Show me want" (mand). The student reaches for the toy. The teacher provides the toy and says "You showed me want, here is the toy."	The teacher and three students are making a cake. The teacher gives two students a turn to hold the mixer. The teacher turns to the third student and says "What do you want?" The student looks expectantly at the teacher. The teacher provides a mand, "Touch 'my turn now.'" The student touches the correct icon. The teacher provides the mixer and says "You told me, 'my turn now'. Now it is Ricky's turn."
Incidental teaching	Several students are eating a snack. The student pulls the teacher to the table. The teacher says "Want what?" The student points to the box of cookies. The teacher provides a cookie and says "Ricky wants a cookie too."	It is a free-choice playtime. The student touches the icon on her board representing "play." The teacher says "Play what?" The student touches the play icon and then the car icon. The teacher moves to the shelf to get the car and says "O.K., Chris wants to play with the car."

expansion on the response (e.g., "Tony wants the big ball"), and the desired material.

Incidental Teaching

In incidental teaching, the interventionist arranges the environment to create the need for students to request materials by placing them out of reach or in visible containers. When the student is verbally or nonverbally requesting a material, the interventionist establishes joint attention with the student and then prompts more elaborate language by using the mand-model procedure or time delay. For example, a student approaches a shelf, looks at the interventionist, and points to a radio. The interventionist follows the student response by using the mand "show me what you want." The student continues to point; the interventionist models the desired response. The interventionist makes a manual sign for music and says to the student "show me, music." The student signs *music* and the interventionist provides the radio, saying, "Here it is. You want to listen to music."

Interrupted Chains

Interrupted chaining is a teaching strategy that involves inserting a communication instructional trial into a routine activity (i.e., chain of behaviors) that the student is completing (Alwell, Hunt, Goetz, & Sailor, 1989). The interrupted chain strategy was shown to be more effective than placing the instructional trial just before the student began a familiar chain of behaviors (Goetz et al., 1985). In addition, students who learned communication skills using the interrupted chain strategy were able to generalize the skills learned to other activities, including those for which no interruption occurred.

To use the interrupted chain strategy, the teacher must first identify the instructional goal. The interrupted chain strategy has been successful in teaching students to use a natural gesture, signs, a "want" card, and a communication book. The teacher then develops a list of behavior sequences that (1) the student engages in at least twice a day, (2) have at least three steps, and (3) are initiated by the student (Alwell et al., 1989). The teacher interrupts the student at various points in these behavior sequences to assess the amount of distress that the interruption precipitates from the student and the student's attempts to complete the behavior chain. The appropriate behavior sequences to use for training cause a moderate level of stress (i.e., the student is motivated to complete the chain) and result in consistent attempts by the student to complete the activity.

When the training sequences have been identified, instruction occurs during the routines when they naturally take place. To interrupt the behavior chain, the teacher can delay presenting a needed item (e.g., spoon to stir cake mix), place a needed item out of reach (e.g., tape player on a high shelf), or block the behavior (e.g., hold the door closed). After the interruption, the teacher waits 5 seconds for a response (e.g., sign *want*, point to needed item, sign *open*). If there is no response, the teacher models the response, physically guides the student through it, and does not let the student finish the routine. The teacher waits for the student to attempt the routine again and interrupts again. If the student responds correctly, the teacher provides reinforcement, gives the student the needed item or removes the block, and allows the student to complete the routine. If the student does not respond correctly, the teacher removes the needed item or removes the student from the situation and does not allow the student to complete the routine.

Conversational Skill Training

Conversational skill training, which was developed to teach students with severe disabilities to initiate and maintain a conversation with peers (Hughes et al., 2000; Hunt, Alwell, & Goetz, 1991; Hunt, Alwell, Goetz, & Sailor, 1990), makes use of a communication book that includes pictures of objects, places, and people associated with activities that the student enjoys and may wish to talk about (e.g., going to the bowling alley). The conversation book should be small enough to be portable and the pictures should be grouped by environments. Topics in the conversation book should be changed weekly.

Peer partners are instructed briefly about their role in the conversation skill training. They should be told to (1) make comments on the pictures in the book, (2) cue the student to take a turn by asking a question, and (3) wait for the student to respond. The peer partner should be given an opportunity to role play the use of the conversation book with the teacher before training begins. The sequence of the turn taking within the conversation skill training is shown in Figure 11–5.

Training the student with severe disabilities involves a most-to-least prompting sequence tailored to the individual student. The teacher may initially verbally prompt the student to initiate (e.g., "Tell Mara about bowling") and then fade the direct verbal prompts to verbal reminders (e.g., "Is there something you want to tell Mara about?"). Some students may initially require a direct verbal prompt plus a gestural prompt (e.g., pointing), which may be faded to the verbal prompt, and then to the verbal reminder. If the

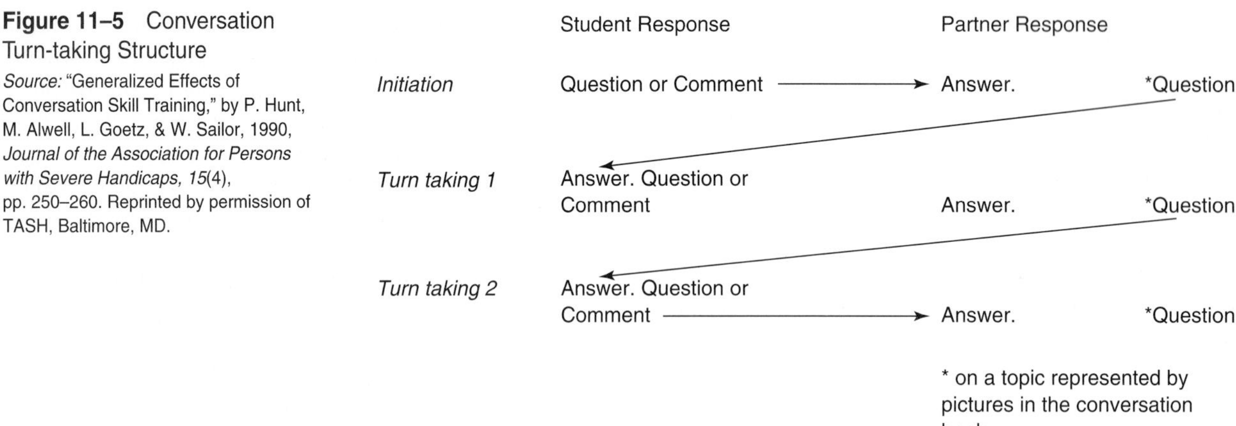

Figure 11–5 Conversation Turn-taking Structure

Source: "Generalized Effects of Conversation Skill Training," by P. Hunt, M. Alwell, L. Goetz, & W. Sailor, 1990, *Journal of the Association for Persons with Severe Handicaps, 15*(4), pp. 250–260. Reprinted by permission of TASH, Baltimore, MD.

student does not respond correctly, increasing assistance should be provided until the student is successful.

Van Dijk Method

There is growing interest among interventionists in the use of the van Dijk method to promote communication development by students with severe disabilities (Lang & Uptmor, 1991; Sternberg & McNerney, 1988). The van Dijk approach was developed in Holland by Jan van Dijk as a communication intervention for students who are deaf and blind. Although there is little empirical research on the efficacy of the procedures and van Dijk does not apply the method to students with severe multiple disabilities (Writer, 1987), educators in this country have begun to apply the principles to students with severe disabilities (Guess & Thompson, 1991; Sternberg & McNerney, 1988; Writer, 1987).

In the van Dijk method the student is moved from an egocentric level of not relating to people or objects to the ability to use communication intentions with others (Lang & Uptmor, 1991). The method involves six major levels of communication development: nurturance, resonance, coactive movement, nonrepresentational reference, deferred imitation, and natural gestures (Writer, 1987). In the first level, nurturance, the caregiver focuses on the development of a warm social bond between himself and the child. In the second level, resonance, the caregiver and the student move together with body-to-body contact. When students are in the resonance level, the caregiver responds to their movements as if they are communicative, rather than attempting to teach specific communication behaviors (Stillman & Battle, 1984). The student moves from a resonance level to coactive movement, where the caregiver and the student move together although they are physically separated. In the coactive stage, complexity is gradually introduced to the movement sequences. The student progresses from the resonance stage of body-to-body contact movements to anticipating the order of a movement sequence and using movement sequences with objects. Anticipation shelves are introduced in the coactive movement stage as a communication device (Sternberg & McNerney, 1988; Stillman & Battle, 1984). Anticipation shelves are a series of boxes arranged horizontally on a shelf. Each box represents a different activity and contains an object that represents that activity (e.g., a bar of soap to represent hand washing). Before the activity begins, the student and the caregiver go to the shelf, pick up the object, and complete the activity. When the activity is completed, the student replaces the object in the box and picks up the object that signals the next activity. The purpose of the anticipation shelves is to evoke anticipatory responses from the student and for the student to understand the representation of activities by objects (Stillman & Battle, 1984).

The fourth level in the van Dijk method is nonrepresentational reference, in which the student develops an understanding of her body parts and, later, the body parts of a doll. At the fifth level, deferred imitation, the student is prompted to imitate the familiar movement actions of the caregiver. Imitative movements usually begin with gross motor movement and progress until the student can imitate limb and hand movement (Writer, 1987). The activities in the imitation stage are conducted within the natural daily routine. The sixth level is the use of natural gestures as communication signals within routines. Natural gestures evolve from a student's experience with the motor qualities of things and first represent what the student does with an object (Sternberg & McNerney, 1988). After the student begins to use a variety of gestures in daily routines, the gestures are gradually shaped into manual signs (Writer, 1987).

Generalization Issues

The generalization of communication skills learned by students with severe disabilities is of great concern. The focus on teaching communication skills in natural contexts and the increased emphasis on milieu teaching strategies represent an effort to instruct communication behavior in a way that results in generalization. Communication instruction is often successful in the instructional setting, but spontaneous use of the instructed communication behavior in other environments is rarely evident (Calculator, 1988; Halle, 1987; Kaczmarek, 1990).

The spontaneous use of communication skills by the learner with severe disabilities is an important outcome. The ability to spontaneously communicate allows the learner to initiate communication about topics that are personally relevant and important and to select the time, place, and conversation partner for social interaction (Kaczmarek, 1990). Halle (1987) defines spontaneous language as language for which an observer cannot identify the controlling conditions.

Halle (1987) addresses the issue of spontaneous communication by defining spontaneity as utterances that occur in the presence of conditions that are not easily discerned. He offers a continuum of controlling stimuli that clarifies the idea of spontaneity (Figure 11–6). Communication is considered more spontaneous when it occurs under conditions that are less easily discerned. This continuum also may be a helpful guide in thinking about the instruction of communication skills and fading of prompts.

On the continuum in Figure 11–6, physical guidance represents the most restricted level of controlling stimuli. Physical guidance is often applied in the early stages of communication training in the use of aided communication systems and natural gestures. The next point on the continuum is modeling. Modeling is frequently used in vocal training or as a less intrusive prompt following physical guidance. Questions or mands are less restricted stimuli that set the occasion for a response from the learner. The last three points on the continuum, presence of objects or events, presence of a listener, and contextual and interoceptive stimuli, describe the diminishing discernability of controlling stimuli to stimuli that are within the setting or the learner and represent spontaneous communication use.

Kaczmarek (1990) addresses the learner's need to select a listener, establish proximity, and obtain attention to deliver a message in a matrix model for teaching spontaneous communication. The ability to perform these skills, described as listener preparatory behavior, gives the learner "more communicative" power to display spontaneous language than the learner who does not (Kaczmarek, 1990, p. 161). These behaviors do not occur in a set sequence, but may vary depending on the environment in which communication is occurring, the response of the listener, and the nature of the message that is being communicated. Contextual variables also influence spontaneous communication. Kaczmarek (1990) suggests the use of a matrix model to understand all the possible contextual and listener preparatory variables that could affect the spontaneous use of a communicative function. An example of the matrix is presented in Figure 11–7.

The matrix can be used for intervention by first assessing the student's abilities within each condition and then by developing an instructional sequence based on the student's entry repertoire. The interventionist can periodically probe in the cells that have not been targeted for intervention to test for generalization. These probes will indicate the conditions that should be targeted for additional training.

Social Skills Instruction

Students with severe disabilities on all levels of communicative functioning need instruction in social exchanges. Skills for instruction may range from early pragmatic skills, such as gaining a listener's attention or taking turns within an interaction, to using social courtesies and maintaining a topic. The determination of skills to target for

Figure 11–6 Continuum of Controlling or Discriminative Stimuli in the Presence of Which Responses Appear More or Less Spontaneous

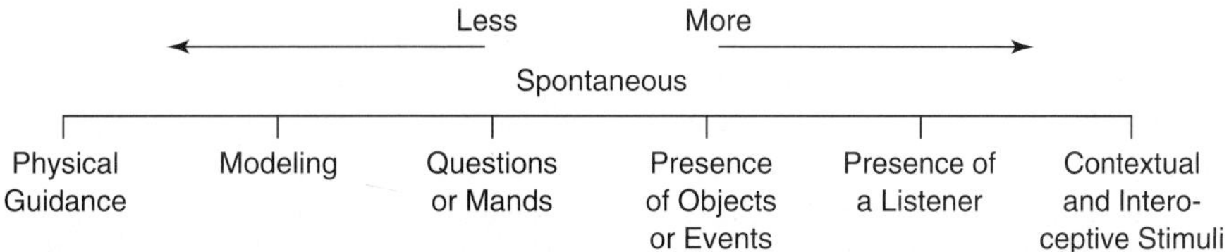

Source: "Teaching Language in the Natural Environment: An Analysis of Spontaneity," by J. W. Halle, 1987, *Journal of the Association for Persons with Severe Handicaps, 12*(1), pp. 28–37. Reprinted by permission of TASH, Baltimore, MD.

Figure 11–7 Example of a Matrix Model Defining a Possible Instructional Universe for Requesting Needed Objects When Materials Needed to Complete a Task Are Not All Accessible

Source: "Teaching Spontaneous Language to Individuals with Severe Handicaps: A Matrix Model," by L. A. Kaczmarek, 1990, *Journal of the Association for Persons with Severe Handicaps, 15*(3), pp. 160–169. Reprinted by permission of TASH, Baltimore, MD.

Listener Preparatory Variables \ Contextual Variables	A	B	C	D
	Incomplete materials given; needed object out of reach			
	needed object in view	needed object in partial view	needed object momentarily in view	needed object out of view
1 Given proximity and attention	Speaker requests desired object			
2 Given proximity, but not attention	Speaker obtains listener's attention and requests object			
3 Given attention, but not proximity	Speaker establishes proximity and requests object			
4 Given no proximity or attention	Speaker establishes proximity, obtains attention, and requests object			

Figure 11–8 Sample Social Story

The students in my class stand in line in the cafeteria. The children know that they must get in the line to get their food. The first thing you do in line is take a tray. Sometimes the trays are hot because they have just been washed. Sometimes they are wet and drippy. I can get in line and take a tray. I put the tray on the shelf and push it as I walk. The next thing you do is pick up silverware. I pick up a silverware pack and put in on my tray. The cafeteria line is sometimes very crowded and noisy. The children may touch each other. They push against me and make me feel squished. The children also talk in loud and excited voices. Sometimes the cafeteria workers will tell the children to be quiet. I can walk behind the child in front of me in the cafeteria line. The cafeteria workers hand the children their plates. Some children say thank you when they get their plate. I watch the cafeteria worker give the plate to the child in front of me. Next I will get a plate. I take the plate and place it on my tray. I push the tray until I get to the drink box. After the child in front of me gets a drink, I will be next. I look in the box and pick my drink. I like to pick orange juice. I put the drink on my tray. I push my tray to the end of the shelf. There is a ticket worker at the end of the shelf. The ticket worker takes the lunch ticket or money from the children. When the child in front of me gives a ticket, I will be next. I give the worker my ticket and then pick up my tray. I carry my tray very carefully to the table.

instruction comes from ecological assessment of how students interact with peers and adults within activities (see Chapter 6). Table 11–1 lists many of the social skills that are important to maintaining a social exchange.

The strategies used for the instruction of social skills range from stimulus-prompting techniques to role playing. Instructional approaches that were identified in Chapter 7 are also applicable to the instruction of targeted social skills. For example, discrete skills (e.g., waving good-bye) may be taught using a most-to-least or least-to-most prompting sequence. Skills that are communicative, for example, saying "I'm sorry," may be taught using the naturalistic teaching procedures described in this chapter as appropriate for instructing language targets. Complex skills (initiating a social interaction to extend an invitation) may require task analysis in addition to selecting an instructional prompting strategy. In addition to the skill acquisition techniques presented in Chapter 7, role playing, script training, peer-mediated interventions, and social stories have been identified as instructional approaches that are specifically designed to promote social skill development (Kamps, Kravits, & Ross, 2002).

Role playing has been used to teach social skills to students who are higher functioning. The first step in teaching through role play is to instruct the student in the skill that should be used. Then the instructor models the skill. The learner is then provided with a role in which the learner can practice the skill with other students or the instructor. After the role play, the instructor guides the student to evaluate her performance of the skill. For example, to teach a student how to politely interrupt a speaker, the instructor develops a role play that includes two students speaking. The target student is instructed that he should "interrupt the speaker politely and ask for directions to the rest room." The students act out the sequence. After the students perform the role play, the instructor asks the students to reflect on what happened and judge if the interruption was polite.

Script training has been used to facilitate social interactions between students with severe disabilities and their peers (Goldstein & Gallagher, 1992; Krantz & McClannahan, 1993). Script training is implemented by prompting students to do or say the components of a scripted activity. For example, Krantz and McClannahan (1993) provided students with autism with a written script of statements and questions that the student with autism could use to engage in a social interaction with a peer. The statements included items such as "(Name), did you like to swing outside today?" and "(Name), do you want to use one of my pencils?" The scripts were constructed immediately before a planned activity so that the script would include the peer names and refer to activities that the students had completed together. To prompt the student with autism to use the script, the teacher guided the student to pick up a pencil and then moved the pencil above the text while reading the statement. Once students began to use the scripts, the teacher faded her manual guidance and moved to the periphery of the classroom during the interaction. After fading manual guidance, the teacher began fading the script by omitting the words in the scripted statement.

Researchers have documented good success in involving peers as instructional agents in teaching social interaction skills (Ostrosky, Kaiser, & Odom, 1993; Windsor, 1995). In peer-mediated interventions, peers are trained to provide social–communicative intervention. Peers have been trained to use strategies that facilitate specific behaviors (e.g., establishing eye contact or making a request) and to use naturalistic strategies to expand on a student's utterance to promote more sophisticated communication or to facilitate attempts at conversational repair (Hunt et al., 1990). There are three steps to implementing a peer-mediated program (Ostrosky et al., 1993). The first step is to provide instruction to the student with disabilities on conversation initiation and response strategies that may be practiced and supported within the peer interaction. The second step is to train the nondisabled peers to use strategies to facilitate the desired interaction behaviors. It is recommended that nondisabled peers who share common interests, enjoy being with the target student, and have natural proximity to each other through shared activities be recruited for providing peer-mediated intervention. The third step for implementing a peer-mediated program is to structure time that brings together the target children and their peers to practice the social interactions with the support and facilitation of adults.

The use of social stories has been recommended for instructing students with autism in learning social skills (Gray, 1995; Gray & Garand, 1993). A social story provides a description of social situations that may be confusing for students with autism and is used to prepare the student to negotiate the social situation more effectively. The social story includes a description of the routine, an identification of the relevant cues, and the responses desired from the student (Gray et al., 1993). Social stories may be used to prepare a student for a new routine (e.g., going to physical education), to define desired social behavior (e.g., raise your hand before talking), or to prepare a child for unexpected situations (a fire drill). Before a social story is developed, the teacher should carefully observe the routine and note the relevant cues that are a part of the activity. It is also important to view the activity from the perspective of the student so that the story will reflect the feelings and reactions of the student. The story should contain descriptive sentences that point out the relevant features of the situation, directive sentences that identify the desired responses of the student, and perspective sentences that provide information on the reactions of others in the target situation. Once a social story is developed, the teacher and parent read the story with the student several times and review the story frequently as the social skill is being learned. Figure 11–8 is a sample social story developed to teach a student how to move through the cafeteria line.

Conclusion

In this chapter, strategies for assessing communication abilities, selecting communication modes, and instructing communication and social skills in natural contexts were presented. The foundation for all these activities must be the belief that all behaviors communicate and that every individual has a right to become a more competent communicator. If these beliefs are in place, the interventionist will continue to seek new ways to understand and teach communication skills.

Questions for Reflection

1. What are some of the environmental variables that the collaborative team may wish to consider in the design of communication intervention plans?
2. What are the positive features of teaching students with severe disabilities multiple modes of communication?
3. What behaviors might be observed in a student who is moving from the perlocutionary stage to the illocutionary stage of development? What strategies would facilitate these behaviors?
4. What might be appropriate instructional goals for a student who is nonsymbolic?
5. What similarities do you see between the discussion in this text of general best practices for instruction and the use of naturalistic teaching procedures for communication development? How do these similarities fit into society's changing view of persons with disabilities?
6. What role does inclusion play in facilitating communication skill development?

References

Alpert, C. L. (1980). Procedures for determining the optimal nonspeech mode with autistic children. In R. L. Schiefelbusch (Ed.), *Nonspeech language and communication: Analysis and intervention* (pp. 389–420). Baltimore: University Park Press.

Alvares, R., Falor, I., & Smiley, L. (1991). Research on nonlinguistic communication functioning of individuals with severe or profound handicaps. In L. Sternberg (Ed.), *Functional communication: Analyzing the nonlinguistic skills of individuals with severe or profound handicaps* (pp. 18–37). New York: Springer-Verlag.

Alwell, M., Hunt, P., Goetz, L., & Sailor, W. (1989). Teaching generalized communicative behaviors within interrupted behavior chain contexts. *Journal of the Association for Persons with Severe Handicaps, 14,* 91–100.

Bates, E. (1979). *The emergence of symbols: Cognition and communication in infancy.* New York: Academic Press.

Biklen, D. (1990). Communication unbound: Autism and praxis. *Harvard Educational Review, 60,* 291–314.

Biklen, D., & Schubert, A. (1991). New words: The communication of students with autism. *Remedial and Special Education, 12,* 46–57.

Bricker, D. (1993). Then, now, and the path between: A brief history of language intervention. In A. P. Kaiser & D. B. Gray (Eds.), *Enhancing children's communication: Research foundations for interventions* (pp. 3–31). Baltimore: Paul H. Brookes.

Broderick, A., & Kasa-Hendrickson, C. (2001). "Say one word at first": The emergence of reliable speech in a student labeled with autism. *Journal of the Association for Persons with Severe Handicaps, 26,* 13–24.

Butterfield, N., & Arthur, M. (1995). Shifting the focus: Emerging priorities in communication for students with a severe intellectual disability. *Education and Training in Mental Retardation, 30,* 41–50.

Butterfield, N., Arthur, M., & Sigafoos, J. (1995). *Partners in everyday communicative exchanges. A guide to promoting interaction involving people with severe intellectual disability.* Sydney: MacLennan & Petty Pty Limited.

Calculator, S. N. (1988). Promoting the acquisition and generalization of conversational skills by individuals with severe disabilities. *Augmentative and Alternative Communication, 4,* 94–103.

Cardinal, D., Hanson, D., & Wakeham, J. (1996). An investigation of the authorship in facilitated communication. *Mental Retardation, 34,* 231–242.

Carlson, F. (1984). *Picsyms categorical dictionary.* Lawrence, KS: Baggeboda Press.

Carr, E. G., McConnachie, G., Levin, L., & Kemp, D. C. (1993). Communication-based treatment of severe behavior problems. In R. Van Houten & S. Axelrod (Eds.), *Effective behavioral treatment: Issues and implementation* (pp. 231–267). New York: Plenum.

Chapman, R., & Miller, J. (1980). Analyzing language and communication in the child. In R. L. Schiefelbusch (Ed.), *Nonspeech language and communication: Analysis and intervention* (pp. 159–196). Baltimore: University Park Press.

Clark, C. R., Davies, C. D., & Woodcock, R. W. (1974). *Standard rebus glossary.* Circle Pines, MN: American Guidance Service.

Coggins, T., & Carpenter, R. (1981). The communication intention inventory: A system for observing and coding children's early intentional communication. *Journal of Applied Psycholinguistics, 2,* 235–251.

Crossley, R., & McDonald, A. (1980). *Annie's coming out.* New York: Penguin Books.

Dennis, R., Reichle, J., Williams, W., & Vogelsberg, T. (1982). Motoric factors influencing the selection of vocabulary for sign production programs. *Journal of the Association for the Severely Handicapped, 7,* 20–33.

Doherty, J. E. (1985). The effects of sign characteristics on sign acquisition and retention: An integrative review of the literature. *Augmentative and Alternative Communication, 1,* 108–121.

Donnellan, A., Mirenda, P., Mesaros, R., & Fassbender, L. (1984). Analyzing the communicative functions of aberrant behavior. *Journal of the Association for Persons with Severe Handicaps, 9,* 202–212.

Downing, J. (1999). *Teaching communication skills to students with severe disabilities.* Baltimore: Paul H. Brookes.

Goetz, L., Gee, K., & Sailor, W. (1985). Using a behavior chain interruption strategy to teach communication skills to students with severe disabilities. *Journal of the Association for Persons with Severe Handicaps, 10,* 21–30.

Goetz, L., & Sailor, W. (1988). New directions: Communication development in persons with severe disabilities. *Topics in Language Disorders, 8,* 41–54.

Goldstein, H., & Gallagher, T. M. (1992). Strategies for promoting the social–communicative competence of young children with specific language impairment. In S. L. Odom, S. R. McConnell, & M. A. McEvoy (Eds.), *Social competence of young children with disabilities* (pp. 189–213). Baltimore: Paul H. Brookes.

Goldstein, H., Kaczmarek, L. A., & English, K. M. (2002). *Promoting social communication: Children with developmental disabilities from birth to adolescence.* Baltimore: Paul H. Brookes.

Gray, C. A. (1995). Teaching children with autism to "read" social situations. In K. Quill (Ed.), *Teaching children with autism. Strategies to enhance communication and socialization.* New York: Delmar Publishers.

Gray, C., Dutkiewicz, M., Fleck, C., Moore, L., Cain, S. L., Lindrup, A., Broek, E., Gray, J., & Gray, B. (Eds.), (1993). *The social story book.* Jenison, MI: Publication of the Jenison, Michigan Public Schools.

Gray, C., & Garand, J. (1993). Social stories: Improving responses of students with autism with accurate social information. *Focus on Autistic Behavior, 8,* 1–10.

Guess, D., & Thompson, B. (1991). Preparation of personnel to educate students with severe and multiple disabilities: A time for change? In L. H. Meyer, C. A. Peck, & L. Brown (Eds.), *Critical issues in the lives of people with severe disabilities* (pp. 391–398). Baltimore: Paul H. Brookes.

Gustason, G., Pfetzing, D., & Zawolkow, E. (1972). *Signing exact English.* Rossmoor, CA: Modern Signs Press.

Halle, J. W. (1984). Arranging the natural environment to occasion language: Giving severely language-delayed children reasons to communicate. *Seminars in Speech and Language, 5,* 185–196.

Halle, J. W. (1987). Teaching language in the natural environment: An analysis of spontaneity. *Journal of the Association for Persons with Severe Handicaps, 12,* 28–37.

Halle, J. W., Marshall, A. M., & Spradlin, J. E. (1979). Time delay: A technique to increase language use and facilitate generalization in retarded children. *Journal of Applied Behavior Analysis, 12,* 431–439.

Harding, C., & Golinkoff, R. (1979). The origins of intentional vocalizations in prelinguistic infants. *Child Development, 50,* 33–40.

Hart, B., & Risley, T. R. (1975). Incidental teaching of language in the preschool. *Journal of Applied Behavior Analysis, 8,* 411–420.

Hughes, C., Rung, L., Wehmeyer, M., Agran, M., Copeland, S. R., & Hwang, B. (2000). Self-prompted communication book use to increase social interactions among high school students. *Journal of the Association for Persons with Severe Handicaps, 25,* 153–166.

Hunt, P., Alwell, M., & Goetz, L. (1991). Interacting with peers through conversation turntaking with a communication book adaptation. *Augmentative and Alternative Communication, 7,* 117–126.

Hunt, P., Alwell, M., Goetz, L., & Sailor, W. (1990). Generalized effects of conversation skill training. *Journal of the Association for Persons with Severe Handicaps, 15,* 250–260.

Hurlbut, B. I., Iwata, B. A., & Green, J. D. (1982). Nonvocal language acquisition in adolescents with severe physical disabilities: Blissymbol versus iconic stimulus formats. *Journal of Applied Behavior Analysis, 15,* 241–258.

Individuals with Disabilities Education Act Amendments of 1997 (IDEA) (1977), 20 U.S.C. 1400 et seq.

Jackson, L. (1993). Elements of a theoretical structure that will support best practices in communication facilitation. *Journal of the Association for Persons with Severe Handicaps, 18,* 143–160.

Johnson, J. M., Baumgart, D., Helmstetter, E., & Curry, C. A. (1996). *Augmenting basic communication in natural contexts.* Baltimore: Paul H. Brookes.

Kaczmarek, L. A. (1990). Teaching spontaneous language to individuals with severe handicaps: A matrix model. *Journal of the Association for Persons with Severe Handicaps, 15,* 160–169.

Kaiser, A. P., Ostrosky, M. M., & Alpert, C. L. (1993). Training teachers to use environmental arrangement and milieu teaching with nonvocal preschool children. *Journal of the Association for Persons with Severe Handicaps, 18,* 188–199.

Kaiser, A. P., Yoder, P. J., & Keetz, A. (1992). Evaluating milieu teaching. In S. F. Warren & J. Reichle (Eds.), *Causes and effects in communication and language intervention* (pp. 9–47). Baltimore: Paul H. Brookes.

Kamps, D. M., Kravits, T., & Ross, M. (2002). Social–communicative strategies for school-age children. In H. Goldstein, L. A. Kaczmarek, & K. M. English (Eds.), *Promoting social communication: Children with developmental disabilities from birth to adolescence* (pp. 239–277). Baltimore: Paul H. Brookes.

Krantz, P. J., & McClannahan, L. E. (1993). Teaching children with autism to initiate to peers: Effects of a script-fading procedure. *Journal of Applied Behavior Analysis, 26,* 121–132.

Lang, L., & Uptmor, E. (1991). Intervention models to develop prelinguistic communication. In L. Sternberg (Ed.), *Functional communication: Analyzing the nonlinguistic skills of individuals with severe or profound handicaps* (pp. 38–56). New York: Springer-Verlag.

Lloyd, L. L., Fuller, D. R., & Arvidson, H. H. (1997). Introduction and overview. In L. L. Lloyd, D. R. Fuller, & H. H. Arvidson (Eds.), *Augmentative and alternative communication: A handbook of principles* (pp. 1–17). Boston: Allyn and Bacon.

MacDonald, J. D., & Gillette, Y. (1986). Communicating with persons with severe handicaps: Roles of parents and professionals. *Journal of the Association for Persons with Severe Handicaps, 11,* 255–265.

McCarthy, C. F., McLean, L. K., Miller, J. F., Paul-Brown, D., Romski, M. A., Rourk, J. D., & Yoder, D. E. (1998). *Communication supports checklist for programs serving individuals with severe disabilities.* Baltimore: Paul H. Brookes.

McLean, L. K., Brady, N. C., & McLean, J. E. (1996). Reported communication abilities of individuals with severe mental retardation. *American Journal of Mental Retardation, 100,* 580–591.

Miller, J., & Allaire, J. (1987). Augmentative communication. In M. Snell, *Systematic instruction of persons with severe handicaps* (3rd Ed., pp. 273–297). Upper Saddle River, NJ: Merrill/Prentice Hall.

Mirenda, P. (1999). Augmentative and alternative communication techniques. In J. Downing (Ed.), *Teaching communication skills to students with severe disabilities* (pp. 119–138). Baltimore: Paul H. Brookes.

Mirenda, P., & Iacono, T. (1990). Communication options for persons with severe and profound disabilities: State of the art and future directions. *Journal of the Association for Persons with Severe Handicaps, 15,* 3–21.

Mirenda, P., & Locke, P. (1989). A comparison of symbol transparency in nonspeaking persons with intellectual disabilities. *Journal of Speech and Hearing Disorders, 54,* 131–140.

Moore, S., Donovan, B., & Hudson, A. (1993). Facilitator-suggested conversational evaluation of facilitated communication. *Journal of Autism and Developmental Disorders, 23,* 541–551.

Musselwhite, C., & St. Louis, K. (1988). *Communication programming for persons with severe handicaps: Vocal and augmentative strategies.* Boston: College-Hill.

Mustonen, T., Locke, P., Reichle, J., Solbrack, M., & Lindgren, A. (1991). An overview of augmentative and alternative communication systems. In J. Reichle, J. York, & J. Sigafoos (Eds.), *Implementing augmentative and alternative communication: Strategies for learners with severe disabilities* (pp. 1–37). Baltimore: Paul H. Brookes.

National Joint Committee for the Communication Needs of Persons with Severe Disabilities. (1992). Guidelines for meeting the communication needs of persons with severe disabilities. *Asha, 34*(Suppl. 7), 2–3.

National Joint Committee for the Communication Needs of Persons with Severe Disabilities. (2002). Access to communication services and supports: Concerns regarding the application of restrictive "eligibility" policies. *Communication Disorders Quarterly, 23*(3), 143–144.

Neel, R. S., & Billingsley, F. F. (1989). *IMPACT: A functional curriculum for students with moderate to severe disabilities.* Baltimore: Paul H. Brookes.

Ostrosky, M. M., & Kaiser, A. P. (1991). Preschool classroom environments that promote communication. *Teaching Exceptional Children, 23,* 6–11.

Ostrosky, M. M., Kaiser, A. P., & Odom, S. L. (1993). Facilitating children's social–communicative interactions through the use of peer-mediated interventions. In A. P. Kaiser & D. B. Gray (Eds.), *Enhancing children's communication. Research foundations for intervention* (pp. 159–186). Baltimore: Paul H. Brookes.

Parette, H. P., Brotherson, M. J., & Huer, M. B. (2000). Giving families a voice in augmentative and alternative communication decision-making. *Education and Training in Mental Retardation and Developmental Disabilities, 35,* 177–190.

Quist, R. W., & Lloyd, L. L. (1997). Principles and uses of technology. In L. L. Lloyd, D. R. Fuller, & H. H. Arvidson (Eds.), *Augmentative and alternative communication: A handbook of principles* (pp. 107–213). Boston: Allyn and Bacon.

Rainforth, B., York, J., & MacDonald, C. (1992). *Collaborative teams for students with severe disabilities.* Baltimore: Paul H. Brookes.

Regal, R. A., Rooney, J. R., & Wandas, T. (1994). Facilitated communication: An experimental evaluation. *Journal of Autism and Developmental Disorders, 24,* 345–355.

Reichle, J. (1991). Defining the decisions involved in designing and implementing augmentative and alternative communication systems. In J. Reichle, J. York, & J. Sigafoos (Eds.), *Implementing augmentative and alternative communication: Strategies for learners with severe disabilities* (pp. 39–60). Baltimore: Paul H. Brookes.

Reichle, J. (1997). Communication intervention with persons who have severe disabilities. *Journal of Special Education, 31,* 110–134.

Reichle, J., Halle, J., & Johnson, S. (1993). Developing an initial communicative repertoire: Applications and issues for persons with severe disabilities. In A. P. Kaiser & D. B. Gray (Eds.), *Enhancing children's communication. Research foundations for intervention* (pp. 105–136). Baltimore: Paul H. Brookes.

Reichle, J., & Keogh, W. J. (1986). Communication instruction for learners with severe handicaps: Some unresolved issues. In R. H. Horner, L. H. Meyer, & H. D. Fredericks (Eds.), *Education of learners with severe handicaps: Exemplary service strategies* (pp. 189–219). Baltimore: Paul H. Brookes.

Romski, M. A., & Sevcik, R. A. (1992). Developing augmented language in children with severe mental retardation. In S. F. Warren & J. Reichle (Eds.), *Causes and effects in communication and language intervention* (pp. 113–130). Baltimore: Paul H. Brookes.

Romski, M. A., & Sevcik, R. A. (1993). Language learning through augmented means: The process and its products. In A. P. Kaiser & D. B. Gray (Eds.), *Enhancing children's communication. Research foundations for intervention* (pp. 85–104). Baltimore: Paul H. Brookes.

Rowland, C., & Schweigert, P. (1989). Tangible symbols: Symbolic communication for individuals with multisensory impairments. *Augmentative and Alternative Communication, 5,* 226–234.

Rowland, C., & Schweigert, P. (1993). Analyzing the communication environment to increase functional communication. *Journal of the Association for Persons with Severe Handicaps, 18,* 161–176.

Sabin, L. A., & Donnellan, A. M. (1993). A qualitative study of the process of facilitated communication. *Journal of the Association for Persons with Severe Handicaps, 18,* 200–211.

Schuler, A. L., Peck, C. A., Willard, C., & Theimer, K. (1989). Assessment of communicative means and functions through interview: Assessing the communicative capabilities of individuals with limited language. *Seminars in Speech and Language, 10,* 51–62.

Sevcik, R., & Romski, M. (1986). Representational matching skills of persons with severe retardation. *Augmentative and Alternative Communication, 2,* 160–164.

Shane, H., & Baskir, A. (1980). Election criteria for the adoption of an augmentative communication system: Preliminary considerations. *Journal of Speech and Hearing Disorders, 45,* 408–414.

Shane, H., & Cohen, C. (1981). A discussion of communicative strategies and patterns by nonspeaking persons. *Language, Speech, and Hearing Services in Schools, 12,* 205–210.

Sheehan, C., & Matuozzi, R. (1996). Validation of facilitated communication. *Mental Retardation, 34*(2), 94–107.

Siegel-Causey, E., & Downing, J. (1987). Nonsymbolic communication development: Theoretical concepts and educational strategies. In L. Goetz, D. Guess, & K. Stremel-Campbell (Eds.), *Innovative program design for individuals with dual sensory impairments* (pp. 15–48). Baltimore: Paul H. Brookes.

Siegel-Causey, E., & Guess, D. (1989). *Enhancing nonsymbolic communication interactions among students with severe disabilities.* Baltimore: Paul H. Brookes.

Sigafoos, J., & York, J. (1991). Using ecological inventories to promote functional communication. In J. Reichle, J. York, & J. Sigafoos, *Implementing augmentative and alternative communication: Strategies for learners with severe disabilities* (pp. 61–70). Baltimore: Paul H. Brookes.

Silverman, F. H. (1980). *Communication for the speechless.* Upper Saddle River, NJ: Prentice Hall.

Skelly, M. (1979). *Amer-Ind gestural code based on universal American Indian hand talk.* New York: Elsevier.

Stephenson, J. R., & Dowrick, M. (2000). Parent priorities in communication intervention for young students with severe disabilities. *Education and Training in Mental Retardation and Developmental Disabilities, 35,* 25–35.

Sternberg, L., & McNerney, C. (1988). Prelanguage communication instruction. In L. Sternberg (Ed.), *Educating students with severe or profound handicaps* (2nd Ed., pp. 311–341). Austin, TX: ProEd.

Stillman, R. D., & Battle, C. W. (1984). Developing prelanguage communication in the severely handicapped. An interpretation of the Van Dijk method. *Seminars in Speech and Language, 4,* 159–170.

TASH. (2002). TASH resolution on the right to communicate. *TASH Connections, 28*(5), 7.

Vanderheiden, G. C., & Lloyd, L. L. (1986). Communication systems and their components. In S. W. Blackstone (Ed.), *Augmentative communication: An introduction* (pp. 49–161). Rockville, MD: American Speech–Language–Hearing Association.

Vazquez, C. (1994). A multi-task controlled evaluation of facilitated communication. *Journal of Autism and Developmental Disorders, 24,* 369–379.

Warren, S. F., McQuarter, R. J., & Rogers-Warren, A. K. (1984). The effects of mands and models on the speech of unresponsive socially isolated children. *Journal of Speech and Hearing Disorders, 47,* 42–52.

Warren, S. F., & Yoder, P. J. (1998). Facilitating the transition from preintentional to intentional communication. In A. M. Wetherby, S. F. Warren, & J. Reichle (Eds.), *Transitions in prelinguistic communication.* Baltimore: Paul H. Brookes.

Weiss, N. (2002). Stop! There's a baby in that bath water: Embracing the critical value of communication and facilitated communication. *TASH Connections, 28*(5), 3–5.

Wetherby, A. M., Cain, D., Yonclass, D., & Walker, V. (1988). Analysis of intentional communication of normal children from the prelinguistic to the multi-word stage. *Journal of Speech and Hearing Research, 31,* 240–252.

Wetherby, A. M., & Prizant, B. M. (1989). The expression of communicative intent: Assessment guidelines. *Seminars in Speech and Language, 10,* 77–90.

Wetherby, A. M., Warren, S. F., & Reichle, J. (Eds.) (1998). *Transitions in prelinguistic communication.* Baltimore: Paul H. Brookes.

Windsor, J. (1995). Language impairment and social competence. In M. E. Fey, J. Windsor, & S. F. Warren (Eds.), *Language intervention. Preschool through the elementary years* (pp. 213–238). Baltimore: Paul H. Brookes.

Woodcock, R. W., Clark, C. R., & Davies, C. O. (1969). *The Peabody rebus reading program teacher's guide.* Circle Pines, MN: American Guidance Service.

Writer, J. (1987). A movement-based approach to the education of students who are sensory impaired/multihandicapped. In L. Goetz, D. Guess, & K. Stremel-Campbell (Eds.), *Innovative program design for individuals with dual sensory impairments* (pp. 191–223). Baltimore: Paul H. Brookes.

Yoder, P. J., & Warren, S. F. (1993). Can developmentally delayed children's language development be enhanced through prelinguistic intervention? In A. P. Kaiser & D. B. Gray (Eds.), *Enhancing children's communication: Research foundations for intervention* (pp. 35–61). Baltimore: Paul H. Brookes.

CHAPTER 12

Providing Behavioral Supports to Improve Challenging Behavior

In this chapter strategies for intervening with challenging behavior are presented. The chapter begins by describing the types of problem behavior that are often targets of intervention programs. Following the description of problem behavior, the importance of viewing behavior from a functional perspective is explained. Problem behavior must be viewed from the orientation that it occurs for a reason and that the teacher must first understand the behavior before an intervention plan can be designed. Strategies for determining why the behavior may be occurring are provided, followed by the steps needed to design a behavior support plan.

Addressing Challenging Behavior

One of the most difficult challenges that teachers encounter is instructing learners who exhibit problem behaviors. Students with severe disabilities often are members of this group. The types of behavior problems that have been observed in persons with severe disabilities include stereotypic, self-injurious, aggressive, and socially inappropriate behavior. Students who have problem behavior that is not effectively resolved may face social isolation, risk of medical complications, and the use of behavior intervention procedures that are highly intrusive.

Current approaches to behavior intervention differ dramatically from earlier views. In the past, behavior interventions focused solely on eliminating behavior, with little consideration given to the context in which the behavior occurred and the need to replace problem behavior with new, appropriate skills. In recent years, behavior interventionists have assessed the function of these behaviors by examining the context in which they occur and linking interventions directly to the assessment. There is also an increased emphasis on considering aspects of an individual's lifestyle and on developing an intervention plan that includes changes in social and ecological conditions that will support meaningful outcomes for the individual. (Carr et al., 2002).

It is important at this point to discuss the beliefs that are the foundation of the approach to problem behavior presented in this chapter. There are two concepts that the interventionist should remember when designing behavior interventions. First, many of these behaviors have a communicative message, and it is essential that the interventionist try to understand and respond to that underlying message. Second, interventions that are designed to simply eliminate a behavior or replace it with another skill while ignoring the entire context in which a problem behavior occurs will not demonstrate long-term effectiveness. The approach that is presented in this chapter is based on a lifestyle perspective (Carr et al., 2002; Evans & Meyer, 1990; Horner et al., 1990; Horner & Carr, 1997; Meyer & Evans, 1993) in which the interventionist examines all aspects of an individual's lifestyle and seeks not only to change behaviors, but also to enhance the lifestyle so that meaningful outcomes will result and be maintained.

In this chapter, strategies for understanding problem behavior and developing intervention programs within a functional approach are presented. The chapter begins with a discussion of the types of problem behavior that may be associated with persons with severe disabilities. Although the topography of the behavior (what the student actually does) does not appear to have a systematic relationship with the reasons why persons with severe disabilities engage in problem behavior, it is relevant to define and describe these categories of behavior (Meyer & Evans, 1989). In the second section the rationale for using a functional approach to intervention for problem behavior is discussed, with research presented to support the method. The third section presents the methods of functional assessment and hypotheses development. The fourth section presents intervention strategies and how they may be used within the behavior support process, and describes how a behavior support plan is developed and applied.

Defining Problem Behavior

Problem behavior can take many forms. An act that may not be considered a problem behavior in one setting, for example, screaming and stamping one's feet at a football game, can be very problematic in a setting such as the classroom. Researchers use classifications to define and describe problem behavior, and these definitions are useful for the purpose of facilitating discourse about such behavior. In this section the major categories of problem behavior are provided to explain how problem behavior has traditionally been viewed. It is important to emphasize that defining a problem behavior by topography (e.g., self-injurious behavior or stereotypic behavior) will not lead directly to a method for reducing the behavior. The following definitions and examples of categories of problem behavior present the terminology that is commonly used to discuss problem behavior.

Stereotypic Behaviors

Stereotypic behaviors are repetitive cycles of behavior that consist of idiosyncratic rhythmic movements of the body or body parts. Many people engage in stereotypic behaviors such as cracking their knuckles, twirling their hair, or swinging their feet. These behaviors become problematic when they occur in such excess that the individual is unable to participate in other activities when engaged in the behavior or when the behaviors result in negative reactions from others. Examples of problematic stereotypic behavior include head weaving, finger flapping, mouthing hands, and rocking.

Self-Injurious Behaviors

Self-injurious behaviors are responses that inflict harm on the individual engaging in the behavior. Examples of such injurious behaviors that have been treated by researchers are head banging, face slapping, eye gouging, and hand biting. Self-injury can be one of the most horrifying categories of problem behavior in persons with disabilities. As a result, interventionists may resort to behavior reduction interventions that are also extreme in nature. Self-injury has been treated with the use of contingent shock, water misting, restraint, and lemon juice in the mouth (Guess, Helmstetter, Turnbull, & Knowlton, 1987). The occurrence of self-injurious behavior is higher (by 10% to 17%) among individuals who are institutionalized (Baumeister & Rollings, 1976; Schroeder, Schroeder, Smith, & Dalldorf, 1978). It also appears to be related to the severity of retardation, indications of neurologic impairments, and the rate of stereotypic behavior (Maisto, Baumeister, & Maisto, 1977).

Aggressive Behaviors

Aggressive and disruptive behavior can be defined as behavior that results in injury or damage to others and/or their property. It often occurs as part of a general tantrum and includes a combination of behaviors (e.g., screaming, crying, destroying property, and attacking others). In addition, some authors include passive–aggressive behavior, such as noncompliance, running away when called, and others, as aggressive acts when they are attempts to countercontrol (Meyer & Evans, 1989).

Inappropriate Social Behaviors

Inappropriate social behavior describes a category of behavior that is regarded as antisocial (Meyer & Evans, 1989). Examples include public masturbation, inappropriate affectionate behavior, laughing hysterically, shouting or swearing, hoarding possessions or food, and inappropriate or irrelevant conversations. These behaviors appear to result from failure to learn more appropriate social skills (Meyer & Evans, 1989).

The current approach to intervening with problem behavior moves beyond a simple identification of the behavior to the selection of a method of intervention. Labeling a behavior (e.g., stereotypic, self-injurious) does little to assist the interventionist in selecting a treatment. For example, one student may engage in aggression because he has an ear infection; another may engage in aggression to express her frustration with a task. A functional approach, in which the relationship of variables to the behavior is individually examined, is most likely to lead to effective intervention (Carr, Robinson, & Palumbo, 1990).

A Functional Approach

Only since the late 1980s have interventionists and researchers stressed the importance of approaching problem behavior from a functional perspective. Before then, behavior modification was used for intervention, but the interventions were usually not developed by analyzing the cause of the behavior (Carr et al., 1990). The concept of a functional approach is simple: before interventions are designed to reduce the occurrence of problem behavior, a functional assessment process is used to determine why the behavior occurs. Thus an intervention can be designed that fits the circumstances surrounding the problem behavior.

Eliminative Approach

Meyer and Evans (1989) used the term *eliminative approach* to describe the use of behavior modification to reduce behaviors without the benefit of a functional assessment. In this approach the interventionist is interested only in eliminating the problem behavior and designs interventions that are focused on behavior reduction. Although this approach appears to be a logical response to problem behavior, several difficulties are inherent in its use. First, it fails to recognize that problem behavior serves a function for the individual (Donnellan, Mirenda, Mesaros, & Fassbender, 1984), and when the means for that function are eliminated, the individual may find an alternative way to express the function, which is often another problem behavior. For example, Bill is a student with severe disabilities who bangs his head frequently. If a functional assessment had been done, the interventionist would have discovered that this behavior occurs when Bill is not engaged in an activity and appears to be an expression of boredom. Because a functional assessment was not done, the interventionist tried a variety of methods to reduce the behavior while increasing the intrusiveness of the methods each time. Finally, the interventionist implemented a behavior reduction program in which Bill was misted with water (from a spray bottle) each time he engaged in head banging. Bill stopped head banging in an effort to avoid the water mist procedure, but within several days he began screaming and biting his hand when he was bored.

A second problem with the eliminative approach is that the problem behavior is often reduced in one setting or with one interventionist, but persists in other situations. For example, Susan bit her hand when an activity became frustrating or when she wished to escape a situation. The teacher implemented a program in which Susan was assisted in raising her hands in the air and then to the side for three repetitions following every incident of hand biting, followed with redirection to the task. Susan stopped biting her hand at school, but continued to exhibit the behavior with increased frequency in the home and in community settings.

An additional problem is that once the behavior change program is phased out the target behavior returns, often with greater intensity. Richard engaged in episodes of extreme aggression when he was not feeling well or was not provided with activities or objects when he requested them. He had hurt several adults and peers by hitting, kicking, and biting them. After an array of treatment approaches, including positive reinforcement and water mist, had been tried, he was treated by being placed in restraints following every episode of aggression. The restraints were permanently fastened to a chair and then placed on his arms, legs, waist, and forehead when he was seated in the chair. His episodes of aggression decreased until efforts were made to decrease the use of the restraints. Within 2 months the aggressive episodes were occurring with the same frequency as before and, in addition, included acts of property destruction.

Finally, interventionists who use the eliminative approach may withhold positive programming or instructing new skills until the problem behavior is controlled (Evans & Meyer, 1985). Often when behavior interventionists or teachers encounter individuals who exhibit high levels of problem behavior, they work on controlling the behavior before shifting their focus to teaching new skills. The eliminative approach is singularly focused on the reduction of problem behavior without considering the need to teach new skills to the individuals and provide them with the support that they need to engage in new patterns of behavior (Evans & Meyer, 1985).

A common feature of behavior intervention programs designed by professionals who are focused solely on behavior reduction is the use of aversive consequences. A wealth of literature documents the use of a great variety of consequences (e.g., electric shock, water mist, slapping, restraint, pinching) that are considered to be aversive (Guess et al., 1987). The use of such consequences in behavior intervention programs has been a controversial issue and the subject of great concern for professionals and professional groups.

In this chapter, only positive approaches to intervening with problem behavior are presented. In a functional approach to behavior intervention, the interventionist focuses on the instruction of new skills and changes that can be made in environments to support appropriate behavior.

Positive Behavior Support

A functional approach to behavior intervention is based on an effort to understand problem behavior before trying to change it (Carr et al., 1990; O'Neill, Horner, Albin, Sprague, Storey, & Newton, 1997). The process of *positive behavior support* is a method for developing an understanding of problem behavior and a behavior support plan that results in behavior reduction and the development of new communication and social skills. Positive behavior support has been developed on the foundational assumption that problem behavior has purpose, and through the discovery of the purpose of problem behavior an effective support plan can be developed to assist the individual in learning new ways to communicate and interact. In positive behavior support, a communication-based approach to intervention is used. Intervention strategies are focused on teaching the individual with disabilities replacement behaviors, while also modifying the environment in ways that make problem behaviors ineffective and irrelevant (Carr et al., 1994; Dunlap, Vaughn, & O'Neill, 1998; Jackson & Panyan, 2002; O'Neill et al., 1997).

Donnellan et al. (1984) used pragmatics to explain the relationship of problem behavior to communication. Pragmatics is the study of language within the social context (Schuler & Goetz, 1981). Within the pragmatics perspective, all behavior is viewed as having a functional message value. For example, if a child approaches her mother with her hand outstretched when her mother is eating a cookie, one would view this behavior as a request for a cookie. The meaning is inferred by viewing the behavior in the social context. If the same child held her hand outstretched while playing in the sandbox with a friend, one might infer that the child is commenting or directing the play interaction. Although the behavior is the same, we infer different meanings by understanding the context in which the behavior occurs.

In positive behavior support, behavior interventions are designed to expand the repertoire of the individual with severe disabilities (Carr et al., 1994; Carr et al., 2002; Donnellan et al., 1984). These interventions are based on determining the message conveyed by the behavior and replacing the behavior with an alternative communication behavior or an alternative response that results in the desired consequences. For example, in a study conducted by Lalli, Casey, and Kates (1995), an assessment procedure was used to discover why several adolescents with moderate mental handicaps and autism engaged in hitting, throwing objects, and self-injurious behavior. They found that the behavior was used to escape the demands of instructional tasks. The experimenters taught the overwhelmed students to request a break from the work by responding "no" to the question "Do you want to work?" Once the students could use the functionally equivalent communication behavior to take a break from work, the researchers taught the students to work longer sequences before taking a break. The problem behaviors dropped to nearly zero, and each student was able to complete the instructional sequence before needing a break.

In addition to teaching new communication skills, the behavior support plan will also involve changes in antecedent conditions to decrease the problem behavior. Through functional assessment, the interventionist will discover when behavior is most likely to occur and what predictors appear to trigger problem behavior. For example, in a study conducted by Vaughn, Dunlap, Fox, Clarke, and Bucy (1997), a child with severe disabilities had extreme problem behavior (self-injury and aggression) when grocery shopping with his mother. He was provided with a picture shopping list of items that he could select and photo albums to look at when waiting in the checkout line.

The functional approach to behavior intervention considers all the aspects of an individual's lifestyle that may lead to problem behavior. In the eliminative approach, the focus of the intervention was mainly on the consequences that maintained a behavior, rather than consideration of the antecedents that might contribute to the behavior. For example, imagine a classroom in which activity choices are limited and students are directed in all their activities. Suppose that a student with severe disabilities in this classroom is unable to expressively communicate in ways that others can understand. When he is directed to an activity that he does not want to do, he becomes aggressive with the teacher to let her know that he does not want to engage in the activity. In this situation, the lack of choices in the classroom has set the stage for the problem behavior to occur. In a functional approach, enriching the classroom with activity choices becomes part of the behavior intervention plan.

Positive behavior support (PBS) may be described as an applied science that seeks to support an individual with problem behavior to achieve a desired quality of life and to minimize his or her problem behavior (Carr et al., 2002; Jackson & Panyan, 2002). It is based on the science of applied behavior analysis, the importance of inclusion and normalization, and person-centered values. PBS is a science based on rigorous and substantive research that has been conducted over the last 20 years (Carr et al., 1999). A synthesis of the research literature revealed that in 26.8% of research studies interventions resulted in 100% reduction of problem behavior and that in 68% of the studies the problem behavior reduction was 80% or better (Carr et al., 1999). These are impressive outcomes when you consider that many individuals with problem behaviors are exposed to numerous intervention approaches with very limited results.

The use of the process of PBS to respond to student's problem behavior became a part of the Individuals with Disabilities Education Act (IDEA) in the reauthorization of the act in 1997 (Turnbull, Wilcox, Stowe, & Turnbull, 2001). The use of PBS is required in two situations for students with disabilities. The first situation requires IEP teams to consider the use of positive interventions and supports to address the problem behavior of a student when that student's behavior may impede his or her learning or that of others. The second situation requires that IEP teams conduct a functional behavioral assessment and formulate a behavior intervention plan or review an existing behavior intervention plan prior to a change in placement due to disciplinary action or removal from the school for more than 10 days. As a result of the IDEA mandates, many school districts have trained school teams in functional behavior assessment and require the development of positive behavior intervention plans for students with disabilities who have problem behavior (Knoster, 2000).

The Process of Positive Behavior Support

The implementation of positive behavior support involves at least three phases: (1) functional assessment, (2) support plan development, and (3) plan implementation and evaluation (Carr et al., 1994; Horner & Carr, 1997; O'Neill et al., 1997; O'Neill, Vaughn, & Dunlap, 1998). The effectiveness of positive behavior support has been documented for students with severe disabilities within classrooms (e.g., Dunlap, Foster-Johnson, Clarke, Kern, & Childs, 1995; Horner & Day, 1991; Kennedy & Haring, 1993) and in the community (e.g., Carr & Carlson, 1993; Frea, 1997; Vaughn et al., 1997). The process of positive behavior support requires the collaboration and participation of all persons who are in a support role for the individual with disabilities. The goal of positive behavior support is the achievement of meaningful lifestyle outcomes. Positive behavior support is focused on providing the individual with problem behavior access to activities, routines, and relationships that are individually important and meaningful. This goal is ambitious and important and can involve an intensive investment of time.

The process of PBS starts with convening the team of stakeholders who are most familiar with the student. This means that family members, teachers, and related service professionals must be a part of the process. Behavior interventions are much more likely to be effective if they are implemented consistently by all caregivers and in all environments. Family members are essential team members. Family members will inform the process by contributing their intimate knowledge of the student and will be the team members who are most likely to ensure that the behavior support plan is implemented in home, community, and future school environments (Lucyshyn, Dunlap, & Albin, 2002). In addition, the team must consider problem behavior at home and in the community, as well as school concerns.

Conducting a Functional Assessment

Because the functional approach to behavior intervention is based on understanding the behavior, the assessment of problem behavior is an essential first step. This assessment is conducted not only to document the behaviors in which the individual engages, but also to develop hypotheses about why the behavior occurs. Before conducting such an assessment, the collaborative team should gain an understanding of the individual's lifestyle.

Lifestyle Understanding

The first step to understanding an individual's behavior is to examine all the conditions and patterns of her life. A collaborative team that wishes to understand the nature of a student's challenging behavior must look into aspects of the student's life that might contribute to the challenging behavior or help to develop a behavior support plan.

When the behavior support plan is developed, changes in the individual's lifestyle are important outcomes. These outcomes cannot be identified without first understanding the student's lifestyle patterns. For example, if the collaborative team is concerned about a student's self-injurious behavior, one outcome they may target is improved health and safety. In addition, they may want the student to be able to experience a broader array of social activities in the community as he becomes less in need of constant supervision.

Lifestyle issues that are particularly relevant to the challenging behavior of individuals with severe disabilities include leisure activities, opportunities for choice making, friendships and social relationships, community activities, health status, and the nature of the classroom, residential, and work environments. Some individuals with severe disabilities have very few leisure activities, little control over their environment, and very few affectionate relationships. When such conditions exist, the team must examine the relationship of these variables to the challenging behavior of the individual. A person (with or without disabilities) whose lifestyle does not include friends or social activities may be expected to be unhappy or to develop undesirable behavior patterns.

One method for examining a student's lifestyle is to use the personal futures planning process described in Chapter 5. It is likely that in an instructional situation the collaborative team is already familiar with the lifestyle issues of the student. If this knowledge is already accessible, the team should ensure that those issues are discussed as part of the functional assessment process.

The methods developed to conduct a functional assessment of problematic behavior can be classified as (1) indirect assessment methods, which include behavioral interviews, checklists, and rating scales; (2) direct observation assessment methods, which rely on observation of the behavior in natural contexts; and (3) experimental analysis, which involves the manipulation of controlling variables to determine the functional relationship of an array of variables to the problem behavior (Lennox & Miltenberger, 1989).

Indirect Assessment Methods

Several tools have been developed to gather information on problem behavior and the context in which it occurs. Behavioral interviews, which are frequently the first step in conducting a functional assessment, provide a series of questions designed to identify and describe the problem behaviors, identify and describe the ecological and consequence events that surround the occurrence of the behavior, and develop initial hypotheses about the functions of the problem behavior (Iwata, Wong, Reardon, Dorsey, & Lau, 1982; Meyer & Evans, 1989; Miltenberger & Veltum, 1988; O'Neill et al., 1997). Questions that are often asked in behavioral interviews include the following:

- What are the problem behaviors?
- Which of the problem behaviors are the most serious?
- What is most likely to occur before the problem behavior?
- What is most likely to occur after the problem behavior?
- Why do you think the individual engages in the behavior?
- What medications is the individual taking?
- What are the eating, sleeping, and activity routines of the individual?
- When is the problem behavior least likely to occur?
- What activities or objects are most preferred by the individual?
- What methods does the individual use to communicate a protest, request an activity or object, and request social attention?
- What intervention strategies have been used in the past to attempt to change the problem behavior?

Another method for collecting information about problem behavior is the use of behavior rating scales and checklists. The Motivation Assessment Scale (Durand & Crimmins, 1988) is designed to provide information to analyze the variables related to self-injurious behavior. This scale lists 16 questions about the nature of the behavior that may identify possible motivators. Once the questions have been answered, the scoring system indicates if the function of the behavior is to escape, to obtain sensory input, to obtain a tangible reinforcer, or to obtain social attention.

Although the Motivation Assessment Scale can be a reliable instrument that is easily implemented, it is limited in the functions of the behavior that it can identify. When it is used to develop initial hypotheses about the functions of behavior, additional observations, interviews, and systematic manipulations may be needed for a comprehensive assessment.

Indirect methods for assessing problem behavior can yield important information in the functional assessment process, but it is important to note that interviews and checklists rely on informants' impressions of the behavior and may be influenced by their personal perspectives (Iwata, Vollmer, & Zarcone, 1990; Lennox & Miltenberger, 1989). It is possible that the interview alone will provide enough information to develop an intervention plan, although it is more likely that direct observation will need to follow the interview. Direct observation of the behavior in naturally occurring contexts can offer important additional information about the nature of the antecedents, behavior, and maintaining consequences.

Direct Observation Assessment Methods

Direct observation assessment involves the observation of behavior and the contexts in which it occurs. ABC analysis is used to record the events that occur before and after the behavior in an effort to understand the variables that are functionally related to the behavior (White, 1971). In an ABC analysis, the observer records the antecedents that are present, the behaviors that follow antecedent events, and the consequences that follow the target behavior. An example of an ABC analysis is provided in Figure 12–1.

When conducting an ABC analysis, the observer should first identify the target behavior that is the focus of the functional analysis. Although many behaviors may be of interest, for accuracy it is important to narrow the scope of the observation. In the antecedent column, the observer lists aspects of the setting, as well as actions and requests of others that may have a relationship to the target behavior. This is followed by a precise description (in the second column) of the observed student's behavior following the antecedent events. The consequences that follow the behavior are noted in the consequence column, where all events that follow the behavior should be described, including actions by others, changes in the setting, and actions by the observed student.

Carr and his colleagues (1994) offer a format for collecting and organizing ABC information that may make the collection and analysis of data easier to manage. They suggest collecting ABC information on index

Figure 12–1 ABC Analysis of Jon's Aggressive Tantrums

Name: Jon
Observer: Rick
Date: May 3, 1993
Target Behavior: aggressive tantrums that include hitting, kicking, and screaming
Observation Setting: classroom, activity time
Time Begins: 9:00 A.M.
Time Ends: 9:25 A.M.

Antecedent	Behavior	Consequence
Teacher directs Jon to go to the shelf and select an activity.	Jon rolls wheelchair to shelf.	Teacher waits for Jon to make toy selection.
Jon reaches for toy Kim is holding. Kim pulls toy to self.	Jon screams and hits Kim.	Teacher reaches for identical toy and gives it to Jon.
Jon takes toy to table.	Jon plays with toy alone.	Teacher watches and moves to another group.
	Jon plays with toy for several minutes.	
Kim brings identical toy to table.	Jon reaches for her toy.	Kim pulls toy to herself.
	Jon screams, hits, and kicks Kim and takes toy.	Teacher runs over and pulls Kim away.
	Jon becomes calm and plays with Kim's toy.	
Teacher says to put toys back.	Jon puts toy under table and head down.	Teacher directs Jon to take the toy to the shelf.
	Jon sits up.	
Teacher tries to physically assist Jon with picking up toy.	Jon screams and hits teacher.	Teacher holds Jon's hands down for 20 seconds.

cards by listing the interpersonal context of the problem behavior, the behavior, and the social reaction to the behavior. Once multiple observations have occurred and multiple index cards have been generated, the index cards are categorized by the hypothesized function of the behavior. To determine the possible function of the behavior, each card is examined and sorted by asking the question "What did the student want to happen as a result of the problem behavior?"

The ABC analysis is a fairly easy method to use, although the accuracy of the assessment is highly dependent on the accuracy of the observer and the objectivity of the recorded events. Because of the potential subjectivity of the measure, the interventionist may want to follow the descriptive information provided in an ABC analysis with more controlled observation techniques, such as the Scatter Plot method and the communicative function observation tool described next.

The Scatter Plot method provides information on the frequency of the behavior within time intervals over the course of a day (Touchette, MacDonald, & Langer, 1985). In this method, a grid is designed that segments time into units on the vertical axis and days across the horizontal axis. Each blank cell represents a frequency of zero occurrences of the problem behavior. If the behavior occurs within the time interval, the cell is marked with a slash to indicate a low frequency or is shaded to indicate a high frequency. The differentiation of high or low frequency is determined before the observation occurs and is based on the nature of the problem behavior that is being observed. An example of a completed Scatter Plot grid is provided in Figure 12–2.

When the grid has been filled with observations, a visual array of the density of the problem behavior and of the times of day that problem behavior occurs is evident. When this information is supplemented with an analysis of the events that occur during these time periods, hypotheses about the relationship of controlling variables to the behavior can be developed.

The Functional Analysis Observation Form shown in Figure 12–3 is an observation tool developed to provide information on the antecedents, behavior, consequences, time, setting, and possible functions of the behavior (O'Neill et al., 1997). It combines the important features of the ABC analysis, scatter plot, and the communicative functions observation tool in one form.

To use the Functional Analysis Observation Form, the observer first records the name of the person being observed and the dates of the observation. The second step is to fill in the times of the observation intervals. Predictable activities (e.g., morning arrival, snack, physical education) may be recorded with the time. If activities are different over the days (e.g., 9:00 on Monday is community-based instruction and on Friday it is physical education), activities may be listed under the setting events/discriminative stimuli column.

The third step is to record the behaviors that will be observed in the behaviors column. The observation form may be used as an event-recording tool to document the occurrence of an episode of a behavior (e.g., crying tantrum) or the frequency of a behavior (e.g., hitting others). When the behavior occurs, the observer records the first instance, placing the number 1 under the behavior that occurred, the setting event or stimuli to which it responded, the observer's impression of the function of the behavior, and the consequences that followed the behavior.

Observations should continue through the day, with behaviors numerically recorded. When a new day of observations begins, the observer makes a hatch mark after the last number assigned to the last behavior recorded that day and then continues the observations and numerical tracking. In this manner, there is a method for tracking what behavior occurred on specified days. Observations should continue until there is a clear pattern to the data suggesting the likely antecedents, functions, and maintaining consequences of the behavior.

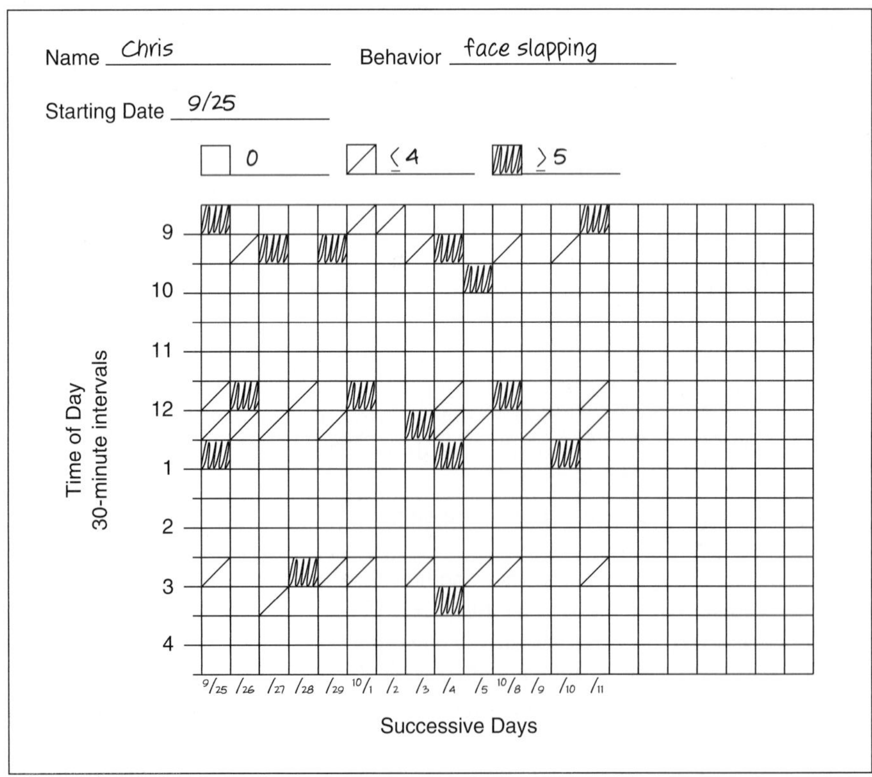

Figure 12–2 Completed Scatter Plot Grid for a Student Who Engages in Face Slapping

Figure 12–3 Functional Analysis Observation Form

Functional Analysis Observation Form

Person: Jean
Dates: 2-20 to 2-21

Time	Behaviors: Screaming	Pinch / Scratch	Rip / Destroy	Settings Events / Discriminative Stimuli: Demand / Request	Difficult Task	Transition (task–task)	Transition (settings)	Interruption	Alone (no attention)	Teacher	Aide	Perceived Functions — Get / Obtain: Don't Know / Unclear	Attention	Desired Item / Activity	Self-stimulation	Escape / Avoid: Demand / Request	Activity ( )	Person	Actual Conseq.: Other / Don't Know	Ignore	Time-out	COMMENTS: (If nothing happened in period, write initials.)
8:30-9:00 H.R.	6	6	6	6							6					6					6	
9:00-10:00 Self-care	1 2 7	1 2		1 2					7	7	1 2	7				1 2			1 7		2	
10:00 11:00 P.E.																						T.R.
11:00-11:30 Office	3		3	3							3					3					3	
11:45 Lunch	8	4	8						4 8		4	4 8							4		8	
12:45 Meal prep	5	5 9	9	5 9						5 9						5 9			5 9			
1:45 Street cross																						T.R.

~~1~~ ~~2~~ ~~3~~ ~~4~~ ~~5~~/~~6~~ ~~7~~ ~~8~~ ~~9~~ 10 11 12 13 14 15 16 17 18 19 20 21 22 23 24 25 26 27 28 29 30 31 32 33 34 35 36 37 38 39 40 41 42 43 44 45 46 47 48 49 50
2-20 2-21

Source: Functional Analysis of Problem Behavior: A Practical Assessment Guide (1st ed.), by R. E. O'Neill, R. H. Horner, R. W. Albin, and K. Storey. Belmont, CA: Wadsworth Publishing Co., Copyright 1990. Reprinted with permission of Wadsworth, a division of Thomson Learning; www.thomsonrights.com. Fax 800-730-2215.

All the direct observation methods described in this section provide the data that allow the observer to make hypotheses about the relationship of variables to problem behavior. To develop a hypothesis or guess about the purpose of the problem behavior, the observer must have information on what the behaviors look like, what factors appear to predict the behavior, and what factors appear to be maintaining problem behavior.

Setting Events

Researchers have discovered that often more distal events (events that don't occur immediately prior to the problem behavior) may affect the individual's likelihood to have problem behavior (Horner, Vaughn, Day, & Ard, 1996). These events are called *setting events* (Bijou & Baer, 1961) or establishing operations (Michael, 1982) and may include fatigue, hunger, environmental irritants, medication, and illness. For example, a student affected by allergies may have slept for only 3 hours the night before school. In the morning, the teacher cues the student to begin a task that the student typically completes without difficulty. On this occasion, the student is tired and does not feel like working. The student pushes the materials away and begins crying when the task is presented.

Hypotheses Development

Hypotheses are informed guesses about why the student engages in the behavior. They are generated through an analysis of the information yielded from the functional assessment process and should be developed to include information about the antecedents that predict the behavior and the consequences that maintain the behavior. Hypothesis statements should include information on the following: (1) the predictors of the problem behavior, (2) what the behaviors look like, (3) the responses that maintain or reinforce the behavior, and (4) the proposed function of the behavior (O'Neill et al., 1997).

O'Neill and his colleagues (1997) describe behavior as serving two major types of functions. Problem behavior may be used to obtain something that is desirable (e.g., object, activity, help, attention) or to avoid something that is undesirable (e.g., attention, tasks, activities). These categories are useful ways to begin sorting out the purpose of problem behavior. Sometimes there is ambiguity about the purpose of the behavior. For example, a student begins a tantrum when the teacher brings out crackers and cheese to make a snack. It may not be clear whether the student wants a different snack or if the student wants to avoid the snack activity. The purpose of the behavior may be identified by asking, "What will make the problem behavior stop?" If the student stops the tantrum when given different choices of a snack, the purpose of the behavior was to obtain a different snack; if the student stops the tantrum when the crackers and cheese are returned to the cabinet, the purpose of the behavior was to avoid the activity. Identifying the consequences that maintain behavior are important clues to the functional purpose of the behavior for the student.

Hypothesis statements should be developed for each behavior and each function that the behavior may serve. It is important to note that some students have problem behavior that serves multiple functions (Carr & Carlson, 1993; Day, Horner, & O'Neill, 1994; Durand & Carr, 1991). For example, a student may use crying and head banging to avoid the task demands of a difficult activity in the classroom and to request the attention of an adult in the lunchroom. Here is an example of a hypothesis statement: "Josh throws materials and screams during the cooking activity to escape the task." When Josh throws materials and screams, adults make him clean up the materials and then pull him away from the activity. Hypotheses may also include information on setting events that may increase the likelihood that a student will have problem behavior. For example, "When Susan has not slept well the night before, she is more likely to hit peers when she becomes frustrated with an assignment." It is important to develop hypothesis statements that are specific and lead directly to an intervention. Vague statements, such as "Susan hits peers when she is angry," will not provide useful information for the development of a behavior support plan.

Experimental Analysis

Sometimes there may be enough ambiguity about a hypothesis that an experimental analysis of the relationship of specified variables to the problem behavior may be conducted to verify the hypotheses. This process, functional analysis, is often used by researchers to confirm the relationship of specific predictors and consequences to problem behavior.

Confirmation of the relationship of variables to behavior can be done by manipulating antecedent and consequent conditions to decipher the meaning of problem behavior. For example, if the hypothesis about tantrum behavior is that the individual is using it to express a desire to escape a particular work activity, conditions can be manipulated to confirm that hypothesis. The interventionist could provide several activities, allow the individual a choice, and then see if the tantrum behavior continues, or the interventionist could systematically present the hypothesized problem task to see if the problem behavior only occurs when that task is presented. A functional analysis to confirm the relationship of identified variables to problem behavior requires at minimum two conditions, one in which the variable of interest is present and one in which it is absent (Iwata et al., 1990). These conditions are then alternated to demonstrate the relationship between conditions and the behavior.

In a study conducted by Dunlap, Kern-Dunlap, Clarke, and Robbins (1991), functional analysis was used to determine the relationship between curriculum features and the severely disruptive behavior of an adolescent female with multiple disabilities. Over a period of 5 weeks, the investigators used a variety of indirect measures and direct observation to develop hypotheses about the student's behavior. The four hypotheses that were developed were (1) that the student was better behaved when engaged in large-motor rather than fine-motor activities, (2) that she did better when activities were brief rather than lengthy, (3) that she did better within functional activities with concrete and preferred outcomes, and (4) that she did better when she had choices about the activities that she was asked to complete.

The four hypotheses were tested using functional analysis. The researchers used rapidly changing reversal designs over 4 days, with one hypothesis tested each day in a 15-minute session. Figure 12–4 shows the results of the functional analysis for the four hypotheses. Once these hypotheses were confirmed, curricular revisions were made in response to the information gained from the functional analysis. The guidelines for changes in the curriculum included short activity sessions when the student was engaged in fine-motor and concentrated academic activity, interspersing fine-motor activities with gross-motor activities, arranging work activities so that the content was meaningful to the student and resulted in concrete outcomes, and providing a menu of choices to the student. These changes resulted in decreases in the student's disruptive behavior and an increase in her on-task responding.

Behavior Support Plan Development

Once hypotheses are developed, a behavior support plan is designed that is comprehensive and multicomponent. The support plan should be broad enough to address issues of lifestyle, ecological variables, immediate antecedents and consequences, and the instruction of new skills. Most of the strategies contained in the support plan will be focused on what adults will do differently that will result in the improved behavior of the student. For many students, the support plan will include new ways to present instruction, curriculum adaptations, teaching students in new ways, responding to behavior in new ways, and the provision of additional supports to the student.

The behavior support plan must be linked to the hypothesis statements that resulted from the functional assessment process. Each hypothesis statement should be linked to support plan strategies that involve changing the predictors of the identified problem behavior, teaching new skills, and creating guidelines for responses to the problem behavior when it occurs. The support plan that is developed should focus on making sure that problem behaviors become irrelevant, inefficient, and ineffective for the student (O'Neill et al., 1997).

Problem behavior is relevant for the student when it is used to achieve a desired consequence. For example, Susan engages in screaming and spitting to get the attention of adults. Susan is in a classroom where students are expected to work on boring tasks without social interaction. In this situation, the teacher can make the problem behavior irrelevant by providing more tasks that are interesting and social interaction. Antecedent or predictor strategies of changing a task, providing curriculum adaptations, providing more frequent attention, or providing more information or predictability are often used to make problem behavior irrelevant. These strategies will not reduce problem behavior by themselves, but are essential elements in the behavior support plan.

Problem behavior is efficient for the student when the use of the behavior gains the desired outcome quickly and with little physical effort. For example, if most of the time when Billy bites his hand the teacher withdraws the activity, the behavior is efficient for Billy. However, if Billy was taught to touch a break card (requiring less physical effort) to immediately obtain a break from an activity, touching the break card becomes more efficient than hand biting. To make problem behavior inefficient for the student, the behavior support team should identify an alternative, more socially appropriate and efficient way for the student to achieve the desired outcome.

Students will continue to use problem behavior when problem behavior is effective (i.e., the student gains the desired outcome). Behavior support plans must include strategies that do not allow the behavior to continue to be effective. This typically involves a withdrawal of the reinforcing consequence (i.e., extinction). A behavior support plan that includes consequence strategies that withdraw the reinforcer must also include instruction on a replacement behavior that results in the same outcome.

Figure 12–4 Results of the Hypothesis-Testing Phase of the Functional Assessment Process Levels of Disruptive Behavior (left) and On-Task Responding (right) Are Shown for Each of the Four Hypotheses.

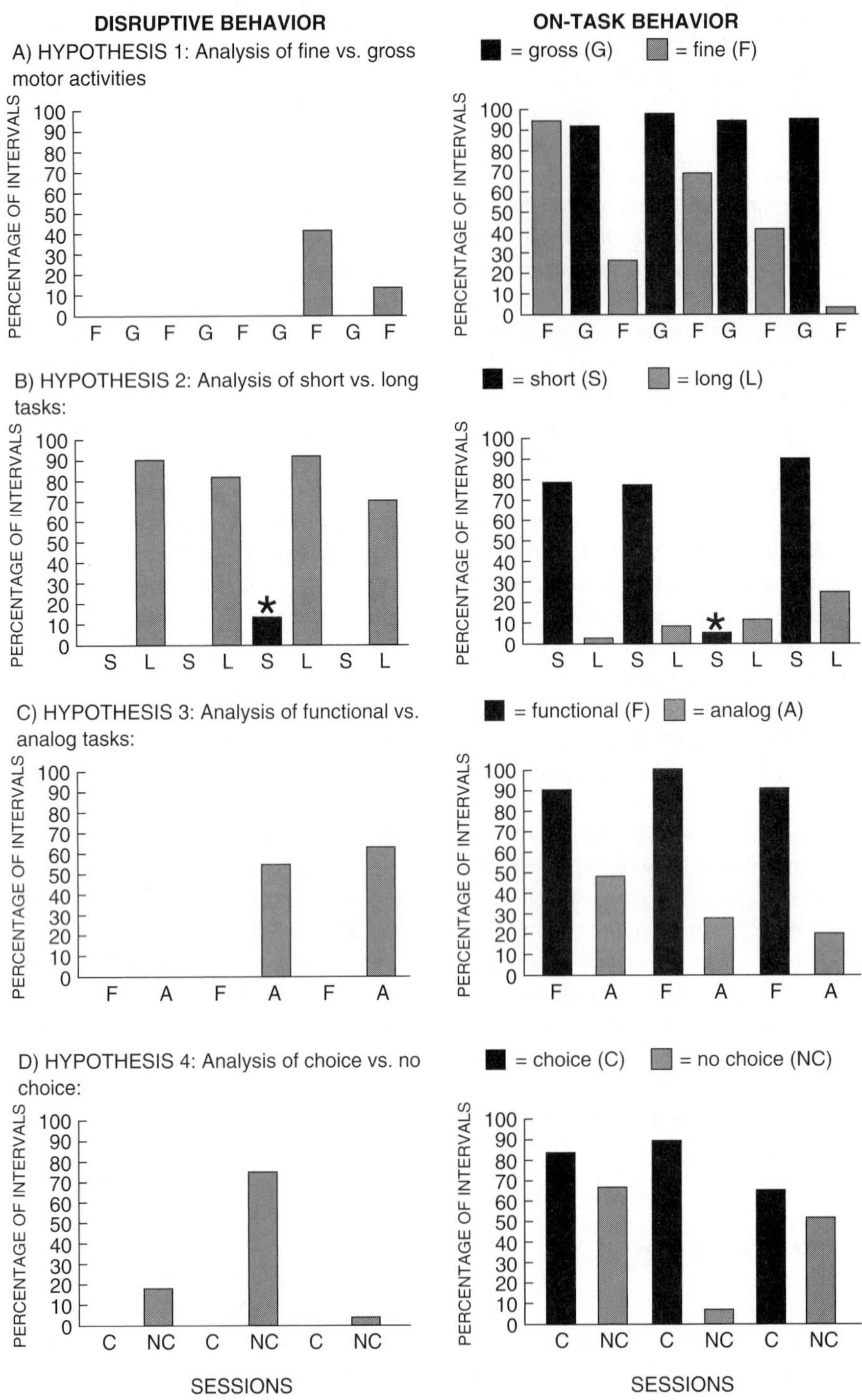

Source: "Functional Assessment, Curricular Revisions, and Severe Behavior Problems," by G. Dunlap, L. Kern-Dunlap, S. Clarke, and F. R. Robbins, 1991, *Journal of Applied Behavior Analysis, 24,* pp. 387–397. Reprinted by permission.

Thus students may be reinforced by using the socially appropriate behavior to gain the outcome.

Teaching Functionally Equivalent Communication Skills

A critical component of the intervention plan is the instruction of new communication skills that are functionally equivalent to the problem behavior. A fundamental rule of positive behavior support is not to attempt to reduce a problem behavior without identifying the behaviors that the student should perform to achieve the desired outcome (O'Neill et al., 1997). To teach the new skill, the teacher must first identify skills that are equivalent to the problem behavior. For example, a student may scream and throw materials to indicate that he wants a break or he may ask for a break by holding up a card with "break" written on it. The selection of the functional equivalent depends on the functional assessment process. If it has been thoroughly conducted, the selection of the behavior to be taught is relatively straightforward. It is important to note that the identification of a functionally equivalent behavior or replacement skill may at times appear as if the behavior support plan is "giving in" to the student. For example, allowing a student to take a break may appear to be counterproductive to teaching a student how to work independently. It is important for the behavior support team to acknowledge that the current approach to "making" a student behave appropriately is not working and to recognize that, by providing the student with alternative ways for expression, problem behavior can be reduced as task engagement is supported through other strategies.

The goal in the selection of a functionally equivalent communication skill is to give the student a more socially acceptable and easily understood mechanism for getting her needs met. When selecting skills to teach, the teacher should select responses that are easy for the student to perform, easy for others to interpret, and usable in a variety of environments. In addition, the teacher must be sure that the new behavior is efficient in achieving the desired response. For example, if a student pushes peers and adults to request a social interaction, the teacher may try to teach him to say "play with me." If the student has difficulty with speech and takes a long time to deliver the phrase, others will not consequate his behavior quickly, and thus he will be likely to continue pushing, which will result in some kind of social response. In this situation, the teacher may want to teach the student a simple gesture, such as patting himself on the chest, and teach others how to respond to the gesture. This gesture may be paired with teaching the verbal request ("play with me"), but initial reinforcement (i.e., social contact) will be delivered on any approximation of the gesture.

When a functionally equivalent skill has been selected, the behavior support team must determine a method of instruction that will result in acquisition and generalization of the skill. It is essential that many opportunities for instruction or skill use be presented and that reinforcement be highly salient and immediate. For example, if a student cries and bangs her head to reject toys and activities, the teacher may decide to teach her to signal protest by using a push-away gesture. But if the only opportunities that are available to use the skill are during free play and center time, it is likely that the acquisition of the skill will be slow and that the problem behavior will persist. The teacher should try to increase the opportunities to use the protest gesture by offering items that she anticipates that the student will reject. Increasing opportunities gives the student more trials of instruction and a higher density of reinforcement for appropriate skill use.

Developing Support Plans

The development of the behavior support plan begins with the development of hypothesis statements and the identification of the functionally equivalent skills that will be taught to the student. In addition, the plan should include antecedent strategies focused on changing the predictors of problem behavior and consequence strategies that make sure that appropriate behavior is reinforced and problem behavior is not effective. The behavior support plan should contain five components: long-term supports, replacement skills (i.e., functional equivalents), prevention strategies (i.e., antecedent and setting event strategies), consequence strategies, and a process for ongoing evaluation of the plan's effectiveness.

In many situations, one individual (such as the teacher or the behavior specialist) is charged with responsibility for designing a behavior support plan. This approach is not desirable for these reasons: (1) functional assessment should involve a variety of individuals to gain a variety of perspectives, and (2) the persons who are involved in day-to-day interactions should be invested in the behavior intervention plan in order to be motivated to carry it out. When a team approach is used to develop an intervention plan, the likelihood of the plan's success is increased.

One of the first tasks of the team is to examine the individual's lifestyle. One method for accomplishing this may be to gather together people who know the individual well (e.g., parents, friends, therapists, teacher) to discuss the patterns of the individual's life. The processes suggested for personal futures planning (Mount & Zwernik, 1988) or lifestyle planning (O'Brien & Lyle, 1987) may be helpful in facilitating this discussion. Meyer and Evans (1989) suggest that the team discuss the individual's history, including an identification of the problem behavior, and then generate a wish list of the ideal program options and life experiences for the individual and a "now list" that includes goals from the wish list that can be implemented immediately.

Once the team has addressed the lifestyle issues of the individual who engages in problem behavior, the behavior support plan can be developed. The creation of the intervention plan is a dynamic process that should include the diverse perspectives of the collaborative team. As the plan is developed, the team should ensure that it:

1. Includes recommendations for lifestyle outcomes.
2. Focuses on the acquisition of skills, rather than on behavior reduction.
3. Is matched to the functional assessment and hypotheses.
4. Includes procedures that are respectful and dignified.
5. Includes strategies that fit with the values, skills, resources, and ecology of the persons who will implement the plan.

Support Plan Components

The first component of the support plan, long-term supports, includes the provision of skill instruction and opportunities for engagement in activities important to achieving the desired lifestyle for the focus individual. For example, if the individual has difficulty with task demands and communicating when she wants a break, a more general instructional program in self-regulation, work skills, and social interaction may be needed. For another student, the provision of opportunities to interact with peers may be important to the development of friendships and social interaction skills. These *long-term supports* are developed by asking, "What are changes that should be made in the focus person's lifestyle to make life more pleasurable and social interactions more positive?" The strategies may include changes in the areas of community integration, employment, or living that are needed to support the individual in the development of new behavior and the reduction of problem behavior.

Long-term supports can only be identified through a process of team discussion and brainstorming. Figure 12–5 provides a list of potential long-term supports that indicates the range of supports that may be considered. It is important for the team to approach the development of this component of the behavior support plan by "thinking outside the box" (Magito-McLaughlin, Mullen-James, Anderson-Ryan, & Carr, 2002). Team members may feel that the student must have appropriate behavior prior to accessing new relationships, environments, or activities. In PBS the emphasis is on supporting the individual with problem behavior to access a quality lifestyle and address the problem behavior (Carr et al., 2002). Students with severe problem behavior often have very restricted and unhappy lives; the goal for long-term support strategies is to reverse these conditions.

The second component of the support plan includes specific details on how functionally equivalent skills will be taught to replace the problem behavior. These *replacement skills* should result in the same outcome as the problem behavior and be easy (i.e., more efficient) for the student to use. One way to identify replacement skills is to examine the communicative skills that already exist in the student's repertoire. Often alternative or augmentative communication devices are used to perform the replacement skill. Sometimes the replacement skill will not be a form of communication expression, but may involve another way to negotiate a difficult situation. For example, a child with autism who does not understand

Figure 12–5 Lifestyle or Long-Term Support Strategies

These strategies are provided as examples of long-term supports

- Enhance peer network
- Enhance daily schedule
- Support development of a hobby
- Support student in developing friendships
- Enhance access to leisure activities
- Support student in self-determination
- Support family in accessing needed resources
- Resolve medical concerns
- Support student in accessing appropriate living situation
- Support student in accessing the community
- Teach student skills to gain access to desired objects, activities, and people
- Enhance student opportunities for choice
- Support student in accessing employment

what is coming next (and acts out to gain the adult's attention and guidance) may be taught to understand the activities of the day using a visual schedule.

The effective instruction of replacement skills is key to the success of the behavior support plan. Once the team selects the replacement skills to be included in the behavior plan, an instructional plan for teaching the skills must be designed. The team should select a systematic instructional strategy, as described in Chapter 7, to use for teaching the new skill. In addition, the team must make a commitment to provide many trials of instruction in the new skill at times when the student is not likely to be engaged in problem behavior. Although you will want to redirect the student to use the replacement skill when he or she is having problem behavior, these occasions are not ideal for instruction. Figure 12–6 provides a list of potential replacement skills to give the team ideas about the types of behaviors or appropriate alternative skills that may serve as functional equivalents to the problem behavior.

The third component of the plan should address antecedents and setting events that may trigger problem behavior. *Prevention strategies* are identified that may reduce the need for the student to use problem behavior (i.e., problem behavior becomes irrelevant). These strategies may include altering the environment, providing additional supports or adaptations, and changing instructional approaches. For example, if a student always exhibits tantrums during transitions from activity to activity, a manipulation of the antecedent should be a part of the plan. A strategy may be to provide the student with a warning that the transition is coming, using a system that the student can comprehend, such as a timer with a bell or a picture schedule. Some teachers feel that this approach is giving in to the student, but it is important to realize that the intervention plan includes ways to decrease the occurrence of the problem behaviors while the student is simultaneously taught new skills. Providing a warning to a student may be a strategy to decrease the occurrence of the problem behavior until he learns new communication or self-management skills and can gradually be taught to handle unexpected changes in activities. Other strategies that may be used to decrease the occurrence of problem behavior are changing the demands of a task to make it less difficult or using prompting techniques to make a task easier, eliminating stimuli that trigger the behavior (e.g., loud music) or providing adaptations that allow the student to avoid triggering stimuli (e.g., transition to a different classroom before the halls fill with students), and embedding trials of difficult tasks within tasks that are easy for the student (Winterling, Dunlap, & O'Neill, 1987).

Figure 12–6 Possible Replacement Skills

These skills represent only an initial list of possible instructional targets. Replacement skills are determined by identifying and matching the function of the problem behavior.

- Request break
- Set work goals
- Request help
- Follow schedule
- Participate in routine
- Make choice
- Self-management
- Teach delay of reinforcement
- Request attention
- Request object
- Request activity
- Initiate social interaction

Figure 12–7 lists many prevention strategies. These strategies are identified through team collaboration. Many teams find that it is helpful to think about problem behavior within routines and activities, list the triggers or antecedents that occasion the problem behavior, and then think of strategies that will eliminate or counteract these triggers. A behavior support plan can include as many prevention strategies as the team is willing to implement with the hope that some combination of the included strategies will be effective. The prevention component of the behavior support plan is very important. The prevention of episodes of problem behavior gives the team the opportunity to provide effective instruction on replacement skills and permits the student to experience positive and rewarding interactions with peers and adults. Prevention strategies are only one component of the behavior support plan and should not be implemented without also teaching new skills and ensuring that problem behavior is ineffective for the student.

Prevention strategies are also important when setting events have been identified that may affect the likelihood that problem behavior may occur. If health issues are a concern (e.g., ear infection), medical remedies should be pursued, although some conditions cannot be eliminated by medical intervention and may persist, such as menstrual discomfort or headaches. If a student is more likely to exhibit problem behavior because of menstrual discomfort, the intervention plan may include a component that is aimed at making her more comfortable during these times (e.g., heating pad, back rub) or decreasing demands in empathy for the student's discomfort.

Figure 12–7 Frequently Used Prevention Strategies

These strategies represent only an initial list of possible strategies. Strategies must be individually determined based on the function of the behavior, the problem behavior context, and student needs.

- Modify task length, modify expectations
- Modify materials
- Modify instructions
- Modify response mode
- Break down task
- Modify seating arrangements
- Reduce distractions
- Provide activity schedule
- Provide clear task prompts
- Provide visual schedule or activity analysis
- Provide adult support and/or assistance
- Select reinforcer prior to activity
- Incorporate student interest
- Self-management system
- Provide peer support and/or assistance
- Add manipulatives
- Provide visual supports
- Follow least preferred with most preferred
- Provide more frequent attention and/or reinforcement
- Contingency for activity completion
- Schedule time with adult or peer
- Schedule access to desired object or event
- Choice of activity, material, and/or partner
- Provide frequent offers of assistance
- Promote active participation
- Use timer or alarm to delay reinforcement
- Rehearse skill or response prior to entry into problem situation

Researchers have suggested five ways to address setting event factors within a behavior support plan (Horner et al., 1996). The first strategy is to minimize the likelihood that the event will occur. For example, making sure a student has a good night's sleep if sleep-iness affects the student's behavior the next day in school. The second strategy is to provide an intervention that neutralizes the effect of the setting event. For example, a student who was prone to problem behavior after becoming overheated on the playground was provided with a cool, wet cloth to wipe his face and a drink of ice water before instruction began. The third strategy is to withhold the activity that provokes problem behavior if the setting event has occurred. For example, in a study conducted by Dadson and Horner (1993), they identified the bus being late as a setting event for a student with severe disabilities. When the student arrived at school in an agitated state because the bus was late, she exhibited tantrums in her first class (P.E.) where she was asked to perform aerobic exercises. The teacher asked the parent to notify the school when the bus was late, and on those mornings aerobic exercises were replaced with stretching exercises (a preferred activity). The fourth strategy is to add prompts that assist a student who is likely to have problem behavior. For example, the teacher can present the task and remind the student periodically, "If you need help, press your buzzer." Finally, a fifth strategy is to increase the reinforcement of the desired behaviors. For example, the teacher may provide more attention or more frequent reinforcement for appropriate engagement.

The fourth component of the plan includes *consequence strategies* for ensuring that problem behavior is no longer effective for the student and that appropriate behaviors are reinforced. Figure 12–8 lists some general strategies that may be used to respond to problem behavior. It is very important for the team to select strategies that will not trigger more problem behavior from the student. For example, if the student becomes more agitated if you provide physical guidance, then you should not include physically guiding the student to engage in the replacement skill. The adult should respond to problem behavior with an affect that is calm, supportive, and firm.

In the following section, more detail is offered on reinforcement strategies and other approaches for responding to problem behavior. Keep in mind that this component of the behavior support plan is only effective when it is implemented with consideration of long-term support, the instruction of replacement skills, and the use of prevention strategies.

Figure 12–8 Consequence Strategies to Consider

These strategies represent only an initial list that the team may wish to consider. The selection of these strategies should ensure that the problem behavior will not continue to work for the student.

- Ignore problem behavior, redirect to use new skill
- Physically guide student to use new skill
- Remove student from problem situation
- Remove problem situation from student
- Protect student from injury or injuring others, redirect to appropriate skill

Reinforcement Strategies

Teachers often use praise or activity reinforcers without individually assessing their reinforcement value to particular students. Reinforcers should be identified for each student, using a systematic assessment process. A simple method for identifying reinforcers is to expose the student to different objects or activities and observe if she interacts with the item, displays positive affect, and tries to retrieve the item when it is removed. It is also important to remember that reinforcers change and that satiation is possible.

When the functional assessment indicates that reinforcement is available and maintaining the problem behavior, a strategy that should be used is to eliminate the reinforcement for the problem behavior and provide reinforcement for an adaptive alternative or appropriate behavior.

Differential reinforcement of other behavior (DRO) is providing reinforcement for not engaging in the target behavior for a specified interval of time. This procedure has been used to intervene with aggression, self-injury, tantrums, self-biting, and a variety of other problem behaviors (Carr, Robinson, Taylor, & Carlson, 1990). To use DRO, the interventionist must first define the target behavior to be changed and take baseline data on the frequency with which the behavior occurs. The next step is to define the time interval to use for the DRO procedure. Donnellan, LaVigna, Negri-Shoultz, and Fassbender (1988) recommend that the selected interval be one-half the interresponse time under baseline conditions. Interresponse time is calculated by observing the behavior and counting the number of times that the behavior occurs within a time interval and then calculating the average length of time between responses. For example, if a student engaged in an average of six tantrums in a 1-hour period, the interresponse time would be one tantrum every 10 minutes. When selecting an interval for reinforcement, the interventionist divides the interresponse time of 10 minutes in half to determine a reinforcement interval of 5 minutes.

After a time interval is selected, the interventionist selects the reinforcement to be used with the procedure and develops a plan to fade the reinforcement. The selected reinforcer should be one that is only available by meeting the criterion of the DRO schedule (Donnellan et al., 1988). Fading the reinforcement can be accomplished by changing the interval schedule. For example, the interventionist may start by using a fixed interval schedule with the DRO procedure and then move to an increasing interval schedule once positive changes in the behavior are established.

The interventionist must also determine the actions to take if the target behavior occurs during the DRO procedure—ignoring the behavior, providing feedback to the student, or using a crisis-intervention procedure if the behavior is very dangerous (Donnellan et al., 1988).

Differential reinforcement of incompatible behavior (DRI) and *differential reinforcement of alternative behavior* (DRA) refer to the reinforcement of behaviors that are topographically different from the target behavior. In DRI the student is reinforced for engaging in a behavior that is physically incompatible with the behavior targeted for reduction. By increasing the targeted incompatible behavior, the target behavior is guaranteed to decrease in frequency (Foxx, 1982).

In using the DRI procedure, it is important to address several variables (Donnellan et al., 1988). First, an alternative behavior should be identified, rather than reinforcing the student for not displaying a behavior. The goal is not passivity, but rather a reduction in the target behavior and an increase in the incompatible or alternative behavior. Second, the more dissimilar the chosen incompatible behavior is to the target behavior, the better the method will work. Third, the identified incompatible behavior and the target behavior must cover the universe of possible behavior. For example, if the student is reinforced for interacting appropriately with others in order to decrease the incompatible behavior of interacting inappropriately by shouting at adults and peers, the universe of possible behavior has been covered. The student can only interact appropriately or inappropriately.

To implement the DRI procedure, the interventionist must first define the target behavior to be reduced. The second step is to identify an alternative behavior that is topographically different and physically incompatible with the target behavior. The alternative behavior and the target behavior should cover the universe of possible behaviors. The third step is to identify the reinforcer to be used for the alternative response and to select a schedule of reinforcement.

Other Consequence Strategies

Response interruption procedures are used to prevent a behavior from occurring (Meyer & Evans, 1989). This can be done through the use of prosthetic devices, by manual blocking, or by cueing the learner. Prosthetic devices have been used to prevent the individual from being able to exhibit a behavior. For example, helmets have been used to prevent individuals who head bang from hitting surfaces, and mittens have been used to prevent an individual from being successful at chewing her fingers. The use of prosthetic devices for this purpose is difficult because they often restrict the movement or sensory awareness of the individual and can be reacted to as if they are aversive. If prosthetic devices are used, every effort should be made to ensure that they do not restrict participation in functional activities, that they are normalized in appearance (e.g., a helmet that is covered by a baseball cap), and that they are not used as a contingent restraint or punishment procedure (Meyer & Evans, 1989).

In manual blocking, a procedure that involves physically blocking the individual from engaging in the target behavior, the interventionist interrupts the behavior by holding the individual's hands down briefly (e.g., when hitting) or preventing contact by blocking the physical action (e.g., hand to head) of the individual. Manual blocking is more effective if a staff person is assigned to shadow the individual when the behavior is likely to occur and to move in and block the behavior when it occurs. This shadow person does not socially interact with the individual, but applies the procedure whenever necessary and reacts to the behavior in a completely neutral manner (Meyer & Evans, 1989).

A cueing procedure may be used if the individual shows signs that indicate that the problem behavior is likely to occur. In this procedure, a verbal and/or physical cue is used to interrupt the behavior chain that leads to the problem behavior. For example, Mary began her tantrums by wringing her hands and reciting the schedule of events that were to occur that day. To prevent the tantrums, her teacher would say to her softly, "It's OK, Mary. Put your hands down. Everything will be fine."

Verbal reprimand is a punishment procedure in which an individual is provided with a firm reprimand following the target behavior. Verbal reprimands can be effective with even very serious behavior when the individual engaging in the behavior is motivated to please others (Meyer & Evans, 1989). A verbal reprimand is not yelling or berating the individual; it is a firm brief statement that is calmly delivered and describes the behavior that the student should engage in (e.g., "No. Hands down. No biting.").

Crisis Intervention Procedures

Crisis intervention procedures may need to be included in the behavior support plan if the student's behavior poses a significant risk to self or others. These procedures only serve to de-escalate the problem behavior and ensure the safety of the student and others; they are not components of the behavior support plan that result in long-term behavior change. Crisis intervention procedures may be needed in the initial days of plan implementation, when previously unidentified triggers set off problem behavior unexpectedly or when episodic setting events occur such as an illness or trauma. If crisis intervention procedures are being used with some frequency, the team should reconvene and evaluate the effectiveness of the behavior support plan. Crisis intervention procedures often involve removing the student from the classroom or problem situation, assisting the student in calming down, or blocking the student from harming himself or others. These procedures often require additional training to ensure that the adult who implements them is able to use the procedures effectively and safely.

Support Plan Evaluation

The final component of the support plan is *evaluation procedures*. It is essential that some method of data collection that provides meaningful information on the effectiveness of the support plan be identified. These measures should assess improvements in the target behavior, the acquisition of the replacement skills, and the achievement of lifestyle outcomes that were identified as important by the behavior support team (Meyer & Evans, 1993). The behavior support process should be regarded as an ongoing endeavor to provide support to the student with challenging behavior. It is likely that students with severe problem behavior will encounter new situations that may trigger new problem behaviors. The team should agree on some mechanism for ongoing communication and monitoring of the behavior support plan, including the integration of the behavior support plan into the student's IEP. In Chapter 9, many strategies were presented for measuring outcomes that are also appropriate for monitoring the success of the behavior support plan.

Comprehensive Interventions

The goal of comprehensive behavioral support is to produce a behavior support plan that is effective across all environments and results in durable and generalized behavior changes (Horner & Carr, 1997). Comprehensive interventions address all the problem behaviors of the individual, are designed to consider all the relevant environments, and are designed to fit with the values, routines, and preferences of the caregivers who will implement the interventions. The notion of *contextual fit* has been proposed to describe the importance of matching behavior intervention strategies to the values, resources, and routines of the persons who will implement the behavior support strategies (Albin, Lucyshyn, Horner, & Flannery, 1996). If a technically sound plan is developed that is not a fit with the persons who must implement the interventions, then it is unlikely that the plan will be implemented or maintained.

The best approach for developing comprehensive interventions applicable to the diversity of environments frequented by the focus individual is to involve the family in all steps of the behavioral support process. Family members can offer unique perspectives and a depth of understanding about the problem behaviors of their child that school personnel do not have. (Lucyshyn et al., 2002). Family members are key informants in the information gathering process. They are able to identify routines and activities that are problematic for the student and can provide important information on the setting events and other factors that may be related to problem behavior.

When family members are involved in the behavioral support process, they become knowledgeable about how the functional assessment process works and why intervention strategies were selected (Lucyshyn et al., 2002). Through their participation in support plan development, their "buy-in" to the importance of the behavior support strategies may be increased. Most importantly, through collaboration with families and other care providers there is an increased likelihood that a truly comprehensive plan is developed.

Figure 12–9 shows a comprehensive support plan developed for an elementary student with autism. This plan is to be implemented in an inclusive elementary school classroom. The plan has been written in a way that is easy for all care providers to understand and implement.

Figure 12–9 Behavior Support Plan for Patrick

Patrick's Behavior Support Plan

The Problem

The purpose of the behavior.

Patrick escapes or avoids transitions and difficult activities by withdrawing, moving around the classroom, running from the classroom, getting out of his chair, throwing instructional materials, and physically resisting the adult. Patrick lacks an understandindg of what is expected of him within activities. When Patrick resists a task or fails to complete his work, adults decrease their demands to prevent further escalation of his problem behavior.

Things to Do All the Time

These strategies will assist Patrick in meeting the demands of difficult activities.

Consistent expectations—Support providers must establish consistent expectations for Patrick's participation in activities. Currently, Patrick is unaware of what he will be asked to do, when it will begin, and when it will end. The use of a picture schedule to inform Patrick of activities and task demands will help Patrick understand expectations. A work sequence for seat work should be established that clearly illustrates the beginning and end of an activity.

Curriculum adaptations—Patrick should be provided with adapted activities that are within the same theme or task that other children are completing. For example, for word families Patrick could match and place the new word with his own personal word list. In math, he could manipulate his own coins on a template to match the amount the teacher demonstrates on the overhead. The expectations of the activity should be clear to Patrick. They should have a visible beginning and end.

Choices—Choices should be given to Patrick throughout the day. Choices could be represented by the picture or by the concrete object. Choices of ways to do an activity should be provided (e.g., "Do you want to do the number puzzle or count objects?") when possible. Choices should be controlled by the adult or a peer tutor (i.e., Patrick should not be allowed to wander until he finds something that he wants).

Peer Support—Peers may be used to support Patrick and help with transitions. The teacher may want to ask for volunteers for a line helper for Patrick each week or month. A child from his table may want to volunteer to be his calender helper. Someone may want to be his lunch buddy. It would be nice to have those helpers not change each day, so that Patrick has a chance to establish a relationship with his peers. Once Patrick becomes more participatory and able to meet task demands, peers may be selected to sit with him during calender, word

Figure 12–9 Continued

family, and math activities and assist him with participation. Peers should be encouraged to interact with Patrick during selected centers.

Short-Term Prevention Strategies

These strategies are used prior to situations that usually evoke resistance from Patrick.

Personal cueing—When Patrick is cued, those prompts need to be personal (i.e., directly given to him in simple language) and understandable (pair with gesture or visual). If the picture schedule is unavailable, prompt Patrick by (1) gaining his attention, (2) showing him a representative object (marker for writing), and (3) giving him a simple direction in a firm tone of voice ("Patrick, write. Time to sit and write.").

Simple language—Patrick continues to have dififiulty understanding complex language. It is especially difficult for him when the classroom is noisy. Use very simple language with Patrick when cueing him. Pair words with gestures (e.g., pat chair and say "Sit. Sit in chair.") or concrete objects. Use simple language when cueing Patrick, but maintain a warm and positive affect.

Picture schedule—The picture schedule should be used to cue Patrick on the activities of the day and transitions. After an activity is over, the facilitator (peer or teacher) should state the activity (e.g., "computer"), say that it is finished while showing him the word finished (e.g.,"computer finished") and take the picture off the schedule, and then show him the next activity (e.g., "Sit at table, journals."). Task demands or the order of work expectations can be illustrated on the picture schedule.

Safety signal—Patrick will be prepared for transitions that are going to be difficult by the use of a safety signal. Support providers will tell him "Patrick, in 2 minutes we will _______" paired with showing him the picture schedule. Then the transition will follow in 2 minutes by the support provider showing him the picture and stating "time for ________". Do not let him delay the transition. Follow through once the cue has been given.

Positive reinforcement—Patrick should receive positive statements about appropriate behavior frequently throughout the day. Support providers need to make a conscious effort to withdraw their reinforcement of his escape behavior (provided through attention) and increase positive reinforcement at other times in the day.

Replacement Skills

Patrick will be taught to ask for a break instead of resisting difficult activities. An important goal is to build his tolerance for hanging in with the activity.

Patrick will be taught to ask for a "break" when a situation becomes intolerable and then allowed to have a brief break from the activity (5 minutes). If the support provider is encountering resistance from Patrick or detects anxiety, he will say "Patrick, want break?" while offering the break card. Then Patrick will be assisted or encouraged to touch the card while repeating "break." Patrick can then move to a designated break area or put his head down on the table, and the support provider will stop activity demands for 5 minutes. If Patrick requests a break independently, provide him with a break. Once Patrick is able to request breaks and does so for several days, begin asking him to hang in for one more time or one more minute and then build up his tolerance.

When the Behaviors Happen

If Patrick has difficulty with task demands, use a language label, "This is hard for you," then follow by asking him if he wants a break or by extending an offer to help (depending on the situation or your perception of his anxiety level).

If Patrick has difficulty with transitions, use a language label, "This is hard for you," then follow with "I'll help you, time for __________" while showing him the picture of the activity.

If Patrick throws a marker, pick it up and place it back in his hand. Give him a simple direction with neutral affect, "Write. Write word."

If Patrick runs from the room, take the picture schedule to him. Redirect him to the activity. If he resists, physically assist him and say "Time for __________. I'll help you."

Always use a visual when redirecting Patrick.

Always tell Patrick the behavior that is expected when redirecting (e.g., "Sit in chair," "Write with marker.").

Figure 12–9 Continued

After a difficult interaction with Patrick, the support provider should take care to approach Patrick in a confident, positive manner.

If Patrick is having a very difficult time in new or unusual situations (e.g., a school assembly), he should be allowed to leave. There is no value in getting in a physical struggle with him. If the situation is intolerable for him (because of sensory overload, lack of awareness of his role), he should be supported and allowed to leave. This is not to punish him, but rather for us to step back from the situation and plan the next time better.

Patrick should never be restrained or physically forced to move. If he pulls away from you or runs away, don't let it become a game. Approach him with confidence, cue him back to an area. Often he can be moved with the firm statement, "I'll help you," and physical guidance to his shoulders and hips.

Conclusion

This chapter presented the rationale and procedures for intervening in problem behavior. What is more difficult to convey, but as important, is the attitude of the interventionist as behavior intervention programs are designed. If the interventionist is to be successful at meaningful behavior change using positive intervention strategies, he or she must be persistent and creative. The methods for determining the functions of problem behavior and the design of intervention plans are only a process. This approach will not provide a cookbook of solutions to problem behavior. The interventionist must use his or her knowledge about the individual and take the individual's perspective to develop an effective intervention plan. It may take many hours of analysis, brainstorming, and problem solving to ultimately develop a behavior plan that is effective and respectful of the individual with disabilities.

Questions for Reflection

1. Why would understanding the history of interventions that have been tried with a student be important to the functional assessment process?
2. How important will knowledge of the student's expressive and communication abilities be in the functional assessment?
3. Think of a behavior of yours that you have successfully or unsuccessfully tried to change. Did you change ecological or setting events? Did you manipulate antecedents or consequences? Did you learn a new skill? If you were successful in changing your behavior, what outcome was the hallmark of your success?
4. If a student engages in behavior that may be dangerous to others, such as hitting or biting, should she be restricted from contact with other students until the behavior changes? Why or why not?
5. Some schools have schoolwide discipline plans, such as going to the office or suspensions after a specified number of rule infractions. Should these consequences also apply to students with severe disabilities? Why or why not?
6. A parent might use corporal punishment at home with a child with severe disabilities and request that the teacher use the same procedures. How would you react to this request?

References

Albin, R. W., Lucyshyn, J. M., Horner, R. H., & Flannery, K. B. (1996). Contextual fit for behavioral support plans. In L. K. Koegel, R. L. Koegel, & G. Dunlap (Eds.), *Positive behavioral support: Including people with difficult behavior in the community* (pp. 81–98). Baltimore: Paul H. Brookes.

Baumeister, A. A., & Rollings, J. P. (1976). Self-injurious behavior. In N. R. Ellis (Ed.), *International review of research in mental retardation* (vol. 6, pp. 59–96). New York: Academic Press.

Bijou, S. W., & Baer, D. M. (1961). *Child development I: A systematic and empirical theory.* Upper Saddle River, NJ: Prentice Hall.

Carr, E. G., & Carlson, J. I. (1993). Reduction of severe behavior problems in the community through a multi-component treatment approach. *Journal of Applied Behavior Analysis, 26,* 157–172.

Carr, E. G., Dunlap, G., Horner, R. H., Koegel, R. L., Turnbull, A. P., Sailor, W., Andeson, J. L., Albin, R. W., Koegel, L. K., & Fox, L. (2002). Positive behavior support: Evolution of an applied science. *Journal of Positive Behavior Intervention, 4,* 4–16.

Carr, E. G., Horner, R. H., Turnbull, A. P., Marquis, J. G., McLaughlin, D. M., McAtee, M. L., Smith, C. E., Ryan K. A., Ruef, M. B., Doolabh, A., & Braddock, D. (1999). *Positive behavior support as an approach for dealing with problem behavior in people with developmental disabilities: A research synthesis.* Washington, DC: American Associastion on Mental Retardation.

Carr, E. G., Levin, L., McConnachie, G., Carlson, J. I., Kemp, D. C., & Smith, C. E. (1994). *Communication-based interventions for problem behavior: A user's guide for producing behavior change.* Baltimore: Paul H. Brookes.

Carr, E. G., Robinson, S., & Palumbo, L. W. (1990). The wrong issue: Aversive versus nonaversive treatment. The right issue: Functional versus nonfunctional treatment. In A. C. Repp & N. N. Singh (Eds.), *Perspectives on the use of nonaversive and aversive interventions for persons with developmental disabilities* (pp. 361–379). Sycamore, IL: Sycamore Publishing Co.

Carr, E. G., Robinson, S., Taylor, J. C., & Carlson, J. I. (1990). *Positive approaches to the treatment of severe behavior problems in persons with developmental disabilities: A review and analysis of reinforcement and stimulus-based procedures.* Seattle, WA: Association for Persons with Severe Handicaps.

Dadson, S., & Horner, R. H. (1993). Manipulating setting events to decrease problem behaviors: A case study. *Teaching Exceptional Children, 25,* 53–55.

Day, M., Horner, R. H., & O'Neill, R. E. (1994). Multiple functions of problem behaviors: Assessment and interventions. *Journal of Applied Behavior Analysis, 27,* 279–289.

Donnellan, A. M., LaVigna, G. W., Negri-Shoultz, N., & Fassbender, L. L. (1988). *Progress without punishment: Effective approaches for learners with behavior problems.* New York: Teachers College Press.

Donnellan, A. M., Mirenda, P. L., Mesaros, R. A., & Fassbender, L. L. (1984). Analyzing the communicative functions of aberrant behavior. *Journal of the Association for Persons with Severe Handicaps, 9,* 201–212.

Dunlap, G., & Fox, L. (1999). A demonstration of behavioral support for young children with autism. *Journal of Positive Behavior Interventions, 1,* 77–87.

Dunlap, G., Foster-Johnson, L., Clarke, S., Kern, L., & Childs, K. E. (1995). Modifying activities to produce functional outcomes: Effects on problem behaviors of students with disabilities. *Journal of the Association for Persons with Severe Handicaps, 20,* 248–258.

Dunlap, G., Kern-Dunlap, L., Clarke, S., & Robbins, F. R. (1991). Functional assessment, curricular revisions, and severe behavior problems. *Journal of Applied Behavior Analysis, 24,* 387–397.

Dunlap, G., Vaughn, B. J., & O'Neill, R. E. (1998). Comprehensive behavioral support: Application and intervention. In A. M. Wetherby, S. F. Warren, & J. Reichle (Eds.), *Transitions in prelinguistic communication* (pp. 343–364). Baltimore: Paul H. Brookes.

Durand, V. M., & Carr, E. G. (1991). Functional communication training to reduce challenging behavior: Maintenance and application in new settings. *Journal of Applied Behavior Analysis, 24,* 251–256.

Durand, V. M., & Crimmins, D. B. (1988). Identifying the variables maintaining self-injurious behavior. *Journal of Autism and Developmental Disorders, 18,* 99–117.

Evans, I. M., & Meyer, L. H. (1985). *An educative approach to behavior problems: A practical decision model for interventions with severely handicapped learners.* Baltimore: Paul H. Brookes.

Evans, I. M., & Meyer, L. H. (1990). Toward a science in support of meaningful outcomes: A response to Horner et al. *Journal of the Association for Persons with Severe Handicaps, 15,* 133–135.

Fox, L., Vaughn, B. J., Wyatte, M. L., & Dunlap, G. (2002). "We can't expect other people to understand": Family perspectives on problem behavior. *Exceptional Children, 68,* 437–451.

Foxx, R. M. (1982). *Decreasing behaviors of severely retarded and autistic persons.* Champaign, IL: Research Press.

Frea, W. (1997). Reducing stereotypic behavior by teaching orienting responses to environmental stimuli. *Journal of the Association for Persons with Severe Handicaps, 22,* 28–35.

Guess, D., Helmstetter, E., Turnbull, H. R., & Knowlton, S. (1987). *Use of aversive procedures with persons who are disabled: An historical review and critical analysis.* Seattle, WA: Association for Persons with Severe Handicaps.

Horner, R. H., & Carr, E. G. (1997). Behavioral support for students with severe disabilities: Functional assessment and comprehensive intervention. *Journal of Special Education, 31,* 84–104.

Horner, R. H., & Day, H. M. (1991). The effects of response efficiency on functionally equivalent competing behaviors. *Journal of Applied Behavior Analysis, 24,* 719–732.

Horner, R. H., Dunlap, G., Koegel, R. L., Carr, E. G., Sailor, W., Anderson, J., Albin, R. W., & O'Neill, R. E. (1990). Toward a technology of "nonaversive" behavioral support. *Journal of the Association for Persons with Severe Handicaps, 15,* 125–132.

Horner, R. H., Vaughn, B. J., Day, H. M., & Ard, W. R. (1996). The relationship between setting events and problem behavior: Expanding our understanding of behavioral support. In L. K. Koegel, R. L. Koegel, & G. Dunlap (Eds.), *Positive behavioral support* (pp. 381–402). Baltimore: Paul H. Brookes.

Iwata, B. A., Vollmer, T. R., & Zarcone, J. R. (1990). The experimental (functional) analysis of behavior disorders: Methodology, applications, and limitations. In A. C. Repp & N. N. Singh (Eds.), *Perspectives on the use of nonaversive and aversive interventions for persons with developmental disabilities* (pp. 301–330). Sycamore, IL: Sycamore Publishing Co.

Iwata, B. A., Wong, S. E., Reardon, M. M., Dorsey, M. F., & Lau, M. M. (1982). Assessment and training of clinical interviewing skills: Analogue analysis and field replication. *Journal of Applied Behavior Analysis, 15,* 191–204.

Jackson, L., & Panyan, M. V. (2002). *Positive behavioral support in the classroom: Principles and practices.* Baltimore: Paul H. Brookes.

Kennedy, C. H., & Haring, T. G. (1993). Combining reward and escape DRO to reduce problem behavior of students with severe disabilities. *Journal of the Association for Persons with Severe Handicaps, 18,* 85–92.

Knoster, T. P. (2000). Practical application of functional behavioral assessment in schools. *Journal of the Association for Persons with Severe Handicaps, 25,* 201–211.

Lalli, J. S., Casey, S., & Kates, K. (1995). Reducing escape behavior and increasing task completion with functional communication training, extinction, and response chaining. *Journal of Applied Behavior Analysis, 28,* 261–268.

Lennox, D. B., & Miltenberger, R. G. (1989). Conducting a functional assessment of problem behavior in applied settings. *Journal of the Association for Persons with Severe Handicaps, 14,* 304–311.

Lucyshyn, J. M., Dunlap, G., & Albin, R. W. (2002). *Families and positive behavior support: Addressing problem behavior in family contexts.* Baltimore: Paul H. Brookes.

Magito-McLaughlin, D., Mullen-James, K., Anderson-Ryan, K., & Carr, E. G. (2002). Best practices: Finding a new direction for Christos. *Journal of Positive Behavior Interventions, 4,* 156–164.

Maisto, C. R., Baumeister, A. B., & Maisto, A. A. (1977). An analysis of variables related to self-injurious behavior among institutionalized retarded persons. *Journal of Mental Deficiency Research, 12,* 232–239.

Meyer, L. H., & Evans, I. M. (1989). *Nonaversive intervention for behavior problems: A manual for home and community.* Baltimore: Paul H. Brookes.

Meyer, L. H., & Evans, I. M. (1993). Meaningful outcomes in behavioral intervention. Evaluating positive approaches to the remediation of challenging behaviors. In J. Reichle & D. P. Wacker (Eds.), *Communicative alternatives to challenging behavior* (pp. 407–428). Baltimore: Paul H. Brookes.

Michael, J. (1982). Establishing operations and the mand. *Analysis of Verbal Behavior, 6,* 3–9.

Miltenberger, R. G., & Veltum, L. (1988). Evaluation of an instruction and modeling procedure for training behavioral assessment interviewing. *Journal of Behavior Therapy and Experimental Psychiatry, 19,* 31–41.

Mount, B., & Zwernik, K. (1988). *It's never too early, it's never too late. A booklet about personal futures planning.* St. Paul, MN: Metropolitan Council.

O'Brien, J., & Lyle, C. (1987). *Framework for accomplishment.* Decatur, GA: Responsive System Associates.

O'Neill, R. E., Horner, R. H., Albin, R. W., Storey, K., Sprague, J. R., & Newton, J. S. (1997). *Functional assessment of problem behavior: A practical assessment guide.* Pacific Grove, CA: Brooks/Cole.

O'Neill, R. E., Vaughn, B. J., & Dunlap, G. (1998). Comprehensive behavioral support: Assessment issues and strategies. In A. M. Wetherby, S. F. Warren, & J. Reichle (Eds.), *Transitions in prelinguistic communication* (pp. 313–341). Baltimore: Paul H. Brookes.

Schroeder, S. R., Schroeder, C. S., Smith, B., & Dalldorf, J. (1978). Prevalence of self-injurious behaviors in a large state facility for the retarded: A three-year follow-up. *Journal of Autism and Childhood Schizophrenia, 8,* 261–270.

Schuler, A. L., & Goetz, L. (1981). The assessment of severe language disabilities: Communicative and cognitive considerations. *Analysis and Intervention in Developmental Disabilities, 1,* 333–346.

Sigafoos, J. (2000). Communication development and aberrant behavior in children with developmental disabilities. *Education and Training in Mental Retardation and Developmental Disabilities, 35,* 168–176.

Touchette, P. E., MacDonald, R. F., & Langer, S. N. (1985). A scatter plot for identifying stimulus control of problem behavior. *Journal of Applied Behavior Analysis, 18,* 343–351.

Turnbull, A. P., & Ruef, M. (1996). Family perspectives on problem behavior. *Mental Retardation, 34,* 280–293.

Turnbull, A. P., & Ruef, M. (1997). Family perspectives on inclusive lifestyle issues for people with problem behavior. *Exceptional Children, 63,* 211–227.

Turnbull, H. R., Wilcox, B. L., Stowe, M., & Turnbull, A. P. (2001). IDEA requirements for use of PBS: Guidelines for responsible agencies. *Journal of Positive Behavior Interventions, 3,* 11–18.

Vaughn, B. J., Dunlap, G., Fox, L., Clarke, S., & Bucy, M. (1997). Parent–professional partnership in behavioral support: A case study of community-based intervention. *Journal of the Association for Persons with Severe Handicaps, 22,* 186–197.

White, O. R. (1971). *A glossary of behavioral terminology.* Champaign, IL: Research Press.

Winterling, V., Dunlap, G., & O'Neill, R. (1987). The influence of task variation on the aberrant behavior of autistic students. *Education and Treatment of Children, 10,* 105–119.

CHAPTER 13

Managing Sensory and Motor Systems

In this chapter techniques are provided that may be used to support students who have motor and sensory disabilities. The chapter begins with a description of motor and sensory development and describes the need for intervention when there are disabilities in these areas. Basic positioning and handling techniques for students with motor disabilities are described, and intervention approaches that may be recommended are explained. A general overview of the impact of hearing and vision impairments on students with severe disabilities is presented, and methods for supporting students with sensory impairments are described.

Addressing Sensory and Motor Challenges

Teachers who work in the field of severe disabilities are encountering an increase among students who may be labeled multiply disabled because they have physical and/or sensory impairments in addition to mental disabilities. This increase may be due to several factors: the increasing number of children who are low birth weight and survive, the use of medical intervention procedures in the neonatal period that affects sensorimotor development, the increase in enrollment of students with multiple disabilities in public schools, and the ability to diagnose sensory impairments in students who in the past were thought to be untestable. Students with multiple disabilities may experience cerebral palsy, skeletal deformities, sensory disorders, seizure disorders, respiratory difficulties, and other medical problems (Orelove & Sobsey, 1996). The needs of such students require that special educators team with professionals from a variety of fields (e.g., physical therapy, occupational therapy, respiratory therapy, nursing) and implement systematic instruction and physical management that are sensitive to the unique needs of the student (Rainforth & York-Barr, 1997).

Collaborative teaming is an essential component of instruction of students with multiple impairments whose unique needs require the expertise of professionals trained in a variety of disciplines (Rainforth & York-Barr, 1997; Romer & Byrne, 1995; Welch & Cloninger, 1995). The term *collaborative teaming* reflects the combination of an integrated therapy approach and transdisciplinary teaming (Rainforth & York-Barr, 1997). In the transdisciplinary team model, team members work across discipline boundaries to train each other in the skills and techniques needed to best meet the needs of the student. The integrated therapy approach adds to the transdisciplinary model by emphasizing that instruction and therapy should take place in natural contexts.

The goal of the collaborative team is to design and implement instructional programs for students with severe disabilities. The team is structured in such a way that decisions are made through consensus with equal participation of all team members, including the family. The team members infuse their discipline-specific knowledge into the design of instructional programs that will provide for the instruction of embedded sensorimotor and communication skills within instructional interventions. Family members on the collaborative team provide their intimate knowledge of their child's development, personality, skills, and needs in different environments. An educational program designed through collaborative teaming offers the student with disabilities the advantages of the knowledge and skills of professionals from diverse disciplines who work together with the family to provide an appropriate program. Educational programs provided by collaborative teams are less likely to duplicate services and are more likely to provide more consistent attention to student needs and integrate discipline-specific knowledge and skills into instructional programs (Albano, Cox, York, & York, 1981).

This chapter presents basic information on the management of sensorimotor and physical disabilities. The chapter begins with a description of the development of the sensorimotor systems and the impact of disability on movement ability. Techniques for facilitating the posture and movement of students are described, and suggestions are given for the provision of systematic instruction that addresses the movement needs of the student. The chapter also describes the effect of sensory impairments on the student with severe disabilities, addressing the needs of the student with sensory impairments and offering techniques for instruction.

The Sensory Systems

People move by integrating the motor and sensory areas of the central nervous and muscular systems (Cusick, 1991). The sensory system integrates information from environmental stimuli, creating complex maps of the person and the environment (Dunn, 1996). The motor system uses these maps to execute movements in response to environmental demands (Dunn, 1996). It is important to understand the interdependence of the motor and sensory systems when designing interventions for students with multiple disabilities. Individuals with multiple disabilities may show evidence of atypical development or involvement in any of these systems. When instructional personnel understand the functioning of the motor and sensory systems, they can adapt activities that build on intact systems and minimize the effects of involved systems (Dunn, 1996).

Sensations from the environment provide the individual with information to facilitate the development of skills. The *somatosensory system* responds to touch input through receptors on the skin (Dunn, 1996). Variations of touch caused by changes in pressure, temperature, duration, and so forth, provide information to the individual about himself or herself and the environment. The *proprioceptive system* responds to the positioning of the body in space and the movement of muscles. Proprioceptive input provides the nervous system with the input needed to create maps of the body as it moves in space. The *vestibular system's* receptor is housed in the inner ear and serves to orient the head in space. When the vestibular receptors are activated through shifts in balance or equilibrium, the vestibular system generates muscle actions to maintain the person in an upright position.

The *gustatory* (taste) and *olfactory* (smell) *systems* use chemical receptors to discriminate sensory input. The *auditory system* uses receptors housed in the ear to process sound, which is used by an individual to map the environment and to communicate with people in the environment. The *visual system* uses receptors housed in the eyeball to decode and transmit images from the environment. It assists the individual in motor movement and depends on the proprioceptive and vestibular systems to interface between the visual and motor systems.

Students with severe disabilities often experience and integrate sensory input in atypical ways. Damage to the central nervous system, specific genetic abnormalities, and the lack of experiences of students with severe disabilities may result in responses to sensorimotor input that are atypical. For example, a student may react to loud noises by being startled or becoming upset; a student may react to soft touches by becoming anxious or withdrawing. When the student responds atypically to sensorimotor input, the teacher must design intervention programs that are appropriate.

Atypical Sensorimotor Responses

The assessment of reaction to sensorimotor input is important in understanding the capacities and skill level of the student. Problem behavior, the avoidance of activities, or the completion of activities in atypical ways may be secondary to a primary difficulty in integrating sensory stimuli. The collaborative team should examine the sensory features of activities that are task analyzed and develop adaptations or learning experiences that will help the student to manage sensory input.

Individuals with multiple disabilities may have limited experience with touch input or may react to touch input in atypical ways. For example, an individual with multiple disabilities may stiffen when touched on the arm or become distressed when feeling cold water. In designing instructional activities, the team should make adaptations based on the student's reactions to these stimuli. For example, the temperature of the water used for hand washing can be adjusted for the student who becomes distressed at contact with cold water. The team may also design instructional activities that specifically use touch input to increase arousal or alertness, to maintain awareness of the body, and to mediate stimulation.

Sometimes a student's difficulty with touch input is characterized as tactile defensiveness or resistance to touching objects and textures. Tactile defensiveness is more appropriately approached as a sensory input difficulty, rather than as intentional noncompliance. Intervention strategies should include a gradual exposure to touch input, reinforcing the student for touch exploration, and providing motivating touch experiences (e.g., an attractive toy, food).

Individuals with multiple disabilities may receive inappropriate proprioceptive input because of the low and/or high tone of their muscles. If the student has difficulty sensing his position in space or has reduced or distorted proprioceptive feedback because of atypical muscle tone, movement may be difficult. The team can develop techniques to generate the muscle tension needed or to decrease muscle tension for the performance of functional movements. For example, a student with low tone may find grasping an eating utensil very difficult. The team can devise techniques to facilitate tone before and during the meal or provide an adaptive utensil that is less challenging to grasp.

Individuals who have difficulty processing vestibular input may react to shifts in position by becoming disoriented, overly excited, and resistive to position changes (Dunn, 1996). Team members who are aware of the effects of movement on the vestibular system of an individual student can design instructional activities and routines that will inhibit disorientation or excitability and enhance the capability of the student to integrate vestibular information. For example, a student who has difficulty bending over because she becomes disoriented or dizzy may have to be supported by an adult so that she can bend down slowly to put on her shoes and socks or may need to be taught an alternative technique, such as placing her shoes on a chair and bringing her foot up to the chair.

Some children with multiple disabilities are placed on restricted diets that result in limited experiences with taste. Students who have hearing or visual disabilities may use their sense of smell to assist them in identifying people, places, and things. Students who have difficulty with gustatory and olfactory input may react to tastes and smells by withdrawing, becoming upset, or becoming excited—or may not react to tastes and smells at all.

In addition to understanding the student's sensory responses, the collaborative team must assess students' motor capabilities and the impact of the disability on motor behavior. In the following section, a description of motor problems and specialized techniques for positioning, handling, and intervention are provided.

The Motor System

The motor system allows the individual to interact with the environment through movement (Dunn, 1996). Movement is used to restore equilibrium when the body has been displaced, to achieve desired actions, and to increase and refine skills. Students with multiple disabilities may have motor impairments due to the extent or location of brain damage.

Muscle Tone

The primary disorder that students with motor impairments may exhibit is abnormal muscle tone (Campbell, 1995). Muscle tone that is lower than the typical range is called *hypotonia;* muscle tone that is higher than the typical range is called *hypertonia.* Some students may have fluctuating muscle tone that changes from very low to high tone. Atypical muscle tone affects a child's ability to produce the muscle contractions needed for posture and movement skills. Muscle tone discrepancies may result in delayed performance of posture and movement skills and/or atypical patterns of movement.

Muscle tone can be modified by using intervention techniques to decrease (inhibit) or increase (facilitate) tone and may also be affected by a number of other environmental or physiological conditions. Medication, environmental noise, interactions, tiredness, mood, and activity are just a few conditions that can affect an individual's muscle tone. Typically, muscle tone can be improved through slow, rhythmic movement and deep pressure. Low tone can be increased by quickly tapping the body part in the direction of the movement or bouncing the individual. The therapist should provide team members with training and ongoing evaluation on specific techniques for inhibiting or facilitating the tone of each student.

Primitive Reflexes

Students with multiple disabilities may also encounter problems with primitive reflexes, which are automatic movement responses to specific stimuli. For example, the rooting reflex is stimulated by brushing an infant's cheek and results in movement of the mouth in the direction of the stimuli. These reflexes act on the sensorimotor system in the first year of life, but may remain present in an older individual with motor impairments. In children who are developing typically, primitive reflexes are present at different points in early development and then disappear as motor development progresses. Because primitive reflexes are automatic movements, they may interfere with the development of functional, volitional patterns of movement.

There are three postural reflexes that most commonly interfere with postural control and movement: the asymmetrical tonic neck reflex (ATNR), the symmetrical tonic neck reflex (STNR), and the tonic labyrinthine reflex (TLR). The ATNR, often called the fencing position, is activated by turning the head to one side, which causes the arm and leg of the side of the body toward which the head is turned to extend. The arm and leg on the side of the body toward which the back of the head is turned are flexed. The ATNR reflex can interfere with feeding, use of the hands in a midline position, and symmetry of the body. For example, a student who has an active ATNR reflex may have difficulty when a switch toy is presented to the side for activation. If the student turns his head to look toward the object, his arm and leg extend, making it difficult to activate the switch. A better way to present the switch toy would be in a midline or when the student is in a side-lying position.

The STNR is activated by bending the neck forward and back. When the neck is bent backward (extended), the arms straighten and the legs bend; when the neck is bent forward (flexed), the arms bend and the legs straighten. The STNR can interfere with crawling, using the arms when sitting, and maintaining a functional sitting position.

The TLR is triggered by the position of the head in relation to gravity. When the individual is supine (placed on her back), an attempt to lift the head results in leg extension. When the individual is in a prone position (placed on her stomach), an attempt to lift the head results in leg flexion. The presence of a TLR keeps the individual from shifting positions when supine or prone. Supine positioning with the head, shoulders, and hips flexed will help decrease or minimize the effects of the TLR.

Posture and Movement

The movements that people perform are composed of a complex array of components. Individuals with physical disabilities who have atypical muscle tone, primitive reflexes, difficulties with postural balance and stability, and deformities may not be able to perform some of the motor components of tasks or may use abnormal posture or movement patterns in performing these tasks. Continued practice of abnormal movement patterns can lead to secondary problems, such as muscle length changes and subsequent orthopedic problems (Campbell, 1989, 1995). Thus early intervention in motor problems is particularly critical.

Early motor development during the infancy period focuses on establishing movement against gravity. For example, an infant learns to lift his head against gravity. These movements are accomplished through muscle contraction. To move the head from side to side requires the activation of the neck muscles and the cocontraction of muscles to maintain postural stability against gravity (Campbell, 1987). If the infant has atypical muscle tone, the movement that results is often atypical. For example, one way that individuals with low tone compensate for the lack of muscle strength in the head and neck is by elevating the shoulders so that less effort is needed to maintain the head erect.

The use of atypical postures is the beginning of a cycle (see Figure 13–1) that results in impaired posture and movement and, for some individuals, permanent deformities. If compensatory motor patterns are allowed to become habitual, they can result in secondary problems of muscle shortening or elongation. These changes in muscle length can result in orthopedic changes or deformities that may be correctable only through surgery (Campbell, 1995).

The goal of the intervention team is to develop a consistent intervention program of positioning, handling, and facilitating movement that elicits more normal muscle tone and facilitates normal posture and movement patterns (Rainforth & York-Barr, 1996). A common approach used to enhance functioning in posture and movement is based on a remedial perspective (Campbell, 1989). In the remedial intervention approach, the individual is assessed by examining current levels of functioning in gross motor milestones and then by determining goals and objectives. In cases in which individuals have disorders that will not respond to remedial interventions because of the severity of the disorder, the quality of previous intervention efforts, or the age of the individual, a compensatory approach may be more effective (Campbell, 1989). In a compensatory approach, the intervention team designs programming that includes strategies to compensate for existing impairments and prevent secondary disorders. The areas of concern for team members are the methods for positioning the individual to prevent secondary disorders (muscle overlengthening or shortening, orthopedic deformities) and to enhance independent functioning and methods for handling the individual that facilitate functional movement and normalized patterns. The next sections present procedures for using appropriate body mechanics while repositioning the individual with physical disabilities, methods for facilitating appropriate posture and movement, and ways to position the individual.

Positioning and Handling

Students with multiple disabilities require an educational program designed with the expertise of a team of professionals, which should include a physical therapist and/or an occupational therapist. These therapists recommend intervention strategies that include preparation to attain tone

Figure 13–1 Cycle of Development of Abnormal Movement

Source: "Integrated Programming and Movement Disabilities" (p. 268), by P. H. Campbell & S. Forsyth, in *Instruction of Students with Severe Disabilities,* Fourth Edition, by Martha Snell. Copyright 1993. Reprinted by permission of Prentice Hall, Inc., Upper Saddle River, NJ.

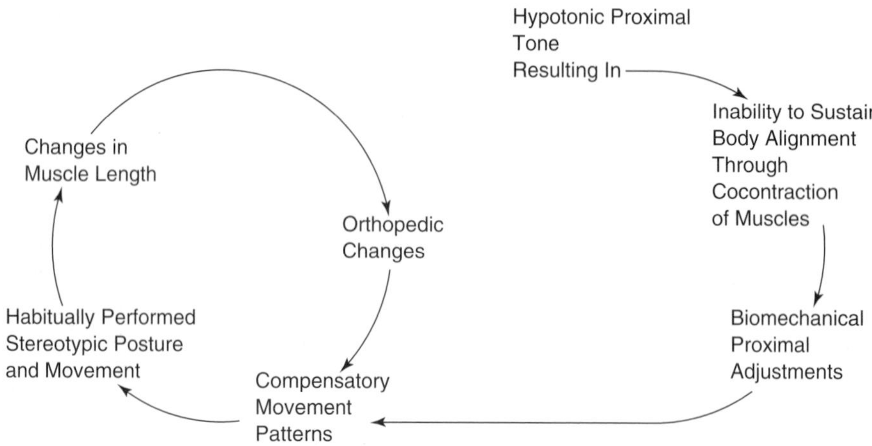

normalization and muscle lengthening for body alignment, control of environmental and sensory influences, inhibition of primitive reflexes, facilitation of movement through space, and maintenance of body alignment and muscle length. Proper procedures for teachers to use are discussed in the following sections, beginning with the use of body mechanics when handling the student with disabilities. It is important that all the procedures described in this chapter be performed only after instruction or training has been provided by the therapist. Teachers place themselves and their students at risk of injury if appropriate guidance has not been received. Subsequent sections include facilitating posture and movement and the use of therapeutic physical management techniques and positioning.

Body Mechanics

It is critically important to the safety of both the lifter and the student with disabilities that good body mechanics be used when lifting and transferring the student. An unsafe lift or transfer can cause permanent damage to the lifter's back and can jeopardize the safety of the student. The most important rule to remember when lifting is to keep the trunk in an erect posture, bending the legs rather than the back. The second rule is to keep the load that is lifted as close to the body as possible and within the safe work zone, which is between the hips and mid-chest.

Before lifting or transferring an individual, the lifter should plan the transfer, arrange the environment so that the transfer can occur easily, and decide if assistance is needed to conduct the lift (Rainforth & York-Barr, 1996). Assistance may be needed if the student is heavy, is unable to assist in the lift or transfer, or has movement patterns that may make handling difficult.

If the student is positioned on the floor, the lifter should squat or kneel beside the child as closely as possible. The lifter should inform the student that he will be lifted and request the student's assistance if he is capable. By informing the student before the lift occurs of what will happen, the student can anticipate the movement, get prepared, and partially participate in the transfer. The lifter should bring the child onto the lap or close to the trunk, distribute the student's weight over the hips, and then conduct the lift. When two adults are needed to conduct the lift, one adult can lift the child's arms and upper body while the other holds the student's hips and legs. Principles for using good body mechanics when lifting are presented in Figure 13–2.

Figure 13–2 Principles of Correct Body Mechanics

Source: Teaching Nontherapists to Do Positioning and Handling in Educational Settings, by N. Cicirello, J. Hyltm, P. Reed, & S. Hall, 1989, Portland, OR: Child Development and Rehabilitation Center Publications, Oregon Health Sciences University. Adapted by permission of CDRC Publications.

1. If the student is able to assist you with the transfer, move at his pace so that he can work with you.
2. If you are unsure of your ability to lift alone, ask someone to help you.
3. When lifting a student, always know his abilities first. Explain what you plan to do before lifting or transferring and encourage the student to assist wherever possible.
4. Assess the environment and make sure your pathway is clear. Arrange equipment and situations so the least amount of work is required.
5. Stay close to the student you are lifting. If necessary, squat or kneel on the floor next to him to gather him up.
6. Maintain a wide, stable base of support by planting your feet flat on the floor and spreading them apart.
7. Line yourself up with the student so that you can maintain a straight back throughout the lift.
8. Never twist your trunk while lifting. Instead, pivot on your feet, keep your back straight, and move your feet, legs, and trunk as a unit.
9. Use your leg muscles when lifting and lowering. Actively tighten your abdominal muscles to establish good pelvic stability and continue to breathe regularly.
10. When two people lift together, make sure the lift is smooth and well-timed to prevent sudden, jerky movements. Plan the lift together and coordinate your movements by counting aloud, "one, two, three."
11. Make sure the student you are transferring feels as secure as possible.

One person can lift and move a student who is small. A student who is spastic (predominantly high tone) and primarily extended should be helped to sit up and assume a symmetrical position before being lifted. A student with a strong extensor pattern should be rolled to the side slightly to make bending her head and hips easier before lifting. One way to pick up the student with an extensor pattern is in a sitting position with his hips and knees bent and arms over the adult's shoulders.

The young student who is athetoid (writhing movement within the muscles) should be lifted by first flexing her hips and legs next to her trunk and gathering her arms across her chest or around her legs. The athetoid child who has uncontrolled and continuous unwanted movements should be provided with steady and firm handling that provides as much stability as possible (Finnie, 1974). The lifter should support the student with one or both arms under her knees. If one arm is under the student's knees, the free arm can be used to secure her arms.

The low-tone child should be provided with steady handling at the shoulders and arms so that it is easier for him to control his head and should be carried in a way that provides adequate stability and support at the hips to encourage him to extend his head and back.

Posture and Movement

Although there are many times when a student must be lifted or carried by an adult, it is essential that students with physical disabilities be helped and encouraged to actively participate in the movement as much as possible. The teacher usually supports and handles the student from key points of control; the head, shoulders, trunk, and pelvis are the areas of the body where abnormal postures and movement patterns are most easily interrupted and more normal postures and movement patterns can be facilitated (Finnie, 1974; Rainforth & York-Barr, 1996).

The touch that the teacher uses when handling the student depends on the student's muscle tone, reaction to tactile stimulation, and the nature of the motor movement. The therapist on the collaborative team should provide team members with guidance on the touch to use with each individual student. In general, a firm, deep touch should be used with students who have high tone or who are hypertonic; a light, active touch should be used with students who are hypotonic or low tone to awaken the muscles and initiate postural adjustments. Quick, light touches cue muscles to move; firm, sustained touches cue muscles to hold a position.

When facilitating a movement, the teacher should first consider where the student's center of gravity is prior to the movement, where the student is bearing weight before the movement, what reactions are desired from the student when a weight shift occurs, which muscles have been properly elongated, what the next movement will be, and the final destination point of the movement. For example, to help move a student from a bench to a sitting position on the floor, the student is first helped to place his hands on the side of the bench and pivot onto his hands so that he turns onto his stomach, and then facilitated to lower himself to his knees. Once on his knees, he is helped to place one hand on the floor and lower his trunk, and then place the other hand on the floor so that he assumes a four-point position on the floor. The student is then facilitated to rotate his pelvis and lower himself into a side-sit position.

Therapists should teach team members the techniques needed to assist students in changing position and in maintaining appropriate postures. Techniques that may be used include (1) rolling a student who exhibits a strong extensor pattern to the side to inhibit the extension, (2) flexing and rotating the student to inhibit extension, (3) stimulating the muscle tone of a low-tone child to elicit participation in movement, and (4) using key points of control to facilitate movement. Therapists should also train team members in techniques to prevent secondary disabilities. These techniques include positioning the student appropriately and providing therapeutic activities intended to maintain muscle length.

Positioning

The student with physical disabilities must be placed in varied positions to (1) promote active participation in activities, (2) prevent the development or progression of deformities and skin breakdowns, (3) provide weight-bearing experiences, (4) facilitate circulatory, respiratory, and digestive functions, and (5) allow mobility. Often individuals who are nonambulatory are positioned in a sitting position for most of the day, which enhances the individual's ability to participate in activities, but may also affect muscle length and spinal musculature that can lead to deformities (Campbell, 1989). Alternative positions must be provided to place the muscle groups that are at risk for muscle overlengthening or shortening into the opposite length (Campbell, 1989). For example, a student who is low tone and spends a large amount of time in an upright position may develop shortened lateral flexors or lower back muscles because she leans to the side or falls forward over the pelvis. This student should also spend time in a supported weight-bearing position (standing or side-lying) that will promote muscle stretching and lengthening.

The positioning of a student can be described as dynamic or static (Rainforth & York-Barr, 1996). Dynamic positioning refers to the use of techniques to modify tone, to stabilize and align body parts, and to facilitate the active movement of the student. Static positioning is performed with adaptive equipment and has the advantage of freeing the team member from having to provide one-to-one assistance.

The collaborative team should decide on the positions that are most appropriate for the student with disabilities. The positions selected should be functional, comfortable, and therapeutic. It is essential that the adaptive equipment selected for use as positioning aids be well fitted to the student. The positions selected for use in the classroom and community must also be age appropriate and functional for the activity. For example, standing and sitting are the most age-appropriate and functional positions for most classroom activities, although a prone or supine position on the floor might be used while reading or during recreational time if nondisabled students assume these positions as well. Rainforth and York (1991) suggest that the team use the following considerations in selecting a position and positioning equipment:

1. What positions do nondisabled peers use when they engage in the activity?
2. Which of these positions allow easy view of and access to activity materials and equipment?
3. Do the positions allow for proximity to peers?
4. Do the positions promote efficient movement as needed to perform the task?
5. What positions provide alternatives to overused postures or equipment?
6. If positioning equipment is required, is it unobtrusive, cosmetically acceptable, and not physically isolating?
7. Is the positioning equipment safe and easy to handle?
8. Is the equipment individually selected and modified to match individual learner needs?
9. Is the equipment available in and/or easily transported to natural environments?

When positions that use adaptive equipment are selected for students, it is helpful to take a Polaroid photograph of the student appropriately positioned. This photograph can be used for reference when he is being positioned and the therapist is not available to monitor correct placement. In addition to having access to such a photograph, the teacher should know why the position is being used, what activities are appropriate for the position, how long the student can remain in the position, if special precautions are associated with the position, and what physical conditions of the student (e.g., placement, pressure points) should be monitored (Cicirello, Hyltm, Reed, & Hall, 1989).

Students with physical disabilities often spend most of the school day in a seated position (Hulme, Poor, Schulein, & Pezzino, 1983). Because adapted wheelchairs do not always meet the physical needs of these students (Rainforth & York-Barr, 1996), educators should have a thorough understanding of the principles of seating so that problems can be minimized.

The optimal position for the pelvis in a seated position is with the hips flexed to 90 degrees and the pelvis symmetrical and tilted slightly forward. The pelvis can be supported in this position by using a lap belt across the hip joint. The weight of the student should be evenly distributed across both buttocks and thighs. A firm seat (rather than a sling) will support the symmetrical positioning of the hip and pelvis. Each thigh should be fully supported, with the seat extending one inch back from the calf (Rainforth & York-Barr, 1996). Students with leg-length differences or a deviation of both legs to one side require a lengthened chair seat to fully support both thighs. The trunk should be held in a symmetrical, midline position. Some students may need to use chest support in addition to the lap belt to hold the trunk upright.

Feet should be positioned flat with the toes forward on a footrest. The footrest should be low enough so that the thighs are resting flat on the seat, but not so low that the feet hang or so high that the thighs are lifted from the seat. Heel straps, when prescribed, help to secure the foot to the footrest. When trays are placed on adapted chairs, they should be high enough that the student can rest his elbows and forearms on the tray without raising his shoulders (Rainforth & York-Barr, 1996). A tray offers the student with poor head and trunk control a surface to lean on and provides greater stability. The tray can also provide a place to support a communication device or serve as a work surface.

A challenge when positioning a student with multiple handicaps upright is maintaining the head in an upright position. The ideal head position is erect with the chin in a tucked position. Some students may benefit from headrests that guide head placement (Fraser, Hensinger, Phelps, & Jacques, 1987); others may need head support equipment that is more elaborate and supports the head completely.

Positioning equipment that provides a structure for supporting the student in a stationary position is commercially available. The collaborative team should discuss the need for positioning equipment and consider the

Figure 13–3 Common Positioning Equipment

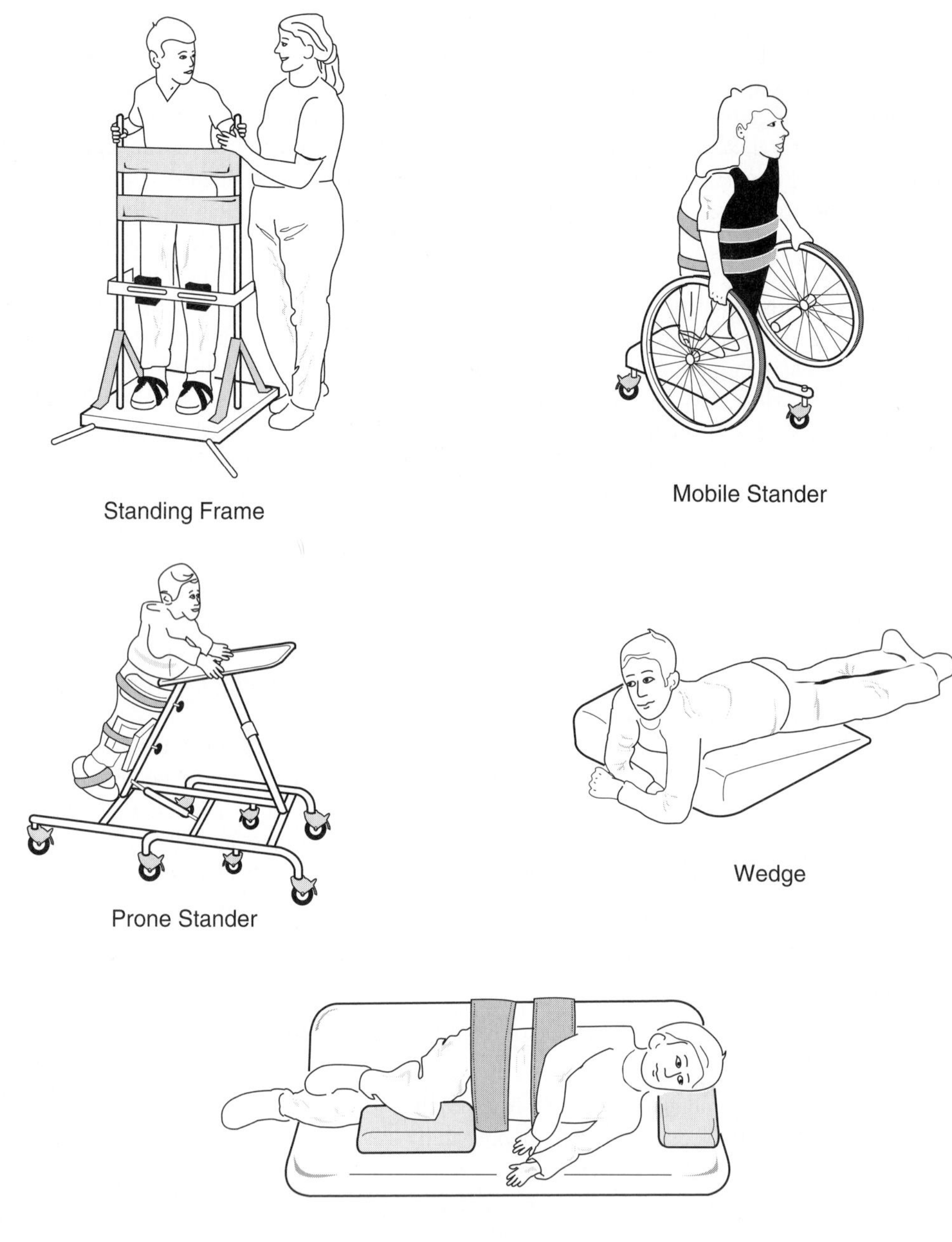

needs for equipment as assistive devices within the IEP process. Some common pieces of equipment are shown in Figure 13–3.

Instructional Programming

In addition to physical management and positioning, individuals with multiple disabilities should be provided with intervention and therapy to help to maintain and develop their motoric skills. In a collaborative team, the person who is with the student during instruction (the teacher or the paraprofessional) is primarily responsible for carrying out intervention plans. Through the collaborative teaming process, therapists work with other team members to select the appropriate approaches for individual students and provide training in the use of intervention techniques. In addition, the family members and educator on the team show the therapist techniques that may be effective and

Figure 13–3 Continued

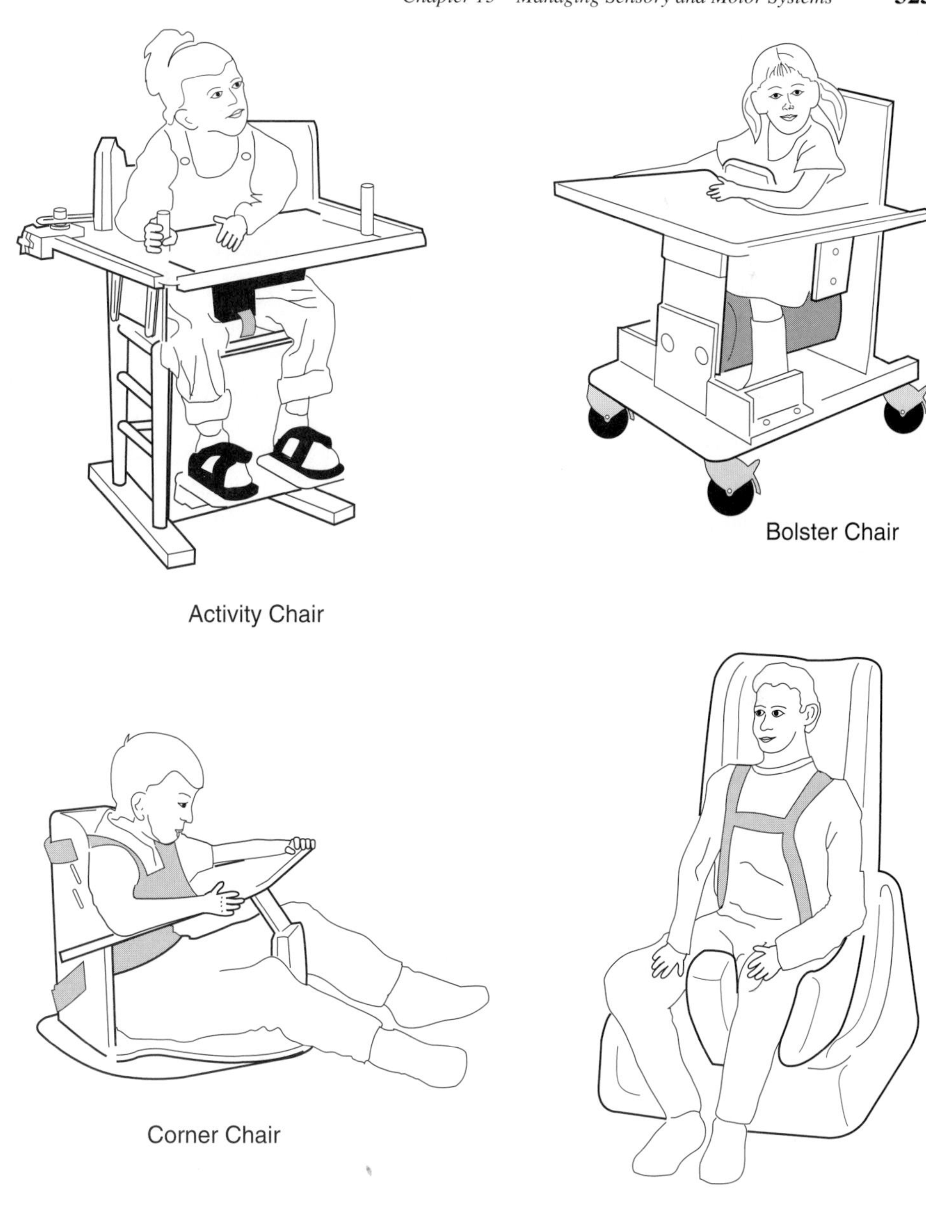

Activity Chair

Bolster Chair

Corner Chair

Large Feeder Seat

evaluate with the therapist the functional utility of proposed interventions. Some common approaches to motor intervention are sensory integration, neurodevelopmental treatment, and behavioral programming.

Sensory Integration

Sensory integration therapy is a neurobiological model of intervention designed to be used with individuals with learning disabilities (Arendt, MacLean, & Baumeister, 1988; Dunn, 1996). Sensory integrative approaches have also been extended to applications with individuals with multiple disabilities, although there is little research documenting benefits for this population (Arendt et al., 1988; Horn, 1991).

Sensory integration, which involves sensory stimulation to the individual to improve the way the brain processes and organizes sensations (Ayres, 1979), is based on the theory that sensory stimulation is necessary to improve the sensory processing capabilities of the brain that are needed for subsequent learning tasks.

Interventions that use a sensory integrative approach may involve adapting a learning activity to provide sensory integrative experiences within the activity or may involve activities that are specifically designed to match the sensory input needs of an individual student. The techniques used may involve rubbing the student with textured items to provide tactile stimulation; moving the child on a therapy ball, in a net, or on a scooter board to provide vestibular stimulation; or positioning the student in a way to accommodate sensory input within a learning activity.

Neurodevelopmental Treatment

Neurodevelopmental treatment (NDT) involves identifying the posture and movement problems of individuals with neurologic dysfunction and designing interventions that decrease the effects of abnormal muscle tone and increase the normal muscle action for functional movement (Bobath, 1980). Intervention strategies that use an NDT approach consist of inhibiting abnormal patterns of posture and movement, normalizing muscle tone, and facilitating equilibrium reactions (Bobath, 1980).

The NDT approach involves direct intervention to affect muscle tone and to guide patterns of posture and movement. The interventionist is first concerned with establishing body alignment and normalized muscle tone. She moves the child through movement patterns that facilitate desired muscle actions and inhibit atypical movement patterns. These patterns are embedded in functional routines and skills. Many therapists report that an NDT approach results in qualitative changes in the student's movement, although little empirical evidence exists to support these claims (Horn, 1991; Stern & Gorga, 1988).

Behavioral Programming Intervention

The behavioral programming approach to motor intervention involves the use of behavioral principles to train motor behavior. The motor skills are taught using prompting, shaping, and contingent reinforcement (Horn, 1991).

In the behavioral programming approach, which is common to educators and psychologists but less familiar to therapists, behavioral principles are used to establish changes in motor behavior. Substantive research supports the use of this approach with students who have multiple disabilities (Ball, McCrady, & Hart, 1975; Filler & Kasari, 1981; Grove & Dalke, 1976; Horn & Warren, 1987; Lee, Mahler, & Westling, 1985; Leiper, Miller, Lang, & Herman, 1981; Richman & Kazlowski, 1977; Skrotzky, Gallenstein, & Osternig, 1978). Through collaborative teaming, therapists and educators can design motor intervention programs that combine knowledge from different disciplines to design maximally effective programs.

Integrated Programming

Regardless of the intervention approach recommended by a therapist, it is critical that intervention techniques be integrated into instructional and activity routines (Campbell, 1995; Craig, Haggart, & Hull, 1999; Giangreco, Prelock, Reid, Dennis, & Edelman, 2000; Rainforth & York-Barr, 1997) and that the strategies used be developed by the collaborative team, including the family. Team members must combine their expertise to develop a functional instructional program that will enhance the student's participation and independent functioning in natural settings. Any adaptations, positions, or therapy techniques selected must be carefully considered with regard to how they can be used in natural environments (including the home and community) by a variety of interventionists. Techniques that require isolated treatment or specialized equipment may not provide enough benefit to outweigh the isolation that will be imposed on the student with severe disabilities. If the techniques, positions, and adaptations selected can be used by a variety of interventionists in a variety of natural environments, positive outcomes are far more likely to occur.

Classroom Support Strategies

The presence of physical impairments that restrict the movement of the student requires that teachers find alternative ways for the student to be involved in activities that require movement or the manipulation of objects. Assistive technology, which ranges from low-tech simple adaptations to high-tech microchip-controlled devices, offers students a wealth of opportunities to actively participate in typical environments (Downing & Demchak, 1996).

Many adaptations that may assist students with physical impairments may be purchased from home health-care stores (e.g., adapted utensils, grasping devices, book holders) or common retail stores (pencil grips, large-number calculators, benches, Velcro). Electromechanical switches may be homemade using materials purchased in an electronics store or are commercially available from many catalogue sources. Switches may be used to activate any device that is operated by a battery or electricity and can be adapted to support individuals who have extremely limited volitional movement. For example, a sip-and-puff switch only requires the ability to control breath and oral movement. Other examples of low-tech adaptations include tape-recorded instructions for nonreaders, visual schedules or communication boards, and handles for objects.

High-tech equipment providing support to individuals with physical impairments has become more available and more affordable. The personal computer provides a wealth of options for instruction and communication. Software programs range from assisting students in learning cause–effect relationships to providing easy access to information and individualized academic instruction. The computer chip has been used to develop augmentative communication systems that range from the very simple (i.e., a few phrases that are easily programmable) and portable to the very complex (i.e., capable of generative conversations with extensive vocabulary).

Peers are a critical source of support to their classmates with physical impairments. Figure 13–4 provides instructions for peers. Peers may provide personal support to students with physical impairments by assisting them with motor movements. For example, a peer may help a student to transfer from the wheelchair into a chair. In addition, peers can take a role in the completion of an activity. For example, if a student can visually make a choice, the peer may then pick up and place the item. If students are giving oral reports in class, a peer may tape-record the report of a classmate with physical disabilities so that her classmate may activate a switch to play the tape recording.

Figure 13–4 Peer Supports for Classmates with Physical Impairments

1. Make eye contact with your classmate before you move his wheelchair or provide assistance.
2. Speak with your classmate using a normal tone of voice. Be careful not to "talk down" because he or she is disabled.
3. Try to get on the level your classmate is on when interacting. Sit down if he or she is in a wheelchair. Get on the floor if he or she is lying on the floor.
4. Offer to help your classmate move from one place to another, but don't overdo. It is important that she has independence. Always ask before assuming she needs help. If your classmate is in a wheelchair, make sure an adult has shown you how to operate it safely.
5. Give your classmate time to talk or use his communication device. Don't become impatient. Ask questions that don't only require yes/no responses.
6. Find ways your classmate can have fun with you. Video games, board games, looking at magazines, talking, and playing on the computer are some things you may be able to do together.
7. Ask the teacher or parent if there is anything you need to be careful about when interacting with your classmate (e.g., seizures, brittle bones), but don't treat your classmate as if he/she could break.
8. Your classmate may need help with grooming activities, eating, or dressing. Do not assume that you can provide the help. Always ask first.
9. Make sure your classmate is positioned where she can see what is going on. Alert your teacher if your classmate can't see the materials.

Sensory Impairments

The prevalence of vision and hearing impairments among persons with severe disabilities is not well determined (Fredericks & Baldwin, 1987; Sobsey & Wolf-Schein, 1996). The accuracy of a prevalence figure is affected by the differences in definitions used by prevalence surveys and differences in sampling procedures (Sobsey & Wolf-Schein, 1996). Despite the difficulty in achieving an accurate estimate of prevalence, it is clear that vision and hearing impairments occur more frequently in individuals with multiple disabilities than in other persons (Sobsey & Wolf-Schein, 1996). The conditions that result in severe and multiple disabilities are frequently related to visual and hearing impairments. Teachers of students with severe disabilities should expect to encounter students with sensory impairments and must be able to work with team members in the assessment of sensory impairments, as well as in determining adaptations that can be made to enhance students' learning potential. In the following sections of this chapter, hearing and visual impairments are described and strategies for assisting the learner with sensory impairments are discussed.

Hearing Impairments

Hearing impairments are described by the type of loss and the degree of impairment. There are four types of hearing loss:

1. *Conductive:* an impairment that results from an obstruction in the pathway from the ear canal to the

inner ear. Sounds may be muffled because they are not transmitted effectively through the hearing system. Conductive losses are caused by otitis media (middle ear infection), ear wax, or a structural abnormality.

2. *Sensorineural:* an impairment that is caused by damage to the inner ear or to the auditory (vestibulocochlear) nerve. Sensorineural losses are usually more severe than conductive losses and are generally permanent. Sensorineural losses are caused by infections, genetic conditions, or ototoxic (harmful to hearing) drugs.
3. *Mixed:* impairments that are both conductive and sensorineural.
4. *Central auditory disorders:* impairments that are caused by damage to the central nervous system in a way that prevents the individual from responding meaningfully to sound.

Degree of hearing loss may be categorized from slight to profound (Herer, Knightly, & Steinberg, 2002). Decibel ranges are used to describe hearing sensitivity. Most people with normal hearing can hear tones of 10 to 20 decibels (dB) in a quiet room (Niswander, 1987).

A slight hearing loss (can hear tones of 15 to 25 dB) may interfere with hearing distant or faint speech. A slight hearing loss commonly occurs with middle-ear infections and typically does not affect the child's development, although frequent episodes of slight hearing loss may pose difficulties for a child in school. A mild loss (25 to 30 dB) results in difficulty in hearing soft speech, distant sounds, and unvoiced consonants (*/s/*, */p/*, */t/*, */k/*, */th/*, */f/*, and */sh/*) (Herer et al., 2002). If a student has a moderate loss (30 to 50 dB), it will be difficult for the student to hear conversations without amplification. A severe loss (50 to 70 dB) precludes hearing conversations, and a profound loss (71 dB or greater) means that the student can only hear very loud sounds (e.g., car horn) and will be unable to discriminate speech sounds.

A teacher may suspect hearing loss by observing behavioral signs such as language delays, poor articulation, poor response to verbal instruction, requests to repeat what was said, distractibility, inattention, failure to localize to sounds, failure to imitate vocalizations, avoidance of tasks with auditory demands, and hyperactivity (Sobsey & Wolf-Schein, 1996). When a hearing loss is suspected, the teacher can use noisemakers and observe responses in an informal testing situation to probe if a hearing loss may be present.

An accurate assessment of hearing loss is typically performed by an audiologist, who may use one of a variety of audiological assessments to determine the extent of the hearing impairment and an intervention plan. Visual reinforcer audiometry (VRA) procedures assess response to sound by pairing a visual stimulus with an auditory signal (Herer et al., 2002). A typical VRA uses a mechanical toy housed in a plexiglas box. An auditory signal is activated and at the same time the box is lit and the mechanical toy is turned on. The child is reinforced for looking at the box by the illumination and the toy. After a few paired trials, the sound is presented and the child is observed to see if he anticipates the appearance of the illuminated toy. If the child turns toward the box, it is assumed that he hears the sound. This procedure may not be effective for children with visual impairments, children who do not localize to sound, and children who are unable to turn their head from side to side (Sobsey & Wolf-Schein, 1996).

The tangible-reinforcer, operant-conditioning audiometry (TROCA) method uses an operant discrimination paradigm for determining hearing ability (Niswander, 1987). TROCA is conducted by using equipment that dispenses a reinforcer when a button is pushed. The individual is reinforced for pressing a lighted bar or button when it is paired with an auditory signal. Once the response is conditioned, the illumination is faded and the auditory stimulus cues the response. This procedure may not be effective with students who have motor delays or cognitive disabilities that inhibit the button-press response or acquisition of stimulus–response relationships (Niswander, 1987).

Auditory brain stem response (ABR) examines the brain-wave response to auditory stimuli. To assess auditory functioning through brain-wave response, three electrodes are attached to the head. These electrodes detect electrical activity and display them on a screen for analysis. The testing requires 30 to 45 minutes to complete and requires that the individual sit or lie motionless. Small children or children who are difficult to test may need to be sedated for the examination. Because the ABR does not require a volitional response on the part of the individual, it is a very powerful assessment technique to use with individuals who are difficult to test. Problems of the ABR include an inability to discern frequency-specific responses, an overestimation of the hearing loss, and difficulty in interpreting the data when the ABR detects no responses to the auditory stimuli (Niswander, 1987).

Another screening measure that has been endorsed as one of the preferred methods to use with infants is evoked otoacoustic emissions (EOAE) (American Academy of Pediatrics, 1999). The EOAE is similar to the ABR in that it is noninvasive, quick (less than 5 minutes), and easy to perform by trained professionals. In the EOAE, a small probe is inserted in the ear canal to detect the otoacoustic emissions that come from the cochlea in response to sound.

Acoustic immitance measures may be used to assess the condition of the eardrum, middle-ear functioning, acoustic reflexes, and the eustachian tubes (Sobsey & Wolf-Schein, 1996). The procedure involves a small probe tip inserted in the ear that emits a low-frequency tone. The tone is transmitted into the middle ear and is reflected to a microphone connected to the probe tip. The magnitude of the reflected tone indicates whether there is an ear mechanism problem. Because these measures require the passive participation of the individual who is being tested, they may not be useful for difficult-to-test individuals (Niswander, 1987).

Adaptive Devices

The most obvious remedy to a hearing problem is to amplify the sound so that it can be heard. There are two types of hearing aids, the air-conduction aid that sends sound through an earmold worn in the ear and the bone-conduction aid that stimulates the skull with a vibrator placed behind the ear (Franklin, 1995). Hearing aids may be placed on the body, over the ear, or in the ear. Body-style aids are typically used with infants and toddlers whose small ears cannot accommodate an ear-level aid, individuals with ear malformations, and older children with limited manual dexterity who can more easily use a body aid (Sobsey & Wolf-Schein, 1996). In-the-ear aids are more frequently prescribed for adults and are not usually recommended for children. Children with hearing impairments should be fitted with an amplification device as soon as the hearing loss is diagnosed (Niswander, 1987). Most individuals can benefit from amplification, although for some persons the hearing aid enables the user only to detect environmental sounds and noises.

Cochlear implants are surgically implanted prostheses that have been designed to provide auditory awareness to individuals who are profoundly hearing impaired. The device involves a microphone that detects sound and feeds it to a processor unit that converts the sound to electrical impulses that are directed into the inner ear and stimulate the auditory nerve. The wearer can hear environmental sounds and sometimes speech, although the words are not discernible.

Vibrotactile communication aids provide alternative sensory input through vibrations on the skin. The devices use a microphone to pick up sounds that are delivered to a small vibrator attached to the arm or finger of the user (Niswander, 1987). The vibratory signals provide information about the pitch, timing, and intensity of the sounds.

Frequency modulation (FM) systems are often used to support the child with hearing impairments in the classroom. Hearing aids amplify all sounds in the environment equally, while an FM system can be used by a classroom teacher to amplify the teacher's voice. This is particularly helpful for deaf–blind students who may have difficulty discerning the teacher's voice from the background noise of the classroom. FM systems involve a microphone worn by the speaker and a receiver attached to the student's hearing aid.

Support Strategies

A critical issue for intervention with students who are severely disabled and hearing impaired is to develop communication skills. Manual sign language may be an appropriate form for receptive and expressive communication skill development, although many students do not have the manual dexterity or cognitive ability to become fluent sign-language users. A discussion of alternative communication systems is provided in Chapter 11.

When a student is hearing impaired, the collaborative team must make an effort to assess the amount of hearing present and design strategies to maximize the use of residual hearing. Sound discrimination, localization, and awareness should be taught within functional activities in the natural environment (Sobsey & Wolf-Schein, 1996).

Simple strategies may be used to support the student with hearing impairments. Speakers should first signal to the student by touching him or moving closer before speaking. Speakers should speak at a normal level of volume at close range, rather than shouting from across the room. It is helpful for the student if the speaker moves in closely, establishes visual contact, and is careful not to obstruct her face when talking so that the student with hearing impairments can gain visual information to help to interpret what is being said. Nondisabled peers should be given information about the student's disability and strategies that they may use to support their classmate. Some basic strategies are listed in Figure 13–5.

Students with hearing impairments should be positioned in the classroom away from background noise and close to the instructor. Classroom noise should be minimized as much as possible, especially when instructions are given. When giving instructions or information, the teacher should use gestures and visual information as appropriate. Most importantly, the teacher should learn how to operate and maintain the student's amplification system.

Figure 13–5 Peer Supports for Classmates with Hearing Impairments

1. Touch your classmate's arm or shoulder before speaking or signing.
2. Ask your teacher to teach you a few signs that will help you communicate with your classmate if your classmate uses sign language (e.g., "Want to go with me?"; "May I sit here?"; "I'd like to work with you.").
3. Watch how your teacher uses visuals or objects to cue your classmate. Use visuals or objects to inform your classmate of the next activity, provide choices, or ask questions.
4. Don't be afraid to get close. Sometimes leaning in to your classmate or speaking in the better ear will enhance your classmate's ability to understand you.
5. Be sensitive about other noise sources. If you are standing near noisy equipment (e.g., next to the copy machine) or if there is a background noise (e.g., humming from the overhead projector fan), it will be more difficult for your classmate to understand you.
6. Don't be afraid to try to communicate in other ways. Use pantomime or visuals (e.g., pictures, objects) to communicate with your classmate if you do not know what else to do.
7. Invite your classmate to be a part of your group. It is hard to make friends when you don't understand what people are saying. Ask your classmate to join you at lunch or to hang out with your group at recess.
8. Find things that you and your classmate can enjoy together. Playing board games, sports, and crafts may be activities that you can both enjoy.

Vision Impairments

Students who are visually impaired experience a restriction in vision of sufficient severity that it interferes with their ability to interpret and use visual input (Scholl, 1986). Definitions of visual impairment are determined by measuring visual acuity in the better eye. Visual acuity can be measured by using an eye chart and determining the distance at which the individual can read letters that a person without visual impairment can read at 20 feet. A visual acuity of 20/20 means that the person has no impairment. A visual acuity with a denominator that is higher, for example, 20/200, indicates an ability to read letters at 20 feet that a person without a visual impairment can read at 200 feet. A visual acuity in both eyes of 20/200 or less with the best visual correction is considered legal blindness. A visual impairment is visual acuity of 20/70 to 20/200. A restriction in the visual field may also be defined as legal blindness when the visual field is determined to be less than 20 degrees in diameter (Hollins, 1989) as compared to a normal visual field of 120 to 150 degrees on each axis (Jose, 1983).

The leading causes of blindness among individuals who are under age 20 are congenital cataracts (clouding of the lens), optic nerve atrophy (degeneration of the optic nerve), and retinopathy of prematurity (damage to the retina due to high concentrations of oxygen used to treat premature infants with respiratory distress) (Ward, 1986). The prevalence of visual impairments among students with other disabilities is much higher than among students without disabilities (Scholl, 1986; Sobsey & Wolf-Schein, 1996). The diagnosis and assessment of a visual impairment involves a physiological examination of the eye and an evaluation of the functional use of vision. These assessment activities are conducted by a vision or eye specialist, ophthalmologist, or optometrist.

Vision Assessment

The following behaviors may cause a teacher to suspect that a student has a visual impairment: moving clumsily in the environment; holding the head down or to the side when moving; shuffling the feet when walking; bumping into objects; finger flicking in front of the eyes; bringing objects to the mouth for exploration; locating objects on sound cues; responding to objects that are shiny or certain colors; overreaching or underreaching when picking up objects; squinting or closing one eye when looking at objects; poking, pressing, or rubbing the eyes; losing interest or avoiding visually demanding tasks; becoming quiet when sounds are presented; and not making eye contact with conversation partners. An informal test for functional vision can be performed by the teacher to determine if further diagnostic assessment should be conducted. Langley and Dubose (1989) provide a checklist (see Figure 13–6) to record information on the student's visual response, reaction to stimuli, the distance and size of objects that the student responds to most consistently, the ability to integrate cognitive and visual information, and the integration of visual and motor processing.

A visual response is assessed by examining the student's pupillary reaction, muscle balance, visual field, blink reflex, and eye preference. Pupillary response is assessed by directing a penlight into the student's eyes and observing whether the pupils constrict and then dilate when the light is removed. The light is flashed into the

Figure 13–6 Functional Vision Checklist

I. Presence and nature of the visual response
- a. Pupillary reaction: __present __absent __R __L
- b. Muscle imbalance: __present __absent __R __L
- c. Blink reflex: __present __absent __R __L
- d. Visual field loss: __present __absent __R __L
- e. Peripheral field loss: __present __absent __R __L
- f. Visual field preference: __present __absent __R __L
- g. Eye preference: __present __absent __R __L

II. Reaction to visual stimuli
- a. Inappropriate visual behaviors: __present __absent
- b. Tracking ability: __present __absent
  __light __objects: __vertical
  __circular __horizontal __oblique
- c. Reaches for toys: __present __absent
  __in front of him __to his right
  __to his left __above eye level
  __below eye level
- d. Shifts attention: __present __absent
  __both sides __one side __R __L
- e. Scanning ability: __present __absent

III. Distance and size of objects and pictures
- a. Locates dropped toy: __present __absent __distance
  __peg or candy
  __inch-cubed blocks __shape chips
- b. Small toy observed: __present __absent __distance
- c. Large toy observed: __present __absent __distance
- d. Objects matched: __present __absent __distance
  __large toys __distance
  __small toys __distance

IV. Integration of visual and cognitive processing
- a. Visual pursuit: __present __absent
- b. Causality: __present __absent
- c. Object permanence: __present __absent
- d. Object concept: __present __absent
- e. Means–ends: __present __absent

V. Integration of visual and motor processing
- a. Approach:
  1. pegs: __visual __tactual reach: __O __U
  2. stacking cone: __visual __tactual reach: __O __U
  3. puzzles: __visual __tactual reach: __O __U
  4. pounding bench: __visual __tactual reach: __O __U
  5. beads: __visual __tactual reach: __O __U
- b. Matching
  1. colored blocks:
     __matches __does not match __near distance __far distance
  2. shapes:
     __matches __does not match __near distance __far distance
  3. pictures:
     __matches __does not match __near distance __far distance

Source: "Functional Vision Screening for Severely Handicapped Children," by B. Langley and R. E. Dubose,1989, in *Dimensions: Visually Impaired Persons with Multiple Disabilities, Selected papers from the Journal of Visual Impairment and Blindness,* pp. 47–51. Reprinted with the permission of the American Foundation for the Blind.

center of the student's eyes to see if the light is reflected in the middle of each pupil. If a deviation is present, it may indicate muscle imbalance. Light perception is assessed by passing a hand across the student's eyes to elicit a blinking response and by flashing the penlight at points above, below, and to the left and right of the student's face to see if he responds to the light and to determine the range of the visual field. The evaluator then sits behind the student and slowly brings the light into the student's visual field while noting the point at which the student turns to look at it. Eye preference can be assessed by holding up a motivating toy and then alternately covering the student's eyes. If one eye is not functional, the student will indicate distress when the functional eye is covered.

The student is observed to determine if any atypical visual behaviors are present, such as eye poking or light filtering with the fingers. Toys or other motivating objects can be used to assess whether the student can track, shift visual attention from one object to another, and scan an array of objects. Objects of various sizes can be used to note the distance and size of the object to which the student will attend. The evaluator can ask a student to match sets of duplicate toys (large and small) that are placed at varying distances to assess the distance that is optimal for vision.

The integration of vision, cognitive, and motor skills is assessed by observing the student interacting with objects. Sensorimotor skills (cognitive skills from birth to 24 months) are assessed to determine the student's developmental level. If there is evidence that a student is at a very early sensorimotor stage of cognitive development, the vision difficulty may be related to cognition, rather than the integrity of the sensory system.

Visual pursuit can be assessed by seeing if the child will watch small objects as they are poured from a container. The cognitive skill of understanding causality can be assessed by scribbling on a large paper and offering the marker to the student. The cognitive skill of object permanence can be assessed by putting a motivating object in a container or hiding it under a cloth and watching the student to see if she searches for the object. Means–ends ability may be assessed by activating an object (e.g., windup toy), letting it wind down, and then watching the student to see if she attempts to reactivate the toy. Visual and motor processing can be assessed in the young child by using a pounding bench or stacking cones and observing if the child underreaches or overreaches as he attempts to place objects in the appropriate place. The ability to match color and configuration can be assessed using shapes or colored blocks at various distances, although for many students more motivating materials may be needed to elicit a response.

Vision Correction

Correction of a visual disorder can be made for some students with visual impairments through surgery or the use of corrective lenses. The presence of multiple disabilities should never be used as an excuse for denying a student visual correction (Cress et al., 1981). If eyeglasses are recommended for a student with severe disabilities, the collaborative team may need to develop strategies that will support the student (e.g., reinforcement procedures, shaping) as she becomes adjusted to wearing them. In addition to correcting vision, the team should design strategies and adaptations that assist the student with visual impairments to maximize the use of her residual vision.

One method for enhancing the use of residual vision is to provide systematic instruction in the use of visual skills. Research has demonstrated that structured vision training can be an effective vision enhancement method (Goetz & Gee, 1987; Mosk & Bucher, 1984; Utley, Duncan, Strain, & Scanlon, 1983; Utley, Roman, & Nelson, 1998). Goetz and Gee (1987) have described a method for instructing functional vision in the context of a functional, community-based curriculum that is discussed later in this chapter.

Support Strategies

Support strategies may be used to accommodate and enhance instruction for students with visual impairments. These strategies must not be universally applied, as each student with vision impairments is unique and will react to these strategies differently (Utley et al., 1998). The vision specialist on the collaborative team should examine all the instructional contexts, instructional routines and demands, and behaviors of the student to determine where support strategies may be used.

An important area to consider is the positioning and posture of the student. Students may turn their body or head away or react to the visual presentation of a stimulus in ways that are linked to their visual condition (Utley et al., 1998). For example, a student with a visual impairment due to rubella may turn her head to view objects. The teacher may feel strongly that the student should look at objects when presented at midline and suggest developing an instructional program focused on shaping this behavior. A more appropriate response may be to explore the reasons why students engage in atypical postures or behaviors and to support the student accessing optimal visual information within tasks.

Some students with visual impairments can discriminate more easily when illumination is provided (Cox &

Dykes, 2001), although some students may need subdued lighting to see (Utley et al., 1998). A good indicator of the student's illumination needs is the student's behavior under varying conditions. If the student squints, turns away, becomes fatigued, or engages in problem behavior when exposed to increased lighting or intense light (e.g., outside in the bright sun), then increased illumination may be problematic. Visors, hats, or light-filtering lenses may be needed for students who react to bright lighting. Teachers should be aware that different kinds of lighting can affect the student. Fluorescent lighting, often used in schools, may pose problems for some students. If supplemental lighting is appropriate for the student, the light is usually placed behind the student, as close to the work space as comfortable, and positioned to prevent shadows on the work surface (Utley et al., 1998).

The work surface for the student should be uncluttered and provide support to the student's forearms to facilitate easy exploration of objects with his hands. Highly reflective work surfaces should be avoided and contrast should be enhanced when possible. Teachers should be aware that acrylic lap trays on wheelchairs can reflect the ceiling light and cause the student discomfort. Contrast can be promoted by placing dark objects on white or light surfaces, using contrasting colors to assist in object finding and discrimination, marking equipment or area boundaries with fluorescent tape, and using a light box when appropriate. Teachers should also position themselves carefully and avoid standing in front of a window or open door so that glare is reduced.

Peers should be provided with information and encouragement to support their classmate with visual impairments. It is important that peers understand their classmate's disability and the ways in which they may encourage the student with visual impairments to feel comfortable in the classroom and in developing friendships. Sample instructions that may be provided to peers are provided in Figure 13–7.

Figure 13–7 Peer Supports for Classmates with Vision Impairments

1. Say your name before you approach your classmate.
2. Speak to your classmate as you would to another peer. Don't worry about using words such as "see" or "look."
3. Offer your upper arm if your classmate needs a guide to move around. Your classmate will hold your upper arm and walk a step behind you. Tell your classmate if you are approaching stairs, change in slope, or curbs. If you bring your classmate to a chair or bench, wait for your classmate to find it or place her hand on it.
4. Give your classmate verbal information about where objects are located when you are in a new environment. Help him find an empty seat in the cafeteria by his friends.
5. Try not to use expressions that are visual in nature when giving directions (e.g., "put it by the green one," "it's over there").
6. Scan the environment and then describe choices to your classmate. For example, in the library there may be choices of where to sit, or at recess there may be different areas where students are gathering.
7. If something funny happens that your classmate can't see or if the teacher changes her facial expression, tell your classmate what is happening.
8. Don't overdo for your classmate. Your classmate can ask for help and would prefer being independent.
9. Be thoughtful about the environment. Close cabinet doors, return materials to their place, push chairs under the table, and avoid creating environmental barriers.
10. Sometimes it is hard to join a group when you can't see the facial expressions of people and how they may react to your approach. Invite your classmate to join your group. Introduce your friends and encourage them to verbally greet your classmate.

Leaders in the field of visual impairments and multiple disabilities have described the curriculum needs of students with visual impairments, including multiple disabilities, as having two major components (Corn, Hatlen, Huebner, Ryan, & Siller, 1995). The first component includes instruction within the curriculum domains that is provided to general education students. Students with visual impairments will need adaptations and assistance within the academic curriculum to be able to understand the visual concepts involved in the lesson or to be able to access information. The second component includes disability-specific issues that are unique to the needs of the learner with visual impairments. The specialized component includes communication skills, orientation and mobility, social interaction skills, independent living skills, recreation and leisure skills, career education, use of assistive technology, and visual efficiency skills. IEPs that are developed for learners with visual impairments should consider each student's instructional needs within these domains.

Functional Vision Training Two components are involved in functional context vision training (Goetz & Gee, 1987; Utley et al., 1998). The first involves teaching visual attention behaviors within tasks that require visual attention for successful performance. For example, the student must visually scan a vending machine to find the coin slot and successfully make a purchase. The second component is to use the systematic instructional procedures of repeated prompting or continuous correction to prompt the student until visual attention occurs.

Five steps are used to develop a functional vision program. The first step is to determine the targeted visual skill. Some skills that may be appropriate to target include orienting to the presence of a stimulus, visual fixation, accommodative convergence, gaze shift, tracking, scanning, and peripheral vision (Goetz & Gee, 1987). The second step is to select the skill contexts that require visual behavior for accurate task performance. The skills selected for functional vision training must be functional, age appropriate, and motivational for the learner.

The third step is to design the instructional program for teaching the vision skill. To decide on a criterion for determining if a student's skill performance is correct or incorrect, the teacher must identify the critical moment that the vision behavior must occur in the task and the duration or accuracy of the visual skill that is needed to perform the task correctly. For example, a student may need to visually scan a box of crackers to find the open tab, but then may not need to visually fixate while opening the box.

When the critical moment is identified, the teaching strategies that will be used to ensure that the student performs the visual behavior are selected. The prompting techniques that are chosen depend on the abilities of the student being taught and the nature of the target skill and skill context. Prompting techniques that have been used with students learning visual behaviors include using physical and tactile cues, auditory cues, and additional visual cues, such as shining a light on an item involved in the task, and interrupting the task until the student performs the required visual behavior (Utley, Goetz, Gee, Baldwin, & Sailor, 1981).

Continuous-loop training procedures are used to make sure that the student understands that successful task performance is contingent on the use of visual skills (Goetz and Gee, 1987; Utley & Nelson, 1992; Utley et al., 1998). In continuous-loop training, instructional trials are repeated until a correct response is achieved. As the student performs the task, he or she is provided with reinforcement for using the visual skill within the motor task. If the student fails to use the visual skill, the instructor interrupts the student and cues him to begin the step again. This is not done in a punitive manner; the teacher should be supportive to the student (Utley et al., 1998). Continuous-loop training or repeated prompting should not be used if the student reacts negatively to the procedures or if its use in community settings is not practical or calls undue negative attention to the learner.

The fourth step of designing a functional vision program is to select the instructional strategies that will be used to teach the functional skill. Once the student is performing the visual skill at the critical moment, a systematic instructional program should be used to ensure competence in performing the functional task. The final step of the functional vision program is to implement and monitor the program that has been designed in Steps 1 through 4.

Orientation and Mobility Skills Students with visual impairments have to be taught how to move safely and purposefully in their environment. These skills are called orientation and mobility skills (Hill, 1986; Welsh & Blasch, 1980). The traditional approach to teaching these skills is based on a developmental model (Hill, 1986) in which individuals are assessed to determine if they understand the concepts that are designated as prerequisites to independent travel skills. Once these concepts are established, training in traveling with a sighted guide, using self-protection techniques, basic cane skills, specific cane techniques, and traveling in outdoor environments is provided (Hill & Ponder, 1976).

A functional approach to orientation and mobility has been implemented for individuals with severe and multiple disabilities (Fazzi, 1998; Gee, Harrell, & Rosenberg, 1987; Joffee & Rikhye, 1991). In a functional approach, travel training is taught without requiring prerequisite skills. The purpose of the functional approach is to give students with severe disabilities the opportunity to travel independently or semi-independently in the environments that naturally call for orientation and mobility skills (Gee et al., 1987).

An orientation and mobility program becomes functional when the skills taught are functional (i.e., immediately useful) and age appropriate, address the student and family needs and preferences, take place in accessible, natural environments, occur with adequate frequency to ensure acquisition, and are likely to be used within daily routines (Fazzi, 1998). Skills that may be taught in a functional approach to orientation and mobility include the use of a sighted guide; self-protection techniques; basic cane skills; diagonal cane skills; touch techniques; wheelchair skills; the use of other adaptive mobility devices; negotiating outside environments, including sidewalk recovery, car access, and street crossings; and negotiating commercial environments, including riding the bus, escalators, and elevators and soliciting assistance (Fazzi, 1998; Gee et al., 1987).

Implementing a functional orientation and mobility program is a process with six phases. The first phase involves a thorough review of assessment information (motor, hearing, and vision skills) and observations of the student when there are natural cues for the performance of the targeted skills. Planned observations can only occur after the orientation and mobility skills to be assessed are targeted and the natural contexts in which the skill is necessary have been identified. For example, the orientation skills of using landmarks and sound localization could be assessed when the student approaches the cafeteria and, hearing the sounds of the cafeteria, turns toward the ramp and reaches for the handrail.

When the performance observations in natural contexts have been completed, the team can select the routes to be used for instruction. Several factors should be considered. The routes of travel selected should be ones that the student encounters on a regular basis, occur when there is an appropriate amount of supervision for instruction, lead to a desirable activity, and be an appropriate length for the practice and use of the targeted skills (Gee et al., 1987).

After the routes are selected for instruction, a task analysis is completed. It includes information on every change in direction, landmarks, cane use, or changes in the hand or foot (Gee et al., 1987). Once the route has been task analyzed, the student is asked to travel the route, and the present level of performance is observed. Baseline information is used to determine where instruction will be necessary, where adaptations should be used, and the instructional techniques that may be appropriate.

The fourth phase of designing an orientation and mobility program is the *context instruction* phase (Gee et al., 1987). Context instruction has been shown to be effective for students with deaf–blindness and other multiple disabilities (Gee, Graham, Oshima, Yoshioka, & Goetz, 1991). In context instruction, the student is assisted to travel the routes with the instructor calling attention to the tactile, auditory, and situational cues. The student is assisted with making turns, holding the cane, and the other movements necessary to complete the route. Gee et al. (1987) suggest that the context instruction phase occur for 5 to 10 days and that a second baseline then be conducted on the student's performance. The rationale for this phase is that many students with severe disabilities may have never experienced the expectation of traveling a route independently. Once an expectation for moving through the environment is established, the student might demonstrate acquisition of some of the skills or be more likely to attempt to travel the route.

Information from the second baseline is used to select the instructional objectives and to design the instructional program. Gee et al. (1987) advise that instruction should begin on the motor skills (turning, cane use) involved in traveling the route, rather than route memory. Modifications on equipment, such as a marshmallow tip cane (Wurzberger, 1980) or a diagonal cane extension (Morse, 1980), and adaptations that make route travel easier (such as printed cards to use for requesting assistance) should be considered to ensure that the student can travel as independently as possible. Once the instructional program is designed, implementation and evaluation of the student's progress is made through ongoing data collection.

Dual Sensory Impairments

Students with severe disabilities who have both hearing and vision impairments have educational needs that present significant challenges for teachers (Fredericks & Baldwin, 1987; Huebner, Prickett, Welch, & Joffee, 1995; Prickett & Welch, 1998). Instructional modifications and adaptations can be made by the collaborative team to support the learner with dual sensory impairments. The first task in developing specific instructional strategies is to assess the extent of the hearing and vision impairment. Most individuals with dual sensory impairments have some functional vision and hearing skills (Fredericks & Baldwin, 1987). The instructional strategies that may be used include enhancing auditory and visual stimuli, using tactile teaching, and targeting visual and auditory skill development within meaningful activities (Downing & Eichinger, 1990). These techniques can be used within the functional curriculum that is currently provided to students with severe disabilities. There is no reason to specialize the instruction of an individual with dual sensory impairments in a way that results in segregated programming or segregated placement (Downing & Eichinger, 1990; Haring & Romer, 1995).

One of the biggest challenges that teachers face in supporting students who are deaf–blind is in the area of communication (Prickett & Welch, 1998). Both receptive and expressive communication is a concern. Deaf–blindness can be considered an information-gathering disability in that these students have extreme difficulty receiving information or extracting information from interactions and activities (Gee, 1994). Teachers must develop strategies for giving the student additional information and helping the student to find information. In addition, the student has limited means for expressive communication.

Two important methods that may be used to communicate with students who are deaf–blind are touch cues and object cues (Engleman, Griffin, Griffin, & Maddox, 1999; Prickett & Welch, 1998). Touch cues are touches to the student's body (e.g., touch lips to signal "time to eat" or touch under the elbow to signal "stand up") that prepare the student to anticipate an action or activity that will follow. Object cues are the provision of an object to the student to signal the next event or a desired action. For students who respond to object cues, other tangible symbols may be used to assist them in understanding the schedule and independently negotiating the routine. The student is taught to associate a miniature object, partial object, or textured material with a specific activity. These symbols can be arranged sequentially on a shelf (see anticipation shelf in Chapter 11) to provide the student with a tangible schedule, or the tangible object may be provided to the student by the adult or peer to cue the next activity (Engleman et al., 1999; Prickett & Welch, 1998).

When designing instruction for students with deaf–blindness, it is important for the teacher to consider the perspective of the student. Students with deaf–blindness may be hesitant to explore the environment and may need additional support and information to feel comfortable in the classroom. Many students with deaf–blindness may appear to be less motivated to learn because they are limited in their awareness of distal activities and interactions. In addition, the student may have an increased need to develop a trusting relationship with the teacher to have the confidence to take risks in the instructional setting (Prickett & Welch, 1998). Students with deaf–blindness may also need more repetitions of information or direct experience to acquire new concepts. The student may also need additional time to take in information, process, and respond (Prickett & Welch, 1998).

Enhancing visual and auditory stimuli is done through modifying materials and material presentation so that students with dual sensory impairments can use their residual hearing and/or visual skills. Adaptations that may be used include enlarging pictures, reducing glare, illumination, presenting stimuli within the student's visual field, using enhanced auditory cues, or positioning the student so that the stimuli are closer. Natural auditory and visual stimuli should also be used to teach the student to attend to stimuli as she completes activity routines. For example, when teaching a student with dual sensory impairments to do laundry, listening for the water flow should be encouraged as a check on the completion of loading the washer, and the slam of the dryer door could serve as an auditory cue that a dryer-loading task sequence has been completed.

Another approach used with students with dual sensory impairments is the movement-based approach described by Jan van Dijk (Writer, 1987). This approach is based on the provision of motor experiences that provide the student with reference points to organize the world and enable the student to communicate and build relationships with others (Writer, 1987). The teacher moves with the students and does activities with her rather than to her. Through the process of these reciprocal movement actions, learning takes place.

Conclusion

This chapter has presented the special concerns associated with students who have multiple impairments. It was stressed that collaborative teaming is essential to developing an appropriate program for students with motor or sensory impairments. It is critical that the collaborative team work together in assessing the sensory and motor capabilities of the student and the design interventions that are appropriate for the home, school, and community. The educator is not expected to be well versed in the techniques of specialized disciplines such as physical therapy or audiology, but is expected to know what questions to ask and how to use the knowledge provided by other disciplines and the family to support the student with multiple impairments.

Questions for Reflection

1. How would the presence of sensory or motor impairments affect the inclusion of a student in general education classes? In community-based instruction? In supported employment?
2. What unique concerns might a family have about the education of their child with a sensory impairment?
3. Many people believe that students who are deaf should be educated in segregated environments where their

peers and teachers understand sign language and will be able to communicate with them. How would you respond to parents who asked you whether you believed that a segregated environment would be a more appropriate placement for their child?

4. Sometimes students with sensory impairments exhibit challenging behavior that has a relationship to the inability to see or hear. Why might this occur?

5. Students with motor impairments often need specialized equipment for positioning. How can teachers in inclusive programs minimize the disruption caused by taking the student in and out of equipment?

6. Make a list of activities that take place in an elementary classroom and then think of adaptations that might be made to accommodate the needs of a student who is hearing or visually impaired.

References

Albano, M., Cox, B., York, J., & York, R. (1981). Educational teams for students with severe and multiple handicaps. In R. York, W. K. Schofield, D. J. Donder, D. L. Ryndak, & B. Reguly (Eds.), *Organizing and implementing services for students with severe and multiple handicaps* (pp. 24–34). Springfield, IL: Illinois State Board of Education.

American Academy of Pediatrics. (1999). Policy statement on newborn and infant hearing loss: Detection and intervention. *Pediatrics, 103*(2), 527–530.

Arendt, R. E., MacLean, W. E., & Baumeister, A. A. (1988). Critique of sensory integration therapy and its application in mental retardation. *American Journal on Mental Retardation, 92,* 401–411.

Ayres, A. J. (1979). *Sensory integration and the child.* Los Angeles: Western Psychological Services.

Ball, T. S., McCrady, R. E., & Hart, A. D. (1975). Automated reinforcement of head posture in two cerebral palsied retarded children. *Perceptual and Motor Skills, 40,* 619–622.

Bobath, K. (1980). *A neurophysiological basis for the treatment of cerebral palsy.* London: William Heinemann Medical Books.

Campbell, P. H. (1987). Programming for students with dysfunction in posture and movement. In M. E. Snell (Ed.), *Systematic instruction of persons with severe handicaps* (pp. 188–212). Upper Saddle River, NJ: Merrill/Prentice Hall.

Campbell, P. H. (1989). Dysfunction in posture and movement in individuals with profound disabilities: Issues and practices. In F. Brown & D. Lehr (Eds.), *Persons with profound disabilities: Issues and practices* (pp. 163–189). Baltimore: Paul H. Brookes.

Campbell, P. H. (1995). Supporting the medical and physical needs of students in inclusive settings. In N. G. Haring & L. T. Romer (Eds.), *Welcoming students who are deaf–blind into typical classrooms. Facilitating school participation, learning, and friendships* (pp. 277–306). Baltimore: Paul H. Brookes.

Cicirello, N., Hyltm, J., Reed, P., & Hall, S. (1989). *Teaching nontherapists to do positioning and handling in educational settings.* Portland: Child Development and Rehabilitation Center Publications, Oregon Health Sciences University.

Corn, A. L., Hatlen, P., Huebner, K. M., Ryan, F., & Siller, M. A. (1995). *The national agenda for education of children and youths with visual impairments, including those with multiple disabilities.* New York: AFB Press.

Cox, P. R., & Dykes, M. K. (2001). Effective classroom adaptations for students with visual impairments. *Teaching Exceptional Children, 33*(6), 68–74.

Craig, S. E., Haggart, A. G., & Hull, K. M. (1999). Integrating therapies into the educational setting: Strategies for supporting children with severe disabilities. *Physical Disabilities: Education and Related Services, 17*(2), 91–109.

Cress, P., Spellman, C., DeBriere, T., Sizemore, A., Northam, J., & Johnson, J. (1981). Vision screening for persons with severe handicaps. *Journal of the Association for the Severely Handicapped, 6,* 41–49.

Cusick, B. (1991). Therapeutic management of sensorimotor and physical disabilities. In J. Bigge (Ed.), *Teaching individuals with physical and multiple disabilities* (pp. 16–49). Upper Saddle River, NJ: Merrill/Prentice Hall.

Downing, J., & Demchak, M. (1996). Determining individual abilities and how best to support students. In J. E. Downing (Ed.), *Including students with severe and multiple disabilities in typical classrooms* (pp. 63–82). Baltimore: Paul H. Brookes.

Downing, J., & Eichinger, J. (1990). Instructional strategies for learners with dual sensory impairments in integrated settings. *Journal of the Association for Persons with Severe Handicaps, 15,* 98–105.

Dunn, W. (1996). The sensorimotor systems: A framework for assessment and intervention. In F. P. Orelove & D. Sobsey, *Educating children with multiple disabilities: A transdisciplinary approach* (3rd Ed., pp. 35–78). Baltimore: Paul H. Brookes.

Engleman, M. D., Griffin, H. C., Griffin, L. W., & Maddox, J. I. (1999). A teacher's guide to communicating with students with deaf–blindness. *Teaching Exceptional Children, 31*(5), 64–70.

Fazzi, D. L. (1998). Facilitating independent travel for students who have visual impairments with other disabilities. In S. Z. Zacks & R. K. Silberman (Eds.), *Educating students who have visual impairments and other disabilities* (pp. 441–468). Baltimore: Paul H. Brookes.

Filler, J., & Kasari, C. (1981). Acquisition, maintenance, and generalization of parent taught skills with two severely handicapped infants. *Journal of the Association for the Severely Handicapped, 6,* 30–38.

Finnie, N. R. (1974). *Handling the young cerebral palsied child at home* (2nd Ed.). New York: E. P. Dutton.

Franklin, B. (1995). Amplification systems. In K. M. Huebner, J. G. Prickett, T. R. Welch, & E. Joffee (Eds.), *Hand in hand. Essentials of communication and orientation and mobility for your students who are deaf–blind* (vol. 11, pp. 39–42). New York: AFB Press.

Fraser, B. A., Hensinger, R. N., Phelps, J. A., & Jacques, K. (1987). Seating systems. In B. A. Fraser, R. N. Hensinger, & J. A. Phelps (Eds.), *A professional's guide: Physical management of multiple handicaps* (pp. 107–136). Baltimore: Paul H. Brookes.

Fredericks, H. D., & Baldwin, V. L. (1987). Individuals with sensory impairments: Who are they? How are they educated? In L. Goetz, D. Guess, & K. Stremel-Campbell (Eds.), *Innovative program design for individuals with dual sensory impairments* (pp. 3–12). Baltimore: Paul H. Brookes.

Gee, K. (1994). The learner who is deaf–blind: Constructing context from depleted sources. In K. Gee, M. Alwell, N. Graham, & L. Goetz (Eds.), *Facilitating informed and active learning for individuals who are deaf–blind in inclusive schools* (pp. 11–31). San Francisco: California Research Institute.

Gee, K., Graham, N., Oshima, G., Yoshioka, K., & Goetz, L. (1991). Teaching students to request the continuation of routine activities by using time delay and decreasing physical assistance in the context of chain interruption. *Journal of the Association for Persons with Severe Handicaps, 16,* 154–167.

Gee, K., Harrell, R., & Rosenberg, R. (1987). Teaching orientation and mobility skills within and across natural opportunities for travel. In L. Goetz, D. Guess, & K. Stremel-Campbell (Eds.), *Innovative program design for individuals with dual sensory impairments* (pp. 127–157). Baltimore: Paul H. Brookes.

Giangreco, M. F., Prelock, P., Reid, R., Dennis, R., & Edelman, S. (2000). Roles of related services personnel in inclusive schools. In R. Villa & J. Thousand (Eds.), *Restructuring for caring and effective education: Piecing the puzzle together* (2nd Ed., pp. 360–388). Baltimore: Paul H. Brookes.

Goetz, L., & Gee, K. (1987). Functional vision programming. In L. Goetz, D. Guess, & K. Stremel-Campbell (Eds.), *Innovative program design for individuals with dual sensory impairments* (pp. 77–97). Baltimore: Paul H. Brookes.

Grove, D. N., & Dalke, B. A. (1976). Contingent feedback for training children to propel their wheelchairs. *Physical Therapy, 56,* 815–820.

Haring, N. G., & Romer, L. T. (1995). *Welcoming students who are deaf–blind into typical classrooms.* Baltimore: Paul H. Brookes.

Herer, G. R., Knightly, C. A., & Steinberg, A. G. (2002). Hearing. Sounds and silences. In M. L. Batshaw (Ed.), *Children with disabilities* (5th Ed., pp. 193–227). Baltimore: Paul H. Brookes.

Hill, E. W. (1986). Orientation and mobility. In G. T. Scholl (Ed.), *Foundations of education for blind and visually handicapped children and youth* (pp. 315–340). New York: American Printing House for the Blind.

Hill, E., & Ponder, P. (1976). *Orientation and mobility techniques: A guide for the practitioner.* New York: American Printing House for the Blind.

Hollins, M. (1989). *Understanding blindness.* Hillsdale, NJ: Lawrence Erlbaum.

Horn, E. M. (1991). Basic motor skills instruction for children with neuromotor delays: A critical review. *Journal of Special Education, 25,* 168–197.

Horn, E. M., & Warren, S. F. (1987). Facilitating the acquisition of sensorimotor behavior with a microcomputer mediated teaching system: An experimental analysis. *Journal of the Association for Persons with Severe Handicaps, 12,* 205–215.

Huebner, K. M., Prickett, J. G., Welch, T. R., & Joffee, E. (1995). *Hand in hand. Essentials of communication and orientation and mobility for your students who are deaf–blind* (vol. 1). New York: AFB Press.

Hulme, J., Poor, R., Schulein, M., & Pezzino, J. (1983). Perceived behavioral changes observed with adaptive seating devices and training programs for multihandicapped, developmentally disabled individuals. *Physical Therapy, 63,* 204–208.

Joffee, E., & Rikhye, C. H. (1991). Orientation and mobility for students with severe visual and multiple impairments: A new perspective. *Journal of Visual Impairment and Blindness, 85*(5), 211–216.

Jose, R. T. (1983). *Understanding low vision.* New York: American Printing House for the Blind.

Langley, B., & Dubose, R. E. (1989). Functional vision screening for severely handicapped children. In *Dimensions: Visually impaired persons with multiple disabilities* (pp. 47–51). Selected papers from the *Journal of Visual Impairment and Blindness.* New York: American Foundation for the Blind.

Lee, J. M., Mahler, T. J., & Westling, D. L. (1985). Reducing occurrences of an ATNR. *American Journal of Mental Deficiency, 89,* 617–621.

Leiper, C., Miller, A., Lang, J., & Herman, R. (1981). Sensory feedback for head control in cerebral palsy. *Physical Therapy, 61,* 512–518.

Morse, K. A. (1980). Modifications of the long cane for use by a multiply impaired child. *Journal of Visual Impairment and Blindness, 74,* 15–18.

Mosk, M., & Bucher, B. (1984). Prompting and stimulus shaping procedures for teaching visual motor skills to retarded children. *Journal of the Association for Persons with Severe Handicaps, 17,* 23–34.

Niswander, P. S. (1987). Audiometric assessment and management. In L. Goetz, D. Guess, & K. Stremel-Campbell (Eds.), *Innovative program design for individuals with dual sensory impairments* (pp. 99–126). Baltimore: Paul H. Brookes.

Orelove, F. P., & Sobsey, D. (1996). Designing transdisciplinary services. In F. P. Orelove & D. Sobsey (Eds.), *Educating children with multiple disabilities: A transdisciplinary approach* (3rd Ed.) (pp. 1–33). Baltimore: Paul H. Brookes.

Prickett, J. G., & Welch, T. R. (1998). Educating students who are deaf–blind. In S. Z. Zacks & R. K. Silberman (Eds.), *Educating students who have visual impairments and other disabilities* (pp. 139–159). Baltimore: Paul H. Brookes.

Rainforth, B., & York, J. (1991). Handling and positioning. In F. P. Orelove & D. Sobsey (Eds.), *Educating children with multiple disabilities: A transdisciplinary approach* (2nd Ed., pp. 79–117). Baltimore: Paul H. Brookes.

Rainforth, B., & York-Barr, J. (1996). Handling and positioning. In F. P. Orelove & D. Sobsey (Eds.), *Educating children with multiple disabilities: A transdisciplinary approach* (3rd Ed., pp. 79–118). Baltimore: Paul H. Brookes.

Rainforth, B., & York-Barr, J. (1997). *Collaborative teams for students with severe disabilities: Integrating therapy and educational services.* Baltimore: Paul H. Brookes.

Richman, J. S., & Kazlowski, N. L. (1977). Operant training of head control and beginning language development for a severely developmentally disabled child. *Journal of Behavior Therapy and Experimental Psychiatry, 8,* 437–440.

Romer, L. T., & Byrne, A. R. (1995). Collaborative teaming to support participation in inclusive education settings. In N. G. Haring & L. T. Romer (Eds.), *Welcoming students who are deaf–blind into typical classrooms. Facilitating school participation, learning, and friendships* (pp. 143–170). Baltimore: Paul H. Brookes.

Scholl, G. T. (1986). What does it mean to be blind? Definitions, terminology, and prevalence. In G. T. Scholl (Ed.), *Foundations of education for blind and visually handicapped children and youth* (pp. 23–33). New York: AFB Press.

Skrotzky, K., Gallenstein, J. S., & Osternig, L. R. (1978). Effects of electromyographic feedback training on motor control in spastic cerebral palsy. *Physical Therapy, 58,* 547–552.

Snell, M. E., & Janney, R. (2000). *Practices for inclusive schools: Collaborative teaming.* Baltimore: Paul H. Brookes.

Sobsey, D., & Wolf-Schein, E. G. (1996). Children with sensory impairments. In F. P. Orelove & D. Sobsey, *Educating children with multiple disabilities: A transdisciplinary approach* (3rd Ed., pp. 411–450). Baltimore: Paul H. Brookes.

Stern, F. M., & Gorga, D. (1988). Neurodevelopmental treatment (NDT): Therapeutic intervention and its efficacy. *Infants and Young Children, 1,* 22–32.

Utley, B., Duncan, D., Strain, P., & Scanlon, K. (1983). Effects of contingent and noncontingent vision stimulation on visual fixation in multiply handicapped children. *Journal of the Association for Persons with Severe Handicaps, 8,* 29–42.

Utley, B., Goetz, L., Gee, K., Baldwin, M., & Sailor, W. (1981). *Vision assessment and program manual for severely handicapped and/or deaf–blind students.* (ERIC Document Reproduction Service No. ED 250 840.) Reston, VA: Council for Exceptional Children.

Utley, B. L., & Nelson, G. L. (1992). Visual–motor efficiency of adults with multiple and visual disabilities: An assessment and intervention model. *Journal of Vocational Rehabilitation, 2*(1), 9–20.

Utley, B. L., Roman, C., & Nelson, G. L. (1998). Functional vision. In S. Z. Zacks & R. K. Silberman (Eds.), *Educating students who have visual impairments and other disabilities* (pp. 371–412). Baltimore: Paul H. Brookes.

Ward, M. E. (1986). The visual system. In G. T. Scholl (Ed.), *Foundations of education for blind and visually handicapped children and youth* (pp. 36–64). New York: American Foundation for the Blind.

Welch, T. R., & Cloninger, C. J. (1995). Effective service delivery. In K. M. Huebner, J. G. Prickett, T. R. Welch, & E. Joffee (Eds.), *Hand in hand. Essentials of communication and orientation and mobility for your students who are deaf–blind* (Vol. 1, pp. 111–145). New York: AFB Press.

Welsh, R. D., & Blasch, B. (Eds.). (1980). *Foundation of orientation and mobility.* New York: American Foundation for the Blind.

Writer, J. (1987). A movement-based approach to the education of students who are sensory impaired/multihandicapped. In L. Goetz, D. Guess, & K. Stremel-Campbell (Eds.), *Innovative program design for individuals with dual sensory impairments* (pp. 191–223). Baltimore: Paul H. Brookes.

Wurzberger, P. (1980). Wurzberger Mobility Aids. 3960 Cottonwood Drive, Concord, CA 94519.

CHAPTER 14

Providing Support for Health and Medical Needs

In this chapter guidelines are provided for managing students' health and medical needs. The chapter gives general guidelines for classroom hygiene practices, dental care, seizure management, skin care, postural drainage, range of motion, medication, and eating difficulties. Procedures for caring for students with tracheostomies, ileostomies, colostomies, and catheters are also provided. The chapter concludes with a discussion of infectious diseases, including HIV.

Supporting Students with Health-Care Needs

The provision of support to students with health-care needs is a prominent issue for teachers of students with severe disabilities (Lehr, 1996; Lehr & Noonan, 1989; Mulligan-Ault, Guess, Struth, & Thompson, 1988; Thomas & Hawke, 1999). As more children who are medically fragile survive the neonatal period and enter the school system, public schools have seen an increase in the number of students with severe disabilities who have health-care needs.

The health-care needs of students with severe disabilities have expanded the role of the special educator. In many school programs, special educators are providing services that have been traditionally viewed as nursing care. Mulligan-Ault et al. (1988) surveyed all the teachers of students with severe and multiple handicaps in Kansas to determine the status of the provision of health services to these students. They found that in over 75% of the classrooms, teachers were monitoring seizures, providing emergency seizure care, engaging in teeth and gum care, and administering medication. In over 50% of the classrooms, teachers were involved in the prevention of skin breakdowns and establishing bowel habits. In 25% to 50% of the classrooms, teachers were involved in the treatment of skin breakdowns, diet monitoring and supplementation, postural drainage (assisting the student in clearing secretions from the lungs), handling and positioning, CPR, shunt care, and percussion (cupping and vibrating the chest to loosen bronchial secretions).

Students with health-care needs have a right to access services under the related services provision of the Individuals with Disabilities Education Act (IDEA) (Katsiyannis & Yell, 2000). School health services are required under IDEA when these services are necessary to assist the student in benefiting from special education. Two important Supreme Court decisions, *Irving Independent School District* v. *Tatro* and *Cedar Rapids Community School District* v. *Garret F.*, have established the standard that school districts must provide health-care services unless a physician is required to administer these services (Katsiyannis & Yell, 2000; Thomas & Hawke, 1999). Both of these cases applied the "bright line test" to decide if health-care services must be provided under IDEA. The bright line test states that if a physician is required to provide the service the school district is not responsible for providing services (Thomas & Hawke, 1999). In the *Tatro* case, the school district was required to provide clean intermittent catheterization to an 8-year-old student with spina bifida every 3 to 4 hours. The *Garret F.* case involved a more complex array of services for the student, including monitoring the student's ventilator, suctioning the tracheotomy, assessing respiration, feeding, repositioning in the wheelchair, and catheterization. In this case, the court considered that many of these services were being provided to other individual students and that the services were necessary for the student to attend school.

The provision of health-care services by school personnel has important implications for school districts, IEP teams, and school employees. Most school districts have established guidelines for the administration of these services and have policies that should be reviewed by the IEP team and individual team members. In many school districts, school nurses or appropriately trained health paraprofessionals implement many of the services that will be discussed in this chapter, although some districts may offer training to the special educator and request that the services be provided by him or her. Many practicing teachers are comfortable performing a variety of health-care procedures and feel that the performance of these procedures is within the scope of their role as a teacher (Mulligan-Ault et al., 1988; Thompson & Guess, 1989). In a survey conducted with members of an organization committed to the education of students with physical handicaps, the most frequent health-care procedure that was conducted in classrooms was tube feedings, followed by catheterization (CIC) and suctioning (Heller, Frederick, Best, Dykes, & Cohen, 2000). Teachers and paraprofessionals were often involved in conducting the health-care procedures of tube feeding, colostomy care, CIC, suctioning, tracheotomy care, ventilator management, providing medications, inhaler or nebulizer administration, oxygen delivery, insulin injections, and blood glucose testing (Heller et al., 2000).

A transdisciplinary approach to the provision of health-care services appears to be the most practical way to meet the needs of individuals (Caldwell et al., 1997; Sobsey & Cox, 1996). The delegation of all health-care services to nursing personnel might lead to the inappropriate clustering of students with medical needs in one classroom or school and to the performance of procedures based on the schedule of the health-service provider, rather than on student needs

(Sobsey & Cox, 1996). Through a transdisciplinary approach, practices and services can be individually tailored to the student's needs. Health-care plans can be developed by the collaborative team, with specific procedures outlined for each student. Classroom personnel can be trained by the nurse or parent on needed health-care procedures. The collaborative team should include at minimum the parent, the school nurse, and the classroom teacher. The team may also be expanded to include the physician, additional teachers, therapists, and other personnel who have daily contact with the student. Issues that the team should address include not only the health-care procedure or medication administration procedure, but also a plan for in-service training of care providers, case coordination responsibilities, and procedures to be used in an emergency.

In this chapter the health-care procedures that teachers of students with severe disabilities should be familiar with are discussed. The first section of the chapter includes guidelines for practices that we describe as therapeutic management. These are low-technology procedures that may be required by students on a daily basis. Subsequent sections offer information on nutrition and feeding, special concerns, and infectious disease. The information offered in this chapter is not meant to be a how-to manual for the implementation of specialized procedures, but to provide basic knowledge for the teacher who may need to seek more detailed information in collaboration with the team before these procedures are carried out in the classroom.

Therapeutic Management

The instruction of students with severe disabilities requires intimate contact between the teacher and student. Often students with severe disabilities require positioning and handling by the teacher for instruction and self-care practices. Teachers may have responsibilities that include toileting assistance and diapering, food preparation, and oral hygiene assistance. Some students with severe disabilities may have no health concerns; others may exhibit the normal range of student illnesses (e.g., colds or flu), and some may have infectious diseases (e.g., HIV, herpes, cytomegalovirus). It is for these reasons that good hygiene practice in the classroom is of particular importance.

Universal Precautions

The Centers for Disease Control recommends that universal blood and body fluid precautions be implemented in classrooms to prevent the transmission of infections and to decrease risk to care providers and students (Porter, Haynie, Bierle, Caldwell, & Palfrey, 1997). The concept of universal precautions implies that all students should be assumed to be infectious for HIV and other blood-borne pathogens (U.S. Department of Health and Human Services, 1989). Staff should wear disposable gloves whenever the direct care of a student involves contact with blood, body fluids, urine, feces, and respiratory infections. A gown or apron should be used if the splattering of body fluids is possible.

Used gloves should be disposed of in a sealed plastic bag that is placed in a second plastic bag and then thrown in the garbage. When spills of body fluids are cleaned up, the teacher should wear gloves and mop up the spill with paper towels or other absorbent material (Porter et al., 1997). After the spill is mopped and the area is cleaned, a solution of one-quarter cup of bleach to one gallon of water should be used to disinfect the area (U.S. Department of Health and Human Services, 1989). Paper towels and gloves should then be double-bagged as described above and placed in the garbage. If clothing, bedding, or towels become contaminated with body fluids or blood, they should be washed in hot water (at least 160°F) and detergent (Porter et al., 1997).

In addition to observing these cautions, classroom personnel must provide an environment that is as clean as possible and that minimizes infection transmission risk. Play surfaces and toys should be washed and then disinfected with bleach solution each day. Trash should be disposed of in plastic bags that are tied and disposed of daily. Soiled clothing and diapers should be placed in sealed plastic bags until they are laundered.

Hand Washing

One of the most important hygiene practices for all personnel who are intimately involved with students is to use appropriate hand-washing procedures. Proper hand washing is critical to prevent the spread of infection and must occur before and after physical contact with a student, after using the toilet, and after contact with items that may carry infection, such as mouthed objects, tissues, or eating utensils. Hands must be washed whether gloves are worn or not and after gloves are removed.

Before washing hands, all textured jewelry on the hands or wrists should be removed and kept off until the contact with the student is completed and hands are rewashed. Hands should be washed with running warm water and soap in a sink that is not used for food preparation. If no running water is available (e.g., on the playground), a towelette or aerosol soap may be used, although running water is preferred to carry contaminants away. Hands should be washed with adequate soap (liquid is preferred), and all skin surfaces at least to the midpoint of the lower arm should be scrubbed. Hands should be rinsed, then dried with a paper towel. A clean paper towel should be used to turn off the faucets. Paper towels should be disposed of in a lined, covered trash receptacle.

Incontinence and Toileting

Toileting and assisting students with incontinent wear can be a high-risk procedure for contamination of the child, support person, and the environment (Taylor & Taylor, 1989). Staff members must wash their hands and put on gloves before assisting students in these activities.

Changing a student's incontinent wear must occur only in a designated area on a changing surface with a disposable covering. Once changing has occurred, the soiled diaper should be placed in a sealed bag and disposed of in a covered trash can. The changing surface must be washed and disinfected after each student. Both the adult and the student must wash their hands before returning to the classroom.

Privacy

When staff members change a student who is soiled, they must be very cautious that the student's privacy is protected. Some schools (and community sites) provide a restroom that is separated from the general men's and women's restrooms for individuals who need attendant care when toileting. If this is not available, arrangements may be made to use a private restroom in another location in the school, such as the office or the clinic. Another option for ensuring privacy is to make an "occupied" sign that may be hung on the outside of the restroom door when the privacy of the student would be compromised if other students are present in the bathroom. For example, if the student is in high school and incontinent it would be very stigmatizing for the student (and uncomfortable for his peers) to be changed in the general restroom. The collaborative team should examine the needs of the student and the options that are available. The student must be provided with a changing area that is both safe and private. If one is not available, the collaborative team should work with school personnel to make sure that arrangements are made to provide an appropriate changing area. The team should resist the temptation to make do with temporary or makeshift accommodations (e.g., a mat on the floor or a cardboard screen).

Safety Issues

Adults must be aware of students' safety and should ensure that all the needed materials (washcloth, incontinent wear, plastic bags) are gathered before placing a student on a changing surface. When assisting a student to the changing surface, the adult must use the appropriate lifting techniques. A student must never be left alone on the changing surface for any amount of time. Students who are capable should be encouraged to assist with the change as much as possible.

Staff who assist students with toileting should also use universal precautions if it is likely that they will have contact with body fluids. If a student needs assistance only with clothing and fasteners, gloves are not necessary. If the student must be assisted with menstrual care or wiping, or is being toilet trained, the adult should wear gloves. Hand washing in a sink that is not used for food preparation must occur before and after assisting students in the bathroom.

Positioning and Transfer

Many students require adapted toilets to accommodate their physical disabilities. Proper positioning on the toilet is critical to safety and aids in elimination. There are three ways that a student in a wheelchair can be transferred to a toilet: forward, sideways, and backward (Bigge, 1991). A forward transfer is made by pushing the wheelchair to the toilet so that the front wheels rest against the base of the toilet. The student's feet are placed on the floor and the student slides onto the toilet facing the back. A backward transfer can occur when the back of the wheelchair is detachable. The wheelchair is pushed against the toilet so that the rear wheels touch the base. When the chair wheels are locked, the back is detached and the student slides backward onto the toilet. To transfer sideways, the wheelchair is placed at the side of the toilet. The chair is locked, and the arm rest on the toilet side is removed. The student then places one hand on the toilet seat and one hand on the wheelchair back and swings her body onto the toilet seat.

Few students with multiple disabilities are able to assist in a transfer from wheelchair to toilet and will need to be assisted by the adult. To assist the student who can bear weight in a standing position, the adult should place the wheelchair in front of the toilet and help the student to stand while holding on to the toilet handrails and pivoting his body to the toilet seat. Other students will need to be lifted from the wheelchair and transferred to the toilet.

Dental Care

Students should be provided with opportunities to brush their teeth after every meal at school. Some students will be learning to brush their teeth independently; others may need complete assistance. The procedure should occur in the most normalized fashion possible (i.e., at the sink and in front of a mirror), although students who are unable to sit or stand at the sink will require different procedures (Graff, Ault, Guess, Taylor, & Thompson, 1990).

To assist the student who cannot brush her teeth at a sink, the student can be in a supine or side-lying position with a towel or basin under the chin. If the student can sit on the floor, the adult can sit behind the student and straddle her head with the adult's thighs while supporting the student's face with one hand and brushing her teeth with the other. If the student can sit at the sink in a wheelchair or chair, the adult can stand or sit behind the student and assist by supporting the student's chin with one hand and brushing with the other.

After the teeth have been brushed, the student's mouth should be rinsed with water. Flossing should occur at least once a day and may also be included as part of the dental hygiene routine at school. The adult should wear gloves when assisting students with toothbrushing and flossing.

Classroom personnel may notice that a student's gums appear sore or swollen or that they bleed during toothbrushing. If this or any other unusual condition is noted, the family and health-care provider must be notified. Special procedures may be indicated for students with oral problems.

Seizure Management

The prevalence of epilepsy ranges from 0.5% to 2% in the general population (Yousef, 1985), with as many as 31% of persons with severe disabilities experiencing seizure disorders (Richardson, Koller, & Katz, 1981). Epilepsy is defined as two or more seizures that occur in the absence of fever, acute disease, or physical injury to the brain (Prensky & Palkes, 1982). A seizure is erratic electrical activity in the brain that affects a part of or the whole body and may involve a loss of consciousness (Scipien, Chard, Howe, & Barnard, 1990).

Seizure Classification

Seizures are classified as either partial or generalized (Behrman, Kliegman, & Arvin, 1996; Weinstein, 2002). Partial seizures are limited to a small area of the cerebral cortex; generalized seizures result from a widespread, diffuse electrical discharge in the central portion of the brain spreading to the cortex and brain stem and affecting other systems of the body (Scipien et al., 1990). The diagnosis of epilepsy is made after the documentation of recurrent seizures. The electroencephalogram (EEG) and imaging methods such as CT (computerized tomography) or MRI (magnetic resonance imaging) scans may be used to assist in the diagnosis of a seizure disorder (Epilepsy Foundation, 2003; Weinstein, 2002).

Tonic–clonic seizures are generalized seizures and occur most commonly. The onset of a tonic–clonic seizure is sudden and may be preceded by an aura (unusual visual or sensory sensation) or a change in appearance or behavior that warns of the impending seizure. During the first phase of the seizure, the tonic phase, the individual falls to the ground and becomes rigid; breathing does not occur, and the person may begin to turn blue (cyanosis). The tonic phase may last from 20 to 40 seconds or longer and is followed by the clonic phase, in which there is shaking of the extremities and generalized twitching. The entire seizure is usually less than 5 minutes long. When the seizure ends, the student may need to sleep, may seem lethargic, and may have a headache, fever, or hypertension. The individual may involuntarily urinate or defecate during the seizure and may awake distressed and embarrassed.

Absence seizures are generalized seizures that are characterized by a brief (5 to 30 seconds) loss of consciousness. The individual usually resumes activity without awareness that the seizure has occurred. Other generalized seizures include myoclonic seizures (repetitive contractions of a muscle), clonic seizures, tonic seizures, and atonic seizures (drop attacks).

Partial seizures may be simple (focal) partial seizures, complex partial seizures, or partial seizures that evolve to secondarily generalized seizures. Simple partial seizures may involve repetitive twitching of the mouth or fingers, dilation of the pupils, or excessive sweating. A focal seizure typically lasts less than 30 seconds and usually involves only one part of the body. Partial complex seizures (also referred to as temporal lobe or psychomotor seizures) may begin with an aura that can be accompanied by strange smells and/or tastes and hallucinations. After the aura, the student may lose consciousness or may engage in stereotyped motor behaviors such as lip smacking, chewing, or picking at clothes. The seizure lasts from 5 to 15 minutes.

Medication

Individuals with seizure disorders are treated with medication that may reduce or inhibit seizure activity. Sometimes total suppression of the seizures cannot occur without medicating the individual so much that daily activity is inhibited. Most students who have seizure disorders receive medication several times a day and will receive medication during school hours. It is vital that medication be administered according to the physician's instructions and that complete dosages be given. Because mixing a medication with food or crushing a tablet or capsule can change the dosage or absorption rate of the medication, strategies used to administer the medication should be approved by the physician or pharmacist. Additional considerations on medication administration and storage are discussed later in this chapter. For many years, medication options were limited to a small number of antiepileptic drugs. In the last decade, many new drugs have been approved by the Food and Drug Administration for use in the United States. The following medications may be prescribed for seizure disorders: Carbatrol, Depakene, Depakote, Diamox, Dilantin, Felbatol, Gabitril, Keppra, Klonopin, Lamictal, Mysoline, Neurontin, phenobarbital, Tegretol, Topamax, Tranxene, Trileptal, Valium, Zarontin, and Zonegran (Epilepsy Foundation, 2003; Weinstein, 2002). Common side effects for many of these medications include fatigue, drowsiness, headache, dizziness, blurred vision, difficulty in thinking, diarrhea, double vision, nausea, and vomiting. Teachers should be aware of the name of the prescribed medication and the side effects to monitor. The *Physician's Desk Reference* or the drug insert that is packaged with the medication should list all the potential side effects.

It is possible for seizures to be evoked by environmental stimuli, such as loud sounds, flashing lights, or extreme temperature changes, or conditions within the student, such as fatigue, stress, and missed meals or fluids. Through careful observation of the student, these events can be noted and avoided in an effort to prevent the seizure activity.

Responding to a Seizure

If a seizure occurs, the adult should remain calm and stay with the student. The student should be placed on her side with a soft object under the head. The area around the student should be cleared of furniture and objects. The adult may loosen student's tight clothing and should *not* place anything in the student's mouth. (Objects placed in the mouth could injure the student or obstruct the airway.) The adult should observe the student carefully and take note of the length of the seizure, color of the student's skin, breathing pattern during the seizure, and movement of the body. Once the seizure is over, the adult should interact with the student to determine her level of awareness or confusion. The student should be checked for incontinence and injuries and then given an opportunity to rest. The length of the seizure and what happened during the seizure should be documented in writing. In addition, the parent or physician may request that staff record other observations (e.g., lethargy, skin color, body temperature).

When a seizure occurs, the student does not require any medical help unless she stops breathing (begin mouth-to-mouth resuscitation), the seizure lasts longer than 5 minutes, she is injured during the course of the seizure, or if this is the first known seizure that she has experienced. Another concern is if the seizure is followed by additional seizures that are so frequent that they appear to be constant. This condition, status epilepticus, requires emergency medical intervention and is treated through emergency anticonvulsant therapy that is usually given intravenously. The staff will become familiar with what is normal for each student and when medical assistance should be requested.

Sensitizing Others

The occurrence of a seizure may be embarrassing to the student with disabilities and frightening or confusing to peers and adults. The collaborative team should discuss procedures that can be used to minimize the impact that seizures may have on others in the school and community. The teacher or parent may wish to inform other students and faculty that the student may have a seizure and provide information on how to react if it occurs. The school may also want to bring in a person from the local epilepsy foundation to educate the student body about seizure disorders. If a seizure occurs when peers are not prepared, they will most likely react with concern for the student. The teacher should reassure them that the student will recover and that there is no imminent danger. If the student is likely to be confused, embarrassed, or incontinent when the seizure ends, the teacher should explain that to the peers and redirect their attention to their activity.

Skin Conditions

Monitoring the skin condition of students with severe disabilities is a concern for staff. Unhealthy skin and skin breakdowns (pressure sores) can occur if the skin is not kept clean and dry, if nutrition is inadequate, if activity is minimal, and if there is continuous pressure on parts of the body (Wong, Hockenberry-Eaton, Wilson, Winkelstein, & Schwartz, 2001). Students with multiple disabilities may be at increased risk for the development of pressure sores because of their lack of activity, difficulty in repositioning themselves, and incontinence.

Staff should monitor students' skin to ensure that sores do not develop and that the skin is kept clean and dry. Pressure sores begin with redness that disappears when the pressure is relieved. If the pressure is not relieved, the skin becomes reddened, hardened, and warmer than the surrounding skin and then develops a sore, which may present drainage. If untreated, the sore continues to deepen. To prevent pressure sores, the student should be checked for redness of the skin in areas that experience pressure as a result of positioning or prosthetic and orthotic equipment. When red areas are noted, the skin must be monitored to see if the redness will disappear (in 20 minutes). If it persists, a health-care provider should be notified.

Staff should also make sure that students are provided with adequate nutrition, hydration, and activity. Students who are at risk for the development of pressure sores should be repositioned every 20 minutes. If a pressure sore is being treated, the staff must conscientiously follow the treatment regimen. Any change in skin condition should be reported immediately to a health-care provider.

Postural Drainage

Some students with severe disabilities experience chronic bronchial and lung problems that result in pooling of secretions in the lungs and bronchi. If the student lacks the muscle control or coordination necessary to effectively cough and clear fluid from the lungs, the physician may recommend postural drainage (Wong, 1997).

Adults who will perform postural drainage must be trained by a health-care provider or parent. The procedure should occur well before (an hour and a half) a meal and should never be done following a meal. The student can be placed on the adult's lap or on a padded incline board. The student is encouraged to breathe deeply. The adult strikes one side of the student's chest with a cupped hand (percussion) for 1 to 2 minutes and then the opposite side of the chest for 1 to 2 minutes. After cupping, the student is encouraged to breathe deeply while the adult vibrates the chest wall. Percussion is performed over the anterior upper and lower lobes, lateral lobes, and posterior lower and upper lobes of the lungs (Scipien et al., 1990). The trainer should demonstrate the proper sites for percussion.

After the postural drainage procedure is completed (20 to 30 minutes), the student should be allowed to rest. Mucus that the student coughs up should be disposed of in a lined garbage container. If the student coughs up yellow, green, or blood-tinged mucus, the health-care provider should be notified. If the student vomits during the postural drainage procedure, care must be taken to remove the vomitus without allowing it to be pulled into the trachea or lungs (Graff et al., 1990).

Passive Range of Motion

Passive joint range-of-motion exercises are performed to prevent joint deformities, aid normalization of muscle tone, and prevent shortening of the muscles. It is termed a passive procedure because the adult performs the movement, rather than the student. These exercises do not strengthen the muscles, but are used to maintain joint mobility.

Passive joint range of motion (ROM) exercises involve the careful flexion and extension of the neck, shoulders, elbows, forearms, wrists, fingers, thumbs, hips, knees, ankles, feet, and toes. The physician, nursing supervisor, or physical therapist should instruct classroom personnel on the movements to perform and the number of times each day that the procedure should be done. Ideally, the adult should seek functional contexts in which to perform the movement (Graff et al., 1990). For example, elbow flexion and extension may be provided in a switch toy activity by flexing and extending the student's elbow so that he can press a switch attached to an age-appropriate, battery-operated toy. Professionals with a medical orientation may not be able to readily identify functional contexts for the performance of passive range of motion. In medical settings, these procedures constitute an activity in themselves. The teacher may have to provide a rationale for the purpose of embedding procedures within functional activities and collaborate with medical team members to determine the appropriate procedures to be used.

It is critical that the staff person who provides the passive range-of-motion exercises understand the appropriate techniques for performing the exercises and the appropriate range of movement for each joint. If muscle resistance is encountered or if the adult attempts to force stretching, the student may experience pain and injury. The student should be relaxed and properly positioned before range-of-motion exercises are performed.

Medication

Students with severe disabilities are more likely than any other population in school to need medication administered during school hours. The most common types of routine medication are anticonvulsants for seizure management, psychotropic medication for treating undesirable behavior, stimulants for hyperactivity or depression, muscle relaxants, and nebulizers or inhalers (Sobsey & Cox, 1996). The prevalence of students with severe disabilities who may be receiving medication ranges from 15% for students labeled trainable mentally disabled (Gadow & Kalachnik, 1981) to 53% of students labeled profoundly mentally disabled (Fox & Westling, 1986). Anticonvulsants and tranquilizers account for the majority of medications prescribed to students with severe disabilities (Fox & Westling, 1986). The administration of medication is the most common health-care procedure provided to students with profound disabilities (Ault, Guy, Rues, Noto, & Guess, 1994). Thus, teachers must become familiar with methods for administering medication and monitoring its effects.

Anticonvulsants

Some commonly prescribed anticonvulsant medications are phenobarbital, Dilantin, Depakene, and Tegretol. The type of medication prescribed is determined by the seizure classification and the medical history of the individual. Reactions may occur from high levels of the drug in the blood, side effects of the medication, or idiosyncratic reactions (Gadow, 1982). The side effects of anticonvulsants may include confusion, dizziness, irritability, impaired learning, drowsiness, and impaired coordination.

Psychotropics

Psychotropic medications include stimulants, major tranquilizers, antidepressants, anxioloytics, and minor tranquilizers; such drugs may be prescribed for the management of hyperactivity or extreme maladaptive behavior, as a sedative, or as a muscle relaxant. The side effects of psychotropic medication can include a reduction of activity, drowsiness, impairment of attention, skin reactions, nausea, and dry mouth. Other very alarming side effects include four disorders that involve the motor area of the brain called the extrapyramidal tract: parkinsonian syndrome, akathisia, acute dystonic reactions, and tardive dyskinesia (Gadow, 1982). In parkinsonian syndrome, the medication user appears depressed, has decreased spontaneous movement, and may walk with a shuffling gait. Akathisia is characterized by motor restlessness. Acute dystonic reactions include the symptoms of facial grimacing, a fixed upward gaze, and an unnatural twisting of the neck. Tardive dyskinesia involves involuntary, repetitive movements such as smacking the lips, tongue movement, movements of the arms, and jerky body movement.

Medication Administration

Because medication administration is critical to the student's medical management and can involve serious side effects, the teacher plays an important role in providing information to the student's family and health-care providers. The administration of medication may be the most common health procedure that students with severe disabilities receive in the schools (Ault et al., 1994). Before medication is administered by school personnel, the information listed in Figure 14–1 should be obtained from the physician.

Some system of ongoing communication should also be established so that the physician is aware of any changes in the student's behavior that may be related to the medication and the dosages that the student is receiving in the classroom. The collaborative team should discuss how information will be relayed to the student's health-care provider. For some students, the teacher may wish to provide the information to the family, who will communicate directly to the physician. In other situations, the teacher or school nurse may be in direct contact with the health-care provider.

Figure 14–1 Information Needed to Administer Medication

1. Medication needed, dosage level, and schedule
2. Purpose of medication
3. Method of administration
4. Precautions about administration (e.g., only after meals or with water)
5. Physician who prescribed the medication
6. Side effects and interaction effects associated with the medication
7. Medication storage information
8. Emergency contact person and phone number

Figure 14–2 Precautions for Medication Administration

1. The caregiver must wash hands before medication administration.
2. Student should be in a relaxed position and calm when receiving medication.
3. Medication can be placed in the student's mouth by spoon, dropper, or plastic syringe or by placing a tablet on the tongue.
4. If the student refuses to take the medication or vomits after administration, the caregiver should wait 20 to 30 minutes and try again.
5. Missed dosages should be recorded and reported to the health-care provider or caregiver.
6. The caregiver should maintain a record of medication administration including the dosage given, the time it was administered, and concerns of which the caregiver or health-care provider should be aware.

It is desirable for medical personnel to administer medications, but when a school nurse is not available for this function, classroom personnel may have to assume the responsibility. Because medication may be in pill, capsule, suppository, or liquid form, teachers and aids should be trained in the appropriate procedures to be used. The precautions for medication administration listed in Figure 14–2 should be noted by school personnel who are involved in medication administration.

Procedures for handling and storing medications in the classroom are also a concern. Some medications need refrigeration and should be kept cold at all times. This may mean that the medication must be stored in a cooler when taken off campus with the student. Classroom personnel should also pay close attention to medication expiration dates. If a medication has expired, it should not be used. Some medications should be stored in a locked cabinet. The collaborative team should discuss ways to ensure that medications are stored safely and are not vulnerable to theft or misuse.

Nutrition and Feeding

Nutrition

The nutritional status of students is a growing concern among educators. Many students have inadequate diets that are nutritionally incomplete. Students with severe and multiple disabilities are at increased risk of nutritional problems. They may need special diets to address their unique nutritional status, require assistance with eating to ensure that an adequate amount of food is safely consumed, and need to be monitored for growth and weight gain (Kedesdy & Budd, 1998).

The collaborative team should develop individual nutrition and feeding plans for students whose nutritional status is a concern. Areas of concern may be the student's medication and its effects on the student's physical status, oral–motor skills, medical conditions that may affect the absorption of nutrients or eating ability, and eating skills or habits.

Many students with severe disabilities may be receiving medications that interfere with the absorption of nutrients; some drugs may cause nausea or decrease the appetite. The collaborative team should review the student's medications for nutritional impact and develop procedures to ensure that malnutrition does not occur.

Several medical conditions may also affect a student's nutritional status. A student who has Prader–Willi syndrome, which is associated with insatiable appetite, will be on a strict diet and must have food intake monitored. A student with a cleft palate may have difficulty with managing food orally and can be at risk for malnutrition because eating is a difficult activity. A student with cerebral palsy may have oral–motor skill difficulties that result in decreased food intake and may be at risk for nutritional problems.

The diet for students who are at risk or have nutritional problems must be monitored by the collaborative team; the basic school lunch is not adequate for many students. Some require diets that provide increased caloric intake. The goal for these students is to add calories, not bulk, to the diet. It is possible that increased calories can result from providing more snacks and several small meals or the assistance needed to ensure adequate intake. For other students, the meal may have to be enriched with an additive (e.g., dry milk, instant breakfast, vegetable oils, dry infant cereal, cheese, peanut butter) to provide increased calories. Supplements in the form of pudding or special drinks that provide increased calories and vitamins also may be a prescribed part of a student's diet.

Team members may also be concerned about the fluid intake of students. Students who are on medication or who have oral–motor difficulties may not have adequate fluid intake; team members should offer them many opportunities to drink and provide diets that are high in water content (e.g., fruit and vegetables). One method for offering liquids throughout the day may be to provide a straw bottle (the kind used by athletes) that is always accessible and filled with water or a preferred drink. If there is a concern about a student's fluid intake, the collaborative team should define the minimal desired intake (based on weight and medical conditions) and develop a tracking system to monitor the student's intake.

The consistency of the diet is a concern for students with oral–motor difficulties. Students who are unable to chew need to be provided a blended diet, and students who are beginning to bite may need to be provided with finger foods and a chopped diet. The consistency of the meal also may be changed to assist the student with oral–motor problems manage food. Blended foods and liquids may be thickened, using cereal, wheat germ, or vegetable flakes, to assist a student who cannot handle thin consistency. Thicker foods and liquids provide more sensory cues and may help the student coordinate oral–motor movements. If the student has very weak tongue and pharynx movements, thick liquids and foods may be more difficult to handle and thinning liquids and foods may be warranted. Any changes in food consistency are part of the overall feeding plan and should be discussed by the collaborative team. Regardless of the diet, the presentation of a meal should be appetizing (e.g., do not mix foods together), and students should be offered choices. Forcing a student to consume foods that are not appealing is not an appropriate practice. The goal of supporting students who have difficulty with nutritional intake is to make meals pleasant and desirable events.

Eating Skills

Students with severe disabilities may have motor difficulties or sensory integration problems that affect their ability to eat. Some of the difficulties that students encounter are described in this section. Diagnosis of feeding problems and the development of a feeding program should be done by the occupational therapist or speech therapist in collaboration with the team (Blasco, 1999).

A *jaw thrust* describes an exaggerated up–down extension of the jaw (Morris & Klein, 1987). Students

Figure 14–3 Hand Placement for Providing Jaw Stability

Source: Pre-feeding Skills, by Marsha Dunn Klein and Suzanne Evans Morrison, Copyright 1987 by Therapy Skill Builders, a division of Communication Skill Builders, Inc., PO Box 420050, Tucson, AZ 85773. Reprinted with permission.

who exhibit an extensor motor pattern or who have oral hypersensitivity may exhibit jaw thrust. Treatment may include (1) reducing the sensory distractions in the feeding environment, (2) providing a better sitting posture, and (3) assisting with jaw closure by providing jaw stability support (Morris & Klein, 1987). Jaw stability support (see Figure 14–3) may be provided by the feeder who is to the side or behind the student by placing the middle finger under the jaw, index finger on the chin, and thumb at the temporomandibular (jaw) joint (Morris & Klein, 1987). If the feeder is in front of the student, she can place the middle finger under the jaw, the index finger at the temporomandibular joint, and the thumb on the chin or below the lower lip (Morris & Klein, 1987).

Jaw clenching describes the movement of the jaw into a tightly clenched position. This may be caused by low tone in the trunk and a poor sitting position, an overstimulating environment, or oral hypersensitivity. Some treatment options include positioning the student appropriately; reducing hypersensitivity by providing firm pressure to the teeth, face, and gums; and using sensory stimulation procedures to normalize the student's response to sensory stimulation.

Jaw retraction describes the retraction of the jaw in a backward direction. This may be related to poor sitting posture, an overstimulating environment, or a motor pattern of hyperextension. Options for intervention include providing a better sitting posture and reducing distracting sensory stimulation in the feeding environment. *Jaw instability* describes the loose movement of the jaw due to lack of muscle tone and joint control. It may be related to hypotonicity and developmental delays or deviations of the oral musculature. Treatment options include activities to build tone in the trunk, stimulation to the muscles that open and close the jaw, and the use of jaw support techniques.

Lack of *lip closure* occurs when there is low muscle tone in the lips, causing food and saliva to drip from the mouth. To increase muscle tone and facilitate lip closure, the adult may pat the lips or stroke around the lips, using a firm, circular motion. Providing jaw stability support may also facilitate lip closure.

A *tonic bite reflex* describes a sudden bite that occurs when the teeth are stimulated by touching them with a finger or a spoon. The tonic bite may be related to an overstimulating environment, oral hypersensitivity, or poor sitting posture. Options for intervention include providing better sitting posture, reducing the stimulation of the feeding environment, and reducing the hypersensitivity that occurs when a finger or a spoon is introduced in the mouth. To reduce hypersensitivity, the adult should wear gloves and begin by sliding her index finger into the student's mouth and applying firm deep pressure to the outer surface of the upper and lower gums (Morris & Klein, 1987). Biting can occur during feeding. A coated spoon or rubber spoon can be used to reduce the hypersensitivity to the spoon. If the student bites on the spoon while it is in his mouth, the adult should wait for the student to release it. Pulling on the spoon will only increase the strength of the bite. The adult can move the student's head into alignment with the body or rock the body gently to reduce overall muscle tension, which will assist the student with the release of the spoon.

Tongue retraction describes the movement of the tongue back into the oral cavity. This may occur with students who have low or high muscle tone, neck hyperextension, or cleft of the hard palate. Proper positioning, including the maintenance of the head in a chin-tucked position, will help decrease tongue retraction. *Tongue protrusion* is the movement of the tongue beyond the border of the gums. A tongue thrust is the forceful protrusion of the tongue from the mouth. Students with low muscle tone may exhibit tongue protrusion. Tongue thrust is typically associated with extensor patterns of movement. Intervention options include appropriate positioning of the student, normalizing tone before positioning for eating, providing a different consistency of food so that tongue protrusion is not needed to move it backward, providing jaw support, presenting the food horizontally at the bottom lip so that the upper lip and a suck are used rather than the tongue, and placing the spoon on the middle of the tongue while pressing evenly downward with a vibratory movement (Morris & Klein, 1987).

If the student's muscle tone is high, *lip retraction* (lips pulled back tightly across mouth) and *pursing* (lips pulled in and puckered to counteract retraction) can occur. Reducing the hypertonicity, working for better sitting posture, and providing a relaxing environment should assist the student to relax the lips.

Some students may exhibit problems with the feeding process that are related to their postural tone, developmental delay, and reflex development. Students who have difficulty with a suckle pattern should be positioned carefully, provided with a quiet mealtime environment, and be given opportunities to suck at different times during the day. The student who does not use mature oral movement patterns when eating soft foods can be provided with jaw control and gentle pressure on the tongue with the spoon as it is placed in the mouth. If a student does not use mature oral movement patterns during cup drinking, the feeder can provide jaw control and thickened liquids to drink that are easier to handle. The student who chokes and gags during the meal should be assessed to determine if a hyperactive gag is present. If so, the occupational therapist can design a program to help the student to develop a more normalized gag reflex. The student may be gagging to communicate that she doesn't like the food that is being offered or that she wants the meal to end. If the behavior is being used for attention and control, the adult should carefully examine the antecedents, consequences, and setting events that occur with the behavior. An intervention plan should be designed to result in behavior reduction based on the function of the behavior (e.g., avoid food), rather than behavior topography (see Chapter 12 for more information). If the student is using the behavior to communicate dislike of a particular food, the adult should ensure that choices are provided. If the student is using the behavior to signal that she is finished eating, the adult may teach the student an alternative way to signal "finished" or may need to systematically teach the student to tolerate more food.

Some students vomit food or liquid during or after a meal. This may be caused by difficulty with digestion that results in refluxing of the stomach contents into the esophagus. Some students are able to tolerate only small quantities of food, and when that point is surpassed, vomiting occurs. If vomiting is occurring, the teacher should refer the student to the physician to explore medical treatment alternatives. The student should be placed in a stander or over a wedge for 30 to 60 minutes after a meal to assist with the digestion. Another option is to provide small meals at shorter intervals in the day.

Positioning

Appropriate positioning is vital to mealtime success for students who have eating difficulties (Snyder, Breath, & DeMauro, 1999). It is most desirable for the student to be upright, provided with adequate trunk stability, with head in an upright and chin-tucked position, and with hips and knees flexed. Good support should be provided for the student, including support under the feet. The most appropriate position is based on the individual student's medical and orthopedic needs and should be determined by the collaborative team. The person who is feeding the student must also be concerned about his or her position. The feeder should be seated with his face at the student's eye level and should also assume a position that allows freedom of movement so that assisting the student will not call for stretching or straining.

Eating Utensils

A variety of adaptive eating utensils are available to support individuals who have difficulty using traditional utensils because of motor challenges (Lowman, 1999). Often these may be purchased in home health-care stores or through specialized equipment catalogs. The most common adaptive utensils and eating equipment are described in Figure 14–4. The decision to use adaptive equipment or utensils for eating should be made by a collaborative team that includes an occupational therapist who is trained in feeding techniques.

Tube Feeding

When students are not able to eat a sufficient amount or are not able to take nourishment orally, tube feeding may be used. In this method, nourishment is provided through a nasogastric (nose to stomach) tube or gastrostomy (stomach) tube.

Tube feedings are fairly simple procedures and may be managed by any person on the team who has received training from a health-care provider. Such training should cover procedures to be used, the student's special health-care needs, and how to implement an established emergency plan. It is desirable to conduct tube feedings at mealtimes and snack times with other students. Some students who are tube fed receive oral feedings as well. Oral feedings are conducted with the guidance of the medical professional or therapist who has designated the procedures to be used.

Students who are tube fed are generally placed in an upright position during the tube feeding and for 1 hour after the feeding. To avoid stomach cramping, the formula should be allowed to reach room temperature before it is used. Unused formula should be refrigerated to prevent bacteria growth.

Nasogastric Tube Feeding

A nasogastric tube (see Figure 14–5) is inserted through the nose, down the esophagus, and into the stomach. Its use is usually a temporary measure to provide nourishment to the student. Students with nasogastric tubes may be provided with nourishment through the bolus method, the intermittent gravity drip method, or the continuous drip method. The bolus method involves a large amount of fluid or formula that is allowed to flow through the tube in several minutes. The intermittent gravity drip method involves dripping the formula slowly from a hanging container for a 20- to 30-minute period. Students who cannot tolerate a rapid presentation of formula may use a continuous drip method, in which the formula is allowed to drip slowly over a 16- to 24-hour period. Infusion pumps that control the presentation of the formula may be used to provide continuous drip feeding. The general procedure to be used for nasogastric tube feeding is provided in Figure 14–6. A health-care provider should train responsible personnel in the procedures to be used and how to implement an established emergency plan.

Gastrostomy Tube Feeding

A gastrostomy is a surgical opening into the stomach through the surface of the abdomen. A tube is used to maintain the opening and to administer food and fluids directly to the stomach (see Figure 14–7). The gastrostomy tube is held in place by a bubble of air or a mushroom tip inside the stomach. The gastrostomy tube extends 8 to 12 inches and has a small removable plug inserted in the end of the tube to keep the stomach contents from flowing out. Some students may have a skin-level tube called a button or gastroport, which protrudes only slightly beyond the abdominal wall and provides increased mobility and comfort. Feeding procedures for the button are almost identical to those for the gastrostomy tube, which are described in Figure 14–8.

Students with gastrostomy tubes may be fed using the bolus, intermittent drip, or continuous drip method. Individual procedures and an emergency plan should be described by the health-care provider who is familiar with the student. Problems that may occur with the gastrostomy site are redness, tenderness, and bleeding. If these signs are present, they should be reported to the health-care provider or parent. It is also possible for the gastrostomy tube to come out. If this occurs, a sterile, dry dressing should be placed over the site, and the health-care provider or parent should be notified immediately. The student is in no imminent danger, although the opening could close in a few hours if another tube is not inserted.

Figure 14–4 Adaptive Utensils and Equipment for Feeding

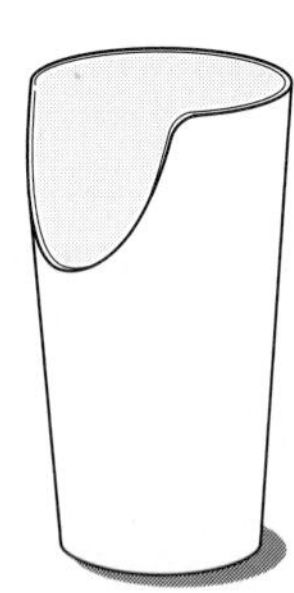

Cut-Out Cup
Cut out allows for proper positioning of head when swallowing

Flow Cup
For drinking when in a semireclined position

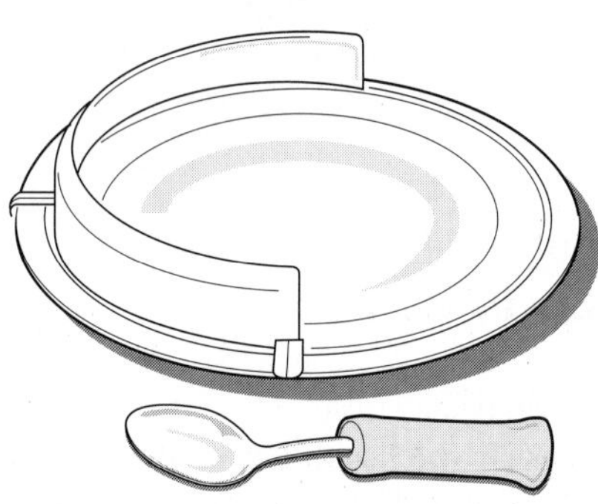

Plate Guard
Assists with scooping

Scoop Dish
Scoop edge that rises gradually

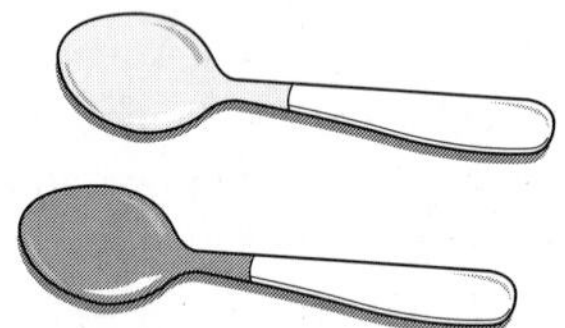

Plastic-Coated Spoon
Protects teeth and lips from edges and minimizes temperature sensitivity

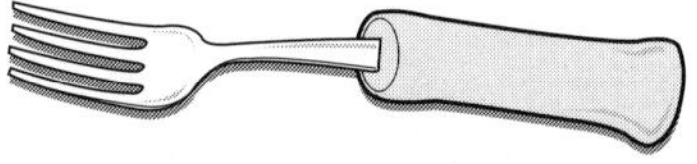

Built-Up Utensils
Assists individuals with difficulties in grasping

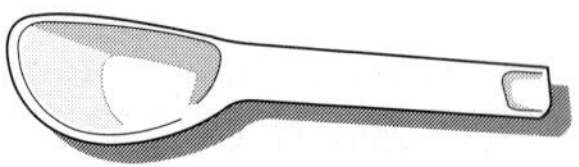

Child's Feeding Spoon
Designed for children starting solid foods

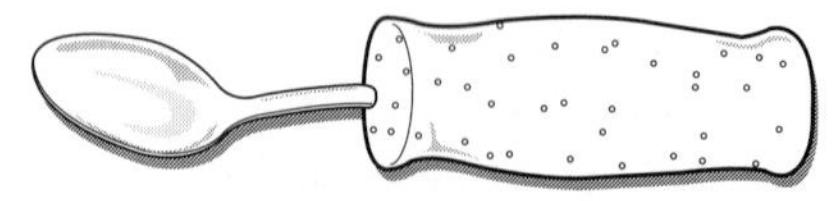

Built-Up Foam Utensils
Assists individuals with limited hand grasp

Figure 14–5 Student with Nasogastric Tube

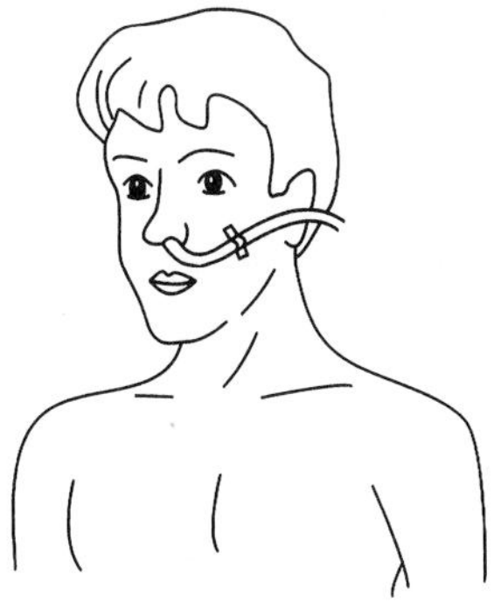

Figure 14–6 Procedure for Nasogastric Tube Feeding

1. Wash hands.
2. Assemble equipment and formula that is room temperature.
3. Position the student.
4. Check the placement of the tube by opening the tube, placing a syringe to the end of the tube, and exerting negative pressure to withdraw stomach contents. Return fluid to stomach. Take the syringe and inject a small amount of air into the stomach while listening to the stomach with a stethoscope. A gurgling or growling sound will be heard if the tube is properly inserted.
5. Remove cap from end of tube and insert syringe for bolus feeding.
6. If using slow drip method or continuous feeding by pump, pour formula into bag and allow to run to tip. Clamp. Hang bag or place in pump. Insert tip of tube into NG tube opening. Open clamp of feeding tube and adjust flow rate.
7. Pour formula into syringe and allow to flow in by gravity. Flow can be regulated by raising or lowering the syringe. Recommended placement height is 6 inches above student's head level.
8. Follow formula with water if recommended.

Source: Developed from *Children Assisted by Medical Technology in Educational Settings: Guidelines for Care,* by M. Haynie, S. M. Porter, and J. S. Palfrey, 1989, Boston: The Children's Hospital, Project School Care. Adapted with permission.

Figure 14–7 Student with Gastrostomy Tube

Special Concerns

Tracheostomy

A tracheostomy is a surgical opening in the trachea to permit the movement of air into the lungs. Tracheostomies may be performed on students who have an obstruction in the upper airway, respiratory distress, or central nervous system disorder that affects the strength and effectiveness of respiratory movements. A tube of plastic or silastic material is placed in the opening and is held in place by cloth ties (see Figure 14–9). The tracheostomy bypasses the normal wetting and filtering actions of the upper airway and thus creates a need to humidify the air that enters the tracheostomy opening (Wong, 1997). Students may have a special tracheostomy mask that provides humidified air directly to the opening, may be attached to a mechanical ventilator, or may need a room humidifier placed near them.

Classroom personnel must be trained to provide tracheostomy care to the student. It is important that all staff members have knowledge of the procedures to be used so that, regardless of who is present, someone will be able to respond in emergency situations. A suction machine is used for cleaning the trachea of secretions that build up in the tracheostomy tube, and this machine must be ready for immediate use at all times; if the equipment

Figure 14–8 Procedure for Gastrostomy Feeding

1. Wash hands.
2. Assemble equipment and formula that is room temperature.
3. Position the child.
4. Remove cap or plug from G-tube and insert a syringe. Draw back plunger to remove any liquid that may be left in the stomach. If instructed, return contents to stomach. If amount of stomach contents is a concern, the feeding may need to be delayed.
5. Clamp the G-tube, remove the plunger from the syringe.
6. Reinsert the syringe, hold at recommended height, unclamp tube, and allow bubbles to escape.
7. If feeding by slow drip or infusion pump, keep tube clamped and prepare formula bag. Allow formula to run to end of feeding tube tip and clamp. Hang bag and insert feeding tube tip into G-tube tip. Unclamp the G-tube. Open clamp of feeding tube and allow to flow. Adjust rate of flow.
8. Pour formula into syringe and allow to flow in by gravity.
9. When feeding is complete, pour in the recommended amount of water to flush the tube.

Source: Developed from *Children Assisted by Medical Technology in Educational Settings: Guidelines for Care,* by M. Haynie, S. M. Porter, and J. S. Palfrey, 1989, Boston: The Children's Hospital, Project School Care.

Figure 14–9 Position of the Tracheostomy Tube

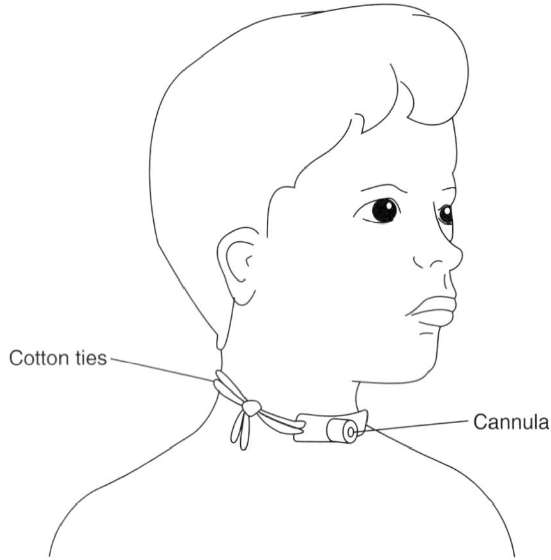

is not operable or present, the student should not attend school until a suction machine is provided. A backup method for suctioning (manual or battery operated) should also be available to be used during all school activities (e.g., on the playground) and during transport.

Suctioning is used to clear the trachea of excessive secretions and mucous plugs. The warning signs that indicate a student needs suctioning are restlessness, difficult breathing, a frightened look, or the sound or presence of bubbles of mucus in the tracheostomy tube (Graff et al., 1990). The procedures used for suctioning are listed in Figure 14–10.

In addition to suctioning, school personnel may also be concerned with cleaning the inner cannula of the tracheostomy, monitoring the skin condition around the stoma, and changing tracheostomy ties and tube. Some tracheostomy tubes are constructed with an inner cannula that can be removed for cleaning. The person removing the inner cannula must wear gloves when conducting the procedure. The inner cannula is then soaked in hydrogen peroxide to loosen the secretions, and the tube is cleaned using a brush or pipe cleaners. The inner cannula is rinsed with water or a saline solution before being replaced in the tracheostomy tube (Graff et al., 1990).

The skin around the stoma must be kept clean and dry. The skin can be cleansed using hydrogen peroxide and water to remove dried or crusted secretions. A dressing may be placed around the tube to soak up excessive secretions. The tracheostomy ties may need to be changed as they become soiled. When changing the ties, the new ties are first threaded and secured before the old ties are cut and removed. Routine replacement of ties should be done at home, although the school must be prepared to conduct the procedure if needed.

It is possible that the tracheostomy tube may need to be changed at school. If the tube comes out, school personnel must be prepared to replace it with a new one. To change a tube, the student is placed on her back with a roll under her neck so that access to the tracheostomy area is easy. The tracheostomy ties are cut and the tube is removed; then the new tube is inserted in the stoma.

Whenever school personnel are involved in tracheostomy care, they must wash their hands and thoroughly clean the equipment that is used. Spare tubes should

Figure 14–10 Procedure for Tracheal Suctioning

1. Wash hands.
2. Assemble needed equipment including a suction backup device.
3. Position student.
4. Open suction catheter or kit without touching the inside of the package to maintain sterility.
5. Fill container with saline solution if recommended.
6. Put gloves on hands. Use dominant hand for handling suction catheter only. Use nondominant hand for manipulating switches, etc.
7. Hold the end of the suction catheter with dominant hand and connect to suction machine tubing.
8. Turn machine on and adjust to prescribed vacuum setting.
9. Encourage the student to cough and take a deep breath. If recommended, place several drops of saline into trachea with nondominant hand.
10. Hold suction catheter 2 to 3 inches from tip and insert tip into saline to test that the suction is functioning.
11. Grasp the catheter connection with nondominant hand and cover vent hole with thumb to suction small amount of saline through catheter.
12. Take thumb off vent hole and gently insert catheter into trachea 1/2 cm. Cover vent hole with thumb and withdraw the catheter.
13. Rotate the catheter gently when withdrawing to reach all of the secretions in the tube. Insertion and withdrawal should be completed within 10 seconds.
14. Allow the student to breathe between suctioning passes.
15. When suctioning is complete, suction saline through catheter to rinse catheter and tubing. Remove gloves and wash hands. Discard used catheter in appropriate receptacle.

Source: Developed from *Children Assisted by Medical Technology in Educational Settings: Guidelines for Care,* by M. Haynie, S. M. Porter, and J. S. Palfrey, 1989, Boston: The Children's Hospital, Project School Care.

be kept in their sealed packages to ensure sterility. Suctioning equipment and other supplies should be checked and replenished daily so that any emergency can be handled immediately.

If the tracheostomy tube becomes blocked, classroom personnel must be poised to take immediate action because the student will be unable to breathe. Suctioning may be used to try to remove the blockage, but if that fails the tracheostomy tube should be removed and a new one inserted. If the student does not begin breathing, CPR procedures for individuals with tracheostomies should be performed (mouth and nose are covered and the rescuer breathes into the stoma). Other difficulties that classroom personnel should respond to are respiratory distress, respiratory infections, and skin infections. Concerns about these conditions must be reported to the designated health-care provider.

Ileostomy and Colostomy

An ileostomy or colostomy redirects the flow of feces in individuals who have obstructions or blockages in the intestines that restrict passage of the intestinal contents. A surgical opening is made and a portion of the intestine is pulled out and secured to the opening in the abdomen (stoma). A pouch or plastic bag is placed over the stoma for the collection of fecal material (see Figure 14–11). In an ileostomy, the stoma is created from a portion of the small intestine (ileum). In a colostomy, the stoma is created from the colon.

If the student has an ileostomy, the consistency of the stool is liquid or pasty and contains digestive enzymes that can be very irritating to the skin (Graff et al., 1990). The student wears a drainable pouch that collects the fecal material as it flows. The pouch must be drained frequently during the day; this is done by placing the student over the toilet and opening the pouch, allowing the material to flow into the toilet. For young children or for students who are unable to sit on the toilet, the pouch can be drained into a receptacle that is later dumped into the toilet. The pouch may also have to be opened periodically to release accumulated gas. The student's health-care provider should train the classroom staff in procedures to be used and the signs and symptoms of possible complications.

A student with a colostomy may have a drainable pouch or may have a regulated elimination cycle and formed feces. These students may have a covering over

Figure 14–11 Student with Ileostomy Bag

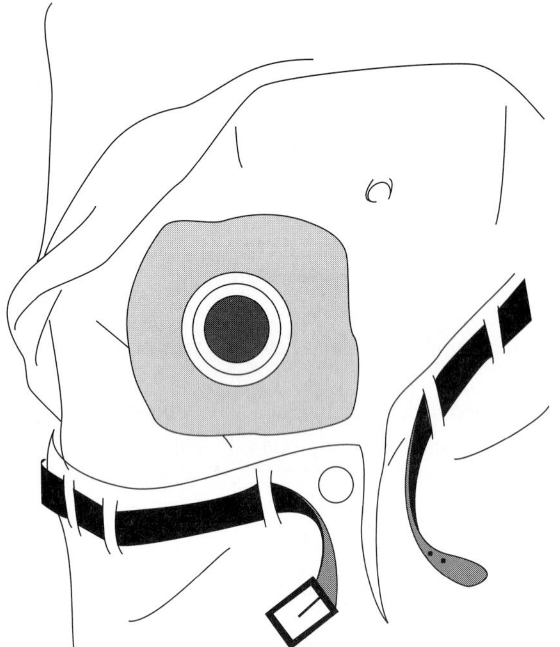

the stoma instead of a drainable bag or may wear a pouch that is not drainable.

Classroom personnel must know the procedures for draining and changing a student's ileostomy or colostomy bag. General procedures are described in Figure 14–12. In addition, classroom staff must be alert to the warning signs that may signal medical problems. Color changes in the stoma (from pink to a dusky or black color), irritation of the skin surrounding the stoma, and difficulty with elimination, diarrhea, or excessive gas must be reported to the parent or health-care provider (Graff et al., 1990).

Catheterization

Students with defects of the spinal cord (e.g., spina bifida) may not be able to voluntarily control bladder functioning and may not have a sense of bladder fullness. Clean intermittent catheterization (CIC) is a technique to empty the bladder through the use of a catheter. Students with the cognitive and motor ability may learn to catheterize themselves; other students will depend on adults for the catheterization procedures.

CIC is performed every 3 to 4 hours. The procedure must be conducted in a location that ensures the student's privacy. The catheterization procedures should be specified by the urologist who has determined that CIC be used. Classroom personnel should be trained by the health-care provider or parent in the procedures for positioning, cleansing the area, inserting the catheter, draining the bladder, removing the catheter, and cleaning the equipment.

The adult assisting with CIC must have clean hands and be wearing gloves. The student may be positioned in a sitting, standing, or reclining position. If the student is a male, the staff person cleanses the penis, using soapy cotton balls and washing toward the base of the penis. The catheter is lubricated and inserted into the urethral opening until there is a flow of urine. When the bladder is emptied, the catheter is removed, washed, rinsed, and dried before being stored for use again.

Figure 14–12 Procedure to Change a Colostomy or Ileostomy Bag

1. Assemble equipment.
2. Wash hands and put on gloves.
3. Empty contents of the bag the student is wearing.
4. Carefully remove the used bag by pushing the skin away from the bag instead of pulling the bag from the skin.
5. Wash the stoma, using a clean cloth or gauze. Cover the stoma and wash the skin around the stoma, using a different cloth or fresh gauze.
6. Inspect the skin for redness, discoloration, rash, or blistering.
7. Pat skin dry and place skin barrier on skin around stoma.
8. Peel off backing from adhesive or apply adhesive to bag.
9. Remove gauze from stoma and discard. Center new bag over stoma.
10. Firmly press bag to skin barrier.
11. Remove gloves and wash hands.

Source: Developed from *Children Assisted by Medical Technology in Educational Settings: Guidelines for Care,* by M. Haynie, S. M. Porter, and J. S. Palfrey, 1989, Boston: The Children's Hospital, Project School Care.

Table 14–1 Infectious Diseases in Group Settings

Disease	*Mode of Transmission*	*Causative Agent*
Upper respiratory infection*	Respiratory	V
Streptococcal sore throat*	Respiratory	B
Otitis media (ear infection)	Respiratory	V or B
Haemophilus influenzae type b	Respiratory	B
Meningitis	Respiratory	V or B
Tuberculosis	Respiratory	B
Hepatitis A*	Oral–fecal	V
Hepatitis B	Body fluid	V
Hepatitis non-A, non-B	Body fluid	V
Shigella diarrhea*	Oral–fecal	B
Salmonella diarrhea*	Oral–fecal	B
Giardia diarrhea*	Oral–fecal	O
Viral gastroenteritis*	Oral–fecal	V
Impetigo	Direct	B
Ringworm	Direct	F
Scabies*	Direct	O
Herpes simplex (cold sore)	Direct	V
Cytomegalovirus (CMV) infection*	Multiple	V
Chickenpox*	Multiple	V
Head lice*	Direct	O
Pinworms	Oral–fecal	O
Acquired immunodeficiency syndrome (AIDS)	Body fluid	V
Conjunctivitis (pinkeye)	Direct	V or B
Mumps	Respiratory	V
Croup	Respiratory	V
Whooping cough	Respiratory	B
Measles	Respiratory	V
German measles	Respiratory	V
Roseola	Direct	V

V, virus; B, bacteria; F, fungus; O, other.
*Frequent occurrence in group settings for children.
Source: Communicable Disease and Young Children in Group Settings (p. 37), by J. M. Taylor and W. S. Taylor, 1989, Boston: Little, Brown and Company. Reprinted by permission.

The female student may be catheterized in a sitting or reclining position. If possible, the student may sit on the toilet with legs straddled. The staff person separates the labia and cleanses the area with soapy cotton balls, washing in a direction from the top of the labia toward the rectum. The catheter is then inserted into the urethra until the urine flow begins. When the bladder is empty, the catheter is removed. If the catheter is to be reused, it is washed and dried.

Infectious Disease

Teachers of students with severe disabilities must be concerned, as all teachers are, with the spread of infectious disease in the classroom. Infectious diseases that are commonly encountered in group-care settings are listed in Table 14–1. Students with severe disabilities may have increased vulnerability to infection if they have other medical conditions or reduced resistance to infection. In addition, the risk of infection spread is heightened when students are incontinent and mouth their hands or objects. School personnel should be aware that hand washing is the single most effective method for the prevention of communicable disease in the classroom.

HIV/AIDS

Human immunodeficiency virus (HIV) is a communicable disease that is a growing concern among many educators. HIV is transmitted through sexual contact, exposure to blood, the sharing of intravenous needles for drug use, and from mother to child perinatally. There is no evidence that transmission of the virus occurs through casual contact (Caldwell & Rogers, 1991). Acquired immune deficiency syndrome (AIDS) is diagnosed when the HIV infection becomes symptomatic. At the early stage of HIV infection, the infected person may show no symptoms.

HIV infection is a worldwide disease and is the leading cause of death in many underdeveloped countries. Children may be at risk for HIV infection through perinatal transmission from an infected mother or blood transfusions or blood products received through 1985 (Lewis & Thomson, 1989). Adolescents may be at risk for HIV infection through sexual activity and shared needles during drug use.

Medical advances have changed the impact of HIV in significant ways in the last decade. The use of highly active antiretroviral therapy (HAART) reduced the mortality rate from AIDS in developed countries by 80% between 1995 and 1998 (Spiegel & Bonwit, 2002). In the United States, voluntary screening of pregnant women has resulted in a decline of mother-to-infant transmission from about 25% to 1% to 2% (Lindegren, Steinberg, & Byers, 2000). Children infected with HIV are likely to have developmental delays, but through the availability of HAART, severe neurodevelopmental problems are rare (Spiegel & Bonwit, 2002).

Special educators may encounter students with AIDS because of the symptomatology of the disease. Clinical manifestations of AIDS in children include parotitis (inflammation of a salivary gland), generalized lymphadenopathy (persistent swelling of the lymph nodes), recurrent bacterial infections, neurologic disease, and developmental abnormalities (Wong, 1997). Children with AIDS who attend child-care and public school programs are more at risk for being infected with a potentially fatal infection from other children than they are for transmitting the HIV infection to others. The decision about placement of a child in a group-care or classroom situation must be made collaboratively by the family and the medical team. Students with HIV or AIDS have the same needs and rights as other students, including the right to attend school and interact with peers. Although HIV/AIDS is an infectious disease, it cannot be easily transmitted in the school setting. Because HIV is a progressive infection, the student with AIDS will have periods of acute episodes of viral and bacterial infection. During these periods, services to students may need to be provided in the home or hospital setting.

Students may not be excluded from public school solely on the basis of their HIV status, and the family is within their legal rights to not notify a school of a student's HIV status. Thus, the safest route is to use universal precautions with the assumption that the HIV status of students in the classroom may not be known. When the HIV status is known, school personnel must protect the student's right to confidentiality. Only staff who have daily and intimate contact with the student may benefit from knowledge of the student's HIV status. An appropriate action would be to request a notification release from the family so that the appropriate personnel can be informed about the student's condition. The most important reason for knowing about a student's HIV status is to be able to fully meet the needs of the student and the family.

The medical management of students with HIV may involve the administration of medication, monitoring of illnesses, and treatment of specific illnesses using prescribed procedures. Teachers should also be aware of the unique educational implications of the disease and the psychosocial needs of the student with HIV or AIDS (Beverly & Thomas, 1997). Students with AIDS may experience neurologic deterioration that will be manifested in the classroom as a loss of skills. Teachers should be prepared to conduct more frequent educational assessment of the student and adjust skill instruction to match the student's developmental needs. Skill instruction also may be affected by long-term hospitalizations and absences from school. In addition to skill loss, students with HIV or AIDS may experience emotional difficulties that must be sensitively addressed by the teacher. Students who have chronic illness often struggle with physical and emotional isolation, rejection from peers, fear of death or serious illness, and depression. The collaborative team should consider the unique emotional needs of the student and the strategies or services that will help the child and family to develop coping skills.

Cytomegalovirus

Cytomegalovirus (CMV) is one of the most common congenital infections of humans (Katz, Gershon, & Hotez, 1998). The manifestations of the disease depend on the age and the immune status of the child, with children infected prenatally manifesting the most serious symptoms. CMV can result in mental retardation, hearing loss, and microcephaly. Postnatal infections occur through contact with urine, semen, and saliva. It is not known if the route of postnatal transmission occurs through oral contact or respiratory exposure. Child-care settings and classrooms where there are many children in diapers and who may be drooling are environments where the spread of CMV to other children, the staff, and their parents is likely. Children who are infected with CMV may shed the virus without displaying any symptoms. Children or staff who become infected may experience mononucleosis-like symptoms or may be asymptomatic. Staff who are pregnant should be extremely cautious about exposure to the virus as they may become unknowingly infected and transmit the virus prenatally to their unborn child. There is no safe and effective antiviral drug available to treat CMV.

Conclusion

The collaborative team is an essential component of an appropriate program for students with health-care needs. The school nurse or health-care provider will not be able to provide direct service to every student with health-care concerns. There are simply not enough health-care personnel in the school systems, and direct service delivery may not be necessary for the majority of students. Students with severe disabilities who have health-care needs should have their needs met as a routine function in their lives. Classroom personnel should treat activities such as administering medications, tube feedings, catheterization, and so forth, as uneventful routines. Also, they should use principles of partial participation and activity-based instruction to embed skill instruction in these activities.

For classroom personnel to shoulder responsibility for health-care procedures, the collaborative team must thoroughly discuss the implications of these procedures and provide adequate training to the persons responsible for them. Sobsey and Cox (1996) recommend that the team develop a school health-care plan as part of the IEP. The plan should list (1) the health-care procedures required, (2) the personnel who will carry out the procedures, (3) a plan for backup if the designated personnel are unavailable, (4) the training needed to carry out the procedure, (5) documentation methods, (6) special precautions, (7) supervision responsibility, (8) equipment and supplies that may be needed, and (9) whom to contact with questions about the procedures.

Before health-care procedures can be performed in the classroom, training must be provided to the responsible classroom personnel. Often this training is best provided by the student's family in collaboration with the school health-care provider. It is very important for all classroom personnel who are in continuous contact with students who have health-care needs to be trained in cardiopulmonary resuscitation, which should only be performed by individuals who are trained. If all classroom personnel are not trained, they must be aware of the nearest CPR-trained person to contact in an emergency.

This chapter emphasizes the importance of carrying out health-care procedures as routine activities that are part of the student's instructional day. The importance of documentation cannot be minimized. The classroom teacher is responsible for documenting what procedures occur and reporting information of interest to the student's family. Information that is critical to the student's continued health and well-being may include the amount of food consumed, seizure activity, when medications were administered, the amounts of elimination, and other information related to the student's health status. A record-keeping system should be developed to ensure that this information is collected and sent home with the student.

Questions for Reflection

1. If one of your students had a special health-care concern or need, what steps would you want to take to ensure that you were providing an appropriate program?
2. What resources are available in your community that may provide information on different health-care and medical needs?
3. What concerns do you feel that families may have when enrolling their son or daughter with medical or health-care needs in public school?
4. Medical conditions exist within the general school population (e.g., asthma, seizure disorders, hemophilia). How are medical conditions complicated by the

presence of mental disabilities and communication problems in students with severe disabilities?

5. How does the presence of health and medical needs affect a student's participation in community-based instruction and inclusion?

6. How might the presence of a contagious condition (e.g., cytomegalovirus or herpes) affect a student's participation in community-based instruction and inclusion?

References

Ault, M. M., Guy, B., Rues, J., Noto, L., & Guess, D. (1994). Some educational implications for students with profound disabilities at risk for inadequate nutrition and nontherapeutic effects of medication. *Mental Retardation, 32,* 200–205.

Behrman, R. E., Kliegman, R. M., & Arvin, A. M. (1996). *Nelson textbook of pediatrics* (15th Ed.). Philadelphia: W. B. Saunders.

Beverly, C. L., & Thomas, S. B. (1997). Developmental and psycho-social effects of HIV in school-aged population: Educational implications. *Education and Training in Mental Retardation, 32,* 32–41.

Bigge, J. L. (1991). *Teaching individuals with physical and multiple disabilities.* Upper Saddle River, NJ: Prentice Hall.

Blasco, P. M. (1999). Collaboration and teams. In D. K. Lowman & S. M. Murphy, *The educator's guide to feeding children with disabilities* (pp. 13–34). Baltimore: Paul H. Brookes.

Caldwell, T. H., Janz, J. R., Alcoulaoumre, D. S., Porter, S., Haynie, M., Palfrey, J. S., Bierle, T., Silva, T., Still, J., Sirvis, B. P., Schwab, N., & Mahoney, A. S. (1997). Entrance and planning for students with special health care needs. In S. Porter, M. Haynie, T. Bierle, T. H. Caldwell, & J. S. Palfrey (Eds.), *Children and youth assisted by medical technology in educational settings* (pp. 41–62). Baltimore: Paul H. Brookes.

Caldwell, M. B., & Rogers, M. F. (1991). Epidemiology of pediatric HIV infection. *Pediatric Clinics of North America, 38,* 1–16.

Cedar Rapids Community School District v. *Garret F.*, 106 F. 3d 822 (8th Cir. 1997).

Epilepsy Foundation. The most frequently asked questions about epilepsy. [Online] Available: http://www.epilepsyfoundation.org/answerplace/faq.html, January 2, 2003.

Fox, L., & Westling, D. L. (1986). The prevalence of students who are profoundly mentally handicapped receiving medication in a school district. *Education and Training of the Mentally Retarded, 21,* 205–210.

Gadow, K. D. (1982). *Children on medication: A primer for school personnel.* Reston, VA: Council for Exceptional Children.

Gadow, K. D., & Kalachnik, J. (1981). Prevalence and pattern of drug treatment for behavior and seizure disorder of TMR students. *American Journal of Mental Deficiency, 85,* 588–595.

Graff, J. C., Ault, M. M., Guess, D., Taylor, M., & Thompson, B. (1990). *Health care for students with disabilities.* Baltimore: Paul H. Brookes.

Heller, K. W., Frederick, L. D., Best, S., Dykes, M. K., & Cohen, E. T. (2000). Specialized health care procedures in the schools: Training and service delivery. *Exceptional Children, 66,* 173–186.

Irving Independent School District v. *Tatro,* 468 U.S. 883 (1984).

Katsiyannis, A., & Yell, M. L. (2000). The Supreme Court and school health services: Cedar Rapids v. Garret F. *Exceptional Children, 66,* 317–326.

Katz, S. L., Gershon, A. A., & Hotez, P. J. (1998). *Krugman's infectious diseases of children* (10th Ed.). St. Louis: Mosby.

Kedesdy, J. H., & Budd, K. S. (1998). *Childhood feeding disorders. Biobehavioral assessment and intervention.* Baltimore: Paul H. Brookes.

Lehr, D. H. (1996). The challenge of educating students with special health care needs. In D. H. Lehr & F. Brown (Eds.), *People with disabilities who challenge the system* (pp. 59–77). Baltimore: Paul H. Brookes.

Lehr, D. H., & Noonan, M. J. (1989). Issues in the education of students with complex health care needs. In F. Brown & D. H. Lehr (Eds.), *Persons with profound disabilities* (pp. 139–160). Baltimore: Paul H. Brookes.

Lewis, K. D., & Thomson, H. B. (1989). Infants, children, & adolescents. In J. H. Flaskerud (Ed.), *AIDS/HIV infection: A reference guide for nursing professionals* (pp. 111–127). Philadelphia: W. B. Saunders.

Lindegren, M. L., Steinberg, S., & Byers, R. H. (2000). Epidemiology of HIV/AIDS in children. *Pediatric Clinics of North America, 47,* 1–20.

Lowman, D. K. (1999). Feeding children with complex health needs. In D. K. Lowman & S. M. Murphy, *The educator's guide to feeding children with disabilities* (pp. 173–188). Baltimore: Paul H. Brookes.

Morris, S. E., & Klein, M. D. (1987). *Pre-feeding skills.* Tucson, AZ: Communication Skill Builders.

Mulligan-Ault, M., Guess, D., Struth, L., & Thompson, B. (1988). The implementation of health-related procedures in classrooms for students with severe multiple impairments. *Journal of the Association for Persons with Severe Handicaps, 13,* 100–109.

Porter, S., Haynie, M., Bierle, T., Caldwell, T. H., & Palfrey, J. S. (1997). *Children and youth assisted by medical technology in educational settings. Guidelines for care* (2nd Ed.). Baltimore: Paul H. Brookes.

Prensky, A. L., & Palkes, H. S. (1982). *Care of the neurologically handicapped child.* New York: Oxford University Press.

Richardson, S. A., Koller, H., & Katz, M. (1981). A functional classification of seizures and distribution in the mentally retarded population. *American Journal of Mental Deficiency, 85,* 457–466.

Scipien, G. M., Chard, M. A., Howe, J., & Barnard, M. U. (1990). *Pediatric nursing care.* St. Louis, MO: Mosby.

Snyder, P. A., Breath, D., & DeMauro, G. J. (1999). Positioning strategies for feeding and eating. In D. K. Lowman & S. M. Murphy (Eds.), *The educator's guide to feeding children with disabilities* (pp. 65–109). Baltimore: Paul H. Brookes.

Sobsey, D., & Cox, A. W. (1996). Integrating health care and educational programs. In F. P. Orelove & D. Sobsey (Eds.), *Educating children with multiple disabilities: A transdisciplinary approach* (3rd Ed., pp. 217–251). Baltimore: Paul H. Brookes.

Spiegel, H. M. L., & Bonwit, A. M. (2002). HIV infection in children. In M. L. Batshaw (Ed.), *Children with disabilities* (5th Ed., pp. 123–139). Baltimore: Paul H. Brookes.

Taylor, J. M., & Taylor, W. S. (1989). *Communicable disease and young children in group settings.* Boston: Little, Brown.

Thomas, S. B., & Hawke, C. (1999). Health care services for children with disabilities: Emerging standards and implications. *Journal of Special Education, 32,* 226–237.

Thompson, B., & Guess, D. (1989). Students who experience the most profound disabilities. In F. Brown & D. H. Lehr (Eds.), *Persons with profound disabilities* (pp. 3–41). Baltimore: Paul H. Brookes.

U.S. Department of Health and Human Services. (February 1989). *Guidelines for prevention of transmission of human immunodeficiency virus and hepatitis B virus to health-care and public safety workers.* Atlanta, GA: Centers for Disease Control.

Weinstein, S. (2002). Epilepsy. In M. L. Batshaw (Ed.), *Children with disabilities* (5th Ed., pp. 493–523). Baltimore: Paul H. Brookes.

Wong, D. L. (1997). *Essentials of pediatric nursing.* St. Louis, MO: Mosby.

Wong, D. L., Hockenberry-Eaton, M., Wilson, D., Winkelstein, M. L., & Schwartz, P. (2001). *Wong's essentials of pediatric nursing* (6th Ed.). St. Louis: Mosby.

Yousef, M. J. (1985). Medical and educational aspects of epilepsy: A review. *DPH Journal, 8,* 3–15.

CHAPTER 15

Teaching Personal Care Skills

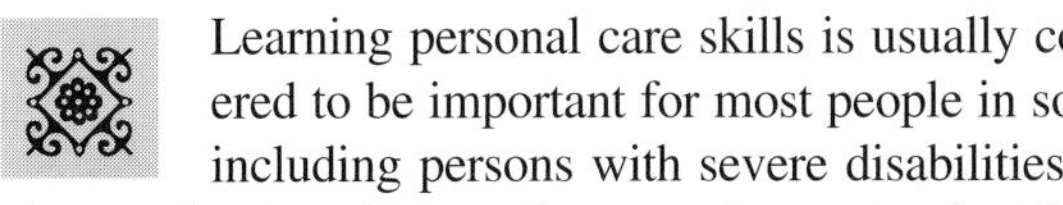

Learning personal care skills is usually considered to be important for most people in society, including persons with severe disabilities. This chapter discusses issues relevant to instruction in this area, including incorporating self-determination opportunities and self-management into the instructional procedure. More depth is provided for instruction in particular areas, including eating skills, toileting skills, learning to dress, and personal hygiene skills.

The Importance of Personal Care

Many personal care (or self-care) skills are required of all individuals to maintain health and to enhance acceptability by others in society. These skills, primarily including feeding oneself, toileting, dressing, and personal hygiene and grooming, are considered to be among the most important instructional objectives for individuals with severe disabilities, especially if they have not acquired the skills to a degree that corresponds to their chronological age (Lent, 1975; Westling & Murden, 1977). Besides being related to one's health and acceptance, these skills are often important to parents or caregivers because they can reduce the amount of assistance required to support the person. They can also increase the person's feeling of self-worth and the perception by others that the individual is competent (Orelove & Sobsey, 1996). Furthermore, because a major objective for educating students with severe disabilities is to increase their opportunity for inclusion into society, attention to these needs is often of paramount importance.

There are several reasons why personal care skills may not have been learned by an age when most people demonstrate them. These include limited fine-motor development, physical or sensory disabilities, reduced social awareness, inadequate learning opportunities, limited cognitive development, or, most likely, a combination of these conditions. In Chapter 14 we discussed ways to provide for the personal needs of individuals with medical conditions that reduced or eliminated their opportunity to eat or toilet in a typical manner. In this chapter we focus on instruction for students who, though they have reduced abilities, can usually learn many functional personal skills. We focus on procedures for teaching self-feeding and related mealtime behaviors, appropriate use of the toilet, self-dressing, hygiene, and grooming skills. Before addressing these areas, however, several general points should be made.

General Considerations

Beginning at about the time that the normalization principle emerged in the 1960s, a great deal of emphasis was placed on the use of applied behavior analysis techniques to teach individuals with severe disabilities to care for their bodily needs, particularly with a focus on toileting (Osarchuk, 1973), self-feeding, and other personal care needs (Westling & Murden, 1977). Most of the studies conducted involved individuals who lived in residential institutions who had few normal learning opportunities. If these persons had been afforded opportunities to grow up in their own homes, in a society that accepted and cared for them, and had attended neighborhood preschools and schools starting at a young age, they may not have gone for so many years without instruction in basic personal skills. Conversely, conditions in society having improved somewhat today, many individuals with severe disabilities have had the experience of a good early home life, early intervention, and appropriate early learning experiences. As a result, they may have less need for intense instruction in the traditional personal care areas than was the case 30 or 40 years ago. In fact, parents often state that other areas of instruction, such as academic skills instruction or the development of social relationships and friendships, are more important than spending much time on personal care skills (Westling, 1996). Thus, although many individuals with severe disabilities require instruction in the personal skills described in this chapter, many do not receive it. Individual determination of need in this area through collaboration with parents is very important.

Ethical Instructional Practices

As you will note from many of the references in this chapter, most of our knowledge and many instructional practices in this area are based on the research that was conducted during the 1960s and 1970s. Some of the methods that were used then, although effective in achieving results, are generally not appropriate today. Our values and practices have changed. A great deal of the instruction in these areas today is in public schools or preschools, as well as in homes and community settings. Instruction in personal care skills often occurs around children and adults without severe disabilities. We will not be working on these skills in isolation from other people or other relevant tasks, but, more appropriately, whenever possible, the skills will be taught in more natural settings and usually within normal daily routines. Therefore, we will not suggest many of the "rapid" training methods that were used years ago to teach new skills, such as self-feeding, toileting, and self-dressing, to persons who had gone for many years without them. Instead, we offer sound instructional procedures, based on the earlier methods, but within the context of what are considered to be best practices today.

The Role of Parents

Many children with severe disabilities today are identified and provided services early in life, either in their own homes, in centers, or in a combination of the two (see Chapter 20). Parents are afforded a number of services that support them in keeping their child at home, and so fewer young children are being placed in institutions or other out-of-home placements. The implication of this change in policy, which occurred during the latter half of the 20th century, is that parents are the first teachers of many important skills, especially personal skills. It is critical for teachers and other professional staff to realize this. In short, they must listen to what parents say is important or not important. Instructional manuals, such as *Steps to Independence* (Baker & Brightman, 1996), are available to assist parents in providing effective home instruction. With such resources or with assistance and support provided by professionals, many parents become very effective in helping their child to achieve many self-care skills.

On the other hand, we cannot assume that parents will be able to teach their children all the skills that they will need. Parents of children with severe disabilities are not superheroes or superparents, simply parents who have children with some uncommon needs. Teachers have often been heard to say, particularly with regard to personal care skills, "If the parents would only do what they need to do, he could learn so much more." While this may well be true, it is nevertheless inappropriate and perhaps unethical. Teachers should teach and collaborate as effectively as possible and not criticize or condemn parents for not meeting their expectations.

When and Where to Teach Personal Care Skills

As a general rule, personal care skills should be taught in natural environments (Freagon & Rotatori, 1982). Teachers should try to provide instruction in these areas at the most natural times (bathroom time, lunch time, going out for P.E., and so on) and in the most natural locations available during the school day. To the extent possible, instruction also should be carried out in the home and in other natural locations outside the school.

With this understanding, it also must be recognized that sometimes divergence from this practice may be necessary. Individuals with severe disabilities who are learning new eating skills, for example, may be too easily distracted and have trouble focusing on the task in a cafeteria setting with many other people. Therefore, at least a portion of their instruction may need to occur in a more private location if it results in better learning. If a separate setting offers no real advantage, then the normal setting should be used. Even if a separate setting is used, there should be opportunity for them to be among their nondisabled peers in the cafeteria whenever possible.

It is also generally recommended that skills be taught in a naturally distributed manner. However, some skills and certain circumstances call for relatively greater concentration on learning so that results might be achieved more quickly. These may be the skills that are deemed most critical by parents, skills that are directly related to health or safety, or skills that have a direct bearing on the acceptance of a student by her peers. Learning to use the toilet is a good example that meets all these criteria. Students who have not acquired this skill, who are at a chronologically appropriate age for using the toilet, and who have no physical limitations that would prevent them from learning to use the toilet may need to practice doing so more than would be called for during a normal daily routine.

Another important consideration is that much of what is being taught (using the toilet, getting dressed and undressed, managing menstrual needs) calls for respecting the student's privacy and dignity. Instruction should not take place in front of other individuals or in any way that is demeaning. Also, ideally, the person providing the instruction should be of the same sex as the person receiving instruction.

The Relation between Personal Care and Self-Determination

According to Wehmeyer (1996), self-determination means "acting as the primary causal agent and making choices and decisions regarding one's quality of life free from undue external influence or interference." Turnbull et al. (1996) believe self-determination to have three key components: motivation, individual skills, and living in a responsive context. These definitions and similar ones imply that, although learning key skills will not alone ensure that an individual can be self-determinative (nor should it), such skills will improve the likelihood of this happening. Although, as Turnbull et al. propose, the context (i.e., the people around the person) must be responsive if an individual is to be self-determining, if the individual has developed skills to the extent he is capable, more responsiveness is likely to occur.

Accepting this premise means that the development of self-care skills and other skills that lead to more personal independence, such as leisure and recreational skills and domestic and community skills (as are discussed in later chapters), is likely to allow a person to be more self-determining. Again, this should not be interpreted to mean that a person who cannot fully develop these skills should not be given the opportunity to become self-determining, but that the skills will contribute to the process and, if formally assessed, will result in a higher rating in the area of autonomy (cf. *The Arc's Self-Determination Scale,* Wehmeyer & Kelchner, 1995).

Being able to take care of many of one's own needs not only allows the student to be more independent but, in the process of teaching these skills, teachers, parents, and therapists can provide many opportunities for the student to exercise self-determination. As discussed in Chapter 2, according to Wehmeyer (1996), the *component elements* of self-determination include the following:

- Choice making
- Decision making
- Problem solving
- Goal setting and attainment
- Self-observation, evaluation, and reinforcement
- Internal locus of control
- Positive attributions of efficacy and outcome expectations
- Self-awareness
- Self-knowledge

Appropriate instruction on self-care skills can improve the student's skills in many of these areas. Making choices about hairstyles or whether to grow sideburns, deciding what to wear to the dance or what to make for lunch, and recognizing the value of good personal hygiene are a few examples of incorporating these self-determination elements into self-care instruction. On the other hand, if we adhere to a rigid self-help curriculum, with our goal being for the student to learn particular skills, we will have missed an important opportunity.

The Need for Collaboration

We have already emphasized the importance of the parents' role in self-care skill instruction. Also, the type or form of care that a person provides for himself or herself is often determined by family and cultural practices (such as eating practices, clothing styles, grooming, etc.). Instruction should not proceed in these areas without knowledge of how the practices are carried out in the home by other members of the family.

The collaborative involvement of other professionals is also important, and the importance increases in direct relation to the severity of the disability (Orelove & Sobsey, 1996). Because of the motor skills required in self-care activities, a PT or OT should provide input about positioning, posturing, oral-musculature functioning, and limb use as these pertain to certain objectives. Likewise, the speech therapist can provide important information about the student's oral-muscular ability as related to eating, and the school nurse or another health-care professional can provide key input about many hygiene needs of students with severe disabilities. A dietician can offer significant advice about nutritional needs and how these can be met through an appropriate diet. Thus, as can be seen, collaboration with team members in this particular instructional area is critical to achieving success.

Tactics for Personal Care Skill Acquisition

In Chapter 7, several tactics were described to teach individuals to acquire new skills. A number of these tactics are especially useful for teaching individuals with severe disabilities to acquire personal care skills. Some of the most commonly used are reviewed here. For more information the reader should review Chapter 7.

One of the most commonly used approaches in teaching self-care skills is graduated guidance. Using this procedure, the teacher guides the learner through a process, such as learning to drink from a cup, by placing his hands over the learner's hands and guiding the learner through the movement. As the teacher feels the student controlling more and more of the movement independently, the teacher reduces the amount of contact being made, allowing the student to control more and more of the movement. McKelvey, Sisson, Van Hasselt, and Hersen (1992) reported a program in which a young girl with dual sensory impairments (deaf and blind) was taught to dress herself using this approach. The teacher guided the child's hands with her own, teaching her to put on her socks, shirt, and shorts. As the student made progress, the teacher exerted less and less control.

Most-to-least prompting is another tactic that is used often, especially with individuals who have very severe disabilities. Instruction begins with several trials or sessions in which the most controlling prompts are used simultaneously with a target stimulus. The controlling prompt is often full physical guidance, with the target stimulus being a verbal cue. After adequate success is achieved with full physical assistance, the instructor uses a less controlling prompt, continuing to provide the target stimulus. For example, instead of fully guiding the person through the task, she may provide partial assistance or guide partially through the task while also giving the verbal direction to complete the task. After three or four levels of assistance have been provided, going from most to least, the student may learn to respond to the request or target stimulus without the use of any more intrusive prompt.

Chapter 7 also described the system of least prompts (or least-to-most prompting), which is particularly useful for chained skills that are broken down into a task analysis. For each step in the task, the instructor has predetermined three to four prompts that can be used, each being slightly more intrusive and controlling than the previous step. If the student does not respond to the least intrusive prompt, the next prompt is given. If there is still no response, the next more intensive level of prompt is given. This continues until, if necessary, a controlling prompt is used, often full physical guidance. This prompt is also used as a correction procedure on any step in which an error occurs.

Three final tactics used to teach some self-care skills are forward chaining, backward chaining, and whole-task approach (Alberto & Troutman, 2002). Again the task is broken down into a series of discrete steps. If a forward chaining approach is used, the teacher focuses on teaching the first step in the chain, using whatever prompting and assistance is necessary to complete the step. Then the teacher may fully assist the student in completing the rest of the steps. After the first step has been mastered, the teacher adds the second step to the instructional sequence. Then the student does the first step independently and instruction is provided for the second step. Every step that is learned is added to the series that the student must do alone at the beginning of each trial before being instructed on the next step. This continues with a new step being added each time that the student masters an additional step. Finally, the entire chain is learned.

Backward chaining reverses the order of instruction so that the student learns the last step in the chain first. After learning it, she learns the preceding (next to the last) step, which is then followed by the final step, which has already been mastered. On all preceding steps, that is those steps that have not been learned, complete assistance is provided by the teacher. As steps are learned, the teacher keeps moving backward on the chain until reaching the first step. At this point the learner initiates the first step and then follows through with the completion of all other steps until reaching the end of the chain.

The backward chaining method was advised by Baker and Brightman (1996) for several self-care tasks. Here is an example that they gave for teaching a child to drink from a cup.

1. Fully guide the cup to the child's mouth with your hands over hers, tilt the cup and allow her to take a swallow, return the cup to the table, remove your hands from hers, and say "good, you're drinking from a cup."
2. Continue as above until just before the cup reaches the table. Then remove your hand from hers, allowing her to place the cup on the table.
3. Next remove your hands from hers when the cup is three-quarters of the way down to the table.
4. Next remove your hands when the cup is halfway down to the table.
5. Then remove your hands when the cup is one-quarter of the way down to the table.
6. Then remove your hands immediately after she has swallowed and let her return the cup to the table.
7. Next assist bringing the cup to her mouth and then let her tip the cup back and take a drink and return it to the table.
8. Next bring the cup up three-quarters of the way and let her complete the rest alone.
9. Continue to remove your hands earlier and earlier on the sequence until the learner can complete the entire series of steps alone. (p. 281)

In this form of instruction, success on each step must be achieved before advancing to the next.

The whole-task approach also uses a task analysis, but at each instructional session the entire task, including every step in the chain, is taught, usually using a least-to-most prompting technique.

As we discuss instruction on specific self-care skills in the sections that follow, the reader will see how one or more of these acquisition tactics could be applied. As indicated in Chapter 7, research suggests that some tactics are more successful than others. However, the teacher must find a tactic that is comfortable and appropriate both for him and the learner. Then data in some form (see Chapter 9) should be collected to document progress or the need to change tactics. In this way, learning is more likely to occur.

Skill Generalization

The importance of skill generalization was covered in Chapter 8. Because most personal care skills of individuals with and without disabilities develop within specific environments, such as the home, and require the use of a limited scope of products, generalization of skills in this area has not been given much consideration. However, it is important that the teacher and other professionals involved in teaching these skills know if there is a need for generalization. Critical to this area, of course, is the ability of the student to carry out skills when and where necessary. It is not sufficient for students to learn to eat correctly at school, only to have to be fed by parents at home, or to be able to use the toilet in the school bathroom, but not in different parts of the community. Teachers need to make sure that the situations and conditions under which they are teaching correspond to those at home and elsewhere to the extent that this is possible. It may also be necessary that parents or caregivers have the opportunity to observe successful methods used in school in order to carry through with them in the home and the community.

Self-Management of Personal Skills

Teachers usually spend a lot of time working on the acquisition of personal care skills. This is particularly true for young children with severe disabilities and for older persons with the most severe disabilities. While this is appropriate and necessary, it is equally important that teachers, parents, and other team members consider the importance of self-managing personal care skills. This will be an important instructional target for persons who have already demonstrated that they can perform the skills when directed to do so by another person (such as a teacher or parent) and who may be in situations in which it is appropriate that they exercise more independence when carrying out skills.

Self-management means that the person is responsible for (1) identifying that it is necessary to do something, (2) doing it, and (3) then checking to make sure it is done and reinforcing himself for doing it. No direct intervention is provided by another person. Pierce and Schreibman (1994) used a picture prompt self-management system to teach three children classified as autistic and moderately to severely mentally retarded to perform different personal care skills. The picture prompts were presented to each child in individual photograph booklets for each different task, with one picture corresponding to one step in the task analysis. The children were taught first to discriminate pictures that indicated a specific part of the task, for example, to point to the picture (out of a group of three) that shows socks. Each child had to learn to successfully point to each picture for each task.

Next the children were taught to choose their own reinforcer, independently turn the pages in the picture book, perform the actions indicated by the pictures, and self-deliver their own reinforcement. Verbal directions and modeling were used to teach appropriate responses. Delayed prompting allowed the children to shift their attention from the teacher to the picture book. After each step of a task was completed, the child was taught to turn the page to find a smiley face on the next page, signaling the completion of the task and that a reinforcer (small edible or toy) could be taken by the child. An example of the task analysis and the pictorial representations for one of the tasks, getting dressed, is presented in Table 15–1.

Once the children learned to perform the task using the picture book, the teacher gradually began to leave the setting so that the picture book was directing the child's performance, rather than the teacher. When the teacher was finally removed from the setting completely, post-treatment and generalization were assessed. The results showed that on-task behavior for each child increased substantially, occurring in almost 100% of the observation intervals, while inappropriate behaviors decreased. Follow-up showed that the skills continued for 2 months after training.

Self-management skills are particularly useful for older persons who are living and working in community settings to improve skills in such areas as personal hygiene. Garff and Story (1998) taught three adults to improve poor hygiene skills that were impeding their acceptance in their employment settings. One man had to learn to monitor being clean shaven. Another had to learn how to make sure he had no food particles on his face or mustache before he went to work. And a woman had to make certain she arrived at work with fresh, clean breath. The adults were taught these skills through modeling and then were provided with checklists in their homes for them to review and check off after completing the steps required for them to arrive at work with proper hygiene. They were evaluated when they arrived at work by their bosses or, in one case, the job coach. The results showed that through the use of the self-monitoring checklists the individuals were able to improve their hygiene status at work.

These studies demonstrate that some individuals with cognitive disabilities can learn to independently perform personal care skills without a teacher or supervisor being

Table 15–1 Task Analysis and Pictorial Representations for the Target Behavior of Getting Dressed

Step	*Behavioral Description*	*Pictorial Representation*
1	Remove pajama top	Child with pajama top raised overhead; picture taken from waist up
2	Retrieve shirt	Shirt on the floor; no other objects in picture
3	Put on shirt	None; above picture signifies this step
4	Remove pajama pants	Child with pajama pants pulled halfway down leg
5	Retrieve pants	Pants on the floor; no other objects in picture
6	Put on pants	None; above picture signifies this step
7	Retrieve socks	Socks on the floor; no other objects in picture
8	Put on socks	None; above picture signifies this step
9	Retrieve shoes	Shoes on the floor with one foot halfway inserted; no other objects in picture
10	Put on shoes	None; above picture signifies this step

Source: "Teaching Daily Living Skills to Children with Autism in Unsupervised Settings through Pictorial Self-management," by K. L. Pierce & L. Schreibman, 1994, *Journal of Applied Behavior Analysis, 27,* p. 473. Copyright 1994 by the Society for the Experimental Analysis of Behavior. Reprinted by permission.

constantly present. This increased level of independence is desirable. It allows the person to do more with less assistance and thus gain more autonomy over his or her own life. Therefore, self-management should be part of the instructional program after skills have been initially acquired whenever possible.

Having considered some factors that are applicable to all areas of personal care instruction, we will now discuss instruction in specific areas. Our discussion is limited by space to some of the more critical areas, including eating and self-feeding, learning to use the toilet, learning to dress oneself, and learning some important personal hygiene skills (personal dental care and menstrual care). For information in additional areas, the reader is referred to Baker and Brightman (1996).

Eating, Self-Feeding, and Other Mealtime Skills

There are few needs more basic to life functioning than eating. If we are to live, we must be able to adequately eat appropriate foods to sustain the body and allow it to function as it should. If there were no other reasons besides this, teaching adequate eating skills to individuals with severe disabilities would be important. However, there are additional concerns because, in the lives of most people, eating is an important social function, as well as a means to keep healthy and stay alive. Mealtimes are often times for relaxation and conversation and for relationships to be nourished just as the body is nourished.

There is a sad history of how many people with severe disabilities have eaten or been fed for many years. Confined often to the back wards of institutions, individuals either were fed or fed themselves without any concern for their dignity or the manner of eating. Greater attention was given to how expeditiously food could be transferred from the outside of a person's body to the inside, with virtually no consideration for the quality of the food, the acceptability of the eating behavior, or the enjoyment of the experience. Feedings through stomach tubes (fistulas) were done many times because they were considered to be cost beneficial, even though they were often not a physical necessity. Feeding a person pureed food while he was lying down and "bird feeding" (holding a person's chin up and pouring the pureed food down the throat) were also quick methods, even though the food often ended up in the lungs instead of the stomach. These tragic incidents have been referred to as "quiet little murders" (Perske, Clifton, McLean, & Stein, 1977). Additionally, because of the nature of the environment, limited time, insufficient food, and inadequate training, when individuals fed themselves, their self-feeding behavior was often characterized by a variety of socially unacceptable behaviors, such as stealing food, eating with their hands, eating directly from plates or bowls, and eating food off the floor (Barton, Guess, Garcia, & Baer, 1970).

Fortunately, with the advent of the normalization principle and the development of effective instructional procedures based on principles of applied behavior analysis, over the years we have witnessed dramatic improvements in the mealtime skills of persons with severe disabilities (Farlow & Snell, 2000; Perske et al., 1977; Westling & Murden, 1977). We also have come to expect that participation in meals by persons with severe disabilities should have no less quality than participation by those without disabilities. Perske and his colleagues (1977) describe the ideal mealtime as having the following characteristics:

- Feeling of comradeship and belonging
- Relaxing and being less defensive
- Communicating in many ways, with voice, eyes, body, taste, smell, and touch
- Laughing and feeling joyful
- Being accepted exactly as you are and being glad you are *you*
- Making choices
- Having all the time you need
- Heightening all the senses
- Feeling full, satisfied, and relaxed
- Taking in nutrition for growth and good health

For persons with severe disabilities to be able to more fully participate and enjoy the type of mealtime experiences that Perske et al. suggest, it is helpful if they can develop certain skills, some relatively basic and others more advanced. Banerdt and Bricker (1978) provide a detailed sequence important for eating, including developing skills related to head, trunk, limb, and sitting control; establishing manual dexterity; and establishing specific eating skills (see Figure 15–1). In the following sections, strategies and tactics for teaching appropriate mealtime skills are described.

Finger-Feeding

The first step in learning to eat independently is using one's fingers to bring food to the mouth. Normally, children start feeding themselves with their hands before they learn to use utensils, typically at the age of about 7 or 8 months. As with other skills, however, this may be delayed in children with severe disabilities. If so, it is a skill that should be taught prior to more advanced mealtime skills, because the ability to bring the hand to the mouth facilitates drinking independently from a cup, feeding oneself with a spoon, and using other utensils.

The best time to work on teaching finger-feeding is at the beginning of the meal when the child is likely to be hungry and is thus motivated to self-feed (Farlow & Snell, 2000). Using foods that the child likes also increases her interest in picking up the food. To get the child to practice the required hand-to-mouth movement, foods that have appeal and stick to the fingers, such as peanut butter, applesauce, cake batter, or whipped cream, might be put on the child's hands (Bigge, 1991). As the child acquires grasping skills, foods that are easy to hold, such as pieces of toast or zweiback, can be used.

Providing the child with many opportunities to eat finger foods is often sufficient to improve the skill. (Teachers and care providers must understand, however, that this is not a neat process, and a great deal of messiness will occur as the child increases his proficiency.) If, however, opportunity alone does not result in acquisition or improvement of finger-feeding, a task analysis should be developed that includes the following steps:

- Reaching to locate the food
- Grasping the food
- Lifting the food from the table to the mouth
- Putting the food into the mouth
- Chewing and swallowing the food

To teach the steps of the task analysis, the teacher may use an approach such as partial and full physical assistance within a system of least prompts procedure or a most-to-least prompts procedure. Graduated guidance may also be used.

Drinking from a Cup

Children normally learn to drink from a cup held by a care provider at about 1 year of age. Soon after this, the typical child is able to hold the cup and drink alone, albeit with some amount of spilling. Children with severe disabilities should be taught to drink from a cup held by another and then from a self-held cup if they are physically capable of doing so.

A flexible plastic cup with a small rim is relatively easy to drink from because it does not impede lip closure. Additionally, because of its flexibility, the teacher can bend it to make it fit the child's lips. If the child has a difficult time tilting her head backward, a section of the top of the cup can be cut away so that the cup can be tilted farther forward without bumping against the child's nose or forehead. Spouted cups that encourage abnormal sucking, brittle plastic cups that might break, and cups that are too large or difficult to handle should not be used.

The cup should be placed gently on the child's lips (not teeth) and tilted gradually to allow the child to take in a small amount of the liquid. While the child is swallowing, the cup should be tilted back but not removed from the lips. The liquid should not be poured into the mouth. Liquids thickened with yogurt, applesauce, or

Figure 15–1 Training Lattice for Establishing Independent Feeding Skills

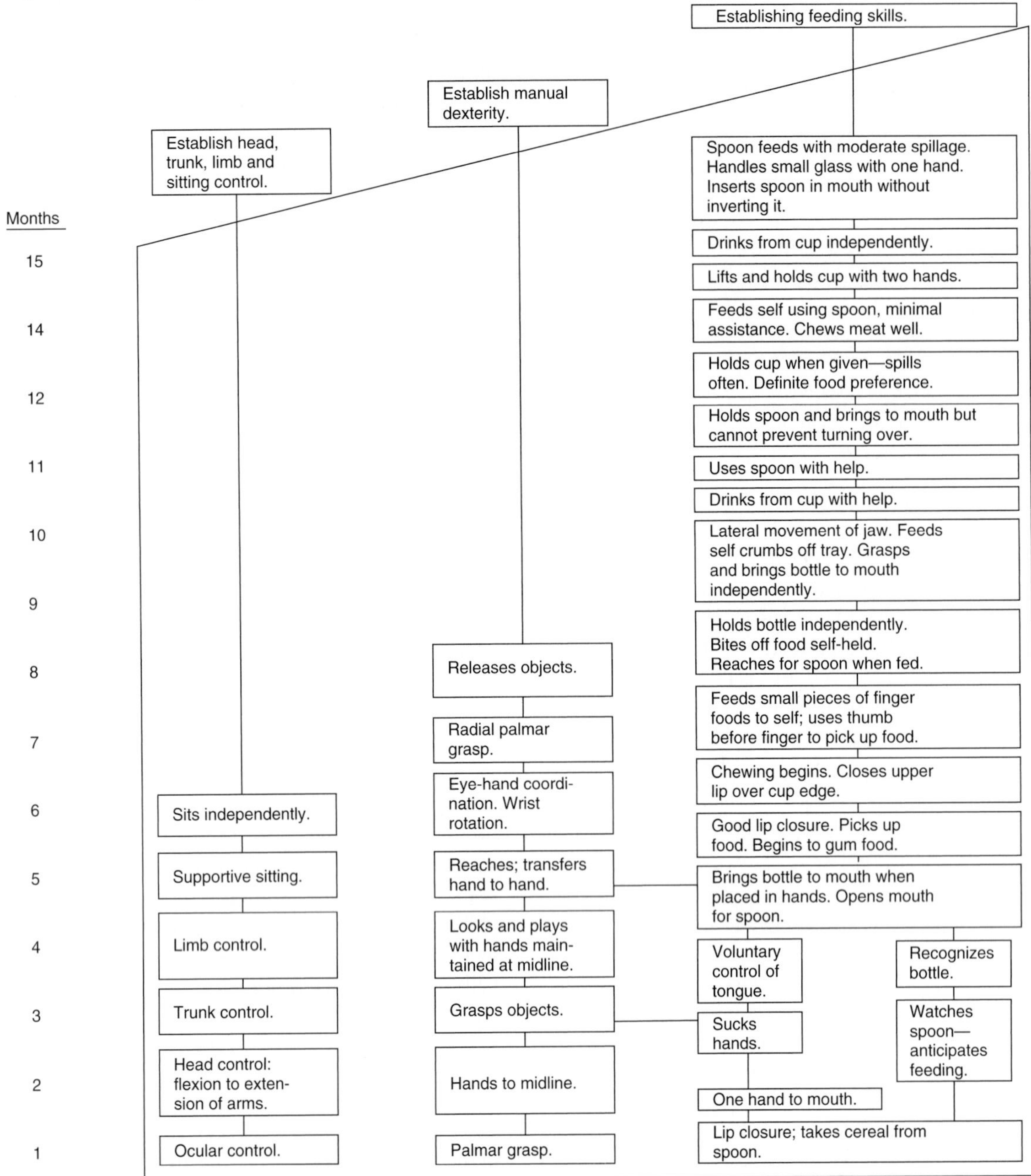

Source: "A Training Program for Selected Self-Feeding Skills for the Motorically Impaired," by B. Banerdt and D. Bricker, 1978, *AAESPH Review, 3,* p. 224. Copyright 1978 by The Association for Persons with Severe Handicaps. Reprinted by permission of TASH, Baltimore, MD.

baby cereal are often easier for the child to handle than regular juice (Alexander, 2001; Orelove & Sobsey, 1996).

When the child can take liquids from a cup held by another with ease, he often starts to ask for a drink by reaching for or touching the cup held by the teacher or care provider. This behavior should always be reinforced and never discouraged. If it does not occur independently, the child's hands should be guided to prompt the behavior. As with all early self-feeding behaviors, a stable, well-supported seating condition makes it easier for the child to grasp and manipulate the cup. Since the behavior consists of one continuous action, a task analysis is not required. For purposes of data collection, teachers may simply count how many sips of liquid the child takes in a certain period of time.

Learning to Eat with a Spoon

Being able to feed oneself with a spoon is an important first step toward becoming an independent eater. The individual who acquires this skill will have a sound basis for developing more advanced mealtime skills. Many students with disabilities acquire this skill like others; that is, they learn it in an incidental manner in the home. Other individuals need to be directly instructed to learn it. If a child or an older student does not eat with a spoon, but has sufficient physical skills and coordination to finger-feed and to grasp and release objects, it should be possible to teach the individual how to eat with the spoon. Many studies have demonstrated that individuals with severe disabilities can learn to eat with a spoon given appropriate instruction (Albin, 1977; Azrin & Armstrong, 1973; Berkowitz, Sherry, & Davis, 1971; Christian, Hollomon, & Lanier, 1973; Groves & Carroccio, 1971; Leibowitz & Holcer, 1974; Lemke & Mitchell, 1972; Miller, Patton, & Henton, 1971; O'Brien & Azrin, 1972; O'Brien, Bugle, & Azrin, 1972; Song & Ghandi, 1974; Zeiler & Jervey, 1968).

Eating correctly with a spoon consists of using the spoon to move the appropriate food (not finger food) from the bowl or plate, with the spoon held right side up, by the handle, in one hand, without spilling any food except back into the container that it came from (O'Brien & Azrin, 1972; O'Brien et al., 1972). Incorrect behaviors include various deviations, such as using hands to eat nonfinger foods, putting too much food on the spoon, spilling food outside the bowl or plate, or holding the spoon incorrectly.

As correct self-feeding behavior is observed, one sees a relatively smooth process of picking up and then holding the spoon, lowering it to the plate or bowl, scooping food, lifting it from the container to the mouth, inserting it into the mouth, removing the food with the lips, lowering the spoon to the food again, and repeating the process in a rhythmic, paced manner. These movements constitute a task analysis of spoon feeding, and the teacher may observe and record correct and incorrect performance of each step. The teacher may use a skill acquisition training procedure such as least-to-most or most-to-least assistance or graduated guidance.

Praising the student for correct responding and giving other appropriate social attention may ultimately eliminate any incorrect responses. If incorrect spoon-feeding behaviors persist, such as excessive spilling or eating with hands when a spoon should be used, they can generally be reduced through a brief (15 to 30 second) time-out from the opportunity to eat. Since food is a natural, unconditioned reinforcer, most individuals have a strong desire to eat. When incorrect behaviors occur, the teacher might say no and then briefly remove the food or pull the learner's chair away from the table. This has generally been shown to be effective in reducing inappropriate behaviors when teaching self-feeding skills (Albin, 1977; Azrin & Armstrong, 1973; Barton et al., 1970; Christian et al., 1973; Martin, McDonald, & Omichinski, 1971; O'Brien et al., 1972).

Learning to Use Other Utensils

Students who have learned to use a spoon competently should be taught and encouraged to use other utensils, primarily forks and knives (for both cutting and spreading), as well as napkins (Azrin & Armstrong, 1973; Nelson, Cone, & Hanson, 1975; O'Brien & Azrin, 1972; O'Brien et al., 1972). The skill acquisition instructional processes for teaching these skills are similar to teaching the student to eat with a spoon. However, two additional tactics can be used.

First, the teacher should teach one new skill at a time (e.g., teach the student how to use a napkin, then a fork, then a knife). When a new utensil is being taught, it should be used initially with only one food item that requires the use of the particular utensil. The new skill should be worked on at the beginning of the meal, if not throughout. Since the student has already learned to use a spoon, there may be a tendency for her to hold the fork or knife incorrectly (i.e., like a spoon). Therefore, the teacher should provide direct instruction on the proper ways to hold utensils for different purposes. Figure 15–2 shows some of these grips. Posting pictures or photographs of correct ways to grip utensils, such as those shown in Figure 15–2, may be helpful (Nelson et al., 1975). Although using a spoon is relatively simple, other forms of utensil use are increasingly complex. The teacher should progress from easier to more difficult skills. The suggested order after spoon use is napkin use, fork use, use of a knife for spreading, and use of a knife for cutting.

Second, after each utensil has been learned, the teacher needs to teach the student which utensils to use for specific needs. The student should learn to discriminate which foods require a spoon as opposed to a fork, and vice versa, and which foods can be eaten with the fingers. The student must also learn that the knife may be used for cutting, spreading butter or condiments, and pushing food

Figure 15–2 Correct Utensil Use: Eating Grip (top), Cutting Grip (center), Spreading Grip (bottom)

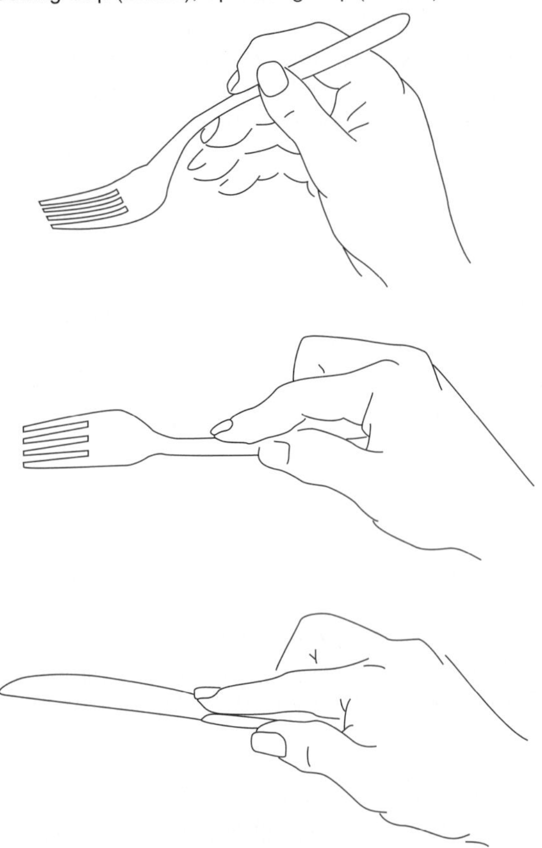

Source: "Training Correct Utensil Use in Retarded Children: Modeling vs. Physical Guidance," by G. L. Nelson, J. D. Cone, and C. R. Hanson, 1975, *American Journal of Mental Deficiency, 80,* p. 115. Copyright 1975 by the American Association on Mental Retardation. Reprinted by permission.

onto the fork, but cannot be used to scoop or spear food. Since by this time students should know *how* to use the utensil, the teacher should be able to focus on prompting and reinforcing the student's correct discrimination to select and use a particular utensil.

Decreasing Inappropriate Mealtime Behaviors

For various reasons, individuals with severe disabilities may display inappropriate mealtime behaviors. Some that may be considered relatively mild include eating foods with hands (not including finger foods), eating too fast or taking bites that are too large, chewing with mouth open, eating with face too close to the plate, spilling food or drinks, using the wrong utensil, playing with food (with or without utensils), holding the utensil incorrectly, putting a napkin on wrong, or not wiping mouth with a napkin when necessary. More serious problems include throwing food or utensils, stealing food from another's plate, eating food directly off the plate (without using hands or utensils), eating food that has fallen on the table or on the floor, smearing food, screaming and pushing the table away, and hitting others (Barton et al., 1970; Henriksen & Doughty, 1972; O'Brien & Azrin, 1972; O'Brien et al., 1972). Additionally, some persons may show a high degree of food selectivity, eating only certain foods and refusing to eat others.

Sometimes, inappropriate behavior occurs because the student has not learned more appropriate behavior. For example, eating with hands is likely to decrease when a student learns to eat correctly using a spoon or other utensil (O'Brien et al., 1972). In other cases, the behavior may occur because of some situation in the environment that prompts the behavior. This may include sitting near someone the student does not like, not having enough food to eat, having undesirable food, or being extremely hungry at the beginning of the meal. Functional assessment of the conditions and communicative intent surrounding the behavior and modifications of instructional practices may result in a decrease in the behavior (see Chapter 12).

It is likely that many of these behaviors, when they exist, have been inadvertently reinforced over the years and thus continue to occur. For example, stealing food or eating food in some inappropriate fashion might be reinforced by the food itself. In such cases, a brief removal and time-out from the food (by taking the food away for 15 to 30 seconds), coupled with a reprimand ("No!") each time that the behavior occurs and then redirecting the student to engage in more appropriate eating behavior may be sufficient to decrease the undesirable behavior. If not, a longer time-out may be necessary (Barton et al., 1970).

Eating too fast may be exhibited by some individuals, and since this may be unhealthy and socially undesirable, it should be corrected. Wright and Vollmer (2002) provided treatment to reduce the rapid eating of an adolescent girl with severe disabilities who ate too fast. The goal was to increase the amount of time between taking bites of food (the interresponse time). This was accomplished by allowing the student to take no more than one bite every 15 seconds. If she tried to take a bite of food too fast, they blocked her attempt and used a verbal prompt to remind her to slow down ("eat slowly"). As a consequence of the intervention, the young woman learned to slow down the bites that she took during meals.

Some persons with cognitive disabilities may refuse to eat foods other than the limited varieties that they prefer. Two approaches may be helpful if this problem occurs: using positive reinforcement for eating undesired foods and gradually changing the foods that are offered from those that are acceptable to others that are not preferred. A 5-year-old boy who refused to eat and met the criteria for "failure to thrive" was described by Kahng, Tarbox, and Wilke (2001). He was dependent on a g-tube for food intake and exhibited aggression and property destruction, as well as food refusal. The treatment of the boy began with identifying preferred items and activities through a preference assessment process (see Chapter 7). Preferred items included certain books and audiotapes. During feeding times, several of the preferred items were given to the child. When he refused to take a bite, expelled food after taking it in his mouth, or engaged in any problem behaviors, the preferred items were removed. As long as he accepted bites of food and ingested them without exhibiting any problem behaviors, he was given access to the preferred items. The treatment resulted in a 100% improvement in taking bites and near elimination of the problem behaviors. His mother and grandmother were also taught to successfully use the same procedure.

Shore, Babbitt, Williams, Coe, and Snyder (1998) used a different approach with four young children with developmental disabilities who would only accept pureed foods, even though medical assessment indicated that they were capable of ingesting foods of denser texture. The main element of the treatment package designed by Shore et al. consisted of a *texture fading procedure*. Using this procedure, they gradually increased the texture density of the food fed to the children from the level that they would accept (pureed) to a targeted level that was more appropriate for their age. For example, one child gradually progressed through this very finely calibrated sequence, which allowed him to move from eating only pureed food to eating food that was finely chopped:

- Pureed texture
- 75% pureed/25% junior
- 50% pureed/50% junior
- 25% pureed/75% junior
- Junior texture
- 75% junior/25% ground
- 50% junior/50% ground
- 25% junior/75% ground
- Ground texture
- Chopped fine texture

Movement to the next, denser texture occurred when the child was 80% successful in eating the current texture. Probes of foods with greater textures were used to determine the appropriate textures for treatment. Along with gradually modifying the texture of the food, the intervention program included praising the children for taking bites and swallowing food and not allowing them to escape when they refused bites (the teacher waited them out and then put the bite of food in their mouths). Participation by an occupational therapist was useful in determining the texture of the food that would be most appropriate for each child.

Teaching Other Appropriate Mealtime Behaviors

Beyond specific eating skills, other mealtime behaviors may be important for instruction depending on a student's current and future needs. Discussing possible needs with a student's parents and other members of the collaborative team may unveil important instructional targets. One such target might be to learn to eat "family style." This includes setting your place at the table, sitting down and putting your napkin on your lap, serving food to yourself from a bowl on the table, passing a bowl of food to another, and clearing away plates and utensils after the meal (Wilson, Reid, Phillips, & Burgio, 1984). If this is the way that the student normally eats at home, these may be important skills to teach. Additionally, since conversations typically occur during meals, attention should be given to working on communication skills. Fine-motor development is another area that can be incorporated into mealtime activities. Finally, consideration should be given to generalization of dining skills to other foods, meals, and locations and with different people. To the extent that skill generalization is important, instructional plans need to be developed for it to occur.

Other Suggestions for Improving Eating

In addition to the tactics described, several additional things that teachers can do to improve eating and mealtime skills of students with severe disabilities (Baker & Brightman, 1996; Orelove & Sobsey, 1996; Westling & Murden, 1977) include:

- Make sure that the child or student is seated appropriately and adequately supported when eating. This is extremely important for students with severe physical disabilities.

- During the initial acquisition of a skill that requires physical guidance, such as learning to eat with a spoon, the learner may have more success if the same person, the teacher or an assistant, always provides the training. Changing the instructor at this point may result in more mistakes. Changes in instructors should be made gradually as the student is progressing.
- Although it is desirable for the student to ultimately eat in a normal integrated environment, some have suggested that initial skills may develop faster without the distractions of the typical school cafeteria. It has been proposed that initial instruction should occur in a quiet area; then, when skills are adequately developed, the student should eat in the cafeteria with the other students. To avoid total isolation during the skills-acquisition stage, however, the student may learn to eat with peers in the classroom, may go to the cafeteria when it is less crowded, or may go to the cafeteria for part of the meal.
- Students' skills increase if they are provided with many opportunities to learn and practice. Having several chances to practice eating and receive instruction during the day is sometimes preferable to having only one or two opportunities. Also, because providing instruction on how to eat without real food being present is not natural and is not likely to have an effect on the student's eating skills, instruction should always be provided during actual eating times (meals and snacks).
- Students acquiring initial skills with different utensils (i.e., using a spoon, fork, or knife) probably do better if there is only one highly desirable food on the plate during instruction. Additional foods can be added as the student's skill increases. Foods should be used for instruction that are desired by the student and suit the instructional need. Finger foods should be easy to grasp and hold, spoon foods should be easy to scoop, and, when learning to use a fork, foods that can be stabbed should be used.
- Some materials are easier to handle than others and may facilitate eating when the student is first learning. For example, simply using large-handled spoons and deeper bowls may help the student learning to feed himself. Plastic bowls that are fastened to the table with suctions will not slip around easily.
- The standard of neatness may need to be very liberal during early stages of learning, but should become gradually stricter as the student progresses. Excessive spilling and other messy behavior should be ultimately eliminated or reduced as much as possible.

Learning to Use the Toilet

Like being able to feed oneself, being able to use the toilet independently and to avoid soiling and wetting oneself helps to maintain good health and increases the social acceptability of an individual. As with self-feeding, school-age individuals with severe disabilities have different skill levels with regard to toilet use. Some are fully independent and require no additional training; others may need reminders to use the toilet or, if directed to a toilet on a regular basis, are able to use the toilet successfully. Some are able to use the toilet, but have difficulty with related skills such as lowering or raising pants, wiping, or washing hands after toilet use. Still others lack the physical ability to use the toilet and need to have bowel and urinary management procedures provided in order to void. Through contact with parents or caregivers and other members of the professional team, the teacher must learn each individual's unique needs related to toileting and provide the appropriate training or the necessary physical management.

Determining Readiness for Toileting

Most children acquire the ability to control their bladders and bowels between 2 and 3 years of age. While it may be expected that many individuals with severe disabilities will learn toileting skills at this age, many do not. For them, sufficient maturity may not occur until they are older. Early studies suggest that the success of training an individual with severe cognitive disabilities to use the toilet is directly related to the individual's mental development and/or chronological age (Osarchuk, 1973). However, these findings are far from conclusive. Factors such as the ability to recognize physical cues, social recognition of the importance of proper toileting behavior, and modeling other children may have more bearing than general developmental level (Farlow & Snell, 2000).

Instead of relying on the individual's chronological or mental age as an indicator of readiness to learn toilet training, other factors may be more indicative of this potential. Three that are very important include:

- Evidence that the individual has a regular pattern of elimination, meaning that she voids at relatively predictable times each day instead of randomly.

- Additionally, the ability of the individual to go for at least 1 or 2 hours without wetting or having a bowel movement. This, along with the previous criterion, suggests that she has attained an adequate degree of voluntary control.
- Finally, the individual is at least 2 1/2 years old. Attempting to train the child before this age is generally too soon, even for a child without disabilities (Farlow & Snell, 2000).

Other individual characteristics that may facilitate the training process include ambulation, fine-motor ability, receptive language, and good visual ability (Foxx & Azrin, 1973). However, these should not be considered prerequisites to training. More important is adequate physiological development, as indicated by the conditions in the previous list. If the parents and teachers have any doubts about physical readiness, a medical examination should precede training.

Teaching Independent Toilet Use

Several tactics based on the principles of applied behavior analysis have been discovered through research to be effective for teaching independent toileting skills to individuals with severe disabilities. These tactics have been widely presented in the research literature (Anderson, 1982; Azrin, Bugle, & O'Brien, 1971; Azrin & Foxx, 1971; Ellis, 1963; Foxx & Azrin, 1973; Giles & Wolf, 1966; Hundziak, Maurer, & Watson, 1965; Kimbrell, Luckey, Barbuto, & Love, 1967; Lancioni, 1980; Mahoney, Van Wagenen, & Meyerson, 1971; Osarchuk, 1973; Smith, 1979; Trott, 1977; Williams & Sloop, 1978). Some of these tactics are no longer considered appropriate because of ethical concerns (e.g., using punishment such as overcorrection for accidents, providing increased amounts of liquids to promote the frequency of urination, spending 6 to 8 hours in the bathroom to be near the toilet); others are effective and allow respect for the dignity of the individual to be maintained. These tactics are presented next.

Pretraining Data Collection

The first step in toilet training requires that data be collected to determine the learner's pattern of urination and bowel movements. The most likely time that the individual will wet or soil his diaper or training pants is obviously the best time for him to be placed on the toilet. A relatively simple chart, such as the partial-interval one presented in Figure 15–3, allows the teacher to record the student's voiding pattern and type of behavior over several days. The more often that checks are made to determine when the student is voiding, the more accurate the teacher's knowledge will be about the time to place the student on the toilet. Therefore, as the chart in Figure 15–3 suggests, checks should be made every 15 minutes followed by an appropriate notation (i.e., dry/clean, wet/soiled); if the teacher places the student on the toilet at some time during this period, it should be noted whether the student urinated or had a bowel movement while on the toilet. Using the chart, the teacher may also note the relation of wetting or bowel movements to drinking or eating by marking on the chart when these behaviors occurred.

During a pretraining baseline period, this data collection should occur without attempts at toileting until a stable pattern of voiding can be identified. In other words, the teacher should learn at what periods of time during the day the student is most likely to wet or have a bowel movement. This may be determined in as few as 3 days, or it may take a week or longer to discern the pattern. This information then confirms that the learner meets the prerequisites listed earlier (has a regular pattern of elimination and can go for an hour or more without voiding) and tells the teacher the best time to put the student on the toilet. It is very important that each time the pants are checked they be changed if they are wet or soiled. This is not only for the comfort of the student, but so that accurate detection will be noted at the next pants check. When checking and changing the learner, the teacher should be sure that no reinforcement is inadvertently given and that a neutral demeanor is maintained at this time.

Learning to Sit on the Toilet

Knowing when the student is most likely to void implies the best time for her to sit on the toilet. (Sometimes it is suggested that males be taught to stand to urinate, but learning to sit for both urinating and having a bowel movement may be easier to teach at first.) If, for example, the chart in Figure 15–3 shows that the student regularly wets between 9:00 and 9:30, this would be an appropriate time for him to be seated on the toilet. However, for some students, sitting on the toilet may be aversive because it is a new and strange experience. If the learner will not willingly sit on the toilet for a period of 5 minutes or longer, it will be necessary to gradually shape this behavior by reinforcing him with praise and social attention for sitting on the toilet for longer and longer periods of time. At first the individual may need to be supported and reinforced

Figure 15–3 Data Collection Form for Toilet Training

Source: Instruction of Students with Severe Disabilities, by M. E. Snell, ©1993, Upper Saddle River, NJ: Prentice Hall. Reprinted by permission.

Toileting/Pants Check Record   Baseline: 9/6 - 9/17   Intervention: 9/20

Name: Jacob   Locations: gym, classroom, north hall, cafeteria, bathrooms

Time	9/6	9/7	9/8	9/9	9/10	9/13	9/14	9/15	9/16	9/17	9/20	9/21	9/22	9/23	9/24	9/27	9/28	9/30	10/1	10/2
8:30		(WB)					(W)	W+	W+	A		W+		W+		W+	(W)	W+	A	(W)
8:45		D		(W)	(W)	W+	D	D	D	B		D	W+	D	W+	D	D	D	B	D
9:00	(W)	D		D	D	D	D	D	D	S	W+	D+	D	D	D	W+	D	D+	S	D
9:15	D	D	(BW)	D	D	D	D	D	D	E	(B)	D	D	D	D	D	D	D	E	D
9:30	D	D	D	(W)	(W)	D	D	(W)	D	N	D	D+	D	D+	D	D+	D+	D+	N	D+
9:45	P.E.	P.E.	P.E.	P.E.	P.E.	P.E.	P.E.	P.E.	P.E.	T	P.E.	P.E.	P.E.	P.E.	P.E.	P.E.	P.E.	P.E.	T	P.E.
10:00	D+	D	(WB)	(W)	W+	D	D	D	(W?)		D	D+	(W)	D+	W+	W+	WB+	D+		WB+
10:15	D	(WB)	D	D	D	D	D	D	D		D	D	D	D	D	D	D	D		D
10:30	D	D	D	D	W-	D	D	D	D		D	D+	D+	D+	D+	D+	D+	D+		D+
10:45	D	D	D	(W)	D	W+	W+	D	D		(W)	D	(W)	D	(W)	D	D	D		D
11:00	W-	D	D	D	D	D	D	W	D		D	D+	D	D+	D	W+	D+	D+		W+
11:15	D	D	(W)	(W)	D	D	D	D	D+		D	D	D	D	D	D	D	D		D
11:30	D	D	D	D	(W)	D	D	D	D		D	D+	D+	D	D+	D+	D	BW+		D
11:45	L	L	L	L	L	L	L	L	L		L	L	L	L	L	L	L	L		L
12:00	D	D	D	D	D	D+	D	D	D		D	B+	B+	D	D	D	D?	D		D
12:15	(WB)	(W)	D	(WB)	W+	(W)	WB+	D	(WB)		D	D	D	B+	WB+	B+	WB+	D-		WB+
12:30	D	D	(WB)	D	D	D	D	B+	D		(WB)	(W)	D	D	D	D	D+			D
12:45	D	D	D	D	D	(BW)	D	D	D		D+	D	D	D+	D+	D	D			D
1:00	D	D	D	D	D	D	D	D	D		D	D	(WB)	D	D	D+	D+	A		D+
1:15	D	D	D	D	D	D	D	D	D		D	D	D	D	D	(W)	D	B		D
1:30	D	(W)	D	D	D	D	D	D	D		D	D+	D	D+	D	D+	D+	S		W
1:45	D	D	D	D	D	D	D	W	D+		D	D	D	D	W-	D	D	E		D
2:00	(BW)	(W)	D	(W)	D	D-	W	D	D+		D	D-	D+	W+	W+	W+	D+	N		D
2:15	D	D	(B)	(WB)	(W)			(W)					W-		D		W-	T		D
2:30					D															
# Self initiations / # Accidents	1/3	0/5	0/5	0/7	2/4	3/2	2/2	2/3	4/2		2/3	9/1	5/3	9/0	7/1	11/1	9/1	7/0		6/2

Key	Student Initiated	Teacher Assisted	Accidents
D = Dry	W+ = Wet on toilet	W– = Wet on toilet	(W) = Wet
L = Lunch	B+ = BM on toilet	B– = BM on toilet	(B) = BM
	D+ = Self-initiated, no elim.	D– = Teacher-initiated, no elim.	

simply for initial sitting. Then, gradually longer periods of sitting (5 seconds, 10 seconds, 15 seconds, . . . , 1 minute) are reinforced until the person becomes accustomed to sitting on the toilet. In the most extreme cases, that is, when the student resists through screaming and temper tantrums, a more gradual approach of just walking into the bathroom and getting near the toilet may need to be reinforced initially to desensitize the student to the environment and the experience. Students should never be held on the toilet while crying or screaming because this indicates that the experience is far too aversive. Instead a very gradual pattern of shaping the child's behavior so that he approaches the toilet should be used. This takes more time but the effect will be more positive.

Learning to Void While on the Toilet

Once the student has learned to sit on the toilet, the idea, of course, is for her to void while there and to stay clean and dry when not there. Three tactics increase the probability of this occurring. The first is for the student to be on the toilet during those times when she is most likely to void (based on the data collected prior to training) and to remain on the toilet long enough for it to occur. When the student does void while on the toilet, much praise and age-appropriate social reinforcement should be given: "Look what you did! That's great! You're going to learn to stay clean and dry!"

The second tactic is to continue the pants checking on a regular basis, just as during the pretraining period, and also to reinforce the student each time a check finds the student clean and dry. For the student to make the association, the teacher may guide the student's hand to his or her crotch area and deliver praise while the student feels the dryness, for example: "You're dry and clean! I'm very proud! Can you feel that you are dry? Very good!" During training, at those times when the student is found to be soiled or wet, the teacher should change him or her immediately and do so without providing any attention or reinforcement. Additionally, mild disapproval may be stated ("I'm very disappointed that you are wet!"), but nothing more.

The third tactic involves the ratio of the time *on* the toilet to the time *off*. The greater the amount of time that the student is on the toilet compared to the time off, the greater the likelihood that urination or a bowel movement will occur while the student is on the toilet. Therefore, in a 15-minute period, if the student is on the toilet for 10 minutes and off for 5, all else being equal, he is twice as likely to go when on the toilet (and be reinforced for it) than when off it. The actual amount of time for being on and off the toilet depends on several factors. Although a 10 minute to 5 minute ratio may work for many students and teachers, for others it may not. The teacher may not be able to get the student on and off the toilet that often, or the student may show resistance to getting off and on so often. For some students, teaching to use the toilet quickly may be a major goal; for others it may not be as critical and more time can be taken. The former situation calls for more opportunities to be on the toilet, but the latter would not, and a schedule such as 10 or 15 minutes on the toilet every hour would be appropriate. Of course, it must be understood that this may decrease the number of on-toilet successes and thus reduce the opportunity for reinforcement, which would lengthen the period of time required for successful learning.

Also related to the speed of acquiring appropriate toileting behavior is the amount of time each day that the teacher and student spend working on this activity. For some it may be possible to commit only 1 hour or so of the school day to toilet training. For example, there may be four 10-minute periods of being on the toilet interspersed with four 5-minute periods of being off. After that time, the teacher does not follow the on–off schedule, but might place the student on the toilet only when urination or a bowel movement is most likely to occur. For others, if toileting skills are a high priority and if conditions warrant it, an on–off schedule may be followed throughout the entire school day. Although this is likely to interfere with other normal daily school routines, it is likely to reduce the total amount of time required for the student to learn to use the toilet. The teacher, parents, and other members of the collaborative team should weigh the positive and negative aspects of more and less intensive toileting schedules before implementing any particular schedule.

During the toilet training period, regardless of the off and on toilet training schedule and the amount of time committed to training, the teacher should continue to collect data as during the pretraining phase, recording the student's condition at each time period when both on and off the toilet. These data indicate if success is occurring and, if not, during what times the student needs to be placed on the toilet, or perhaps placed for longer periods of time. If the teacher wishes to chart the data, this can be done by placing the total "correct" and "incorrect" occurrences for the day or the training time on a chart (see Chapter 9).

Success at toileting occurs when the student voids when on the toilet and not when off the toilet most of the time. Although 100% success is naturally preferable, it is to be expected that accidents will occur. If these start to occur with some frequency, the teacher needs to return to data collection and the toilet training procedure as described earlier. However, if the accidents are infrequent, the teacher should simply change the student without any fanfare and expect her to use the toilet appropriately in the future.

Teaching Skills Associated with Toileting

Several skills typically associated with toileting should be considered for instruction as the student is learning to use the toilet. These skills include walking to the bathroom, lifting or lowering the toilet seat as necessary, lowering outer pants or lifting skirt or dress, lowering underpants, sitting on the toilet, wiping after voiding, standing up, pulling up underwear, pulling up pants or lowering skirt or dress, washing hands with soap and water, drying hands, and returning to the previous location outside the bathroom. Each or any of these could be included as instructional targets, task analyzed, and taught during toilet training periods, using the skill acquisition methods described in Chapter 7.

Whether skills such as these are taught simultaneously with toileting skills depends on factors that should be considered by the teacher and the planning team. The student may be too young or not yet have adequate motor skills to learn some of the related tasks. The teacher may be toilet training several students simultaneously and may not have time to teach all related skills to all students learning to use the toilet. In contrast, it may be judged that it is essential for the student to learn all or certain related skills. Regardless, there are two considerations to keep in mind. First, toilet training provides a natural opportunity to teach related skills; but, second, if for whatever reason it is not possible to teach these skills simultaneously, toilet training may still proceed with the teacher fully assisting the student to carry out all the related behaviors.

Using the Toilet Independently

When the student with severe disabilities begins to go in the toilet instead of in his pants or diapers, a major step has been achieved. The student can then be taken or directed to the bathroom to use the toilet at the times determined by the previously established schedule. In this way, the habit of using the toilet is strengthened and, along with pressure on the bowel or bladder, the toilet will ultimately gain influence as the stimulus prompting bowel movements or urination to occur.

It will always be necessary to direct some individuals with severe disabilities to the toilet on a regular schedule. For others, the need to use the toilet is communicated by their facial expression or by indicative acts such as touching their genital area or pulling at the crotch of their pants. In cases such as these, the teacher and others must be vigilant and respond appropriately to prevent subsequent accidents. The teacher also may attempt to teach the student an alternative way to communicate the need to go to the bathroom, using either verbal language, a manual sign, or a picture or symbol when she feels the urge to void.

The greatest degree of toileting independence occurs if and when the individual can reliably indicate the need to go to the toilet or simply goes to the toilet without being told when the need arises. The teacher may prompt this by teaching the student, when possible, to communicate the need to use the toilet whenever the student actually goes to the bathroom. One way to do this may be through a constant time delay procedure (see Chapter 7).

Using constant time delay, when it is time for the student to go to the bathroom or when the student's behavior indicates a need to go, the teacher says, "Do you need to go to the bathroom? Say 'bathroom' " (or "sign bathroom," or "point to bathroom"). After several such occurrences, using the principles of time delay, the teacher delays the final prompt. That is, the question is asked and a 4- or 5-second delay occurs before prompting the student to say, sign, or point to the symbol for bathroom. Ultimately, the internal sensation experienced by the student results in the communicative act instead of the teacher's question, and at this point the student is able to indicate his need as other students do.

Teaching to Use the Toilet in Different Settings

Initial toilet training often occurs in one setting, for example, the bathroom in or nearest to the classroom. However, the student must learn to use various bathrooms, for example, bathrooms at home, in different parts of the school, or in different community settings. Success in learning to use different bathrooms depends on the continuity of treatment across settings and the participation of the various individuals who provide supervision and support in these settings (Dunlap, Koegel, & Koegel, 1984).

The most likely way to ensure that the student has toileting success in different areas is to arrange coordinated training practices. The intent is that those providing supervision in the various sites will follow essentially the same plan as the teacher in the primary training site. This can occur if (1) there is contact with the supervisors, teachers, or trainers in additional areas to initiate coordination, (2) the student carries written instructions to secondary support persons to help to maintain consistency across settings, and (3) there is phone contact or other regular contact between the primary teacher and others to help to maintain coordination and consistency (Dunlap et al., 1984). Of course, as the learner gains greater toileting independence, opportunity to practice in a variety of bathrooms will promote generalization.

Other Suggestions for Improving Toileting

The basic procedures for teaching someone to use the toilet should result in toileting success for many students. The following suggestions may add to this success.

- The parents' desire to have their child learn to use the toilet is an important factor; if the parents feel this is an important goal, it will be easier to coordinate efforts between home and school, and the child may learn more quickly.
- The teacher should attempt to determine the time pattern that exists between eating and elimination. This physiological relationship will help the teacher to know when the student is most likely to need to be directed to the toilet or when she might signal the need to go.

- The most difficult part of learning to use the toilet is going for the first time while sitting on the toilet and without training pants or a diaper on. This presents a completely different sensation to the student than he has experienced before. When it does occur, much social reinforcement should be given.
- If a teacher cannot devote an extensive amount of time to toilet training each day, shorter periods can be used. Successful toileting during these periods will help toileting to occur more easily after it has been learned in an initial time period.
- Parents who report that their children are bedwetters should be informed that daytime control is typically achieved before nighttime control. If bedwetting continues after day control has been learned, parents may eliminate it by (1) making sure the child uses the toilet before going to bed, (2) withholding caffeine drinks including coffee, tea, and cola during the evening, (3) waking the child before the parents' bedtime to use the bathroom, (4) checking the bed for wetness periodically during the night and if it is wet, awakening the individual, cleaning her, changing the bed, and requiring the use of the toilet before she returns to bed, and (5) praising and reinforcing the individual after a dry night (Azrin, Sneed, & Foxx, 1974; Mohr & Sharpley, 1988).

Learning to Dress

A third major area of personal self-care is learning to dress and undress oneself. Students with severe disabilities who can manage putting on and taking off articles of clothing at appropriate times during the day have to rely less on others and therefore are more independent. For this reason, the ability to dress and undress oneself is often considered an important objective for students with severe disabilities. Additionally, more advanced, related skills such as buying clothes, selecting clothes for daily wear, and caring for clothing are sometimes considered important objectives for instruction (Wilcox & Bellamy, 1987). Targeting specific skills related to the process of dressing should be given due consideration by parents, teachers, and other members of the team.

Selecting Skills to Teach

When deciding what specific dressing skills should be taught, consideration should be given to three factors: current and future needs, normal dressing skills sequence, and physical ability.

Current and Future Needs

It is very important to determine what dressing or undressing skills the student needs in his current life to increase independence and decrease dependence on others. For example, if a student's parents say that the morning routine would be less hectic if their child could take off pajamas and put on socks and underwear and a dress or pants and a shirt, it suggests that these skills should be made primary instructional targets. For others, it may be helpful to learn to put on or take off sweaters and coats so that going out to play or coming in for dinner could be done without the involvement of a parent or caregiver.

Additional thought may need to be given to dressing skills needed for the immediate future. If colder weather is coming, if the student is moving to a different climate, if the student is learning a job that requires different clothing, or if an important social event is on the horizon that requires special dressing, any of these conditions could imply that certain dressing skills should be learned.

Normal Dressing Skills Sequence

Although not always the most important factor, particularly for older students, members of the collaborative team should be aware of the normal pattern of dressing that occurs among most children who do not have disabilities. Typically, dressing skills begin at about 12 months with cooperative acts such as holding out an arm to have a shirt put on or a foot to have a sock or shoe put on. From this point the child progresses until, by the age of 4 years, she can pretty well dress and undress with only a little assistance (Orelove & Sobsey, 1996). Table 15–2 provides a sequence of dressing skills as they normally develop. Note that many undressing skills occur before dressing skills. Also, in accordance with general developmental patterns, skills requiring gross-motor movements typically precede those requiring fine-motor movements. It is not always appropriate to follow a normal developmental dressing sequence, but in some cases it is, particularly with younger individuals who have mastered few or no skills.

Physical Ability

Some students will very likely not be able to learn independent dressing skills. This is particularly true for students with the most severe disabilities or those who have both cognitive and physical disabilities. Still, this does not mean that they cannot learn any useful dressing skills or that no effort should be made to teach them some skills. Instead, consideration should be given to teaching skills that allow them to participate as fully and mean-

Table 15–2 Normal Developmental Sequence of Dressing Skills

Approximate Age	*Dressing Skill*
12 months	Begins to cooperate by holding out foot for shoe, arm for sleeve
12–18 months	Begins to remove hat, socks, and mittens
2 years	Removes unlaced shoes, socks, and pants
2 1/2 years	Removes all clothing Can put on socks, shirt, coat
3 years	Undresses rapidly and well Dresses, except for heavy outer clothing
4 years	Dresses and undresses with little assistance

Source: Educating Children with Multiple Disabilities: A Transdisciplinary Approach (3rd ed., p. 359), by F. P. Orelove and D. Sobsey, 1996, Baltimore: Paul H. Brookes Publishing Co. Reprinted by permission.

ingfully as possible in dressing and undressing processes. An occupational therapist is able to provide critical assistance in this area. An example of this was reported by Reese and Snell (1991), who taught students with multiple physical and sensory disabilities how to take coats and jackets off and put them on. In performing these skills, the students performed many steps in the task analysis, and the teacher assisted with those steps that the students were physically unable to do. The task analyses for the three students are presented in Figure 15–4. Note that the teacher's involvement was individually determined for each task for each student.

Assessing Dressing Ability

An overview assessment of the student's current dressing and undressing abilities can be determined by interviewing parents or caregivers. As an aid to this procedure, adaptive behavior scales or commercial check sheets that itemize different skills can be used (see Chapter 6). Baker and Brightman (1996) have provided an inventory for dressing skills, as well as for other self-care skills.

Once the dressing skills to be taught have been determined, as with other skills, it is important to assess the student to see what specific abilities he has with the articles of clothing to be taught (Farlow & Snell, 2000). As with most other skills that will be taught, the teacher should first conduct a task analysis and then ask the student to perform the task. As the student attempts to do so, the teacher records performance on each step, noting whether the student can perform the step independently. Three to five days of such observation and recording should indicate to the teacher the exact deficiencies that exist in the student's dressing or undressing ability for specific articles of clothing. After these baseline data have been collected, the teacher may begin instructional activities, continuing to record progress as he does so.

Instructional Strategies for Teaching Dressing

After the teacher has conducted the initial assessment, the instructional intervention may start. As the instruction proceeds, the teacher should continue to collect data on the student's performance. If several students are in need of the same instruction, for example, learning to put on a coat or sweater, group instruction may be provided. Regardless of whether one individual or several are being taught, however, the teacher must select effective instructional strategies. The available literature in the area of teaching dressing skills to persons with severe disabilities has provided various instructional strategies and tactics of great utility (Azrin, Schaeffer, & Wesolowski, 1976; Diorio & Konarski, 1984; Kramer & Whitehurst, 1981; Martin, Kehoe, Bird, Jensen, & Darbyshire, 1971; McKelvey et al., 1992; Minge & Ball, 1967; Reese & Snell, 1991; Young, West, Howard, & Whitney, 1986).

Order of Instruction

Dressing skills have been taught to persons with severe disabilities in three ways described earlier in the chapter: the whole-task approach, the forward chaining approach, and the backward chaining approach. All three require teaching the steps listed in the task analysis, but the nature of the instruction is very different. The whole-task approach has been recommended previously (see Chapter 7) and is

Figure 15–4 Task Analyses for Dressing Skills for Students with Cognitive and Physical Disabilities

Lynn
Jacket/Coat Off

1. Take jacket/coat off left shoulder
2. Bend left elbow
3. Take elbow out of sleeve opening
4. Grasp left sleeve with right hand
5. Take left arm out of sleeve
6. Lean forward
7. Bring jacket/coat from behind to right side
8. Shake jacket/coat off right arm
9. Hang jacket/coat on hook

Jacket/Coat On

1. Take jacket/coat off hook
2. Place jacket/coat on your lap, hood/collar next to stomach with inside facing up

*(T) Place left hand into sleeve opening

3. Place right hand into other sleeve opening
4. Lean forward
5. Raise right arm up and over head
6. Pull sides of jacket/coat down

Anne
Jacket/Coat Off

1. Grasp sleeve with preferred hand
2. Bend arm of opposite hand
3. Take arm out of sleeve
4. Grasp remaining sleeve
5. Bend sleeved arm
6. Take arm out of sleeve

Jacket/Coat On

*(T) Place jacket/coat on child's lap, hood/collar next to stomach with inside facing up

1. Place hands in sleeve openings simultaneously
2. Raise arms
3. Flip garment over head
4. Straighten arms

*(T) Pull coat down at sides

Kari
Jacket/Coat Off

1. Grasp right sleeve with left hand
2. Bend right elbow
3. Take right arm out of sleeve
4. Grasp left sleeve with right hand
5. Bend left elbow
6. Take left arm out of sleeve

Jacket/Coat On

*(T) Place jacket/coat on child's lap, hood/collar next to stomach with inside facing up

1. Place hands in sleeve openings at the same time
2. Raise arms
3. Lean forward
4. Flip jacket/coat over head
5. Straighten arms
6. Pull jacket/coat down at sides

Source: "Putting On and Removing Coats and Jackets: The Acquisition and Maintenance of Skills by Children with Severe Multiple Disabilities," by G. M. Reese and M. E. Snell, 1991, *Education and Training in Mental Retardation, 26,* pp. 398–410. Copyright 1991 by the Division on Mental Retardation and Developmental Disabilities, The Council for Exceptional Children. Reprinted by permission.

recommended here for most situations as well. This approach requires that at every instructional session the teacher instruct the student in every step of the task analysis. The steps that the student cannot perform, either independently or with assistance, are performed for the student by the teacher. In this way the student experiences the entire chain of behavior occurring in a natural order. The previous discussion provides information about the forward and backward chaining methods. The following sequence would be used as a backward chaining approach to putting on pants (Mori & Masters, 1980):

1. Place the trousers on the student pulled up to hips; have the student pull them up the rest of the way.

2. Place the trousers on the student pulled up to the thighs; have the student pull them up the rest of the way.
3. Place the trousers on the student pulled up to the knees; have the student pull them up the rest of the way.
4. Place both feet in the trousers and allow them to lie around the ankles; have the student pull them up all the way.
5. Place one foot in the trousers; require that the student place the other foot in and pull the pants up around the waist.
6. Have the learner put both feet in the trousers and pull them all the way up around the waist.

Prompting Strategies

As discussed in Chapter 7 and earlier in this chapter, various instructional prompting strategies may be used during skill acquisition. For dressing instruction, two approaches have been dominant: graduated guidance and the system of least prompts.

Instructional Materials

Although most instruction on dressing skills naturally calls for the use of the student's regular clothes, for some particularly difficult parts of the dressing process, temporary modifications may be helpful. Realizing, for example, the difficulty associated with various motor movements (putting arms in sleeves, legs in pants), the use of clothing that is one or two sizes too large during early phases of instruction is suggested. This allows the student to get into and out of garments more easily. After success is experienced with these movements, the teacher then reduces the size of the clothes, in one or two steps, to the student's actual size (Orelove & Sobsey, 1996).

The same principle can be applied to different features of clothing, such as using larger buttons and then gradually reducing their size (Kramer & Whitehurst, 1981). Because students with severe disabilities typically have difficulty with fine-motor skills, working with objects that are larger and thus easier to grasp, such as larger buttons, zippers, laces, clasps, or other clothing components, is initially easier than working with smaller items. As students become more skilled at manipulating these larger items, they can be replaced with smaller and smaller ones.

In some cases the parents and professionals (teacher, occupational therapist) may agree that the time that it will take the student to learn to manipulate certain aspects of clothing, such as shoelaces, is simply too long. In other cases, the physical ability of the student may be inadequate for certain tasks. For example, the student may lack adequate motor skills to tie a shoe and may be getting older, and more critical skills may be necessary for functioning in the near future. In these types of situations, a decision may be made to use different clothing materials or different types of clothes. Shoes that have Velcro straps instead of laces, for example, may be worn, and the student may then have greater success in learning to put them on with no or little assistance.

Some commercially available devices have been built to provide practice for dressing skills; they come in various shapes and typically contain buttons, snaps, and zippers. Their use is not suggested because they are not natural. Students might improve their fine-motor skills by working on them, but they would not necessarily be able to transfer these skills to actual clothes.

Dressing and Students with More Severe Disabilities

Some students with more severe disabilities or students who have multiple disabilities, as indicated previously, are not able to carry out all the functions of dressing even if there is adequate time and appropriate instructional practices have been used. In these cases, additional modifications in the dressing process should be provided (Heller, Bigge, & Allgood, 2001; Orelove & Sobsey, 1996; Reese & Snell, 1991). An occupational therapist should provide assistance in planning instructional processes and determining the most effective strategies for teaching the student or involving the student through partial participation.

Since many of these individuals are nonambulatory, they should be appropriately positioned for dressing activities—in a sitting position if possible, with their back against the teacher's chest if necessary. The student may also be dressed while lying in a side-lying position with appropriate supports; lying flat on the back is generally the most difficult way for the student to participate in the dressing activity.

Partial participation should be encouraged whenever the student can control her movements to do so. For this reason, the teacher needs to conduct a task analysis for these students and give them the opportunity to participate, to the extent that they can, on each step of the task. On some steps, they may be able to complete the movement independently; on others, the teacher will have to provide full physical assistance. Nevertheless, it is extremely important to encourage as much participation as possible.

Teachers should also look for other ways to construct a dressing task that may make it easier for the student with more severe disabilities. A task analysis need not be constructed in the order in which it typically occurs for nondisabled individuals. It is generally better to stress satisfactory completion of the function of a task, instead of adherence to the common form of the task. For example, Heller et al. (2001) describe an uncommon process for putting on a coat:

> Flipping a coat over one's head is a technique often used by students with coordination or weakness problems. The student lays the garment flat on her lap, the floor or a table. The collar should be near her body with the front of the coat on top and the lining showing. The student can then push both arms into the sleeves or push the involved arm in first and the other arm second. Ducking the head forward while extending the arms over the head is next. Finally the coat is slipped into place when the student shrugs her shoulders and pulls down with her arms. (p. 552)

Working with parents and occupational therapists, teachers may devise several additional ways to facilitate dressing.

Besides varying the way in which the student may put clothes on, parents may also be advised to purchase for their children with multiple disabilities clothes that are more comfortable and better meet their unique needs. Heller et al. (2001) suggest expandable neck openings and stretchable fabrics, large zipper tabs, large buttons that are loosely sewn on, Velcro fastenings, and large hook-and-eye fasteners that are easy to see. Students who wear leg braces may need full-length crotch openings in the inseam that can be fastened with zippers or Velcro. Wide pant legs also may be helpful. An individual who uses full-length crutches may benefit from double-stitched underarm seams. Pants and culottes are often more comfortable and modest for girls and women in wheelchairs than are skirts or dresses. Also for individuals in wheelchairs, a wool cape can provide warmth in cold weather and can also be taken off and put on more easily than a coat or jacket. Table 15–3 provides additional suggestions for modifying clothing for students with multiple severe disabilities.

Teaching Skills Related to Dressing

As with other skills, dressing should be taught as much as possible in relation to other skills, as part of a natural sequence of activities whenever possible and in the context of teaching other skills. For example, in the discussion on teaching toileting skills it was pointed out that this is an appropriate opportunity to also teach associated dressing skills. Other times of the day also provide opportunities, for example, arriving at school in the morning, going out to and coming in from outside play activities, dressing for physical education, changing clothes for different work activities, putting on smocks for art activities, and getting ready to go home in the afternoon. While teaching dressing skills, the teacher can also teach various incidental skills and thus increase the efficacy of instruction. For example, the color, size, and weight of the material might be taught. The concepts of right and left, back and front, top and bottom, and in and out can be taught in an incidental, natural fashion.

Students with more advanced abilities may have already learned many of the more basic dressing skills, but it may be appropriate to teach them other skills, particularly related to choice making and self-determination. One very important such skill is appropriate clothing

Table 15–3 Specific Suggestions for Modifying Clothing

Problem or Disability	*Suggested Solutions*
Difficulty with pullover shirts or sweaters	Use garments of stretchable knits Use elasticized necklines Open seams under arms and at sides Use Velcro dots along seam lines Use large sleeve openings
Difficulty with cardigans, jackets,or front-opening shirts	Use garments of stretchable knits Select styles with fullness in back (add gathers,action pleats, gussets) Use large sleeve openings Use smooth, nonslippery fabrics
Difficulty with pants or pull-on skirts	Sew loops at waistband Use elasticized waistbands
Difficulty with socks	Use tube socks Sew loop tabs at top sides of socks
Crutches	Add fabric patches to underside Line garment Choose knit or stretch fabric Select longer shirttails Use overblouses or sweaters
Long leg braces or cast	Choose pants legs loose enough to fit over braces or cast Apply long zipper to inside seam

Source: Educating Children with Multiple Disabilities: A Transdisciplinary Approach (3rd ed., p. 367), by F. P. Orelove and D. Sobsey, 1996, Baltimore: Paul H. Brookes Publishing Co. Reprinted by permission.

selection. For example, Nutter and Reid (1978) taught women with cognitive disabilities how to select color-coordinated clothes that met community standards of normalcy. They did so by teaching them to match appropriate-colored blouses to selected slacks. Obviously, this type of skill is important. Individuals who can dress themselves have even more independence if they select the types of clothes that they should wear. Besides color coordination, learning to select clothes for different types of weather, different occasions, and different seasons may also be important skills related to dressing.

Other Suggestions for Improving Dressing

Some final general suggestions for teaching dressing skills to students with severe disabilities include the following:

- It is generally easier to teach undressing before dressing. If appropriate (i.e., if undressing and dressing are both to be taught), the teacher should teach undressing first in order to give the student initial success with the experience.
- The same principle (i.e., easier before more difficult) should also be applied to other dressing skills when appropriate. For example, it is easier to teach putting on shoes than putting on socks, pants are easier to put on than shirts, and button shirts are easier than pullover shirts.
- The student may have preferences for wearing certain articles of clothing. If the teacher can learn from the parent what these are, these pieces may be used during instruction to heighten the student's interest and motivation.
- Although teaching should occur at natural times of the day, the more often instruction is offered, the faster the skill will be learned. For particularly difficult skills, short periods of massed practice instruction may be appropriate.
- For some students, it may be necessary to work on their attention to the task, as well as on the task itself. This may be done by reinforcing them for looking at the clothes for greater periods of time and then reducing the frequency of reinforcement after adequate attending skills have been developed. The teacher should not, however, attempt to teach attending before teaching dressing, because this would fractionalize the skills too much.
- As with other skills, brief periods of time-out may be sufficient to reduce inappropriate behaviors during dressing instruction periods.
- A well-dressed individual is often reinforced for his attire. Students learning to dress should always be naturally reinforced for looking nice after they finish a dressing skill. This reinforcement should occur in the presence of others.
- Teachers should always know what parents are working on, and vice versa, in the area of dressing. Using the same procedures to practice dressing skills both at home and at school will hasten the learning process.
- When learning skills, practice in using different types of clothing of the same form (different types of sweaters) in different locations will increase skill generalization.

Learning Personal Hygiene and Grooming Skills

Personal hygiene and grooming skills include the things a person does to (or for) his or her body on a regular basis to maintain health and an acceptable standard of personal presentation, such as bathing or showering; washing hands and face; brushing teeth, flossing, and using mouthwash; shaving; using deodorant; washing and drying hair; using rollers or a curling iron; using cologne, perfume, and powder; combing or brushing hair; taking care of menstruation; and using cosmetics (Baker & Brightman, 1996; Wilcox & Bellamy, 1987). Some of these activities are very important for health purposes; others are important for self-expression or for developing personal appeal. Obviously, it is not possible to discuss all these here. However, basically, the procedures for most are similar to procedures that were discussed in Chapter 7 and throughout this chapter. Assessment must be conducted to determine what skills the person needs and the degree to which they exist. If it is desirable to teach them, a task analysis should be constructed along with a format for data collection. Finally, a systematic means of instruction must be developed, including a plan for generalization.

Two critical skills for hygiene purposes that are often neglected when instructing persons with severe disabilities are personal dental care and menstrual care for young women. These skills are discussed here in some detail.

Personal Dental Care

Students with severe disabilities, like other people, need to maintain proper oral hygiene. In many cases this is even more significant than in the general population, because an individual's disabilities may directly or indirectly lead to inordinate dental problems. Poor motor control and muscle tone, mouth breathing, tooth grinding, finger sucking, and tongue thrusting are common among students with severe disabilities and may lead to periodontal disease and malocclusion (Acs, Wai Ng, Helpen, & Rosenberg, 2002). Additional problems may be caused by the buildup of plaque, resulting in gum disease, dental decay, and cavities. This is sometimes compounded by the use of drugs to control seizures that have a side effect of excessive gum growth, infection, and bleeding. The best approach to dealing with such problems is through preventive maintenance, that is, caring for the teeth and gums as well as possible to prevent or reduce dental problems (Acs et al., 2002; Coffee, 1977).

Research has demonstrated that many students with severe disabilities can learn to brush their teeth or assist in the process of toothbrushing (Abramson & Wunderlich, 1972; Horner & Keilitz, 1975; Snell, Lewis, & Houghton, 1989). The instructional methods are similar to those used to teach others self-care skills, beginning with a task analysis of the process. The task analysis used by Horner and Keilitz (1975) is presented in Figure 15–5.

A graduated guidance or system of least prompts method can be used to guide students through each step of the toothbrushing task. Horner and Keilitz used the latter, which included the following prompts: (1) no help, (2) verbal instruction, (3) demonstration and verbal instruction, and (4) physical guidance and verbal instruction if necessary. Even students who lack the ability to self-conduct many of the steps of toothbrushing can often still participate. Note the task analysis used by Snell et al. (1989) presented in Figure 15–6. Students who had severe physical disabilities were able to participate in dental care by opening their mouth and holding it open, rinsing the mouth, and turning the head back and forth to assist in wiping the mouth.

Whether students with severe disabilities require more or less assistance to effectively brush their teeth,

Figure 15–5 Description of Toothbrushing Skills

Source: "Training Mentally Retarded Adolescents to Brush Their Teeth," by D. R. Horner and I. Keilitz, 1975, *Journal of Applied Behavior Analysis, 8,* p. 303. Reprinted by permission.

1. *Pick up and hold the toothbrush.* The student should turn on the water and pick up the toothbrush by the handle.
2. *Wet the toothbrush.* The student should continue to hold the toothbrush, placing the bristles under the running water for at least 5 seconds. Then, the student should turn off the running water and lay the toothbrush down.
3. *Remove the cap from the toothpaste.* The student should place the tube of toothpaste in his least-preferred hand, unscrew the cap with the thumb and index finger of his preferred hand, and set the cap on the sink.
4. *Apply the toothpaste to the brush.* The student should pick up the toothbrush by the handle, hold the back part of the bristles against the opening of the toothpaste tube, squeeze the tube, move the tube toward the front bristles as toothpaste flows out on top of the bristles, and lay the toothbrush on the sink with the bristles up.
5. *Replace the cap on the toothpaste.* The student should pick up the toothpaste cap with the thumb and index finger of the preferred hand, screw the cap on the toothpaste tube, which is held in the least-preferred hand, lay the tube of toothpaste down, and with the preferred hand pick up the toothbrush by the handle.
6. *Brush the outside surfaces of the teeth.* The student should brush the outside surfaces of the upper and lower teeth on both sides and in the center of the mouth, using either an up and down or back and forth motion, for at least 30 seconds.
7. *Brush the biting surfaces of the teeth.* The student should brush the biting surfaces of the upper and lower teeth on both sides and in the center of the mouth, using a back and forth motion, for at least 30 seconds.

Figure 15–5 Continued

8. *Brush the inside surfaces of the teeth.* The student should brush the inside surfaces of the upper and lower teeth on both sides and in the center of the mouth, using a back and forth motion, for at least 30 seconds.
9. *Fill the cup with water.* The student should lay the toothbrush down, pick up the cup, place it under the faucet, turn on the water, fill the cup, and turn off the water.
10. *Rinse the mouth.* The student should spit out any excess toothpaste foam, take a sip of water, hold it in the mouth, swish it around in the mouth, and spit it out. If any toothpaste foam remains, the procedure should be repeated.
11. *Wipe the mouth.* The student should pull a tissue from the container (or pick up a hand towel) and dry his mouth.
12. *Rinse the toothbrush.* The student should pick up the toothbrush by the handle, turn on the water, and place the bristles under the running water until the bristles are free of toothpaste (any toothpaste not removed by the water may be dislodged by drawing the fingers across the bristles), turn off the water, and lay the toothbrush down.
13. *Rinse the sink.* The student should turn on the water, rub around the inside of the sink with the hand to wash any residue of toothpaste or toothpaste foam down the drain, and turn off the water.
14. *Put the equipment away.* The student should put the toothpaste and toothbrush in the proper storage place. (If a glass and hand towel are used, these should be placed in the proper place.)
15. *Discard the disposables.* Any used paper cups and tissues should be placed in a waste receptacle.

a thorough brushing should occur at least once a day. Additionally, students should learn to floss and to use mouthwash if they are physically able to do so. Some students may lack the fine-motor skills required for flossing or may have a tendency to swallow the mouthwash or the toothpaste. In these cases the teacher should attempt to teach the student as much as possible and do for the student those things that he simply cannot do, unless these needs are adequately handled at home.

For students who must have oral hygiene provided for them by another person, several suggestions are noteworthy (Acs et al., 2002; Coffee, 1977). If there is a problem with swallowing toothpaste or mouthwash, these products may be omitted and only water used. It is actually more important to adequately brush all the surfaces of the teeth at least once a day than to use toothpaste. Also, children who have very sensitive teeth or gums may have their teeth thoroughly cleaned with a warm wet washcloth or gauze pad. One thorough cleaning per day is better than several less adequate attempts. Additional suggestions made by Coffee (1977) include the following:

- The five surfaces of each tooth must be cleaned. The side surfaces that cannot be reached by toothbrush must be flossed.
- A soft, nylon-bristled toothbrush is the best to use. Toothbrushes with enlarged or adapted handles may be easier to handle for some students. An occupational therapist should be consulted to assist with this need.
- A systematic brushing pattern should be used to avoid missing any surface areas.
- Brushing should be done with a gentle back-and-forth or circular motion, with the bristles held at a slight angle to tooth surfaces.
- Each brushing should be followed with flossing, stretching the floss across fingers or using a floss holder and cleaning the inside surfaces of each tooth.
- A commercial plaque-disclosing solution should be used to identify areas that have been missed.
- Assistance should be sought from the school nurse or occupational therapist to learn how to get the student

Figure 15–6 Task Analysis of Toothbrushing

Toothbrushing Discriminative stimuli (teacher) "Brush your teeth."		Task steps (Student and teacher)
Presents toothbrush		1. Open your mouth wide.
Inserts toothbrush		2. Keep it open (5 sec).
	Teacher:	a. Brushes outside of upper left teeth, back to front.
		b. Brushes cutting edge of upper left teeth, back to front.
Removes toothbrush		3. Close your mouth (lips touch).
Presents toothbrush		4. Open your mouth wide.
Inserts toothbrush		5. Keep it open (5 sec).
	Teacher:	a. Brushes outside of lower left teeth, back to front.
		b. Brushes cutting edge of lower left teeth, back to front.
Removes toothbrush		6. Close your mouth (lips touch).
Presents toothbrush		7. Open your mouth wide.
Inserts toothbrush		8. Keep it open (5 sec).
	Teacher:	a. Brushes outside of upper right teeth, back to front.
		b. Brushes cutting edge of lower right teeth, back to front.
Removes toothbrush		9. Close your mouth (lips touch).
Presents toothbrush		10. Open your mouth wide.
Inserts toothbrush		11. Keep it open (5 sec).
	Teacher:	a. Brushes outside of lower right teeth, back to front.
		b. Brushes cutting edge of lower right teeth, back to front.
Removes toothbrush		12. Close your mouth (lips touch).
Rinsing Discriminative stimuli (teacher) "Rinse your mouth."		Task steps (Student & teacher)
Squirts water into student's mouth; holds bowl under chin		1. Drop your head (chin to chest).
		2. Spit (water drops from mouth into bowl).
Removes bowl		3. Lift your head up.
Wiping Discriminative stimuli (teacher) "Wipe your mouth."		Task steps (Student & teacher)
Holds paper towel at the middle of student's mouth		1. Turn your head to one side (turns midline to cheek and back to midline).
		2. Turn your head to other side (turns midline to cheek and back to midline).
Removes paper towel and places in trash		

Source: "Acquisition and Maintenance of Toothbrushing Skills by Students with Cerebral Palsy and Mental Retardation," by M. E. Snell, A. P. Lewis, and A. Houghton, 1989, *Journal of the Association for Persons with Severe Handicaps, 14,* p. 218. Reprinted by permission of TASH, Baltimore, MD.

to open her mouth and hold it open if doing so is normally a problem. Often, slight pressure on the jaw can be used to open the mouth, and two or three gauze-covered tongue blades can be used to hold the mouth open. In some cases, students may learn to hold the mouth open for short periods of time so that brushing or flossing can occur (Snell et al., 1989).

- The student should be encouraged to look in a mirror to see her clean teeth after brushing and should be reinforced for practicing good oral hygiene.

In addition to brushing and flossing, healthful eating habits, fluoridation, and regular dental care can greatly reduce diseases of gums and teeth (Acs et al., 2002). Snacks should include fresh vegetables and nuts if the student can handle them; and if the local water is not fluoridated, fluoride tablets or fluoridated mouthwash or toothpaste can be used. Early visits to the dentist may begin at 1 year of age.

Menstrual Care

A key need for young women is to learn how to manage their own menstrual care independently. As with other personal care areas, this may be taught at home by parents or caregivers, but there is sometimes a need for it to be taught in school. Naturally, the teacher should have a high level of communication with the student's home if it is deemed necessary to provide instruction in this area at school. In some cases, the young woman may be instructed primarily at home, and the teacher's role may be to provide advice about instructional procedures.

Two methods may be used to provide instruction, and it is suggested that input from parents or caregivers and other team members be solicited on the method to be used. This is very important; different individuals have different opinions on the appropriateness of each approach (Epps, Prescott, & Horner, 1990). One method is to provide direct instruction to the student both during menses and during role-playing activities in which sanitary napkins and underwear have been stained with red dye, food coloring, or nontoxic theater blood. The second method is to use large adult dolls and miniature clothes, underwear, and napkins to demonstrate appropriate personal care during menses (Epps, Stern, & Horner, 1990; Richman, Ponticas, Page, & Epps, 1986; Richman, Reiss, Bauman, & Bailey, 1984).

The primary objective of both approaches is for the student to recognize that there is a need to respond appropriately when the underwear and/or the sanitary napkin is stained. In the role-playing situation the student is taught to go into the bathroom, check her underwear and pad (if she is wearing one), and, if the pad or underwear is stained, to remove them and dispose of them properly, wash hands, obtain clean underwear and another pad, and put them on. Several learning opportunities need to be provided with the student experiencing both needing to change the underwear and/or pad and having no need to make a change, that is, when no stain exists. Of course, training should occur when the student is having her period, but role playing can also be used to increase the frequency of instruction. When this is done, the instructional process begins with the young woman donning prestained underwear or pad. In both the real situation and the role-playing situation, the student is cued to "check your pants."

Teaching menstrual care through the use of dolls has been shown to be a successful approach in at least one study (Epps, Stern, & Horner, 1990). The advantage of this approach is that several young women can be given the simulated instruction simultaneously, and then self-use of the skill can be carried out at home or in private. Using this approach, the teacher needs to create all the materials in miniature form and then, as with the first method, teach the students how to respond to the different situations.

Again, regardless of the approach used, it is critical that parental or caregiver permission and cooperation be sought. Of course, for ethical reasons the training should be provided by a professional woman. If the teacher is male, a female counterpart should be sought to provide instruction. If the school nurse is female, she is the ideal individual to provide the training.

Other Suggestions for Improving Hygiene and Personal Grooming

When teaching any hygiene or personal grooming skill, the following general suggestions are recommended:

- This is probably the instructional domain that calls for the most cooperation and interaction with the home. The teacher should know what is considered important and what idiosyncratic features of instruction should be used to coordinate with what is done in the home.
- Many skills in this area bear on the health of an individual and should not be ignored if there is a need for instruction.
- Most people normally engage in grooming activities to be socially accepted, as well as to have good health. Teachers and others should make sure

a strong dose of positive, age-appropriate social reinforcement follows appropriate grooming behavior.

- Students who have had many personal care skills provided for them in the past may be uncomfortable when initially being taught to take care of these needs themselves. The teacher may need to move gradually but surely in these areas.
- Learning personal care skills is a private matter, and training should be conducted in private, natural locations and with respect for the needs of the individual.
- Safety should also be a concern when students are learning skills in this area. Toxic material that could be ingested should be avoided, and even nontoxic material, such as mouthwash, should be carefully monitored. The teacher should also be extremely careful about water temperature when teaching washing and bathing.

Conclusion

There is nothing more personal than the way we go about caring for our bodily needs. Not only does it help us to stay healthy, but it also allows us to make a statement about ourselves to everyone with whom we come in contact. Most of us learned how to take care of our personal needs in an incidental way, following, for the most part, the patterns of behavior typical of our parents, family, and culture.

For several reasons, many people with severe disabilities must be specifically taught such things as how to use the toilet appropriately or how to brush their teeth. For some, even given direct instruction, complete learning may not be possible. Individuals with the most significant disabilities may be able to manage only partial participation as someone else directly assists them in carrying out a great deal of the task. Nevertheless, learning as much as possible to care for one's personal needs is important, because it allows people to be more a part of their families, their circle of friends, and their society.

We also cannot forget the importance of self-determination and self-management when students are learning personal care skills. The opportunity to determine for oneself the particular way to comb or brush hair, for example, or the brand of deodorant or soap to use, can be very significant in a person's life. When individuals are more involved in the decisions that are made about how to take care of themselves, it is likely that they will extend greater efforts to do so. Similarly, students, to the extent possible, should be taught to manage their daily personal skills themselves. Putting on your jacket before going outside when the teacher tells you to is one thing; knowing that the outside air is cool and thus you need to find your jacket and put it on is another. If the student is capable of learning to be responsive in this way, we should teach him to do so. Then we are putting the emphasis on "personal" as much as on "care."

Questions for Reflection

1. In comparison to other skills that might be important for students with severe disabilities to learn, how do self-care skills compare? When should you *not* focus on these skills?
2. In the interest of increasing self-determination, should individuals have the right not to learn or practice certain self-care skills?
3. Do you believe most persons with severe disabilities can learn to use self-management to maintain appropriate self-care skills? What procedures would be helpful?
4. What other skills (besides eating skills) could be learned during mealtimes?
5. In what type of environment do you like to eat? Do you think persons with severe disabilities would like to learn to eat appropriately in this type of environment?
6. What ethical guidelines should be developed for working with individuals, particularly those who are older, on private activities such as toilet training or menstrual care?
7. What are some natural times and places to teach dressing skills during the day? How about in the regular classroom?
8. How does a person's dressing ability relate to his participation in various social activities?
9. In what ways might students without disabilities play important roles when students with severe disabilities are learning self-care skills?

References

Abramson, S. E., & Wunderlich, R. A. (1972). Dental hygiene training for retardates: An application of behavioral techniques. *Mental Retardation, 10*(3), 6–8.

Acs, G., Wai Ng, M., Helpen, M. L., & Rosenberg, H. M. (2002). Dental care: Promoting health and preventing disease. In M. L. Batshaw (Ed.), *Children with disabilities* (5th Ed., pp. 567–578). Baltimore: Paul H. Brookes.

Alberto, P. A., & Troutman, A. C. (2002). *Applied behavior analysis for teachers* (6th Ed.). Upper Saddle River, NJ: Merrill/Prentice Hall.

Albin, J. B. (1977). Some variables influencing the maintenance of acquired self-feeding behavior in profoundly retarded children. *Mental Retardation, 15*(5), 49–52.

Alexander, R. (2001). Feeding and swallowing. In J. L. Bigge, S. J. Best, & K. W. Heller (Eds.), *Teaching individuals with physical, health, or multiple disabilities* (4th Ed., pp. 504–535). Upper Saddle River, NJ: Merrill/Prentice Hall.

Anderson, D. M. (1982). Ten years later: Toilet training in the post-Azrin-and-Foxx era. *Journal of the Association for the Severely Handicapped, 7*(2), 71–79.

Azrin, N. H., & Armstrong, P. M. (1973). The "mini-meal"—A method for teaching eating skills to the profoundly retarded. *Mental Retardation, 11*(1), 9–13.

Azrin, N. H., Bugle, C., & O'Brien, F. (1971). Behavioral engineering: Two apparatuses for toilet training retarded children. *Journal of Applied Behavior Analysis, 4,* 249–253.

Azrin, N. H., & Foxx, R. M. (1971). A rapid method of toilet training the institutionalized retarded. *Journal of Applied Behavior Analysis, 4,* 89–99.

Azrin, N. H., Schaeffer, R. M., & Wesolowski, M. D. (1976). A rapid method of teaching profoundly retarded persons to dress. *Mental Retardation, 14*(6), 29–33.

Azrin, N. H., Sneed, T. J., & Foxx, R. M. (1974). Dry-bed training: Rapid elimination of childhood enuresis. *Behaviour Research and Therapy, 12,* 147–156.

Baker, B. L., & Brightman, A. J. (1996). *Steps to independence: Teaching everyday skills to children with special needs* (3rd Ed.). Baltimore: Paul H. Brookes.

Banerdt, B., & Bricker, D. (1978). A training program for selected self-feeding skills for the motorically impaired. *AAESPH Review, 3,* 222–229.

Barton, E. S., Guess, D., Garcia, E., & Baer, D. (1970). Improvements of retardates' mealtime behaviors by timeout procedures using the multiple baseline technique. *Journal of Applied Behavior Analysis, 3,* 77–84.

Berkowitz, S., Sherry, P. J., & Davis, B. A. (1971). Teaching self-feeding skills to profound retardates using reinforcement and fading procedures. *Behavior Therapy, 2,* 62–67.

Christian, W. P., Hollomon, S. W., & Lanier, C. L. (1973). An attendant operated feeding program. *Mental Retardation, 11*(5), 35–37.

Coffee, L. (1977). Planning daily care for healthy teeth. In R. Perske, A. Clifton, B. M. McLean, & J. I. Stein (Eds.), *Mealtimes for severely and profoundly handicapped persons: New concepts and attitudes* (pp. 119–122). Baltimore: University Park Press.

Diorio, M. S., & Konarski, E. A. (1984). Evaluation of a method for teaching dressing skills to profoundly mentally retarded persons. *American Journal of Mental Deficiency, 89,* 307–309.

Dunlap, G., Koegel, R. L., & Koegel, L. K. (1984). Continuity of treatment: Toilet training in multiple community settings. *Journal of the Association for Persons with Severe Handicaps, 9,* 134–141.

Ellis, N. R. (1963). Toilet training and the severely defective patient: An S–R reinforcement analysis. *American Journal of Mental Deficiency, 68,* 98–103.

Epps, S., Prescott, A. L., & Horner, R. H. (1990). Social acceptability of menstrual care training methods for young women with developmental disabilities. *Education and Training in Mental Retardation, 25,* 33–44.

Epps, S., Stern, R. J., & Horner, R. H. (1990). Comparison of simulation training on self and using a doll for teaching generalized menstrual care to women with severe mental retardation. *Research in Developmental Disabilities, 11,* 37–66.

Farlow, L. J., & Snell, M. E. (2000). Teaching basic self-care skills. In M. E. Snell & F. Brown (Ed.), *Instruction of students with severe disabilities* (5th Ed., pp. 331–408). Upper Saddle River, NJ: Merrill/Prentice Hall.

Foxx, R. M., & Azrin, N. H. (1973). *Toilet training the retarded.* Champaign, IL: Research Press.

Freagon, S., & Rotatori, A. F. (1982). Comparing natural and artificial environments in training self-care skills to group home residents. *Journal of the Association for the Severely Handicapped, 7*(3), 73–86.

Garff, J. T., & Story, K. (1998). The use of self-management strategies for increasing appropriate hygiene of persons with disabilities in supported employment settings. *Education and Training in Mental Retardation and Developmental Disabilities, 33,* 179–188.

Giles, D. K., & Wolf, M. M. (1966). Toilet training institutionalized severe retardates: An application of behavior modification techniques. *American Journal of Mental Deficiency, 70,* 766–780.

Groves, I. D., & Carroccio, D. F. (1971). A self-feeding program for the severely and profoundly retarded. *Mental Retardation, 9*(3), 10–12.

Heller, K. W., Bigge, J., & Allgood, P. (2001). Adaptations for personal independence. In J. L. Bigge, S. J. Best, & K. W. Heller (Eds.), *Teaching individuals with physical, health, or multiple disabilities* (4th Ed., pp. 536–565). Upper Saddle River, NJ: Merrill/Prentice Hall.

Henriksen, K., & Doughty, R. (1972). Decelerating undesired mealtime behavior in a group of profoundly retarded boys. *American Journal of Mental Deficiency, 72,* 40–44.

Horner, D. R., & Keilitz, I. (1975). Training mentally retarded adolescents to brush their teeth. *Journal of Applied Behavior Analysis, 8,* 301–309.

Hundziak, M., Maurer, R. A., & Watson, L. S. (1965). Operant conditioning in toilet training severely mentally retarded boys. *American Journal of Mental Deficiency, 70,* 120–124.

Kahng, S. W., Tarbox, J., & Wilke, A. E. (2001). Use of a multicomponent treatment for food refusal. *Journal of Applied Behavior Analysis, 34,* 93–96.

Kimbrell, D. L., Luckey, R. E., Barbuto, P. F., & Love, J. G. (1967). Operation dry pants: An intensive habit training program for the severely and profoundly retarded. *Mental Retardation, 5*(2), 32–36.

Kramer, L., & Whitehurst, C. (1981). Effects of button features on self-dressing in young retarded children. *Education and Training of the Mentally Retarded, 16,* 277–283.

Lancioni, G. E. (1980). Teaching independent toileting to profoundly retarded deaf–blind children. *Behavior Therapy, 11,* 234–244.

Leibowitz, M. J., & Holcer, P. (1974). Building and maintaining self-feeding skills in a retarded child. *American Journal of Occupational Therapy, 28,* 545–548.

Lemke, H., & Mitchell, R. D. (1972). Controlling the behavior of a profoundly retarded child. *American Journal of Occupational Therapy, 26,* 261–264.

Lent, J. R. (1975). Teaching daily living skills. In J. M. Kauffman & J. M. Payne (Eds.), *Mental retardation: Introduction and personal perspectives* (pp. 246–274). Upper Saddle River, NJ: Merrill/Prentice Hall.

Mahoney, K., Van Wagenen, R. K., & Meyerson, L. (1971). Toilet training of normal and retarded children. *Journal of Applied Behavior Analysis, 4,* 173–181.

Martin, G. L., Kehoe, B., Bird, E., Jensen, V., & Darbyshire, M. (1971). Operant conditioning in the dressing behavior of severely retarded girls. *Mental Retardation, 9*(3), 27–30.

Martin, L., McDonald, S., & Omichinski, M. (1971). An operant analysis of response interactions during meals with severely retarded girls. *American Journal of Mental Deficiency, 76,* 68–75.

McKelvey, J. L., Sisson, L. A., Van Hasselt, V. B., & Hersen, M. (1992). An approach to teaching self dressing to a child with dual sensory impairment. *Teaching Exceptional Children, 25,* 12–15.

Miller, H. R., Patton, M. E., & Henton, K. R. (1971). Behavior modification of a profoundly retarded child: A case report. *Behavior Therapy, 2,* 375–384.

Minge, M. R., & Ball, T. S. (1967). Teaching self-help skills to profoundly retarded patients. *American Journal of Mental Deficiency, 71,* 864–868.

Mohr, C., & Sharpley, C. F. (1988). Multi-modal treatment of nocturnal enuresis. *Education and Training in Mental Retardation, 23,* 70–75.

Mori, A. A., & Masters, L. F. (1980). *Teaching the severely mentally retarded: Adaptive skills training.* Germantown, MD: Aspen Systems Corporation.

Nelson, G. L., Cone, J. D., & Hanson, C. R. (1975). Training correct utensil use in retarded children: Modeling vs. physical guidance. *American Journal of Mental Deficiency, 80,* 114–122.

Nutter, D., & Reid, D. H. (1978). Teaching retarded women a clothing selection skill using community norms. *Journal of Applied Behavior Analysis, 11,* 475–487.

O'Brien, F., & Azrin, N. H. (1972). Developing proper mealtime behaviors of the institutionalized retarded. *Journal of Applied Behavior Analysis, 5,* 389–399.

O'Brien, F., Bugle, C., & Azrin, N. H. (1972). Training and maintaining a retarded child's proper eating. *Journal of Applied Behavior Analysis, 5,* 67–72.

Orelove, F. P., & Sobsey, D. (1996). *Educating children with multiple disabilities: A transdisciplinary approach* (3rd Ed.). Baltimore: Paul H. Brookes.

Osarchuk, M. (1973). Operant methods of toilet behavior training the severely and profoundly retarded: A review. *Journal of Special Education, 7,* 423–437.

Perske, R., Clifton, A., McLean, B. M., & Stein, J. I. (Eds.). (1977). *Mealtimes for severely and profoundly handicapped persons: New concepts and attitudes.* Baltimore: University Park Press.

Pierce, K. L., & Schreibman, L. (1994). Teaching daily living skills to children with autism in unsupervised settings through pictorial self-management. *Journal of Applied Behavior Analysis, 27,* 471–481.

Reese, G. M., & Snell, M. E. (1991). Putting on and removing coats and jackets: The acquisition and maintenance of skills by children with severe multiple disabilities. *Education and Training in Mental Retardation, 26,* 398–410.

Richman, G. S., Ponticas, Y., Page, T. J., & Epps, S. (1986). Simulation procedures for teaching independent menstrual care to mentally retarded persons. *Applied Research in Mental Retardation, 7,* 21–35.

Richman, G. S., Reiss, M. L., Bauman, K. E., & Bailey, J. S. (1984). Teaching menstrual care to mentally retarded women: Acquisition, generalization, and maintenance. *Journal of Applied Behavior Analysis, 17,* 441–451.

Shore, B. A., Babbitt, R. L., Williams, K. E., Coe, D. A., & Snyder, A. (1998). Use of texture fading in the treatment of food selectivity. *Journal of Applied Behavior Analysis, 31,* 621–633.

Smith, P. S. (1979). A comparison of different methods of toilet training the mentally handicapped. *Behaviour Research and Therapy, 17,* 33–43.

Snell, M. E., Lewis, A. P., & Houghton, A. (1989). Acquisition and maintenance of toothbrushing skills by students with cerebral palsy and mental retardation. *Journal of the Association for Persons with Severe Handicaps, 14,* 216–226.

Song, A. Y., & Ghandi, R. (1974). An analysis of behavior during the acquisition and maintenance phases of self spoon feeding skills of profound retardates. *Mental Retardation, 12*(1), 25–28.

Trott, M. C. (1977). Applications of Foxx and Azrin toilet training for the retarded in a school program. *Education and Training of the Mentally Retarded, 12,* 336–338.

Turnbull, A. P., Blue-Banning, M. J., Anderson, E. L., Turnbull, H. R., Seaton, K. A., & Dinas, P. A. (1996). Enhancing self-determination through group action planning: A holistic emphasis. In D. J. Sands & M. L. Wehmeyer (Eds.), *Self-determination across the lifespan: Independence and choice for people with disabilities* (pp. 237–256). Baltimore: Paul H. Brookes.

Wehmeyer, M. L. (1996). Self-determination as an educational outcome: Why is it important to children, youth, and adults with disabilities? In D. J. Sands & M. L. Wehmeyer (Eds.), *Self-determination across the lifespan: Independence and choice for people with disabilities* (pp. 15–34). Baltimore: Paul H. Brookes.

Wehmeyer, M. L., & Kelchner, K. (1995). *The Arc's self-determination scale.* Arlington, TX: The Arc National Headquarters.

Westling, D. L. (1996). What do parents of children with moderate and severe disabilities want? *Education and Training in Mental Retardation and Developmental Disabilities, 31,* 86–114.

Westling, D. L., & Murden, L. (1977). Self-help skills training: A review of operant studies. *Journal of Special Education, 12,* 253–283.

Wilcox, B., & Bellamy, G. T. (1987). *The activities catalog: An alternative curriculum for youth and adults with severe disabilities.* Baltimore: Paul H. Brookes.

Williams, F. E., & Sloop, E. W. (1978). Success with a shortened Foxx–Azrin toilet training program. *Education and Training of the Mentally Retarded, 13,* 399–402.

Wilson, P. G., Reid, D. H., Phillips, J. F., & Burgio, L. D. (1984). Normalization of institutional mealtimes for profoundly rettarded persons: Effects and noneffects of teaching family style dining. *Journal of Applied Behavior Analysis, 17,* 189–201.

Wright, C. S., & Vollmer, T. R. (2002). Evaluation of a treatment package to reduce rapid eating. *Journal of Applied Behavior Analysis, 35*, 89–93.

Young, K. R., West, R. P., Howard, V. F., & Whitney, R. (1986). Acquisition, fluency training, generalization, and maintenance of dressing skills of two developmentally disabled children. *Education and Treatment of Children, 9*(1), 16–29.

Zeiler, M. S., & Jervey, S. S. (1968). Development of behavior: Self-feeding. *Journal of Consulting and Clinical Psychology, 32*(2), 164–168.

CHAPTER 16

Teaching Leisure and Recreational Skills

In this chapter the importance of teaching students leisure and recreation skills is discussed. The chapter provides guidelines on how to select and teach leisure skills and emphasizes the development of skills that may be used in inclusive environments.

The Importance of Recreation Skills

The leisure and recreation curricular domain involves the instruction of skills that students may use for enjoyment and entertainment in their free time. *Leisure* is defined as freedom from occupation, spare time, unoccupied time; *recreation* means refreshment from weariness, any pleasurable interest, amusement. Recreation has been identified as a major curricular domain in addition to community, vocational, and domestic skills.

Instruction of recreation skills is particularly important for students with severe disabilities because of their limited skill repertoires and difficulty in accessing environments and peers. Teachers of students without disabilities do not typically address recreation skill development outside physical education, library skills, and art and music instruction; they are usually assured that the recreation needs of their students are met outside school hours or during the more informal parts (e.g., free play, after school) of the day. Unfortunately, an assumption that students with severe disabilities can meet their recreation needs without instruction cannot be made, so a systematic approach to the development of recreation skills must be provided. In this chapter the importance of recreation as a curricular domain is presented, along with strategies for teaching recreation skills. The chapter provides a detailed discussion on how to select appropriate recreation and leisure activities, with an emphasis on choice, age appropriateness, and peer interaction. In addition, the issues surrounding friendship development are discussed.

Recreation Skill Instruction

What would your life be without recreation time? Many of us complain about the fast pace of our society, which leaves little time to "play." The time for leisure pursuits is highly valued in our society. If you think about your life without leisure time you might describe it as boring, stressful, and lonely. Most people use recreation time to build friendships with others, relax, keep physically fit, explore interests, and learn new skills and as a diversion from work time.

People with severe disabilities often have large blocks of time with nothing to do. Because they may be limited in mobility and in access to others, they spend a large amount of time waiting for someone to assist them. The time available for leisure pursuits is not an issue; it is usually the lack of opportunities to engage in recreation activities and the lack of recreation skills that are barriers to leisure activities. Researchers have expressed concern that a majority of adults with disabilities spend their free time at home or within solitary activities (Sparrow & Mayne, 1990; Wehman, Schleien, & Kiernan, 1980).

Recreation skill instruction is important for individuals with severe disabilities for many of the same reasons that it is important to all other persons in society. Recreation is fun, provides opportunities for social affiliation, increases physical fitness, and offers a satisfying way to spend one's free time. In addition, participation in play activities and training in play skills have been related to increases in skills in other domains (Schleien, Heyne, & Dattilo, 1995; Vandercook, 1991; Voeltz & Apffel, 1981; Voeltz, Wuerch, & Wilcox, 1982). Many recreational and leisure skill activities create opportunities for persons with severe disabilities and nondisabled peers to practice social interaction and communication behaviors and to develop friendships (Schleien, Meyer, Heyne, & Brandt, 1995).

Recreational and leisure activities help to eliminate unstructured or "down" time; they provide for constructive use of free time. An increase in play skills has been related to a decrease in negative and inappropriate social behavior (Gaylord-Ross, 1980; Schleien, Kiernan, & Wehman, 1981). Moreover, an increase in the constructive use of leisure time may reduce the need for supervision by others and enhance the independence of individuals with severe disabilities.

In the past, recreational programs for individuals with severe disabilities were segregated and often not responsive to the preferences of the person (Moon, 1994; Schleien et al., 1995). For example, a swimming or camp program may have been the only opportunities offered within a community. When segregated recreational programs were the only opportunities offered, there was little focus on the need to teach individuals leisure skills that could be used in a variety of environments or to develop the social support needed to help individuals with disabilities to participate in leisure activities with nondisabled persons.

In the last decade, the emphasis on inclusion and normalization has changed the approach to teaching recreational skills. The goal of leisure instruction is to assist individuals with severe disabilities to acquire the skills and supports needed to engage in a variety of recreational activities in the community and with nondisabled persons

(Schleien et al., 1995). In addition, there is an emphasis on matching the preferences of the individual to the recreational skills and activities selected (Cipriano, 1998; Dattilo & Rusch, 1985).

Recreation as a Related Service

The Individuals with Disabilities Education Act (PL 101-476) allows for the provision of recreation as a related service to be provided in the student's Individual Educational Program (IEP). Under IDEA, recreation as a related service includes the following components:

1. *Assessment of recreation and leisure functioning.* A comprehensive assessment of the student's leisure skills, abilities, interests, and attitudes provides the basis for developing instructional goals.
2. *Leisure education.* Systematic instruction is provided to enhance the student's recreation skill development, recreation participation (decision making and planning), and knowledge of recreation options and to promote participation in recreational activities.
3. *Therapeutic recreation services.* Recreation is used to habilitate or rehabilitate the student's cognitive, social, emotional, physical, and functional well-being. Therapeutic recreation involves individualized assessment, development of goals and objectives, implementation of intervention, and the evaluation of student progress.
4. *Recreation programs in school and community agencies.* The provision of recreation services that promote the inclusion of students with disabilities in school and community activities and programs.

In IDEA, a Certified Therapeutic Recreational Specialist is identified as the qualified professional to provide recreation as a related service. This professional may work with a student with severe disabilities in a variety of ways, from conducting assessments, identifying goals, providing training to educators and families, providing direct instruction to the student, to identifying recreation resources within the community (Heyne, 1998). Recreation as a related service can provide the student with essential skills for the development of leisure interests and abilities that provide students with opportunities for community and social participation and integration. In addition, therapeutic recreational services can be used as a functional tool to support the development of social, emotional, and physical objectives in the student's IEP. As the student approaches the secondary school transition years, recreation and leisure education should become focused on assisting the student in developing the skills necessary to locate, plan, and engage in recreation and leisure activities that will promote physical health and a sense of well-being and provide opportunities for social interaction and friendship development.

Selecting Recreation Activities

The recreation activities selected for instruction must be individually determined, using the same process for developing individualized objectives in the other curricular domains. The definition of recreation includes the components of amusement and relaxation, concepts that are individually determined. For example, one individual may enjoy playing basketball; another may prefer collecting baseball cards. Personal preference is a critical feature of determining the recreational skills that are taught. Teachers cannot simply teach skills that match the materials available in their classrooms or assume that a recreational curriculum can be determined for a group of students without individualization.

In addition to personal preference, the teacher should select recreational activities that are chronologically age appropriate and provide interaction opportunities with nondisabled persons. The activities selected also should be ones that can be adapted for active participation by the individual with disabilities and be used in a variety of environments currently and in the future. The leisure skills curriculum should include leisure activities that have life value in terms of independence and integration. Leisure activities in which the individual can participate without assistance should be a priority, as should activities that promote integration into the community.

Families must be partners in the selection of the leisure skills and recreation activities that will be taught. Family preference for and access to the activities proposed are essential to what leisure skills are taught (Moon, 1994; Voeltz & Apffel, 1981). Skills targeted for instruction should be ones that have potential for lifelong leisure pursuit. Families will have important perspective about leisure activities that are culturally valued by them, affordable, and that can be maintained at home. Questions that the teacher may want to ask family members to identify potential activities are listed in Figure 16–1.

Nondisabled peers are a useful resource in determining age-appropriate recreation activities. The popularity of different activities may change over time. It is more desirable to teach a student a recreation activity that will facilitate social inclusion because it is valued by nondisabled

Figure 16–1 Home Leisure Questions

1. What does your child do during his or her free time after school?
2. What does your child do during his or her free time on the weekends?
3. What recreation activities does your child do with the family?
4. What recreation activities does your child do with neighbors and friends?
5. What are your child's favorite recreation activities?
6. What are the favorite recreation activities of your family?
7. Do special problems occur for your child during these activities?
8. What recreation activities do you think your child may want to try?
9. What community recreation activities (e.g., scouts, after-school, little league, etc.) would you like to see your child become involved in?

peers. An open-ended peer interest questionnaire can provide parents, educators, and others with useful information to develop age-appropriate activities. York, Vandercook, and Stave (1990) developed a two-page recreation/leisure questionnaire that can be used or modified for any age group. The questionnaire consists of the following seven open-ended, short-answer questions:

1. What are some of your favorite after-school, evening, and weekend recreation/leisure activities that you do by yourself, with your family, and with your friends?
2. If you use any type of equipment during your leisure time, what do you like to use?
3. What magazines do you like to read or browse through?
4. If you have a favorite music group and rock star, who are they?
5. If you like to play cards or board games, which are your favorites?
6. If you have hobbies that you enjoy, what are they?
7. If you could get any two items for your birthday, what would you want?

It is important not to approach the selection of recreation activities for students with severe disabilities in a conventional way. Family members and teachers may have difficulty in thinking beyond the array of activities that have been traditionally offered to individuals with disabilities (Modell & Valdez, 2002). Swimming, woodworking, plant care, and bowling are examples of activities that are easily adapted for individuals with disabilities and, as a consequence, they may be the options that are thought of first. Playing pinball (Hill, Wehman, & Horst, 1982; Vandercook, 1991), photography (Giangreco, 1983), and playing darts (Schleien, Wehman, & Kiernan, 1981) are examples of activities that can be done alone or with a group and in a variety of environments that may be appealing to individuals with disabilities and their peers.

A variety of common leisure preferences of students in elementary, middle, and high school are listed in Figure 16–2. This list is not meant to be exhaustive, but was developed to demonstrate the array of options that are available. The activities in the list are categorized by eight major leisure curriculum categories developed by Bender, Brannan, and Verhoven (1984): play and games, sports and physical development, camping and outdoor activities, nature study, hobby activities, craft activities, arts activities, and educational, entertainment, and cultural activities.

Assessing Student Preference

Although we have stressed the importance of using student preference in determining potential leisure activities, it may be difficult to determine preference because of the student's limited communication skills and his lack of experience with a variety of activities. A student's initial reaction may be one of apprehension but, after repeated exposure, he may find the activity very pleasurable.

Schleien et al. (1995) provide an inventory that may be used to determine student leisure preferences. The Student Interest Inventory (see Figure 16–3) is based on the assumptions that an individual's feelings are reflected in outward behaviors and that these outward behaviors are related to her interest and enjoyment of activities (Wuerch & Voeltz, 1982). For example, if the student smiles and vocalizes when assisted in playing a computer game, the teacher would determine that the computer

Figure 16–2 Sample Recreation Activities

Play and Games	Sports and Physical	Camping and Outdoors	Nature Study	Hobby Activities	Craft Activities	Art Activities	Educational, Entertainment, Cultural
Elementary							
• puzzles • tag • hide and seek • card games (UNO, Go Fish) • board games (Sorry, Jr. Monopoly)	• swimming • T ball • soccer • tumbling	• camping • day hikes	• bird watching • shell collecting • nature walks • pet care	• card collecting • comic collecting • action figures • doll collection	• T-shirt art • ceramics • models	• painting • clay • coloring • puppet shows • musical instruments	• reading • recreation courses • scouts • zoo • park
Middle School							
• board games • card games • video games • computer games • catch	• karate • softball • basketball • jogging • swimming	• camping • hiking • canoeing/ boating • snorkeling	• pet care • gardening • aquariums • rocks	• stamp collecting • coin collections • comic collections	• bead work • leather craft • tie dye • sewing	• musical instruments • painting • dance • drama	• listen to music • parties • shopping • sports events
High School							
• pool/billiards • cards • darts • video games • computer games	• bowling • jogging • tennis • aerobics	• canoeing/ boating • camping • backpacking • cooking outdoors	• gardening • pet care • bird watching • plant identification • astronomy	• poster collections • button collections • jewelry collections • records/cd's	• candle making • stitchery • jewelry craft	• drawing • musical instruments • dance • mime • drama	• listen to music • attending plays • art shows • concerts • shopping • dating • sports events

Figure 16–3 Student Interest Inventory

Student: ____________________

Instructions: For each activity, answer each question by placing the number of the description that best matches the child's behavior in the appropriate box for that activity.						
	Activity					
	Date					
	Rater					
A. For this child's usual level of interest in play materials, he or she is: 1. Not as interested as usual 2. About as interested as usual 3. More interested than usual						
B. For this child's usual level of physical interaction with materials (pushing control buttons, turning knobs, putting things together, etc.), he or she is: 1. Not as busy as usual 2. About as busy as usual 3. Busier than usual						
C. For this child's usual affective behaviors (smiling, signs of enjoyment, etc.), he or she seems to be: 1. Enjoying this less than usual 2. Showing about the same amount of enjoyment as usual 3. Enjoying this more than usual						
D. For this child's usual level of "looking" or visual regard of an activity, object, or person, he or she is: 1. Not looking as much as usual 2. Looking as much as usual 3. Looking more often or longer than usual						
E. Compared to this child's usual behavior during a short period of time with minimal supervision, he or she is: 1. Engaging in more negative behavior than usual 2. Engaging in about the same amount of negative behavior as usual 3. Engaging in less negative (or off-task) behavior than usual						
Activity Interest Scores: *Total the numbers in each column*		______	______	______	______	______

Source: Lifelong Leisure Skills and Lifestyles for Persons with Developmental Disabilities by S. J. Schleien, L. H. Meyer, L. A. Heyne, and B. B. Brandt, 1995, Baltimore: Paul H. Brookes Publishing Co. Reprinted by permission.

game is a preferred activity. Conversely, if the student withdraws or sleeps during an activity, a lack of interest in the activity may be assumed.

It is important to realize that analyzing student behavior to determine preferences can be a little tricky. For example, think about a student who closes his eyes and becomes very relaxed when activating a tape player with a music tape. Should the teacher assume that it is a preferred activity or a boring one? Obviously, more information would be needed to determine preference. The teacher might want to examine the student's response to different types of music as one method of determining the meaning of the response. The teacher might also compare the reaction to the tape player to the student's reaction to known preferred and nonpreferred activities.

What about the student who reacts to all new activities in a manner that appears to signal dislike? Repeated sampling of a variety of activities may be necessary to overcome the initial resistance to something new. Participation in activities should not be forced or coerced; the activity should be offered several times in a gentle and supportive manner to determine if it holds interest for the student.

Student response to activities may also be determined by nonessential components of the activity. For example, a student who has difficulty with auditory stimulation may enjoy playing a hand-held video game if the noise is turned off. A student who has difficulty with close contact with others may not be able to handle participating in a basketball game, but may do well with "one on one." The person assessing preferences should use information on the student's reaction to stimuli and current behavior patterns to offer variations of activities that match the student's needs. Once preference is determined, the issue of changing student response to components of the activities can be handled through instruction.

A related difficulty in assessing preference is student attachment to objects or activities that are not age appropriate and are used in a manner that is stereotypic. Teachers may feel that these attachments constitute preference and be reluctant to direct students to other activities. For example, a student may select a tambourine when offered a variety of materials and then shake the tambourine in a stereotypic manner for a prolonged duration. What we see in this example is not a student selecting a leisure activity, but rather a person engaging in stereotypic behavior. Students who engage in such excess behavior should be taught appropriate leisure skills so that the acquisition of a leisure behavior can serve as a replacement for the stereotypic behavior. When selecting options for leisure activities, the teacher may want to analyze the stereotypic behavior to determine the sensory features of the material that the student uses and then look for leisure activities that include these sensory components. For example, a student who repeatedly picks at cloth (blankets, towels, upholstery) to separate the fibers may be taught rug hooking, which involves the repeated practice of pulling yarn strands tightly. Another alternative is to shape the stereotypic behavior so that it occurs within normalized conditions. For example, shaking a tambourine is appropriate when it occurs with music and in the context of playing instruments. The teacher may wish to teach the student to demonstrate the behavior in situations in which the behavior is appropriate.

Leisure Activity Goal Areas

Once the teacher has identified potential recreational activities or leisure skills, a selection must be made about what skills or activities to teach. Demchak (1994) has developed a form that provides a mechanism for evaluating activities across multiple considerations to determine what should be targeted for instruction (see Figure 16–4). In addition, Ford et al. (1989) have identified five major goal areas in the recreation/leisure domain and suggest that students participate in activities in each of these:

1. School and extracurricular activities
2. Activities to do alone at home and in the neighborhood
3. Activities to do with family and friends at home and in the neighborhood
4. Activities to do with family and friends in the community
5. Physical fitness

Teachers should determine potential instructional goals for activities in each of these areas while ensuring that the activities selected will require active participation by the student.

School and Extracurricular Activities

The school is a rich resource for leisure activities that are planned and informal. Recreational goals should target the existing opportunities to provide students with disabilities opportunities to learn and practice leisure skills with their peers. Leisure activities that may occur in the school include participating in sports, playing musical instruments, taking part in craft and art activities, playing board and card games, reading books

Figure 16–4 Form for Evaluating Potential Recreational Activities

Name: ______________________ Date: ______________

Completed by: ______________________________

Directions: List each recreational activity and the setting in which each activity will occur. Score a 1 for each "yes" answer and a 0 for each "no" answer. Total your answers for each activity.

Activity and Setting:				
1. Are nondisabled peers present in the setting?				
2. Do nondisabled peers participate in the activity?				
3. Is it likely that nondisabled peers will interact with the student in the activity?				
4. Can the person participate in the activity with a minimum of assistance or supervision by specialized personnel (e.g., special education teacher)?				
5. Can the least intrusive, natural prompts and contingencies be used, if needed, to help the person to participate in the activity?				
6. Is the setting appropriate for the chronological age of the student?				
7. Are the materials appropriate for the chronological age of the student?				
8. Is the activity appropriate for the chronological age of the student?				
9. Have repeated observations verified that this is a preferred activity for the individual?				
10. Is the individual presented with a choice at the onset of the activity?				
11. Can the individual self-initiate this activity or be taught to do so?				
12. Is it a preference of the family or caregiver that the individual participate in this activity?				
13. If needed, can the rules be adapted to allow participation?				
14. If needed, can the materials be adapted or prosthetics be used to allow participation?				
15. If needed, can personal assistance strategies be used to allow participation?				
16. Can the person partially (or independently) participate in the activity?				
17. Is the person able to meet any financial costs associated with the activity?				
18. Is the person able to obtain the necessary materials, equipment, and clothing to enable participation?				
19. Is transportation to and from the activity available?				
20. Is the setting accessible?				
21. Are the setting and activity safe for the person?				
22. Is the activity one that is useful in current and future environments?				
Totals				
Activity				
Setting				

Source: "*Helping Individuals with Severe Disabilities Find Leisure Activities,*" by M. A. Demchak, *Teaching Exceptional Children, 27,* 1994, 48–53.

and magazines, playing computer games, attending special events and assemblies, and hanging out with friends. In addition, the school may offer organized extracurricular activities such as sports teams, collector clubs, hobby clubs, special interest lessons (e.g., ceramics, ballet, computer), after-school programs, and scout programs.

Activities to Do Alone

Leisure activities that the student can perform alone are as important as activities that involve peers. Students with severe disabilities find that there are many times at home when someone cannot interact with them when they would benefit from being able to entertain themselves. In addition, sometimes an individual prefers to be alone and would benefit from leisure skill instruction to use this time for amusement and relaxation.

Activities that a student may perform alone include reading books and magazines, playing computer or video games, listening to music, working on craft and hobby projects, interacting with and caring for pets, and organizing collections (e.g., arranging baseball cards). Adaptations of equipment (e.g., microswitches, page turners) and activity expectations (e.g., arranging baseball cards involves placing them from a box into card sleeves in random order) allow the student to complete the activity independently.

Social interaction with nondisabled peers is an important aspect of leisure activities.

Activities to Do at Home and in the Neighborhood

The teacher should look for a match between leisure activities that can be taught at school and activities that are available in the home and neighborhood. Activities that occur across environments are more desirable instructional targets because the student will have more opportunities to practice the skill. Activities that occur in the home and neighborhood are usually very similar to those available during free time in school; examples include playing card games, playing board games, playing computer and video games, playing ball (basketball, kickball, soccer) or frisbee, listening to music, and using playground or riding (e.g., bikes, wagons) equipment.

Activities to Do in the Community

Leisure activities that occur in the community may also be activities that are targeted for community-based instruction. For example, using the public library, eating at a fast-food restaurant, and shopping may be considered by many individuals to be leisure activities, in addition to being important community skills. Other community activities might include attending special events and performances and using public parks and recreation facilities. Teachers should look for opportunities to use community-based instruction to teach skills that match the leisure opportunities that the student has when not in school. If going to the mall is a frequent community leisure experience offered to the student with disabilities, the teacher may want to include instruction in that setting as a component of community-based instruction. Many families may want their child to enjoy community leisure experiences, but are unsure of how to make adaptations or how to provide the supports that the student needs to enjoy the experience. The teacher can be an important resource in helping families to design the supports that a student may need to more fully participate in those activities.

Activities for Physical Fitness

Many noncompetitive physical fitness activities may be appropriate leisure activities for students with disabilities. Running in community "fun" runs, aerobics and slimnastics, yoga, dance, skipping rope, walking, riding bicycles, skating, and swimming are just a few activities that may be performed by people of all ages and ability levels. In addition, many activities in the recreational/leisure domain involve fitness as a primary component. The crux of the inclusion of physical fitness in leisure skill components for individuals with severe disabilities is the person's active participation. Learning is more effective when people are actively involved in the instructional activity. The ability for individuals with significant physical challenges to participate often relies on the physical adaptation of materials. For example, a student with severe disabilities may need the support of a float or a kickboard to participate in swimming. A student may be able to use a tennis racket if the handle is modified so that it is easier to grasp or if the handle is attached to the hand using a specialized device or straps.

Educators must systematically identify the materials and activities that foster active involvement of individuals with severe disabilities. In cases in which independent active participation is not occurring, cooperative participation with a peer can facilitate skill acquisition. Cooperative participation could be used for a soccer game by assigning a peer buddy to assist a student with severe disability in goal keeping or by having the student in a wheelchair throw in foul balls.

Some students may appear so limited in physical ability that physical fitness is not an option. In these cases, the definition of physical fitness should be thought of in a broader sense. A student who has an arm extension response may learn a switch activation program that helps to maintain the physical skill of arm extension and allows the student to access a radio or computer for a leisure activity.

Choice-Making Issues

Dattilo (1992) has stressed the importance of including choice-making skills in leisure education programs. Some researchers have used adaptive switches connected to different leisure materials to show that students with multiple disabilities can demonstrate their preferences for activities (Dattilo & Mirenda, 1987; Realon, Favell, & Lowerre, 1990; Wacker, Berg, Wiggins, Muldoon, & Cavanaugh, 1985). For example, the teacher might connect a radio, a video game, and a computer to different switches. He can then determine the student's preference by observing the devices the student activates and the amount of time the student is engaged in the activity.

Instructional goals that focus on choice making may include the use of switches or augmentative communication systems for selecting an activity. Other instructional goals related to choice may be for students to make a selection and then follow through with the activity, to make a selection and invite a peer to join, or to plan leisure activities for the week.

Students with severe disabilities may have to be taught how to express their preferences for leisure activities (Bambara and Ager, 1992; Browder, Cooper, & Lim, 1998). In a study conducted by Browder et al. (1998) adults with severe disabilities and profound mental retardation were taught to use symbols to express their preferences for activity choices. The method they used for instruction can be used within classrooms for students who do not have a means to express their leisure preferences.

To teach preference selection, the teacher must first determine the activity preferences of the student. This can be done through observation or using the form provided in Figure 16–3. Once preferences have been determined, the teacher should select a symbol to represent the activity. The complexity of the symbol (e.g., photo or object) is determined by the student's cognitive, communicative, and sensory abilities. Once the target symbol has been identified, it is presented to the student with irrelevant distractors. Irrelevant distractors are other symbols that are not related to the preferred activity. For example, you may present a game cartridge for playing Nintendo with the distractors of a pencil and a sock. The student is then prompted to make a selection using the systematic prompt hierarchy that is most appropriately matched to the student's skill level and the instructional context (see Chapter 7 for more information). Once the student makes a symbol selection, the teacher follows with the activity. The student must be provided with many opportunities to use the labels to make requests and the teacher should continue to teach the student additional symbols. If the student appears to shift in her preference of activities, the teacher should honor these preference changes.

Social Interaction

It is critical to teach students with severe disabilities the skills that they need to play with peers if there is an expectation for them to engage in leisure activities with peers. Knowing the skill of how to perform the leisure activity is only one part of what students will need to know to have successful play or leisure exchanges. For example, a student may learn to play a game, but is unable to wait for her turn when two or more players join the game. Teachers must include the important social interaction skills of initiating play, taking turns, and interacting with peers while they are teaching the student to perform an activity.

Social interaction skill instruction should be embedded in all leisure activities. Meyer, Cole, McQuarter, and Reichle (1990) have identified a hierarchy of social skills to consider within leisure skills instruction. The student should learn to start or join an interaction with a peer. For example, the student should be able to greet a peer and then extend an invitation to play. As the student becomes more sophisticated, the student should be able to initiate an interaction with a peer that is unfamiliar to him or join a group of peers. The student should learn to manage his own behavior without needing instructions from others. For example, the student should be able to set a goal and feel gratification for reaching the goal or should be able to delay immediate gratification to get a desired reward later. The student should learn to follow the rules, guidelines and routines of others. For example, often rules are posted for the use of recreation equipment or areas in the community. The student may need to learn to follow the directions given by an adult or peer in the environment or learn to follow rules in the absence of an authority. The student should learn to provide positive and negative feedback to others. For example, in a social interaction the student could provide positive regard to a peer by clapping his hands or shouting. In contrast, when the student dislikes something that has occurred, she needs to be taught how to appropriately express the sentiment.

It may be important to teach the student how to obtain information from and respond to relevant situational cues in the environment. For example, the student may need to learn to orient his body or materials to interact with a peer, or the student may need to learn to attend to contextual cues to gain information before acting (e.g., judge the space needed to lay out a jigsaw puzzle). The student may need to be taught how to provide information and assistance to others, for example, how to direct a friend's attention to an event or an object; or a student may need to be taught how to provide help to a peer who needs assistance. The student may also need instruction in how to accept assistance from peers. For example, the student may need instruction in how to use a help symbol to let a peer know that he needs help with an activity.

We have already addressed the importance of choice making and providing the student with a mechanism for expressing a preference. The student may also have to be taught how to appropriately express a protest or how to cope with negative situations. For example, a student may need to learn how to cope with not winning a game or performing a skill with accuracy. The student may also need to be taught ways to terminate an interaction or withdraw from a situation. For example, a student may need instruction in how to signal that she is leaving a game with a peer.

A common approach to teaching social skills within activities is to include them in the task analysis. Gaylord-Ross, Haring, Breen, and Pitts-Conway (1984) taught a student with autism to socially interact with peers in the context of playing a hand-held video game, using a Walkman, and chewing gum. The task analyses for these sequences are shown in Figure 16–5.

Instructional Methods

When the priority activities and goals have been identified by the teacher, the family, and the student, several important decisions remain before instruction can begin. The teacher must decide where the instruction will occur, with whom the activity will occur, and how often instructional sessions will be scheduled. It is prudent to select activities and skills for instruction that can be performed in multiple environments. This will ensure that optimal opportunities to practice and generalize the skill will be available.

The nature of the activity influences where the optimal site for instruction will be. Instruction should occur in the most natural environment, although many activities can take place in both the school and home environments. Activities like learning to play a computer game are not as dependent on special environmental cues as are others, such as playing basketball or using a fast-food restaurant. If instruction occurs in an environment other than the environment in which the behavior is expected to be used, generalization procedures should be used in instruction, and generalization to the natural environment should be assessed (Ford et al., 1989).

In choosing the optimal instructional site for learning a leisure skill, the opportunity for receiving instruction with peers who are not disabled is a basic part of the decision (Ford et al., 1989). For example, the student could be taught to play a board game in the school's media center with two eighth graders, instead of participating in the same activity with a teaching assistant in the special education classroom. It is important for the student to learn from peers and to have an opportunity to get to know others and to develop friendships. The attractive atmosphere of the media center with student activity and movement may increase the student's interest in the board game.

Unfortunately, for some students with severe disabilities the opportunities to use a leisure skill at school may be limited somewhat. General education students spend much of their school day engaged in academic instruction. As a consequence, the teacher may have to offer structured instructional sessions (i.e., using systematic instructional techniques) and follow instruction with practice sessions with nondisabled peers. In a study conducted by Collins, Hall, and Branson (1997), general education peers provided generalization sessions for students with moderate disabilities who were learning a variety of leisure skills within their self-contained classroom. The students with disabilities were able to increase and generalize their leisure skills, and the peer volunteers enjoyed getting to know the students from the special education classroom.

Figure 16–5 Task Analyses for Social Skills Training

[a]AS = student with autism, NS = nonhandicapped student.

[b]Applies only to AS, who will write on a notebook the words that he or she was saying and display the notebook to the NS.

Source: "*The Training and Generalization of Social Interaction Skills with Autistic Youth,*" by R. J. Gaylord-Ross, T. G. Haring, C. Breen, and F. Pitts-Conway, 1984, *Journal of Applied Behavior Analysis, 17,* pp. 198–199. Copyright 1984 by the *Journal of Applied Behavior Analysis.* Reprinted by permission.

Pacman

1. AS approaches NS.[a]
2. AS establishes one meter proximity.
3. AS establishes a face-forward orientation.
4. AS says, "Hi."
5. AS waits for response.
6. AS says, "Want to play?"
7. AS waits for response. AS finds someone else if NS does not indicate willingness to play. AS then begins sequence at step 1 again.
8. AS turns on game.
9. AS hands game to NS.
10. AS watches NS play.
11. AS receives game from NS.
12. AS reads NS's score.
13. AS turns off game.
14. AS turns game on to reset score to zero.
15. AS plays game.
16. AS reads own score.
17. AS offers game to NS. If NS accepts, play continues in alternating fashion. When NS indicates that she or he is finished, AS takes game back.
18. AS says, "Bye."

Walkman

1. AS approaches MS.
2. AS establishes one meter proximity.
3. AS establishes face-forward orientation with NS.
4. AS says, "Hi."

The nature of schools and classroom structures presents challenges when instructing leisure skills (Schleien, Heyne, et al., 1995). The teacher must identify both the appropriate time and place for leisure skill use. In elementary schools where centers are often used for instruction, a center may be constructed that offers leisure instruction time or activities. Elementary schools are more likely to have free play or recess, during which students can be provided with instruction and leisure activity materials.

In middle schools, students may be introduced to a home room period or a "club" period during which they are not engaged in instruction. This may be a period during which leisure instruction could occur. The collaborative team may also want to examine the electives offered in the school and build leisure opportunities within these courses. For example, electives of drama, music, band, home economics, or art may more easily accommodate leisure skills instruction. High schools can be large, complex environments that upon first glance do not seem easily adapted to leisure instruction. Homeroom may be one environment where leisure skill instruction can occur. The collaborative team should also carefully consider elective courses and seek courses that may provide an appropriate context for leisure instruction. For example, a class in multimedia art may offer an opportunity for a student who is working on some simple art skills. Course requirements can be adjusted so that the student is enrolled for the purpose of instruction in leisure skills, peer interaction, communication skills, and other relevant objectives.

Figure 16–5 Continued

5. AS waits for response.
6. AS says (and writes[b]), "Want to listen?"
7. AS shows radio to NS. If NS is not interested in interacting, AS approaches another student (step 1).
8. AS turns on radio.
9. AS adjusts volume to level 6.
10. AS hands headphones to NS.
11. AS puts on headphones.
12. AS selects rock and roll station.
13. AS remains in proximity to NS until termination of interaction by NS.
14. AS says "Bye."

Gum

1. AS approaches NS.
2. AS establishes one meter proximity.
3. AS establishes a face-forward orientation.
4. AS says "Hi" to NS.
5. AS waits for a response.
6. AS says (and writes[b]), "What are you doing?"
7. AS waits for a response.
8. AS says (and writes[b]), "Want some gum?" and shows pack of gum.
9. If NS says yes, AS hands pack of gum to NS.
10. NS hands pack back to AS.
11. AS selects a stick of gum and chews it until the end of the interaction.
12. AS remains in one meter proximity to NS for at least 30 seconds or until the end of interaction.
13. AS says "Bye" when NS terminates the interaction.

Electives that are commonly offered in high schools that may offer leisure instructional opportunities include aerobics, dance, weight training, chorus, painting, computer graphics, drama, team sports, and personal fitness. In addition to examining electives, the collaborative team may have to creatively search for other opportunities to teach and practice leisure skills. For example, students may arrive before school and congregate in the cafeteria. This may be a time to teach a student to play a game with peers. Another opportunity may be during lunch periods. Perhaps the student with disabilities could have two lunch periods, one for lunch and another to engage in a leisure activity with peers. These opportunities will have to be identified by observing the other high school students, their activities and interests. High schools also offer many after-school clubs that could be a mechanism for practicing leisure skills and developing friendships or companions who would be available for after-school leisure activities.

The acquisition and generalization of the leisure skill depends on how frequently instruction occurs.The activities selected should allow for instruction to occur with enough frequency that the student will make significant gains over the school year (Ford et al., 1989). An instructional goal that targets a leisure activity that only occurs weekly for a student who needs daily, repeated practice to learn will not be mastered and should be replaced with skill instruction in an activity with more opportunities for instruction and practice.

When the instructional goal has been defined, skill instruction can begin. The systematic procedures used to teach all other skills also apply to the instruction of leisure skills. The following are some additional hints for instruction that are specific to leisure skill instruction:

1. Determine the natural cues that are used to prompt a leisure activity. The adult should not say "Jim, play basketball" when the natural cue given to typical peers is "You can have free time now."
2. Use the most natural reinforcer possible that matches the activity. It would be inappropriate and stigmatizing to a student to say "Good, you threw the frisbee." A more acceptable form of praise may be "Cool, look how far the frisbee went."
3. Be very cautious about getting in the way of peer interactions. Often an adult is needed to begin a leisure activity, but then she should retreat into the background as soon as possible. If the adult is in the middle of the interaction, the nondisabled peer does not have the opportunity to engage the student with disabilities in his own way.
4. Some students with disabilities may need the support of an adult throughout an activity with a peer. In these cases, the adult should try to remain in the background and encourage peer interaction by prompting interactive behavior or by interpreting the communication efforts of the student with disabilities to the nondisabled peer.
5. Leisure activities should be fun. The adult who is instructing the student with disabilities should model the affective expressions of joy or pleasure! Setting the stage for having fun should include a relaxed pace of instruction, unobtrusive forms of data collection, positions that the student prefers, and the relaxed interactional style of the instructor.

Partial Participation

The principle of partial participation was introduced in 1982 by Baumgart et al. and is an important idea for helping teachers to create and implement effective educational programming for students with severe disabilities. In age-appropriate settings, students with severe disabilities may be unable to participate as fully and effectively as other students involved in an activity and, therefore, adaptations to facilitate active participation must be considered.

The principle of partial participation was proposed to ensure that even those students who are currently unable to acquire the functional skills needed to completely participate in the activities of their lives can still partially participate. As teachers have implemented the concept of partial participation, they have made some errors that should be avoided (Ferguson & Baumgart, 1991).

Partial participation is not defined as presence in an activity. Students should be active participants, rather than passive observers. Activities that use partial participation must be community and family referenced. Partial participation does not imply that the recreational or leisure activity does not have to be meaningful to the student and responsive to his learning needs. Partial participation in functional activities should occur throughout the day in a curriculum that is activity based and meaningful.

When partial participation is being implemented, the student should not have to do so much of an activity that she misses opportunities to move on to other activities. For example, it may seem important for a student to learn to put her own materials away, unless doing so is so physically difficult and time consuming that she cannot keep up with her peers as they move to another activity. A student with disabilities should work to increase skill development, but should not be forced to perform a skill "all by herself" to the point that it is burdensome or image damaging.

Ferguson and Baumgart (1991) describe four strategies that explain the core of partial participation.

Strategy 1: Achieving active instead of passive participation. Ferguson and Baumgart (1991) report that using a "practice abilities" logic for instruction helps students to build skills in the context of activities. The teacher must determine ways to maximize the students' opportunities for practicing the behaviors that they currently possess, however small and inconsistent. Although they may not be able to complete a movement independently, they may contribute to a movement or continue a movement that they have been helped to begin. In addition, active participation may enhance the image of the students with disabilities to nondisabled peers. For example, a student might kick a ball that is placed next to his wheelchair to participate in a kickball game and then be pushed by a peer to the bases. A student with disabilities might be assisted to pick up a puzzle piece and encouraged to place the piece in the area where it fits, before a peer fits the piece in its place.

Strategy 2: Use multiple perspectives. Teachers should use family- and community-referenced strategies to build a functional curriculum focused on participation in activities, rather than isolated skill development. Instructional assessment should be broadened in scope to include other measures, such as a student's enjoyment of an activity or a rating by peers of the student's participation. This means that proficiency at leisure skill performance should not be the teacher's primary concern. Other ways to assess leisure skill outcomes include the length of time that a student is engaged in an activity, the affect of the student while engaged, or the evaluation by peers of whether the student is having fun.

Strategy 3: Use information from multiple sources for curriculum planning to avoid piecemeal participation. Leisure activities should be a part of an activity-based, functional curriculum that is comprehensive and meaningful to the students.

Strategy 4: Enhance the student's image and achieve interdependence by facilitating participation. Teachers may need to shift instructional choices when the situation suggests that performance gaps will not change or will not need to change. They should offer opportunities for students with severe disabilities to depend on their more able partners to help with parts of the activity that are difficult, time consuming, or burdensome. For example, in card playing, a person with limited grasping and reaching ability might use eye gaze to choose the card she wishes her nondisabled partner to discard. The activity is more normalized and thus more enjoyable to all participants when the natural flow of the activity remains constant. This also enhances the self-image of the student with severe disabilities about his ability to participate in normal, age-appropriate activities.

Adapting Activities

The concept of adaptations is usually related to the design and usage of materials and devices, but it may also be expanded to include adapting skill sequences and rules, using personal assistance to increase participation, modifying the physical and social environment, and choosing or creating materials and devices that meet a student's individual needs (Baumgart et al., 1982).

When determining whether to use an adaptation and what adaptations should be used, several factors must be considered (Bishop, Eshilian, & Falvey, 1989):

1. Does the activity have a valid goal? If an activity takes place frequently, several adaptations may be necessary to lead to greater independence. The effort expended to make such adaptations is valid if practice of the skill is provided on a regular basis. Extensive adaptations may not be cost effective for activities that are performed infrequently.
2. Does the activity require an adaptation for the individual to succeed? There must be a balance between the goal of independence and fostering dependence on the use of adaptations. Students need to use their motor skills as much as possible, but in promoting normalization with nondisabled peers, speed of response and uninterrupted play may be just as important. For example, in playing some computer games with a nondisabled peer, using a microswitch adaptation to compete helps the student to display an equal amount of speed and accuracy and normalizes the student with disabilities in the eyes of his peers.
3. What adaptation is most appropriate? There are many types of adaptations. The optimal adaptation allows for greater participation and control over one's environment and compensates for factors that may impede independent performance. The student's current skills, strengths, weaknesses, and motivation should also be taken into account when determining an appropriate adaptation. The usage and maintenance of the adaptation must also be considered. If an adaptation may not be reliable or easily replaced, it may not be appropriate for use.
4. Does the adaptation fit the student? Adaptations that are selected should match the positions that students prefer and the dominant motor movements.
5. Is the adaptation safe? The fit and function of any adaptation must be continually evaluated.

In addition, the adaptation should be evaluated for continued need by the student. Adaptations and special equipment are used to enhance physical abilities, but fading the use of the special devices as soon as possible leads to more normalized appearance and functioning.

A variety of adaptations has been developed by researchers to assist the active involvement of students with disabilities in leisure activities. Some equipment adaptations are using a cable release and tripod to adapt taking pictures with a camera, using a tee so that a student can hit a softball, using enlarged pieces for a table game, and using a microswitch to operate a computer or video game. Activities have also been modified so that students with disabilities may participate, including having others keep score for a student who is bowling, changing the Go Fish card game so that a peer looks for the match and the student with disabilities activates a tape-recorded Go Fish message when prompted, and using a designated runner for a student in a wheelchair who is playing softball.

Adaptations may be made for almost any activity, only limited by creativity, finances, and mechanical ability. Teachers who need assistance in thinking of adaptations may want to consult peers, other professionals in the classroom, or family members for ideas. People who are somewhat removed from the situation often can see possibilities that the person who is most intimate with the student may miss. Ideas for adaptations can also be found in catalogs from companies that sell assistive devices and patient-care supplies. Companies that sell microswitches also are good resources for ideas and equipment.

Community Recreation Opportunities

The inclusion of individuals with severe disabilities into community recreation programs is a relatively new concept that is not widely practiced. The Americans with Disabilities Act (P.L. 101–336), which prohibits discrimination in employment, transportation, public services, and communication, also forbids discrimination in community recreation programs.

This legislation is helpful in gaining access to recreation programs, but access is not all that is needed. Appropriate supports must be provided if individuals with severe disabilities are going to be successful and to benefit from these programs. Schleien, Green, and Heyne (1993) describe three approaches for establishing the inclusion of individuals with disabilities into community recreation programs. The first approach is the reverse mainstreaming model, which involves programs that are designed for persons with disabilities, but also include nondisabled individuals. The advantage of the reverse mainstreaming model is that programs are basically designed for persons with disabilities and their needs are assured of being met. The major disadvantage of reverse mainstreaming is the disproportionate number of participants who are disabled, which does not enhance integration or friendship development.

The second model is the integration of an existing program for nondisabled participants. The advantages are that persons with disabilities are included in a natural proportion and there is potential for development of peer friendships. The main disadvantage is that the staff may not be trained to work with individuals with disabilities.

The third approach is through programs that meet the needs of all persons in the community. These programs are collaboratively designed by persons trained in therapeutic recreation and those who provide general recreation programs. Unfortunately, not many communities have developed such programs, and many families are left with trying to achieve the integration of their child into a community recreation program or requesting that programs for individuals with disabilities be expanded to include nondisabled persons.

As teachers and parents seek to identify appropriate community recreation programs, they should attempt to identify the level of commitment to inclusion that exists in the recreation program (Schleien & Rynders, 1998). Interviews with program administrators can provide information on administrative policies and practices that support inclusion efforts. Specifically, the teacher or parent should seek to identify if the commitment to inclusion is central to the provision of services (e.g., stated in the mission statement, evident in the program brochure), if resources are adequate to promote inclusion, and if recreation staff have the skills to support individuals with severe disabilities. Written descriptions of program options and an observation of program activities should reveal if the program offers modifications for physical accessibility and the provision of age-appropriate activities. In addition, the teacher or parent should seek to determine if the program is prepared to meet the individual preferences and needs of the individual with disabilities.

Hamre-Nietupski et al. (1992) describe the efforts of one community to provide a summer recreation program for elementary-age children that included students with severe disabilities. The development of the program involved (1) surveying community recreation options, (2) approaching community recreation programs, (3) obtaining funding, (4) publicizing the program, and (5) collaborative planning of activities that met the needs of all students. In-service was provided to the recreation staff that presented the rationale for inclusion, descriptions of the students who would be included, plans for partial participation and adaptations, and ways to facilitate peer interactions. Nondisabled children were also prepared for the inclusion of the students with disabilities through formal presentations that introduced the students and informal modeling throughout the summer program.

Strategies for Families

It is very important that families promote leisure skill development and offer opportunities for leisure skill activities after school. Families may need the teacher's assistance in determining how to find appropriate activities or how to teach activities at home. When assisting families, it is important to ask about the following: (1) what activities the family engages in, (2) what activities they want to participate in but are unable to due to the skill level or behavior of their child, and (3) what barriers they identify (financial, health issues, transportation, safety) that may affect accessing preferred leisure activities (Schleien, Meyer et al., 1995). In addition, the family should identify leisure activities that they would like their child to participate in independently of other family members.

Figure 16–6 Community Recreation/Leisure Opportunities

Boy Scouts Girl Scouts 4-H Club Boys Club Girls Club Gymboree Recreation sports leagues (e.g., soccer, softball, basketball, football) Personal sports instruction (e.g., horseback riding, tennis, golf, swimming, gymnastics, dance) Community recreation programs (e.g., art, sports, crafts, music, pet care, dance, collecting, fitness clubs) YMCA (e.g., swimming, crafts, fitness)	Library (e.g., computer use groups, story hour, reading clubs) Community theater groups Summer and holiday camp programs (offered by YMCA, private groups, community recreation centers, children's museums, science museums) Agriculture Extension Office (e.g., gardening, forestry, bird watching, animal care) Sierra Club Inner City Outings for Children Children's events at parks, zoos, museums, community agencies

Once families have discussed their preferences, the teacher can help them to identify leisure activity opportunities and strategies for supporting their children. For example, the teacher may send home a list of neighborhood recreation center activities or provide the family with the phone number of the recreation center. Sometimes the family may need guidance in how to approach a program director about including the child with disabilities. The teacher can help the parent to talk through an explanation of her child's disability and her goals in including the child within the program or activity. Figure 16–6 provides a list of possible community organizations or programs that offer after-school leisure opportunities.

If a family would like to teach the child a leisure skill at home, but are uncertain about how to begin, the teacher may offer to provide a demonstration of instructional techniques. Another mechanism for demonstrating how to teach a skill is to videotape a demonstration of instruction and send the videotape home with the student. Families may also appreciate assistance in determining when to teach a skill and in planning how to organize routines or family activities that accommodate leisure skill instruction. The teacher should consider offering these types of supports to the family. Many families are reluctant to place any additional demands on their child's teacher, especially ones that do not appear to be school related.

Developing Friendships

The development of friendships has not traditionally been included as a goal in a leisure education program for individuals with disabilities. Prior to the current emphasis on inclusion and supports in the community, human service workers did not give much thought to supporting social relationships. It has only been in the most recent years that professionals have directed their attention to promoting friendships among students with severe disabilities and their peers (Geisthardt, Brotherson, & Cook, 2002; Haring, 1992; Lutfiyya, 2001; Turnbull, Pereia, & Blue-Blanning, 1999). Because the concept of friendship is difficult to define and the promotion of friendships is a new area of interest, little empirical work is available to guide professionals. Most published work in this area comprises narrative and descriptive information on how specific friendships have been developed and maintained (Forest, 1987; Geisthardt et al., 2002; Perske, 1988; Strully & Strully, 1985; Turnbull et al., 1999).

Friendship is important to everyone across the life cycle. Friendships in the early childhood years provide children with play partners, companions, and peers to share affection. Through play, children learn essential social, language, and play skills. Adolescents spend a significant amount of time with their friends and affiliate with friends who share similar interests and experiences. Close friends give us the opportunity to meet our needs for intimacy and affection (G. Allan Roeher Institute, 1990). It seems that all people need at least one special friend to talk with and share their feelings. When intimacy and affection are denied for long periods of time, people develop feelings of frustration and rejection. Close friendships make people feel valued and important. To understand the importance of friendship, we can examine our own lives. Our friends are the people with whom we share our feelings, thoughts, secrets, and life stories. When we want to celebrate, have fun, or receive support in a crisis, we look for our friends to be there. Now imagine your life with no friends in it.

Friendships can develop when people have proximity to each other and adequate opportunity to become acquainted (Grenot-Scheyer, Coots, & Falvey, 1989; Lutfiyya, 2001; Rubin, 1980). Most parents take for granted that their children will have friends in their lives. Parents of children with disabilities are unable to count on the natural development of friendships, because many students with severe disabilities do not have the proximity to typically developing peers and may not have the skills needed to initiate and establish relationships (Forest & Pearpoint, 1992; Geisthardt et al., 2002). People with disabilities usually have family and human service workers in their lives, but very few friends (Green & Schleien, 1991).

Leisure education is a natural context for the development of friendships (Schleien, Green, & Stone, 2002). Although professionals cannot program friendships, they can create the opportunities that may foster and support the development of peer relationships (Grenot-Scheyer et al., 1989; Perske, 1988).

Proximity and shared experiences seem to be a foundation for friendship development (Lutfiyya, 2001; Salisbury & Palombaro, 1998). Although establishing friendships is not guaranteed in these situations, students cannot build relationships unless they have access to each other. Teachers can provide proximity and shared experiences by planning leisure activities that bring students together on a regular basis. They can also plan activities that encourage students to express their interests and discover their peers' interests. Students with disabilities can be assisted to share their interests through augmentative communication, presentations by a family member, or slides and photographs that depict the student with disabilities in activities that she enjoys.

Closer friendships may develop when students and peers have opportunities to share activities after school and on weekends. In research studies that have examined the friendships of children with disabilities at home, many children had limited interactions with peers or potential friends (Geisthardt et al., 2002). Parents who are successful in facilitating friendships engage in the following strategies to promote their child's access to potential friends (Geisthardt et al., 2002; Turnbull et al., 1999):

1. Finding opportunities in the community for their child to be with other children
2. Encouraging others to accept the child with disabilities
3. Applying the principle of partial participation to their child's engagement in activities
4. Arranging play dates with other children
5. Getting to know the neighbors
6. Making indoor and outdoor play spaces available and accessible
7. Enrolling the child in the neighborhood school

The classroom teacher can offer assistance to the family in promoting the development of friendships. The teacher may have to take an active role in facilitating access to peers by suggesting that peers exchange phone numbers or by letting family members know about peers who are developing a relationship with their child. Sometimes families will want support in planning parties or recreation activities in which peers can be invited to participate. Teachers may also offer to provide families with information on how to bridge and promote peer interactions or how to adapt activities so that children without disabilities can include their child in their play. Parents may also want assistance with the design of play spaces or the identification of play activities that will promote peer interaction.

The teacher should strive to establish a supportive classroom environment that will foster friendship development (Salisbury & Palombaro, 1998; Schaffner & Buswell, 1992). In classrooms where teachers establish a culture of caring, encouraging students to interact in supportive ways, friendships are more likely to be established between students with disabilities and their peers (Grenot-Scheyer, Staub, Peck, & Schwartz, 1998). Teachers can create a classroom culture of caring by having classroom discussions about feelings, friendship development, and how students treat each other and by involving the students in problem-solving ways to support their peers with disabilities.

Many students may need some form of friendship facilitation from an adult or competent peer. Facilitation is ensuring that the student with disabilities is provided with the encouragement, opportunities, and assistance to develop friendships (Schaffner & Buswell, 1992). For example, when a teacher structures a classroom activity using cooperative learning (see Chapter 9), students are being provided opportunities for social interaction and friendship development. Teachers can encourage friendship development by helping other students to understand the student's disability, efforts to communicate, or behavior. For example, Matt is a student who has low muscle tone and is nonverbal. When he wants to interact with someone, he tends to lean into them and smile. His sixth-grade teacher interprets these actions to another student by saying, "Matt is leaning on you because he likes you. Maybe you could share the book you are reading with him."

Friendship Skills

Stainback, Stainback, and Wilkinson (1992) identified behaviors that may be taught to students who lack friends to encourage others to be supportive and friendly toward them. Some of these behaviors are the following:

1. *Demonstrating a positive interaction style.* Students who are positive, attentive, and encouraging to others are more likely to be included by others. Students who like and support others are more likely to be supported by peers (Rubin, 1980). Teachers can assist students with severe disabilities in having a positive interaction style by teaching them interaction skills such as the ability to give "high fives" as a greeting or how to listen to others as they speak. Teachers may want to address interaction issues in designing communication systems by providing a mechanism for the student with disabilities to inquire "How are you?" or "Are you having fun?"
2. *Communicating areas of interest.* Friendships are built around areas of compatibility. Students who can communicate about their interests and express interest in learning about other people's favorite activities are more likely to build relationships with others. Teachers should help students with severe disabilities to express their interests to their peers. One way to do this is by programming communication devices or providing communication symbols to reflect a student's interests (e.g., "Do you like race cars?"). Other ways are to find activities that will match the student's interests with peers who share the same interests.
3. *Taking the perspective of others.* Students who are able to listen to others and show sensitivity to their feelings are more able to contribute to a friendship relationship. It is important for teachers to realize that the student with disabilities must be able to be a sensitive friend to peers. Teachers can interpret the feelings of the nondisabled peer for a student with disabilities who may not pick up on subtle cues (e.g., "Bobby is disappointed. He lost the game") and provide the student with disabilities with the skill or mechanism to share empathy (e.g., say or sign "I'm sorry").
4. *Providing support.* Students who can provide support and encouragement to others who are in need are better prepared for a reciprocal relationship. One way that peers support one another is by inquiring about important events such as birthdays or the outcome of an exam. Teachers can help students with disabilities to be supportive by prompting them to remember friends' birthdays by making cards or by saying "Happy birthday."
Communication devices can be programmed with a message that says, "How did you do on the test?" or "Is everything OK?"
5. *Demonstrating trustworthiness and loyalty.* To solidify a budding relationship, the student must demonstrate trustworthiness and loyalty to the friend. Teachers should respect the loyalty of one friend to another and not try to artificially force the interaction of a student with disabilities with a variety of peers.
6. *Using conflict resolution skills.* The student must be able to express and defend his needs and rights without compromising the needs and rights of peers.

One way to teach friendship skills is to discuss them and then encourage students to think of real-life situations in which they can use the skills. The teacher observes the students in social interactions and then discusses their progress in developing the skills. The issues surrounding friendship and friendship skills development can also be infused in a variety of other classes (e.g., social studies, reading) and class activities (e.g., group projects, classroom rules discussions).

In Chapter 10, the development of Circles of Friends was discussed as a way to support the inclusion of students with disabilities with their nondisabled peers. The circles strategy is used to build a network of friends who will support the student in developing relationships and in becoming integrated in the school community (Forest, 1987).

Friendships with Disabled Peers

Many people enjoy the support of others who share the same circumstances. Support networks of people who share an interest, cause, or the same oppression are abundant in most communities (e.g., political parties, National Organization of Women, NAACP). Adults with disabilities have described friendship with and the support of others with disabilities as very important in their lives (Huemann, 1993).

Although there is a very strong emphasis in this text on teaching students recreation and leisure skills so that they may build relationships with their nondisabled peers and have fun in community environments, there is no intention to exclude the possibility that friendships with peers who have disabilities may also be important. That may seem counter to many of the themes in this text. Note that there is no mention of Special Olympics in this chapter. This was an intentional omission; Special Olympics is viewed by some as a segregated fitness activity that promotes undesirable and undignified images of people with disabilities. Developing a friendship with a peer because she shares similar circumstances is an act of choice by the student with severe disabilities, rather than a situation that develops because there are no other opportunities.

Connections with other peers with disabilities in informal friendships or in advocacy groups such as People First can offer students with disabilities opportunities to share experiences and problems with someone else who has been there. Huemann (1993) summarizes this issue well:

> At the end of the day, I feel that as disabled people we must feel good about ourselves and be able to choose our friends, and if we choose to spend most of our time outside of work with disabled people, that should not be considered "an inappropriate model." We must have the ability and the opportunity to choose from a broad group of the people with whom we truly feel most comfortable, which can change over time, the same way nondisabled people choose their friends. (p. 246)

Conclusion

In the past, students with severe disabilities were offered opportunities for recreation and leisure activities only in segregated programs. In the last decade, there has been an increased emphasis on the inclusion of individuals in the community and with that comes the promise of recreation opportunities with nondisabled peers.

The role of the teacher is not only to prepare the student for integrated recreation activities outside the school, but also to provide opportunities for fulfilling leisure activities with peers during the school day. The teacher must remember that the ultimate goals for all students in the recreation and leisure curriculum are fitness, friendship, and, most of all, fun. The instructor must keep a student-centered focus. The curriculum must be based on the student's interests, as well as his instructional needs. Age-appropriate environments and inclusive situations with nondisabled peers will facilitate normalization and personal happiness. If students are allowed to choose activities from their own interest inventories and have friends with common interests with whom to participate, the instructor will see more active participation from these students. If the teacher is able to combine all the components for an inclusive recreation/leisure curriculum through adaptations, peer support, and student choices, the ultimate goals of fitness, friendship, and fun will naturally occur.

Questions for Reflection

1. What leisure activities do you most enjoy? Can you think of ways that these activities might be adapted for a person who is physically disabled? Nonverbal?
2. Are activities such as Special Olympics, horseback riding for the disabled, and therapeutic swimming important to leisure instruction? What feedback would you give a family who asked you about their child's participation in these types of activities?
3. In high school, important leisure activities may be dating, hanging out, playing sports, and participating in clubs. How can a secondary teacher ensure that a student with disabilities will be included in these leisure activities?
4. How do you select your friendships? What behaviors may indicate that a student with disabilities wants to be a friend to a peer?
5. Think about your own leisure preferences. How did these preferences develop and change as you grew older? In what ways have your peer relationships influenced your leisure preferences? How can teachers promote a student's awareness of her peers' leisure interests?
6. If you were to include a student with severe disability in a community recreation activity (e.g., a community run or a golf tournament), what preparation should occur before the event? How would you ensure that other participants would accept the individual with disabilities?

References

Bambara, L. M., & Ager, C. (1992). Using self-scheduling to promote self-directed leisure activity in home and community settings. *Journal of the Association for Persons with Severe Handicaps, 17,* 67–76.

Baumgart, D., Brown, L., Pumpian, I., Nisbet, J., Ford, A., Sweet, M., et al., (1982). Principle of partial participation and individualized adaptions in education programs for severely handicapped students. *Journal of the Association for Persons with Severe Handicaps, 7*(2), 17–27.

Bender, M., Brannan, S. A., & Verhoven, P. J. (1984). *Leisure education for the handicapped.* San Diego, CA: College-Hill Press.

Bishop, K. D., Eshilian, L., & Falvey, M. A. (1989). Motor skills. In M. A. Falvey (Ed.), *Community-based curriculum: Instructional strategies for students with severe handicaps* (2nd Ed., pp. 229–254). Baltimore: Paul H. Brookes.

Browder, D. M., Cooper, K. J., & Lim, L. (1998). Teaching adults with severe disabilities to express their choice of settings for leisure activities. *Education and Training in Mental Retardation, 33,* 228–238.

Cipriano, R. E. (1998). An individualized person-centered approach to therapeutic recreation services. *TASH Newsletter, 24*(4), 6–87.

Collins, B. C., Hall, M., & Branson, T. A. (1997). Teaching leisure skills to adolescents with moderate disabilities. *Exceptional Children, 63,* 499–512.

Dattilo, J. (1992). Recreation and leisure: A review of the literature and recommendations for future directions. In L. H. Meyer, C. A. Peck, & L. Brown (Eds.), *Critical issues in the lives of people with severe disabilities* (pp. 171–193). Baltimore: Paul H. Brookes.

Dattilo, J., & Mirenda, P. (1987). An application of a leisure preference assessment protocol for persons with severe handicaps. *Journal of the Association for Persons with Severe Handicaps, 12,* 306–311.

Dattilo, J., & Rusch, F. (1985). Effects of choice on behavior: Leisure participation for persons with severe handicaps. *Journal of the Association for Persons with Severe Handicaps, 11,* 194–199.

Demchak, M. A. (1994). Helping individuals with severe disabilities find leisure activities. *Teaching Exceptional Children, 27,* 48–53.

Ferguson, D. L., & Baumgart, D. (1991). Partial participation revisited. *Journal of the Association for Persons with Severe Handicaps, 16,* 218–227.

Ford, A., Davern, L., Meyer, L., Schnorr, R., Black, J., & Dempsey, P. (1989). *The Syracuse community-referenced curriculum guide for students with moderate and severe disabilities.* Baltimore: Paul H. Brookes.

Forest, M. (1987). *More education integration.* Downsview, Ontario: G. Allan Roeher Institute.

Forest, M., & Pearpoint, J. (1992). Families, friends, and circles. In J. Nisbet (Ed.), *Natural supports in school, at work, and in the community for people with severe disabilities* (pp. 65–86). Baltimore: Paul H. Brookes.

G. Allan Roeher Institute. (1990). *Making friends: Developing relationships between people with a disability and other members of the community.* Downsview, Ontario: G. Allan Roeher Institute.

Gaylord-Ross, R. (1980). A decision model for the treatment of aberrant behavior in applied settings. In W. Sailor, B. Wilcox, & L. Brown (Eds.), *Methods of instruction for severely handicapped students.* Baltimore: Paul H. Brookes.

Gaylord-Ross, R. J., Haring, T. G., Breen, C., & Pitts-Conway, F. (1984). The training and generalization of social interaction skills with autistic youth. *Journal of Applied Behavior Analysis, 17,* 229–247.

Geisthardt, C. L., Brotherson, M. J., & Cook, C. C. (2002). Friendships of children with disabilities in the home environment. *Education and Training in Mental Retardation, 37,* 235–252.

Giangreco, M. (1983). Teaching basic photography skills to a severely handicapped young adult using simulated materials. *Journal of the Association for the Severely Handicapped, 8,* 43–49.

Green, F. P., & Schleien, S. J. (1991). Understanding friendship and recreation: A theoretical sampling. *Therapeutic Recreation Journal, 25*(4), 29–40.

Grenot-Scheyer, M., Coots, J., & Falvey, M. A. (1989). Developing and fostering friendships. In M. A. Falvey (Ed.), *Community-based curriculum: Instructional strategies for students with severe handicaps* (2nd Ed., pp. 345–358). Baltimore: Paul H. Brookes.

Grenot-Scheyer, M., Staub, D., Peck, C. A., & Schwartz, I. S. (1998). Reciprocity and friendships: Listening to the voices of children and youth with and without disabilities. In L. H. Meyer, H. Park, M. Grenot-Scheyer, I. S. Schwartz, & B. Harry (Eds.), *Making friends. The influence of culture and development* (pp. 149–167). Baltimore: Paul H. Brookes.

Hamre-Nietupski, S., Krajewski, L., Riehle, R., Sensor, K., Nietupski, J., Moravec, J., et al. (1992). Enhancing integration during the summer: Combined educational and community recreation options for students with severe disabilities. *Education and Training in Mental Retardation, 27,* 68–74.

Haring, T. G. (1992). Social relationships. In L. H. Meyer, C. A. Peck, & L. Brown (Eds.), *Critical issues in the lives of people with severe disabilities* (pp. 195–217). Baltimore: Paul H. Brookes.

Heyne, L. A. (1998). Teaching students to play. *TASH Newsletter, 24*(4), 10–12.

Hill, J., Wehman, P., & Horst, G. (1982). Toward generalization of appropriate leisure and social behavior in severely handicapped youth: Pinball machine use. *Journal of the Association for the Severely Handicapped, 6*(4), 38–44.

Huemann, J. E. (1993). A disabled woman's reflections: Myths and realities of integration. In J. A. Racino, P. Walker, S. O'Connor, & S. J. Taylor (Eds.), *Housing, support, and community: Choices and strategies for adults with disabilities* (pp. 233–249). Baltimore: Paul H. Brookes.

Lutfiyya, Z. M. (2001). Personal relationships between people with and without disabilities. *TASH Connections, 27*(10), 26–27.

Meyer, L. H., Cole, D. A., McQuarter, R., & Reichle, J. (1990). Validation of the Assessment of Social Competence (ASC) for children and young adults with developmental disabilities. *Journal of the Association for Persons with Severe Handicaps, 15,* 57–68.

Modell, S. J., & Valdez, L. A. (2002). Beyond bowling: Transition planning for students with disabilities. *Teaching Exceptional Children, 34*(6), 46–52.

Moon, M. S. (1994). *Making school and community recreation fun for everyone.* Baltimore: Paul H. Brookes.

Obermayer, L. (2001). Friendship is a two-way street. *TASH Connections, 27*(10), 23.

Perske, R. (1988). *Circles of friends: People with disabilities and their friends enrich the lives of one another.* Nashville, TN: Abingdon Press.

Realon, R., Favell, J. E., & Lowerre, A. (1990). The effects of making choices on engagement levels with persons who are profoundly multiply handicapped. *Education and Training in Mental Retardation, 25,* 299–305.

Rubin, Z. (1980). *Children's friendships.* Cambridge, MA: Harvard University Press.

Salisbury, C. L., & Palombaro, M. M. (1998). Friends and acquaintances: Evolving relationships in an inclusive elementary school. In L. H. Meyer, H. Park, M. Grenot-Scheyer, I. S. Schwartz, & B. Harry (Eds.), *Making friends. The influence of culture and development* (pp. 81–104). Baltimore: Paul H. Brookes.

Schaffner, C. B., & B. E. Buswell (1992). *Connecting students: A guide to thoughtful friendship facilitation for educators and families.* Colorado Springs, CO: PEAK Parent Center.

Schleien, S. J., Green, F. P., & Heyne, L. A. (1993). Integrated community recreation. In M. E. Snell (Ed.), *Instruction of students with severe disabilities* (4th Ed., pp. 526–555). Upper Saddle River, NJ: Merrill/Prentice Hall.

Schleien, S., Green, F., & Stone, C. (2002). Making friends within inclusive community recreation programs. *TASH Connections, 28*(7/8), 16–23.

Schleien, S. J., Heyne, L., & Dattilo, J. (1995). Teaching severely handicapped children: Social skills development through leisure skills programming. In G. Cartledge & J. Milburn (Eds.), *Teaching social skills to children: Innovative approaches* (3rd Ed., pp. 262–290). Boston: Allyn and Bacon.

Schleien, S. J., Kiernan, J., & Wehman, P. (1981). Evaluation of an age-appropriate leisure skills program for moderately retarded adults. *Education and Training of the Mentally Retarded, 16,* 13–19.

Schleien, S. J., Meyer, L. H., Heyne, L. A., & Brandt, B. B. (1995). *Lifelong leisure skills and lifestyles for persons with developmental disabilities.* Baltimore: Paul H. Brookes.

Schleien, S. J., & Rynders, J. E. (1998). Inclusive recreation: A parent's guide to quality. *TASH Newsletter, 24*(4), 18–19.

Schleien, S. J., Wehman, P., & Kiernan, J. (1981). Teaching leisure skills to severely handicapped adults: An age-appropriate darts game. *Journal of Applied Behavior Analysis, 14,* 513–519.

Sparrow, W. A., & Mayne, S. C. (1990). Recreation patterns of adults with intellectual disabilities. *Therapeutic Recreation Journal, 24*(3), 45–49.

Stainback, W., Stainback, S., & Wilkinson, A. (1992). Encouraging peer supports and friendships. *Teaching Exceptional Children, 24*(2), 6–11.

Strully, J., & Strully, C. (1985). Friendship and our children. *Journal of the Association for Persons with Severe Handicaps, 10,* 224–227.

Turnbull, A. P., Pereira, L., & Blue-Banning, M. (1999). Parents' facilitation of friendships between their children with a disability and friends without a disability. *Journal of the Association for Persons with Severe Handicaps, 24,* 85–99.

Vandercook, T. (1991). Leisure instruction outcomes: Criterion performance, positive interactions, and acceptance by typical high school peers. *Journal of Special Education, 25,* 320–339.

Voeltz, L. M., & Apffel, J. A. (1981). A leisure activities curricular component for severely handicapped youth: Why and how? *Viewpoints in Teaching and Learning, 57,* 82–93.

Voeltz, L. M., Wuerch, B. B., & Wilcox, B. (1982). Leisure and recreation: Preparation for independence, integration, and self-fulfillment. In B. Wilcox & G. T. Bellamy (Eds.), *High school programs for severely handicapped students.* Baltimore: Paul H. Brookes.

Wacker, D. P., Berg, W., Wiggins, B., Muldoon, M., & Cavanaugh, J. (1985). Evaluation of reinforcer preferences for profoundly handicapped students. *Journal of Applied Behavior Analysis, 18,* 173–178.

Wehman, P., Schleien, S., & Kiernan, J. (1980). Age appropriate recreation programs for severely handicapped youth and adults. *Journal of the Association for the Severely Handicapped, 5,* 394–407.

Wuerch, B. B., & Voeltz, L. M. (1982). *Longitudinal leisure skills for severely handicapped learners: The Ho'onanea curriculum component.* Baltimore: Paul H. Brookes.

York, J., Vandercook, T., & Stave, K. (1990). Recreational and leisure activities: Determining the favorites for middle school students. *Teaching Exceptional Children, 22,* 10–13.

CHAPTER 17

Teaching Appropriate Academic Skills

Many students classified as having a severe disability, particularly those considered to have moderate mental disabilities and many classified as having autism, can learn basic or even more advanced academic skills. This chapter addresses teaching academic skills, particularly methods for teaching literacy skills and functional arithmetic skills.

Issues Related to Academic Instruction

Educational programs for students with severe disabilities often emphasize instructing students in the functional skills necessary for life in the home and community. Other chapters have discussed the importance of these skills and ways in which they should be taught. In addition to these skills, however, we should consider the importance of academic instruction for many students with severe disabilities. Most children and adolescents have traditionally learned academic skills, ranging from basic reading to calculus, in school. However, any discussion of academic skills for students with severe disabilities raises questions like the following:

- To what extent are students with severe disabilities capable of learning traditional academic subjects such as reading, writing, and arithmetic?
- Will these skills be functional for students with severe disabilities? How will they be applied to meeting students' needs?
- Is it appropriate to teach academic skills for reasons other than their functionality?
- When in their school career will students be in most need of learning academic skills? When will they be most capable of learning these skills?
- Where is the most appropriate location for delivering academic instruction? In the special classroom? In the regular classroom?
- What type or form of curriculum will be appropriate?
- What instructional techniques might be successful?

And with recent legislation, most importantly,

- To what degree and in what way should students with severe disabilities participate in the general curriculum?

For many years there was a fundamental assumption that individuals whose measured intelligence fell at or below the level of moderate mental retardation (IQ < 55) could not be expected to acquire any skills requiring cognitive abilities. They were referred to as being "trainable mentally retarded," implying that they might be capable of learning some nonacademic skills, but they were not capable of more sophisticated learning (Kirk, 1972). Furthermore, people often questioned teaching academic skills because of the need to focus on relevant functional skills during the school years. Because the relevance of some academic skills is not always apparent, it may be appropriate to question spending valuable instructional time teaching them.

We suggest, however, that there are appropriate circumstances for teaching academic skills and there are relevant and important academic skills that should be taught. Techniques for academic instruction are discussed in this chapter. However, first we should consider some of the issues raised above.

Who Can Learn Academic Skills?

Although all students with severe disabilities can learn relevant skills that will increase their opportunities to participate in normal life activities, most research on academic learning has demonstrated that individuals within the traditional range of *moderate mental disabilities* (IQ approximately 40 to 55) have the ability to learn useful academic skills (Baroody & Snyder, 1983; Browder & Lalli, 1991; Browder & Xin, 1998; Conners, 1992; Rynders & Horrobin, 1990). Therefore, teachers can generally assume that students functioning at this level of cognitive ability are viable candidates for learning fundamental academic skills. However, although one's initial thought may be to include only individuals at this level when providing academic instruction, four qualifiers should be mentioned. First, the learning potential of individuals should never be underestimated. If there is any question about a person's ability to learn relevant academic skills in some form, it would probably be best to err on the side of attempting instruction, rather than discounting potential and making no attempt at instruction. Second, as discussed below, there are different levels of academic instruction. If a student is not successful at one level, perhaps she will have success at another. Third, although traditional academic learning in some areas (such as reading) and in some ways (such as sight word or phonics learning) may have a low probability of success, some modifications in instructional procedures (such as using symbols instead of words) might lead to success. And, fourth, although some students may not be able to verbally express what they know, understand, and appreciate, it may well be that some students with severe disabilities may nevertheless enjoy literacy experiences presented to them in different formats.

Levels of Academic Curricula

Some authorities have recommended that academic curricula for students with severe disabilities should be multileveled in difficulty (Browder & Snell, 1993; Ford et al., 1989). Depending on various conditions, such as a student's needs, abilities, age, time remaining in school, and student and parent desires, the student may be appropriately placed in an academic curriculum drawn from several options.

The first option is to place the student in the general academic curriculum provided to students without disabilities. A placement of this nature is most likely to be successful in the earlier school years (K–3) because there is often a wide range of instruction in early education; in addition, the discrepancy between the abilities of students with and without disabilities is relatively narrow (Ford et al., 1989). As the individual with disabilities grows older and the curricular emphasis becomes more abstract, the appropriateness of much of the regular curriculum decreases.

The second alternative is to provide an academic curriculum that is parallel to the general curriculum, but emphasizes only selected components of the general curriculum. For example, a student in a reading program might be focusing on sight-word identification skills, increasing reading fluency, and answering comprehension questions, instead of using a dictionary and learning about the card catalog in the library. In arithmetic, students may spend more time on computational skills and solving reasoning problems and little or no time on activities such as decimals and writing Roman numerals. Ford et al. (1989) referred to this as a *regular-adapted* or *streamlined curriculum.*

The regular-adapted curriculum may be appropriate for many children during the early to middle elementary years, but as students grow older (or for some younger students who are not succeeding with the regular-adapted curriculum), concern must be raised about the extent to which such skills will serve students as they participate in activities in their homes and communities. Skills such as reading, writing, and understanding words in natural environments, handling money, and telling time increase in significance as the student's world grows larger. At that time there is often a need to shift to a *functional* or *limited academic curriculum* (Browder & Snell, 1993; Ford et al., 1989). In the functional curriculum the instructional targets are based on the student's current and future environmental needs as determined through ecological inventories.

For many students, functional curricular targets may be taught in a more or less traditional academic manner. That is, in a regular classroom setting, students can learn to read their unique sets of words, handle money appropriately, and so forth, and later practice these skills in natural environments. For other students, those whose cognitive disabilities are more significant, instruction on such skills outside the contexts in which they will ultimately be applied will not be very meaningful. These students are more likely to benefit from academic instruction when it is what Ford et al. (1989) referred to as *embedded-functional instruction,* that is, when it is presented as the students are learning other functional skills in appropriate contexts. When an embedded-functional curriculum is used, academic prostheses (such as money that has been pre-counted and placed in a marked envelope for paying for food at a restaurant) is often helpful for the student (Browder & Snell, 1993).

Defining Functional Academic Instruction

Functional academics are areas of instruction that are meant to serve the individual in his current and future life. When one thinks of the types of academic skills that are actually needed to operate daily and to experience a relatively good quality of life, there are actually very few. There is the need to read and understand select words that allow us to do things like order from a menu or catch the right bus, write notes to ourselves to remind us to do some things or to convey to others our thoughts or needs, count out an adequate amount of money to pay for movie tickets and popcorn, or know what time it is so we won't be late for work or miss our favorite TV show. The ability to do these things and carry out similar activities largely dictates the nature of functional academic instruction.

Participation in the General Curriculum: Moving beyond Functional Instruction

Is functional academic instruction sufficient for students with severe disabilities? Certainly it is important, but as we saw in Chapter 2, IDEA '97 called for students with disabilities to participate in the general curriculum to the extent possible as well as to be tested at the end of the year when other students are required by state laws to take mandated tests. To some extent the requirement of *accessing the general curriculum* challenges the notion that students with severe disabilities should be limited to functional academic skill instruction. It requires that collaborative IEP teams give consideration to the appropriateness of these students engaging in the general curriculum. In Chapter 2 we discussed a decision-making process that will help team members to make an appropriate decision (Wehmeyer, Lance, & Bashinski, 2002; Wehmeyer, Lattin, and Agran, 2001; see Figure 2–1).

In doing so, some professionals will find it useful to look at recent thinking and research on this topic. One important area that deserves attention is participation in literacy instruction and activities (Katims, 2000; Kliewer & Biklen, 2001; Kliewer & Landis, 1999; Ryndak, Morrison, & Sommerstein, 1999). The position taken by these researchers and writers is that we have been too limited in focusing only on functional skills and need to explore ways in which students with severe disabilities can be participants in literate communities. They maintain that often schools overlook a person's potential and interest in literacy. This thought might be expanded to other academic areas, such as social studies, science, and art.

We may also often overlook learning academic skills for the sake of fun and pleasure. If we analyze our own reading, writing, and counting behavior, for example, or that of an adolescent or a child, we may note that we often apply our skills for pastime pursuits. Reading magazines, newspapers, or supermarket tabloids is often done for recreational purposes and being able to do so enhances one's quality of life. Keeping a diary or writing notes and letters to those we care about can be a nice way to spend an afternoon or evening. Keeping score when bowling, golfing, or playing cards allows us to enjoy these games more. A great number of examples of applying even relatively basic academic skills to various fun activities can be imagined. Although teachers are often concerned about how particular academic skills are applied in functional ways, they should also consider how these skills can be used in fun ways.

Academic skills might also serve other functions, such as helping individuals with disabilities to manage their own behavior or improve certain social skills (Browder & Minarovic, 2000; Krantz & McClannahan, 1998). In these ways academic skills become mediators for improving appropriate behavior in other learning domains.

Location of Academic Instruction

Considering the desirability of including students with severe disabilities in general education classrooms and assuming that many students will be learning academic skills at levels somewhat different from those of their nondisabled classmates, we need to know how to manage instruction in the regular classroom so that all benefit. Although this presents a challenge, general and special educators can work together in many ways to provide a high quality of instruction for all students. Procedures for doing so are presented briefly in the final section of this chapter. Chapter 10 is devoted fully to including students with severe disabilities in regular classrooms.

Summary of Issues Related to Teaching Academic Skills

It is arguable that the most important skills for individuals with severe disabilities are not academic in nature. It should also be realized that academic instruction, even instruction primarily of a functional nature, is likely to be of benefit to students who are functioning within the moderate range of mental disabilities. However, underestimating the ability of students in special education has more often been a problem than overestimating it. As with other areas of learning, academic instruction should be approached with a view that all students can learn skills to some degree, and so the teacher must find the appropriate level, need, and interest for each student. Many parents feel that it is very appropriate for their children to learn academic tasks (Hamre-Nietupski, Nietupski, & Strathe, 1992), and many general educators feel that some academic skills are important for students with disabilities to learn in order to work in inclusive classrooms (Hanrahan, Goodman, & Rapagna, 1990). Therefore, the importance of learning these skills should be given due attention.

Having students with different levels of academic ability in the regular classroom can be a challenge even for skilled teachers. However, the benefits of including children with disabilities in typical classes warrant that the challenge be accepted and successfully addressed.

Teaching Literacy Skills

For most individuals with severe disabilities, historically, there has been little emphasis on teaching literacy skills. Most of the practice and research in this area has focused on learning to read single words by sight. To a lesser extent, there have been attempts to teach phonics skills, oral reading from books, comprehension skills, writing skills, spelling, and literacy in more comprehensive contexts (Browder & Lalli, 1991; Browder & Xin, 1998; Conners, 1992; Erickson, Koppenhaven, & Yoder, 1994; Katims, 2000). In the following sections we focus on the most traditional approaches to instruction in the area of reading for students with severe disabilities, that is, teaching sight words. We begin by looking at the importance of the words to be taught and then at ways that they can be taught. Commercial materials that may be useful and applications of computer programs are briefly discussed. After discussing this approach and related methods of instruction, we examine more recent thoughts and trends in literacy instruction.

What Students Should Learn to Read

Teaching basic reading skills requires the identification of materials that the learner needs to learn to read. In most cases, when teaching reading to students with moderate mental disabilities, the material should include high-frequency words that the student can learn to identify by sight and read in various important contexts. Although many of these may be drawn from basic reading lists, such as those of Fry (1957, 1972) or Dolch (1950), more relevant lists may be constructed from meaningful environments. Based on their review of literature, Browder and Xin (1998) reported that sight word instruction has been used to teach students to read words to help them to achieve grocery shopping, do household chores, follow instructions for cooking and other daily tasks, read product warning labels, and read signs during community recreational activities. As suggested by this research, teachers should put emphasis on teaching words that occur in the students' natural environments. When conducting an ecological inventory of a student's environments, attention should be given to the words in the environments that will allow the student to operate in this setting. In this vein, Ford et al. (1989) identified various opportunities for reading and writing in the school, for both functional activities and for pleasure. Several of these opportunities are listed in Table 17–1. Analyses of other environments yield similar results. For example:

- Cuvo and Klatt (1992) identified signs in community settings that later served as instructional targets for the individuals that they were teaching.
- Schloss, Alexander, Hornig, Parker, & Wright (1993) and Collins, Branson, and Hall (1995) taught students to read words necessary for preparing meals.
- Collins and Stinson (1995) taught students to read words that were on the warning labels of different products.
- Krantz and McClannahan (1998) taught two children with autism to read and say words ("look" and "watch me") that would prompt others to engage in social and communicative interactions with them.
- Browder and Minarovic (2000) taught young adults with moderate mental retardation to first read sight words and then to use the words to prompt themselves to complete specific jobs in their places of competitive employment.

Differentiating the words to be learned based on the age of the student may also be important (Feinberg, 1975). For children, Feinberg suggested that words appropriate for reading instruction could be those that are naturally spoken and heard by children, that is, an extension of their natural language. For those closer to the adult years, however, Feinberg recommended words that would best allow them to operate successfully in community settings, such as *men, woman, ladies, exit, entrance, enter, in, out, stop, push, pull, emergency, danger, walk, don't walk, wait, up, down, bus stop, keep out, keep off,* and *no smoking.* Feinberg (1975) also pointed out that it is important to teach sight words in various contexts in order for the concepts to be learned.

Regardless of the particular source of the words, after they are identified for instruction, they should be arranged and then taught in sets; typically, these sets include two to ten words with an average of about four per set (Browder & Xin, 1998). The grouping of the words should be in a logical order, but there is no definitive rule for doing so. Some teachers group them based on their appearance in different settings (e.g., grocery store words, words in the bowling alley); in other cases they are grouped as they appear in books that the student will read. What is important is that word groups be identified for instruction.

When the student masters one set by being able to read all the words correctly to a preset criterion, say for three days in a row, the next group of words may be introduced. Although the new words are learned as a group, time should be set aside, perhaps one or two days a week, for students to review all previously learned words so that the learning will be maintained.

Instructional Methods for Teaching Sight Words

The most common method for teaching sight words is for the teacher to print the target words clearly on plain index cards, using a black felt-tip pen to form block letters, and then show the words, one at a time, to a student or a group of students, having them read one word at a time. During each daily instructional session, the entire set of words (e.g., two to ten) is studied. Until a word has been learned, it is modeled by the instructor. After several episodes, the student should be able to say the word when he sees it. Several variations that have been found to improve the

Table 17–1 Reading and Writing Opportunities

School Level	*For Pleasure*	*For Functional Use*
Elementary school: reading	Looking at books during free time Checking out books from the library Listening to stories read aloud (by peers, by teacher, by librarian) Participating in structured reading time Reading self-composed stories aloud to classmates Reading books	Following sequence cards for classroom jobs Reviewing daily lunch menu Reviewing daily schedule Managing weekly/monthly calendar Using communication booklet Reading portions of newsletters or notes to take home Reading signs, posters, and bulletin boards Following recipe for snack preparation
Elementary school: writing	Writing stories or drawing pictures to illustrate messages Writing cards and letters Constructing photo albums and writing captions Writing journals	Writing name on school projects Writing name on card to check out library book Filling out emergency cards and other forms that require name, address, and telephone number Leaving notes or messages for a friend or teacher Signing up for a classroom job
Middle school and high school: reading	Looking at books during free time Checking out books from the library Participating in structured reading program in English class or reading lab	Following sequence cards at job site Following written daily schedule Reading the weekly cafeteria menu and menus in restaurants Managing weekly/monthly calendar Using communication booklet Looking at school newspaper Reading signs, posters, and bulletin boards Following recipe in home economics class Identifying labels on items in store
Middle school and high school: writing	Writing collection of stories Writing cards and letters Constructing photo album or essay with captions Writing journals, diaries	Writing name on belongings (papers, books) Writing name on library cards Writing name on sign-up sheets Filling out forms requiring identifying information Leaving notes or messages for friends or teacher Writing events/reminders on personal calendar Writing grocery lists Writing address and phone number down for friend

Source: The Syracuse Community-Referenced Curriculum Guide for Students with Moderate and Severe Disabilities (p. 98), by A. Ford, R. Schnorr, I. Meyer, J. Black, and P. Dempsey, 1989. Baltimore: Paul H. Brookes Publishing Co. Reprinted by permission.

effectiveness of this approach are discussed in the sections that follow. You will note the application of several of the skill acquisition procedures discussed in Chapter 7.

Constant Time Delay

A simple and effective technique for teaching sight words is to apply a constant time delay (CTD) procedure. Using this method, the teacher gives an attentional cue, presents the word on a flashcard, and waits 4 or 5 seconds for the student to say the word. If the student does not respond, the teacher models the word for the student to repeat. To initially help the students to learn the words, on the first several trials or the first one or two sessions of instruction, the teacher will use a zero-second delay between showing the word on the card and modeling the word. While showing the written word on the card, the teacher says "what word?" or "read, please" as a verbal cue to get the student to respond and then immediately say the word; when the student repeats the word, she is reinforced by the teacher. After a few such zero-second delay sessions, the teacher waits for several seconds and then supplies the word if the student has not said it. If the student says the word before the prompt, the teacher provides strong reinforcement. A milder form of reinforcement is used when the student does not say the word until after the prompt has been given. If an error occurs either before or after the prompt, the teacher prompts the correct response.

The straightforwardness of the CTD procedure for teaching sight words makes it an ideal method for use by paraprofessionals in inclusive classrooms or for use by peer tutors. There is often concern that students with cognitive disabilities in regular classrooms will not receive instruction geared to their needs. However McDonnell, Johnson, Polychronis, and Risen (2002) developed a program in which paraprofessionals used CTD to teach students with moderate mental disabilities either to read sight words or to state the definition of terms at times during the regular class sessions when they were not engaged in other class activities. Working with four middle school boys, the paraprofessionals used CTD to teach the boys words relevant to the general education classes that they were taking. The paraprofessionals taught the words to the students during down times, that is, right at the beginning or end of an activity, during transitions between activities, and when there was a lull in an ongoing activity. Each boy learned three sets of five word groups (either reading them or defining them) during the study. Likewise, Miracle, Collins, Schuster, and Grisham-Brown (2001) taught five adolescent peers without disabilities to teach sight words to four students with moderate to severe mental disabilities using CTD. After the peers were taught to use the CTD procedure, they taught the students with disabilities for 20 to 30 instructional sessions. The progress achieved by the students with disabilities when tutored by their peers was compared to their progress when taught by the teacher using the same procedure. The results showed that three of the four students learned the words as well from their teenage peers as they did from the teacher. What is most significant about this study is that the amount of time it took to teach the peers how to use CTD was approximately 90 minutes. With this relatively small investment of time with the peer instructors, the teacher was able to greatly increase the instructional time for the students with disabilities, as well as enhance their opportunity to spend time with their nondisabled peers.

A substantial amount of research supports the use of CTD as an effective means of teaching sight words to individuals with moderate mental retardation (Browder & Lalli, 1991; Browder & Xin, 1998; Collins et al., 1995; Gast, Ault, Wolery, Doyle, & Belanger, 1988; Gast, Wolery, Morris, Doyle, & Meyer, 1990; Koury & Browder, 1986; Lalli & Browder, 1993; Schloss et al., 1993). Because of the ease with which it can be implemented, it is often recommended as the primary tactic for teaching sight words.

Progressive Time Delay

The teacher can also use progressive time delay (PTD), a variation of CTD, by starting with a shorter delay period between showing the word and saying it (prompting the correct response if the student does not read the word), but then extending the delay by increasing it every session by 1 or 2 seconds. Using this method, instead of having a constant time delay of 4 or 5 seconds, the teacher starts with a zero delay on the first day (just as with constant time delay), but then uses a 2-second delay on session 2, a 4-second delay on session 3, 6 seconds on session 4, and so on, until reaching an 8- or 10-second delay (Ault, Gast, & Wolery, 1988; Browder, Hines, McCarthy, & Fees, 1984).

The theoretical advantage of PTD as a sight word reading instructional method is that it allows more time for the student to try to read the word. Although PTD has been used successfully in some studies (e.g., Collins & Stinson, 1995), it is more cumbersome for the teacher to use, requires more time, and has not been found to be more effective than CTD (Ault et al., 1988; Browder & Lalli, 1991). Still, it may be useful for teaching students with less developed cognitive ability or for teaching longer or more complex words.

System of Least Prompts

The principle of providing only as much prompting as necessary to get the student to read the word is also a viable technique for teaching sight words. Using this method, the teacher begins by developing a series of prompts that are applied in an order of increasing assistance if the student does not read the word correctly when shown the card. Using the system of least prompts requires the teacher to show the word to the student and, after ensuring that the student is looking, to deliver a sequence of prompts such as the following:

1. The teacher says "read this" and then waits 4 seconds. If the student does not respond correctly (i.e., does not respond at all or says the wrong word),
2. The teacher says "read this" and also verbally describes the word (e.g., if the word is *milk,* the teacher might say "this is something white that we drink"). If the student still does not respond,
3. The teacher repeats "read this" and shows the student a picture of the item.
4. Finally, if the student does not respond correctly, the teacher says, "Read this . . . milk, say milk."

This procedure is intended to get the student to respond correctly with the least amount of assistance. While it has been shown to be effective, it may not actually be any more effective than CTD and takes more time to implement (Gast et al., 1988).

Pairing Pictures with Sight Words

The abstract nature of the configuration of words—linking abstract symbols together to form a meaningful unit—can result in difficulty in correct responding by students with mental disabilities. It may be helpful if, when words are initially presented, they are presented on cards or pages paired with pictures of what the words represent. Since the picture is likely to have more inherent meaning, there is a higher probability that the student will learn to respond to it faster than he will to a word. Obviously, this approach requires the material to be altered by attaching a picture or drawing one on the card. The instructional delivery uses one of the methods above (e.g., CTD) to teach the student to respond to the word–picture pair.

Ultimately, the student may be able to transfer attention from the picture to the word and thus read the word when it is seen without the picture (Barudin & Hourcade, 1990; Dorry & Zeaman, 1973, 1975; Entriken, York, & Brown, 1977; Miller & Miller, 1971; Singh & Solman, 1990). There is one major concern with this method. A *blocking effect,* may occur meaning that the transference of attention by the student from the picture to the word may not be sucessful. In fact, because the picture is likely to have greater attentional value, transferring attention may be very difficult (Didden, Prinsen, & Sigafoos, 2000; Singh & Solman, 1990). Therefore, the teacher might need to devise a *fading procedure* that ultimately (over several sessions) results in the picture being completely faded while the word remains on the card. This change in the stimulus requires that the student shift attention gradually from the picture to the word (Browder & Lalli, 1991; Lalli & Browder, 1993). Figure 17–1 displays how this process may be applied.

Because of the time required to prepare the material (several cards would be required for each word, as shown in Figure 17–1), this approach may not be as efficient as other methods. On the other hand, it may help students who are otherwise having difficulty interpreting the written word.

Figure 17–1 Example of Using a Pairing and Fading Procedure to Teach Sight Words

Embedding Sight Words in Pictures and Figures

This approach is very similar to the pairing method, but with an important distinction: the word to be learned is *embedded* in the figure that represents it (or there is a figure embedded in the word), instead of simply being paired with it (Miller & Miller, 1968, 1971; Worrall & Singh, 1983). The advantage of this method over the pairing method is that the student does not have to make an overt shift of attention away from the figure and to the word. Because of this, the embedded arrangement tends to be more effective than only pairing the word and the picture (Conners, 1992). Again, however, as with pairing, it is necessary to gradually fade the figure until only the word remains. Figure 17–2 provides an example of this process.

Using Symbols and Pictures Instead of Words

It is possible for some students with mental disabilities to learn to read symbols or pictures (see them and state the word that they represent) even if they cannot actually learn to read sight words (Brady & McLean, 1996). Sym-

Figure 17–2 Example of Using Embedding and Fading to Teach Sight Words

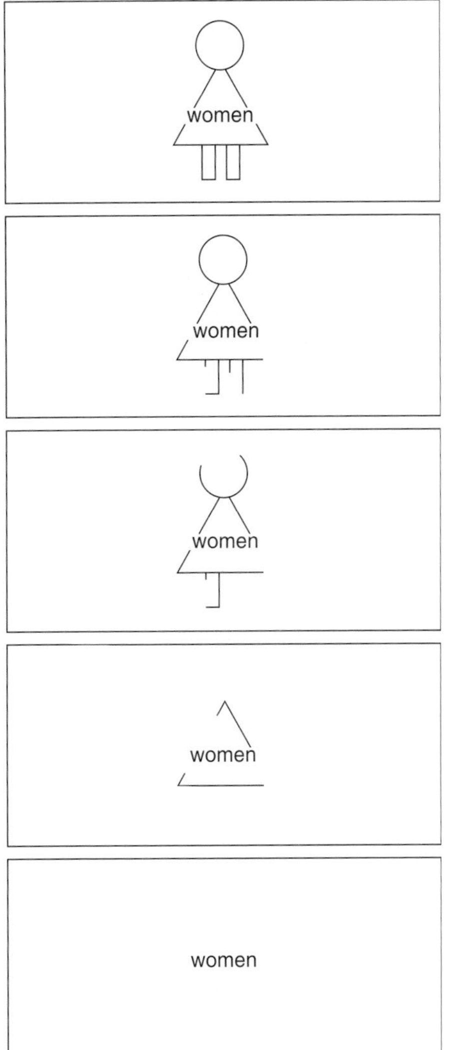

bols, line drawings, pictures, or photographs may be placed in sequence in order for the student to "read" a story to someone. They may also be used to provide cues to the student for completing the steps in a particular task (House, Hanley, & Magid, 1980; Roberson, Gravel, Valcante, & Maurer, 1992). In some cases, students may be able to use the symbols or pictures to generate their own sentences.

When pictures or symbols are used in this way, they are not faded out and therefore remain as the symbolic unit that is being interpreted. There are two disadvantages to using this approach. First, only the student and a few other people will know the meaning of the pictures or symbols. Second, the student will not be able to respond to real words when they appear in the natural environment. Of course, the advantage of the approach is that the student who has not been able to learn to read words can still learn to "read."

Teaching Word Analysis (Phonics) Skills

Although most reading instruction for students with moderate mental disabilities has focused on teaching whole words, several efforts have been made to teach students to analyze the sounds of the letters in words and thus be able to sound out unknown words without having to rely on visual memorization of the entire word. Furthermore, research suggests that using phonics skills is more related to developmental level than to intelligence level (Conners, Carr, & Willis, 1998). Students who can use phonics skills are at an advantage because they then have the potential for deciphering unknown words that they might encounter in the future (Nietupski, Williams, & York, 1979). It should be realized, however, that this is a time-consuming undertaking. Because the time and effort required to teach phonics to a level of generalizable applicability is substantial, it may be better to spend instructional time teaching individual words.

A preferred strategy would most likely be a combination of approaches in which a functional list of sight words is first taught, perhaps 100 to 200 words, followed by an attempt at teaching word analysis (Conners, 1992). If this process is undertaken, the following methods are likely to be helpful.

Teaching Letter Names and Sounds

The first step in the process of teaching phonics skills is generally to teach the names of the letters. This process can be undertaken using a flashcard method or alphabet sets until all letter names are committed to memory. It is not actually necessary for students to know the names of the letters in order to know their sounds, but this is the most conventional way.

The next step is to teach individual letter sounds and letter combinations. The teacher first models the letter sounds for the students and has them repeat them. When students can demonstrate that they can imitate letter sounds, they should then be able to indicate whether the sounds that they hear are the same or different (Nietupski et al., 1979). These skills (modeling sounds and being able to indicate whether two sounds are the same or different) is used with both individual letter sounds and with combined letter sounds.

Next, students must learn to hear and combine separate letter sounds into one sound. This may be easier if they first learn to blend together words heard separately (e.g., *dog . . . house, doghouse*), then syllables heard separately (e.g., *hap . . . py, happy*), and finally letter sounds heard separately (e.g., *b . . . l, bl*) (Hoogeveen & Smeets, 1988).

The process of teaching phonics skills should continue in an orderly fashion by teaching certain letter combinations in sets. Nietupski et al. (1979) used the following sequence:

1. Say single consonant sounds to a preset criterion level. The sounds were taught in this order: set 1: *b, d, m, t, w;* set 2: set 1 plus *c, g, h, n, p;* set 3: set 2 plus *f, j, l, r, s;* set 4: set 3 plus *k, v, x, y, z.*
2. Say short vowel sounds to criterion.
3. Read vowel–consonant (VC) combinations (*an, up, of*).
4. Read consonant–vowel–consonant combinations (*sat, beg, rip*).

Ford et al. (1989) proposed that the extensive sequence of phonics skills listed in Figure 17–3 be used after a basic sight word vocabulary has been acquired.

Using Games to Teach Phonics Skills

At each phase of instruction, Nietupski et al. (1979) reported that the use of various games helped students with moderate mental disabilities to learn phonics sounds. The games included *sound bingo* (marking the sounds on cards as they were heard); *chutes and ladders* board games (roll dice, move to the position, say the sound or move back to your original position); *phonics concentration* (find and label pairs of the same sounds); and *word wheels* (form and say new words by spinning the word wheels). This last game is displayed in Figure 17–4. Other teacher-made phonics games may also be helpful.

Using Visual Prompts to Teach Letter Sounds

Students who have difficulty remembering the sounds of particular letters may do better if picture cues are embedded in, or used to accentuate, particular letters, similar to the procedure used with recognizing sight words. This can be done in two ways. One way is to incorporate a picture with a letter that represents the sound that the letter makes (Hoogeveen, Smeets, & Van der Houven, 1987). An example is incorporating a picture of a snake around the letter *S,* as displayed in Figure 17–5. As with the use of pictorial prompts with words, it is important to gradually fade the prompt so that the student ultimately associates the letter sound with the actual letter without the prompt (see Figure 17–6). As students learn individual letter sounds, they can be taught to combine them either with or without the continued use of the prompts, but the prompts eventually need to be eliminated.

A second approach is similar to the first except that, instead of using a picture to represent the sound of the letter, the picture represents an object whose *initial sound* is the same as the sound of the letter (Hoogeveen, Smeets, & Lancioni, 1989). For example, if the teacher wants to teach the long *e* sound (ee), a picture of an eel with the letter *e* embedded in it is presented to the student and he is taught to say "eeeeel." Ultimately, the teacher will help the student drop the undesired part of the sound and say "ee" when the picture of the eel with the letter *e* was shown. Finally, the picture is faded over five or more steps, leaving only the *e,* and the student says this sound. Individual letter sounds could then be combined to create new words and syllables.

These approaches suggest that with careful planning and program development some students with moderate mental disabilities can learn letter sounds. However, the procedures are elaborate, and if letter sounds are not being learned at an adequate rate using these approaches or other methods of skill acquisition (such as time delay or a system of least prompts), time and effort might be better spent on learning more whole words.

Teaching Oral Reading from Books

Oral reading skills allow students to go beyond reading individual whole words or sounding out words by letter sounds to reading entire sentences, paragraphs, or multiword passages from books. In most initial learning processes reported in the literature, these books have been limited to basal readers, but they may also include various magazines, storybooks, or other books that contain vocabulary within the students' learning potential. Most students without disabilities begin reading from books while they are acquiring basic sight words and initial phonics abilities. Students with moderate mental disabilities should also have such initial skills or at least be able to read by sight most of the words in the books to be read.

Oral reading from books should allow the student to improve the speed of reading and also acquire new vocab-

Figure 17–3 Sequence of Reading Skills for Instructing Students with Severe Disabilities

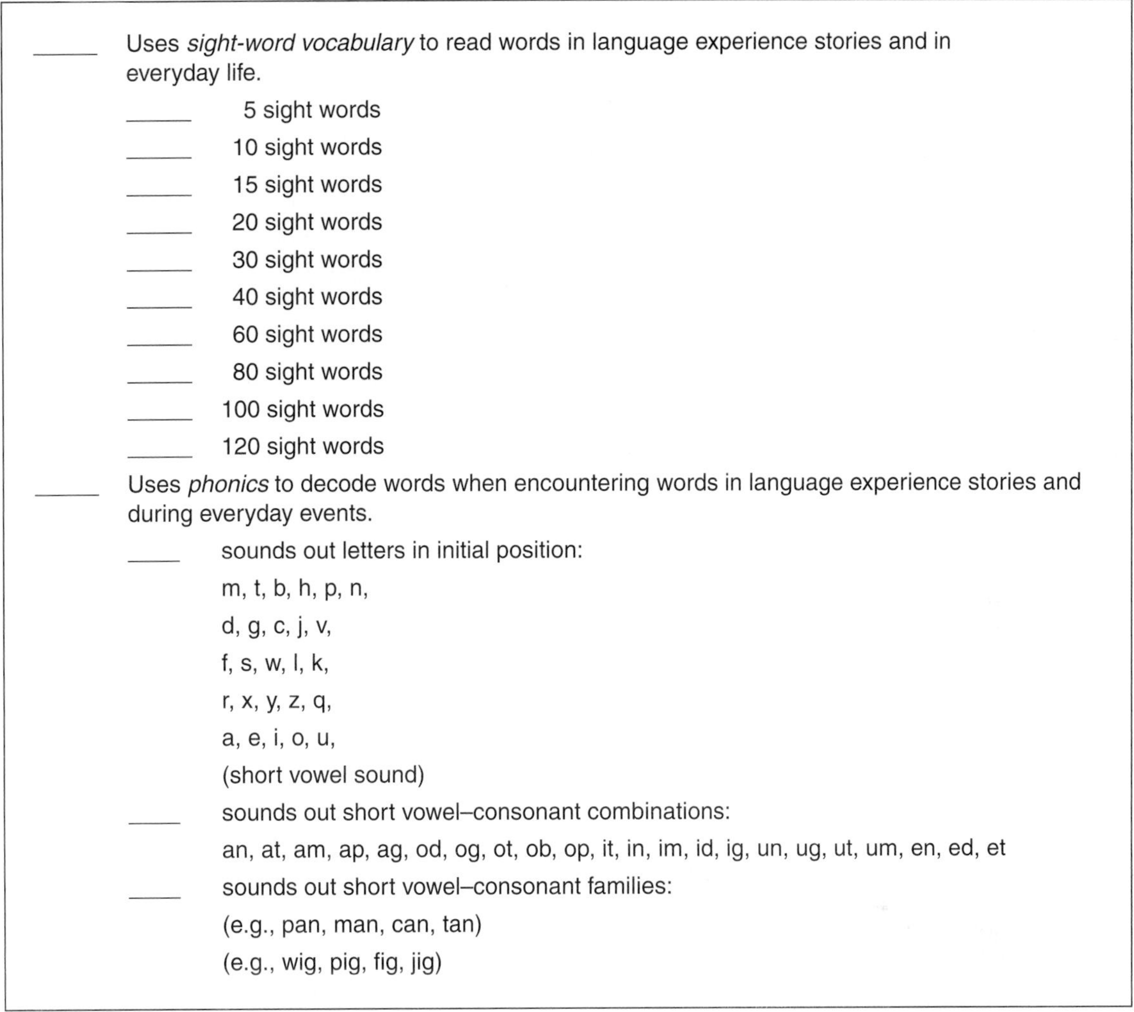

_____ Uses *sight-word vocabulary* to read words in language experience stories and in everyday life.

- _____ 5 sight words
- _____ 10 sight words
- _____ 15 sight words
- _____ 20 sight words
- _____ 30 sight words
- _____ 40 sight words
- _____ 60 sight words
- _____ 80 sight words
- _____ 100 sight words
- _____ 120 sight words

_____ Uses *phonics* to decode words when encountering words in language experience stories and during everyday events.

- _____ sounds out letters in initial position:
  m, t, b, h, p, n,
  d, g, c, j, v,
  f, s, w, l, k,
  r, x, y, z, q,
  a, e, i, o, u,
  (short vowel sound)
- _____ sounds out short vowel–consonant combinations:
  an, at, am, ap, ag, od, og, ot, ob, op, it, in, im, id, ig, un, ug, ut, um, en, ed, et
- _____ sounds out short vowel–consonant families:
  (e.g., pan, man, can, tan)
  (e.g., wig, pig, fig, jig)

Source: The Syracuse Community-Referenced Curriculum Guide for Students with Moderate and Severe Disabilities (pp. 112–114), by A. Ford, R. Schnorr, L. Meyer, J. Black, and P. Dempsey, 1989, Baltimore: Paul H. Brookes Publishing Co. Reprinted by permission.

(continued)

ulary words. It can also serve as a basis for learning to sound out new words. The following tactics have been found helpful in improving the oral reading ability of students with moderate mental disabilities.

Preview of Material

Taking time to preview a story or passage before it is read may help students to read with fewer errors during oral reading. Previewing consists of discussing the story with the student by talking about the title, looking at and discussing any pictures that may appear in the text, introducing new words and phrases that will appear and talking about their meaning, and answering any questions about the story that students may have before they read (Singh & Singh, 1984). This process takes relatively little time and is one that many students enjoy and benefit from. One positive by-product of previewing is that it can involve all students, even those who cannot read the text.

Positive Practice

Often when students are reading orally and they miss a word by reading it incorrectly or not reading it at all, the teacher supplies the word and the student continues reading. If, instead of allowing the student to continue immediately, the teacher asks the student to say the word five times while looking at it, on subsequent occasions

Figure 17–3 Continued

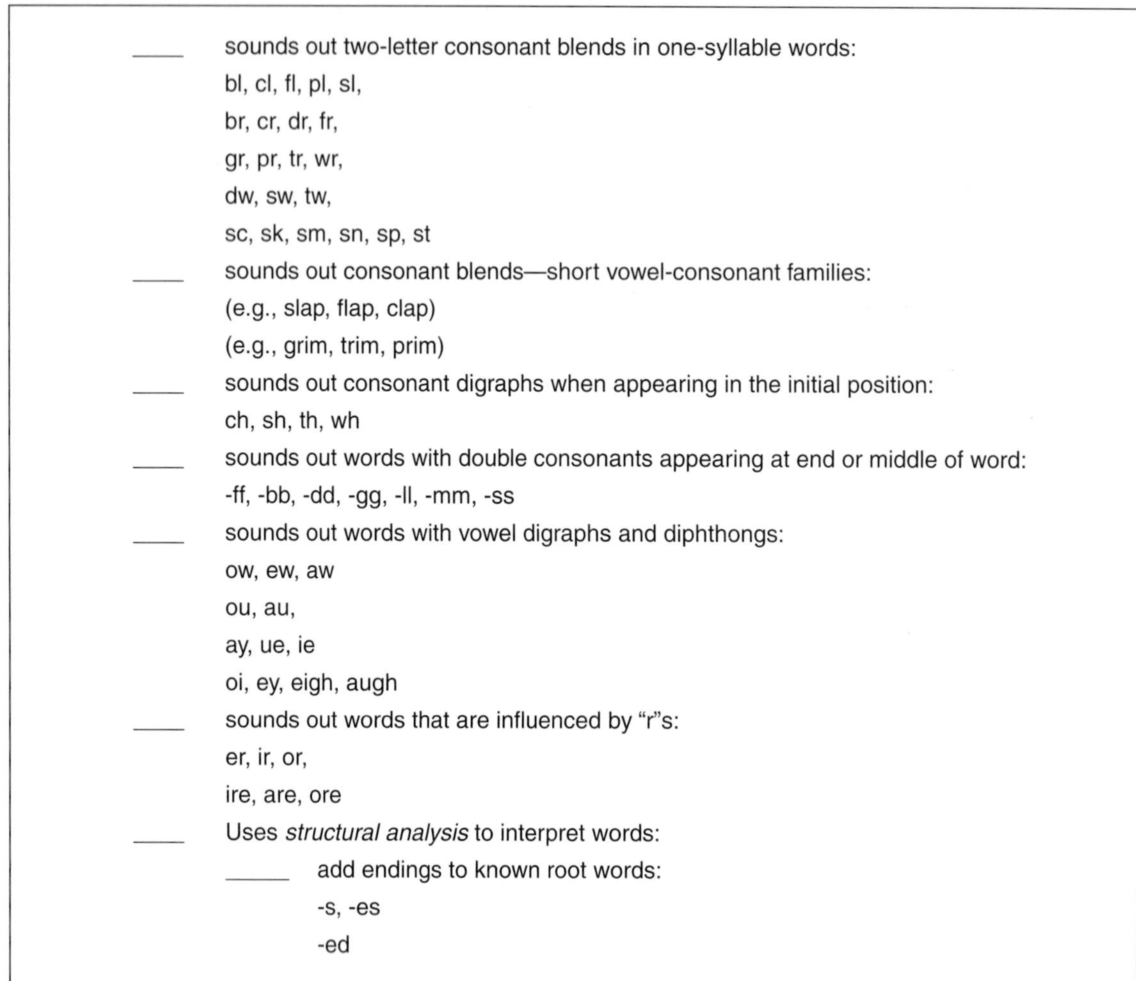

____ sounds out two-letter consonant blends in one-syllable words:
bl, cl, fl, pl, sl,
br, cr, dr, fr,
gr, pr, tr, wr,
dw, sw, tw,
sc, sk, sm, sn, sp, st

____ sounds out consonant blends—short vowel-consonant families:
(e.g., slap, flap, clap)
(e.g., grim, trim, prim)

____ sounds out consonant digraphs when appearing in the initial position:
ch, sh, th, wh

____ sounds out words with double consonants appearing at end or middle of word:
-ff, -bb, -dd, -gg, -ll, -mm, -ss

____ sounds out words with vowel digraphs and diphthongs:
ow, ew, aw
ou, au,
ay, ue, ie
oi, ey, eigh, augh

____ sounds out words that are influenced by "r"s:
er, ir, or,
ire, are, ore

____ Uses *structural analysis* to interpret words:

 _____ add endings to known root words:
 -s, -es
 -ed

(continued)

the student will be less likely to miss the word when it appears again in the story (Singh & Singh, 1988).

Word Analysis Skills

Some students are able to sound out words by looking at the individual letters or letter combinations. If teachers help with this process during oral reading, rather than simply saying the word that has been omitted or read incorrectly, students may be more likely to read the word correctly on subsequent appearances (Singh & Singh, 1985).

Pictures and Context Clues

Some oral reading errors may be avoided by teaching students to use available information to figure out the word (Entriken et al., 1977). If a student knows the sound of the first letter of the word, he may be able to determine what the word is by looking at pictures in the story or by recalling information provided in the narrative. Considering such information as this may help the student who has basic phonics skills.

Students who can read orally from books have the potential to become functional in their reading and to be able to read for both need and pleasure; those who can advance to this level should be given adequate instruction in the reading process. The instructional goals should be to acquire a greater vocabulary, read faster, and make fewer errors at increasingly higher reading levels. Words read correctly and incorrectly are discrete behaviors that can be counted and charted, using the procedures described in Chapter 8. By keeping these kinds of records, the teacher can monitor students' progress.

Figure 17–3 Continued

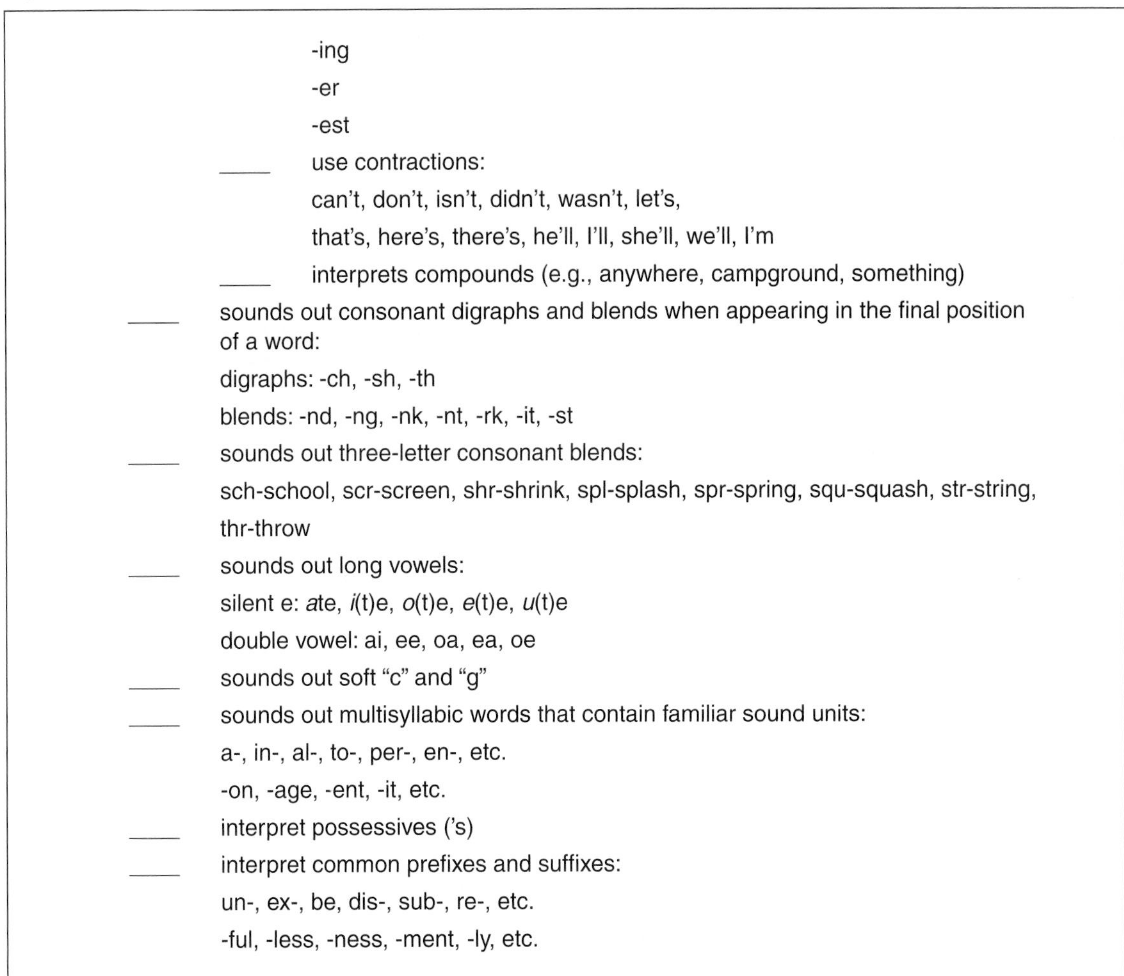

-ing

-er

-est

____ use contractions:

can't, don't, isn't, didn't, wasn't, let's,

that's, here's, there's, he'll, I'll, she'll, we'll, I'm

____ interprets compounds (e.g., anywhere, campground, something)

____ sounds out consonant digraphs and blends when appearing in the final position of a word:

digraphs: -ch, -sh, -th

blends: -nd, -ng, -nk, -nt, -rk, -it, -st

____ sounds out three-letter consonant blends:

sch-school, scr-screen, shr-shrink, spl-splash, spr-spring, squ-squash, str-string,

thr-throw

____ sounds out long vowels:

silent e: *a*te, *i*(t)e, *o*(t)e, *e*(t)e, *u*(t)e

double vowel: ai, ee, oa, ea, oe

____ sounds out soft "c" and "g"

____ sounds out multisyllabic words that contain familiar sound units:

a-, in-, al-, to-, per-, en-, etc.

-on, -age, -ent, -it, etc.

____ interpret possessives ('s)

____ interpret common prefixes and suffixes:

un-, ex-, be, dis-, sub-, re-, etc.

-ful, -less, -ness, -ment, -ly, etc.

Using Commercial Materials to Teach Reading

Commercially produced instructional materials have often been used successfully to teach reading to students with moderate mental disabilities. Three are described here: the Edmark Reading Program, material from the Attainment Company, and the DISTAR Reading Program.

The Edmark program is based on the process of visual discrimination. Students learn first to simply point to an isolated word when it is said by the teacher. They then learn to point to the word as it appears in increasingly complex arrays of words. After target words can be accurately identified, the students learn to say the word as they see it. As they progress, they learn to identify and read more and more sight words. Walsh and Lambert (1979) found the Edmark program to be more effective than a picture-fading technique for recognizing, matching, and identifying words.

The Edmark program comes both in a traditional format and as software and is available from Riverdeep (http://www.riverdeep.net/edmark/). At the Web site, the program is described as follows:

> The Edmark Reading Program is designed for students with learning or developmental disabilities and those who have not succeeded with other reading methods. For 30 years, this trusted program has been highly regarded by teaching professionals as "the one that works," allowing most nonreaders to master basic reading skills. The Edmark Reading Program uses a whole-word approach, with short instructional steps, consistent repetition, and positive reinforcement to ensure that students experience immediate success. Multiple learning modalities are incorporated into this highly effective process with a variety of lesson formats that keep students motivated and involved. Graphics,

Figure 17–4 A Word Wheel Game

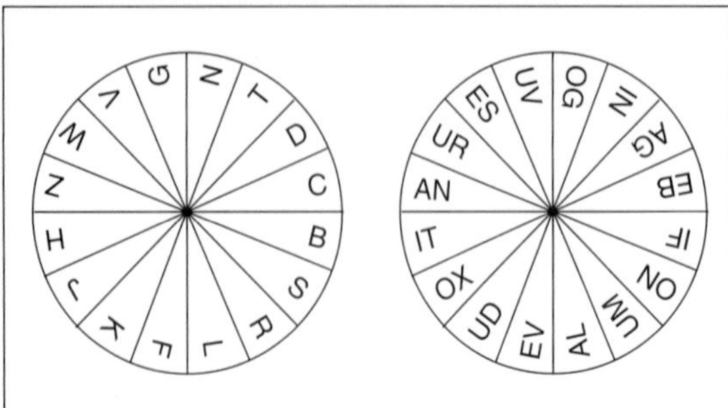

Source: "Teaching Selected Phonic Word Analysis Skills to TMR Labeled Students," by J. Nietupski, W. Williams, and R. York, 1979, *Teaching Exceptional Children, 11,* p. 80. Copyright 1979 by The Council for Exceptional Children. Reprinted by permission.

> content, and presentation are appropriate for readers of all ages. Graphics can be turned off for adult or older students.
>
> At five- and ten-word intervals, review and test activities are provided, allowing teachers to test student knowledge of learned words. Management tools and automatic record keeping allow teachers to individualize student learning and track progress.
>
> The Level 1 software version teaches 150 words chosen from the Dolch Word List for first-grade readers, as well as "-s," "-ed," and "-ing" endings, capitalization, and punctuation. Students can click on individual words or whole sentences to hear them read aloud. From the beginning, students find success with a process that teaches sight recognition of a word, introduces its meaning, provides comprehension activities, and uses the word in story context.

The Attainment Company (http://www.attainmentinc.com) offers materials that combine pictures and words to teach students practical skills such as daily planning, meal selection, shopping, cooking, grooming, and housekeeping. According to their Web site, one of their materials, *Practical Practice Reading Series*, is designed to teach essential reading skills in the context of everyday life situations. It is targeted toward students, grades 4 to 12, who read at a third- to fourth-grade level and combines reading instruction with life skill training. The program uses everyday materials for reading content, including newspapers, ads, coupons, catalogs, schedules, directories, and guides. Six reproducible books include The Newspaper, Labels & Packages, Ads & Coupons, Directories & Guides, Catalogs, and Filling Out Forms.

The DISTAR program uses a direct instruction approach to teach a series of phonics skills that have been carefully sequenced. The student must master each skill before moving on to a new one. The teacher follows an instructional script that includes cues that are to be provided to the students and the error-correction techniques. Students are instructed in small groups and reinforced for correct responses. The instruction is very quickly paced. Although DISTAR was designed primarily for students with mild disabilities with poor reading skills, it has also been used with some success for students with moderate mental disabilities (Bracey, Maggs, & Morath, 1975; Gersten & Maggs, 1982). Commercial DISTAR reading programs are available online at http://www.abiva.com.ph/SRA.HTML.

Teaching Comprehension Skills and Applying Reading Skills in Real Settings

Besides teaching sight words and oral reading skills, it is also important to teach comprehension skills to students with cognitive disabilities and how to use these skills in real-world conditions. Although comprehension has been evaluated in some studies, with only a few exceptions, little has been done to specifically teach students to understand, interpret, or act on what they have read (Browder & Lalli, 1991; Browder & Xin, 1998; Erickson et al., 1994). It will not be sufficient simply to have students read words individually or even read them in texts. Nor does the ability to sound out new words mean that the student understands what she is reading or is able to use the skills in a beneficial way. Instead, the utility or pleasure of reading will come from the ability to gain meaning from what has been read. This may range from knowing that *ball* represents an object that we can toss around, that a list of groceries indicates what should be selected in a grocery store, or that someone's interesting experiences may be understood by reading about them in a magazine.

There are several possible ways to develop or improve the reading comprehension skills of students with mental disabilities. One way is to teach them to

Figure 17–5 Example of Using a Picture around a Letter to Teach the Letter Sound

Source: "Establishing Letter–Sound Correspondence in Children Classified as Trainable Mentally Retarded," by F. R. Hoogeveen, P. M. Smeets, and J. E.Van der Houven, 1987, *Education and Training in Mental Retardation, 22*(2), p. 80. Copyright 1987 by the Division on Mental Retardation and Developmental Disabilities, The Council for Exceptional Children. Reprinted by permission.

Figure 17–6 The Gradual Transition from the Pictorial Cue Snake to the Letter *s* (10 Steps)

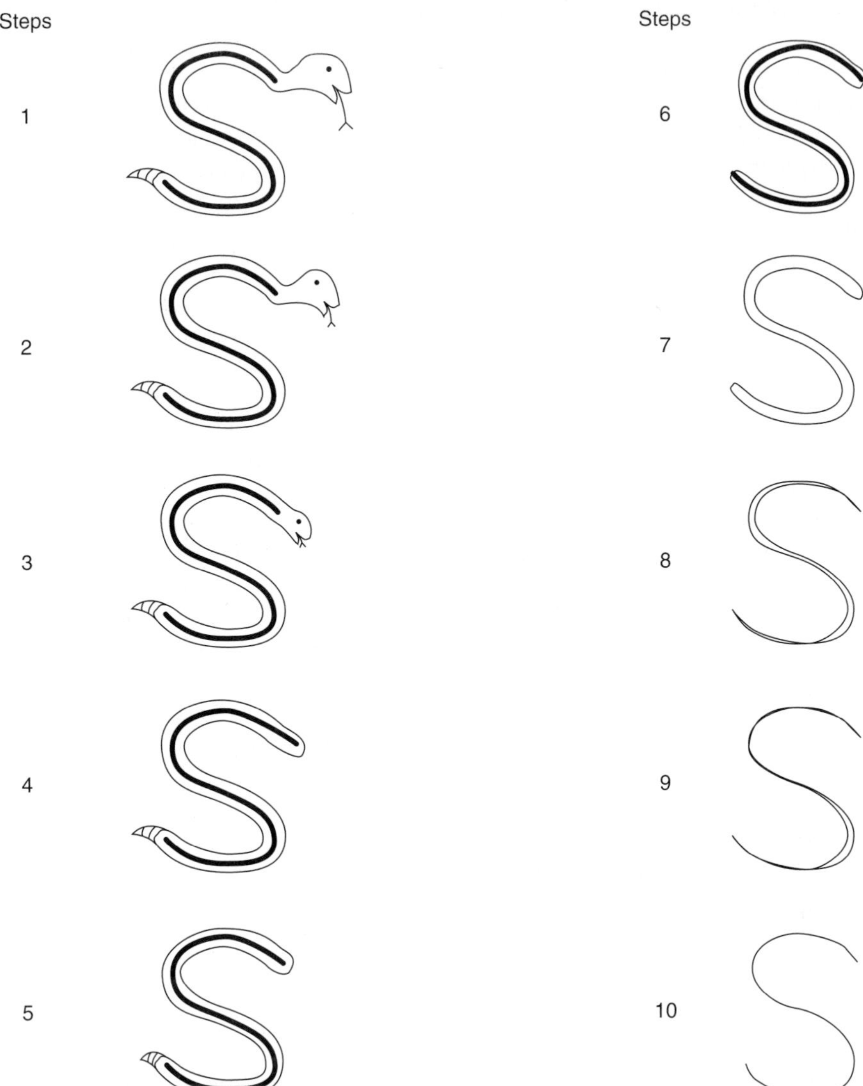

Source: "Establishing Letter–Sound Correspondence in Children Classified as Trainable Mentally Retarded," by F. R. Hoogeveen, P. M. Smeets, and J. E. Van der Houven, 1987, *Education and Training in Mental Retardation, 22*(2), p. 82. Copyright 1987 by the Division on Mental Retardation and Developmental Disabilities, The Council for Exceptional Children. Reprinted by permission.

read certain materials and then to act out or follow the directions stated or implied by the material. In one study, for example (Brown & Perlmutter, 1971), students learned to read words that indicated the location of a penny in a specially built cabinet (e.g., *in front, behind, on top*) and then responded to the directions by correctly locating the penny. To do this successfully, they had to understand what the words meant. In a similar study, students were taught to say the names of objects, read the written name, and then demonstrate that they understood that the written word represented an object by touching it when it appeared in an array of objects (Brown et al., 1972).

Acting out written activities could range from following relatively simple directions, such as the above, to much more complicated activities. An excellent example of this was provided in a study by Browder and Minarovic (2000). In this study, young adults with moderate mental retardation first learned to read sight words and then to use the words to prompt themselves to complete specific jobs in their places of employment. Each participant had regular competitive jobs, but they were not performing well by independently completing certain aspects of their jobs. Browder and Minarovic identified the problems that the adults were having and created four to five sight words for each person that could be associated with initiating the jobs. For example Carl, who worked in a grocery store, was assigned the words *sweep* (sweep the storefront), *bag* (bag groceries), *carts* (collect the carts from the parking lot), *restock* (put stock on shelves), and *fill bags* (replace bags at the checkout). Following the identification of the words, each person was taught to read the words using progressive time delay. After they could read the words, they were taught to connect the words with the job activities. They had to read the word on a list, go to the area where the job was to be performed, and explain what the word meant with regard to completing the activity. Finally, the participants had to demonstrate that they could use the list of prompt words and complete their tasks independently. Ultimately, all of the participants learned to read the words, demonstrate what they meant with regard to the job task, and then complete the task. Their accomplishments were validated by substantial increases in their job ratings by their employers.

Another way to demonstrate comprehension is for students to respond orally to questions about signs or directions that they have just read. Cuvo and Klatt (1992) asked students to read certain community signs that had been learned and then asked them to "tell me what you would do if you saw the sign." The signs included "Not an Exit," "Service," "Sorry, We're Closed," "Cashier," "NO SHOES, NO SHIRT, NO SERVICE!" and "Shoplifters will be prosecuted." Particularly in situations in which it is impractical for students to actually do what the sign is directing, they could instead verbally describe the actions that they would take, such as Cuvo and Klatt had their students do. Thus, they could demonstrate how well they understood the information that the sign was conveying.

Oral responses to questions about stories can also demonstrate comprehension. Teachers can develop their own questions about the content of stories read by students if questions are not supplied as part of the story. These questions should allow the student to demonstrate knowledge of the main facts about the story by answering questions about who, what, when, where, and why. Such questions might also be answered in writing by some students with moderate mental disabilities, which would be another method to teach and evaluate reading comprehension. Domnie and Brown (1977) taught students to write answers to who, what, and where questions by gradually progressing them through several phases of instruction. Students first learned to read up to 90 sight words and then learned to copy 40 potential components that would be necessary to answer the questions. Next, they read the sight words that they had learned within the contexts of stories and also read questions about the stories. Finally, they learned to write the answers to the questions about the stories, successfully demonstrating comprehension of what they had read.

It may be possible to teach comprehension in an incidental manner as students are learning to read words by sight. This can be done by using a method such as constant time delay or progressive time delay to teach the sight words and also telling the student the meaning of the word that he has just read when reinforcing the student for the correct answer. Later the student can be assessed to determine if the meaning has been learned. The effectiveness of incidental instruction for comprehension learning has been demonstrated in several studies:

- Collins, Branson, and Hall (1995) taught students with moderate mental retardation sight words that were on the labels of cooking products. Incidental instruction was used to teach the definitions of the words by stating the meaning of the word when reinforcing the student for reading the word correctly. Probes for both acquisition and generalization demonstrated that the participants learned how to read the words and learned the meanings of many of the words through the less structured, incidental teaching method.
- Collins and Stinson (1995) selected words for instruction that were contained on warning labels. Students with moderate mental retardation were taught in pairs to read the words as sight words using progressive time delay. The meanings of the words were taught incidentally by telling the meanings when giving positive reinforcement to the students for correctly reading the sight words. Through this incidental procedure, a number of the students learned the definitions of the words. However, students failed to generalize reading the words when they were shown the words on actual warning labels in grocery stores.
- Singleton, Schuster, and Ault (1995) reported teaching community signs to two students with moderate mental disabilities using simultaneous prompting procedures. A picture of the community sign was held up and simultaneously the teacher said "What sign?" If the student correctly repeated the answer within 5 seconds, the teacher praised the student and, when doing so, also gave the meaning of the sign ("Good job! Exit means go out!"). The

researchers found that the students learned to see and say all the sign words and also learned incidentally the meaning of the words that had been embedded in the reinforcement.

- Gast, Doyle, Wolery, Ault, and Farmer (1991) used progressive time delay and the system of least prompts to teach recipe words and simultaneously taught the meaning of the words in an incidental manner. To do this, they embedded the related information in the prompt hierarchy or in the reinforcement that followed correct responses. The incidental information was presented by either showing an action picture representing the word or using a gesture to represent the action of the word. For example if the student saw and read the word *stir* the teacher would say "Yes, that's right, this is stir" while showing an action picture or a gesture of "stir."

Regardless of the approach selected, it is important for the teacher to give students the opportunity to display their knowledge of what they have comprehended in the words that they have read and sometimes to demonstrate correct actions in response to written words. Many students with moderate mental disabilities are able to read words, but do not fully comprehend what they have read or how they should respond to them in their environment. This critical part of reading instruction should not be overlooked if reading is to be a part of a student's curriculum.

Teaching Writing

Teaching writing to students with moderate mental disabilities should be considered a parallel learning activity to teaching reading. Words targeted for writing should be some of the same words that the student is learning to read or has already learned, and, as with reading, the writing activities should be both functional and recreational. The mechanics of writing generally are considered to be less cumbersome when letters are formed in manuscript style rather than cursive, and the possibility of using word processors should also be considered, as this may be easier and more efficient for some students.

What Students Should Learn to Write

Various potential writing opportunities, both for pleasure and functional purposes, that occur in the school environment are presented in Table 17–1. As can be seen, functional activities tend to require very specific writing targets (such as writing one's name, address, and phone number), whereas pleasurable writing activities allow for more creativity and personal expression (such as writing stories, cards or letters, and journals).

Functional writing should focus on skills that are required in natural environments. For example, at a relatively young age, children must learn to write their name on school papers, even if the papers contain no other written words (e.g., pictures or worksheets). During the early school years (K–3), it is not uncommon for children without disabilities to write only their first name or their first name and the initial of their last name. This type of skill, then, is an appropriate writing target for a student with a moderate mental disability.

As students get older, functional writing calls for writing that meets key needs in environments other than the classroom. These needs might include notes to remind oneself of certain activities, shopping lists, or travel directions to get from one place to another. The teacher must be knowledgeable about these needs and develop the functional writing skills necessary to meet them. The student must learn to write the content in a format that she can read and understand and that is suitable for the event. Consider, for example, writing directions to take a bus from one's home to downtown. It would not be useful for the student to write down words or abbreviations that could not be comprehended independently. Nor would it be sufficient for a student to learn to write directions on a chalkboard, but not on a piece of paper that could be folded and put in a pocket. During instruction, the teacher must therefore be certain that the student can write what is necessary in an appropriate format and then read and comprehend it.

Besides writing functional information, students with moderate mental disabilities should be taught and encouraged to write for fun or leisure purposes. This has several benefits. It can provide age-appropriate recreational activity, help to develop or improve social interactions, and naturally improve reading and writing skills. At an early age, students can learn to express themselves through symbols. For some, these symbols may be pictures, for others they may be simple words (e.g., "Mom I love you" or "Happy Father's Day"). As students progress, their personal writing activities may become more extensive and complex. Notes to friends, letters to pen pals, scrap books, journals, and letters to the editor are a few examples of leisure writing activities that can be undertaken by students with moderate mental disabilities. Specific desirable writing activities can be determined through initial assessment when interviewing parents or the student.

Expanding Writing Content

Words targeted for writing instruction, including those for both functional and recreational writing, can be the same words identified for reading, using any of the reading instructional methods described previously. Sight words or words in books that the student has learned or is learning, or a subset of the most important words, can be used to develop word sets that the student can learn to spell and write. As with the reading process, learning to write the words can be based on either the whole-word configuration or a word-analysis approach, depending on a student's ability.

A useful method for teaching both reading and writing skills to students with moderate mental disabilities is the language experience approach (Ford et al., 1989). This procedure, which is relatively easy to implement, considers reading and writing to be natural extensions of spoken language. The teacher asks each student to tell a brief story or describe a recent event. For example, students may talk about a recent field trip with their class or a recreational outing with their family. As the student tells what happened, the teacher uses a large blank chart paper to write down word for word what is being said. Several sentences are written in this way. The teacher points to and reads the words that have been written, the student is asked to read them, and the teacher helps him when a word is not known. This narrative is practiced until the student can read it and then write it, first copying the words and then writing them from memory. Practice on individual words can also be done by transferring them to flashcards. This has the negative effect of taking the words out of context, but the positive effect of allowing the student to learn the words without relying on contextual cues. As a result, the student may learn to read the words in other contexts and use them to write new sentences. Language experience is useful not only for teaching reading and writing skills, but also for improving speaking and language skills. It is desirable because most students may participate at their own level of language, speech, reading, or writing.

Another method for improving writing skills, as well as language and reading skills, is shared writing (Mather & Lachowicz, 1992). Although developed primarily for children with mild disabilities, it may also be useful for individuals with moderate mental disabilities. The process is relatively simple: the teacher and the student (or two or more students without the teacher) work together, taking turns to write the same story. The process begins with the writers identifying a topic that they will write about. Then they take turns writing different elements of the story (words, sentences, or paragraphs). The elements need not be the same for both (or all) writers. For example, the teacher could write a sentence, and the student could write one word. After each writes a portion, the words are read by the teacher and then the student, with the teacher helping when necessary.

Using the shared writing approach, the teacher can control the vocabulary that she wants the student to learn to read and also prompt the student to write new words. Writing errors made by the student may be corrected incidentally when the teacher writes an addition to the story.

Teaching Writing Mechanics

Often students with moderate mental disabilities learn to form letters correctly by first tracing them and then copying them. To do this, they must be able to hold a pencil correctly and use the pencil to make controlled marks on paper. If writing exercises are to be realistic, they must be undertaken using words that students need to read and write in their daily lives. In other words, students should not work on letter formations in isolation.

Some letters may be more difficult for students to form than others; some students may have significant difficulties forming any letters. In such cases, a more structured teaching method may be required. Such a method has been described by Vacc and Vacc (1979). These authors suggested the use of specific verbal cues along with visual models to help students to form each letter. The verbal cues include five basic directions, all of which begin with the cue to *touch*; for example, touch, pull; touch, cross; touch, slant; touch, slide; and touch, dot. The cues as they are applied to specific letters are presented in Figure 17–7.

Using these cues, Vacc and Vacc suggested nine steps for teaching letter formation. They proposed that students practice these steps for each letter, one at a time, before moving on to the next. The steps are the following:

1. The teacher presents the letter and says the letter name.
2. The teacher demonstrates writing the letter, using verbal cues while making the letter strokes.
3. The student traces a sandpaper letter, using verbal cues while making the letter.
4. The student writes the letter in sand, using verbal cues while writing.
5. Holding chalk, student writes the letter in air, using verbal cues.

Figure 17–7 Verbal Cues for Manuscript Letters

A	touch slant, touch slant, touch cross
B	touch pull, touch slide around, touch slide around
C	touch slide up and around
D	touch pull, touch slide around
E	touch pull, touch cross, touch cross, touch cross
F	touch pull, touch cross, touch cross
G	touch slide up and around, touch cross
H	touch pull, touch pull, touch cross
I	touch pull
J	touch pull and slide
K	touch pull, touch slant, touch slant
L	touch pull, touch cross
M	touch pull, touch slant, touch slant, touch pull
N	touch pull, touch slant, touch pull
O	touch slide up and all the way around
P	touch pull, touch slide around
Q	touch slide up and all the way around, touch slant
R	touch pull, touch slide around, touch slant
S	touch slide and slide
T	touch pull, touch cross
U	touch pull and slide, touch pull and slide OR touch pull and slide and straight up
V	touch slant, touch slant
W	touch slant, touch slant, touch slant, touch slant
X	touch slant, touch slant
Y	touch slant, touch slant, touch pull
Z	touch cross, touch slant, touch cross

Source: "Teaching Manuscript Writing to Mentally Retarded Children," by N. N. Vacc and N. A. Vacc, 1979, *Education and Training of the Mentally Retarded* (Dec.), p. 288. Copyright 1979 by the Division on Mental Retardation and Developmental Disabilities, The Council for Exceptional Children. Reprinted by permission.

6. Student writes the letter on chalkboard, using verbal cues.
7. Holding pencil, student writes the letter in air, using verbal cues.
8. Student writes the letter on paper, using verbal cues.
9. Student writes the letter on paper without using verbal cues.

For many people, learning to write only manuscript letters is sufficient, and this is generally the case for persons with moderate mental disabilities. It is possible to teach some of these students to write using cursive letters, but most likely this would not increase the speed of writing or reduce errors and therefore is not usually considered a high priority.

In some situations it may be desirable to teach students to use word processors. This requires that students be able to learn the basic procedures necessary for operating the necessary equipment, for example, to give the appropriate commands or to put paper in the machine. Beyond that, students need to learn to find and hit the appropriate keys on the keyboard. Calhoun (1985) reported success using typewriters with adolescents with mild mental disabilities. Their typing (which used the "hunt and peck" approach) started out very slowly when compared to writing words with a pencil. However, after only 10 days of practice on the typewriters, their speed got three times faster and became comparable to their rate of handwriting, and they made more strokes correctly and fewer errors per minute when using the typewriter.

Teaching Spelling

Efforts undertaken by teachers to teach students with moderate mental disabilities to spell words tend to be very limited. Typically, the words that students must learn to write are related to some of the activities we have already discussed, such as making a grocery list or writing the directions for using public transportation. When students are directed to compose notes such as these, they are often given models from which to copy down the words.

Although students' cognitive limitations and associated memory problems may make learning to spell many words difficult, it might be useful for some students to memorize the spelling of some words for the same reasons that other persons learn how to spell, so that they can write without relying on prompts provided by someone else or by a dictionary. The question is to what extent is learning to spell possible and how functional might the skill be? Reading words and spelling them require two very different skills. Reading requires that one provide a single response to a cluster of abstract symbols, whereas spelling requires just the opposite.

Nevertheless, some attempts at teaching spelling may prove beneficial. One approach to begin with may be the use of anagram spelling. Stromer, MacKay, Howell, and McVay (1996) conducted experiments using computer programs to teach spelling to an adult with moderate mental retardation and one with a severe hearing disability. In the first study, the individual learned to match pictures to printed words on a computer, and vice versa. The person then learned to spell the words represented by the pictures using an anagram spelling procedure that required that the correct letters be selected from an array of letters on the computer. Finally, the person learned to write the words corresponding to the pictures on a piece of paper. In the second experiment, the individual extended the findings in the first experiment by learning to write words representing pairs of objects that were presented and then retrieving objects that were represented by the written words after a delay of time. The study demonstrated that learning to spell using anagrams—selecting the correct letters from an array—can lead to written spelling of pictures and objects.

Although this is a very limited finding, it suggests that spelling may be a possible skill for some individuals with moderate mental disabilities. It also suggests that the use of anagrams from which the student must select the right letters might be a useful place to begin.

Expanding Literacy Instruction and Participation for Students with Severe Disabilities

Katims (2000) traced the history of literacy instruction for individuals with mental retardation over a 200-year period and noted the various approaches that had been used in efforts to teach reading, writing, and spelling skills, many of which have been discussed in the previous sections. Katims also analyzed several contemporary textbooks to assess the information provided about the relative abilities of persons with cognitive disabilities to learn literacy skills and the methods used to teach them. He concluded that most instructional approaches have been behavioral and, although they have been successful in teaching discrete skills (e.g., students can read individual words and sometimes respond to them), they have not provided opportunities for students with cognitive disabilities to experience the larger world of connected text and true literature. He pointed out that most reviews of research on reading abilities of students with mental retardation have found that their skills are less than what would be predicted based on their mental ages. One possibility of this, according to Katims, is that "Attempts at literacy instruction for people with mental retardation have generally focused on the teaching of isolated mastery of a linear set of subskills, which rarely engage students with well constructed, connected texts containing multiple sentences" (Katims, 2000, p. 11). He argued that, since students do not progress rapidly in the attainment of these isolated skills, they never progress to a point of being sufficiently immersed in literature with associated opportunities to use literacy for communication, obtaining information, or pleasure. Katims urged that teachers use a more comprehensive approach to literacy instruction that does not simplify it to the level of learning discrete words, but that allows a multitude of interwoven skills to be taught and opportunities to participate more fully in literacy experiences. He says that, currently, there appears to be a "serious lack of literacy optimism for people with mental retardation" (Katims, 2000, p. 12).

Others have made the same or a similar argument. Kliewer and Landis (1999) challenged the notion that children with moderate to severe cognitive disabilities should be excluded from literate communities. Instead, they maintained, these students should be given opportunities to develop levels of literacy skills and appreciation to the extent of their unique capacities and through different symbolic systems. They hypothesized that our thoughts about the abilities of individuals with cognitive disabilities are based on what they referred to as "institutional understanding." Accordingly, assumptions about persons are generally tied to standardized measures of development (i.e., developmental levels or intelligence quotients). From this context, they argued that presumptions are made by educators about the individual's readiness, or ability to acquire reading and writing skills. These presumptions typically lead to not providing the opportunity for the student to become engaged in learning activities that foster literacy skills or appreciation or to limiting learning to a program of reading functional sight words. In contrast, when each student is approached individually with an effort to determine what form of comprehension and expression the person is capable of, then a "local understanding" of the person may develop that leads to opportunities for engagement and thus better enhances the chance of a student acquiring literacy skills and participating in literate communities.

As suggested by these positions and similar positions of others (e.g., Kliewer & Biklen, 2001; Ryndak et al., 1999), some in the field are questioning whether instruction in basic, functional skills is sufficient for students with severe disabilities. They suggest that the development of more sophisticated literacy skills are possible and should be encouraged. This raises several important questions: Are students with severe disabilities able to acquire a greater breadth and depth of literacy skills than many have thought possible in the past? If so, in what ways might they demonstrate these skills? Also, how can teachers, parents, caregivers, and advocates facilitate the acquisition of these skills?

Broadly speaking, literacy skills include reading, writing, speaking, and listening. In the most traditional sense, these skills occur through development and learning and within a hierarchal sequence. In other words, more basic skills, such as reading readiness, precede more complex skills, such as naming letters, knowing letter sounds, reading words, and blending sounds. Since these skills are often taught in such a sequence, many children with cognitive disabilities do not advance very far because the pace of their learning falls behind that of other children, they are assumed to have insufficient intellectual ability to progress, and thus they are placed in instructional programs that focus on more basic or functional skills. But some are questioning whether this typical occurrence inhibits these individuals from participating to the degree possible in the world of literacy. This questioning is strengthened by the legal requirement under IDEA Amendments of 1997 that all students with disabilities be given access to the general curriculum to the extent possible. Much of the general curriculum of states and local school districts includes literacy skill development. If students are to participate in some form in the general curriculum, then acquisition of literacy skills to the extent possible is an important goal for them.

In the following sections we examine some studies in which skills in the area of literacy by students with severe disabilities have been demonstrated to be more extensive than those discussed earlier in the chapter. Readers may find that, at least for some persons classified as having severe disabilities, there is the potential for greater literacy participation and progress.

In a relatively early report of literacy instruction for people with severe disabilities, Mirenda (1992) described the instructional reading activities of two adults with severe physical disabilities. Larry, a 20-year-old man with severe spastic cerebral palsy, learned to read stories from newspapers and magazines that were rewritten at a first-grade level. He and his mother picked out the stories together, and they were rewritten by his instructor. (His favorite topics included serial killers, executions, and natural disasters.) After the stories were rewritten, they were previewed, and new or unfamiliar words were explained. Larry then read the story quietly while the instructor followed his eyes. Phonics was worked on within the context of the story. *Yes* and *no* questions were presented to check his comprehension. The second individual described by Mirenda (1992) was Mary Lou, a 39-year-old woman who also had severe cerebral palsy. In stark contrast to the interest of the first student, this woman's favorite reading was the Bible. She learned to read out loud from a children's Bible written at the second- to third-grade level. Phonics was again worked on within the context of the reading material, and rereading was done to build fluency. Additional activities included listening to the Bible being read at home, use of questioning to increase inferential thinking and comprehension, and spelling practice.

In another report, Erickson and Koppenhaver (1995) developed a model literacy program for children with severe disabilities in a self-contained special class. The program that they describe served eight elementary school-age students with severe disabilities who had "untestable" IQ scores. The children all had severe speech and language problems and severe physical disabilities. Before the program began, their IEPs had focused on fine-motor skills and self-help skills.

The literacy program developed by Erickson and Koppenhaver used computers and several peripheral devices to facilitate communication. *Light technology* also was used, including communication boards with pictures and line drawings and tape players. An "integrated, child-centered, transdisciplinary" approach was used and classroom activities were designed to be "language rich and meaningful." Therapeutic needs were incorporated into the classroom academic instruction. Physical positioning, for example, was designed to match academic instruction, and academic instruction was offered within therapy sessions. Technology was used to provide alternative response modes when necessary. After a morning group time, students worked on individual computers on language arts and math skills. In the afternoon, additional group activities were held. One favorite was acting out favorite books. Cooking was another. Large recipe charts and corresponding communication boards were used.

Throughout the day, children had the opportunity to interact with print and became "emergent readers and writers." They learned letter names and letter–sound correspondence and common words within their environment and could comprehend text that was read to them. As the program progressed, more emphasis was placed on child-directed and constructive approaches and included more writing and more directed reading in small groups and individually. Reading material included a variety of trade books, basal readers, and computer programs. Emphasis was placed on reading words, comprehension, and spelling words.

Although the authors were pleased with the direction of the program and the progress of the students, they were regretful of the fact that it was housed in a self-contained special class. They were supportive of inclusive programs and felt that the technology used in this segregated classroom could be implemented within a regular classroom. (Methods for teaching academic skills to students in regular classrooms are discussed later in the chapter and are also presented in more detail in Chapter 10.)

Kliewer and Biklen (2001) challenged the notion that students with severe disabilities could not participate meaningfully in literacy activities by examining forms of symbolic expression and understanding in the lives of several persons with severe disabilities. Three of the individuals they came to know and the literacy skills they manifested were as follows:

- Steven was 16 years old and attended a special school. He was diagnosed as having autism and mental retardation. Steven had a great interest in butterflies and, according to his respite care worker, had read every book in the library about them. His reading method was a bit uncommon in that he would sit on the floor and open three books at the same time and read one page in each before turning the pages in all three and continuing. The authors were dismayed to discover that there was nothing on Steven's IEP about learning reading skills. The school teachers maintained that Steven may be able to decode, but not to process, what he read. But based on his interest in butterflies, the authors disagreed, believing that he not only read, but understood and enjoyed what he read.
- Rebecca was 11 years old and also diagnosed as having autism and severe mental disabilities. She was in a sixth-grade inclusive classroom, but often exhibited serious behavior problems, mainly self-stimulation or self-injurious behaviors. Because Rebecca didn't speak and because the other students in the class wanted to interact with her, they decided to "do notes." (Pass notes to her and then read them to her and ask for her reaction.) They found that Rebecca focused completely on the note reader and ceased all inappropriate behavior when engaged in note reading activity. Although it was not clear how much Rebecca comprehended, this type of interaction led to the creation of communication symbols for Rebecca that could be passed by her as notes. In one year, Rebecca progressed from being considered nonsymbolic to interacting symbolically with her classmates.
- Kimberly was a 13-year-old with multiple disabilities, including visual disabilities, who participated in an inclusive classroom that was very oriented toward literature-based instruction. It was decided that if she was going to be a participating member of the class a way had to be found for Kimberly to be involved in literacy activities. To accomplish this, her parents began to send notes telling about recent activities that their daughter had been involved in. The notes spurred questions from the teachers and the complexity of both the questions and the answers increased. Ultimately, Kimberly developed keyboarding skills and demonstrated relatively sophisticated writing skills.

To gain knowledge of the actual symbolic abilities of persons with severe disabilities, Kliewer and Biklen (2001) stress that there must be an intimate association (a "local understanding") between the individual and the individual's teacher, whether the teacher is actually a school teacher, a parent, or an advocate. This relationship allows a better understanding of the individual's symbolic and literate interests and skills to develop and lies in stark contrast to what the authors refer to as an "institutional" relationship. The authors stated:

> Thus, individuals with severe disabilities are commonly found stalled at a readiness stage where proof of intellect is demanded, an exceedingly difficult task when symbol use is profoundly restricted. In contrast to convention, our observations suggested that teachers who effectively supported the development of symbolic capacities in individuals with disabilities acted on a recognition that social engagement (i.e., students meaningfully interacting with others around them) drives the development of internalized symbolic capacities (i.e., symbolic abilities that allow people to meaningfully interact with others around them). (p. 5)

In a different but related study, Kliewer and Landis (1999) interviewed 14 teachers who were either general education or special education teachers, asking them to document their experiences with children with moderate to severe disabilities who had initially been rejected from opportunities to learn to read or write or enjoy literature, but who had subsequently had such opportunities and had benefited from them. One story that was told was about the experience of Josh.

Josh was a nine-year-old boy enrolled in a general education classroom who was classified in the range of severe mental retardation. When the teachers discussed the need for the class to develop reading comprehension skills ("What is the main idea? How does it relate to what has been read? What do we think is going to happen?"), the question arose as to how Josh should participate. The response to this question resulted in various ways in which Josh should be involved in learning literacy skills. Kliewer and Landis (1999) described one class activity:

> For instance, during one reading period the children in his group were paired and shared the chapter reading between themselves. Josh too had a partner who sat next to his wheelchair and who did the spoken reading. As his partner turned the pages of her own book, she would flip Josh's pages which were clipped to a tilted board. Was he reading along? "We really don't know where his reading level is at, but I know he can read and does read," insisted his teacher.

Kliewer and Landis argued that the teachers made an assumption that Josh *was* literate and *would* participate in literacy instruction. Because of this assumption, they took certain steps. Josh was placed in a group with a reading partner, the group formed a social context in which Josh had a space, and Josh was provided with a symbol system that allowed him to participate to the degree that he was able. In this way Josh was able to work on developing literacy skills, but also on developing social and communication skills.

Finally, we note a case study by Ryndak et. al., (1999) that described the experiences of a young woman named Melinda whom they observed over a 7-year period of her life. When the story was told, Melinda was in her early 20s, but the described events and their impact were of her life from that of a child, through adolescence, and into young adulthood. The authors demonstrated that the circumstances brought on by inclusion in regular classes in junior high school, high school, and college resulted in the acquisition and use of literacy skills by Melinda.

Until she was 15 years old, Melinda attended school in separate special education classes. In the last month of the seventh grade, when Melinda was 15 years old, the school district, with some reluctance, agreed to place Melinda in a regular classroom. Her inclusive placement was continued in the following year and then, for the most part, through high school and then in a private college for 2 years.

Problems in the separate special classes were attributed by the authors to learning activities that were either too difficult, too easy, too boring, or too irrelevant for Melinda. Because her progress on this work was always limited, she continued to repeat the same work over and over again, year in and year out. Her mother stated, "Her life didn't have opportunity. There was no sense of optimism, no sense that she could have something like a career, or that she could have experiences similar to other kids" (Ryndak et al., 1999, p. 9). Besides not being interested in the low-level academic work, when she was in the special class, Melinda demonstrated relatively immature social skills and several behavior problems. Her parents maintained that she was frustrated because of the lack of opportunities to socialize and interact with nondisabled peers in the schools.

After placement in inclusive classes, Ryndak et al. reported that Melinda's participation in various social and academic activities improved and she began to show progress in her literacy skills. Instructional content in the inclusive classes included aspects of the general curriculum that were most pertinent to Melinda's abilities, needs, and interests, as well as special skills addressing her functional needs. This latter instruction was gradually interwoven into general education activities and addressed in daily school routines. Most importantly, expectations for what Melinda could accomplish began to increase. As her mother stated, "Melinda finally had exposure to curriculum, instead of skill development in isolation" (Ryndak et al., 1999, p.13).

Melinda's progress in inclusive classrooms was especially noted in the area of literacy. She demonstrated growth in her spoken articulation and vocabulary, expressed interests in areas such as history, and became sufficiently able to explain her disability to her classmates. She improved her reading and writing skills as well. She learned how to listen and take notes in regular classes, demonstrated improved handwriting skills, read study versions and summaries of plays (by Shakespeare) and other stories, and prepared posters for presentation in her classes. To facilitate her writing, she learned numerous functional vocabulary words, used word banks developed for specific topics, and learned to work cooperatively with classmates to edit and refine written products using either a computer or on regular paper.

Ultimately, Melinda progressed to a point where she was able to make presentations at conferences and meetings, address her state's general assembly to discuss why students with disabilities should be included, and write an article for her college newspaper. Most importantly, Melinda learned to accept and enjoy the life she had. According to the authors,

> Finally, Melinda began to accept the concept that she did not have to know everything that her peers knew, or do things in the same manner as them, in order to be accepted, belong, and be valued. With this realization, Melinda accepted the fact that she needed assistance to learn, and that receiving assistance to acquire new skills led to greater independence in later life. (Ryndak et al., 1999, p.18)

What do these reports tell us about individuals with cognitive disabilities, literacy, and their participation in the general curriculum? What implications do they hold for teachers?

To begin, we need to recognize that these case studies are descriptive in nature. They are qualitative studies of individuals or small groups of individuals. Thus the extent to which these outcomes can be generalized is unknown. However, the studies clearly indicate that some persons labeled as severely disabled can demonstrate literacy skills that before were not considered possible or meaningful. Equally important, key people in their world were able to recognize these skills, encourage them, and foster more extensive learning.

The implication for teachers should be that we need to explore and try to move beyond our current levels of achievement. Although we know that learning individual sight words is often possible and that these words can help people to operate in meaningful ways, deeper involvement in literacy activities may be of interest and relevance to students with severe disabilities. Instead of limiting instruction, creative explorations should be taken to expand into more complex and, perhaps, interesting literacy activity. Kliewer and Landis (1999) stressed the importance of not making assumptions about students based on an "institutional understanding." Instead they recommended that teachers:

- Engage in "critical self-reflectivity" about what students are able to achieve.
- Look at cases where persons with intellectual disabilities have been able to demonstrate literacy skills.
- Support literacy learning for all students and, if failure appears to occur, not blame the student but seek different instructional approaches.
- Surround all children with a symbolic and literate milieu and facilitate their participation in it.
- Avoid grouping and instructing students based on categorical labels and presumed levels of development and ability.

Summary of Approaches to Teaching Literacy Skills

It is apparent from the research literature that students with moderate mental disabilities can learn to read whole words, sometimes use word analysis skills, and comprehend the meaning of what they have read in different ways. Students with more severe cognitive disabilities can often learn to "read" pictures that have greater iconic value as symbols than individual letters or whole words and sometimes read more abstract symbols that represent single words. This is not to imply that every student needs to learn reading skills or that reading skills are essential for daily living. However, the fact that many students can learn these skills and that the skills can increase their participation in life activities in both fun and functional ways suggests that sight word reading instruction be considered in the development of individual educational plans.

Teaching writing is a natural extension of teaching reading, which is itself an extension of spoken language. The writing skills that the student develops can be used for functional purposes and for leisure or recreational pursuits. Some or all the words that the student is learning to read will also be targets for developing writing skills. Increased writing opportunities can be developed by increasing reading opportunities and also by using language experience and shared writing methods.

Many students can learn the mechanical skills for forming letters by seeing the teacher form the letters, tracing over the letters, and copying the letters. Some students may require more structured input, and this may be provided by the teacher giving verbal cues to help the student to form letters properly. The ability to learn how to spell words is difficult for students with moderate disabilities because of the required memorization. However, they may be able to learn to spell some words, and learning to spell by presenting letters in an array (anagram spelling) might be helpful.

Most exciting in this area of learning is the possibility of some students with severe disabilities becoming involved and learning literacy skills that have not been thought possible or appropriate in past years. Although some may question the extent to which students with severe disabilities may benefit for literacy instruction, it is apparent from the case studies available that some students will develop literacy skills and, maybe more important, will enjoy the literacy experiences included in their curriculum. And isn't this much of what participating in these types of activities should be about?

Teaching Arithmetic

Like reading, writing, and other literacy skills, arithmetic is a basic area of academic instruction in schools. And also like these skills, arithmetic skills can add significantly to the quality of a person's life. Being able to determine if you have enough money to buy a soda and a magazine and if the store will be open long enough for you to make the purchase require fundamental math skills that many individuals with cognitive disabilities can acquire. Teachers must be aware of appropriate goals and objectives for learning arithmetic skills and the instructional methods that will help to achieve them.

Arithmetic instruction for students with moderate mental disabilities should focus on at least three areas of learning:

1. Acquiring basic concepts and skills
2. Applying skills to handling money
3. Applying skills to time management

Instruction in each of these areas is discussed in the sections that follow.

Acquiring Basic Concepts and Skills

The application of fundamental arithmetic skills is improved by an understanding of some basic concepts about numbers and quantities. Although authorities in the past concluded that individuals with moderate mental disabilities have only rote arithmetic skills (e.g., the ability to memorize single-digit addition), several studies have challenged this conclusion, reporting that these individuals often have the ability to acquire generalized arithmetic concepts (Baroody, 1987, 1988, 1996; Baroody & Snyder, 1983; Caycho, Gunn, & Siegal, 1991; Mastropieri, Bakken, & Scruggs, 1991). These concepts tend to be developed by persons with moderate mental disabilities in about the same way as they are developed by nondisabled children, although generally at a later chronological age. Learning these skills to the extent possible in the elementary school years will help students to acquire more applied skills later. Critical concepts and basic skills include the following.

Counting Word Sequence

This skill consists of saying numbers in their appropriate order, beginning with 1 and counting to some target number, for example, 100. After memorizing the numbers 1 through 13, students may be able to continue counting, using numerical logic.

Enumeration and Cardinality

Students demonstrate this by being able to count a set of objects (using 1 to 1 correspondence), saying the number of each object as it is counted, and knowing that the last number that they say in the count represents the number of objects in the set. Various sets of objects need to be used to promote generalization.

Order Irrelevance Principle

This concept requires students to realize that the order in which they count the objects in a set does not change the total number.

$N + 1 > N$ Rule

The purpose of counting is to be able to compare quantities of objects contained within sets. Students must learn that numbers counted later in a sequence represent greater quantities than numbers counted earlier.

Addition and Subtraction

These basic skills are learned initially when students develop methods to determine the sum or difference of two numbers by using a counting strategy. Typically, students begin with one number in the problem and, starting with its cardinal value, add to it or subtract from it by counting forward (or backward) the number of times represented by the second number. For example, given the problem 5 + 3, the student might say: "5 and 3 more; that's 5, 6 (that's 1), 7 (that's 2), 8 (that's 3). 5 and 3 is 8." Often students use their fingers or other concrete objects and may also devise their own strategies for adding or subtracting.

Commutativity Principle

Students who understand the commutative nature of numbers realize that the order in which numbers are added together (3 + 2 vs. 2 + 3) does not affect the outcome.

In their 1983 study, Baroody and Snyder examined the ability of several adolescents with moderate mental disabilities to perform various number tasks, such as those just listed, and found that the students had the ability to perform correctly on several task. Those that were more difficult included applying the rule that $N + 1$ is greater than N and using the principle of commutativity in addition. Based on their findings, Baroody and Snyder recommended the following:

1. Except for the first several numbers (up to 13), counting should not be taught by rote, but in terms of the structure of the numbers. Rote counting results in errors occurring in the teens and the decades. Understanding the rules that govern the order of numbers can help to avoid errors. For students to learn more advanced skills, such as enumeration, the $N + 1 > N$ rule, addition, and estimation, they must master oral counting.
2. The ability to count objects accurately (enumerate) is another important basic skill that presents difficulty to some students. Students must be given practice in both counting objects within sets and producing the number of objects requested.
3. Students must learn to compare sets of objects and know which has more and which has fewer. Because students may not realize that the count sequence can be used to compare sets, practice in this skill is important. The process is easier if the student learns what numbers come after other numbers (the N after rule).
4. Some students with moderate mental disabilities have the ability to use unique self-developed strategies to add and subtract accurately. If the teacher discovers that students have such abilities, they should be encouraged to use them. Various game activities give students the opportunity to develop these types of skills.

In support of this last point, Baroody (1996) investigated the effects of instruction followed by practice on self-invented addition strategies by individuals with mild to moderate mental disabilities. He pointed out that it is generally assumed that these individuals are passive learners, that they can learn by rote, but that they cannot engage in their own active learning processes. Baroody challenged this idea by teaching children with mild and moderate mental retardation to use a basic addition procedure and then observed if they would use a more advanced procedure that they discovered on their own. The students, between 6 and 20 years of age, were taught to add using *direct modeling* throughout most of a school year. The direct modeling consisted of using concrete objects to count out individual addends (e.g., $3 + 5$) and then counting them together to get the sum. The students learned to use this strategy and also to generalize it to a new set of problems. More importantly, they developed shortcuts that allowed them to calculate faster. The most common strategy developed by the students (without direction or instruction) was to use their fingers to count instead of the concrete objects with which they had learned. Furthermore, a number of children developed automatic addition, having memorized facts without direct instruction to do so. A few students developed more advanced strategies, including a keeping-track process that allowed them to count from the endpoint of one sum to the final sum without using concrete objects.

Concrete Materials

Initial instruction on counting, addition, and subtraction requires the use of concrete, manipulative materials. Flexer (1989) and Paddock (1992) stressed the importance of using units (single items) that could be grouped into sets of 5 and/or 10 to develop a mental model for understanding quantities. Flexer proposed the use of 5- and 10-frames such as displayed in Figure 17–8. Recognizing and being able to identify the number of objects as they appear within the frames is intended to help students to acquire an image of the number that will become significant and easier to recall than items that appear only as unrelated units. This recognition of the number structures is intended to reduce the need for counting each item when adding or subtracting and to develop the concept of place values (Flexer, 1989).

After students acquire skills in oral counting, enumeration, and cardinality; recognizing quantities; and the concepts of greater than and less than, they may use the manipulatives to begin developing concepts of addition and subtraction. Using the frames proposed by Flexer, the addition of two numbers can be taught by using the following steps:

1. Place two 5-frames with different numbers of objects in them side by side.
2. Move objects from one frame to another to fill missing cells.
3. Place the frames together and read the sum.

This procedure is pictured in Figure 17–9. For subtraction, the process would require these steps:

Figure 17–8 Configurations of Numbers with 5- and 10-Frames

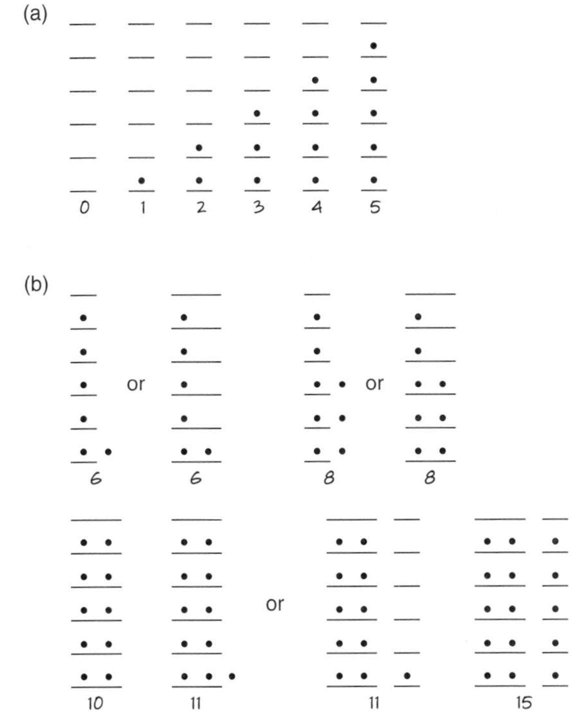

(a) 0 1 2 3 4 5

(b) 6 or 6 8 or 8

10 11 or 11 15

Source: "Conceptualizing Addition," by R. Flexer, 1989, *Teaching Exceptional Children, 21*(4), p. 23. Copyright 1989 by the Council for Exceptional Children. Reprinted by permission.

1. Identify the total from which a smaller amount will be subtracted and place this number in a frame.
2. Identify the number to be subtracted and remove it from the first frame and into another one.
3. Read the number of items remaining in the first frame.

Baroody (1993) also stressed the importance of using manipulatives; however, he suggested that not all manipulatives may be equally effective. Baroody contrasted the use of sticks to Cuisenaire rods and recommended that teachers use the number sticks. The Cuisenaire rods may not be as effective because they do not match the child's number concepts. Instead, they represent continuous quantities that must be measured instead of counted. They do not present a link between a concrete model of numbers and their symbolic representation. On the other hand, by using number sticks that link together discrete individual units to form the total quantity (see Figure 17–9), the student can see that the stick is made of discrete units. They can also build their own number sticks with interlocking blocks and can confirm the number represented by the stick by counting the units. In addition to counting and learning initial number concepts, number sticks can be used in early problem-solving activities and performing arithmetic operations.

Figure 17–9 The Addition of Numbers Using 5- and 10-Frames

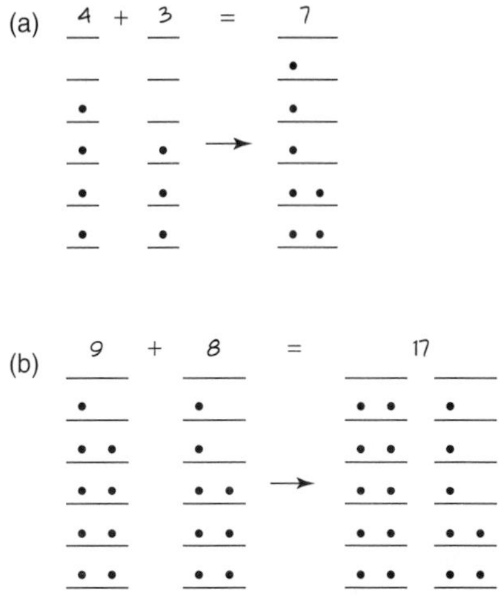

(a) 4 + 3 = 7

(b) 9 + 8 = 17

Source: "Conceptualizing Addition," by R. Flexer, 1989, *Teaching Exceptional Children, 21*(4), p. 24. Copyright 1989 by The Council for Exceptional Children. Reprinted by permission.

The development of initial concepts and skills by students with mental disabilities during the early school years may lead to more advanced arithmetic skills such as addition and subtraction with regrouping, multiplying, dividing, estimating, graphing, measuring, and other skills. Students with the ability to learn such skills should be encouraged to do so. They are best served by a regular or regular-adapted arithmetic curriculum (Ford et al., 1989). If students' progress does not continue at an adequate pace, however, as they approach the middle and high school years, instructional efforts should be devoted to more functional math skills, particularly using money and telling time.

Applying Skills to Handling Money

Comprehensive money management requires an array of skills. Browder and Grasso (1999) proposed that five skills are most important:

1. Knowing how much money one has
2. Knowing how to gain access to one's money (banking skills)
3. Knowing how much money one can spend (budgeting skills)
4. Knowing how to spend money (comparing prices, purchasing)

5. Knowing how to use money to make more money (saving and investing)

In a more immediate context, more essential skills are required: identifying the cost of an item or the total cost of several items; determining if one has enough money to purchase the item(s); and, if so, selecting the necessary amount of money from what is available to pay for the item(s) (Ford et al., 1989). If there is more than one item, the individual must be able to add the separate prices and calculate a total cost. The person also must be able to decide if he has enough to make the purchase, and this requires an understanding of quantities (in this case of money) being more or less than other quantities. Along with these skills, students may need to learn the names or identity of different coins and paper currency and their corresponding values.

Several studies have demonstrated that students with moderate mental disabilities can learn to develop such skills (e.g., Bellamy & Buttars, 1975; Borakove & Cuvo, 1976; Cuvo, Veitch, Trace, & Konke, 1978; Lowe & Cuvo, 1976). Many methods have used multiple instructional steps to help students to achieve basic purchasing skills. For example, Bellamy and Buttars (1975) used these steps to teach students with moderate mental disabilities to purchase a single item costing less than one dollar:

- Students learned to count to 100 by ones, fives, tens, and twenty-fives.
- Students learned to read all prices on price cards or tags between one cent and one dollar.
- Students learned to identify coins by touching a coin when the teacher says its name.
- Students learned to count out the amount of money as identified on individual price cards.

Most students with cognitive disabilities can learn skills like these or even more sophisticated skills. In a comprehensive review of research on instruction in money management for persons with mental disabilities, Browder and Grasso (1999) demonstrated that students with different degrees of mental disabilities could learn purchasing skills if provided with sufficient skills or supports. Some types of support commonly provided are described in the following sections.

Number Line Strategy

A number line can be a helpful tool for students to determine if they have enough money to purchase an item (Ford et al., 1989; Frank, 1978). The student determines

Figure 17–10 Using a Number Line

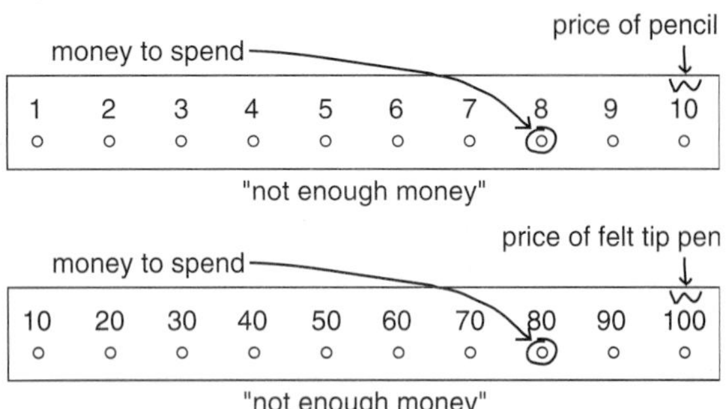

Source: The Syracuse Community-Referenced Curriculum Guide for Students with Moderate and Severe Disabilities (p. 121), by A. Ford, R. Schnorr, L. Meyer, J. Black, and P. Dempsey, 1989, Baltimore: Paul H. Brookes Publishing Co. Reprinted by permission.

the price of an item and marks that amount on the number line; she then counts the money that she has and marks the amount on the money line. The student then compares the two amounts; if the mark indicating the amount of money that the student has is to the right of the mark indicating the cost, the student knows that it is possible to make the purchase. Figure 17–10 demonstrates the application of number line strategy.

Ford et al. (1989) recommended that number line skills be learned sequentially in the following order:

- Learning to purchase items with pennies (items costing 1 to 10 cents)
- Learning to purchase items between 1 and 10 cents, using a dime
- Using dimes to purchase items up to a dollar
- Learning to purchase items up to a dollar, using quarters
- Learning to purchase items up to a dollar, using two quarters and five dimes
- Learning to purchase items up to a dollar, using nickels
- Learning to purchase items up to a dollar, using various combinations of coins: quarters + nickels; dimes + nickels; quarters + dimes + nickels.

After students have mastered the use of the number line with coins, the strategy should be taught using singles, fives, tens, and twenty-dollar bills, following a sequence similar to the one for coins. Ford et al. (1989) stressed the importance of using price tags that correspond to the real cost of real items. They also noted that students must learn to add a little more to the cost for taxable items. When the cost of an item falls between two marks on the number line, students must learn to estimate where a price falls in order to mark the appropriate spot on the line (e.g., 34 cents).

Calculators

Many students with moderate mental disabilities are able to learn to use calculators, and their use is likely to improve the accuracy and efficiency of calculations (Horton, 1985; Koller & Mulhern, 1977; Matson & Long, 1986). Calculators might be especially practical when students are learning to purchase multiple items, for example, when shopping in a grocery or department store (Ford et al., 1989; Matson & Long, 1986). A procedure for using them, based on subtraction, has been described by Ford et al:

- The student determines the money available for spending by counting it.
- The amount is entered on the calculator. (Ford et al. recommend that the decimal point be omitted, e.g., entering 100 for one dollar.)
- When an item to be purchased is found, the student presses the minus sign on the calculator.
- The student finds the price of the item and enters it, again disregarding the decimal point.
- The student presses the equal sign.
- After each such entry, the student checks the display on the calculator to determine if there is enough money remaining to purchase an additional item.
- If the display indicates the amount of money remaining is less than zero the student should realize that he does not have enough money.

As with the use of the number line strategy, the use of a calculator should begin with limited amounts of money and relatively few items and increase to more money and more items. Again, teachers should remember that students need to account for taxes. One way to do this is to determine the maximum amount of sales tax that could be applied to the total amount of money that the student has to spend and to teach the student to subtract this amount from the total before entering item amounts. A tax table could be written on a card for the student to determine this amount (Ford et al., 1989).

Other Money-Handling Tactics

Many students can acquire basic arithmetic skills and learn to use number lines and calculators to gain greater independence in their lives by making purchases in various community settings. For some students, particularly those with more severe cognitive disabilities, however, the use of these devices may be too difficult. If this is the case, the teacher may be able to teach them to use other money-handling techniques (Ford et al., 1989).

One possibility is to provide students with predetermined amounts of money for certain purchases. The money is placed in an envelope, and the student learns to give the envelope to a particular individual at a specific time in order to make a purchase. As students progress in this skill, they may learn to select an appropriate envelope from a group packaged together in a purse or backpack. In this way, they can make a purchase at one location, then select another envelope to make another purchase, and so on. The envelopes should be marked or coded in some fashion to help students to make the correct selection and purchase.

Students may also learn to use coin displacement cards or coin books, which are available commercially or may be made by the teacher and can be used in different ways. In one way, pictures or drawings of certain items (e.g., a soda or a bus fare) are displayed on the card, along with either indentations in which the required coins may be inserted or true-size pictures of the necessary coins. The student must learn to select from the coins that she possesses the ones that match the requirement for the purchase. This is a match-to-sample activity and therefore does not require the student to know the name of the coin or the amount that it represents. However, students must learn to make a correct match.

If students can read numbers, the cards can be used more generically by having different price amounts affixed to different cards or pages without pictures of particular items. Once again, indentations or pictures of coins are included. When the student sees or hears the price of a particular item, the card representing that amount is found, and the student selects the coins that match those on the card.

Students may make purchases using single dollar bills (even if they do not know the value of coins or bills) if they can count the single bills and round up, using the *next dollar strategy.* Using this procedure, the student takes an item or items to a cashier along with several dollar bills. The cashier calculates the amount and tells the student what it is. The student adds one additional dollar to the dollar amount that is heard and gives this amount to the cashier. For example, if the student is told the amount is $4.86, then he would count out five one-dollar bills and give them to the cashier, who would then return the change to the student. Browder and Grasso (1999) reported that the next dollar strategy was one of the most successfully taught skills to help students to determine the amount of money to pay for their purchase.

Another approach is for students to classify objects according to where they fall within a particular cost range. Gardill and Browder (1995) taught individuals with mental retardation and behavioral disabilities to use this strategy by matching fixed amounts of money to classes of items with similar costs. The amounts included 75 cents (three quarters), one dollar (a one dollar bill), and five dollars (a five dollar bill). For each of these there were several items that cost that amount or less. For example, the 75 cents could be used to make purchases from vending machines, the dollar could be used to buy a snack in a store, and the five dollars could be used to purchase a lunch. The idea was that the student did not have to count the money, but could select the amount necessary to purchase the item according to the class in which it was included. Students were first taught to match the amount of necessary money to pictures of items within the class that also showed the necessary amount. The amount required was then removed, and they had to select the amount based only on the picture. Finally, they had to select the amount based on the need to purchase a real item.

Although these strategies do not allow students to be as independent as using number lines or calculators would, they afford the opportunity to participate in activities that call for money handling. Because of this, they are useful when students have difficulty acquiring more advanced skills.

In summarizing the research on money management skills, Browder and Grasso (1999) stated the following:

> The research on purchasing found in this review demonstrated that individuals with all levels of mental retardation made independent purchases. This capacity for independence was often fostered by focusing on the most essential skills and simplifying the academic demands of money use. The most essential skill in using money to make a purchase is to give the correct amount of tender to the cashier. In contrast, skills such as naming coins and paper currency, matching equivalent money amounts, and counting change are not essential to making a transaction independently. (p. 304)

This suggests that teachers should carefully examine the money management skills that they teach to ensure that the most critical and significant are given priority. Based on the reviewed research, Browder and Grasso made the following recommendations:

1. Begin with instruction on purchasing. This introduces the student to the purpose of money and lets the student appreciate the natural consequences of learning to use money.
2. Simplify the academic demand related to money use, or use skills the student has already acquired. For students with very limited cognitive abilities, preselected amounts of money may be used; students with more ability may learn to use more sophisticated skills, such as the next dollar strategy, using a calculator, or writing a check.
3. Direct instructional tactics such as constant time delay or system of least prompts may be necessary for teaching money use skills.
4. Plan for skill generalization. Teach students to use money in different contexts and different ways. This may be done in different community settings, through the use of simulations, or through role-playing activities.
5. Expand instruction so that students can learn more advanced money management skills, such as budgeting, banking, using ATMs, keeping a checkbook, and planning purchases.

Applying Skills to Time Management

Being able to tell time allows individuals to identify when certain events occur during the day. Thus they can predict when something is going to occur, when it will start, and when it will end and regulate their lives in a corresponding manner. Being able to tell time and to manage one's life accordingly allows a person to have greater independence. For this reason, when possible, it is important for persons with intellectual disabilities to learn how to tell and manage time.

To know what time it is, a person must be able to understand the numbers on a clock and what these numbers mean in two dimensions: hours and minutes. Additionally, it is necessary for the person to understand the language of telling time, for example, "ten after," "a quarter till," "nine thirty," and so forth. Although we typically take this skill for granted, learning to tell time is a relatively complicated cognitive task. Even so, many students with moderate mental disabilities can learn to do so given appropriate instruction. Instructional procedures useful for teachers have been described by Ford et al. (1989) and by Smeets, Van Lieshout, Lancioni, and Striefel (1986).

Learning to Tell Time

Using a large clock or an accurate facsimile, the teacher should teach students how to tell time by employing an instructional plan such as the following. Sufficient trials should be allotted for each step so that the student can learn the requirement of the step accurately.

- Students learn to read the hour. The teacher removes the minute hand and uses the hour hand (the little hand) to point to different numbers. The students learn to say "It is __ o'clock."
- After students can read the hour, the teacher replaces the minute hand and leaves it pointing to 12. The hour hand is moved to point to different numbers. As it points, the students should say, "It is __ o'clock."
- Next, students learn to read the time at half past the hour. The teacher moves the hour hand halfway between various numbers and moves the minute hand to point to the 6. The students read the time, using different, appropriate statements: "It's 6:30," "It's half past 8," "It's 30 minutes after 4," and so forth. Some students may benefit from counting the individual minutes (1 to 30) in order to understand why they are saying " __:30," or "30 minutes after __."
- After students have mastered the above skill, they should be given several opportunities to read the time at both the hour and the half-hour. This is important because they need to learn to discriminate between the two.
- When students can reliably read the time at the hour and half-hour, the quarter-hour before and after the hour should be introduced. The minute hand should be placed appropriately and the hour hand should be placed just a little before or a little after the hour, depending on the time that is to be read. It is important that the placement of the hands be as accurate as possible in order for correct discrimination and generalization to occur. Once again, students learn to say the time, using several appropriate phrases: "It's 15 after 3," "It's a quarter till 7," "It's 11:15," and so forth.
- Once again, maintenance and discrimination training must be used to practice all the clock configurations studied thus far: the time on the hour, half past the hour, and a quarter-hour before and after the hour.

Most stores, offices, businesses, schools, and other community settings open and close on the hour, the half-hour, or at quarter-hours. Jobs and recreational events also usually begin and end at such times. If students are successful in learning to tell time to this degree of accuracy, they will have accomplished a significant skill. All the remaining indications of time can be stated by the student in terms of approximations without indicating the exact number of minutes. For example, students can learn to read a clock that shows between 1 and 8 minutes after the hour by saying, "It is a little after __." Similarly, they can learn to read clocks and say, "It's almost __:30," or "It's just past __:45," and so forth.

Students who can learn to read the time more accurately by referring to the exact number of minutes should continue the sequence in the following order:

- After students can discriminate and read the time on the hour and half-hour and 15 minutes before and after the hour, they should be taught 5 and 10 minutes before and after the hour. It will be necessary to position the hands on the clock precisely and allow many practice opportunities.
- Success with the above step requires discrimination instruction that allows the student to practice telling time on the hour; at 5, 10, and 15 past the hour; on the half-hour; and 15, 10, and 5 minutes before the hour.
- The remaining major time configurations to be identified are 20 and 25 minutes before and after the hour. When these have been learned, discrimination practice should again be instituted, because it will continue to be important for the student to learn to vary the verbal statements used to tell time and to hear the variations in order to understand them.

Each progressive step has brought the student closer to being able to read, tell, hear, and understand time with greater degrees of accuracy. With adequate progress to this point, it may be appropriate to teach students to understand minutes and seconds and thus have a more complete understanding of time, clocks, and watches.

It can be expected that students will have various difficulties as they learn to tell time. For many individuals with cognitive disabilities, the ability to discriminate is relatively difficult. Smeets et al. (1986) found that when the hour hand was situated between two numbers the students often made reference to the incorrect number. For example, 1:15 might be misread as 2:15. They also had difficulty in discriminating before and after, that is, "10 till" was sometimes read as "10 after." But still they found that with adequate instruction all their students were able to learn time-telling skills.

Learning to Manage Time

Being able to tell time does not necessarily mean that students will use these skills as normally required. Teachers and others should provide ample opportunities for students to say the time and then respond according to what the time calls for. For example, class schedules may show that physical education begins at 10:15. Individual students can be asked to inform the teacher when the clock says 10:15 so that everyone will know when it is time to go to P.E. Ultimately, it may be expected that natural environmental contingencies will maintain the skill, but, until that happens, emphasis should be placed on telling and managing time. Given adequate ability, students should ultimately learn how to tell and understand time, estimate time needs, predict when something is expected to occur, and solve problems related to the use of time (Ford et al., 1989).

Students with less ability can also acquire some time-management skills even though they cannot read a watch or clock face to tell time. Since using time correctly means that we can tell what time it is and simultaneously know what is to happen at that time, some students can acquire this skill by learning to match the time on the clock with a certain activity that should occur at that time. This can be facilitated through the use of picture cues. This technique requires a figure representing the activity and a clock face showing the time for the activity to appear on the same chart, card, or page. When the student sees that the time on the clock or watch matches the time on the chart, she learns to engage in the activity that is also represented on the chart. This task requires the ability to match the real time with that beside the figure and then engage in the activity, which is somewhat less complex than actually being able to read a clock or watch.

If students cannot acquire a skill such as this, instructional efforts on time management should focus on getting the student to recognize sequences of events in relation to each other and to environmental cues (Ford et al., 1989). For example, students could learn that when others start gathering their belongings the school day is nearly over and it is almost time to go home. In this way, even though students do not acquire skills for reading or responding to clock time, they learn broad concepts of time and the organization of events in their day.

Whether a student uses a watch or clock to tell time, uses pictures or figures to help, or learns to understand the relation between environmental cues and activities, a number of natural opportunities when these skills may be practiced are listed in Table 17–2.

Summary of Strategies for Teaching Arithmetic

During the elementary school years, students with moderate mental disabilities may do well in the acquisition of basic arithmetic skills. To the extent that they can have success learning these skills, instruction should be provided that focuses on basic concepts and uses a variety of concrete instructional materials. As with reading and writing, during the younger years, students with cognitive disabilities are closer to their nondisabled peers in terms of their academic ability than they are later in life. Therefore, instructional time might be best spent teaching arithmetic skills similar to (if not the same as) those being taught to children without disabilities.

Ultimately, however, when the student reaches the middle school years (or sooner for children with more severe disabilities), the focus of instruction must shift to arithmetic skills more directly applicable to everyday life. The primary areas of instruction at this time are learning to use money and to tell and manage time. The extent of success achieved by students on learning basic arithmetic skills and concepts will likely bear on how well students

Table 17–2 Time-Management Opportunities

Elementary School	*Middle and High School*
Responds to bells or other cues for arrival and departure	Responds to bells or other cues for passage between classes
Uses class calendar to determine which day it is, what activities are planned, and so forth	Uses personal calendar to keep track of birthdates and other special dates, events that are planned, and so forth
Follows classroom schedule of daily activities	Follows personal schedule of classes for day and week
Uses wall clock and/or watch to manage time throughout day	Uses wall clock and/or watch to manage time throughout day
	Uses timer during home economics class to monitor cooking activities
	Manages time card at job site
	Manages time as needed in community situations (e.g., bus use, arrival, breaktime, and departure from job site)

Source: The Syracuse Community-Referenced Curriculum Guide for Students with Moderate and Severe Disabilities (p. 154), by A. Ford, R. Schnorr, L. Meyer, J. Black, and P. Dempsey, 1989, Baltimore: Paul H. Brookes Publishing Co. Reprinted by permission.

can learn these more functional skills. However, even if students have not been able to acquire many of the basic arithmetic concepts, they may learn some skills related to handling money and managing time. These should be taught, practiced, and applied so that the student can become as competent as possible in their use.

Teaching Academics in the Regular Classroom

Inclusion of students with severe disabilities in regular classroom settings is an important goal. Strategies and tactics for doing this were discussed previously in Chapter 10, and therefore in this section only a brief description of how some of these approaches can be used to teach academic skills is provided. Because regular classrooms are the primary sites for academic instruction, it makes sense that much academic instruction for students with disabilities should occur in the regular classroom. Many instructional goals and strategies discussed in this chapter can be used in regular class settings if special and general educators work together and employ the cooperation of other professionals, paraprofessionals, and students. Some ways to do this are described in the following sections.

Cooperative Learning

Cooperative learning allows several students to work together toward a common goal. Each student uses his skills to contribute to the group. Students do not have to have the same level of ability nor do they need to be working on the same skill or objective as long as they are working together to achieve a goal designated by the instructor. This format allows a student with a disability to work on academic skills targeted for him while the other students work at their own skill levels (Johnson & Johnson, 1986, 1989; Putnam, Rynders, Johnson, & Johnson, 1989).

There are several ways students with cognitive disabilities can work on academic skills in a regular classroom setting in a cooperative learning arrangement. For example, they might read part of the text containing words that they know, write down some key words during an activity, say the beginning and ending time of an experiment, or count objects or add them together.

Incidental Learning and Observational Learning

Teaching students with disabilities in groups can provide the opportunity to take advantage of incidental learning and observational learning opportunities. For example, when giving students feedback about their reading performance within a small group, incidental learning can be used to embed related information (such as the definition of words) into the feedback. Students can also be encouraged to observe the learning opportunities of other students and in this way may acquire additional information through observational learning, such as learning additional sight words (Collins et al., 1995; Collins & Stinson, 1995; Gast et al., 1990; Schoen & Ogden, 1995).

Parallel Learning Activities

Parallel or alternative learning activities occur in the regular classroom and are related to the primary class activities, but are designed to meet the instructional needs and abilities of students with disabilities. Ford and Davern (1989) provided several examples of such activities. One was of two boys with disabilities in the fourth grade who developed and operated a hot chocolate business along with other class members. The students without disabilities worked on applying the math skills that they were learning; the two students with disabilities worked on learning their individually determined skills: one using a calculator and the other matching coins to a number card.

Multilevel Curriculum

In a multilevel curriculum, the area of instruction includes objectives at several different levels (to accommodate students of different abilities) within the same learning exercise (Giangreco & Putnam, 1991). For example, some students might be working on single-digit addition using concrete materials, others might be working on multidigit addition without regrouping, and others could be working on multidigit addition with regrouping. A multilevel curricular approach could be applied easily within a cooperative learning model.

Curriculum Overlapping

Curriculum overlapping is similar to the multilevel curriculum, but the instructional activities do not all have to be within the same instructional domain (Giangreco & Putnam, 1991). The implication is that for most students in a class the learning activity may be one thing; for others, it may be another. This fits well into the cooperative learning model. For example, some students might practice their writing skills from a model while others are working on writing a play.

Individual Tutoring

Within the activities of the regular classroom, the student with disabilities may receive individual or small-group instruction from a general education or special education teacher, a paraprofessional, or a peer (Giangreco & Putnam, 1991). This form of instructional activity is most appropriate at the initial acquisition of specific academic skills, for example, when the student is first learning to read a section of a book with new words or is carrying out a new arithmetic exercise. After the student has shown the ability to perform the task, she may practice it in another format in the regular classroom. Studies have shown that peer tutors can be effective in teaching both reading skills (Collins et al., 1995; Collins & Stinson, 1995) and arithmetic skills (Vacc & Cannon, 1991).

Considerations for Delivering Instruction in the Regular Classroom

It is possible for students with disabilities to acquire many skills in the regular classroom, including different types of academic skills. Success, however, depends largely on the ability of special educators and general educators to work cooperatively (see Chapter 10). Both must participate in planning and implementing instruction for all children, those with and without disabilities, if the process is to be effective.

Unfortunately, sometimes students are placed in regular classrooms, but are there only physically, not truly participating or learning anything of relevance. This is not much better than being in a segregated environment. The procedures described in general terms earlier and in more detail in Chapter 10 are designed to avoid this outcome. As integration progresses, teachers will find many new and innovative ways to make it work successfully.

Conclusion

The importance of academic skills for individuals with severe disabilities varies. Some, primarily those whose cognitive disabilities are more moderate, will have more success at learning traditional academics than others, particularly those who have more severe or profound mental disabilities. It is important that those who acquire academic skills be able to apply them to daily life or use them to improve the quality of life. Those whose ability to learn academic skills is more limited need either to learn skills that can be immediately and directly applied or to learn how to operate as successfully as possible without academic skills.

Often it is difficult to determine precisely how much a student might be able to learn. Students may seem to show poor ability because they lack motivation or because they have not been given the opportunity to learn. Additionally, students' learning potential may change over time as they become older and acquire more life experience. Teachers should not assume a person's ability or inability, particularly if it is based on his or her diagnostic label. During the process of initial assessment, the teacher will have plenty of opportunity to determine both needs and abilities. Even beyond this time, the teacher, along with the other members of the collaborative team, should consider the appropriateness of teaching academic skills and the nature of the skills to be taught. The most important academic skills are those that will allow the student to function and enjoy life more in the environments in which he or she participates. The choice of words, sentences, signs, menus, directions, or books the student should learn to read should be determined in this way. So should writing needs and money-handling and time-telling skills. When these determinations are made, fun and leisure should be considered, just as should functional and work activities. Traditional academic skills can bring pleasure to life, and students should be taught with that in mind.

Questions for Reflection

1. What feelings or concerns might parents of children with moderate mental disabilities have about academic instruction?
2. How could academic instruction affect inclusion in the regular classroom?
3. Describe some important nonfunctional academic instructional objectives.
4. What factors should be considered when developing the reading material for a student with moderate mental disabilities?
5. What are some ways in which a student with moderate mental disabilities can participate in a classroom in which whole language is used? What are some academic and some nonacademic ways?

6. Why do you think more teachers have used a skills-based approach rather than a whole language approach with students with moderate mental disabilities?

7. In what ways might the Internet or other forms of technology be used to improve literacy skills?

8. How can a person's quality of life be affected by basic arithmetic skills?

9. How do you believe most students with moderate mental disabilities feel about receiving academic instruction?

References

Ault, M. J., Gast, D. L., & Wolery, M. (1988). Comparison of progressive and constant time delay procedures in teaching community-sign word reading. *American Journal of Mental Retardation, 93,* 44–56.

Baroody, A. J. (1987). Problem size and mentally retarded children's judgment of commutativity. *American Journal of Mental Deficiency, 91*(4), 439–442.

Baroody, A. J. (1988). Number comparison learning by children classified as mentally retarded. *American Journal on Mental Retardation, 92,* 461–471.

Baroody, A. J. (1993). Introducing number and arithmetic concepts with number sticks. *Teaching Exceptional Children, 26*(1), 7–11.

Baroody, A. J. (1996). Self-invented addition strategies by children with mental retardation. *American Journal on Mental Retardation, 101,* 72–89.

Baroody, A. J., & Snyder, P. M. (1983). A cognitive analysis of basic arithmetic skills of TMR children. *Education and Training of the Mentally Retarded, 18*(4), 253–259.

Barudin, S. I., & Hourcade, J. J. (1990). Relative effectiveness of three methods of reading instruction in developing specific recall and transfer skills in learners with moderate and severe mental retardation. *Education and Training in Mental Retardation, 21,* 286–291.

Bellamy, T., & Buttars, K. L. (1975). Teaching trainable level retarded students to count money. *Education and Training of the Mentally Retarded, 10,* 18–26.

Borakove, L. S., & Cuvo, A. J. (1976). Facilitative effects of coin displacement on teaching coin summation to mentally retarded adolescents. *American Journal of Mental Deficiency, 81,* 350–356.

Bracey, S., Maggs, A., & Morath, P. (1975). The effects of a direct phonics approach in teaching reading with six moderately retarded children: Acquisition and mastery learning stages. *Exceptional Child, 22*(2), 83–90.

Brady, N. C., & McLean, L. K. (1996). Arbitrary symbol learning by adults with severe mental retardation: Comparison of lexigrams and printed words. *American Journal on Mental Retardation, 100,* 423–427.

Browder, D.M., & Grasso, E. (1999). Teaching money skills to individuals with mental retardation: A research review with practical applications. *Remedial & Special Education, 20,* 297–309.

Browder, D. M., Hines, C., McCarthy, L. J., & Fees, J. (1984). A treatment package for increasing sight word recognition for use in daily living skills. *Education and Training of the Mentally Retarded, 19,* 191–200.

Browder, D. M., & Lalli, J. S. (1991). Review of research on sight word instruction. *Research in Developmental Disabilities, 12,* 203–228.

Browder, D. M., & Minarovic, T. J. (2000). Utilizing sight words in self-instruction training for employees with moderate mental retardation in competitive jobs. *Education and Training in Mental Retardation and Developmental Disabilities, 35,* 78–89.

Browder, D. M., & Snell, M. E. (1993). Functional academics. In M. E. Snell (Ed.), *Instruction of students with severe disabilities* (4th Ed., pp. 442–479). Upper Saddle River, NJ: Merrill/Prentice Hall.

Browder, D. M., & Xin, Y. P. (1998). A meta-analysis and review of sight word research and its implication for teaching reading to individuals with moderate and severe disabilities. *Journal of Special Education, 32,* 130–153.

Brown, L., Jones, S., Troccolo, E., Heiser, C., Bellamy, T., & Sontag, E. (1972). Teaching functional reading to young trainable students: Toward longitudinal objectives. *Journal of Special Education, 6,* 51–56.

Brown, L., & Perlmutter, L. (1971). Teaching functional reading to trainable level retarded students. *Education and Training of the Mentally Retarded, 6,* 74–84.

Calhoun, M. L. (1985). Typing contrasted with handwriting in language arts instruction for moderately mentally retarded students. *Education and Training of the Mentally Retarded, 20,* 48–52.

Caycho, L., Gunn, P., & Siegal, M. (1991). Counting by children with Down syndrome. *American Journal on Mental Retardation, 95*(5), 575–583.

Collins, B. C., Branson, T. A., & Hall, M. (1995). Teaching generalized reading of cooking product labels to adolescents with mental disabilities through the use of key words taught by peer tutors. *Education and Training in Mental Retardation and Developmental Disabilities, 30,* 65–75.

Collins, B. C., & Stinson, D. M. (1995). Teaching generalized reading of product warning labels to adolescents with mental disabilities through the use of key words. *Exceptionality, 5,* 163–181.

Conners, F. A. (1992). Reading instruction for students with moderate mental retardation: Review and analysis of research. *American Journal on Mental Retardation, 96*(6), 577–597.

Conners, F. A., Carr, M. D., & Willis, S. (1998). Is the phonological loop responsible for intelligence-related differences in forward digit span? *American Journal on Mental Retardation, 103,* 1–11.

Cuvo, A. J., & Klatt, K. P. (1992). Effects of community-based, videotape, and flash card instruction of community-referenced sight words on students with mental retardation. *Journal of Applied Behavior Analysis, 25*(2), 499–512.

Cuvo, A. J., Veitch, V. D., Trace, M. W., & Konke, J. L. (1978). Teaching change computation to the mentally retarded. *Behavior Modification, 2,* 531–548.

Didden, R., Prinsen, H., & Sigafoos, J. (2000). The blocking effect of pictorial prompts on sight-word reading. *Journal of Applied Behavior Analysis, 33,* 317–320.

Dolch, E. W. (1950). *Teaching primary reading* (2nd Ed.). Champaign, IL: Garrard Press.

Domnie, M., & Brown, L. (1977). Teaching severely handicapped students reading skills requiring printed answers to who, what and where questions. *Education and Training of the Mentally Retarded, 12*(4), 324–331.

Dorry, G. W., & Zeaman, D. (1973). The use of a fading technique in paired-associate reading vocabulary with retardates. *Mental Retardation, 11*(6), 3–6.

Dorry, G. W., & Zeaman, D. (1975). Teaching a simple reading vocabulary to retarded children: Effectiveness of fading and non-fading procedures. *American Journal of Mental Deficiency, 79,* 711–716.

Entriken, D., York, R., & Brown, L. (1977). Teaching trainable level multiply handicapped students to use picture cues, context cues, and initial consonant sounds to determine the labels of unknown words. *AAESPH Review, 2,* 169–190.

Erickson, K. A., & Koppenhaver, D. A. (1995). Developing a literacy program for children with severe disabilities. *The Reading Teacher, 48,* 676–687.

Erickson, K. A., Koppenhaven, D. A., & Yoder, D. E. (1994). *Literacy and adults with developmental disabilities* (NCAL Technical Report TR 94-15). The Center for Literacy and Disability Studies, University of North Carolina at Chapel Hill. (ERIC Document Number ED 377 340.)

Feinberg, P. (1975). Sight vocabulary for the TMR child and adult: Rationale, development, and application. *Education and Training of the Mentally Retarded, 10*(4), 246–251.

Flexer, R. (1989). Conceptualizing addition. *Teaching Exceptional Children, 21*(4), 21–24.

Ford, A., & Davern, L. (1989). Moving forward with school integration: Strategies for involving students with severe handicaps in the life of the school. In R. Gaylord-Ross (Ed.), *Integration strategies for students with handicaps* (pp. 11–31), Baltimore: Paul H. Brookes.

Ford, A., Schnorr, R., Meyer, L., Davern, L., Black, J., & Dempsey, P. (1989). *The Syracuse community-referenced curriculum guide for students with moderate and severe disabilities.* Baltimore: Paul H. Brookes.

Frank, A. R. (1978). Teaching money skills with a number line. *Teaching Exceptional Children, 10*(2), 46–47.

Fry, E. (1957). Developing a word list for remedial reading. *Elementary English, 33,* 456–458.

Fry, E. (1972). *Reading instruction for classroom and clinic.* New York: McGraw-Hill.

Gardill, M. C., & Browder, D. M. (1995). Teaching stimulus class to encourage independent purchasing by students with severe behavior disorders. *Education and Training in Mental Retardation and Developmental Disabilities, 30,* 254–264.

Gast, D. L., Ault, M. J., Wolery, M., Doyle, P. M., & Belanger, S. (1988). Comparison of constant time delay and the system of least prompts in teaching sight word reading to students with moderate retardation. *Education and Training in Mental Retardation, 25,* 117–128.

Gast, D. L., Doyle, P. M., Wolery, M., Ault, M. J., & Farmer, J. A. (1991). Assessing the acquisition of incidental information by secondary-age students with mental retardation: Comparison of response prompting strategies. *American Journal on Mental Retardation, 96,* 63–80.

Gast, D. L., Wolery, M., Morris, L. L., Doyle, P. M., & Meyer, S. (1990). Teaching sight reading in a group instructional arrangement using constant time delay. *Exceptionality, 1,* 81–96.

Gersten, R. M., & Maggs, A. (1982). Teaching the general case to moderately retarded children: Evaluation of a five year project. *Analysis and Intervention in Developmental Disabilities, 2,* 329–343.

Giangreco, M. F., & Putnam, J. W. (1991). Supporting the education of students with severe disabilities in regular education environments. In L. H. Meyer, C. A. Peck, & L. Brown (Eds.), *Critical issues in the lives of people with severe disabilities* (pp. 245–270). Baltimore: Paul H. Brookes.

Hamre-Nietupski, S., Nietupski, J., & Strathe, M. (1992). Functional life skills, academic skills, and friendship/social relationship development: What do parents of students with moderate/severe/profound disabilities value? *Journal of the Association for Persons with Severe Handicaps, 17*(1), 53–58.

Hanrahan, J., Goodman, W., & Rapagna, S. (1990). Preparing mentally retarded students for mainstreaming: Priorities of regular class and special school teachers. *American Journal on Mental Retardation, 94,* 470–474.

Hoogeveen, F. R., & Smeets, P. M. (1988). Establishing phoneme blending in trainable mentally retarded children. *Remedial and Special Education, 9*(2), 46–53.

Hoogeveen, F. R., Smeets, P. M., & Lancioni, G. E. (1989). Teaching moderately retarded children basic reading skills. *Research in Developmental Disabilities, 10,* 1–18.

Hoogeveen, F. R., Smeets, P. M., & Van der Houven, J. E. (1987). Establishing letter–sound correspondence in children classified as trainable mentally retarded. *Education and Training in Mental Retardation, 22*(2), 77–84.

Horton, S. (1985). Computational rates of educable mentally retarded adolescents with and without calculators in comparison to normals. *Education and Training of the Mentally Retarded, 20,* 14–24.

House, B. J., Hanley, M. J., & Magid, D. F. (1980). Logographic reading by TMR adults. *American Journal of Mental Deficiency, 85,* 161–170.

Johnson, D. W., & Johnson, R. T. (1986). Mainstreaming and cooperative learning strategies. *Exceptional Children, 52*(6), 553–561.

Johnson, D. W., & Johnson, R. T. (1989). Cooperative learning and mainstreaming. In R. Gaylord-Ross (Ed.), *Integration strategies for students with handicaps* (pp. 233–248). Baltimore: Paul H. Brookes.

Katims, D. S. (2000). Literacy instruction for people with mental retardation: Historical highlights and contemporary analysis. *Education and Training in Mental Retardation and Developmental Disabilities, 35,* 3–15.

Kirk, S. A. (1972). *Educating exceptional children* (2nd Ed.). Boston: Houghton Mifflin.

Kliewer, C., & Biklen, D. (2001). "School's not really a place for reading": A research synthesis of literate lives of students with severe disabilities. *Journal of the Association for Persons with Severe Handicaps, 26,* 1–12.

Kliewer, C., & Landis, D. (1999). Individualizing literacy instruction for young children with moderate to severe disabilities. *Exceptional Children, 66,* 85–100.

Koller, E. Z., & Mulhern, T. J. (1977). Use of a pocket calculator to train arithmetic skills with trainable adolescents. *Education and Training of the Mentally Retarded, 12*(4), 332–335.

Koury, M., & Browder, D. M. (1986). The use of delay to teach sight words by peer tutors classified as moderately mentally retarded. *Education and Training of the Mentally Retarded, 21,* 252–258.

Krantz, P. J., & McClannahan, L. E. (1998). Social interaction skills for children with autism: A script fading procedure for beginning readers. *Journal of Applied Behavior Analysis, 31,* 191–202.

Lalli, J. S., & Browder, D. M. (1993). Comparison of sight word training procedures with validation of the most practical procedure for teaching reading for daily living. *Research in Developmental Disabilities, 14,* 107–127.

Lowe, M. L., & Cuvo, A. J. (1976). Teaching coin summation to the mentally retarded. *Journal of Applied Behavior Analysis, 9,* 483–489.

Mastropieri, M. A., Bakken, J. P., & Scruggs, T. E. (1991). Mathematics instruction for people with mental retardation: A perspective and research synthesis. *Education and Training in Mental Retardation, 26*(2), 115–129.

Mather, N., & Lachowicz, B. L. (1992). Shared writing: An instructional approach for reluctant writers. *Teaching Exceptional Children, 25*(1), 26–30.

Matson, J. L., & Long, S. (1986). Teaching computation/shopping skills to mentally retarded adults. *American Journal of Mental Deficiency, 91,* 98–101.

McDonnell, J., Johnson, J. W., Polychronis, S., & Risen, T. (2002). Effects of embedded instruction on students with moderate disabilities enrolled in general education classes. *Education and Training in Mental Retardation and Developmental Disabilities, 37,* 363–377.

Miller, A., & Miller, E. E. (1968). Symbol accentuation: The perceptual transfer of meaning from spoken to printed words. *American Journal of Mental Deficiency, 73,* 200–208.

Miller, A., & Miller, E. E. (1971). Symbol accentuation, single-track functioning, and early reading. *American Journal of Mental Deficiency, 76,* 110–117.

Miracle, S. A., Collins, B. C., Schuster, J. W., & Grisham-Brown, J. (2001). Peer- versus teacher-delivered instruction: Effects on acquisition and maintenance. *Education and Training in Mental Retardation and Developmental Disabilities, 36,* 373–385.

Mirenda, P. (1992). *Literacy instruction for persons with severe disabilities.* Paper presented at the Conference of the Association for Persons with Severe Handicaps, San Francisco.

Nietupski, J., Williams, W., & York, R. (1979). Teaching selected phonic word analysis skills to TMR labeled students. *Teaching Exceptional Children, 11*(4), 140–143.

Paddock, C. (1992). Ice cream stick math. *Teaching Exceptional Children, 24*(2), 50–51.

Putnam, J. W., Rynders, J. E., Johnson, R. T., & Johnson, D. W. (1989). Collaborative skill instruction for promoting positive interactions between mentally handicapped and nonhandicapped children. *Exceptional Children, 55*(6), 550–557.

Roberson, W. H., Gravel, J. S., Valcante, G. C., & Maurer, R. G. (1992). Using a picture task analysis to teach students with multiple disabilities. *Teaching Exceptional Children, 24*(4), 12–15.

Ryndak, D.L., Morrison, A.P., & Sommerstein, L. (1999). Literacy before and after inclusion in general education settings: A case study. *Journal of the Association for Persons with Severe Handicaps, 24,* 5–22.

Rynders, J. E., & Horrobin, J. M. (1990). Always trainable? Never educable? Updating education expectations of children with Down syndrome. *American Journal on Mental Retardation, 95,* 77–83.

Schloss, P. J., Alexander, N., Hornig, E., Parker, K., & Wright, B. (1993). Teaching meal preparation vocabulary and procedures to individuals with mental retardation. *Teaching Exceptional Children, 25*(3), 7–12.

Schoen, S. F., & Ogden, S. (1995). Impact of time delay, observational learning, and attentional cuing upon word recognition during integrated small-group instruction. *Journal of Autism and Developmental Disorders, 25,* 503–519.

Singh, N. N., & Singh, J. (1984). Antecedent control of oral reading errors and self-corrections by mentally retarded children. *Journal of Applied Behavior Analysis, 17,* 111–119.

Singh, J., & Singh, N. N. (1985). Comparison of word-supply and word-analysis error correction procedures on oral reading by mentally retarded children. *American Journal of Mental Deficiency, 90,* 64–70.

Singh, N. N., & Singh, J. (1988). Increasing oral reading proficiency through overcorrection and phonic analysis. *American Journal on Mental Retardation, 93,* 312–319.

Singh, N. N., & Solman, R. T. (1990). A stimulus control analysis of the picture-word problem in children who are mentally retarded: The blocking effect. *Journal of Applied Behavior Analysis, 23,* 525–532.

Singleton, K. C., Schuster, J. W., & Ault, M. J. (1995). Simultaneous prompting in a small group instructional arrangement. *Education and Training in Mental Retardation and Developmental Disabilities, 30,* 218–230.

Smeets, P. M., Van Lieshout, R. W., Lancioni, G. E., & Striefel, S. (1986). Teaching mentally retarded students to tell time. *Analysis and Intervention in Developmental Disabilities, 6,* 221–238.

Stromer, R., Mackay, H. A., Howell, S. R., & McVay, A. A. (1996). Teaching computer-assisted spelling to individuals with developmental and hearing disabilities: Transfer of stimulus control to writing tasks. *Journal of Applied Behavior Analysis, 29,* 25–42.

Vacc, N. N., & Cannon, S. J. (1991). Cross-age tutoring in mathematics: Sixth graders helping students who are moderately handicapped. *Education and Training in Mental Retardation, 26*(1), 89–97.

Vacc, N. N., & Vacc, N. A. (1979). Teaching manuscript writing to mentally retarded children. *Education and Training of the Mentally Retarded* (Dec.), 286–291.

Walsh, B. F., & Lambert, F. (1979). Errorless discrimination and picture fading as techniques for teaching sight words to TMR students. *American Journal of Mental Deficiency, 83,* 473–479.

Wehmeyer, M. L., Lance, G. D., & Bashinski, S. (2002). Promoting access to the general curriculum for students with mental retardation: A multi-level model. *Education and Training in Mental Retardation and Developmental Disabilities, 37*(3), 223–234.

Wehmeyer, M. L., Lattin, D., & Agran, M. (2001). Achieving access to the general curriculum for students with mental retardation: A curriculum-decision making model. *Education and Training in Mental Retardation and Developmental Disabilities, 36*, 327–342.

Worrall, N., & Singh, Y. (1983). Teaching TMR children to read using integrated picture cuing. *American Journal of Mental Deficiency, 87,* 422–429.

CHAPTER 18

Teaching Community and Domestic Skills

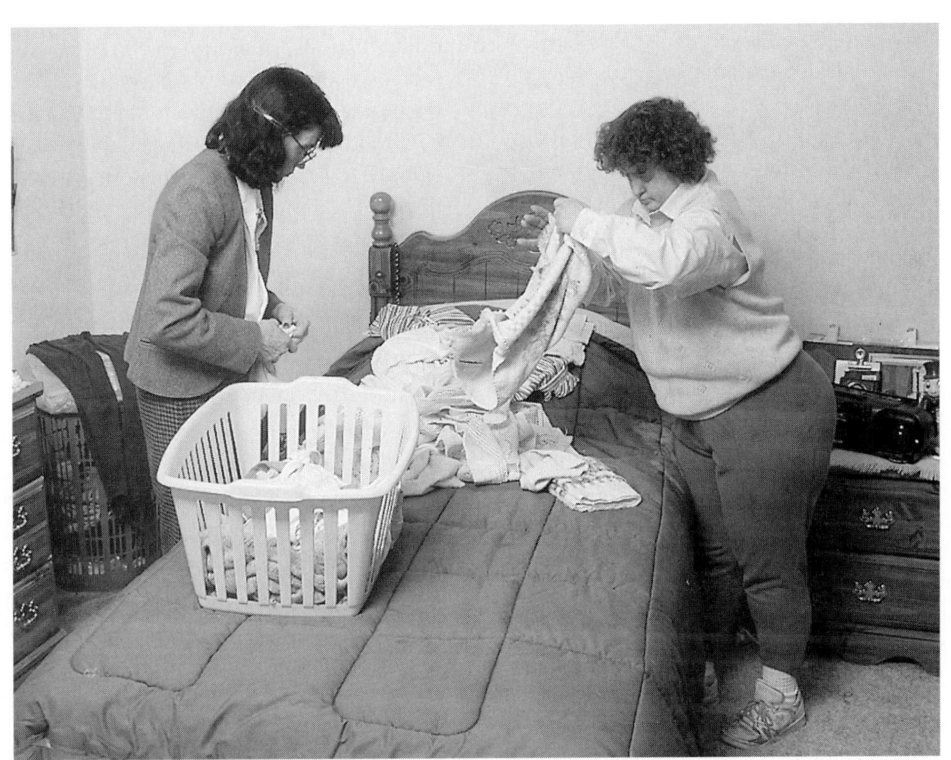

Several considerations about teaching skills for functioning in community and home settings are discussed in this chapter. Specific methods are presented for teaching skills for operating in grocery stores and restaurants, using vending machines, teaching pedestrian skills and using public transportation, preparing food, completing different household chores, and using a telephone.

Why Teach Community and Domestic Skills?

Many important life skills are learned incidentally by most people. Shopping for clothes and groceries, using buses and laundromats, preparing meals, and making phone calls are a few examples. We generally do not take courses or receive formal instruction on how to perform the tasks and subtasks incorporated in these activities, but learn them through less formal experiences. As we learn them, we learn to apply basic skills such as language, reading, writing, arithmetic, and appropriate social behavior. Most of the time we acquire these skills by accompanying and observing parents, siblings, relatives, or friends as they perform the tasks in home and community settings.

For several reasons, however, persons with severe disabilities do not learn skills of this kind to a level commensurate with their age in the same informal ways as many others (Brown et al., 1983). Obviously, cognitive limitations reduce the ability to attain, synthesize, remember, and use information correctly in appropriate settings. Also, as discussed in Chapter 8, generalization of skills is often a problem, meaning that even if students learn skills in one setting they may have difficulty using them in another. These problems are multiplied by the fact that the tasks are often relatively complex, requiring the student to complete many steps in a functional order. Because of these conditions, direct instruction in nonschool settings is often necessary if students with severe disabilities are going to learn domestic and community skills. Traditional classroom instruction in these areas is insufficient in most cases to ensure that the skills will be used and learned.

Including Nondisabled Peers in Community Learning

Despite its importance, there are two problems with taking students out of their schools for community-based instruction. First, instruction that occurs outside the typical school environment often results in the separation of students with severe disabilities from their peers. Even though learning community skills may be important from the teacher's perspective, if they are not really important to the person who is learning them and to the significant individuals in this person's life, this separation is difficult to justify. Second, because students with cognitive disabilities may benefit from participation in the general curriculum (Wehmeyer, Lance, & Bashinski, 2002; Wehmeyer, Lattin, & Agran, 2001), and are encouraged by IDEA to do so, leaving the classroom to learn in the community decreases the amount of time that they can devote to participating in academic learning.

Still there is a sense among many that we should not abandon teaching functional community and domestic skills, especially when they are relevant to students' needs. To try to determine the relative value of inclusion and community-based instruction, Agran, Snow, and Swaner (1999) conducted a survey of middle school and high school special education teachers to assess their opinions regarding this issue. The participants were asked to rate the relative value of each approach with regard to its impact on students with severe disabilities. The results indicated that the teachers saw strong values in both types of instruction. A majority (53%) saw inclusion as offering increased opportunities for social interactions, 79% felt that it increased the students' acceptance by others, and 77% said that it increased social interactions and friendships. However, similar benefits were reported as an effect of community-based instruction: 77% said that students with disabilities had increased opportunities in the community to interact with nondisabled peers, 55% said that their students had made friends or been invited to social events because of community experiences, and 79% said that students had increased their independence. Finally, 91% of the teachers agreed that inclusion was somewhat helpful or very helpful in preparing students with severe disabilities for postschool life, whereas 77% agreed that community-based instruction helped their students to be better prepared and successful in postschool life. The authors concluded that teachers clearly saw the value of both inclusion and community-based instruction for students with severe disabilities.

Taking a similar position, Billingsley and Albertson (1999) argued that these students still need to receive instruction in learning functional skills for use in the home, community, and other areas of their lives. The strongest argument for instruction in these areas is that persons who are more able to care for their personal needs are perceived as more competent and thus are better accepted by other individuals. Billingsley and Albertson stated, "We contend . . . that quality of life depends on multiple factors, one of which is competence in typical, functional skills that are performed throughout typical days by typical individuals. The problem . . . is that, in our desire to include all children in general education settings and programs, we may have begun to discount the importance of those skills" (p. 298).

But is it necessary that we make a decision between instructing students with disabilities outside the school and including them with their peers in relevant learning activities? Kluth (2000) contends that it is not. She notes that there is a history of community learning for both students with and without disabilities and proposes that in unified school systems (in which special education and general education are merged) all students could learn together in meaningful *community-referenced* activities. She gives specific examples of joint participation in work experience, research teams, and service learning activities.

Such arrangements could prove to be very beneficial to all students. In the following sections we look at the specific needs for community and domestic learning often identified for students with severe disabilities and how this learning can be achieved.

General Procedures Related to Teaching Community and Domestic Skills

Several procedural matters that must be considered to provide community and domestic instruction are discussed in the next several sections.

Who Should Participate in Community and Domestic Instruction?

Students who require direct instruction to learn most chronological age-appropriate community and domestic skills are usually good candidates for community instruction. Most of the time this group consists of older students in the middle school or high school years, but younger students may also participate if parents and collaborative team members feel that it would be beneficial for them. Particularly during the elementary school years, however, it is more desirable for students to spend their time with their peers in typical school activities instead of in nonschool instruction. If elementary-age students are to be taught community skills, the nature and degree of their community instruction should be appropriate for their age. For example, 8-year-olds do not usually shop for groceries, but they may go with older siblings to the movies, and so the necessary skills for this type of community participation could be targeted for instruction (Morse, Schuster, & Sandknop, 1996).

Partial Participation

Students should not be eliminated from community-based instruction because of the severity of their disability, but should have instructional targets identified that allow them to increase their participation. Everyone has the right to be as active as possible in home and community settings, including people with very severe (i.e., profound) mental disabilities and multiple disabilities. There are many ways to participate partially but meaningfully in community settings. Although most research on community instruction has ignored the inclusion of these individuals (Snell & Browder, 1986; Westling & Floyd, 1990), they may participate in various ways in community and domestic activities. Helmstetter (1989) stressed three points about the involvement of individuals with the most severe disabilities in community activities:

1. There should be emphasis on partial participation as opposed to no participation at all. For example, a student who cannot perform all the steps necessary to operate a vending machine may be able to press a button to make a selection.
2. Various adaptations to material and equipment may be made to allow for partial participation. For example, a student who might have difficulty changing the television station at home could have all the remote-control buttons covered except for the one to change the channel. Although the student has poor motor control, she can still participate meaningfully by having better control over channel selection.
3. Participation in various community activities can give parents and teachers information about a student's preference for different environments. By watching facial reactions, body tone, and behavioral reactions, an observer can draw inferences about a student's likes and dislikes. This information can then be used to determine in which environments and activities the student would like to participate.

Where to Teach Community and Domestic Skills

Given the learning characteristics of students with severe disabilities, it should be understood that much of the instruction for skills appropriate for application in homes and community settings must be directly instructed in these settings. Students with severe disabilities are taught certain skills in actual settings to increase the probability that they will learn and be able to demonstrate these skills in natural contexts and in response to natural cues. School-based instruction on community skills, even in well-designed simulations, generally has not been found to be effective when tests for generalization to community settings have been conducted. The literature has reported successful community-based instruction occurring in restaurants, grocery stores, department stores, banks, and various recreational settings and in teaching students to use vending machines, automatic banking machines, public transportation, and safe pedestrian skills (Westling & Floyd, 1990). These and similar settings in individual communities are primary settings for instruction.

Likewise, instructional programs have been developed for teaching students to function adequately in their homes. However, teaching students in their actual homes may present more difficulty than does teaching in community settings because of several important distinctions. First, the community settings in which students are taught are open to the public, and there are generally few or no limitations on teaching students with severe disabilities in them (Aveno, Renzaglia, and Lively, 1987). On the other hand, parents of students with severe disabilities may not care for the idea of teachers coming into their home to teach domestic skills to their children, even though they may consider the skills important. This issue may be raised in sessions with parents, but teachers should not usually expect that parents will want them to teach in their homes.

Second, even if doing so were possible, it would not necessarily be a good idea to teach individuals in their parents' private homes. Since out-of-school instruction generally takes place in small groups, working in the home of a particular student requires the other students to learn in environments not natural to them. This will likely reduce the effectiveness of instruction because it would not necessarily generalize to their own home.

Third, at the age when it is becoming increasingly important for students to acquire domestic skills (during adolescence) students are usually getting closer to the day when they will move away from their parents' home into a supported apartment setting, a group home, or some other type of shared residence. In this setting, the washing machines, stoves, bathrooms, and so on, may be different from those found in the student's current home. Therefore, even if teaching skills at home were possible, they might not generalize well to the individual's postschool residence.

For these reasons, the most logical place to teach domestic skills might be the high school home economics classroom or perhaps the cafeteria, although they are not natural environments. For many students, it is possible to teach these skills when they are participating in regular home economics classes. In this setting, the special educator and the general educator can work together to ensure that students are learning domestic skills as indicated by their IEP, as well as relevant skills from the general curriculum.

One alternative to providing domestic instruction in the regular school setting is to provide training for domestic skills in actual apartments or homes specifically developed for such training (Freagon et al., 1983; Livi & Ford, 1985; Sands, Able-Boone, Margolis, 1995). Freagon and her colleagues described a home site that was designed to teach domestic skills to students with severe disabilities who were between the ages of 18 and 21. Students learned various chores associated with independent living and took turns staying over on three successive long weekends to learn independent living skills. The program served up to 20 students a year and was judged very successful for preparing students for natural home environments. The setting and learning activities described by Livi and Ford (1985) were similar. An important finding by Livi and Ford, however, was that the skills learned in their nonschool Domestic Training Site (DTS) did not generalize well to the students' own homes until the stimulus conditions within the DTS were modified to be more similar to those found in the homes.

Sands et al. (1995) described the LITE program that made it possible for students to live in an apartment for 8 weeks during the summer preceding graduation from high school. Students worked at job sites during the day and learned domestic and recreational skills during the evening and on the weekend in one of the three or four apartments rented for the program, which was supported by interagency funding. Many skills were taught both formally and informally, such as cooking, money management, household management, personal management, knowledge of community resources, and social and recreational activities. Central to the philosophy of the program, individual choice of activities was encouraged and expected. Some parents of the students became more supportive of independent or semi-independent living arrangements for their young adult children because of the experience.

Notwithstanding the merits of these programs, their limitations must be taken into account. Besides problems with generalization, there are two additional drawbacks to nonschool sites developed explicitly for teaching domestic skills. Again, they segregate students from their nondisabled peers; and, second, they must be financed by someone. Typically, most school districts cannot be expected to fund such a site although, as Sands et al. showed, interagency agreements are possible.

Determining Target Sites and Skills

Although it has been found that persons with severe disabilities participate in a range of home and community activities (Aveno, 1987), teachers should expect a great deal of variability in what students need to learn and where they need to learn it. It should not be assumed that there is a universal set of community and domestic skills that students must learn. Professionals should discuss with parents, the student, and other family members what community sites are important for instruction.

Determining Operational Skills to Be Taught

After determining instructional target sites, the teacher must visit the community and domestic settings where instruction is to take place to conduct an analysis, or ecological inventory, of what skills must be learned in the setting (see Chapter 6). The operational skills targeted (those that are basic to the completion of the task) should be specific to the settings in which the skills are taught. The teacher should observe nondisabled individuals in the setting, walk through the activity that the student is expected to learn, and write down the steps in the appropriate sequence, which should include both operational skills and associated skills (see next section) clustered together. Task analyses or functional routines (see Chapter 7) should be written as guides for instructional activities (Snell & Browder, 1986).

In at least two cases, a full list of operational skills is not an appropriate instructional goal. First, individuals with the most severe disabilities should have learning goals individually determined that allow them to participate in functional and meaningful ways. Second, young children should have goals designed for them based on their chronological age. Usually, these do not consist of completing major functions typical of adults, but are roles appropriate for children.

Determining Associated Skills to Be Taught

In addition to the skills required for completing a specific task in a community setting (i.e., operational skills), teachers, parents, and other team members should target related or associated skills for instruction in the setting. Language, social, physical, and academic skills that are a part of the student's instructional needs should be incorporated into skill clusters that are to be taught, thus forming a functional routine. For example, Westling, Floyd, and Carr (1990) focused on both operational and social skills when teaching adolescents with moderate and severe mental disabilities to shop in a department store. These skills are listed in Figure 18–1.

Figure 18–1 Social Skills Taught as Part of Department Store Shopping

Responds appropriately to accidents.
Asks for help when necessary.
Says "thanks" when assistance is provided.
Waits turn at checkout counter.
Greets cashier appropriately.
Says good-bye appropriately.

Source: Adapted from "Effect of Single Setting versus Multiple Setting Training on Learning to Shop in a Department Store," by D. L. Westling, J. Floyd, and D. Carr, 1990, *American Journal on Mental Deficiency, 94,* pp. 616–624. Copyright 1990 by the American Association on Mental Retardation. Reprinted by permission.

Developing Instructional Plans

Each group or cluster of skills to be taught requires an instructional procedure that will result in skill acquisition and generalization. Most instruction in community settings calls for teaching the whole skill sequence during each instructional episode as opposed to teaching isolated skills (Snell & Browder, 1986). As indicated above, the first step in an instructional plan is to develop the task analysis or functional routine, including both operational and associated behaviors (see Chapter 7). After the components of the task have been written, the teacher must determine the natural cues that are present in the environment that the student must learn to attend to in order to complete each part of the task. Additionally, the teacher must determine the instructional prompts that he will present when the student does not respond to the natural cues. A system of least prompts or time constant time delay (see Chapter 7) is often effective (Snell & Browder, 1986).

Regardless of the prompting system used, it is very important that the teacher reference the student to the natural cues in the environment in order that these stimuli, and not the prompts provided by the teacher, ultimately become the cue for the student's behavior (Ford & Mirenda, 1984). For example, using constant time delay, the teacher places the student at a certain location in the setting where the available cues call for a particular action (e.g., being in front of an empty washing machine in a laundromat with a load of dirty clothes should adequately prompt the student to put the clothes in the washing machine). During an initial instructional phase, the teacher points out the student's location and all the key aspects of the environment and demonstrates what the student is expected to do. On subsequent occasions, once in the environment, the teacher waits for a brief time before using instructional prompts to allow the natural stimuli to have an effect.

Planning for Skill Generalization

Most of the time it will be necessary for the student to learn generalizable community skills so that she can apply the skills in different community settings or in a variety of circumstances. Strategies for achieving skill generalization were discussed in Chapter 8. Although some researchers have reported students learning to generalize without specific training to do so, most of the time spontaneous generalization does not occur (Westling & Floyd, 1990). This being so, teachers usually need to devise instructional strategies to help to achieve generalization. The most effective approach identified to date is the general case method, which was discussed in Chapter 8. Its application in teaching community skills consists of identifying all the specific community settings of a particular type in which the student might need to operate and then training him to operate in a sufficient number of the settings that reflect the range of discriminative stimuli and responses necessary to perform in any setting.

While skill generalization is often an important instructional goal, in some cases of instruction for community participation, it may not be. For example, quality of life may be very good even though an individual learns to use only one bank or to check out videos or DVDs from only one movie rental store. This, in fact, is often the case among individuals who do not have severe disabilities. The assessment and planning procedures discussed in Chapters 5 and 6 will help to determine how much generalization of community skills is necessary.

Implementing Instruction in Community Settings

Teaching students in community settings is often considered by teachers to be more interesting and stimulating than teaching in traditional school settings, because it is easier for the students to see the relevance of the instruction and the direct benefit of students learning relevant skills (Westling & Fleck, 1991). However, providing instruction in nonschool settings requires some special considerations (Test & Spooner, 1996).

Teacher–Student Interactions

When teaching in community settings, the style of interaction with students must be somewhat different from that normally used in schools. It is important that the teacher should interact as naturally as possible so that both students and teacher fit normally and unobtrusively into the setting. Verbal directions should be made in conversational tones, reinforcement should be very subtle, and correction of incorrect or inappropriate behavior should not be loud or harsh.

Instruction should follow the written sequence of skills and utilize the instructional tactic or tactics that have been decided on (e.g., time delay or system of least prompts). Again, for most students, it is important that the teacher work toward ultimately allowing natural environmental cues to control the occurrence of the behaviors and eliminating the delivery of verbal, visual, or physical prompts. When the student no longer requires artificial prompts to complete the skill sequence in the community, the teacher should begin to gradually fade her presence. This can be accomplished, for example, by slowly increasing the distance that the teacher is following along behind the student. This type of action is important, because the student needs to learn to adequately complete the task without the teacher's presence and, by doing so, become more self-reliant.

Number of Students per Instructional Session

Teachers should limit the number of students being instructed in community settings to two or three per session for several reasons. First, objectives for students must be individually determined. It is unlikely that more than a few students will need to learn the same skills in the same setting. Generally, it is inappropriate to take students to a community setting for instruction if the setting has not been identified through the process assessment and planning as one in which instruction should occur. Students going en masse to community settings simply for the sake of going somewhere off campus are actually taking a field trip, and while field trips have benefits, they should not be confused with providing functional community-based instruction.

Second, it is important to limit the number of students to avoid negative attention that might be drawn to a large group of students with disabilities. Gathering many individuals with severe disabilities together in one place often results in attitudes of pity and patronization, certainly something we want to avoid. People working in and using community settings are not likely to arrive at conclusions of individual competence and ability if a large group consisting only of individuals with disabilities comes into the place and proceeds through it in a haphazard fashion. Learning in community settings by individuals without disabilities, which as stated earlier is generally incidental, usually occurs in small natural groups, for example, a parent and a child, an adult and a few children, or a small group of preadolescents or adolescents. A small group in most community settings looks natural, is likely to receive a more natural response, and therefore should be the grouping pattern of choice when teaching students with severe disabilities.

How Often to Provide Instruction

The schedule of community instruction should allow the students to be in the settings two or three times per week, at least when the skill is being initially learned. This should provide adequate opportunity for them to learn target skills without forgetting them from one visit to another. After the skill is learned, trips to the community setting might be reduced to a level that is relatively natural for the setting, as long as the frequency of visits is adequate for the skill to be retained by the student. It is never advisable to visit one type of community setting for a certain period of time, say 6 to 9 weeks, stop the visits, and then begin to visit other settings. In other words, sometimes teachers might want to approach community-based instruction using a "units of instruction" or "thematic" approach (i.e., "This six weeks we will be visiting banks because we are doing a unit on banking. During the next six weeks we will visit shoe stores."). This is not how people normally use community settings nor is it how they learn to use them. Therefore, this approach to community-based instruction should give way to more natural schedules of visits.

Using Prosthetic Aids

Sometimes students with disabilities can learn to be more independent in community settings by using prosthetic devices that help them to accomplish certain skills that otherwise are too difficult or would take a long time to learn. Many individuals without disabilities also use these types of devices; for example, many people use shopping lists to help them to remember what they need to buy at the grocery store.

Figure 18–2 Devices That Can Help in Community Learning Settings

- Written list of items to buy.
- Picture list of items to buy.
- Prewritten messages on card to store employees: "I would like to buy______."
- Clock/watch faces drawn on cards with indications when to come, go, leave, stay, etc.
- Picture list of activities to complete (task analysis) within a setting.
- Card stating learner's name, school, home address, and phone number.
- Prerecorded messages for store employees stating what is desired.
- Money cards showing different amounts required for different purchases.
- Numberlines and/or calculators.

Certainly, these types of devices and others also can be useful for persons with severe disabilities. In Chapter 17, number lines, coin cards, and calculators were described to assist students in making purchases during shopping routines. Figure 18–2 lists additional devices that may be helpful for some students with disabilities.

Using Simulated Community Settings in Schools

Over the years many teachers have attempted to teach functional community-referenced skills to students with severe disabilities by creating simulations of community settings in their classrooms. For example, teachers might create a make-believe bus for students to learn to ride or a grocery store for them to shop in. Although the intentions are good, most research does not support the use of simulated settings as effective approaches when used exclusively (Westling & Floyd, 1990).

If simulations are to be effective, at least two conditions must exist. First, the simulations must contain stimuli very close to those which students must learn to respond to in actual community settings. This may be done by bringing real items into the classroom or using slides projected on the wall to create life-size simulations. If the material does not re-create the stimulus conditions and cues that exist in the natural environment, it is not very likely to be effective.

The second condition is that training in simulated conditions has a chance of being effective only if it is paired with training in the actual settings. Teachers may find that instruction that is alternated between actual community settings and school-based simulations may be an effective instructional practice. Again, though, the importance of the simulation clearly representing the real environment should not be ignored.

In some cases teachers create simulations of parts of the nonschool environment so that a specific set of skills may be taught and then practiced in the community setting. This can be especially useful if the skill is one that a student is having particular difficulty with and/or one that may be improved with massed practice. It can also be useful if the specific part of the community setting environment is one that the student could not use very frequently in the actual community for one reason or another. For example, a grocery store checkout line complete with a cash register and racks of tabloid newspapers may be placed in the classroom to teach the steps required for checking out of the grocery store (McDonnell, Horner, & Williams, 1984). Another example would be creating a simulated automatic teller machine (ATM) to teach the tasks required for taking money out of an account (Shafer, Inge, & Hill, 1986). Obviously, because it is not easy for students to get a great deal of practice in these types of unique settings, well-developed simulations may be useful (Morse et al., 1996). Again, however, adequate community training cannot rely solely on simulations; actual community-based site training will always be necessary.

Using Technology to Create Simulations

Some researchers have found that technology can be used to create tenable simulated conditions that, when used in conjunction with actual community settings, can lead to functional learning. For example, Branham, Collins, Schuster, and Kleinert (1999) used constant time delay (CTD) to teach three adolescents with moderate disabilities three different community skills: cashing a check, crossing a street, and mailing a letter. The CTD procedure was used in combination with three different instructional arrangements that were compared: classroom simulation plus community-based instruction (CBI), videotape instruction plus CBI, and simulation plus videotape plus CBI. All three instruction techniques allowed students to learn the targeted skills, but classroom simulation and CBI turned out to be the most efficient in terms of instructional time required to achieve criterion. Nevertheless, the use of the video images was the most innovative. It presented students with a still frame of a step in the task analysis and asked them to describe verbally the activity to be undertaken. After describing the steps when presented with the video still images, the students were able to transfer learning to actual performance in the community.

Another innovative approach using technology to facilitate simulation learning was conducted by Mechling, Gast, and Langone (2002). They noted that aisle signs within grocery stores can be a useful way for people to locate items as they are shopping, but this skill has not often been taught to individuals with mental disabilities. Instead, they are usually given a list of pictures or words and taught how to move through the store to find the items. Realizing that recognizing the signs in grocery stores could be helpful, Mechling et al. decided to try to teach persons with cognitive disabilities to read these signs to help them find desired items. While doing this, the researchers also wanted to find out if the students could learn to read the signs if they were taught using computer-based video instruction as a simulation, instead of actually taking the individuals into the stores to teach the signs. Working with four adolescents with moderate mental disabilities, Mechling et al. taught them to read the words on the video display and then gave them a list of items to see if they could use the signs in the stores to find the items. After students were taught in their classrooms using video instruction, they went into real grocery stores to determine if their skills had generalized.

The computer-based video instruction used by Mechling et al. was unique. First the researchers developed a list of 12 targeted words contained on aisle signs (e.g., "cat food"). They then went into stores and videotaped the progression of a person moving through the stores, stopping to look at and video record the aisle signs, some of which contained the targeted words and some of which did not. When an aisle sign was recorded that had a targeted word, they continued to progress down the aisle and, after finding an appropriate item on the aisle, they videotaped it being picked up a placed in the cart. During video instruction, the student was given a list of words (with corresponding pictures) and then sat in front of the video monitor and watched while "walking" through the store. When an aisle was reached, a still picture of the aisle sign appeared, and the student had to recognize if one of the targeted words from the list appeared on the sign; if so, the student could tap the screen to continue down the aisle to search for the item. When the camera pointed to the item, the student had to touch it and mark it of this list. A system of least prompts was used to help the students to learn correct responding.

The researchers found that the students were able to generalize into actual grocery stores from what they had learned to do through the video instruction. They learned the targeted words and how to correctly identify them on aisle signs in actual grocery stores and then go down the aisles to find the desired items (the actual brand was considered irrelevant). The study demonstrated that, for at least some students with moderate mental disabilities, it is possible to create video simulations, teach appropriate responses to them in traditional instructional settings, and then apply the skills in real-life settings.

Providing Concurrent Instruction in School

In addition to simulations, other classroom-based instruction might help students to achieve in community settings. Verbal instructions as to how to perform in the community settings and role playing have been shown to contribute to community-based learning (Aeschleman & Schladenhauffen, 1984). Skills to be learned in the community sometimes require (or are enhanced by) academic skills and, when this is the case, instruction in these skills should occur at school. Since such skills and related instructional practices were discussed in the previous Chapter 17, they will not be repeated here.

Evaluating Community Skills

When community skills are identified for instruction, including the desired degree of generalization, the *criterion of ultimate performance* should be determined. For some students, particularly younger students and those with more severe disabilities, total completion of a particular task may not be appropriate or possible. In these cases, participation based on chronological-age expectations or meaningful partial participation may be the ultimate goal. For many students, however, particularly those who are older, the goal for them will often be to perform the community-based task independently.

Using the direct measurement data collection procedures described in Chapter 9, the teacher should monitor and record the student's performance on a frequent basis. This will allow the teacher to make necessary adjustments in the instructional process if adequate progress is not being made. When the student reaches the desired criterion, the teacher should reduce the frequency of instruction and instead provide adequate practice so that the skill is retained.

For students whose performance criterion is complete independence on a task, either in one setting or generalized to several settings, it is necessary that the skills be tested without the student receiving any assistance or support. For these students, it is very important that the teacher gradually fade all instructional prompts so that the student learns to complete the task alone and without assistance.

Ultimately, the teacher should devise a means whereby the student can be unknowingly observed by someone that the student does not know. The purpose of this secret observation is not to spy on the student, but to determine if the task can be undertaken without the presence or assistance of the teacher or another support person. This type of assessment should take place in all settings in which independent performance is desired.

Securing Adequate Funds for Community Instruction

One problem that is often related to providing community instruction is the availability of money for learning to ride the bus, buying various items, eating in restaurants, and carrying out other activities in the community. When teachers intend to initiate community instruction, they must consider from where the money will come.

Undoubtedly, the most legitimate source of money is the school or school district. The instructional goals that the students are working to achieve are of consequence and have been identified by parents and members of the planning team as important for students to learn. Schools should have in their budgets adequate funds to support community-based instruction. To offset this cost, teachers and school administrators should realize that many traditional instructional materials are simply inappropriate and money should not be wasted on them.

Unfortunately, there may not be money in the budget for community-based instruction and, even if there is, it may not be enough. Alternative or supplemental funds are sometimes needed. One source of these funds is through traditional school fund-raising activities (car washes, bake sales), but this is not generally recommended for two reasons. First, it is easy for this type of event to turn into a "help the handicapped" charity event. Second, it casts community training as some type of extracurricular activity and, of course, this is not what it is.

A more appropriate alternative is to use the family's money to shop for items that they will need anyway. Another is to shop for teacher's needs from shopping lists that they provide. Similarly, a shopping service could be provided for elderly individuals who have difficulty getting into the community as often as they would like. Of course, all this requires coordination, but it could be a source of revenue that would provide some important learning experiences.

Teaching Community and Domestic Skills in the Most Meaningful Way

When all the different skills that one may need in the community and the home are considered, we realize that there is much that can be taught and learned. One way to approach this task is to avoid teaching skills in isolation, but instead to teach them in a way that is natural and that maximizes the effect of the instruction, that is, to teach related skills together. Teaching skills in this way means we look at them as they would normally occur over a day, a week, or several weeks.

Consider, for example, students who need to learn goals related to shopping, preparing food, cleaning up after a meal, using community transportation, and crossing streets safely. The teacher may find on the student's educational plan a list of goals to be met in each of these areas, but these goals may be approached in very different ways. The most desirable approach is for the teacher to provide instruction so that the tasks have some relation to each other. First, plan the meal, prepare a shopping list, decide where to shop, and then learn about the public transportation that will take you there. The process continues until ultimately the students have had instruction directed at completing each goal, concluding with completing the meal and cleaning up afterward.

This approach is not suggested in order that school will become "fun" or "watered down" for students with severe disabilities, but instead so that environmental cues will have greater meaning and skills will be seen as relevant. If it happens that the experience is also enjoyable, so much the better.

In the following sections, learning to function in different settings and to use different skills will be discussed. It should be kept in mind that, in practice, the preferred approach to instruction is one in which the activities are related in a meaningful and functional way.

Community Settings and Activities

Many of the possible settings in which community instruction may occur are listed in Figure 18–3, and typical tasks that often require instruction in the community at large are suggested in Figure 18–4. Although it is understood that skills and settings must be individually determined, it may be expected that many of the settings in Figure 18–3 and activities in Figure 18–4 are often targets for instruction for students with severe disabilities. Of course, other settings and skills may also be appropriate for instruction, depending on the student and the nature of the local community.

Community instruction also presents an important opportunity to teach students social skills. Acquisition and generalization of these skills increases the acceptance of individuals with severe disabilities in various settings and helps them to function more appropriately in these settings. Some important skills that many students need to learn are listed in Figure 18–5.

Although it is not possible to address instructional practices appropriate for all community settings and skills, suggestions for teaching skills for four conditions are presented next: grocery stores, restaurants, vending

Figure 18–3 Community Settings in Which Instruction May Occur

Grocery stores	Cafeteria restaurants
Department stores	Vending machines
Fast-food restaurants	Banks
Public transportation	Bowling alleys
Pay telephones	Pinball machines
Automatic tellers	Movie theaters
Miniature golf	Churches, synagogues, temples
Video games	Barber shops/hair salons
Theaters & concerts	Recreation centers
Museums	Post office
Public parks	Skating rink
Doctors/dentists	Club meetings (Scouts)
Public library	Friend's house
Public swimming pool	
Sporting events	
Convenience stores	
Regular restaurants	

Figure 18–4 General Skills for Community Participation

Crossing the street	Putting on seat belt
Paying for items	Telling time
Preparing shopping lists	

Figure 18–5 Social Skills Appropriate for the Community

Being wary of strangers	Requesting assistance from store employees
Greeting others appropriately	Ending conversations appropriately
Keeping appropriate distance when speaking	Not asking personal or embarrassing questions
Apologizing for mistakes	Refrain from inappropriate touching of others
Refrain from touching items not to be purchased	Waiting in line for turn
Controlling emotions/temper	Following community rules (e.g., "don't litter")
Sitting quietly when necessary	
Keeping appointments on time	
Earning and saving money	

machines, and pedestrian skills and public transportation. These are discussed because they have a relatively high frequency of use.

Grocery Stores

Many teachers have taught students with severe disabilities to shop in grocery stores, and many researchers have documented some effective practices (Aeschleman & Schladenhauffen, 1984; Haring et al., 1987; Horner, Albin, & Ralph, 1986; Matson, 1981; Matson & Long, 1986; McDonnell et al., 1984; Morse & Schuster, 2000; Nietupski, Welch, & Wacker, 1983; Sarber, Halasz, Messmer, Bickett, & Lutzker, 1983). (See Morse et al. [1996] for a review of many of these studies). Most students who need to learn grocery-shopping skills are adolescents or young adults. Some relevant suggestions for teaching students to shop in grocery stores are presented here.

Students need to prepare a shopping list or have one prepared for them before they enter the store. This list should consist of items desired by the student or parents and required for use in the home. Picture shopping lists that may be homemade or purchased commercially can be used for students who cannot read words. The student must carry an adequate amount of money and needs to know how to use a number line or a calculator (as described in Chapter 17) to determine if he has enough money to make the desired purchase.

The task analysis developed by the teacher guides the student's activity through the store. Many of the previously listed references have task analyses that may serve as models, but the most appropriate one is individually designed. The task analysis calls for the student to enter the store, get a shopping cart, select the appropriate items as indicated by the list, go to the checkout line, pay for the groceries, and carry them out of the store. Details are listed depending on the student's needs. Along with the operational behaviors, the teacher probably needs to focus on social behaviors. This is true in grocery stores as well as in various other community settings. Figure 18–5 lists some of the more common social behaviors that may be important instructional targets; others may be developed by the planning team.

The natural cues in the setting need to be referenced by pointing them out to the student during the initial stages of the instructional process and then delaying instructional prompts so that the student learns to respond to the naturally present cues. For example, the shopping baskets at the entrance of the store should ultimately serve as the cue to take a basket and start searching for the first item. As the student enters different parts of the store, other cues can be pointed out.

Students do better if they are taught to shop in a systematic fashion, going up one aisle and down another and from one side of the store to the other. This helps them to learn the location of items and ultimately decreases the amount of time required for shopping. Persons with very significant disabilities may participate in grocery store shopping in several ways. As they go up and down aisles with parents, teachers, or cohorts, they may indicate choices of items by looking at different products and pointing to them or reaching for them. Some individuals may be able to push a cart or drop items into it. When checking out, they may be able to place items on the counter and hand money or a credit card to the cashier (Helmstetter, 1989).

Several classroom activities may help the student to improve her ability to shop in the grocery store. These include developing shopping lists based on household needs and menus; learning to match the pictures or words on the shopping list to the actual items; learning to read sight words found in grocery stores, particularly on signs that mark specific aisles; practicing money skills; using the calculator or the number line system; scanning and selecting sale items in newspaper ads and cutting out appropriate coupons; and practicing the social skills that may be targeted for instruction in the grocery store.

Although grocery shopping is an activity that is more important for older individuals, the planning team might receive input from parents that a younger child requires some instruction in this activity. When this is the case, the instructional targets need to be made age appropriate. Typically, younger children "help" their parents as they take a shopping cart, select items, and so forth. It is likely that social behavior targets are important instructional objectives for younger children with disabilities, just as they are for young children without disabilities in grocery stores.

Restaurants

Today more than ever, many people are routinely eating several meals a week in restaurants, and so these settings should be considered important community locations where individuals with severe disabilities must learn to function. Several studies have been conducted documenting effective instructional practices in restaurants (Marholin, O'Toole, Touchette, Berger, & Doyle, 1979; McDonnell & Ferguson, 1988; Storey, Bates, & Hanson, 1984; Van den Pol et al., 1981).

Restaurants in which students need to learn to operate can vary, suggesting that the required skills will be different depending on the setting. Fast-food restaurants are different from traditional restaurants in which one sits down and orders food, and both are different from cafeteria-style restaurants. The specific type of restaurant in which the student needs to learn to function is best determined by the parent, and perhaps the student, through the planning process. It should be realized, however, that success in one particular type of restaurant does not necessarily mean that the individual knows how to function in other types. Again, it is important for the teacher to visit the particular restaurants in which skills will be taught and conduct task analyses.

In a traditional restaurant, the student must learn to enter, wait to be seated or select a seat (depending on the sign in the entry foyer), interact with the wait staff, look at a menu, make a selection, place an order, eat the meal appropriately, ask for the check, leave a tip, pay the check at the cash register or through the waiter, and leave through an appropriate exit. In a fast-food restaurant, the student must wait in line to place an order, review the menu on the wall over the front counter, order when it is her turn, pay for the food, take the tray with the food to the table, eat appropriately, and finish by cleaning off the table and taking the wrappings and the tray to the receptacle. Cafeterias call for the patron to locate the end of the line moving through the food display area, select appropriate items from each food section, place the items carefully on the tray as they are delivered, pay for the items, and take the items to a table.

Some of these skills may be within the ability of students with more severe disabilities. If not, the student may still partially participate. Helmstetter (1989) suggested that students could learn to order by looking at pictures of foods held up by peers or by handing the waiter or counter attendant a picture of the desired food. Of course, there are many eating skills that the individual can work on in restaurants. A person with very severe disabilities may also participate by learning to use the restroom to wash up before eating and by paying the bill when leaving the restaurant.

Perhaps more than in other community settings, the display of appropriate social behavior is necessary in restaurants. It is important for students to learn to interact with hosts, wait staff, meal companions, and other patrons in the restaurant. Students also need to learn suitable table manners, utensil usage, appropriate conversational voice levels, and other skills that allow them to mix comfortably with other customers in the restaurant.

Instructional procedures for teaching operational and social behaviors for functioning in restaurants are like those described for grocery stores. Again, it is important for the teacher to fade instructional prompts so that the student learns to rely on the natural cues in the setting. Ultimately, for students whose goal is to acquire total independence, the teacher needs to arrange for the student to visit the restaurant independently and to follow through on all aspects of the procedure, successfully consuming a meal without assistance.

Several concurrent school-based activities can help students to learn to function in restaurants. Money skills are important, particularly in determining what items on a menu can be afforded and selecting the correct amount to pay for them. Reading menus or recognizing key food words can also be useful. For both restaurants and grocery stores, basic information on the nutritional value of different foods can be taught in the context of useful community skills. Many skills can be taught at breakfast and lunch time in the school cafeteria: table manners, ordering food, carrying trays, paying for food, waiting in line, and others.

Although being able to use basic academic skills is helpful, many students who cannot do so can still learn to function adequately in restaurants by using some alternative skills. For example, students who cannot read or order verbally from a menu may be able to recognize key words on menus and point to them to indicate what they want.

If they cannot discriminate particular words, they may carry pictures of certain favorite foods in small wallet-size picture books or even a prewritten food order to indicate their desired items. Likewise, being able to handle money is desirable, but if a student cannot do so he may still be able to function with some independence in a restaurant by having predetermined amounts of money placed in an envelope to give the counter attendant, waiter, or cashier when paying for the food.

If it is determined through assessment and planning that restaurant skills are desired learning goals, it is important to consider some unique characteristics of the student. Different students may be at different levels of self-feeding skill acquisition (e.g., properly handling a fork or a knife); some may require some form of assistance when eating. Students who have food allergies, are on special diets, or require their food to be prepared in a certain way should learn what to order and not order in restaurants. Other students may have a tendency to order the same item each time and will need to be prompted to order different items at least on occasion so that they can benefit from a more complete experience.

As with grocery stores, most young children do not use restaurants independently, but may do so with their parents or older siblings or friends, and so preadolescent individuals may warrant instruction on appropriate restaurant use. Most of the skills that they need are proper eating and social skills, as opposed to more independent skills, such as selecting, ordering, and paying for food. Instructional targets might include waiting and walking with parents or an accompanying adult; sitting properly; using napkins, utensils, straws, and so forth, correctly; occupying self appropriately before the food arrives (often by drawing or coloring with restaurant-supplied material or playing on the restaurant's playground equipment); eating properly; speaking at an appropriate volume; and communicating needs and desires effectively.

Vending Machines

It cannot be said with certainty, but it may be that vending machines are used by more people than stores or restaurants. Certainly, there are many of them in most modern environments, and they are used to dispense items ranging from food and drink to toys, stamps, and more. It should not be surprising then that several researchers have studied ways to teach the required skills for individuals with severe disabilities to use vending machines (Browder, Snell, & Wildonger, 1988; Nietupski, Clancy, & Christiansen, 1984; Sprague & Horner, 1984). The ability to use at least some vending machines adds convenience to persons' lives and perhaps gives them access to items that are not otherwise readily available.

As with other community skills, it is important for the teacher to determine if this particular skill is of current or future importance in the lives of the students being taught. In this process, the teacher also must determine the extensiveness of the skills required and how generalizable they need to be. For some individuals, opportunities to use vending machines may be limited, and thus they need to learn how to use only one or two types. It may be more important to focus on other community skills. For others, however, those who have greater mobility in the community, for example, there may be a need to learn to operate all different types of vending machines. Obviously, the level of skills required and the amount and type of instruction are different depending on different needs.

The basic process for using a vending machine begins with deciding that something in a machine is desirable and determining that the machine that is needed is present or in the vicinity. (The order in which these decisions are made is not particularly important.) A process of familiarizing the student with vending machines and what they contain might be undertaken by teachers in an incidental manner around the school and community. Experience with family members and other students will help the student to understand the nature, purpose, and contents of the machines.

When planning instruction, the teacher must begin with knowledge of how much generalization is desired. Assuming that the student is to learn to operate any vending machine that might be encountered, the teacher should use the general case method of instruction as described in Chapter 8. Using this method, Sprague and Horner (1984) taught their students to use several different vending machines that varied by the types of stimuli presented (types of items displayed, amount of money required, directions) and in the types of responses required (where to insert money, where to press the button, where to retrieve the items). They were able to teach students how to select any food or beverage item that cost between 25 and 75 cents from any appropriate vending machine in their community. Teachers teaching generalized vending machine use should vary the machines that they use for instruction to maximize generalization.

When the teacher has determined the types of machines to be learned, the task analysis for each machine is conducted. Each analysis will include similar steps that require the user to select an appropriate amount of money, insert the money in the machine, press the button or activate the machine in an appropriate manner, obtain the item from the machine, and check to see if there is any change. Individual actions from this list may be isolated and targeted for instruction to allow partial participation for students with the most severe disabilities.

The two most difficult aspects of making a vending machine purchase may be determining what is to be bought and handling money adequately to make the purchase. The first problem may be dealt with by teaching the student to use a prosthetic card or booklet that lists by word or picture the various items contained in the machine. The student can then preview the contents of the machine and point to or circle the item on the card before attempting to make a purchase and then match the identified item with the button or lever on the machine that allows it to be dispensed. The second problem requires that the student identify the price of the item, select the required amount of money, and insert it into the machine. Again, this could be facilitated by using a booklet or card that shows various amounts of money (e.g., 50 cents) matched with depictions of the coins that equal the amount. The student then has to select the coins that match the picture from a pocket, wallet, or purse. The student also could use a number line to determine if she has a sufficient amount of money. Naturally, the more advanced the student's money skills, the less need there is for using such aids. In addition, the more familiar the student becomes with certain machines, the easier and more automatic it is to make desired purchases from vending machines.

One thing about vending machines that students who use them must ultimately learn is that they sometimes do not operate correctly. Certainly, this is a frustration that many have experienced. When it occurs, teachers should take the opportunity to teach students that they should not continue to put money into the machine and that, if there is a nearby proprietor of the machine, this person should be told about the problem.

Pedestrian Skills and Public Transportation

Regardless of the community settings used, there is always a need to travel to get to them. This may require simply walking from a nearby street corner after being dropped off or walking from home, school, or work, or, if the distance is too great for walking, the individual may need to use public transportation such as a city bus. Although young children, both with and without disabilities, are usually accompanied by an older, more competent person when traveling around the community, adolescents are often expected to demonstrate local travel skills independently. Research suggests that some persons with severe disabilities can learn pedestrian skills (Horner, Jones, & Williams, 1985; Marchetti, McCartney, Drain, Hooper, & Dix, 1983; Vogelsberg & Rusch, 1979), the appropriate use of public transportation, specifically buses (Coon, Vogelsberg, & Williams, 1981; Marchetti, Cecil, Graves, & Marchetti, 1984; Neef, Iwata, & Page, 1978; Sowers, Rusch, & Hudson, 1979; Welch, Nietupski, & Hamre-Nietupski, 1985), and what to do if they get lost in the community (Taber, Alberto, Hughes, & Seltzer, 2002).

The most critical pedestrian skill requires an individual to cross the street at the appropriate time to avoid traffic. To be safe, the student must learn to cross at different types of intersections and must be 100% correct in his attempts. Until the student can do this consistently, supervision is required.

The instructional intersections may be uncontrolled, or they may be controlled by traffic lights, walk–don't walk signs, or stop signs. Traffic conditions may be light or heavy, the direction of the traffic may be one or two ways, and the street may have two lanes or more (Horner et al., 1985). Other variations in the conditions of intersections that exist in local communities must also be identified and incorporated into the training sessions.

When learning to cross, students must learn to attend to the correct stimuli for the particular type of intersection and then make a decision as to whether to cross depending on the status of the stimulus. Verbal directions and cues are required initially, but then, as with other learning situations, these are faded out by the teacher so that the student learns to attend to the natural cues and does not rely on the teacher's prompting. Students who cannot learn to cross independently can participate by pushing the button for walking if there is one, by watching for the light to change, and then by walking independently or semi-independently or assisting in pushing their wheelchairs.

After the student has learned to cross the street safely, further walking to a particular location can be learned through practice. The procedure requires that the student learn to identify landmarks that indicate that she is progressing satisfactorily along the route. For some students, written directions or a map may be helpful; for others, repeated practice is the best instructional technique. Once again, as the student acquires more independence on the skill, the teacher should fade his presence so that the student can walk independently.

In addition to learning to walk to certain locations, the independence of students with severe disabilities is increased if they can learn to use public transportation. The operational skills involved require that the student learn to recognize the bus to be taken by identifying its number or route sign; board the bus; pay the fair, using coins or tokens; take a seat; identify the stop where she is to get off and signal the bus driver to stop if necessary (by pulling the cord); get off the bus; and proceed by walking. If the student has difficulty in recognizing the bus or the name of the street at which she wants to get off, written words, numbers, or picture cues (pictures taken by the teacher as she learned the route) may be carried and used as prompts. Whenever bus riding skills are being taught, it is suggested that round trips be used so that the student can learn the way back to the origin, as well as the way to the designated target.

As with other community-based learning activities, there are some skills associated with the use of public transportation that students with the most severe disabilities may find difficult. Again, this is no reason to exclude these students from developing key skills in this area. For example, they might learn to purchase a ticket by handing their money to the driver or depositing the money or ticket as they proceed through the turnstile; they may learn to get on and off the bus or train as independently as they are able; they can find an empty seat; and they can sit appropriately and ride until they are directed to get up and get off at a particular stop.

The training procedures for teaching bus riding skills to most students consist of the instructor accompanying the student to the bus stop and providing the verbal directions and cues necessary for the student to complete each step in the task. As trials progress, the teacher should use time delay prompting by waiting an adequate amount of time for the student to respond to the natural cues. When the student has achieved criterion by completing all the steps in the task for several days without cues from the teacher, the teacher (with the parents' and school administrator's permission) should allow the student to take the bus independently. To be able to maintain a safety net, however, the teacher may enlist an ally unknown to the student to see that the trip is safely completed. This person should be aboard the bus when it picks up the student.

Although some studies have shown some effectiveness by creating simulated conditions in classrooms to teach pedestrian skills and bus riding, it is doubtful that this type of training alone will ever be sufficient for the student to learn adequately. At the very least, assessment of the skill needs to occur in actual settings. It is suggested that, for the time and effort required to create the simulated conditions in the school, the teacher would make wiser use of time by teaching students in actual situations. If simulations are to be used, it might be best to use videotapes or slides showing the bus that the student is to board, the street sign where he is to get off, and traffic signs and conditions signaling whether to cross the street.

Safety Issues in Community Activities

Individuals who learn to use community facilities, who can walk through their community, or who can use public transportation will have acquired much independence. However, because there is a clear element of danger associated with being in and traveling independently in the community, certain commonsense safety skills are very important. Students must learn to be wary of strangers and not interact with them except to subtly greet them as they proceed. They should be able to recognize police and public safety officers and know that they can get help and protection from them when necessary. They should realize that well-lighted places where there are many people are generally safe and that isolated and dark areas should be avoided. They should always carry identification that includes the names and phone numbers of persons to be contacted in an emergency. In addition, students should learn to practice relevant social skills when traveling through the community. Acting in a way that suggests one is not competent may serve to invite danger.

A problem of concern for many parents and teachers is that students with severe disabilities may get lost while in the community. For example, an individual with cognitive disabilities may go to a mall, but not be able to find the way back to the bus stop. To counter this challenge, Taber et al. (2002) conducted a study in which they taught middle school students with moderate cognitive disabilities how to use cell phones to contact a support person in case they got lost. Taber et al. reasoned that, with advances in technology, pay phones are becoming less common as more people acquire their own cell phones. After the researchers taught the students to use the phones, they tested the program by taking several of them to different settings and letting them get "lost" in order to see if they could make the contact correctly.

In the first phase of the study, Taber et al. (2002) constructed a task analysis of the steps to be taken to use a cell phone. While in the school building, participants learned to complete the steps through instruction using a five-step, least-to-most prompting system (independent, verbal, verbal and gesture, verbal and model, and verbal and guidance). Next they were taught to stay in one location (still in the school), look around to see if they saw someone they knew (the teacher or an assistant), and, if they didn't, to use the cell phone to call the contact person. Making the call required that they take out a small card on which the appropriate phone number was written and then use the cell phone to call. When the call was answered, the student was to say that he or she was lost, describe the surrounding area, answer questions about the area, and then hang up, but leave the phone on in case the contact person needed to call back. In the second phase, after the students learned to use the phones successfully in the school, the teachers took them to community settings to practice. In these settings, the same procedure that the students had successfully achieved in the school was used, except the teacher removed herself from each student's immediate line of view while the student made the call. After three successful attempts, the last phase of the study occurred. In this phase, the teacher took each student into a new community setting and gave the student a phone and the card with the number on it. The teacher reminded the student to use the phone to contact a support person if he got lost. At an opportune time, the teacher then slipped away from the student, leaving him with no person he knew in sight. If the student did not make a call within five minutes, the teacher returned. However, a secondary observer whom the student did not know was always watching the student to ensure safety.

Five of six students who participated in this final generalization phase of the study successfully made the phone call when they thought that they were lost. One student withdrew from school before she could be tested in the final phase. The authors therefore demonstrated that many students with moderate mental disabilities can learn to recognize when they are lost and use a cell phone to contact someone to assist them in this emergency situation. They warned however, that learning to use the cell phones was difficult for some of the students and that students required instruction to learn the meaning of the concept of "lost." That is, not all the students could readily discriminate between being lost and not being lost.

Domestic Skills and Activities

Just as students need to learn to operate independently in community settings, they also need to learn to perform various domestic chores to be more independent. The domestic activities listed in Figure 18–6 represent daily or weekly activities that are typically required by persons living in their own homes. Once again, it is important to understand that not all individuals with severe disabilities need to learn to perform all these tasks. Tasks that may be more suitable for those with the most severe disabilities are listed in Figure 18–7. It should also be realized that the importance of specific household tasks may vary from family to family. For some students with severe disabilities, some of the tasks listed in Figures 18–6 and 18–7 may not be considered very important. More significant ones are usually be those that allow the person more freedom. Therefore, instruction for three such sets of skills are discussed here: preparing meals and snacks, performing household chores, and using a telephone.

Figure 18–6 Skills Often Required for Domestic Activity

- Preparing snacks and meals
- Cleaning up after meals
- Doing laundry
- Straightening & picking up
- Cleaning bathroom
- Cleaning refrigerator
- Using a telephone
- Planning appointments
- Making beds
- Dusting
- Responding to fire alarm
- Washing car
- Abiding by various safety rules

Preparing Meals and Snacks

Individuals who are able to prepare food or to contribute to any degree in its preparation will be able to use their skills in several ways: to sustain themselves, as a form of leisure activity, as a way to save money (by not needing to dine out all the time), and as a mechanism for appropriate social interaction (Schuster, 1988). Preparing food plays an important part in a normal life routine. Various studies of individuals with mild, moderate, and severe mental disabilities have reported that these individuals can learn to prepare a variety of foods, such as jello, hot chocolate, hot dogs, baked chicken, roast beef, spaghetti, broiled fish, fried eggs, boiled eggs, toast, cheese toast, boiled vegetables, and various other food items (Browder & Snell, 1993; Schuster, 1988).

The instructional process for teaching food preparation skills is much like other instruction. The teacher must begin by communicating with the parents to determine if cooking or other food preparation skills should be taught and, if so, what specific food items the student should learn to prepare. Often parents look on these skills as being particularly useful, even for preadolescent children, because they allow their children to handle chores that previously the parent had to take care of, for example, fixing a sandwich to take for lunch or preparing a snack after school. Many parents indicate that learning such a functional skill is helpful to them as well as to their child.

Depending on the age of the student, it may be desirable for the food preparation process to include meal planning. Students who are older should be given the opportunity not only to learn how to prepare food, but also

Figure 18–7 Domestic Skills for Students with the Most Severe Disabilities

Source: Adapted from "Curriculum for School Age Students: The Ecological Model," by E. Helmstetter, 1989, in F. Brown and D. H. Lehrer (Eds.), *Persons with Profound Disabilities: Issues and Practices,* Baltimore: Paul H. Brookes. Used with permission.

Bathroom: Clean mirror, clean counter tops, pick up clothing and place in hamper.
Kitchen: Scrape plates for washing, load into dishwasher, operate dishwasher or do parts of the process, sort and put away clean dishes, prepare or participate in meal preparation.
Bedroom: Make bed or assist, straighten room.
Utility room: Separate clothes for washing, wash clothes or assist in the process, remove clothes from dryer.
General housekeeping: Dust furniture surfaces, vacuum, take out trash.

how to decide on the food to be prepared. The meal-planning component should capitalize on the opportunity to teach students about nutrition, food groups, and balanced meals and allow them to indicate which foods they would like to prepare for particular meals. When planning meals, students may find it more practical to plan entire meals that include an entree, vegetables, bread, salad, drink, and dessert. Such meals could be listed on cards for subsequent use. For example, if students plan to prepare broiled chicken for dinner, they can pull the "broiled chicken" card; all the necessary food items are listed on it. Some authors have also suggested that using prepackaged frozen foods might be more desirable than "cooking from scratch" because the packages provide all the parts of a meal in the correct proportions, promote choice making, and allow more independence (Wilcox & Bellamy, 1987). As a follow-up to planning, students can practice grocery-shopping skills as they purchase the food at their local grocery store.

Having planned and gathered the necessary food for preparation, the teacher should develop a task analysis for food preparation, whether the task is making sandwiches or cooking a roast. The basic elements of the analysis should include selecting a recipe (if one is to be used), gathering the food items together, gathering the equipment necessary for the preparation (pots, pans, plates, glasses, utensils, etc.), opening the food items, measuring and mixing items as called for by the recipe, turning on the stove or oven, placing food on the stove or in the oven (or in the microwave), stirring the food if required, taking the food off the stove or out of the oven, and serving the food. More detailed cooking task analyses have been provided by Sobsey (1987) for cooking with a microwave, frying, baking, boiling, broiling, making sandwiches, making coffee or tea, and cleaning up after preparing food.

Given that the food to be prepared is relatively simple and involves only a few steps, individuals with severe disabilities may be able to learn the task after several instructional sessions. Many researchers, however, have found that learning occurs more easily and faster if the student can follow a recipe. Although complete formal recipes generally are too difficult to read, they can be simplified by using a list of key words and/or drawings to serve as cues for each step in the food preparation task. About half of the studies on teaching food preparation skills used some type of picture recipe cards or books (Schuster, 1988).

When picture (or word) recipes are used, the pictures (and/or the words) are arranged so that they serve as a cue to the student as to what must happen next in the preparation sequence. For example, the first card might show a picture of all the ingredients and necessary equipment sitting on a kitchen table, the second would show the first ingredient being emptied into the first bowl, and so on, until the process is complete. One very practical arrangement is for the cards to be hooked together in a booklike format so that they can be flipped as they are completed, with the newly displayed card providing the cue for the next step. The food item or the meal is complete when the student has progressed through the entire recipe book.

The instructional tactic that seems to be most efficient and effective is the constant time delay procedure (Schuster, 1988; Schuster, Gast, Wolery, & Guiltinan, 1988; Schuster & Griffin, 1991). As described in Chapter 7, following the presentation of a stimulus, the instructor waits for a brief period of time (e.g., 5 seconds) and then uses a controlling prompt to get the student to perform the behavior if he has not already done so. When preparing food, the teacher begins by giving a general activity direction, for example, "You're probably hungry; why don't you make a sandwich for yourself?" Then the teacher observes to see if the student starts on the sequence as called for by the task analysis. If this is not done within 5 seconds, the teacher gives the controlling prompt for the first step, "Get out the bread and peanut butter and jelly." The completion of each step of the task analysis is considered the cue for the next step. If the student does not initiate the next step in 5 seconds, the teacher then prompts the student, for example, "Open the peanut butter jar and spread some on one piece of bread." After several sessions, the controlling prompt is delayed, and the student learns to initiate the step before being told to do so and ultimately is able to perform all the steps independently. The use of a picture recipe provides the student with a more concrete cue as to what is expected to occur. In other words, instead of the only cue being the completion of the previous step in the task analysis, the student learns to flip the page and be prompted by the picture that indicates the next step. For longer food preparation tasks, this may be helpful.

During food preparation times, the teacher should take advantage of the natural opportunity to teach related skills, including washing hands before cooking and washing dishes, wiping counter tops, and sweeping the floor afterward.

Performing Household Chores

Living independently or semi-independently means that an individual must assume responsibility for several household chores or share responsibilities with other people. A typical family may have one person whose primary job is to cook, another to clean up afterward, someone to do the laundry, another to take out the trash, someone else to clean the floors, and so on. In some homes these chores are permanently assigned to individuals, and in others the chores might be rotated on a weekly or monthly basis.

As with many activities, household chores are likely to change with the age of the individual. Although young children may have responsibilities such as putting their dirty laundry in the hamper, they most likely are not required to operate the washer and dryer. Also, chores may be divided based on the preferences of family members. Some may like to do one thing but not another, and so cooperative agreements are established so that each person's duty is less burdensome.

It should not be expected that families of individuals with severe disabilities are any different with regard to the need for completing household chores. Additionally, it can be assumed that as the individual grows older and closer to the time of completing school, more instruction is required so that more independence can be developed. Through the assessment and planning process, teachers should determine what chores can be learned that better allow the student to function in the family and, as the student grows older, what should be learned that will help with greater independence as an adult.

As is seen in Figures 18–6 and 18–7, a host of household duties may be required. Additional duties can be found in other sources (Ford et al., 1989; Sobsey, 1987; Wilcox & Bellamy, 1987). Based on interviews with parents, the teacher may determine which household chores should be targeted for instruction. Again, it is important to realize that not all students need to learn all chores. Skills taught in the home economics classroom or elsewhere at school that are not needed or desired at home are soon forgotten, and the instructional time will have been wasted for the student and teacher.

After the instructional targets have been identified, the teacher must task analyze them into sequential steps. For many household tasks, this process has already been undertaken and is available in published materials (Sobsey, 1987; Wilcox & Bellamy, 1987), and the teacher may need to make only slight modifications. The instructional procedures for teaching household chores are similar for teaching other skills (see Chapter 7). Although the teacher has several approaches to choose from, constant time delay is the one that appears to be easiest to use and results in the fastest learning of household chores, such as using a washer and dryer (Miller & Test, 1989).

An important consideration when teaching household chores is the likelihood of the student's being able to perform the chores at home after learning them at school (Livi & Ford, 1985). It would be more desirable for the initial learning to occur at home, but this may not be possible. On the positive side, however, the teacher typically does not need to plan instruction that results in unlimited generalization because the student is living in only one home (at least for the time being). However, if the skill does not generalize at least to the one location where it is needed (i.e., the student's home), it will not be practical. Therefore, it is critical that the teacher arrange the instructional environment for teaching so that the stimulus conditions during instruction are as similar as possible to those in which the student will need to demonstrate the skill. Close communication between home and teachers can better ensure that similar brooms, mops, detergents, and other such items are being used. Undoubtedly, however, the school will not be able to purchase appliances for the school that are the same as in everyone's home. This being the case, the only way that the student can learn to use the models that are in the home is to receive instruction on them. Parents need to understand the basic problem of generalization and why their child may have difficulty at home while performing well in school on household chores.

Using a Telephone

The opportunity to communicate with individuals who are not physically present by using the telephone is one that we generally take for granted. It allows us to have immediate contact with others and therefore to have greater freedom, independence, and happiness and, when necessary, it may help us to be safe. In this world of immediate communications, individuals who do not know how to call others or receive telephone calls are at a disadvantage. It is suggested, therefore, that telephone skills are a very important goal for many individuals with severe disabilities.

The various skills for using the telephone can be divided into five categories: making telephone calls using a standard phone; making phone calls using a pay phone; making calls using a cell phone; answering the phone; and engaging in telephone conversation. Each of these five skill areas consists of several subskills, which are listed in Figure 18–8. These skills and subskills are based on several reports that have appeared in the literature (Horner et al., 1987; Karen, Astin-Smith, & Creasy, 1985; Leff, 1974, 1975; Risley & Cuvo, 1980; Smith & Meyers, 1979; Taber et al., 2002).

Teaching students with severe disabilities to use the phone should be preceded by determining which of the skills in Figure 18–8 are most appropriate. For some, it may be most important simply to learn to answer the phone properly. Others may need to learn to use the phone to make contact with another specific individual. For others still, learning to engage appropriately in conversation is the desired goal. Students who are learning to participate in various community activities might need to learn to use a telephone to call businesses to get certain information ("What time does the movie start?") or to call a friend to see if she wants to go to the movie.

Making Calls from a Standard Phone

As with the other skills discussed in this chapter, teaching students to use telephones should occur in natural environments and at natural times when possible. For obvious reasons, however, this may not be possible and the use of real phones may be restricted to testing for skill acquisition and generalization. Basic skill training will probably need to occur using phones not connected to the actual system.

Many people maintain a list or a small personal phone book of numbers that they frequently call. This commonly used device is also useful for students with severe disabilities. The book can identify by name (or picture) persons or places that are called with some regularity (Leff, 1974, 1975). Students who have difficulty transferring recognition of the number in their book to the number to be dialed can learn to block out the numbers, unveiling them one at a time while dialing each number as it appears.

Students who have adequate verbal skills should be able to learn without difficulty how to express an appropriate greeting to the person being called. A more difficult skill, however, may be learning to differentiate between a ring and a busy signal at the other end of the line, and so an adequate amount of practice needs to be devoted to this. Learning how to leave an appropriate message on an answering machine also takes practice, requiring the student to leave his name, phone number, and a brief message. Students who cannot accomplish this need to be taught to simply hang up and call at a later time.

Making Calls from a Pay Phone

Students who can use a standard telephone should have little difficulty learning to use a pay phone, except that they may have to learn to deal with more distractions when using a phone in a public area. In addition, they need to learn to select the appropriate coins and insert them before dialing or when the message says to do so. If selecting a coin and inserting it into the slot presents a problem, a coin equivalence card can be used. Students should also be taught how to retrieve the coin if the line is busy or if no one answers, and it is also important for them to learn to wait a specified amount of time before repeating their call or taking some alternative action.

Making Calls Using a Cell Phone

Taber et al. (2002) point out that cell phones are becoming more common and in many areas are being used much more often than pay phones. It is not unreasonable for many individuals with severe disabilities to be able to acquire and use cell phones just as they are used by others. The mechanics of using a cell phone are fairly well known and are listed in Figure 18–8 for the sake of reference.

Two issues, however, need to be kept in mind that make cell phones a little different from other phones. First, they tend to be smaller that traditional phones or pay phones. Thus, persons who have difficulty with fine-motor skills may find them somewhat awkward to use. Second, because they are not attached to a wall, table, or desk by a cord, they are easier to lose. Such problems can

Figure 18–8 Skills for Using a Telephone

Making calls from a standard phone
Identify the number to be called.
Pick up the receiver and listen for a dial tone.
Dial the number, listen for ringing or busy signal.
Engage in greeting, hang up if phone is busy, or leave message if there is an answering machine.

Making calls from a pay phone
Identify the number to be called.
Select the appropriate coins to insert into the pay phone.
Pick up the receiver and continue as for a standard phone.

Making calls using a cell phone
Turn on the phone.
Dial the number or find the prestored name and/or number and press the call button.
Talk on the phone.
Press the button to end the call when the conversation is finished.
Leave the phone on or turn off if appropriate.
When finished using for the day, recharge the phone.

Answering the phone
Pick up the phone when it is ringing.
Greet caller and ask for whom the call is if caller does not say. Determine if the call is for you. If so, engage in conversation.
Determine if another person being called is there; if so, tell the caller to wait one minute and notify the person.
Determine if the person is there; if not, tell caller and volunteer to take message. Write down name and phone number of caller.
Determine if the person has the wrong number. Ask what number was called. Tell person if number is different.

Engaging in telephone conversation (when making a call)
Determine the purpose of the call: to report an emergency, to get information, to give information, to have a conversation?
Tell the person why you are calling: "This is an emergency. . . ."
"I am calling to find out. . . ."
"I wanted to let you know. . . ."
"I just wanted to chat. Do you have time now?" Provide details of the message.
End the conversation after purpose is achieved by saying thank you, you're welcome, or nice talking to you, as appropriate.

Engaging in telephone conversation (when receiving a call)
Identify yourself, "Hello, this is. . . ."
Ask why the person is calling: "What can I do for you?" "What are you calling about?" "Why did you call me?"
Provide information as requested; engage in conversation.
Conclude conversation appropriately: "Good-bye." "Thanks for calling." "Call again." "Glad I could help."

and do happen to many people, and it is a slight risk to take for the convenience that cell phones provide.

Answering the Phone

Although answering the phone may seem a relatively simple task, its difficulty is better understood when we realize, as Figure 18–8 shows, how many variations can occur with regard to the calling party and what she wants (Karen et al., 1985). A call to the student per se is relatively easy to handle, and the student can proceed to engage in conversation. But another type of call requires a series of decisions and may be more difficult. When teaching students to answer the phone, the teacher must present the student with opportunities to practice all variations of possible incoming calls: calls for the student, calls for someone else who is present, calls for someone who is normally at the number called but who is not present, and calls to the wrong number.

Different skills are required depending on the nature of the call. The most important and the one requiring the most instructional time is learning to take a message. If students are expected to learn this, that is, if it is important in their current or future life situation, they need to learn how to write down the name of the caller, the time he called, and the phone number. A brief message may also be required, although standard office phone message forms may be used so that the student can simply check the appropriate message. Even though such skills are within the ability of many individuals with cognitive disabilities, they require a substantial amount of instruction and practice.

Engaging in Telephone Conversation

When learning to make phone calls, in addition to learning how to dial numbers, students must learn to identify the purpose of the call and, from that, the type of conversation they will have when the person answers the phone. When calling friends for simple conversation, this is not so important because friends can discuss anything and can call for no particular purpose. However, when calling to get or give specific information, students must know what to say. They also must know how to respond to what is said. The teacher should outline a number of situations for incoming phone calls and also for making calls. Scripts should be developed that allow the teacher and other students to "call in" and to answer calls. There should also be a list of various practice calls to be made to businesses, friends, and services. Before making practice calls, students should be asked to state why they want to make the call, what they intend to ask or say, and how they will respond to questions asked of them.

One very important area of training is making emergency (911) phone calls. This should be taught to all students who are learning to use the telephone. The skills are relatively straightforward, assuming that the student can recognize an emergency situation. They must dial 911 (or the local emergency number), give their name and address, and state the nature of the emergency. If possible, they should learn to stay on the line until help arrives.

The most effective way for teaching telephone skills is through role playing. Verbal prompts and models are probably the best type of instructional tactics and may be systematically faded as students' skills increase with practice. Instruction on the use of the phone should occur several times a week. Training telephones, available from most local phone companies, should be used. As skills develop, they should be used in natural settings whenever possible. One way to do this is for teachers to incorporate telephone activities into community-based activities. For example, when students are in the department store, they might call other businesses to see what time they close or what time they open the next day.

Issues Related to Community-Based Instruction

Few people would argue with the need for students with severe disabilities to learn relevant community and domestic skills, but it must be realized complicated issues related to teaching them must be considered.

School Administrative Policies

Providing community-based instruction requires that students be taken off the school campus, raising questions about instructional schedules, teaching assignments, liability, and transportation. Clearly, some school administrative policies may make it difficult to take students off campus for instruction, and such policies should be studied and modified to the extent possible if nonschool instruction is to occur. In other cases, though, school policy makers and administrators have realized that providing instruction in actual settings in which skills must be used is an important part of the educational process for students with severe disabilities, and nonschool instruction has become an integral part of school life.

If students are to leave the school grounds for instruction, some authorities suggest that administrative practices and normal school scheduling procedures be employed to better accommodate this strategy (Baumgart & VanWalleghem, 1986; Hamre-Nietupski, Nietupski, Bates, & Maurer, 1982; Nietupski, Hamre-Nietupski, Houselog, Donder, & Anderson, 1988). Their suggestions include the following:

- Peers without disabilities and volunteers can be used to assist in instructional activities in community settings.
- Team teaching should be used so that one teacher can accompany students into community settings while another remains in school providing instruction to other students.
- Paraprofessionals can be used effectively both in the school and in nonschool instruction.

- Other professionals providing related services can occasionally accompany students and teachers to nonschool settings to assist in teaching skills and providing therapeutic services in natural settings.
- Heterogeneous groupings of students, including students without disabilities as well as those with less severe and more severe disabilities, are preferable to homogeneous groupings.
- Consultant teachers can help with planning, site identification, scheduling, and some instructional activities.
- Implementation of nonschool instruction can be staggered across students, beginning at different times for different students. Ultimately, all students whose educational plan calls for community or domestic instruction will need to be provided this instruction.
- Liability and insurance issues should be reviewed by school administrators to ensure that there is adequate coverage. Since many school districts have provided nonschool instruction for several years now, it is suggested that risk issues do not pose a major barrier to such procedures.
- All school employees engaged in nonschool instruction should know first aid and the school's policy for handling emergency situations.

Relation of Other Instruction to Community Instruction

The relationship of community instruction to other aspects of the student's curricular or therapeutic needs must be considered. How does the importance of community and domestic skills compare to the importance of academic skills? How, when, and where should physical therapy, occupational therapy, or communication therapy be provided to improve the student's functioning and application of skills in these areas? Will instruction in nonschool settings interfere with the provision of therapy?

Although these questions seem to propose that conflicts exist, in many cases they are not major problems. Community instructional goals, academic goals, and therapeutic needs may often be addressed in multiple environments. Students may practice many academic skills in community settings and then go back to the classroom to work on academic skills that will help them in the community. Likewise, many therapeutic goals can be worked on in natural, nonschool environments. What is important is for parents and professionals to work cooperatively to identify goals and then to determine proportionally how much time should be spent in various environments—the school, community, and home—to achieve the goals.

One way in which the value of community or domestic skills can be increased is to use incidental and observational learning techniques to increase the benefit of the activities to the participating students. As pointed out in Chapter 7, these methods do not provide instruction directly, but, nevertheless, students can often benefit from them. For example, consider the following studies.

- Smith, Collins, Schuster, and Kleinert (1999) taught table-clearing skills to four adolescents with moderate to severe mental disabilities. Students were taught to clean the tables using the system of least prompts, and all were successful in learning to do so. But, additionally, the students were asked to observe as the instructor prepared the materials for cleaning the table and also put them away. While completing these tasks, the instructor described each step in the tasks. Pre- and postassessments showed that the students were able to learn most of the steps in the tasks for preparing the materials for table cleaning and also for putting them away, even though they were not taught directly to do so.
- Taylor, Collins, Schuster, and Kleinert (2002) used the system of least prompts (SLP) to teach laundry skills to four teenagers with moderate mental disabilities, while simultaneously using incidental instruction to teach them sight words associated with doing laundry. During the instructional session to teach the laundry skills, the teacher taught each student a set of eight sight words relevant to doing the laundry (e.g., cycle, detergent, fabric, rinse). The words, referred to as "nontargeted information," were taught incidentally when the teacher was reinforcing a student for completion of a step. Not only did the students learn, maintain, and generalize the skills necessary for washing and drying their clothes, but they also learned and maintained more than 80% of the words taught through incidental instruction.
- Fiscus, Schuster, Morse, and Collins (2002) taught four children with moderate to severe cognitive disabilities to prepare snacks at school. As they were

teaching the food preparation skills, they embedded different types of instructive feedback into the prompting and feedback components. During the prompting, if it was necessary for the teacher to use a controlling prompt, the teacher read a sentence directing the student to complete the task while pointing to the words as she read them and then modeled the step for the student. When delivering a consequence, either reinforcing the student for a correct response or correcting an error, the teacher again read the words in the sentence as she was pointing to them. Afterward she recorded the student's response and then gave the second type of instructive feedback, which was to show the student a kitchen utensil (one not used by the student to prepare the snack) and name the utensil. Three of the four students learned to prepare three snacks and three of the four students learned either to read some of the words or to recognize them when presented in an array with distracter words. All four students learned to name or recognize the cooking utensils.

These studies all clearly indicate that, as a teacher is providing instruction on important community or domestic skills, the effect of their instruction can be multiplied. To do this, related skills can be taught by directing students to observe another or by embedding incidental instruction into the targeted skill training. The outcome is that students often learn not only one skill, but also all or parts of an additional skill.

Conclusion

Learning community and domestic skills is necessary for students with severe disabilities and should be included on the educational plans for most students. The most effective site of instruction for these skills is outside the typical classroom setting, either in community settings, homelike environments, or actual homes. Providing out-of-school instruction is uncommon for some teachers, and it may take a little while for teachers to become comfortable with the process (Westling & Fleck, 1991), but the effort will be worthwhile.

This instruction should not be mistaken for field trips or in any other way be considered an instructional frill. It provides for many students the opportunity to develop skills that will give them more independence and a better quality of life. Of course, the more the instruction intermeshes with students' needs, the more worthwhile it will be. This is why community and domestic instruction must be individually prescribed.

Removing students from inclusive classrooms and reducing beneficial participation in the general curriculum is a serious issue that must be taken into account when providing nonschool instruction. Some, such as Kluth (2000), propose that students without disabilities, as well as those with disabilities, can gain great educational benefit from participation in community learning activities. We certainly encourage this to occur whenever possible. It is likely to increase the relevance of schooling for all students.

Questions for Reflection

1. What is the relative importance of students with severe disabilities learning skills for use in community and domestic settings?
2. Why should teachers provide training in natural community settings and not simply construct simulations in the classroom? To what degree might simulations be helpful?
3. Give examples of how school-based instruction can assist in developing functional community and domestic skills.
4. Besides those listed in Figure 18–2, what other aids might be used to assist functioning in community settings?
5. Describe an afternoon of community-based instruction that might incorporate different objectives being learned in different settings.
6. Why might it be better for students to learn to prepare complete sets of foods (snacks or meals) instead of individual items?
7. Besides some of the partial participation activities described in this chapter, what other types of activities might be appropriate for students with the most severe disabilities in different settings?
8. What are some ways that community and domestic instruction can be provided without separating students with severe disabilities from other students?

References

Aeschleman, S. R., & Schladenhauffen, J. (1984). Acquisition, generalization and maintenance of grocery shopping skills by severely mentally retarded adolescents. *Applied Research in Mental Retardation, 5*, 245–258.

Agran, M., Snow, K., & Swaner, J. (1999). A survey of secondary level teachers' opinions on community-based instruction and inclusive education. *Journal of the Association for Persons with Severe Handicaps, 24*, 58–62.

Aveno, A. (1987). A survey of activities engaged in and skills most needed by adults in community residences. *Journal of the Association for Persons with Severe Handicaps, 12*, 125–130.

Aveno, A., Renzaglia, A., & Lively, C. (1987). Surveying community training sites to insure that instructional decisions accommodate the site as well as the trainees. *Education and Training in Mental Retardation, 22*, 167–175.

Baumgart, D., & VanWalleghem, J. (1986). Staffing strategies for implementing community based instruction. *Journal of the Association for Persons with Severe Handicaps, 11*, 92–102.

Billingsley, F. F., & Albertson, L. R. (1999). Finding a future for functional skills. *Journal of the Association for Students with Severe Disabilities, 24*, 298–302.

Branham, R. S., Collins, B. C., Schuster, J. W., & Kleinert, J. S. (1999). Teaching community skills to students with moderate disabilities: Comparing combined techniques of classroom simulation, videotape modeling, and community-based instruction. *Education and Training in Mental Retardation and Developmental Disabilities, 34*, 170–181.

Browder, D. M., & Snell, M. E. (1993). Daily living and community skills. In M. E. Snell (Ed.), *Instruction of students with severe disabilities* (4th Ed.). Upper Saddle River, NJ: Prentice Hall.

Browder, D. M., Snell, M. E., & Wildonger, B. A. (1988). Simulation and community-based instruction of vending machines with time delay. *Education and Training in Mental Retardation, 23*, 175–185.

Brown, L., Nisbet, J., Ford, A., Sweet, M., Shiraga, B., & York, J. (1983). The critical need for non-school instruction in programs for severely handicapped students. *Journal of the Association for the Severely Handicapped, 8*, 71–77.

Coon, M. E., Vogelsberg, R. T., & Williams, W. (1981). Effects of classroom public transportation instruction on generalization to the natural environment. *Journal of the Association for the Severely Handicapped, 6*, 46–53.

Fiscus, R. S., Schuster, J. W., Morse, T. E., & Collins, B. C. (2002). Teaching elementary students with cognitive disabilities food preparation skills while embedding instructive feedback in the prompt and consequent event. *Education and Training in Mental Retardation and Developmental Disabilities, 37*, 55–69.

Ford, A., & Mirenda, P. (1984). Community instruction: A natural cues and corrections decision model. *Journal of the Association for the Severely Handicapped, 9*, 79–88.

Ford, A., Schnorr, R., Meyer, L., Davern, L., Black, J., & Dempsey, P. (1989). *The Syracuse community-referenced curriculum guide for students with moderate and severe disabilities.* Baltimore: Paul H. Brookes.

Freagon, S., Wheeler, J., Hill, L., Brankin, G., Costello, D., & Peters, W. M. (1983). A domestic training environment for students who are severely handicapped. *Journal of the Association for the Severely Handicapped, 8*, 49–61.

Hamre-Nietupski, S., Nietupski, J., Bates, P., & Maurer, S. (1982). Implementing a community based education model for moderately/severely handicapped students: Common problems and suggested solutions. *Journal of the Association for the Severely Handicapped, 7*(4), 38–43.

Haring, T., Kennedy, C., Adams, M., & Pitts-Conway, V. (1987). Teaching generalization of purchasing skills across community settings to autistic youth using videotape modeling. *Journal of Applied Behavior Analysis, 20*, 89–96.

Helmstetter, E. (1989). Curriculum for school age students: The ecological model. In F. Brown & D. H. Lehrer (Eds.), *Persons with profound disabilities: Issues and practices.* Baltimore: Paul H. Brookes.

Horner, R. H., Albin, R. W., & Ralph, G. (1986). Generalization with precision: The role of negative teaching examples in the instruction of generalized grocery item selection. *Journal of the Association for Persons with Severe Handicaps, 11*, 300–308.

Horner, R. H., Jones, D. N., & Williams, J. A. (1985). A functional approach to teaching generalized street crossing. *Journal of the Association for Persons with Severe Handicaps, 10*, 71–78.

Horner, R. H., et al. (1987). Acquisition of generalized telephone use by students with moderate and severe mental retardation. *Research in Developmental Disabilities, 8*, 229–247.

Karen, R. L., Astin-Smith, S., & Creasy, D. (1985). Teaching telephone answering skills to mentally retarded adults. *American Journal of Mental Deficiency, 89*, 595–609.

Kluth, P. (2000). Community-referenced learning and the inclusive classroom. *Remedial and Special Education, 21*, 19–27.

Leff, R. B. (1974). Teaching the TMR to dial the telephone. *Mental Retardation, 12*(2), 12–13.

Leff, R. B. (1975). Teaching TMR children and adults to dial the telephone. *Mental Retardation, 13*(3), 9–11.

Livi, J., & Ford, A. (1985). Skill transfer from a domestic training site to the actual homes of three moderately handicapped students. *Education and Training of the Mentally Retarded, 20*, 69–82.

Marchetti, A. G., Cecil, C. E., Graves, J., & Marchetti, D. C. (1984). Public transportation instruction: Comparison of classroom instruction, community instruction, and facility grounds instruction. *Mental Retardation, 22*, 128–136.

Marchetti, A. G., McCartney, J. R., Drain, S., Hooper, M., & Dix, J. (1983). Pedestrian skills training for mentally retarded adults: Comparison of training in two settings. *Mental Retardation, 21*, 107–110.

Marholin, D., O'Toole, K. M., Touchette, P. E., Berger, P. L., & Doyle, D. A. (1979). I'll have a Big Mac, large fries, large coke, and apple pie, . . . or teaching adaptive community skills. *Behavior Therapy, 10,* 249–259.

Matson, J. L. (1981). Use of independence training to teach shopping skills to mildly mentally retarded adults. *American Journal of Mental Deficiency, 86,* 178–183.

Matson, J. L., & Long, S. (1986). Teaching computation/shopping skills to mentally retarded adults. *American Journal of Mental Deficiency, 91,* 98–101.

McDonnell, J. J., & Ferguson, B. (1988). A comparison of general case in vivo and general case simulation plus in vivo training. *Journal of the Association for Persons with Severe Handicaps, 13,* 116–124.

McDonnell, J. J., Horner, R. H., & Williams, J. A. (1984). Comparison of three strategies for teaching generalized grocery purchasing to high school students with severe handicaps. *Journal of the Association for Persons with Severe Handicaps, 9,* 123–133.

Mechling, L. C., Gast, D. L., & Langone, J. (2002). Computer-based video instruction to teach persons with moderate intellectual disabilities to read grocery aisle signs and locate items. *Journal of Special Education, 35,* 224–240.

Miller, U. C., & Test, D. W. (1989). A comparison of constant time delay and most-to-least prompting in teaching laundry skills to students with moderate retardation. *Education and Training in Mental Retardation, 24,* 341–351.

Morse, T. E., & Schuster, J. W. (2000). Teaching elementary students with moderate intellectual disabilities how to shop for groceries. *Exceptional Children, 66,* 273–288.

Morse, T. E., Schuster, J. W., & Sandknop, P. A. (1996). Grocery shopping skills for persons with moderate to profound intellectual disabilities: A review of the literature. *Education and Treatment of Children, 19,* 487–517.

Neef, N. A., Iwata, B. A., & Page, T. J. (1978). Public transportation training: In vivo vs. classroom instruction. *Journal of Applied Behavior Analysis, 11,* 331–344.

Nietupski, J., Clancy, P., & Christiansen, C. (1984). Acquisition, maintenance, and generalization of vending machine purchasing skills by moderately handicapped students. *Education and Training of the Mentally Retarded, 17,* 91–96.

Nietupski, J., Hamre-Nietupski, S., Houselog, M., Donder, D. J., & Anderson, R. J. (1988). Proactive administrative strategies for implementing community based programs for students with moderate/severe handicaps. *Education and Training in Mental Retardation, 23,* 138–146.

Nietupski, J., Welch, J., & Wacker, D. (1983). Acquisition, maintenance and transfer of grocery item purchasing skills by moderately and severely handicapped students. *Education and Training of the Mentally Retarded, 18,* 279–286.

Risley, R. M., & Cuvo, A. J. (1980). Training mentally retarded adults to make emergency phone calls. *Behavior Modification, 4,* 513–516.

Sands, D. J., Able-Boone, H., & Margolis, H. (1995). Live-in training experience (LITE): A transition program for youth with disabilities. *Teaching Exceptional Children, 27*(2), 19–23.

Sarber, R. E., Halasz, M. M., Messmer, M. C., Bickett, A. D., & Lutzker, J. R. (1983). Teaching menu planning and grocery shopping skills to a mentally retarded mother. *Mental Retardation, 21,* 101–106.

Schuster, J. W. (1988). Cooking instruction for persons labeled mentally retarded: A review of literature. *Education and Training in Mental Retardation, 23,* 43–50.

Schuster, J. W., Gast, D. L., Wolery, M., & Guiltinan, S. (1988). The effectiveness of a constant time delay procedure to teach chained responses to adolescents with mental retardation. *Journal of Applied Behavior Analysis, 21,* 169–178.

Schuster, J. W., & Griffin, A. K. (1991). Using constant time delay to teach recipe following skills. *Education and Training in Mental Retardation, 26,* 411–419.

Shafer, M. S., Inge, K. J., & Hill, J. (1986). Acquisition, generalization and maintenance of automated banking skills. *Education and Training of the Mentally Retarded, 21,* 265–272.

Smith, M., & Meyers, A. (1979). Telephone-skills training for retarded adults: Group and individual demonstrations with and without verbal instruction. *American Journal of Mental Deficiency, 83,* 581–587.

Smith, R. L., Collins, B. C., Schuster, J. W., & Kleinert, H. (1999). Teaching table cleaning skills to secondary students with moderate/severe disabilities: Facilitating observational learning during instructional downtime. *Education and Training in Mental Retardation and Developmental Disabilities, 34,* 342–353.

Snell, M. E., & Browder, D. M. (1986). Community referenced instruction: Research and issues. *Journal of the Association for Persons with Severe Handicaps, 11,* 1–11.

Sobsey, D. (Ed.) (1987). *Ecological inventory exemplars.* Edmonton: University of Alberta, Department of Educational Psychology.

Sowers, J., Rusch, F. R., & Hudson, C. (1979). Training a severely retarded young adult to ride the city bus to and from work. *AAESPH Review, 4*(1), 15–23.

Sprague, J. R., & Horner, R. H. (1984). The effects of single instance, multiple instance, and general case training on generalized vending machine use by moderately and severely handicapped students. *Journal of Applied Behavior Analysis, 17,* 273–278.

Storey, K., Bates, P., & Hanson, H. B. (1984). Acquisition and generalization of coffee purchase skills by adults with severe disabilities. *Journal of the Association for Persons with Severe Handicaps, 9,* 178–185.

Taber, T. A., Alberto, P. A., Hughes, M., & Seltzer, A. (2002). A strategy for students with moderate disabilities when lost in the community. *Research and Practice for Persons with Severe Disabilities, 27,* 141–152.

Taylor, P., Collins, B. C., Schuster, J. W., & Kleinert, H. (2002). Teaching laundry skill to high school students with disabilities: Generalization of targeted skills and non-targeted information. *Education and Training in Mental Retardation and Developmental Disabilities, 37*(2), 172–183.

Test, D. W., & Spooner, F. (1996). *Innovations: Community-based instructional support.* Washington, DC: American Association on Mental Retardation.

Van den Pol, R. A., Iwata, B. A., Ivancic, M. T., Page, T. J., Neef, N. A., & Whitley, P. F. (1981). Teaching the handicapped to eat in public places: Acquisition, generalization and maintenance of restaurant skills. *Journal of Applied Behavior Analysis, 14,* 61–69.

Vogelsberg, R. T., & Rusch, F. R. (1979). Training severely handicapped adolescents to cross partially controlled intersections. *AAESPH Review, 4,* 264–273.

Wehmeyer, M. L., Lance, G. D., & Bashinski, S. (2002). Promoting access to the general curriculum for students with mental retardation: A multi-level model. *Education and Training in Mental Retardation and Developmental Disabilities, 37*(3), 223–234.

Wehmeyer, M. L., Lattin, D., & Agran, M. (2001). Achieving access to the general curriculum for students with mental retardation: A curriculum decision-making model. *Education and Training in Mental Retardation and Developmental Disabilities, 36,* 327–342.

Welch, J., Nietupski, J., & Hamre-Nietupski, S. (1985). Teaching public transportation problem solving skills to young adults with moderate handicaps. *Education and Training of the Mentally Retarded, 20,* 287–295.

Westling, D. L., & Fleck, L. (1991). Teachers' views of community instruction. *Teacher Education and Special Education, 14,* 127–134.

Westling, D. L., & Floyd, J. (1990). Generalization of community skills: How much training is necessary? *Journal of Special Education, 23,* 386–406.

Westling, D. L., Floyd, J., & Carr, D. (1990). Effect of single setting versus multiple setting training on learning to shop in a department store. *American Journal on Mental Deficiency, 94,* 616–624.

Wilcox, B., & Bellamy, G. T. (1987). *The activities catalog: An alternative curriculum for youth and adults with severe disabilities.* Baltimore: Paul H. Brookes.

PART 5

Special Considerations

CHAPTER 19

Using Technology to Enhance Teaching and Learning

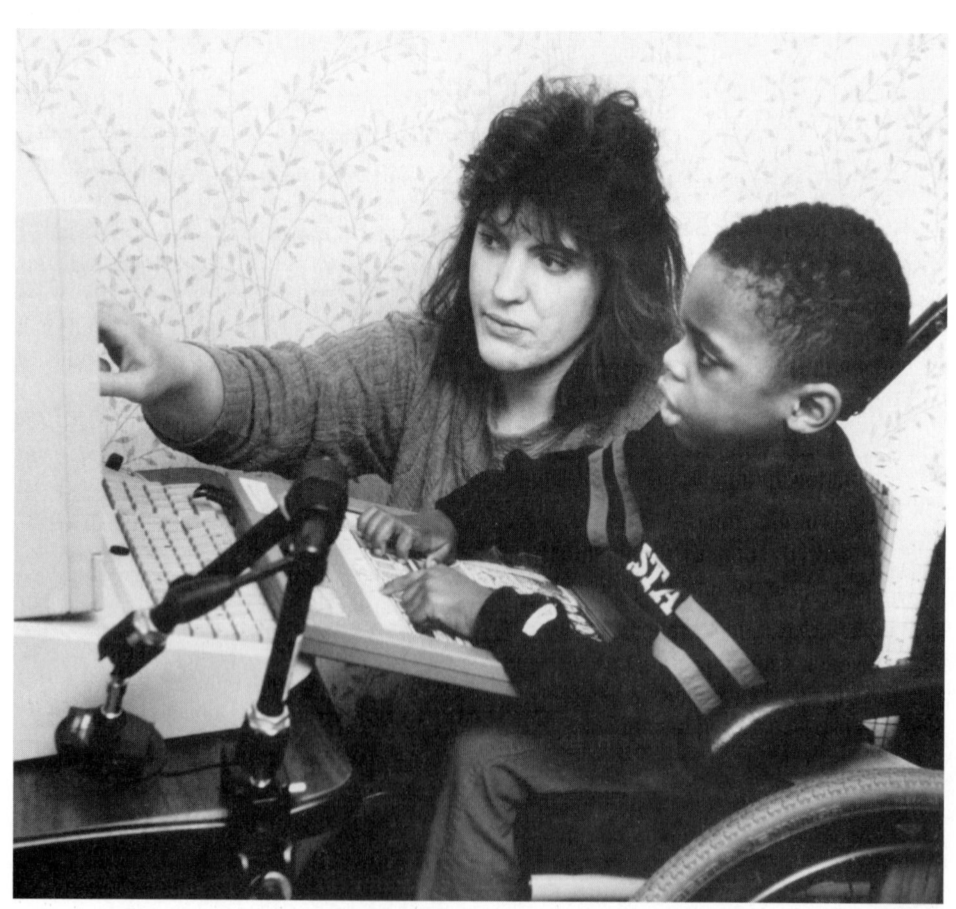

Many of the needs of individuals with severe disabilities can be better met through the appropriate use of assistive technology (AT). Just as we all find that living and learning is made considerably easier thanks to advances in technology, people with disabilities are likewise benefited through various AT devices and the provision of AT services related to their use. But we also need to keep in mind that, just as with us, technology for students with severe disabilities is not a magic carpet. They will still face many challenges associated with their disabilities. Technology does not increase cognitive abilities, improve personal or social skills, or make someone physically stronger or more able. But many AT devices and services will help individuals with severe disabilities to negotiate their way more easily through many social and physical environments and to achieve many skills and overcome numerous obstacles that might otherwise impede them.

Assistive Technology Devices and Services

A line of federal laws, beginning with the 1988 Technology-Related Assistance for Individuals with Disabilities Act (or the Tech Act, P.L. 100-407); the Technology-Related Assistance for Individuals with Disabilities Act Amendments of 1994 (P.L. 103-218); the Assistive Technology Act of 1998 (P.L. 105-394), and the Individuals with Disabilities Education Act, 1997 Amendments, have made provisions for *assistive technology devices* and *assistive technology services*. According to these laws, an AT device is "any item, piece of equipment, or product system, whether acquired commercially off the shelf, modified, or customized, that is used to increase, maintain, or improve functional capabilities of a child with a disability." Additionally, the law defines AT services as "any service that directly assists a child with a disability in the selection, acquisition, or use of an assistive technology device." According to IDEA '97, there are several types of AT services for which students with disabilities are eligible:

- the evaluation of the needs of such child (with disabilities), including a functional evaluation of the child in the child's customary environment;
- purchasing, leasing, or otherwise providing for the acquisition of assistive technology devices by such child;
- selecting, designing, fitting, customizing, adapting, applying, maintaining, repairing, or replacing of assistive technology devices;
- coordinating and using other therapies, interventions, or services with assistive technology devices, such as those associated with existing education and rehabilitation plans and programs;
- training or technical assistance for such child, or, where appropriate, the family of such child; and
- training or technical assistance for professionals (including individuals providing education and rehabilitation services), employers, or other individuals who provide services to, employ, or are otherwise substantially involved in the major life functions of such child.

It is important to note the laws do not simply recognize the importance of AT *devices*, but also the critical need for providing AT *services* that better enable students, their family members, and the professionals who work with them to make the best use of the devices. This is done through the AT services listed previously.

But who is eligible for AT devices and services? For public school students, IDEA '97 requires that during an IEP session the IEP planning committee must "consider whether the child requires assistive technology devices and services." This means that for each student eligible for special education services the committee must deliberate about how an AT device might help a student during his educational program. If the device is necessary for the student to receive a "free and appropriate" education, then it must be provided by the school district at no cost to the parents. However, because of the expense associated with more complex, high tech assistive devices, the necessity of a device is often a point of contention between schools and parents (Parette, 1997; Reed and Best, 2001).

Assistive Technology Devices for Students with Severe Disabilities

A wide range of AT devices may be beneficial to students with various types and degrees of disabilities. The devices may be relatively simple or very complex. Reed and Best (2001) categorized the types of devices according to the functions that they might serve in the following manner:

- Writing
    - Mechanics of writing
    - Computer access
    - Composing written material
- Communication

- Reading, studying, and math
  - Reading
  - Learning and studying
  - Math
- Recreation and leisure
- Activities of daily living
- Mobility
- Control of the environment
- Positioning and seating
- Vision
- Hearing

As the list implies, AT devices may address needs in a multitude of areas, some of which are appropriate for students with severe disabilities, some of which may not be. Key areas of need for students with severe disabilities and examples of devices within these areas are listed in Table 19–1. The devices are listed from the simple to the more complex. Those that are more complex, especially in the area of communication, may be beyond the ability level of persons with relatively more severe cognitive disabilities.

Literally thousands of AT devices may be beneficial to individuals with disabilities, certainly far too many to be listed in this chapter. However, an excellent resource for reviewing available devices can be found at *www.abledata.com*. According to their Web site, "ABLEDATA is a federally funded project whose primary mission is to provide information on assistive technology and rehabilitation equipment available from domestic and international sources to consumers, organizations, professionals, and caregivers within the United States." ABLEDATA is sponsored by the National Institute on Disability and Rehabilitation Research (NIDRR), which is part of the Office of Special Education and Rehabilitative Services (OSERS) of the U.S. Department of Education. The ABLEDATA database contains information on more than 29,000 assistive technology products (over 19,000 of which are currently available). As noted at the Web site, "the database contains detailed descriptions of each product including price and company information. The database also contains information on non-commercial prototypes, customized and one-of-a-kind products, and do-it-yourself designs." The Web site advises that "to select devices most appropriate to your needs, we suggest combining ABLEDATA information with professional advice, product evaluations, and hands-on product trials. ABLEDATA does not produce, distribute or sell any of the products listed in their database, but provides information on how to contact manufacturers or distributors of products."

Although we often think of all technology devices as being rather sophisticated, they can be divided into high-tech and low-tech categories. Parette (1997) provides a list of examples of both types that could be used by individual with cognitive disabilities. These are presented in Table 19–2.

Individuals with severe disabilities can benefit from AT devices and services in several ways. Often noted improvements are in the areas of interpersonal relations, sensory abilities and cognitive capabilities, communication skills, motor performance, self-maintenance, leisure, and productivity. The extensive range of AT items, equipment, or systems may increase, maintain, or improve the functional abilities of students with disabilities (Parette, 1997).

Unfortunately, students with cognitive disabilities, especially those with more severe disabilities, tend to be provided with fewer AT devices and services than students with milder disabilities. Derer, Polsgrove, and Rieth (1996) conducted a survey of special education teachers (of students with various types of disabilities) in three different states (Indiana, Kentucky, and Tennessee) regarding the use of assistive technology devices by their students. The teachers reported that they used AT devices with 34% of their students, primarily with students with learning disabilities, communication disorders, and/or mental retardation, but also with students with visual disabilities and physical disabilities. The most frequently used devices were for students with milder disabilities. These included computers (usually Apple computers), academic software, tape recorders, and videos. As might be expected, less frequently used AT devices were for students with more severe disabilities. These included communication boards, alternative keyboards, electronic adapters, mechanical adapters, positioning devices, transportation devices, and adapted switch toys.

Two additional studies by Wehmeyer (1998, 1999) support the finding of underuse of AT devices by individuals with cognitive disabilities. In the first report by Wehmeyer (1998), the *Assistive Technology Use Survey* was used in a national survey to determine the use of AT devices by adults with mental retardation. Data were collected from 1,218 families that included an adult with mental retardation. Wehmeyer asked about the *use* of AT devices and the *need* for devices to facilitate individuals in five areas: mobility, hearing and vision, communication, home adaptation and access, and environmental control. Questions were asked about AT devices and also the use of personal computers, sources of funding for technology devices, assessment for the use of technology devices, information about how to use the device, and

Table 19–1 Continuum of Assistive Devices in Select Functional Areas

Communication

- Communication board, book with pictures, objects, letters, words
- Eye gaze board, frame
- Simple voice output device (e.g., BIGmack, Cheap Talk, Voice in a Box, MicroVoice, Talking Picture Frame)
- Voice output device with levels (e.g., 6 Level Voice in a Box, Macaw, Digivox)
- Voice output device with icon sequencing (e.g., AlphaTalker II, Vanguard, Chatbox)
- Voice output device with dynamic display (e.g., Dynavox, Speaking Dynamically with laptop computer, Freestyle)
- Device with speech synthesis for typing (e.g., Cannon Communicator, Link, Write:Out Loud with laptop)

Activities of Daily Living

- Nonslip materials to hold things in place
- Universal cuff, strap to hold items
- Color-coded items for easier locating and identifying
- Adaptive eating utensils (e.g., foam handle on utensils)
- Adaptive drinking devices (e.g., cup with cut-out rim)
- Adaptive dressing equipment (e.g., button hook, reacher)
- Adaptive devices for hygiene
- Adapted bathing devices

Mobility

- Walker
- Grab rails
- Manual wheelchair
- Powered mobility toy (e.g., Cooper Car, GoBot)
- Powered scooter or cart
- Powered wheelchair with joystick, head switch, or sip-puff control

Control of the Environment

- Light switch extension
- Use of Powerlink and switch to turn on electrical appliance (e.g., radio, fan, blender)
- Radio, ultrasound, remote-controlled appliances

Positioning and Seating

- Nonslip surface on chair to prevent slipping (e.g., Dycem)
- Bolster, rolled towel, blocks for feet
- Adapted, alternative chair, sidelyer, stander
- Custom-fitted wheelchair or insert

Source: "Assessment for Assistive Technology," by P. Reed, and S. Best, 2001. In J. L. Bigge, S. J. Best, and K. W. Heller (Eds.), *Teaching Individuals with Physical, Health, or Multiple Disabilities* (4th Ed., pp. 149–194), Upper Saddle River, New Jersey: Merrill/Prentice Hall. Adapted by permission of Pearson Education, Inc.

satisfaction with the device. If respondents indicated that the family member with mental retardation did not use a particular device in one of the five areas, they were asked if such a device would be beneficial. If the answer was yes, the respondent was asked what barriers prevented use of technology devices.

Wehmeyer (1998) found that AT devices were used most frequently to assist with mobility (12.7%, of the respondents), and the most commonly used mobility device was a wheelchair. AT devices were used in the other areas by *less than 10%* of the individuals: 8.9% used devices to assist with vision or hearing (e.g., glasses or hearing aids), 4.9% used communication devices (usually nonspeech touch and point systems or picture systems), 9.7% had home adaptations (e.g., extra wide doors, handrails, ramps), and 5.5% used devices to facilitate environmental control (e.g., adapted utensils or eating devices). However, in two areas, communication and environmental control, the percent of family members with mental retardation who the respondents said *could benefit* from devices if they could get them, *exceeded the percent who had them.* The large majority of individuals who used AT devices were very satisfied or somewhat satisfied with the evaluation and training provided for using the device (i.e., AT services).

Wehmeyer (1998) also examined barriers to acquiring and using devices for those individuals who said their family member could benefit from one or more, but who

Table 19–2 Examples of Low- and High-Tech Devices for Persons with Mental Retardation and Developmental Disabilities

Low-Tech Devices	*High-Tech Devices*
Adaptive switches to allow access to battery-operated toys, electrical systems, or electronic systems	Computers for educational tasks, recreation, communication; and environmental control
Cell systems, such as buzzers, or loop tapes to communicate short messages	Augmentative and alternative communication devices which use synthetic or digitized speech
Communication boards, notebooks, folders to communicate a wider variety of messages	Powered mobility devices to enable the individual to independently move about in the environment
Activity frames or objects stabilized by Velcro, Dycem, elastic and other materials	Environmental control systems which use, infrared, radio frequency, ultrasound, or AC power line control scheme
Adapted books to facilitate participation in story time or reading	Advanced switches, such as those which detect eye or muscle movements
Adapted eating utensils to enable more effective self-feeding	Modified or alternative keyboards and other computer adaptations
Jigs, elongated levers for on/off switches, and other adaptations to allow gross- or fine-motor control, designed for specific work tasks and needs	Braille printers and text-to-speech devices to enable access to information
Tactile enhancement such as using raised lines on pictures or to label clothes	Computerized visual amplification systems
Talking, lighted, or enlarged clocks and calculators to optimize use of these devices	Powered lifts and transfer systems

Source: "Assistive Technology Devices and Services," by H. P. Parette, 1997. *Education and Training in Mental Retardation and Developmental Disabilities, 32,* 267–280. Reprinted with permission of Council for Exceptional Children.

did not have one. The most commonly identified barriers were the cost of the products and lack of information about the products. This finding was true regardless of the particular device purpose. In a separate question, Wehmeyer asked about the use of a computer by the family member with mental retardation. Twenty-three percent of the respondents said that their family member used a computer either inside or outside the home. Most of the computer use was for leisure and recreational activities or for educational activities, with negligible numbers using the computer for household financing or budgeting or work-related activities.

Wehmeyer (1998) concluded that "generally, adults with mental retardation underutilize assistive technology devices" (p. 48), but that about the same number of people who currently use the device could benefit from it if it was made available to them. Lack of information and cost of devices appeared to be the main reasons why more persons with mental retardation did not use the devices. The same could be said about the use of personal computers. As a side issue, Wehmeyer pointed out that computer programs are generally not designed for people with mental retardation. Existing programs are either too complex or, if not, they are not age appropriate.

In a second similar study, Wehmeyer (1999) assessed the extent of use of AT devices by *students* with mental retardation and barriers to use. Again the *Assistive Technology Use Survey* was used and was answered by 516 family members of students with mental retardation from 45 states and the District of Columbia. The purpose of this survey was the same as the first, but with a focus on students instead of adults. In this study, Wehmeyer found that the most frequently used devices included wheelchairs, picture-based communication devices, touch-or-point communication systems, hearing aids, walkers, and synthesized speech communication devices. A relatively small number of individuals reported that in the area of home adaptation extra wide doors, hand rails, ramps, and raised toilets had been installed. In the environmental control independent/living area, the most commonly used devices were adapted toys, switches for recreational or leisure activities, and adapted utensils and eating devices. A large majority of respondents (83%) indicated that the family member with mental retardation "had access to or used" a computer. Computers were used mostly in schools and homes, but very little in other living situations, recreational settings, or work settings.

As in the first study, several barriers to the use of potentially helpful assistive technology devices were identified. The most common were the cost of devices and lack of information about them. Less common barriers included lack of assessment for using the device, complexity of the devices, lack of training in how to use the device, and availability of the device. For those using technology devices, the most to least common sources of funding included personal funding, funding by schools, private insurance funding, government funding, and funding through donations. As with the first study, Wehmeyer (1999) concluded that assistive technology devices are underutilized by persons with mental retardation and that many individuals who could benefit from certain devices did not have them.

Identification of Specific AT Devices and Services for Students with Severe Disabilities

For AT devices to be used most effectively, it is critical that the most appropriate device be found to meet the student's need in the context in which the student will use the device. Because so many devices exist, it may be tempting to simply select a device "off the shelf" or contrive a device because it seems as though it would be useful to the student. However, several authorities have noted the importance of undergoing a thoughtful and detailed process to find the most appropriate device and to put it into service with the student in a way that best assures its correct use and to avoid the relatively common phenomenon referred to as *technology abandonment*. Recommendations for achieving success with the use of AT devices have been made by Hutinger, Johanson, and Stoneburner (1996), Parette (1997), Parette, Hourcade, and VanBiervliet (1993), Reed and Best (2001), and Todis (1996). These are summarized next.

Involve the Collaborative Team in the Decision-Making Process

When considering the need for an assistive device, the collaborative team should collectively have enough knowledge to make a decision. This means that at least one person on the team should have some knowledge about available devices or types of devices in different areas and how a device might help the student to achieve goals and objectives if current progress is inadequate. Other members of the team should have knowledge about the student's curriculum (the special or general education teacher) and about the student's functioning in other areas, including physical ability (a physical or occupational therapist), language development (a speech–language pathologist), and any other areas of development that may be pertinent, such as visual ability (a vision specialist). Of course, most importantly, parents or caregivers should be involved in the decision-making process.

Determine the Specific Needs of the Student for the Device and the Goals of Using the Device

Selection of an AT device should be in response to a clearly defined goals and objectives with the intention of enhancing skills. For example, when considering acquiring an alternative or augmentative communication device (AAC) for a student, it might be noted that the student needs a way to greet other students and to express a few needs and feelings. Also the student currently expresses himself intentionally, but uses incomprehensible verbalizations. Consequently, the other students don't always know what he is trying to say.

Consider Student Characteristics, Including Abilities Related to the Use of a Specific AT Device and Preference for a Device

Different AT devices have different levels of complexity and use requirements that should be considered in light of the student's abilities. Depending on the type of device that is needed, the collaborative team must take into consideration the student's cognitive, physical, sensory, and social abilities. Whenever possible, the student's preference for a device should also be given attention. Interviews with the student and parent and the student's previous experience with AT devices can be helpful in determining preferences and abilities. Also, whenever possible, children and family members must have an opportunity for hands-on use of a device to determine if it is appropriate prior to purchase. Many local and state agencies have loan programs from which devices may be borrowed for trial use.

Determine Where the Device Is to Be Used

In most cases the team will need to consider where a device will be used before selecting a particular device. Although some devices may be appropriate for use in only one setting, others may be useful or necessary for several settings, including the classroom, other parts of the school, at home, and in some community settings. This implies that the transportability of the device, its size, and its durability, among other factors, must be considered. Decision makers should also be sensitive to the issue of how an AT device may draw attention to the disabilities of an individual. A device that may not be noticed in a special class or even accepted in a regular classroom may draw unfavorable attention in some community settings.

Determine How Long the Device Is to Be Used

Some AT devices are suitable for relatively short periods of time, such as an assistive feeding device for a young child, whereas others may be expected to last longer, such as an AAC device. Items that are intended to serve a person for a longer period of time should be able to "grow" with the individual. For example, an AAC device with a limited range of symbols or icons to point to or verbal messages to express may be suitable for a short term, but may render the device less useful as the individual expands her potential for greater vocabulary. An AT device that becomes useless after a brief period of use has less value than one that can be adapted to grow with the student.

Especially for AAC Devices, Determine with Whom the Device Will Be Used

When the AT device being considered is a communication device, it is important for the team to consider the targets of the individual when he uses a device. If the target audience is limited, for example, a few friends, classmates, and family members, these select individuals can be instructed in the meaning of the signs, icons, or expressions that can be indicated by the device. If the audience is broader or even unlimited, the production of the device must be relatively clear and unambiguous. Devices vary with regard to the length and complexity of the message that they can deliver. A low-tech device requires the user to point to or select each symbol that he wishes to link together to express a message and then the listener must comprehend or infer meaning. Some high-tech devices can be programmed to produce more lengthy messages when one symbol is touched and more complex messages when multiple symbols are touched (Sigafoos & Iacono, 1993).

Determine How Well the Device Must Operate

How fast must the device operate? How durable must it be? And to what degree or breadth must the device perform? In some situations, speed is important. AAC devices that convey a message after a target has passed are not very useful. A mobility device that is suitable only for indoor use will not allow a person access to community settings. Hearing aids with inadequate amplification will not facilitate hearing.

Determine the Reliability of the Device

Likewise, a device in need of constant repair will not be often used or will soon be abandoned. It is important for the team to consider the reliability and repair records of devices. The "product review forum" at abledata.com is a good location to acquire product information. Additionally, others in a school district who have had experience with a device can attest to its quality.

Consider Practical Constraints in Acquiring the Device and Determine if They Can Be Adequately Addressed

Specifically, the team must consider different funding sources for the device, the availability of the device or equipment, and how long it may take to arrive. Team members should also consider who will teach the student to use the device and interact with others, such as family members, about the use of the device. Does this individual have the necessary skills and time to teach the use of the device? With any AT device, training must be provided to personnel who will assist the student with the device. This is part of the AT service requirement and professionals should expect training and support for the use of specific devices. However, this means time must be allocated for professional training.

Consider the Real Cost of the Device

The real cost of a device or system should be considered, including cost of the device; cost associated with assembling the device; cost of special batteries and parts; maintenance requirements; and additional devices necessary to operate the device. Some equipment, especially those requiring batteries or power packs, may be costly to maintain.

Consider the Response to the Device Within the Student's Family and Cultural Contexts

Finally, a great deal of thought must be given as to how the AT device will affect the family of the individual with disabilities on a daily basis. Consideration should be given to how the AT device will be used within the family and what affect it might have on family activities, routines, and resources. In doing this, additional attention needs to be given to the family's cultural milieu. Not all cultures or all families will view an AT device in an entirely positive light, and this must be understood by team members. Without the support of the family for the use of a device, it almost certainly will not be fully utilized.

Parette (1997) stated that "to most effectively match assistive technology devices and services with any individual with a disability, team members must consider five parallel domains: (a) user characteristics, (b) family issues, (c) cultural factors, (d) technology features, and (e) service system considerations" (Parette, 1997, p. 271). Table 19–3 lists some of the more important considerations in these areas.

Two of the most critical factors related to the use of AT devices are the extent to which the device is used outside the school, that is, in the home and community, and the financial considerations related to acquiring and maintaining the device. These two topics are more extensively discussed in the following sections.

Use of AT Devices in Family and Cultural Contexts

Family participation is critical when making decisions about AT devices and services because there is a need to recognize realistic conditions in which the device is expected to be used. Without this knowledge, a good match might not be formed or the device may not be used to the greatest extent possible, or perhaps not at all. Parette and Brotherson (1996) have developed a comprehensive four-domain model for involving families in

Table 19–3 Domains of Influence to Be Considered by Assistive Technology Team Members

User characteristics	Performance levels (from assessment data) Age Gender Current devices used, past experiences, and preferences Academic and vocational aspirations Desire for independence Training needs and willingness to receive training Changes in user characteristics across time
Technology features	Range and availability of devices Potential to enhance user performance levels Real cost Ease of use Comfort Dependability Transportability Longevity and durability Adaptability Comparability with other devices Safety features Availability for hands-on demonstrations Repair considerations
Family concerns	Changes in activities, routines, and resources Effect on family interaction patterns Degree of expectations for independence
Cultural factors	Compatibility of device with cultural values Extent to which device calls attention to user in social and public settings Extent to which dependence or independence is valued Developmental expectations for the acquisition of skills Perception of disability
Service system issues	Cost Community usage of device Protection from theft and damage Training

Source: "Assistive Technology Devices and Services," by H. P. Parette, 1997. *Education and Training in Mental Retardation and Developmental Disabilities, 32*, 267–280. Reprinted with permission of Council for Exceptional Children.

an AT assessment and planning process. The four domains are:

1. The child (needs, capability, goals)
2. The family (perceptions, definition of quality of life, needs, resources, strengths, styles, and preferences)
3. Technology factors (demands placed on the child and the family, opportunities that are presented by the AT)
4. Service system factors (limitations, demands, and resources available to the family)

The comprehensive assessment strategy should consider the linkages between all these factors, and interactions should be held with family members to consider specific issues within each domain.

The impact of a device within the family routine needs to be assessed for various possible outcomes. For example, the device can affect communication within the family, change family member's roles and activities, and create new demands for family members. Additionally, many AT devices require parents or caregivers to be trained in their operation and maintenance. This is considered an essential AT support service, but it requires additional time and effort on the part of family members. Even though an AT device may improve mobility, communication, or other skills for an individual, it may limit family interaction or cause a family to become more isolated. Without being given adequate prior consideration, these changes can add stress to the family and its members (Parette & Brotherson, 1996; Parette, VanBiervliet, & Hourcade, 2000).

Minority children with severe disabilities and their families warrant special attention. Kemp and Parette (2000) reported that minority families are often treated differently by professionals with regard to providing AT devices and services for their children and that minority children with disabilities seem to use AT devices less often than their European American counterparts. They also reported that minority parents are less involved in decision making about AT devices and services than are other parents. According to Kemp and Parette, "Historically, minority parents have fought service systems in our country that have denied equitable rights to their children. In spite of legislation to correct past practices of prejudice and discrimination, minority families must still function in a system that often displays negative attitudes toward poverty and diversity." This condition is further exacerbated by the fact that many schools or school districts that serve predominately poor students and their families lag significantly behind those serving middle- and upper-middle-class students in terms of the resources that they can offer.

Another problem with the use of AT devices by children within minority families is that the families may often feel that the advantages of the devices do not outweigh the stigma that may be associated with them in their community. For example, a child may be able to communicate more effectively using an AAC device, but the device itself may be perceived by family members as drawing unfavorable attention toward the child. Different cultures may react differently to AT devices or have a different view on the use of AT devices. In some cultures, for example, extended family members play an important role and should be given consideration with regard to their opinions about AT devices. "Failure to consider cultural values may result in the provision of a device that is neither wanted nor used by the student and the family in the home and the community environments." (Parette, 1997, p. 273).

To better serve children from minority families with AT devices and service, Kemp and Parette (2000) emphasize the need to first provide more information to the families about the devices, services, training, and funding options. Professionals also need to find a realistic way to involve family members in the decision-making process about the use of AT devices, but in doing so they should realize that many minority individuals tend to view the professional as the "expert" and rely less often on their own opinions and attitudes. Kemp and Parette suggest that professionals ask themselves the following questions about the family and its culture:

- Does the family want the AT device in the home setting?
- If so, is AT device usage congruous with family needs and goals?
- Will changes in routines and responsibilities result when using the AT device?
- Are families willing and able to accept these changes?
- Will siblings have access to the AT device?
- Will training and supports (in the native language when appropriate) be provided for effective use of the AT device in the home?
- Does the family (both immediate and extended) feel that the child's use of AT is important?
- Will use of the AT device draw unnecessary or negative attention to the child?
- Will use of the AT device increase the child's opportunities for interactions in the community?
- Has the family been involved in initial conversations on AT to find out what their options are?

- Has the family been informed of the advantages and disadvantages of the AT device?
- Have discussions with the family involved their input and not only the input of professionals?
- Does the family believe that their input is valued and taken into consideration?
- Has the family been allowed to process how the use of AT will affect them in terms of their family and extended community?
- Are the cultural and belief systems of the family taken into consideration when AT is discussed?
- Has the family been exposed to and experimented with various AT devices that are being considered for the child?

Notwithstanding the potential of AT devices and services, many families find the vast world of AT one that is difficult to navigate. Some families may come to AT planning meetings with inaccurate notions regarding AT devices. For example, they may believe that, once a child has an AT device, the child should be able to demonstrate desired skills immediately (Parette, VanBiervliet, & Hourcade, 2000). Therefore, it is helpful that parents be given accurate information about the role of AT for their child and directed to useful sources of information. Several useful Web sites are available for parents and professionals alike to explore. Table 19–4 lists Web sites that contain practical information and that have links to numerous other Web sites. Additionally, all states have assistive technology projects, and their Web sites are easily accessible.

Despite the importance of family participation in identifying and acquiring appropriate AT devices and services, their participation is not commonplace. Parette and Hourcade (1997) conducted a national survey of states and territories in the United States to determine assessment practices used to prescribe AAC devices for young children with disabilities. They were particularly interested in determining the extent of family involvement

Table 19–4 Web Sites on AT

Organization and URL	*Organization's Description (as reported on its Web site)*
ABLEDATA http://www.abledata.com/	ABLEDATA is a federally funded project whose primary mission is to provide information on the assistive technology and rehabilitation equipment available from domestic and international sources to consumers, organizations, professionals, and caregivers within the United States. We are sponsored by the National Institute on Disability and Rehabilitation Research (NIDRR), which is part of the Office of Special Education and Rehabilitative Services (OSERS) of the U.S. Department of Education. The ABLEDATA database contains information on more than 29,000 assistive technology products (over 19,000 of which are currently available), from white canes to voice output programs. The database contains detailed descriptions of each product including price and company information. The database also contains information on non-commercial prototypes, customized and one-of-a-kind products, and do-it-yourself designs. To select devices most appropriate to your needs, we suggest combining ABLEDATA information with professional advice, product evaluations, and hands-on product trials. We do not produce, distribute or sell any of the products listed on the database, but we will provide you with information on how to contact manufacturers or distributors of these products. We also do not produce any type of catalog.
RESNA: Rehabilitation Engineering and Assistive Technology Society of North America http://www.resna.org/	RESNA is an interdisciplinary association of people with a common interest in technology and disability. Our purpose is to improve the potential of people with disabilities to achieve their goals through the use of technology. We serve that purpose by promoting research, development, education, advocacy, and the provision of technology and by supporting the people engaged in these activities. RESNA's membership ranges from rehabilitation professionals to consumers. All members are dedicated to promoting the exchange of ideas and information for the advancement of assistive technology.
Assistive Technology Industry Association (ATIA) http://www.atia.org/	ATIA is a not-for-profit membership organization of organizations manufacturing or selling technology-based assistive devices for people with disabilities or providing services associated with or required by people with disabilities. Among its primary goals was the establishment and continuation of an assistive device technology conference to be held on the East Coast of the United States, initially in 1999 and thereafter on an annual basis. The purpose of such a conference is generally to provide a forum for education and communication to professional practitioners serving those with disabilities (teachers, occupational therapists, rehabilitation counselors, physicians, psychologists, speech–language pathologists, etc.), with the overarching goal of providing enhanced benefits and opportunities to people with disabilities.

in the prescription and provision of high-tech AAC assistive technology practices for young children with disabilities. State agency Part H administrators (or their designees) were asked to complete a survey regarding practices used in the state, with particular questions asking about the importance of family involvement. Twenty-eight responses provided usable information.

Parette and Hourcade (1997) found that factors such as "the device's ability to improve the child's functional performance" and "the identification of the funding streams" were reported most often to be "considered to a great extent," but that family-related factors were not considered in many states. Such factors included the additional responsibilities to be taken on by family members, how the device might restrict family activities, or the ability of the family to cope with the stress that might be associated with the use of a high-tech device. They noted that, if family factors are not considered in the prescription of ACC devices, technology abandonment may occur, with the device not being used as intended or used at all.

Funding of AT Devices and Services

Wehmeyer (1998, 1999) found that one of the most common reasons that persons with cognitive disabilities often do not use AT devices is because of the cost. Undoubtedly, this is true with many other persons with disabilities, both students and adults. However, it is important to understand two points. First, if it is determined by an IEP committee that a student with a disability needs an AT device, the Individuals with Disabilities Education Act Amendments of 1997 requires that the school system provide such a device without cost to the parents. IDEA '97 specifically requires the IEP team to evaluate a student's need for AT devices and services in developing a student's IEP. There are three sections in the IEP where the role and contributions of AT may appear; (1) the proposed annual goals and short-term objectives, (2) required supplementary aids and services, and (3) related services necessary for the student to benefit from FAPE.

But the second point is equally important: public schools will likely be resistant to funding items that are expensive in times of funding shortages. They may also only fund items that are limited to school use, a serious limitation for devices that would be useful in multiple settings (Kemp, Hourcade, & Parette, 2000; Parette, 1997). Furthermore, even when IEP team members recognize the tremendous potential of AT to benefit students with disabilities, they may not pursue the issue further because they may not know how to access or pay for AT devices and services. Securing the funding necessary for these often expensive resources is a common frustration. In fact, funding is often the biggest barrier to acquiring AT devices and services (Kemp et al., 2000).

Because of the funding issue, different avenues have been developed to address the problem. In passing the most recent tech act, the Technology-Related Assistance for Individuals with Disabilities Act of 1998 (P.L. 105-394), Congress created alternative funding approaches to assist individuals in acquiring AT devices and services. Under the 1998 act, all states are eligible for long-term federal funding to support their assistive technology programs. Title III of the act created alternative financing mechanisms that may include the following:

- Low-interest loan fund
- Interest buy-down program
- Revolving loan fund
- Loan guarantee or insurance program
- Program operated by a partnership among private entities for the purchase, lease, or other acquisition of assistive technology devices or services
- Another mechanism that meets the requirements of this title and is approved by the secretary

School professionals and parents should be aware that AT funding is available through a variety of sources, including IDEA, Medicaid programs, Developmental Disabilities initiatives, the Department of Vocational Rehabilitation, and private insurance. The actual source of funding depends on different factors, such as why the device or service is needed, the age of the individual, and the financial resources of the family. For example, in general, for school-aged students, schools (through IDEA) are responsible for any assistive technology used primarily for educational purposes. Funding for AT used to help to gain meaningful employment for students aged 16 and over might be obtained through the local Department of Vocational Rehabilitation. Funding for any AT device proposed as a medical necessity should be accessed through private insurance or Medicaid (Kemp et al., 2000). Kemp et al. offer the following summary of funding sources:

> *Medicaid programs as a funding source for assistive technology.* Medicaid was developed in 1965 to provide medical assistance for individuals and families with low incomes and resources. Medicaid programs vary considerably from state to state. The Medicaid Amendments for Special

Education Related Services of 1988 allow each state the option of including a variety of reimbursable services within that state's Medicaid plan, including special education and related services. Schools wishing to take advantage of Medicaid funding to provide AT for students with disabilities should refer students and their families to their local Medicaid office.

School Health and Related Services (SHARS) Program. The SHARS program allows school districts to obtain Medicaid reimbursement for specific services provided to students who are Medicaid eligible and are receiving special education and related services. For school districts to apply for Medicaid reimbursement under the SHARS program, a student must be eligible for Medicaid services. Additionally, AT devices and services must be deemed medically necessary and related to a child's IEP.

Early Periodic, Screening, Diagnosis, and Treatment (EPSDT) Program. In addition to SHARS, students with disabilities may receive AT devices and services through a second Medicaid program known as Early Periodic, Screening, Diagnosis, and Treatment (EPSDT). EPSDT was established under the Medicaid Early and Periodic Screening, Diagnosis, and Treatment Amendments of 1989 (P.L. 101-238) and targets children from birth to age 21 who are eligible for, or who are presently receiving, Medicaid services.

Developmental Disabilities Assistance and Bill of Rights Act Amendments of 1987. Although IDEA and Medicaid remain the two major providers of assistive technology, there are several other options. Federal funds for AT support are available to states through the Developmental Disabilities Assistance and Bill of Rights Act Amendments of 1987 (P.L. 100-146). Through this legislation, states are assisted in the provision of direct services to persons who incur a chronic or severe disability prior to age 18 or, in some states, age 22. Each state has its own plan for service delivery. Persons eligible to receive services are individuals with developmental disabilities. Services provided through this program are usually broad based and on an individualized basis. Most services are provided to children from age 5.

Vocational rehabilitation. Assistive technology services for transition-age students may include items necessary to prepare the student for job training, independent living, employment, social and recreational activities, and further education. The agency legally responsible for providing the services identified in the Individual Transition Plan will remain financially responsible for providing any associated AT services that the student requires. In addition, if the AT is being used to gain meaningful employment, the local Department of Vocational Rehabilitation can help to fund the device.

Private insurance as a funding source for assistive technology. In addition to federal and state funding sources, parents can access AT through private insurance The IDEA regulations also authorize the use of a parent's private insurance. However, school districts cannot require parents to use this funding source. Thus its use must be strictly voluntary on the part of the parents. Private insurance may dictate the type and degree of AT equipment covered.

Philanthropic and charitable organizations. Several organizations are available that provide support services for persons with disabilities. Many times these organizations provide grants to families so that they can acquire devices and services.

Because of the 1998 Tech Act, all states have developed technology assistance programs for persons with disabilities. The Web sites of these states can be assessed through RESNA (http://www.resna.org/). Professionals and parents who cannot determine sources of funding for AT devices and services through their local school districts should contact their state's assistive technology office for additional information. The University of Washington Center for Technology and Disability Studies (UWCTDS, http://uwctds.washington.edu/index.htm), which is a part of the Washington Assistive Technology Alliance (WATA, http://wata.org/), is an excellent example of a state agency that provides useful information about AT funding for both individuals and schools.

Effectiveness of AT Devices and Services

A number of reported studies and cases have demonstrated the potential of AT to affect the lives of persons with severe disabilities. A sampling of these reports is contained in this section. They allow us to see the effectiveness of AT devices and services as well as the problems. First we look at two long-term qualitative studies (Hutinger et al., 1996; Todis, 1996) that provide us with insight into the nature of successful use of AT devices.

In a rather extensive study, Hutinger et al. (1996) reported the effects of the use of various types of AT devices on the learning and development of 14 children with multiple disabilities over a 2-year period. Their overall conclusion was that by the end of the study all the children were able to accomplish new tasks that they had been unable to do previously because of the nature and severity of their disabilities. They also noted that one of the greatest areas of improvement by the children was in the area of social and emotional development.

Hutinger and her colleagues (1996) used a case study approach to document the impact of various types of adaptive devices on children. All the children were classified as having multiple disabilities. Their disabilities included various combinations of cerebral palsy, seizure disorders, visual impairments, learning disabilities, and severe mental retardation. At the beginning of the study, the children ranged in age from just under 3 years to almost 12 years of age. Data about the progress of the children were collected primarily through observations and the recording of notes describing critical behaviors such as vocalizations, social interactions, level of independence, and affective expressions. In addition to the observations, interviews were conducted with family members and with the professional staff that worked with the children.

Different children benefited in different ways from the use of different devices. For example:

- Anne, who was 5 years old and had cerebral palsy at the beginning of the study, needed assistance to participate in her favorite activities. She learned to use a Liberator (an electronic portable direct selection or scanning communicator designed for use by individuals with speech and language disabilities) at home for meaningful communication and at school during structured language lessons and also during "calendar" time. Anne's mother reported that the greatest benefit was that Anne came to be seen by adults as a child with information to share, rather than a helpless infant.
- Eric was 8 years old at the beginning of the study and had motor and communication disabilities due to cerebral palsy. He used several AT devices, including an Apple II GS computer with an Adaptive Firmware Card, a motorized wheelchair, various adaptive utensils, and a Touch Talker. Eric's teachers and family members agreed that Eric had benefited from the use of adaptive devices by improving his problem-solving skills, attention to tasks, social and emotional skills, and independence.
- Gary was 7 years old and experienced developmental delays in motor skills and expressive language due to brain damage. Gary's language delay caused frustration because it interfered with his social interactions; therefore, his parents were interested in exploring an augmentative communication system. With a combination of private and public school communication therapy, Gary learned to operate a Liberator, which allowed him to participate in classroom activities. As a result, his teacher reported that he became more interactive, confident, and happier at school. His mother said his social and cognitive abilities had also increased.

Overall, Hutinger et al. (1996) reported that "Across developmental areas, the greatest gains reported by both parents and staff were in the area of emotional outcomes, including enhanced self-concept, independence, social interaction, cooperation, and exploratory play" (pp. 26–27). The researchers found that equipment in the schools were purchased by the schools and included computers that ranged from an Apple II+ to a Macintosh LC II. Peripheral devices included switches, joy sticks, TouchWindow, PowerPad, the Echo, the Muppet Learning Keys, the Unicorn Expanded Keyboard, the Adaptive Firmware Card or Ke:nx, electronic switch-operated toys, typewriters, calculators, and switch input loop tapes. Equipment at home was purchased with funds from insurance companies, community fund-raising groups, equipment loan programs, philanthropic agencies, grants, and personal funds. Most of the equipment in the homes consisted of older-model Apple computers with a few peripherals for alternative access. Hutinger et al. also found that funding for AT devices was limited in both schools and homes, and insufficient training of school staff and parents was also a problem. Other problems were with the hardware and software and a lack of collaboration. Several were problems associated with all 14 children. These included the following:

- There were no comprehensive technology plans.
- There were no ongoing technology reassessments.
- When placements changed, receiving staff often lacked training in the use of technology.
- There was much variability in the quality of the equipment, software, and maintenance.
- Technology was not considered in transitions plans.

- Unless the equipment was owned by the family, it did not follow the child as he or she moved through the educational system.
- The availability of appropriate equipment was not a consideration for placement in the receiving program.
- There were discrepancies between families and staff regarding expectancies for technology objectives.

Based on their observations, Hutinger and her colleagues made these recommendations:

- More effort should be placed on staff development and adequate funding for the use of technology devices.
- Technology applications must be integrated into children's daily lives, as opposed to being used to develop isolated skills.
- A team approach to assessment and planning is needed to maximize the use of technology devices. Parents and professionals should reach a consensus on necessary technology devices and technology goals.
- The equipment needs to follow the child throughout the school environment, or similar equipment needs to be located in different locations.
- Parents need information about various devices and how to purchase the devices.
- The school system should support staff and family members in using and troubleshooting technology devices. A technology specialist knowledgeable about the needs of students with disabilities should provide this support.
- Equipment should be maintained and repaired in a timely fashion.
- Budgets need to include funds for upgrading equipment.
- Training for professionals about technology should be built into their working time, or they should be compensated for receiving training.
- Child-size products should be developed by equipment providers.
- More software is needed for problem solving and for use in daily life, rather than just for drill and practice, and should be useful for children with and without disabilities.
- Health insurance for families of children with disabilities should allow funds to be used for technology that will allow children to participate in daily living activities.

In another 2-year qualitative study, Todis (1996) assessed various perspectives on the impact of AT devices used by 13 students with severe disabilities. The students were between 4 and 20 years of age and used devices ranging from motorized wheelchairs to AAC devices. Todis examined the impact of the devices from the views of the students with disabilities, their parents, their peers, and different professionals and paraprofessionals who worked with them. Among her more important findings were these factors that resulted in the AT devices consistently meeting students needs:

- Student and family goals formed the basis of the student's educational program. The acquisition and use of the AT device were tied directly to the student's academic, social, and personal goals.
- Students, family, and educators worked as a team to select, obtain, implement, and monitor the AT device. Communication about all aspects of the student's educational program was frequent and honest.
- Devices and equipment that were worn out or outgrown were replaced.
- Glitches were viewed as inevitable, but were dealt with quickly and systematically by the team.

"In short," stated Todis (1996), "when AT was successful, devices were regarded as tools students needed to accomplish their educational goals. The IEP process and the multidisciplinary team were used to make decisions about and to monitor AT, like any other aspect of the student's program" (p. 51).

Todis (1996) also reported factors that were perceived to impede the effective use of AT. Parents, for example, sometimes initially viewed AT devices as indications that their child would not acquire skills in a more normal fashion or that they might lose acquired skills because of the use of the AT device. Some parents felt that the introduction of an AT device meant that professionals were giving up on their students. Other parents looked at AT devices as magic bullets that would permit their child to overcome their limitations. "The parents' conviction that the device holds the key to their child's school progress and social acceptance can become the focus of a student's school program, and sometimes become a source of home–school conflict for months or years." Conflicts are often based on parents' perspectives that educators lack interest in the device, hold a low opinion of the student's potential to succeed using the device, or lack adequate training and knowledge about the device.

Special educators observed and questioned by Todis (1996) seemed for the most part to be willing to try AT devices if they felt that the students would benefit through better access to school settings, learning, and interaction opportunities. Their willingness and enthusiasm could change to frustration, however, when various issues occurred when using the devices. For example, rearranging classrooms and modifying furniture for wheelchair accessibility, providing maintenance for wheelchairs, figuring out how to offer switch access for a computer, locating and loading software, and dealing with sundry glitches could consume a great deal of teacher time.

Finally, Todis (1996) reported problems with AT devices from the point of view of the students who used them, as well as from their peers without disabilities. She noted that there is typically a "physical cost" associated with using AT devices, especially AAC devices, and that sometimes this cost can be frustrating and hamper communicative and social interactions. However, the problem is often ignored by professionals working with the student, and the student is encouraged (or required) to continue to use the device even though a faster response may be possible (for example, smiling or waving instead of using an AAC device to say "Hi"). The rationale is that with practice the student will become faster at using the device, but, in the meantime, significant opportunities for interactions are being passed by and the student with disabilities is left socially stranded as peers without disabilities move on to the next event. Todis concluded that, although AT offers a great deal of potential for facilitating interactions with a student's environment, professionals also need to be aware of how they may have a counterintuitive effect as well.

Some studies have examined the acquisition of specific skills as an outcome of using specific AT devices (e.g., Carey & Sale, 1994; Daniels, Sparling, Reilly, & Humphry, 1995; Davies, Stock, & Wehmeyer, 2002). Daniels et al. evaluated the effectiveness of teaching two young children with profound mental disabilities (ages 2 and 3½ years) to use the "Big Red" switch to activate either electric toys (a drumming bear and a hopping rabbit) or computer programs that featured brightly colored flashing pictures. A timer device was used with the switch to maintain activation of the devices after the switch had been pressed.

The researchers were interested in determining if "contingent learning" would occur, that is, if the different audiovisual responses would differentially affect the children's responding, as well as their attention and orientation to the devices. After providing physical assistance to teach the children to hit the switch, they observed the response patterns of the children. If the children did not respond within a minute after they were placed in front of the switch and the connected device (either the toys or the computer program) or did not respond for a minute after a previous activation, the researcher provided physical assistance. The researchers recorded both assisted and independent responses.

Daniels et al. (1995) found that indeed the children did learn to activate the switch, exhibiting many more independent activations than those requiring assistance. They also found that the children responded differently to the different attachments. Whereas the younger child seemed to prefer the toys more (i.e., activated the switch more when it was attached to the toys rather than to the computer), the older child exhibited the opposite response. But both children showed an overall higher level of independent responses when the attachments were alternated, indicating that having variation in the attachments was an important feature in maintaining switch activation. Additionally, increased levels of independent switch activation were associated with increased levels of attention. Although it is not possible to say that the switch activation caused the attention, or vice versa, it is clear that the two were associated, and the researchers suggested that this implies that, whenever possible, independent switch activation should be encouraged.

In Project FIT (Full Inclusion through Technology), Carey and Sale (1994) attempted to facilitate the inclusion of seven students with severe disabilities by using lightweight notebook computers as mobile, personal communication devices. Carey and Sale conducted a very extensive assessment procedure to determine the vocabulary that would be appropriate for each student, the type of input device that would work best for each (keyboard, modified keyboard or switches), the type of desired output (visual words or auditory output), and the best way to mount the computers and devices for individual students for physical interaction.

Students were taught to make selections of icons presented on the screen using different arrangements and activation procedures. The icons could be presented one at a time for scanning, and the student could activate a choice when a desired icon appeared; or two, four, or more choices (up to 20) could be presented on the screen at one time, and a direct selection or scanning procedure could be used to allow the student to select the desired icon. Under some icons, once the student made an initial selection, a submenu of additional related icons appeared. For students with visual disabilities, audio scanning could be used with the computer verbalizing the icon being presented.

A variety of input devices were possible. Besides the standard keyboard and mouse, switches or other commercial devices could be used, including trackballs, touch tablets, and joysticks, and special devices such as button switches, wobble switches, sensor switchers, and puff-and-sip switches. Color-coded plastic keyboard overlays were also used. Most output was done using audible output. For example, if the student selected a water glass icon, the output might be "Could I have a glass of water please."

Communication needs had to be determined. Baseline communication abilities and potential needs were determined through conversations with teachers and parents. These persons and others, including teacher aides, occupational and physical therapists, and speech–language pathologists, provided input that was useful for designing individual systems. Typical communication needs included initiating communication, greeting peers, indicating a need for assistance, indicating distress, or responding to questions. Other information was equally important. "The various therapists provided important information on the student's potential physical limitations in operating or transporting equipment, range of motion, visual and aural impairments, and strategies for instruction. Parents added to the list of receptive and expressive vocabulary and suggested additional communication needs at home" (Carey & Sale, 1994, p. 63). Additional information was gleaned from students' school records. Following this input, the researchers evaluated the students with regard to their ability to use different input and output devices, which led to an optimal starting point for each student. This starting point consisted of adding new vocabulary to what students already knew, placing the input device in the most accessible and operable location (considering possible visual and motor limitations, range of motion, strength) and then adjusting its sensitivity.

Carey and Sale (1994) offered numerous other insights and caveats. Students' visual acuity, field of vision, and range of motion dictated placement of equipment, including the computer screen, keyboard, mouse, switch, or other device. Placement of the equipment around the student had to take into account potential *technology isolation.* That is, the student may be so surrounded by equipment intended to facilitate inclusion that he becomes more isolated than included. They recommended placing devices so that nondisabled peers could use them to interact with the person with severe disabilities. Some students may express themselves by knocking everything off their wheelchair tray or table top. Care had be taken to secure equipment that might be subjected to this type of responding. Switch sites that placed switches on students' bodies had to be eliminated because inadvertent switch activation was caused by seizures, flexions, and extensions. Parents were essential for providing useful information on their children's history, habits, likes and dislikes, communication needs, health problems, aptitudes, and personalities. Parents also "often provided the encouragement we needed to find more options and alternatives when we were at a loss for how to proceed" (Carey & Sale, 1994, p.69).

Davies et al. (2002) described a unique AT device designed to increase the independence of persons with cognitive disabilities in community settings and demonstrated its effectives through an empirical study. The device, referred to as a Visual Assistant, was described by the authors as follows:

> Visual Assistant is a multimedia training program designed to run on the Windows CE platform that allows a special needs user to view step-by-step pictures along with audio instructions on the computer at his or her own pace. Audio instructions and digital pictures can be created to customize the system to provide self-directed training on a wide variety of tasks. Tasks are task analyzed according to the specific training and support needs of each individual user. Individual pictures and audio instructions are then integrated into the task for each discrete step in the task. Each task can be represented on the palmtop computer screen with an icon that users press to initiate task instructions. After a task is selected, the picture for the first step is displayed and the last audio instruction is played. The user then presses a "done" button after they complete the step. This then loads the next step picture and the user presses a "play" button to hear the associated audio instruction. (pp. 212–213)

Davies et al. (2002) tested their device with 10 adults with cognitive disabilities whose measured IQs were between 39 and 72. They had these persons complete two similar tasks, one when using the palmtop personal assistance device and one without. Using the device resulted in significantly fewer errors and required less prompts from the supervisor of the individuals.

Finally, two brief case reports demonstrate the power of AT for individuals with severe disabilities (Lode, 1992; Cavalier & Brown, 1998). Carol Lode (Lode, 1992) described the different ways AT devices assisted her daughter Sierra from when she was 3 years old until she was 9. Her story demonstrates the power of AT and the effect it can have on a parent's outlook for a child. But she also notes that it was not an easy journey.

Sierra had severe cerebral palsy and was quadriplegic and nonverbal. Early estimates of Sierra's cognitive abilities were quite pessimistic, but Sierra's parents were not sure of their validity. At 3 years of age, Sierra was taught to use a cheek switch to activate battery-operated toys. She quickly demonstrated that she had the concept of "cause and effect," but became bored with the activity, so it was suggested that she move on to a light scanning board that could be controlled by the cheek switch. Since Sierra loved dolls, doll clothing and doll activities were cut out and placed on squares of the scanning board, and Sierra learned "lickety-split" to choose the outfit or activity for the doll. Her mother wrote, "We were all ecstatic, and the feedback from her play partners was great."

From this activity, Sierra learned to use an electronic augmentative communication device with icons that could be selected to activate a child's voice output. According to her mother, "Within a month, Sierra was having great success with it. It was unbelievable; if I had even a tad of lingering doubts about Sierra's cognitive abilities, they were now completely gone." But Sierra's AT-aided progress did not stop. She learned to operate a battery-powered wheelchair and ultimately was finding her way all over her school and the playground. An Apple IIGS computer was acquired with a peripheral device that allowed an alternative way to access the keyboard. Her electronic speech device was interfaced with the computer and she learned to use her preprogrammed vocabulary to develop stories and add graphics to them. She acquired numerous software programs and learned to activate and enjoy them using her single-switch device. At the end of 3 years of preschool, Sierra was placed in a regular kindergarten program where she was deemed to be "academically and socially competitive with her peers." As she progressed in years, she progressed in her academic skills, learning reading, spelling, and math skills. But as her mother explained, her progress socially was just as important: "Equally rewarding were the friendships that evolved during that year. Sierra's relationship with seven wonderful little girls formed a tight bond of 'kindred spirits.' Within this circle of friend, Sierra's disabilities disappear and she is just 'Sierra.' She has all their names on her keyboard and they have elected her president of their 'Girls Club.' "

Sierra's progress in school continued largely due to the access gained to academic and social opportunities afforded by AT devices. But her mother also noted that their were many problems. "There were many pot holes along the way, the biggest of which was funding. Other problems were time, energy, frustration, impatience, lack of technical support, lack of moral support, glitches, crashes, maintenance and repair to name a few." But she concluded, 'I can say unequivocally that it was all worth it' " (Lode, 1992).

Finally, in a most intriguing case study, Cavalier and Brown (1998) told the story of Sue, a woman with profound mental retardation and severe cerebral palsy who learned how to use her limited verbal ability to control her environment. Sue was a 42-year-old woman who lived in a residential institution. She was nonambulatory and had severe cerebral palsy; her records reported a measured IQ of 19. Sue had very few skills, but could make several distinct vocalizations that approximated the words "for," "move," "ray," and "be." (The researchers also taught her to verbalize a sound close to "off."). Cavalier and Brown (1998) wanted to develop an assistive technology system that would give Sue some degree of choice making and the ability to manipulate her environment at will in order to increase her independence. To do this, they decided to use a microcomputer equipped with speech-recognition capabilities connected to an environmental control unit. (Speech-recognition software allows a computer to operate from human speech, just as it responds to a keyboard or a mouse. Environmental control technology allows the computer to control electrical appliances to which it is connected.) Cavalier and Brown wanted to answer several questions: Could Sue learn to vocalize with sufficient consistency for her voice to be recognized? Could she learn the connection between her vocalizing and causing a specific device to be activated? Could she learn that different vocalizations differentially affected different devices? If she learned to activate a device, could she learn the concept of deactivation? If she became a more active person in controlling her environment, would she show different emotions?

Using the "words" Sue could express, the researchers connected them to four appliances that they determined through interviews produced effects that Sue found pleasurable. These included videotapes of pages of her favorite stories being read allowed, a vibrating massage pad on which she could lay, a favorite radio station, and a videotape of telegrams from her family. Here is their report of the first day of the experiment:

> Sue was in a large activity room, positioned on a rolling gurney wheelchair with a TV monitor within easy view above her. Before this research, she vocalized none of the five sounds with great frequency. On the first day that "for" and the videotaped storybooks were linked, the clinical staff were tense with anticipation. Sue did not disappoint them. Over the course of the afternoon, the first few times that she emitted a "for" type of vocalization and the storybooks turned on above her, she appeared to be mildly entertained. Nothing about her demeanor or responding, however, indicated that she thought that she had anything to do with their activation. One time, however, she said the word and then glanced directly at the monitor. When the storybooks appeared, she suddenly erupted into shrieks of joy and animated squeals. She frantically struggled to twist her body onto its side to wave to others around her, with her eyes darting back and forth between them and the monitor, as if to beckon them to see what she had done. This celebration continued for a considerable length of time. (Cavalier and Brown, 1998, p. 62)

As the experiment continued, the researchers systematically linked Sue's vocalization with the other favored outcomes and also taught her to say "off" to terminate a device. Sue learned that she could decide what she wanted to see and activate or deactivate a device using the words that she could say. After all the cause-effect conditions were learned, Sue could be seen distributing her time of engagement with the visual activities somewhat equally over a period of time just as anyone else might do.

But learning to control her choices of leisure viewing was only one result of the study. Cavalier and Brown (1998) reported that the residential staff started to react to Sue's new abilities and resultant emotions in an unpredictable manner: they wanted her to acquire greater control over other aspects of her environment. They suggested that she be taught to choose when she would like to have visitors in her room and how she would like to participate in the kitchen. They also proposed that the system be developed to allow Sue to talk so that she could "choose what she wants to say." The researchers reported that the relatively minor changes in what Sue could do had a profound impact on those around her.

> These requests (of the residential staff) seem to imply a major shift in their attitudes about Sue's capability of doing things for herself and even about her right to be a part of the life around her. Largely as a result of these changes, Sue has now moved to a less restrictive environment, a group home, near her family in West Texas, where she is actively involved in family and community activities on a daily basis. (Cavalier and Brown, 1998, p. 62)

Sue's story, as reported by Cavalier and Brown (1998), and other documented cases of success clearly indicate the value of AT devices and services. Not only can individuals acquire communication skills and other functional abilities, but they can also gain a sense of independence and greater control over their lives. What is more important, those around them can begin to appreciate that they are capable individuals.

Limitations of AT Devices and Services and Needed Directions

The current power of assistive technology is apparent, and there is certainly a great deal of potential for its advancement. It can help to achieve many of the values-based outcomes that we have discussed throughout this text. But it is important to realize that numerous challenges and barriers are associated with the use of AT, and these must be resolved at an individual and societal level if we are to be as successful in using AT devices as is possible. Most of these have been discussed throughout the chapter. The major issues are highlighted here in a summative fashion.

Funding

Although IDEA '97 entitles students with disabilities to be considered for use of AT devices and services and gives them the right to such if necessary for them to have a "free and appropriate education," the cost of some items can be extremely high. When this is the case, school systems that are almost constantly short of funding will try to avoid purchasing equipment. If they do acquire the equipment, they will not always allow it to be taken home where it can be used in natural contexts.

Therefore, parents will often need to find a way to finance AT devices themselves. They may look to government funding sources such as Medicaid, private insurance, or charitable organizations to help them to find the money they need. This takes a great deal of time and effort and can be demoralizing and frustrating. Some parents are likely to give up their search for assistance, which means that their child may not make as much progress as possible.

School districts and human service agencies may not be able to provide all the funds that are needed, but they can serve an important service to families if they make information about funding sources readily available and comprehensible. With support of this nature, parents may be much more likely to be successful in finding the resources provide their child with the needed equipment.

Teamwork, Family, and Cultural Understanding

No one has such an extensive knowledge of assistive technology that they can prescribe and implement the use of any AT device available, not experts, not teachers, and certainly not parents. While all professionals should learn as much as possible about the various AT devices, especially those that may benefit their students, there will always be gaps in their knowledge. The best way to deal with individual shortcomings is to work as part of a team. Although we have stressed this need earlier and throughout this book, we feel it is especially critical in the field of assistive technology.

An essential part of the teamwork is that which can be offered by family members. Perhaps unlike any other aspect of education for students with severe disabilities, acquiring the thoughts and ideas of parents and other family members is critical when attempting to use assistive technology devices. Most AT devices are of greatest value in the home and community, and this makes it essential that professionals understand how devices will affect families and the cultural milieu of the student.

Adequate Assessment and Related Services

While investing in devices per se is important, devices without services will not be sufficient. First, extensive effort must be made to make sure that a device is usable and functional for the student. The device must help the student to achieve goals and objectives, but, to do so, a good fit must exist between the student's skills and abilities and those required to operate the device.

Since the student will be using the device, there is a clear need to invest adequate time in teaching the student how to use it. But there is also often a need for key individuals to learn how to operate, maintain, and repair the device. AT services call for a training program for these individuals so that they can provide support, assistance, and interaction with the student as needed.

Like all human-made material, AT devices break down. This is to be expected. But part of the AT services call for readily available repairs. Unfortunately, many times a nonfunctioning AT device means the end of AT support. Thus the gains made by the student will be lost and additional gains will not be made. Therefore, it is critical that plans be made for what to do when the device breaks, is outgrown, or cannot be used for any other reason.

Personnel Training and Support

Although we hope this chapter has served as an introduction and overview of the potential of AT devices and service, no chapter or book can provide all the information that a teacher may need to be facile with the use of AT devices. Several studies have shown that many special education teachers are not skilled in the use of different devices and, what is worse, do not have an interest in acquiring information or helping their students to use AT devices.

This should not be an option. Teachers of students with severe disabilities should take at least one course in assistive technology and should continue their education through readings, searching the Internet, and attending workshops and staff development sessions. Even though there are many limits and flaws in many current devices, the overall power of devices to positively influence the lives of students with severe disabilities requires that teachers gain necessary knowledge and develop positive attitudes about its use.

Continuity and Context

Finally, AT devices and services should not be considered as isolated aspect of educational services, but must be prescribed for use in the context of important goals and objectives for students. In this vein, devices and services should not be hit and miss, but should be built into the educational plan with an eye toward long-term use and outcomes.

One of the most important implications is that, during transitions from one grade level to the next, one school to the next, or one agency to the next, careful planning should occur regarding current AT devices and services and how they will be extended, modified, or changed for the future setting. Once success has begun to be achieved, there should be a plan and an expectation that it will continue.

Conclusion

The development of assistive technology devices has accelerated in recent years and undoubtedly new devices will continue to appear. These devices, along with the services necessary to have them be used successfully, hold promise for a better quality of life for many persons with severe disabilities. It is a bit disheartening to note, however, that available devices are not being used to the extent possible. Hopefully parents, professionals, and administrators will note this shortcoming and work to remedy it. As reported in this chapter, there are some very good sites on the Internet where available devices can be found and their benefits can be explained.

Certainly funding is an issue. Even though laws say the devices and services should be available, in poor economic times needs are often not met. Still, there are many alternatives for funding, and these alternatives should be explored by local personnel and agencies desiring to provide devices and services to individuals with disabilities.

Case studies indicate that many persons with severe cognitive disabilities have the potential to achieve more if they are provided with appropriate devices. Certainly the key word here is *appropriate:* there must be a good fit between the device, the student's needs, and the student's abilities. Additionally, consideration must be give to the environments in which the devices will be used and the people in those environments, including family members, teachers, and other school personnel, and members of the community. Of course the provision of support services, both for the student and for key persons in his or her environments, is critical.

The benefits of various assistive devices and services is only beginning to be recognized. It is likely that sooner, rather than later, these benefits will become more commonplace.

Questions for Reflection

1. List some of the common AT devices presented in this chapter and conduct a review of them using abledata.com.
2. Explain the type of assessments that should be conducted before implementing the use of an AT device.
3. What factors tend to be associated with the successful use of AT devices?
4. Why is it important to consider family and cultural issues related to the use of AT devices?
5. Evaluate the Web sites provided in this chapter and others as sources of information about AT devices.
6. What are the major problems associated with the use of AT devices?

References

Carey, D. M., & Sale, P. (1994). Notebook computers increase communication. *Teaching Exceptional Children, 27*(1), 62–69.

Cavalier, A. R., & Brown, C. C. (1998). From passivity to participation: The transformational possibilities of speech-recognition technology. *Teaching Exceptional Children, 30* (6), 60–65.

Daniels, L. E. Sparling, J. W., Reilly, M., & Humphry, R. (1995). Use of assistive technology with young children with severe and profound disabilities. *Infant–Toddler Intervention, 5*, 91–112.

Davies, D. K., Stock, S. E., & Wehmeyer, M. L. (2002). Enhancing independent task performance for individuals with mental retardation through use of a handheld self-directed visual and audio prompting system. *Education and Training in Mental Retardation and Developmental Disabilities, 37*, 209–218.

Derer, K., Polsgrove, L., & Rieth, H. (1996). A survey of assistive technology applications in schools and recommendations for practice. *Journal of Special Education Technology, 13*(2), 62–80.

Hutinger, P., Johanson, J., & Stoneburner, R. (1996). Assistive technology applications in educational programs of children with multiple disabilities: A case study report on the state of the practice. *Journal of Special Education Technology, 13*(1), 16–35.

Kemp, C. E., Hourcade, J. J., & Parette, H. P. (2000). Building an initial information base: Assistive technology funding resources for school-aged students with disabilities. *Journal of Special Education Technology, 15*(4), 15–24.

Kemp, C. E., & Parette, H. P. (2000). Barriers to minority family involvement in assistive technology decision-making processes. *Education and Training in Mental Retardation and Developmental Disabilities, 35*, 384–392.

Lode, C. (1992). How technology assists my daughter to compete in the mainstream of life. *Exceptional Parent, 22*(8) 34, 41.

Parette, H. P. (1997). Assistive technology devices and services. *Education and Training in Mental Retardation and Developmental Disabilities, 32*, 267–280.

Parette, H. P., & Brotherson, M. J. (1996). Family participation in assistive technology assessment for young children with mental retardation and developmental disabilities. *Education and Training in Mental Retardation and Developmental Disabilities, 31*, 29–43.

Parette, H. P., & Hourcade, J. J. (1997). Family issues and assistive technology needs: A sampling of state practices. *Journal of Special Education Technology, 13*(3), 27–43.

Parette, H. P., Hourcade, J. J., & VanBiervliet, A. (1993). Selection of appropriate technology for children with disabilities. *Teaching Exceptional Children, 25*(3), 18–22.

Parette, P., VanBiervliet, A., & Hourcade, J. J. (2000). Family-centered decision making in assistive technology. *Journal of Special Education Technology, 15*(1), 45–55.

Reed, P., & Best, S. (2001). Assessment for assistive technology. In J. L. Bigge, S. J. Best, & K. W. Heller (Eds.), *Teaching individuals with physical, health, or multiple disabilities* (4th Ed., pp. 149–194). Upper Saddle River, New Jersey: Merrill/Prentice Hall.

Sigafoos, J., & Iacono, T. (1993). Selecting augmentative communication devices for persons with severe disabilities: Some factors for educational teams to consider. *Australia and New Zealand Journal of Developmental Disabilities, 18*(3), 133–146.

Todis, B. (1996). Tools for the task? Perspectives on assistive technology in educational settings. *Journal of Special Education Technology, 13(*2), 49–61.

Wehmeyer, M. L. (1998). National survey on the use of assistive technology by adults with mental retardation. *Mental Retardation, 36*, 44–51.

Wehmeyer, M. L. (1999). Assistive technology and students with mental retardation: Utilization and barriers. *Journal of Special Education Technology, 14*(1), 48–58.

CHAPTER 20

Meeting the Needs of Young Children

This chapter describes practices in early childhood special education and procedures that may be used to meet the unique needs of infants, toddlers, and preschoolers and their families. The chapter includes information on assessment practices, developing individualized family support plans, service delivery arrangements, instructional strategies, and supporting the transitions of young children and their families.

Special Education Programs and the Law

The Individuals with Disabilities Education Act Amendments of 1997 (IDEA, 1997; P.L. 105-17) provides early intervention programs to young children with special needs and their families. In 1986, Public Law 99-457, an amendment to P.L. 94-142, extended all of the rights and protections of P.L. 94-142 to 3- to 5-year-old children with disabilities and created a discretionary program to assist states in developing early intervention programs for families and their children who are at risk or disabled from birth up to age 3 years.

Section 619 of IDEA provides assistance to states to provide special education and related services to children with disabilities aged 3 through 5. Children are eligible for services if they have diagnoses of mental retardation, hearing impairments, speech or language impairments, visual impairments, severe emotional disturbance, orthopedic impairments, autism, traumatic brain injury, other health impairments, or specific learning disabilities. In addition, children aged 3 through 9 are eligible for services (at the discretion of the state and local educational agency) if they have been identified as experiencing developmental delays in one or more of the following areas: physical development, cognitive development, communication development, social or emotional development, or adaptive development.

Part C of IDEA provides services for infants and toddlers with disabilities or developmental delays or who are at risk for disability. The purpose of early intervention programs is to enhance the development of infants and toddlers and to minimize the need for subsequent special education services as they reach school age. In addition, early intervention services are designed to enhance the capacity of families to meet the special needs of their infant or toddler.

Historical Development

The roots of the field of early childhood special education can be found in the establishment of kindergarten, nursery school, special education, and compensatory education programs (Gargiulo & Kilgo, 2000; Peterson, 1987). The establishment of kindergarten and nursery school programs provided the foundation for the concept that young children may benefit from early education, and the special education movement established the rights of children with disabilities to a public education. But it was the compensatory education program that introduced the concept of early intervention through the establishment of Head Start programs (Bricker, 1989; Peterson, 1987).

Head Start, which began in the late 1960s in the social–political climate of the civil rights movement and the War on Poverty, was established to provide 3- and 4-year-old children who were environmentally at risk with an intervention designed to improve their health and their physical, social, and emotional well-being; improve their mental processes and skills; and establish a climate of expectations that would enhance the child's ability to be successful in school (Bricker, 1989).

Research on the effects of Head Start published as the Westinghouse Study (Cicirelli, Evans, & Schiller, 1969) dampened the enthusiasm for the program by reporting that summer Head Start gains did not persist in the early grades and that full-year programs were more effective in producing lasting cognitive gains. Parents, however, felt that the programs were valuable. Three ideas emerged from the Westinghouse Study analysis that have had an impact on the design of current early intervention efforts. These concepts are that interventions must begin earlier and last longer if they are going to be effective, that intervention should not stop abruptly when the child enters public school, and that support of families should be an area of focus for early intervention programs. Later research documented that a "sleeper effect" could be detected in the later elementary grades in which Head Start graduates showed superior academic achievement in comparison to a control group (Zigler & Yale Research Group, 1976).

The expansion of early intervention programs to include children with disabilities was initiated to improve the outcomes of individuals who could be considered disadvantaged and might later become a burden to society. Parallel to societal concern about the future of disadvantaged children was the civil rights movement, which focused on the provision of equal opportunity to all. The civil rights approach to providing services may be a stronger factor in accounting for the expansion of services to young children with severe disabilities, rather than the cost–benefit perspective (Westlake & Kaiser, 1991). Young children with severe disabilities are not likely to have their needs for continued support ameliorated through early intervention. The goals of early intervention programs were to maximize the child's developmental outcomes, prevent the establishment of secondary disabilities, provide support to families, and diminish the costs of institutionalization and other services needed if early intervention had not been provided (Bricker, 1989).

Efficacy Research

Research on the efficacy of early intervention programs for children with severe disabilities is difficult to interpret given the methodological flaws of the majority of studies (Dunst & Rheingrover, 1981). In addition, much of the research on early intervention is also conceptually flawed (Dunst, 1986). In the majority of studies, early intervention is defined globally as an independent variable, and developmental outcome (measured by changes in developmental or intellectual quotient) is used as the primary dependent measure. This approach is problematic in that early intervention is not a well-defined construct and can be comprised of varying levels of support and services. The use of developmental changes in the child as the primary dependent variable neglects to consider the effects of early intervention programs on the family. Dunst (1986) states that early intervention should be conceptualized as "an aggregation of the many types of help, assistance, and services" (p. 122) and suggests that researchers move from the question of "Does early intervention work?" to "What dimensions of early intervention are related to different outcome measures?" (p. 124). This approach to evaluating the efficacy of early intervention programs is based on an ecological or social systems view. From this perspective, early intervention programs are viewed as comprising a broad array of supports and services that may affect both the child and the family in a variety of ways. A social systems view of early intervention programs looks beyond the goal of changing a child's developmental status to assisting families in developing the resources and skills that they need to support their child's development and participation in normalized life experiences. Bailey et al. (1998) proposed that early intervention programs examine the following questions when addressing program evaluation and efficacy:

1. Does the family see early intervention as appropriate in making a difference in their child's life? In their family's life?
2. Does the family have a positive view of professionals and special service system?
3. Did early intervention enable the family to help their child to grow, learn, and develop?
4. Did early intervention enhance the family's perceived ability to work with professionals and advocate for services?
5. Did early intervention assist the family in building a stronger support system?
6. Did early intervention help to enhance an optimistic view of the future?
7. Did early intervention enhance the family's perceived quality of life?

Goals of Early Childhood Special Education Programs

Bailey and Wolery (1992) have described seven broad goals for early childhood special education programs:

1. To support families in achieving their own goals
2. To promote child engagement, independence, and mastery
3. To promote development in key domains (e.g.,motor, cognition, communication, daily living, and social)
4. To build and support children's social competence
5. To promote the generalized use of skills
6. To provide and prepare for normalized life experiences
7. To prevent the emergence of future problems or disabilities

These goals do not appear to be unique to young children with disabilities; we could say that they apply to all students with severe disabilities. Early intervention programs are unique because the population of concern is very young, which has a significant impact on how interventions are structured. Bailey (1989) presented an analysis of the differences between intervention programs that are designed for infants and toddlers, for preschoolers, and for elementary-school-age children with disabilities. This is shown in Table 20–1.

This chapter presents issues concerning the characteristics of young children, the family-centered approach of early childhood special education, and the design of intervention programs for young children. Within each of these areas of concern, strategies for providing appropriate programs to young children with severe disabilities are presented.

Teaching Young Children

A distinguishing feature of early intervention and preschool programs is that they typically serve a diverse group of children and families. Under IDEA, services

Table 20–1 A Comparison of Interventions with Infants, Preschoolers, and Elementary-Age Children with Special Needs

Domain	*Infants and Toddlers (0–36 months)*	*Preschoolers (36–60 months)*	*Elementary (5–12 years)*
I. Characteristics of children			
Population parameters	Noncategorical; developmentally delayed, conditions that typically result in delay, at risk of substantial delay; results in wide range of ability levels and types of handicaps	Noncategorical; wide range of ability levels and handicaps (some states, however, will choose categorical descriptions)	Categorical; more restricted range of ability levels and disability types; formal eligibility criteria
Goals for intervention	Behavior and motor organization, differentiated responses to environmental cues, cause and effect, early communication and social skills, attachment	Cognitive, self-help, social, fine motor, communication, behavior, toy play, gross motor	Reading, spelling, mathematics, appropriate social behavior
Schedule regularity	Low; almost entirely determined by infant	Moderate; some adult determination of schedules, but requires flexibility depending on children's needs and interest	High; preset routine and time allocation for tasks; very little in the way of child-initiated activities.
Endurance	Short; interactions typically last less than 2–3 minutes	Moderate; interactions may last 5–15 minutes	Long; interactions may last 30 minutes to 2 hours
Motivation	Must come from inherent appeal of material or activity; based on infant's interest	Begin to follow adult expectations, but high-interest toys and activities are critical	Based on adult expectations for compliance; reliance on self-regulation and response to rules
II. The intervention context			
Context of teaching	Parent–child interaction; feeding, bathing, diapering, and dressing routines; object play	Object play, peer interactions, adult–child interactions, routines	Classroom instruction, written materials
Sites for intervention and services	Homes, day care centers, family day homes, specialized developmental centers, developmental evaluation centers, hospital settings (NICU, pediatrics ward)	Specialized developmental centers and classrooms, day care centers, homes, developmental evaluation centers, hospital settings	Elementary schools (regular classroom, resource room, self-contained classroom)
Responsible agencies	Mental health centers, hospital public health services, private day care, specialized nonprofit agencies, public school	Public school, mental health, Head Start, day care	Public school
Team functioning	Often involves multiple professionals from multiple agencies; considerable role overlap, requiring extensive communication and coordination	Moderate blending of roles, but work in isolation is possible	Differentiated and specific roles, isolation likely
III. Family role			
Mandated family role	Essential and family-focused; IFSP requires documentation of family needs and strengths, a statement of family goals, and the provision of family services, including case management	Very important; IEP provisions pertain, all parents' rights protected, and parent training encouraged when necessary	Important; IEP provisions pertain, all parents' rights protected

Source: "Issues and Directions in Preparing Professionals to Work with Young Handicapped Children and Their Families," by D. B. Bailey, 1989, in J. J. Gallagher, R. M. Clifford, and P. Trohanis (Eds.), *Policy Implementation and P. L. 99–457: Planning for Young Children with Special Needs* (pp. 101–102), Baltimore: Paul H. Brookes Publishing Co. Reprinted by permission.

may be provided to children under a developmental delay category until age 9, and the early intervention program provided through Part C allows states to provide services to children who are determined to be at risk of substantial developmental delay. This flexibility allows for a noncategorical approach to service delivery. Young children with severe disabilities and their families are usually served by programs for children and families with a variety of needs.

The age of the population being served by early intervention programs has a profound impact on the nature of services that are provided. In the early childhood stage of development, young children move from the infancy stage of exhibiting behavior that is restricted, uncoordinated, and primarily reflexive to independently responding to environmental demands as preschoolers. Developmental changes occur in the context of the social environment (Lewis, 1984). Infants learn through interactions with caregivers and the environment that they can act on the world. Developmental changes in cognitive, sensory, and motor development allow them to interact with the environment in increasingly sophisticated ways.

Transactional Approach

Young children with severe disabilities do not spontaneously exhibit the rapid developmental growth that is seen with typically developing children. Thus the focus of early intervention is to promote development within the context of interactions with caregivers and the environment (Wolery, 2000). A transactional perspective (Sameroff & Chandler, 1975) offers a way to approach early intervention that is based on the theory that the individual and the environment are interdependent and constantly interacting. Interventions based on a transactional perspective are not concerned only with the attainment of developmental skills; they also view the achievement of developmental milestones in the broader context of the behavior, beliefs, and values of all the players in the system (Sameroff & Fiese, 1990). This is a somewhat different approach from the educational model applied for school-age children. In programs for school-age children, educators bring the student to school and teach skills in the context of interactions with peers and the community. In programs for young children, interventionists design ways to support the development of the child in the context of interactions with the caregiver and the environment.

Instructional Activities

The capacity of young children for direct intervention also has an influence on the design of early intervention programs. In programs for students who are school age, an effort is made to maintain a high level of active engagement in instruction in an instructional day that can last from 5 to 7 hours. Although active engagement is a goal of early intervention, young children, especially young children who may have medical concerns or multiple disabilities, have very low thresholds for continual engagement. Activities that are designed for young children must be brief and based on the child's interest. As a consequence, the early interventionist must be able to embed instruction in playful or child-motivating activities that can be applied throughout the day by a variety of caregivers. Young children have little to gain from intensive, didactic training sessions scheduled by the adult. Instruction must occur when the child is ready and last only as long as the child can tolerate.

Instructional Content

The nature of what is taught to young children is different from what is taught to older individuals with severe disabilities. Instructional goals are more likely to contain very early developmental skills. The focus of infant intervention may be to teach an infant to mediate his behavior states, basic motor movements, and contingent responsiveness. These goals are taught in reciprocal exchanges that are meaningful to the infant. The goals for young children are developmentally based, although an emphasis is placed on teaching the skills in meaningful routines in the same way that we teach older individuals with severe disabilities. A functional curriculum is also a concern of early interventionists. Instructional goals developed for young children should center around the types of skills that are functional in a variety of environments and that lead to greater independence. Skill instruction occurs in routine and meaningful activities, rather than in isolated, situation-specific contexts.

Family Support

In addition to providing intervention to young children, the early interventionist is concerned with providing support to families. The expressed focus on supporting families is different from the traditional role that educators have assumed for school-age children. In IDEA, the involvement of families in the development of an IEP is clearly specified for 3- to 5-year-olds and in the development of the IFSP for birth to 2-year-olds. This approach to family involvement goes beyond teaching parents techniques to facilitate the development of the child. It is broadly aimed at providing positive support to caregivers and family members as the critical context for the child's development (Kaiser & Hemmeter, 1989). In a family-centered approach to early intervention, the family's needs and desires determine the provision of resources and services (Dunst, Johanson, Trivette, & Hamby; 1991; Trivette & Dunst, 2000; McWilliam et al. 1998). Early interventionists work as the agent of the family to strengthen the family's capacity to provide for the child.

Family-Centered Approach

The term *family-centered* describes an approach to early intervention that is consumer driven and focused on enhancing the competencies of families to support the development of their children (Bailey et al., 1998; Dunst et al., 1991). In early intervention there has been an evolution of ways to consider families and their roles in the early intervention program (Bricker, 1989). The first stage, professionally controlled, did not consider the family at all in the evaluation of the child or in the design and implementation of the intervention program. In the second stage, family involvement, families were recognized as important to the child's progress, and interventionists made an effort to include them in the IEP process and requested that parents carry out treatment plans in the home. In the third stage, family focused, early interventionists regarded understanding the family as fundamental to the focused approach, the assessment of family needs as they relate to the child were a concern, and IFSP or IEP goals were mutually selected by the family and professionals (Dunst et al., 1991).

The family-centered approach is markedly different from the earlier ways that professionals viewed families. In a family-centered approach, family needs and desires determine what services are provided. The goal of early intervention is to provide the resources and supports that strengthen the family's capacity to meet their needs (Dunst et al., 1991; Trivette & Dunst, 2000). The words *empowerment* and *enablement* reflect the spirit of the family-centered approach (McGonigel, 1991). In early intervention, empowerment means that families are supported in a way that results in a feeling that they are in control and that positive changes that occur are the result of their strengths and abilities (Dunst, Trivette, & Deal, 1988). Enablement is used to describe the process of finding ways for families to use their competencies or to acquire new competencies to meet their needs (Dunst et al., 1988).

A family-centered approach is important for several reasons (Bricker, 1989). First, the family spends more time with the child than the early interventionist. Any intervention that is delivered is far more powerful if the family is involved, and interventions designed in response to a family-identified need are far more likely to be carried out at home. Second, it is economically more sound to empower the family to find ways to coordinate resources to meet their unique needs than for one agency to try to coordinate and deliver all the services. Third, families have a legal right to be participants in the design of interventions for their child. Embracing a family-centered approach means that parents will be fully informed and integrally involved in their child's program. Finally, the design of an early intervention program will be far more relevant and appropriate if it is done with an understanding of and respect for the family who is involved.

The adoption of a family-centered approach requires the early interventionist to use a social-systems perspective of the family and understand that the family is a social unit embedded in other social networks (Dunst et al., 1988). The ability of a family to fulfill their role in supporting their child's development involves far more than their relationships with their child or the information that they have about the child; it is contingent on the family's role demands, stresses, and supports from other units in their social system (Brofenbrenner, 1975). Thus, the adoption of a family-centered approach broadens the focus of early intervention from the child to the family. The emphasis of the focus on the family is not to find problems in the family system, but to assist families in identifying their strengths, needs, and sources of support and in the achievement of the resources that they desire (Dunst et al., 1988).

Inherent in a family-centered approach are new roles for professionals. The early interventionist must be willing to move beyond the traditional role of working only with the child and be able to become a consultant, resource, enabler, mobilizer, mediator, and advocate for the family. Most important, the early interventionist must be able to actively and reflectively listen to families, allowing them to guide the intervention. The roles of the early interventionist in a family-centered approach are described in Figure 20–1.

Individualized Family Service Plan

The configuration of services and supports is formalized in the IFSP process. Although the IFSP is similar to an IEP in terms of intervention goals for the infant or toddler, it

Figure 20–1 The Roles of the Early Interventionist in a Family-Centered Approach

Empathetic Listener	The early interventionist must be able to use active and reflective listening in interactions with families.
Teacher/Therapist	The early interventionist must be able to address family and child needs in the design of interventions that will enhance the developmental status of the child and the competence of the family.
Consultant	The early interventionist must be able to provide information and opinions in response to requests made by the family or their social network members.
Resource	The early interventionist must be able to share information about different sources of support and resources with the family.
Enabler	The early interventionist must be able to create opportunities for families to become skilled at obtaining resources and supports they need.
Mobilizer	The early interventionist must be able to link the family with others who can assist in gaining access to needed resources and supports.
Mediator	The early interventionist must be able to mediate the interactions between different agencies and support network members in a manner that promotes cooperation.
Advocate	The early interventionist must be able to provide the family with knowledge of the rights of families and children and how to negotiate with policy makers.

Source: Enabling and Empowering Families: Principles and Guidelines for Practice, by C. J. Dunst, C. M. Trivette, and A. G. Deal, 1988, Cambridge, MA: Brookline Books. Copyright 1988 by Brookline Books, Inc. Reprinted by permission.

differs significantly in the area of family involvement and concerns, as described in Chapter 5.

The process involves far more than the generation of an IFSP. Before an IFSP can be developed, the early intervention professionals and the family must work together to determine the priorities and needs of the family. The principles that underlie the IFSP process have been identified by McGonigel (1991) and are listed in Figure 20–2.

Initial Contact

The IFSP process begins with the initial contact between the family and the early intervention agency. During the initial contact the family should be introduced to the concept of a family-centered approach. This means that a child's developmental status, family's income level, or some other agency criteria does not drive what services are considered for the family. Early intervention services that are allowed under Part C include family training, counseling, and home visits; special instruction; speech pathology and audiology; occupational therapy; physical therapy; psychological services; service coordination services; medical services for the purpose of diagnosis and evaluation; screening and assessment services; health services needed to help the child to benefit from other services; social work services; vision services; assistive technology; and transportation costs. At this stage, the early intervention team should seek to determine family needs and priorities in order to offer services that are family centered. Some families come to an early intervention program with prior experience in working with professionals (e.g., in a hospital setting) and may have a clear vision of what they want; other families may not be aware of the available services. It is important at this stage in the IFSP process to inform families of the services that may be available, but to do so in a way that does not communicate that their needs in other areas are not a concern to the early intervention team.

Planning the Assessment

After the first contact is made, the family and professionals should plan the assessment process. The early inter-

Figure 20–2 Principles Underlying the IFSP Process

- Infants and toddlers are uniquely dependent on their families for their survival and nurturance. This dependence necessitates a family-centered approach to early intervention.
- States and programs should define "family" in a way that reflects the diversity of family patterns and structures.
- Each family has its own structure, roles, values, beliefs, and coping styles. Respect for and acceptance of this diversity is a cornerstone of family-centered early intervention.
- Early intervention systems and strategies must honor the racial, ethnic, cultural, and socioeconomic diversity of families.
- Respect for family autonomy, independence, and decision making means that families must be able to choose the level and nature of early intervention's involvement in their lives.
- Family–professional collaboration and partnerships are the keys to family-centered early intervention and to successful implementation of the IFSP process.
- An enabling approach to working with families requires that professionals reexamine their traditional roles and practices and develop new practices when necessary—practices that promote mutual respect and partnerships.
- Early intervention services should be flexible, accessible, and responsive to family-identified needs.
- Early intervention services should be provided according to the normalization principle; that is, families should have access to services provided in as normal a fashion and environment as possible and that promote the integration of the child and family within the community.
- No one agency or discipline can meet the diverse and complex needs of infants and toddlers with special needs and their families. Therefore, a team approach to planning and implementing the IFSP is necessary.

Source: "Philosophical and Conceptual Framework," by M. J. McGonigel, 1991, in M. J. McGonigel, R. K. Kaufman, and B. H. Johnson (Eds.), *Guidelines and Recommended Practices for the Individualized Family Service Plan* (2nd Ed., p. 9), Bethesda, MD: Association for the Care of Children's Health. Reprinted by permission.

vention team will assess the child, and Part C requires that the child be assessed by a multidisciplinary team composed of persons with training in the appropriate methods and procedures. Another activity to be completed in this stage is identifying family concerns, priorities, and resources. This is an activity that is not familiar to most early interventionists and that should be approached with sensitivity and caution.

Part C of IDEA does not require that family strengths and needs be formally assessed. Families who participate in early intervention programs are not under an obligation to provide information on aspects of their family life that they do not wish to share. Moreover, the identification of family concerns, priorities, and resources should be based on the family's determination of which aspects are relevant to supporting their child's development (Bailey et al., 1998; Kaufmann & McGonigel, 1991; McWilliam et al., 1998).

Formal and informal measures have been used with families to assist them in identifying their concerns, priorities, and resources. Informal measures may be more appropriate in that they can be developed to yield information on both family strengths and needs. The use of more formal measures developed for clinical settings and that have a pathological orientation are not recommended for early intervention. These types of instruments are highly intrusive and may cause families to feel as if they have problems or deficits (Slentz & Bricker, 1992).

Partnering with Families in the Assessment Process

Prior to the development of the IFSP, early intervention professionals conduct a variety of assessments (see discussion in later section of this chapter) to develop an understanding of the child's strengths, abilities, developmental concerns, and intervention needs. This process should be conducted in full partnership with the family (Neisworth & Bagnato, 2000; Woods & McCormick, 2002).

Parents offer unique and critical expertise to the assessment process (Neisworth & Bagnato, 2000). The family is often the sole source of information about the child's longitudinal development. In addition, the family has a perspective about their child's development that is uniquely their own and should be considered independently of other perspectives or evaluations. In addition, family members are the only source of information about the family system, resources, structure, and circumstances. These variables must be considered in the design of early interventions.

Collaboration with families is fostered when early intervention systems are arranged in ways that families can easily access services and understand the process for enrolling in the program and receiving services. Practices that are helpful are offering easy access to screening activities, providing a single point of contact for making arrangements for assessment activities and receiving updates, and providing family information on the values and services of the program in user-friendly formats (e.g., video, brochure). When professionals meet with families to plan the assessment, they should work with the family in determining what assessments will be used, the situations of assessment that will be most appropriate, and the family's desired role in the assessment process. Families should be actively involved in the assessment (e.g., facilitate interactions, present items, conduct observations) if they choose. Prior to the development of assessment reports, the results of the assessment should be discussed with the family as a full, participating member of the collaborative team. Professionals can promote the family's sense of membership in the collaborative team by sharing information in respectful and reciprocal ways, providing time for questions and review, responding to family questions with sincerity, and eliminating the use of jargon or acronyms that may be unfamiliar to the family (Woods & McCormick, 2002).

Developing the IFSP

When the assessment activities have been completed, the team should meet with the family and discuss the results. Once the child assessment activities and family concerns and priorities have been identified, the early intervention team, composed of the family, service coordinator, and other relevant program staff, should identify the outcomes desired from the early intervention. This is accomplished by developing the IFSP.

The IFSP should be viewed as a dynamic document that represents an ongoing process. The form of the written IFSP is not as important as the collaboration and interactions that occur in the process, although the IFSP must include some required features, as described in Figure 20–3.

The first step in developing the IFSP is to determine the desired outcomes of the early intervention. Outcome statements are not behavioral objectives. In keeping with

Figure 20–3 Required Components of the Individualized Family Support Plan (IFSP)

1. Statement of the infant's or toddler's present levels of physical development, cognitive development, communication development, social or emotional development, and adaptive development.
2. Statement of family's resources, priorities, and concerns relating to enhancing the development of the child.
3. Statement of the major outcomes expected to be achieved for the infant or toddler and the family and the evaluation criteria, procedures, and time lines.
4. Statement of the early intervention services necessary to meet the needs of the infant or toddler and the family including the frequency, intensity, and method for delivering the services.
5. Statement of the natural environments in which early intervention services shall be provided and a justification for services (if any) that will not be in a natural environment.
6. The projected dates for the initiation of services and the anticipated duration.
7. The identification of the service coordinator who will be responsible for the implementation of the plan and coordination with other agencies and persons.
8. The steps to be taken to support the transition of the toddler with a disability to preschool or other services.

Source: Individuals with Disabilities Education Act Amendments of 1997. Individuals with Disabilities Education Act Amendments of 1997 (IDEA) (1997), 20 U.S.C. 1400 et seq.

the family-centered approach, outcome statements should come from the family, be written in the family's language (Kramer, McGonigel, & Kaufman, 1991), and should list the changes the family wants for themselves and their child.

When outcomes have been identified, the team should examine the resources available from the family, the early intervention program, and the community to contribute to the achievement of the outcomes (Kramer et al., 1991). At this point in the process, knowledge of family strengths and resources is critical. The goal for the professionals on the team is to build on and use family strengths and resources for accomplishing outcomes, rather than to try to provide all the needed resources.

The identification of strategies and activities designed to accomplish outcomes is a natural extension of the discussion of strengths and resources (Kramer et al., 1991). When they have been identified, criteria for the achievement of the outcome and a time line for evaluation are established. It is important to emphasize that this is not the end of the IFSP process. The IFSP should be reviewed and revised as frequently as needed. Early intervention programs must resist the temptation to ritualize the IFSP process or the document or to establish procedures that may inhibit the intended family-centered philosophy of the process.

The Intervention Context

The environments that serve as the context of interventions are very diverse. Professionals may work in the home, community childcare programs, public school early childhood classrooms, developmental centers, and hospitals. Programs designed for infants and toddlers are more likely to deliver services in the home, community, or a hospital. IDEA places emphasis on the delivery of early intervention services in natural environments by requiring documentation of the use of natural environments in the IFSP. Programs for 3- to 5-year-olds often use a classroom approach, bringing the children into a center for instruction.

The role of the professional is different in each of these settings. In home-based programs, the professional works directly with the family and supports them in meeting their needs and the developmental needs of their child. In center-based programs, the professional must coordinate instruction of a small group of children for an extended period of time and, in addition, must also find a way to maintain a family focus and support the family in meeting their needs, although they may not be involved in the program on a daily basis. A combination of center- and home-based approaches is helpful in providing an intensity of services to the child and maintaining the involvement of the family (Bricker, 1989). The role of the professional is also different when she provides services in a hospital or community childcare program, where the primary caregivers are typically not the early interventionists. In these settings, the early interventionist functions as a consulting team member, designing interventions collaboratively and providing caregivers with the support and skills that they need to support the child's development.

Natural Learning Opportunities

There has been growing interest among researchers about how to define and optimize the use of natural environments in the early intervention for young children with disabilities (Dunst, Hamby, Trivette, Raab, & Bruder, 2000; Dunst, 2001). An implicit value in early childhood special education is that early intervention should be conducted within the ecology of the child and in consideration of the child's interactions with others in the natural environment (Sandall, McLean, & Smith, 2000). This value is reflected in a policy mandate to implement early intervention services for children in birth to 3 programs in the "natural environment." These values have encouraged researchers to examine what learning opportunities occur in natural environments for the purpose of providing guidance to early interventionists.

A national survey was distributed to 3,300 parents and caregivers of young children with or at risk for developmental delays to develop an understanding of the learning opportunities that existed in the course of family and community life (Dunst et al., 2000). Through these surveys, family members and caregivers identified 22 categories of activities that offered natural learning opportunities for their young children, as listed in Figure 20–4.

The categories of activity settings provide a rich description of all the experiences that offer learning opportunities for young children. These natural learning opportunities should be considered as prime learning contexts for the child and regarded as important learning opportunities by the early interventionists. This is not to suggest that the early interventionist's presence is required in these situations, but rather to encourage the early interventionist to broaden his or her perspective about the learning opportunities available to children and families. Early interventionists can work with families to identify the learning opportunities available to their child (by examining and listing family activities within the 22 categories) and to develop an intervention plan to

Figure 20–4 Home, Family, and Community Activities That Are Learning Opportunities

- Family routines (chores, errands)
- Parenting routines (mealtimes, bedtime)
- Child routines (toileting, picking up toys)
- Literacy activities (reading a book, telling stories)
- Physical play (ball, riding bike)
- Play activities (art, games)
- Entertainment activities (dancing, singing)
- Family rituals (prayer, family meetings)
- Family celebrations (holiday dinners, birthday)
- Socialization activities (picnics, play dates)
- Gardening activities (yardwork, planting)
- Family excursions (car rides, errands)
- Family outings (eating out, shopping)
- Play activities (playgrounds, play groups)
- Community activities (festivals, parades)
- Outdoor activities (nature walks, camping)
- Recreational activities (swimming, fishing)
- Children's attractions (zoo, park)
- Art and entertainment activities (children's museum, library)
- Church and religious activities (Sunday school, synagogue)
- Organizations and groups (gymnastics, children's clubs)
- Sports (soccer, baseball)

Source: "Everyday Family and Community Life and Children's Naturally Occurring Learning Opportunities," by C. J. Dunst, D. Hamby, C. M. Trivette et al., 2000, *Journal of Early Intervention, 23.* Adapted by permission.

maximize these opportunities as intervention contexts for the child (Dunst, Bruder, Trivette, Raab, & McLean, 2001). For example, a child in Florida may visit the beach with his family on a regular basis. The child particularly enjoys this experience and is actively engaged in playing in the sand and water. The early interventionist, in partnership with the family, develops strategies that the parent can use to maximize these learning opportunities to support the child's intervention goals. The interventionist examines the activities of the beach (digging in sand, having a picnic, building a castle, picking up shells, splashing in the water) to identify ways that the child's targeted goals can be taught and practiced.

Interagency Collaboration and Teaming

The unique needs of the young child and the varied contexts in which intervention occurs result in a heavy emphasis on collaboration between agencies and professionals. Thus the early interventionist may need to function as a team member on a multiagency team and/or a collaborative team. The goals of a multiagency team may be to assess the needs of families and young children, provide interventions to families and children, assess the array of services available to families and children, and coordinate resources to provide programs. The multiagency team is almost always multidisciplinary and involves the challenges that emerge when professionals from different backgrounds work together. Teaming across agencies also results in the challenges that surface when agencies with different organizational structures, missions, and funding sources attempt to collaborate.

The goals of the collaborative team may be to assess the needs of the child and family, develop and implement an intervention plan for the child and family, evaluate the effectiveness of interventions, and support the child and family during transition. In addition, all of these activities must be carried out in the family-centered framework.

To establish effective teams, the philosophy and principles that underlie the purpose of the team should be a topic of discussion. Key skills needed by professionals on early intervention teams are a family-centered philosophical approach, effective communication skills, and skills related to team process and decision making (Bailey, 1991).

Assessment in Early Intervention

Assessment in early intervention programs is used to (1) screen and identify children who may be in need of services, (2) diagnose the nature and extent of developmental delay, (3) develop a program plan, and (4) evaluate the effectiveness of the intervention program. The assessment practices used by early interventionists must be sensitive to the unique characteristics and needs of very young children and their families. The complex needs and abilities of young children with severe disabilities require assessment practices that use multiple measures, derive information from multiple contexts, and examine multiple developmental domains (Neisworth & Bagnato, 1988).

The Individuals with Disabilities Education Act (IDEA) calls for the development of an IFSP and IEP based on an assessment of children's current level of development and family strengths and needs. The early interventionist is typically involved in assessing the functioning level and individual instructional needs of a child, assessing family needs and strengths, and monitoring the ongoing progress of the families and children served by the early intervention program.

Curriculum-Based Assessment

Curriculum-based assessment measures are used to determine a child's current abilities, derive instructional goals, and track a child's progress along a continuum of objectives. Some curriculum-based assessment measures that may be useful for young children with severe disabilities are the Carolina Curriculum for Infants and Toddlers with Special Needs (Johnson-Martin, Jens, Attermeier, & Hacker, 1991); The Carolina Curriculum for Preschoolers with Special Needs (Johnson-Martin, Attermeier, & Hacker, 1990); Assessment, Evaluation, and Programming System (AEPS) Measurement for Birth to Three Years (Bricker, 1992); Early Intervention Developmental Profile (Schafer & Moersch 1981), and the Hawaii Early Learning Profile (Furono et al., 1979).

Infant Learning: A Cognitive–Linguistic Intervention Strategy (Dunst, 1981) is an assessment and intervention system based on Piagetian theory of cognitive development. The system uses the Uzgiris–Hunt Infant Psychological Development Scale to determine the child's abilities in the sensorimotor period of cognitive development and then provides intervention suggestions based on the child's developmental stage. The scale uses a process approach to assessment that examines changes in the child's reaction to stimulus events to determine his cognitive stage (Neisworth & Bagnato, 1988). This approach is very flexible and allows the interventionist to use toys and situations that the child will find attractive and motivating.

Judgment-Based Assessment

Judgment-based assessments are clinical judgment devices that collect and quantify clinical observations (Neisworth & Bagnato, 1988). Such assessments offer a way to measure qualitative traits and behaviors, such as consolability, temperament, motivation, and self-control, that are important to interventionists, but not often measured by traditional assessment devices. The Carolina Record of Individual Behavior (Simeonsson, Huntington, Short, & Ware, 1982), which measures the behavioral style of young children with severe disabilities, is designed to allow parents and professionals to rate their perceptions of the child's social orientation, frustration, activity, reactivity, object orientation, endurance, and stereotypic behavior.

Interactive Assessment

Interactive assessment examines the social interactions of the caregiver and child. These measures are particularly useful for early interventionists who are providing home-based intervention. Scales that may be used to assess caregiver–child interaction are the Parent Behavior Progression (Bromwich, 1981); the Teaching Skills Inventory (Rosenberg, Robinson, & Beckman, 1984); and the Maternal Behavior Rating Scale (Mahoney, Powell, & Finger, 1986).

Norm-Based Assessment

Norm-based assessments are used to compare a child's developmental skills to a normative group; they describe the child's level of functioning, predict her developmental outcome, and place her in a diagnostic category (Neisworth & Bagnato, 1988). Norm-based scales allow you to compare a child's developmental level to the average child, but they are not helpful in evaluating progress and provide little guidance in determining the instructional program for a child with severe disabilities. Norm-based scales that are frequently used by early interventionists are the Battelle Developmental Inventory (Newborg, Stock, Wnek, Guidubaldi, & Svinicki, 1988) and the Bayley Scales of Infant Development (Bayley, 1969).

Systematic Observation

Early interventionists find that a valuable tool in determining educational goals and evaluating child progress is the use of systematic observation. Although early interventionists deal with very young children and families, an ecological approach to determining intervention targets can be very helpful (Gargiulo & Kilgo, 2000). The procedures are the same as those used in conducting ecological inventories and constructing a functional curriculum for older students. Moreover, the use of systematic observation to track the developmental progress of children is of paramount importance. No other measure is as dynamic and sensitive to behavior change.

Instructional Programs for Young Children

Instructional programs for young children with severe disabilities should consist of systematic instruction embedded in the context of age-appropriate activities, just as we have recommended for the school-age student with severe disabilities. However, for young children the primary activity is play with a caregiver, toys, or peers. Early childhood educators, who have recognized the importance of play in the programs that they design for infants and young children who are typically developing, believe that the primary vehicle for promoting learning is child-initiated, child-directed, teacher-supported play (Hanline & Fox, 1993). The teacher's role is to arrange the environment to encourage play and to support children as they are playing in a way that promotes skill development. The components of best practices in early childhood education programs are described in Bredekamp & Copple (1997).

Developmentally Appropriate Practice

Developmentally appropriate practice (DAP) is defined as providing interventions that are (1) individually appropriate, (2) age appropriate, and (3) based on knowledge of the social and cultural contexts in which children live. Early educators use their knowledge of child development in conjunction with their knowledge of individual children and their culture to plan a curriculum that supports the child's development.

Children should be supported by the adult as they engage in play.

A developmentally appropriate curriculum focuses on all areas of a child's development through an integrated approach. The process of learning is emphasized, rather than the creation of a product. The activities and materials used in the curriculum are concrete and relevant to children's daily lives. The environment is prepared by the teacher to encourage active exploration and interaction with adults, peers, and materials. Teachers facilitate children's learning by asking questions, adding more complex materials, and making suggestions to children as they work with materials or activities. Adults provide children with many opportunities to make choices and time to explore through active involvement. Infants and toddlers are given opportunities to use self-initiated repetition to practice newly acquired skills. Activities for the preschooler include dramatic play materials, wheeled toys, art activities, puzzles, blocks, and simple stories. Worksheets and isolated drill activities are not considered appropriate.

In developmentally appropriate programs, adult–child interactions are characterized by adults responding to children immediately, warmly, and directly. Adults provide varied opportunities for children to participate in two-way communication and respond to children by identifying and elaborating on their feelings, perceptions, interests, and activities. In early childhood special education, the role of the adult is much more intrusive. Young children with severe disabilities often need to be positioned or assisted with movement and to have their communication facilitated or interpreted; they need more intrusive, systematic instructional techniques. The DAP framework is viewed by early educators as a dynamic approach to curriculum development and implementation that accommodates these more intrusive approaches if they are needed by individual children (Bredekamp & Copple, 1997; Kostelnik, 1992).

Activity-Based Instruction

The concept of activity-based instruction can be applied to young children with severe disabilities in the manner discussed (see Chapter 10) for school-age students. Bricker and Cripe (1992) describe an activity-based approach as "a child directed, transactional approach that embeds intervention on children's individual goals and objectives in routine, planned, or child-initiated activities, and uses logically occurring antecedents and consequences to develop functional and generalizable skills" (p. 40). The context for the activity-based approach, which is a play-based environment, is the same as that used for typically developing young children (Davis, Kilgo, & Gamel-McCormick, 1998; Hanline & Fox, 1993).

The adoption of an activity-based approach to instruction means that instruction will be delivered from a normalized perspective by providing the same activities to children with disabilities that are provided to typically developing children and using instructional procedures that are only as intrusive as necessary (Bailey & McWilliam, 1990). The implementation of an activity-based approach begins with the identification of functional and generative target skills (Bricker & Cripe, 1992). Although typical early childhood experiences are used for the context of instruction (e.g., sandbox play, easel painting), the skills selected for instruction should focus on the development of generalized motor, communication, cognitive, self-help, and social skills that will lead to independent functioning. For example, it would be inappropriate to have an instructional goal of painting a picture at the easel. A more appropriate goal would be to grasp a variety of objects. Then the skill of grasping could be instructed when the child attempted to easel paint, in addition to a variety of other activities. Once the instructional goals are selected, the early interventionist uses an activity–skill matrix to determine opportunities for embedding skill instruction within activities (Davis et al, 1998; Grisham-Brown & Hemmeter, 1998; Hanline & Fox, 1993).

The activities selected for instruction can be routine, planned, or child initiated. Routine activities occur daily in a predictable sequence—washing hands before meals, picking up toys before moving to another activity, and putting on outer clothing before going outside—and offer practical opportunities to use motor, communication, social, and cognitive skills. Planned activities are child-relevant activities that are fun and interesting and also create opportunities for specific skill development. An example of a planned activity might be a cooking activity during which the child with disabilities is prompted to reach and grasp, pour ingredients into a bowl, and take turns. Child-initiated activities are ones that children express an interest in or introduce. An example of a child-initiated activity is a child walking to a swing to indicate that he wishes to get on and be pushed. These types of activities should be used by the early interventionist to embed instruction or guided practice on targeted skills.

Figure 20–5 presents an activity–skill matrix for Trina, a preschooler with severe disabilities. Trina's goals include lifting her head up and maintaining it in an upright position, reaching and grasping for objects, initiating social interactions by vocalizing to peers and adults, maintaining attention to an activity, engaging in turn taking, and indicating preferences by looking at a desired object. In Trina's preschool program she learns these skills in a play-based curriculum with typical peers. Much of Trina's schedule includes large blocks of time when children are free to select activities. Trina is assisted to make an activity selection by an adult or peer. When she begins an activity, the adult follows her lead and embeds systematic instruction within the selected context.

Naturalistic Teaching Procedures

Naturalistic teaching is an approach to instruction that is easily accommodated in a play-based classroom. Naturalistic teaching procedures fall within the framework of DAP in that they are based on child interest and promote child exploration (Davis et al., 1998; Rule, Losardo, Dinnebeil, Kaiser, & Rowland, 1998). Fox and Hanline (1993) describe how naturalistic teaching may be used to teach young children with disabilities cognitive, preacademic, motor, and presymbolic skills in a developmentally appropriate preschool classroom.

The teaching episode begins with child selection of an activity or a toy. If it is difficult to determine what activity the child is interested in, the teacher takes the child to the various centers and observes her behavior. Signs of interest may include smiling, relaxation of tone, manipulation of materials, and vocalizing. Another way to provide choices is to offer representational objects for selection of play centers (e.g., a block to represent blocks or a plate to represent the dramatic area) or a picture board that displays the activities for selection.

Once the child has made a selection, the teacher joins the child in the play activity and provides focused attention by (1) modeling the desired target behavior and/or identifying peers who are engaging in the target behavior, (2) verbally labeling the behavior, and (3) looking expectantly at the child. If the child does not respond to the focused attention cues, the teacher should provide a verbal cue in the form of a question (e.g., "Do you want a block?"). If the child does not respond to the question, the teacher provides a mand (instruction) to engage in the behavior (e.g., "Pick up the block"). If the child does not respond correctly to the mand, the teacher provides physical assistance to perform the skill. An example of the naturalistic teaching procedure for teaching a child with severe disabilities to put objects in a container, give an object on request, and manipulate objects with two hands is shown in Figure 20–6.

Figure 20–5 Activity–Skill Matrix for Trina, a Preschooler with Severe Disabilities

	Skills to Be Taught					
Time/Activity	**Lift Head**	**Reach & Grasp**	**Initiate Social Interactions**	**Indicate Preferences**	**Maintain Attention**	**Turn Taking**
9:00-9:10 arrival with Dad	look at teacher or peer	pull out cubby for belongings	vocalize or smile a greeting			
9:10-10:15 center time (choice of blocks, micro-spheric sociodramatic, macro-spheric sociodramatic, quiet area, art/fluid materials)	within chosen activity	with materials of choice	with peer in play	a. in activity selection b. when peers offer objects	time spent in play activity	exchange of toys/materials in play
10:15-10:40 transition to snack/handwashing & toileting/snack	a. standing at sink b. sitting in chair	a. soap b. towel c. spoon d. cup	with peers at snack	when offered drink & snack items		
10:40-11:30 outdoor activities (choice of water play, sand play, sociodramatic, riding toys, climbing)	within chosen activity	with materials of choice	with peers in play	a. in activity selection b. when peers offer objects	time spent in play activity	exchange of toys/materials in play
11:30-12:15 transition to lunch/handwashing & toileting/lunch	a. standing at sink b. sitting in chair	a. soap b. towel c. spoon d. cup	with peers at lunch	when offered drink & meal items		

Figure 20–5 Continued

12:15-12:30 lunch clean-up/ toileting/tooth brushing/transition to quiet activity of choice	a. standing at sink b. sitting in chair	a. soap b. towel c. toothbrush d. play material or book	with peers in activity	a. in activity selection b. when peers offer objects	time spent in activity	exchange of toys/materials in activity
12:30-12:45 group storytime/songtime or quiet centers	sitting on rug or sitting at center	materials in center	within group activity	a. in activity selection b. when peers offer objects	time spent in activity	exchange of toys/materials in activity
12:45 nap time or quiet centers (books, fine motor manipulatives)	not addressed unless awake; if awake, goals are addressed as in 9:10-10:15 center time					
1:15 transition to outside with toileting or continue napping	not addressed unless awake; if awake, goals are addressed as described					
1:25 continue napping or outdoor centers	not addressed unless awake; if awake, goals are addressed as in 10:15-10:45 outdoor activities if sleeping, toileting clusters (as indicated at 1:15) occur at 1:50					
2:00 review of the day	sitting on rug		within group activity		time spent in activity	exchange of materials in activity
2:15 depart with child care provider	look at teacher/peer/ child care provider	receive home notebook	vocalize or smile a greeting			

Source: "Learning within the Context of Play: Providing Typical Early Childhood Experiences for Children with Severe Disabilities," by M. F. Hanline and L. Fox, 1993, *Journal of the Association for Persons with Severe Handicaps, 18,* pp. 121–129. Reprinted by permission of TASH, Baltimore, MD.

Figure 20–6 Examples of Naturalistic Teaching Procedure

Target One: Puts object in container	**Target Two: Gives object on request**	**Target Three: Manipulates object with both hands**
1. The teacher, Josh, and his peers are playing in the housekeeping area, pretending to cook dinner. Josh is watching a peer place plastic green beans into a pan that is on the stove. The teacher looks at the peer engaging in the target behavior, turns to Josh with an expectant look, and waits for a response. If Josh does not respond in 4 seconds, the teacher provides a comment on the peer's engagement in the target behavior (e.g., "Japre is putting beans in the pan.").	1. The teacher, Josh, and his peers are playing in the block area with blocks and small plastic zoo animals. Josh is seated on the floor alongside a pile of blocks. The adult begins to hand blocks one at a time to the peers. They are using the blocks to build an enclosure in which to put the animals. When Josh looks at the teacher handing blocks to his peers, the teacher turns to Josh with an expectant look, and waits for a response. If Josh does not respond in 4 seconds, the teacher provides a comment on her engagement in the target behavior (e.g., "I'm handing blocks to your friends.").	1. The teacher, Josh, and peers are outdoors engaging in water play. The water table is equipped with small plastic dolls, baby bottles, and washcloths. Some of the children are washing the dolls, some are dripping water on their arms with a washcloth, and others are feeding the dolls. Josh is watching a child who is holding her doll with two hands, dipping it in and out of the water. The teacher looks at the peer engaging in the target behavior, turns to Josh with an expectant look, and waits for a response. If Josh does not respond in 4 seconds, the teacher provides a comment on the peer's engagement in the target behavior (e.g., "Kathryn is using her hands to dip her baby doll.").
2. If Josh does not respond to the comment on the peer's engagement in 4 seconds, the teacher provides a verbal cue in the form of **a question** (e.g., "Do you want to take a turn putting beans in the pan?").	2. If Josh does not respond to the comment in 4 seconds, the teacher provides a verbal cue in the form of **a question** (e.g., "Do you want to give Andy a block?").	2. If Josh does not respond to the comment on the peer's engagement in 4 seconds, the teacher provides a verbal cue in the form of **a question** (e.g., "Do you want to dip a baby doll?").
3. If Josh does not respond to the question in 4 seconds, the adult provides **a mand** to engage in the target behavior (e.g., "Josh, take a turn, please. Put the beans in the pan.").	3. If Josh does not respond to the question in 4 seconds, the adult provides **a mand** to engage in the target behavior (e.g., "Josh, take a turn, please. Give Andy a block.").	3. If Josh does not respond to the question in 4 seconds, the adult provides **a mand** to engage in the target behavior (e.g., "Josh, take a turn, please. Use your hands to dip the baby.").
4. If Josh does not respond to the mand in 4 seconds, the adult provides **physical assistance** to engage in the target behavior.	4. If Josh does not respond to the mand in 4 seconds, the adult provides **physical assistance** to engage in the target behavior.	4. If Josh does not respond to the mand in 4 seconds, the adult provides **physical assistance** to engage in the target behavior.
5. The skill is **reinforced** by affirmation of the child's engagement in the target behavior by the adult (e.g., "This is fun! We're putting beans in the pan with Japre.").	5. The skill is **reinforced** by affirmation of the child's engagement in the target behavior by the adult (e.g., "I like playing with blocks with you and your friends.").	5. The skill is **reinforced** by affirmation of the child's engagement in the target behavior by the adult (e.g., "We're dipping the baby. Isn't this fun?").

Source: "A Preliminary Evaluation of Learning within Developmentally Appropriate Early Childhood Settings," by L. Fox and M. F. Hanline, 1993, *Topics in Early Childhood Special Education, 13,* pp. 308–327.

The Importance of Systematic Instruction

The instruction of young children with severe disabilities within developmentally appropriate, early childhood classrooms may be a challenge for early educators and the professionals who support them (e.g., early childhood special educator). The child with a severe disability often encounters challenges with instructional engagement, play with peers, communication, and movement. It is critically important that the following three tenets of child-focused interventions are always practiced (Wolery, 2000, p. 31):

1. Adults design environments to promote children's safety, active engagement, participation, and membership.
2. Adults individualize and adapt practices for each child based on ongoing data to meet children's changing needs.
3. Adults use systematic procedures within and across environments, activities, and routines to promote children's learning and participation.

In this chapter we have described a new instructional prompting approach, naturalistic instruction, that is particularly well suited to young children. In addition to naturalistic instruction, all the skill acquisition and generalization approaches discussed in earlier chapters are applicable to young children with severe disabilities. We emphasize this point to make clear that instruction must be planned, systematic, and monitored, even when instruction occurs within the play and routines of young children.

Many of the demonstrations in the literature on systematic (but naturalistic) strategies may be used to promote the learning of children with the most severe disabilities within normalized early childhood classrooms. Activity schedules may be used to assist young children with autism in understanding routines and how to move from one activity to another (Massey & Wheeler, 2000; Schwartz, Billingsley, & McBride, 1998). Providing children with conspicuous choices has assisted children in maintaining engagement and reducing problem behavior (Reinhartsen, Garfinkle, & Wolery, 2002; Schwartz et al., 1998). In addition, the use of embedded instruction has demonstrated that systematic instruction within the activities of an early childhood classroom can result in the acquisition of important learning outcomes for children whose development is severely delayed (Horn, Lieber, Li, Sandall, & Schwartz, 2000; Hwang & Hughes, 2000; Sandall & Schwartz, 2002).

Environmental Arrangements

Environments for preschoolers, infants, and toddlers are arranged in ways that are safe and nurturing and support the development of skills. Young children should not be required to sit at tables and engage only in teacher-selected activities. The environments provided to young children with severe disabilities should be very similar to those provided for typically developing children.

Classrooms for young children are usually large, open rooms with activity areas defined by low bookcases or storage shelves, which make it easy for an adult to have a view of the entire classroom while providing the children with defined spaces for their activities (Bredekamp & Copple, 1997; Twardosz, Cataldo, & Risley, 1974). The barriers around activity areas should be arranged to allow for ease of movement from one activity to another.

The classroom should be furnished with child-sized furniture, including tables, chairs, and toilets. Appropriate adaptive seating equipment should be available for each child who has specialized seating needs. It is important that adaptive seating or positioning equipment allow the child to access activity areas and to be at the same level as his peers. For example, it is not appropriate to use an adaptive chair that raises the child with disabilities above his peers; the physical separation will hinder social interaction opportunities. In addition to child-size furniture, the classroom should have a personal storage space for each child.

Displays used to decorate the classroom should be relevant to children and reflect an acceptance of diverse cultures and individuals. Wall displays and bulletin boards should be placed where children can see them and should include products from the children. When commercial displays are used (e.g., bulletin-board kits), the teacher should be careful to select those that reflect multicultural values. Some displays reinforce stereotyped images of other cultures (e.g., Native Americans as Indians with tomahawks), abilities (e.g., children with disabilities not participating actively), and gender (e.g., girls playing house and boys building with blocks).

The activity areas typically provided in classrooms for young children are arts and craft area, dramatic play area, blocks, fluid play, manipulatives, and reading. In addition, it is important to provide a quiet, comfortable area for children who need a break and an area where parents have a bulletin board or message book for home–school communication. A typical classroom arrangement is shown in Figure 20–7.

Materials should be stored in activity areas so that they are easily accessible to children and on open shelves

Figure 20–7 Room Arrangement

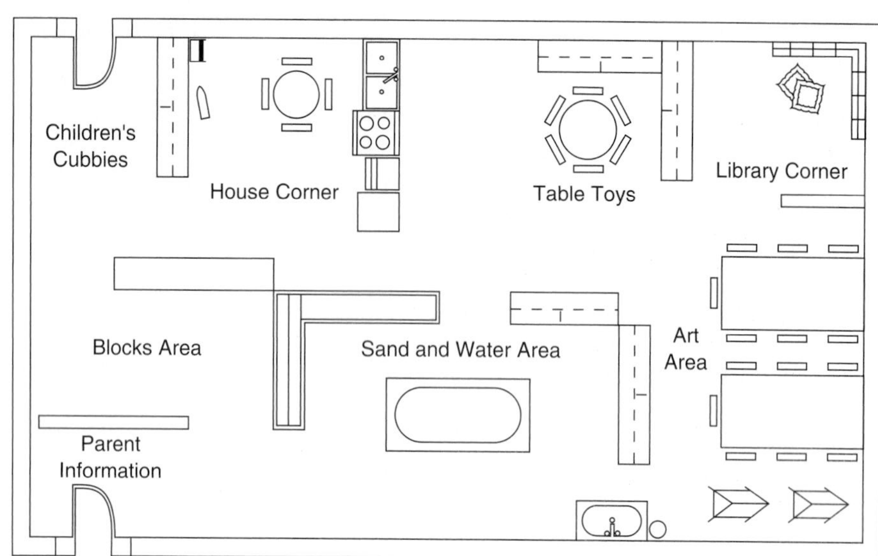

Source: "Activity-Based Instruction," by T. Udell, 1992. In J. Peters, C. Bunse, L. Carlson, L. Doede, G. Glasenapp, K. Hayden, C. Lehman, T. P. Templeman, and T. Udell (Eds.), *Supporting Children with Disabilities in Community Programs* (p. 23), 1992, Monmouth, OR: Teaching Research Publications. Copyright 1992 by The Teaching Research Division. Reprinted by permission.

or in clear bins so that they are visible to the children. Storage containers can be labeled with pictures of the items that belong in them to facilitate putting materials away after use. The number of materials available in each activity area is of importance. When too few toys are provided, children have difficulty playing together. Some teachers may feel that providing only one of each toy will teach children to share, but very young children, and especially children who have social development delays, are not ready to share or play cooperatively until they are 4 or 5 years old. It is better to have enough duplicates of each item for the number of children who are expected to play in the activity center. For example, if you expect four children to play in the dramatic play area, you should provide four hats or four shopping baskets.

Blocks

Block areas should provide enough blocks so that several children can work together. Bender (1978) suggests that 60 to 80 blocks be provided in a block area that is designed to accommodate several children. In addition to blocks, small people, vehicles, and animals should be provided to facilitate the building of structures and pretend play. The block area is an appropriate activity area for children who are not yet engaging in pretend play. Young children with severe disabilities can engage in "putting in and taking out" play sequences, knocking down structures, and other skills as they are embedded in play activities with peers.

Dramatic Play

Dramatic play areas are usually noisy and should be located away from the quiet area or reading area. It should include dress-ups and props for acting out real-life roles, and dolls of different ethnic backgrounds, kitchen equipment, telephone, tea sets, a mirror, and other dramatic play props should be available as well. Teachers often change the content of the dramatic play area to reflect different community environments, such as a hospital, a restaurant, or an office, that are relevant to the children in the classroom. Although young children with severe disabilities may not yet understand the concept of dressing up, they can work on embedded skills within play sequences with their peers. For example, a child with severe disabilities may put dishes in and out of the toy sink while practicing the skills of grasp and release and social interactions with a peer.

Arts and Crafts

The arts and crafts area typically provides easel painting, cutting and pasting activities, and markers with paper. This area offers children the opportunity to practice fine-motor skills and engage in creative construction activities.

Children with severe disabilities may need adaptive equipment, such as a built-up handle on a paintbrush or material adaptations, such as taping the paper to the table, to facilitate their engagement in these activities.

Sand and Water

Sand and water play are considered fluid play activities and can take place outdoors or indoors. The sand or water table can also be filled with rice or dried beans to vary the experiences offered to children. Other options for fluid play include bathing a doll in a small dishpan, playing with toy boats in water in a small wading pool, and sand play on a cafeteria tray with cookie cutters for imprinting shapes. Fluid play activities are very soothing to some young children; however, other children may have difficulty with containing the fluids. For children who have difficulty with fluid play, offering them a more controlled fluid experience, such as pouring water from a pitcher into a bowl or washing a doll in a small pan may be an appropriate first step (Wolfgang & Wolfgang, 1992).

Computers

Computers are a common learning center in most early childhood programs. Children in early childhood classrooms may use computers for literacy experiences (writing notes, writing stories, publishing work), for art or drawing, to gain new information by accessing developmentally appropriate sites on the World Wide Web, to learn and practice preacademic skills, and to engage with software that enriches the curriculum content of the classroom (Haugland, 2000). Each month, new software that is high quality and developmentally appropriate becomes available for use by families and educators. The National Association for the Education of Young Children supports the use of computers in the classroom when "technology is integrated into the regular learning environment and used as one of the many options to support children's learning" (NAEYC, 1996).

Computers can be "powerful tools" for children with disabilities (NAEYC, 1996). Computers can offer these children opportunities to engage in activities that may not be accessible otherwise, such as reading a story, making music, or drawing a picture (Judge, 2001). Children with physical challenges may use an adapted switch or touch screen to activate and interact with the computer. Computer centers should be evaluated to make sure that the child with severe disabilities can easily access (through appropriate positioning) and operate (through adaptive equipment if necessary) the computer.

Manipulatives

The manipulatives area provides puzzles, counting markers, beads to string, small building blocks such as Legos or Bristle Blocks, lotto, lacing boards, parquetry sets, and pegboards for children's construction play. This area should not be viewed as a preacademic area where "real" teaching occurs, but only as another area where children learn through play and exploration. This is also an appropriate area to house a computer. When properly outfitted with a switch or touch screen, a computer can provide a wealth of exploratory learning experiences for children with severe disabilities. Computer software that encourages the discovery of simple cause-and-effect relationships as well as concept development is useful in the preschool classroom.

Reading

In the reading center, quality children's literature and a comfortable place to read should be provided. Books should be displayed on shelves with their covers clearly visible so that children will be encouraged to explore them. The reading area could also include a puppet theater, Language Master, or tape recorder with books on tape. Children with disabilities may need adaptive equipment to turn pages, hold a book, or activate the tape recorder.

Making Adaptations

In every activity center, adaptations may have to be made to accommodate children with severe disabilities. Rosenberg, Clark, Filer, Hupp, & Finkler (1992) describe a process by which the barriers to active participation are examined and interventions occur to increase the participation of the child with disabilities. The process begins by analyzing how much the child participates and identifying the factors that lead to low participation. Then interventions are designed that (1) increase the child's skills, (2) identify alternative behaviors that can be used, (3) modify the environment, or (4) adapt the activity to circumvent the barrier. For example, a child with physical disabilities who has difficulty using regular blocks can be provided with magnetic blocks on a cookie tray.

Electromechanical switch toys might also be used to increase active participation by children with severe disabilities (Lane & Mistrett, 2002). The preschool teacher may want to include an activity center of switch toys or integrate them into centers as appropriate. For example, it may be appropriate to have a switch toy of cars on a track in the block center and a switch attached to a "spin art" toy in the arts and crafts center.

If the child with severe disabilities uses an augmentative device or alternative communication, the teacher should examine all play centers to determine how augmentative communication can be embedded within play activities (DiCarlo, Banajee, & Stricklin, 2000). For example, if the child is a sign language user, the classroom teacher should teach all children key signs that go with thematic units or materials in the center. If the child uses picture symbols, choice boards and visual schedules may be developed for each center, offering the child multiple opportunities for expression with peers. In a similar manner, voice output communication devices should be programmed with the words and phrases that are likely to be needed to play in each center.

Infant Intervention

Many early intervention programs do not provide classroom programs for infants and toddlers, but do provide home-based early intervention in the child's home or child-care setting. In such situations, an activity–skills matrix can still be used to organize the instruction of skills in routine, planned, and child-initiated activities (Cripe & Venn, 1997). The design of the activity–skill matrix should occur in collaboration with the caregiver and should be responsive to the caregiver's schedule and time demands. Routine activities in the home are activities such as diapering, feeding, dressing, and bath time. Child-initiated activities are activities such as play interactions or requests for attention. Planned activities could be reading stories, a walk in the stroller, or play time. An activity–skill matrix for Sita, a 12-month-old with severe disabilities, is shown in Figure 20–8.

In some home-based programs the early interventionist works primarily with the child, while the caregiver observes and learns techniques that can be used to facilitate the child's development. A recent trend is for interventionists to provide support to the caregiver as the caregiver interacts with the child (Mahoney & Powell, 1988; McCollum & Stayton, 1985). Because the caregiver is with the child more than the interventionist, supporting and guiding the caregiver's interactions with the child may be a more effective practice. Moreover, the quality of the caregiver–infant relationship is critical to the development of the child. Programs designed with a focus on the caregiver–infant relationship are the Transactional Intervention Program (Mahoney & Powell, 1988), the ECO model (McDonald & Gillette, 1986), and the Hanen Program (Manolson, 1992).

Figure 20–8 Home Activity–Skill Matrix for Sita

	Skills to Be Taught				
Time/Activity	**Stand Independently**	**Objects in Containers**	**Take Turn in Social Game**	**Imitate "Ma" "Ba"**	**Extend Arms to Request**
Play time	by table by shelf	toys away toys in containers	peek-a-boo tickle game	vocal play	to get in lap to be picked up
Feeding				vocal play	to get in high chair
Diapering	before lifting to changing table		tickle game	vocal play	to get down
Bath time	before lifting into tub	toys in/out tub	peek-a-boo bath game tickle game	vocal play	to get out
Dressing	before lifting to changing table		peek-a-boo tickle game	vocal play	to get down
Walk in stroller	before placing in stroller	toys in/out of bag	social games when resting	vocal play	to get in/out of stroller

Inclusion and Young Children

The inclusion of young children with disabilities is important for legal, educational, and moral reasons, as described in Chapter 10. Much of the research that supports the feasibility and benefits of inclusion programs was conducted with young children (Peck, Furman, & Helmstetter, 1993). Despite the clear rationales for providing inclusive programs and the wealth of literature that supports inclusion, programs face professional and bureaucratic barriers that impede implementation (Guralnick, 2001; Odom & McEvoy, 1990; Wolery, 1996).

A significant barrier to inclusive programs for preschoolers with disabilities is that schools are not typically serving nondisabled children of the same age. Similar problems exist for agencies that serve infants and toddlers in early intervention programs. Often they have no access to typically developing children. A solution to the difficulty is for early intervention programs to work with programs that are serving typically developing children (i.e., child-care centers, Head Start, family day-care providers, and play groups).

In programs that have made a commitment to work with other agencies in the provision of inclusive programs, a new set of challenges can emerge. Issues that may need to be addressed include the differences in the educational philosophy of early educators and early childhood special educators, lack of experience of early educators in teaching young children with disabilities, and the need to provide related services within the early childhood program. Progress in these areas requires extensive preservice and in-service training, as well as administrative support, including state-level support of systems change (Odom & McEvoy, 1990).

Some schools provide experiences for interactions with nondisabled peers by using mainstreaming or reverse mainstreaming options. Young children with disabilities may be mainstreamed with kindergarten children, or kindergarten children may spend time in the classroom with preschoolers with disabilities. Some school districts operate Head Start programs or early intervention programs for at-risk children and their families that offer opportunities for interaction with age-matched peers.

Providing opportunities for the inclusion of infants and toddlers is even more challenging. Hanline and Hanson (1989) suggest that the inclusion of infants and toddlers with typically developing children can occur by capitalizing on opportunities available in the community, which may include playgroups, infant–toddler swimming classes, child care, family events and festivals, and story hour at the library. To implement the inclusion of infants and toddlers with disabilities in these situations, the developmental needs, family needs, and health and safety concerns for the child must be considered. Hanline and Hanson (1989) support a flexible approach to providing inclusive programs with inclusion experiences being designed to meet the individual needs of each child.

Transition Issues

Families with young children who are severely disabled experience transitions that team members can help them to manage. Predictable transitions may include discharge from the neonatal intensive care unit (NICU), moving from an early intervention program to a preschool program, and moving from preschool to kindergarten.

Transitions are often very difficult for families (Hanson et al., 2000). Transitions involve the emotional challenges of leaving a program or service provider that is familiar and confronting a set of new procedures, professionals, and practices. The difficulty of transition is compounded when families have developed a strong emotional bond with their current provider or service program.

Transition planning involves a set of procedures that can be used to assist the family and the child in experiencing a smooth transition. Because transition planning is perceived by families and professionals as an essential service to families in early intervention programs, IDEA specifies that each IFSP must document that steps should be taken to support the transition of the 3-year-old child to the preschool program. Part C requires that the family participate in the development of the transition plan and that a conference be held with the local educational agency (if the family approves) to discuss the transition to preschool at least 90 days before the child is eligible for preschool services. Transition planning includes a discussion with the parents about future placements and other related matters, procedures to prepare the child for changes in service delivery, and, with parental permission, the transmission of information about the child to the receiving program.

Preparation for Transition

There are basic general procedures that most programs use to prepare for transitions, although different programs may use a variety of ways to conduct the procedures (Hains, Fowler, & Chandler, 1988; Hanline, 1993; Hanline & Knowlton, 1988; Lazzari, 1991). The first step in preparing for a transition is to identify the receiving program or agency. The family or the sending program may then initiate a referral to the new program. The family may be prepared for the transition to the new program by learning about the services that may be offered, the procedures that the receiving agency will use to provide services (e.g., IEP meetings), and their legal rights. Prior to the transition, a new evaluation is performed on the child, with family permission, to determine current levels of functioning. When the transition involves an array of program options, the family may be encouraged at this point to visit these programs. The sending program may provide parents with information (e.g., what to look for in a preschool program) to assist the family with site visits.

Typically, the transition involves a discharge conference (e.g., from the NICU) or eligibility staffing (e.g., into a public school preschool). A staff person from each of the sending and receiving programs should attend these meetings to exchange information and to keep open lines of communication between agencies. Information helpful to the receiving program is provided by the sending agency with parental permission. Once the transition is complete, the sending agency provides a follow-up contact.

Each transition involves a different set of parental concerns and requires variations of the procedures. In the following sections, information relevant to transitions from the NICU, infant and toddler program, and preschool program is provided.

Transition from the Neonatal Intensive Care Unit

The discharge of the infant with severe disabilities from the NICU to home can be a time of great parental concern and stress. The family's concerns may include adjusting to caring for an infant with specialized medical, physical, and nutritional needs; locating and accessing services in the community; and managing the day-to-day care of the child (Hanline & Deppe, 1990). A supported and planned transition may help families with the discharge and the adjustment to caring for the infant at home.

One way to provide a smooth transition is for the hospital or early intervention service provider to assign a professional to be a support person for the family when the child is in the NICU and when the child goes home. When the child is in the NICU, this person can help the family understand the roles of the professionals who are involved in the infant's care and assist in gathering the information and supports that the family needs in coping with their situation. In planning for the discharge, the support person can assist the family in developing questions that they have about bringing their child home. Many infants leave the NICU already linked with an agency that will provide early intervention services. If this occurs, the support person can prepare the family for the IFSP meeting by explaining the process and purpose. In addition to the IFSP meeting, the support person should attend the preparation sessions on nutritional and medical management of the infant at home with the family (Hanline & Deppe, 1990).

When the discharge has occurred, the support person can help the family to respond to the child's needs (Hanline & Deppe, 1990). The family may have questions about caregiving routines, their child's developmental status, and resources and services available in the community. Once the family has been successfully linked to an early intervention program, the role of the support person can be diminished.

Transition from the Early Intervention Program to Preschool

The transition from an early intervention program to a preschool program typically occurs when the child is 3 years old. Planning for the transition should occur several months before that day. The first step is to build a transition planning team composed of the family, the family's service coordinator, professionals who work with the family and the child, and other service providers who have frequent contact with the family. Transition planning occurs within the IFSP meeting because Part C of IDEA mandates that transition concerns be addressed in the IFSP.

Transition planning begins by identifying the transition date for the child and the tasks that should be accomplished prior to the transition. Some of these tasks are contacting the receiving program, making the referral, visiting program options, updating the child's evaluation information, preparing the family for developing an IEP, meeting with the receiving program, and transferring information and records to the receiving program (Hanline & Knowlton, 1988).

The transition team should remember that the goal of transition planning is to minimize the difficulties that the child and family experience with the change of service agencies. The team should discuss anticipated problems that could occur with the transition and develop strategies to minimize them. For example, if the child has a gastrostomy feeding tube, the team may wish to offer to train the receiving programs in the proper procedures to use. In addition, the early interventionist may want to conduct an ecological inventory of the preschool classroom to anticipate skill demands that she can begin to prepare the toddler to manage. For example, if children in the preschool classroom are expected to make a choice of an activity before moving to a center, the toddler teacher may want to introduce that procedure in her classroom.

It is permissible for a preschool program to continue to use an IFSP instead of the IEP for 3- to 5-year-olds (if permitted by state guidelines and approved by the family). If this does not occur, families must be prepared for participating in the IEP process. Hanline and Knowlton (1988) offered families a book that describes the referral, IEP, and placement procedures. In addition, they showed families a videotape of a mock IEP meeting and discussed the video with them. Another strategy that may be used to prepare the family for their first IEP meeting is to guide them in determining what goals and services they wish to request for their child. A person from the early intervention program should attend the IEP meeting and eligibility staffing to provide support to the family and to maintain a collaborative relationship with the receiving program.

Transition to Kindergarten

The transition to kindergarten brings a change in the curriculum and, potentially, in the amount of inclusion that can be provided to the child with severe disabilities. In some programs, children move from a program for preschoolers with disabilities to a full-inclusion classroom. Other children may be offered opportunities for integration from a special education classroom. The prospect of inclusion should not be a new idea that parents must be prepared for, although for many families this will be the case. Thus families may need information on why inclusion is important and how inclusive programs are structured.

Several early childhood special educators have written about the need to identify the skills required in kindergarten to prepare preschoolers to function independently in these classrooms (Hains, Fowler, Schwartz, Kottwitz, & Rosenkoetter, 1989; Johnson, Gallagher, Cook, & Wong, 1995; McCormick & Kawate, 1982; Vincent et al., 1980). These skills, which have been called "kindergarten survival skills," include following rules and routines, expressing wants and needs, cooperating with others, complying with directions given by an adult, sharing materials with a peer, socializing with peers, taking turns, interacting verbally with adults and peers, focusing attention on the speaker, and making decisions (Noonan & McCormick, 1993).

For many young children with severe disabilities, the mastery of such skills before kindergarten is not realistic. The intent of identifying kindergarten survival skills is for the preschool teacher to gain knowledge about the kindergarten curriculum and to prepare students for the expectations of the kindergarten classroom. Another tactic, which fits with this intent, is to conduct an ecological inventory of the kindergarten program so that appropriate goals can be identified and adaptations planned so that the child with severe disabilities can participate actively in the kindergarten classroom (Fowler, Schwartz, & Atwater, 1991).

A kindergarten classroom can be very different from a preschool classroom. Often the number of children is greater, the school day is more structured, and the program is less flexible. Families should have an opportunity to visit a kindergarten classroom before the transition so that they will be able to anticipate these differences. A visit to a kindergarten classroom also will assist the family in actively participating in the development of the IEP. All the IEP team will need to understand the demands of the kindergarten classroom before designing the IEP. Both the preschool teacher and the receiving teacher should be present at the IEP meeting so that an exchange of information and collaborative planning can occur.

Conclusion

In this chapter the rationale for and design of early childhood special education programs for young children with severe disabilities were presented. Many aspects of providing programs for young children are different due to the young age of the child and the need to provide programs in a variety of settings. Most important, early intervention programs embrace the philosophy of a family-centered approach that is supported through early intervention legislation.

Despite the unique features of early intervention programs, the foundation of these programs should be the principle of normalization (Bailey & McWilliam, 1990). Young children with severe disabilities should be provided services in normalized environments and be taught using procedures that are least intrusive but result in skill acquisition. Most important, families of children with disabilities should be helped to determine and obtain the supports and resources that they need in the community to nurture their child's development.

Questions for Reflection

1. Are there features of the IFSP that, if adopted, could enhance the IEP for students with severe disabilities?
2. What skills are important for the early interventionist to have for working in such close collaboration with families?
3. What are some issues that the collaborative team could face when working with families from diverse cultures?
4. What do you think the benefits and difficulties are when implementing home-based instruction?
5. In what ways might the achievement of inclusion be easier in early childhood programs than in school-age programs?
6. How would *functional instruction* be defined for an infant or toddler?

References

Bailey, D. B. (1989). Issues and directions in preparing professionals to work with young handicapped children and their families. In J. J. Gallagher, R. M. Clifford, & P. Trohanis (Eds.), *Policy implementation and P.L. 99-457: Planning for young children with special needs* (pp. 97–132). Baltimore: Paul H. Brookes.

Bailey, D. B. (1991). Building positive relationships between professionals and families. In M. J. McGonigel, R. K. Kaufmann, & B. H. Johnson (Eds.), *Guidelines and recommended practices for the Individualized Family Service Plan* (2nd Ed., pp. 29–38). Bethesda, MD: Association for the Care of Children's Health.

Bailey, D. B., & McWilliam, R. A. (1990). Normalizing early intervention. *Topics in Early Childhood Special Education, 10,* 33–47.

Bailey, D. B., McWilliam, R. A., Darkes, L. A., Hebbeler, K., Simeonsson, R. J., Spiker, D., et al. (1998). Family outcomes in early intervention: A framework for program evaluation and efficacy research. *Exceptional Children, 64,* 313–328.

Bailey, D. B., & Wolery, M. (1992). *Teaching infants and preschoolers with disabilities* (2nd Ed.). Upper Saddle River, NJ: Merrill/ Prentice Hall.

Bayley, N. (1969). *Bayley scales of infant development.* New York: Psychological Development.

Bender, J. (1978). Large hollow blocks: Relationship of quantity to block-building behaviors. *Young Children, 34,* 17–23.

Bredekamp, S., & Copple, C. (1997). *Developmentally appropriate practice in early childhood programs.* Washington, DC: National Association for the Education of Young Children.

Bricker, D. D. (1989). *Early intervention for at-risk and handicapped infants, toddlers, and preschool children* (2nd Ed.). Palo Alto, CA: Vort Corp.

Bricker, D. D. (1992) *AEPS measurement for birth to three years.* Baltimore: Paul H. Brookes.

Bricker, D. D., & Cripe, J. J. W. (1992). *An activity-based approach to early intervention.* Baltimore: Paul H. Brookes.

Brofenbrenner, U. (1975). Is early intervention effective? In B. Friedlander, G. Sterrit, & G. Kirk (Eds.), *Exceptional infant: Vol. 3. Assessment and intervention* (pp. 449–475). New York: Brunner/Mazel.

Bromwich, R. (1981). *Working with parents and infants: An interactional approach.* Baltimore: University Park Press.

Cicirelli, V., Evans, J., & Schiller, J. (1969). *The impact of Head Start: An evaluation of the effects of Head Start on children's cognitive and affective development.* Report to the U.S. Office of Economic Opportunity by Westinghouse Learning Corporation and Ohio University. Washington, DC: Government Printing Office.

Cripe, J. W., & Venn, M. L. (1997). Family-guided routines for early intervention services. *Young Exceptional Children, 1*(1), 18–26.

Davis, M. D., Kilgo, J. L., & Gamel-McCormick, M. (1998). *Young children with special needs: A developmentally appropriate approach.* Boston: Allyn and Bacon.

DiCarlo, C., Banajee, M., & Stricklin, S. B. (2000). Embedding augmentative communication within early childhood classrooms. *Young Exceptional Children, 3*(3), 18–27.

Dunst, C. J. (1981). *Infant learning: A cognitive–linguistic intervention strategy.* Allen, TX: DLM/Teaching Resources.

Dunst, C. J. (1986). Overview of the efficacy of early intervention programs. In L. Bickman & D. L. Weatherford (Eds.), *Evaluating early intervention programs for severely handicapped children and their families* (pp. 79–147). Austin, TX: Pro-Ed.

Dunst, C. J. (2001). Participation of young children with disabilities in community learning activities. In M. J. Guralnick (Ed.), *Early childhood inclusion: Focus on change* (pp. 307–336). Baltimore: Paul H. Brookes.

Dunst, C. J., Bruder, M. B., Trivette, C. M., Raab, M., & McLean, M. (2001). Natural learning opportunities for infants, toddlers, and preschoolers. *Young Exceptional Children, 4*(3), 19–25.

Dunst, C. J., Hamby, D., Trivette, C. M., Raab, M., & Bruder, M. B. (2000). Everyday family and community life and children's naturally occurring learning opportunities. *Journal of Early Intervention, 23*, 151–164.

Dunst, C. J., Johanson, C., Trivette, C. M., & Hamby, D. (1991). Family-oriented early intervention policies and practices: Family centered or not? *Exceptional Children, 58,* 115–126.

Dunst, C. J., & Rheingrover, R. (1981). An analysis of the efficacy of infant intervention programs with organically handicapped children. *Evaluation and Program Planning, 4,* 287–323.

Dunst, C. J., Trivette, C., & Deal, A. (1988). *Enabling and empowering families: Principles & guidelines for practice.* Cambridge, MA: Brookline Books.

Fowler, S. A., Schwartz, I., & Atwater, J. (1991). Perspectives on the transition from preschool to kindergarten for children with disabilities and their families. *Exceptional Children, 58,* 136–145.

Fox, L., & Hanline, M. F. (1993). A preliminary evaluation of learning within developmentally appropriate early childhood settings. *Topics in Early Childhood Special Education, 13,* 308–327.

Furono, S., O'Reilly, K., Hosaka, C., Inatsuka, T., Allman, T., & Zeisloft, B. (1979). *Hawaii early learning profile.* Palo Alto, CA: Vort Corp.

Gargiulo, R. M., & Kilgo, J. (2000). *Young children with special needs*. Albany, NY: Delmar.

Grisham-Brown, J., & Hemmeter, M. L. (1998). Writing IEP goals and objectives: Reflecting an activity-based approach to young children with disabilities. *Young Exceptional Children, 1*(3), 2–10.

Guralnick, M. J. (2001). *Early childhood inclusion: Focus on change*. Baltimore: Paul H. Brookes.

Hains, A. H., Fowler, S. A., & Chandler, L. K. (1988). Planning school transitions: Family and professional collaboration. *Journal of the Division for Early Childhood, 12,* 108–115.

Hains, A. H., Fowler, S. A., Schwartz, I. S., Kottwitz, E., & Rosenkoetter, S. (1989). A comparison of preschool and kindergarten expectations for school readiness. *Early Childhood Research Quarterly, 4,* 75–88.

Hanline, M. F. (1988). Making the transition to preschool: Identification of parent needs. *Journal of the Division for Early Childhood, 12,* 98–107.

Hanline, M. F. (1993). Facilitating integrated preschool service delivery transitions for children, families, and professionals. In C. A. Peck, S. L. Odom, & D. D. Bricker (Eds.), *Integrating young children with disabilities into community programs* (pp. 133–146). Baltimore: Paul H. Brookes.

Hanline, M. F., & Deppe, J. (1990). Discharging the premature infant: Family issues and implications for intervention. *Topics in Early Childhood Special Education, 9,* 15–25.

Hanline, M. F., & Fox, L. (1993). Learning within the context of play: Providing typical early childhood experiences for children with severe disabilities. *Journal of the Association for Persons with Severe Handicaps, 18,* 121–129.

Hanline, M. F., & Hanson, M. J. (1989). Integration considerations for infants and toddlers with multiple disabilities. *Journal of the Association for Persons with Severe Handicaps, 14,* 178–183.

Hanline, M. F., & Knowlton, A. (1988). A collaborative model for providing support to parents during their child's transition from infant intervention to preschool special education public school programs. *Journal of the Division for Early Childhood, 12,* 116–125.

Hanson, M. J., Beckman, P. J., Horn, E., Marquart, J., Sandall, S. R., Greig, D., et al. (2000). Entering preschool: Family and professional experiences in this transition process. *Journal of Early Intervention, 23*, 279–293.

Haugland, S. W. (2000). What role should technology play in young children's learning? Part 2. Early childhood classrooms in the 21st century: Using computers to maximize learning. *Young Children, 55*(1), 12–20.

Horn, E., Lieber, J., Li, S., Sandall, S., & Schwartz, I. (2000). Supporting young children's IEP goals in inclusive settings through embedded learning opportunities. *Topics in Early Childhood Special Education, 20*, 208–223.

Hwang, B., & Hughes, C. (2000). Increasing early social–communicative skills of preverbal preschool children with autism through social interactive training. *Journal of the Association for Persons with Severe Handicaps, 26*, 18–28.

Individuals with Disabilities Education Act Amendments of 1997 (IDEA) (1997), 20 U. S. C. 1400 et seq.

Johnson, L. J., Gallagher, R. J., Cook, M., & Wong, P. (1995). Critical skills for kindergarten: Perceptions from kindergarten teachers. *Journal of Early Intervention, 19,* 315–327.

Johnson-Martin, N. M., Attermeier, S. M., & Hacker, B. J. (1990). *The Carolina curriculum for preschoolers with special needs.* Baltimore: Paul H. Brookes.

Johnson-Martin, N. M., Jens, K. G., Attermeier, S. M., & Hacker, B. J. (1991). *The Carolina curriculum for infants and toddlers with special needs* (2nd Ed.). Baltimore: Paul H. Brookes.

Judge, S. L. (2001). Integrating computer technology within early childhood classrooms. *Young Exceptional Children, 5*(1), 20–26.

Kaiser, A. P., & Hemmeter, M. L. (1989). Value-based approaches to early intervention. *Topics in Early Childhood Special Education, 8,* 72–86.

Kaufman, R. K., & McGonigel, M. J. (1991). Identifying family concerns, priorities, and resources. In M. J. McGonigel, R. K. Kaufman, & B. H. Johnson (Eds.), *Guidelines and recommended practices for the individualized family service plan* (2nd Ed., pp. 47–55). Bethesda, MD: Association for the Care of Children's Health.

Kostelnik, M. J. (1992). Myths associated with developmentally appropriate programs. *Young Children, 47,* 17–23.

Kramer, S., McGonigel, M. J., & Kaufman, R. K. (1991). Developing the IFSP: Outcomes, strategies, activities, and services. In M. J. McGonigel, R. K. Kaufman, & B. H. Johnson (Eds.), *Guidelines and recommended practices for the individualized family service plan* (2nd Ed., pp. 57–66). Bethesda, MD: Association for the Care of Children's Health.

Lane, S. J., & Mistrett, S. (2002). Let's play! Assistive technology interventions for play. *Young Exceptional Children, 5*(2), 19–27.

Lazzari, A. M. (1991). *The transition sourcebook: A practical guide for early intervention programs.* Tucson, AZ: Communication Skill Builders.

Lewis, M. (1984). Developmental principles and their implications for at-risk and handicapped infants. In M. Hanson (Ed.), *Atypical infant development* (pp. 3–17). Baltimore: University Park Press.

Mahoney, G., & Powell, A. (1988). Modifying parent–child interaction: Enhancing the development of handicapped children. *Journal of Special Education, 22,* 82–96.

Mahoney, G., Powell, A., & Finger, I. (1986). The maternal behavior rating scale. *Topics in Early Childhood Special Education, 6,* 44–56.

Manolson, A. (1992). *It takes two to talk.* Toronto, Ontario, Canada: The Hanen Center.

Massey, N. G., & Wheeler, J. J. (2000). Acquisition and generalization of activity schedules and their effects on task engagement in a young child with autism in an inclusive pre-school classroom. *Education and Training in Mental Retardation, 35,* 326–335.

McCollum, J., & Stayton, V. (1985). Infant/parent interaction: Studies and intervention guidelines based on the SIAI model. *Journal of the Division for Early Childhood, 9,* 125–135.

McCormick, L., & Kawate, J. (1982). Kindergarten survival skills: New directions for preschool special education. *Education and Training of the Mentally Retarded, 17,* 247–252.

McDonald, J. D., & Gillette, Y. (1986). Communicating with persons with severe handicaps: Roles of parents and professionals. *Journal of the Association for Persons with Severe Handicaps, 11,* 255–265.

McGonigel, M. J. (1991). Philosophy and conceptual framework. In M. J. McGonigel, R. K. Kaufman, & B. H. Johnson (Eds.), *Guidelines and recommended practices for the individualized family service plan* (2nd Ed., pp. 7–14). Bethesda, MD: Association for the Care of Children's Health.

McGonigel, M. J., Kaufman, R. K., & Johnson, B. H. (1991). A family-centered process for the individualized family service plan. *Journal of Early Intervention, 15,* 46–56.

McWilliam, R. A., Ferguson, A., Harbin, G. L., Porter, P., Munn, D., & Vandiviere, P. (1998). The family-centeredness of individualized family service plans. *Topics in Early Childhood Special Education, 18,* 69–82.

National Association for the Education of Young Children (1996). NAEYC position statement: Technology and young children—ages three through eight. *Young Children, 51*(6), 11–16.

Neisworth, J. T., & Bagnato, S. J. (1988). Assessment in early childhood special education. In S. L. Odom & M. B. Karnes (Eds.), *Early intervention for infants and children with handicaps: An empirical base* (pp. 23–49). Baltimore: Paul H. Brookes.

Newborg, J., Stock, J. R., Wnek, L., Guidubaldi, J., & Svinicki, J. (1988). *Battelle developmental inventory.* Allen, TX: DLM Teaching Resources.

Noonan, M. J., & McCormick, L. (1993). *Early intervention in natural environments: Methods and procedures.* Pacific Grove, CA: Brooks/Cole Publishing Co.

Odom, S. L., & McEvoy, M. A. (1990). Mainstreaming at the preschool level: Potential barriers and tasks for the field. *Topics in Early Childhood Special Education, 10,* 48–61.

Peck, C. A., Furman, G. C., & Helmstetter, E. (1993). Integrated early childhood programs: Research on the implementation of change in organizational contexts. In C. A. Peck, S. L. Odom, & D. D. Bricker (Eds.), *Integrating young children with disabilities into community programs* (pp. 187–205). Baltimore: Paul H. Brookes.

Peterson, N. L. (1987). *Early intervention for handicapped and at-risk children.* Denver, CO: Love Publishing.

Reinhartsen, D. B., Garfinkle, A. N., & Wolery, M. (2002). Engagement with toys in two-year-old children with autism: Teacher selection versus child choice. *Research and Practice for Persons with Severe Disabilities, 27,* 175–187.

Rosenberg, S., Clark, M., Filer, J., Hupp, S., & Finkler, D. (1992). Facilitating active learner participation. *Journal of Early Intervention, 16,* 262–274.

Rosenberg, S., Robinson, C., & Beckman, P. (1984). Teaching skills inventory: A measure of parent performance. *Journal of the Division for Early Childhood, 8,* 107–113.

Rule, S., Losardo, A., Dinnebeil, L., Kaiser, A., & Rowland, C. (1998). Translating research on naturalistic instruction into practice. *Journal of Early Intervention, 21,* 283–293.

Sameroff, A. J., & Chandler, M. J. (1975). Reproductive risk and the continuum of caretaking casualty. In F. D. Horowitz, M. Hetherington, S. Scarr-Salapatek, & G. Siegel (Eds.), *Review of child development research* (vol. 4, pp. 187–244). Chicago: University of Chicago Press.

Sameroff, A. J., & Fiese, B. (1990). Transactional regulation and early intervention. In S. J. Meisels & J. P. Shonkoff (Eds.), *Handbook of early childhood early intervention* (pp. 119–149). Cambridge, MA: Cambridge University Press.

Sandall, S., McLean, M. E., & Smith, B. J. (2000). *DEC recommended practices in early intervention/early childhood special education.* Longmont, CO: Sopris West.

Sandall, S., & Schwartz, I. S. (2002). *Building blocks for teaching preschoolers with special needs.* Baltimore: Paul H. Brookes.

Schafer, D. S., & Moersch, M. S. (Eds.) (1981). *Developmental programming for infants and young children.* Ann Arbor: University of Michigan Press.

Schwartz, I. S., Billingsley, F. F., & McBride, B. M. (1998). Including children with autism in inclusive preschools: Strategies that work. *Young Exceptional Children, 1*(2), 19–26.

Simeonsson, R. J., Huntington, G. S., Short, R. J., & Ware, W. B. (1982). The Carolina record of individual behavior: Characteristics of handicapped infants and children. *Topics in Early Childhood Special Education, 2,* 43–55.

Slentz, K. L., & Bricker, D. (1992). Family-guided assessment for IFSP development: Jumping off the family assessment bandwagon. *Journal of Early Intervention, 16,* 11–19.

Trivette, C. M., & Dunst, C. J. (2000). Recommended practices in family-based practices. In S. Sandall, M. E. McLean, & B. J. Smith (Eds.), *DEC recommended practices in early intervention/early childhood special education* (pp. 39–46). Longmont, CO: Sopris West.

Twardosz, S., Cataldo, M. F., & Risley, T. R. (1974). Open environment design for infant and toddler day care. *Journal of Applied Behavior Analysis, 7,* 529–546.

Vincent, L. J., Salisbury, C., Walter, G., Brown, P., Gruenewald, L. J., & Powers, M. (1980). Program evaluation and curriculum development in early childhood special education: Criteria of the next environment. In W. Sailor, B. Wilcox, & L. Brown (Eds.), *Methods of instruction for severely handicapped students* (pp. 303–328). Baltimore: Paul H. Brookes.

Westlake, C. R., & Kaiser, A. P. (1991). Early childhood services for children with severe disabilities: Research, values, policy, and practices. In L. H. Meyer, C. A. Peck, & L. Brown (Eds.), *Critical issues in the lives of people with severe disabilities* (pp. 429–458). Baltimore: Paul H. Brookes.

Wolfgang, C. H., & Wolfgang, M. E. (1992). *School for young children: Developmentally appropriate practices.* Boston: Allyn and Bacon.

Wolery, M. (1996). Early childhood special and general education. In R. A. McWilliam (Eds.), *Rethinking pull-out services in early intervention* (pp. 185–215). Baltimore: Paul H. Brookes.

Wolery, M. (2000). Recommended practices in child-focused interventions. In S. Sandall, M. E. McLean, & B. J. Smith (Eds.), *DEC recommended practices in early intervention/early childhood special education* (pp. 29–37). Longmont, CO: Sopris West.

Woods, J. J., & McCormick, K. M. (2002). Toward an integration of child- and family-centered practices in the assessment of preschool children: Welcoming the family. *Young Exceptional Children, 5*(3), 2–11

Zigler, E., & Yale Research Group. (1976). *Summary of findings from longitudinal evaluations of intervention programs.* New Haven, CT: Yale University Press.

CHAPTER 21

Transition Planning and Adult Issues

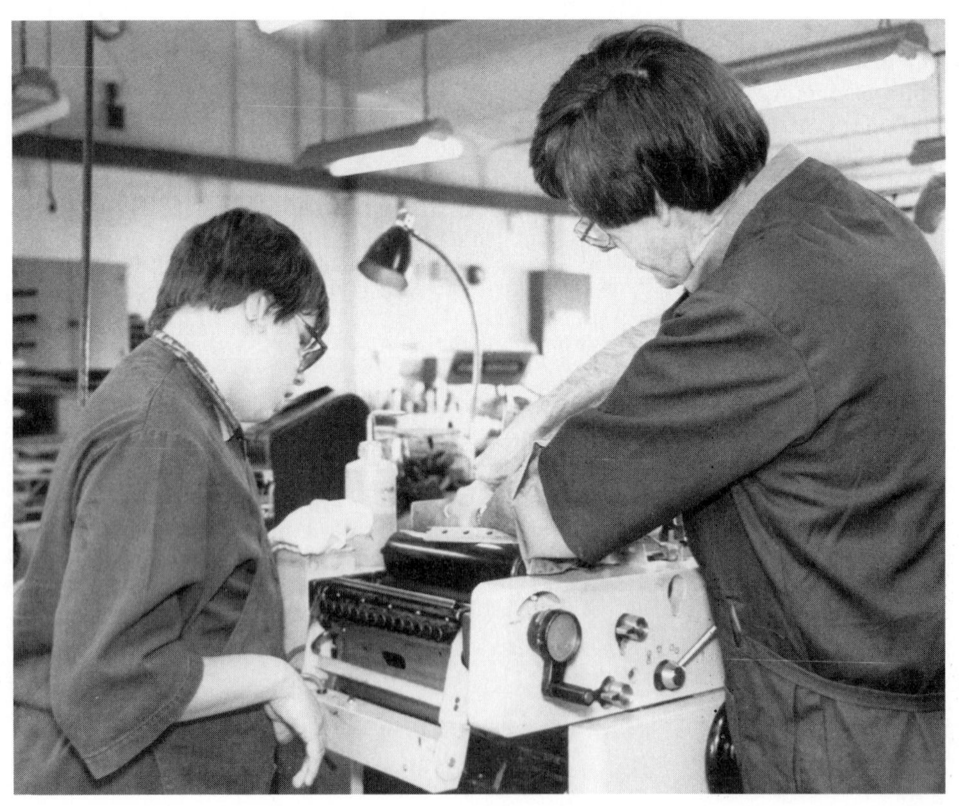

In this chapter issues associated with the movement of the student with disabilities from high school to the adult world are addressed. The chapter provides information on how to prepare for transition, the development of the transition individual education plan, and issues for consideration in the support of the student with severe disabilities in high school.

The Importance of Transition Planning

One of the most difficult transitions that students with severe disabilities and their families face is leaving the public school system and entering the adult world. The transition from school to adulthood involves major adjustments for the student with disabilities. Issues of importance are where the individual will live and work and how access to peers for friendship and leisure opportunities will be provided. In addition, the student's family will be leaving a public school system that offers services on an entitlement basis and entering an adult service system that operates on the basis of eligibility. This means that employment and living opportunities are not guaranteed for every individual and that families face many unknowns when they plan for their child's future.

Transition planning is a process designed to prepare for the inevitable exit of the student from the public school program (West et al., 1999). In transition planning, the school, family, and community work together with the student to anticipate and prepare for adulthood activities. Aspects considered in this planning process are the student's employment and financial independence, living arrangements, mobility, peer and community relationships, and self-esteem (Wehman, 2001).

Two concepts are fundamental to transition planning and the development of a transition curriculum. These concepts, self-determination and natural supports, are principles that should guide the thinking and actions of the collaborative team. These principles will assist the collaborative team in developing transition supports focused on providing students with disabilities a full life within the community.

Self-Determination

The transition experience for an adolescent leaving high school and entering adulthood is the process of self-determination. As young adults leave high school, they make decisions about employment, further education, living arrangements, and social relationships. These decisions may be facilitated by the adults in parental or mentor roles, but usually stem from the interests and preferences of the young adult. It is desirable that young adults with severe disabilities also experience self-determination.

Self-determination has been described as "acting as the primary causal agent in one's life and making choices and decisions regarding one's quality of life, free from undue external influence or interference" (Wehmeyer, 1992, p. 305). Self-determination develops over the life span and is associated with reaching adulthood. In the last 25 years the disability rights movement has been focused on the broad outcome of allowing persons with disabilities the right to the opportunity to be self-determined (Hughes & Agran, 1998). Issues such as accessibility, employment rights, community living, inclusive schooling, mobility, and personal care assistance all stem from the desire of individuals with disabilities to access the activities and lifestyle that they desire. A person can be said to be self-determined when their actions reflect autonomy, self-regulation, empowerment, and self-realization (Wehmeyer, 1996). A person who is self-determined has control over his or her own life and is able to advocate for the quality of life that is desired.

Self-determination is what is desired for all adults. Schooling should be designed to foster the ability of all students to become self-determined adults. In general education, students without disabilities are taught the prerequisite skills that prepare them for technical careers or further education. Students are provided with increasing opportunities for decision making and are expected to assume more personal responsibility as they grow older. The fostering of self-determination occurs implicitly within the schooling and parenting experience. For students with severe disabilities, the promotion of self-determination should be explicitly addressed. (Agran, Blanchard, & Wehmeyer, 2000). There is no implicit model for providing students with disabilities increasing autonomy or independence. Often, the contrary occurs. Teachers and parents neglect to address issues of independence until the student's graduation is impending and decisions must be made about adult living.

Promoting Student Self-Competence

An important task for educators is to promote the attitudes, perceptions, and skills necessary for students to act as causal agents in their lives. As students enter into high school, a transition curriculum should be focused on fostering the student's abilities to make choices, set goals, and engage in problem solving.

The curriculum should address not only the student's ability to make decisions about school, but should focus on the comprehensive lifestyle domains of school, home, and community. Teachers and families must work in partnership to provide the student with adequate opportunities to make choices in their lives and to participate within the community (Brown, Gothelf, Guess, & Lehr, 1998; Wehman, 2001; Wehmeyer, 1998).

Fostering the self-determination of students with severe disabilities may seem difficult, especially if a student does not use conventional forms of communication or has significant cognitive challenges. Strategies for instructing students with the most severe disabilities to develop skills of self-determination include teaching students to make choices, developing self-initiated behavior, supporting expressive communication, understanding student preferences, and providing the student with mechanisms to communicate preference, and using positive behavioral support to provide students with conventional and appropriate forms of communication to replace problem behavior (Brown et al., 1998). The student with severe disabilities may always need support and may not be capable of independent performance. But this should not imply that self-determination is not possible (Wehmeyer, 1998).

The job coach provides training and support to the employee with disabilities.

Natural Supports

An important change in the conceptualization of how to best support individuals with disabilities has occurred in the last decade. In the past, disability service providers were paid to provide services that supported individuals with disabilities to work and live. If support was needed, the next step was to locate the funding and a paid provider. No thought was given to the supports that may already be in place within a work setting, school, or community.

The concept of natural supports refers to reliance on the persons within typical environments and the use of typical activities for support, instead of relying on specialized services and personnel (Nisbet, 1992). Although the concept of natural supports appears to be simple, the process of using natural supports requires a radical change in how the delivery of specialized services has been implemented.

The concept of natural supports has been applied to supporting coworkers with disabilities, individuals with disabilities living in their own homes, and students within inclusive classrooms. The use of natural supports in employment has been discussed and debated the most in the literature (DiLeo & Luecking, 1995; Hagner, 1996; Mank, 1996; Nisbet & Hagner, 1988; Test & Wood, 1996). Early efforts at obtaining job placements involved marketing the benefits of supported employment to potential employers and assuring them of their minimal involvement. This practice may restrict the inclusion and participation of workers with disabilities. In recent years, business management has begun to recognize the need to support all workers. Job developers and job coaches should identify and use those resources for individuals with severe disabilities. This calls for a new framework of support that involves the teaching of supported employment techniques (precise instruction, supervision, job analysis, and self-management strategies) to supervisors and coworkers. Employment specialists and job coaches could provide assistance to company training programs and use existing assistance programs to provide needed job supports (Rhodes, Sandow, Mank, Buckley, & Albin, 1991).

Nisbet and Hagner (1988) suggest that, before placement of a worker with disabilities, work environments should be examined to determine the available natural supports and social interactions so that supported employment efforts can build on what is already in place. One option for providing support and supervision to workers may be to use coworkers rather than the job coach.

In a study conducted by Lee and colleagues (1997), two models for training employees with severe disabilities were examined. The researchers examined the social interactions of workers with disabilities and their coworkers in their employment at a Pizza Hut Restaurant. One group of workers had been trained by a job coach, and the second group of workers had been trained by managers who had been taught to mentor the new workers and foster natural supports. The workers with severe disabilities who had been trained in the mentor model had significantly more reciprocal social interactions when compared to workers trained by a job coach. These data suggest that a model of natural support may be beneficial in promoting the social interaction and integration of employees with severe disabilities.

In community living, individuals with disabilities have relied on neighbors, roommates, or personal care attendants (hired by the individual with disabilities) to provide assistance with daily living skills, community access, and transportation (Kennedy, 1993; Klein, 1992; Shoultz, 1993). For example, an individual with physical disabilities who needs assistance with bathing and dressing may receive daily personal care assistance in his own apartment from someone, rather than living in a residential center where daily care attendants are hired as staff.

The use of natural support in inclusive schooling describes the use of support structures (persons, activities) that exist for nondisabled students in the inclusion of the student with disabilities. For example, peers are asked to assist a student with mobility difficulties rather than use a paraprofessional. Cooperative learning strategies may be used to ensure the inclusion of children who are on different learning levels rather than relying solely on individualized instruction. The use of natural supports for inclusive schooling is discussed in detail in Chapter 10.

Postschool Outcomes

As the student's remaining time in high school becomes limited, the collaborative team is challenged to provide the instruction and experiences that will lead to optimal postschool outcomes. In the last 25 years, many changes have occurred in society that broaden the opportunity for a full adult lifestyle within the community. Students with severe disabilities do not have to settle for an adult life in segregated work environments or institutional living. Although there are no entitlement programs for adults with disabilities, many social service agencies have successfully supported adults with disabilities in living, working, and enjoying a rich social life within the community.

The following postschool outcome areas should be considered for the student with disabilities. It is particularly important that the collaborative team consider all domains of the student's lifestyle, as well as the student's preferences and interests, and build a transition plan that will help the student to achieve a full adult life.

Supported Employment

A primary area of emphasis for students in secondary programs is vocational training. Only in recent years has the employment of students with severe disabilities been a realistic expectation. This change in expected outcomes has developed through the provision of longitudinal vocational training in the school system and opportunities for supported employment. Before such opportunities for real work in the community were available, students with severe disabilities were often relegated to adult activity programs or sheltered workshops or sat at home after graduation from high school.

Supported employment, which provides paid work to individuals with severe disabilities who may need support or supervision, was designed to meet the needs of persons who have not been traditionally eligible for rehabilitation services and who may need ongoing support because of the severity of their disability.

The supported employment model was developed in response to the inadequacy of the traditional approach to employment services. In the past the options available to persons with disabilities were competitive employment, sheltered workshops, and work activity programs. The traditional model was conceptualized as a continuum, with individuals moving from sheltered work situations to jobs in the community as their skill level increased. In reality, few persons with severe disabilities ever moved beyond the sheltered situations. In addition, sheltered work situations provided very low wages and limited contact with nondisabled persons.

Supported employment is valued over other work programs (e.g., sheltered workshops, work activity programs) because it offers workers with disabilities the support that they need to work in the community in real jobs with nondisabled coworkers. In the evaluation of supported work programs, supported employees have stated that they prefer their jobs to sheltered work programs and value their relationship with their job coach. They have stated that job coaches help them not only to learn the job, but also to learn appropriate behavior and to advocate for themselves in situations other than work (Test, Hinson, Solow, & Keul, 1993). They also experience increase of wages (Cimera, 1998; Thompson, Powers, & Houchard, 1992; Tines, Rusch, McCaughrin, & Conley, 1990).

Recent research on supported employment and individuals with severe disabilities has demonstrated that some individuals with severe disabilities achieve high-quality outcomes in terms of work wages, typicalness, and social integration and that their success seems to be related to training efforts with their nondisabled coworkers (Mank, Cioffi, & Yovanoff, 1998). Data also indicate that it is more beneficial to provide coworker training in small groups, rather than formal training sessions and to include specific information on the supports needed by a particular individual with the disability. General disability awareness training was not found to be related to worker wage or social integration outcomes (Mank, Cioffi, & Yovanoff, 1999).

Traditional practice in vocational education for students with severe disabilities was to provide training in a variety of work skills (e.g., sorting, assembling, packaging) to prepare for eventual vocational training. The rationale was that students should learn to sort objects or complete simple assembly projects to develop the prerequisite skills needed for employment. But because the skills that were taught had little or no relationship to jobs in the community, this type of prevocational training did not increase a student's employability. Students with severe disabilities must be taught functional skills in natural settings and with materials that will be used by the student. For example, students who live in a community where there are potential jobs in a hospital and in several shopping malls should not be trained to do assembly tasks. The most efficient method of instruction is to use the community environment and the tasks involved in the job for training.

In high school a large portion of the instruction should occur in community environments and employment sites. Some authors have recommended that by high school half the day should be spent in vocational training (Hutchins & Renzaglia, 1990). Once the high school student is eligible, the curriculum also should consist of paid employment experiences in the community. The goal for a high school vocational program is to provide students with experiences in a range of employment situations so that they graduate with several paid work experiences on their résumé.

Supported Living

As individuals with disabilities were moved from the institution to the community, many residential service providers developed residential placements as a continuum of services (Klein, 1992; Racino, Taylor, Walker, & O'Connor, 1993). Individuals who had intensive support needs were typically placed in larger congregate living situations where direct care staff and nursing services were available. Individuals with less intensive needs, if they met an eligibility criteria, were placed in smaller, more homelike settings where they could be responsible for their own daily care.

In recent years, the field has moved away from a continuum of services for residential living to person-centered approaches for supporting individuals to live in the community (Klein, 1992; Racino, 1995; Racino et al., 1993). In a person-centered approach to residential living, the concepts of providing housing and providing support are separated. No longer would a service agency own the facility, employ the staff, and provide the support services. The following elements characterize the housing and support approach: (1) the focus is on people, not programs, (2) supports are provided wherever a person may live, (3) individuals have choices in housing, home location, and roommates, (4) there are opportunities for home ownership or leasing, (5) supports are individualized and flexible, (6) "getting to know the person" is a valued assessment strategy, (7) services are focused on building natural supports, and (8) individuals are given choices about who provides services (Racino & Taylor, 1993).

In the housing and support approach, creative strategies are used to provide the level of supports necessary for an individual, and housing arrangements are individually determined. For example, an individual may live in a home shared with nondisabled roommates, owned or leased by their guardian or themselves, or shared with paid support providers. Support options may include a personal attendant, live-in support providers, or technological adaptations and communication devices that facilitate independent living. In a study that compared the experiences of supportive living participants compared to participants who received traditional residential supports, supportive living was not shown to be more expensive. Moreover, participants in supportive living were more likely to engage in activities in the community, experience a wider variety of activities, and do preferred activities more frequently (Howe, Horner, & Newton, 1998).

Community Participation

When individuals with disabilities lived in segregated, congregate living facilities and spent their days in sheltered workshops or activity programs, there was little contact with others in the community. Typically, ventures into the community consisted of facility-wide outings or field trips. An important element of the housing and support approach is community inclusion and participation.

Nondisabled individuals engage in many activities in the community that are critical to domestic living and bring them in contact with other people. Mundane tasks such as grocery shopping, picking up the dry cleaning, banking, using public transportation, and going to the drug store are all activities during which you interact with other persons in the community. In the past, when individuals lived in sheltered, segregated environments, these activities were conducted by staff. As the collaborative team examines options for community living and participation, these activities should be considered as important to the student's independence and self-determination. Many individuals with severe disabilities need assistance with these activities, but this assistance should not preclude their active participation in daily tasks that bring them into the community and in contact with neighbors and friends.

Also, many activities of community participation offer social opportunities or comprise the social life of many people. For example, faith community (e.g., church, synagogue) activities offer a rich milieu of spiritual support, community service, social support, and social activities. For some people, participation in political advocacy organizations (e.g., National Organization for Women), interest groups (e.g., Sierra Club), or neighborhood associations provides opportunities for developing relationships with individuals who share similar interests.

Recreation and Leisure

The development of recreation and leisure opportunities and skills is important to most adults. Of course, what defines recreation and leisure is highly individualized. Some adults may love to shop and view shopping as a leisure pursuit. Others may despise shopping and seek to engage in spectator events within the community and on television. Most communities offer a wealth of recreation and leisure opportunities with a variety of experiences for the individual with disabilities. It is not necessary to develop specialized programs or seek out recreational programs designed solely for individuals with disabilities.

The first step to developing recreation and leisure outcome goals is to identify the student's interests. Many students may not have been exposed to many choices of hobbies, interests, or activities. (Modell &Valdez, 2002). High school may be a time during which new leisure and recreation pursuits can be identified and students with disabilities can be supported by their peers and families in exploring them. Interest areas may be hobbies (crafts, collecting, gardening), clubs (music, games, social service, arts), spectator events (sports, music, films, theater), sports (fishing, golfing, basketball), community events (fairs, festivals, concerts), and activities that can occur alone or with friends (reading, video games, cooking, listening to music). Once a student's interest areas have been identified, the collaborative team can examine the student's support or instructional needs to fully develop these interests so that they may be maintained postschool.

Postsecondary Education and Training

Some students with severe disabilities will continue instruction past their enrollment in high school. Technical schools, trade schools, community colleges, and continuing education community classes all may offer opportunities for ongoing education and training. These options should be identified within transition planning. Activities or strategies that facilitate the identification or enrollment in these options should be considered within transition planning.

Postsecondary schooling may also be an option for the student who has completed 4 years of high school but is still eligible for public schooling. An increasing number of programs offer schooling in postsecondary settings (community colleges and college campuses) to students with severe disabilities who are age 18 to 21 (Grigal, Neubert, & Moon, 2001; Hall, Kleinert, & Kearns, 2000). The provision of this option allows students to continue to receive their public education within a setting that is chronologically age appropriate (Fisher & Sax, 1999; Tashie, Malloy, & Lichtenstein, 1998). These programs are typically staffed by public-school-supported special educators who ensure that the student receives appropriate instruction including inclusion in college electives (as appropriate), vocational skills training, recreation skills instruction, and community-based instruction. The postsecondary setting offers a full range of options for a variety of instructional situations and opportunities for social integration with same-age peers.

Social Relationships

Families are greatly concerned about the potential social isolation of their adult child with disabilities. Attending school everyday offers many opportunities for developing friendships that may not be so obvious or easy to access in adult life. It is very important to consider the contexts available for developing friendships when the student leaves school and to identify the skills that the student must develop to initiate and maintain social relationships.

The collaborative team should carefully examine the desires of the student in friendship development, the kind of friends that she most enjoys, and the opportunities that will be available in postschool activities to maintain or build relationships. For example, the team may consider two potential job opportunities and decide on the job that also provides rich social interactions, rather than the job in which the student will work in isolation. The team may also want to consider teaching the student skills that are critical to the development and maintenance of relationships. For example, a student may need to be taught how to call a friend on the phone or how to respond to an invitation.

Transition Services

The importance of transition services was legislatively recognized when Public Law 94-142 was reauthorized and expanded under PL 101-476, the Individuals with Disabilities Education Act (IDEA), in 1990. In the reauthorization of IDEA in 1997, the age at which a statement of transition needs must be included in the student's IEP was changed from age 16 to 14. At age 16 the IEP must also include a statement of interagency responsibilities or any needed linkages for transition services if appropriate. Transition services are addressed in IDEA in the following way (PL 101-476, 20 U.S.C. 1401 [a][19]):

> Transition services means a coordinated set of activities for a student, designed within an outcome-oriented process, which promotes movement from school to post-school activities, including post-secondary education, vocational training, integrated employment (including supported employment), continuing and adult education, adult services, independent living or community participation. The coordinated set of activities shall be based upon the individual student's needs taking into account the student's preferences and interests and shall include instruction, related services, community experiences, the development of employment, and other post-school adult living objectives and, when appropriate, acquisition of daily living skills and functional vocational evaluation.

When planning a student's transition, these principles should guide the nature of the planning process and program (Steere, Pancsofar, Wood, & Hecimovic, 1990). A first priority must be to include students and their families as equal and collaborative partners. The decisions as to where an individual should work and live cannot be made without the full involvement of the family and recognition of the preferences of the student. Transition planning should not be regarded as an additional aspect of an appropriate program, but should serve to direct curricular efforts. Students with severe disabilities must be provided with a program that results in the acquisition of functional, community-referenced skills. The emphasis of transition planning should be on preparing supports for the student, rather than focusing on preparing the student to meet the eligibility criteria of existing situations. This emphasis requires that the planning team work collaboratively in an ongoing partnership with adult service and funding agencies. Finally, a major goal of the team should be to ensure that each student graduates into paid community employment. Transition planning efforts should result in employment experiences that allow each student to attain an improved quality of life.

Halpern (1993) has proposed that teams consider broad dimensions when attempting to develop a variety of life goals for students in transition. He has identified the life domains of physical and material well-being, performance of adult roles, and personal fulfillment as areas of concern when considering outcomes for students in transition. These quality-of-life domains, presented in Figure 21–1, can be used to structure and evaluate a student's transition program.

Figure 21–1 Quality-of-Life Domains

Physical and Material Well-Being

- physical and mental health
- food, clothing, and lodging
- financial security
- safety from harm

Performance of Adult Roles

- mobility and community access
- vocation, career, employment
- leisure and recreation
- personal relationships and social networks
- educational attainment
- spiritual fulfillment
- citizenship (e.g., voting)
- social responsibility (e.g., doesn't break laws)

Personal Fulfillment

- happiness
- satisfaction
- sense of general well-being

Source: "Quality of Life as a Conceptual Framework for Evaluating Transition Outcomes" by A. Halpern, 1993, *Exceptional Children, 59,* 486–498.

For example, the domain of physical and material well-being includes the basic outcomes of physical and mental health; food, clothing, and lodging; financial security; and safety from harm. These outcomes should be viewed by the transition program as basic entitlements and the "minimal conditions" that should be met (Halpern, 1993, p. 490). The outcomes in the domain of performance of adult roles include a variety of opportunities that should be considered by the transition program to ensure that all aspects of an individual's life are addressed. Finally, the domain of personal fulfillment should be examined as an essential outcome in both the planning and evaluation of a transition program.

Families as Partners in the Transition Process

The transition to adulthood is a very difficult time for families of students with disabilities (Callahan & Garner, 1997; Thorin, Yovanoff, & Irvin, 1996; Whitney-Thomas & Hanley-Maxwell, 1996). Families struggle with wanting to create opportunities for their child's independence, while being concerned about their child's health and safety (Thorin et al., 1996). They want their child to have a life that is separate from the family, but are concerned that their adult child have a good life rich with experiences and the caring of others (Thorin et al., 1996). Families are particularly concerned about where their children will live and if they will be socially isolated as adults (Hanley-Maxwell, Whitney-Thomas, & Pogoloff, 1995; Westling, 1996; Whitney-Thomas & Hanley-Maxwell, 1996).

In a qualitative study of the transition experiences of nine students with severe disabilities, Cooney (2002) found that transition meetings were rarely conducted in a way that promoted the meaningful participation of family members or the student with disabilities. The researcher found that the young adults were able to articulate their desires for postschool working and living clearly and that their parents were optimistic about a promising adulthood. The researcher described the parents as approaching transition "inductively," with a focus on their child's strengths and the creation of opportunities that built on her strengths. In contrast, school professionals were described as approaching transition "deductively," with a basic skepticism about whether the student could achieve the transition goals. School team members looked for a match between the student's skill level and a program and judged many options as not viable if there was not a match. The author concluded that these students experienced a transition that was "done to them," rather than being engaged in the transition process.

It is of utmost importance that the concerns of the family are recognized and addressed in transition planning (Grossi, Regan, & Regan, 1998; Turnbull & Turnbull, 1996; Westling, 1996). Often school personnel are narrowly focused on the importance of assisting the student with being ready for employment and neglect the broader issues of community living and participation. It is critical that school personnel work closely with families and seek to understand the unique and individual concerns of the family as they think about their child's transition to adulthood.

The teacher must offer a variety of mechanisms to establish rapport with families. Once rapport and trust are established, the dialogue on family concerns about their child's future can occur. Teachers may want to consider the strategies listed in Figure 21–2 for promoting family involvement. It is important for teachers to remember that each family may connect with the school in a different way and may be comfortable with some activities and not others. Some families will want to read articles or books about transition issues. Other families may enjoy attending meetings at the school where topics relating to adult issues are discussed. A family may appreciate receiving a list of community adult service providers that they may contact to find out about services and programs.

In a survey of families who are culturally and linguistically diverse (CLD), researchers found a gap between the perception of school personnel about the involvement of CLD families in transition planning activities and the self-report of the family (Geenen, Powers, & Lopez-Vasquez, 2001). The research indicated that parents and professionals were in general agreement about the importance of a variety of transition activities. CLD parents, in comparison to European American families placed a higher value on the importance of talking to their child about transition, helping their child prepare for postsecondary schooling, teaching the child about family culture, teaching the child to care for his or her disability, and teaching the child to use public transportation independently. The CLD parents rated themselves as highly engaged in transition planning, but reported low participation in school-based planning meetings. Professionals rated CLD parents as having a low level of involvement in transition activities.

This research demonstrates some of the challenges of promoting parent involvement. Professionals must broaden their perception of what it may mean to "be involved" and realize that participation in school-based meetings is not the only vehicle for involvement. It is possible that for CLD families the launching of their child into adulthood is a community and family activity,

Figure 21–2 Promoting Family Involvement in Transition Planning

1. Provide meetings on transition issue for families
2. Connect the family with a family who has successfully moved through the transition process
3. Provide social events where families may meet each other
4. Arrange visitations to agencies that provide adult services
5. Lend videotapes or provide readings that explain adult issues and support strategies
6. Maintain informal contact with families
7. Provide the family with information on the student's social, academic, and vocational achievements
8. Assist families with identifying friendly peers for after-school social activities
9. Make sure families are aware of school social events and family activities
10. Encourage family and friends to attend planning meetings
11. Ask families to use their social networks to identify employment opportunities
12. Assist families in scheduling person-centered planning meetings
13. Identify community social, leisure, and recreational opportunities
14. Help families identify strategies to build the student's social network
15. Assist families in developing instructional and support strategies to use at home and in the community.

rather than an experience planned by the school. School personnel should examine their presumptions and efforts at developing partnerships with families before assuming that a family is not involved or uninterested in the transition process. Ideally, transition planning meetings should occur in a manner that is most comfortable for the students with disabilities and their family members.

Person-Centered Planning

Person-Centered Planning meetings offer a powerful mechanism for developing a vision for the student's future and for identifying persons who can provide support (see Chapter 5). Personal Futures Planning may be used prior to transition planning to develop an understanding of the student's preferences and to organize natural supports (Callahan & Garner, 1997; Hagner, Helm, & Butterworth, 1996; Kregel, 1998; Whitney-Thomas, Shaw, Honey, & Butterworth, 1998). When Person-Centered Planning meetings are held prior to the development of a transition IEP, families may participate more in the transition IEP meeting and be more satisfied with their involvement in the process (Miner & Bates, 1997).

The teacher can initiate a Person-Centered Planning meeting using the processes described as Personal Futures Planning (Mount & Zwernick, 1988), Essential Lifestyle Planning (Smull & Harrison, 1992), Planning Alternative Tomorrows with Hope (PATH) (Pearpoint, O'Brien, & Forest, 1993), or Making Action Plans (MAPS) (Forest & Pearpoint, 1992) by describing the process to the family and sharing literature about the process and outcomes. In most communities, adult service agencies are familiar with Person-Centered Planning processes and should be able to participate or be a resource in planning the meeting. Teachers need to remember that Person-Centered Planning is an informal, collaborative, and creative process focused on articulating a vision for an individual and creating a circle of support. It is unlike meetings that are school based and regulated by bureaucratic processes or paperwork. Person-Centered Planning meetings are typically conducted in an informal setting; involve friends, family and professionals; examine all aspects of an individual's life; and are considered an ongoing process.

Developing the Transition Individualized Education Plan

The scope of the transition IEP is purposefully broad, covering the full range of adult life domains and addressing in particular the problems that students with disabilities encounter in their adult life. Preparing for the transition to adulthood challenges the collaborative team to think deeply about the lifestyle of the student once he graduates from high school. The collaborative team should consider preparation of the student for work, community living, community participation, recreation and leisure, and social relationships. IDEA states that the transition services must represent coordinated activities. Coordinated activities are activities that complement each other and may be provided by different individuals and agencies. For example, a student may enroll in a career exploration course offered by the school that includes paid work experiences during the last 2 years of high school enrollment and be supported in an after-school job by an adult service agency that will continue to provide supports after graduation. IDEA explicitly addresses the need for identifying and connecting with agencies that can provide supports and services to the student with disabilities.

The transition IEP maintains familiar components of the traditional IEP (e.g., identifying long-term goals and short-term objectives), but also differs in important ways. First, the student must be invited to attend the IEP. The step is to ensure that students have an opportunity to express their preferences and interests and are encouraged to engage in self-advocacy. Second, the transition activities identified must be based on the student's preferences or interests. This further reinforces the notion that self-determination is a critical process in the transition of the student to adulthood. Finally, the transition IEP requires that the collaborative team address a broader vision than just educational goals for 1 year. The statement of needed transition services is to project what services will be needed to reach the desired postschool outcomes of the student with disabilities.

It is critically important that the student have a voice in the transition planning process (Thoma, 1999; Thoma, Rogan, & Baker, 2001; Wehmeyer, 2001; West et al., 1999). Although a student with severe disabilities may not be able to independently run a transition meeting, every effort should be made to establish a partnership with the student, promote the active involvement of the student, assist the student in contributing using communication and decision-making supports, and ensuring that interactions are respectful of the student. Figure 21–3 provides some ideas about how to promote the full participation of the student in the meeting. It is still very common that transition planning meetings are adult directed, paperwork driven, and scheduled to meet the needs of the professionals. In addition, communication with the student occurs more as an afterthought, with little preparation to ensure that the student can be actively involved (Thoma, Rogan, & Baker, 2001).

Before the transition IEP meeting occurs, the student's teacher and family members should be engaged in preparation activities. The teacher or collaborative team should become familiar with community resources and services, determine the student's present level of performance, identify who should be involved in the transition IEP meeting, determine the best dates and times to convene the meeting, send out written notification for the meeting, help the student to prepare for her role in the meeting, and participate in a process for identifying the preferences, interests, and dreams of the student for adult living.

The family can prepare for the meeting by preparing their child for participation in the meeting, assisting their child in developing a vision for the future, and thinking about the types of supports that they will be able to provide their child during and after the transition. It is very helpful for the family to gather and organize background information on the student and the student's history or experiences in work and the community. In addition, the family should become aware of services that exist in the community. During the transition IEP, very difficult topics will be discussed. The family will participate with the student and the collaborative team in thinking about the kind of job that the student may have after high school, where the student will live, how he will get around in the community, and how he will become part of the community and develop social relationships. It is helpful for the family to prepare for these topics by participating in a personal futures plan meeting or holding a family meeting where these topics are discussed with important family members and friends. The teacher should take an active role in helping the family to prepare for the transition IEP. The teacher may suggest visits to community agencies, could share articles or videos about important adult considerations (e.g., community living, supported employment), or may offer to connect a family with another family who has moved through the transition period and is experiencing successful community-based supports for their adult child.

Postschool Outcomes

The transition IEP includes a statement of postschool outcomes for each transition activity area. The transition areas include instruction in academic or vocational skills, community experiences, employment, postschool adult living skills, daily living skills, and functional vocational evaluation. Postschool outcome statements should be written from the student's perspective and be based on the student's preferences. The outcomes statements should be clearly and concisely written and be individualized, reflective, and futuristic statements that represent the student's desires. Postschool outcomes should describe what the student hopes to achieve 1 to 3 years posthigh school graduation. Here are examples of postschool outcome statements:

> "Juanita wants to live in an apartment with a roommate that she likes in an apartment building near her parents' home."

Figure 21–3 Strategies to Promote Student Participation in the Transition Planning Meeting

1. Ask the student to select the time and location of the meeting.
2. Have the student identify the persons to invite to the meeting. If the student needs support in the decision, provide photos of persons that the student might select or visual representations of topic areas that the student may want to discuss (employment, recreation, living).
3. Provide the student with an opportunity to role play what will occur in the meeting.
4. Support the student in meeting preparation (e.g., sharpening pencils, providing tablets, selecting a snack, making coffee).
5. Arrange the room so that the student sits in the position of meeting leader (head of the table).
6. Have the student pass out forms, documents, etc.
7. Refer to the meeting as being "(name of student)'s meeting."
8. Redirect team members if they talk about the student as if he or she is not present.
9. Provide a mechanism for the student to share his or her history and desires for the future. The student could operate a PowerPoint presentation depicting photos of his or her current situation and desires for the future or show a video made by the student and his or her family.
10. The student could use photos to communicate his or her desires or select photos to indicate his or her choices.
11. Bring the "maps" or illustrations from a person-centered planning meeting that was held before the transition planning meeting.
12. Use first person when writing goals. Confirm each goal with the student verbally before writing the goal on the plan.
13. Avoid discussion of skill deficits; focus on capacities, interests, and choices. When areas of difficulties are discussed, maintain respect for the student. For example, many people without disabilities openly acknowledge their personal challenges and preferences (e.g., "I don't like paperwork," "I'd rather work alone").
14. Use chart paper to illustrate the discussion or major points so that the student can follow along.
15. Once goals are developed, discuss transition services as supports that may be provided to the student. For example, the vocational rehabilitation counselor might say to the student "Joe, I'd be glad to work with you in finding a job that matches your interest in computers."

"I want to join a running club and go to community fun runs. I want to go to my family's church and participate in the adult choir."

"I want to be employed full time as a veterinary assistant."

Annual Goals and Objectives

Each postschool outcome will yield annual goals that indicate what will be accomplished in a 1-year time period. For example, Juanita stated that she wanted to live in an apartment. Annual goals for Juanita include learning how to prepare simple meals, to grocery shop, and to handle household emergencies. For every annual goal, a present level of performance should be stated that describes what the student is able to do, likes to do, or needs to work on. Short-term objectives are written for each annual goal. These objectives are the skills that the student must learn to meet the annual goal. For example, Juanita has an annual goal of learning how to prepare simple meals. Her short-term objectives include: Juanita will make a casserole using canned ingredients and the oven; Juanita will make a salad using fresh produce and bottled salad dressing; and Juanita will make a frozen dinner using the microwave.

Each objective should include an evaluation criteria for determining if the objective was met and the person responsible for implementing the objective. In the transition IEP, the person responsible for meeting the objective is not always the educator. The person responsible may be from a service agency or may be the family member who agrees that the objective will be taught at home or within the community. For example, Juanita's meal preparation objectives may be taught in home economics and in the home environment.

As the goals and objectives are developed, the transition services needed by the student will become clear. These services should not be driven by what the program wishes to provide to secondary students, but must be individually determined and driven by student preferences for postschool outcomes. There may be some areas for which no transition services are needed for the student. If no services are needed, a statement addressing why services are not needed should be included. The statement of needed transition services should also identify the participating agency's responsibilities or the linkages that are critical to the student's transition.

Teaching the Secondary Student

Secondary schools are concerned with the development of young adults into successful and independent adults. As a consequence, they offer a diversity of curriculum experiences and activities that provide a context for teaching the student with severe disabilities many of the skills needed for transition. Most secondary schools include work experiences, technical skills, basic academic programs, and special interest courses. The collaborative team should examine the transition needs of the student and then identify instructional contexts where those services or instructional supports can be provided.

Consider the instruction of Janice, a 17-year-old student with severe disabilities who is beginning her junior year in high school. When Janice graduates from school she wants to continue her employment at the Veterinary Hospital. Currently, she assists with feeding, grooming, and walking animals who are boarded. She would like to learn additional skills so that she may be employed as a veterinary assistant. Janice will live at home after graduating, although her family would like her to eventually purchase a mobile home and live with a roommate on her family's property. Janice has two good friends at her high school who will be going to college. She wants to maintain these friendships, but realizes that she will need to meet new friends. Janice wants to remain active in her family's church and would like to volunteer in the church's day-care program on Sunday and join the adult choir. Janice wants to be able to take the bus to work, shop for herself, and do her own banking.

The collaborative team examined the transition goals of Janice and her short-term objectives and created this schedule for her junior year. Janice will enroll in a home economics class where she receives instruction in meal preparation. She is also enrolled in a veterinary assistant course where she is supported by her peers and is provided with an individualized adapted curriculum to learn basic veterinary assistant skills. Janice loves to sing and will continue to pursue her interest in singing by enrolling in chorus. She will also enroll in an early childhood education course that provides students with training for work in early childhood programs. Janice will be taught basic skills of child care and emergency procedures for working with young children through an adapted curriculum and peer support. For two periods at the end of her high school day, Janice works at the Veterinary Hospital. A job coach assists her in learning skills on the job and teaches coworkers how to provide Janice with support and instruction in new work tasks. Janice will be learning how to take the bus to the Veterinary Hospital from her high school.

Janice's family is also actively involved in her transition support. They will be helping her to become independent in her daily living skills by teaching her household chores, asking her to prepare one meal a week, and assisting her with cashing her weekly paycheck at the bank. In addition, the family will seek opportunities for Janice to attend school-sponsored events (concerts, plays, pep rallies) with her friends. Janice's family will assist her in signing up for the adult choir at church and applying to help in the church day-care program. Her family will identify other events or activities in the community to which Janice can ride the bus, providing her with additional practice in using the bus independently.

The secondary teacher may feel a sense of urgency about the instructional needs of the student and the critical importance of preparation for adulthood. This urgency should not lead to providing instruction in isolation of typical peers or in contexts that are not natural. Through collaboration and creative thinking, contexts of instruction can be identified that will offer the secondary students the opportunity to learn skills with their nondisabled peers and enjoy the typical experiences of high school.

Vocational Instruction

The thrust of vocational programs for students with severe disabilities is to prepare them for eventual work placement in the community. Sowers and Powers (1991, p. 3) have identified the critical components of successful vocational programs to be the following:

1. Identify and train for jobs and tasks that reflect the local community job market.
2. Train work-related skills that are critical to job success.
3. Train students in community settings.
4. Use systematic instructional procedures to train students.
5. Identify adaptive strategies that will increase student independence.
6. Reconceptualize staff roles and organizational-structures.
7. Involve parents in the vocational preparation of their children.
8. Establish paid employment for students before they leave school.
9. Coordinate and collaborate with adult service programs.

Preparation for living and working in the community can begin as early as preschool and elementary school. For example, in the preschool classroom, students with severe disabilities can be taught that there are activity periods and then clean-up periods and that individuals are responsible for putting away their belongings and materials. These skills are used by all workers and are important to adult functioning.

In the elementary school, teachers can begin to prepare students for work by assigning them classroom chores or school jobs. Students may be responsible for classroom pet or plant care, assisting in the office or cafeteria, working in the media center, and doing tasks assigned by the teacher (e.g., stacking chairs, passing out books, collecting lunch money). At this time, community-based instruction also begins, with students learning individualized objectives that enhance independence and participation in relevant community environments (see Chapter 20).

In middle school, preparation for work in the community receives more attention. Teachers should assess the school to determine potential work sites that are relevant to jobs in the community. For example, filing and photocopying, which may be skills required in jobs that are potential supported employment placements, are tasks that are done in the school in multiple environments (e.g., office, media center, department office) and could be used for work-skill instruction. Other jobs may be found in the media center, computer room, attendance office, cafeteria, and office. Examples of relevant tasks are delivering messages, computer entry, cleaning, answering phones, and sorting mail. In the middle school, the emphasis of the vocational program should include assessing work opportunities in the community, assessing student job preferences, determining adaptations that may be needed to perform tasks, and teaching job skills (Sowers & Powers, 1991).

A major component of the high school vocational program is to provide students with disabilities with community work experience, career exploration, and the transition into employment that matches a student's preferences. Before job matching can occur, evaluation of both student needs and employment opportunities must take place (Hutchins & Renzaglia, 1990).

The evaluation of employment opportunities can be conducted by talking to the city or county employment agency, visiting businesses in the community, and/or surveying businesses in the community to establish what employment opportunities exist. From these contacts, the employment specialist or teacher can generate a task pool of potential jobs that may be appropriate for the supported employment of individuals with severe disabilities. A sample task pool is provided in Table 21–1. Once a task pool is developed, some jobs can be eliminated because they are not a match to the student's capabilities or interests. The task pool developed should be viewed as a dynamic list that will need to be updated as the local job market changes.

Once a task pool is identified, student needs should be assessed to determine a match between individual students and particular jobs. Factors to include in the assessment of student needs are the student's and the family's preferences, task-related and work-related skills, and supervision or support needs in a potential placement.

Community Work Experience

To provide high school students with community work experience, the secondary teacher should identify sites that match the task pool that was generated. The purpose in doing this is to develop a list of work experience sites that can serve as employment training sites and offer opportunities for students to gain experience in tasks that relate to jobs in the community. Often the employment teacher will use just one community site to train a group of students because it is easier to supervise and transport them. When this model is used, the employment teacher should try to ensure that the students are well dispersed in

Table 21–1 Generic Task Pool for Students with Physical and Multiple Disabilities

Tasks	*Examples/Descriptions*
Typing	Type membership cards at banks, associations, clubs, libraries. Type file folder labels. Type addresses on mailing labels or envelopes.
Computer Data Entry	Input customer, patient, client information for businesses and medical offices, and billing, inventory information for same. Input mailing list information for associations and commercial businesses.
Word Processing	Word process memos and letters. This occurs in almost any office. It requires ability to read cursive writing.
Filing	Place papers in individual file folders, placing folders in file drawers, and retrieving files. Complexity varies depending on file system.
Phone Answering	In small, informal offices one person may answer phone and then tell coworkers they have a call. Larger and more formal offices will include putting callers on hold and transferring calls. Typically will require taking messages (usually written, but potentially recording messages).
Photocopying	Few businesses are without a photocopy machine. The type of copying done varies among companies. Some only need copies of single-page documents; others need large documents and books or manuals. In most cases the person who photocopies is also responsible for collating (if it is not done by the machine) and stapling.
Collating/Stapling	Companies that perform a large amount of photocopying or have materials printed elsewhere may hire persons to collate and staple. Examples include print shops, direct mail businesses, associations.
Mail Preparation	Includes folding letters, stuffing envelopes, placing labels and stamps on envelopes, running a postage meter machine.
Packaging	Packaging products in manufacturing or distribution businesses. Type of product and packaging process will vary greatly.
Unpackage/Price	Most stores require merchandise received from distributors to be unpackaged (in some cases repackaged for sale) and a price tag or label placed on it. Pricing may be done by hand or with price gun. May also include placing the items on shelves.
Delivery	Deliver food for a restaurant, items from central supply or pharmacy to floors in hospital, fax messages that come in on central machine, documents from one office to other offices (e.g., legal documents from law office to courthouse).
Assembly/Light	Electronics assembly is a common type of light manufacturing task. There are hundreds of other products assembled in large and small businesses in most communities.
Light Cleaning	Most offices desire some light clean-up and straightening in addition to the more heavy cleaning done by a janitorial service. For example, banks need to have someone straighten up the lobby a couple of times a day.
Microfilming	Microfilming is becoming less prevalent due to the advent of computers. However, some businesses still employ microfilming for recordkeeping. Some banks microfilm checks. Hospitals and government offices also typically maintain microfilm records.

Source: Vocational Preparation and Employment of Students with Physical and Multiple Disabilities (p. 30), by J. Sowers and L. Powers, 1991, Baltimore: Paul H. Brookes Publishing Co. Reprinted by permission.

the site and have opportunities to learn several tasks (Sowers & Powers, 1991). The rotation of students in various employment training sites is part of the student assessment process. The goal in providing such rotations is to assess student preferences and work behavior to discern the employment situations that offer the best match to individual students.

Before placing a student, the Fair Labor Standards Act (FLSA) Section 14 compliance specialist in the regional U.S. Department of Labor, Wage, and Hour Division office should be contacted to determine if the student should be paid in the work placement (Moon, Kiernan, & Halloran, 1990). For a student not to be paid as a worker, the following six criteria must be met (U.S. Department of Labor, 1962):

1. The training, even though it includes actual operation of the facilities of the employer, is similar to that given in a vocational school.
2. The training is for the benefit of the trainees or students.
3. The trainees do not displace regular employees, but rather work under their close observation.
4. The employer who provides the training derives no immediate advantage from the activities of the

Table 21–2 Direct Service Strategy Definitions, Procedures, and Decision Rules

Support Strategy	*Procedures*	*Decision Rules*
Task analysis—Analysis of the stimulus and response requirements of each step in a task across the range of variability that occurs in the specific conditions in which the task is performed.	• Establish efficient task design. • Identify task-related stimulus for each response. • Articulate steps in terms of employer criteria. • Identify all conditions and variations. • Identify errors that occur. • Identify variations in criteria.	• Complete after-job analysis. • Use in response to documented performance problems. • Analyze errors and error patterns to provide efficient assistance. • Criteria for mastery must be based on performance according to employer criteria across all relevant conditions encountered.
Self-management—The use of systems that enable the user to gain control of environmental events and/or work behaviors. Self-management is further defined by the particular component emphasized, antecedent cue regulation, self-monitoring, or self-recruited feedback.	• Define the performance requirement, i.e., some specific form of initiation, monitoring or feedback. • Select and teach a system that emphasizes the appropriate component. • Use standard instructional procedures (task analysis, assistance, reinforcement and error correction) to document that the user knows how to manipulate the system.	• Determine when to initiate by analyzing dependence and/or trainer presence. • System must be individualized for the target worker and job site. • Systems should be as unobtrusive as possible. • Systems should be easy for target worker, employment training specialist, and employer to operate, maintain, and adapt over time. • Decisions regarding fading or withdrawing the system depend on obtrusiveness of the system, time involved in use, and worker and employer preference.
Productivity programming—Rate increase programs help target workers perform units of work according to time criteria specific to the task and work rate. Pacing programs help target workers identify varying environmental conditions that require different performance rates.	• Identify rate requirements for each task (beginning in job analysis). • Identify the frequency with which the pace changes. • Document the rate(s) at which the worker is able to perform. • Set incentives for increases in rate. • Select or identify cues for differences in pace. • Teach workers to respond to pacing cues.	• Rate issues depend on a system for identifying employer standards across varying production demands. • Task modification may increase productivity. • Self-managed systems can help workers increase rates of production and/or identify environmental cues requiring changes in pacing. • Criteria need to be validated for the job site according to the actual conditions the target worker encounters. • Production criteria change should therefore be assessed over time.
Community-referenced behavior management—Functional analysis to determine the relationship between difficult behavior (or classes of behavior) and events in the person's environment in order to apply an intervention that meets the unique demands of the individual, job site, and behavior under analysis.	• Observe and assess the individual in as many natural settings as possible. • Identify a range of stimulus conditions within and across environments. • Develop and test hypotheses regarding stimulus control factors. • Design a model for desired and excess responses. • Continue to analyze the behavior and presence or absence of various stimuli.	• Functional analysis should be used when extinction procedures are not successful. • Many individuals with challenging behaviors have little experience in employment settings. More natural stimuli may control more appropriate responses and obviate the need for intervention. • Support must be adequate for individuals with challenging behaviors. • Criteria need to be based on individual dignity, safety, security, and job site standards.

trainees, and on occasion the employer's operations may actually be impeded.

5. The trainees or students are not necessarily entitled to a job at the conclusion of the training period.

6. The employer and the trainees understand that the trainees or students are not entitled to wages for the time spent in training.

If these criteria are not met, there is an employment relationship, and the student must be paid minimum wage even if the work experience is part of the IEP or transition plan.

Instructional Strategies

The instruction of vocational skills is broader than teaching students with severe disabilities to perform work tasks. Work-related skills such as punching in on

Table 21–2 Continued

Support Strategy	Procedures	Decision Rules
Social skill training–The development of specific behaviors that occur in the context of interactions that take place in specific work sites.	• Identify specific activities and events and the social interactions involved. • Assess target worker participation and performance in these events. • Analyze targeted skills across the range of variation encountered in the work place. • Select performance alternatives. • Model the skill and allow the target worker to practice. • Shape, reinforce, and fade assistance.	• Target workers' preference in selecting activities and performance alternatives is critical. • Task analyses and/or self-management can be of assistance to the target worker and the trainer. • Social competence refers to perceived adherence to cultural rules. Coworker orientation and support can be invaluable.
Communication training–Development of the modality or type of system used, the form or rules, and the content of the "language."	• Identify job-related communication requirements. • Designate a communication modality or system. • Ensure that critical communication requirements are covered. • Add work-related and social content as needed. • Test for ease of use. • Train the worker, coworker, and employer to operate the system.	• Existing and highly technical systems may not enable the worker to communicate with coworkers, employers, and the public. • Systems and content should be introduced as needed. • Systems should be easy for the target worker, employment training specialist, coworkers, and employer to use, maintain, and adapt over time. • Due to skill and/or experiential deficits, some workers with no apparent communication disorders may need communication training.
Mobility training–Enabling a target worker to gain access to areas that are critical for worker performance and socialization in and around the workplace.	• Identify environments in which the individual has optimum mobility. • Identify the amount and range of mobility required for the job. • Match mobility strategies to demands of the job. • Identify discrepancies and make modifications. • Teach the target worker, coworkers, and the employer to optimize mobility.	• Job match is the first issue. • The person must learn to enjoy full access to work and social opportunities. • Shaping and sensitization may help some individuals overcome reticence. • Due to skill and/or experiential deficits, some individuals with no apparent mobility impairments may need mobility training. • Coworker orientation and training can help target workers feel welcome in new settings.

Source: Supported Employment, Models, Methods, and Issues 1st Edition by Rusch. © 1990. Reprinted with permission of Wadsworth, a division of Thomson Learning: www.thomsonrights.com. Fax 800 730-2215.

the time clock and gathering materials and social behavior such as greeting coworkers and interacting on breaks are instructional issues in addition to work-task skills.

The use of a task analysis is fundamental to the instruction of work tasks. In task analysis the job is broken down into meaningful and measurable steps, and instruction begins once an initial task analytic assessment have been conducted (see Chapter 6). Other instructional methods that may be used to teach students work-related skills and social behaviors have been described by Buckley, Mank, and Sandow (1990) and are presented in Table 21–2. Strategies that teachers have used for skill acquisition and generalization in other domains apply to achievement of work tasks and work-related behavior (Storey, Sandow, & Rhodes, 1990).

Some instructional issues should receive careful attention when teaching students work skills. The use of reinforcers should be carefully approached, with particular attention paid to using natural reinforcers and a reinforcement schedule that does not inhibit work progress. For example, the use of praise for each work step may call undue attention to the employee and may serve to reduce his productivity. An alternative strategy may be to use exchangeable reinforcers such as checks on a card or tokens that can be exchanged at break time for a tangible reinforcer or to solicit feedback. Another issue is the fading of the instructor as quickly as possible. The teacher's presence must be systematically faded so that the employee is able to rely on the cues of the workplace, rather than on the instructor (Chadsey-Rusch, 1990).

Many students with severe disabilities will need the support of adaptations to perform job tasks. Sowers and Powers (1991) have identified six major ways to approach adapting a job or task to meet the needs of the student:

1. Redesign the task to eliminate the difficult steps.
2. Provide the individual with disabilities with an alternative way to perform the task or task component.
3. Rearrange the environment to eliminate barriers or to increase worker productivity.
4. Reposition equipment to enhance worker performance.

Figure 21–4 Job Design Analysis Form

Source: Vocational Preparation and Employment of Students with Physical and Multiple Disabilities (p. 123), by J. Sowers and L. Powers, 1991, Baltimore: Paul H. Brookes Publishing Co. Reprinted by permission.

JOB DESIGN ANALYSIS FORM

Task *Preparing to enter data* Staff *Steve*

Site *Acme Insurance* New Employee *Beth*

Step	Physical difficulties	Discrimination difficulties
Obtain disk from disk holder.	Holder located on high shelf. Beth cannot reach.	20 disks in holder. Coding of disks complicated. Beth will have difficulty identifying the one to use.
Remove disk from sleeve.		
Insert disk into drive.		
Push switch in back of compter to turn on.	Switch is located in back of machine. Beth will not be able to reach it.	

Figure 21–5 Design Strategy Ideas

Source: Vocational Preparation and Employment of Students with Physical and Multiple Disabilities (p. 126), by J. Sowers and L. Powers, 1991, Baltimore: Paul H. Brookes Publishing Co. Reprinted by permission.

DESIGN STRATEGY IDEAS

Task Preparing to enter data — Worker Beth

Difficult step Push switch to turn on computer — Site Acme Insurance

Strategy type	Specific design strategy ideas
Eliminate step	Have someone else turn on computer for her.
Alternative response strategy	
Rearranging environment	Have table on which computer is placed pulled away from wall so Beth could move her chair behind it and turn it on.
Repositioning equipment	
Environmental cues	
Assistive devices–special	Buy and install switch that fits on side of computer—available at all computer stores.
Assistive devices–generic	Buy a power cord—plug into computer and place on the floor.
Assistive devices–constructed	

5. Teach the worker to use environmental cues (e.g., picture prompts, tape-recorded instructions) to assist them through the task.
6. Provide an assistive device that allows the worker to manipulate materials or operate equipment needed in the task. (pp. 112–117)

Sowers and Powers (1991) have provided processes that can be used to approach job design systematically. The first step is to task analyze the job and then identify the steps that the worker may have difficulty with, using the job design analysis form shown in Figure 21–4. When the areas of difficulty have been identified, design modifications and adaptations are selected (see the example in Figure 21–5). After design changes have been made, a new task analysis is constructed that includes task modifications, and the individual is trained to perform the task.

Conclusion

In this chapter the importance of transition planning and postschool outcomes was discussed. The process of transition involves outcomes in vocational preparation, community access, leisure, relationships, spiritual fulfillment, participation in the community, and a sense of well-being. Transition planning is a process for anticipating the needs of the student in the adult world and preparing for that eventual outcome. One of the most important aspects of transition planning is the collaboration with the family and with agencies that will provide supports to the young adult. Transition planning requires that the teacher think more broadly about lifestyle outcomes and develop linkages with persons in the community who can provide ongoing supports and services to students with disabilities as they enter adulthood.

Questions for Reflection

1. What may be a family's greatest worries as their son or daughter with severe disabilities approaches graduation from high school?
2. Will planning for transition assist families in resolving their worries or might it heighten their anxiety?
3. In what ways can students with disabilities participate in the transition plan?
4. How will changes in society's acceptance of persons with disabilities affect postschool outcomes for students with severe disabilities?
5. How can the outcomes of personal fulfillment and satisfaction be measured for a student with severe disabilities?
6. Who in the family and community should participate in transition planning? Why?

References

Agran, M., Blanchard, C., & Wehmeyer, M. L. (2000). Promoting transition goals and self-determination through student self-directed learning: The self-determined learning model of instruction. *Education and Training in Mental Retardation and Developmental Disabilities, 35*(4), 351–364.

Brown, F., Gothelf, C. R., Guess, D., & Lehr, D. H. (1998). Self-determination for individuals with the most severe disabilities: Moving beyond chimera. *Journal of the Association for Persons with Severe Handicaps, 23,* 17–26.

Buckley, J., Mank, D., & Sandow, D. (1990). Developing and implementing support strategies. In F. R. Rusch (Ed.), *Supported employment: Models, methods, and issues* (pp. 131–144). Sycamore, IL: Sycamore.

Callahan, M. J., & Garner, J. B. (1997). *Keys to the workplace. Skills and supports for people with disabilities.* Baltimore: Paul H. Brookes.

Chadsey-Rusch, J. (1990). Social interactions of secondary-aged students with severe handicaps: Implications for facilitating the transition from school to work. *Journal of the Association for Persons with Severe Handicaps, 15,* 69–78.

Cimera, R. E. (1998). Are individuals with severe mental retardation and multiple disabilities cost-efficient to serve via supported employment programs? *Mental Retardation, 36*(4), 280–292.

Cooney, B. F. (2002). Exploring perspectives on transition of youth with disabilities: Voices of young adults, parents, and professionals. *Mental Retardation, 40*(6), 425–435.

DiLeo, D., & Luecking, R. (1995). The risks of misapplying natural supports in the workplace. *Supported Employment Infolines, 6*(8), 4–5.

Fisher, D., & Sax, C. (1999). Noticing differences between secondary and postsecondary education: Extending Agran, Snow, and Swaner's discussion. *Journal of the Association for Persons with Severe Handicaps, 24*, 303–305.

Forest, M., & Pearpoint, J. (1992). Commonsense tools: MAPs and circles. In J. Pearpoint, M. Forest, & J. Snow (Eds.), *The inclusion papers: Strategies to make inclusion work* (pp. 52–57). Toronto, Ontario, Canada: Inclusion Press.

Geenen, S., Powers, L. E., & Lopez-Vasquez, A. (2001). Multicultural aspects of parent involvement in transition planning. *Exceptional Children, 67*(2), 265–282.

Grigal, M., Neubert, D. A., & Moon, M. S. (2001). Public school programs for students with significant disabilities in postsecondary settings. *Education and Training in Mental Retardation and Developmental Disabilities, 36*(3), 244–254.

Grossi, T. A., Regan, J., & Regan, B. (1998). Consumer-driven training techniques. In P. Wehman & J. Kregel (Eds.), *More than a job. Securing satisfying careers for people with disabilities* (pp. 119–147). Baltimore: Paul H. Brookes.

Hagner, D. C. (1996). "Natural supports" on trial: Day 2799? *Journal of the Association for Persons with Severe Handicaps, 21,* 181–184.

Hagner, D., Helm, D. T., & Butterworth, J. (1996). "This is our meeting": A qualitative study of person-centered planning. *Mental Retardation, 34,* 159–171.

Hall, M., Kleinert, H. L., Kearns, J. F. (2000). Going to college! Postsecondary programs for students with moderate and severe disabilities. *Teaching Exceptional Children, 32*(3), 58–65.

Halpern, A. (1993). Quality of life as a conceptual framework for evaluating transition outcomes. *Exceptional Children, 59,* 486–498.

Hanley-Maxwell, C., Whitney-Thomas, J., & Pogoloff, S. M. (1995). The second shock: A qualitative study of parents' perspectives and needs during their child's transition from school to adult life. *Journal of the Association for Persons with Severe Handicaps, 20,* 3–15.

Howe, J., Horner, R. H., & Newton, J. S. (1998). Comparison of supported living and traditional residential services in the state of Oregon. *Mental Retardation, 36*(1), 1–11.

Hughes, C., & Agran, M. (1998). Introduction to the special section: Self-determination: Signaling a systems change? *Journal of the Association for Persons with Severe Handicaps, 23,* 1–4.

Hutchins, M. P., & Renzaglia, A. M. (1990). Developing a longitudinal vocational training program. In F. R. Rusch (Ed.), *Supported employment: Models, methods, and issues* (pp. 365–380). Sycamore, IL: Sycamore.

Individuals with Disabilities Education Act Amendments of 1997 (IDEA) (1997), 20 U.S.C. 1400 et seq.

Kennedy, M. J. (1993). Turning the pages of life. In J. A. Racino, P. Walker, S. O'Connor, & S. J. Taylor (Eds.), *Housing support, and community: Choices and strategies for adults with disabilities* (pp. 205–216). Baltimore: Paul H. Brookes.

Klein, J. (1992). Get me the hell out of here: Supporting people with disabilities to live in their own homes. In J. Nisbet (Ed.), *Natural supports in school, at work, and in the community for people with severe disabilities* (pp. 277–339). Baltimore: Paul H. Brookes.

Kregel, J. (1998). Developing a career path: Application of person-centered planning. In P. Wehman & J. Kregel (Eds.), *More than a job. Securing satisfying careers for people with disabilities* (pp. 71–91). Baltimore: Paul H. Brookes.

Lee, M., Storey, K., Anderson, J. L., Goetz, L., & Zivolich, S. (1997). The effect of mentoring versus job coach instruction on integration in supported employment settings. *Journal of the Association for Persons with Severe Handicaps, 22*(3), 151–158.

Mank, D. (1996). Natural support in employment for people with disabilities: What do we know and when did we know it? *Journal of the Association for Persons with Severe Handicaps, 21,* 174–177.

Mank, D., Cioffi, A., & Yovanoff, P. (1998). Employment outcomes for people with severe disabilities: Opportunities for improvement. *Mental Retardation, 36*(3), 205–216.

Mank, D., Cioffi, A., & Yovanoff, P. (1999). Impact of coworker involvement with supported employees on wage and integration outcomes. *Mental Retardation, 37*(5), 383–394.

Miner, C. A., & Bates, P. E. (1997). The effect of person centered planning activities on the IEP/transition planning process. *Education and Training in Mental Retardation, 32,* 105–112.

Modell, S. J., & Valdez, L. A. (2002). Beyond bowling: Transition planning for students with disabilities. *Teaching Exceptional Children, 34*(6), 46–52.

Moon, M. S., Kiernan, W., & Halloran, W. (1990). School-based vocational programs and labor laws: A 1990 update. *Journal of the Association for Persons with Severe Handicaps, 15,* 177–185.

Mount, B., & Zwernick, K. (1988). *It's never too early, it's never too late: A booklet about personal futures planning.* St. Paul, MN: Metropolitan Council.

Nisbet, J. (1992). *Natural supports in school, at work, and in the community for people with severe disabilities.* Baltimore: Paul H. Brookes.

Nisbet, J., & Hagner, D. (1988). Natural supports in the workplace: A reexamination of supported employment. *Journal of the Association for Persons with Severe Handicaps, 13,* 260–267.

Pearpoint, J., O'Brien, J., & Forest, M. (1993). *PATH: A workbook for planning positive possible futures.* Toronto, Ontario, Canada: Inclusion Press.

Racino, J. A. (1995). Community living for adults with developmental disabilities: A housing and support approach. *Journal of the Association for Persons with Severe Handicaps, 20,* 300–310.

Racino, J. A., & Taylor, S. J. (1993). "People First": Approaches to housing and support. In J. A. Racino, P. Walker, S. O'Connor, & S. J. Taylor (Eds.), *Housing, support, and community. Choices and strategies for adults with disabilities* (pp. 33–56). Baltimore: Paul H. Brookes.

Racino, J. A., Taylor, S. J., Walker, P., & O'Connor, S. (1993). Introduction. In J. A. Racino, P. Walker, S. O'Connor, & S. J. Taylor (Eds.), *Housing, support, and community. Choices and strategies for adults with disabilities* (pp. 1–30). Baltimore: Paul H. Brookes.

Rhodes, L., Sandow, D., Mank, D., Buckley, J., & Albin, J. (1991). Expanding the role of employers in supported employment. *Journal of the Association for Persons with Severe Handicaps, 16,* 213–217.

Shoultz, B. (1993). Regenerating a community: The story of Residential, Inc. In J. A. Racino, P. Walker, S. O'Connor, & S. J. Taylor (Eds.), *Housing, support, and community. Choices and strategies for adults with disabilities* (pp. 281–298). Baltimore: Paul H. Brookes.

Smull, M., & Harrison, S. B. (1992). *Supporting people with severe reputations in the community.* Alexandria, VA: National Association of State Mental Retardation Program Directors.

Sowers, J., & Powers, L. (1991). *Vocational preparation and employment of students with physical and multiple disabilities.* Baltimore: Paul H. Brookes.

Steere, D., Pancsofar, E., Wood, R., & Hecimovic, A. (1990). *The principles of shared responsibility.* Hartford, CT: Institute of Human Resources.

Storey, K., Sandow, D., & Rhodes, I. (1990). Service delivery issues in supported employment. *Education and Training in Mental Retardation, 26,* 53–63.

Tashie, C., Malloy, J. M., & Lichtenstein, S. J. (1998). Transition or graduation? Supporting all students to plan for the future. In C. J. Jorgensen (Ed.), *Restructuring high schools for all students: Taking students to the next level* (pp. 234–259). Baltimore: Paul H. Brookes.

Test, D. W., Hinson, K. B., Solow, J., & Keul, P. (1993). Job satisfaction of persons in supported employment. *Education and Training in Mental Retardation, 28,* 38–46.

Test, D. W., & Wood, W. M. (1996). Natural supports in the workplace: The jury is still out. *Journal of the Association for Persons with Severe Handicaps, 21,* 155–173.

Thoma, C. A. (1999). Supporting student voice in transition planning. *Teaching Exceptional Children, 31*(5), 4–9.

Thoma, C. A., Rogan, P., & Baker, S. R. (2001). Student involvement in transition planning: Unheard voices. *Education and Training in Mental Retardation and Developmental Disabilities, 36*(1), 16–29.

Thompson, L., Powers, G., & Houchard, B. (1992). The wage effects of supported employment. *Journal of the Association for Persons with Severe Handicaps, 17,* 87–94.

Thorin, E., Yovanoff, P., & Irvin, L. (1996). Dilemmas faced by families during their young adult's transitions to adulthood: A brief report. *Mental Retardation, 34,* 117–120.

Tines, J., Rusch, F. R., McCaughrin, W., & Conley, R. W. (1990). Benefit–cost analysis of supported employment in Illinois: A statewide evaluation. *American Journal on Mental Retardation, 95,* 44–54.

Turnbull, A. P., & Turnbull, H. R., III (1996). Self-determination within a culturally responsive family systems perspective. Balancing the family system mobile. In L. E. Powers, G. H. S. Singer, & J. Sowers (Eds.), *On the road to autonomy. Promoting self-competence in children and youth with disabilities* (pp. 195–220). Baltimore: Paul H. Brookes.

U.S. Department of Labor (1962). *Field operations handbook* (6/21/62-10b10-10b11). Washington, DC: Author.

Wehman, P. (1992). *Life beyond the classroom: Transition strategies for young people with disabilities.* Baltimore: Paul H. Brookes.

Wehman, P. (2001). *Life beyond the classroom* (3rd Ed.). Baltimore: Paul H. Brookes.

Wehmeyer, M. L. (1992). Self-determination and the education of students with mental retardation. *Education and Training in Mental Retardation, 27,* 303–314.

Wehmeyer, M. (1996). Self-determination for youth with significant cognitive disabilities: From theory to practice. In L. E. Powers, G. H. S. Singer, & J. Sowers (Eds.), *On the road to autonomy. Promoting self-competence in children and youth with disabilities* (pp. 115–133). Baltimore: Paul H. Brookes.

Wehmeyer, M. (1998). Self-determination and individuals with significant disabilities: Examining meanings and misconceptions. *Journal of the Association for Persons with Severe Handicaps, 23,* 5–16.

Wehmeyer, M. L. (2001). Self-determination and transition. In P. Wehman, *Life Beyond the Classroom* (3rd Ed., pp. 35–60). Baltimore: Paul H. Brookes.

West, L. L., Corbey, S., Boyer-Stephens, A., Jones, B., Miller, R. J., & Sarkees-Wircenski, M. (1999). *Integrating transition planning into the IEP process* (2nd Ed.). Reston, VA: Division of Career Development and Transition, a division of The Council for Exceptional Children.

Westling, D. L. (1996). What do parents of children with moderate and severe disabilities want? *Education and Training in Mental Retardation, 31,* 86–114.

Whitney-Thomas, J., & Hanley-Maxwell, C. (1996). Packing the parachute: Parents' experiences as their children prepare to leave high school. *Exceptional Children, 63,* 75–87.

Whitney-Thomas, J., Shaw, D., Honey, K., & Butterworth, J. (1998). Building a future: A study of student participation in person-centered planning. *Journal of the Association for Persons with Severe Handicaps, 23,* 119–133.

Name Index

Subject Index

UNIVERSITY OF WALES, NEWPORT
LIBRARY
AND
INFORMATION
SERVICES
CAERLEON